P9-CMF-574
PUBLIC LIBRARY
Given
In Memory of
Lillie Bell Askew
Arnold
by
Judge Edwin Arnold, Sr.
Memorial

THE

WAR OF THE REBELLION:

A COMPILATION OF THE

OFFICIAL RECORDS

OF THE

UNION AND CONFEDERATE ARMIES.

PREPARED UNDER THE DIRECTION OF THE SECRETARY OF WAR, BY BVT. LIEUT. COL. ROBERT N. SCOTT, THIRD U. S. ARTILLERY,

AND

PUBLISHED PURSUANT TO ACT OF CONGRESS APPROVED JUNE 16, 1880.

SERIES I—VOLUME VI.

WASHINGTON:
GOVERNMENT PRINTING OFFICE.
1882.

CHAPTER XV.

OPERATIONS ON THE COASTS OF SOUTH CAROLINA, GEORGIA, AND MIDDLE AND EAST FLORIDA.

August 21, 1861–April 11, 1862.

SUMMARY OF THE PRINCIPAL EVENTS.

Aug. 21, 1861.—Brig. Gen. Roswell S. Ripley, C. S. Army, assigned to command of the Department of South Carolina.*

Brig. Gen. John B. Grayson, C. S. Army, assigned to command of the Department of Middle and East Florida.

Oct. 10, 1861.—Brig. Gen. E. Kirby Smith, C. S. Army, assigned to command of the Department of Middle and East Florida. (Revoked.)

21, 1861.—The expedition under command of Brig. Gen. Thomas W. Sherman, U. S. Army, sails from Annapolis, Md., for the South Carolina coast.

22, 1861.—Brig. Gen. James H. Trapier, C. S. Army, assigned to command of the Department of Middle and East Florida.

26, 1861.—Brig. Gen. Alexander R. Lawton, C. S. Army, assigned to command of the Department of Georgia.†

29, 1861.—The Sherman expedition sails from Hampton Roads, Va.

Nov. 5, 1861.—The coasts of South Carolina, Georgia, and East Florida, constituted a department, under command of General Robert E. Lee, C. S. Army.

7, 1861.—Forts Beauregard and Walker, Port Royal Bay, S. C., captured by U. S. Navy.

8, 1861.—General Robert E. Lee, C. S. Army, assumes command of the Department of South Carolina, Georgia, and East Florida.

Reconnaissance on Hilton Head Island, S. C.

10–11, 1861.—Expedition from Hilton Head to Braddock's Point, S. C.

16, 1861.—Capt. D. N. Ingraham, C. S. Navy, assigned to duty in Charleston Harbor, S. C.

24, 1861.—Union forces occupy Tybee Island, Ga.

Dec. 6–7, 1861.—Expedition to Port Royal Ferry and Beaufort, S. C.

17, 1861.—Evacuation of Rockville, S. C., by the Confederate forces.

Skirmish on Chisolm's Island, S. C.

20, 1861.—Stone fleet sunk at the entrance to Charleston Harbor, S. C.

Jan. 1, 1862.—Engagement at Port Royal Ferry, Coosaw River, S. C.

11, 1862.—The Department of Key West, Fla., constituted, under command of Brig. Gen. John M. Brannan, U. S. Army.

---

* On the 27th of May, 1861, Brig. Gen. G. T. Beauregard, being relieved from duty in the State of South Carolina, relinquished to Governor Pickens the command of the State volunteer forces, and transferred to Col. R. H. Anderson the command of the Confederate forces in Charleston Harbor and its vicinity. See Beauregard to Pickens, May 27, 1861, Vol. I, Series IV.

† He had been commanding the District of Savannah, Ga., since April 17, 1861.

Jan. 16, 1862.—Naval descent upon Cedar Keys, Fla.
20, 1862.—Second stone fleet sunk at the entrance to Charleston Harbor, S. C.
22-25, 1862.—Expedition to Edisto Island, S. C.
26-28, 1862.—Reconnaissance to Wilmington Narrows, Ga.; naval engagement.
Feb. 6, 1862.—Reconnaissance to Wright River, S. C.
10, 1862.—Skirmish on Barnwell's Island, S. C.
11, 1862.—Edisto Island, S. C., occupied by Union forces.
15, 1862.—Action at Venus Point, Ga.
23-26, 1862.—Reconnaissance on Bull River and Schooner Channel, S. C.
28, 1862.—Florida expedition sails from Warsaw Sound.
March 3, 1862.—General Robert E. Lee, C. S. Army, called to Richmond, Va.
3, 1862.—Amelia Island, Fla., evacuated by the Confederate forces.
4, 1862.—Amelia Island, Fla., occupied by the Union forces.
4, 1862.—Maj. Gen. John C. Pemberton, C. S. Army, assumes command of the Department of South Carolina, Georgia, and East Florida.
7-11, 1862.—Reconnaissance up the Savannah River and to Elba Island.
12, 1862.—Jacksonville, Fla., occupied by the Union forces.
13, 1862.—General Robert E. Lee charged with the conduct of military operations in the armies of the Confederacy.
14, 1862.—Maj. Gen. John C. Pemberton, C. S. Army, assigned to command of the Department of South Carolina and Georgia.
Brig. Gen. James H. Trapier, C. S. Army, assigned to command of the Department of Middle and East Florida.
15, 1862.—The States of South Carolina, Georgia, and Florida constituted the Department of the South, to be commanded by Maj. Gen. David Hunter, U. S. Army.
19, 1862.—Col. W. S. Dilworth, Florida, assigned to the command of the Department of Florida, vice Trapier, ordered to Alabama.
19-24, 1862.—Reconnaissance on May River, S. C.
20-24, 1862.—Operations near Bluffton, S. C., including affairs at Buckingham and Hunting Island.
23, 1862.—Affair at Smyrna, Fla.
28, 1862.—Reconnaissance near the mouth of Saint Augustine Creek, Ga.
29, 1862.—Affair on Edisto Island, S. C.
30-31, 1862.—Affairs on Wilmington and Whitemarsh Islands, Ga.
31, 1862.—Maj. Gen. David Hunter, U. S. Army, assumes command of the Department of the South.
April 5, 1862.—Occupation of Edisto Island, S. C., by the Union forces.
7, 1862.—Major-General Pemberton's command extended over Middle and Eastern Florida.
8, 1862.—Brig. Gen. Joseph Finegan, C. S. Army, assigned to command of the Department of Middle and Eastern Florida.
9, 1862.—Jacksonville, Fla., evacuated by the Union forces.
10, 1862.—Skirmish near Fernandina, Fla.
10-11, 1862.—Bombardment and capture of Fort Pulaski, Ga.

NOVEMBER 7, 1861.—Capture of Forts Beauregard and Walker, Port Royal Bay, S. C., by the United States Navy.

REPORTS, ETC.

No. 1.—Brig. Gen. Thomas W. Sherman, U. S. Army, with proclamation.
No. 2.—Brig. Gen. Thomas F. Drayton, C. S. Army, of the bombardment of Forts Walker and Beauregard.
No. 3.—Col. John A. Wagener, First Artillery, South Carolina Militia, of the bombardment of Fort Walker.

No. 1.

Reports of Brig. Gen. Thomas W. Sherman, U. S. A., with proclamation.

HEADQUARTERS EXPEDITIONARY CORPS,
Port Royal, S. C., November 8, 1861.

SIR: I have the honor to report that the force under my command embarked at Annapolis, Md., on the 21st October, and arrived at Hampton Roads, Va., on the 22d. In consequence of the delay in the arrival of some of our transports and the unfavorable state of the weather the fleet was unable to set out for the Southern coast until the 29th, when, under convoy of a naval squadron, in command of Commodore DuPont, and after the most mature consideration of the objects of the expedition by that flag-officer and myself, it was agreed to first reduce any works that might be found at Port Royal, S. C., and thus open the finest harbor on the coast that exists south of Hatteras. It was calculated to reach Port Royal in five days at most, but in consequence of adverse winds and a perilous storm on the day and night of the 1st November the fleet arrived at Port Royal bar not till the 4th, and then but in part, for it had been almost entirely dispersed by the gale, and the vessels have been straggling in up to this date. The transport steamers Union, Belvidere, Osceola, and Peerless have not arrived. Two of them are known to be lost, and it is probable that all are. It is gratifying, however, to say that none of the troop transports connected with the land forces were lost, though the Winfield Scott had to sacrifice her whole cargo and the Roanoke a portion of her cargo to save the lives of the regiments on board. The former will be unable to again put to sea. The vessels connected with the naval portion of the fleet have also suffered much and some have been lost.

After a careful reconnaissance of Port Royal Bay it was ascertained that the rebels had three field works of remarkable strength, strongly garrisoned, and covered by a fleet of three gunboats, under Captain Tatnall, late of the U. S. Navy, besides strong land forces, which the rebels were concentrating from Charleston and Savannah. The troops of the rebels were afterwards ascertained to have been commanded by General Drayton. One of the forts, and probably the strongest, was situated on Hilton Head, and the other two on Phillip's Island. It was deemed proper to first reduce the fort on Hilton Head, though to do this a greater or less fire might have to be met from the batteries on Bay Point at the same time. Our original plan of co-operation of the land forces in this attack had to be set aside, in consequence of the loss, during the voyage, of a greater portion of our means of disembarkment, together with the fact that the only point where the troops should have landed was from 5 to 6 miles (measuring around the intervening shoal) from the anchoring place of our transports—altogether too great a distance for successful debarkation with our limited means. It was therefore agreed that the place should be reduced by the naval force alone.

In consequence of the shattered condition of the fleet and the delay in the arrival of vessels that were indispensable for the attack it had to be postponed until the 7th instant. I was a mere spectator of the combat, and it is not my province to render any report of this action, but I deem it an imperative duty to say that the firing and maneuvering of our fleet against that of the rebels and their formidable land batteries was a master-piece of activity and professional skill that must have elicited the applause of the rebels themselves as a tactical operation. I think that too much praise cannot be awarded to the science and skill exhibited by the flag-officer of the naval squadron and the officers connected with his ships. I deem the performance a masterly one, and ought to have been seen to be fully appreciated. After the works were reduced I took possession of them with the land forces. The beautifully constructed work on Hilton Head was severely crippled and many of the guns dismounted. Much slaughter had evidently been made there, many bodies having been buried in the fort, and some 20 or 30 were found some half a mile distant.

The island for many miles was found strewed with arms and accouterments and baggage of the rebels, which they threw away in their hasty retreat. We have also come into possession of about forty pieces of ordnance, most of which is of the heaviest caliber and the most approved models, and a large quantity of ammunition and camp equipage.

It is my duty to report the valuable services of Mr. Boutelle, [C. A.] assistant in the Coast Survey, assisting me with his accurate and extensive knowledge of this country. His services are invaluable to the Army as well as to the Navy, and I earnestly recommend that important notice be taken of this very able and scientific officer by the War Department.

I am, very respectfully, your obedient servant,

T. W. SHERMAN.

Brigadier-General, Commanding.

ADJUTANT-GENERAL U. S. ARMY,

Washington, D. C.

[Inclosure.]

PROCLAMATION.

To the People of South Carolina :

In obedience to the orders of the President of these United States of America I have landed on your shores with a small force of national troops. The dictates of a duty which, under these circumstances, I owe to a great sovereign State, and to a proud and hospitable people, among whom I have passed some of the pleasantest days of my life, prompt me to proclaim that we have come amongst you with no feelings of personal animosity; no desire to harm your citizens, destroy your property, or interfere with any of your lawful rights or your social and local institutions, beyond what the causes herein briefly alluded to may render unavoidable.

Citizens of South Carolina, the civilized world stands appalled at the course you are pursuing; appalled at the crime you are committing against your own mother—the best, the most enlightened, and heretofore the most prosperous of nations. You are in a state of active rebellion against the laws of your country. You have lawlessly seized upon the forts, arsenals, and other property belonging to our common country and within your borders. With this property you are in arms and waging a ruthless war against your constitutional Government, and thus threatening the existence of a Government which you are bound by the terms of a solemn compact to live under and faithfully support. In doing this you are not only undermining and preparing the way for totally ignoring your own political and social existence, but you are threatening the civilized world with the odious sentiment that self-government is impossible with civilized man.

Fellow-citizens, I implore you to pause and reflect upon the tenor and the consequences of your acts. If the awful sacrifices made by the devastation of our property, the shedding of fraternal blood in battle, the mourning and wailing of widows and orphans throughout our land, are insufficient to deter you from further pursuing this unholy war, then ponder, I beseech you, upon the ultimate but not less certain results which its much further progress must necessarily and naturally entail upon your once happy and prosperous State. Indeed, can you pursue this fratricidal war and continue to imbrue your hands in the loyal blood of your countrymen, your friends, your kinsmen, for no other object than to unlawfully disrupt the confederacy of a great people—a confederacy established by your own hands—in order to set up, were it possible, an independent government, under which you can never live in peace, prosperity, or quietness?

Carolinians, we have come among you as loyal men, fully impressed with our constitutional obligations to the citizens of your State. Those obligations shall be performed as far as in our power. But be not deceived. The obligation of suppressing armed combinations against the constitutional authorities is paramount to all others. If in the performance of this duty other minor but important obligations should be in any way neglected, it must be attributed to necessities of the case, because rights dependent on the laws of the State must be necessarily subordinate to military exigencies created by insurrection and rebellion.

T. W. SHERMAN,
Brigadier-General, Commanding.

HEADQUARTERS EXPEDITIONARY CORPS,
Port Royal, S. C., November 8, 1861.

—

HEADQUARTERS EXPEDITIONARY CORPS,
Hilton Head, S. C., November 11, 1861.

SIR: In addition to my report of the 8th instant, and after a more perfect examination into details, I have to state that the number of pieces of ordnance which have fallen into our hands is fifty-two, the bulk of which is of the largest caliber, all with fine carriages, &c., except eight or nine, that were ruined by our fire, which dismounted their pieces. A complete inventory of the amount of public property captured is being prepared and will be duly furnished. Besides the wreck of small-arms, &c., thrown away by the rebels in their hasty retreat, as stated in my last, a light battery of two fine 12-pounder howitzers has been found to have been abandoned near the ferry, about 6 miles distant. I have also ascertained by examination that the flight of the rebels extended to Braddock's Point, at the south end of the island, and about 15 miles distant, the fort at that point being deserted and its guns spiked. It has one 10-inch columbiad and two 5½-inch guns.

On clearing out the fort at Hilton Head the dead body of Dr. Buist, formerly an assistant surgeon in the Army, was found in one of the galleries leading from the terre-plein to a caponiere, he having been killed by the explosion of a shell and buried by the falling in of a parapet. He was the principal surgeon of this fort.

The effect of this victory is startling. Every white inhabitant has left the island. The wealthy islands of Saint Helena, Ladies, and most of Port Royal are abandoned by the whites, and the beautiful estates of the planters, with all their immense property, left to the pillage of hordes of apparently disaffected blacks, and the indications are that the panic has extended to the fort on the north end of Reynolds' Island, commanding the fine anchorage of Saint Helena Sound. Of this, however, I shall have satisfactory information in a few days. I am now in the occupation of the forts at Hilton Head, the two on Phillip's Island, and the one at Braddock's Point. The task of unloading our vessels will be a very slow and difficult operation, in consequence of the extended shallow shores, until wharves can be constructed; nevertheless it is expected to be able to leave here with a large force as soon as our defenses are fully under way, to further carry out the grand objects of the expedition.

I am, very respectfully, your obedient servant,

T. W. SHERMAN,
Brigadier-General, Commanding.

The ADJUTANT-GENERAL U. S. ARMY,
Washington, D. C.

No. 2.

Report of Brig. Gen. Thomas F. Drayton, C. S. Army, of the bombardment of Forts Walker and Beauregard.

HDQRS. PROV. FORCES, THIRD MIL. DIST., DEPT. S. C.,
Camp Lee, Hardeeville, November 24, 1861.

SIR: I have the honor of presenting my official report of the engagement on the 7th instant between the Federal fleet, numbering fifteen war steamers and gunboats, and Forts Walker and Beauregard, upon Hilton Head and Bay Point, at the entrance of Port Royal Sound. The fleet was commanded by Capt. S. F. DuPont, flag-officer of the South Atlantic Blockading Squadron, and the troops on board the transports by Brigadier-General [T. W.] Sherman. The distance between the forts is by Coast Survey two and five-eighths miles.

The enemy's fleet had been collecting in our waters since the morning of the 4th instant, and had increased in the afternoon to thirty-two war steamers and transports. On receiving a dispatch to this effect from Col. William C. Heyward, commanding the troops at Camp Walker, I left my headquarters in Beaufort and repaired by steamer to Bay Point, which I reached at 6 p. m., passing on the way the ever-watchful little fleet of Flag-Officer [Josiah] Tatnall, C. S. Navy.

After remaining in consultation until 1.30 a. m. with Col. R. G. M. Dunovant, commandant of the post, I took my departure, leaving him such general instruction as the uncertain mode and direction from which an attack might be expected would permit. I then visited Commodore Tatnall, and after an interchange of views took leave, crossed over to Hilton Head Island, landed there at daylight on the 5th, and immediately dispatched a courier to Braddock's Point, south end of the island, ordering Captain Stuart's company, of Ninth Regiment, to march on Fort Walker, and embark thence to strengthen Captain Elliott's gunners in Fort Beauregard. This company did not leave on the 6th, as proposed, as Captain Sapard, of the steamer Edith, failed to comply with his orders to carry it across early in the morning. They were dispatched, however, by the first steamer at my disposal on the 7th, and before they had reached half way across the bay they were cut off from Bay Point by the advancing fleet of the enemy, and obliged to seek shelter in Skull Creek, where Captain Stuart disembarked his whole command in safety.

On inspecting Fort Walker shortly after my arrival I found twenty guns, of various caliber, mounted upon the ramparts, thirteen of which were on the channel battery, viz, one 10-inch columbiad in the center, flanked to the right by five 32-pounders and one 9-inch Dahlgren rifled cannon, and to the left by six other cannon in the following order: One 32-pounder, one 8-inch columbiad, three 42-pounders, and one rifled 24-pounder; north bastion, one 32-pounder; south bastion, one 32-pounder, one 8-inch howitzer, and one long 12-pounder; south flank of bastion, one navy 32-pounder; demi-lune, two 24-pounders; redan, one navy 8-inch howitzer. Of these eight guns one in the north bastion and two in the south flank could occasionally be used against the ships of war. The rest were for the land defense.

To man the guns within the fort and for an infantry reserve outside we had, until re-enforcements came from Savannah on the afternoon of the 6th, two companies of Colonel Wagener's First Regiment Artillery, South Carolina Militia, numbering 152 men; three companies of Colonel Heyward's Ninth [Eleventh] Regiment South Carolina Volunteers, 210 men; four companies of Col. R. G. M. Dunovant's Twelfth Regiment South Carolina Volunteers, under Major Jones, 260 men. Total, 622 men.

There were stationed on the beach at Camp Lookout, 6 miles off, Capt. I. H. Screven's Mounted Guerrillas, numbering 65, who acted as scouts and couriers.

About 9 o'clock a. m. of the 5th, Commodore Tatnall, who had boldly attacked the enemy's gunboats on the previous day, again gallantly steamed out to exchange shots with them, but he was met by too large a force, and therefore retired slowly behind our forts. The enemy followed, and engaged both batteries for about forty-five minutes, with no other injury than 3 men slightly burned in Fort Beauregard from the explosion of a caisson struck by a rifle shell.

On the 6th instant the fleet and transports, which had increased to about forty-five sail, would probably have attacked us had not the weather been very boisterous. In the afternoon about 4 o'clock we received our first re-enforcements from Georgia, 450 infantry, under command of Captain Berry, C. S. Army, and Captain Read's battery of two 12-pounder howitzers and 50 men.

I have reason for supposing that this assistance would have arrived sooner, for General A. R. Lawton, commanding provisional forces in Georgia, wrote from Savannah to Col. W. C. Heyward on the 4th instant, 8.30 p. m., as follows: "From a dispatch received to-day from General Ripley I infer that you (Col. W. C. Heyward) have been sufficiently re-enforced from his command until the plans of the enemy shall be more fully developed."

Two hours after the gallant Georgians came to the rescue I received the welcome intelligence that Colonel De Saussure's Fifteenth Regiment South Carolina Volunteers, 650 strong, had landed at Seabrook's Wharf, upon Skull Creek, and were close at hand.

At last the memorable 7th dawned upon us bright and serene, not a ripple upon the broad expanse of water to disturb the accuracy of fire from the broad decks of that magnificent armada about advancing in battle array to vomit forth its iron hail with all the spiteful energy of long-suppressed rage and conscious strength. At 9.25 a. m. one 9-inch Dahlgren gun opened fire upon the —— gun steamship Wabash, flag-ship of Capt. S. F. DuPont, which led the van, closely succeeded by fourteen other large steamers and gunboats.

The shell from the Dahlgren exploded near the muzzle, and was harmless. Other shots followed from both forts, and soon the fire became general on land and water. In spite of our fire, directed with deliberation and coolness, the fleet soon passed both batteries apparently unharmed, and then returning delivered in their changing rounds a terrific shower of shot and shell in flank and front.

Besides this moving battery, the fort was enfiladed by two gunboats anchored to the north off the mouth of Fish Hall Creek, and another at a point on the edge of the shoals to the south. This enfilading fire on so still a sea annoyed and damaged us excessively, particularly as we had no gun on either flank of the bastion to reply with, for the 32-pounder on the right flank was shattered very early by a round shot, and on the north flank for want of a carriage no gun had been mounted. After the fourth fire the 10-inch columbiad bounded over the limber and became useless. The 24-pounder rifled cannon was choked while ramming down a shell, and lay idle during nearly the whole engagement. The shells for the 9-inch Dahlgren were also too large. The fourth shell attempted to be rammed home could not be driven below the trunnions, and was then at great risk discharged.

Thus far the fire of the enemy had been endured and replied to with the unruffled courage of veterans. At 10.30 our gunners became so fatigued that I left the fort, accompanied by one of my volunteer aides, Capt. H. Rose, and went back to Captain Read's battery (one and three-quarter miles in the rear of the fort) and brought the greater part of his men back to take the places of our exhausted men inside the fort. It was while thus engaged with Captain Read's company that Col. W. H. Stiles rode up and reported his regiment about 2 miles off. I instantly directed my aide, Lieutenant Drayton, to accompany Colonel Stiles to the road along which his regiment was advancing, and to station it in position by the side of the other Georgia troops. On entering the fort with Captain Read's company they were cordially greeted by both officers and men.

The vigorous attack from the fleet continued unabated, with still no decided damage to any of their ships. About 12.30 p. m. I again went out of the fort with my assistant adjutant-general, Captain Young, for the purpose of mustering together the infantry and reserves, and have them in readiness for any eventuality. Before leaving, however, I turned over the command to Colonel Heyward, with directions to hold out as long as any effective fire could be returned.

Having mounted our horses, we rejoined the troops near Hospital No. 2. I received information through one of the vedettes that a steamer and small boats were sounding close to the beach. I detached Captain Berry, with three companies of his battalion, under the guidance of Capt. Ephraim Barnard, volunteer aide, to watch the enemy, beat them back if they attempted to land, and give notice if he wanted support. I then, with some of my staff, rode to collect together the other troops, who, through ignorance of our island roads, had lost their way and had not yet come up.

On the road leading to wharf on Skull Creek, about one and one-fourth miles from Fort Walker, I unexpectedly met General Ripley and staff. Saluting him, I inquired if he visited the island to assume command, and whether he wished to go back with me into the fort. He said no, but that he would return to Coosawhatchie to collect and bring back two or three regiments to my support. We then moved from under the fire of the ships to the shelter of some myrtles, where we could not be seen. I then stated to him the incidents of the morning; how the men had fought, that the day was going against us, and I was then collecting my forces for any emergency that might arise; and, if compelled to defend the island, it should by retained to the last extremity. We then parted, he taking the road toward the ferry and I in pursuit of the purposes which brought me out of the fort.

On reaching my reserves at Hospital No. 2 I learned that the enemy had ceased making soundings and had gone back to sea, whereupon I dispatched Captain Read to order Captain Berry to return from the beach.

Two o'clock had now arrived, when I noticed our men coming out of the fort, which they had bravely defended for four and a half hours against fearful odds, and then only retiring when all but three of the guns on the water front had been disabled, and only 500 pounds of powder in the magazine, commencing the action with 220 men inside the fort, afterwards increased to 255 by the accession from Read's battery. These heroic men retired slowly and sadly from their well-fought guns, which to have defended longer would have exhibited the energy of despair rather than the manly pluck of the true soldier.

The defense of this post involved a twofold preparation: first to repel the attack from the fleet, and secondly an assault by the beach from the troops upon the transports. By the beach we had to provide against an attack from the north under cover of the bluff south of Fish Hall Creek, and from the south by the beach under cover of the woods, between where a picket of 25 men were posted, under Capt. Paul H. Seabrook, and lastly by the road leading from the beach to the second hospital. To guard against surprise either by Fish Hall Creek or by the beach, when I was returning to the fort with a portion of Captain Read's company, I at the same time led up Colonel De Saussure's regiment to the hollow west of the road and directed them to lie down. They were perfectly masked from the fire of the fort, but not from that of the fleet, for the watchmen at the mast-heads gave notice of their position, compelling Colonel De Saussure after a short time to fall back under a heavy fire to a less dangerous locality.

Had the intrenched camp, with store-houses and magazines, been made in time several lives and large quantities of public property might have been saved; but it was impossible to have made this within the short time and with the diminutive force at my disposal, for on my arrival at headquarters in Beaufort, on the night of the 17th October, the number of troops at Camp Walker was but 362, afterward increased on the 24th to 622 by the accession of four companies under Major Jones, of Twelfth Regiment South Carolina Volunteers. To this may be added the engineer force of some 60 men, who, with the soldiers, worked incessantly day and night. As for evidence of what they accomplished: The 8-inch columbiad on the water front was only mounted on the 1st November, one 8-inch howitzer in the salient of the south bastion, mounted on the 4th; one 32-pounder on the right flank of bastion, mounted on the 5th; one 8-inch howitzer mounted on a ship carriage; embrasure cut through parapet of demi-lune on the night of the 5th; covered way and hot-shot furnace for 42-pounders, constructed of earth and dry masonry, on the morning of the 6th, together with wads of moss and hay for same; splinter-proof, occupying only one-half terre-plein behind the principal traverse, was finished on the morning of the engagement (7th instant), the material not having arrived before the 4th instant.

The retreat was commenced about 3 p. m. toward Ferry Point, about 6 miles off, Colonel De Saussure's regiment and Capt. I. Read's company of artillery bringing up the rear. At 1.30 a. m., by the aid of Commodore Tatnall's fleet, the steamers St. Johns and Edisto, and three large flats, capable of holding 150 men each, the troops were all safely embarked without provisions, no ammunition but what was contained in the cartridge-boxes (the 100,000 cartridges I had made requisition for, and been anxiously expecting, not having reached us until after the battle), and fearing that our retreat would be cut off by the enemy's gunboats at Skull Creek, no other alternative was left but to leave the island and concentrate upon the main-land, where we would be enabled to fight the enemy on more equal terms should he venture beyond the protection of his fleet and attack us there.

The muskets captured by the enemy, with the exception of some ten or fifteen, were those left in the fort, shattered by shot and shell, others left in camp belonging to men on sick leave, or to those engaged in heating hot-shot furnaces two days before the fight, and some boxes of arms which had been left on the wharf the night before the battle, belonging to the sick men of Colonel De Saussure's regiment, who had been left behind at Lightwood Knot, and which could have been saved, with a box of swords, if the captains of the steamers Edisto and St. Johns had not refused to take them on board when directed to do so.

To Captain Tatnall, flag-officer C. S. Navy, and the officers and men of his little fleet, I cannot too highly express my admiration of their intrepidity and hardihood in attacking the enemy's gunboats on the 4th and 5th instants. These encounters, by interrupting their soundings and the location of their buoys, no doubt prevented our being attacked on Tuesday, the 5th instant, before our re-enforcements reached us. I must also acknowledge the assistance extended to us by the gallant commodore with his boats on the night of our retreat from the island.

FORT BEAUREGARD.

The attack upon the fort, though not so concentrated and heavy as that upon Walker, was nevertheless very severe. Its armament was nineteen guns, of which the following, viz, one 8-inch Rodman, bored to 24-pounder and rifled; two 42-pounders; one 10-inch columbiad; two 42-pounders, reamed to eight inches, and one 32-pounder in hot-shot battery, were the only guns capable of being used against the fleet.

The force on Bay Point was 640 men, commanded by Col. R. G. M.

Dunovant, Twelfth Regiment South Carolina Volunteers. Of the above, 149 garrisoned Fort Beauregard, under the immediate command of Capt. Stephen Elliott, jr., Beaufort Volunteer Artillery, Company A, Ninth Regiment South Carolina Volunteers. The infantry force of Colonel Dunovant's regiment was intrusted with the protection of the eastern part of the island, and of the defense of the bastion line at the Island Narrows, where an attack was expected from the enemy.

Knowing how small a force Captain Elliott had to command his batteries, I ordered, as soon as I reached Hilton Head, on the 5th instant, Captain Stuart's company (Hamilton Guards), Ninth [Company E., Eleventh] Regiment South Carolina Volunteers, to march upon Fort Walker from Braddock's Point, and take thence the steamer Edith for Bay Point, but the failure of Captain Sapard, of the Edith, to fulfill his appointment at the hour designated, prevented me from supporting Captain Elliott as I desired. But on Thursday morning, 7th instant, having obtained the steamer Emma, I dispatched Captain Stuart's company in her to Fort Beauregard. The rapid advance of the enemy's fleet, however, to the attack on the batteries cut off and compelled her, at the risk of being intercepted, to turn back and seek shelter in Skull Creek, on the shores of which Captain Stuart's company safely disembarked and joined me in the afternoon; and here again was exhibited another act of heroism on the part of our veteran commodore, who to save the Emma interposed his own frail flag-steamer between her and the advancing flag-ship of Commodore DuPont, drawing upon himself her entire broadside, and thus diverting this huge leviathan temporarily from her course, secured the safety of the Emma at the peril of his own vessel.

The non-arrival of any re-enforcements at Camp Walker until the night of the 6th instant also prevented me from sending the four companies of the Twelfth Regiment South Carolina Volunteers, under Major Jones, to the support of the other six companies of the regiment at Bay Point.

For the details of the engagement at this post, the notable examples of bravery, the general good conduct, their well-timed retreat in the direction indicated by the dotted red lines on the map appended,* I beg leave to refer you to the official reports of Colonel Dunovant and Captain Elliott. But among the many officers and men honorably noticed on this occasion in the official report of Colonel Dunovant, none of them are so justly entitled to well-merited encomium as Capt. Stephen Elliott, the commander of the fort. Others may have exhibited an equal amount of cool bravery in front of the foe, but his opportunities enabled him to surpass all his brother officers in the skillful arrangement of his defenses, superb condition of his batteries, and in the high discipline which he had imparted to his model company, the creature of his own indefatigable exertions.

The delays and dangers incident to the manner in which troops and supplies of all kinds were landed at the forts of Port Royal and the absence of all means of retreat in case of disaster had attracted my most serious attention immediately after I assumed command at Beaufort, on the evening of the 7th instant. I immediately took steps for remedying the first and providing for the last.

With the double object of landing supplies in all weather at Bay Point, and at the same time of furnishing the means of retreat beyond the range of the enemy's guns, I directed one of my volunteer aides, Capt. T. R. S. Elliott, to make an examination of the adjacent creeks

---

*Not found.

to the north of the fort. He reported that about 3 miles from the mouth of Moss Creek there was a depth of water sufficient for steamers drawing 7 feet at low water, and that from thence a causeway of 300 yards over the marsh might easily be made, and furnish a sure means of transportation, and thus avoid the losses and delays which had previously occurred in landing from the steamers into flats upon the beach.

From the point above indicated in Moss Creek flats were to have been provided and stationed to convey the soldiers in case of emergency across the creek, thence by land to Station Creek, where other flats were to be placed for the same object as at Moss Creek. Landing at Saint Helena the transit to White Hall Ferry opposite Beaufort was comparatively safe.

On Hilton Head I also commenced repairing the wharf at Seabrook's Landing, on Skull Creek, with a view of transporting stores to Fort Walker when the weather was too boisterous to land them in the surf. The completion of the wharf was prevented, however, by the unexpected attack of the enemy, though in its incomplete state it had already been put to successful use.

I succeeded, however, in obtaining from Charleston two flats and two troop boats, and from Savannah three large flats, capable of containing 150 men each, which reached Jenkins' Island Ferry in time to assist in embarking our troops on the night of the retreat. Three other smaller ones were sent at the same time to White Hall Ferry, which assisted in performing the same good offices for Colonel Dunovant's command. The rest of the scheme, for want of time and flats, could not be carried out in the manner I intended.

For the purpose of sending messages between Forts Walker and Beauregard, and thence to my headquarters at Beaufort, I had prepared, by the assistance of Captain Lynah, another of my aides, a number of signal flags, the designs of which had already been prepared and painted, and only needed a few more days to have been put into operation.

In alluding as I have to these matters I do not mean to reflect upon any person, or to say these pressing wants could have been supplied anterior to the period when I entered upon my new duties. My design has been to exhibit the condition in which I found my command, and to show that I have left no effort untried to improve it.

Notwithstanding the prompt measures adopted by Colonel Dunovant to effect his retreat in the direction of the Narrows, it is surprising that, with the knowledge possessed by the enemy (through Mr. Boutelle and others connected with the Coast Survey), his retreat had not been intercepted by gunboats passing up towards Beaufort, and mine by other steamers taking the passage through Skull Creek towards the ferry landing. Why they did not adopt this course must be left to time to explain.

Casualties.—The following is a correct list of killed, wounded, missing, and prisoners:

Command.	Killed.	Wounded.	Captured.	Missing.	Aggregate.
Fort Walker	10	20	......	......	30
Fort Beauregard	......	13	......	......	13
15th South Carolina	1	15	......	......	16
Sick in hospital	......	......	3	......	3
Command not stated	......	......	......	4	4
Total	11	48	3	4	66

The heads of the quartermaster's and commissary's departments, Maj. E. Willis and Capt. C. D. Owens, have discharged their several duties with economy and fidelity. The reports hereunto appended of these officers and of their assistants show how unwearied and earnest were their efforts to save the public property left at the headquarters in Beaufort. I must likewise make honorable mention of Col. W. C. Heyward, Ninth [Eleventh] Regiment South Carolina Volunteers, who commanded in Fort Walker and its vicinity, and who during the battle made the best use of the means at his disposal. Col. John A. Wagener, First Regiment Artillery South Carolina Militia, supported by Maj. Arthur M. Huger, of the same regiment, was placed in the immediate command of all the batteries, nine of which, upon the water front, were manned by the German Artillery, Companies A and B, Capts. H. Harms and D. Werner, First Regiment Artillery South Carolina Militia, all of whom fought under the flag of their adopted country with an enthusiasm which could not have been surpassed had they been fighting in defense of their own fatherland.

The remaining four batteries on the left flank of the water front were under the direction of Capt. Josiah Bedon, Ninth [Eleventh] Regiment South Carolina Volunteers. The flanking and rear guns of the fort were manned by detachments from Captain Bedon's, Canaday's, and White's companies, Ninth [Eleventh] Regiment South Carolina Volunteers. Maj. F. D. Lee, South Carolina Engineers and constructing engineer of Fort Walker, not only fought gallantly at the batteries, but afforded valuable assistance at other points in the work during the contest.

Capt. Joseph A. Yates, Battalion South Carolina Artillery, and acting ordnance officer, was zealous in the execution of all the duties assigned to him. Toward the close of the fight he was severely wounded, but has since recovered, and is again ready in another field to resist all marauders that may approach our shores. Dr. Ogier and his able assistants, Drs. W. C. Ravenel, and William Elliott, a volunteer from Savannah, Ga., were present, and rendered efficient service in the hospitals. I cannot but regret the painful wound which has been the cause of the resignation of Dr. Ogier as medical director in my military district.

In conclusion, I cannot but express my high appreciation of the gallant behavior of my aides, Capt. Henry E. Young and Lieut. J. E. Drayton, as also that of the gentlemen comprising my volunteer staff, Capts. L. Cheves, H. Rose, E. Lynah, J. E. Eddings, J. I. Middleton, jr., and Joseph A. Huger. The names of the officers and men not mentioned in my report will be found deservedly mentioned in the official reports of the colonels of regiments, commandants of batteries, and chiefs of the general staff.

I have the honor to be, respectfully, yours,

THOS. F. DRAYTON,
Brigadier-General, Commanding.

Capt. L. D. WALKER,
Assistant Adjutant-General, Charleston, S. C.

[Indorsement.]

HDQRS. PROV. FORCES, DEPT. SOUTH CAROLINA,
Charleston, November 19, 1861.

It might be proper to remark upon the within report and some probably inadvertent inaccuracies, or to give a report of movements and orders from these headquarters and instructions given after news was received that the enemy's fleet was intended for Port Royal and how they were carried out and followed. I deem, however, that no good would result to the service from a discussion of these points at this time; and requesting that, should it be thought proper to publish this report, it should be published with this indorsement, it is respectfully forwarded.

R. S. RIPLEY,
Brigadier-General, Commanding.

No. 3.

Report of Col. John A. Wagener, First Artillery, South Carolina Militia, of the bombardment of Fort Walker.

CHARLESTON, *November* 11, 1861.

SIR: In consequence of our fatiguing retreat from the island of Hilton Head I am only now able to render you my official report of that disastrous day, together with the returns, in part only, as I have not been able to obtain the reports of Captains Bedon, Canaday, and White, of Colonel Heyward's regiment, which I would beg you to receive through Colonel Heyward.

On Thursday morning, the 7th instant, the fleet which had been watching us for days began to move in such a manner that I had the long roll beat immediately, and in one and a half minutes every cannoneer was at his post. The armament of the fort was divided into batteries and served as follows, viz:

Right channel battery: Nos. 1, 2, 3, 4, and 5, German Artillery, Company B, Capt. H. Harms. Center channel battery: Nos. 6, 7, 8, and 9, German Artillery, Company A, Capt. D. Werner. Left channel battery: Nos. 10, 11, 12, and 13, Company C, Ninth [Eleventh] Regiment South Carolina Volunteers, Capt. Josiah Bedon. These were the front batteries, all under command of Maj. A. M. Huger, First Artillery, South Carolina Militia.

The flanking and rear guns were manned by detachments from Captains Bedon's, Canaday's, and White's companies, Ninth [Eleventh] Regiment, under the command of Captain Canaday. The reserve was under charge of Captain White. The first gun (32-pounder rifle), which was loaded with a percussion shell, I directed myself, but unfortunately the shell exploded directly in front of the muzzle.

The battle opened, I think, a few minutes before 9 o'clock a. m. The enemy had chosen a day which was entirely propitious to him. The water was as smooth as glass. The air was just sufficient to blow the smoke of his guns into our faces, where it would meet the column of our own smoke and prevent our sight, excepting by glimpses. The sailing vessels of our opponents were towed by his steamers, and thus could maneuver on the broad expanse of Port Royal with the accuracy of well-trained battalions. No sooner did we obtain his range than it would be changed, and time after time rechanged, while the deep water permitted him to choose his own position, and fire shot after shot and shell after shell with the precision of target practice. Most unfortunate for us was the mistake of the engineers, which I had pointed out before the battle, of having failed to establish a battery on the bluff which commanded our flank. The enemy having taken position in the mouth of the creek exposed us to a raking fire, which did us the greatest damage, dismounting our guns and killing and wounding numbers of our men.

Major Huger reports to me as follows, viz:

Up to some minutes after 9 o'clock a. m. the firing was very slow, the range being too great. About that time, however, the enemy reached a position in front of the batteries at about one and a quarter miles range at easy speed, delivering a slow but well-directed fire, and evidencing their determination to pass beyond, which I endeavored by a rapid fire of shell and hot shot to prevent, but the long range and moving objects did not let me succeed. In a few minutes several of the enemy's ships passed well beyond us. Three of them took position to enfilade our batteries from our northwest flank, while others, which had not yet got into action, assumed direction opposite our southeast front, and their largest ship (the Minnesota) returned down our front, delivering a beautifully accurate fire at short range, supported at rather longer range by the fire of two other large ships of war. So soon as these positions had become established the fort was fought simply as a point of honor, for from that moment we were defeated, excepting perhaps by providential interference.

Our guns were fought, nevertheless, with determination and skill, and did a great deal of damage to the enemy. About 11 o'clock it was reported to me that the Bay Point batteries had been silenced, whereupon we determined that we would have to fight so much harder, and I am proud to say our men were equal to the exigencies of the occasion. Between 12 and 1 o'clock I was knocked down by a piece of shell, and a good deal stunned. I sent for Major Huger and transferred the command of the fort to him, to enable me to get a few moments' rest. By a little after 1 o'clock Major Huger informed Colonel Heyward, commanding the island, that the ammunition was nearly gone. It was thereupon determined by the order of the general commanding to evacuate the works. Three sections of the German Artillery, under Captain Harms, Lieut. F. Melchers, and Orderly Bischoff, were detailed to continue a slow fire while the wounded were removed, and the garrison was ordered to retreat by dispersion. Near 2 o'clock Major Huger ordered the last detachment from their guns.

By this time the field in our rear was covered with the shells of the enemy, and it is by the intervention of God's providence only that not more were lost. The fort was gone, but our honor was saved. Of the channel battery only three guns were in condition to have continued the fight, which would have been hopeless under any circumstances. A retreat was consequently ordered. On reaching Bluffton, the general commanding was kind enough to order our battalion here with expressions of approval, for which I respectfully tender him my thanks.

I beg leave to inclose you a return of our killed and severely wounded. The slightly wounded have not been mentioned, for they are very numerous. The general commanding will concur with me that this has been one of the hardest-fought fields on record, and I would be very grateful to him for the public expression of his opinion, to set the tongue of slander at rest and encourage our citizen soldiery. I beg leave also respectfully to bring to his notice the names of the following officers and men who have particularly distinguished themselves by acts of heroism, viz: Major Huger, the bravest of the brave; Lieut. [J. E.] Heape, of Captain Bedon's company, whom I saw myself save a poor, severely-wounded soldier in the terrible shell-fire of the enemy while crossing the field in retreat; Mr. Carlsen, of the German Artillery, who replaced the Confederate flag on the rampart in a storm of shot and shell; Private Julius Wagener, a boy only fifteen years of age, who replanted our noble Palmetto banner on the ramparts, whence it had been shot down—I would not have mentioned his name, he being my own son, but for the opinion that he may hereafter become very useful to his country; Private Geilfuss, German Artillery, who brought away the Palmetto flag, and was otherwise heroically attentive to his duties.

I deem, besides, specially deserving the notice of the general commanding Major Barnwell and Captains Yates and Read, of the Regular Army; Major Lee, of the engineers; Col. Gaston Allen, who kindly acted as my special aide, and my entire staff, who did their duty well.

I may further mention as deserving of great praise Captain Bedon and his officers and Captain Harms and his officers, Captain Werner and his officers, especially Lieutenant Melchers, who fired the last gun. Private Heidenreich and Corporals Petersen and Stelljes, of the German Artillery, deserve to be praisefully mentioned, likewise several members of the Ninth [Eleventh] Regiment, whose names I have not been able to remember. Captains Canaday and White and their officers, Lieutenant Scanlan, of the ordnance, and Sergeants Cameron and Bruggermann, have also done well. Indeed, where all were heroes, with very few exceptions, it is the voice of our country only which is strong enough to proclaim their "well done."

The entire force in the works consisted of 220 men, as detailed by my special alarm regulations, and these had to resist an overpowering array of seventeen war vessels, with nearly 400 guns of the best and heaviest caliber. All the guns, as is usual in sand batteries, worked hard, adding much to the labor of the men, who had already worked hard and enjoyed little or no rest for several days preceding. I had great reason to be grateful to Captain Read's regulars for their brave and valuable aid.

Under the circumstances of our retreat nothing whatever could be saved by the men. They had been working at the guns in most cases in shirt sleeves; the sand had covered their knapsacks and muskets, sometimes two or three feet deep, and very few arms were therefore brought off and very few knapsacks and clothing saved. They are entirely destitute, and should be cared for by the State. The officers have also lost all, in some cases even their swords. The Confederate flag was rent into so many shreds that no piece could be found. The Palmetto flag, however, has been brought home, decorated with many a token of the enemy's wrath.

The battle of Port Royal, it is true, has been lost, but the enemy, I sincerely believe, have paid very dear for their success, and we may console ourselves with the conviction that we have not only done our duty manfully under the most terrific circumstances, but that we have for five hours defended a position against the most scientific and bravest seamen which one of our best generals and engineers had pronounced untenable.

I am, sir, most respectfully, your obedient servant,

JOHN A. WAGENER,

Colonel First Artillery, S. C. M., late Comdt. Fort Walker.

Capt. H. E. YOUNG, *Assistant Adjutant-General.*

No. 4.

Report of Col. William C. Heyward, Eleventh South Carolina Infantry, of the bombardment of Fort Walker.

HDQRS. NINTH REGIMENT S. C. VOLS.,*
THIRD MIL. DIST., DEPT. SOUTH CAROLINA,
Camp Lee, November 16, 1861.

SIR: On the morning of Thursday, the 7th November, I was placed in command of Fort Walker, Col. J. A. Wagener and Maj. A. M. Huger

* This organization is borne on the Confederate registers as the Eleventh Regiment.

having the immediate command of the batteries, assisted by Captain Yates and Maj. John Barnwell. The enemy opened fire upon us about 9 a. m., which was briskly returned by us until many of our guns were either disabled by them or rendered useless by various accidents. The two rifled guns failed, in consequence of it being found impossible to force down the shells, after two or three discharges. The 10-inch gun at the fourth or fifth discharge was rendered useless. Two of the 42-pounders were also rendered useless.

About 2 p. m., finding the fire of our batteries had nearly ceased, I inquired of Major Huger where Colonel Wagener was. He informed me that the colonel had been stunned by the bursting of a shell, and that he (Major Huger) was then in command of the battery. On consulting with him it was determined that Mr. L. Cheves and myself (Mr. Cheves acting as aide to General Drayton) should proceed to the magazine and inquire into the state of the ammunition. On reaching the door we were met by Lieutenant Scanlan, who reported that there were about ten or eleven rounds for 32-pounders left. On returning and reporting this to Major Huger it was decided that, as we could fight no longer with any hope of success, one or two guns should still be served slowly until all the wounded could be removed, and then to evacuate the fort. This was fortunately accomplished with but little additional loss, and the retreat to Buckingham Ferry commenced.

For particulars respecting the officers and men of my own regiment on duty in the fort I refer you to the reports of Capt. Josiah Bedon and Capt. D. S. Canaday. The list of killed and wounded has already been sent in by my adjutant. Colonel Wagener's report, I presume, will furnish all the necessary information respecting his regiment. I regret that my report should be so short, but without a room for myself, with very little convenience for writing, constant applications for leave of absence, noise and confusion about me, I find it impossible to write more.

Yours, respectfully,

WM. C. HEYWARD,
Colonel Ninth Regiment South Carolina Volunteers.

Capt. H. E. YOUNG,
Assistant Adjutant-General.

Captain Bedon and Lieuts. J. E. Heape, J. J. Guerard, and W. A. Boyle behaved with distinguished bravery during the whole action. Mr. Joseph A. Huger and Mr. Hugh Rose, aides to General Drayton, rendered great assistance and displayed great coolness.

No. 5.

Report of Col. W. D. De Saussure, Fifteenth South Carolina Infantry, of the bombardment of Fort Walker.

CAMP LEE, *November* 17, 1861.

SIR: In compliance with instructions from the general commanding, I beg leave to make the following report of casualties in the Fifteenth Regiment South Carolina Volunteers at the battle of Fort Walker, on Hilton Head Island, on the 7th of November, 1861.*

*Nominal list, omitted, shows 2 officers (Lieuts. Z. E. Suggart and James Norris) killed, and 2 officers and 12 enlisted men wounded, but see statement of casualties on p. 12.

As the command was all day under the eye of the general I deem it unnecessary to report its operations during the engagement, but cannot close without bringing to the notice of the general commanding that Col. Randolph Spaulding, of Georgia, attached himself to Company B of this regiment, and fought throughout the day as a private in the ranks.

Respectfully submitted.

W. D. DE SAUSSURE,
Colonel Fifteenth Regiment South Carolina Volunteers.

Capt. H. E. YOUNG,
Assistant Adjutant-General.

No. 6.

Report of Maj. Francis D. Lee, South Carolina Engineers.

NEW RIVER BRIDGE, *December* 4, 1861.

SIR: In obedience to instructions I have the honor of submitting the following report of the defenses of Hilton Head up to the time of the bombardment of Fort Walker, November 7, 1861:

As Chief of Engineers S. C. A., I received instructions during the month of May, 1861, from General Beauregard, then commanding provisional forces in South Carolina, to carry into execution the defensive works on this coast. The general location of these defenses, together with the number and character of guns to be employed, was designated by General Beauregard, and the immediate necessity of the early completion of the proposed works was urged upon those in authority.

In the month of June I received an appropriation of $15,000, and with this limited means at my disposal commenced the works at Port Royal, Captain Gregorie, S. C. A., being charged with the construction of Fort Beauregard at Bay Point. Shortly after the commencement of this work Maj. J. H. Trapier, C. S. Engineers, having been charged with the engineering work in this State, and by order of the governor having transferred to Major Trapier the corps then under my command, I was instructed to proceed to Hilton Head and carry into execution the defensive work at that point.

I immediately on the receipt of this order organized a party of artisans, and leaving Charleston July 1, 1861, reached Hilton Head on the 3d of the same month. The labor necessary for the conduct of the work was to be immediately furnished by the planters of the vicinity, but owing to some delays in the issuing of the order no laboring force was put at my disposal for three weeks after my arrival at Hilton Head.

In the mean time I designed and laid out the proposed work, a sketch* of which accompanies this report. The armament of the water front, as ordered by General Beauregard, consisted of seven 10-inch columbiads, and my plans were arranged for such a battery. The interior slopes of the water battery were consequently intended for seven circular traverses against enfilading fire. The labor having arrived, the work was rapidly pressed forward, and by September 1, 1861, was ready to receive its armament. In place of receiving seven 10-inch guns, but one could be procured, together with one 10-inch columbiad, model bored to a 32-pounder and rifled; one 8-inch columbiad, model bored to a 24-pounder and rifled; one 8-inch columbiad; nine navy 32-pounders; three navy

---

* To appear in Atlas.

42-pounders; three navy 8-inch howitzers; two 24-pounders; two 42-pounder carronades, and two long English 12-pounders. Thirteen of these, viz, one 10-inch columbiad; one 10-inch columbiad, pattern bored to a 32-pounder and rifled; one 8-inch columbiad, pattern bored to a 24-pounder and rifled; one 8-inch columbiad; six navy 32 pounders, and three navy 42-pounders, being in all 13 guns, were ordered to be placed on the water front.

This involved the necessity of subdividing the spaces allotted to the guns in this battery, and consequently placing them in such near proximity as effectually to prevent the construction of traverses against enfilading fire. The salient of the bastions of the fort on the land side, and also of the demi-lune, were arranged for circular traverses, some of which were sent me; but, the necessary chassis and carriages never having arrived, I was forced to make use of two spare carriages, viz, one low navy carriage—to suit which an embrasure had to be cut through the salient of the demi-lune on the eve of the engagement—and one barbette carriage, the latter of which was placed in the salient of the south bastion, but with a limited traverse segment.

Two 8-inch navy howitzers were mounted on these carriages. The third 8-inch howitzer, intended for the salient of the north bastion, was never mounted, no carriage having arrived for it. Besides these, one navy 32-pounder was mounted on the exterior angle of each bastion, and one long English 12-pounder, *en embrasure*, was placed in the shoulders, to enfilade the curtain face of the work. One of these last was afterwards removed for beach defense. Besides the 8-inch howitzer two 24-pounders, *en barbette*, were mounted in the demi-lune.

For beach defense two heavy shell guns were designated to occupy the two exterior flanking works, which commanded the beach approaches on both sides, and to give a cross-fire on the front of the glacis, or, more properly, cover face to the water front of the works. In place of these, two light carronades arrived a short time before the bombardment, but without carriages or chassis. They were therefore simply buried in the sand to such depth and with such directions as to enable us to have at least one fire in the event of an attempt to storm the work. In addition to these the 12-pounder from the north bastion was placed in such position as to sweep the beach by the approach from the south. The ditches on the water front not being protected by bastions, I arranged caponieres, constructed of palmetto logs, pierced for two tiers of musketry, approached by galleries leading under the parapets from the interior of the fort. These completed the ditch defenses, and enabled us, in the event of the enemy attempting to cross the ditch at any point, to pour in a cross-fire of canister and ball. As a protection to the land batteries of the fort I constructed a heavy traverse longitudinally to the work, and to insure against casualties from shot and shell bursting in the parade I arranged small traverses in rear of each gun of the water battery, sufficiently low, however, as to offer no obstacle to the passage of such shell as might graze the parapet of the water front.

It was my purpose to construct a splinter-roof over the entire place of arms between the principal traverse and the curtain of the work, and had ordered all the necessary material for that purpose. My requisitions for a steamer to transport the same some 30 miles were, however, not complied with, and I was enabled to cover in only about one-third of the proper space, and then by bringing ranging timber by hand nearly 2 miles, and by working day and night.

The magazine of the work was large and complete, and so protected that, though an enormous amount of shot and shell was fired against it, it remained at the close of the action as strong and secure as before the fight. No permanent hot-shot furnace was constructed, but a portion of the material for one which had been ordered arrived a few days before the action, and from it a temporary one was constructed on Tuesday, November 5. This work was well and rapidly executed by my artisans while under the fire of the enemy, and I feel it my duty to call to your attention the cool bravery of Mr. Patterson and the artisans under him in executing my orders under the most trying circumstances. Besides the above-mentioned temporary furnace a portable one had arrived some time before the bombardment, but of exceedingly limited capacity. In connection with the fort it was proper to construct a line of infantry works about 2 miles to the south, and also a battery at the outlet of Skull Creek into Broad River; but, for reasons over which I had no control, these works were never carried into execution.

Such was the condition of the defenses at Hilton Head on the morning of November 7, 1861. As an offensive work, Fort Walker proved itself unequal to the immense force brought against it. As a defensive work, it accomplished its purpose by so well protecting the lives of the garrison that after sustaining an incessant fire of shot and shell for nearly five hours but 10 of the garrison were reported killed. This number would, I believe, have been materially lessened had the traverses on the water front been practicable.

At the close of the engagement the fort had received but little damage, although hundreds of shot and shell were buried in the parapets and traverses.

I have the honor to be, very respectfully, your obedient servant,

FRANCIS D. LEE,
Major, Engineers, S. C. A.

Capt. H. E. YOUNG,
Assistant Adjutant-General, Hardeeville.

No. 7.

Report of Capt. Josiah Bedon, Eleventh South Carolina Infantry, of the bombardment of Fort Walker.

CAMP LEE, *November* 12, 1861.

SIR: The following is respectfully submitted as a report of the part taken in the defense of Fort Walker, on the 7th instant, by Company C, of this regiment:

The company was posted in the battery at 7.30 o'clock a. m. Five guns were assigned the company—one rifled 24-pounder, under my immediate charge; three 42-pounders, under charge of Lieuts. J. E. Heape, J. J. Guerard, and W. A. Boyle, respectively; one 32-pounder in left bastion of the fort. The rifled gun and the three 42-pounders were on the left front of the fort.

Early in the engagement, which commenced about 9.30 o'clock a. m., the rifled gun and one of the 42s became disabled. Late in the action another 42-pounder became disabled. The remaining 42 and one 32 pounder were served until the ammunition failed. About 2.30 o'clock p. m. we were ordered to evacuate the fort. My company retired in good order, bearing with them their arms.

Two men were slightly wounded, Privates G. Munroe and T. Hudson, and 3 taken prisoners, who were sick in hospital.

I beg leave respectfully to call your attention to the gallant conduct of Lieutenant Heape, who had charge of a 42-pounder until disabled and afterwards took charge of a 32-pounder in the left bastion of the fort, as also that of Lieutenants Guerard and Boyle. The sergeants who were chiefs of pieces acted with great coolness and bravery.

Very respectfully, your obedient servant,

JOSIAH BEDON,
Captain Company C, Ninth [*Eleventh*] *Regiment S. C. Vols.*

Lieut. E. W. FRASER,
Adjutant Ninth [*Eleventh*] *Regiment S. C. Volunteers.*

No. 8.

Report of Capt. D. S. Canaday, Eleventh South Carolina Infantry, of the bombardment of Fort Walker.

HDQRS. NINTH [ELEVENTH] REGIMENT S. C. VOLS.,
Camp Lee, November 12, 1861.

SIR: The following is respectfully submitted as a report of the part taken in the defense of Fort Walker on the 7th instant by detachments from Companies F and H, of this regiment, under my command:

There were six guns under my charge—one 32-pounder on the right flank of the fort, two in the right bastion of the fort, one a 32-pounder and the other a 24-pounder. The remaining three were in the redan, two 24-pounders and one 32-pounder howitzer. Lieuts. F. B. Appleby and T. E. Raysor, of Company H, were in charge of the guns in bastion and redan, and acted with coolness and bravery. But two of the guns could be used in the action, as the others could only be used in land defense. One 32-pounder was disabled by solid shot early in the engagement. The other 32-pounder was served until ammunition gave out.

The officers and men acted with bravery and coolness. One private in Company F (Burnett) was killed; Corporal O. Quin and Privates I. Martin and William Hudson slightly wounded. In Company H were wounded in the arm Corporal E. T. Howell, and slightly in the thigh Private P. Heaton. The remainder of my company and of Company H were acting as infantry outside the fort. Missing from my company (H) Private J. Judah, and from Company F Privates James Bryant and James Colson.

We were ordered to evacuate the fort about 2.30 o'clock p. m., and the detachment retreated in good order, carrying with them their arms, except those which were shot to pieces by the enemy's fire.

Very respectfully, your obedient servant,

D. S. CANADAY,
Captain Company H.

Lieut. E. W. FRASER,
Adjutant Ninth [*Eleventh*] *Regiment S. C. Volunteers.*

No. 9.

Statement of Capt. C. D. Owens, Assistant Commissary of Subsistence, C. S. Army.

OFFICE A. C. S., THIRD MIL. DIST., DEPT. S. C.,
Camp Lee, November 23, 1861.

SIR: On the morning of the 7th November I received, through Maj. E. Willis, quartermaster, your orders to report to you at Fort Walker, and accordingly left Beaufort at 5 o'clock a. m.; arrived at Fort Walker, Hilton Head, and reported to you at 8 o'clock p. m. On the receipt of your orders to proceed to Charleston with steamer Emma for supplies I made the necessary arrangements to do so, and started in a yawl-boat for the steamer Edisto, in order to be transferred to the Emma, then engaged in landing troops at Bay Point. The steamers were compelled by the fire of the enemy to take refuge in Skull Creek, and the steamer Emma I afterwards learned continued on to Savannah. Our boat, in consequence, was compelled to return to the island, and I found it impossible, for that day at least, to carry out your instructions. Since that time you are aware of all that has transpired in my department. In reference to the stores left at Beaufort I would beg leave to call your attention to the report of my chief clerk, Mr. Baya, a copy of which I inclose.* I feel satisfied that Mr. Baya made every exertion in his power to have the stores removed to a place of safety, and his failure to do so was from causes entirely beyond his control.

I am, sir, very respectfully, your most obedient servant,

C. D. OWENS,
Captain, P. A., and A. C. S.

Brig. Gen. THOMAS F. DRAYTON.

No. 10.

Report of Mr. H. T. Baya, Clerk in Confederate Subsistence Department.

HARDEEVILLE, S. C., *November* 23, 1861.

SIR: In accordance with your instructions I left Beaufort on Wednesday morning, in the steamer General Clinch, with provisions, to be landed at Hilton Head and Bay Point. On our way down, having met the steamer John A. Moore, with a portion of the Fifteenth Regiment on board, bound for Hilton Head, and unable to continue the passage owing to the severity of the wind, we took the troops off of her on board the steamer General Clinch, and proceeded to Seabrook's Landing, on Hilton Head Island, and landed them. The provisions for that post were also safely landed there. Capt. S. Simmons, the commissary of the post, to whom the provisions were marked, not being at the landing, I sent the invoices to him under care of Capt. E. I. Dawson, quartermaster of the Ninth [Eleventh] Regiment South Carolina Volunteers. At the landing in question I met Capt. C. Tracy, of General Drayton's staff, to whose attention I called the landing of the provisions. At about 9 p. m. we started on our mission to Bay Point, and laid quietly at anchor about 3 miles from the fort until about daylight the following morning (November 7), when we steamed up to quite near the fort (the usual place of landing,) and began landing provisions for the point in two lighters. Capt. A. E. Rabb, the commissary of the post, being absent, I sent a messenger to him asking his presence. He soon came down to the point of landing, when I informed him of the object of my mission, and handed him your letter containing invoices. He desired me to hurry with the landing, and he would sign receipts for the goods as soon as he could check off the invoices.

In the midst of the landing the fleet of the enemy's vessels, which were then at anchor near the bar, appeared to be in motion, and soon after came in and began the fight. On their approach we stopped the landing of provisions, hoisted anchor, and stood towards Beaufort, where we arrived at about 1 p. m. I there found the people under intense excitement, the mass of whom were making preparations to go to some place of safety on the main-land, they fully believing that the enemy

---

* See No. 10, following.

would take possession of the town that night. After considerable anxious thought I concluded it would be best to have what stores we had in Beaufort on board of the steamer General Clinch, but in making inquiry as to whether she would take them, I found that the steamer was almost filled with the various and voluminous properties of the citizens, who were eagerly taking advantage of any and every method to get their things away; and, again, the supply of wood was very short; so much so, that the captain of the boat had to knock down the whole line of fence extending from the wharf to the street, that he might take and use it for fire-wood. He did not wish to overload the boat, as it would make it more difficult for him to reach Charleston, almost overloaded as he then was, and thus, there being no other mode of moving them, they had to remain as they were.

At about 8 p. m. I packed up all of our papers and had them taken on board of the steamer General Clinch, but soon took them off and had them carried to the quartermaster's quarters, determining to remain until the last moment. We had already heard that our troops were retreating, and had been advised by many (who appeared to be conversant with the geography of the country) that we had better send any of our valuable articles over on the main-land. We still held on until advised by both Captain Pope and Captain Elliott to go. We packed two carts with both the quartermaster's and commissary's papers, and I, in company with Mr. Caldwell, of the quartermaster's department, started in charge of the papers for Pocotaligo. While crossing the town three rockets were fired and the alarm bell was rung to announce the approach of the enemy. This was about 12 o'clock, and the alarm was so great that the few remaining in the town immediately left, leaving the place quite deserted. On the road out we were passed by several, who informed us that the enemy were making their way up Broad River to cut off communication by Port Royal Ferry to the main-land; but this, like other reports, proved false. We arrived at Pocotaligo about 9.30 or 10 o'clock on Friday morning, and remained until Saturday morning, when Mr. Tuomey, of the quartermaster's department, and myself started with a mule and cart for Beaufort, with the determination to get away any of the public property that we could, and if we were unable to do so to fire it.

Arriving at the ferry, our mule being unfit to take us to Beaufort, we endeavored to procure horses, but were unable to do so, and thus returned to Pocotaligo, where I remained until Sunday afternoon, when, General Ripley offering his special train for our accommodation, with mules, carts, and papers we arrived at Hardeeville, and on Monday, the 11th, reported in person, with papers, to you.

I am, sir, very respectfully, your obedient servant,

H. T. BAYA.

Capt. C. D. OWENS,
P. A. and A. C. S., Hardeeville, S. C.

No. 11.

Report of Col. R. G. M. Dunovant, Twelfth South Carolina Infantry, of the bombardment of Fort Beauregard.

HEADQUARTERS TWELFTH REGIMENT S. C. VOLS.,
Camp Lee, Pocotaligo, November 16, 1861.

SIR: On the 26th of October last I assumed command of the forces stationed on Bay Point Island, consisting of three companies of the

Ninth [Eleventh] Regiment, to wit: The Beaufort Artillery, Capt. Stephen Elliott; Colleton Rifles, Captain Anderson, and Captain [J. J.] Harrison's company of infantry; six companies of the Twelfth Regiment South Carolina Volunteers, to wit, Company A, Captain [W. H.] McCorkle; Company C, Captain [H. C.] Davis; Company D, Captain [E. F.] Bookter; Company E, Captain Hinson; Company F, Captain [Hayne] McMeekin, and Company I, Captain [N. B.] Valandingham, and a small detachment of Captain Screven's company of Beaufort Guerillas, under Lieutenant Youmans. My staff consisted of Lieut. W. H. Talley, adjutant; Dr. E. B. Turnipseed, surgeon; Capt. T. I. Bell, quartermaster; Capt. E. A. Rabb, commissary; Rev. C. B. Betts, chaplain, and Mr. Robert Chisolm, volunteer on staff. The entire force on the island, inclusive of field, staff, and company officers, was 619. Lieutenant-Colonel Barnes, of the Twelfth Regiment, was placed in command of the six companies of that regiment and Captain Anderson's company, then at the Narrows. Captain Elliott was assigned to the command of the work known as Fort Beauregard with his own company and Captain Harrison's. The detachment of Captain Screven's company was ordered to report directly to me.

Monday, the 4th instant, the enemy's fleet made its appearance early in the morning, and crossing the bar came to anchor to the south of and opposite the island, but made no further demonstration of an attack on our position during that day.

In the afternoon Commodore Tatnall, with three small steamers, attacked the nearest of the enemy's vessels, and after sustaining a heavy fire and replying most gallantly, retired slowly up the river.

Tuesday morning, in view of the uncertainty of the point and mode of attack, the following disposition was made of the companies of the Twelfth Regiment: Companies A and D were posted in rear of a range of sand hills, distant about 200 yards from Fort Beauregard, for the purpose of protecting that work in case of an attempt of the enemy to land; Companies C and E took position near Captain Anderson's company at the Narrows, and Companies F and I were held at the camp of the regiment, being about equidistant between the detachments, so as to support either.

Between 7 and 8 o'clock Commodore Tatnall's steamers again advanced and engaged the enemy, who met the attack in such numbers and with such weight of metal that the little steamers were compelled again to retreat above the forts. The enemy followed, firing upon the steamers till within range of our guns, when Fort Beauregard joined in the conflict, and drew a heavy fire of shot and shell, principally the latter, upon that work and the other portions of the island occupied by our troops. This engagement lasted nearly two hours, when the enemy's fleet withdrew and assumed very nearly its former position opposite our island, which it retained for the remainder of the day.

The only casualties on our part were those stated in Captain Elliott's report, herewith transmitted, as resulting from the explosion of a caisson.

The unfavorable state of the weather prevented any further action of the enemy on Wednesday. Thursday morning, however, the wind lulled, and the water was unusually smooth. Of this the enemy availed himself, and at 8.30 a. m. the fleet of war vessels, headed by what is supposed to have been the Minnesota, bore towards the northwest, till, reaching the main channel, they moved directly towards our batteries. As soon as they came within range Fort Beauregard opened upon the vessel in advance, which, being seconded by Fort Walker and replied to by the enemy, the action became general. About the time of the first movement of the fleet it having been reported to me that barges filled with troops were leaving the transports, which still occupied their position opposite the camp, in anticipation of an attempt to effect a landing in that vicinity, I ordered Companies C and E, which had been withdrawn on Wednesday, back to a point near the earthwork at the Narrows, retaining at the camp the four remaining companies of the Twelfth Regiment. After, however, having made a careful personal observation of the movements of the enemy, and in view of their steady advance and heavy fire upon the western end of the island, I changed the arrangement of the force, throwing the four companies at the camp in the rear of the sand hills before referred to near Fort Beauregard, and withdrew within supporting distance the two companies of the Twelfth at the Narrows. Thus the troops remained for several hours under a heavy fire of shot and shell, during which they exhibited great coolness and promptness in obedience to orders. Nothwithstanding the protection afforded by the sand hills many shot and shell fell around them, but fortunately without inflicting injury of any kind. The batteries at Fort Beauregard were worked with great gallantry, skill, and energy, and the highest praise is due to Captain Elliott and his command for the manner in which they discharged their important trust.

About 2 p. m. the fire of the enemy upon our batteries was slackened and redoubled against Hilton Head. A little after 3 o'clock it was reported to me by Adjutant Talley that a boat was leaving one of the fleet for the shore of Hilton Head amid loud cheers from the former and that Fort Walker was silent. I at once proceeded to Fort Beauregard, and, after the colloquies accurately detailed by Captain Elliott in his report, ordered him to make arrangements for retreat from the fort towards the Narrows.

I then returned and issued the necessary orders for the evacuation of the island, and the force moved in good order towards the eastern portion of the island. The only line of retreat lay across the strip of land known as the Narrows, scarce 50 yards wide and 1,000 long, to the main body of Eddings' Island, which itself is but an extensive swamp, entirely impenetrable save by a trail known to few, and of such extreme difficulty as to preclude the possibility of transporting baggage of any kind beyond what could be borne on the shoulders of the men. Of the character of the route and the consequent impracticability of transportation I had been fully advised, and therefore did not undertake the removal of camp equipage, stores, or heavy baggage. Nor did I think it prudent to destroy such property by fire, inasmuch as the retreat was at best of doubtful feasibility, and the nature of the movement would have been thereby revealed to the enemy, and its success still further jeoparded, if not entirely frustrated.

I believe that in consequence of the manner in which the evacuation of the island was effected it was unknown to the enemy until it had been fully accomplished, and this conviction is strengthened by their failure to take advantage of the entire command of Station Creek and Beaufort River to cut off the retreat at Jenkins' Landing, and especially at White Hall Ferry. The body of the command reached the landing at Station Creek and crossed to Dr. Jenkins' plantation during the night, and after resting a short time at the latter place resumed the march for Beaufort, where it arrived early Friday morning. The town was deserted by the white population, and no representative of the quartermaster's or commissary's departments, or other person in authority, could be found. I was therefore under the necessity of assuming the responsibility of taking for the use of the troops such provisions and necessaries as their condition imperatively demanded, and had I known the amount and nature of the stores might have saved much public property, which has probably fallen into the hands of the enemy. I proceeded with the command to Port Royal Ferry, and thence to this place, regarding the latter as an important point of defense, and at the same time one from which I could readily open communication to procure the necessary supplies for my command. In consequence of the intricacy and difficulty of the line of retreat, some officers and men, detained by their duties, lost their way, but all these have since rejoined their respective companies. There is but one man whom I am under the necessity of reporting as missing. As to the particulars of this case I refer you to the accompanying report of the efficient surgeon of the Twelfth Regiment, herewith submitted. Some muskets were left, but only those which had been drawn for enlisted men, who were at the time absent by reason of the severe epidemic which had thinned our ranks during the previous month.

No soldier threw away his arms. In regard to the manner in which the retreat was arranged and effected, justice to myself and others requires that I should add a word of explanation. Having received no instructions as to the mode in which the island of Bay Point should be defended, nor of the contingencies upon which it should be abandoned, with no arrangement for receiving orders, by means of signals or otherwise, from headquarters, and totally without information of any plan devised or facilities provided for the retreat of my command in case of disaster, I felt that these circumstances imposed upon me the obligation of endeavoring to secure some means of evacuating the island in the event such a step should become necessary, Accordingly, the state of facts above referred to continuing, on Tuesday I went in person to Captain Elliott, who perhaps was more familiar with the localities than any other person, and after learning from him, in answer to my inquiries, that a retreat was practicable through Eddings' Island, if boats and flats could be secured to take the forces across Station Creek, I instructed him to select some prudent and trusty person to superintend the collection of the necessary means of transportation at the landing on Edding's Island. The Rev. Stephen Elliott was chosen to discharge this important duty, and left on Thursday morning for that purpose. Fortunately Capt. Thomas Hanckel, Mr. Henry Stuart, and Mr. W. H. Cuthbert, of Beaufort, had already secured a large number of flats at Dr. Jenkins' Landing, for the purpose of taking them to some point on Eddings' Island for our relief. Mr. Elliott informed them of the plan agreed upon, and thus, through the co-operation of these gentlemen and the valuable assistance of Captain Tripp and his command, the evacuation of the island was effected. I communicated the plan of retreat to none save Captain Elliott, the adjutant, and the quartermaster.

Lieutenant-Colonel Barnes, commanding the greater portion of the infantry, was prompt and energetic in executing the orders for the movements of his immediate command. From the nature of the attack the forces at Fort Beauregard were the only active participants in the engagement, and I cannot close this report without drawing special attention to the high qualities of the officer exhibited by Captain Elliott, commanding that work. Compelled from the necessities of our position to act the part of engineer, ordnance officer, and commander of the fort, he exhibited an energy and intelligence in preparing the batteries for the fight which were only equaled by the gallantry and firmness of the defense.

All the members of my staff did their duty. Adjutant Talley, Captain Bell, quartermaster, and Rev. C. B. Betts, the chaplain, frequently sent with orders to various parts of the island during the bombardment, executed their trust in a manner entirely satisfactory to me.

Lieutenant Youmans and his detachment were efficient in the performance of the part assigned them. To Lieutenant Johnson, of the Beaufort Artillery, the command is under obligations for valuable services rendered at the ferry across Station Creek, and to Capt. Thomas R. Elliott for similar aid in passing White Hall Ferry.

The reports of Captain Elliott and Surgeon Turnipseed* are herewith respectfully submitted.

Very respectfully, your obedient servant,

R. G. M. DUNOVANT,
Colonel Twelfth Regiment South Carolina Volunteers.

Capt. H. E. YOUNG,
Assistant Adjutant-General.

No. 12.

Report of Capt. Stephen Elliott, jr., Beaufort Artillery, of the bombardment of Fort Beauregard.

HEADQUARTERS BEAUFORT VOLUNTEER ARTILLERY,
November 13, 1861.

SIR: Having been assigned to the command of Fort Beauregard by Colonel Dunovant, commanding the post, I beg leave to submit the following report:

The garrison consisted of Beaufort Volunteer Artillery (Company A, 83 men) and Captain Harrison's company (Company D, 66 men), both of Colonel Heyward's Ninth [Eleventh] Regiment South Carolina Volunteers. To the former was intrusted the main work (thirteen guns); to the latter the hot-shot battery (three guns) and the sand battery (two guns).

On Monday, the 4th instant, the enemy appeared and anchored within the bar 4 miles below the fort. On Tuesday morning, at 7.30 o'clock, five gunboats came within range and opened upon us with heavy guns, throwing spherical and rifle shell with accuracy. One of these struck a caisson, causing it to explode, and thereby injuring slightly one of the gun detachments. I replied, but found the range too great for successful firing, and at 9.15 o'clock a. m. the enemy withdrew, having been struck several times. On Wednesday, the weather being boisterous, the enemy remained quiet.

On Thursday, pursuant to an order previously received from Colonel Dunovant, I dispatched the chaplain of the Ninth [Eleventh] Regiment to Saint Helena, for the purpose of providing transportation in case it should be necessary and prove practicable to retire. At 8.30 a. m. fifteen of the enemy's sail formed in line and steamed up the harbor, engaging us at 9.15 o'clock. These were subsequently joined by four others. Having passed the batteries, they turned to the left and southwards, and repassed near the Hilton Head shore. This circuit was performed three times, after which they remained out of reach of any except our heaviest guns. The last gun from my battery was fired at 3.35 p. m., being the eighth to which the enemy had not replied. A few moments

---

*The surgeon's report not found.

afterwards Colonel Dunovant entered the fort and said to me, "Captain Elliott, what is the condition of things over the river?" I replied, "Fort Walker has been silenced, sir." "By what do you judge?" "By the facts that the fort has been subjected to a heavy enfilade and direct fire, to which it has ceased to reply; that, the vessels having terminated their fire, the flag-ship has steamed up and delivered a single shot, which was unanswered, and that thereupon cheering was heard from the fleet." "Then, sir, it having been proved that these works cannot accomplish the end for which they were designed—that of protecting the harbor—you will prepare to retire from a position from which our retreat may readily be cut off, and which our small force will not enable us to hold against a land attack." I then prepared my command for a retreat, destroyed the greater part of the powder, spiked the guns, and an hour later took up the line of march for Eddings' Island.

Our fire was remitted during those intervals when passing down on the farther side of the river, as the ships were too distant. This cessation afforded a respite to the cannoneers, already fatigued by labors properly belonging to the Engineer and Ordnance Departments. At all other times it was kept up with shot and shell. One of the columbiads was fired 57 times; the other not quite so often. The position of the hot-shot guns in the main battery was such that, when unmasked, the ships were too far distant to be reached by any elevation the guns were susceptible of. They were therefore used but sparingly, but hot shot were fired from two 42-pounders on the front face. The flag-ship was supposed to be on fire more than once.

Our fire was directed almost exclusively at the larger vessels. They were seen to be struck repeatedly, but the great distance—never less than 2,500 yards—prevented our ascertaining the extent of injury. The wooden fuses for the 8-inch shell were very defective, generally igniting the charge a few seconds too soon. The paper fuses were more reliable. It had been found during the engagemant on Tuesday that the rifle shell could not without much difficulty be forced down after one or two discharges. They had therefore in the interim been refitted. The gun, however, exploded at the thirty-second discharge, slightly wounding every man of the detachment. No other cause can be assigned except that the gun, after being fired several times in rapid succession, was loaded and allowed to remain. As it became cool it may have contracted upon the shell, and hence the explosion.

The hot-shot battery, manned by Captain Harrison's company, fired a few rounds, but the great severity of the cannonade in an exposed position drove the men from the guns. Some of his men afterward assisted me in the main work, among whom Sergeant Edenfield deserves to be mentioned with praise. The Beaufort Artillery behaved with coolness under a heavy fire, as is attested by the fact that no accident attributable to carelessness occurred at their guns. Instances of conspicuous bravery might be mentioned, but it would be unfair to eulogize a few when the majority did their duty.

Previous to the engagement the members of this corps contributed each according to his talent to the efficiency of the whole, but especially zealous and untiring were Privates S. E. Scanlan and I. E. Falbin in preparing ammunition and placing the battery in order. In this connection I must mention with honor Captain Harrison's company, who for months before cheerfully gave me their assistance. I must also thank the companies of Colonel Dunovant's command, who labored to make my position more secure. Honor is due to Midshipmen Maffit and Read, who with coolness and courage gave me valuable aid whenever it was required.

The following is a list of the wounded of the Beaufort Artillery: Capt. S. Elliott, in the leg, by a fragment of rifled gun; Sergt. B. W. Sloman, in the hand, by the same; Privates Fripp, Hamilton, Wilcox, Perryclear, and Joyce, by same; Sergeant Stuart, by recoil of columbiad; Private M. W. Fripp, by the same; Privates William Elliott and F. M. Murdaugh, by explosion of caisson—all slightly. Of Captain Harrison's company, Privates T. and I. E. Crews lost each an arm by the premature discharge of a gun.

I am, sir, with respect, your obedient servant,

STEPHEN ELLIOTT, JR.,
Captain of Beaufort Artillery.

First Lieut. WILLIAM H. TALLEY,
Adjutant of Twelfth Regiment.

No. 13.

Statement of Messrs. John Tuomey and Henry C. Robertson, of occurrences at Beaufort, S. C., November 7 and 8, 1861.

QUARTERMASTER'S OFFICE PROVISIONAL FORCES,
THIRD MILITARY DISTRICT, DEPT. S. C.,
Camp Lee, November 24, 1861.

About 4 o'clock on the morning of the 7th instant Capt. Joseph A. Huger arrived at our quarters in Beaufort, S. C., with instructions from Brigadier-General Drayton to Maj. E. Willis, quartermaster Third Military District, Department of South Carolina. Major Willis, with Captain Huger, left Beaufort about 5 o'clock a. m. in steamer Emma for Fort Walker, Hilton Head. Twelve o'clock noon same day written orders were received from Brigadier-General Drayton to Major Willis, authorizing the purchase of 2,000 feet of lumber to repair Skull Creek Bridge; also a gang of carpenters, and to send to Fort Walker, Hilton Head, immediately, six barrels of powder, then in the arsenal in Beaufort.

Major Willis having been ordered to report at Hilton Head, the orders were opened, the lumber purchased from Mr. Cockroft, carpenters engaged, and powder shipped all ready to start, when the Confederate steamers Huntress, Captain Morris, and Lady Davis, Captain Rutledge, left, after setting fire to the two light-ships about three miles below Beaufort. The enemy were then reported to be in possession of Broad River and Port Royal Harbor, all communication cut off, and our troops were retreating to the main-land, having abandoned the batteries at Hilton Head and Bay Point. The powder was immediately taken out of the steamer and taken charge of by Mr. Robert Chisolm and Mr. McKee, of Beaufort, who kindly had it taken to a place of safety from the enemy. It is now at Mr. Heyward's plantation, near Pocotaligo. The carpenters were dismissed and sent to Charleston; the raft of lumber left in Beaufort. Then, with the assistance and advice of Capt. Thomas M. Hanckel, of Brigadier-General Ripley's staff, and Capt. Carlos Tracy and Capt. Thomas R. S. Elliott, of Brigadier-General Drayton's staff, the two steamers, Beauregard and Mary Frances, ordered by Captain Willey, of Savannah, Ga., were dispatched forthwith to White Hall Ferry (Ladies Island) with flats to bring over the troops then retreating from Bay Point, consisting of a portion of Col. R. G. M. Dunovant's command (Twelfth Regiment South Carolina Volunteers) and Beaufort Artillery, Capt. S. Elliott.

The most intense excitement prevailed in Beaufort amongst some of the citizens. They threw up rockets about 11.30 or 12 o'clock at night, as to indicate the approach of the enemy. We immediately packed up all the papers and books we could get and sent them in charge of Mr. Caldwell to Pocotaligo, Mr. H. C. Robertson and the undersigned awaiting the arrival of the troops from Bay Point, whom we furnished transportation for.

On the morning of 8th instant, about 4 o'clock, a report was then in circulation that communication was cut off at Port Royal Ferry. Feeling anxious for the safety of what books and papers we had saved, as they were important, we left Beaufort about 4 o'clock a. m. on foot for about three and a half miles.

Previous to our leaving Beaufort we had all the sick men in the hospital cared for, about 16, who were kindly treated by Capt. C. M. Morris, of steamer Huntress, and taken to Charleston. The medicines and brandy left in Beaufort for Drs. Johnson and Prioleau were taken charge of by Col. R. G. M. Dunovant, as he gave me to understand.

I am, very respectfully,

JOHN TUOMEY.

Capt. H. E. YOUNG,
Assistant Adjutant-General.

I certify that the above is a correct statement of things that transpired at Beaufort, S. C.

HENRY C. ROBERTSON.

NOVEMBER 8, 1861.—Reconnaissance on Hilton Head Island, S. C.

Report of Capt. Q. A. Gillmore, U. S. Corps of Engineers.

OFFICE OF CHIEF ENGINEER E. C.,
Hilton Head, S. C., November 8, 1861.

SIR: In obedience to your directions of this date to proceed on a reconnaissance of Hilton Head Island, or so much thereof as I could examine, returning to headquarters on the same day, I have to report a completion of the day's operations under the escort promised to me, to wit, the Seventh Connecticut Regiment, 900 strong, Colonel Terry commanding.

The regiment was placed at my disposal at 11 o'clock a. m., when I at once set out upon the reconnaissance, the principal object of which was to proceed across the island to Seabrook, on Skull Creek, a distance of 6 miles, by the nearest practicable route, and locate suitable positions for batteries to control the inland water communications by way of Skull Creek between Savannah and Charleston.

As no advance had been made from our position on Hilton Head since we came in possession yesterday evening, and as nothing certain was known of the position and movements of the enemy since he was driven from the work, I deemed it proper to exercise great caution against surprise, and accordingly requested Colonel Terry to cover the advance of the main body of escort by skirmishers. Over a very considerable portion of the route we took to Seabrook Point—the one running through the woods beyond General Drayton's plantation, as distinguished from the one near the shore—skirmishers could not be deployed, as both sides of the road are lined by an impenetrable jungle. Our progress was necessarily quite slow. We reached Seabrook Landing about 2 o'clock p. m.

without encountering any of the enemy or any white person whatever. From what I can gather from negroes, there are no rebel troops on any of the northern portions of Hilton Head Island.

About 300 of them, with some wounded, passed over the road last night about the time we were disembarking. They were under the influence of a terrible panic; knapsacks, haversacks, canteens, cartridge-boxes, &c., were found scattered over the road and on the wharf at Seabrook, where the hasty embarkation took place. We also found at the landing a number of rifled muskets and bayonets. There is near the wharf, some in store and some outside, a considerable quantity, say fifteen or eighteen large wagon loads, of valuable commissary supplies, such as bacon, hard bread, sugar, rice, corn, vinegar, &c. We brought back two wagon loads of these articles, which Colonel Terry will account for. Had my orders admitted of it I would have remained at Seabrook with half the escort until boats could have been dispatched from headquarters under convoy to bring off the commissary stores. At Seabrook an excellent position for a battery, elevated some 12 or 15 feet above the level of the river, to sweep and control the Skull Creek channel, has been selected. The river at that point is about one-fourth of a mile inside, and is skirted on the farther side by a marsh, which enlarges the distance between the firm ground on the opposite shore to half a mile or a little more.

I caused soundings to be taken across the stream at half tide, finding two fathoms at the end of Seabrook wharf, three fathoms a short distance out, and a good 5-fathom anchorage in the middle of the stream.

A battery of five or six heavy guns at Seabrook would be quite sufficient to close this inland water passage between Charleston and Savannah, but to secure it against a *coup de main* I would recommend an inclosed work of strong relief and of sufficient capacity for 1,000 men, with guns on the gorge and with suitable flanking arrangements, should be commenced immediately. It should mount fifteen guns, at least, of all calibers. The route over which I passed is practicable for heavy artillery and heavy transportation generally, but materials can best be taken to Seabrook by water. The wharf there requires some repairs.

On my return I increased the guard at General Drayton's plantation at the request of the officer in charge there. I found no public property or papers at General Drayton's, with the exception of two letters already in your possession.

There is no post-office at Seabrook. I have to acknowledge the cordial and efficient co-operation of Colonel Terry in carrying out the objects of the reconnaissance.

Very respectfully, your obedient servant,

Q. A. GILLMORE,
Captain of Engineers, Chief Engineer E. C.

Brigadier-General WRIGHT,
Commanding Forces on Hilton Head, S. C.

NOVEMBER 10–11, 1861.—Expedition from Hilton Head to Braddock's Point, S. C.

Report of Capt. Q. A. Gillmore, U. S. Corps of Engineers.

U. S. ENGINEER OFFICE,
Hilton Head, S. C., November 12, 1861.

SIR: I have the honor to report that I accompanied Brigadier-General Wright on a night expedition to Braddock's Point, leaving Hilton

Head on the evening of the 10th instant and returning on the afternoon of the following day. We reached Lawton's plantation about midnight, where our escort, composed of five companies of the Seventh Connecticut Volunteers, Colonel Terry commanding, was halted until 4 o'clock in the morning. By the road Lawton's place is nearly 4 miles from Braddock's Point. At 4 o'clock the march was resumed, and the column reached the point where the road strikes the beach just at the break of day, where another halt was ordered. When it became light enough to reconnoiter a single company was sent forward for that purpose. The report soon came back that the place appeared to be abandoned, when General Wright and staff went forward.

A battery of one 24-pounder gun, old pattern, was found behind an irregular parapet. It was on a siege carriage. A battery of one 10-inch columbiad, on a new wrought-iron carriage and a good wooden platform with iron traverse circle, was found. The parapet at this point is of considerable length (263 feet), and contains within it a good magazine and some little ammunition. A well-constructed parapet, containing two 24-pounder guns, old pattern, was found. It contained a good magazine. Some few rounds of balls, grape and canister, were scattered on the beach outside the parapet, apparently left behind in the haste of embarkation or for the want of the means of transportation. Near this battery is a good garrison sling-cart, and all the finished parts of wooden columbiad platform, full circle. Three ordinary "A" tents were left standing, which were probably all that the garrison had, as extensive preparations existed for protecting troops from the inclemency of the weather by means of poles erected on the ground and covered with branches of trees.

Braddock's Point cannot be held by us without a considerable force (except by the active co-operation of the fleet), so as to enable us to control the Calibogue Sound. To hold it with this end in view the point should be occupied in force, and strong guards stationed at the point where the cross-road at Lawton's and the one above it debouch upon the eastern shore.

Very respectfully, your obedient servant,

Q. A GILLMORE,
Captain and Chief Engineer.

Brig. Gen. THOMAS W. SHERMAN,
Commanding Division, Hilton Head, S. C.

NOVEMBER 24, 1861.—Occupation of Tybee Island by the Union forces.

Report of General Robert E. Lee, C. S. Army.

HEADQUARTERS, *Savannah, November* 29, 1861.

SIR: On Sunday last, 24th instant, the enemy crossed Savannah Bar with five of his vessels, and made a lodgment on Tybee Island. Subsequently three other vessels joined them, and the force on Tybee Island was re-enforced. Five vessels, one of them a frigate, said to be the Sabine, now lay inside of the bar north of Tybee Island. They are 3 or 4 miles from Fort Pulaski, within range of whose guns they have not yet approached. The force on Tybee Island is reported to be large, but I am unable to state it. No demonstration of their purpose has yet been made further than the occupation of the island.

The preparation and arrangement of Fort Pulaski ordered on my first arrival have progressed slowly, but I do not think the passage of the river can be forced. Fort Jackson is now armed, and its defenses have been strengthened, and forms an interior barrier. The channel of the river has also been blocked up.

The force in the Savannah River is believed to be part of that from Port Royal Harbor.

I have the honor to be, your obedient servant,

R. E. LEE,
General, Commanding.

Hon. J. P. BENJAMIN,
Secretary of War, Richmond, Va.

DECEMBER 6-7, 1861.—Expedition to Port Royal Ferry and Beaufort, S. C.

Reports of Col. William E. Martin, C. S. Army, with preliminary correspondence.

HEADQUARTERS MOUNTED REGIMENT,
Pocotaligo, November 25, 1861.

Capt. T. A. WASHINGTON,
Aide-de-Camp, Coosawhatchie, S. C.:

CAPTAIN: I have the honor of inclosing copies of the following papers:

A. General Ripley's order, date November 16.
B. Memorandum by myself.
C. Reports to General Ripley, November 19.
D. Letter to F. H. Harleston, aide-de-camp, November 22.
E. Extract from a letter of General Ripley, November 24.

I hope you will pardon the trouble of asking your attention to these papers. I am embarrassed about the duty devolved upon me, because I do not know whether my coadjutor, Captain Pope, appointed to the command jointly with myself, has abandoned the project; and whether he has or has not, I am at a loss to know whether General Lee would approve the execution of the only order practicable for cavalry—the operations on Port Royal Island and separate movement. If the matter had been confided to me solely I would have attempted that portion of it before this time. I feel bound to wait for the co-operation of Captain Pope a reasonable time. My doubts are whether I have a right to wait any longer. These doubts it is my anxious desire to have resolved by an expression of opinion from headquarters, and it is to solicit your assistance in obtaining it that I venture to invite your kind assistance.

In the exercise of the discretion with which I am intrusted I would not now ask advice if the matter were not complicated by the joint operation contemplated and now apparently impracticable. I am anxious to gratify the public expectation for action on Port Royal Island immediately. I think the objects of the expedition can be attained in safety as far as that island is concerned, and I would be gratified by permission to proceed in its execution. May I beg the favor of you, therefore, under the circumstances, to favor me with advice from General Lee, if you think it proper to request it.

I have the honor to be, captain, very respectfully, your obedient servant,

WM. E. MARTIN,
Colonel Mounted Regiment.

[Inclosure A.]

HEADQUARTERS PROVISIONAL FORCES, DEPT. S. C.,
Tulafinny, November 16, 1861.

Col. WILLIAM E. MARTIN,
Commanding Mounted Regiment:

COLONEL: You will proceed as quickly as possible to organize four or more parties, to be composed of volunteers from your command and such citizens as you can induce to give their services to the country, to proceed, in such manner as you may determine upon and direct, into that section of country which is now in possession of the enemy, to take such steps as may be fit and proper for the removal and escape of citizens of South Carolina or their slaves, and for the protection of the material property which may be in the vicinity, and to prevent its falling into the hands of the enemy. Should it be necessary, you are authorized to destroy all cotton which is in that district of country, to prevent its being made use of by the enemy, but where the owner of the property is present let him be consulted. On no account, however, let it fall into the hands of the enemy if your force can prevent it. Much discretion must be left to you in carrying out these orders, but first secure all property, next prevent the enemy from getting possession of cotton.

I am, very respectfully, your obedient servant,

R. S. RIPLEY,
Brigadier-General, Commanding.

P. S.—Should you be unable from any circumstance to carry out this order in full, carry it out as far as possible.

[Indorsement.]

I have seen the within order and approve of it. I suggested it to General Lee, because I consider the property now in possession of the enemy and because its destruction weakens the enemy.

F. W. PICKENS.

[Inclosure B.]

NOVEMBER 16, 1861.

On the next day I was shown by Captain Pope orders from General Ripley assigning the captain to the command of two or more parties in the expedition, and directing the movements to be made in conjunction with and simultaneous with mine.

[WM. E. MARTIN,
Colonel Mounted Regiment.]

[Inclosure C.]

CAMP MARTIN, NEAR POCOTALIGO, S. C.,
November 19, 1861.

Brigadier-General RIPLEY, *Charleston, S. C.:*

GENERAL: Referring to your orders for penetrating into the islands held by the enemy, I have the honor to report that, in consequence of Captain Pope's intimate knowledge of the topography of these islands and the navigation for reaching them and his capabilities as an officer, I intrusted to him the details of the plan for reaching Saint Helena, while I determined, in conjunction with Major Oswald, to take charge of a strong column of cavalry for operations on Port Royal Island. Your orders directed the duties to be performed by volunteers from my command and such citizens as could be induced to give their aid. On my return to camp, after an absence of twenty-eight hours (my visit to the city being partly to see my sick family and partly to make arrangements for the expedition), I found the first impediment in the way by the discovery of the whole plan being known and openly talked about among the planters; indeed, in several instances, under my own observation, they spoke of it in promiscuous assemblages as if it were an ordinary topic of conversation. Fearing the information would reach the enemy, I determined to act promptly. Captain Pope undertook to confer with the island planters and ascertain how many of them could be induced to co-operate with us. Here we have both experienced a great disappointment, as we have scarcely met with a man who was willing to lend his aid and the knowledge of navigation essential to the enterprise. The water transportation to Saint Helena would be in boats and flats by oars, occupying, under the most favorable circumstances of weather and tide, fully two hours. If cavalry were to be transported the flats would take horses with their riders, and I was unwilling, with my knowledge of the difficulty and danger of transporting cavalry in open water and in flats without aprons, to risk any horses and men but those belonging to Captain Tripp's company, in which the troopers and horses are accustomed to such mode of transportation. I regret to be obliged to inform you that with two or three exceptions this company refused to volunteer. Having no infantry, I was thus left to the volunteers from my command. I have purposely avoided calling on them until the expedition was ripe for execution, but I have no doubt of being able to get the requisite number. As it was deemed expedient by you and Captain Pope, and I fully concurred in the opinion, that the movement should be simultaneous, I have not deemed it advisable to make the descent upon Port Royal until the remaining portion of the expedition was ready, especially as that island is still and is likely to continue accessible to us, the enemy not being in sight of it and not having drawn cotton and provisions from it up to this time. I have been obliged to make this full narration to inform you fully of the causes which have led to a suspension of our proceedings for the present.

This will be handed to you by Captain Pope, who will explain matters more fully. In the mean time I hope the circumstances will justify in your estimation the suspension we deem necessary. As soon as we are prepared to be successful we will use every exertion to carry out your orders in their spirit and letter.

I have the honor to be, general, yours, most respectfully,

WM. E. MARTIN,
Colonel Mounted Regiment.

[Inclosure D.]

CAMP NEAR POCOTALIGO, *November* 22, 1861.

Capt. F. H. HARLESTON,
Aide-de-Camp, Charleston, S. C.:

CAPTAIN: On the 19th instant I submitted to General Ripley a detailed report of the causes which retarded the execution of his order of [the] 16th, relative to an expedition to the islands in possession of the enemy. In that report I stated that Captain Pope, who was assigned to the command of one or more parties by General Ripley, had gone to headquarters to confer with the general relative to the further prosecution of the scheme, and I gave my reasons for awaiting the issue of their conference. I refer you to the communication for a full explanation.

I have heard nothing since from Captain Pope, and I do not know whether he is still prosecuting his plans or has returned to his command at Stono, nor where to address him. I feel very anxious to discharge the obligation imposed upon me by the order, and I am at a loss whether I should wait longer upon Captain Pope. Under these circumstances may I ask the favor of you to mention the subject to the general, and to confer with Captain Pope, if he is in Charleston, and ask him to let me have his views or inform me whether he has gone to Stono? I am disposed to execute the scheme as to Port Royal Island and without waiting longer, and I would be most happy to be relieved from the suspense at present.

I have the honor to be, very respectfully, your obedient servant,

WM. E. MARTIN,
Colonel Mounted Regiment.

[Inclosure E.]

[Extract from a letter from General Ripley in reply.]

NOVEMBER 24, 1861.

* * * * * * *

As regards the execution of the order relative to operations on Port Royal you are to use your own discretion.

* * * * * * *

—

HEADQUARTERS MOUNTED REGIMENT,
Pocotaligo, S. C., December 5, 1861—3 p. m.

GENERAL: I wrote to Captain Elliott yesterday that you desired his presence with mine at your headquarters to know the details of the expedition to Port Royal Island. I have just learned that after the receipt of the letter Captain Elliott went over with 25 men and has partly executed his mission, and had not returned when last heard from. I send this by a special messenger, to inquire if you will approve of my starting immediately with a detachment of 30 or 40 men to support Captain Elliott and complete the work. If you will favor me with a reply by telegraph it will expedite my departure.

I have the honor to be, general, very respectfully, your obedient servant,

WM. E. MARTIN,
Colonel Mounted Regiment.

Major-General LEE, *Coosawhatchie, S. C.*

—

HEADQUARTERS MOUNTED REGIMENT,
Pocotaligo, S. C., December 9, 1861.

GENERAL: At 9 p. m., 5th instant, I received a telegram from you, authorizing me to proceed to Port Royal Island to complete the burning of the cotton commenced by Capt. Stephen Elliott. As it was advisable to cross the ferry about dark, I started next day at 12 m., sent forward scouts to Beaufort to report to me at the ferry. They did so, and the information from the town was brought (down to sundown) that there was no enemy on the island.

At 6 p. m. I crossed the ferry with 10 men, under a lieutenant, with two guides—Capt. O. Barnwell and Dr. Hasell—leaving the remainder of the detachment of about 50 men to follow me, under the command of Major Oswald, of my regiment. It was my intention to enter the town and meet Major Oswald 2 miles this side and commence the burning back towards the ferry. I had provided an additional mode of egress from the island in case of pursuit by crossing with flats to Page's Point, on the main-land. In this I was aided by Captain Maffit, Colonel Jones, and Major Sams. I will mention for your information, in passing, that 11 men can be crossed at the regular ferry with their horses in fifteen minutes with the flat in use.

I proceeded until within three-quarters of a mile from Beaufort. When at the distance of about thirty yards we received the fire of about thirty muskets, as I suppose, of the enemy. The order to halt from the enemy, with oaths and curses, was followed up instantly by their discharge. I am obliged, with much pain, to say that the whole detachment and the guides retreated instantly, with the exception of one man. I saw but one discharge from our retreating party, and that seemed to be in the air. The exception to which I refer was a private [of] Captain Bostick's company, the Allendale Mounted Guard. At the discharge his horse dashed forward and he checked him about ten paces in advance of me. He then fired one barrel of his gun and snapped the other three times. I then heard him complaining of the retreat of our detachment, adding, "Their guns (the pickets') are all discharged, and we could have captured them all if the men had not run away." As he is one of my soldiers I must do him the justice of mentioning his name, although he is my son—Private Vincent F. Martin. The retreat of the detachment was so nearly simultaneous with the flashing of the guns, that the men informed me that they did not hear my orders to them to halt, which I gave, intending to form an advance. I recalled Private Martin after one or two minutes, and we rode down the way our men had retreated to the distance of seventy-five yards, or thereabouts, and, one of us on either side of the road, we listened for half an hour for sounds in both directions. We heard no sounds except the discharge of sixty or seventy guns in the town or outskirts about half an hour after the firing on us.

I then rode on with the soldier above mentioned in a walk all the way to the ferry in momentary expectation of meeting first the advance guard and then the main body, but was disappointed, and when I reached the ferry the whole detachment was on the opposite side.

Major Oswald, in his report, informs me of the following:

About 5 miles from the ferry we met one of the advance detachment at full speed crying out, "The colonel is killed," and he rushed on past the men. The major ordered his column to advance to revenge their colonel, but they did not move. Others came at the same speed from the direction of Beaufort, also stating the death of the colonel and that there was a wounded man behind. Major Oswald then again ordered his men to advance to succor this wounded man. This man came up immediately, but did not halt from his speed, although ordered to do so by Major Oswald. He turned out to be Capt. O. Barnwell, who was wounded in the arm—a flesh wound—badly. With him all Major Oswald's detachment, except about 20, retreated. The officers collected around Major Oswald, and he inquired if they were willing to go on, but met with no encouragement. He then called for volunteers, but received but one, Private Edward Bostick, of the Allendale Mounted Guard, who replied he would follow him to the death to revenge the colonel. Major Oswald then, finding he could accomplish nothing, ordered a retreat, which he conducted in good order, crossing the ferry, where I ascertained they were.

Major Oswald's conduct was all I knew it would be in a brave and judicious officer. He mentions in his report that Capt. W. G. Green, of the Salkehatchie Guerrillas, was cool and collected, and was willing to advance, but that in his (the captain's) judgment it was not advisable.

I did not recross the ferry, but remained on the other side with Private Martin, and ordered them to recross. This they did at 12 midnight with the utmost alacrity, cheering me with the utmost enthusiasm. From this moment I am spared the pain of recording anything more to their discredit. I conducted the column to a plantation on the road to Beaufort, and bivouacked until daylight about 2 miles from the ferry.

Early in the morning I moved the column to within 4 miles of Beaufort, when I called for volunteers to go into the town. I wanted but 8, but nearly all the detachment volunteered. I ought to have added that at the ferry, my guides having left me, I sent over for volunteers to Captain Barnwell's and Captain Smith's Company, but received only one—a Mr. Givens. The detachment of volunteers passed round the head of Saltwater Creek to within 2 miles of Beaufort, and within the lines of the enemy's pickets, and exchanged shots with them. They were commanded by Captain Smart, of the Allendale Mounted Guard, an officer whose conduct has won my respect by the manner in which he discharged the duty assigned to him. Privates Edward Bostick, V. F. Martin, B. T. Lawton, J. E. Bailey, and J. A. Owens, of his company; Sergt. Maj. Marion Green, and Charles Jones and Shepherd, of Green's company, and the guide, J. C. Givens, above named, constituted his party.

Mr. Givens' and Mr. Shepherd's services as guides were meritorious and valuable to me until I left the island.

On the return of my pickets from the enemy's lines I divided the column into two detachments, and taking charge of one, and assigning the other to Major Oswald, we proceeded respectively to the waters around the island where the plantations lie and burned all the cotton, except where the quantity was too inconsiderable to destroy the building or where the owners were engaged in removing it. I have reason to suppose but little cotton remains on the island. Where the cotton was in the dwelling-houses, or its destruction involved the loss of valuable buildings, it was thrown out and rendered valueless.

The two detachments united at a rendezvous near the ferry, and crossed at 10 p. m. on [the] 7th instant, the men having been almost incessantly in the saddle for thirty-four hours, with but two meals, which they carried in their haversacks.

I have no casualties to men or horses in my command to report, and, regretting the necessity of so lengthy a communication, I have the honor to be, general, very respectfully, your obedient servant,

WM. E. MARTIN,
Colonel Mounted Regiment.

Major-General LEE, *Coosawhatchie, S. C.*

P. S.—I omitted to state, on my arrival within half a mile of the ferry, on my way to cross over from this side, I concealed my men in a dense thicket and allowed no negroes to pass; that when I bivouacked on the plantation beyond the ferry I guarded every negro house and the country around, and that at all times, after the pickets fired on us, I took every negro who was passing into custody, and that all opportunity of conveying intelligence of our movements was cut off.

DECEMBER 17, 1861.—Evacuation of Rockville, S. C., by Confederate forces.

REPORTS.

No. 1.—Brig. Gen. R. S. Ripley, C. S. Army.
No. 2.—Col. J. L. Branch, Rifle Regiment.
No. 3.—Capt. T. G. Budd, quartermaster Rifle Regiment.

No. 1.

Report of Brig. Gen. R. S. Ripley, C. S. Army.

HEADQUARTERS SECOND DISTRICT SOUTH CAROLINA,
Charleston, S. C., December 30, 1861.

CAPTAIN: I have the honor to inclose herewith the report of Colonel Branch and accompanying papers [Nos. 2 and 3] relating to [the] retreat from Rockville. I also inclose copy of the orders given to Colonel Branch from these headquarters when he occupied John's Island. I should have forwarded these papers earlier, but that I deemed, considering the organization of the troops, that a report on the subject could not very materially benefit the service.

I am, very respectfully, your obedient servant,

R. S. RIPLEY,
Brigadier-General, Commanding.

Capt. T. A. WASHINGTON,
Assistant Adjutant-General, Coosawhatchie, S. C.

[Inclosure.]

SPECIAL ORDERS, No. 217. } HDQRS. PROV. FORCES, SEC'D MIL. DIST.,
Charleston, S. C., November 25, 1861.

I. Colonel Branch's regiment of rifles, South Carolina militia, will take post on John's and Wadmalaw Islands as soon as possible. One battalion of the regiment will land at John's Island Ferry, and leaving one company at that point in charge of the ferry and boats, which will accompany the command, will proceed to the interior of the island. The other battalion, with the headquarters, will proceed to Rockville, and take post in observation at that point.

II. The regiment will move with as little baggage as possible, and on no account will the strict regulation allowance of transportation be exceeded.

III. The different commands and detachments will be kept in light marching order, and move from point to point, as may be directed by the colonel or commanding officer, the object being to familiarize the officers and troops with the locality, as well as to give protection to the inhabitants.

IV. Colonel Branch is authorized to employ such guides as may be necessary, and if possible, until cavalry can be furnished him, to mount a small force of his command to keep up his communications.

V. The regiment will take fifteen days' rations of small stores, but the principal part of the subsistence will be purchased in the vicinity.

VI. After having made a thorough reconnaissance of the island, Colonel Branch will report to these headquarters upon the strength of the position and the disposition of his command. He will meantime keep himself in communication with the post near Church Flats, and be ready, if necessary, to support it by any means in his power.

* * * * * * *

By order of Brigadier-General Ripley:

F. H. HARLESTON,
Aide-de-Camp.

No. 2.

Report of Col. John L. Branch, Rifle Regiment.

HEADQUARTERS REGIMENT OF RIFLES,
Camp Evans, December 22, 1861.

CAPTAIN: I have the honor to submit the following statement of facts and reasons which governed me in the removal of this command from its late encampment near Rockville:

On Tuesday, the 17th instant, about 4.30 p. m., it was reported to me that four of the enemy's vessels had crossed the bar or were in sight, and firing shells. I at once prepared to make observations for myself, and saw the vessels, one considerably in advance of the others, coming up the Edisto River. I ordered the regimental line to be formed without knapsacks and marched out of camp, supposing that a fire of shells would at once be opened upon it. This was not done, however, and the advanced steamer continued up the river, while the others stopped near the entrance of the Bohicket Creek (about one and a half miles from Rockville) into the Edisto.

On this river and the several bold creeks connected therewith are many places where troops could be landed, and by a forced march to our rear gain possession of the only two bridges (Church and Bugby) connecting Wadmalaw with John's Island, and thereby cut off my entire command, 292 rifles. Having no means of ascertaining whether or not such would be the action of the enemy—five of my mounted officers being absent—I ordered the regiment to fall back to this point as a better position for defense. It is needless to say that had no demonstration been made to cut us off from John's Island, no retreat, save beyond the range of [the] enemy's shells, would have been ordered, unless a very heavy force had been landed at Rockville.

The commissary's report will show the losses sustained in his department, and the report of the quartermaster, whose activity and energy in the duties of his office deserve the highest commendation, will set forth the condition of the transportation and account in some measure for those losses.

I have the honor to be, with great respect, your obedient servant,

JOHN L. BRANCH,
Colonel Regiment of Rifles.

LEO. D. WALKER,
Assistant Adjutant-General, Department of South Carolina.

No. 3.

Report of Capt. T. G. Budd, Quartermaster Rifle Regiment.

HEADQUARTERS RIFLE REGIMENT,
Camp Evans, S. C., December 23, 1861.

DEAR SIR: I beg leave to report in as concise form as possible the circumstances interesting my department at the retreat from the vicinity of Rockville on the evening of the 17th instant:

You will bear in mind the lapse of time from the first alarm to the appearance of four of the enemy's ships did not exceed twenty minutes. At the first intimation of an attack I had the teams promptly harnessed. The ammunition wagon first moved off, next followed the surgeon's wagon with medical stores. Two wagons were sent to the commissary store-house and loaded with the most valuable and necessary provisions. One spring cart was loaded with various articles out of my store-rooms, and the four remaining wagons, with the other spring cart, were loaded with knapsacks and blankets, in accordance with your orders. On these wagons were placed other articles of a private character, in opposition to my express orders to the contrary, as it was impossible to supervise in person the loading of each. All the wagons were then taken in charge by the regiment and retreated to Bogle Place, about four and a half miles distant. The first three of them unloaded were returned to camp and again dispatched with tents. Two other wagons returned and were also dispatched with tents and commissary stores.

At this period our scouts reported the enemy as having landed on the wharf at Rockville, and you instructed me to turn back the other wagons, which were returning to camp for the purpose of saving the remainder. At my request Quartermaster-Sergeant Green visited a neighboring plantation for the purpose of obtaining additional transportation. He secured one team, on which was placed the property of the field and staff, or so much of it as was saved.

You are aware of the repeated applications I have made to the brigade quartermaster for transportation sufficient to move the regiment, and the loss realized by the retreat was due to the small capacity and limited number of wagons I could control. The commissary stores lost, consisting of about thirteen days' rations of grist, sugar, and bread, were too bulky for rapid movement, owing to the size of the packages (hogsheads and tierces), even had I the necessary wagons.

I will also call your attention to the anxiety I had expressed to you that large wall-tents should be furnished for the storing of commissary and quartermaster's stores. These had been refused at headquarters after my repeated applications for them, and after my having brought to the notice of the brigade quartermaster (with a request that he would read my remarks at headquarters) that if they were not sent my responsibility for the loss occasioned by having the stores in advance of the regiment ceased. Great delay was occasioned by the inferiority of the team harness, as they continually broke, and also from many of the mules given me in exchange for the horses which had been taken for artillery service in the city, [which] were wild and unbroken. Eight of them would not draw or lead, and on the retreat broke loose from the wagons to which they were hitched; 2 have since been recovered and 6 are still in the woods.

I am satisfied that had the proper transportation been furnished, together with other appliances actually necessary to the regiment, all the quartermaster's and commissary stores, as well as other property, would have been saved. You are well aware I have often complained to you of the want of those articles essential to the perfect organization of my department, and the difficulty I experienced in getting my orders filled or a response to my applications.

My assistants, Quartermaster-Sergeant Green and Private Adam, rendered good service in making the loss light as posssible under the adverse circumstances attending the retreat, and I feel indebted to each of them for their active co-operation.

In conclusion, I may add the loss realized is much less than at first anticipated.

I am, dear sir, your respectful and obedient servant,

T. G. BUDD,
Quartermaster First Regiment Rifles.

Col. JOHN L. BRANCH, *Commanding.*

DECEMBER 17, 1861.—Skirmish on Chisolm's Island, S. C.

Report of Brig. Gen. Isaac I. Stevens, U. S. Army.

HEADQUARTERS DISTRICT OF PORT ROYAL,
Beaufort, S. C., December 18, 1861.

SIR: In pursuance of my directions Lieutenant Porter, Eighth Michigan Regiment, took a party last evening across the Coosaw River, and surprised a picket on Chisolm's Island. I found an intelligent negro as guide. The party started at 9.30 o'clock, crossed the Coosaw, got in the rear of the picket, attacked it, and took the whole party of 6 prisoners. Two were wounded. They belonged to the Fourteenth Regiment South Carolina Volunteers, Colonel [James] Jones commanding, and their names are J. P. Longford, L. M. Longford, B. Mathis, John Mates, M. W. Jennings (wounded), and Corporal J. Y. Longford (wounded).

I have not been able to elicit much information from them. They state, however, that theirs is the only regiment stationed at Garden's Corner, and that there are no pieces of artillery there. They have been in the Confederate service about four months; have received no pay. They stated that the common people had been led into the war by the leaders; that they volunteered to prevent being drafted. They (the prisoners) believe the whole difficulty grows out of a misunderstanding. Their leaders, however, were very determined.

I am, sir, very respectfully, your obedient servant,

ISAAC I. STEVENS,
Brigadier General, Commanding.

Capt. L. H. PELOUZE,
Assistant Adjutant-General, Port Royal, S. C.

DECEMBER 20, 1861.—Sinking of the Stone Fleet at the entrance to Charleston Harbor, S. C.

REPORTS.

No. 1.

Report of General Robert E. Lee, C. S. Army.

HEADQUARTERS, COOSAWHATCHIE, S. C.,
December 20, 1861.

SIR: It has been reported to me by General Ripley that the enemy brought his stone fleet to the entrance of Charleston Harbor to-day, and sunk between thirteen and seventeen vessels in the main ship channel. The North Channel and Maffit's Channel are still open. This achievement, so unworthy any nation, is the abortive expression of the malice and revenge of a people which it wishes to perpetuate by rendering more memorable a day hateful in their calendar. It is also indicative of their despair of ever capturing a city they design to ruin, for they can never expect to possess what they labor so hard to reduce to a condition not to be enjoyed. I think, therefore, it is certain that an attack on the city of Charleston is not contemplated, and we must endeavor to be prepared against assaults elsewhere on the Southern coast.

I have the honor to be, your obedient servant,

R. E. LEE,
General, Commanding.

Hon. J. P. BENJAMIN,
Secretary of War, Richmond, Va.

No. 2.

Report of Maj. Thomas M. Wagner, S. C. Artillery.

FORT SUMTER, CHARLESTON HARBOR,
February 12, 1862.

SIR: In obedience to instructions, I have the honor to submit the following report of the sinking of the stone fleet at the entrance of Charleston Harbor:

On the afternoon of December 18 a large increase to the blockading squadron was observed. The majority of vessels appeared to be old whaling and trading vessels. On the 19th, the weather being bad, not much progress was made in their preparations for sinking. A few of the vessels were stripped. By dawn on the morning of the 20th great activity was observed; fifteen vessels were placed in line more or less direct across the main ship channel, about 4 miles south-southeast of Fort Sumter and 3 miles east-southeast of the light on Morris Island. By evening all had been stripped, dismasted, and sunk. From the observations made the vessels appeared to have been placed in a single irregular line, with intervals of 100 feet, making a distance of about 3,500 feet in extent from shoal to shoal, and completely occupying the channel. The vessels commenced to settle immediately, and at the end of a week but little was to be seen of any of their hulls. They have now entirely disappeared. Large portions of the wrecks have from time to time come ashore. The position of the blockading squadron has, however, prevented any accurate survey being made.

On January 20 another fleet came to anchor off the port. They took up their position in a line extending from the entrance of the north channel southwardly to the main ship channel. The vessels were mostly of a smaller class than those of December. They were fourteen in number—barks and brigs. They were stripped and towed northwardly to their positions, which was on the south edge of the shoal known as the Rattle Snake, and opposite the entrance of the Maffit Channel, with the exception of one vessel, which was placed on the eastern edge of the shoal about two and a half miles east of the other vessels and between the Shoal and the Long Island Beach.

The line extended from north to south, and, by measurement, six miles and a half east-northeast of Fort Sumter. The place has been carefully noted on the chart of the harbor at Fort Sumter. The first four vessels to the north of the line were sunk on the western end of the Rattle Snake in shoal water, the balance in 4 or 5 fathoms water, and in the track of vessels entering Charleston Harbor by Maffit's Channel.

The operations on both occasions were superintended by six armed steamers and a sailing frigate.

I have the honor to be, very respectfully, your obedient servant,

THOMAS M. WAGNER,
Major, S. C. Artillery, Commanding Fort Sumter.

Capt. LEO. D. WALKER,
Assistant Adjutant-General.

JANUARY 1, 1862.—Engagement at Port Royal Ferry, Coosaw River, S. C.

REPORTS, ETC.

No. 1.—Brig. Gen. Thomas W. Sherman, U. S. Army, with congratulatory orders.
No. 2.—Brig. Gen. Isaac I. Stevens, U. S. Army.
No. 3.—Col. William M. Fenton, Eighth Michigan Infantry.
No. 4.—Lieut. Col. James L. Fraser, Forty-seventh New York Infantry.
No. 5.—Col. James H. Perry, Forty-eighth New York Infantry.
No. 6.—Maj. David Morrison, Seventy-ninth New York Infantry.
No. 7.—Lieut. William St. George Elliott, Seventy-ninth New York Infantry.
No. 8.—Col. B. C. Christ, Fiftieth Pennsylvania Infantry.
No. 9.—Lieut. Col. Thomas S. Brenholts, Fiftieth Pennsylvania Infantry.
No. 10.—Col. Daniel Leasure, One hundredth Pennsylvania Infantry.
No. 11.—Lieut. William S. Cogswell, Fifth Connecticut Infantry, Signal Office.
No. 12.—Lieut. Henry S. Tafft, Fifteenth Massachusetts Infantry, Signal Office.
No. 13.—Letter from Maj. Albert J. Myer, Signal Officer, U. S. Army.
No. 14.—Return of casualties in Union forces.
No. 15.—Congratulatory orders from Maj. Gen. George B. McClellan, U. S. Army.
No. 16.—Brig. Gen. John C. Pemberton, C. S. Army.
No. 17.—Brig. Gen. Daniel S. Donelson, C. S. Army.
No. 18.—Col. James Jones, Fourteenth South Carolina Infantry.
No. 19.—Lieut. Col. Dixon Barnes, Twelfth South Carolina Infantry.
No. 20.—Maj. Cadwalader Jones, Twelfth South Carolina Infantry.
No. 21.—Col. William E. Martin, Mounted Regiment.
No. 22.—Return of casualties in Confederate forces.

No. 1.

Reports of Brig. Gen. Thomas W. Sherman, U. S. Army, with congratulatory orders.

HEADQUARTERS EXPEDITIONARY CORPS,
Port Royal, S. C., January 2, 1862.

SIR: As the Vanderbilt leaves to-morrow morning, I deem it proper to inclose to you a letter of instructions to General Stevens, commanding second brigade of this division, of December 30.

The simple object of this dash was to destroy the batteries which the enemy appeared to have erected on the Coosaw River for the obstruction of the navigation and the passage of that stream, and also to punish him for the insult in firing upon the steamer Mayflower on her recent passage through that stream for the purpose of sounding the depth of the channel. The affair succeeded perfectly, and the enemy were driven out of their batteries, the batteries demolished, and property found there brought away or destroyed with little or no loss of life on our side. After the object of the movement was executed General Stevens, agreeably to his instructions, returned to Port Royal Island.* As soon as his report reaches me it will be duly forwarded.

Very respectfully, your obedient servant,

T. W. SHERMAN,
Brigadier-General, Commanding.

General L. THOMAS,
Adjutant-General U. S. A., Washington, D. C.

[Inclosure.]

HEADQUARTERS EXPEDITIONARY CORPS,
Port Royal, S. C., December 30, 1861.

GENERAL: Agreeably to the conversation already had with you, it is designed to cross a force over the Coosaw River on the morning of the 1st, and seize upon the enemy's batteries at the ferry and other points on that river. According to our understanding, you will be able to land from 1,500 to 2,000 men suddenly from the means of transportation at your disposal. These men can probably be landed above the Brick-yard at a convenient place for making a dash at the ferry fort. A small force should also cross at Seabrook at the proper time, or certainly attempt to do so. Commodore DuPont will furnish some gunboats and gun-launches, to be commanded by Capt. C. R. P. Rodgers, U. S. Navy, with whom you must consult and co-operate. Two of these gunboats will probably take up a position near you and above the Brick-yard. The other two will probably enter Whale Branch at the proper time, and advance towards the ferry. The time for crossing the troops above the Brick-yard is prompt daylight, when the gunboats there will be prepared to cover your storming party.

The gunboats at Whale Branch I would recommend to enter the branch as soon as it is sufficiently light to see, and proceed up the stream, and when approaching Seabrook the force you will have at that point should then attempt to cross under their fire and seize upon and destroy whatever may be found there. A sufficient force I recommend to move straight upon the fort from the first-mentioned landing and seize it by storm or escalade, whilst probably a larger force should maintain a covering position on its right, but not so extended as to prevent the fire of the gunboats raking any of the enemy's force coming from Garden's Corner without hitting our own men.

When the fort is fully in possession of our men, and not till then, a signal agreed upon beforehand should make the fact unmistakably known to all the gunboats, when those boats I would recommend, if possible, should speedily close in towards the fort and effectually cover it whilst our men are removing or destroying the guns and other property.

It is unnecessary to say that a corps of pioneers, &c., should be ready to destroy, burn, &c.

The above are only calculated as hints in the management of the affair, but, after all, the success must depend mainly upon the judgment of yourself and able coadjutors, who must necessarily be governed in a great measure by circumstances. It must be understood, however, general, that the object of this dash is simply the destruction of the enemy's

*See also Sherman to McClellan, January 2, 1862, in "Correspondence, etc.," p. 214.

batteries, and no advance must be made beyond what is necessary to effect that object. It is unnecessary to assure you that a deviation from this injunction would at the present time harm us more than the advantage of destroying their batteries.

Very respectfully, your obedient servant,

T. W. SHERMAN,
Brigadier-General, Commanding.

Brigadier-General STEVENS,
Commanding at Beaufort, S. C.

HEADQUARTERS EXPEDITIONARY CORPS,
Port Royal, S. C., January 4, 1862.

SIR: I have the honor to forward herewith the report of Brigadier-General Stevens of the affair at Port Royal Ferry on the 1st instant, and referred to in my communication of the 2d. It having been reported to me that the enemy had erected batteries at Port Royal Ferry and at the landing opposite Seabrook, which report having been confirmed by General Stevens' pickets, and especially by the reports of officers who had long been watching the progress of these works, that seven guns of heavy caliber had been mounted in the former and probably some in the latter, and which seemed to be still more strongly confirmed from the fact of large numbers of the enemy being habitually seen in that vicinity, the object of this movement was to storm these works by a small portion of our troops and bring away or destroy the cannon and other property. Hence my instructions to General Stevens, a copy of which has already been forwarded. In consequence of the presumed nature of the works and their armament, their position relative to the points of landing of the storming parties, I applied to Flag-Officer Du Pont for a few gunboats to assist in the operation, which he cheerfully furnished, and placed under the command of Commander C. R. P. Rodgers.

The idea was to carry the works, of whatever nature they were found to be, by storm. In consequence of the difficulty of maneuvering gunboats in so narrow and tortuous a river as the Coosaw under the fire of forts, these boats, whilst covering the rear of our storming party, were to have remained in reserve until the works at the ferry were in possession of the stormers, and were then to close in from both directions and cover the works from the assaults of the enemy whilst the storming party were carrying off or destroying the artillery and other property.

This plan appears to have been well carried out. Although we were somewhat disappointed in the amount of artillery found in the forts and the state of progress the Confederates had yet made with their batteries, the maneuver will be found from General Stevens' report to have met with complete success, and, still more, to have proved that our inexperienced troops will behave well in critical situations, to which they are very soon to be doubly exposed. The fine co-operation of the naval forces under that able and indefatigable officer Commander C. R. P. Rodgers is deserving of all praise, and I am also happy to have the opportunity to add the important service and the zeal and intelligence of the signal officers connected with the expedition, as stated by General Stevens.

General Stevens, to whom the command of this expedition on the part of the land forces was intrusted, is too well known to the country for his extensive official acquirements, his indomitable zeal and energy, to even attempt enlarging upon them here. The prompt and complete execution of his orders and its clever and happy result are all that need be mentioned.

Very respectfully, your obedient servant,

T. W. SHERMAN,
Brigadier-General, Commanding.

General L. THOMAS,
Adjutant-General U. S. Army, Washington, D. C.

GENERAL ORDERS, No. 1. } HEADQUARTERS E. C.,
Hilton Head, S. C., January 7, 1862.

The general commanding desires to express his gratification at the good conduct exhibited by the troops under command of Brigadier-General Stevens when engaged on the 1st instant in capturing and destroying the enemy's batteries on the Coosaw River.

The conduct of this affair confirms him in the conviction that our troops, when ordered to march ahead, will know no obstacle, and will promptly and in good order penetrate wherever ordered.

The thanks of the commanding general are specially due to Brigadier-General Stevens for the energy and good judgment evinced in the preparation and prosecution of this affair.

To Flag-Officer DuPont, commanding blockading squadron, and to Commander C. R. P. Rodgers, commanding the naval portion of this expedition, and the officers and men under his command, the thanks of the country and the Army are likewise due. The energy, alacrity, and efficiency which supported the land forces on this occasion, though nothing more than what could have been expected from that distinguished branch of the service, will ever be gratefully remembered.

By order of Brig. Gen. T. W. Sherman:

L. H. PELOUZE,
Captain Fifteenth Infantry, Acting Assistant Adjutant-General.

No. 2.

Report of Brig. Gen. Isaac I. Stevens, U. S. Army.

HEADQUARTERS SECOND BRIGADE EXPED'Y CORPS,
Beaufort, S. C., January 3, 1862.

SIR: I have the honor to report, for the information of the commanding general, the complete success of the joint expedition of which the land forces were placed under my command, and the return of the several regiments to their respective encampments. The object of the joint expedition was to seize and destroy the enemy's batteries on the main opposite Port Royal Island, bring away the guns and other property, but not to engage the enemy except in the accomplishment of this object, and not to advance into the interior.

To effect it Commodore DuPont furnished five gunboats, under the command of Capt. C. R. P. Rodgers, U. S. Navy, to operate with the land forces, which consisted of my own brigade and the Forty-seventh and Forty-eight New York Regiments of General Viele's brigade. The plan was for three of the gunboats to operate from Coosaw River and two from Broad River, both entering the Port Royal channel, and moving the former towards the ferry and the latter towards Seabrook. A force was at early dawn to effect a landing at some convenient point on the right, move rapidly towards the fort, whilst simultaneously should operate from the ferry and from Seabrook.

On the 31st instant, leaving two companies of the Roundhead [One hundredth Pennsylvania] Regiment as a guard for the town and depot of Beaufort, and one company at the cross-roads, 3 miles from this place, to relieve the two companies of the Fiftieth Pennsylvania Volunteers there on duty, I advanced the remaining eight companies of the Roundhead Regiment to the advanced posts on the island. I withdrew, at the same time, seven companies of the Seventy-ninth New York (Highlanders) from these advanced posts for the operation on our right. At Seabrook two companies of the Highlanders and two companies of the Roundheads, under Captain Elliott, of the Highlanders, were to cross the river, land on the main, destroy the enemy's works, and bring away his guns and other property. At the ferry one company of Highlanders and four companies of the Roundheads were to observe the enemy and cross over should circumstances favor it. At the point running down from the ferry opposite to the Brick-yard Ransom's two guns of Hamilton's battery were placed to cover the advance of the land party and to act according to circumstances. The entire remaining force, consisting of seven companies of Highlanders, Major Morrison; the Eighth Michigan, Colonel Fenton; Fiftieth Pennsylvania Volunteers, Colonel Christ; the Forty-seventh New York, Lieutenant-Colonel Fraser, and the Forty-eighth New York, Colonel Perry, were destined to form the land party, to operate against the enemy's left.

Ever since my occupation of this island I had taken great pains to collect every boat and flat that could be found, and in consequence had already at Seabrook and the ferry transportation enough to cross the two bodies of troops in position there. These boats I caused to be prepared for their work. I sent up all the boats and flats I had at Beaufort and could find at other points on the nights of the 30th–31st, to a secure and good landing on the creek which flows into the Coosaw at the Brick-yard and well up the creek, so as to be screened from the observation of the enemy, and from this point I designed by one embarkation to cross to the main that portion of the party which belonged to my own brigade.

At 12 m. of the 31st Captain Rodgers, in command of the naval portion of the expedition, arrived with the Ottawa and the Pembina, and towards night was joined by the Hale, the force destined to operate from the Coosaw, and we arranged the details of the joint operation, and especially agreed upon the signals which would enable us to act in concert in engaging the enemy. About dark Colonel Perry, Forty-eighth New York, and Lieutenant-Colonel Fraser, Forty-seventh New York, arrived from Hilton Head. They were ordered to follow the gunboats, effect a landing at the Adams house, and act in co operation with the party which were to cross the river in flat-boats.

It was expected that the landing from the flat-boats would have been made at daylight, and that the gunboats, creeping up the Port Royal channel at night-fall of the 31st to within a short distance of the Brick-yard, and passing through that channel at daylight, would appear in the Coosaw shortly afterwards, and thus aid in the advance of the land forces. These forces were, in crossing the river, to be accompanied by four launches, under the personal command of Captain Rodgers, each launch having a 12-pounder gun, and when the landing was effected they were to move towards the ferry *pari passu* with the advance of the land forces. This plan was in substantial points carried out. Four companies, however, of the Fiftieth Pennsylvania, under the command of Lieutenant-Colonel Brenholts, were moved directly from the town of Beaufort by means of flats collected in that vicinity on the 31st, and the flats collected in the Brick-yard Creek were found insufficient to embark the six companies of the Fiftieth Pennsylvania, which had therefore to wait till the boats were sent back.

In the night of the 31st and 1st I visited all the troops and positions on the island, and at 3.30 o'clock was with all the troops at the place of embarkation, which I superintended in person. At the first break of day we were under way, viz: seven companies of Highlanders, four companies of the Fiftieth Pennsylvania, and the entire Michigan regiment. This side of the Brick-yard met Captain Rodgers and his four launches, and immediately pushed for the opposite shore. Meanwhile the gunboat Ottawa had made her appearance. I landed at about 8 o'clock at a good landing place below the cotton-gin and some 3 miles below the Adams house, and immediately sent back boats to take off Colonel Christ's command, with orders to land them at the Adams house. I found also that the Eighth Michigan was still waiting in the creek, having misunderstood my orders. I sent word to them to push at once to the Adams house, and turned off in the same direction all the flats which had not come up, and with five companies of the Highlanders, and the four companies of the Fiftieth Pennsylvania, consisting of about 500 men, and with two howitzers from the boats under the command of Lieutenant Irwin, U. S. Navy, I commenced my march. We moved rapidly and in good order, employing the Highlanders as skirmishers and the howitzers to drive off small parties of the enemy. We observed them at several points, but without noticing the few shots they fired at us we pushed to the Adams house, where we arrived after a very fatiguing march at about 11 o'clock.

It was some two and a half hours before I was able to resume the movement with the remaining forces. At 1.30 o'clock I formed my order of march, and avoiding the main road, but pushing across the open field, I marched for the fort. The Highlanders were in advance, preceded by two companies thrown out as skirmishers. The two howitzers of the Navy followed. The support were the regiments of Colonel Christ and Colonel Fenton, and the Forty-seventh and the Forty-eighth New York constituted the reserve, under Colonel Perry. Now the signals came most beautifully and effectively into use. All the commands bore the flag which had been agreed upon, viz, a ground of white and blue. The signal officer, Lieutenant Tafft, was with the skirmishers, communicating constantly with his colleague, Lieutenant Cogswell, on board the Ottawa. The concert of action thus established was absolutely perfect. The skirmishers marched steadily on, followed at proper intervals by the entire command, moving in column of companies or divisions or by flank, according to the ground. The shells from the gunboats tore through the woods just in advance of the skirmishers. They had well passed the position taken by the enemy in the woods when he opened his battery upon our columns. I got my command into the position I desired before the troops ascertained that it was not the fire of the boats but the fire of an enemy. It was exceedingly well adapted to the ground and favored my getting information by means of skirmishers. Nor was it possible for the enemy, although in large force, to make a flank movement against me without my being able in season to make my dispositions to repel it. The two regiments, the Forty-seventh and Forty-eighth New York, were formed in line on the right, and about at right angles to the remainder of the line. The Eighth Michigan and Fiftieth Pennsylvania were formed in line in the center, and the Highlanders in column of companies, with their skirmishers in position, constituted the left.

I now ordered Colonel Fenton to send forward skirmishers from his regiment, the Eighth Michigan, to feel the enemy, and, if circumstances favored, to seize the battery. He first sent three companies to the front and left, under Lieutenant-Colonel Graves, and soon four companies to the front and right, under Major Watson, the flanks resting under cover of the woods, which extended to our right and ran down quite closely to our left. These companies advanced in most admirable order, pushed forward rapidly, plunged under a heavy fire of musketry into the woods at a double-quick, and engaged the enemy. The firing showed that he was in large force. I at once ordered Colonel Perry to push skirmishers from his right along the skirt of woods, and Colonel Christ, with one wing of his regiment, to move well to the front and left in column of companies and push skirmishers to the rear of the enemy's position. My object in these several dispositions was to ascertain the force of the enemy, the particular character for the passage of troops of the wooded country in which the enemy lay concealed, and to carry out the plan which I had formed of interposing the bulk of my force between him and his battery, and thus compel the latter to surrender.

These orders were obeyed with great alacrity and without a moment's delay. Both bodies moved forward and engaged the enemy. Colonel Christ's movement was very opportune. It drove back the skirmishers on our left, and enabled the skirmishers of Fenton and Perry to fall back and give information of the condition of the field; for, be it remembered, our men had gained positions from which they could not be dislodged, and rendered certain the feasibility of my plan of attack. Indeed, the cheers at this moment from all portions of our line showed that our troops looked upon the day as theirs. The progress of our troops had been observed from the mast-heads of the gunboats, who threw shells over their heads into the ranks of the enemy. At this moment I received word that the skirmishers of the Highlanders, never once halting, had pushed on and entered the fort almost simultaneously with the force from the front under Colonel Leasure. The enemy's fire had ceased for some fifteen minutes, and I gave orders for moving the whole command into the fort, where we arrived at about 4.30 o'clock. Here I met both Colonel Leasure, who was placed by me in command of the front and of the special movement from the ferry, and Captain Elliott, who commanded the crossing party at Seabrook, and learned of the complete success of the latter. The gunboats, the Seneca, Captain Ammen, and the Ellen, Captain Budd, entered Whale Branch, as originally intended, and opened fire upon the battery opposite Seabrook. Captain Elliott crossed with his party and found a battery ready for guns, but no guns in position, and after destroying the works returned to Seabrook.

Captain Rodgers most kindly sent on shore a 12-pounder howitzer gun, under the command of Lieut. J. H. Upshur, and kept there one of the howitzers which had accompanied our march by land under Acting Master Louis Kempff. One of the wheels of the other howitzer had been broken a short time before reaching the fort. Night signals were also specially arranged to communicate with the gunboats.

Just before dark Lieutenant Lyons came in from the pickets, bringing word that he had met a flag of truce, and that the officer bearing it asked for permission to take off their dead. The gunboats were about firing a few shells into the woods where the skirmishers of the enemy had been observed. The firing was immediately stopped, and I sent Lieutenant Lyons back twice, granting a truce of one hour for that purpose, but he did not on either occasion find the flag. The gunboats were now brought into position on either side of the ferry and placed suitably to cover our operations, and I at once proceeded to make the proper dispositions for the night, established a strong picket force, with the entire Roundhead regiment as a reserve, and had the ferry properly prepared for the return of the troops.

My post and brigade quartermaster, Capt. William Lilley, in this business was most efficient, for he, entirely in the night, absolutely restored the old ferry, ropes, windlass, and all, and with the assistance of two of my staff, Lieutenant Cottrell, Eighth Michigan, and Lieutenant Lyons, Fiftieth Pennsylvania, made arrangements for the most rapid and most orderly recrossing of the troops. The use of the ferry was required early in the morning for the passage of wagons and the 12-pounder and its carriage, which was the only one piece of ordnance found in the fort.

About 9 o'clock the work of crossing the troops commenced. The passage-way is about 550 feet wide. The whole force of 3,000 men, with their horses, was over at 12 o'clock. It was not less orderly than rapid. The enemy was in considerable force in the woods back of our position, watching our movements. The shell from the gunboats kept him very quiet. At 12 o'clock I myself crossed with the last of the forces, having caused the buildings in the vicinity of the fort to be burned and the fort to be leveled sufficiently for all practical purposes.

I cannot close this report without congratulating the commanding general and the country on the good conduct of the troops under my command, none of whom, except the Highlanders, had ever been under fire before, and on the perfect success of the expedition, placed by him, so far as regards the land forces, in my hands. Looking to the marches by land and the movements by water, looking to the very considerable combination involved in the final concentration of troops, it is a little remarkable that every departure in detail from the original plan, and indeed every accident, seemed only to further it. We effected in flat-boats, manned by negroes alone and without the aid of a single employé, a landing on the enemy's shore, having to cross in our boats a space of 3 miles. We moved to our point not along the main road, but across the fields and along paths shown us by negroes picked up upon the shore. We engaged the enemy on our own and not on his field. We gave him fair challenge of battle. Every regiment of my command was, through its skirmishers, brought into contact with him. He kept under cover, fell back from his position, and yielded the field to us. Our troops have confidence in themselves and faith in the bayonet.

This, in brief, is the history of the expedition and its *morale*, to be shown, I trust, more signally on future fields. Moreover, this is the first occasion the system of signals invented by Major Myer has been tested in actual battle. I claim for the signal officers of my staff—Lieutenant Tafft and Lieutenant Cogswell—the merit of showing the code to be a perfect success, and myself the good fortune of commanding on the occasion.

Says Lieutenant Cogswell, who was on board the Ottawa:

Permit me, before closing, to call your attention to the able and efficient manner in which Lieutenant Tafft managed the signals on shore. During the whole march from

Adams' Landing to the ferry he so managed it that only for a few minutes was he so situated that he could not instantly open communication, though in order to accomplish this he was frequently exposed to the direct fire of the enemy.

I must also express my warm acknowledgments and high appreciation of the services of the Navy. Captain Rodgers on all occasions responded to my requests. The working of the gunboats in the narrow channel of Port Royal and the handling of the guns was most masterly and most beautiful. The signaling was perfect throughout. The whole operation reflects the highest credit upon the Navy and upon the officers and men specially engaged in it. I repeat, my whole command, as well as myself, will mark with a white stone the day of this fraternal and patriotic co-operation. In saying that the troops under my command behaved with great coolness and constancy, I only say what every man observed. I will not particularize, except to say that the skirmishers of the Highlanders first met the enemy, and those of the Eighth Michigan came into the severest contact with him. This regiment has been and still is a great sufferer from sickness, but it showed that loyal steel from the frozen North has fire and power against the enemies of our country.

I must return my acknowledgments to the several members of my staff, to my assistant adjutant-general, Capt. Hazard Stevens, who is referred to in the highest terms in the accompanying reports; to Lieutenant Porter, Eighth Michigan Regiment, who, by means of the negroes, guided my force all the way from the first landing to the ferry (in this he was assisted by Lieutenant Taylor, Roundhead Regiment); to Lieutenant Lyons, Fiftieth Pennsylvania Volunteers, who organized the transportation on flat-boats, in which duty Lieutenant Cottrell, Eighth Michigan, rendered service; to Captain Fuller, assistant quartermaster, for valuable aid in his department and on my staff; and to Lieutenant Holbrook, who volunteered and served most acceptably as aide throughout. Dr. Kemble, the brigade surgeon, was very efficient. He examined in person, under fire, the ground occupied by our skirmishers, and personally superintended the bringing off of our wounded men. I am under very special obligations to my post and brigade quartermaster, Capt. William Lilley, who was indefatigable in preparing for the expedition and efficient in furthering it. He furnished the crews of negroes for the flats and removed the 12-pounder gun and carriage to Beaufort. At midnight he remounted it, took it across the ferry early in the morning, and brought it into Beaufort before night, taking along with him a wagon load of three-inch plank, and making eight bridges on the road. The large ferry-boat itself, with all its appurtenances, is now safely laid away at Beaufort in his charge, for use on future occasions.

The loss of my brigade is one killed, one missing, and nine wounded, as per surgeon's report, herewith appended;* in addition to which 3 men were slightly wounded of the Forty-eighth Regiment. Among the wounded is Major Watson, of the Eighth Michigan Regiment, a most excellent officer, and who gallantly commanded in the late affair. The enemy's loss must have been very considerable from our skirmishers alone, and still heavier from the shell practice of the Navy. We buried 3 of their men and have 1 of their wounded men in our hands.

A reconnoitering party I sent out to-day landed at the Adams house, examined the battle-field, and went to the ferry. They found and buried 1 of our missing men, known to have been wounded, and the only one killed, and encountered but one small scouting party of 6 mounted men of the enemy.

---

* Embodied in No. 14.

The negroes all report that there are no troops this side of Garden's Corner. This party consisted of 20 men of the Eighth Michigan, under the command of Captain Ely.

From the observations made from the mast-heads of the gunboats and those made on the field, I estimate the force of the enemy at about 3,000 men, and from information obtained to-day they had 2,000 more within two hours' march. The force which I moved from the Adams house was about 2,500 men, which, with the command of Leasure and of Elliott, made my whole force 3,000 men.

I append the sub-reports; and, in conclusion, I hope the general commanding may be gratified with our celebration of New Year's Day.

I am, sir, very respectfully, your most obedient,

ISAAC I. STEVENS,
Brigadier-General, Commanding Land Forces.

Capt. L. H. PELOUZE,
Assistant Adjutant-General Exped'y Corps, Port Royal, S. C.

No. 3.

Report of Col. William M. Fenton, Eighth Michigan Infantry.

HEADQUARTERS EIGHTH MICHIGAN REGIMENT,
Main-land, Port Royal Ferry, January 1, 1862—8 p. m.

SIR: I have the honor to report that, in compliance with your order, this regiment was safely landed at the Adams house, on main-land, having effected the crossing in flat-boats from Brick-yard Point, Port Royal Island, and took up the line of march towards the enemy's battery at this place at 1 o'clock p. m. On our approach towards the ferry we were ordered to attack as skirmishers a masked battery which opened fire on us from the right. I immediately detached the first two and the tenth companies, and directed their march to the left and front of the battery. This was followed by four additional companies to the right and front. The fire of the battery with shells continued on our line until the skirmishers reached the right, when it was turned on them, and on their approach, right, left, and front, to within 50 to 100 yards of the enemy's position, a fire of musketry was opened upon them. The force of the enemy as well as the battery was concealed to a considerable extent by trees, brush, and underwood, but appeared to consist of two mounted howitzers, supported by a regiment or more of infantry and some cavalry. The skirmishers were measurably protected in brush and furrows, and continued their fire upon the enemy, which was returned by volleys of musketry and shells from the battery. Our fire was well directed and seemed to be effective. One mounted officer, who appeared to be very active, was seen to fall from his horse, at which the troops on the enemy's right were thrown into confusion. Their position seemed to be changing to the rear, and as our skirmishers were called off and the regiment formed in line the enemy's fire ceased. The regiment was then marched to its position in line of battle in rear of the fort at this point. Lieutenant-Colonel Graves led on the left and Major Watson the right of skirmishers. The major, in leading on his line, received a severe flesh wound in the leg. I have to report that officers and men behaved with admirable bravery and coolness.

The loss of the enemy from the well-directed fire of our skirmishers cannot be less than 40. Our loss is 7 wounded, 2 missing.

I have the honor to be, very respectfully, your obedient servant,

W. M. FENTON,
Colonel Eighth Michigan Regiment.

Brigadier-General STEVENS.

No. 4.

Report of Lieut. Col. James L. Fraser, Forty-seventh New York Infantry.

HEADQUARTERS FORTY-SEVENTH REGIMENT N. Y. S. V.,
Hilton Head, January 3, 1862.

CAPTAIN: Pursuant to orders from Brigadier-General Viele, I embarked with my regiment on board the United States steamboat Boston on or about noon Tuesday, December 31, 1861, and was ordered by General Sherman to report to Brigadier-General Stevens at Beaufort, where we arrived at, say, 6 p. m., remaining on board off said place until, say, 7 a. m., the morning following, when we started for Port Royal Ferry, arriving some few miles this side, and landed by means of surf-boats. Upon landing of the right wing orders were received to march. Taking my position on the left of Colonel Perry, Forty-eighth New York, and under his orders we advanced, and arriving at the woods, was ordered by Colonel Perry to reconnoiter with my regiment, and give all information as regards the position of the enemy. Discovered a rifle-pit. The right flank company, being skirmishers, fired, and instantly routed the enemy, holding said pit, when orders came from Colonel Perry to return to the fort. During the night the regiment was detailed on picket and fatigue duty.

At, say, 11 a. m. on the morning of January 2, 1862, the regiment crossed Port Royal Ferry and marched to Beaufort, went on board the United States steamboat Boston, and remained off said place all night. Sailed for Hilton Head early in the morning of January 3. Landed by means of surf-boats, and returned to the camp in fine spirits, and am happy to inform you that none of my regiment were either wounded, killed, or taken prisoner.

I am, sir, your obedient servant,

JAMES L. FRASER,
Lieutenant-Colonel, Comdg. Forty-seventh Regiment N. Y. Vols.

Capt. HAZARD STEVENS,
Assistant Adjutant-General, General Stevens' Brigade.

No. 5.

Report of Col. James H. Perry, Forty-eighth New York Infantry.

HEADQUARTERS FORTY-EIGHTH REGIMENT N. Y. VOLS.,
Hilton Head, S. C., January 3, 1862.

CAPTAIN: I beg leave respectfully to submit for the information of the general commanding the following report of the participation of my command in the affair at Port Royal Ferry on the 1st instant:

On account of some delay on the part of the Forty-seventh New York,

I detained my column at Adams' plantation (the place of landing) until the latest moment, and finally commenced the march before the arrival of two companies of that regiment. I had advanced perhaps three-quarters of a mile, when I received an order from the general to bring forward my command with the greatest expedition. We immediately advanced at double-quick until we overtook the supporting column, when I received notice of the existence of a battery threatening our right flank, and was ordered to attack and capture it. In obedience to the order, I immediately deployed my column, and forming double line of battle advanced upon the position of the enemy, the Forty-eighth New York, under command of Lieutenant-Colonel Barton, leading, supported by the Forty-seventh New York, under the command of Lieutenant-Colonel Fraser.

When my first line was fairly under fire at long range it was halted under shelter of the timber and protected by the inequalities of the ground, and I sent forward two companies of skirmishers, with orders to ascertain the exact position of the battery, the best method of approaching it, the number of its guns, and with what force it was supported. The skirmishers were met by a sharp fire of artillery and musketry, but they went forward steadily and rapidly, and soon reported to me that a marsh covered the front of the enemy's position, and that they had at least four guns, supported by a heavy force of infantry. I then advanced the Forty-seventh New York for the purpose of maneuvering upon the left flank and gaining the rear of the enemy before attacking in front. The Forty-seventh pressed through the timber, and had gained a position well on the left and rear, and their advance had exchanged a few shots with the enemy, when I received the general's order to retire, the battery on the river having been taken and the object of the expedition accomplished. I drew off my men without loss. Three members of the Forty-eighth Regiment were slightly wounded, but not a man was disabled or rendered unfit for duty.

I am happy to add that the men and officers of my command behaved with great steadiness and resolution, obeying the word of command under fire as if they had been on drill.

Very respectfully,

J. H. PERRY,

Colonel Forty-eighth Regiment New York Volunteers.

No. 6.

Report of Maj. David Morrison, Seventy-ninth New York Infantry.

HDQRS. SEVENTY-NINTH REGIMENT (HIGHLANDERS),
Beaufort, S. C., January 3, 1862.

GENERAL: I have the honor to submit to you my report of the part taken by the Seventy-ninth (Highlanders) with the expedition on the 1st instant under your command:

Agreeably to orders received on the afternoon of the 31st ultimo, I moved seven companies of my regiment, consisting of the 1st, 2d, 3d, 4th, 5th, 7th, and 8th companies, to the creek leading to the Brick-yard, reaching that point at 5 o'clock p. m., where they bivouacked for the night. At 4 a. m. on the morning of the 1st instant I received orders to embark in boats, seven in number, furnished by Lieutenant Lyons. Having accomplished this satisfactorily, I proceeded down the creek leading to the Brick-yard, and was there joined by five large man-of-war launches, manned by sailors and armed with howitzers, who conveyed us to the point directly opposite on the main-land, known as —— Landing, where we arrived about 8 o'clock a. m. and disembarked.

By your orders I immediately advanced a party of skirmishers to scour the woods in the vicinity, which was done without opposition from the enemy. I then formed the battalion and advanced, sending forward two companies, the 4th and 5th, as skirmishers, and took the road leading to the Adams plantation. We were accompanied by a party of sailors, with two small brass howitzers, and arrived there about noon. This operation was under the immediate direction of Capt. Hazard Stevens, the assistant adjutant-general. After resting about half an hour I was ordered to take up the position in advance, leading to the enemy's fort at Port Royal Ferry. I advanced about half a mile and halted until receiving further orders, which were given by Captain Stevens, viz, to send forward skirmishers and advance. I detailed for this purpose the 4th and 8th companies, who at once took up their position as such at about a quarter of a mile in advance of the main body of the battalion. The order was then given to move, which was done in gallant style. The men were eager to tackle the enemy, and it was with difficulty I could restrain them from pushing forward. Having advanced about the distance of 1 mile the enemy opened fire upon us from a battery in the woods on our right flank, some of the shells falling in our midst, but happily without doing any injury, my men remarking that "their shells were warranted not to kill."

I continued to advance, and took up a position within half a mile of the fort, and rested for some time until I received orders from you to advance and occupy the fort, which had already been taken possession of by my skirmishers, who exchanged a few shots with the retreating foe. I entered the fort and found it evacuated by the enemy, leaving behind them one cannon, spiked. I am happy to be able to report that the whole operation was conducted without loss.

In closing my report I deem it my duty to bring before your notice the exemplary and soldierly conduct of the Highlanders, every one acting as if on parade, and confident that their general would lead them to victory. Captain Stevens' noble conduct excited our admiration, and their confidence and attachment to him are none the less than towards yourself.

Respectfully submitted by, general, your most obedient servant,

DAVID MORRISON,

Major, Commanding Seventy-ninth Highlanders.

General ISAAC I. STEVENS.

No. 7.

Report of Lieut. William St. G. Elliott, Seventy-ninth New York Infantry.

SEABROOK'S FERRY, *January* 2, 1862.

SIR: I have the honor to report that the body of troops assigned me for duty on January 1, instant, were in position along the bank of the river opposite Barnwell's Island before daybreak, awaiting the arrival of the gunboats. About 8 o'clock I manned a boat and went down Whale Branch to meet the vessels on their way up the river, as I was anxious to communicate with them in relation to a code of signals I had instructed two men in for the purpose of properly directing the gunboats' line of fire. I met them about 1 mile below, and went on board the Seneca and communicated my wishes to Captain Ammen, who very kindly gave me all the assistance in his power. I suggested that a few shell should be thrown into the enemy's works opposite Seabrook's Ferry and then a number back in the woods to the right and left. I had no idea at any time that there were more troops than one picket stationed at their works, but apprehended a concealed force in the woods to the right. At a given signal from me the troops, who until now lay concealed in the bushes, manned the flat-boats in the following order: 1st, 9th Company, and, 2d, 6th Company Highlanders; Company B and Company C, Roundheads. I led the way in a small boat. The tide, fortunately, was very high, and I could thus take the flats directly across 200 yards of marsh that intervened between the river and the enemy's works. The companies landed in regular succession, except Company C, Roundhead regiment, which I did not think it necessary to land. We found the work, as we expected, abandoned, with evidences of a hasty retreat of but a small party of men. The works were nearly completed, and were intended for one large sea-coast gun and a field battery. The magazine was rather out of proportion to the size of the works, being amply large enough for a fort of six heavy pieces. The works were admirably masked and pretty well constructed. I threw out a semicircular line of pickets, who reported small bodies of the enemy some distance in the interior. I gave orders for the entire destruction of the work and the felling of trees, while I started in my boat for Stewart's plantation, formerly the headquarters of a rebel picket, and situated about half a mile from Port Royal Ferry. I made a successful landing, and searched for late papers and letters or other property of service to the Army. I found none of the former, and all of the latter is now in possession of Captain Stevens, assistant adjutant-general.

From this point I had a very good view of the batteries at Port Royal Ferry and I found them quite deserted. This must have been three hours before possession was taken of the place by the troops under Colonel Leasure. I should have immediately gone there had I known officially that another column was approaching from the right. I returned to my command, and finding the work of destruction about finished, with the exception of all the trees, and not having sufficient axes for the purpose, I withdrew the troops after some trouble, as the tide had fallen and the flats were floating in an adjacent creek, the troops consequently being obliged to march some distance through heavy mud. I relanded my command at Seabrook's without further difficulty.

Truly and respectfully,

W. ST. G. ELLIOTT,
Commanding Left Column.

Brig. Gen. ISAAC I. STEVENS.

No. 8.

Report of Col. B. C. Christ, Fiftieth Pennsylvania Infantry.

BEAUFORT, S. C., *January* 2, 1862.

SIR: I respectfully submit the following: According to Special Orders, No. —, I left our encampment at Beaufort at 5.30 o'clock p. m. December

30, 1861, with four companies of my command, viz, C, E, F, and K, and proceeded along the shell road in the direction of Port Royal Ferry to the cross-roads, where I was joined by Companies D and H. We then proceeded along the shell road to the 6-mile post, where we bivouacked until 2.30 o'clock a. m. January 1, 1862, when I again took up my line of march, under the direction of a guide, to a point on Coosaw Creek. From this latter point I was ordered by the general commanding to a point called the Brick-yard, on the upper end of Port Royal Island, and as soon as boats were furnished me to push across Coosaw River and land at the Adams house, where I arrived at 12.30 p. m., and immediately formed a junction with Companies A, B, G, and I, under command of Lieutenant Colonel Brenholts, who had reached this point from Beaufort by boats. The whole regiment then took their position in the center of the brigade, and proceeded with it under heavy cannonading of the enemy over a narrow causeway and along a road leading to the fort at Port Royal Ferry. When within three-quarters of a mile of the fort I was ordered to move with the right wing of my command on the enemy's right, with a view to support Colonel Fenton, of the Eighth Michigan, who was gallantly leading his command in the face of a battery on the enemy's left. I accordingly moved forward, taking the precaution to throw out small skirmishing parties, the better to watch the movements of the enemy and to guard against surprise. After moving forward about 300 yards my advance was fired upon by the enemy from a wood on our left. I called in my skirmishers, and immediately put my command on a double-quick until within good musket range, when I discovered from 400 to 500 of the enemy forming in line of battle and evidently preparing to give us a warm reception. I, however, anticipated his movement, and before his line was completed mine was formed and ready for action. I immediately commenced firing, and I believe with telling effect, for at the third volley the enemy broke and beat a hasty retreat towards the woods.

I again rapidly pushed forward, with a view to cut off his retreat and prevent a junction with the main body, when I was arrested in my further progress by shells from our gunboats, which now came pouring in among them, making sad havoc in their already decimated ranks. After firing one more volley at their broken and disordered ranks we retired about 200 yards out of range of the gunboats, and were subsequently ordered to take a position near the fort, where we bivouacked for the night, and to-day, January 2, recrossed the Coosaw, and reached our encampment at 5 o'clock p. m.

Although the whole of my command were within range of the enemy's cannon for a half hour and a portion of them within 100 yards of a detachment of his (the enemy's) infantry, and for some time sustained a heavy fire, I have no killed to report and none wounded save M. Weidenhammer, of Company E, a slight wound on the right foot, and Ensign Herbert, wounded in the leg by a spent piece of shell.

I cannot close this report without expressing my decided approbation of the conduct of both officers and men of my command—to the officers for anticipating almost every order, thereby rendering my portion of the work comparatively easy, and to the men for their strict attention and prompt compliance with every command.

All of which is respectfully submitted.

B. C. CHRIST,
Colonel, Commanding Fiftieth Regiment Pennsylvania Volunteers.

Capt. HAZARD STEVENS, *Assistant Adjutant-General.*

No. 9.

Report of Lieut. Col. Thomas S. Brenholts, Fiftieth Pennsylvania Infantry.

BEAUFORT, S. C., *January* 3, 1862.

SIR: I have the honor to submit the following report of the movements and operations of that portion of your regiment which was placed under my command on the afternoon of December 31, 1861:

Soon after you had taken up your line of march I received an order through the assistant adjutant-general to form my command and march them to the wharf at Beaufort, where we were rapidly embarked in six flat-boats. In accordance with my instructions, I then reported for further orders to General Stevens, and, these being received, I pushed off with my command, consisting of Companies A, B, G, and I, under the guidance of Corporal Hurst, and after a long and laborious passage reached the Ottawa, where I conferred with Captain Rodgers, commanding the fleet, and after leaving with him several negroes acquainted with the channel we pushed on, making but slow progress, the tide setting swiftly against us, and finally reached the Brick-yard, where we were informed that the place of rendezvous was farther on, at a point which we reached, after the most arduous rowing, about 2 o'clock on the morning of the 1st January, 1862. The Highlanders here embarking in accordance with the orders of the general commanding, who was himself on the ground, we followed them, and between the hours of 6 and 7 effected an unopposed landing on the enemy's shore. Here, preceded by skirmishers from the Highlanders, by the boats' crews with howitzers, and immediately by the Highland regiment, we took up our line of march for the ferry, seeing none of the enemy but a small party who were convoying a wagon, and from whom we received a few harmless shots, up to the time of our being joined by yourself while we were lying in the rear of the house known as Adams'.

In conclusion, I would express my entire satisfaction with the conduct of the officers and men under my command.

Very respectfully,

THOMAS S. BRENHOLTS,
Lieutenant-Colonel, Commanding.

Col. B. C. CHRIST.

No. 10.

Report of Col. Daniel Leasure, One hundredth Pennsylvania Infantry.

FORT AT PORT ROYAL FERRY, *January* 1, 186?.

GENERAL: Pursuant to your orders I dispatched two companies of my command, viz, Company B, Captain Dawson, and Company C, Captain Cornelius, to report to Captain Elliott, of the Seventy-ninth New York Regiment (Highlanders), in command at Seabrook, on yesterday; last night at 8 o'clock Lieutenant-Colonel Armstrong to a well-masked position south of the Stewart house, near Port Royal Ferry, with four companies, viz, Company A, Captain Templeton; Company G, Captain Brown; Company I, Captain Squiers, and Company M, Captain Campbell, where he remained perfectly concealed from the enemy until he received orders to move over the ferry. With Company D, Captain Hamilton, and Company K, Captain Van Gorder, I remained in reserve at the headquarters of Major Morrison, of the Seventy-ninth New York

Regiment, until 8 o'clock this morning, when I placed them under charge of Major Leckey, with instructions to remain till ordered forward, and detain all teams and carriages, as well as all spectators, at that point till I gave orders for them to be permitted to advance.

At 8.30 o'clock I joined Lieutenant-Colonel Armstrong, and selected a point of observation at the fort, where with a strong glass I could observe the operations of the enemy in front and on either side alongshore. At that hour the enemy could be seen in force in and about the fort and for some distance in its rear. I counted about 200 men in the fort at that time, and the number to the rear I computed at four times that number, but there was evidently a force of cavalry secreted in the forest still farther to the rear, as I could observe mounted men in considerable numbers passing the interstices of the woods. At that time the enemy seemed unconscious of any attack impending, for my own force in front was effectually concealed, save the ordinary sentinels of the Seventy-ninth, which were posted as usual, and there was no evidence of any approach visible from the fort.

At 9 o'clock one of the enemy's pickets came hastily in from the eastward, and immediately the forces in and about the fort fell into line, and the artillerists manned the guns, and gave them a direction to command the approach by water from the east. At 9.30 heavy firing on the west announced that the gunboats Seneca and Ellen were approaching from Broad River and shelling the batteries as they advanced. This seemed to disturb the occupants of the fort a good deal, and they changed the range of their guns to command the approach by water from that direction. In a few minutes (say twenty) the firing to the east announced the approach of the gunboats Pembina, Ottawa, and Hale, and a look in that direction revealed those boats, or at least two of them—the Ottawa and Pembina—covering the landing of troops in small boats from a transport lying at anchor about 4 or 5 miles to the east of the ferry. At 10 to 10.30 o'clock the firing on the west was very heavy, and as the boats approached nearer and nearer and the shells began to explode in the woods along the shore and far back towards the interior the enemy's infantry began to leave the trenches, and seek an open field to the east and rearward of the fort, where they lay down in the deep furrows amongst the weeds.

At this stage of affairs I ordered Lieutenant Marshall, commanding Company K, of the Seventy-ninth New York Regiment (who was for the time being with his command attached to my command), to send an orderly to the position occupied by one of his pickets alongshore eastward, to communicate, if possible, the position of the enemy's infantry to the commanding officer of the nearest gunboat. In about half an hour the Hale steamed up and fired several shells with great precision into the field, and the enemy ran off in all directions inland, and I saw no more of them. Seeing the works apparently deserted, and fearing the low tide might beach the flat-boats, I sent some men into them, with instructions to place them well afloat at low tide. On seeing this some 20 or 30 artillerists in the fort ran out a field piece so as to command the boats, and, not wishing to precipitate matters or draw their fire unnecessarily, I recalled the men, and at this juncture the officer in command of the Pembina arrived, and reported to me that you were on the farther shore, with the troops accompanying you, as indeed I had observed for some time; and, further, that the gunboats would run up shortly and shell out the fort. I now instructed Coxswain Connor, who had been assigned to me by Captain Fuller, to hold a party of watermen, 6 in number, from Company M, in readiness to put the boats into the ferry at a moment's notice. Shortly after the gunboats on both sides approached and began to throw shells into the fort. As soon as the gunboats began to approach the enemy withdrew one or two field pieces and hastily sent them up northward, and also attempted to remove a heavy siege gun; but they seemed to encounter some difficulty, and they abandoned it with much precipitation on the bursting of a shell from the Ottawa, which fell in close proximity.

I now observed your skirmishers of the Seventy-ninth New York Regiment approaching carefully along the coast about a mile eastward of the fort, and judging that a rapid concentration of the forces was your aim, I ordered Lieutenant-Colonel Armstrong to advance the first detachment, Company M, Captain Campbell, to the ferry, to be followed by Company D, Captain Hamilton, and Company K, Captain Van Gorder, under charge of Major Leckey, and I attended to getting off the boats as rapidly as possible to meet them. Through the efficient aid of Coxswain Connor, whom I take this opportunity of recommending to your favorable notice, the boats were at the ferry at the proper moment, and Lieutenant-Colonel Armstrong immediately embarked and crossed over with his detachment, and on reaching the fort he found it entirely abandoned by the enemy, and took possession of it, and sent Captain Campbell with a portion of his command to make a reconnaissance to the northward. Captain Campbell soon came upon the enemy in retreat, and received their fire without any damage, and returned it without knowing with what effect. The enemy, about 50 in number, continued to retreat, and a detachment of Captain Campbell's company, while deploying in the order of skirmishers to the right, came upon about 40 of the enemy guarding the approach to a hospital. The enemy fired upon Captain Campbell's men without effect, and on their returning the fire two of the enemy fell, as I afterwards learned, mortally wounded, and died instantly. Before this I had arrived with the rest of my command, and a portion of the Seventy-ninth New York Regiment had also arrived, and in a short time you also arrived with your entire force, and the day was won.

I am happy in being able to report favorably of my command, and also to recommend to your favor Lieutenant Marshall, in command of Company K, of the Seventy-ninth New York Regiment, for the time being attached to my command. His intimate knowledge of the locality and ready co-operation deserve, as they have received, my warmest thanks, which I very respectfully submit.

Your most obedient servant,

DANIEL LEASURE,

Colonel Roundhead Regiment Pennsylvania Volunteers.

ISAAC I. STEVENS,

Brigadier-General, Commanding Second Brigade E. C.

No. 11.

Reports of Lieut. William S. Cogswell, Fifth Connecticut Infantry, signal officer.

BEAUFORT, S. C., *January* 3, 1862.

GENERAL: Agreeably to your instructions, received on the 31st instant, I reported to Captain Rodgers, on board the Ottawa, for signal service. Communication was first opened with your command on the main-land at Adams' Landing about 11 o'clock in the morning of the 1st instant, and was carried on without interruption until our troops had all recrossed to Port Royal Island, on the morning of the 2d instant. By means of the signals the position of the enemy, your own movements and wishes, were promptly communicated to Captain Rodgers, enabling him to render you assistance, which otherwise would, I think, have been impossible. This is, as far as I am aware, the first time this system of signaling has been used in action. I flatter myself that it has proved successful, and trust that it will meet with your approval.

Permit me, before closing, to call your attention to the able and efficient manner in which Lieutenant Tafft managed the signals on shore. During the whole march from Adams' Landing to the ferry he so managed it that only for a few minutes was he so situated that he could not instantly open communication, though in order to accomplish this he was frequently exposed to the direct fire of the enemy.

All of which is respectfully submitted.

WM. S. COGSWELL,
Lieutenant in charge of Party attached to Second Brigade.

General ISAAC I. STEVENS.

BEAUFORT, S. C., *January* 4, 1862.

MAJOR: I hereby transmit the following report of signal operations:

During the first of last month General Stevens occupied Beaufort, and as soon as possible after our arrival stations were built and communication opened with headquarters on Hilton Head, since which time the line has been constantly employed in the transmission of messages.

On the 31st of last month I was notified by General Stevens of an expedition to surprise and take possession of a battery of the enemy, and received orders to report to Captain Rodgers, on board the gunboat Ottawa, for signal duty.

On the morning of the 1st instant I accompanied Captain Rodgers, who went with the launches to cover the landing of our forces.

After our troops had landed I returned to the Ottawa, and opened communication with the shore at Adams' Landing (a point about a mile and a half from the first landing, but in order to reach it the troops had to make a circuit inland, and were hid from the shipping by thick woods) about 11 o'clock, from which time until all our forces had recrossed to Port Royal Island, on the morning of the 2d instant, communication was uninterrupted. The distance from Adams' Landing to the ferry is about 2 miles (the ferry is where our troops remained overnight and crossed the next morning); the shore is swampy, and heavy woods come down nearly to the water, with occasional openings. In these woods the enemy were posted, and through them our forces had to fight their way to the battery at the ferry. By means of your signals Captain Rodgers was kept constantly informed of the position of the enemy and the disposition of our troops, and was thus enabled to direct his fire with precision and without fear of injuring our own men.

Nothing could be more perfect than the manner in which we were able to transmit communications; it exceeded my expectations entirely. During the whole march, which occupied some four hours, I do not think there was more than ten minutes during which we could not transmit messages instantly. Both General Stevens and Captain Rodgers were pleased to express their appreciation of the importance of your system of signals, commending it very highly. Without its assistance I do not think the fleet would have been able to have rendered the great service it did and our land forces would have met much greater resistance.

In conclusion, permit me to congratulate you upon the success of the expedition and the part your signals took in it.

I am, sir, very respectfully, your obedient servant,

WM. S. COGSWELL,
Lieutenant, Acting Signal Officer Second Brigade E. C.

Maj. ALBERT J. MYER.

No. 12.

Reports of Lieut. Henry S. Tafft, Fifteenth Massachusetts Infantry, signal officer.

HEADQUARTERS SECOND BRIGADE E. C.,
Beaufort, S. C., January 3, 1862.

GENERAL: I have the honor to report that, agreeably to your instructions, I accompanied the expedition under your command to the mainland, and was present during the engagement with the enemy near Port Royal Ferry on the 1st instant; that during the whole time your requests to the commander of the gunboats were successfully transmitted by the system of signals invented by Major Myer. The firing from the gunboats was in this manner done in entire concert with you, and therefore proved the more effective, as the various positions of the enemy were thus made known to Captain Rodgers, commanding gunboats. My signal flag, carried by myself, was repeatedly fired upon when in presence of the enemy. Without egotism, I claim the honor for Lieutenant Cogswell (who was on gunboat Ottawa) and myself of being the first signal officers who have performed signal duty under fire upon the battle-field since the adoption of the system into the service of the United States; whether successfully or not I of course leave to your judgment.

Very respectfully, your obedient servant,

HENRY S. TAFFT,
Lieutenant, Signal Officer.

Brigadier-General STEVENS,
Commanding Second Brigade.

HEADQUARTERS SECOND BRIGADE E. C.,
Beaufort, S. C., January 4, 1862.

MAJOR: I have the honor to report that I was present and took part in the battle of Port Royal Ferry on the 1st instant, Lieut. William S. Cogswell being on board gunboat Ottawa, acting in concert with me.

General Stevens (commanding our troops) directed all the firing from the gunboats during the battle through the signal officers, naming different points where their shells should be thrown, when to cease firing, when to open fire, &c., thus enabling the gunboats to use their artillery with as much precision as though they were upon the field, and consequently creating terrible slaughter among the enemy.

I had before the battle caused to be made some two dozen flags, blue and white

White
Blue

, to be carried by our troops, to prevent any mistakes by firing upon each other, and also to assist the firing from the gunboats, which I believe was a great assistance, and effectually prevented any such unfortunate errors.

Lieutenant Cogswell and myself had also arranged a simple code for certain messages, which enabled us to work with surprising quickness, and by so doing added still more to the success of your system of signaling. I believe that an impromptu code can always be arranged by signal officers for use upon any important occasion of this kind, and when they know their ground, which will prove of immense service. I found in this manner that I could send a message from the battle-field to Lieutenant Cogswell between the discharges of artillery, when the smoke lifted, which could not otherwise have been done.

My flag was repeatedly fired upon, the enemy seeming to understand its use and importance. Their battery, which was concealed in the woods, threw canister and shell directly across the field in which I was stationed, and, although they struck all around and near me, neither myself nor the man with me (Sergeant Ried) were hurt.

My feet were first upon the shore of the main-land of South Carolina, the signal flag the first to wave, and it was kept constantly flying during the whole engagement.

At 10 p. m. I returned to Beaufort with a dispatch for General Sherman, at Hilton Head, announcing our success, and Lieutenant Town immediately went back to the ferry to act in my place in case of necessity.

I believe that the very great assistance rendered by the use of your system of signals aided very materially in gaining a victory for us, and that fact I also think is fully impressed upon the mind of the general commanding, as well as upon the officer commanding the gunboats.

Very respectfully, your obedient servant,

HENRY S. TAFFT,
First Lieut. Fifteenth Mass. Regt. Vols., Actg. Sig. Off. E. C.

Maj. ALBERT J. MYER,
Commanding Signal Corps.

No. 13.

Letter from Maj. Albert J. Myer, Signal Officer, U. S. Army.

OFFICE OF THE SIGNAL OFFICER, A. P.,
Washington, D. C., January 14, 1862.

SIR: I have the honor to submit to the general commanding the Army the inclosed letter of special mention from General Stevens, the official report of Commander C. R. P. Rodgers, commanding naval forces, in the recent action at Port Royal Ferry, and the official reports of Lieuts. Henry S. Tafft and William S. Cogswell, acting signal officers of the Army, engaged in that action.

The gallantry, good conduct, and services rendered by First Lieut. William S. Cogswell, Fifth Connecticut Volunteers, and First Lieut. Henry S. Tafft, Fifteenth Massachusetts Volunteers, acting signal officers, having been of a character which has elicited the official approbation and mention of the officers commanding both the land and the naval forces, I desire to bring their names to the especial notice of the general commanding the Army.

I am, sir, very respectfully, your obedient servant,

ALBERT J. MYER,
Signal Officer, Major, U. S. Army.

Brig. Gen. S. WILLIAMS,
Assistant Adjutant-General, Army of the Potomac.

[Inclosure.]

U. S. FLAG-SHIP WABASH,
Port Royal Harbor, S. C., January 3, 1862.

SIR: * * * Lieutenant Cogswell, a signal officer of the Army, was directed to report to me for duty, and furnished me with the means of constantly communicating with General Stevens with a facility and rapidity unknown to the naval service. I take this opportunity of recommending that the code of signals invented by Major Myer be at once introduced into the Navy.

I have the honor to be, very respectfully, your obedient servant,

C. R. P. RODGERS,
Commander.

Flag-Officer S. F. DUPONT,
Commanding South Atlantic Blockading Squadron.

[Inclosure.]

HEADQUARTERS SECOND BRIGADE E. C.,
Beaufort, S. C., January 3, 1862.

DEAR SIR: I desire to express my great confidence in your code of signals from my actual experience on the field of battle, and to call your attention to the great skill and merit of the signal officers of my command, Lieutenant Tafft and Lieutenant Cogswell. In my official report of the affair at Port Royal Ferry on New Year's Day I have stated that the signaling was a perfect success. It was indeed an extraordinary success. So far as I am advised, this is the first time it has been tested in actual battle.

It affords me the greater satisfaction to be able to give this testimonial from the circumstance that I had faith in your code from the beginning, as you will well remember, and lent my humble name in favor of your appointment to your present position.

Truly, your friend,

ISAAC I. STEVENS,
Brigadier-General, Commanding.

Maj. ALBERT J. MYER,
Signal Officer of the Army, Washington City.

No. 14.

Return of casualties in the Union forces at Port Royal Ferry, S. C., January 1, 1862.

[Compiled from records of Adjutant-General's Office.]

Command.	Killed.		Wounded.		Missing.		
	Officers.	Enlisted men.	Officers.	Enlisted men.	Officers.	Enlisted men.	Aggregate.
8th Michigan	......	2	1	6	......	1	10
48th New York	......	......	......	3	......	......	3
50th Pennsylvania	......	......	......	2	......	......	2
Total	......	2	1	11	......	1	15

No. 15.

Congratulatory orders from Major-General McClellan, U. S. Army.

GENERAL ORDERS, No. 99. } HDQRS. OF THE ARMY, A. G. O., *Washington, November 14, 1861.*

The Major-General Commanding announces to the Army with sincere pleasure, 1st, the brilliant reduction of the forts in Port Royal harbor, by the officers and sailors of our gallant fleet, under command of Flag-Officer S. F. DuPont, the utter rout of the enemy, the capture of the town of Beaufort, and the landing of Brig. Gen. T. W. Sherman's army on the coast of South Carolina; 2d, the victory achieved by Brig. Gen. William Nelson at Pikeville, Ky., in which, after two days' hard fighting, the rebels were completely defeated and put to flight; and, 3d, the daring attack made by Brig. Gen. U. S. Grant, with an inferior force, on the rebels at Belmont, Mo., and the signal defeat of the latter, with a loss of all their artillery, baggage, and means of transportation.

The Major-General Commanding cannot too highly extol the steadiness, courage, and admirable conduct displayed by officers, sailors, and soldiers alike in these several engagements. He commends them to the imitation of the whole Army.

By command of Maj. Gen. George B. McClellan:

L. THOMAS,
Adjutant-General.

No. 16.

Report of Brig. Gen. John C. Pemberton, C. S. Army.

HEADQUARTERS FOURTH MILITARY DIST. S. C.,
Pocotaligo Station, S. C., January 10, 1862.

SIR: I have the honor to inclose herewith official reports from Brig. Gen. D. S. Donelson, Provisional Army; Col. James Jones, Fourteenth Regiment South Carolina Volunteers; Lieut. Col. D. Barnes, Twelfth Regiment South Carolina Volunteers, and Maj. C. Jones, Twelfth Regiment South Carolina Volunteers, of their respective operations against the enemy in the affair on the Coosaw River on the 1st instant.

About 9.30 a. m. on that day, hearing heavy and rapid firing, I moved with as much dispatch as possible from my headquarters near Pocotaligo Station towards the direction whence it appeared to proceed. On reaching the camp of the Twelfth South Carolina Regiment, located where the Sheldon road and that from Page's Point and Cunningham's Bluff intersect the Port Royal road, I found that no positive information had been received as to the precise points whence the cannonading proceeded.

Towards 12 m. I received the first dispatch from Col. James Jones, commanding Fourteenth South Carolina Volunteers, stating that the enemy was landing in strong force at Chisolm's Landing, and shortly after another informing me that there was an evident intention of landing a large force from Chisolm's to Port Royal Ferry. I immediately directed Colonel Jones to have the siege howitzer and the long 12-pounder iron gun on siege carriage (the only two guns of greater caliber than 6-pounder field pieces which I had been able to place in position on the Coosaw River) in readiness to be removed from the intrenchments at the ferry should their safety be threatened by the enemy's advance on our left. I will here remark that the 12-pounder referred to, being very heavy and not equipped for transportation, was unfortunately, but accidentally, overturned in a ditch in the act of removal. The heavy fire from the enemy's gunboats rendered it impracticable to extricate it without the risk of too great a loss of life. It was therefore spiked and left. I also directed Colonel Jones to move towards the enemy at once, and to attack him the moment an opportunity should offer, and, if compelled to fall back, to do so fighting. In addition to his own regiment, Colonel Jones had under his command a section of Captain Leake's Virginia battery, which on several occasions during the day was effectively employed against the enemy's columns, under Captain Leake in person. Forty cavalry, under Major Oswald and Captain Evans, and four companies of the Twelfth South Carolina Volunteers, Lieutenant-Colonel Barnes commanding) Colonel Dunovant being in attendance at the session of the State Convention in Columbia), were moved forward with as much dispatch as possible. Colonel Barnes arrived in time to assist in opening the first fire on the enemy's forces.

To the reports of these officers (Colonel Jones and Lieutenant-Colonel Barnes) I respectfully refer for details of the operations of their respective corps, though during the engagement Lieutenant-Colonel Barnes acted under the immediate orders of his superior.

A large portion of the Tennessee brigade, under Brigadier-General Donelson, and Thornton's Virginia field battery were also ordered forward to the support of Colonel Jones. They did not, however, reach the field in time to take part in the action; though moved with the utmost promptitude, the brigade was disappointed in its desire to meet the enemy. I respectfully refer to General Donelson's report, herewith.*

During the day and succeeding night I was in frequent communication with Maj. C. Jones, commanding a detachment of three companies of his regiment (Twelfth South Carolina Volunteers) and a section of Leake's battery, near Page's Point, and in observation of Cunningham's Bluff. The enemy, though expending a large number of shot and shell, did no further damage than to burn the wood work of a battery which I was about completing, but for which I had not been able to obtain guns. Major Jones' report is respectfully forwarded herewith.

Although the enemy did not land in force at Page's Point or Cunningham's Bluff, it was entirely practicable for him to have done so under cover of his gunboats at any time. This compelled me to hold in reserve a sufficient force to meet him on the road in those directions; or, should he so select, on that to Mackay's Point, where a landing was equally feasible, and would have taken my advanced troops in rear, should he succeed in forcing his way. For these reasons no other troops than those mentioned were advanced, though others were held in readiness at a moment's notice.

Colonel Martin's cavalry corps acted during the day principally as pickets and vedettes, the colonel himself rendering efficient service as my aide-de-camp when his other duties permitted.

Our troops evinced from first to last a laudable desire to meet the enemy whenever and wherever it could be done upon anything like equal terms. On every occasion of his attempt to advance beyond the cover of his gunboats he was driven back or his troops dispersed. At no time during his occupation of the river bank did he leave their protection, and finally, when withdrawing to the island, did so under a fire from his vessels almost as heavy as that under which he had landed.

I also transmit herewith reports of killed and wounded; many of the latter were slight, by far the larger portion of the casualties being from the shells of the fleet; yet, from all the information I have been able to obtain, I am convinced the enemy's loss at least equaled our own.

My aide-de-camp, Lieut. J. H. Morrison, Provisional Army, was necessarily engaged during the day in office duties. I am much indebted to my volunteer aides-de-camp, Messrs. J. Huguenin and George Elliott.

To the officers whose reports are transmitted herewith I have to return my thanks, and through them to those under their immediate command. Also to Surgeon Turnipseed, Twelfth South Carolina Volunteers, for his untiring professional zeal, as well in the field as in the camp.

I am, sir, very respectfully, your obedient servant,

J. C. PEMBERTON,
Brigadier-General, Commanding Fourth Mil. Dist. S. C.

Capt. T. A. WASHINGTON,
Assistant Adjutant-General.

No. 17.

Report of Brig. Gen. Daniel S. Donelson, C. S. Army.

BRIGADE HEADQUARTERS,
Pocotaligo, S. C., January 5, 1862.

GENERAL: I refer you to the inclosed report of Col. James Jones, of the Fourteenth Regiment South Carolina Volunteers, which I found at my quarters last night, of all that transpired in the engagement of the forces under his command with the enemy at Port Royal Ferry on the 1st instant.

I reached the encampment of Colonel Jones between the hours of 4 and 5 p. m. the 1st instant; proceeded about 200 yards, after a moment's halt, to a point in the woods near the Kean's Neck road. Here I halted my command, which consisted of eight companies of the Eighth Tennessee Regiment, the Sixteenth Tennessee Regiment not having come up, until I could make a personal reconnaissance by going into the field in which the Chaplin house was situated, with the view to taking position and to co-operate with the forces of Colonel Jones. I saw upon entering this field our troops falling back along the road leading from the Chaplin house perpendicularly to the Kean's Neck road, near the point I had stationed the Eighth Tennessee Regiment. The troops of Colonel Jones, without halting, passed to his camp.

Here, after making the acquaintance of Colonel Jones, I ordered the whole force to halt. I found at once the enemy's shells could do us much injury without any ability on our part to return the enemy's fire; they, the enemy in the field, having previously retired, under cover of their gunboats, out of sight.

It being now near sundown, I ordered the entire command to fall back to a point out of the range of the enemy's gunboats. During all this time, both at the camp of Colonel Jones and on the march to the rear to take position, there was a quick and constant firing by the enemy. No casualty happened, the shells falling to our right. They ceased firing just at dark.

I have omitted to say that before getting to Colonel Jones' camp, Colonel Martin, commanding regiment of cavalry, rode up, introduced himself, and gave me the direction to lead my Eighth Regiment Tennessee Volunteers to the point occupied by them until he and myself could survey the open field through which Colonel Jones' regiment was then retiring. We thus remained until they passed into the Kean's Neck road, near the point of location of the Eighth Tennessee Regiment.

At this moment, in the preparation of this report, I received the inclosed official report of Lieutenant-Colonel Barnes, of the Twelfth Regiment South Carolina Volunteers, who commanded a detachment of four companies of said regiment in the action with the enemy on the 1st instant at Port Royal Ferry.

All of which is respectfully submitted.

I am, with high respect, your obedient servant,

D. S. DONELSON,

Brigadier-General First Brigade, Fourth Mil. Dist. of S. C.

Brigadier-General PEMBERTON,

Commanding Fourth Military District South Carolina.

No. 18.

Report of Col. James Jones, Fourteenth South Carolina Infantry.

HEADQUARTERS FOURTEENTH REGT. S. C. VOLS.,
Tomotley, S. C., January 4, 1862.

GENERAL: In obedience to instructions I have the honor to report the following occurrences of the 1st instant:

My camp was pitched on the road from Garden's Corner to Port Royal Ferry, 1 mile from the latter place, and where a road diverges eastward at nearly a right angle with the Port Royal Ferry road leading into Kean's Neck, and nearly parallel with and about a mile distant from Coosaw River. At the termination of the causeway of the ferry, on the northern bank of the Coosaw River, an earthwork was thrown up to prevent a crossing at that point, armed with two siege guns (a howitzer and 12-pounder gun), under the command of Lieutenant Webb, the 12-pounder being manned by an inexperienced detail from my regiment, and supported by a section of Captain Leake's field battery.

Two of my companies were sent out on picket duty—one (Company B) commanded by Captain [A. P.] West, at Adams' place, two and a half miles distant, on the Kean's Neck road; and the other (Company

H), commanded by Captain [Ed.] Croft, at a church 2 miles farther on the same road, and near the bridge and causeway leading into Chisolm's Island, with orders to guard the bridge and causeway above referred to, and with orders to send out pickets and scouts into Chisolm's Island. Two other companies were at the ferry, to support the battery there, leaving but six companies at my camp.

About 7 o'clock on the morning of the 1st instant, Captain Croft communicated the intelligence to me that the enemy had landed in force on Chisolm's Island. He estimated the number at two regiments, as he saw a long column advancing with two regimental stands of colors and two pieces of artillery. Soon after this (about 7.30 o'clock) Captain West dispatched a courier to me, with the information that the enemy had landed at Adams' place and were advancing in strong force to the Kean's Neck road. I ordered forward Lieutenant-Colonel [Samuel] McGowan, with three companies of my regiment, commanded by Captains [W. J.] Carter, [A.] Perrin, and [D. C.] Tomkins, and one gun of Captain Leake's section, to support Captain West, whom he met at about one and a half miles, retiring in good order towards my camp, when he formed his line of battle. I withdrew my two companies from the earthwork at the ferry, and, assisted by Major [W. D.] Simpson, with the five companies commanded by Captains [W. L.] Wood, [J. N.] Brown, [R. S.] Owens, [H. H.] Harper, and [M. C.] Taggart, took post near Chaplin's house, to intercept any column that might attempt to pass along the margin of the river to the ferry, and at the same time to be in supporting distance of Lieutenant-Colonel McGowan.

No attempt was made on the part of the enemy to advance in any direction—probably waiting for a sufficient tide to allow his gunboats to advance—until 12.30 p. m., when the gunboats began to move up slowly towards the ferry and to throw shells rapidly, when a message from Lieutenant-Colonel McGowan informed me that the enemy were advancing along the Kean's Neck road.

Regarding the earthwork at the ferry now unimportant, as the enemy had effected a landing at another point, I ordered Captain Leake and Lieutenant Webb to withdraw their guns from that position, Captain Leake to bring his gun to Lieutenant-Colonel McGowan's line, and I proceeded with my five companies also to his support.

Soon after I arrived at Lieutenant-Colonel McGowan's line my other company (Captain Croft's)—which had been posted at the church on the Kean's Neck road, and, on account of the landing of the enemy at Adams', could not return by that road—made a circuitous march by another road, in obedience to my instructions, and joined the regiment.

The whole regiment was then put in line of battle, the left resting on Captain Leake's section of his battery, placed in the road, and the right extending towards the river as far as I deemed practicable. I had just got into position when Major Oswald, of Colonel Martin's regiment, reported to me with 42 mounted men, and I directed him to take post upon my left. Almost at the same time Lieutenant-Colonel Barnes, of the Twelfth Regiment South Carolina Volunteers, reported with four companies of that regiment, and I directed him to return to Chaplin's house (the position I had left) and to guard to the river bank.

The enemy, instead of advancing, as I supposed he would do, along the Kean's Neck road, to attack my camp, and the only route by which he could bring up his artillery, left his artillery in his rear, and advanced close along the river bank and across the adjacent fields and woods, creeping along opposite his gunboats, five of which steamed slowly on, throwing shells in advance of and over his troops.

As soon as his column advancing by the margin of the river could be seen Captain Leake opened upon it, scattering it right and left and driving it out of view, down the slope, to the marsh; and when those advancing across the fields appeared before my right wing, I opened fire upon them with musketry, dispersing and driving them back to the river, under shelter of their gunboats.

When I became satisfied that the enemy would not advance by the Kean's Neck road I changed my position to Chaplin's house, near the ferry, in support of Lieutenant-Colonel Barnes' command; but when I arrived with the head of my regiment at that point I saw that I was too late to accomplish any useful purpose. The enemy had reached the earthwork at the end of the causeway in large force, and were protected by the guns of three steamers in the river near the bulkheads of the ferry. I then withdrew the whole command to my camp, to wait for further orders from general headquarters.

On arriving at my camp I met you at the head of the Eighth Regiment Tennessee Volunteers, and placed myself under your orders.

I cannot state with certainty the loss of the enemy, but I have reason to believe it was considerable in killed and wounded. Wherever we met him we invariably drove him from the field in confusion to the protection of his gunboats. We saw many dead upon the field and captured 2 prisoners, badly wounded, both of whom have since died.

I was not only satisfied, but highly gratified, with the conduct of all my officers and men during the engagement. Their coolness and enthusiasm were admirable.

I herewith transmit a complete list of the casualties* in my regiment. I also transmit two orders received during the engagement from the general commanding the Fourth Military District of South Carolina.†

I have the honor to be, general, very respectfully, your obedient servant,

JAMES JONES,
Colonel, Commanding Fourteenth Regiment S. C. Vols.

Brig. Gen. D. S. DONELSON,
Commanding First Brigade, Fourth Military District S. C.

No. 19.

Report of Lieut. Col. Dixon Barnes, Twelfth Regiment South Carolina Infantry.

TOMOTLEY, S. C., *January* 5, 1862.

GENERAL: I transmit herewith the report of Lieut. Col. D. Barnes of the affair at Port Royal on the 1st instant.

I have no remarks to make on it except to correct the distance of my line from my camp at the time the lieutenant-colonel reported to me, which is probably immaterial; but the line was about 1 mile from my camp instead of half a mile, as stated by Lieutenant-Colonel Barnes.

I am, general, very respectfully, your obedient servant,

JAMES JONES,
Colonel, Commanding Fourteenth Regiment S. C. Vols.

General D. S. DONELSON,
First Brigade, Fourth Military District South Carolina.

---

* Embodied in No. 22, p. 75.

† Not found.

[Inclosure.]

HEADQUARTERS TWELFTH REGIMENT S. C. VOLS.,
January 4, 1862.

SIR: I submit the following report of the part performed in the recent affair at Port Royal Ferry by the detachment of the Twelfth Regiment, under my command:

Between 1 and 2 p. m. of the 1st instant I left Camp Pemberton, near Garden's Corner, with Adjutant Talley and four companies of the Twelfth Regiment, to wit: Company A, Captain [W. H.] McCorkle; Company B, Captain [John L.] Miller; Company G, Lieutenant [John M.] Moody; and Company I, Lieutenant [H. W.] Campbell, under orders from the brigadier-general commanding the Fourth Military District to proceed to join the Fourteenth Regiment in resisting the reported advance of the enemy from Chisolm's Point, where it was said they had landed in force.

On reaching the camp of the Fourteenth Regiment, at the junction of the road leading to Kean's Neck with the Port Royal Ferry road, I ascertained that the earthworks at the ferry had been abandoned, and that the Fourteenth Regiment, with some of the pieces, had advanced down the former road, leaving a small guard, with a howitzer, at the camp. I followed with my command, the direction being nearly parallel to the river and within easy range of the heavy guns of the enemy's vessels; but we came up with Colonel Jones' regiment about a half mile from their camp without having sustained any loss from the few shells which were fired. That regiment was then filing off from the road to the right, and upon reporting to Colonel Jones I was informed that the enemy were advancing on the right, and was ordered to countermarch to a gate-way some 300 yards to the rear, from which a road extended directly towards the river, and thus to gain a position to the right of that occupied by the Fourteenth Regiment. On reaching the gate-way indicated I discovered that the road to which I had been directed ran through the middle of an extensive cotton field, bounded on our right by the Port Royal Ferry road and on the left for some 200 yards by a wood of small pines, into which the Fourteenth Regiment had filed, and beyond that wood, on the left, by a rail fence, which separated the cotton field from other open lands. Directly in front of the gate-way, about a quarter of a mile distant, a ridge, whereon stood a dwelling and outbuildings (known as Chaplin's), and which was partially covered with trees and undergrowth, extended from the Port Royal Ferry road, on the right, to a considerable distance beyond the fence referred to, on our left.

My detachment marched from the gate to the left, crossing the cotton field diagonally, so as to advance nearer to the position of the Fourteenth Regiment, and at the same time gain a point between its right and the river. This we did, and formed in line under cover of the fence, our right resting near the ridge. The Fourteenth Regiment was hidden from us by the intervening growth of pines, but to the front of our line the view was unobstructed for a considerable distance. Through this open area we soon saw the enemy advancing as skirmishers upon the right of the Fourteenth Regiment, apparently in ignorance of our position. That regiment opened fire, and immediately afterward I ordered my detachment to advance. They responded promptly, with a cheer, and, leaping the fence, we advanced at a run, firing upon the enemy. They returned the fire, wounding 2 of our men, and fled, screening themselves behind a point of woodland to our right. The firing from the Fourteenth Regiment also ceased; and it having been reported to me by a few men of Company B, posted on the ridge to our right to observe the movements of the enemy in that direction, that they were moving down towards the ferry between our right and the river, I proceeded to deploy one company, and subsequently the remaining three, along the ridge at right angles to the line of our former position, and about 100 yards farther to the right. We had scarcely gained this ground before the enemy were seen advancing directly towards our new front, and shortly afterwards a body of them appeared towards our right, at a gate on the Port Royal Ferry road. The right of our line fired upon the body of men at the gate, who gave way and ran precipitately, and about the same time our left fired upon those near our front. These latter also disappeared among the thick growth of pine, and the fire of the enemy ceased entirely.

I now ordered the detachment forward into the wood which covered the eminence. We had, however, advanced but a few paces, when Colonel Jones rode up to our line, and I then saw the regiment of the latter and another regiment, which I afterwards learned was the Eighth Tennessee, advancing to our support, marching by a flank along the road through the cotton field in our rear. At this moment the enemy's gunboats opened a heavy fire of shell, and the whole force was ordered to fall back. While returning through the field my detachment lost 1 killed and 2 wounded. This loss resulted from the enemy's shells exclusively, their infantry making no further demonstration whatever.

Throughout the affair Adjutant [W. H.] Talley rendered me great assistance in the execution of the various movements, and did his duty in every respect in a manner entirely satisfactory to me.

Surgeon Turnipseed joined the command a short time before we first fired upon the enemy, and entered at once upon the discharge of the duties of his position. His services were valuable, especially in the removal of the wounded from the field while it was still under fire of the enemy.

The conduct of the whole command was good. They obeyed orders promptly, and exhibited enthusiasm when the prospect was presented of meeting the foe face to face upon a fair field of battle.

I forward herewith the report of Surgeon Turnipseed.*

I am, very respectfully, your obedient servant,

D. BARNES,

Lieutenant-Colonel, Comdg. Detachment Twelfth Regt. S. C. Vols.

Lieutenant READY,

Adjutant Fourteenth Regiment South Carolina Volunteers.

No. 20.

Report of Maj. Cadwalader Jones, Twelfth South Carolina Infantry.

PAGE'S POINT, S. C., *January* —, 1862.

SIR: In obedience to your orders I proceeded from Camp Pemberton, at 10 o'clock on the 1st instant, to Page's Point, and took command of the forces at this place. They consisted of three companies of the Twelfth Regiment South Carolina Volunteers (Colonel Dunovant), to wit: Captain [E. F.] Bookter's, Captain H. C. Davis' (Lieutenant [J. W.] Delleney commanding), and Captain T. F. Clyburn's company; also

---

*Embodied in No. 22, p. 75.

one section of Captain Leake's Virginia artillery, Lieutenant Leake commanding.

I found the command well placed, under direction of E. F. Bookter, senior captain. On my arrival a heavy cannonading from two of the enemy's gunboats, chiefly in the direction of the Island battery (not yet completed), was going on. I immediately sent a small detachment to this battery, which reported that the enemy had burned it and made their escape. Very soon another of the enemy's gunboats came in sight from the direction of Cunningham's Bluff and lay off Page's Point. The three gunboats then commenced a heavy fire of shells in all directions—I supposed with a view of effecting a landing. I immediately moved the command under a considerable shelling, but without loss, to a point of safety about three-fourths of a mile from the boats, where I remained during the day. About 4 o'clock the enemy threw on shore some 20 men, under protection of their guns. They remained a short time and returned to their boats. At night I fell back to the springs, and at about 2 o'clock in the night I sent forward a detachment of 15 men, under command of Lieutenant Roseborough, and burned all the cotton and corn on the Point. This was effected in the face of the enemy, who lay in their gunboats off Page's Point during the night.

In the morning I returned to my former position. The boats of the enemy were still off the Point, where they remained without attempting to land, but passing occasionally in the direction of Cunningham's Bluff, until the afternoon, when they left. At the same time I observed the enemy leave Port Royal Ferry, as reported at the time.

I have the honor to be, very respectfully, your obedient servant,

CAD'R JONES,
Major, Twelfth Regiment South Carolina Volunteers.

Brigadier-General PEMBERTON.

No. 21.

Reports of Col. William E. Martin, Mounted Regiment.

HEADQUARTERS MOUNTED REGIMENT,
January 4, 1861, [1862.]

GENERAL: I avail myself of your suggestion to-day relative to the action of the 1st merely to report that a detachment of my regiment, under Maj. G. W. Oswald, reported to Colonel Jones early in the day, and participated in the engagement with their double-barreled guns and navy revolvers; that I was detained by General Pemberton at his headquarters, and it was in carrying orders for him that I had the pleasure of meeting you, and my local knowledge, which I have diligently acquired, enabled me to point out the way through the woods which you followed. Further, I have only to add that after the engagement I, with Colonel McGowan, rode at full speed to the causeway near the enemy's position, ascertained the condition of the wounded, and with the same gentleman and Dr. Turnipseed and some soldiers returned and brought away the wounded in a wagon, the enemy shelling us while so engaged.

Respectfully submitted.

W. E. MARTIN,
Colonel Mounted Regiment.

Brigadier-General DONELSON.

HEADQUARTERS MOUNTED REGIMENT,
Heywood, January 4, 1862.

SIR: I have the honor to report that on the 1st instant I received orders from Brigadier-General Pemberton to send a detachment of forty cavalry to report to General Jones, near the ferry. The detachment was under Captain Evans, as commander of the company, and Major Oswald, of my regiment. The detachment continued to act as a reserve, though engaged occasionally with the enemy's skirmishers, whom they assisted in driving back, the double-barreled gun and navy revolver having proved useful. General Pemberton directed me to remain at his headquarters.

At 3 p. m. he sent me to the scene of action to observe and report. On my way I overtook General Donelson with one of his regiments and led them to position by the general's request. I had no other part in the affair, except that soon after our regiments retired to the cover of the wood I proposed to Lieutenant-Colonel McGowan, of Jones' regiment, to reconnoiter the field in search of our wounded. This we did, advancing on horseback at [full] speed to the spot in the causeway, where the shell exploded which did us the principal damage.

This was within 100 yards of the enemy's position at Chaplin's house. Having found the wounded, we returned with Dr. Turnipseed, of Dunovant's regiment, and a few soldiers, and with a wagon we brought the wounded away under the shells of the enemy aimed at us and the wagon containing the wounded.

I have no casualties to report in my command.

Respectfully submitted.

WM. E. MARTIN,
Colonel Mounted Regiment.

Lieut. J. H. MORRISON,
Assistant Adjutant-General, Fourth Military District S. C.

No. 22.

Return of casualties in the Confederate forces at Port Royal Ferry, S. C., January 1, 1862.

Command.	Killed.		Wounded.		Aggregate.	Remarks.
	Officers.	Enlisted men.	Officers.	Enlisted men.		
12th South Carolina	......	1	......	4	5	
14th South Carolina	1	6	1	19	27	Lieut. J. A. Powers, killed.
Martin's regiment	......	......	......	......	......	No casualties.
Total	1	7	1	23	32	

JANUARY 16, 1862.—Naval descent upon Cedar Keys, Fla.

Reports of Brig. Gen. J. H. Trapier, C. S. Army.

HEADQUARTERS PROVISIONAL FORCES,
DEPARTMENT EAST AND MIDDLE FLORIDA,
Fernandina, Fla., January 20, 1862.

CAPTAIN: On the 16th instant the enemy, in a steamer armed with five guns, made a descent upon the harbor and village of Cedar Keys.

Having burned seven small vessels in the harbor, which were loading with cotton and turpentine (with the intention, information of which had doubtless been conveyed to the enemy, of running the blockade), and also the wharf of the Florida Railroad, which has its Gulf terminus at that point, and several flat cars belonging to the same road, he withdrew and went to sea. There was posted at this place a small force, consisting of a lieutenant and 22 men, belonging to the Fourth Regiment Florida Volunteers, placed there as a sort of police force, to protect the inhabitants of the Key (some 80 or 100 persons) against any disturbance from bands of marauders. The lieutenant and 14 privates were taken prisoners, but 4 of the latter were subsequently released for reasons set forth in one of the papers,* which I have the honor to forward herewith (as information) to the commanding general. The rest of the men made their escape. There were three old guns which had been in battery on one of the Keys of the group, but which had been condemned after inspection by Maj. J. G. Barnwell, inspector-general of this military department, as unserviceble. They were never removed, however, as not being worth the removal, neither the guns nor their carriages. These guns the enemy, nevertheless, is said to have spiked.

It is said that some of the inhabitants of the Key were required to sign an oath not to take up arms against the Government of the (so-called) United States during the present war.

I must not omit to mention a circumstance which reflects high credit upon Commander Emmons. Three negroes escaped from the Key and went out to his steamer; they were all ordered back forthwith.

I am, very respectfully, your obedient servant,

J. H. TRAPIER,
Brigadier-General, Commanding.

Capt. T. A. WASHINGTON,
Assistant Adjutant-General, Coosawhatchie, S. C.

HEADQUARTERS PROVISIONAL FORCES,
DEPARTMENT EAST AND MIDDLE FLORIDA,
Tallahassee, Fla., January 31, 1862.

CAPTAIN: I have the honor to acknowledge the receipt to-day of a letter from the general commanding, under date January 27, from Coosawhatchie. Referring to the late affair at Cedar Keys, the general says:

> It seems that the commanding officer, with almost his entire force, were taken prisoners in daylight by the crew of a man-of-war. I desire to know the circumstances attending the capture. Was any resistance made? If not, why did not the guard escape?

In reply to all which I have the honor respectfully to submit the following statement: No official report of the affair has reached me of course, the only commissioned officer of the guard having been taken prisoner. I learn, however, through sources entitled to credence, that no resistance whatever was attempted, and for the reason that protest against it was made by a portion of the citizens of the Key upon the ground that it would be hopeless, and could only result, by drawing the fire of the war vessel, in a useless destruction of property and shedding of blood—perhaps the blood of women and children. The guard did attempt to escape and was captured in the act. They embarked on

* Inclosed papers not of sufficient importance for publication.

board of a flat-boat, with no other means of propulsion than poles. When they had reached mid-channel, their poles being too short to reach the bottom, they were left at the mercy of the tide, by which they were swept out, and fell easy victims into the hands of the enemy.

If it is said that better and surer means of escape ought to have been furnished them in the event of an attack from an irresistible force, I answer that my letter-book contains an order, dated December 23, 1861, to the brigade quartermaster, to charter a steamer of 125 tons burden, for purposes of transportation between the Key and the main-land, and the records of this office show that this officer did his duty, and that the boat was chartered. Why she was not in place I know not. If it be asked why so small a force was left upon the Key, I answer that it was all that could be spared from more important points, and that even this was in contravention, to some extent, of the instructions (by telegraph) from the commanding general. By these instructions I was directed to order all the Florida troops to Fernandina. In compliance with them, given when an attack was hourly expected at the latter point, I ordered the two companies then stationed at Cedar Keys to Fernandina.

In a few days after their removal, and when it had become obvious that Fernandina was not then to be the object of attack, I received a paper from Cedar Keys, signed by a number of its inhabitants, setting forth their fears that certain persons who had been arrested there as traitors, and released afterwards for want of sufficient testimony to convict, would, prompted by motives of revenge, now that the troops were withdrawn, avail themselves of the opportunity thus afforded to wreak their vengeance upon their accusers, and requesting, therefore, that a guard of 20 or 30 men might be sent for their protection, I took the responsibility of promptly complying with the petition.

I have the honor to be, very respectfully, sir, your obedient servant,

J. H. TRAPIER,
Brigadier-General, Commanding.

Capt. T. A. WASHINGTON,
Assistant Adjutant-General, Coosawhatchie, S. C.

JANUARY 22-25, 1862.—Expedition to Edisto Island, S. C.

REPORTS, ETC.

No. 1.—Brig. Gen. Nathan G. Evans, C. S. Army.
No. 2.—Col. P. F. Stevens, Holcombe Legion, C. S. Army.
No. 3.—Instructions from General Evans to Colonel Stevens.

No. 1.

Report of Brig. Gen. Nathan G. Evans, C. S. Army.

HEADQUARTERS THIRD MILITARY DISTRICT,
Adams Run, S. C., January 25, 1862.

CAPTAIN: I have the honor to report that the expedition under Col. P. F. Stevens, Holcombe Legion, has succeeded in capturing about 50 negroes on Edisto Island, several of whom are the negroes that attacked my pickets at Watt's Cut. I think after a due investigation, should any of the negroes be convicted, they should be hanged as soon as possible at some public place as an example. The negroes have evidently been incited to insurrection by the enemy. I have now as prisoners several negroes, who say they can identify the men who attacked the pickets. I will keep all the negroes till the investigation is through, and would earnestly request instructions from the general commanding. The negro fellows not implicated directly I propose to iron heavily and work them under guard on the causeway now being made at Church Flats. Colonel Stevens will probably arrive to-day with the remainder of the negroes.

Very respectfully, your obedient servant,

N. G. EVANS,
Brigadier-General, Commanding.

Capt. T. A. WASHINGTON,
Assistant Adjutant-General, Charleston, S. C.

No. 2.

Report of Col. P. F. Stevens, Holcombe Legion, C. S. Army.

HEADQUARTERS THIRD MILITARY DISTRICT,
Adams Run, S. C., January 28, 1862.

CAPTAIN: Inclosed I have the honor to submit the report of Col. P. F. Stevens, Holcombe Legion, commanding the expedition to Edisto Island. The negro men captured I have now under guard at this place. The women and children I have sent to the workhouse in Charleston. As five of the negroes have confessed themselves as being the party that attacked my pickets on Jehossee Island, I would respectfully ask instructions as to their disposition, as it is unsafe to return them to their owners unless they be obligated to submit them to a trial for their lives, and in case of acquittal to be removed from this district.

Very respectfully, your obedient servant,

N. G. EVANS,
Brigadier-General.

Capt. T. A. WASHINGTON,
Assistant Adjutant-General, Coosawhatchie, S. C.

[Inclosure.]

HEADQUARTERS HOLCOMBE LEGION,
Camp Walsh, January 27, 1862.

CAPTAIN: I have the honor to submit the following report:

Pursuant to orders from the general commanding, at 6.30 a. m. on Wednesday, the 22d instant, I proceeded with a detachment to cross the Dawho on an expedition to Edisto Island. My force was 120 infantry and 65 cavalry, composed of detachments from Captain Blair's company (attached to the Legion), Company A and Company C of the infantry, and Company A and Company B of the cavalry. Major Palmer was in command of the cavalry, while I took the more immediate charge of the infantry. The Rev. Mr. Baynard accompanied me as guide.

After considerable delay at the inconvenient ferry near Mr. Grimball's (three-quarters of a mile long) and at the bridge over Watt's Cut, between Jehossee Island and Edisto, I left the cut about 3.30 p. m. and began my march on Edisto. About a mile from Watt's Cut we passed

Dr. William Bailey's place—Old Dominion; found some potatoes; corn-house burnt, together with two or three other outbuildings; 1 horse and 1 mule shot, supposed to have been killed by the pickets on Saturday in a field near by; 1 horse reported wounded. The detachment of cavalry thrown in advance examined the next plantation to the south-east of the road and reported no provisions, but the ruins of the corn-house still smoking. About 3 miles from the cut, just at the crossing of the Edisto Ferry road, at Mr. William Whaley's place, found 4 negroes—Joe and his wife—belonging to Mr. Whaley, and in charge of the place; Bill, belonging to W. G. Baynard, these all old and infirm, and Peter, belonging to Henry Seabrook. Peter's manner being very insubordinate, and his holding one hand in his pocket exciting suspicion, he was seized, searched, and tied on the discovery of a sharp knife in the pocket where he had kept his hand. Old Joe, on interrogation, confessed to having heard of the attack of Saturday, and said he could lead us to the rendezvous of the attacking party. Mounting some 30 infantry behind as many cavalry, I proceeded with this force, added to the cavalry, to the point—Miss Mary Seabrook's—under guidance of Joe, but no trace of the negroes could be discovered. The dwelling-house had been very little used by the negroes, and their own houses deserted for a length of time. Returning to Whaley's, I spent the night there. At Mr. Whaley's we found some 400 bushels of corn and a few pigs.

On the 23d sent Peter, under guard, to the pickets at Watt's Cut with 1 horse and saddle; took 1 mule and cart and moved down the main road towards Mr. Townsend's. One detachment of cavalry covered my front, while another visited the places on either side of the road. The detachment on the south and east of the road soon found a party of negroes, some 10 in number, whom I ordered to be taken into custody, and, through a fortunate misunderstanding of the order, they were sent immediately back to Watt's Cut; I therefore cannot report their names or place of capture. Moving slowly until past the Episcopal Church, my advanced party captured Paul, belonging to the estate of James Clark; Penny, his wife, and Victoria, his child, belonging to Mr. Henry Bailey, and on his place. One mule and cart were taken from this place. Under guidance of Paul I directed my march towards Point of Pines, in which locality he said a number of negroes were assembled.

Arrived at Mr. Edward Whaley's place, a number of negroes were taken in the house and yard. They had assembled here from all points. While securing these several others were taken in the adjoining roads and fields, some in buggies, some on horseback, and some in carts. Leaving a guard over the negroes taken, I moved on, under guidance of Paul, to Mr. Hopkinson's place, while a small party, under Messrs. Elliott and Curry (I omitted to state that at Jehossee these gentlemen reported to me by order of the general commanding), proceeded to Mr. Berwick Legaré's place.

By this time the alarm had been given, and the negroes were on the move for the lower part of the island; the number captured was therefore less than it would otherwise have been. A number were seen by Messrs. Elliott and Curry making their escape. Crossing a long foot-bridge from Hopkinson's to Mr. Edward Seabrook's, several negroes were taken at the latter place. Our party was there joined by Major Palmer, who, with his detachment, had passed through a number of plantations, among others those of Mr. Evans Eddings, Mr. Lastree, and one belonging to the estate of Berwick Legaré. At these places he had either captured or pursued negroes, and our hands were now quite full of prisoners. The infantry being in rear, as not able to move with the celerity of the cavalry, compelled to move rapidly in order to be ahead of the alarm which was now spreading, I could not stop to take notes as to the names of the negroes or their owners.

The alarm must have been communicated in some way to the gun-boat, which was now seen approaching Mr. Seabrook's place. Leaving a picket there I proceeded to assemble the command, which was scattered over the three places last mentioned, and covering the march of the captured negroes, I moved back to Edward Whaley's, where I left the negroes under guard, and taking the infantry moved rapidly back to Seabrook's to resist a landing, which seemed imminent. On the march two shells were thrown at the Seabrook house, but by the time my party came up the boat had retired. Night closing in, I quartered the infantry at Mr. Seabrook's and carried the cavalry to Whaley's.

I regret to state that at the Legaré and Seabrook places 3 negroes were either shot or drowned and a fourth wounded; 2 women and 1 man ran into the water, and, refusing or failing to come out, were fired upon and disappeared beneath the water.

Early on the 24th I dispatched the captured negroes under guard, with orders to the lieutenant that they were to be reported to the general commanding. I then proceeded with my force to the neighborhood of Mr. Townsend's. Stopping at Major Murray's, I endeavored, with a field glass, to examine Eddingsville, but could discover no signs of any persons in the village.

In the mean time Major Palmer, who had gone to Townsend's, returned with 5 negroes, and reported, on their statement, that the enemy were landing in our rear at Point of Pines. As I had heard one or two shells fired in that direction, I presumed they had thrown these to cover the landing, and thinking it prudent to secure my retreat in case the party should be greatly superior to my own, I dispatched the cavalry to cover the road by which the enemy was to approach, while I endeavored to pass it. Having passed this road, and the cavalry reporting no enemy landed, I concluded that, as I had visited nearly the entire island, my command greatly fatigued, provisions scarce, and my return so far begun, I had better continue my march home. The infantry reached Mr. Aiken's summer house about 4 o'clock, after a march of some 15 miles, or thereabouts. Spending the night on Jehossee, I returned to camp about 4 o'clock on Saturday.

The result of the expedition was the capture of some 80 negroes, men, women, and children. I brought off 9 mules, 10 horses, 5 colts, 8 carts, 1 two-horse wagon, 2 carriages, and 1 buggy. The mules and carts I thought might do for public service, and the same for the horses. The colts were bought by some of the men. The carriages were used in transporting the sick and the children. The buggy was bought by a Mr. Price, who accompanied the expedition. The colts and some of the horses not being available for public service, the parties capturing them are desirous of purchasing at reasonable prices. The mules will make good teams for army transportation.

From my observation and the report of my men I think there is very little provision on the island, and only a small portion of that can be removed.

I burned about 300 or 400 bushels of corn and a little cotton, as follows: Mr. Lastree's, about 200 bushels of corn; Mr. Berwick Legaré's, near Eddings', about 100 bushels of corn; Mrs. Martha M. Whaley's, about 125 bushels of corn; Mr. W. G. Baynard's, small quantity of cotton and hay.

The upper portion of the island is completely deserted, and this expedition has, I think, driven off the island nearly all the able-bodied negroes, according to the information gathered. I think the negroes are congregated in large numbers on Botany Bay, in the vicinity of the fort. They have destroyed the bridges connecting Botany Bay and Eddingsville with the main island. Should it be desirable, I recommend that a force of 300 men be sent to Botany Bay, provided with the means of repairing the bridge which separates it from Edisto, and under instructions to make a surprise at night, when the gunboats cannot use their artillery. By this means I think nearly the entire force of negroes, numbering, according to accounts, some thousand, may be captured. From the confessions of some of the negroes taken, I think several of the party were concerned in the attack made on our pickets on Saturday last.

By permission of the general commanding I have this morning dispatched a foraging party to obtain provisions from Mr. William Whaley's place.

The stock taken in the expedition is now in the hands of my quartermaster, subject to the order of the general commanding.

In conclusion, I beg leave to mention particularly the energy, activity, and efficiency of Major Palmer, to whose exertions I think the success of the expedition greatly due.

I also mention with pleasure the patient and cheerful endurance of all my men, who, amid cold, rain, and a lack of provisions, were ready and prompt in every call made upon them.

Very respectfully,

P. F. STEVENS,
Colonel Holcombe Legion.

Capt. W. H. ROGERS,
Acting Assistant Adjutant-General.

No. 3.

Instructions from General Evans to Colonel Stevens.

HEADQUARTERS THIRD MILITARY DISTRICT,
Adams Run, January 21, 1862.

COLONEL: I received a report last night that the negroes on Edisto Island attacked at 12 m. yesterday our pickets at the summer house. I wish to capture the party and check this insurrection. The negroes have evidently been armed by the enemy, who are no doubt lurking in the rear. I send you an order to go to-morrow with 100 infantry and a company of cavalry to attack the party. Captain Miller has been instructed to furnish every assistance, and will probably have the flats in position for you. You had better send your regimental quartermaster to fix the bridge over the cut. Should you not be able to cross the cavalry, you can dismount a portion and leave the balance as a guard. Send word to your pickets at Bennett's Point to keep a sharp lookout and to send word to Captain Perrin. The battery at Pineberry will receive orders to fire into any craft that should attempt to cut you off. I wish you to take four days' rations, and to advance with caution as far on the island as possible, making a thorough reconnaissance, and find out the position of the enemy. Should you find him in strength and position as would warrant a successful attack, you will attack and drive him at least under cover of his guns.

Captain Miller reports that there is a considerable quantity of potatoes and some corn on the island. You will destroy all you possibly can with your party. All negroes taken will be brought over to the main-land to be sent to jail. Should any attempt to escape, they will be shot. On your return make a written report of your operations.

Very respectfully, your obedient servant,

N. G. EVANS,
Brigadier-General, Commanding.

Col. P. F. STEVENS,
Commanding Holcombe Legion.

[Inclosure.]

SPECIAL ORDERS, No. 10. } HEADQUARTERS SECOND MIL. DIST. S. C.,
Charleston, January 21, 1862.

I. An expedition to act against the enemy in North Edisto will proceed to Seabrook's Island without delay.

Captain Ives, engineer, C. S. Army, will have charge of the attack, being informed of the desires of the brigadier-general commanding, and his directions will be obeyed accordingly.

Capt. Alfred Rhett, S. C. artillery, will have charge of the firing party, and will receive instructions to open fire from Captain Ives. Col. Clement H. Stevens, volunteer aide-de-camp, will detail from the unattached troops in camp near the junction of Wappoo and Stono Rivers such infantry force as is requisite for support.

II. Lieut. H. K. Stevens, C. S. Navy, is detailed as ordnance officer, and will report and communicate with Captains Ives and Rhett.

III. The commander of the different parties will report to Captain Ives for duty on engineer service until in action, and receive instructions from that officer in the absence of other orders, the duty having been performed.

By order of Brigadier-General Ripley:

LEO. D. WALKER,
Assistant Adjutant-General.

JANUARY 26-28, 1862.—Reconnaissance to Wilmington Narrows, Ga., and naval engagement.

REPORTS.

No. 1.—Brig. Gen. Horatio G. Wright, U. S. Army.
No. 2.—General Robert E. Lee, C. S. Army.

No. 1.

Report of Brig. Gen. Horatio G. Wright, U. S. Army.

HEADQUARTERS,
Hilton Head, S. C., January 29, 1862.

CAPTAIN: In pursuance of the instructions of the general commanding, dated the 21st and 25th instant, I proceeded on the morning of the

26th, with the transports carrying my command, in company with the gunboats, to Warsaw Sound, Ga., where we arrived and anchored about 2 o'clock the same day. The naval portion of the expedition, commanded by Capt. Charles H. Davis, U. S. Navy, was composed of the gunboats Ottawa, Capt. T. H. Stevens; the Seneca, Captain Ammen; the Isaac H. Smith, Captain Nicholson; the Potomska, Captain Watmough; the Ellen, Captain Budd; the Western World, Captain Gregory, and two armed launches, with their crews, from the Wabash, under the command of Capt. C. R. P. Rodgers, U. S. Navy.

It was arranged between Captain Davis and myself that two companies of troops should be placed on board the gunboats, and that the latter should proceed to reconnoiter the passage known on our maps as Wilmington Narrows. Accordingly the next morning, the troops having been taken on board, the gunboats proceeded up the Narrows, leaving the transports at anchor in the sound. I accompanied Captain Davis, in the Ottawa. No obstruction to our progress was met with, or any signs of an enemy discovered, before reaching a position in the Narrows between the plantations marked on our sketches as Scriven's and Gibson's. At this point the passage forks, and it was discovered that the one leading to the right was obstructed by a double line of piling of heavy timber, near which we anchored.

Soon after anchoring I went on shore with Captain Rodgers, of the Navy, to examine the lower of the three plantations, taking with us, to cover the landing, the two large launches, each carrying a boat howitzer, and to serve as skirmishers after landing 20 men from the troops were taken, to act in connection with the launches' crews, which were armed with rifles. The place was found to be utterly deserted, with no evidence of its having been occupied for weeks and perhaps months. All the movable property of every description had been carried off. No signs of life were visible. Soon after our return on board, however, a party of some 5 or 6 men were seen from one of the gunboats, who were dispersed by a shot from the vessel.

The following morning, the 28th, I started in a small boat with Lieutenant Barnes, of the Wabash, temporarily with the launches, to examine the Narrows above the piles. Lieutenant Barnes had been over the same ground the evening before, with the black pilot Isaac, to a point which the latter represented as within a short distance of the entrance into Saint Augustine Creek. We proceeded a little farther only, as we came to fast land, where it was probable that pickets would be stationed, and, as we confidently believed, close to the junction of the two creeks. The banks up to this point were of soft mud, rendering it impracticable to land, and overgrown with high grass, which made it difficult to see the surrounding country. We took carefully the bearings of the different reaches of the creek, and, as often as we could see them, of surrounding objects. The soundings nowhere showed a less depth of water than 20 feet, and the width is sufficient for any of the gunboats. The piling above referred to was therefore the only obstacle to the passage of the gunboats so far as we penetrated, and this it is no doubt practicable to remove.

Just as we were preparing to return we perceived the rebel gunboats, five in number, coming down from Savannah, and soon after reaching our vessels the enemy appeared to be within the Savannah River. Our gunboats at once opened fire, as did those under the command of Capt. John Rodgers, on the other side of the Savannah River. The leading rebel boat, bearing a flag-officer's pennant, was soon apparently quite disabled, and, turning back, made her way slowly to Savannah in company with one of the others. The remaining three proceeded on to Fort Pulaski. All were represented to have had barges in tow. In the afternoon, while Captain Rodgers and myself were on shore at the plantation of Scriven and Gibson, the three rebel boats last referred to returned up the river, and the firing recommenced, but the boats got past apparently without serious damage, and reached Savannah. This firing, though no part of the plan, was very instructive in connection with any project for cutting off Fort Pulaski by batteries on Wilmington Island or by gunboats lying at or below the obstructions. It showed conclusively to my mind that steamers might run the gauntlet, not without danger, but without any serious risk, even under so heavy and well-directed a fire as that delivered by our gunboats. The position from which to cut off communication between the fort and Savannah by way of the river must therefore be sought higher up.

The plat of the courses of the stream would indicate that it empties directly into the Savannah River, and not into Saint Augustine Creek, as had been supposed, and other circumstances would seem to confirm this conclusion, though contrary to some of the evidence obtained. However this may be, there is no doubt that the stream we followed gradually approaches the river, from which it can be separated only by a narrow strip of marsh at the point reached by us in the boat. A position might, therefore, be taken up by the gunboats, after removing the obstructions, from which the river might be commanded, and it is quite possible that the headland alluded to as just above the point reached by us would permit the establishment of a battery which would command both the Saint Augustine Creek and the Savannah River.

Wilmington Island, as a simple military position, is, in my judgment, of no importance whatever, and any troops landed there could be of no real service. But should it be decided to cut off all communication by the Savannah River, either by gunboats stationed above or by the establishment of the battery alluded to, or by both, then the occupation of the island becomes a matter of high importance, as in this way only can the line of communication with our base be kept open. Should it therefore be decided to intercept the river communication in this way, or to use the passage in any ulterior movements on Savannah, I would recommend the occupation of the island in force; otherwise not. The portion of the island above Gibson's is marshy for one and a half to two miles back from the bank of the creek, and therefore no battery could, I think, be established by the enemy at any point above Gibson's which could seriously annoy our gunboats. The portion of the island below the plantation is also marshy.

Having made the reconnaissance as above detailed, the gunboats returned to Warsaw Sound, and after consultation with Captain Davis, whose orders required him to return and report, I thought it best to return with him and report in person. I accordingly arrived here in the Ottawa just before sunset this evening, leaving the transports and the three other gunboats at anchor in the sound. I should have stated our nearest approach to Fort Pulaski was within long range—say 2 miles—while the distance from the fort to our anchorage near the obstructions was much greater and entirely beyond range.

Very respectfully, your obedient servant,

H. G. WRIGHT,
Brigadier-General, Commanding.

Capt. L. H. PELOUZE,
Asst. Adjt. Gen., Hdqrs. Exped'y Corps, Hilton Head, S. C.

No. 2.

Report of General Robert E. Lee, C. S. Army.

SAVANNAH, GA., *January* 29, 1862.

GENERAL: I have the honor to report, for the information of the Secretary of War, that five [?] days since it was discovered that the enemy were at work removing the obstructions placed in Wall's Cut. This cut is the pass between Daufuskie River and Wright River, in South Carolina, and forms part of the inland communication between Savannah River and Port Royal Harbor. This communication traverses an extensive marsh, is crooked, shallow, and difficult of navigation, and though it was apparent that unless protected by batteries any artificial obstructions may be removed, yet as the marsh is too soft and impassable to admit the construction of a battery, it was the only obstacle that could be opposed to its navigation. The obstruction consisted of the hull of a large schooner, sunk in the narrowest and shoalest part of the cut, with rows of piles driven across on each side. A similar obstruction was placed in Wilmington Narrows, a small creek west of the Savannah, connecting Wilmington River and Saint Augustine Creek. Day before yesterday seven of the enemy's gunboats were discovered at Wall's Cut and six in Wilmington Narrows. They had reached the obstructions in each stream, and were apparently endeavoring to work through. Flag-Officer Tatnall, with his gunboats, descended the Savannah River and boldly engaged them, but the range and caliber of their guns were so superior to his, that after an hour's trial he had to haul off, as he found that while their shot and shell were falling around him, his shot fell short of them. His boats were, however, unharmed. Their position was such as to disturb the passage of the Savannah, and the boat plying between the city and Fort Pulaski received three shots through her upper works. If the enemy succeed in removing the obstacles in Wall's Cut and Wilmington Narrows, there is nothing to prevent their reaching the Savannah River, and we have nothing afloat that can contend against them. The communication between Savannah and Fort Pulaski will then be cut off. The latter is supplied with four months' provisions, and we must endeavor to defend the city. To-day I have caused to be sunk in Wilmington Narrows the floating dock of this city. I hope this passage at least will be effectually obstructed.

I am, &c.,

R. E. LEE,
General, Commanding.

General S. COOPER,
Adjutant and Inspector General, Richmond, Va.

FEBRUARY 6, 1862.—Reconnaissance to Wright River, S. C.

Report of Maj. Oliver T. Beard, Forty-eighth New York Infantry.

HILTON HEAD, S. C., *February* 6, 1862.

GENERAL: I have the honor to report that the reconnaissance ordered by you of Wright River, its tributary creeks, and the land adjacent thereto, together with the new fortifications and raft in the Savannah River, has been made.

Accompanying this report and necessarily forming a part thereof are maps of the section of country embraced in the reconnaissance.*

The soundings or depths of water as shown in these maps were made with a great deal of care and noted at the particular part of the rivers where made, so that there might be no error as to the particular location of any soundings. They were always made rather under than over the mark, but especial care was taken to have them precise and so note them.

It will be perceived that the course of Wright River is not precisely as laid down in the charts in the engineers' hands. The courses as they are here laid down are made up from notes at each turn and bend of the river, being guided solely by a pocket compass. I think that in this manner I have been enabled to show very nearly the true course of the river and its tributaries much more accurately than they are laid down in other maps. There are many more trees on Hog Marsh Island than are laid down on the accompanying map, but all those not so laid down are palmetto, and those on that island grow out of the marsh, their base being surrounded by water during high tides. The trees shown on this island are scrub pines, and are found in clumps on small dry spots scattered about through the marsh. These dry spots vary in diameter from 20 to 100 feet, no one spot being found larger than the maximum mentioned. The island cannot be used for military purposes.

The woods laid down north of Wright River are noted as taken from three points of observation—1st, from the top of a large and high rice-barn on the bank of the Savannah River; 2d, from the several points of Wright River and its upper tributaries, where soundings were made; and, 3d, from Red Bank, on New River. These observations showed the heavy timber, which in that vicinity always grows on dry ground, to continue in an irregular line, unbroken except by plantations from Red Bank, on New River, to the Union causeway near Lunbridge's plantation. There are a large number of cotton plantations embraced in this region, especially in that portion of it nearest New River. Leaving this, the character of the soil gradually changes, until from being a sandy clay at Red Bank it becomes at Lunbridge's a porous, black, light loam, which is the only kind of soil used for the culture of rice.

The rice plantations which are noted east of the Union causeway are of this character. An examination of the soil here shows that it looks very much like the *débris* of decayed trees and roots; very much of it is indeed nothing else. All this land is below the level of high tides, dikes thrown about the various fields preventing overflow. All these fields are very much cut up with ditches and canals; so much so as to be impassable by either cavalry, artillery, or infantry in face of an enemy. The ditches are useless except as so many barriers, but all the canals might be used as rifle-pits, and all the dikes for the same purpose, or to plant artillery behind, the soil being dry enough for this purpose. Though these plantations are surronnded on the front and rear by swamps, the canals entering them from bordering rivers or creeks afford easy access to the dry ground on them.

There are about 15,000 bushels of rice on the plantations which I visited. The negroes have mostly all been moved up the country. The new rebel earthworks on an island in the Savannah River is completed. Two guns were mounted on Sunday last, the third was in the shears, while a

* Not found.

steamer was lying alongside the island with two more guns evidently intended to be landed. All the persons seen at work here were negroes.

The raft which is near this point I found to be between 600 and 800 feet long and from 20 to 30 feet wide, extending across the channel at this part of the river. Portions of the raft have been daubed with some substance, probably tar or pitch. On the entire raft there is perhaps as much as six or eight cords of what is commonly called cord-wood. This has become scattered about the raft in all directions, until now there are scarcely two sticks together in any one point. Four piles have been driven near the eastern end of the raft. I could see none on the western.

The pile-driver which was reported as being in the vicinity of the raft for about two weeks was doubtless at work driving piles at the Fort Jackson wharf, as I could plainly see that new piles have been recently driven there. The map of the raft and fort will show my idea, but I am firmly convinced that this raft was never designed to be used for any purpose at any point below the north end of Elba Island. I am also of the opinion that it is not intended to be moved from the present position except in case of an attack upon Fort Jackson. It is a harmless thing and very poorly gotten up.

I think that an addition has been made to the southerly end of Fort Jackson, as noted by the line A B C, on map No. 2. This seems to be a wall, I think, of square logs, the ends buried in the ground, and fitting very nicely together. The face A C has eight openings in it, and the face C B has sixteen openings and a door; these, I think, are for rifle purposes.

The barbette guns on the fort have been covered over with logs and dirt. In the rebel camp below Fort Jackson I should judge there are about 700 persons. No other camps could be seen between that and Augustine Creek, nor above the fort toward Savannah, nor are there any camps on the Carolina side between the causeway and Wright River, on the Savannah, except 12 men about one-half mile up the causeway.

The rebel camp near New River does not probably contain over 200 persons, as there were not fires for over that number.

On New River, at Box's, a bluff makes in, running about one-half mile on the river and thence extending back, according to the report of a negro on the place, to Bluffton. This is the only dry ground met on the right bank of New River, as far as I was enabled to observe.

On the left bank of the river, the first dry firm ground is met at Red Bank, extending along the river about $1\frac{1}{4}$ miles; a swamp borders this on the north, and this is followed by another bank of dry land, extending about three-fourths of a mile along the river. No more firm ground is met for 5 miles up the river. At Red Bank there is a beautiful open plain of about 600 acres; this is skirted by a wood, which continues until the swamp is again met, about $1\frac{3}{4}$ miles from the open plain. There are, however, some upland cotton plantations in this area.

Very respectfully, your obedient servant,

O. T. BEARD,
Major, Forty-eighth New York Volunteers.

Brig. Gen. THOMAS W. SHERMAN,
Commanding Expeditionary Corps.

FEBRUARY 10, 1862.—Skirmish on Barnwell's Island, S. C.

REPORTS.

No. 1.—Brig. Gen. Isaac I. Stevens, U. S. Army.
No. 2.—Capt. Gordon Z. Dimock, Fiftieth Pennsylvania Infantry.

No. 1.

Report of Brig. Gen. Isaac I. Stevens, U. S. Army.

HEADQUARTERS SECOND BRIGADE, EXPED'Y CORPS,
Beaufort, S. C., February 11, 1862.

SIR: I have to report for the information of the commanding general that a party of the enemy landed on Barnwell's Island last night and made an attack on our pickets. Lieutenant Foot, in command of the pickets, held his ground till re-enforced by Captain Dimock with a portion of his command from Seabrook, when the whole force pushed forward and drove the enemy to his boats. It was a very handsome affair, exceedingly creditable to all engaged, and gives convincing proof that the command is wide awake and ready for emergencies.

I will particularly call the attention of the commanding general to the good conduct of Captain Dimock and Lieutenant Foot, Fiftieth Regiment Pennsylvania Volunteers, on the occasion.

A copy of Captain Dimock's report is herewith inclosed.

I am, sir, very respectfully, your obedient servant,

ISAAC I. STEVENS,
Brigadier-General, Commanding.

Capt. L. H. PELOUZE,
Acting Assistant Adjutant-General E. C., Hilton Head, S. C.

No. 2.

Report of Capt. Gordon Z. Dimock, Fiftieth Pennsylvania Infantry.

SEABROOK, *February* 11, 1862.

Last night about 10 o'clock I was startled by the report of several guns on Barnwell's Island. I took a row-boat full of Company D and went over, leaving word for my command to follow—part immediately and part should there be more firing. Went on a double-quick to causeway. Saw men on the farther end of the causeway in the underbrush and the glistening of several bayonets. As we came they retired more into the shade. Lieutenant Foot, with 3 men, advanced on the causeway to reconnoiter, followed by 10 or 15 more, who advanced in parties of 3, at intervals of one or two rods, with directions, if fired upon, to fire and lie down on the sides of the causeway to load. As they approached the farther end of the causeway they saw 3 or 4 men, and fired upon them. They continued to advance, while I brought up the main force in parties of 9 and 10, so placed in the shade as to cover the retreat of the skirmishers and check the advance of the rebels. Having passed beyond the trees and underbrush at the farther end of the causeway, I left a small force there and took a double-quick to the next causeway. As we passed the negro houses one negro exclaimed, "Great many rebels down there, sir." As we approached the next causeway skirmishers were again thrown out, led by Lieutenant Foot. Passing cautiously through the bushes at this end of the causeway, they proceeded across the causeway until they were approaching the farther end. They were ordered to halt by a voice behind the bushes. At the second command he stepped out and fired. The shot was promptly returned, and my whole command started forward on a double-quick. Two men were seen running to the left of Little Bull Island, and several were heard to run forward and to the right. We then proceeded cautiously through the hedge at the farther end of the causeway into the open field, and deployed skirmishers right and left to the hedges, while a party took a double-quick for the next causeway. Sentinels were placed at each end of the second causeway, and the third causeway crossed in the same cautious manner. When we got through the bushes to the shore of Broad River it was evident that two boats had just left the beach, and their wake was visible on the surface of the still water. One very large wake was seen, very rough in its center, and the sound of wheels turning in the water could be heard beyond Mackay's Point. Company B was left in detachments at the Trescott house, first causeway, and negro houses.

The pickets heard a noise in the field beyond the marsh to the left of the road before the firing, and the negroes' dogs, which are usually very noisy at the least stir, were not heard to bark. We examined the field to the left of the road, and could find numerous tracks in the soft mud between the cotton rows. The tracks of a bare foot were also seen, supposed to be the track of a negro guide. Tracks in the field south of the negro houses were observed going both east and west, presumed to have been made by the rebel party having turned out into the field to avoid the negro houses and the dogs.

When the attacking party appeared on the farther end of the first causeway they were halted by the picket three times. At the third command they discharged a whole volley at the pickets. The pickets fired their pieces, and continued to load and fire whenever a rebel could be seen.

Fires were seen on the main-land in the field west of the fort, as if there might be a small encampment there. It might be fire in the woods.

Nothing else of interest occurred.

Respectfully,

G. Z. DIMOCK,
Captain, Commanding at Seabrook.

Major OVERTON.

FEBRUARY 11, 1862.—Occupation of Edisto Island, S. C., by the Union forces.

Report of Col. Henry Moore, Forty-seventh New York Infantry.

HDQRS. FORTY-SEVENTH REGT. N. Y. S. V. TROOPS,
Edisto Island, S. C., February 15, 1862.

SIR: Pursuant to Army Regulations, page 104, paragraph 716, I take the earliest opportunity to inform you, both by letter and by chart, of the occupation of this island by the force under my command.

Pursuant to Special Orders, No. 69, I was ordered by General T. W. Sherman, of the expeditionary corps, to proceed to this point, on North Edisto River, and establish this post. After some reconnoitering I finally located myself at this place, known as Point of Pines, only 25 miles from Charleston. The enemy are all around us. By the aid of light-draught gunboats, which I am expecting daily from Port Royal, to keep them at bay, if troops sufficient, say at the most 10,000, could be forwarded here, in less than three days we could be in Charleston. I consider this point the great key to Charleston, and trust this point will meet with your immediate consideration, as time may be everything to us in the premises.

I am, general, very respectfully, your most obedient servant,

HENRY MOORE,
Colonel, Commanding Post.

L. THOMAS,
Adjutant-General, Washington, D. C.

FEBRUARY 15, 1862.—Action at Venus Point, Ga.

REPORTS.

No. 1.—Brig. Gen. Thomas W. Sherman, U. S. Army.
No. 2.—Brig. Gen. Egbert L. Viele, U. S. Army.

No. 1.

Report of Brig. Gen. Thomas W. Sherman, U. S. Army.

HEADQUARTERS EXPEDITIONARY CORPS,
Port Royal, S. C., February 17, 1862.

SIR: A rebel steamer, the Ida, ran by our battery on the Savannah River on the 14th instant for Fort Pulaski. The guns had not been worked nor the ranges obtained. On the next day she attempted to return, and four of Tatnall's gunboats came down from Savannah to cover her. They were all sent back to their places of departure, and one of them seriously crippled.

I inclose herewith the copy of General Viele's report on the subject.

Very respectfully, your obedient servant,

T. W. SHERMAN,
Brigadier-General, Commanding.

The ADJUTANT-GENERAL U. S. ARMY,
Washington, D. C.

No. 2.

Report of Brig. Gen. Egbert L. Viele, U. S. Army.

HEADQUARTERS U. S. FORCES,
Savannah River, February 16, 1862.

SIR: I have the honor to report that the batteries on Venus Point were attacked at 3 o'clock p. m. on yesterday by four rebel gunboats with a view of effecting a passage from Fort Pulaski for the rebel steamer then at that place. After an engagement of one hour the rebels were driven off, the flag steamer being disabled and taken in tow, and the steamer that attempted the passage of the river returning to Fort Pulaski. The guns were manned by the Third Rhode Island detachment, under Captain Gould, and effectively worked. There was no loss on our side.

Very respectfully, your obedient servant,

EGBERT L. VIELE,
Brigadier-General, Commanding.

Capt. L. H. PELOUZE,
Acting Assistant Adjutant-General.

FEBRUARY 23-26, 1862.—Reconnaissance up Bull River and Schooner Channel, S. C.

Report of Brig. Gen. Isaac I. Stevens, U. S. Army.

HEADQUARTERS SECOND BRIGADE, EXPED'Y CORPS,
Beaufort, S. C., February 27, 1862.

SIR: I have to report, for the information of the commanding general, that in pursuance to instructions from these headquarters Captain Ely, Eighth Regiment Michigan Volunteers, and commanding on Ladies and Saint Helena Islands, with 22 men of his own company and that of Lieutenant Doyle, and accompanied by Lieutenants Doyle, Badger, and Brown, all of the Eighth Michigan Regiment, left Ladies Island on the morning of Sunday, February 23, to make an examination of Bull River and the enemy's force in that vicinity. The party employed three row-boats. The services of a negro belonging to Robert Barnwell, who had lately come down the river, were secured as guide. From Coosaw Island another negro, named Cyas, was obtained, who subsequently proved of great service from the intimate knowledge he possessed of the country under examination.

Captain Ely reports substantially as follows: After leaving Ladies' Island at Brick-yard Point, and passing down the Coosaw to the mouth of Bull River, a distance of 9 miles, he ascended the stream to Schooner Channel. He then proceeded up Schooner Channel until he came to the mouth of the creek which passes by Willmar's Island. There he landed, placed his men under cover of the woods, and with a small party passed over the island and found it entirely uninhabited. Starting at nightfall he passed up the creek to near within 80 rods of its intersection with North Wimbee River, which is about 12 miles from the mouth of Bull River. Here he left the bulk of his party, and in his own boat, with only 3 men, passed into and up the North Wimbee branch to the landing at Barnwell's plantation, a mile distant. This landing is on the right bank. This point was entirely unguarded. He landed, examined the shore for some distance, and visited Robert Barnwell's plantation. There he found an old plantation negro, who came to Robert Barnwell's from Pocotaligo by way of Garden's Corner on the 22d instant, and who reported that he saw but few troops at the latter place, probably not a hundred all told; that the greater part of the troops had been withdrawn to Pocotaligo, and that the boats at the bridge near Garden's Corner were guarded by 2 men. These boats were row-boats and flats, at least fifty in number (some negroes estimated the number as high as one hundred). Captain Ely also met another negro, who had come down from Walterborough the same day with a loaded team. From him he learned that the nearest picket, composed of 6 men, was $1\frac{1}{2}$ miles distant, at the fork of the roads connecting respectively with Garden's Corner and Combahee Ferry. He likewise said he had seen no soldiers between that point and the ferry.

With this information Captain Ely brought his whole party together at the Robert Barnwell Landing, placed them under cover, and with his 3 men and a negro guide started for the Combahee Ferry. He kept in the woods, passed within 40 or 50 rods of the pickets at the cross-roads, and pushed about 1 mile beyond there, where the country became so densely wooded and was so intersected by streams and marshes that Captain Ely was unable to proceed farther. He learned, however, that the principal force of the enemy, estimated at possibly 300 men, is stationed at Combahee Church, about 2 miles from the ferry, on the Garden's Corner road, and that to the left of the ferry there are two pieces of artillery, placed behind an earthwork and covered with pine brush.

On his return he proceeded to Bush Church, examined the country in its vicinity, and, favored by the woods in its immediate vicinity, passed entirely around it. At Bush Church he found only about 30 men, quartered in the church itself. They stationed pickets a quarter of a mile down toward the Chisolm Landing, on the Coosaw, and about the same distance up the road toward Port Royal Ferry. Their headquarters are some 1½ miles in rear of the Adams Landing, and the force there is about the same as at Combahee Church.

Captain Ely also examined the country between Stuart's plantation and Bush Church. It consists of open woods and fields, and furnishes the best route to Bush Church from the river. At Stuart's troops should be landed to operate against Bush Church. The distance is only 1 mile. Edward Barnwell has a plantation a mile below Stuart's. All these plantations are on the right bank of the river. From Robert Barnwell's place a causeway leads to Bush Church. A wide gap has been made in it, through which boats can pass, and which compelled Captain Ely to make a long detour up the river to reach the latter place. Boats can go above Robert Barnwell's to Potter's.

Captain Ely could easily have surprised and captured the pickets at Bush Church, and both he and his command felt some inclination to attempt it. His instructions were, however, to get information, and he found no difficulty in controlling his command.

In the morning, before the break of day, Captain Ely returned to his men and boats, crossed back to the channel from whence he came undiscovered by any of the enemy, and returning came in sight of Field's Point, where he discovered a few men at work apparently repairing the fort, and on the left bank of the Combahee River were extensive rice fields on fire, which in the evening were visible at a long distance.

The enemy's force, as far as Captain Ely could learn, is in that direction very small at the present time. Many of the picket stations have been taken up lately. The Combahee Ferry is made passable by flats, so that teams pass over as on a bridge. Captain Ely reached Brickyard Point on the morning of February 26, and was therefore absent two days and three nights.

The reconnaissance of Captain Ely does him great credit, and has resulted both in verifying and adding to the information already obtained. I have instructed him to continue his reconnaissances, looking particularly to the Ashepoo River. The above account is nearly in his own words, and I have adopted the above form in order to incorporate with the details of his written report details which I have gathered from him on a personal conference.

I am, sir, very respectfully, your most obedient,

ISAAC I. STEVENS,
Brigadier-General, Commanding.

Capt. L. H. PELOUZE,
Actg. Asst. Adjt. Gen., Exped'y Corps, Hilton Head, S. C.

MARCH 3, 1862.—Evacuation of Amelia Island, Fla., by the Confederate forces.

REPORTS.

No. 1.—Brig. Gen. James H. Trapier, C. S. Army.
No. 2.—Col. Edward Hopkins, Fourth Florida Infantry.

No. 1.

Report of Brig. Gen. James H. Trapier, C. S. Army.

HEADQUARTERS PROVISIONAL FORCE,
Tallahassee, Fla., March 28, 1862.

MAJOR: In consequence of the illness of Col. Edward Hopkins, Fourth Regiment Florida Volunteers, the officer in command of the post at Amelia Island at the time of its evacuation by our troops, I have had no official report from him. I have the honor, however, to submit for the information of the commanding general the following narrative of the events attending that operation, which, derived from sources entitled to credence, may be regarded as altogether authentic:

On the evening of February 23 I received by telegraph orders from General R. E. Lee, then commanding the military department in which Middle and East Florida are embraced, dated February 19, to withdraw from the islands, securing the artillery, &c. This order was extended forthwith, at the hands of a special messenger, to the officer commanding the post at Amelia and Talbot Islands and to Col. Charles H. McBlair, Provisional Army, commanding the batteries, with instructions to dismantle the batteries with all possible expedition and caution, and then to withdraw the troops and abandon the post.

On the fourth day after this order was received at Amelia Island the enemy made his appearance simultaneously in the inland passage between Cumberland Island and the main-land (having come in at Saint Andrew's Sound) and off the main entrance into Cumberland Sound, the principal approach from the sea to the town of Fernandina. At this time there had been dismounted, and in great part removed from the island, all the guns that bore upon this approach. These were the most effective batteries, and without them it was deemed by the officers in council that it would be fruitless to attempt the defense of the place. The order was accordingly given for the troops to retire from the island, which they did in good order and without the loss of a single man. The garrison from the adjacent island (Talbot) was withdrawn with equal success.

Of heavy ordnance upon these islands there were, including a battery of field pieces, 33 guns. Of these, 18 were saved, thus showing a loss of but 15 guns, a fact which, in view of our very limited means of transportation and the extreme difficulty of removing heavy ordnance, or, indeed, ordnance of any description, over sand hills, reflects, in my judgment, high credit upon the officers to whom was assigned this arduous duty; and besides the guns, there were saved also all the powder and most of the shot and shell, some of the carriages, implements, &c. When it is remembered that all this was accomplished in four days and nights, under the most adverse circumstances, no other conclusion can be formed than that the utmost energy, industry, and vigor were exhibited by both officers and men.

Five of the guns were, however, I regret to add, subsequently lost.

They had been placed at Saint John's Bluff, on the Saint John's River, with the purpose of putting them in battery there for the defense of that river. The enemy's prompt movements in that direction rendered it impossible to remove them, as it was my intention to have done, in pursuance of the orders from headquarters, dated March 1, 1862, which required that all the troops in this military department, except such as might be necessary for the defense of the Apalachicola River, should be ordered to report to General A. S. Johnston.

From the above it appears that our entire loss in and consequent upon the evacuation of Amelia Island is 20 guns and some stores of the quartermaster and commissary departments, though no considerable amount of either. The capture under false pretenses of Lieutenant-Colonel Holland and 5 men and his subsequent restoration has been already reported in my letter of the 19th instant.

I am, major, very respectfully, your obedient servant,

J. H. TRAPIER,
Brigadier-General, Commanding.

Maj. T. A. WASHINGTON,
Assistant Adjutant-General, Pocotaligo, S. C.

[Indorsement.]

HEADQUARTERS DEPARTMENT S. C. AND GA.,
Pocotaligo, S. C., April 6, 1862.

This report is respectfully referred to War Department. Although East and Middle Florida has been constituted a separate department, reports and returns continue to be made to these headquarters.

J. C. PEMBERTON,
Major-General, Commanding.

No. 2.

Report of Col. Edward Hopkins, Fourth Florida Infantry.

HEADQUARTERS FOURTH REGIMENT FLORIDA VOLS.,
Lake City, Fla., March 30, 1862.

SIR: Your order to evacuate the island of Amelia was received on Tuesday, February 25. In accordance with that order I consulted fully with Colonel McBlair, commander of the batteries, as to the best method of effecting the important duty specially assigned him. I furnished him such details of men as were deemed necessary, and, in short, all things which our position would admit of.

On Saturday, March 1, I ordered Capt. J. M. Martin, Marion Artillery, to place his battery 2 miles beyond the railroad bridge, on the mainland, leaving a strong guard to protect the same, and to return with the rest of his command to the island, which he did, and rendered me important service to the end. I also directed Captain Owens, commanding Marion Dragoons, to take his horses to the position assigned the artillery and return (the necessary guard excepted) to the island. This dismounted corps, under its efficient commander, was useful to me throughout.

I had previously caused the citizens of Fernandina to be notified that ample transportation would be furnished all who desired to leave the city; that orders had been issued for that purpose. Finding that the citizens paid no attention to this notice, I issued, on Saturday, March 1, a written notice, to wit, that on Sunday, March 2, at 10 a. m., a special train would leave the city expressly for the transportation of all women and children desirous of leaving. But little heed seemed to have been given to the second admonition.

No demonstration beyond the usual blockade was made by the enemy until Sunday, March 2, about 9 a. m. A bark, bearing French colors, appeared in the offing and hoisted signals for a pilot, whereupon Lieut. Col. D. P. Holland went out to her with a white flag, taking with him 6 soldiers of the Fourth Florida Regiment. She proved to be a Federal vessel, and they were captured by the perfidious craft and taken off. I have the happiness to state that they have since been released and are again at their post.

About 10 o'clock the same day several ships hove in sight, bore down near the bar, and anchored. It became evident that an attack would be made on Monday, the 3d. Our position was critical. As the enemy had full view of my quarters, it was necessary that the usual camp quiet should prevail.

It was not until 6.30 p. m. that I issued the order to break camp and transport everything to the railroad depot. This was effected by 2 o'clock next morning.

At an early hour in the night I received a dispatch from Colonel Styles, saying that from nineteen to twenty-one of the enemy's gunboats were in Saint Andrew's Sound, of which fact Colonel McBlair was duly notified. In consequence of this information he very properly placed his command *en route* for the city, where it arrived about 1.30 o'clock in the morning.

At 1 o'clock on Monday morning I repaired to town, and at 2.30 a. m. ordered all the troops (three companies of the Fourth Regiment Florida Volunteers excepted) to take up the line of march to the main-land. These three companies I retained for the protection of the citizens and for the more speedy removal of our equipage. No trains were permitted to go beyond 2 miles from the railroad bridge. The rush for succor and aid was perplexing. Duty on one side and commiseration for the sufferers rendered my position very distressing.

At 12 m. I was informed that four of the enemy's gunboats had come around the north end of Cumberland Island and entered the sound.

At 1 o'clock it was reported to me that they were moving across, whereupon I ordered the companies to file across the bridge, and at 2 p. m., in company with Colonel McBlair, I left Fernandina. It was now that all trains should have been removed to a place of safety, and no difficulty would have occurred. The three companies behaved well. There was no confusion; not the slightest. The train fired into was not injured.

On Tuesday, at 4 a. m., I ordered Second Lieutenant Deakle, of Company C, Fourth Regiment, to burn the trestle-work on the side next the main-land, which he accomplished, under fire of the enemy's gunboats, without loss. You are aware, sir, my orders restricted me entirely to my immediate command, Colonel McBlair having full charge of the batteries.

In conclusion, I will add that nothing was lost belonging to my command. My ill-health prevented an earlier report, as well as one more full and complete.

Most respectfully, your obedient servant,

E. HOPKINS,

Colonel, Commanding Fourth Regiment Florida Volunteers.

R. H. ANDERSON,

Major and Assistant Adjutant-General.

MARCH 4, 1862.—Occupation of Amelia Island, Fla., by the Union forces.

Reports of Brig. Gen. Horatio G. Wright, U. S. Army.

HEADQUARTERS THIRD BRIGADE, EXPED'Y CORPS,
Fernandina, Fla., March 5, 1862.

GENERAL: I have the honor to inform you that the combined navy and army expedition is in possession of Fernandina and the military defenses on Amelia Island, and also of the batteries on the south end of Cumberland Island.

Our occupation was a bloodless one, the rebels having evacuated on the first suspicion of our approach all the strong defenses on which they had lavished so much time and labor, removing, so far as time permitted, guns, stores, and troops. They, however, left behind no less than fourteen guns, all of large caliber.

The town is nearly deserted of inhabitants, many of whom left reluctantly, in obedience to the orders of the rebel authorities.

So far as I can gather from the conflicting statements of the citizens left behind, the rebel force here has exceeded 5,000 men. A detailed report will be submitted hereafter.

Very respectfully, your obedient servant,

H. G. WRIGHT,
Brigadier-General, Commanding.

General THOMAS W. SHERMAN,
Commanding Expeditionary Corps, Hilton Head, S. C.

HEADQUARTERS THIRD BRIGADE, EXPED'Y CORPS,
Fernandina, Fla., March 13, 1862.

GENERAL: Your letters of the 10th and 12th instant were received this evening, through Mr. Boutelle, U. S. Coast Survey, and I hasten to reply by the steamer Ben De Ford, which leaves early to-morrow morning. The Saint John's expedition is still absent, and I have received no official information in regard to it since the 11th, at which time the vessels had not succeeded in passing the bar of that river. I learn, however, through contrabands and others who have come in, that the enemy has deserted everything as high up as Jacksonville, and has burned a portion of that town; that there are no troops nearer than Baldwin, and but few there, the Mississippi regiment having been sent to Tennessee and most of the Florida troops to Tallahassee. I infer, therefore, that the capture of Saint Augustine will not require a formidable demonstration, but that the place will surrender on the approach of the gunboats. Should there be any indications of resistance there, which I do not expect, I will add to the land force already sent. As you will have learned by one of my late letters, it is doubtful whether the place is garrisoned even. The ordnance captured here amounts to sixteen pieces in all, two having been found in a battery beyond the railroad bridge, which had not, however, been mounted. The battery was nearly completed. No powder of any moment was left behind. Three large sling-carts were left in good condition and a fourth partly burned. We shall need the ammunition and other stores estimated for by Lieutenant Tardy. I shall retain the whole force now here until the result of the expedition now absent is accomplished, or until I hear further from you. I believe, from present information, that at least one regiment and the battery may be sent back soon, if you desire it, still retaining an adequate garrison at this point.

Very respectfully, your obedient servant,

H. G. WRIGHT,
Brigadier-General, Commanding.

General THOMAS W. SHERMAN,
Commanding Exped'y Corps, Hdqrs. Hilton Head, S. C.

[Indorsement.]

General Wright will be instructed to put the place in as good a state of defense as his means will permit, so that it can be held by a regiment or less. He is also instructed to have a detailed estimate made for the thorough completion of Fort Clinch, and submit the same at as early a day as practicable.

T. W. SHERMAN.

MARCH 7-11, 1862.—Reconnaissance up the Savannah River and to Elba Island.

Report of Lieut. Col. John H. Jackson, Third New Hampshire Infantry.

HEADQUARTERS THIRD REGIMENT N. H. VOLS.,
Port Royal, S. C., March 13, 1862.

I have the honor to report that in compliance with instructions received from Brig. Gen. T. W. Sherman, March 7, I left this camp at 6 p. m. on that date, and proceeded to Seabrook with 20 officers and 371 men, with Surgeon Moulton and 4 hospital attendants. I arrived at Seabrook at 8 p. m., and found there six boats, two of them of small size. I made every effort to obtain more boats, and after waiting an hour Captain Dunbar arrived from Hilton Head with four boats, making ten boats with which to transfer my command to Daufuskie Island. The boats were crowded full, and I was compelled to leave behind Company A, with 2 officers, and a part of Company F, with 1 officer, a total of 91 men and 3 officers. Just as we were about to leave Seabrook, Captain Dunbar was taken sick, and I placed the whole charge of the boats and boatmen with Lieutenant Cornelius, of Company D, who discharged his duties in a prompt and efficient manner during the whole time of our absence. We left Seabrook at 10 p. m., some of the boats leaking badly. When I arrived opposite Buckingham's Ferry, and several times before reaching there, I was fired on by rebel pickets. I found we had lost our way, and having no countersign, were being fired on by our own pickets as well as by the rebels. I thought it advisable to land and wait till daylight, it then being very dark. Quite a number of shots were fired at us, none hitting either the men or boats.

It was 2 in the morning when I landed, two of the boats not coming up till daylight, having lost their way during the night. At daylight I started again, having procured a guide—Private Alonzo Borden, Company I, Forty-fifth Pennsylvania Volunteers. At 7.30 a. m. we came up with the two boats we had missed during the night, and at 9 a. m.

I landed on Daufuskie, marched 5 miles, to General Viele's quarters, and reported to him at 12 o'clock. After landing I sent the boats to Engineer's Wharf, at the upper end of the island. General Viele ordered me to encamp and wait further orders. During the evening Companies A and F arrived from Seabrook on the Mayflower, she coming from Hilton Head with commissary stores, and having taken them on board when passing Seabrook.

The next morning (Sunday, the 9th) I was ordered to embark and proceed to Savannah River, with my entire command, on a reconnaissance. I proceeded to Savannah River and some distance up the river, without seeing any signs of rebel pickets. I then returned and landed at the battery opposite Jones' Island, letting the men leave the boats a short time to rest them. While there a rebel steamer came out of San Augustine Creek in sight of our batteries and steamed up the river towards Savannah. Our batteries opened on them, making some good line shots, though they did not appear to strike the steamer, but they quickened her speed. After resting a short time I crossed to Jones' Island. As the boats were heavily laden and the tide low I could not pass down Mud River. I therefore landed the men and sent the boats around to the opposite side of the island to join me there. From there I again embarked, and returned to Daufuskie.

The next morning (Monday, 10th) I received orders from General Viele to take one day's rations and with all my command make a reconnaissance of Elba Island, which I proceeded to do, accompanied by Major Gardiner, of the Seventh Connecticut Volunteers, and Captain Liebenau, of General Viele's staff. We left the landing known as the Engineer's Wharf at 9.45 a. m. in small boats, which were taken in tow by the steamer Mayflower to the point of Jones' Island (on Mud River) known as Sears' Landing, arriving there at 12 o'clock. From thence we proceeded in our boats, heavily laden as they were, against wind and tide, through Mud River, across the Savannah River, to a point on Elba Island opposite to and below the mouth of Mud River, where I landed, accompanied by Major Bedel, of the Third New Hampshire Volunteers, Major Gardiner, and Captain Liebenau. I at once saw the impracticability of landing my whole force, as the tall reeds and grass on the lower portion of the island had been burned, thus leaving us a fair mark for any of the enemy's steamers, should any of them (attracted by the large force under my command in small boats crossing the Savannah in daylight) have thought best to come down and attack us. I left the force there under the command of Captain Plimpton, with instructions to officers in command of the several different boats to allow no man to land, but each officer and soldier to remain seated in the boats, covered by the shores of the island, and instructing the officers in charge, as soon as any black heavy smoke became visible beyond them, to pull directly for Mud River, so as to be under the cover of the guns from our batteries and those of the Western World; to leave a small boat for us, or if this was not practicable, to take all the boats, leaving us on the island.

After these instructions I divided our small force landed, by giving Major Bedel 6 men, and instructions to proceed across to the opposite side of the island, scattering his men, and thence to the upper end, while with Major Gardiner, Captain Liebenau, and 6 men I proceeded on our course on this side, expecting to join Major Bedel at the upper end of the island. We separated to start upon our several courses at 1.45 p. m., and after traveling two hours and a quarter and crossing several small streams we came to the point of land, the extreme end of the island, looking towards the mouth of Wright River. On a point of land above the mouth of said river we saw a large store-house, or factory, with the windows closed, and no signs of any picket, although 2 men were seen, apparently unarmed.

From this point we proceeded directly across the island to the opposite side. Here we found the ruins of two houses, with one high brick chimney standing. From this point we could look directly up a stream across which there seemed to be a bridge, with heavy, strong abutments, as if intended for guns to be placed upon. Upon these abutments men could be distinctly seen at work, but what they were doing or if guns were in position at this place we were unable to see, as the afternoon sun shone directly against us and, shining upon the water, impaired our view. Near the bridge, on the side towards us, were three steamers lying at anchor (these were black) and one white steamer under way inside of the bridge. On the right-hand side were two vessels, schooner-rigged. It was impossible to tell whether they were steamers or sailing vessels. I then proceeded to the above-mentioned chimney, from which point I plainly saw houses, appearing to be store-houses, apparently filled with men, some of whom were distinctly seen lounging in the windows, but could see no signs of a battery. While resting ourselves, we saw a sail-boat well filled with men—some sailors and some soldiers, about 20 in all—leave one of the steamers and shape their course for this point. We at once proceeded to return to our boats. After a fatiguing tramp of one hour and a half one of the corporals who accompanied us saw a sail passing down the river. He reported the fact to me. We then ascertained that it was a boat from the steamer Western World, with Captain Gregory and Surgeon Moulton, of the New Hampshire Third, who were in search of us alongshore, thinking from our protracted absence we had lost our way. The captain immediately took us on board, and we proceeded to join the forces of my command, lying in boats at the lower end of the island.

On arriving there we found Major Bedel returned with the men of his command and 4 of those of mine. He reports that after crossing the island and proceeding up the southerly side opposite Saint Augustine Creek, on the upper point of which he discovered a picket of 5 men, they were within range, but his instructions were not to fire upon any pickets, but to keep themselves hidden. After traveling an hour and a half he found a stream, which it was impossible to cross. He followed the course of the stream inland until he reached the head of the stream, where he lost his way, owing to the thickness and height of the rushes, when, finding evening approaching, he returned to the boats. Upon my joining the forces in the boats, we proceeded to camp, where we arrived at 8 o'clock p. m.

The next morning (Tuesday, 11) I received orders from General Viele to prepare to return to Hilton Head, with the understanding that the Mayflower was to bring the troops and tow the boats. Between 3 and 4 o'clock p. m., and after the men had been standing in the rain some time, we were notified that we must return in our boats, and as it was impossible to get all the men in the boats, I sent the boats around to the point (Egg Point), where we first landed on the island, and marched the men down there. It was dark when we arrived there, and the tide running out and a strong head wind blowing, I found it impossible to get home that night. I then took two companies across the river to Lawton's plantation, on Hilton Head Island, and sent the boats back to join the other boats. I left Major Bedel with the remaining four companies, with instructions to return to Hilton Head as soon as practicable. The next morning early Major Bedel landed with two companies at Lawton's plantation. The remaining two companies went to Seabrook in the boats, and marched from there to this camp yesterday noon. Between 9 and 10 o'clock a. m. I left the plantation with the four companies there and arrived here in camp at 1 p. m. Every man that left the camp with me has returned. Five men are sick and in their quarters, and 1 was sent to the hospital on our return. The remainder of the men are in good health and spirits.

With great respect, this report is respectfully submitted.

JOHN H. JACKSON,
Lieutenant-Colonel, Commanding Third New Hampshire Vols.

To COMMANDING OFFICER,
Port Royal, S. C.

MARCH 12, 1862.—Occupation of Jacksonville, Fla., by the Union forces.

Report of Brig. Gen. Horatio G. Wright, U. S. Army.

HEADQUARTERS THIRD BRIGADE, EXPED'Y CORPS,
Fernandina, Fla., March 15, 1862.

CAPTAIN: I have the honor to report that I have just learned from my aide-de camp, Lieutenant Hubbell, who accompanied the expedition to the Saint John's River, that the batteries at the mouth of the river and at Saint John's Bluff were abandoned on the approach of the gunboats, and that Jacksonville was evacuated by the rebels before our forces reached the town. Jacksonville was occupied by six companies of the Fourth New Hampshire on the 12th instant. Seven saw-mills, 4,000,000 feet of lumber, a large hotel, four or five private dwellings, the railroad depot, and the gunboat in process of construction and nearly ready for launching were burned by the rebels on their evacuation of the place.

A portion of the gunboats, having with them one company of the Fourth New Hampshire Regiment, went to Saint Augustine, which the rebel forces had deserted on the first appearance of the expedition on the Florida coast. The inhabitants of the town are represented to have hailed with joy the arrival of our forces and their relief from the oppressive rule of the rebel authorities. At Jacksonville many of the inhabitants are still remaining, though considerable numbers had gone when our troops landed.

I shall endeavor to visit Jacksonville, and perhaps Saint Augustine, to-morrow, after which I will report more in detail.

Very respectfully, your obedient servant,

H. G. WRIGHT,
Brigadier-General, Commanding.

Capt. L. H. PELOUZE,
Act. Asst. Adjt. Gen., Hdqrs. E. C., Hilton Head, S. C.

MARCH 20-24, 1862.—Operations near Bluffton, S. C., including affairs at Buckingham and Hunting Island.

REPORTS, ETC.

No. 1.—Lieut. Col. John H. Jackson, Third New Hampshire Infantry.
No. 2.—Brig. Gen. Thomas F. Drayton, C. S. Army.
No. 3.—Maj. John B. Willcoxon, Phillips Legion.
No. 4.—Capt. Carlos Tracy, volunteer aide-de-camp.
No. 5.—Miscellaneous orders and correspondence.

No. 1.

Report of Lieut. Col. John H. Jackson, Third New Hampshire Infantry.

HEADQUARTERS THIRD NEW HAMPSHIRE VOLUNTEERS,
Hilton Head, S. C., March 25, 1862.

SIR: I have the honor to report that, in compliance with Special Orders, No. 67, March 18, 1862, I proceeded on the 19th, with 24 officers and —— enlisted men, on a reconnaissance in force on May River, running between the islands of Bull and Savage and the main-land. Accompanying the battalion from my regiment was a detachment from the Third Rhode Island Volunteers, with a 12-pounder howitzer, under the command of Lieutenant Morrow, who conducted himself in a manner deserving my thanks, and materially assisted me in all my movements during the five days I was gone.

I left my camp at this place at 2 p. m., and arrived at Seabrook at 3.30 p. m., and had all but one company embarked at 4 o'clock, filling what boats I had, fifteen in number, one leaking so badly I had to leave it behind. The field piece I embarked in a scow we found at Seabrook and towed it with one of our large boats. Soon after leaving the wharf it began to grow dark and to rain, and the wind blew hard, so as to endanger the safety of our field piece, the scow being low in the water. After an hour and a half's rowing, I thought best to land a short time until the weather became somewhat calmer, and landed at Dr. Frank Pope's plantation, on Hilton Head Island. The men found shelter in the buildings, and at 2.30 o'clock in the morning of Thursday, the 20th, we again embarked, and about daybreak landed on a hard beach at Dr. James Kirk's plantation, on the main-land, and 1 mile from Bluffton.

I had previously sent two companies under command of Captain Randlett to the White house, on Ephraim Baynard's plantation, opposite the lower end of Pinckney Island, to drive in or capture the picket stationed there. Immediately after landing, the command remaining with me, I threw out Captain Plimpton's company as skirmishers in the direction of the above plantation, to assist Captain Randlett, and to ascertain what other pickets there were near there, and, if possible, to capture them.

Immediately after landing we could see cavalry pickets in the woods skirting the plantation. I immediately had the field piece brought up and fired three shells into the wood, scattering the enemy. As I had not made preparation to advance far into the interior, I drew off my command, and dropped down to Colonel Seabrook's wharf and plantation, on Bull Island, opposite the main-land. After landing that portion of my command I proceeded to Baynard's plantation, and found that 4 rebel pickets had been captured. Captain Plimpton's company, under command of Lieutenant Ela, had cut off their retreat, and being hemmed in on all sides, they surrendered without resistance.

On arriving, I disarmed them of their rifles and long knives, with which they were armed, and carried them across to Buckingham's Ferry, Hilton Head Island, and delivered them over to an officer of the Forty-fifth Pennsylvania Volunteers, commanding the picket there stationed, and requested him to send them to headquarters, which he did. With my command I then proceeded to Bull Island. That afternoon I was notified that there was a strong force on the main-land, and having made up my mind to visit Bluffton, I sent to headquarters for another piece of artillery, which I received Friday afternoon.

Friday morning, having got some information that led me to believe there was a picket on Savage Islands, on the side towards the main-land, I determined to reconnoiter those islands thoroughly. I embarked my command and landed them on Savage Islands, thoroughly examined them, but found no pickets. On the main-land opposite, the cavalry pickets were visible narrowly watching our movements, apparently expecting us to land on the main-land above Bluffton. At 1.30 o'clock, I started on my return to Bull Island. In the morning, before starting, I was notified by our picket that the enemy had that morning burned all the buildings (about fifteen in number) on Kirk's plantation, where we landed yesterday. On our passage to Savage Islands we were frequently fired on by the rebel pickets. On our return they again fired on us, and when opposite Kirk's I ordered my men to return the fire, which they did, firing as each boat came abreast the plantation. After passing beyond rifle range we could see a cluster of the horsemen apparently gathered around some wounded or killed companion, as they dismounted. Most of our shots reached the shore, but whether we succeeded in hitting the enemy or not I could not ascertain.

That night I received another piece of artillery from headquarters, with men to man it. Next morning, after putting one of the guns in a position to command the landing at Kirk's, I embarked the men and landed at the same place as on Thursday, the 20th, driving in the pickets. I then threw out two companies as skirmishers, and after advancing a short distance into the wood sent forward two companies more to support them, under command of Captain Plimpton, acting major. Lieutenant Morrow having got his field piece in position, I left a few men, with an officer, to assist him, and advanced the remainder of my force towards Bluffton. In advancing I found cross-roads, where I left detachments to prevent the enemy getting into our rear.

We arrived at Bluffton at 12 o'clock, driving the pickets through the town and a short distance [beyond], but finding it impossible to cut them off, abandoned the pursuit. I found the town entirely deserted, with the exception of 3 old negroes, who informed me there had been no artillery there, and there was no evidence of any or of any earthworks there or some distance up the river. The nearest approach to artillery was an old dismounted iron gun on the bluff near the church and on the bank of the river. I examined the town thoroughly, to be sure there were none of the rebels secreted. I found none, and neither arms nor ammunition. The town had been apparently only occupied as a headquarters for pickets during the past three months.

One of the rebel pickets, in endeavoring to escape, could not get his horse to start for some reason or other. He was in sight of our advance, but at long-range distance, and after endeavoring for a few minutes to urge his horse into a run and being unsuccessful, left his horse and blankets and ran for the woods, which he reached without further harm from us. The horse was a good one, and, with a mule taken from Bull Island, I have turned over to Colonel Reynolds, Government agent at this place, and have his receipt for them. After a thorough examination of the town I drew in my command, and retired rapidly and in good order without any attack from any quarter, and returned in the boats to Bull Island.

The officers and men behaved like good soldiers, moving steadily and quietly to and from the town; remained in ranks while in the town (with the exception of such squads as were ordered to examine the various houses), and in every way conducted themselves in a meritorious manner.

I visited the islands near Bull Island, finding a number of cattle, sheep, and hogs, and evidences that the enemy obtained some of their fresh provisions from these islands. As we were short of rations, I had a few of the cattle killed and properly distributed among my command.

On Monday, at 3 p. m., I returned to Hilton Head. All the boats, with the exception of three, are at Seabrook in good order. These three leaked badly from the start, and I had them sent to the wharf at Hilton Head for repairs. All my command have returned in good health and without one accident.

With great respect, your obedient servant,

JOHN H. JACKSON,
Lieutenant-Colonel, Commanding Third New Hampshire Vols.

Col. ENOCH Q. FELLOWS,
Third New Hampshire Volunteers, Commanding Post.

No. 2.

Reports of Brig. Gen. Thomas F. Drayton, C. S. Army.

HEADQUARTERS SIXTH MILITARY DISTRICT,
Hardeeville, S. C., March 23, 1862.

CAPTAIN: Major Willcoxon, commanding cavalry of Phillips Legion at Bluffton, reported to me yesterday afternoon [at] 3 p. m. that he had been driven back from Bluffton about 3 miles, and the enemy—could not say how many—[were] a mile and a half in his front, at Mr. James Pope's gate. I immediately sent forward to ascertain the facts, following on myself shortly after. The enemy were in the position stated by Major Willcoxon, but fell back again upon Bluffton and retired thence about 9 p. m.

I have moved troops forward and will take such position with others as I hope will enable me to cut off or drive back into the river any of the invaders, should they venture as far up the public road as they did yesterday. The enemy came up to Red Bluff yesterday in a steamer and shelled the woods in the vicinity. I have no further official account than this.

Captain Ives informed me that he was ready to supply me with torpedoes, but had no powder. I have made a requisition upon General Ripley for 1,200 pounds of blasting powder, the better qualities being so scarce.

The telegram of the major-general commanding has been received, and I will accordingly apply to General Lawton for the two regiments from Georgia, which will enable me to move forward and act in concert with the other regiments of my command, who are known to each other and are well drilled.

The whole command has been very much fatigued by their forced march of the other night—20th instant.

Major Willcoxon reports that the enemy landed at Hunting Island in ten barges.

Respectfully, yours,

THOS. F. DRAYTON,
Brigadier-General, Commanding.

Capt. J. R. WADDY,
Assistant Adjutant-General, Pocotaligo, S. C.

HEADQUARTERS SIXTH MILITARY DISTRICT,
Hardeeville, S. C., March 24, 1862.

SIR: I beg to submit to the consideration of the major-general commanding the accompanying papers in regard to the enemy's landing in the vicinity of Bluffton on the 20th and 22d instant.

No. 1, report of Major Willcoxon, Phillips Legion, Georgia Volunteers, at Bluffton, of the landing on the 20th instant, together with No. 2, additional report of above, stating loss of 4 pickets; No. 3, copies of dispatches from Major Willcoxon concerning landing on 22d instant; No. 4, report of Major Willcoxon in reference to landing of enemy on 22d instant; No. 5, report of Capt. Carlos Tracy, volunteer aide-de-camp, of the landing, &c., on 22d instant.

The examination of witnesses was made by Captain Tracy in the presence of Major Willcoxon without any contradiction by that officer of the testimony given by the officers and men eye-witnesses of the facts and circumstances stated.

Major Willcoxon no longer occupies a separate command, and I trust that under a new and severer discipline no such confused reports of the position and numbers of the enemy will again be forwarded like those which have so lately ended in harassing marches and disappointment to the troops.

I have the honor to be, very respectfully,

THOS. F. DRAYTON,
Brigadier-General.

Capt. J. R. WADDY,
Assistant Adjutant-General, Pocotaligo, S. C.

No. 3.

Reports of Maj. John B. Willcoxon, Phillips Legion.

BLUFFTON, S. C., *March* 20, 1862.

DEAR SIR: This morning at day the enemy landed a regiment at Buckingham and one at Hunting Island, with a battery of artillery. As we approached Hunting Island to attack the enemy they opened their artillery on us, so that we could not approach them nearer than the gate. The enemy that landed at Buckingham advanced to the church. There our skirmishers met, and after a few shots on either side the enemy retired through the woods towards Hunting Island. The enemy has made no advance as yet from Hunting Island. We are fearful that we lost 4 pickets (as they have not yet returned), belonging to Captain Daniels' company. I have scouts watching the movements of the enemy.

Our wagons left here this morning with our baggage for the fork of the South May River road or Colonel Jones' camp.

Yours, respectfully,

JNO. B. WILLCOXON,
Major, Commanding at Bluffton.

General DRAYTON.

HEADQUARTERS CAVALRY BATTALION PHILLIPS LEGION,
Camp at Stony Place, S. C., March 23, 1862.

SIR: In answer to the communication to you from brigade headquarters, dated March 23, asking for my official report of yesterday's engagement with the enemy, &c., I report as follows:

About 11 a. m. the pickets stationed at Hunting Island reported that ten or twelve boats or barges had landed (four at Hunting Island and six or eight above), and that each of said boats contained 50 to 100 men, and that they were advancing on Bluffton in two columns, one column by the gate and one around by the beach or bluff. About the same time, or soon thereafter, another picket reported that four boats had landed at Baynard's negro quarters. I then dispatched Captains Du Bignon's and Rich's companies, consisting of some 20 men each (the others of said companies on picket and sent to relieve the same), to meet the enemy on Hunting Island road, at the same time dispatching Pucket's company to the Seabrook Church to support the picket.

Captains Du Bignon's and Rich's companies were soon engaged by the enemy, and not having force sufficient to check his advance, I, after sharp firing for a short time, ordered them to fall back, at the same time, seeing that Pucket's company was about being cut off, ordered it to fall back by Fording Island road. I then fell back to Pope's lane, and, dismounting, advanced to meet the enemy, who was now in town and still advancing on us; and seeing that our horses were much exposed and we liable to be cut off from our horses, I ordered my men to mount, and then retreated to the end of Mr. Crowell's lane, at which point our horses could be sheltered under cover of the wood, and we having the benefit of attacking the enemy in his advance through an open field.

Lieutenant Milhollin and a few men, having been left in the rear to watch and report the advance of the enemy, reported that he had fallen back. Lieutenant Milhollin was then ordered to follow them up and report their movement; and after returning late in the evening reported no enemy in or about Bluffton.

During the skirmish the enemy wounded two of our horses, one of which has since died and the other rendered unfit for duty, and during the time captured a horse belonging to one of the recruits of Captain Rich's company; the said recruit not being with the company, he having no arms.

Mr. Farr's store-house and dwelling-house broken open; also the post-office and dwelling on the same lot; but do not know anything about what was taken out, not knowing what was in either house; no public stores being [were] lost. Some 50 or 60 bushels of corn were left in town, but no damage other than stated heard of. This morning at day Lieutenant Milhollin, with 20 men, was sent out and reconnoitered to Hunting Island, but found no enemy.

Respectfully submitted.

JNO. B. WILLCOXON,
Major, Commanding Cavalry Phillips Legion.

Lieut. Col. S. JONES, Jr.,
Commanding Legion.

CAVALRY BATTALION PHILLIPS LEGION,
March 24, 1862.

You are hereby notified that four pickets belonging to the Green Rifles, lately under my command at Bluffton, are missing, and I am fearful they were captured by the enemy on the morning of the 20th instant.

Yours, respectfully,

JNO. B. WILLCOXON,
Major, Commanding Cavalry Phillips Legion.

Lieut. Col. S. JONES, Jr.

HDQRS. CAVALRY BATTALION PHILLIPS LEGION, GA. VOLS.,
Stony Place, S. C., March 24, 1862.

SIR: In answer to the request of Brigadier-General Drayton, as per note of J. I. Middleton, aide-de-camp, 23d instant, I report the following:

About daylight on the morning of the 20th instant the pickets from Hunting Islands and Buckingham reported the enemy landing at those two points, as verbally reported. I then ordered Captain Du Bignon's company to Hunting Island, the officer in command of which dispatched a courier to inform me that one regiment and one piece of artillery had landed. The courier reported one regiment and one battery. The officer of the pickets, after relieving them, reported to me (cannot state at what hour) that about one regiment had landed at Buckingham. I then made my written report from that of those two officers.

Respectfully submitted.

JNO. B. WILLCOXON,
Major, Commanding Cavalry Phillips Legion.

HENRY A. YOUNG,
Assistant Adjutant-General.

No. 4.

Report of Capt. Carlos Tracy, volunteer aide-de-camp.

HEADQUARTERS SIXTH MILITARY DISTRICT,
Camp Lee, March 23, 1862.

SIR: In compliance with instructions from Brigadier-General Drayton, delivered at New River Bridge about 8 p. m. yesterday, that I should proceed to Major Willcoxon, commanding in the vicinity of Bluffton, and acquaint myself as accurately as I could with the facts of the reported landing and advance of the enemy on that day into and from the village of Bluffton, I proceeded towards that place, and found Major Willcoxon, with his command, 2 miles this side of Bluffton. I learned from Major Willcoxon that the enemy—reported shortly before by his scouts to him and by him to the major-general commanding as having retired from Bluffton—had returned. I inquired if this fact had been reported to Brigadier-General Drayton, but found it had not been, because, as Major Willcoxon stated, he had not the countersign, and besides did not know if the report was true.

I got Major Willcoxon to call before me the men of his command who could give me information of the movements of the enemy since the afternoon of the 21st instant. A commissioned and a non-commissioned officer and several privates were examined by me in the presence of Major Willcoxon. I learned from these that on the afternoon of the 21st eight boats had returned from the direction of Box's (eight had been reported at Box's on that morning), and that two steamers (scouts could not say if they were gunboats) had come up to one of the islands near the Hunting Islands with four small boats with some men in them in tow; that the enemy that night had burned a small house at or near Buckingham Point; that on the morning of the 22d eleven small boats proceeded up towards the Hunting Islands. Eight of these kept the opposite shore, passed the Hunting Islands, and were not seen afterwards. They probably landed at or near the edge of Bluffton. Three landed at the Hunting Islands. The vedettes rapidly retired to Bluffton from the Hunting Islands and the enemy entered the village. Soon after that some of our men were fired upon without knowing that the enemy was coming. One man, who was near, said about 100 of the enemy had been seen by him advancing by the bluff. Another said he had seen about 12 men at the back of the village, and that there were others, how many he could not say; that our men rapidly retired; that the enemy advanced at the double quick until they reached the edge of the village on this side, and last fired upon us, as Major Willcoxon stated, from a grist-mill, which is said to be about the last house this end of the village and about three-quarters of a mile from the farther end of Pope's lane; that the enemy, after firing upon us, retired at the double-quick from this end of the village, and were not seen, as far as I could learn, from this time, which must have been about 9.20 a. m. At that hour they had entered the village; that a detachment of 20 men, under Lieutenant Milhollin, had late in the evening entered the village, found no damage done, except to the contents of two stores, said to have had in them liquor and tobacco, and conversed with a negro man, who had some of their property in his charge, who stated, on delivering up these articles safely, that he had never seen any Yankees. The negro lived at this end of the village; that this detachment had commenced scouting towards the Hunting Islands (it was then dark), when a sergeant and two men saw a man lying in the road with his head towards them; that he was snapped at by the sergeant and a man, when he turned across the road and another man then joined him from the bushes and laid himself down alongside of him. Our men then fired and retired. One of them declared (this was reported of him; he was on picket at the investigation) that he saw two more of the enemy come up to the men lying in the road, and that one gun was fired by the enemy. The sergeant evidently did not believe that a gun had been fired or that two others had joined those in the road.

No further scouting was done up to the time of my arrival at Major Willcoxon's camp.

Being satisfied that if these objects in the road were men they were drunken stragglers of the enemy, I advised Major Willcoxon to send an intelligent officer and 20 or more men to reach Bluffton by daylight and rapidly scout towards the Hunting Islands, and stated that I thought by so doing he could capture such drunken stragglers of the enemy as had not gone off in their boats. I had no doubt the sober men of the expedition had left the evening before. Major Willcoxon said he had already determined to send out such a party in the morning. I learned who was to lead the party, and got him to say that he would report to me in person at New River Bridge this morning.

I returned to New River Bridge, where I was to report to you, last night at 2 a. m.

This morning Lieutenant Milhollin, who led the scouting party, reported to me that he made the scout as expected; that no enemy was on the main-land anywhere near Bluffton, and that he had ascertained from satisfactory evidence that the objects seen and fired at by the sergeants and the two men last night, and on which was based the supposition that the enemy had returned to Bluffton, were branches of trees.

Respectfully, CARLOS TRACY,
Aide-de-Camp.

HENRY E. YOUNG,
Assistant Adjutant-General.

P. S.—Major Willcoxon stated that he supposed the force of the enemy to be from 300 to 400 men.

No. 5.

Miscellaneous orders and correspondence.

HDQRS. DEPT. OF SOUTH CAROLINA AND GEORGIA,
Pocotaligo, S. C., March 20, 1862.

Brig. Gen. MAXCY GREGG,
Commanding Fourth Military District, Jericho, S. C.:

GENERAL: The general commanding the department directs that you will hold the Fourteenth Regiment South Carolina Volunteers, Colonel Jones, prepared and ready to move at a moment's notice. He also directs that the regiment should be lightly equipped and not encumbered by equipage, &c. You will, if possible, hold them in readiness, with three days' rations in their knapsacks.

By order of Major-General Pemberton:

J. R. WADDY,
Assistant Adjutant-General.

HDQRS. DEPT. OF SOUTH CAROLINA AND GEORGIA,
Pocotaligo, S. C., March 20, 1862.

Brig. Gen. MAXCY GREGG:

The major-general commanding the department directs that you move forward Colonel Jones' five companies near Tomotley, to the works on Bee Creek. They will proceed from Pocotaligo Station to Coosawhatchie by railroad. Transportation will be furnished immediately at Coosawhatchie. They will leave the cars and proceed by road to Bee Creek. Captain Thornton's light battery of artillery, Virginia volunteers, has been ordered to Grahamville, S. C. Replace Colonel Jones' five companies by a corresponding number from Colonel Dunovant's Twelfth Regiment South Carolina Volunteers.

By order of Major-General Pemberton:

[J. R. WADDY,]
Assistant Adjutant-General.

HDQRS. DEPT. OF SOUTH CAROLINA AND GEORGIA,
Pocotaligo, S. C., March 20, 1862.

Brig. Gen. MAXCY GREGG,
Commanding Fourth Military District:

GENERAL: If the Tennessee regiment has moved you need not move Colonel Jones' regiment, but hold it in readiness in case it is wanted, and relieve the pickets by cavalry and such other troops as may be most convenient, if you are required to move Colonel Jones. If said regiment should be moved the general will endeavor to move it by rail.

The general leaves in a few moments for Hardeeville, S. C. Communicate by telegraph.

I am, general, very respectfully,

J. R. WADDY,
Assistant Adjutant-General.

HDQRS. DEPT. OF SOUTH CAROLINA AND GEORGIA,
Pocotaligo, S. C., March 20, 1862.

Brigadier-General DONELSON,
Commanding Fifth Military District, Stony Creek, S. C.:

GENERAL: The major-general commanding department directs that all the Tennessee troops, except the ones at the heavy guns on the Coosawhatchie River, advance at once by the public road towards New River Bridge. Those advancing from Grahamville, if forced to fall back, will do so by the same road on which they advanced to the intrenchments on the Honey Hill road.

By order of Major-General Pemberton:

[J. R. WADDY,]
Assistant Adjutant-General.

HDQRS. DEPT. OF SOUTH CAROLINA AND GEORGIA,
Pocotaligo, S. C., March 20, 1862.

Brigadier-General GREGG,
Commanding Fourth Military District, Jericho, S. C.:

GENERAL: I am directed by the major-general commanding the department to countermand the order just issued in reference to movements of troops in your district. Captain Thornton will be advised accordingly.

By order of Major-General Pemberton:

[J. R. WADDY,]
Assistant Adjutant-General.

HDQRS. DEPT. OF SOUTH CAROLINA AND GEORGIA,
Hardeeville, S. C., March 20, 1862—8.45 p. m.

Brigadier-General DONELSON,
Commanding Fifth Military District of South Carolina:

GENERAL: I wish you to move forward to the head of the Fording Island road, leading from Buckingham Ferry, with Captain Latham's battery. One company will be left at the heavy guns on Coosawhatchie River. Colonel Jones is ordered to move five companies to the intrenchment near Bee Creek. You will not, however, await his arrival, but move at once. The five companies of your brigade now at Camp Pemberton will proceed to Grahamville and occupy the camp now established. No tents will be taken except those from Camp Pemberton. Leave the one company at Coosawhatchie, as also those in Grahamville. I wish you to move as speedily as possible. If the companies have arrived from Camp Pemberton you can take them with you also.

Very respectfully, your obedient servant,

J. C. PEMBERTON,
Major-General, Commanding.

HDQRS. DEPT. OF SOUTH CAROLINA AND GEORGIA,
Hardeeville, S. C., March 21, 1862.

Brig. Gen. THOMAS F. DRAYTON,
Commanding Sixth Military District of South Carolina:

GENERAL: I consider that there is a sufficient number of troops now in hand and near Bluffton to capture or drive the enemy from his position at Hunting Island. This you will endeavor to do, if not already done, on the receipt of this communication. In consequence of the representations of a courier (dispatched to me by telegraph) and subsequent statements by Major Willcoxon, Georgia volunteers, I have been induced to order forward many more troops than enough to accomplish this object, and I desire you to carry out my orders, though this should not reach you until after daylight.

Very respectfully, your obedient servant,

[J. C. PEMBERTON,]
Major-General, Commanding.

HDQRS. DEPT. OF SOUTH CAROLINA AND GEORGIA,
Hardeeville, S. C., March 21, 1862.

Brigadier-General DONELSON,
Comdg. Fifth Mil. Dist. S. C., Head of Fording Island Road:

GENERAL: The general commanding directs that as soon as your men are rested you return with your command to the positions previously designated for your brigade.

Very respectfully, your obedient servant,

——— ———,
Captain and Ordnance Officer.

HDQRS. DEPT. OF SOUTH CAROLINA AND GEORGIA,
Pocotaligo, S. C., March 22, 1862.

Col. R. G. M. DUNOVANT,
Twelfth Regiment South Carolina Volunteers, Stony Creek, S. C.:

COLONEL: The major-general commanding the department directs that you move the eight companies of your regiment now stationed near Stony Creek immediately to Pocotaligo Station, where they will take the cars and proceed to Grahamville Station, S. C.; from thence you will proceed as speedily as possible to Grahamville by public road. You will equip your men with arms, ammunition, and three days' provision in their haversacks. The enemy are reported advancing from Bluffton, S. C.

By order of Major-General Pemberton:

R. W. MEMMINGER,
Assistant Adjutant-General.

HDQRS. DEPT. OF SOUTH CAROLINA AND GEORGIA,
Pocotaligo, S. C., March 22, 1862.

Brig. Gen. MAXCY GREGG,
Commanding Fourth Military District:

GENERAL: As information has again been received of the landing of the enemy at Bluffton, the major-general commanding directs that you hold your command in readiness to move, if necessary. Colonel Dunovant's regiment will move by railroad.

I am, general, very respectfully,

J. R. WADDY,
Assistant Adjutant-General.

HDQRS. DEPT. OF SOUTH CAROLINA AND GEORGIA,
Pocotaligo, S. C., March 22, 1862.

Brigadier-General DONELSON,
Commanding Fifth Military District:

GENERAL: As information has been again received of the landing of the enemy at Bluffton, the major-general commanding directs that you hold your command in readiness to move, if required, at once.

I am, general, very respectfully,

J. R. WADDY,
Assistant Adjutant-General.

MARCH 23, 1862.—Affair at Smyrna, Fla.

Report of Col. W. S. Dilworth, commanding forces of the Department of East and Middle Florida.

HDQRS. PROVISIONAL FORCES, DEPT. E. AND M. FLA.,
Tallahassee, Fla., April 4, 1862.

MAJOR: I have to report a most successful skirmish, which took place at Smyrna on [the] 23d ultimo—Capt. D. B. Bird, Third Regiment Florida Volunteers, C. S. [Army], commanding post, the skirmishers commanded by Captain Strain, Third Regiment, and Lieutenant Chambers, of Captain Owens' independent troop of cavalry.

The enemy landed, or attempted to land, from gunboats Penguin and Henry Andrew in launches, when our men fired into them. The enemy retreated to the opposite side of the river and abandoned their launches, five in number.

Captain Bird reports 7 killed, 3 prisoners, and about 30 wounded. Among the killed were Captain Mather, of the Henry Andrew, and Lieutenant Budd, of the Penguin. A runaway negro also was captured, who had piloted the enemy into the inlet to Smyrna, and who was to be hanged.

This skirmish I regard as quite a success; not a man on our side killed or wounded.

Smyrna is the place where arms, &c., for [the] Confederate States have been landed, and the enemy were seeking to capture them. The enemy are preparing to advance from Jacksonville to Baldwin to cut them off there.

I have the honor to subscribe myself, respectfully, your obedient servant,

W. S. DILWORTH,
Colonel, Commanding.

Maj. T. A. WASHINGTON,
Assistant Adjutant-General, Pocotaligo, S. C.

MARCH 28, 1862.—Reconnaissance near the Mouth of Saint Augustine Creek, Ga.

REPORTS.

No. 1.—Brig. Gen. Egbert L. Viele, U. S. Army.
No. 2.—Maj. Oliver T. Beard, Forty-eighth New York Infantry.

No. 1.

Report of Brig. Gen. Egbert L. Viele, U. S. Army.

DAUFUSKIE ISLAND, S. C., *March* 30, 1862.

GENERAL: I inclose a report from Major Beard. This is the third report on the iron-clad vessels. In case the vessels of the Navy are withdrawn, I can suggest no other plan than supplying their place with schooners armed with rifled guns and howitzers, and occupied by an infantry force—one in Mud River, one in Wright River, one at mouth of New River, and one in Cooper River. No batteries on land can possibly be erected to accomplish the results that would be obtained by these floating batteries.

Very respectfully, your obedient servant,

EGBERT L. VIELE,
Brigadier-General.

General THOMAS W. SHERMAN,
Commanding Expeditionary Corps.

No. 2.

Report of Maj. Oliver T. Beard, Forty-eighth New York Infantry.

BATTERY HAMILTON, GA., *March* 28, 1862.

CAPTAIN: I have the honor to report that I this day made a reconnaissance of the land about the mouth of Saint Augustine Creek. The best view was obtained from the summit of the upper Coast Survey station, on Elba Island. I send you a sketch of observations. The only rebel pickets about the mouth of Saint Augustine are stationed at the points indicated. In case of an attempt to cut them off their only chance of escape would be by swimming the bayou.

The rebels clearly visit Elba Island, coming low down. The following is an exact copy of a document found on the island: "The Glynn Guards have been in gunshot of you, you damned scoundrels, and examined your quarters. We invite you ashore; we have no navy." I give it for what it is worth. The rebels have no fort erected at the head of Wilmington Narrows. A large black square object is to be seen in the river opposite Fort Jackson. It looks like a floating battery. Anchored in the stream, below the fort, there is a steamer with two large schooners, one on either side. I think they are both armed, and intended to be towed into action in that shape, as the schooners would in a measure protect the machinery of the steamer.

Very respectfully, your obedient servant,

O. T. BEARD,
Major, Commanding.

Capt. J. H. LIEBENAU,
Assistant Adjutant-General.

MARCH 29, 1862.—Affair on Edisto Island, S. C.

REPORTS.

No. 1.—Brig. Gen. Nathan G. Evans, C. S. Army, commanding Third Military District of South Carolina.

No. 2.—Col. P. F. Stevens, Holcombe Legion.

No. 3.—Maj. F. G. Palmer, Holcombe Legion.

No. 4.—Lieut. James Salvo, Washington Light Artillery.

No. 1.

Report of Brig. Gen. Nathan G. Evans, C. S. Army, commanding Third Military District of South Carolina.

HEADQUARTERS THIRD MILITARY DISTRICT S. C.,
Adams Run, S. C., March 30, 1862.

CAPTAIN: About two weeks since it was reported to me that the enemy had advanced from Edisto Island and had occupied Little Edisto Island, with the probable intention of effecting a crossing at the Edisto Ferry or at Pineberry. I sent a reconnoitering party, consisting of Henry Seabrook, Edward W. Seabrook, Joseph S. Whaley, Joseph Seabrook, and Dr. Hanahan, privates in the Marion Artillery, who willingly undertook to ascertain the position and strength of the enemy.

After three days' work Edward Seabrook reported to me that the enemy had a grand guard of four companies stationed on the northern extremity of Edisto and Little Edisto Islands. This position of the enemy was also reported to me by Col. P. F. Stevens, commanding the Holcombe Legion, after a conference with whom I determined to attack the enemy, and directed Colonel Stevens to make the necessary arrangements, and that the expedition would be under his immediate command.

On Thursday morning, 27th instant, Colonel Stevens reported that the arrangements for crossing the river, &c., were ready.

On the morning of the 28th instant I gave Colonel Stevens the written instructions (a copy of which is herewith transmitted, marked A). About dark the entire force—the infantry of the Holcombe Legion (343); cavalry, dismounted (75); the Enfield Battalion (230); and the reserve (four companies), Lieutenant-Colonel Moore's battalion—crossed the Dawho River on a bridge of flats at Pineberry. The section of the Washington Artillery and cavalry detachment, mounted, crossed in a flat at Aiken's Mill before sunset, and the force assembled at Governor Aiken's winter residence on Jehossee Island.

After duly organizing his command, Colonel Stevens, leaving the four companies of Lieutenant-Colonel Moore's battalion as a reserve at Aiken's residence, marched his command to Edisto Island about 3 a. m.

On the morning of the 29th instant, crossing Watt's Cut, he proceeded to a place known as the Old Dominion, where the first pickets of the enemy were met, who were immediately attacked, killing one and mortally wounding another (since dead).

Agreeably to my instructions, he divided his command into three columns, one with orders to charge the bridge over the Little Edisto River and capture the company stationed on Little Edisto Island, one in direction of Baynard's, to prevent being cut off, as well as to prevent re-enforcements coming from the main body of the enemy, and another to attack the company at Mr. Whaley's place. These dispositions were faithfully and gallantly executed by Colonel Stevens, who had admirably effected all his arrangements before the movement commenced. I also placed a reserve of four companies of Colonel Moore's battalion at Pineberry, on the main-land, to guard the bridge of flats, as well as to be ready to support the attacking force if required.

About sunrise I crossed over the Edisto River and took my position on Jehossee Island, to be convenient to throw over more troops and to take command should the necessity occur. About 7 a. m. Colonel Stevens sent me a dispatch that he had progressed as far as Mr. Whaley's place, and had driven the enemy to their artillery, and would await further instructions.

Thinking the enemy were in too large a force to be met by his divided command, I immediately ordered him to effect his retreat, and sent forward four companies of the reserve to cover his crossing over Watt's Cut. The retreat was conducted in good order, and the majority of his command had arrived at Pineberry by 9 a. m. On account of the non-arrival of the flats sent for his use, Major Palmer and his command were retarded, and did not arrive until near 11 a. m.

In closing my report I would call the attention of the general commanding to the dauntless conduct of Major Palmer and his command. Crossing the bridge over the Little Edisto River, in obedience to his instructions he burned the bridge in his rear and vigorously charged the enemy, determined to conquer or die in the defense of his country.

To Col. P. F. Stevens I am greatly indebted for the skill and gallantry with which he conducted the expedition, to which is due its entire success.

For individual instances of gallantry and devotion to our cause I beg leave to refer to the accompanying reports.

To my personal staff great credit is due. Capts. Ralph Elliott and W. Seabrook and Mr. Samuel Cary were engaged during the night in transmitting, under great difficulty, my orders. Asst. Surg. James Evans was on Jehossee Island, prepared to render every assistance to the wounded. The guides (Edward W. Seabrook, Henry Seabrook, Joseph Seabrook, Joseph S. Whaley, and Dr. Hanahan, of the Marion Artillery) conducted the several columns and rendered valuable assistance by their thorough knowledge of the country.

Very respectfully, your obedient servant,

N. G. EVANS,

Brigadier General, Commanding Third Military Dist. S. C.

Capt. J. R. WADDY,

Assistant Adjutant-General, Pocotaligo, S. C.

[Inclosure A.]

HEADQUARTERS THIRD MILITARY DISTRICT S. C.,

Adams Run, S. C., March 28, 1862.

COLONEL: Proceed to-night to Edisto Island with the infantry force of your Legion, the Enfield Battalion, a section of the Washington Artillery, and a small detachment of cavalry, and attack the companies of the enemy said to be on Little Edisto Island at the Old Dominion, and also at the places of Messrs. Bailey and Whaley. You will attack these companies vigorously, charge the force on Little Edisto, destroying the bridge over the Little Edisto River after your passage, and drive the enemy off the island. You will place a reserve at Aiken's Mill, with orders to join you at the shortest notice. Another reserve will be held to assist you at Pineberry. You will use every precaution not to be cut off. For this purpose send a strong picket in the direction of Baynard's. Send also word to the pickets at Bear Island to inform you of the approach of any vessel coming up the South Edisto. Should you capture any prisoners, you will hurry them off to the reserve at Pineberry. Should you deem it practicable to pursue the enemy beyond Whaley's, at the forks of the roads, you will immediately advise me at Pineberry, stating the condition and position of the enemy. Should you encounter a superior force in numbers too great to engage, you will effect your retreat in good order to Aiken's Mill or to Pineberry, either way you should deem advisable and the most safe.

Very respectfully, your obedient servant,

N. G. EVANS,

Brigadier-General, Commanding.

Col. P. F. STEVENS,

Commanding Expedition.

No. 2.

Report of Col. P. F. Stevens, Holcombe Legion.

HEADQUARTERS HOLCOMBE LEGION,

March 29, 1862.

CAPTAIN: I have the honor to report that, pursuant to orders from Brig. Gen. N. G. Evans, commanding, I last night moved from Jehossee, about 3 a. m., on an expedition to Edisto Island, with the following force, viz: The Enfield Battalion, 230 strong, Maj. P. Nelson, commanding; a detachment of cavalry, Holcombe Legion, dismounted, 75 men; Companies B and F, Holcombe Legion, 81 men; Companies A, C, D, E, G, and H, or rather portions of each, 261 men, commanded by Majors Palmer and Garlington.

Major Nelson, throwing out skirmishers from Captain Blair's company (A) of his battalion, crossed Watt's Cut first, supported by Lieutenant-Colonel Shingler, with whose command I was principally in position. Moving forward without opposition until near Old Dominion, the enemy's picket there first challenged, when an interchange of shots took place between them and our advance. Moving on past Old Dominion, if I remember aright, a second interchange of shots took place between our advance and the enemy, when I discovered that the head of the column had taken the wrong direction for Bailey's house, which I had determined to attack with this portion of my force.

After the delay thus caused, our guide having placed the advance on the correct road, the march was continued to Bailey's without interruption. On reaching that place it was found deserted. The alarm of the picket and the delay incident to missing the way probably gave the enemy time to escape, as one of the prisoners, subsequently taken, stated that there was a company at that point and two companies at Baynard's. Moving on from Bailey's to Whaley's, on reaching the main road we were fired on from the woods on the road-side, but fortunately without any loss on our side. The enemy retiring from the woods, we moved on until near Whaley's, when, several discharges of artillery being heard at that point and the roll of the enemy's drums being also heard from two points beyond Whaley's, I deemed it prudent to retire, as my retreat over the long causeway would have been very disastrous in the face of artillery.

Returning to the cut, we found that at the first fire our skirmishers had killed one of the pickets and wounded a second, We there found four muskets. Bringing the wounded and the dead man to Jehossee, I buried the latter and dispatched the wounded man to Pineberry. I understand that he has since died.

The second part of the command, under the guidance of Mr. Seabrook, and the command of Majors Palmer and Garlington, taking a by-path, moved rapidly to Little Edisto Bridge, receiving the fire of pickets and moving steadily forward. At the bridge the enemy offered considerable resistance, but charging in the face of the fire the bridge was carried. Leaving a detachment to destroy the bridge, the main party pushed on for the house of Hanahan. There was considerable resistance on the part of the enemy, but being finally broken, our party captured 19, as follows: First Lieut. John McElhaney, Corporal Samuel Moorhead, and Noah Fisher, Samuel Campbell, James Steffey, Andy Farren, John L. Taylor, Abr. D. Coy, Nicholas Cameron, Westley Cameron, Robert Crytzer, and L. L. Thompson, all members of Company F, Fifty-fifth Pennsylvania Regiment; Issac Ream, W. E. Garlinger, John Mars, John Werning, Thomas Lockard, Christian Whitaker, and a sergeant* (name unknown, sent to hospital wounded), of Company H, same regiment. One man was found killed on the field, said to be a non-commisioned officer.

Of our entire command, one private in the cavalry, Kinsler Davis, of Company B, was slightly wounded in the leg; Private Henderson, of Company I, was shot through the arm, and Private Chapman, of Company C, was slightly wounded in the head.

Crossing his men and prisoners in a small boat found at Hanahan's, Major Palmer got off safely to Jehossee. The flats sent by Lieutenant Bates did not arrive until late, thereby greatly retarding the retreat of Major Palmer.

I cannot too highly commend the gallantry and daring of Majors Palmer and Garlington, crossing to an island and shutting themselves

* Silas Golliplier.

thereon, determined to conquer the enemy, no matter what his force. The duty assigned them was most handsomely performed.

Respectfully,

P. F. STEVENS,
Colonel Holcombe Legion.

Capt. A. L. EVANS,
Assistant Adjutant-General.

P. S.—I omitted to mention that there was a strong reserve posted partly at Pineberry and partly at Aiken's Mill, on Jehossee. This reserve consisted of Lieutenant-Colonel Moore's second battalion South Carolina volunteers. I will send Major Palmer's report. Moore's battalion had four companies at Pineberry and four companies at Aiken's Mill.

Respectfully,

[Inclosure.]

HEADQUARTERS HOLCOMBE LEGION,
Camp Blair, S. C., March 31, 1862.

CAPTAIN: I have the honor to report the following articles captured in the late expedition to Edisto: 9 muskets and 7 bayonets; 2 rifled muskets and 2 bayonets; 17 sets of accouterments; 397 cartridges and caps; 9 nipple-wrenches; 12 wipers; 1 sword of First Lieutenant McElhaney, now in possession of Capt. W. J. Smith, to whom it was surrendered; 1 sword, now in possession of Captain Crawley.

Respectfully,

P. F. STEVENS,
Colonel Holcombe Legion.

Capt. A. L. EVANS,
Assistant Adjutant-General.

P. S.—I forward also one letter mentioning the force on the island and the descriptive list of Company F, Fifty-fifth Regiment Pennsylvania Volunteers.

No. 3.

Report of Maj. F. G. Palmer, Holcombe Legion.

HEADQUARTERS HOLCOMBE LEGION,
Camp Blair, S. C., March 30, 1862.

COLONEL: In pursuance of your orders, as soon as Colonel Shingler's command crossed Watt's Cut, I moved my command, composed of the following companies, Captains Smith's, Crawley's, Bomar's, Maffett's, Heller's, Roebuck's, and Bishop's, the two latter under the command of Lieutenants Wright and Bishop, numbering in all 260 men, across the cut, and moved rapidly forward until I arrived near the Old Dominion house, when, under the guidance of Edward and Henry Seabrook, I filed to the left and rear of the house, throwing out Captain Smith's company, of 22 men, as an advance, and one platoon of Captain Crawley's company to support it. Striking a direct course through the field for the bridge across Little Edisto River by a path known only to the Seabrooks, we moved forward as rapidly as the darkness of the night and the nature of the ground would admit. Arriving at the bridge, we drove in the enemy's pickets, which I found stationed there, and having crossed over I left our chaplain, the Rev. Mr. McCollough, and Mr. Irwin, who had volunteered to me for the expedition, with Captain Bishop's company, under the command of Lieutenant Bishop, to destroy it, and ordered Lieutenant Wright to remain there as a support until the destruction of the bridge had sufficiently progressed to cause any attempt at throwing re-enforcements across both difficult and hazardous; then he (Lieutenant Wright) was to rejoin me with his command. It was my intention, after crossing the bridge, to divide my force, and to place one portion under the command of Major Garlington, which would proceed up the main road to Hanahan's house, the headquarters of the enemy, on Little Edisto, and I, with the other portion, would move along a by-path across the field by a more direct route; but after a consultation with Major Garlington we deemed it prudent not to divide our force, as it was necessary to leave two companies at the bridge, in consequence of the combustible material which had been prepared for setting it on fire failing to reach us in time.

Striking a direct course for Hanahan's house we pushed forward at the double-quick, but had not proceeded more than a quarter of a mile before we succeeded in capturing 3 prisoners, who, upon being questioned, asserted that they had one regiment upon Little Edisto Island. Having Captains Smith's and Crawley's companies in front, and not knowing where the enemy was stationed, I ordered Captain Bomar to throw his company to the right and make a reconnaissance in that direction. He had not proceeded far when the enemy opened fire upon him from behind a ditch and bank about 100 or 150 yards off, which fire was promptly returned by his company. I immediately ordered Captains Maffett and Heller to the support of Captain Bomar. Our men, succeeding in getting under cover of the bank, opened a sharp fire upon the place from which the fire of the enemy proceeded, and soon drove them from their position; but not being able to see, on account of the density of the fog, and supposing their main force at the house when they retired, I took it for granted they had fallen back to that position, and in the mean time Captains Smith and Crawley came up with 14 other prisoners, which they had captured.

I then ordered Major Garlington, with Captains Maffett's and Heller's companies, to attack the house, and the remainder of the force to support the attack. With a yell and at the double-quick they charged the house, but to their astonishment found only two or three of the enemy, who fled at their approach and escaped under cover of a dense fog.

The forces left for the destruction of the bridge, having accomplished their object, rejoined me shortly after I had taken possession of the house, but too late to take part in the skirmish.

Having executed your orders in reference to the attack upon the enemy, and not seeing the flats which were ordered to be sent to me there, I immediately commenced crossing the prisoners and troops in a small boat, capable of carrying only 5 persons, which I found at the landing. I was therefore obliged to land on the opposite shore, from which place we had to march through a marsh about three-fourths of a mile in length.

Not being able to make an examination of the ground on which the skirmish took place, I am unable to give an exact account of the loss the enemy sustained. I know only of 1 being killed, 1 wounded and captured, together with 18 privates and non-commissioned officers and 1 first lieutenant, all of the Fifty-fifth Pennsylvania Regiment; making a total of 21 in killed, wounded, and captured. We also took some arms, accouterments, and baggage, but not being able to bring them off, most of the things were destroyed. I was obliged, on account of the sickness of one of the prisoners, to leave him.

I have the satisfaction of reporting that my command sustained no loss, and only 2 men slightly wounded, 1 belonging to Captain Bomar's and the other to Captain Bishop's companies.

I take pleasure in stating that the officers and men under my command behaved in a prompt, gallant, and meritorious manner, and upon which the success of the expedition depended.

Before closing my report I must call your attention particularly to the gallant part taken by Maj. A. C. Garlington, not only in rendering me invaluable assistance by his counsels, but by being prominently engaged in extending and attending to the prompt execution of every order I gave; also to the active part taken by Mr. McCollough and Mr. Irwin in the faithful discharge of the duty I assigned them, upon which the safety of the command depended.

I have the honor to remain, yours, respectfully,

F. G. PALMER,
Major Holcombe Legion.

Col. P. F. STEVENS,
Commanding Expedition to Edisto, S. C.

P. S.—The Seabrooks not only rendered me invaluable assistance as guides, but took an active part in the skirmish we had with the enemy.

[Indorsement.]

HDQRS. HOLCOMBE LEGION, CAMP BLAIR, S. C.,
March 31, 1862.

CAPTAIN: I have the honor to forward the above report of Major Palmer. In explanation of one or two points I would state that among the 21 killed, wounded, and captured, as mentioned by Major Palmer, there was 1 prisoner sick in the house, and he was the one left.

I would also call especial attention to the gallantry of Messrs. McCollough and Irwin at the bridge. While they were engaged in destroying the bridge a portion of the enemy, escaping from Major Palmer's party, attempted to cross the bridge, but were driven back, Messrs. McCollough and Irwin encouraging and directing Company I during the skirmish. While holding the bridge two officers approached from Whaley's side (Big Edisto). They were fired on by a party under charge of Mr. Irwin, and one of the officers was seen to fall and struggle upon the side of the road. He was not seen to rise again. The other fled. Mr. Irwin is under the impression the officer was of high rank, as indicated by his dress, and his impression is that he was killed.

I forward the report of Lieutenant Salvo, commanding detachment of Washington Artillery.

Respectfully,

P. F. STEVENS,
Colonel Holcombe Legion.

Capt. A. L. EVANS,
Assistant Adjutant-General.

No. 4.

Report of Lieut. James Salvo, Washington Light Artillery.

CAMP SALVO, S. C., *March* 30, 1862.

SIR: I have the honor to report that, having received orders from Colonel Stevens at 1 p. m. Friday, 28th instant, to cross with my section of the Washington Light Artillery to Jehossee Island, in compliance therewith I left this camp at 1.30 p. m. with the two pieces, one 6-pounder gun and one 12-pounder howitzer, for Grimball's Landing, which we reached at 2.30 p. m.

There I waited till sunset with the view of precluding the enemy from observing our movements, and also because the tide was more favorable at that hour for effecting a landing on the other side. I then passed my command over in three flats to Governor Aiken's Landing, on Jehossee Island.

Here, moving a short distance along the road, I halted till 2.30 a. m. of Saturday, the 29th instant, and then taking a negro guide moved down to the Little Edisto River, and took up a position directly opposite to Hanahan's house, on Little Edisto Island. In this position I waited for the burning of the bridge which joined Big Edisto to Little Edisto, the signal for me to take my part in the engagement, which the rattle of musketry and the shouts of the combatants soon gave me to understand had now commenced.

Darkness seemed to linger later than usual, and I was afraid that the contest would be decided before it became light enough for me to render any assistance with the artillery. And when at last the daylight shone I found that a dense fog prevailed and entirely intercepted my view of the opposite shore, so that even the tops of the trees on Little Edisto were invisible. This unfortunate condition of affairs lasted until the engagement was over, effectually cutting me off from taking any share in it, and preventing my seeing even the signal for me to open fire.

After the firing had all ceased, having previously heard it in the direction of Hanahan's house, besides much shouting there, too, showing that our men had got there, I came to the conclusion that the fight at this point had been decided in our favor, and so, according to previous instructions, I sent the howitzer with orders to report to Colonel Shingler at Watt's Cut; but before it got there our troops had all recrossed to Jehossee Island, and being met by Colonel Shingler on the road, he ordered it to cross over to the main.

Shortly afterwards I received orders to the same effect, and in compliance therewith returned to Aiken's Landing with the other piece, and embarking the section, reached Grimball's Landing at 11.30 a. m. and this camp at 2 p. m., the pieces, horses, and men unscathed and in good condition.

I have the honor to remain, your obedient servant,

JAMES SALVO,

Lieut., Commanding First Section Washington Light Artillery.

Adjutant DU BOSE, *Holcombe Legion.*

MARCH 30-31, 1862.—Affairs on Wilmington and Whitemarsh Islands, Ga.

REPORTS.

No. 1.—Brig. Gen. Quincy A. Gillmore, U. S. Army.
No. 2.—Col. Rudolph Rosa, Forty-sixth New York Infantry.
No. 3.—Brig. Gen. Alexander R. Lawton, C. S. Army.

No. 1.

Report of Brig. Gen. Quincy A. Gillmore, U. S. Army.

HEADQUARTERS TYBEE ISLAND, GA., *April* 1, 1862.

GENERAL: I send herewith a report from Colonel Rosa, commanding the Forty-sixth New York, from which regiment the hulk in Lazaretto

Creek receives its crew. One of his guard boats and 17 men, sent out daily from the hulk, have been taken by the enemy. They were attacked apparently by a large scouting party. I have always recommended that position to be held by a gunboat. At the time the very poor substitute of an old hulk was resorted to no gunboat was available, I suppose. The position is by no means secure from attack in small boats, of which the enemy is known to have a good supply in Saint Augustine Creek and adjacent waters. The hulk when first sent there was intended principally to prevent small steamers communicating with Fort Pulaski through Turner's Creek, and not to guard McQueen's Island Marsh against the approach of foot passengers, on which extra and extended duty the boat and guard were lost. I urgently recommend that the services of a gunboat in Wilmington Narrows be at once secured. I do not consider the property (guns and ammunition) on Goat's Point safe from a foray without this precaution.

I recommended some days ago to General Viele and also to General Sherman to picket McQueen's Island from Bird Island battery, to which place it is convenient. I could put some siege and field guns in position on Goat's Point (screened from view from the fort) to cover Lazaretto Creek and send out every evening a boat guard from that point up the creek to remain out twenty-four hours. A small steamer like the Mayflower or Honduras is wanted here very much. If no gunboats can be had the steamer is indispensably necessary, and could be armed. This would help matters some by placing her near the hulk. I have made repeated applications for a steamer, but thus far without success. I sent this afternoon to Warsaw Sound, requesting that a gunboat from that place be sent up Wilmington Narrows until advices can be had from division headquarters. The messenger has not returned. Should the hulk be overpowered our batteries against Fort Pulaski would be exposed to a very annoying fire from her. The place should be held by us securely.

I trust these matters will command your immediate attention.

Very respectfully, your obedient servant,

Q. A. GILLMORE,
Brigadier-General, Commanding Post.

Brig. Gen. H. W. BENHAM,
Comdg. First Division, Dept. of the South, Beaufort, S. C.

No. 2.

Report of Col. Rudolph Rosa, Forty-sixth New York Infantry.

SHIP MONTEZUMA,
Gibson Cut, April 1, 1862.

GENERAL: In accordance with your orders, I arrived here on Saturday evening with a detachment of 30 men and 2 commissioned officers from the Forty-sixth Regiment. On Sunday I made a reconnaissance on Whitemarsh and Wilmington Islands, pushing in both cases out to Thunderbolt and Saint Augustine Creeks, opposite to Thunderbolt and Carston Bluff batteries. Nothing remarkable occurred, excepting that the small stern-wheel steamer did show herself near to our boats left at Gibson's, in the Oatland Creek, which is not spiked, and turned back after receiving three of our musket shots from a point of land. For particulars apply preliminary to Lieutenant Metzner.

On returning, I learned that, by an unaccountable hallucination of the lieutenant left in command of the Montezuma, the German Dannenfelser and 2 men had been allowed to visit Wilmington Island, and were missing. On Monday morning it was ascertained by a patrol that they had been on Dannenfelser's farm, and left there at 12 o'clock, Sunday, for the Montezuma. The usual boat guard was then left opposite Hunter's farm, and a relief was sent for them towards the afternoon. Guard boat and relief are now missing unaccountably, together with 2 commissioned officers and 35 enlisted men. I shall stay here until further news. I just sent Captain Hinckel to the three gunboats in Warsaw Sound for the purpose of inducing one of them to make a trip up to Gibson's farm and the spikes across Wilmington Narrows.

I most respectfully propose to send 50 men, with 2 commissioned officers and two days' rations, to-night for another reconnaissance in Wilmington, and for ascertaining the fate of the guard boat. If the Forty-sixth Regiment is to give the men, then I most respectfully suggest Captains Schwickart and Paulsackel, with 25 men, from their respective companies each. By the sayings of Dannenfelser and of the negro whom I sent along great rewards ($12,000) have been offered for removing from the fort the garrison. Perhaps an organized great patrol of row-boats lays in Turner's Creek, and it would be desirable to have a steamboat there doing duty during the last period of the siege. Our boats are transports, but not swift enough for military service, and the distance is too great.

By reconnaissances I have got the conviction that the intercourse between the fort and Savannah can be stopped only by taking a position on the water between Turner's and Scriven's, near to the spikes. All the other terrain is a net-work of creeks, passable for small boats, and of the most complicated features. To have a picket on the shore of the south channel, relieved from this place, I found entirely unfeasible, useless, and dangerous. Perhaps from Bird's Point it would be more suitable.

Please find inclosed some papers. The one referring to Dannenfelser shows all traces of genuineness, and talks greatly for the presumption that he is no traitor.

If one or two spacious and easy-moving row-boats could be sent—if so, at once. Send also a dozen of good oars.

Yours, most respectfully,

RUDOLPH ROSA,
Colonel Forty-Sixth Regiment.

Brigadier-General GILLMORE,
Commanding Post, Tybee Island, Ga.

[Indorsement.]

Since I received the above, Colonel Rosa sends word that the 2 officers and 17 of the men (one boat party) have returned to the hulk. The other boat party was fired into and taken.

Q. A. GILLMORE.

No. 3.

Report of Brig. Gen. Alexander R. Lawton, C. S. Army.

HEADQUARTERS DEPARTMENT [DIST.] OF GEORGIA,
Savannah, Ga., April 5, 1862.

CAPTAIN: I have the honor to report that on two successive nights, March 30 and 31, scouting parties were sent to Whitemarsh and Wilmington Islands from the Thirteenth Georgia Regiment, Colonel Douglass, which were entirely successful, killing 1 and capturing 18 of the enemy, 2 of whom have since died. They also captured a barge with a 6-pounder. We had but 1 man wounded, and it is feared that he will not recover. The scouting party was under the immediate command of Captain Crawford, Thirteenth Georgia Regiment, who conducted it with skill and gallantry, and all the officers and men under his command exhibited the most commendable courage and enterprise.

I regret further to report that on the occasion of a subsequent expedition to Wilmington Island, for the purpose of ascertaining the position of the enemy and attacking him if there, Assistant Surgeon Beasly was shot through the leg by a mistake of our own men and had both bones broken. There is reason to hope, however, that he will recover with as little injury as possible.

I am, captain, very respectfully, your obedient servant,

A. R. LAWTON,
Brigadier-General, Commanding.

Capt. J. R. WADDY,
Assistant Adjutant-General.

APRIL 5, 1862.—Occupation of Edisto Island, S. C., by Union forces.

Report of Col. Enoch Q. Fellows, Third New Hampshire Infantry.

HEADQUARTERS U. S. FORCES,
North Edisto, S. C., April 5, 1862.

GENERAL: I have the honor to report that the reconnaissance contemplated last evening for to-day has been made and proved very satisfactory. I have taken possession of the entire island, and have not as yet seen the enemy. The Third Regiment New Hampshire Volunteers and two pieces of artillery are stationed at the farther part of the island. I think our position is secure, and do not apprehend any danger. The Third New Hampshire Volunteers will be re-enforced immediately by the Forty-seventh New York Volunteers, the Fifty-fifth Pennsylvania Volunteers being held in reserve. Two gunboats of light draught would be of great value to us here as a means of defense. The Crusader draws too much water to be able to run around in the creeks. Gunboats of light draught will be able to pass around the island, therefore keeping the enemy at bay, and securing all necessary positions. The steamer Boston arrived at this post this p. m. The sloop of war Dale is still in Saint Helena Sound. I am not fully prepared to give you a full detail of the different positions now held by our forces, but will make a full report soon. Colonel Moore has permission to visit Hilton Head, leaving Major Kane in command, who is fully competent. The Ben DeFord returns to Hilton Head early to-morrow. A line of communication is kept up with the outposts by means of the cavalry. I will make a further report to-morrow.

I am, general, very respectfully, your obedient servant,

E. Q. FELLOWS,
Colonel Third New Hampshire Volunteers, Commanding Post.

APRIL 9, 1862.—Evacuation of Jacksonville, Fla., by Union forces.

REPORTS.

No. 1.—Brig. Gen. Horatio G. Wright, U. S. Army, with orders, &c.
No. 2.—Secretary of War to the House of Representatives.
No. 3.—Col. W. S. Dilworth, commanding District of Middle and East Florida.

No. 1.

Report of Brig. Gen. Horatio G. Wright, U. S. Army, with orders, &c.

HEADQUARTERS, STEAMER COSMOPOLITAN,
Port Royal Harbor, S. C., April 13, 1862.

CAPTAIN: I have the honor to report, for the information of the general commanding the Northern District, that, in obedience to the instructions contained in his letter of the 2d instant [following], I have withdrawn the troops from Jacksonville, taking with me all the stores and other public property, and likewise removing property belonging to the enemy, consisting in part of two 8-inch columbiads, with chassis and carriages, and three field pieces, with their carriages. Some few captured articles, for which we had not room on the transports, were destroyed.

General Benham's letter was received by me on the 6th instant. On the 7th, preparations for withdrawing were begun by embarking the public stores, and on the 8th, at 12 m., the troops were marched on board, and the embarkation was completed by about 2 p. m. the same day. Owing to the heavy wind which had sprung up during the morning, it was impossible to get all the transports clear of the wharf until near sunset—too late to move safely very far down the intricate channel of the river that night—and it was therefore determined by the senior naval officer and myself to lay off the town until morning. This I was more willing to do as it took from our movement all appearance of a hasty retreat.

At 6 a. m. on the 9th the transports, convoyed by the gunboats Ottawa, Capt. Thomas H. Stevens, senior naval officer; Pembina, Capt. J. P. Bankhead, and the Ellen, Captain Budd, proceeded down the river, reaching Mayport, near the mouth, at about 2 p. m., but too late for passing over the bar, on account of the state of the tide. Here I took on board one company of the Fourth New Hampshire Regiment, which had been stationed at the batteries abandoned by the enemy, and as our means of transportation did not permit of our carrying off the guns, they were destroyed and their carriages and platforms burned, as were also the small buildings thereat.

At 3 p. m. on the 10th, the tide serving, the transports passed the bar, the steamer Belvidere proceeding to Saint Augustine and the Cosmopolitan to Fernandina. Stormy weather detained the steamers at Fernandina until this morning, which place we left at about 7.30 o'clock.

The troops in garrison at Jacksonville were the Ninety-seventh Pennsylvania Regiment, six companies of the Fourth New Hampshire Regiment, and two sections of Hamilton's battery, under the command of Captain Ransom. Under the general instructions of General Benham, I have disposed the force as follows: The Ninety-seventh Pennsylvania Regiment and Ransom's battery to Hilton Head, four companies of the Fourth New Hampshire Regiment, including the one at Saint John's

Bar, to Saint Augustine, and the remaining three companies of the regiment to Fernandina. The garrison at Saint Augustine now consists of seven companies of the Fourth New Hampshire Regiment, and that at Fernandina of the Ninth Maine Regiment, three companies of the Fourth New Hampshire Regiment, and one company of the volunteer engineers. The necessity for the withdrawal of the troops from Jacksonville is to be regretted. A considerable number of the inhabitants had avowed themselves publicly in favor of our cause, and, encouraged by the proclamation issued by General Sherman to the people of East Florida, had been active in their efforts to organize a State and city government. These persons could not remain behind with their families with any safety, the enemy having threatened the lives of all who should show us the least favor or even remain in town after our occupation, and I accordingly brought off all such as desired to go, taking also such of their property as the limited transportation at my command permitted. Many of these people have abandoned all, and are without other means than the worthless paper currency in circulation before our arrival. Their condition not only appeals strongly to our sympathies, but they have a claim to present assistance from the Government to which they profess to be attached, and which owes them aid and protection. I could see no way in which these people could be subsisted at Fernandina, where most of them were landed, except by issues from Government supplies, for the purchase of which many of them, as before remarked, have no money. I have accordingly instructed the commander of the post to cause provisions to be issued to such as need them, not exceeding one ration per day to each person of twelve years old and over, and a half ration to those under that age, the provisions thus issued to be paid for by those having money. This arrangement will, I hope, be continued so long as the necessity for it exists.

To Capt. Thomas H. Stevens, senior naval officer in the Saint John's River, I desire to express my obligations for his efficient aid in the embarkation of the troops and in convoying them down the Saint John's River, and to Capt. J. P. Bankhead, U. S. Navy, commanding gunboat Pembina, for his valuable assistance in hauling the transports off the wharf at Jacksonville after the troops were on board, which, in consequence of the wind, could not have been accomplished without assistance. I would also acknowledge the obligations I am under to Captain Stevens for his cordial co-operation during the time the troops were in occupation of Jacksonville.

Very respectfully, your obedient servant,

H. G. WRIGHT,

Brigadier-General, Commanding Third Brigade.

Capt. A. B. ELY,

Asst. Adjt. Gen., Hdqrs. N. Dist., Hilton Head, S. C.

—

HEADQUARTERS, *Jacksonville, Fla., March* 31, 1862.

Capt. LOUIS H. PELOUZE,

Actg. Asst. Adjt. Gen., Hdqrs. E. C., Hilton Head, S. C.:

CAPTAIN: Reports from various sources more or less reliable have been received within the past few days of an intention upon the part of the enemy to make an attack upon this place, and on Saturday, the 29th, it was reported by persons coming into the lines that his forces were at Three Mile Creek and prepared to attack the town. To ascertain the truth of the report I ordered five companies of the Fourth New

Hampshire Regiment to make a reconnaissance of that vicinity, and in order to see that nothing which should be done should be omitted I accompanied the party myself. We examined the country as far as the creek and pushed the advance some three-quarters of a mile beyond without seeing anything of the enemy, but we learned that a party (horse and foot, numbering 100 perhaps in all) had been in that vicinity earlier in the day and had turned off to their right.

Yesterday two companies sent out from the Ninety-seventh Pennsylvania Regiment scoured the country up to and somewhat beyond the run without meeting any signs of the enemy.

To-day reports of a concentration of troops in our front have come in from various persons. At first I was inclined to view them as repetitions of previous rumors, but I have since received intelligence in which I place considerable confidence to this effect:

1st. That the order for the evacuation of East Florida and the transfer of the troops to other localities has been rescinded, and that Governor Milton has been placed in command of all the rebel forces within the State.

2d. That troops were being assembled at the Six Mile Run, or Creek, and that they were to move to the Three Mile Run and take up position at once.

3d. That the forces just alluded to are as follows:

The 3d Florida Regiment	700
The 4th Florida Regiment	1,000
The 5th Davis Cavalry	650
The 1st Florida Battalion	350
Total	2,700

4th. That orders had been issued to return to this section of the State the First and Second Florida Regiments, relieving them by Georgia troops. Where these regiments are I am unable to ascertain with certainty; some say at Pensacola, others in Virginia.

I shall, of course, hold this point to the last against any force that may be brought by the enemy, and am entirely confident, with the aid of the gunboats now here, of making a successful defense; yet I must impress upon the general commanding our isolated condition and the disparity between the forces numerically which the enemy can bring against us, as detailed above, and the troops under my command at this point. I would therefore most urgently apply to the general commanding for an increase to the force now at this post of at least two regiments. Should this re-enforcement be sent, it should be furnished with the necessary subsistence. The two sections of the light battery under Captain Ransom are already here.

We are getting up a work on the approaches to mount three or four guns, but it cannot be in condition for defense for several days.

Very respectfully, your obedient servant,

H. G. WRIGHT,
Brigadier-General, Commanding.

HEADQUARTERS, *Jacksonville, Fla., April* 2, 1862.

Capt. LOUIS H. PELOUZE,
Actg. Asst. Adjt. Genl., Hdqrs. E. C., Hilton Head, S. C.:

CAPTAIN: Since the date of my last report I have used every effort to ascertain, through individuals coming in, the strength and position of the enemy's forces in this vicinity, and after sifting and comparing the information obtained I am pretty well satisfied that the estimate then presented is not far from the truth. I would, however, state that instead of First and Second Regiments of Florida troops being returned to the State, two Georgia regiments are to be sent here in their place, and that General Anderson, who has been at Pensacola under Bragg, is to command the rebel forces in East Florida. I trust the commanding general may be able to send the re-enforcements I asked for, and if a few cavalry could be added it would leave nothing to be wished for.

Very respectfully, your obedient servant,

H. G. WRIGHT,
Brigadier-General, Commanding.

HDQRS. THIRD BRIGADE, EXPEDITIONARY CORPS,
Jacksonville, Fla., April 2, 1862.

Col. W. G. M. DAVIS,
Commanding Provisional Forces of East Florida,
Camp Langford, East Florida:

COLONEL: After a careful consideration of the propositions presented in your communication of the 1st instant, brought in by Mr. Oscar Hart, under a flag of truce, I have to make the following reply:

1st. That permission to Mr. Hart to have interviews with any citizens of Jacksonville in regard to their leaving the city cannot be granted, nor can I permit him to collect transportation for the conveyance of persons desirous to leave our lines. The propriety of this decision you, as a military man, will readily recognize.

2d. That the policy announced in my note of yesterday, of permitting the removal from Jacksonville of such persons as may desire to leave our lines to join their families or to reside in the interior of the State, will be continued, and that on application to these headquarters such permission will be granted as will carry them safely beyond our lines. We do not profess to wage war upon women and children, nor upon quiet, unoffending citizens; but, on the contrary, have done all in our power for the protection of their persons and property.

In announcing this policy I have to express the hope that it will be reciprocated by yourself in permitting the free return to Jacksonville of such persons as may desire to come back to their homes. I desire further to say that the forces under my command are instructed to carry on all operations according to the rules of civilized warfare, and that any outrages upon unarmed and unoffending citizens will be punished to the full extent of the law.

From the representation made to me of your character as an officer and a gentleman I am sure you will be governed by a similar spirit.

Very respectfully, your obedient servant,

H. G. WRIGHT,
Brigadier-General, Commanding.

HDQRS. NORTHERN DISTRICT, DEPT. OF THE SOUTH,
Hilton Head, S. C., April 2, 1862.

Brig. Gen. HORATIO G. WRIGHT,
Commanding U. S. Forces, Jacksonville, Fla.:

SIR: In view of the fact of the already too extended line of operations of our forces in this district, the major-general commanding the department directs that you make preparations for the early withdrawal of your forces from Jacksonville, Fla., the exact time and manner of which is left to your own judgment, the proper precautions being taken to avoid the appearance of a retreat; to bring off all your stores and supplies, and have the withdrawal completed within some two or three days after the receipt of this order. Your attention will then be directed to the proper re-enforcing of Saint Augustine and Fernandina. At the former place it is believed that at least 600 men may be necessary, though perhaps you may deem it expedient that 700 or 800 should be left, or, say, a small regiment, if you have one, under a judicious and reliable commander.

At Fernandina it is believed that 900 to 1,000 men will be sufficient, but 1,200 may, in your judgment, be necessary; which force you will select and place under a proper commander. Return yourself to this place with the balance of your command, unless you should feel that it was of great importance to the safety of Fernandina that you should continue for the present at that post. It being the intention to hold permanently the posts of Saint Augustine and Fernandina, you will distribute your supplies of provisions, ammunition, &c., between these two posts, leaving the supply for the longer time at Saint Augustine, if practicable, to the extent of some 50 or 60 days for the provisions, your troops, if possible, being so shipped at Jacksonville as to avoid any necessity for a transfer before reaching that place. It is the desire of the commander of the department that you should notify the people of Jacksonville on leaving that place that it is his intention to have all the aid and protection afforded to the loyal inhabitants of the interior of Florida that is practicable from the posts above named for the security of their persons and property and for the punishment of outrages, and that you should notify all persons in that vicinity that we hold them responsible for the preservation of order and quiet, being fully determined that any outrages upon persons or property contrary to the laws and usages of war shall be visited fourfold upon the inhabitants of disloyal or doubtful character nearest the scene of any such wrongs when the actual and known perpetrators cannot be discovered. As Commodore DuPont promises that his gunboats shall remain in the Saint John's River, it is very possible that this force may be sufficient, with proper efforts on the part of the inhabitants themselves, for the security of that city.

Lieutenant Tardy is directed to go in the boat which carries this, for the purpose of accompanying the re-enforcements to Saint Augustine, that he may there put such repairs as can be conveniently added for its defense, change traverse circles from the water battery to the interior work, &c.

Very respectfully, your obedient servant,

H. W. BENHAM.

Brigadier-General, Commanding.

—

HEADQUARTERS, *Jacksonville, Fla., April* 3, 1862.

Capt. LOUIS H. PELOUZE,

Actg. Asst. Adjt. Gen., Hdqrs. Ex. Corps, Hilton Head, S. C.:

CAPTAIN: If East Florida is to be permanently occupied by United States forces, it is desirable and, indeed, necessary that certain civil offices should be promptly filled. Questions are constantly arising which should not be left to the decision of the military commander, as they belong to a civil and not a military jurisdiction, and require a knowledge of law which officers commanding troops are not presumed to possess. I would therefore suggest that the Government be recommended to appoint a district judge and marshal, to reside at Jacksonville, to take cognizance of all cases arising under the civil Federal jurisdiction; and as a convenience to the inhabitants of the place and the United States troops in the vicinity, I would suggest the propriety of the appointment of a postmaster for Jacksonville, for Fernandina, and for Saint Augustine, all of which places are in possession of our land and naval forces. I presume that the necessity for the establishment of a proper civil authority by the Federal Government is as fully appreciated by the commander of the naval forces as by myself; indeed, I understand from him that he will address a communication to the flag-officer upon that subject.

It gives me pleasure to state what is only an act of justice to Captain Stevens, of the Ottawa, commanding the naval forces in the Saint John's, that he has rendered every aid in his power to my command, and that in our counsels and our acts there has been an entire harmony of sentiment.

Some of the citizens of the vicinity, whom I believe to be loyal to the Union, have already brought or desire soon to bring in cotton and other products of their plantations and ship them to the North for sale. The orders so far received do not seem to be applicable to such cases, and I have the honor to request specific instructions in the matter.

Very respectfully, your obedient servant,

H. G. WRIGHT,
Brigadier-General, Commanding.

HEADQUARTERS THIRD BRIGADE,
NOTICE.] *Jacksonville, Fla., April* 7, 1862.

In accordance with orders issued by the general commanding the Department of the South, the troops will be withdrawn from this place, and I am directed by him to notify the people of Jacksonville that it is his intention to have all the aid and protection afforded to the loyal inhabitants of the interior of Florida that is practicable for the security of their persons and property and for the punishment of outrages, and that he holds all persons in that vicinity responsible for the preservation of order and quiet, being fully determined that any outrages upon persons or property contrary to the laws and usages of war shall be visited fourfold upon the inhabitants of disloyal or doubtful character nearest the scene of any such wrongs, when the actual and known perpetrators cannot be discovered. The undersigned trusts that, inasmuch as the unoffending citizens of this place have been treated with the utmost forbearance by our forces, it will not be necessary to carry out the intention expressed in the last clause of the above notice.

H. G. WRIGHT,
Brigadier-General, Commanding.

HEADQUARTERS THIRD BRIGADE,
Jacksonville, Fla., April 8, 1862.

Lieut. Col. LOUIS BELL,
Comdg. Fourth N. H. Regiment, Saint Augustine, Fla.:

COLONEL: The major-general commanding the department having directed the abandonment of Jacksonville as a military post and the re-enforcement of the garrison at Saint Augustine, I send by the Belvidere four companies of your regiment and the regimental quartermaster to report to you. There will also be delivered at the same time subsistence and forage for about sixty days and 60,000 rounds of cartridges (caliber .69), for all of which Quartermaster Kelly has receipted. The remaining three companies of your regiment, under Major Drew, will go to Fernandina, to re-enforce the garrison at that point. The post at the mouth of the Saint John's, at which Captain Sleeper, Fourth New Hampshire Volunteers, with his company, is now stationed, will also be abandoned. What the arrangements in regard to commands and brigades will be I am unable to say at present. Until further instructions are received you will therefore consider yourself as the commander of the post at Saint Augustine, and make your reports to the headquarters of General Benham, commanding the Northern District. Captain Ransom's battery, likewise on the Belvidere, is to proceed to Hilton Head on that vessel without delay. Please afford the steamer all dispatch in unloading. I shall advise that the Belvidere or some other light-draught steamer be sent back to ply between Fernandina and Saint Augustine. I go to Hilton Head with the Ninety-seventh Pennsylvania Regiment.

Very respectfully, your obedient servant,

H. G. WRIGHT,

Brigadier-General, Commanding.

HEADQUARTERS THIRD BRIGADE,

Fernandina, Fla., April 10, 1862.

Lieut. Col. H. BISBEE, Jr.,

Ninth Maine Regiment, Commanding Post, Fernandina, Fla.:

COLONEL: Three companies of the Fourth New Hampshire Regiment, now on board the Cosmopolitan, are to be added to the garrison of your post, and I have instructed their commander, Maj. J. D. Drew, to report to you. As it is desirable that companies of the same regiment be kept together so far as possible, you will relieve those of the Ninth Maine, now at Fort Clinch, by these three companies of the Fourth New Hampshire Regiment. In withdrawing the forces from Jacksonville it was necessary for the security of such of the inhabitants as had given free exhibition to their Union sentiments to remove also, and I have brought them with me, with such of their effects as our means of transportation permitted. To these people you will assign such of the vacant houses in Fernandina as may be needed for their temporary homes, and, as many of these people have lost their all and will not have the means of purchasing provisions, you are authorized to furnish them from the Government supplies at the post to the extent necessary, not exceeding one ration to each person of twelve years old and over and a half ration to those under that age. Such persons among them as have the means of paying for their subsistence must of course do so. Provisions supplied under this authority must be regularly issued, and you should appoint an officer to superintend the same, if necessary, and to make the proper returns therefor.

I shall proceed to Hilton Head with the Ninety-seventh Pennsylvania Regiment, and as I am not sure what arrangements will be adopted in regard to commands, brigades, &c., you will make your reports and returns, till further orders, to the headquarters of the Northern District. Requisitions for supplies will be made to the same headquarters.

Very respectfully, your obedient servant,

H. G. WRIGHT,

Brigadier-General, Commanding.

No. 2.

Report of the Secretary of War to the House of Representatives.

WAR DEPARTMENT,
Washington, D. C., April 28, 1862.

SIR: In answer to the resolution of the House of Representatives, passed on the 24th instant, directing the Secretary of War to communicate to the House all the facts and circumstances within his knowledge in regard to the late evacuation of Jacksonville, Fla., by the troops of the United States, I have the honor respectfully to state that, conceiving it to be the province of the President to direct this Department what facts in relation to military operations shall be communicated, he instructs me to say that Jacksonville was evacuated by the orders of the commanding general of that department for reasons which it is not deemed compatible with the public interest at present to disclose.

Very respectfully, your obedient servant,

EDWIN M. STANTON,
Secretary of War.

Hon. GALUSHA A. GROW,
Speaker of the House of Representatives.

No. 3.

Report of Col. W. S. Dilworth, commanding District of Middle and East Florida.

HDQRS. DISTRICT OF EAST AND MIDDLE FLORIDA,
Tallahassee, Fla., April 15, 1862.

CAPTAIN: I have the honor to report to the commanding general the evacuation of Jacksonville by the enemy, which was done on the 9th instant.

When the enemy first occupied Jacksonville, and while all the Florida troops were retreating in confusion and disorder, I, as colonel of the Third Regiment Florida Volunteers, ordered a part of my regiment to advance in the direction of Jacksonville, and took a position within 10 miles of the city, with only 250 effective men. Soon I had eight companies of my regiment with me. After making a thorough reconnaissance of the city, I became convinced that I could not attack the city without heavy loss and could be driven out by the enemy's gunboats. I then determined to commence a system of annoyances, by attacking their pickets, foraging parties, &c. I made a successful attack on the picket near the city of Jacksonville, killing 4 and taking 3 prisoners, when I was ordered to take command of the district. Colonel Davis was then ordered to the command of the forces near Jacksonville, and has most successfully carried on the system which I commenced, and which has resulted in their evacuation of the place. Colonel Davis I regard as an efficient officer, and commend him to your favorable consideration.

I have further to report that after the evacuation the enemy returned, under a flag of truce, and were permitted to land 52 negroes, which were taken in charge by the commander of the post.

I inclose a list of prisoners taken near Jacksonville, and ask instructions as to what disposition will be made of them.

I also ask permission to exchange three of them for three of ours which were taken at Santa Rosa, near Pensacola, and are here on parole. This exchange could be made at Fernandina. I inclose reports of Colonel Davis, reporting the capture of these prisoners.*

I have the honor to subscribe myself, your obedient servant,

W. S. DILWORTH,
Colonel, Commanding.

Capt. T. A. WASHINGTON,
Assistant Adjutant-General, Pocotaligo, S. C.

APRIL 10, 1862.—Skirmish near Fernandina, Fla.

REPORTS.

No. 1.—Lieut. Col. H. Bisbee, jr., Ninth Maine Infantry.
No. 2.—Col. W. G. M. Davis, First Florida Cavalry.

No. 1.

Report of Lieut. Col. H. Bisbee, jr., Ninth Maine Infantry.

HEADQUARTERS,
Fernandina, Fla., April 27, 1862.

Report in case of a party of men belonging to Company I, Ninth Maine Regiment, captured by the enemy on the 10th of April, 1862.—Names of the party: Orderly Sergt. Richard Webster, Corp. James W. Bowman, Privates Isaac Whitney, John E. Kent, Alonzo B. Merrill, C. Wesley Adams, taken prisoners; Private Ansel Chase, killed.

At the time the above party were captured and killed Company I was doing picket duty at the railroad bridge which spans the creek separating Amelia Island from the main-land. They were captured at what is known in this vicinity as the Judge O'Neal place, which is about two miles and a half from the railroad bridge. The captain of the company (S. D. Baker) allowed this party of men on the 7th of April to remain at said Judge O'Neal place to protect the wife of one Mr. Heath, whom I held in arrest at the time, and who was living at O'Neal's house. Captain Baker left the party at said place without reporting it to his commanding officer, doing it as an act of kindness and sympathy for Mrs. Heath, and, as his men daily frequented the vicinity with impunity, did not think that he was doing a wrong act or exposing his men. On the same day (7th of April) Private William W. Lunt, of Company I, Ninth Maine Regiment, deserted, went to the enemy's lines, and, it is supposed, reported to the enemy that this party of men was stationed at Judge O'Neal's.

On Thursday, 10th of April, Captain Baker sent 2 men to order the party in, who found the dead body of 1 man, that from appearances had been shot that day, and the remainder of the party taken prisoners.

Very respectfully,

H. BISBEE, JR.,
Lieutenant-Colonel Ninth Maine Regiment.

Brig. Gen. H. W. BENHAM,
Commanding First Division, Southern Department.

---

*Not found.

No. 2.

Report of Col. W. G. M. Davis, First Florida Cavalry.

HDQRS. PROVISIONAL FORCES EAST FLORIDA,
Camp Langford, Fla., April 12, 1862.

CAPTAIN: I have the honor to report, for the information of the colonel commanding the department, that Capt. William M. Footman, of Company F, First Florida Cavalry, in charge of a detachment of 40 men (same corps), sent by me to watch the movements of the enemy near Fernandina and to repel any effort made to leave the island of Amelia for the main-land in such small parties as he might be able to cope with, in the execution of such orders encountered two men on the railroad, who had landed from a hand car, and made them prisoners without resistance.

In a short time afterwards he found a party of 5 men at the house of Judge O'Neal. One of the party, offering resistance, was killed, and the rest then made prisoners. The whole of the prisoners were sent here by Captain Footman, and I have sent them by the train to-day, under a guard of 5 men, to be delivered to you at Tallahassee.

I desire particularly to commend the conduct of Captain Footman, who has on this occasion, as he has at all times, proved himself a zealous, intelligent, and efficient officer.

I am about to increase Captain Footman's force to 100 men. He will be assisted by parties of citizens should he at any time need them, and I look for good news from him before long. He will alarm the enemy and keep them confined to the island.

I remain, very respectfully, your obedient servant,

W. G. M. DAVIS,
Colonel, Commanding Regiment.

Capt. I. S. CROSS,
Actg. Asst. Adjt. Gen., Dept. Middle and East Florida.

APRIL 10-11, 1862.—Bombardment and capture of Fort Pulaski, Ga.

REPORTS.

No. 1.—Maj. Gen. David Hunter, U. S. Army.
No. 2.—Brig. Gen. Henry W. Benham, U. S. Army.
No. 3.—Brig. Gen. Egbert L. Viele, U. S. Army.
No. 4.—Lieut. P. H. O'Rorke, U. S. Corps of Engineers, of condition of the works of investment on February 28, 1862.
No. 5.—Brig. Gen. Quincy A. Gillmore, U. S. Army, of operations against Fort Pulaski, January 28–April 11, 1862.
No. 6.—Surg. George E. Cooper, U. S. Army.
No. 7.—Maj. Gen. John C. Pemberton, C. S. Army.
No. 8.—Brig. Gen. Alexander R. Lawton, C. S. Army.

No. 1.

Report of Maj. Gen. David Hunter, U. S. Army.

HEADQUARTERS DEPARTMENT OF THE SOUTH,
Fort Pulaski, Cockspur Island, Ga., April 13, 1862.

SIR: The flag of our country waves over Fort Pulaski. I summoned the garrison to surrender at sunrise on the morning of the 10th instant.

Immediately on receiving their refusal, at 8 a. m., we opened fire, the bombardment continuing without intermission for thirty hours. At the end of eighteen hours' firing the fort was breached in the southeast angle, and at the moment of surrender, 2 p. m. on the 11th instant, we had commenced preparations for storming.

The whole armament of the fort—47 guns, a great supply of fixed ammunition, 40,000 pounds of powder, and large quantities of commissary stores, have fallen into our hands; also 360 prisoners, of whom the officers will be sent North by the first opportunity that offers.

The result of this bombardment must cause, I am convinced, a change in the construction of fortifications as radical as that forshadowed in naval architecture by the conflict between the Monitor and Merrimac. No works of stone or brick can resist the impact of rifled artillery of heavy caliber.

Too much praise cannot be given Capt. Q. A. Gillmore, U. S. Engineers (acting brigadier-general), the officer immediately in charge of our works on Tybee Island, for his industry, skill, and patriotic zeal. Great credit is also due to his assistants, Lieut. J. H. Wilson, U. S. Topographical Engineers, and Lieut. Horace Porter, of the Ordnance Department. I have also to gratefully acknowledge the services of Capt. C. R. P. Rodgers, U. S. Navy, who, with 100 of his men from the Wabash, under command of Lieutenant Irwin, did nobly at the guns.

Our gallant volunteers, under the scientific direction of Captain Gillmore, displayed admirable energy and perseverance in the construction of the earthworks on Tybee Island, and nothing could be finer or more impressive than the steadiness, activity, skill, and courage with which they worked their guns in battery. When I receive the reports of the officers now immediately in command—Brig. Gen. H. W. Benham and Acting Brigadier-General Gillmore—a statement more in detail will be immediately forwarded; but I cannot close without expressing my thanks to both these officers, and the hope that Acting Brigadier-General Gillmore may be confirmed in the position of brigadier-general, to which in this bombardment he has established such deserving claims.

I am happy to state that our loss was but one man killed, the earthworks of our batteries affording secure protection against the heaviest fire of the enemy. The loss of the enemy has been stated as three severely wounded.

I have the honor to be, sir, most respectfully, your very obedient servant,

DAVID HUNTER,
Major-General, Commanding.

Hon. E. M. STANTON,
Secretary of War, Washington, D. C.

HEADQUARTERS DEPARTMENT OF THE SOUTH,
Tybee Island, Ga., April 10, 1862.

To the COMMANDING OFFICER, *Fort Pulaski:*

SIR: I hereby demand of you the immediate surrender and restoration of Fort Pulaski to the authority and possession of the United States. This demand is made with a view to avoiding, if possible, the effusion of blood which must result from the bombardment and attack now in readiness to be opened.

The number, caliber, and completeness of the batteries surrounding you leave no doubt as to what must result in case of your refusal; and as the defense, however obstinate, must eventually succumb to the assailing force at my disposal, it is hoped you may see fit to avert the useless waste of life.

This communication will be carried to you under a flag of truce by Lieut. J. H. Wilson, U. S. Army, who is authorized to wait any period not exceeding thirty minutes from delivery for your answer.

I have the honor to be, sir, very respectfully, your most obedient servant,

DAVID HUNTER,
Major-General, Commanding.

No. 2.

Reports of Brig. Gen. Henry W. Benham, U. S. Army.

HDQRS. FIRST DIV., NORTH'N DIST., DEPT. OF THE SOUTH,
Fort Pulaski, Cockspur Island, Ga., April 12, 1862.

SIR: I have the honor to report the conclusion of the operations of the siege of Fort Pulaski, in Savannah River, Georgia, which have resulted in the capture of that fort and its armament and the unconditional surrender of the effective force of the garrison, amounting to 361, of whom 24 were officers, besides about 18 who were sick and wounded. This siege is, as I would remark, the first trial, at least on our side of the Atlantic, of the modern heavy and rifled projectiles against forts erected and supposed to be sufficiently strong prior to these inventions, almost equaling, as it would appear, the revolution accomplished in naval warfare by the iron-clad vessels recently constructed. These operations, with the cordial assistance and co-operation of the naval forces under Flag-Officer S. F. DuPont, have been accomplished by a portion of the troops of my division, for the most part under the immediate direction of Capt. Q. A. Gillmore, Corps of Engineers, acting brigadier-general and chief engineer of the siege, to whose report (copy of which respectfully forwarded herewith) I have the honor to refer for the details of the operations.

Immediately after our arrival in this department, as you are aware, I visited Tybee Island on the 31st ultimo, and carefully inspected the works being erected there for the direct attack upon this fort, which had been well advanced by General Gillmore, under the directions of that faithful and judicious officer Brig. Gen. T. W. Sherman, my predecessor in this district. These works consisted of eleven batteries, prepared for thirty-five to thirty-seven pieces of heavy ordnance, extending along an oblique line of about one and a half miles in length, opposite the southeast face of the fort, the extremities of this line being at distances, respectively, of about 1 and 2 miles from the fort. They were placed with great skill and judgment, and constructed properly, and with as much strength and regularity as the circumstances of the case would permit, and the care and forethought of the engineer in providing for the proper supply of ordnance and other stores that might be needed is worthy of especial mention, the whole arrangement at Tybee Island meeting my entire approval.

Desiring, however, to obtain, if possible, a concentric fire upon the work, I endeavored to arrange with General Viele, commanding at Daufuskie Island, to accomplish this object, directing him upon the 6th instant to place a battery on Long Island, to attack the gorge of the fort on the west, and after a second visit to him, on the 9th, to construct another, if practicable and the distance were not too great, upon Turtle Island on the north, the object being mainly the moral effect of an encircling fire rather than the expectation of any serious effect upon the walls at that distance. From some cause, however, the heavy ordnance for these batteries did not arrive in time, and the lighter pieces most available and placed in position on Long Island served rather as a diversion than for any serious demonstration upon the work.

The main attack upon the work, as you are aware, commenced upon the morning of the 10th instant, at about 7.30 o'clock, and immediately after the refusal of its commander to surrender according to your summons previously sent. Being present yourself at or between our batteries for the greater portion of the day during the contest between these batteries and the fort, you are, of course, personally aware of the great efficiency with which these batteries were served, and of the successful commencement of the breach at the southeast angle of the fort on that day. You are also aware of the efficient and accurate firing of the guns from the fort, directed as they were with great precision, not only at our batteries, but even at the individual persons passing between them or otherwise exposed. The fire on our part, though delayed at first by the necessity for obtaining the proper ranges, was kept up with such vigor that over 3,000 projectiles, varying in size from the 13-inch mortar shell to the 30 pounder Parrott shot, were thrown at the fort during the first day.

At evening, as it was necessary to guard against the possibility of attack from the Wilmington marshes, a force of some two regiments was stationed upon the ridges of land adjacent—one immediately in rear of the upper batteries and one on a ridge running towards Tybee River; and to give General Gillmore an opportunity for the rest which he required, I arranged with him to remain myself at the batteries in general charge of the forces during the first half of the night, directing at the same time that the shells should be thrown at the fort every ten or fifteen minutes during the night, for the purpose of fatiguing the garrison. This shell practice, especially during the early part of the night, while the moon was up, was reported to be most successful, or fully as accurate as by daylight.

As a principal battery of one James and five Parrott guns near the fort appeared not to have been so successfully served as was possible during the day, and as a detachment of 100 seamen from the Navy, under Lieutenant Irwin, had been kindly furnished to us by Flag-Officer DuPont, at the suggestion of Capt. C. R. P. Rodgers, which had unfortunately reached us too late for the first assignment to the batteries, I directed that a portion of this battery should be placed in the hands of this command, and the remainder, with suitable men, to be under Captain Turner, assistant commissary of subsistence, late of the First Artillery, U. S. Army, and now chief commissary of your staff, and the James and three of the Parrott guns were assigned to the naval detachment accordingly.

At about 7 on the morning of the 11th the fire opened on both sides with great vigor and accuracy, the certainty as to direction and distance being greatly beyond that of the previous day, especially on the part of the enemy, there being scarcely any exposure of our force that did not draw a close shot, while the embrasures and parapets of our batteries were most accurately reached. At about 10 to 11 a. m. I visited all the batteries, finding each of them most efficiently served, especially the small mortar batteries nearest the fort, the batteries just referred to in charge of the Navy and Captain Turner, and the columbiad batteries under Captain Pelouze. I found that an embrasure at the breached point, which was much enlarged on the previous day, was now opened to fully the size of the recess arch, or some 8 or 10 feet square, and the adjacent embrasures were rapidly being brought to a similar condition. At about noon the whole mask and parapet wall of the casemate first injured fell into the ditch, raising a ramp quite visible to us, and soon after the corresponding parts of the adjacent casemate began to fall, the Parrott and James shot passing entirely through (as we could see) the heavy timber blindage in rear of the casemates to the rear of the magazine on the opposite (northwest) angle of the fort.

In this state of things I felt sure that we would soon be able to peel off the whole scarp wall from the front of the casemates of the southeast front, making a breach greatly larger than the small garrison could defend, with probably another smaller breach upon the opposite side, and I at once determined that if the resistance was continued it would be best and entirely practicable to storm the fort successfully within thirty to forty hours, and I had given directions to General Gillmore to have suitable scaling-ladders prepared for the purpose, and was arranging for the proper forces, boats, &c., when, at about 2 p. m., we discovered a white flag thrown up, and the rebel flag, after filling out to the wind for a few minutes at half-mast, came slowly to the ground. I then directed my assistant adjutant-general, Capt. A. B. Ely, to leave for the fort, but finding soon after your own adjutant-general, Major Halpine, at the batteries, I commissioned him, accompanied by Captain Ely, to proceed there with the terms I proposed—simply those of your first note—demanding the surrender of the garrison and all the armament and weapons; no other modification to be allowed than that they should have as favorable terms as are given by our Government in this war. General Gillmore reaching the upper batteries soon after, and appearing to desire it, and as his services most eminently merited that his wishes should be gratified, I authorized him also to pass over to accept the surrender of the fort, and the terms assented to by him are essentially those dictated by me, excepting, perhaps, those relating to the disabled men, who would otherwise have been a burden to us, and by the return of these I have endeavored to provide by a letter from Colonel Olmstead, the rebel commander, for the receiving of a like number of men of the Forty-sixth New York Regiment, captured from Tybee about two weeks since.

I have now in closing but the pleasing duty of reporting upon the instances of individual merit that have come under my observation during this siege, which reports must necessarily be brief where so many have done so well.

To the kind and cordial co-operation of the naval forces, under Flag-Officer DuPont, I feel that our highest thanks are due, for it was only by their assistance that we have been enabled to completely isolate the fort from the hope of succor and relief, while the ready supply of ordnance stores and other material most needed by us at the last moment has been of great value, and the battery manned by their detachment, under Lieutenant Irwin, I have the pleasure of stating, was one of the most efficiently served against the fort during the action, a supervision being kept over it constantly by Capt. C. R. P. Rodgers in person, an officer who, an acquaintance of more than twenty years assures me, is without a superior either in our own or any other service.

To Acting Brig. Gen. Q. A. Gillmore, captain of engineers, the highest praise is due for the exercise of his great professional skill and judgment and his laborious industry in arranging and personally superintending all the general preparations and all the details of the actual siege, which have resulted so successfully, showing how eminently worthy of the position and rank in which his previous commander, General Sherman, had placed him, as far as was in his power, and which rank I would respectfully ask your interest for the confirmation of by the President. Captain Pelouze, acting inspector-general of the department; Captain Turner, chief commissary of the department; Lieutenant Porter, of the U. S. Ordnance Department, and Lieutenant Wilson, Topographical Engineers, all in charge of batteries, rendered most zealous and efficient service, which their previous military education has so well fitted them for. Lieut. P. H. O'Rorke, of the U. S. Engineers, acting as assistant engineer to General Gillmore, was also most energetic and useful.

Of your own department staff I had the pleasure of noticing repeatedly under fire most actively engaged Major Halpine, assistant adjutant-general; Lieutenant Smith, acting assistant adjutant-general; Major Hough, most especially zealous; Major Wright; Captains Thompson and Dole; and Lieutenants Stockton, Hay, and Kinzie, your aides, not only complying with your own directions, but ready to aid me at all times when needed.

Lieutenant-Colonel Hall, of the Volunteer Engineer Regiment, deserves most special commendation for his activity, zeal, and general usefulness at all times, by night and by day, by which he constantly rendered most valuable services, as did the battalion of his fine regiment during the siege and previously; and Captain McArthur, of the Eighth Maine Regiment, being highly praised by different officers, who witnessed his successful management of his men at the batteries, deserves my commendation.

The companies of the Third Rhode Island Artillery, under Captain Tourtellott, served their guns most efficiently; and the Seventh Connecticut Regiment, under Colonel Terry, very ably manned the batteries which they had most laboriously constructed, so that I designated them (as I was pleased to find had been, unknown to me, the previous selection of General Gillmore) for the honor of being the first to garrison the surrendered fort.

Of my personal staff, my senior aide, Lieut. A. B. Ely, acting assistant adjutant general, was constantly with me when not occupied otherwise by my direction, still showing most eminently every qualification, as he had done previously, for the responsible position for which I had selected him, and Lieut. S. N. Benham, my junior aide, and H. F. Hawkes, acting aide, were ready and prompt in the discharge of their duties. Colonel Serrell, of the Volunteer Engineer Regiment, acting temporarily on my staff, showed great zeal and activity throughout the action.

I would respectfully recommend, in relation to the commander of the garrison of the fort, Col. Charles H. Olmstead, whose gallant conduct as an enemy and whose courtesy as a gentleman are entitled to all consideration, that, should you deem it proper, the courtesy of the return of his own sword should be extended to him. His defense, I would remark, was continued until almost the latest limit possible, for a few hours more of our fire would, to all appearance, have sufficed for the destruction of the magazine and a larger portion of the fort, while another day would, in any event, have unavoidably placed the garrison at the mercy of a storming column from our command.

I have the honor to be, sir, very respectfully, your most obedient servant,

H. W. BENHAM,
Brigadier-General, Comdg. N. Dist., Dept. of the South.

Maj. CHARLES G. HALPINE,
Assistant Adjutant-General, Department of the South.

HDQRS. NORTH. DIST., DEPT. OF THE SOUTH,
Tybee River, Georgia, April 11, 1862.

SIR: I have the satisfaction of inclosing to you herewith the terms of surrender of Fort Pulaski, as arranged this day by Acting Brig. Gen. Q. A. Gillmore, whom I dispatched to the fort for that purpose immediately after the appearance of the white flag from that fort at about 2 p. m. this day, the anniversary of the opening of the fire upon Fort Sumter by the rebels last year. The terms agreed to by Col. C. H. Olmstead, the rebel commander of the fort, are essentially those dictated by myself, and such as I trust will meet your approval, from my previous communication with you on this subject.

With much congratulation to you on this first success in your present department, I have the honor to be, most respectfully, your obedient servant,

H. W. BENHAM,
Brig. Gen. Comdg. N. Dist., First Div., Dept. of the South.

Maj. Gen. D. HUNTER, U. S. A.,
Commanding Department of the South.

[Inclosure.]

FORT PULASKI, GA., *April* 11, 1862.

SIR: I have the honor to transmit herewith the terms of capitulation for the surrender to the United States of Fort Pulaski, Ga., signed by me this 11th day of April, 1862. I trust these terms will meet your approval, they being substantially those authorized by you as commander of the district.

The fort hoisted the white flag at a quarter before 2 o'clock this afternoon, after a resistance since 8 o'clock yesterday morning to the continuous fire of our batteries. A practicable breach in the walls was made in eighteen and a half hours' firing by daylight.

I have the honor to be, very respectfully, your obedient servant,

Q. A. GILLMORE,
Brig. Gen. Vols., Comdg. U. S. Forces at Tybee Island, Ga.

Brig. Gen. H. W. BENHAM,
Comdg. N. Dist. Dept. of the South, Tybee Island, Ga.

Terms of capitulation agreed upon for the surrender to the forces of the United States of Fort Pulaski, Cockspur Island, Ga.

ARTICLE 1. The fort, armament, and garrison to be surrendered at once to the forces of the United States.

ART. 2. The officers and men of the garrison to be allowed to take with them all their private effects, such as clothing, bedding, books, &c.; this not to include private weapons.

ART. 3. The sick and wounded, under charge of the hospital steward of the garrison, to be sent up under a flag of truce to the Confederate lines, and at the same time the men to be allowed to send up any letters they may desire, subject to the inspection of a Federal officer.

Signed this the 11th day of April, 1862, at Fort Pulaski, Cockspur Island, Ga.

CHAS. H. OLMSTEAD,
Colonel First Vol. Regt. of Georgia, Comdg. Fort Pulaski.
Q. A. GILLMORE,
Brig. Gen. Vols., Comdg. U. S. Forces, Tybee Island, Ga.

[Indorsement.]

I authorized these terms, subject to your approval.

H. W. BENHAM,
Brigadier-General.

Major-General HUNTER.

HDQRS. NORTH'N DIST. DEPT. OF THE SOUTH,
Hilton Head, S. C., April 16, 1862.

MAJOR: I have the honor to inclose herewith a copy of the report of General Viele, giving an account of the operations of the troops under his command at and near Daufuskie Island, as connected with the environment and reduction of Fort Pulaski.

The principal labors of this command, as connected with the bombardment itself, have been already referred to in my report upon that subject, of the 12th instant, as would have been the other matter referred to in General Viele's paper, had it been received before my report was completed.

Although the investment was made more complete and perfect, as I therein stated, by the assistance of the naval forces—by whom, as I learn, the telegraphic communication to Fort Pulaski was destroyed—yet it is undoubted that the formidable operations for the accomplishment of this object on the main line of communication by the two channels of the Savannah River were accomplished by the incessant watchfulness and arduous labors of General Viele's command; and for this purpose there were prepared upon each of two marsh islands—frequently overflowed at the high spring tides—a strong battery of eight or nine guns, or seventeen in all, with the suitable magazines and splinter-proofs to protect the material and men, and in one case, for the proper security of the works, a causeway road was required of over one-half mile in length, for the passage of the ordnance and material, which of itself—with the construction of the parapets, &c., of the batteries—was a work of extraordinary labor and exposure, and meriting the highest commendation to all the officers and men engaged.

For all the other details of the duties performed by this command, which were of great utility in the prosecution of this investment and siege, I respectfully refer to the report of General Viele himself.

Very respectfully, your obedient servant,

H. W. BENHAM,
Brigadier-General, Commanding.

Maj. CHARLES G. HALPINE,
Assistant Adjutant-General, Department of the South.

No. 3.

Reports of Brig. Gen. Egbert L. Viele, U. S. Army.

HEADQUARTERS U. S. FORCES,
Savannah River, *April* 11, 1862.

SIR: I have the honor to submit the following report of the operations of the troops under my command in connection with the investment and reduction of Fort Pulaski.

The plan of operations assigned to me comprised the erection of batteries on the Savannah River, to cut off communication between the fort and the city of Savannah, from which supplies of ammunition and men were drawn, and to establish batteries on the islands adjacent to the fort, against the gorge and left flank, with which, in conjunction with the batteries on Tybee Island, the fort could be reduced. The expedition for these purposes was fitted out at Port Royal, and consisted of a detachment of the Third Rhode Island Artillery, a detachment of Volunteer Engineers, a battalion of the Eighth Maine Regiment Volunteers, and the Sixth Regiment Connecticut Volunteers, the Forty-eighth New York Volunteers, and a full supply of heavy ordnance and intrenching tools.

A full reconnaissance and report had previously been made by Lieut. J. H. Wilson, Topographical Engineers, of the water communications with the Savannah River, by which it was developed that the rebels had sunk the hulk of a brig, securely fixed in its position by means of heavy piles in what is known as Wall's Cut, an artificial channel connecting Wright River (one of the outlets of the Savannah) with Bull River, which last, by its connection, forms a direct communication with the harbor of Port Royal, thus serving as a thoroughfare between that harbor and Savannah.

The removal of the hulk was the first thing to be accomplished, and was intrusted to Maj. O. T. Beard, Forty-eighth New York Volunteers, who, with the aid of a company of the Volunteer Engineers, and by means of mechanical appliances, suggested by his own ingenuity, succeeded after three weeks of unremitting night labor, and in close proximity to the rebel forces, in removing the piles and hulk from the channel, so as to admit of the passage of gunboats and light-draught steamers. This being accomplished, the expedition proceeded to the north end of Daufuskie Island, at which point a camp and depot were established for operations in the Savannah.

Reconnaissances for suitable locations for the batteries were then made under the superintendence of Captain and Acting Brigadier-General Gillmore, during which the telegraphic communication between Fort Pulaski and Savannah was cut, and the wires, both land and submarine, removed for about the distance of 1 mile. Venus Point, on Jones Island, on the north side of the Savannah, and the upper end of Long Island, in the Savannah River, were recommended as the most feasible positions to be occupied. These islands, as well as all others in the river, are merely deposits of soft mud on sand shoals, always covered at high tide and overgrown with rank grasses.

The occupation of points so unfavorable for the erection of batteries was rendered still more difficult by the presence in the Savannah of a fleet of rebel gunboats, constantly passing and always on the alert. To have floated the ordnance in the flat-boats in which it had been placed into the Savannah River would have exposed it to capture by the gunboats. To move it over the swamps seemed almost impossible, while at the same time it would be constantly exposed to view from the river. The alternative was adopted of moving the armament of one battery by hand at night on shifting tram-ways across Jones Island, and it was accomplished on the night of the 11th of February. A drenching storm added to the difficulties, the men often sinking to their waists in the marsh, and the guns sometimes slipping from the tram-ways. By morning the guns were in position on the river, and the next day resisted, with unfinished platforms and without cover, an attack from the rebel gunboats, disabling them and driving them off.

Three days after another battery was erected on Bird Island, in the Savannah, under cover of the battery on Jones Island. Bird Island was selected in preference to the upper end of Long Island, as affording a more uninterrupted command of the south channel of the river. Since the erection of the batteries the works have been completed on both islands, the one on Jones Island being called Fort Vulcan, and that on Bird Island Battery Hamilton, and although the material of which they are composed (mud highly saturated with water) is of the most unfavorable description, they are both most creditable specimens of field works, and evidence of the great labor and perseverance of the troops under most trying circumstances, the fatigue parties always standing in water twenty-four hours.

The positions selected for batteries to aid in the reduction of the fort were the lower end of Long Island and the south side of Turtle Island. As these two points were directly under the fire of the fort it was deemed advisable to delay the erection of the batteries until those on Tybee Island were ready to open. Hence it was not until the night before the bombardment commenced that they were thrown up. The intrenchments were completed, but before the guns were all in position the fort surrendered unconditionally. The mortar battery on the lower end of Long Island did good execution. It was gallantly served during the entire bombardment by a detachment of the Third Rhode Island Artillery, under Lieutenants Turner and Tisdale, receiving the most constant and heaviest fire from the fort of all the batteries erected, without in the slightest degree diminishing its activity.

In reporting the results accomplished I have to refer to the services rendered by the staff of General Sherman, without whom the work could not have been performed. These officers were, Captain and Acting Brigadier General Gillmore, chief engineer; Capt. John Hamilton, chief of artillery; Lieut. J. H. Wilson, Topographical Engineers; Lieutenant Porter, Ordnance Corps, and Lieutenant O'Rorke, Engineer Corps. Hesitating at no amount of exposure or fatigue, they succeeded by their individual examples in inspiring the men with that energy and zeal which could alone have led them to accomplish the arduous labor required. I am also greatly indebted to the services of Captain Sears, of the Volunteer Engineers, and to Capt. J. H. Liebenau, assistant adjutant-general. The accompanying sketch exhibits the positions of the batteries.

Very respectfully, your obedient servant,

EGBERT L. VIELE,
Brigadier-General, Commanding.

Maj. CHARLES G. HALPINE,
Assistant Adjutant-General.

—

DAUFUSKIE ISLAND, *April* 14, 1862.

GENERAL: The accompanying report was prepared for you on the 11th, and was yesterday sent to Tybee, or rather Pulaski, hoping to find you there. I did not receive your note of the 11th until yesterday (13th) afternoon. I think the report covers all the ground, and will send it as I had written it.

With regard to the sortie, a couple of men prowling around from the fort the day before we opened saw the mortar, which had not been quite placed in position before the party was overtaken by daylight, they (the party) having withdrawn to escape observation, concealing a few cartridges which they had brought down with the mortar. These were found and carried off by the two men, who must have been in a great hurry, as they did no damage otherwise. The position of the Long Island battery seemed almost under the walls of the fort, and the men were very much exposed. Nevertheless, although over 50 shots were fired at them, some striking the parapet and some bursting over their heads, no one was injured. The marks of the shell from this mortar I saw on the gorge yesterday, and if I had had time to get heavy guns in position I should have had a fine opportunity to do a great deal of execution.

Very respectfully, your obedient servant,

EGBERT L. VIELE,
Brigadier-General.

General BENHAM,
Commanding, &c.

No. 4.

Report of Lieut. P. H. O'Rorke, U. S. Corps of Engineers, of condition of the works of investment on February 28, 1862.

DAUFUSKIE ISLAND, S. C., *February* 28, 1862.

SIR: In compliance with your directions, I have the honor to submit the following report, showing the amount of work accomplished and the present condition of the batteries on Jones and Bird Islands:

About the 7th of this month it was determined by you to wait no longer the long delayed entrance of the naval force into the Savannah River. It was at the same time directed that a battery should be planted, under cover of the night, at Venus Point, on Jones Island, at the earliest practicable moment. The next day the proposed battery was staked out, and on the same evening an attempt was made to transport the guns and material to the landing on Mud River. This movement, after the greatest exertions to carry it into execution, had to be abandoned for that night, in consequence of the severe storm which came up and the extreme darkness of the night. The attempt was made again on the ensuing night, and was most successful. Five Parrott guns and an 8 inch siege howitzer were landed on Jones Island, and two of the guns were moved about 200 yards towards their intended positions. Four platforms were laid the same night, two others commenced, and a magazine built. As it was not deemed expedient to show ourselves in the daytime, the work was suspended until the next night. The following morning saw our guns in position and ready for action.

Fatigue parties were now set at work to throw up a parapet as rapidly as possible, and by night a parapet 8 feet wide and about 3 feet high was thrown up in front of the guns. At the same time a thin covering of earth was thrown around the magazine, in addition to the sand bags which had been placed around it at first. In consequence of the softness of the mud of which the island is made, it was found impossible to make the parapet sufficiently high at once or to give it a regular shape. The first occasion for using the guns showed that the platforms furnished by the Ordnance Department were too narrow to allow them to be traversed sufficiently. Immediate steps were taken to provide the lumber necessary to enlarge the platforms. A grillage was formed of logs, and upon these planks were laid, increasing the width to 20 feet. Some of the lumber used had to be transported from the Winfield Scott, and other pieces obtained by pulling down houses on Daufuskie Island.

The subsequent engagement with the gunboats of the enemy showed that our platforms were now sufficiently wide and firm. The spring tides now coming on, the whole island was covered with water, and our efforts were immediately directed to the completion of a level around the work. After having the battery twice flooded this was accomplished. The work for some days could now be prosecuted only at low water, and then with great difficulty, in consequence of the softening of the surface. Since then the work has been progressing constantly, though slowly.

There is now a parapet around the work over 1,000 feet in length, from 6 to 10 feet thick, differing on different faces, and from 3 to 4 feet high. The magazine is covered on top by 5 feet of earth and sand bags, and on the sides by about 10 feet in thickness of the same material. It is not entirely completed. A board walk has been built about 6 feet in rear of the platforms, to extend the whole length of the work, with other walks leading from this to the platforms. A good wheelbarrow road has been made across the island by laying poles about 2 feet apart and placing boards upon them. Some of the lumber last brought from Hilton Head has been applied towards making the garrison as comfortable as possible.

About the 19th of this month it was decided by you that a battery should be placed on the north end of Bird Island. It was staked out the next day, and the same night the guns and material were taken from Daufuskie Island to that point and landed. On the following day the platforms were laid and the guns put in position. Since then the levee has been built around the work, and in addition to this another has been built for the protection of the camp of the infantry supports against high tides. A magazine has also been built here, and secured as far as practicable. A strong wind prevented our flats from being towed backward and forward for two or three days, and consequently has prevented us from supplying the battery with sufficient lumber up to this time. Some of the platforms have begun to sink, and will have to be relaid. Profiles have been put up on this battery, and it is steadily progressing. Timbers for the foundation of the platform for the columbiad have been got out of the houses pulled down on this island, and are ready as soon as transportation can be had for them.

Very respectfully, your most obedient servant.

P. H. O'RORKE,
Lieutenant of Engineers, U. S. Army.

Brig. Gen. EGBERT L. VIELE,
Commanding U. S. Forces on Savannah River.

No. 5.

Reports of Brig. Gen. Quincy A. Gillmore, U. S. Army, of operations against Fort Pulaski, January 28–April 11, 1862.

HEADQUARTERS, *Fort Pulaski, Ga., April* 12, 1862.

SIR: I have the honor to report that the several batteries established on Tybee Island, to operate against Fort Pulaski, opened fire on the morning of the 10th instant, at 8.15 o'clock, commencing with the 13-inch mortars. When the range of these pieces had been approximately obtained by the use of signals, the other batteries opened in the order previously prescribed in General Orders, No. 17, from these headquarters, hereunto appended as part of this report,* so that by 9.30 o'clock all our batteries, eleven in number, had commenced their work. The breaching batteries opened at 9.30. With the exception of four 10-inch columbiads, dismounted at the outset by their own recoil in consequence of their having been supplied with unsuitable pintles, and from very serious defects in the wrought-iron chassis, which will be noticed more fully in my detailed report, all the pieces were served through the day.

With few exceptions, strict regard was paid to the instructions laid down in orders for regulating the rapidity and direction of the fire. At dark all the pieces ceased firing except two 13-inch mortars, one 10-inch mortar, and one 30-pounder Parrott, which were served through the night at intervals of twenty minutes for each piece. The only plainly perceptible result of this cannonade of ten and a half hours' duration (the breaching batteries having been served but nine and a half hours) was the commencement of a breach in the easterly half of the *pan-coupé* connecting the south and southeast faces, and in that portion of the southeast face spanned by the two casemates adjacent to the *pan-coupé*. The breach had been ordered in this portion of the scarp so as to take in reverse through the opening the magazine located in the angle formed by the gorge and north face. Two of the barbette guns of the fort had been disabled and three casemate guns silenced. The enemy served both tiers of guns briskly throughout the day, but without injury to the *matériel* or *personnel* of our batteries. The result from the mortar batteries was not at all satisfactory, notwithstanding the care and skill with which the pieces were served.

On the morning of the 11th our batteries again opened a little after sunrise with decided effect, the fort returning a heavy and well-directed fire from its barbette and casemate guns. The breach was rapidly enlarged. At the expiration of three hours the entire casemate next the *pan-coupé* had been opened, and by 11 o'clock the one adjacent to it was in a similar condition. Directions were then given to train the guns upon the third embrasure, upon which the breaching batteries were operating with effect, when the fort hoisted the white flag. This occurred at 2 o'clock. The formalities of visiting the fort, receiving its surrender, and occupying it with our troops consumed the balance of the afternoon and evening.

I cannot indulge in details, however interesting and instructive, in this hasty and preliminary report, but the pleasing duty of acknowledging the valuable services of the officers and men under my command during the laborious and fatiguing preliminaries for opening fire, as well as during the action, I do not feel at liberty to defer.

The labor of landing the heaviest ordnance, with large supplies of ordnance stores, without a wharf, upon an open and exposed beach remarkable for its heavy surf, taking advantage of the tide night and day; the transportation of those articles to the advance batteries under cover of night; the erection of seven of the eleven batteries in plain view of Fort Pulaski and under its fire; the construction over marshy ground in the night-time exclusively of nearly 1 mile of causeway resting on fascines and brush-wood; the difficult task of hauling the guns, carriages, and chassis to their positions in the dark over a narrow road bordered by marsh by the labor of the men alone (the advance batteries being 2½

* Embodied in report following.

miles from the landing); the indomitable perseverance and cheerful deportment of the officers and men under the frequent and discouraging incidents of breaking down, miring in the swamp, &c., are services to the cause and country which I do not feel at liberty to leave unrecorded. An idea of the immense labor expended in transporting the ordnance can be gained from the fact that 250 men could hardly move a 13-inch mortar loaded on a sling-cart.

Another circumstance deserving especial mention is that twenty-two of the thirty-six pieces comprised in the batteries were served during the action by the troops who had performed the fatiguing labors to which I have referred above. They received all their instruction in gunnery at such odd times as they could be spared from other duty during the week preceding the action. The troops who participated in all the heavy labor were the Forty-sixth New York Volunteers, Col. Rudolph Rosa; the Seventh Connecticut Volunteers, Col. Alfred H. Terry; two companies of the New York Volunteer Engineers (Captain Graef and Lieutenant Brooks), under command of Lieut. Col. James F. Hall; two companies of the Third Rhode Island Artillery, Captains Mason and Rogers, and a small detachment from Company A, Corps of Engineers, under Sergt. James E. Wilson. Colonel Terry and Lieutenant-Colonel Hall entered most zealously upon the discharge of their varied duties.

A detachment from Colonel Rosa's regiment, under Captain Hinckel, have occupied since the 22d of February an advanced and very exposed position on Lazaretto Creek, by which boat communication between Fort Pulaski and the interior was cut off. Several interesting reconnaissances of Wilmington Island were made by Captain Hinckel, one of which, commanded by Colonel Rosa, developed some useful information. Lieut. Horace Porter, of the Ordnance Department, has rendered signal, important, and indispensable services. Besides discharging most faithfully the special duties of ordnance officer, he directed in person the transportation of the heaviest ordnance, and drilled and instructed the men in their use, laboring indefatigably night and day. He was actively engaged among the batteries during the action. Lieut. James H. Wilson, Corps of Topographical Engineers, joined my command eleven days before the action, and did good service in instructing the artillerists. He rendered efficient service with the breaching batteries on the 10th and 11th. Capt. L. H. Pelouze, Fifteenth Infantry, U. S. Army, and Capt. J. W. Turner, of the Commissary Department, U. S. Army, members of General Hunter's staff, volunteered for the action, and did good service in the batteries.

I am under obligations to Commander C. R. P. Rodgers, U. S. Navy, and a detachment of sailors under Lieut. John Irwin, U. S. Navy, for skillfully serving four seige guns in Battery Sigel on the 11th.

Lieut. P. H. O'Rorke, Corps of Engineers, and Adam Badeau, esq., volunteered, and served on my staff as aides during the 10th and 11th. Sergt. J. E. Wilson, of Company A, Corps of Engineers, Regular Army, did excellent service in mounting the heavy guns and getting them ready for action. He commanded Battery Burnside during the action. No mortar battery was served more skillfully than his.

I will close this preliminary report with some general deductions from absolute results, without going into details or reasons.

1. Mortars (even the 13-inch sea-coast) are unreliable for the reduction of works of small area, like Fort Pulaski. They cannot be fired with sufficient accuracy to crush the casemate arches. They might after a long time tire out any ordinary garrison.

2. Good rifled guns, properly served, can breach rapidly at 1,650 yards'

distance. A few heavy round shot, to bring down the masses loosened by the rifled projectiles, are of good service. I would not hesitate to attempt a practicable breach in a brick scarp at 2,000 yards' distance with ten guns of my own selection.

3. No better piece for breaching can be desired than the 42-pounder James. The grooves, however, must be kept clean. Parrott guns throwing as much metal as the James would be equally good, supposing them to fire as accurately as the 30-pounder Parrott.

I append to this report a map,* giving the positions of our several batteries and the orders issued, assigning the detachments to the batteries, and regulating the direction and rapidity of the firing.

Very respectfully, your obedient servant,

Q. A. GILLMORE,
Comdg. U. S. Forces, Tybee and Cockspur Islands, Ga.

Lieut. A. B. ELY,
A. A. A. G., N. D., Dept. of the South, Hilton Head, S. C.

HEADQUARTERS U. S. FORCES,
Tybee and Cockspur Islands, April 23, 1862.

GENERAL: You showed me General Viele's report of the operations of his command on the Savannah River. As I was present with his forces as General Sherman's chief engineer until after the Venus Point battery was established, I have, in compliance with General Totten's request and with General Sherman's knowledge, furnished a report of those operations, and shall accompany my report of the siege of Pulaski with an accurate map of the Savannah River.* I am very desirous that there shall be no conflict or discrepancy in the records. This is my excuse for calling your attention to some portions of General Viele's report, which must have left his hands without having been closely inspected by him. The points to which I refer are—

1st. One impression conveyed in the report is that the obstructions in Wall's Cut were removed by General Viele's command, when in fact Major Beard, Forty-eighth New York, then the provost-marshal at Hilton Head, was secretly sent out by General Sherman to do this work, with a company of engineers, more than three weeks before the investing force left Port Royal or General Viele was assigned to their command. The obstructions were removed on January 13, two weeks before General Viele's troops left Port Royal.

2d. The length of the road across Jones Island, over which the Venus Point guns were carried, is represented on the general's map as considerably longer than the distance from Fort Pulaski to the 10-inch mortar on Long Island, which opened on the fort the last day of the siege, while in fact it is not much over one-half as long. In other words, the Jones Island causeway is about three-quarters of a mile long, while the distance from Fort Pulaski to the mortar referred to is over one mile and a quarter, according to Coast Survey charts. The mortar was not at the extreme lower end of the island. The effect is to unduly exaggerate the labor of building the road and the danger of serving the mortar. According to statements of Colonel Olmstead and his officers after the surrender not a single shell from Long Island reached the fort; a circumstance which might have been foreseen by a reference to the table of range for 10-inch siege mortars.

---

* To appear in Atlas.

3d. The map represents a battery on Turtle Island, while in fact none was placed there.

A desire to secure historical accuracy in the records of this siege alone induces me to make these statements, which you are at liberty to make such use of as you think proper.

Very respectfully, your obedient servant,

Q. A. GILLMORE,
Brigadier-General, Commanding.

General H. W. BENHAM,
Comdg. North'n Dist., Dept. of the South, Hilton Head, S. C.

HEADQUARTERS DEPARTMENT OF SOUTH CAROLINA,
Hilton Head, S. C., October 20, 1865.

SIR: I have the honor to submit the following report, compiled from my original report to the Chief Engineer, of operations against Fort Pulaski, Ga., resulting in its capitulation to the United States forces under my immediate command on the 11th day of April, 1862:

The two accompanying maps* are deemed necessary to a full understanding of the report.

This success so fully demonstrated the power and effectiveness of rifled cannon for breaching at long distances—at distances, indeed, hitherto untried and considered altogether impracticable, thus opening a new era in the use of this most valuable and comparatively unknown arm of service—was obtained with such singularly strict adherence to the details of the project as originally submitted by me in the previous December, and has withal in its developed results such an important bearing upon the character of our harbor and frontier defenses, that I feel called upon to enter into some details.

The transfer to another field of labor of Brig. Gen. T. W. Sherman, lately in command of the forces on this coast, under whose auspices the project for the reduction of Fort Pulaski was pushed forward to within a few days of its final accomplishment, renders it proper that this report should refer to the preliminary operations directly connected with the siege.

In the capacity of chief engineer on General Sherman's staff I was present with the investing forces under General Viele when the Savannah River was closed above the fort by the establishment of the battery on Venus Point, Jones Island, on the night of the 11th of February last. I took no part in the erection of the Bird Island battery, opposite Venus Point. These two batteries effectually closed the Savannah River.

In the double capacity of engineer and commander of the forces I was charged with the offensive operations on Tybee Island, where the batteries for the reduction of the work were to be established, and also with the completion of the investment by the blockade of the Wilmington Narrows and Lazaretto Creek passage.

The data for this report will therefore be taken in a measure from my private journal and from official correspondence and orders.

Fort Pulaski.—Fort Pulaski is situated on Cockspur Island, Georgia, latitude 32° 2′ north and longitude 3° 51′ west from Washington, at the head of Tybee Roads, commanding both channels of the Savannah River. The position is a very strong one. Cockspur Island is wholly a marsh, and is about one mile long and half a mile wide.

---

* To appear in Atlas.

Fort Pulaski is a brick work of five sides or faces, including the gorge, casemated on all sides, walls 7½ feet thick, and 25 feet high above high water, mounting one tier of guns in embrasures and one *en barbette*. The gorge is covered by an earthen outwork (demi-lune) of bold relief.

The main work and demi-lune are both surrounded and separated by a wet ditch. Around the main work the ditch is 48 feet wide; around the demi-lune, 32 feet.

The communication with the exterior is through the gorge into the demi-lune over a draw-bridge, and then through one face of the demi-lune over the demi-lune ditch by another draw-bridge. The scarp of the demi-lune and the entire counterscarp of main work and demi-lune are revetted with good brick masonry.

At the time of the siege it contained 48 guns, of which 20 bore upon the batteries on Tybee, viz, five 10-inch columbiads, five 8 inch columbiads, four 32-pounders, one 24-pounder Blakely rifle, two 12-inch and three 10-inch sea coast mortars. A full armament for the work would be 140 guns.

On the 29th of November I was directed by General Sherman to make an examination of Tybee Island and Fort Pulaski, and to report upon the propriety of occupying and holding that island and upon the practicability (and, if deemed practicable, the best method) of reducing Fort Pulaski. I reported as follows:

HEADQUARTERS CHIEF ENGINEER'S OFFICE,
Hilton Head, S. C., December 1, 1861.

Brig. Gen. THOMAS W. SHERMAN,
Commanding Expeditionary Corps, Hilton Head, S. C.:

SIR: Agreeably to your orders, I proceeded in the steamer Ben DeFord, on the afternoon of the 29th ultimo, to Tybee Island, to make a military reconnaissance of that locality. The enemy had a battery on Warsaw Sound, whose exact position was unknown. The exact position of the battery controlling Warsaw Inlet has no bearing on the prominent points to which my attention was directed, namely, the propriety of occupying and holding the first Tybee Island and the practicability (and, if deemed practicable, the best method) of reducing Fort Pulaski. I deemed the reduction of that work practicable by batteries of mortars and rifled guns established on Tybee Island. I think it probable that a nearer position, on firm ground (although very shallow, and therefore ill-adapted to mortars and sunken batteries), can be found on the island west of Tybee. I would establish these batteries from 20 to 25 yards apart, one gun or one mortar in each, behind the ridge of sand on the shore westward from the light-house. I would sink the mortar batteries as low as the water would permit, and the guns sufficiently low to leave a high parapet in front. On the sides and rear of each I would have a high mound of earth, and I would cover each with a horizontal bomb-proof shelter of logs covered with earth and supported by logs planted vertically in the ground. The embrasures for the guns should be deep, narrow, and of very little splay. I estimate that, after once obtaining the range, five-eighths of the shells from the mortars can be lodged inside the fort. I would have enough mortars to throw one shell a minute into the fort, and as many guns as mortars. For landing the ordnance required I would have built two or three large flat-bottomed bateaux or scows, such as are commonly used on rope ferries. I think these could be built here.

There are now probably at Fort Pulaski 700 good troops. About 200 landed yesterday, and the Navy officers informed me that at least 500 have entered the fort within the last three days, while some (probably raw recruits or portions of the Home Guards) have gone away. It may be their design to land on Tybee and hold the west end of it, to prevent the erection of batteries against the fort. I therefore recommend the immediate occupation of Tybee Island by one good regiment until the question of attempting the reduction of Fort Pulaski be determined.

I learned while at Tybee that offers have been made by negroes to burn two of the principal bridges on the railroad between Charleston and Savannah. One of these bridges is said to be nearly 2 miles long. In a military point of view its destruction would be of great value to us, and I recommend the subject to your attention.

Very respectfully, your obedient servant,

Q. A. GILLMORE,
Captain, and Chief Engineer Expeditionary Corps.

The armament proposed for the several batteries is given in the following communication:

OFFICE OF CHIEF ENGINEER EXPEDITIONARY CORPS,
Hilton Head, S. C., December 5, 1861.

Brig. Gen. THOMAS W. SHERMAN,
Commanding Expeditionary Corps, Hilton Head, S. C.:

SIR: Should it be determined to attempt the reduction of Fort Pulaski from Tybee Island, I recommend the following armament for the batteries, inclusive of pieces held in reserve to replace those dismounted or otherwise rendered unserviceable:

Ten 10-inch sea-coast mortars; ten 13-inch sea-coast mortars; eight heavy rifled guns of the best kind, to be used some against the barbette guns of the fort and some against the walls; eight columbiads for firing solid shot principally, some of them to fire shells, in case it be found practicable to drop them in or explode them over the fort. The mortars should each have 900 rounds of shell, the guns and columbiads the same number of rounds of solid shot, and the columbiads 300 rounds of shell besides. It would be well to have a 15-inch columbiad, if one can be obtained.

Very respectfully, your obedient servant,

Q. A. GILLMORE,
Captain, and Chief Engineer Expeditionary Corps.

The project set forth in the foregoing communications received General Sherman's sanction at once, with some slight modifications as to the number and caliber of the mortars to be used, and was forwarded to Washington and approved there. Information was in due time received that orders to prepare and forward the ordnance and ordnance stores had been issued. For months, therefore, preceding the fall of Pulaski, its reduction from Big Tybee, favored by a thorough investment, formed one of General Sherman's approved plans, awaiting only the action of others in sending the necessary supplies for its completion. The Forty-sixth Regiment New York Volunters, Col. R. Rosa, was sent to occupy Big Tybee Island early in December.

Operations for investing the place by the erection of batteries on the Savannah River above the work were set on foot about the middle of January, 1862. It was known to General Sherman before that time that gunboats of medium draught could enter the river above Fort Pulaski without encountering any batteries on the south side through Warsaw Sound, Wilmington Narrows (or Freeborn's Cut), and Saint Augustine Creek, and on the north side through New River, Wall's Cut, and either Wright or Mud Rivers.

Wall's Cut is an artificial channel, narrow but deep, connecting New and Wright Rivers, and has for years been used in making the inland water passage between Charleston and Savannah. This cut the enemy had obstructed by an old hulk and numerous heavy piles, as ascertained about the 1st of January by Lieut. J. H. Wilson, of the Topographical Engineers. These obstructions had all been removed by a detachment of our engineer troops, under Major Beard, Forty-eighth Regiment New York Volunteers, secretly sent from Hilton Head by General Sherman for that purpose. The piles were sawed off on a level with the bottom of the stream, and the hulk was swung around against the side of the cut, leaving ample room for the passage of transports and gunboats. The opening of Wall's Cut, which required four days and four nights to effect, was reported to the Navy on the 14th January, in order that the gunboats might enter the Savannah River and cover us in the erection of our investing batteries. At this time the enemy's gunboats were daily passing up and down the river.

Mud River is navigable at high spring tide for vessels of 8½ to 9 feet draught. Wright River Bar has about 11½ feet of water at ordinary high tide. The Wright River passage rendered it necessary to approach to within about 2 miles of Fort Pulaski.

After the removal of the Wall's Cut obstructions a joint expedition of land and naval forces for the investment was organized by General Sherman and Commodore DuPont. This expedition consisted of one regiment of infantry (the Forty-eighth New York Volunteers), two companies of the New York Volunteer Engineers, and two companies of the Third Rhode Island Volunteer Heavy Artillery, with 20 guns of all caliber, viz, two 8-inch siege howitzers, four 30-pounder Parrotts, three 20-pounder Parrotts, three 12-pounder James rifles, and eight 24-pounder field howitzers, and was accompanied by three gunboats. The troops were to rendezvous at Daufuskie Island, where we already had three companies of the Seventh Connecticut Volunteers, under Major Gardiner, guarding Wall's Cut. They had been posted there on January 13. The land force was in readiness at Hilton Head soon after the middle of January. Various causes delayed the expected naval co-operation, so that no gunboats passed Wall's Cut until the 28th of January. The naval forces were commanded by Commander John Rodgers, U. S. N.; the land forces by Brigadier-General Viele. Another mixed force, approaching by way of Warsaw Sound, presented itself on the south of the Savannah River, in Wilmington Narrows (or Freeborn's Cut), at the same time, the land force being commanded by Brig. Gen. H. G. Wright and the gunboats by Fleet Captain Davis.

On the afternoon of January 28 a reconnaissance was made by me of Mud River and the Savannah River shore of Jones Island. Venus Point, on the margin of the Savannah, was selected as the position for one of the investing batteries. The line for a road or causeway over the marsh between Venus Point and Mud River was also located. Its length was nearly 1,300 yards. This causeway or corduroy was never completed.

Jones Island is nothing but a mud marsh, covered with reeds and tall grass. The general surface is about on the level of ordinary high tide. There are a few spots of limited area, Venus Point being one of them, that are submerged only by spring tides or by ordinary high tides favored by the wind, but the character of the soil is the same over the whole island. It is a soft unctuous mud, free of grit or sand, and is incapable of supporting a heavy weight. Even in the most elevated places the partially dry crust is but 3 or 4 inches in depth, the substratum being a semi-fluid mud, which is agitated like jelly by the falling of even small bodies upon it, like the jumping of men or ramming of earth. A pole or an oar can be forced into it with ease to the depth of 12 or 15 feet. In most places the resistance diminishes with increase of penetration. Men walking over it are partially sustained by the roots of reeds and grass, and sink in only 5 or 6 inches. When this top support gives way they go down from 2 to 2½ feet, and in some places much farther. A road or causeway of some kind across Jones Island from Mud River to Venus Point was deemed necessary and determined upon at the outset, even if the guns should not have to be carried over it, as the means of getting speedy succor to the Venus Point battery in case of attack; Daufuskie Island, 4 miles distant, being the nearest point where troops could be kept for that purpose.

On the 29th of January Lieutenant O'Rorke, of the Engineers, was dispatched by me in a small boat to examine Long and Elba Islands, in the Savannah River. Major Beard, Forty-eighth New York Volunteers, accompanied him. They entered the Savannah River via Cunningham Point at the lower end of Jones Island, pulled up the Savannah, stopping several times on Long and Elba Islands, and went around the west end of the latter to within about 2 miles of Fort Jackson. Lieutenant

O'Rorke reported the upper end of Long Island favorable for batteries, the surface being fully as high as that at Venus Point.

The following extracts from my journal furnish a portion of the history of the operations on Jones Island and the Savannah River for the investment of Fort Pulaski, and may be properly introduced into this report:

Extracts from journal of Brigadier-General Gillmore, chief engineer Expeditionary Corps.

February 1, 2, 3, *and* 4.—The two engineer companies on Daufuskie Island, commanded by Captain Sears, were employed in cutting poles for a causeway on Jones Island from Mud River to Venus Point, and for the engineer wharf on Daufuskie Island, New River.

On the 4th, the wharf, with 8 feet of water at low tide, was completed. Ten thousand poles, 5 to 6 inches in diameter and 9 feet long, had been cut on Daufuskie Island, and 1,900 of them deposited at the wharf. The men of the Forty-eighth New York and Seventh Connecticut Volunteers transported the poles on their shoulders, the average distance carried being 1 mile. At the suggestion of Captain Sears I had a swath cut and cleared of reeds and grass across the upper end of Jones Island, to prevent the enemy burning the island over.

Navy officers were engaged in sounding Mud and Wright Rivers. No certainty as yet that the gunboats will enter the Savannah River. Mud River has about one and one-half feet of water in it at the extreme low tide, with a very soft (almost semi-fluid) bottom. Soundings in Wright River are not completed yet.

February 5 *and* 6.—Nothing specially new. Engineer force engaged in cutting poles, filling sand bags on Daufuskie Island, building a temporary wharf of poles and sand bags on Mud River, and constructing a wheelbarrow track of planks laid end to end from Venus Point to Mud River Wharf. The Forty-eighth New York, Seventh Connecticut Volunteers, and a portion of the engineer forces engaged in transporting poles and planks and carrying filled sand bags from Daufuskie Island to Jones Island (a distance of about 4 miles) in row-boats.

February 7 *and* 8.—Finished temporary wharf on Mud River. Carried several hundred filled sand bags across to Venus Point; also a quantity of planks and other battery materials. Had the balance of the engineer materials required for the Venus Point battery put into lighters, so as to be ready whenever the gunboats should move. There appears to be no immediate prospect of their moving.

February 9.—I visited Commander Rodgers to consult in regard to his moving into the Savannah. He said he intended to attempt the Mud River passage that night on the high tide. The signal for his starting would be one note from his steam-whistle. Returned to Daufuskie and consulted with General Viele and Captain Hamilton, the chief of artillery. It was arranged that the flats, with the guns and ammunition on them, should be towed by the steamer Mayflower through Wall's Cut and up Mud River into the Savannah, just behind the gunboats. They were accordingly taken in tow in the evening after dark from the engineer wharf. The night was windy, rainy, and very dark. The Mayflower, after several attempts, failed to reach Wall's Cut, and cast anchor near the spot she started from. The gunboats did not move on account of the weather.

February 10.—The gunboats Pembina and Unadilla are at anchor in Wright River, near Wall's Cut. The gunboat Hale has taken up position in Mud River about 200 yards to the eastward of the temporary wharf, in order to protect the landing and cover us if driven back. Captain Hamilton quite ill from last night's exposure in the Mayflower. I consulted with General Viele in the afternoon, and it was determined to establish the Venus Point battery at once, and wait no longer for the gunboats to go ahead of us. Orders from General Sherman to that effect were subsequently received that same evening, also to effect this by landing the guns on Jones Island from Mud River and hauling them over the marsh instead of towing them into the Savannah in flats, as first contemplated. Major Beard, Forty-eighth New York Volunteers, and Lieut. J. H. Wilson, Topographical Engineers, volunteered to assist Lieut. Horace Porter, the ordnance officer, in getting the flats into Mud River and the guns on shore and into position. Accordingly the flats with the guns were towed by our row-boats up the river against the tide and landed without accident. Two of them were taken about 300 yards into the marsh by Lieutenant Wilson. The Forty-eighth New York Volunteers furnished the fatigue parties, which had already been twenty-four hours at work on Jones Island and were very much exhausted. Deeming it impossible to get the guns over that night, I directed them to be covered with reeds and grass, to prevent their discovery by the enemy, and left there until the following night.

During the night of the 10th, Lieutenant O'Rorke, of the Engineers, with a party of volunteer engineers, commenced the magazine and gun platforms at Venus Point.

The party concealed their work at daybreak (11th) and withdrew. The platforms were made by raising the surface 5 or 6 inches with sand, carried over in bags. On this sand foundation thick planks at right angles to the line of the battery were laid, nearly, but not quite, in contact with each other. At right angles to these, deck-planks were laid, giving a platform 9 by 17 feet. The floor of the magazine was 20 inches above the natural surface, and rested on sand bags.

February 11.—Continued getting battery and road materials to Jones Island during the day. Early in the evening I went to Jones Island with fresh men, to finish the labor of getting the guns over. Lieutenants Wilson and Porter and Major Beard took charge of the fatigue parties as before. The work was done in the following manner: The pieces, mounted on their carriages and limbered up, were moved forward on shifting runways of planks about 15 feet long, 1 foot wide, and 3 inches thick, laid end to end. Lieutenant Wilson, with a party of 35 men, took charge of the two pieces in advance, one 8-inch siege howitzer and a 30-pounder Parrott, and Major Beard and Lieutenant Porter, with a somewhat larger force, of the four pieces in the rear, two 20 and two 30 pounder Parrotts. Each party had one pair of planks in excess of the number required for the guns and limbers to rest upon when closed together. This extra pair of planks being placed in front, in prolongation of those already under the carriages, the pieces were then drawn forward with drag-ropes one after the other the length of a plank, thus freeing the two planks in the rear, which in their turn were carried to the front. This labor is of the most fatiguing kind. In most places the men sank to their knees in the mud, in some places much deeper. This mud being of the most slippery and slimy kind and perfectly free from grit and sand, the planks soon became entirely smeared over with it. Many delays and much exhausting labor were occasioned by the gun-carriages slipping off the planks. When this occurred the wheels would suddenly sink to the hubs, and powerful levers had to be devised to raise them up again. I authorized the men to encase their feet in sand bags to keep the mud out of their shoes. Many did this, tying the strings just below the knees. The magazines and platforms were ready for service at daybreak. Lieutenant Wilson got his two pieces into position at 2.30 a. m. and Major Beard and Lieutenant Porter their four pieces at 8.30 a. m. on the 12th. At 3 a. m. Lieutenant Wilson started back to General Viele, on Daufuskie, to report the success.

February 12.—After giving directions for the fresh relief to be put to work in throwing up a dike around the battery to keep out the spring tides, which were beginning to flow, I returned to Daufuskie Island. The high tide to-day came within 8 inches of the surface at Venus Point.

February 13, 14, 15.—Various causes, particularly the weather, delayed the establishment of the battery on Long Island. On the morning of the 13th the rebel steamer Ida passed down by Venus Point under full steam. Nine shots were fired at her, striking her astern, all but one. Elevation good, but not enough allowance made for speed of vessel. I was not in the battery at the time. All the pieces, except one 30-pounder, recoiled off the platforms. These were at once enlarged to 18 by 17½ feet. On the afternoon of the 14th three rebel gunboats came down the river and opened fire on the battery, taking a position about 1 mile distant. Battery fired about 30 shots. One of the vessels was struck. The boats then withdrew.

February 16.—The steamer Ida, which ran the battery on the 13th, left Fort Pulaski and returned to Savannah, via Lazaretto Creek, Wilmington Narrows, Turner's Creek, and Saint Augustine Creek.

February 17.—I returned to Hilton Head, by General Sherman's order, leaving Lieutenant O'Rorke with General Viele, with written instructions concerning the engineering operations to be carried on.

The foregoing extracts from my journal are all that bear directly upon the operations on the Savannah above Fort Pulaski. I did not return there on duty. I soon received official information, however, that a second battery, consisting of one 8-inch siege howitzer, one 30-pounder Parrott, one 20-pounder Parrott, and three 12-pounder James rifles, was established on Bird Island, just above Long Island. This was done on the night of February 20, the flats, with the guns, ammunition, &c., on them, being towed up Mud River and across the Savannah by row-boats. Lieutenant O'Rorke, of the Engineers, was present as engineer officer, and Lieutenant Porter as ordnance officer. Capt. John Hamilton, General Sherman's chief of artillery, was also present.

On the 19th of February I was ordered by Brig. Gen. T. W. Sherman to Big Tybee Island, to place it "in a thorough state of defense against approach from Wilmington Narrows and Lazaretto Creek, to prevent all approach by water, and blockade the channel," thereby completing the investment, and also to "commence operations for the bombardment of Fort Pulaski."

The absolute blockade of Pulaski dates from the 22d of February, at which time I stationed two companies of the Forty-sixth New York Volunteers, with a battery of two field pieces, on Decent Island, Lazaretto Creek. This force was subsequently placed on board an old hulk, anchored in Lazaretto Creek, about 2¼ miles from Fort Pulaski. One 30-pounder Parrott was then added to the battery. A small guard boat, mounting a Navy 6 pounder, was posted considerably in advance of the hulk, to intercept messengers attempting to reach Fort Pulaski by way of McQueen's Island Marsh. On the 31st of March the guard boat and 18 men were captured by a large scouting party of the enemy, who suddenly appeared on Wilmington Island. After this the services of the gunboat Norwich, Captain Duncan, were secured in Wilmington Narrows, to assist the blockade.

It was found impossible to perfectly isolate the work. In order to appreciate the difficulty and even impracticability of securing, with ordinary means, the complete blockade of a place like Fort Pulaski, it is necessary to understand something of the topography of the position.

The Savannah River, from its mouth on Tybee Roads to its confluence with Saint Augustine Creek, 8 miles above, is skirted on both sides by low marsh islands, submerged by spring tides, covered with a thick growth of reeds and tall grass, and cut up by numerous small, tortuous creeks and bayous. With light boats that can be hauled over the marsh by hand from creek to creek small parties familiar with the locality can with comparative security find their way over these marshes in the night, and avoid guards and pickets. It was known that messengers passed to and from the fort in this way quite frequently. Several of these were caught. One of them started from the fort and made his escape to Savannah, just after the white flag was raised, on the day of the surrender.

On the 21st of February the first vessel with ordnance and ordnance stores for the siege arrived in Tybee Roads. From that time until the 9th of April all the troops on Tybee Island, consisting of the Seventh Regiment Connecticut Volunteers, the Forty-sixth Regiment New York Volunteers, two companies of the Volunteer Engineers, and, for the most of the time, two companies of the Third Rhode Island Volunteer Artillery, were constantly engaged in landing and transporting ordnance, ordnance stores, and battery materials, making fascines and roads, constructing gun and mortar batteries, service and depot magazines, splinter and bomb proof shelters for the relief of cannoneers off duty, and drilling at the several pieces.

The armament comprised 36 pieces, distributed in eleven batteries, at various distances from the fort, as shown in the following table:

1. Battery Stanton, three heavy 13-inch mortars, at 3,400 yards.
2. Battery Grant, three heavy 13-inch mortars, at 3,200 yards.
3. Battery Lyon, three heavy 10-inch columbiads, at 3,100 yards.
4. Battery Lincoln, three heavy 8-inch columbiads, at 3,045 yards.
5. Battery Burnside, one heavy 13-inch mortar, at 2,750 yards.
6. Battery Sherman, three heavy 13-inch mortars, at 2,650 yards.
7. Battery Halleck, two heavy 13-inch mortars, at 2,400 yards.
8. Battery Scott, three 10-inch and one 8-inch columbiad, at 1,740 yards.
9. Battery Sigel, five 30-pounder Parrotts and one 48-pounder James (old 24-pounder), at 1,670 yards.
10. Battery McClellan, two 84-pounder James (old 42-pounder) and two 64-pounder James (old 32-pounder), at 1,650 yards.
11. Battery Totten, four 10-inch siege mortars, at 1,650 yards.

Each battery had a service magazine capable of containing a supply of powder for about two days' firing. A depot powder magazine of 3,600 barrels' capacity was constructed near the Martello Tower, which was the landing place for all the supplies. Serious difficulties were encountered in making a road sufficiently firm to serve for this heavy transportation.

Tybee Island is mostly a mud marsh, like other marsh islands on this coast. Several ridges and hummocks of firm ground, however, exist upon it, and the shore of Tybee Roads, where the batteries were located, is partially skirted by low sand banks, formed by the gradual and protracted action of the wind and tides. The distance along this shore from the landing place to the advanced batteries is about 2½ miles. The last mile of this route, on which the seven most advanced batteries were placed, is low and marshy, lies in full view of Fort Pulaski, and is within effective range of its guns. The construction of a causeway resting on fascines and brush-wood over this swampy portion of the line; the erection of the several batteries, with the magazines, gun platforms, and splinter-proof shelters; the transportation of the heaviest ordnance in our service by the labor of men alone; the hauling of ordnance stores and engineer supplies, and the mounting of the guns and mortars on their carriages and beds had to be done almost exclusive y at night, alike regardless of the inclemency of the weather and of the miasma from the swamps.

No one except an eye-witness can form any but a faint conception of the herculean labor by which mortars of 8½ tons' weight and columbiads but a trifle lighter were moved in the dead of night over a narrow causeway, bordered by swamps on either side, and liable at any moment to be overturned and buried in the mud beyond reach. The stratum of mud is about 12 feet deep, and on several occasions the heaviest pieces, particularly the mortars, became detached from the sling-carts, and were with great difficulty, by the use of planks and skids, kept from sinking to the bottom. Two hundred and fifty men were barely sufficient to move a single piece on sling-carts. The men were not allowed to speak above a whisper, and were guided by the notes of a whistle.

The positions selected for the five most advanced batteries were artificially screened from view from the fort by a gradual and almost inperceptible change, made little by little every night, in the condition and appearance of the brush-wood and bushes in front of them. No sudden alteration of the outline of the landscape was permitted. After the concealment was once perfected to such a degree as to afford a good and safe parapet behind it less care was taken, and some of the work in the batteries requiring mechanical skill was done in the daytime, the fatigue parties going to their labor before break of day and returning in the evening after dark. In all the batteries traverses were placed between the pieces. With two exceptions (Batteries Lincoln and Totten) the magazines were placed in or near the center of the battery, against the epaulement, with the opening to the rear. An ante-room for filling cartridge bags was attached to each. The magazines for the Batteries Lincoln and Totten weie located in the rear of the platforms.

For revetting the sides of the traverses and epaulements fascines, hurdles, brush, and marsh sods were used. Marsh sods form the best revetment for sandy soil. All the others allow the sand to sift through them to such an extent as to become a serious annoyance to the men serving the pieces.

In order to diminish as much as possible the labor of forming the parapets in front of the pieces the foundation timbers of all the gun and mortar platforms were sunk to high-water mark. This brought them in many cases to within 6 or 8 inches of the substratum of soft clay. To secure them against settlement the lateral as well as vertical dimensions usually adopted for platforms were considerably enlarged.

On the 31st day of March Major-General Hunter assumed command of the Department of the South, and Brigadier-General Benham, of the Northern District thereof, comprising the States of South Carolina, Georgia, and a part of Florida. During the week which followed these generals visited Tybee Island at separate times, and inspected the siege works and batteries there established. No change or modification of any of the works was suggested by either.

On the afternoon of April 9 everything was in readiness to open fire. Generals Hunter and Benham had arrived the evening before with their respective staffs.

The following general orders, regulating the rapidity and direction of the firing and the charges and elevation of the pieces of each battery, were issued. As the instructions then given were, with one or two trifling exceptions, adhered to with remarkable fidelity throughout the action, they are inserted here in full, to save the necessity of further reference to them:

GENERAL ORDERS, No. 17. } HEADQUARTERS U. S. FORCES, *Tybee Island, Ga., April 9, 1862.*

The batteries established against Fort Pulaski will be manned and ready for service at break of day to-morrow. The signal to begin the action will be one gun from the right mortar of Battery Halleck (2,400 yards from the work), fired under the direction of Lieut. Horace Porter, chief of ordnance. Charge of mortar, 11 pounds; charge of shell, 11 pounds; elevation, 55 degrees; length of fuse, 24 seconds. This battery (two 13-inch mortars) will continue firing at the rate of fifteen minutes to each mortar alternately, varying the charge of mortars and the length of fuse so that the shells will drop over the arches of the north and northeast faces of the work and explode immediately after striking, and not before.

The other batteries will open as follows, viz, Battery Stanton (three 13-inch mortars, 3,400 yards distant) immediately after the signal, at the rate of fifteen minutes for each piece, alternating from the right. Charge of mortars, 14 pounds; charge of shell, 7 pounds; elevation, 45 degrees; length of fuse, 23 seconds; varying the charge of mortar and length of fuse as may be required. The shells should drop over the arches of the south face of the work and explode immediately after striking, but not before.

Battery Grant (three 13-inch mortars, 3,200 yards distant) immediately after the ranges of Battery Stanton have been determined, at the rate of fifteen minutes for each piece, alternating from the right. Charge of shells, 7 pounds; elevation, 45 degrees; charges of mortars and length of fuse to be varied to suit the range, as determined from Battery Stanton. The shells should drop over the south face of the work and explode immediately after striking, but not before.

Battery Lyon (three 10-inch columbiads, 3,100 yards distant), with a curved fire, immediately after the signal, allowing ten minutes between the discharges for each piece, alternating from the right. Charge of gun, 17 pounds; charge of shell, 3 pounds; elevation, 20 degrees, and length of fuse, 20 seconds; charge and length of fuse to vary as required. The shells should pass over the parapet into the work, taking the gorge and north face in reverse, and exploding at the moment of striking or immediately after.

Battery Lincoln (three 8-inch columbiads, 3,045 yards distant), with a curved fire, immediately after the signal, allowing six minutes between discharges for each piece, alternating from the right. Charge of gun, 10 pounds; charge of shell, 1½ pounds; elevation, 20 degrees, and length of fuse, 20 seconds. Directed the same as Battery Lyon, upon the gorge and north face in reverse, varying the charge and length of fuse accordingly.

Battery Burnside (one 13-inch mortar, 2,750 yards distant) firing every ten minutes from the time the range is obtained for Battery Sherman. Charge of shell, 7 pounds; elevation, 45 degrees; charge of mortar and length of fuse varying as required from those obtained for Battery Sherman. The shells should drop on the arches of the north and northeast faces, and explode immediately after striking, but not before.

Battery Sherman (three 13-inch mortars, 2,650 yards distant) commencing immediately after the ranges for Battery Grant have been determined, and firing at the rate of fifteen minutes for each piece, alternating from the right. Charge of shell, 7 pounds elevation, 45 degrees; charge of mortar and length of fuse to be fixed to suit the range, as determined from Battery Grant. The shells should drop over the arches of the north and northeast faces.

Battery Scott (three 10-inch and one 8-inch columbiads, 1,740 yards distant) firing solid shot, and commencing immediately after the barbette fire of the work has ceased. Charge of 10-inch columbiads, 20 pounds; elevation, 4½ degrees. Charge of 8-inch columbiad, 10 pounds; elevation, 5 degrees. This battery should breach the *pan-coupé* between the south and southeast faces, and the embrasure next to it, in the southeast face, the elevation to be varied accordingly; the charge to remain the same. Until the elevation is accurately determined each gun should fire once in ten minutes; after that every six or eight minutes.

Battery Sigel (five 30-pounder Parrotts and one 48-pounder James, old 24-pounder rifled, 1,670 yards distant) to open with 4¾-seconds fuses on the barbette guns of the fort at the second discharge from Battery Sherman. Charge for 30-pounder, 3½ pounds; charge for 45-pounder, 5 pounds; elevation, 4 degrees for both calibers. As soon as the barbette fire of the work has been silenced this battery will be directed with percussion shells upon the walls, to breach the *pan-coupé* between the south and southeast faces, the elevation to be varied accordingly, the charge to remain the same. Until the elevation is accurately determined each gun should fire once in six or eight minutes; after that every four or five minutes.

Battery McClellan (two 84 and two 64-pounders James, old 42 and 32 pounders rifled, 1,650 yards distant) opens fire immediately after Battery Scott. Charge for 84-pounder, 8 pounds; charge for 64-pounder, 6 pounds; elevation for 84-pounder, 4¼ degrees, and for the 64-pounder, 4 degrees. Each piece should fire once every five or six minutes after the elevation has been established. Charge to remain the same. This battery should breach the work in the *pan-coupé* between the south and southeast faces and the embrasure next to it in the southeast face. The steel scraper for the grooves should be used after every fifth or sixth discharge.

Battery Totten (four 10-inch siege mortars, 1,650 yards distant) opens fire immediately after Battery Sigel, firing each piece about once in five minutes. Charge of mortar, 3½ pounds; charge of shell, 3 pounds; elevation, 45 degrees, and length of fuse, 18½ seconds. The charge of mortar and length of fuse to vary so as to explode the shells over the northeast and southeast faces of the work. If any battery should be unmasked outside the work, Battery Totten will direct its fire upon it, varying the charge and length of fuse accordingly. The fire from each battery will cease at dark, except especial directions be given to the contrary. A signal officer at Battery Scott, to observe the effect of the 13-inch shells, will be in communication with other signal officers stationed near Batteries Stanton, Grant, and Sherman, in order to determine the range for these batteries in succession.

By order of Brig. Gen. Q. A. Gillmore:

W. L. M. BURGER,
First Lieutenant, Volunteer Engineers, and Actg. Asst. Adjt. Gen.

Just after sunrise, on the morning of the 10th, Maj. Gen. David Hunter, commanding the department, dispatched Lieut. J. H. Wilson, of the Topographical Engineers, to Fort Pulaski, bearing a flag of truce and a summons to surrender. To this demand a negative answer was returned.

The order was given to open fire, commencing with the mortar batteries, agreeably to the foregoing instructions.

The first shell was fired at a quarter past 8 o'clock a. m. from Battery Halleck. The other mortar batteries opened one after the other, as rapidly in succession as it was found practicable to determine the approximate ranges by the use of signals. The guns and columbiads soon followed, so that before half past 9 a. m. all the batteries were in operation, it having been deemed expedient not to wait for the barbette fire of the work to be silenced before opening with Breaching Batteries Scott and McClellan.

The three 10-inch columbiads in Battery Scott were dismounted by their own recoil at the first discharge, and one of those in Battery Lyon, from the same cause, at the third discharge. The gun-carriages were the new iron pattern, while the pintles and pintle-crosses belonged to the old wooden carriages, and were unsuitable. They were all, except one in Battery Scott, subsequently remounted and served.

As the several batteries along our line, which was 2,550 yards in length, opened fire one after another, the enemy followed them up successively with a vigorous though not at first very accurate fire from his barbette and casemate guns. Subsequent inquiry showed that he knew the exact position of only two of our batteries—Sherman and Burnside. These were established just above high-water mark, on low ground, void of bushes or undergrowth of any kind. During their construction no special attempt at concealment had been made after once securing good parapet cover by night work.

Great surprise and disappointment were expressed by all experienced officers present at the unsatisfactory results obtained with the 13-inch mortars. Although the platforms were excellent and remained for all useful purposes intact, and although the pieces were served with a fair degree of care and skill, not one-tenth of the shells thrown appeared to fall within the work—an estimate that was afterwards found to be rather over than under the correct proportion. Whether this inaccuracy is due to the fact that no cartridge-bags were furnished for the mortars, to inequalities in the strength of the powder, to defects inherent in the piece itself, or to these several causes combined, remains yet to be ascertained. It is suggested that the earnest attention of the proper department be directed to this subject.

By 1 o'clock in the afternoon (April 10) it became evident that the work would be breached, provided our breaching batteries did not become seriously disabled by the enemy's fire. By the aid of a powerful telescope it could be observed that the rifled projectiles were doing excellent service, that their penetration was deep and effective, and that the portion of the wall where the breach had been ordered was becoming rapidly honey-combed.

It also became evident before night, on account of the inefficiency of the mortar firing, that upon breaching alone ending perhaps in an assault, we must depend for the reduction of the work.

In order to increase the security of our advanced batteries a tolerably brisk fire against the barbette guns of the fort was kept up throughout the day. Probably from 15 to 20 per cent. of the metal thrown from the breaching batteries on the 10th was expended in this way.

As evening closed in, rendering objects indistinct, all the pieces ceased firing, with the exception of two 13-inch mortars, one 10-inch mortar, and one 30-pounder Parrott, which were served throughout the night at intervals of fifteen or twenty minutes for each piece. The object of this was to prevent repairs of the breach or the filling of the casemates in rear of it with sand bags or other material.

I extract as follows from my preliminary report to Brigadier-General Benham, dated April 12, 1862:

The only plainly perceptible result of this cannonade of ten and a half hours' duration (on the 10th), the breaching batteries having been served but nine and a halt hours, was the commencement of a breach in the easterly half of the *pan-coupé* connecting the south and southeast faces, and in that portion of the southeast face spanned by the two casemates adjacent to the *pan-coupé*.

The breach had been ordered in this portion of the scarp so as to take in reverse, through the opening formed, the powder magazine, located in the angle formed by the gorge and the north face.

Two of the barbette guns of the fort had been disabled and three casemate guns silenced.

The enemy served both tiers of guns briskly throughout the day, but without injury to the *matériel* or *personnel* of our batteries.

* * * * * * *

On the morning of the 11th, a little after sunrise, our batteries again opened fire with decided effect, the fort returning a heavy and well-directed fire from its casemates and barbette guns. The breach was rapidly enlarged. After the expiration of three hours the entire casemate next the *pan-coupé* had been opened, and by 12 o'clock the one adjacent to it was in a similar condition.

Directions were then given to train the guns upon the third embrasure, upon which the breaching batteries were operating with effect, when the fort hoisted the white flag. This occurred at 2 o'clock.

The formalities of visiting the fort, receiving its surrender, and occupying it with our troops, consumed the balance of the afternoon and evening.

During the 11th about one-tenth of the projectiles from the three breaching batteries were directed against the barbette guns of the fort. Eleven of its guns were dismounted, or otherwise rendered temporarily unserviceable.

The garrison of the fort was found to consist of 385 men, including a full complement of officers. Several of them were severely, and one fatally, wounded.

Our total loss was 1 man killed. None of our pieces were struck.

I take pleasure in recording my acknowledgment of the hearty, zealous, and persevering co-operation afforded me by the officers and men under my command, not only during the 10th and 11th, when all more or less forgot their fatigue in the excitement and danger of the engagement, but throughout the exhausting and unwholesome labors of preparation, occupying day and night a period of nearly eight weeks.

The entire available strength of the command was on guard or fatigue duty every twenty-four hours.

The details for night work were always paraded immediately after sunset, and were usually dismissed from labor between 1 and 2 o'clock in the morning, although circumstances frequently required parties to remain out all night.

In unloading the ordnance and ordnance stores advantage was always taken of favorable tide and weather day and night.

There is one circumstance connected with this siege which appears to deserve special mention, and that is, that with the exception of a detachment of sailors from the frigate Wabash, who served four of the light siege pieces in Battery Sigel on the 11th, we had no artillerists of any experience whatever. Four of the batteries were manned by the Third Rhode Island Volunteer Artillery, who were conversant with the manual of the pieces, but had never been practiced at firing. All the other pieces were served by infantry troops, who had been on constant fatigue duty, and who received all their instructions in gunnery at such odd times as they could be spared from other duties during the week or ten days preceding the action.

Instructions had been given by General Benham to place a mortar battery on the lower end of Long Island and two 10-inch columbiads on Turtle Island, in order to obtain a reverse fire on the work. These batteries were to have been erected and manned by detachments from General Viele's command. One 10-inch siege mortar was therefore placed on Long Island, and was served on the 11th April by a detachment commanded by Major Beard, Forty-eighth New York Volunteers. It was entirely ineffective on account of the distance—nearly 1,900 yards. The idea of Turtle Island battery was not carried into effect, and no pieces were landed there.

Throughout the siege Col. Alfred H. Terry, Seventh Regiment Connecticut Volunteers, and Lieut. Col. James F. Hall, commanding battalion of New York Volunteer Engineers, were conspicuous for the zeal and perseverance with which they discharged the varied duties to which they were assigned.

Captain Hinckel, with one company of the Forty-sixth Regiment New York Volunteers and a small battery, occupied for eight weeks, with credit to himself and command, an advanced and exposed position on a hulk in Lazaretto Creek, cutting off boat communication in that direction between Fort Pulaski and the interior.

Lieut. Horace Porter, of the Ordnance Department, rendered important and valuable service. Besides discharging most efficiently the special duties of chief of ordnance and artillery, he directed in person the transportation of nearly all the heavy ordnance and instructed the men in its use. He was actively engaged among the batteries during the action.

Capt. Charles E. Fuller, assistant quartermaster, served with me four weeks, assuming during that time the entire charge of unloadiug the ordnance and ordnance stores from the vessels; a duty which he discharged with a success worthy of special notice.

Lieut. James H. Wilson, Topographical Engineers, joined my command eleven days before the action, and was assigned to duty as instructor of artillery. He rendered valuable service in that capacity, and also at the breaching batteries on the 10th and 11th.

Capt. Louis H. Pelouze, Fifteenth U. S. Infantry, and Capt. J. W. Turner, commissary of subsistence, U. S. Army, members of Major-General Hunter's staff, volunteered for the engagement, and were assigned to the command of batteries, where their knowledge and experience as artillerists proved of great value.

On the 11th two pieces of Battery Sigel were served by a detachment from the Eighth Regiment Maine Volunteers, under Captain McArthur, of that regiment. The men had all served exclusively as infantry, and received their first artillery drill from Captain Turner and Lieutenant Wilson under a severe fire. They readily adapted themselves to their new duties, and served their guns creditably.

Capt. F. E. Graef and Lieut. T. B. Brooks, commanding respectively the two companies (D and A) of Volunteer Engineers, were indefatigable in the discharge of their duties as engineer officers, which required them to be out with the working parties every night.

I am under obligations to Commander C. R. P. Rodgers and Lieut. John Irwin, U. S. Navy, for skillfully serving with a detachment of sailors four siege guns in Battery Sigel on the 11th.

Lieut. W. L. M. Burger, of the regiment of New York Volunteer Engineers, served with zeal and efficiency as my adjutant-general during the operations on Tybee Island.

Lieut. P. H. O'Rorke, of the Corps of Engineers, and Adam Badeau, esq., volunteered to serve as my aides on the 10th and 11th, and rendered valuable assistance.

The services of Sergt. James E. Wilson, of Company A, Corps of Engineers, deserve special mention, and largely contributed towards getting the breaching batteries ready for service. Sergeant Wilson commanded Battery Burnside during the action.

To Major-General Hunter and Brigadier-General Benham, commanding respectively this department and district, I am under obligations for the official courtesy with which they allowed the project for reducing the fort, which was planned and all but executed before they assumed their commands, to be carried out in all its details without change or modification.

GENERAL OBSERVATIONS.

The three breaching batteries—Sigel, Scott, and McClellan—were established at a mean distance of 1,700 yards from the scarp walls of Fort Pulaski.

The circumstance, altogether new in the annals of sieges, that a practicable breach, which compelled the surrender of the work, was made at that distance in a wall 7½ feet thick, standing obliquely to the line of fire and backed by heavy casemate piers and arches, cannot be ignored by a simple reference to the time-honored military maxims that "Forts cannot sustain a vigorous land attack," and that "All masonry should be covered from land batteries."

A comparative glance at the status of military science as regards breaching prior to the invention of rifled cannon will enable us to form a tolerably correct estimate of the importance to be attached to the results developed by this improved arm of the service. A standard military work furnishes the following extract:

> An exposed wall may be breached with certainty at distances from 500 to 700 yards, even when elevated 100 feet above the breaching battery; and it is believed that in case of extreme necessity it would be justifiable to attempt to batter down an exposed wall from any distance not exceeding 1,000 yards; but then the quantity of artillery must be considerable, and it will require from four to seven days' firing, according to the number of guns in battery and the period of daylight, to render a breach practicable.

During the Peninsular war breaching at 500 to 700 yards was of frequent occurrence, and at the second siege of Badajos fourteen brass 24-pounders breached an exposed castle wall backed by earth alone, and consequently much weaker than a scarp sustained in the rear by heavy piers and arches, in eight hours, at a distance of 800 yards.

Experiments of breaching with rifled guns have recently been made. I shall notice two cases:

In August, 1860, experiments with Armstrong's rifled guns were made against a condemned martello tower at Eastbourne, on the coast of Sussex, England. The tower was of brick, fifty-six years old, and designed for one gun, the wall being 7½ feet thick at the level of the ground and 5¾ thick at the spring of the vault, which was 19 feet above the ground. It was 31½ feet high, 46 feet exterior diameter at the bottom, and 40 feet at the top. The pieces used against it were: one 40-pounder of 4¾-inch caliber, one 82-pounder of 6-inch caliber, and one 7-inch howitzer, throwing 100-pound shells. A practicable breach, 24 feet wide, including most of the arch, was made with an expenditure of 10,850 pounds of metal, at a distance of 1,032 yards. The projectiles expended were: 40-pounder gun, 20 solid shot, 1 plugged shell, 43 live shells; 82-pounder gun, 19 solid shot, 8 plugged shells, 36 live shells; 7-inch howitzer, 2 plugged shells, 29 live shells.

Projectiles that failed to hit the wall are excluded from the above table.*

General Sir John Burgoyne, in his report upon these experiments, says:

> Trials were subsequently made to breach a similar tower from smooth-bored 68 and 32 pounders at the same range of 1,030 yards, and the result may be deemed altogether a failure, both accuracy of fire and velocity of missiles being quite deficient for such a range. At 500, or perhaps 600, yards the superiority of the rifled ordnance would probably have been very little, if any.

Experimental siege operations for the instruction of the Prussian army, comprising the demolition of the defective and obsolete fortifications at

* Reference is to table on the map showing position of the batteries, &c., to appear in Atlas. The table shows that 4,079 shell and 914 shot were fired.

Juliers, were carried on in the month of September, 1860, especially with reference to the effect of rifled breech-loading guns.

The following brief summary of the breaching experiments is taken from the report of Lieut. Col. A. Ross, Royal Engineers:

Four 12-pounder iron guns and two 12-pounder brass guns, weighing, respectively, 2,700 pounds and 1,300 pounds, throwing a conical ball weighing 27 pounds, and fired with a charge of 2.1 pounds, at 800 Prussian paces (640 yards), made a practicable breach 32 feet wide in a brick wall 3 feet thick, with counter-forts 4 feet thick, 4 feet wide, and 16 feet from center to center, the wall being 16 feet high, and built *en décharge*, after firing 126 rounds. The first six rounds are omitted from this calculation, as they did not strike the wall, the wall being entirely covered from the guns. No difference was observed between the effects of the brass and the iron guns. The bursting charge of the shells was fourteen-fifteenths of a pound. The penetration was 15 inches.

Six 6-pounder guns, four of iron and two of cast steel, weighing, respectively, 1,300 and 800 pounds, throwing a conical shell weighing 13 pounds, and firing with a charge of 1.1 pounds, at 50 paces, made a practicable breach 70 feet wide, in precisely the same description of wall as that above described, after firing 276 rounds, the battery being situated on the counterscarp opposite the wall. No difference was observed between the effects of the cast steel and iron guns. The bursting charge of a shell was half a pound. The penetration of the first single shot averaged 18 inches.

Four 24-pounder iron guns, weighing between 53 and 54 hundredweight, throwing a shell weighing 57 pounds and firing with a charge of 4 pounds, at a distance of 60 yards made a practicable breach 62 feet wide in a loop-holed brick wall 24 feet high and 6½ thick after firing 117 rounds, the wall being seen from the battery. The bursting charge of the shell was 2 pounds. The penetration of the two first single shots was 2½ and 3 feet.

The same guns, after firing 294 rounds with the same charges and at a distance of 96 yards, made a breach 46 feet wide in a brick wall 40 feet high and 12 feet thick at the foot, with a batter of about 4 feet. The wall was 12 feet thick, and built *en décharge*, with counter-forts 6 feet wide and 16 feet from center to center, and connected by two rows of arches, one above the other. The penetration of the first single shot was 3 feet and 3½ feet. All the above-mentioned guns were rifled breach-loaders.

It is impossible to institute a very close comparison of the relative value of rifled and smooth-bore guns for breaching purposes from any data which experience has thus far developed.

The experiments at Eastbourne, hereinbefore mentioned, are the only ones on record where they have been tried side by side to the extent of actual breaching against the same kind of masonry and at the same distance. We have seen how on that occasion the rifles were a complete success, while the smooth-bores were an utter failure.

At Fort Pulaski an excellent opportunity was afforded on the scarp wall near the breach for obtaining the actual penetration of the several kinds of projectiles. An average of three or more shots for each caliber was taken, giving the following results, which may be relied upon as correct:

Table of penetrations in a brick wall, as determined at the siege of Fort Pulaski, Ga., April, 1862.

Kind of gun.	Distance from wall.	Kind and weight of projectiles.	Elevation.	Charge.	Penetration.
	Yards.		°	*Lbs.*	*Ins.*
Old 42-pounder, rifled	1,650	James, 84 lbs., solid	4¼	8	26
Old 32-pounder, rifled	1,650	James, 64 lbs., solid	4	6	20
Old 24-pounder, rifled	1,670	James, 48 lbs., solid	4½	5	19
Parrott rifled gun	1,670	Parrott, 30 lbs., solid	4½	3½	18
Columbiad (10-inch), smooth bore	1,740	Parrott, 128 lbs., solid round	4½	20	13
Columbiad (8-inch), smooth bore	1,740	Parrott, 68 lbs., solid round	5	10	11

The above table indicates very prominently, although it affords no exact means of measuring, the great superiority of rifle over smooth-bore guns for purposes requiring great penetrating power.

Against brick walls the breaching effect of percussion shell is certainly as great as that of solid shot of the same caliber. They do not penetrate as far by 20 to 25 per cent., but by bursting they make a much broader crater. Such shell would doubtless break against granite walls without inflicting much injury.

Sir W. Dennison, from a comparison of the several sieges in Spain during the Peninsular war, estimated that a practicable breach at 500 yards could be made in a rubble wall backed by earth by an average expenditure of 254,400 pounds of metal fired from smooth-bore 24-pounders for every 100 feet in width of breach—equal to 2,544 pounds of metal for ever linear foot in width of breach.

Before we can draw any comparison, however imperfect, between this estimate and the results obtained at Fort Pulaski, it is necessary to make certain deductions from the amount of metal thrown from the breaching batteries used against that work, as follows:

First. For the shots expended upon the barbette guns of the fort in silencing their fire.

Second. For 10 per cent. of Parrott projectiles, which upset from some defect which I know from personal observation has been entirely removed by the recent improvements of the manufacturer.

Third. For nearly 50 per cent. of the 64-pound James shot, due to the fact that one of the two pieces from which they were thrown had by some unaccountable oversight been bored nearly one-fourth of an inch too large in diameter, and gave no good firing whatever. Making these deductions, it results that 110,643 pounds of metal were fired at the breach.

The really practicable portion of the breach was of course only the two casemates that were fully opened, say 30 feet in aggregate width; but the scarp wall was battered down in front of three casemate piers besides, and had these piers not been there, or had the scarp been backed by earth alone, as was generally the case in Spain, the practicable portion of the opening would have been from 45 to 50 feet wide. Calling it 45 feet, the weight of metal thrown per linear foot of breach was 2,458 pounds, against 2,544 per linear foot in the Peninsular sieges. Had the fort held out a few hours longer this difference would have been much greater, for the wall was so badly shattered to the distance of 25 or 30 feet each side of the breach that the opening could have been extended either way with a comparatively trifling expenditure of metal. On repairing the work 100 linear feet of the scarp wall had to be rebuilt.

It must be borne in mind that at Fort Pulaski only 58 per cent. of the breaching metal was fired from rifled guns, the balance being from smooth-bored 8-inch and 10-inch columbiads (68 and 128 pounders) of Battery Scott.

It may therefore be briefly and safely announced that the breaching of Fort Pulaski at 1,700 yards did not require as great an expenditure of metal, although but 58 per cent. of it was thrown from rifled guns, as the breaches made in Spain with smooth-bores exclusively at 500 yards. In the former case the wall was good brick masonry, laid in lime mortar, and backed by heavy piers and arches; in the latter, rubble masonry, backed by earth.

A knowledge of the relative value of heavy round shot, 10-inch for example, and elongated percussion shells from lighter guns, say James 64-pounders (old 32-pounders), in bringing down the masses of brick masonry cracked and loosened by the elongated solid shot, is a matter of some importance, considering the vast difference in the amount of labor required to transport and handle the two kinds of ordnance. The penetration of the percussion shell would exceed, and its local effect would at least equal, that of the solid round shot. The general effect of the latter, within certain ranges, is a matter for consideration.

My own opinion, based principally upon personal observation, corroborated by the reports of experiments made in Europe, may be stated in the following terms:

First. Within 700 yards heavy smooth bores may be advantageously used for breaching, either alone or in combination with rifles.

Second. Within the same distance light smooth bores will breach with certainty, but rifles of the same weight are much better.

Third. Beyond 700 yards rifled guns exclusively are much superior for breaching purposes to any combination of rifles and heavy or light smooth bores.

Fourth. Beyond 1,000 yards a due regard to economy in the expenditure of manual labor and ammunition requires that smooth bores, no matter how heavy they may be, should be scrupulously excluded from breaching batteries.

Fifth. In all cases when rifled guns are used exclusively against brick walls at least one-half of them should fire percussion shells. Against stone walls shell would be ineffective.

For breaching at long distances the James and Parrott projectiles seem to be all that can be desired. The grooves of the James gun must be kept clean at the seat of the shot. This is not only indispensably necessary, but of easy and ready attainment, by using the very simple and effective scraper devised on the principle of the searcher for the pieces we employed against Pulaski. This scraper consists of a number of steel springs or prongs, one for each groove, firmly attached by screws to the cylindrical part of a rammer-head, and flaring like a broom, so as to fit closely into the grooves. About half an inch of the lower end of each prong is bent out at right angles. The prongs being compressed by a ring, to which a lanyard is attached, when entering the bore spring out firmly into the grooves when the ring is removed, and clean them thoroughly as the scraper is drawn out.

The failure of the James shot, as reported on two or three occasions by apparently good authority, is probably due to neglect in this particular. There were no failures in our firing, except as before mentioned, with the 32-pounders (carrying a 64-pound shot), that had been bored too large.

Although the James projectiles are surrounded when first made by greased canvas, there is believed to be an advantage in greasing them again at the moment of loading. This was done in our batteries against Fort Pulaski. As the Parrott projectiles receive their rotary motion from a ring of wrought-iron or brass which surrounds the lower portion of the cylinder, and which does not foul the grooves while engaging them, no special precaution to prevent fouling need be taken with the Parrott guns.

With heavy James or Parrott guns the practicability of breaching the best-constructed brick scarp at 2,300 to 2,500 yards with satisfactory rapidity admits of very little doubt. Had we possessed our present knowledge of their power previous to the bombardment of Fort Pulaski, the eight weeks of laborious preparation for its reduction could have been curtailed to one week, as heavy mortars and columbiads would have been omitted from the armament of the batteries as unsuitable for breaching at long ranges.

It is also true beyond question that the minimum distance, say from 900 to 1,000 yards, at which land batteries have heretofore been considered practically harmless against exposed masonry, must be at least trebled, now the rifled guns have to be provided against.

The inaccuracy of the fire of the 13-inch mortars has already been adverted to. Not one-tenth of the shells dropped inside of the fort. A few struck the terre-plein over the casemate arches, but, so far as could be observed by subsequent inspection from below, without producing any effect upon the masonry. Whether they penetrated the earth work to the roofing of the arches was not ascertained.

Two or three striking in rapid succession into the same spot over an arch might be expected to injure it seriously, if not fatally. Such an occurrence would, however, be rare indeed. Against all, except very extraordinary casualties, it would be easy for a garrison to provide as they occurred, by repairing with sand bags or loose earth the holes formed in the terre-plein by shells.

We may therefore assume that mortars are unreliable for the reduction of a good casemated work of small area, like most of our sea-coast fortifications.

As auxiliary in silencing a barbette fire, or in the reduction of a work containing wooden buildings and other exposed combustible material, mortars may undoubtedly be made to play an important part.

For the reduction of fortified towns or cities, or extensive fortresses containing large garrisons, there is perhaps no better arm than the mortar, unless it be the rifled gun, firing at high elevations.

To the splinter-proof shelters constructed for the seven advanced batteries I attribute our almost entire exemption from loss of life. We had 1 man killed by a shell from one of the mortar batteries outside the fort, which was the only casualty.

The demoralizing effect of constant and laborious fatigue duty upon the health and discipline of troops, particularly upon such as are unused to the privations of war, like our volunteers, who can but slowly adapt themselves to the stinted comforts of a campaign, is a subject which demands the earnest attention of commanding officers in the field.

Upon regular troops, to whom the drill in their special arm has to a certain extent become a second nature, who are accustomed to the vicissitudes of the field and familiar with expedients and make-shifts to secure comfort, the bad effects of excessive labor and constant interruption of drill are of course less apparent.

With the average of our volunteer regiments every alternate day should be devoted to drill, in order to keep them up to a fair standard of efficiency.

Very respectfully, your obedient servant,

Q. A. GILLMORE,
Major-General Volunteers.

To the ADJUTANT-GENERAL U. S. ARMY,
Washington, D. C.

No. 6.

Report of Surg. George E. Cooper, U. S. Army.

MEDICAL DIRECTOR'S OFFICE, DEP'T OF THE SOUTH,
Hilton Head, S. C., April 14, 1862.

SIR: Herewith inclosed I transmit the list of casualties which occurred among the United States forces during the attack on Fort Pulaski, Ga.

Though the professional services of the surgeons were fortunately but little needed, I cannot but state that great credit is due to Dr. Francis Bacon, surgeon of the Seventh Connecticut Volunteers, for his voluntary presence in the batteries nearest to the work being assailed from the opening of the fire until the surrender of the fort, as well as to Brigade Surgeon Craven for the energy shown by him in the performance of the duties belonging to his position during the action.

Respectfully, your most obedient servant,

GEO. E. COOPER,
Surgeon, U. S. Army, Medical Director Dept. of the South.

Maj. CHARLES G. HALPINE,
Assistant Adjutant-General, Department of the South.

[Inclosure.]

List of casualties occurring among the United States forces during the siege of Fort Pulaski, Ga., on April 10 and 11: [killed] Thomas Campbell, private, Company H, Third Rhode Island Artillery. There were a few slight injuries received by the cannoneers during the action, but none were reported as unfitting the men for the performance of their duties.

GEO. E. COOPER,
Surgeon, U. S. Army, Medical Director Dept. of the South.

No. 7.

Report of Maj. Gen. John C. Pemberton, C. S. Army.

HDQRS. DEP'T OF SOUTH CAROLINA AND GEORGIA,
Pocotaligo, S. C., April 11, 1862—11.40 p. m.

General LEE, *Richmond, Va.:*

I have just received the following telegraph from General Lawton:

General J. C. PEMBERTON:

A messenger from Pulaski reports that the fort surrendered at 2 o'clock to-day; seven breaches in the wall; all barbette guns dismounted, and three shots had entered the magazine.

I left Savannah at 5.30 p. m. At that time all was believed to be right. Four regiments have been ordered to Tennessee. I should have them replaced. Martial law should be proclaimed from Savannah to Augusta, inclusive.

J. C. PEMBERTON.

No. 8.

Report of Brig. Gen. Alexander R. Lawton, C. S. Army.

HEADQUARTERS DEPARTMENT [DIST.] GEORGIA,
Savannah, Ga., April 14, 1862.

CAPTAIN: I have the honor to report that the enemy opened fire on Fort Pulaski early on the morning of the 10th instant, as was evident from the rapid and continuous firing and bursting of shells, which could be seen from the city of Savannah and other accessible points of observation. As communication with the fort was cut off, my knowledge of what occurred during the first day's bombardment was derived exclusively from distant views and the sound of the guns. The firing continued during the entire day and at intervals during the night.

On the night of the 10th I attempted to communicate with the fort by a small boat, for the purpose of conveying to it a man detailed on signal service, who had recently arrived, under orders, from Richmond. He was carried there by Corporal Law, of the Phœnix Riflemen, stationed at Thunderbolt, who had successfully communicated with the fort more than once before since the steamers had been cut off.

It was observed that the fire on both sides ceased about 2 p. m. on the 11th, and these two men returned to the battery at Thunderbolt about 8 o'clock that evening. The only detailed information I have is derived from the verbal statement of these two men. They represent that they reached the fort about 6 o'clock on the morning of the 11th, in the midst of a heavy fire both from the fort and the enemy; that soon after their arrival a breach was made in the wall at the southeast angle, nearest the Tybee Island, and that before the fort surrendered this breach was wide enough to drive a four-horse team through; that the wall, which embraced seven casemates in succession, was nearly all knocked down, and that all the barbette guns which could play on their batteries at Tybee [Island] had been disabled; that several shots had been fired into the magazine. They further represent that 4 men had their arms or legs broken; none others seriously wounded, and none dead at the time they left. They further state that the ships were not engaged at all, but that all the firing was from batteries on Tybee [Island], chiefly from a battery of Parrott guns at King's Landing, the nearest point of Tybee [Island] to the fort. As these men constituted no part of the garrison, they were advised by Colonel Olmstead to make their escape, if possible.

In reporting the statements of these two men I must express my belief that they gave an exaggerated account of the injury done to the fort, owing, perhaps, to the very exciting circumstances under which they must have entered and left it. It is truly painful to be left without any more definite or reliable details, but it is quite certain that Pulaski has fallen, as the enemy's flag has been distinctly seen flying above the ramparts, and I consider it my duty to give you these statements as they were made to me. As there have been no returns received from Fort Pulaski for some time, I cannot give you the precise strength of the garrison. It consisted, however, of five companies, numbering a little over 400 men, and commanded by Col. C. H. Olmstead. The armament consisted of five 10-inch columbiads, nine 8-inch columbiads, three 42-pounders, three 10-inch mortars, one 12-inch mortar, one 24-pounder howitzer, two 12-pounder howitzers, twenty 32-pounders, and two 4½-inch (Blakely) rifled guns, with 130 rounds of ammunition per gun.

I am, captain, very respectfully, your obedient servant,

A. R. LAWTON,
Brigadier-General, Commanding.

Capt. J. R. WADDY,
Assistant Adjutant-General, Pocotaligo, S. C.

CORRESPONDENCE, ORDERS, AND RETURNS RELATING TO OPERATIONS ON THE COASTS OF SOUTH CAROLINA, GEORGIA, AND MIDDLE AND EAST FLORIDA FROM AUGUST 21, 1861, TO APRIL 11, 1862.

UNION CORRESPONDENCE, ETC.

WAR DEPARTMENT, *August* 2, 1861.

Brig. Gen. THOMAS W. SHERMAN:

GENERAL: You will proceed to New York immediately and organize, in connection with Captain DuPont, of the Navy, an expedition of 12,000 men. Its destination you and the naval commander will determine after you have sailed. You should sail at the earliest possible moment.

THOMAS A. SCOTT,
Assistant Secretary of War.

AUGUST 2, 1861.

Approved:

A. LINCOLN.

WAR DEPARTMENT,
Washington, August 11, 1861.

Brig. Gen. THOMAS W. SHERMAN:

SIR: You will proceed to the capitals of the States of Connecticut, Rhode Island, Massachusetts, New Hampshire, and Maine, and confer with the governors of those States on the subject which I have verbally communicated to you, and which is conveyed to the governors also in the letters herewith placed in your hands, and which you are requested to deliver. You will then proceed to New York City, as heretofore instructed.

Very respectfully,

THOMAS A. SCOTT,
Assistant Secretary of War.

[Inclosure.]

WAR DEPARTMENT,
Washington, August 10, 1861.

General T. W. Sherman, having been charged with the preparation of an expedition to rendezvous on Long Island Sound, will, on the part of this Department, consult with you as to the troops which can be earliest made available for this service.

Very respectfully, your obedient servant,

THOMAS A. SCOTT,
Assistant Secretary of War.

Their excellencies the governors of Maine, New Hampshire, Massachusetts, Connecticut, and Rhode Island.

NEW YORK, *August* 20, 1861.

Col. E. D. TOWNSEND,
A. A. G., U. S. A., Hdqrs. Army, Washington, D. C.:

SIR: In conformity to verbal instructions of the 10th instant I have delivered in person the letters placed in my hands by the honorable

Secretary of War to the governors of Maine, New Hampshire, Massachusetts, Rhode Island, and Connecticut, and conferred with each of them on the subject of my mission. Their excellencies were animated with a very commendable interest in the success of rendezvousing the force on Long Island, and feel a deep solicitude that the Government should extend its efforts even in different directions from those already commenced.

I have ascertained that the probable number of men that can be concentrated on Long Island by September 5 from the above States, with a little increase of energy, is: Maine, three regiments; New Hampshire, two regiments; Massachusetts, five regiments; Rhode Island, one regiment; Connecticut, two regiments; or about 13,000 men.

Some of these regiments will contain men peculiarly well adapted to the nature of the service required, but unless some means outside of the camp on Long Island be taken to make heavy artillerists, this force will be entirely deficient in that element, which the nature of our operations will render of the first importance. Any deficiency, therefore, of "regular" artillerists should be made up of men from these regiments sent to some of our forts for instruction in that particular arm.

But, in consequence of recent orders from the War Department to the governors, the force above, considered available for the expedition, is to be diverted to Washington City, and it now, therefore, remains for the Department to decide from whence and when this expedition is to be organized. The time set by the Cabinet for the expedition to leave is rapidly approaching, and, even with the greatest dispatch, it will already be impracticable to prepare it within that time. The rumored threats of the enemy on the Potomac but only necessitate the greater dispatch of this expedition.

Very respectfully, your obedient servant,

T. W. SHERMAN,
Brigadier-General, U. S. Army.

HEADQUARTERS OF THE ARMY,
Washington, D. C., August 27, 1861.

[General THOMAS W. SHERMAN:]

SIR: Your letter of the 20th instant having been submitted to the Secretary of War, I now inclose herewith letters to be delivered or forwarded by you to the several governors to whom they are addressed. You will observe the former quota from Massachusetts is reduced from five to three regiments, and three regiments are now called for from New York, in the hope of thus hastening the organization of the force to be under your command.

Very respectfully, &c.,

E. D. TOWNSEND,
Assistant Adjutant-General.

[Inclosures.]

WAR DEPARTMENT,
Washington, August 27, 1861.

SIR: This will be sent you by Brig. Gen. Thomas W. Sherman, U. S. A., who has heretofore communicated with you on the project of concentrating in a camp of instruction a number of regiments of United

States volunteers. As late emergencies may have somewhat interfered with this object, I have now to renew the request that you will put —— regiments, as soon as they can be prepared for service, under the orders of General Sherman, who will indicate the place of rendezvous.

I am, sir, very respectfully, your obedient servant,

SIMON CAMERON,
Secretary of War.

(Copy sent to the governor of Maine, three regiments; governor of New Hampshire, two regiments; governor of Massachusetts, three regiments; governor of Rhode Island, one regiment; governor of Connecticut, two regiments; governor of New York, three regiments.)

WAR DEPARTMENT,
Washington, August 27, 1861.

His Excellency E. D. MORGAN,
Governor of New York:

SIR: This will be handed you by Brig. Gen. Thomas W. Sherman, who will explain to your excellency the purpose of the Department in requesting that three of the New York regiments first prepared for service may be put under the orders of General Sherman as soon as they can be made ready. I will also request your excellency to send the next three New York regiments which may be ready, after those above indicated, to Fort Monroe, Old Point Comfort, Va., and the Department will take it as a favor if you will inform it of your action in these matters.

I have the honor to be, very respectfully, your obedient servant,

SIMON CAMERON,
Secretary of War.

GENERAL ORDERS, No. 1.

HEADQUARTERS U. S. FORCES,
New York, September 9, 1861.

I. The following-named officers are announced upon the staff of the commanding officer:

Maj. H. G. Wright, U. S. Engineers, chief engineer.

Capt. John McNutt, U. S. Ordnance, chief ordnance officer.

Capt. Rufus Saxton, Quartermaster's Department, U. S. Army, chief quartermaster.

Capt. Michael R. Morgan, Commissary of Subsistence, U. S. Army, chief commissary.

Lieut. Silas Crispin, U. S. Ordnance.

Assistant Surgeon Chas. A. McCall, Medical Department, U. S. Army.

Lieut. George Merrill, volunteer aide.

Lieut. James Magner, volunteer aide.

II. The camp at Hempstead Plains will be designated and known as Camp Winfield Scott.

* * * * * * *

IV. Brigadier-General Viele, having been assigned to duty with this command, will take post at Camp Winfield Scott.

* * * * * * *

T. W. SHERMAN,
Brigadier-General, Commanding.

HEADQUARTERS U. S. FORCES,
New York, September 13, 1861.

Capt. RUFUS SAXTON,
Assistant Quartermaster, U. S. Army:

SIR: You will provide transportation in good, sound, and safe steamers for fourteen regiments of infantry from this place to localities not to be designated in the contract; said transportation to be ready to leave on the 5th of October. Besides the troops above mentioned, but in connection therewith, are to be transported some 1,400 tons of ordnance and ordnance stores, and the commissary and quartermaster's stores, horses, &c., that will be hereafter turned over to you for that purpose.

Sufficient water must be provided for the men and horses for at least fifteen days, and proper and ample arrangements for cooking, &c., for the whole force. As it is very uncertain when the steamers can be discharged, and as some of them may be required for some time after reaching their destination, without any facilities or means of recoaling, the largest amount of coal must be taken, without prejudice to the stipulated cargo. No stipulation, however, should be made to keep the transports over fifteen days, and indeed this clause had better be left out altogether if practicable. Should it prove advantageous to the public interest to have a couple of these vessels in readiness by the 1st of October, in consideration of the immensity of your material and the difficulty of depositing it, you are authorized to do so, but the public economy must be consulted and adhered to in every contract.

Very respectfully, your obedient servant,

T. W. SHERMAN,
Brigadier-General, Commanding.

HEADQUARTERS OF THE ARMY,
Washington, September 14, 1861.

Brig. Gen. THOMAS W. SHERMAN, U. S. A.,
New York City, N. Y.:

General Scott says: "Come here with all your command without delay, leaving the smallest guard necessary to protect your camp."

E. D. TOWNSEND,
Assistant Adjutant-General.

EXECUTIVE MANSION, *September* 18, 1861.

Hon. SECRETARY OF WAR:

MY DEAR SIR: To guard against misunderstanding I think fit to say that the joint expedition of the Army and Navy, agreed upon some time since, and in which General T. W. Sherman was and is to bear a conspicuous part, is in nowise to be abandoned, but must be ready to move by the 1st of or very early in October. Let all preparations go forward accordingly.

Yours, truly,
A. LINCOLN.

GENERAL ORDERS, No. 5. } HEADQUARTERS EXPEDITIONARY CORPS,
Washington, D. C., September 19, 1861.

The command will for the present be divided into three brigades, to be composed and commanded as follows:

First Brigade, Brigadier-General Viele.—The Forty-sixth, Forty-seventh, and Forty-eighth New York, the Eighth Maine, and the Third New Hampshire Regiments.

Second Brigade, Brigadier-General ———.—The two remaining Maine regiments, the remaining New Hampshire, and one of the Massachusetts regiments.

Third Brigade, Brigadier-General Wright.—The two Connecticut regiments and the first two Massachusetts regiments that arrive.

The Rhode Island regiment is reserved for special service and will be disposed of hereafter.

T. W. SHERMAN,
Brigadier-General, Commanding.

EXECUTIVE DEPARTMENT,
Hartford, Conn., September 20, 1861.

Hon. SIMON CAMERON,
Secretary of War, Washington:

SIR: I telegraphed you on the 17th and 18th instant, and would now repeat the dispatch, by saying that the Sixth Regiment Connecticut Volunteers left New Haven for Washington on the 17th instant with 974 men, rank and file, and the Seventh Regiment left on the 18th instant with about 1,000 men. Under the direction of General Sherman I fitted the regiments with only five wagons and two ambulances and a corresponding number of horses to each.

I am, dear sir, yours, with high regard,

WM. A. BUCKINGHAM.

EXECUTIVE DEPARTMENT,
Albany, N. Y., September 21, 1861.

Hon. SIMON CAMERON,
Secretary of War:

SIR: I have the honor to inform you that, in accordance with your telegraphic message of the 14th instant, received on the evening of that day, in the words following—

WAR DEPARTMENT,
Washington, September 14, 1861.

Governor MORGAN,
Astor House:

Secure transportation to-day, and forward immediately to Washington the three regiments intended for Sherman and all others that you can possibly send. Give them arms and start them. Sherman has been ordered here with all his force. Let me know immediately what you can do.

SIMON CAMERON,
Secretary of War—

I have dispatched six infantry regiments to Washington, commanded and of the strength, respectively, as near as can be ascertained at this moment: Forty-seventh New York, Colonel Moore, 662; Forty-eighth New York, Colonel Perry, 950; Forty-sixth New York, Colonel Rosa, 675; Forty-third New York, Colonel Vinton, 750; Forty-ninth New York, Colonel Bidwell, 800; Fiftieth New York, Colonel Stuart, 864. The first three were being organized for Brigadier-General Sherman, to be sent to his camp at Hempstead. The remaining three regiments would have been sent to General Wool at Fortress Monroe, agreeably to orders of 27th August, but for the above dispatch. I also forwarded on Sunday last ten rifled cannon, with carriages, caissons, harness, and shot, taking Major Hagner's receipt therefor, to be replaced. I have not yet heard of the safe arrival of this battery.

The regiments forwarded are not all of the requisite strength, nor was it possible to send them in proper condition and comply with your telegraphic dispatch herein copied. I propose to retain recruiting the forces now in the State until near or quite full regimental organizations can be made therefrom and proper equipment can be provided, as the apprehended danger of an attack does not now, I believe, exist at Washington. It would be well for the General Government to direct the several departments of United States officers on duty in this State to fill promptly my requisitions, obey all orders, and to afford every facility in their power in aid of my efforts in supplying the General Government with troops; also to give me authority to continue the raising of regiments or batteries without limit until revoked, or, if in your judgment you deem it necessary and proper to fix a limit, let it be for twenty infantry regiments, additional to those called for, and the proper proportion additional of artillery and cavalry. I do not propose that this call should be public. I am sure it should not be, yet I need the power, as all present requirements, judging from present appearances, are quite sure to be filled. I also desire that, disregarding specifications and forms, the Government should send without delay a competent person to purchase horses in this State, Vermont, or elsewhere near by, for all the purposes required, whether for artillery, cavalry, or ambulance service. Horse equipments, sabers, and bugles are needed immediately. The inspection of horses should be here, and the delivery of them here. Inspection at Washington will greatly embarrass matters. They will be wanted for drilling purposes sooner than they can be purchased and delivered.

Colonel Bailey's regiment at Elmira will consist of ten batteries; the guns, carriages, caissons, shot, harness, and uniforms for the men will be ready, and there will be no finer regiment in the service. He is almost discouraged, as he does not get detached from the United States service, and horses, horse equipments, sabers, and bugles are indispensable, and no ability to procure the former under the restrictions in the horse specifications, and the latter I have been informed would be provided by the Government. At this moment there is less difficulty in getting soldiers than arms. May I ask your immediate attention to the several subjects to which this communication relates?

Faithfully and truly, yours,

E. D. MORGAN.

[Indorsement.]

The within letter of Governor Morgan is referred to the Quartermaster-General, with the request that he will reply to that portion which refers to purchasing horses.

By order: J. LESLEY, JR.

COMMONWEALTH OF MASSACHUSETTS, EXEC. DEPT.,
Boston, Mass., September 23, 1861.

Brigadier-General SHERMAN, U. S. A.:

GENERAL: His excellency Governor Andrew directs me to write you that he expects you to exert all the personal effort within your power to secure to your command the contingent which you expect from Massachusetts, and prevent it from being diverted to General Butler or any other officer. His excellency pledged to you his own personal efforts to secure to you the first regiments whose organization should be completed in the State after the dispatch to Washington of the five regiments which were forming when you first visited Boston. Those five regiments are all now in the field in active service, and the three which he conceives rightfully to belong to your command (being the three which will next be completed) are General Wilson's two regiments, now encamped at Springfield, *i. e.*, the Twenty-second and Twenty-third, and the Twenty-fifth Regiment, now encamped at Worcester. Other regiments can be furnished General Butler in proper time, and neither he nor any other commander ought to be allowed to divert from you these three regiments, which are yours almost by right. His excellency, so far as he can influence the matter, proposes to assign to General Butler the regiment being raised by Colonel Jones (the Twenty-sixth), who is a townsman and a personal and political friend of General Butler, and also an Irish regiment, whose organization is in progress. There can be no just pretense on which your claim to the Twenty-second, Twenty-third, and Twenty-fifth can be disputed; but as it is probable that it may, nevertheless, be drawn into question, his excellency relies upon you, for your own sake, to assist him to maintain it. The Twenty-second is already full, and it will be ready to move at the beginning of next week—certainly by October 1. The Twenty-third and Twenty-fifth are also in an advanced state of progress.

I have the honor to be, very truly, your obedient servant,

A. G. BROWNE, JR.,
Captain and Military Secretary.

EXECUTIVE DEPARTMENT,
Boston, Mass., September 23, 1861.

Brig. Gen. THOMAS W. SHERMAN:

GENERAL: Since the accompanying letter was written his excellency Governor Andrew has received a telegram from the office of the Secretary of War as follows:

Select the regiments yourself for Sherman, and supply him first.

THOMAS A. SCOTT,
Acting Secretary of War.

I have the honor to remain, yours, very truly,

THOS. DREW,
Assistant Military Secretary.

HEADQUARTERS EXPEDITIONARY CORPS,
New York, September 27, 1861.

Capt. RUFUS SAXTON,
Assistant Quartermaster:

SIR: The vessels chartered to transport the fourteen regiments are to form two divisions, to move and act together or separately, as the circumstances may require.

Division No. 1 is to accommodate 8,000 men, the ordnance and ordnance stores, provisions, and material for a certain locality, the amount of which will be furnished you by the chief ordnance officer and commissary.

Division No. 2 is to accommodate, say, 5,000 men, with the ordnance and ordnance stores, provisions, and material for another locality, the amount of which will also be furnished you by the same officers.

The light guns and their carriages complete, with their ammunition, are to be so placed on the transports that they can be got off at a moment's notice for immediate action. The regimental commissaries will have sufficient supplies furnished them for the voyage, so that the bulk of the supplies will remain intact during the voyage. The surf-boats are to be so secured that they can be launched with safety at a moment's notice.

A transport must be fitted up mainly for the purpose of transporting the horses, and the greatest security afforded them by proper stalls and slings. A sufficient quantity of disinfectants must be taken along to insure health on board each vessel.

The shipping of so large a quantity of supplies and the necessary distribution of it among so many vessels will demand a great deal of care and system to prevent misplacement and delay in getting at the proper stores wanted at the period of landing, as well as to prevent losses, and you are authorized to employ all the assistance necessary to effect these important ends. The most of the staff officers of the command being necessarily employed with their brigades in Washington City, it will require the utmost exertion and management on your part to get this expedition fitted out within the time designated, and you are authorized to call on Colonel Tompkins for any assistance he can render, and if that is insufficient, to employ responsible agents to assist you in the work.

Very respectfully,

T. W. SHERMAN,
Brigadier-General, Commanding.

WAR DEPARTMENT,
Washington, October 5, 1861.

Maj. Gen. JOHN E. WOOL,
Commanding Fort Monroe:

Please select 1,000 active men from the lot of fugitive contrabands now on hand at Fort Monroe, and prepare them to accompany General Sherman's expedition to the Southern coast. Have them ready to embark by the 15th of October. General Sherman will provide transportation.

I have the honor to be, very truly, yours,

THOMAS A. SCOTT,
Acting Secretary of War.

SPECIAL ORDERS, No. 10. } HEADQUARTERS EXPEDITIONARY CORPS,
Washington, D. C., October 5, 1861.

I. Surg. George E. Cooper, Medical Department, U. S. Army, is hereby announced as medical director to this command.

II. Brigadier-General Viele's brigade will continue its movement to Annapolis, as before directed.

III. Brig. Gen. H. G. Wright will move his brigade to Annapolis at the earliest possible moment. The Ninth Maine and the Fourth New Hampshire Regiments are assigned to this Third Brigade and will move with it, taking the place of the two Massachusetts regiments not arrived.

General Wright will apply to the headquarters of the Army of the

Potomac for the necessary transportation of baggage, property, and supplies.

IV. The Second Brigade of this division will be composed of the Massachusetts regiment daily expected in New York, the Eighth Michigan, the Fiftieth Pennsylvania and the Roundhead Pennsylvania Regiments. The Massachusetts regiment will embark at New York, and the three remaining regiments now in Washington will march as soon as practicable to Annapolis, under their brigade commander. In the event of no brigade commander being assigned to this brigade before that time, it will march on Wednesday morning, 9th instant, under the command of its senior colonel.

The headquarters of the Army of the Potomac will be applied to for transportation of baggage, property, and supplies.

V. Hamilton's light battery of artillery will march at once to Annapolis and report to the commanding officer of the expedition.

VI. All the above-mentioned troops will be in position, with all brigade and staff officers at their posts, on Thursday, the 10th instant, in readiness for embarkation.

VII. The position at Annapolis will be taken up with fifteen days' supply of subsistence and forage.

VIII. The movements above directed will be conducted by the brigade commanders, who will arrange their own transportation, and, to avoid interference, Brigadier-General Wright's brigade will leave not later than Tuesday morning, 8th instant, and the Independent brigade positively on Wednesday morning.

IX. The embarkation will be made in accordance with orders hereafter published.

X. Brigade commanders will enforce a strict compliance with the regulation for allowance of personal baggage.

By command of Brig. Gen. T. W. Sherman:

JUSTUS STEINBERGER,
Assistant Adjutant-General.

WAR DEPARTMENT, *October* 14, 1861.

Brig. Gen. THOMAS W. SHERMAN,
Commanding Expedition to the Southern Coast:

SIR: In conducting military operations within States declared by the proclamation of the President to be in a state of insurrection you will govern yourself, so far as persons held to service under the laws of such States are concerned, by the principles of the letters addressed by me to Major-General Butler on the 30th of May and the 8th of August, copies of which are herewith furnished to you.* Special directions adapted to special circumstances cannot be given. Much must be referred to your own discretion as commanding general of the expedition. You will, however, in general avail yourself of the services of any persons, whether fugitives from labor or not, who may offer them to the National Government. You will employ such persons in such services as they may be fitted for—either as ordinary employés, or, if special circumstances seem to require it, in any other capacity, with such organization (in squads, companies, or otherwise) as you may deem most beneficial to the service; this, however, not being a general arming of them for military service. You will assure all loyal masters that Congress will provide just compensation to them for the loss of the services of the persons so employed.

---

* See under these dates in Vol. I, Series III, pp. 282, 402.

It is believed that the course thus indicated will best secure the substantial rights of loyal masters and the proper benefits to the United States of the services of all disposed to support the Government, while it will avoid all interference with the social systems or local institutions of every State, beyond that which insurrection makes unavoidable and which a restoration of peaceful relations to the Union under the Constitution will immediately remove.

Respectfully,

THOMAS A. SCOTT,
Acting Secretary of War.

HEADQUARTERS OF THE ARMY,
Washington, October 14, 1861.

Brig. Gen. THOMAS W. SHERMAN,
U. S. Volunteers:

SIR: You have been selected to command the land portion of a joint expedition with a naval squadron, and selected on account of its importance. A short letter of general instructions you have already received from the War Department, and are fully impressed with the principal objects of the expedition. Wishing to leave you a wide margin of discretion, I have but little to add, and that little relates to the principles which govern co-operation in joint expeditions. No land officer can be subjected in strictness to the orders of any sea officer until placed on ship to serve as a marine, and no sea officer under the orders of a land officer unless placed in some fortification to assist in its defense or before it to assist in its capture. But land troops embarked in vessels of war for transportation merely will be considered, in respect to naval commanders, as passengers, subject, of course, to the internal regulations of the vessel.

Cordiality and deference on the part of our land forces towards those of our Navy in the service in question need scarcely to be urged. Hearty reciprocity cannot fail to be the result. To this end free and frequent conferences between the joint commanders are recommended. Accordingly the President, Commander-in-Chief of the Army and Navy, requires and expects the most effective and cordial co-operation between the commanders of the expedition, their officers and men, and will hold all, in proportion to rank, to a strict and severe responsibility for any failure to preserve harmony and to secure all the objects of the joint expedition.

You will take care to maintain strict order and discipline among your troops, not to neglect opportunities of making the prescribed returns to the Adjutant-General, and to report to him every incident of importance that may occur to your command.

I am, with great respect,

WINFIELD SCOTT.

GENERAL ORDERS, No. 11. } HEADQUARTERS EXPEDITIONARY CORPS,
Annapolis, Md., October 14, 1861.

The following-named officers are announced upon the staff of the general commanding:

Capt. Louis H. Pelouze, Fifteenth Infantry, acting assistant adjutant-general.

First Lieut. George Merrill, U. S. volunteers, aide-de-camp.

Capt. Rufus Saxton, assistant quartermaster, U. S. Army, chief quartermaster.

Capt. Michael R. Morgan, commissary subsistence, U. S. Army, chief commissary.

Capt. Quincy A. Gillmore, U. S. Engineers, chief engineer.

Capt. John McNutt, Ordnance Department, chief of ordnance.

Surg. George E. Cooper, Medical Department, U. S. Army, medical director.

By order of Brig. Gen. T. W. Sherman:

L. H. PELOUZE,
Captain, Fifteenth Infantry, Act. Asst. Adjt. General.

GENERAL ORDERS, No. 13. } HEADQUARTERS EXPEDITIONARY CORPS, *Annapolis, Md., October* 15, 1861.

The following instructions are promulgated for the information and guidance of the troops composing this command:

I. The troops will embark on the transports, which will be specially assigned to brigades and regiments. The senior officer on board each transport will assign each company, when embarked, its position, and see that each man has been assigned a place or bunk, which assignment will remain permanent while on board.

II. The arms, accouterments, and knapsack of each man will be disposed of with a view to convenience and security, and the ammunition, in cartridge-boxes, will be so placed as to be entirely secure from fire.

III. Every precaution will be taken against fire. Smoking between decks or in the cabins will be prohibited. No lights will be permitted between decks, except such ship-lanterns as may be directed to be suspended in secure positions.

IV. As transports on sea voyages can carry but a limited supply of water, every precaution will be taken to prevent waste or its unnecessary use. The daily allowance per man, including that required for cooking purposes, will be limited to one gallon, and the allowance for each horse to three gallons. This quantity may be reduced by the senior officer on each transport, if deemed necessary.

V. A sufficient guard will be mounted daily, with side-arms, and so posted as will best prevent fire and any improper use of water.

VI. No arm will be loaded on board of transports without proper orders. Both arms and ammunition will be kept in a serviceable condition, and at all times in readiness for use at a moment's notice. Reserve ammunition will be deposited in a safe position, the master of the transport to be consulted as to its location.

VII. The master of each transport will be requested by the senior officer on board to provide wind-sails sufficient to keep the men below decks comfortable at all times.

VIII. Much attention will be paid to the cooking. Such arrangements will be made with the masters of transports as will insure a regular supply of meals to all. The caboose will be kept free of all persons not sent to it on duty. Fancy cooking—such, for instance, as frying meats and dough in fat—is prohibited. Soups, boiled meats, and hard bread compose the true and healthy diet of the soldier on transports at sea.

IX. The Quartermaster's Department will supply the proper disinfecting agents to secure the comfort and health of the command.

By order of Gen. T. W. Sherman:

L. H. PELOUZE,
Captain, Fifteenth Infantry, Act. Asst. Adjt. General.

WASHINGTON, *October* 17, 1861.

General THOMAS W. SHERMAN, *Annapolis:*

If General McClellan should consent to spare the New York Seventy-ninth Regiment to join your expedition with General Stevens, do you want them, and have you transportation for them? Answer immediately.

THOMAS A. SCOTT.

ANNAPOLIS, *October* 17, 1861.

Hon. THOMAS A. SCOTT,
Assistant Secretary of War:

Have received your dispatch. I want the Highlanders (Seventy-ninth), and I have transportation. Send them on immediately.

T. W. SHERMAN.

WAR DEPARTMENT, *October* 17, 1861.

General MCCLELLAN:

If Generals Stevens and Sherman want the New York Seventy-ninth to go with expedition, can you spare them without serious loss or inconvenience? Please answer.

THOMAS A. SCOTT.

CAMP GRIFFIN, *October* 17, 1861.

Hon. THOMAS A. SCOTT,
Assistant Secretary of War:

I gave General Sherman all the regiments he asked for. At least two of those originally intended for him, and promised to me, have been diverted from me. The artillery promised me to replace Hamilton's battery have not been given to me. I will not consent to one other man being detached from this army for that expedition. I need far more than I now have to save this country, and cannot spare any disciplined regiment. Instead of diminishing this army, true policy would dictate its immediate increase to a large extent. It is the task of the Army of the Potomac to decide the question at issue. No outside expedition can effect the result. I hope that I will not again be asked to detach anybody.

GEO. B. MCCLELLAN,
Major-General, Commanding.

GENERAL ORDERS, No. 15. } HEADQUARTERS EXPEDITIONARY CORPS,
Annapolis, Md., October 17, 1861.

The embarkation of the troops of this division will commence immediately and in accordance with the following order and assignment:

I. First Brigade, Brigadier-General Viele, commanding.

Third Regiment New Hampshire Volunteers to steamer Atlantic.

Forty-sixth Regiment New York Volunteers to steamer Webster.

Forty-seventh Regiment New York Volunteers to steamer Roanoke.

Forty-eighth Regiment New York Volunteers to steamer Empire City.

Eighth Regiment Maine Volunteers to steamer Ariel.

The horses and wagons pertaining to the First Brigade are assigned to the steamers Belvidere and Philadelphia.

II. Second Brigade, Brig. Gen. I. I. Stevens, commanding.

Roundhead Regiment Pennsylvania Volunteers to steamer Ocean Queen.

Five companies of the Fiftieth Regiment Pennsylvania Volunteers to steamer Ocean Queen.

Five companies of the Fiftieth Regiment Pennsylvania Volunteers to steamer Vanderbilt.

Eighth Regiment Michigan Volunteers to steamer Vanderbilt.

The horses and wagons pertaining to the Second Brigade are assigned to the steamer Ben De Ford.

III. Third Brigade, Brig. Gen. H. G. Wright, commanding.

Fourth Regiment New Hampshire Volunteers to the steamer Baltic.

Sixth Regiment Connecticut Volunteers to the steamers Marion and Parkersburg.

Seventh Regiment Connecticut Volunteers to the steamer Illinois.

Ninth Regiment Maine Volunteers to the steamer Coatzacoalcos.

The horses and wagons pertaining to the Third Brigade are assigned to the steamer Baltic.

IV. Hamilton's light battery to steamer Ericsson.

V. The Battalion of Volunteer Engineers (now at Fortress Monroe, Va.) to the steamer Star of the South.

VI. The regiment of Rhode Island volunteers (now at Fortress Monroe, Va.) to the steamer Cahawba.

VII. Division headquarters to the steamer Atlantic and the horses pertaining thereto to the steamer Ericsson.

VIII. Each brigade commander will select from the transports assigned to his brigade the one upon which the headquarters will embark, the name of the transport thus selected to be reported to these headquarters.

IX. The horses and equipments of mounted officers will, as far as practicable, be so placed as to be disembarked at the shortest notice.

X. Brigade commanders will issue and enforce such orders as will effectually prevent any person not belonging to the military organization from embarking on their transports, and will prevent any stores from being shipped but the necessary provisions and supplies, including the authorized allowance of camp and garrison equipage.

XI. No sutler but the one appointed by the Secretary of War will be recognized in any manner or received on board the transports belonging to this command.

By order of General T. W. Sherman:

L. H. PELOUZE,
Captain, Fifteenth Infantry, Actg. Asst. Adjt. General.

GENERAL ORDERS, No. 16.
HEADQUARTERS EXPEDITIONARY CORPS,
Annapolis, Md., October 17, 1861.

It is confidently expected that General Orders, No. 15, current series, from these headquarters will be enforced with vigor and promptitude. The officers concerned will infuse into their men a spirit of energy adequate to the occasion; they will see that their respective commands move with life and alacrity; that all work is so systematized that every man and body of men may work to advantage.

Each officer and man will apply his every effort to the task set before him, and will exhibit at all times and upon all occasions that spirit of energy and industry so essential in every well-disciplined command and without which successful war cannot be prosecuted.

Whilst the general commanding expects in this way the support of his command, he regrets to say that he has recently noticed a few instances of a lax, loose, and lazy bearing on the part of a few men when on duty. This spirit, if generally diffused, would ignore all usefulness and destroy all prospects of successful operations.

Commanders should at once bring to their official notice all cases of this nature, and if shame will not bring the offender to a sense of duty, punishment must be resorted to.

II. All horses and wagons that the chief quartermaster decides cannot be taken on the transports will be transferred to the quartermaster of the post, with the requisite invoices.

By order Brig. Gen. T. W. Sherman:

L. H. PELOUZE,
Captain, Fifteenth Infantry, Actg. Asst. Adjt. General.

WASHINGTON, *October* 18, 1861.

General THOMAS W. SHERMAN, *Annapolis, Md.:*

Your dispatch of yesterday received and shown to General McClellan. I have promised him to not break his army here without his consent.

I do not think I shall go to Annapolis.

A. LINCOLN.

GENERAL ORDERS, No. 19. } HEADQUARTERS EXPEDITIONARY CORPS, *Steamer Atlantic, October* 23, 1861.

This command will sail for its destination in a very few days, under convoy of a naval squadron, commanded by Commodore DuPont. The transports will move in three columns and in rear of the main body of the squadron. The transports belonging to the First Brigade will compose the right column, those of the Second Brigade and the Third Rhode Island Regiment the center, and those of the Third Brigade and the Battalion of Volunteer Engineers the left column. Each vessel will retain its order in column, and the columns will move in parallel lines, equidistant, regulating from the right. The sail vessels and other transports inadequate to the task of sailing with the fleet will be towed by such steamers as the chief quartermaster may designate. Commodore DuPont, in co-operation with the land forces, has kindly made such an arrangement of his fleet as will secure the transports from unnecessary diffusion, and all senior officers on transports and masters of vessels will enter into the spirit of and conform to these arrangements, a plan of which will be duly given.

II. The general commanding announces to the expeditionary corps that it is intended to make a descent on the enemy's coast, and probably under circumstances which will demand the utmost vigilance, coolness, and intrepidity on the part of every officer and man of his command. In consideration of the justness and holiness of our cause, of the ardent patriotism which has prompted the virtuous and industrious citizens of our land to fly to their country's standard in the moment of her peril, he most confidently believes that he will be effectually and efficiently supported in his efforts to overthrow a zealous, active, and wily foe, whose cause is unholy and principles untenable.

III. On the approach of the transports to the place of disembarkment each brigade commander will anchor his transports as near each other as practicable, and will at the proper time superintend the disembarkment of his brigade. The surf-boats, with other means for disembarkment on hand, are believed to be capable of landing at once from 3,000 to 4,000 men. The surf-boats are of different sizes. Two of the largest may take the officers and men of a company of 100 men; two of the next size a company of 70 men, and so on in proportion. The other means of transportation may take the remainder of a brigade, with probably one or two sections of field artillery.

IV. The disembarkment will be made in three lines. The first line will be the brigade of General Wright, flanked by two sections of Hamilton's light battery, and accompanied by the squad of Regular Sappers and Miners, and two companies of Serrell's volunteer engineers, with a sufficient supply of intrenching tools and sand bags. The second line will be the brigade of General Stevens, and, if necessary, accompanied by a section of Hamilton's battery and two field pieces, to be manned by a company of the Third Rhode Island Regiment. The reserve will be composed of General Viele's brigade, the remaining portion of Serrell's volunteer engineers, and the Third Rhode Island Regiment, and will be disposed of according to circumstances.

V. The boats of not only each company, but of each regiment and brigade, will land abreast as far as practicable, and in the order of battle. The utmost effort will be made to effect the landing in that order. Should it be found impracticable to land immediately from the lighters, then the surf-boats, when emptied, will immediately proceed to the rapid landing of the men from the lighters, and as soon as the whole line is landed all the boats will return and bring forward in like manner the troops of the second line, and so with the reserve.

VI. The general officers and commanders of battalions, &c., will be furnished in time with the plan of descent and the particular order of battle. It is probable that the first line will have to conquer the ground on which to establish itself, and, if opposed by greatly superior numbers, to maneuver, and perhaps to momentarily intrench. If not seriously opposed, the first line, after overcoming immediate difficulties, will continue to drive backward the enemy, but will not venture beyond supporting distance from the shore before the landing of the general commanding or without his special orders.

VII. The commanding officer of the naval squadron has kindly consented to furnish 300 sailors to assist in launching and manning the surf-boats, and he appeals to the patriotism of the masters, mates, and sailors of the several transports to furnish an additional number of coxswains and oarsmen. Any deficiency of oarsmen in surf-boats will be supplied from the platoons on board of these respectively, so that each boat, when ready, may be rapidly rowed ashore. The soldier oarsmen will land and form with their platoons.

VIII. General and field officers, with their respective staffs, will endeavor to obtain landing boats for themselves, with the necessary coxswains and oarsmen from the transports and other hired vessels of the fleet.

IX. The senior officer of the troops on board each transport will arrange with the master for voluntary helps of this kind which may be needed and can be given, and will make a special report to these headquarters as early as practicable of the assistance thus rendered.

X. As soon as the landing shall have been effected the surf and other landing boats will revert to the chief quartermaster for immediate supplies.

XI. The sick and non-effective men will remain on board the several transports until provision can be made for them on shore. The non-effectives will be specially charged with the care of the sick, under directions to be left by the respective medical officers.

XII. Medical officers, excepting one from each brigade, to be designated by the respective brigade commanders, will land with the troops. The three medical officers left afloat will, under the directions of the medical director, divide the duty of visiting all the sick on board, including those of the Third Rhode Island Regiment and the Battalion of Volunteer Engineers.

By order of Brig. Gen. T. W. Sherman:

L. H. PELOUZE,
Captain, Fifteenth Infantry, Actg. Asst. Adjt. General.

CIRCULAR.] HEADQUARTERS EXPEDITIONARY CORPS,
U. S. F. Wabash, October 26, 1861.

In consequence of the present unexpected delay in putting to sea, on account of unfavorable weather, it is considered indispensable to impress upon the minds of all commanding officers of troops on transports the strict necessity of conforming to orders heretofore given, respecting cleanliness and the economy in the use of water.

To still further secure the command from an eventual want of water, all steam transports will, whilst lying still, be occupied in condensing as much water as practicable.

It is probable that some of the transports will hold their troops from twenty to thirty days.

All commanding officers will see the necessity of having everything in readiness for a prompt debarkation. The field artillery particularly will have its guns, carriages, horses and harness ready to disembark without unnecessary delay. All obstructions on board preventing this promptness must be removed as soon as the transports get to sea.

Every transport, as well as the troops on board, must be ready to sail at any moment, when the proper signals are given.

By order of Brig. Gen. T. W. Sherman:

L. H. PELOUZE,
Captain, Fifteenth Infantry, Actg. Asst. Adjt. General.

HEADQUARTERS EXPEDITIONARY CORPS,
Hampton Roads, October 27, 1861.

General M. C. MEIGS,
Quartermaster-General U. S. Army, Washington, D. C.:

The unexpected delay of the expedition at this point, owing to the stormy and unfavorable state of the weather for our light vessels and tugs, will, it is very much to be apprehended, produce a failure in our supply of water.

Our horses have already been on board some thirteen days and men a week. Although all the vessels were loaded with all the water they could carry, some of the transports are already reduced to a supply for nine days.

Major Belger has been written to, with an urgent request for him to forward immediately to this place 200,000 gallons, and as we shall leave here the very first favorable moment, the post quartermaster will have sealed instructions for the water transports, directing to what point they shall proceed.

The resources of Fort Monroe are not at our disposal, even if they had more water than they want themselves.

Will you please to instruct Major Belger to promptly send forward the water asked for? The weather is such that Commodore DuPont decides it yet unsafe for our fleet to put to sea.

Very respectfully, your obedient servant,

T. W. SHERMAN,
Brigadier-General, Commanding.

HEADQUARTERS DEPARTMENT OF VIRGINIA,
Fort Monroe, October 28, 1861.

Hon. SIMON CAMERON,
Secretary of War:

SIR: By special messenger I would inform you that the expedition under the command of Brigadier-General Sherman is still in Hampton Roads. Brigadier-General Sherman has been here since Tuesday last. On his arrival, in order to hasten his departure, I gave him a large amount of supplies, among others 350,000 rounds of cartridges. It appears that his ammunition was stored at the bottom of his ships, and could not be got at short of four days. To prevent this delay I granted him the ammunition, which leaves me less than 100 rounds to each man of my command, which I earnestly request that you will have increased to the number delivered to Brigadier-General Sherman with as little delay as practicable. When I gave the ammunition I was under the impression that the expedition would leave immediately. It is now nearly seven days since the general received the ammunition, and the fleet is still in port, and when it will sail is more than I can tell. I am now furnishing ten days' rations for the soldiers, and for the same reasons assigned for the ammunition furnished, that their rations are stowed where they cannot be got at without several days' delay. I will venture to assert that a worse-managed expedition could not well be contrived. Every opportunity has been given the rebels to be prepared to meet them at any point on the coast. Among other opportunities a deserter from the fleet, a petty officer (the party referred to I find upon inquiry to be Mr. Hale, a young officer connected with the Navy, and, I believe, a relative of Secretary Welles, a native of Virginia), carried with him the signal book, and, as he said, a knowledge of the destination of the expedition.

My object, however, in making this communication is to hasten a supply of ammunition for small-arms. In supplying Brigadier-General Sherman's command, I have not now 100 rounds for each man remaining in store. I would again call your attention to the garrison of Fort Monroe. I am deficient in artillerists, both in officers and men. I could not man more than ten guns. I made a special report on this subject to Lieutenant General Scott, 26th instant.

I have the honor to be, very respectfully, your obedient servant,

JOHN E. WOOL,
Major-General.

Abstract from return of the Expeditionary Corps, commanded by Brig. Gen. Thomas W. Sherman, for October 28, 1861.

Commands.	Present.				
	Officers.		Men.		Aggregate.
	For duty.	Total.	For duty.	Total.	
Division staff	26	26	25	25	51
First Brigade	185	192	3,682	3,796	3,988
Second Brigade	137	141	3,015	3,196	3,337
Third Brigade	147	153	3,574	3,747	3,900
Troops not brigaded	61	62	1,242	1,315	1,377
Total	556	574	11,538	12,079	12,653

Organization of the Expeditionary Corps, commanded by Brig. Gen. Thomas W. Sherman, U. S. Army, October 28, 1861.

First Brigade.

Brig. Gen. EGBERT L. VIELE.

8th Maine, Col. Lee Strickland.
3d New Hampshire, Col. Enoch Q. Fellows.
46th New York, Col. Rudolph Rosa.
47th New York, Col. Henry Moore.
48th New York, Col. James H. Perry.

Second Brigade.

Brig. Gen. ISAAC I. STEVENS.

8th Michigan, Col. William M. Fenton.
79th New York, Lieut. Col. William H. Nobles.
50th Pennsylvania, Col. B. C. Christ.
100th Pennsylvania, Col. Daniel Leasure.

Third Brigade.

Brig. Gen. HORATIO G. WRIGHT.

6th Connecticut, Col. John L. Chatfield.
7th Connecticut, Col. Alfred H. Terry.
9th Maine, Col. Rishworth Rich.
4th New Hampshire, Col. Thomas J. Whipple.

Troops not brigaded.

1st New York Engineers, Col. Edward W. Serrell.
3d Rhode Island, Col. Nathaniel W. Brown.
3d U. S. Artillery, Battery E, Capt. John Hamilton.

CIRCULAR.] HEADQUARTERS EXPEDITIONARY CORPS,
U. S. F. Wabash (off Port Royal, S. C.), Nov. 4, 1861.

The general commanding has the unparalleled gratification to congratulate the officers and men of his command upon their safe arrival at this point, after a most perilous and tempestuous passage from Hampton Roads.

Some vessels probably have been lost, but it is believed that the hand of Providence has saved the lives of all. For this let us be thankful to the Ruler of our destinies, in whom we must ever trust for protection.

Soldiers! Let the dangers you have encountered and the anxieties you have experienced be an incentive to a greater exertion on your part in the holy cause in which you are engaged. The eyes of your country are upon you. She expects you to conquer. Deceive not her expectations. Be cool and determined. Act only at the command of your officers, and be prompt to do so. Be not led away by a vain and spontaneous enthusiasm, nor restrained by a want of willingness or alacrity. Let your officers judge when you are to act; to do otherwise would lead to confusion and disgrace. Some of you have not had proper opportunities for instruction; let coolness, firmness, and the cold steel take the place of better instruction.

Soldiers! You are contending against an enemy who depreciates your manhood, who denies that your prowess is equal to his. Belie this sentiment, or you will disgrace yourselves and your nativity.

By order of Brig. Gen. T. W. Sherman:

L. H. PELOUZE,
Captain, Fifteenth Infantry, Actg. Asst. Adjt. General.

HILTON HEAD,
Port Royal, S. C., November 9, 1861.

GENERAL: I have the honor to report the arrival at this place of all the vessels which I chartered in New York, having on board General Sherman's entire command, with the greater part of the supplies. For your approval of the care exercised in the selection of vessels for the transportation of troops, I wish to mention that we rode out one of the severest gales which have occurred on this coast for a long time without losing a single man.

The fleet left Hampton Roads on the 29th of October. On the 1st of November it encountered a heavy gale, which scattered it in every direction. The quartermaster's steamer (Winfield Scott, Captain Seldy) lost all her cargo, and was so much injured that she can never leave this port. The quartermaster's steamer (Union) with stores, it is reported, went ashore on the South Carolina coast, and was lost; her crew taken prisoners. The steamers Peerless and Osceola, sent by Colonel Tompkins from New York, with cattle, were lost. The crew of the Peerless was saved. The steamer Belvidere, from Baltimore, with horses, was compelled to put back to Hampton Roads, having thrown overboard a portion of her horses. On the 3d of November the fleet arrived at this place. It gives me great pleasure to report that so far the expedition has been a complete success. We are now in complete possession of the finest harbor in the South, where the largest ships can enter and ride at anchor in safety. In the heart of the richest part of the cotton district, with direct and easy communication by water inland with Charleston and Savannah, it possesses unrivaled advantages for a quartermaster's and naval depot, and in the future a great commercial city must grow up here.

A place of such importance cannot be held for any great length of time without large re-enforcements. All the stores have now to be landed through the surf; a laborious, tedious operation, detaining these large ships a long time in discharging their cargo. Economy requires that a substantial wharf should be built. I have made a requisition on Colonel Tompkins for a steam pile-driver and scow and the plank necessary to cover the pier. If this meets your approval, I hope that Colonel Tompkins may be directed to send them as soon as practicable.

The water ships have arrived. The brilliant victory gained by the naval fleet enabled the troops to land much sooner than was expected when the request for water was sent, and rendered our wants in this respect less pressing than they would have been under other circumstances. An abundance of good water can be had by sinking wells.

In order to insure regularity and promptness in forwarding supplies to the troops, I would respectfully call your attention to the propriety of keeping two or three first-class steamers like the Atlantic and Baltic running constantly between this place and New York.

Contraband negroes are coming in in great numbers. In two days

150 have come in, mostly able-bodied men, and it will soon be necessary to furnish them with coarse clothing.

With great respect, your obedient servant,

R. SAXTON,
Captain, U. S. Army, Assistant Quartermaster.

[Indorsements.]

NOVEMBER 15, 1861.

Respectfully referred to the Secretary of War. The requisition for pile-driver has been approved. The safe escape of all the vessels engaged by Captain Saxton did credit to his care and judgment.

There should be a regular line of large steamers between New York and Port Royal now running as transports. I know of none better than the Atlantic and Baltic, and I suggest the propriety of purchasing instead of chartering for the consideration of the Department of War.

Respectfully,

M. C. MEIGS,
Quartermaster-General.

NOVEMBER 16, 1861.

I read the indorsement to the Secretary, who decides that the Baltic and Atlantic may be purchased. Requested Mr. Tucker to see to this.

M. C. MEIGS,
Quartermaster-General.

GENERAL ORDERS, No. 24. } HEADQUARTERS EXPEDITIONARY CORPS, *Hilton Head, S. C., November 11, 1861.*

The general commanding is pained to know that some of the troops of his command have, without orders, invaded the premises of private individuals and committed gross depredations upon their property, and what he considers a matter of still graver character and most prejudicial to the discipline of the command and the interests of the service is, that some commissioned officers (it is hoped but few) have not only connived at these outrages, but have actually participated in them.

The rights of citizens to be secure in their property and the character of the American Army are too important to allow such transactions to go unrebuked. The first duty of the soldier is the protection of the citizen. The political character of the citizen is not to be judged and weighed in this manner by the soldier, and there must be by him no molestation of his lawful rights. The Government alone is to decide how far the present unfortunate condition of this portion of the country is to authorize or demand a departure from the well-settled principles of American law.

Brigade commanders and all other commanding officers will at once see that these depredations cease, and endeavor to ascertain the names of the perpetrators, that they may be brought to justice.

All horses, cattle, and other private property which have been taken off any of the plantations and now in the hands of officers or soldiers, will be immediately surrendered to the chief quartermaster, who will cause an inventory to be taken of the same, stating, if practicable, to whom the property belongs, and make a report to these headquarters.

II. All public property left by the enemy, such as muskets, accouterments, &c., and now in the hands of soldiers or citizens, will be immediately turned over to the chief ordnance officer, Lieut. Francis J. Shunk.

III. All persons found outside the pickets without a pass will be arrested and reported to these headquarters.

By order of Brigadier-General T. W. Sherman:

L. H. PELOUZE,
Captain, Fifteenth Infantry, Actg. Asst. Adjt. General.

HEADQUARTERS EXPEDITIONARY CORPS,
Hilton Head, S. C., November 15, 1861.

The ADJUTANT-GENERAL U. S. ARMY,
Washington, D. C.:

SIR: I have the honor to report that, in consequence of the difficulty and great amount of labor in landing our stores, some delay must necessarily occur in continuing operations. This delay is as distasteful to us as it must be to the authorities at Washington. In the mean while a matter of the first importance is to erect proper defenses at Hilton Head as well as to strengthen the land side of the fort, to the end of securing this important point with the least number of men. This is being done, and a plan of the same will be furnished as soon as it can be prepared.

In conducting operations here two modes suggest themselves:

First, to hold Hilton Head and Phillip's Island with a strong force, and proceed with a sufficient force, in connection with the naval fleet under Commodore DuPont, and open another important harbor. This would be carrying out the original and actual object of the expedition, as I understand it, and for which object only our means have been provided.

Second, to occupy the points first mentioned as well as Beaufort as a base of operations, and act thence on a line of operations embracing Port Royal Island and the road to Pocotaligo, the nearest point of the Savannah and Charleston Railroad, into the southern counties of the State, threatening Savannah, &c., or to operate from the base of Hilton Head through the interior creeks and channels leading into the Savannah River below Savannah and near Fort Jackson, thus laying siege to Savannah and cutting off Fort Pulaski.

For these last operations the former would require more land transportation than we are provided with, and the latter would require an outfit of boats, that we are also insufficiently provided with. The former would also require a small cavalry force. The only course, therefore, at present is, notwithstanding the apparent opening for more brilliant operations, the first and original plan.

The surrounding country evacuated by the whites, as described in my last, has upon it an abundance of valuable property, including ungathered crops and cotton mostly gathered. I have directed all the means of transportation, such as boats, scows, wagons, &c., to be collected for the use of the Army; but in regard to other private property, such as can be made of no injury to us in the operations of the enemy, I have directed not to be interfered with. This, however, is a difficult matter, and there exists too great a propensity to rob and pillage the houses and plantations left in charge only of the blacks. I hope to receive instructions on this point; that is, in a country entirely deserted by its white inhabitants, all of whom are known to be disloyal, how far I am to authorize the appropriation of private property.

Very respectfully, your obedient servant,

T. W. SHERMAN,
Brigadier-General, Commanding.

GENERAL ORDERS, No. 29. } HDQRS. EXPEDITIONARY CORPS, *Hilton Head, S. C., November* 15, 1861.

* * * * * * *

III. The fort on Hilton Head will be known as Fort Welles, and the one on Bay Point, heretofore called Fort Beauregard, will be known as Fort Seward.

* * * * * * *

By order of Brig. Gen. T. W. Sherman:

L. H. PELOUZE,
Captain, Fifteenth Infantry, Actg. Asst. Adjt. General.

HEADQUARTERS EXPEDITIONARY CORPS,
Hilton Head, S. C., November 17, 1861.

The ADJUTANT-GENERAL U. S. ARMY,
Washington, D. C.:

SIR: I have the honor to report that the position of the forces here necessitates the most active operations during the coming winter, the climate and localities of these islands rendering it impracticable to carry on operations upon them after April next. We have now possession of the valuable harbors of Port Royal and Saint Helena. One more will probably be in our possession in a short time. A fort should be constructed on Hunting Island, to secure that important roadstead of Saint Helena. After well securing these important points, and establishing a firm base from which to operate inland, there will not be left a very large force disposable for internal operations. I would therefore recommend that an additional force of 10,000 men be sent to this point as early as practicable, and among them some regular troops, including some companies of artillery, for garrisoning the forts; the volunteer force not being adapted to the artillery service.

We shall require three or four steamers, drawing not over 9 feet, and capable of conveying 800 or 1,000, for operations in the rivers and creeks, and a couple of ferry-boats, drawing not over 5 or 6 feet of water, would be of the greatest advantage. We would require also about 100 row-boats, capable of carrying from 40 to 50 men each, with kedges and oars. A few of them should be large enough and so constructed as to transport pieces of artillery with their carriages, including siege guns. I also take the liberty of recommending that the light-ship formerly stationed at the entrance of Port Royal channel be replaced, and that the light-house on Hunting Islands, Saint Helena Sound, be relighted. It is my duty also to recommend that some more engineer officers be sent here. The duties of that corps are too important and too extended to be left to the few we have here. It is also important to have at least three more ordnance sergeants here for the several artillery stations, the two heretofore furnished having been absorbed at Forts Welles and Seward.

Very respectfully, your obedient servant,

T. W. SHERMAN,
Brigadier-General, Commanding Expeditionary Corps.

GENERAL ORDERS, No. 32. } HEADQUARTERS EXPEDITIONARY CORPS, *Hilton Head, S. C., November* 17, 1861.

The following troops will be put in readiness to embark, as follows:

Forty-sixth Regiment New York Volunteers on the steamer Empire City.

Forty-seventh Regiment New York Volunteers on the steamer Star of the South.

Forty-eighth Regiment New York Volunteers on the steamer Cahawba.

Eighth Regiment Maine Volunteers on the steamer Ariel.

Third Regiment New Hampshire Volunteers six companies on the steamer Daniel Webster and four companies on the steamer Marion.

Two companies of the Regiment of Volunteer Engineers on the steamer Oriental.

Three companies of the Third Regiment Rhode Island Volunteers on the steamer Matanzas.

By order of Brig. Gen. T. W. Sherman:

L. H. PELOUZE,
Acting Assistant Adjutant-General.

HEADQUARTERS EXPEDITIONARY CORPS,
Hilton Head, S. C., November 25, 1861.

The ADJUTANT-GENERAL U. S. ARMY,
Washington, D. C.:

SIR: I have the honor to report that we have found stowed away on Ladies Island two light-house apparatus, including lamps and reflectors, with a large quantity of oil. I thought it best to turn the same over to Commodore DuPont, as he has better facilities for keeping them safe and secure than we have. He had before one also which he found at Beaufort.

It having been learned by a reconnaissance sent to the neighboring island that the forts on Tybee Island had been deserted by the rebels, I informed Commodore DuPont of the same, whereupon he yesterday started some gunboats down there, and discovered it to be a fact. We have therefore another light-house, which should be relighted at once.

Very respectfully, your obedient servant,

T. W. SHERMAN,
Brigadier-General, Commanding.

HEADQUARTERS EXPEDITIONARY CORPS,
Hilton Head, S. C., November 25, 1861.

The ADJUTANT-GENERAL U. S. ARMY,
Washington, D. C.:

SIR: Our scouts have found the fort on Ladies Island covering the Coosaw River, which was deserted by the rebels at the time of the capture of this place. The scouts spiked the guns, but we shall remove them as soon as practicable to this place. Our scouts have been up into the vicinity of Port Royal Ferry, and discovered that the advanced outpost of the enemy is at that point and that their main body is at Pocotaligo. There is another large force also collecting at Grahamville, nearer to Savannah, and also on the railroad, the advance post of which is at Bluffton, a small village some 10 or 14 miles from here. The object of these forces is undoubtedly to protect the railroad and cover the interior of the State against our invasion in that direction, which, from all the information I can gather, they are daily expecting.

I have already briefly referred to our facilities, or rather want of facilities, for such an operation, and the propriety of confining ourselves with our present means to establishing a firm and secure base on the coast, and thus be prepared for any ulterior movements inland that the service may demand.

Very respectfully, your obedient servant,

T. W. SHERMAN,
Brigadier-General, Commanding Expedition.

OFFICE CHIEF TOPOGRAPHICAL ENGINEER E. C.,
Hilton Head, S. C., November 25, 1861.

Capt. LOUIS H. PELOUZE,
Fifteenth Infantry, Acting Assistant Adjutant-General:

SIR: In accordance with instructions from General Sherman, I have examined the ferries from this island to the main-land, situated at Ferry Point and Spanish Wells, and have to report as follows:

The distance from Ferry Point to the large white house opposite is 2,714 yards, or 1.54 miles. The landing on this side is tolerably good, the slope of the beach being sufficiently abrupt to allow small boats to land, and vessels of 15 feet draught to come within 50 yards of the shore; but from the intermixture of sand and mud it is hardly firm enough for anything but infantry to march upon. The shape of the point and the approaches to it are such that a small body of men could easily prevent the landing of a hostile force. A flat or marsh 600 yards wide, at the large white house, extends entirely around the south point of the main-land between May River and the small creek on the east side of the ferry, thus rendering the debarkation of troops in numbers on the main impracticable. At high tide small boats can be run over the flat in front of the house and infantry landed, but at low tide the only means of approaching the shore is by a small slough running nearly east through the flat. In this way one or two boats at a time can be pushed to within 200 yards of the house, but the men can only reach the solid ground by bogging through the mud. The negroes living on the adjacent plantations inform me that this ferry is only used at high tide, and at such times men, horses, and carriages can be crossed in light-draught scows.

Spanish Wells is situated opposite the mouth of May River. It has a good landing, on a tolerably firm sand beach, and deep water at 50 yards from shore. The first landing on the main is up May River, distant about 5 miles, at a point in front of the farm-houses of Mrs. Calk. At this place boats of considerable draught can lie alongside the shore, and land men by putting out the ordinary stage-planks. The channel all the way is deep enough for boats drawing 15 feet. This place is in every way suitable for a steam ferry. Its communications with Hilton Head are by the usual roads of the island.

The rebel picket of six or eight horsemen did not attempt to resist our landing at Buckingham Ferry, but fled upon our approach. Shortly afterwards the cotton-house on an adjoining plantation, said to belong to a Mr. Baynard, was observed to be on fire, and later in the evening one owned by Mrs. Calk was also set on fire and burned. The pickets on the main-land, stationed at the places of exit, seemed to be intended to keep the negroes from running off rather than to prevent our approach.

I am, sir, very respectfully, your obedient servant,

J. H. WILSON,
First Lieut., Top. Eng., Chief Top. Eng. Exp'y Corps.

HDQRS. OF THE ARMY, ADJUTANT-GENERAL'S OFFICE,
Washington, November 27, 1861.

Brig. Gen. THOMAS W. SHERMAN, U. S. A.,
Port Royal, S. C.:

SIR: Your letters of the 11th,* 15th, and 17th instant have been received. Four additional regiments have been ordered to join your command. The General-in-Chief desires you, through your quartermaster, to seize all cotton and other property which may be used to our prejudice. The cotton and such other articles as may not be required for the use of your command will be shipped by return transports to the quartermaster in New York, there to be sold on public account. The services of negroes will be used in picking, collecting, and packing cotton, as well as in constructing defensive works, &c. Private property of individuals should not be interfered with, unless it be of military utility under the circumstances you mention, and you will be justified in taking measures to prevent pillage or any outrage so far as the exigencies of the service will permit, no matter what relations the persons or property may bear to the United States Government.

I am, sir, very respectfully, your obedient servant,

L. THOMAS,
Adjutant-General.

HEADQUARTERS EXPEDITIONARY CORPS,
Hilton Head, S. C., November 27, 1861.

ADJUTANT-GENERAL U. S. ARMY,
Washington, D. C.:

SIR: For the want of an engineer officer (one being sick, one engaged on a reconnaissance on Saint Helena Sound, and the remaining one necessarily employed here) I went down to Tybee Island last evening, and this morning made a sufficient reconnaissance of that island as to ascertain its general topography and the range of the enemy's guns on Fort Pulaski. I find it not impossible to reduce Pulaski from this island, though it will be a work of time. Mortar and breeching batteries may be constructed so as not to be very seriously annoyed by their guns. I find that their casemate guns will hardly range to the island, while their barbette guns will explode shells upon the island with certainty and considerable accuracy. A further reconnaissance will be made as soon as an engineer officer can be spared.

Not hearing from the Department to-day as to our future operations, (as the Bienville has just returned), I shall have to act from my own judgment alone, or be the cause of a delay in operations that will militate seriously to our disadvantage on account of the rapidity of time that must be made use of to avoid being caught by earliness of spring. In order, therefore, to meet the wants of the operations of this portion of the Army, I have to request that as much cavalry, not exceeding a regiment, ten regiments of infantry, and one regiment of regular artillery be sent here as soon as practicable. The steamboats, ferry-boats, and small boats required were mentioned in my letters of the 17th and 21st. It would be of the greatest advantage in having a small force of regular infantry to leaven the mass of raw volunteers of which this command is composed.

I have also to call the attention of the Department to the proportions

---

*See capture of Fort Walker, &c., p. 5.

we are developing in these operations. Our coast is becoming more and more extended. The operations of the engineer, ordnance, and artillery departments are of the greatest importance. We have not officers enough to manage them, particularly with raw troops, where every man must be instructed to avail anything. I recommend that three more engineer officers, two ordnance officers, and several artillery officers be sent here at once. The want of direction among our raw hands, a direction which the few officers here cannot sufficiently give, is a serious cause of delay in everything we undertake to do. I also ask that an officer of the Quartermaster's Department, of rank and great experience, be sent to control the operations of that department here. A good pontoon bridge would also be desirable here.

Very respectfully, your obedient servant,

T. W. SHERMAN,
Brigadier-General, Commanding.

HEADQUARTERS EXPEDITIONARY CORPS,
Port Royal, S. C., December 4, 1861.

General LORENZO THOMAS,
Adjutant-General U. S. Army, Washington, D. C.:

SIR: Since my letter of the 27th ultimo Tybee, Island has been thoroughly examined, and I inclose herewith a copy of the report of the engineer, Captain Gillmore, whose opinion is in accordance with my own as to the feasibility of shelling Fort Pulaski, and, if not demolishing it, of rendering it untenable. I am about occupying that island with a regiment, and as soon as practicable shall mount some sea-coast guns in the work near the light-house, so as to secure the channel entering the river in the absence of naval vessels.

The reduction of Fort Pulaski will require an armament from the North, and I inclose herewith the amount of ordnance we shall require, which I beg may be forwarded to Tybee Island at the earliest practicable moment, in charge of an active and experienced ordnance officer, if a suitable artillery officer cannot be obtained; for I repeat from former communications that, this command being composed of raw volunteers and a dearth of experienced and instructed officers, an impossibility now exists of obtaining proper hands to direct.

The shelling of Pulaski may have an important effect in favor of some other movement that it might be possible to carry on at the same time.

Very respectfully, your obedient servant,

T. W. SHERMAN,
Bigadier-General, Commanding,

[Inclosure.]

HEADQUARTERS CHIEF ENGINEER OFFICER E. C.,
Hilton Head, S. C., December 1, 1861.

Brig. Gen. THOMAS W. SHERMAN,
Commanding Expeditionary Corps, Hilton Head, S. C.:

SIR: Agreeably to your orders I proceeded in the steamer Ben DeFord, on the afternoon of the 29th ultimo, to Tybee Island, to make a military examination of that locality. We arrived at the Tybee light-house about 7 p. m., when I called upon the senior naval officer present, and made arrangements with him for disembarking my escort (three companies of the Fourth New Hampshire Volunteers, under Major Drew) at

7 o'clock on the following morning. There was some delay in landing, so that I was not ready to commence the work of the day before 9 a. m.

I first endeavored to determine the prominent topographical features of the island, and found that at high water it is nearly divided into two parts by a marsh, or rather two marshes, which make up from the inlet or creek which bounds the island on the southwest. This marsh, or a great part of it, is slightly submerged at high tide, and is difficult to pass even at low water. Men might pick their way across it, but troops could not maneuver on it. To pass from the northwest point of the island, opposite Fort Pulaski, to the southeast part, at the mouth of the inlet, I found it necessary to come back within 300 yards of the light-house.

On the west end of Tybee Island, opposite Fort Pulaski, a parapet for infantry 100 yards long has been thrown across the neck of land to prevent troops from approaching from the direction of the light house. West of this troops have been encamped in bush tents. In a southwesterly direction on the other side of the creek the land appears to be low and marshy, except a small area in a southerly direction from the earthwork, occupied by a house. Returning to the old tower near the light-house, I took its principal dimensions and those of the unfinished earthwork which surrounds it. The tower is built of shell concrete; its walls are 10 feet thick, and it is three stories in height. The first story is 9 feet high, with but one opening (4 feet wide) to the exterior. In it is a good magazine 6 by 7 feet and 7 feet high, with brick walls $3\frac{1}{3}$ feet thick. The second story is about 9 feet high, and has one communication with the exterior. It is on the west side. The third story is pierced with twelve loop-holes, at equal distances apart, 1 by 1 foot at the throat and 2 by 2 feet on the exterior. Four fire-places exist on this story. Above the floor covering the third story the wall is carried up flush with the inside, so as to form a breast-height 4 feet thick and $4\frac{1}{2}$ feet high.

The tower is surrounded by an unfinished field work, which could with little labor be made a strong position, that would control the principal entrance to Savannah River, and thus render efficient services to the blockade in case the fleet should be driven off by stress of weather. One or two siege guns could be mounted on the tower.

I give a rough sketch of the tower and its surroundings.

I proceeded to the southern point of the island along the main shore and thence up the inlet on the southwest, in order to get a near view, if possible, of the battery which controls Warsaw Inlet. My guide (Mr. Ferguson, of the steamer Flag) is of opinion that this battery contains four guns and is located on the second Tybee Island, as it had been firing seaward the day before, when he was on the south point of North Tybee, and had a very good opportunity to judge. A large derrick, plainly visible, with all its rigging, had been erected since he last saw it. I am unable to say whether he is correct or not, and three naval officers with whom I conversed could furnish me with no positive information on the subject. Its thorough examination can only be made by using boats, either directly from the sea or by passing over to the second Tybee Island. To do this would have detained me from Hilton Head all of to-day and a portion of (perhaps all of) to-morrow, as the pilot of the Ben DeFord requires daylight to navigate his ship in. My hurried departure on Friday left my duties here in a condition that would not warrant so lengthy an absence. I therefore thought it proper to report to you for further orders.

The exact position of the battery controlling Warsaw Inlet has, however, no bearing on the prominent points to which my attention was directed in your verbal instructions, viz, the propriety of occupying and holding the first Tybee Island, and the practicability (and, if deemed practicable, the best method) of reducing Fort Pulaski. I deem the reduction of that work practicable by batteries of mortars and rifled guns established on Tybee Island. I think it probable that a nearer position on firm ground (though very shallow, and therefore ill-adapted to mortar and sunken batteries) can be found on the island west of Tybee. I would establish these batteries from 20 to 25 yards apart, one gun or one mortar in each, behind the ridge of sand on the shore, westward from the light-house. I would sink the mortar batteries as low as the water would permit, and the guns sufficiently low to leave a high parapet in front. On the sides and rear of each I would have a high mound of earth, and I should cover each with a horizontal bombproof shelter of logs, covered with earth, and supported by logs planted vertically in the ground. The embrasures for the guns should be deep, narrow, and of very little splay. I estimate that after once obtaining the range five-eighths of the shells from mortars can be lodged inside of the fort. I would have enough mortars to throw one shell a minute into the fort, and as many guns as mortars. The batteries should operate day and night. For landing the ordnance required for these operations I would have built two or three broad flat-bottomed bateaux or scows, such as are commonly used on rope ferries. I think these could be built here.

There are now probably at Fort Pulaski 700 good troops. About 200 landed yesterday, and the Navy officers informed me that at least 500 have entered the fort within the last three days, while some (probably raw recruits or portions of the Home Guard) have gone away. It may be their design to land on Tybee and hold the west end of it, to prevent the erection of batteries against the fort. I therefore recommend the immediate occupation of Tybee Island by one good regiment until the question of attempting the reduction of Fort Pulaski be determined.

I learned while at Tybee that offers have been made by negroes to burn two of the principal bridges on the railroad between Charleston and Savannah. One of these bridges is said to be nearly two miles long. In a military point of view its destruction would be of great value to us, and I recommend the subject to your attention.

Very respectfully, your obedient servant,

Q. A. GILLMORE,
Captain, and Chief Engineer Expeditionary Corps.

[Indorsement.]

Approved, and I fully concur in the plan of Captain Gillmore for reducing Fort Pulaski, except possibly the use of rifled guns, until their effect has been more fully tested. All that can be done with guns is to shake the walls as far as practicable in a random manner. As the nearest distance at which batteries can be constructed is 1½ miles from Pulaski, if rifled guns are found to be non effective at that distance, which is certain if it is discovered that the shot will not strike point foremost, then I think that a few 10-inch columbiads may be used in addition to the mortars, for they may be employed with solid shot for direct fire against the walls or as mortars for the interior.

It is impracticable to establish batteries nearer Pulaski than above stated, whether on Tybee or the island west of it. A few days before this reconnaissance I drew the fire of the fort, and ascertained that their casemate guns came a little short of the shore at the position of the fort constructed on the narrow neck which Captain Gillmore describes, but that their barbette guns effectually shell the shore. Now, as you proceed west, you are constantly shortening the line between the island and Pulaski. In a word, though guns will be of much importance to assist in the work, yet if the place is to be reduced, it is to be done with mortars of the heaviest caliber, and if it should even turn out that the bombproofs cannot be ruptured, the place can be made untenable.

Respectfully submitted.

T. W. SHERMAN,
Brigadier-General, Commanding.

DECEMBER 4, 1861.

HEADQUARTERS EXPEDITIONARY CORPS,
Hilton Head, S. C., December 6, 1861.

Col. RUDOLPH ROSA,
Commanding Forty-sixth New York Volunteers:

COLONEL: The commanding general directs that you take post with your regiment on North Tybee Island with as little delay as practicable, and at once take up a defensive position, so as to hold the entire island. Your men will occupy as quarters the buildings near the light-house, and you will establish a camp on the clear ground near the light-house, always keeping out pickets at the salient points of the island. Your attention is particularly called to the narrow neck of land west of the light-house, as a point which should always be guarded. The work thrown up by the enemy at this point should be torn down to the ground as soon as possible, and, to avoid the effects of the fire from Fort Pulaski, this should be done in the night. You must take every precaution against being surprised, and in the mean time take particular care that the works thrown up about the light-house are not injured or defaced in any way, as guns are to be mounted in them as soon as they can be got there. You will take particular care of your supplies, and see that they are not in any way wasted or destroyed. You will see that vessels sent there are unloaded as soon as possible and sent back to this place. You will keep these headquarters informed of all passing events.

Very respectfully, your obedient servant,

L. H. PELOUZE,
Captain, Fifteenth Infantry, Acting Assistant Adjutant-General.

CAMP NINTH MAINE REGIMENT,
December 6, 1861.

Capt. LOUIS H. PELOUZE,
Acting Assistant Adjutant-General, Sherman's Command:

As directed, on Thursday, October [November] 28, with three companies from this regiment, I relieved Captain Ely at Graham's plantation, and posted pickets at points most advantageous for observation and defense. There had been none previously posted on Baynard's plantation, on the point at Spanish Wells, on account of its distance from the reserve; but I judged it expedient to station a small force there, with a horse, in order to bring me word if anything important should occur.

The picket at that point reports that on Sunday night, December 1, at about 2 o'clock, a boat filled with armed men, apparently, came from the direction of Hunting Island, with the seeming intention of entering

Broad Creek. On hailing and receiving no reply they fired upon the boat, when considerable confusion ensued, the boat turning and rowing rapidly back.

On Saturday I made a reconnaissance of Pinckney Island and vicinity. From Muddy Point, the western extremity of the island, I saw the rebel picket at Topping Landing, on the main, scarcely a rifle-shot distance. From negroes who came over that day I found that they have mounted pickets at Fort Point, 3 miles above Topping Landing, at the junction of Mackay's Creek and Broad River; also at Hog Bluff, 1 mile below Topping Landing; at Buckingham, or Ferry Landing, and on Hunting Island, so called—in reality a peninsula, extending into Skull Creek in a northeasterly direction from Bluffton.

On Monday I reconnoitered Bull's Island. There is a large quantity of corn and cotton there, about 200 head of cattle, and 100 sheep; also a small steam-engine, in good repair, of about 8-inch cylinder and 18-inch stroke. I learned that the rebels constantly come over in the night, in small parties, and carry off the stock. Negroes are constantly coming from the main, and report the rebel force in and about Bluffton to be 400, two companies of which are infantry, composed mostly of boys and old men; the remainder mounted.

On Tuesday night John and Rollin Kirk, brothers, and a Mr. Pinckney, landed on Pinckney Island, for the purpose of taking off the stores; but the negroes getting off in boats and raising an alarm, they left the island without accomplishing their object.

Very respectfully, your obedient servant,

SABINE EMERY,
Major, Commanding Detachment.

HEADQUARTERS DISTRICT OF PORT ROYAL,
Beaufort, S. C., December 8, 1861.

Brig. Gen. THOMAS W. SHERMAN,
Commanding Expeditionary Corps, Hilton Head, S. C.:

GENERAL: At 8.30 o'clock I moved forward towards the ferry with Hamilton's section, under Lieutenant Ransom, and 600 infantry. Captain Burket is now proceeding cautiously, with 100 men, in the same direction, and is about 4 miles from this point. My information is that the enemy are on the island, with 140 cavalry and 100 infantry. It is reported that Captain Barmode was wounded in the arm in the affair of pickets night before last.

I am, sir, very respectfully, your most obedient servant,

ISAAC I. STEVENS,
Brigadier-General, Commanding.

HEADQUARTERS DISTRICT OF PORT ROYAL,
Beaufort, S. C., December 8, 1861.

Lieut. Col. BRENHOLTS,
Commanding Detachment, Port Royal Ferry:

SIR: In command of the three companies of the Fiftieth Pennsylvania Regiment which have been assigned to you, you will move at 5 o'clock to-morrow morning, proceed to Port Royal Ferry, and relieve Lieutenant-Colonel Armstrong, now stationed there. Tents will not be required, as there are buildings sufficient for the accommodation of your command. You will observe closely the ferry, the adjacent main, and the shores of Port Royal Island on either hand. You will send small parties, each under the charge of an officer, to the neighboring plantations, to ascertain the amount of transportation, forage, and provisions they will supply to this command, and will take the necessary measures to save them for its use. It is said the navigation of the river separating the island from the main has been obstructed, both above and below the ferry, by piles driven across. Ascertain the facts and stop further proceedings of the kind. You will take every precaution to guard against surprise; will endeavor to send in daily reports, noting carefully everything you learn in regard to the several points to which your attention has been called.

Truly and respectfully, your most obedient,

ISAAC I. STEVENS,
Brigadier-General, Commanding.

HEADQUARTERS DISTRICT OF PORT ROYAL,
Beaufort, S. C., December 9, 1861.

Brig. Gen. THOMAS W. SHERMAN:

GENERAL: I have received information that since my visit to Port Royal Ferry yesterday the Confederates have commenced the erection of a battery on the main near by, and at a distance of about 1,000 yards from the firm land on the island. I shall at daylight to-morrow morning have the two guns of Hamilton's battery in position, and I shall open fire upon the Confederates. In the event they persist in the construction of the battery I will most urgently ask that a gunboat be sent to the same general vicinity, to co-operate with the land force. It is the manifest purpose of the Confederates to close the passage. Shall a movement be made with the re-enforcement, or perhaps with troops which they can replace, to seize the railroad crossing on Broad River and silence it by works? This would involve crossing the Port Royal Ferry and occupying the main. I will, at all events, stop further proceedings in the defense of the passage between Port Royal and the main, and await your further instructions.

I am, very respectfully, your most obedient servant,

ISAAC I. STEVENS,
Brigadier-General, Commanding.

HEADQUARTERS EXPEDITIONARY CORPS,
Port Royal, S. C., December 10, 1861.

General LORENZO THOMAS,
Adjutant-General U. S. Army, Washington, D. C.:

SIR: I have the honor to report that Otter Island has been occupied by six companies, with an armament sufficient for the protection of Saint Helena Sound and our right flank from any incursions of the enemy by the way of the Ashepoo River and South Edisto from the direction of Charleston.

I have also to report that Tybee Island is now in the occupancy of one regiment, and that an armament is being prepared sufficient to cover the channel leading into Savannah River. This armament, however, is independent of that required for the reduction of Fort Pulaski. I have also to report that I have occupied Port Royal Island with General Stevens' brigade. I very much regret the necessity of this measure, as, although fully convinced of its untenability by the enemy, he has commenced against us a system of blockade by constructing piles and stockades across the Coosaw River, washing the northern and western sides of the island, and thus intercepting the navigation around the island. General Stevens has driven off his pickets, and now holds both sides of Port Royal Ferry. This island can be held by a small force, and I hope to be able to make use of part of that brigade for other movements. At the same time I repeat my former recommendation for more troops here and some cavalry.

The enemy's line can be considered strategically as occupying the country from Ossabaw Sound through Savannah and the important places on the Charleston and Savannah Railroad, viz, Hardeeville, Grahamville, Coosawhatchie, Pocotaligo, and so on to the left. Some point on this line should be struck soon, but nothing but the development of circumstances and the quantity and kind of means in hand will fully solve the important question.

Very respectfully, your obedient servant,

T. W. SHERMAN,
Brigadier-General, Commanding.

P. S.—Three regiments of Pennsylvanians have arrived—one of them without arms.

HEADQUARTERS DISTRICT OF PORT ROYAL,
Beaufort, S. C., December 10, 1861.

Brigadier-General SHERMAN,
Commanding Expeditionary Corps:

GENERAL: Lieutenant Ransom and the section of Hamilton's battery under his command moved at 3 o'clock this morning, and I followed with two members of my staff, Acting Aides-de-Camp Lusk and Taylor, of, respectively, the Highlanders and Fiftieth Pennsylvania, a half hour afterwards. We reached the ferry at daylight. I found, however, on careful examination that the Confederates had not commenced the erection of any works since our occupation of the island. After an examination of the country adjoining the ferry, especially of the old ferry at Seabrook, a mile and a half to the westward of the present ferry, I determined to take positive possession of both sides of the existing ferry, especially as an effort had been made during my absence at Seabrook to fire the ferry building on the island side. Lieutenant Ransom, bringing, under my direction, his battery into position at Stuart's place, fired four shots and dispersed the enemy's pickets, and Lieutenant-Colonel Brenholts, commanding the detachment at the ferry, advanced immediately a picket of 12 men to the ferry, and took possession of both banks, with some four boats. These have since been secured. A small block-house commanding the ferry on the main was destroyed. I left the battery at the ferry, with instructions to return to-morrow, unless, after conference with Lieutenant-Colonel Brenholts, Lieutenant Ransom should be satisfied from the unexpected developments of circumstances he ought to remain at the ferry. In this event he was promptly to advise me by messenger.

I have had the points carefully examined where it was alleged stockades were being built to close the channel. East of the ferry the attempt was actually made, but nothing was accomplished. I have, with the assistance of my aides and scouting parties, examined nearly all portions of the island to-day. The conduct of the troops is exemplary, and there will be considerable additions made to our stock of quartermaster's stores.

I am, sir, very respectfully, yours, most obediently,

ISAAC I. STEVENS,
Brigadier-General Commanding.

HEADQUARTERS U. S. AGENCY,
Dr. Jenkins' Plantation, Saint Helena Island, December 10, 1861.

Brig. Gen. ISAAC I. STEVENS,
Commanding Second Brigade Expeditionary Corps:

SIR: I send you herewith copies of the letters of Brig. Gen. T. W. Sherman and Chief Quartermaster Expeditionary Corps R. Saxton, captain, U. S. Army, appointing me agent for the United States Government "to take possession of all the cotton, commissary and quartermasters' stores, and all public property that I may find in any part of the State of South Carolina deserted by the inhabitants"; also a copy of my letter appointing James A. Suydam my assistant, with full authority with myself. I have taken possession of all the property on Saint Helena, Ladies, and Cat Islands, and have directed Lieutenant Hamilton, of the Fifth Company, and Lieutenant Graham, of the Eighth Company, Seventy-ninth Regiment New York State Militia, to collect and deliver to me all the property on those islands. Mr. Suydam will establish his headquarters at Beaufort, for the purpose of taking possession of all the property, as directed in my instructions.

Respectfully, yours, &c.,

WM. H. NOBLES,
United States Agent.

[Inclosures.]

HEADQUARTERS EXPEDITIONARY CORPS,
Port Royal, S. C., December 3, 1861.

WILLIAM H. NOBLES, Esq.:

SIR: The inhabitants of the deserted islands having been warned of the destruction of their property by the negroes and invited to return and take charge of their plantations, with a promise of ample protection to all loyal citizens, and such invitation and promise of protection having been set at naught by their refusal to return and by several instances of ordering their cotton to be burned, I deem it proper to take steps for the preservation of as much of this article as practicable, in order that such disposition may be made of it as the Government may direct. You are therefore appointed an agent of the United States Government to collect and put into store, at the most convenient points occupied by the United States troops, such quantities of cotton as you may find in any part of the State of South Carolina deserted by the inhabitants. A correct and explanatory statement will be made by you weekly to the headquarters, showing the amount of cotton stored, its quality, whether baled or unbaled, from whose plantation obtained, and all o her information which in your judgment may be necessary to convey a correct idea of its value and the fixing of its ownership, so that the Government will not be at a loss to dispose of the questions of its disposition or of remuneration to its owners if such questions should arise.

You will employ negroes in picking, collecting, and packing the cotton, who on your vouchers, properly made out and certified to, will be paid by the Quartermaster's Department. Your services will be compensated by allowing you 6 per cent. on the market value of the cotton stored as above.

Very respectfully, &c.,

T. W. SHERMAN,
Brigadier-General, Commanding.

OFFICE CHIEF QUARTERMASTER EXPED'Y CORPS,
Fort Welles, S. C., December 6, 1861.

I hereby appoint James Adrian Suydam my assistant in the execution of the above orders from Brigadier-General Sherman and Captain Saxton and of all future orders from their departments to me as agent for the United States Government, his orders and directions to be obeyed as mine, and his acts as agent to be recognized by me.

WM. H. NOBLES,
United States Agent.

HEADQUARTERS DISTRICT OF PORT ROYAL,
Beaufort, S. C., December 10, 1861.

WILLIAM H. NOBLES, Esq., *Collector of Cotton:*

SIR: I have received your letter and inclosures of this date, claiming that you are authorized to take possession of the cotton in the deserted portions of South Carolina, and also of all other public property. The instructions of Brigadier-General Sherman clearly give you authority to collect, gin, and pack cotton. I am not advised of the extent of your authority in regard to quartermaster and commissary stores. The letter of instructions of Captain Saxton does not give the information. I have, however, to inform you that I have taken military possession of Ladies Island, and shall proceed to collect and take charge of such quartermaster and commissary stores as my parties may take possession of—not interfering, however, with your operations in collecting cotton on that island or the quartermaster or commissary stores you have already collected.

I shall not permit you to establish an agency at Beaufort, or to interfere in any way with the steps already taken by the commanding general to collect the cotton and the quartermaster and commissary stores on Port Royal Island and its dependencies.

I am, sir, very respectfully, your most obedient,

ISAAC I. STEVENS,
Brigadier-General, Commanding.

PORT ROYAL, S. C., *December* 10, 1861.

General MEIGS,
Washington, D. C.:

DEAR GENERAL: After the representations of the medical director, and my own observations as to the great number of deaths here and the continued sickness among the troops, I gave the quartermaster directions to put up a temporary hospital to accommodate 300 men. This is not a healthy climate; not near as healthy as the Potomac. The actual temperature has but little to do with it; it is the deadly malaria that arises from the swamps and the very sudden changes from hot to frosty cold. The mortality here is alarming, considering the season of the year. I have not directed any temporary barracks, and of course they will not be constructed without directions from Washington. The hospital will not cost much. It is to be single story and very temporary.

Beaufort will answer for the sick we may have there, but it will be absolutely necessary to have one here, especially in the summer, and this point must be occupied, for the whole safety of the harbor depends on it and Bay Point. The thing was so absolutely necessary, that I gave Captain Saxton his directions, I presume, before he wrote to you on the subject. It will cost but little more than an ordinary store-house of the same dimensions.

Our labor here is enormous. Thus far the negroes have rendered us but little assistance. Many come in and run off. They have not yet been organized to an extent we desire. The large families they bring with them make a great many useless mouths. Before long—after they have consumed all they have on the plantations—they will come in in greater numbers, and no doubt will give us many laborers; but where we get one good, able-bodied man, we have five to six women and children. They are a most prolific race.

In fitting out this expedition an opportunity for marching rapidly into the interior was not anticipated. The object was to seize on two important points of the coast and hold them for the protection of our blockading squadron. Therefore no more transportation was taken along than sufficient for the purposes of wood, water, and drayage of quartermaster and commissary stores, and only boats enough to assist in landing. Indeed, the number and description of boats I had nothing to do with; that was left to Captain DuPont. I have always regretted this, as we would have been far better off had we relied entirely on ourselves and not had to trust to the Navy. I am at times perfectly helpless without the Navy, and had I not depended on them, I have not a doubt but we would have been able to land at the time of the fight, and, if not assisted in reducing the work, at least have taken the whole garrison prisoners.

Captain DuPont always insisted that he would be able to and would put us ashore, but two things prevented: First, the loss of all his ferry-boats; and, second, his failure to supply me, according to promise, with oarsmen from his ships. I repeatedly asked him, when in New York, if there would be any uncertainty in his fulfilling that promise, and if there were the least I desired to know it then, in order to take measures to provide for it in time. He repeatedly assured me there was none, and that he would see that I was landed. So you see that I have been completely at his mercy. I never wish again, general, to co-operate. It is a thankless task.

As it turned out, I was compelled to agree not to attempt a landing. Had I known how things were to turn out, I should have made quite different arrangements in many things, and, among them, should have come down here equipped perfectly, independent of the Navy.

We have now a wide field before us, but we want boats, cavalry, and more force. The enemy's line extends from the Ossabaw Inlet through Savannah and upon the railroad beyond Pocotaligo, and we have to choose on which point of that extended and well-garrisoned line to make a main attack, which point must depend on the amount and description of means at our disposal.

We have not yet gone down to F——. The Navy had to send for more ammunition, and we have been constantly employed on our depot and base. Events multiply, and it is impossible to say exactly what we shall do or how we shall do it. Had I the means, I would have been on the Charleston and Savannah Railroad long ere this. Movements on water, through winding and shallow creeks, with men unaccustomed to boats, is slow, tedious, and ticklish, and I have got to see my way pretty clear now before attempting it.

It is hoped that a plenty of boats will be soon sent here.

Very truly, yours,

T. W. SHERMAN.

HEADQUARTERS EXPEDITIONARY CORPS,
Port Royal, S. C., December 14, 1861.

General LORENZO THOMAS,
Adjutant-General U. S. Army, Washington, D. C.:

SIR: I have the honor to submit the following to the consideration of the General-in-Chief and to the War Department:

The object of this expedition was to seize upon at least two important points of our Southern coast, and hold the same for the protection of our blockading squadron when compelled to seek a harbor, as well as to create something of a diversion in favor of our armies in the field. After the taking of Port Royal it was intended to proceed to Fernandina and get possession of that harbor, but in consequence of circumstances unnecessary here to particularly relate that part of the expedition has not yet been accomplished, and, although I have been for some time prepared for it, a still further delay arises from the fact that the gunboats of the Navy have first to be occupied in the work of disposing of the stone fleet just arrived from the North; but our operations resulting from the capture of Port Royal have become so developed as to lead to the occupation of Saint Helena Sound, the Tybee, and, in short, to the full possession of the coast from South Edisto to Tybee, and to which may be added Warsaw and Ossabaw Sounds, which, if not yet occupied by us, have been deserted by the enemy.

In the mean time there is a formidable strategic line formed and forming in our front, its right resting on Green Island, in Vernon River, passing by Thunderbolt, or Augustine Creek, at both of which places there are earthworks mounted with heavy guns, through Fort Jackson, Savannah, and thence along the line of the Savannah and Charleston Railroad indefinitely towards Charleston, this line having its principal bodies of troops between Vernon River and Savannah, at Savannah, Hardeeville, Grahamville, Coosawhatchie, Pocotaligo, Saltketcher, &c., and its most advanced posts at Pulaski, New River Bridge, Bluffton, Port Royal Ferry, &c. The object of this line appears to be to resist an invasion of the main-land, and not to attack the occupied coast, which, from all that can be learned, the enemy have concluded they cannot maintain, and given up all idea of doing so. It may be hence inferred that the main object of the expedition has been already accomplished, and that the point of Fernandina is now of so secondary a character as to render it not only almost insignificant, but the operation of taking it actually prejudicial to the great work which the development of circumstances appears to have set before us.

I am aware of the good effect that the capture of this place would have on the public mind, but the military is the only point of view that should be taken of it. It is no point from which to operate, and will probably fall of itself the moment Savannah is occupied by our forces, and therefore the resources of the Navy and Army here should be husbanded for a more important operation, viz, the attack of the enemy's line the moment preparations can be made.

The precise point of the hostile line to be struck and mode of attack cannot now be specifically set out without first knowing the means to be placed in our hands, and must therefore be left to time and circumstances; but in my judgment, with the necessary means, Savannah should be the point, and to be accomplished somewhat in this way: Pulaski to be vigorously shelled, as already recommended in a former communication; at the same time the gunboats of the naval squadron to shell out the garrisons of the forts on Vernon and Augustine Rivers, to be closely followed up by the landing of the land forces in the vicinity of Montgomery and Beaulieu, thus taking Augustine River, Fort Jackson, and Savannah in reverse; this operation to be connected at the same time with one from this point on Bluffton, New River Bridge, and Hardeeville, to get effectual possession of the railroad crossing the Savannah River, and prevent re-enforcements arriving at Savannah from the center and left of their line. A small head of column shown at Port Royal Ferry would have its effect in aiding this demonstration. I am firmly convinced that an operation of this sort would not only give us Savannah, but, if successful and strong enough to follow up the success, would shake the so-called Southern Confederacy to its very foundation.

Not knowing precisely what forces the enemy may have available, it is difficult to estimate for the men and means necessary to the success of this operation. But I must modify the terms of my letter of the 27th November, which did not look to this precise operation, and recommend that the one "regiment of cavalry, one regiment of regular artillery, ten regiments of infantry, and one pontoon bridge" be extended to "one regiment of cavalry, one regiment of regular artillery, and twenty regiments of infantry, and as many pontoon bridges as can be sent here." An addition to our armament will also be required to enable us to carry on a siege, if necessary, for which the ordnance officer will make requisition. I do not say but the thing can be done with less troops, but it would be better to have too many than too few, particularly as any success should be followed up rapidly and with sufficient force. I must, at the risk of being considered importunate, again repeat the necessity of having some more experienced staff officers, particularly a quartermaster of rank and great experience, artillery officers, and, if they cannot be had, ordnance officers.

All our work, which is immense, is done by volunteer soldiers, and it all drags for the want of a sufficient number of able directors. The negro labor expected to be obtained here is so far almost a failure. They are disinclined to labor, and will evidently not work to our satisfaction without those aids to which they have ever been accustomed, viz, the driver and the lash. A sudden change of condition from servitude to apparent freedom is more than their intellects can stand, and this circumstance alone renders it a very serious question what is to be done with the negroes who will hereafter be found on conquered soil.

Very respectfully, your obedient servant,

T. W. SHERMAN,

Brigadier-General, Commanding.

HEADQUARTERS EXPEDITIONARY CORPS,
Port Royal, S. C., December 15, 1861.

General LORENZO THOMAS,
Adjutant-General U. S. Army, Washington, D. C.:

SIR: For the information of the proper authorities, and for fear lest the Government may be disappointed in the amount of labor to be gathered here from the contrabands, I have the honor to report that from the hordes of negroes left on the plantations but about 320 have thus far come in and offered their services. Of these the quartermaster has but about 60 able-bodied male hands, the rest being decrepit, and women and children. Several of the 320 have run off. Every inducement has been held out to them to come in and labor for wages, and money distributed among those who have labored. The reasons for this apparent failure thus far appear to be these:

1st. They are naturally slothful and indolent, and have always been accustomed to the lash; an aid we do not make use of.

2d. They appear to be so overjoyed with the change of their condition that their minds are unsettled to any plan.

3d. Their present ease and comfort on the plantations, as long as their provisions will last, will induce most of them to remain there until compelled to seek our lines for subsistence.

Although comparatively few have thus far come in, it is therefore probable that in time many will, and if they are to be received and taken care of, some provision should be made to cover them. They are a prolific race, and it will be found that for every able-bodied male there will be five to six females, children, and decrepit. It is really a question for the Government to decide what is to be done with the contrabands.

Very respectfully, your obedient servant,

T. W. SHERMAN,
Brigadier-General, Commanding.

P. S.—Besides those who have come in there are many still on the plantations employed in gathering cotton.

HEADQUARTERS SECOND BRIGADE, EXPED'Y CORPS,
Beaufort, S. C., December 16, 1861.

Captain LOUIS H. PELOUZE,
Actg. Asst. Adjt. Gen. E. C., Port Royal, S. C.:

SIR: I inclose, for the information of the brigadier-general commanding, reports received from Col. B. C. Christ last evening and early this morning, in regard to affairs at Port Royal Ferry, and also a report from Mr. Rockwell,* received early this morning.

From these reports it will appear that the channel of the river is not obstructed sufficiently to prevent the passage of the lighter-draught gunboats, and that the enemy has no guns in position. I have endeavored to make all portions of the command vigilant and attentive, especially at the ferry, and am having nightly careful inspections of the pickets and camps in that quarter.

The gunboat which went up Port Royal River day before yesterday did not proceed to the ferry, but made the main-land some three and one-half miles to the right of or below the ferry, and yesterday morning was anchored off of Lane's Point, Ladies Island. At 8 o'clock last evening

*Not found.

I sent a dispatch to the captain of the gunboat, urging him to proceed to the ferry, but on its arrival, about 11 o'clock, at the point, the gunboat had left and gone in the direction of Saint Helena Sound. Such is the report of Lieutenant Lyons, who bore my dispatch.

I will again urge with all possible earnestness that a gunboat be sent without delay up Broad River and through the Port Royal passage, and if this meets your approval, I trust you may succeed in getting Commodore DuPont to dispatch one to-day. I shall telegraph to this effect this morning.

It is my purpose to go to the ferry in the course of an hour or two, and may remain there until to-morrow evening; but I shall make arrangements to have your dispatches forwarded without delay.

I am, sir, very respectfully, your most obedient servant,

ISAAC I. STEVENS,
Brigadier-General, Commanding.

[Inclosure No. 1.]

HEADQUARTERS PORT ROYAL FERRY,
December 15, 1861.

General ISAAC I. STEVENS,
Commanding Port Royal District:

SIR: I have to report that no demonstration of a hostile character has occurred on the part of the enemy since my last dispatch, save a report (verbally) from Captain Elliott, Company I, Seventy-ninth New York Regiment, that 400 men appeared last evening on the shore occupied by the enemy about 1 mile above Seabrook. Captain Elliott reports, through Major Morrison, that he mounted a log on two cart-wheels and ran it on the beach, which had the effect to scatter the enemy in all directions.

Lieutenant Colonel Brenholts, accompanied by Lieutenant Kellogg, Company K, Fiftieth Pennsylvania Regiment, with four men, left Port Royal Ferry yesterday morning at 9 o'clock and proceeded down the river (on our right) 2½ miles, taking soundings of the channel 1½ miles below the ferry (on right). Stockades were driven and timber sunk, so as to leave but 7 feet of water in the channel at low tide, but the obstruction does not extend half way across the river. Our side of the channel is clear (the enemy from some cause or other having abandoned the work before finishing it). I wish it distinctly understood that I am correct in this, that not one-half the channel is obstructed; that the obstructions are all on the enemy's side, and, if necessary, could be easily removed; further, that Lieutenant-Colonel Brenholts reports outside of the obstructions a channel 112 feet wide, with 12 feet of water at low tide and 19 feet of water at high tide. This is reliable, and, so far as our observations extend, no other obstructions exist in the channels.

Our pickets are so posted as to command the shore from Seabrook to a point opposite a brick-yard 2½ or 3 miles below the ferry (our right), said brick-yard being separated from that portion of the island we occupy by a stream, supposed to be the outlet of the stream crossed by a bridge 4 miles from Beaufort. Discovered that the point on which the brick-yard is located is occupied by a detachment from the Eighth Michigan Regiment, under Captain Elder. Pickets have been posted from the point last indicated to Seabrook, and every precaution taken to guard against surprise. I would add that on the opposite shore, 2 miles below the ferry (our right), what was supposed at first to be a picket station of the enemy on a more careful examination proves to be an entire regiment. Nothing further or more definite than that contained in my previous dispatch has been ascertained relating to the guns supposed to be mounted opposite to and commanding the causeway.

The outer pickets (on our right) report that this morning at 8 o'clock a white steamer landed on the enemy's shore about 3½ or 4 miles below the ferry (our right), and remained there about one hour; what it unloaded, if anything, or what it took on board, they cannot say.

All of which is respectfully submitted.

B. C. CHRIST,
Col. Fiftieth Regt. Pa. Vols., Comdg. Port Royal Ferry.

[Inclosure No. 2.]

HEADQUARTERS PORT ROYAL FERRY,
December 15, 1861—9 o'clock.

General ISAAC I. STEVENS,
Commanding Port Royal District:

SIR: Your dispatch just received. Have no knowledge of pile driving to the left (or right) of the ferry. The party who gave you the information must have mistaken the chopping of wood for the driving of piles. I am certain that it is not so. They cannot (*i. e.*, the enemy) do anything, from Seabrook down to 2½ miles on the right of the ferry, but our pickets must see them, either day or night. No pickets asleep on post last night have been reported to me. I will inquire into the matter, and if any pickets have been guilty of neglect of duty they will be promptly arrested and their names reported to headquarters as soon as practicable.

Very respectfully, your most obedient servant,

B. C. CHRIST,
Col. Fiftieth Regt. Pa. Vols., Comdg. Port Royal Ferry.

PORT ROYAL, S. C., *December* 19, 1861.

General MCCLELLAN,
Commanding U. S. Army, Washington, D. C.:

DEAR GENERAL: I have received your kind letter of the 5th,* and hasten to say that I think that the trip to Fernandina is lost for the present. I have been in readiness for some time, keeping all the vessels destined thither waiting for the Navy to be ready, but have found that the latter has a new job on its hands, viz, the convoying and sinking the vessels of the stone fleet; also, for reasons already given in an official letter, I believe that the public interests will be much advanced by deferring it now—it has been postponed so long. It was unfortunate that the naval fleet had to send for more ammunition after the affair of Port Royal, as Fernandina would have been taken then without much trouble, and no doubt it could be easily taken now; but it has been re-enforced, and fresh artillery sent there. It has a garrison of about 1,300 men and four forts, one of which is on Cumberland Island. Fort Clinch, though never yet finished, has a partial armament. We have understood that Brunswick has quite a large garrison, but cannot find out any particulars.

Commodore DuPont thinks he will be ready for Fernandina in a week or two, but I am inclined to believe that the wants of Tybee and Saint Helena will divide him too much until those places are made perfectly secure. Already the Georgians are making serious threats on Tybee,

* Not found.

and I had to send General Wright down there yesterday with another regiment, and DuPont has sent three of his gunboats, in addition to two vessels he had there. Tatnall is busy reconnoitering with his fleet, and Pulaski has been filled with men during the past few days. They may probably make a desperate effort to retake it before our guns are up, but every care will be taken that they do not.

I have opened the passage around Port Royal Island, which the enemy attempted to close, but their batteries fired into our boat and hit her once, doing no damage.

As it will be some time before proper preparations can be made for Savannah, I am inclined towards seizing upon the south end of the Charleston and Savannah Railroad as soon as I can get the cavalry. To do this I must be sure of success, for it is quite a vital point in our success on Savannah. I think it can be done at a dash, properly executed, but then the security of our communications will have to be looked to against forays from Coosawhatchie, a point on the railroad strongly fortified. I have tried to get this railroad destroyed, but thus far without success, though our party has not returned.

As to the point of Charleston, of which you desire me to speak, I will have the pleasure of writing you in a day or two. If we are to operate inward, I think another light battery here very necessary, as well as a regiment of cavalry and infantry, as stated in my official communication.

Very truly and respectfully,

T. W. SHERMAN.

FORT WELLES, HILTON HEAD, S. C.,
December 20, 1861.

General M. C. MEIGS:

MY DEAR GENERAL: I have received your letter informing me that all my requisitions on Colonel Tompkins were to be filled. I shall use every endeavor to carry out your views with regard to economy.

I have thus far and shall continue to erect buildings of most temporary character, consistent with utility.

Immediately upon the reception of your first, I took steps to collect the cotton, and was so far successful as to send about the value of $30,000 of it by the steamship Atlantic, consigned to Colonel Tompkins.

By the Vanderbilt, which has just arrived, came the agent of the Treasury Department, and I have turned the whole business over to him. He finds the parties all organized, in successful operation, so that he will have little to do but take the credit of collecting a couple millions dollars' worth of cotton.

I very much wish, general, that you would visit Port Royal. It is but seventy hours' sail from New York City, and your stay here could be governed entirely by the time at your disposal. I think you would be able to get a better idea of its wants and of our successes already achieved or in prospect than any I could give by letter. The steamship Atlantic will leave New York in a few days after this reaches you for this place. I am very sure that your visit would prove pleasant to yourself and advantageous to the service. I have endeavored to carry out your suggestions with regard to burning the bridges, with what success the future may disclose. Some of my contrabands inform me that they have been expecting that Charleston would be burned, and they think the negroes did it.

General Sherman has strengthened the occupation of Tybee Island by an additional regiment, and guns are being put in position bearing on Fort Pulaski; the garrison in that place is about 2,000.

I think before long we shall have accounts of the burning of Savannah. I do not think, however, that we can advance upon either it or Charleston without re-enforcements.

With great respect, I am, general, yours, sincerely,

R. SAXTON.

PORT ROYAL, S. C., *December* 21, 1861.

Hon. SIMON CAMERON,

Secretary of War:

SIR: You will pardon me for writing to you in this direct manner, but the newspapers of the country appear in some degree dissatisfied that we have not moved ahead, and it may be that the Government shares in this feeling.

I have for a long time been ready to move to Fernandina, but the Navy is not, even now; after the commodore had waited for his ammunition from the North a new job fell upon his hands: the convoying and sinking the stone fleets. And it is now so uncertain when the Navy will be ready, that my attention has been turned off from that expedition to objects which the development of circumstances is bringing about, and have kept the Department duly advised of my acts and my views.

The operations on the main and towards Savannah were not anticipated in preparing the expedition. We have no cavalry yet, and are not sufficiently supplied with field artillery. We came prepared to take possession of certain harbors and fortify them; that is all. All the boats furnished were prepared by Commodore DuPont, only sufficient, or what were thought to be, for landing purposes. It must therefore be easily seen that any move of our troops into the interior of South Carolina, under the circumstances, was a sheer impossibility. I could long ago have landed and established part of my force on the main, but I have particularly avoided doing anything of the kind until I can ascertain what means are to be furnished me for moving onwards. There are several points to be chosen, and it would not answer to reveal that point to the enemy before I am ready to immediately follow up the movement. No one is more anxious than myself to push on and crush out this rebellion, but there is some judgment and proper prudence to be exercised in this matter. I do not desire to initiate a failure.

Our base is now well, very well, established, and am ready to move as soon as I can get some cavalry and proper re-enforcements to insure and follow up success.

The point of Savannah is now the point, but, to say nothing of the public interest, my own professional reputation would not permit me to make dashes without object and without lasting result. The work before us is a great one. It requires thought, system, and prudence.

I have presumed to write you thus, as I am pained to believe that there is a growing distrust among a portion of the people as to the activity and usefulness of this portion of the Army.

The amount of labor and activity here I would gladly submit to the judgment of the most enlightened men. We have done all that men can properly do under the circumstances.

With the highest respect, your most obedient servant,

T. W. SHERMAN,

Brigadier-General, Commanding.

HEADQUARTERS EXPEDITIONARY CORPS,
Port Royal, S. C., December 22, 1861.

General LORENZO THOMAS,
Adjutant-General U. S. Army, Washington, D. C.:

SIR: I have just been informed by Commodore DuPont that a reconnaissance, under Commander Drayton, with the gunboats Pawnee and Seneca, has discovered that the rebel forts at both South and North Edisto are abandoned and guns withdrawn. He also states that a camp of 500 men, in the vicinity of North Edisto, left with their arms on the approach of the gunboats, leaving tents, provisions, and camp equipage in his possession.

I think it would be well to occupy Edisto Island, and would do so with part of my own forces were it not necessary to remain here as much concentrated as possible, to be ready for movements already contemplated. Troops pushed up towards Stono Inlet at this time would produce a good effect at Charleston.

From all the information I can gather the South Carolinians are strongly fortifying Charleston Neck and James Island, on the Stono River, and are removing some of the guns from Fort Sumter and the islands for that object, evidently supposing that Charleston is to be attacked by land.

Very respectfully, your obedient servant,

T. W. SHERMAN,
Brigadier-General, Commanding.

PORT ROYAL, S. C., *December* 23, 1861.

General GEORGE B. MCCLELLAN, U. S. A.:

DEAR GENERAL: I have not yet been able to see Commodore DuPont, but have thought somewhat of the Charleston problem, which is rather difficult to solve, and will demand much thought; but the premises on which much of the data must be based are that the South Carolinians have long come to the conclusion that Charleston is to be attacked by land. Some time ago they removed several of the barbette guns from Sumter and guns from the island batteries to place on the Neck. They have abandoned Edisto Island entirely and removed the guns to some works they have thrown up on the Stono—I believe three in number, including the one at the mouth. Several vessels have been sunk in this river. They are making, therefore, a desperate effort to prevent a landing on James Island. What they have done on the north side of Charleston I have not learned. Without looking at the thing satisfactorily, yet I am inclined to the opinion that the easiest way to take or destroy the city is by the route of Sullivan's and Morris Islands, erecting batteries there, carrying Moultrie, seizing on Point Pleasant (making a demonstration by Bull's Bay, if necessary), and reducing Sumter, then bringing forward the Navy and shelling the city, assisted by mortar batteries on land, if necessary; but the objection will now arise to this that the channel has been stopped up by a stone fleet. If so stopped, of course this mode would not be so convenient, though it will be very possible to shell Charleston from Sumter and Point Pleasant and other points that will readily be seized upon when Sumter has fallen. I have heard it said, however, by officers of the Navy that, if found necessary for the gunboats to enter Charleston Harbor, it can yet be done. As soon as I can get Captain DuPont's views I will write again.

I believe that the South Carolinians are under the conviction that we are about to strike their center by Port Royal Ferry. We want to keep up the delusion, and if I only had some cavalry would feel justified in moving the bulk of our force to the southern end of the railroads and shutting off South Carolinia from Savannah, and preparing the way to effectually take the city by the southern route. I have written also for another battery of light artillery.

Very respectfully and truly,

T. W. SHERMAN.

WAR DEPARTMENT,
Washington, December 26, 1861.

Brig. Gen. THOMAS W. SHERMAN,
Commanding, Port Royal, S. C.:

GENERAL: Your letter of the 21st is received. You are correct in your belief "that there is a growing distrust among a portion of the people as to the activity and usefulness of this (your) portion of the Army." I do not share in that distrust, for my confidence in your ability is very great. I must confess, however, that I am constrained to believe that all the operations of our Army have been too much delayed, and that there has been too great a desire to avoid responsibility rather than force the enemy into early action. The fact seems to be overlooked that while we are preparing our enemy is also engaged in preparation, and that, being in his own country, he can do so much more rapidly than ourselves. It will give me much pleasure to hear from you frequently. I shall be especially glad at this time to know the actual force under your command, the number of troops you need, and the kind of which you are most in want. You refer in your letter to a want of cavalry. This is the first intimation I have had that any were needed by you. Let me know the number required and they shall be sent at once, as well as any other force that you may deem necessary.

At this distance from the field of your operations this Department will not attempt to give you specific instructions. You will have to rely upon your own judgment, in which I have every confidence; but let me add that I trust you will soon be able to accomplish something. Winter is now half over; spring is coming, and our forces must soon be useless in a region so far south.

I am, general, very respectfully and truly, yours,

SIMON CAMERON,
Secretary of War.

PORT ROYAL, S. C., *December 26, 1861.*

General MCCLELLAN, U. S. A.,
Washington, D. C.:

GENERAL: I have been unable to get Commodore DuPont to investigate with me the problem of Charleston, and, as time is important, I have conferred with Captain Gillmore on the subject confidentially, and after the most serious deliberation of his views and my own have come to the conclusion that but two modes suggest themselves as practical operations:

First. In the preliminary taking of Sullivan's and Morris Islands and the reduction of Sumter from these two points. When Sumter is reduced, the naval fleet to pass into the harbor and shell the city, with assistance, possibly, of the Army, that will have obtained possession of Point Pleasant in the mean while. When the city is thus reduced the country around will probably become abandoned, and a base thus formed for further offensive operations.

Second. In operating by Stono Inlet and Stono River, getting possession of James Island, and shelling the city from the northern side of the island, leaving Sumter and Moultrie intact, to fall of themselves.

The difficulty in operating on this line consists in the preparations the enemy have made on Stono River for the defense of James Island. So far as I have been able to learn they consist of two forts near or at the mouth—one near its junction with Wappoo Creek and one at Guerin's Ferry. Several vessels, too, have been sunk in the river at points not yet ascertained. Now that the channels entering Charleston Harbor have been blocked up by stone vessels (except Maffitt's Channel, the shoalest) the first plan seems impracticable—at least until nature opens a new channel, which time alone can determine. The operation will probably have to be confined to the second plan, assisted, probably, by a demonstration by way of Bull's Bay; and if a landing can be effected on fast land not far from the mouth of the Stono, after the taking of the forts near the mouth, a victorious battle fought on James Island will enable us to plant siege batteries in a position for the effectual shelling of Charleston. At a rough estimate I should consider the means necessary to be 20,000 infantry, 1,000 cavalry, two light batteries, thirty siege pieces, with a sufficiency of 8 and 10 pounder mortars. Two or three pontoon bridges also would be necessary for operating about the Stono and James Island.

If the railroad to the north is to be so cut as to open that side to demonstrations from the north, I would diminish the assailing force at least one-third.

I inclose the views of Captain Gillmore, to which I have agreed in most points.

Very truly, yours,

T. W. SHERMAN.

P. S.—I am still waiting to hear from you in the way of re-enforcements. I really do not consider it prudent to make a grand attack on the main without cavalry. The enemy has a plenty of it. Would prefer vastly my general plan carried out, as expressed in official letter of the 14th instant, but, to quiet the public mind, which is getting furious, would make a dash on the railroad at once if I had cavalry to assist me and boats enough.

[Inclosure.]

OFFICE OF CHIEF ENGINEER EXPEDITIONARY CORPS,
Hilton Head, S. C., December 25, 1861.

Brig. Gen. THOMAS W. SHERMAN,
Commanding Expeditionary Corps, Hilton Head, S. C.:

SIR: In response to your verbal directions to me I have the honor to submit a plan, or rather the prominent features of a plan, for obtaining possession of the city of Charleston, S. C.

Three projects for attaining this object naturally suggest themselves for our examination, viz:

1st. By way of Morris and Sullivan's Islands, involving the reduction of Forts Sumter and Moultrie, Johnson, and Castle Pinckney, and the subsequent bombardment of the city. The fall of Forts Sumter and Moultrie would insure the success of this project if the Navy could cooperate with us afterwards.

2d. By way of Stono Inlet and River and James Island, taking Fort Johnson, and leaving Forts Sumter, Moultrie, and Castle Pinckney on the right for the time being. We could not occupy Fort Johnson, however, until Sumter had been reduced.

3d. By way of Bull's Bay, leaving all the forts in the harbor on the left, and taking the city in the rear by Wando and Cooper Rivers.

The Bull's Bay project presents the greatest difficulties in the way of land and water transportation; would probably for other reasons be the most difficult of execution, and I therefore would not recommend a principal attack in that direction. A feint there in force would in my opinion very materially second the initial steps of any offensive operations on James Island via Stono River.

As between the other two projects I distinctly favor that by James Island for the following prominent reasons, without going into details, viz:

First. The recent blockade of the channels leading into Charleston Harbor by old hulks. Although it will most likely eventuate in opening one good channel for vessels of moderate draught, it will, for some time to come at least, practically exclude any effective co-operation of the Navy in a direct attack from the sea;

Second. The complete success of the first project (by first reducing the forts) would neither give us the possession of Charleston as the objective point nor a good base of operations, unless we had all of James Island also; while,

Third. If we have James Island we command and can even hold the city, and of course secure all the real advantages which its possession is supposed to confer, even if the forts in the harbor (that is, Sumter and Moultrie) remain in the hands of the enemy.

Fourth. The attack by James Island would render it necessary for the Navy first to shell out the battery or batteries on Stono Inlet and River, so as to secure to us the undisputed command of those waters up to the first good landing place on the island, probably Turnbull's. Having a footing on the island, we would have to fight a battle for its possession. If beaten, a position on the south of the island could be maintained against very great odds, even in the absence of any active assistance from the Navy.

It would be equally necessary to fight and gain this battle on James Island in order to hold and occupy Charleston, even if we first captured the harbor *per se* by reducing the forts by a siege. Once in possession of James Island and holding the sea, the forts fall into our hands in due time as a matter of course. The reduction of Fort Sumter, or even Fort Moultrie, with an investment by water only, is a matter of no small moment.

As an isolated movement, not really seconded by descent on other important points of this coast, I would consider the following force sufficient to carry this project by James Island into effect. Our knowledge of the extent of the preparations against such an attempt by us is quite meager, and radical modifications of this plan may be necessary so far as it relates to the proportion of the different arms when a thorough reconnaissance shall have placed us in possession of more facts. I should consider the following as simply a near approximation to what is required, viz: 14,000 infantry, 1,000 cavalry, 12 pieces light artillery (two light batteries), 20 siege guns, with a large proportion of 20-pounder and 30-pounder Parrott guns.

Very respectfully, your obedient servant,

Q. A. GILLMORE,

Captain, and Chief Engineer Expeditionary Corps.

PORT ROYAL, S. C., *December* 27, 1861.

General GEORGE B. MCCLELLAN,
Commanding U. S. Army:

DEAR GENERAL: The Ocean Queen arrived yesterday with a mail, but brought no news of any cavalry. Had I cavalry and another light battery this would be a fine opportunity to strike for the railroad and cut off Savannah, and thus prepare ourselves for operations south of it.

It is absolutely necessary to do something here soon, without waiting for our armament for P—— L—— S——. The rebels are exceedingly active. They are erecting earthworks around Port Royal Island—one, I understand to-day, on the Ashepoo, above Otter Island, and another below Thunderbolt, on Skidaway Island, making two on this last island. In a word, they are erecting a cordon of earthworks, armed with heavy cannon, a certain distance from the coast, just far enough back to avoid fire from gunboats.

I shall try to organize a dash on the forts about Port Royal Island, and also to the railroad, if not running too much risk without cavalry and artillery. It will require much consideration. It would not do to sustain here a defeat. We are badly in want of boats, too.

We are quite secure here now. The place is well fortified, and can be held by 2,500 or 3,000 men against any force that can be brought against it. Had I the means, now is the time to do something. These fellows are getting stronger and stronger every day.

Very truly, yours,

T. W. SHERMAN.

HEADQUARTERS EXPEDITIONARY CORPS,
Port Royal, S. C., January 2, 1862.

Maj. Gen. GEORGE B. MCCLELLAN, U. S. A.,
Washington, D. C.:

GENERAL: I ordered a dash on the enemy's batteries opposite Port Royal Island, but no doubt you will have perceived the object of advancing no farther, which the public will not. I want to make no real movement in that direction, yet I want the enemy to think I do, which he evidently does. I want to make a great dash on the north side of Savannah River, thus occupying the road to that city, the whole country between Broad River and Savannah River, and the southern end of the railroad, and at the same time, if found practicable, the islands in this river north of Pulaski.

But to do this I must have a regiment at least of cavalry and at least another strong battery of light artillery. Circumstances are developing themselves wonderfully here. The time has come to act; every day's delay now is a sad loss.

Let me take possession of that country now, and the siege of the south of Savannah will be comparatively light and easy. I think Pulaski need not be shelled. I can cut it off, I think.

Important information has been obtained with regard to the topography of the country about Savannah River which we never knew before. I hope to lay the whole subject before you in an official and topographical form as soon as it can be prepared. But we are so hard pushed for proper engineers that they have no time for office work.

I think a terrible blow struck here will aid your important work most materially, but we must have cavalry and light artillery. You, general, are to be the savior of this country, if it is saved. Let me aid you in the work. But I must act militarily, and not to please the superficial and nonsensical views of the public press, by which I have been soundly berated for not playing the militiaman and egotistical soldier.

I am, general, yours, truly,

T. W. SHERMAN.

OFFICE CHIEF TOPOGRAPHICAL ENGINEER E. C.,
Hilton Head, S. C., January 2, 1862.

Capt. LOUIS H. PELOUZE,
Fifteenth Infantry, A. A. A. G. Hdqrs. E. C., Hilton Head, S. C.:

SIR: In accordance with the verbal instructions of the general commanding I have made an examination of the land and water between the Cooper and Savannah Rivers, and have to report as follows:

The communications between Cooper and New Rivers by the channel around the north side of Long Pine Island are practicable and comparatively easy at all times for vessels of 10 or 12 feet draught. Soundings to a distance of 2 miles beyond Box's plantation were made, and show nowhere less than 18 feet water. From this fact and those referred to in my former report (evidence of the negroes, tides, &c.) there is no doubt that boats of the draught mentioned can pass up New River to or even beyond Red Bluff or Whitehead's Landing.

From Bloody Point, the western extremity of Daufuskie Island, through Bull or New River to Wall's Cut and thence both by Wright and Mud Rivers to the Savannah, accurate soundings were made. They show a sufficient depth of water through the lower entrance of Wright River for gunboats of 15 feet draught, but from the cut to the Savannah by the Mud River Channel only boats of 6 or 7 feet draught can pass at full flood tide. The former route conducts into the ship channel of the Savannah about 2 miles above Fort Pulaski, the latter about 6. Wall's Cut is straight, about 250 yards long, and has a water-way of near 100 feet. At the distance of 120 yards from either end a bark 90 feet long and 24 feet beam has been sunk; beyond her three rows of square piles have been firmly driven into the bed of the stream from side to side. Originally the bark was placed directly athwart the channel, completely obstructing it, but she is at present lying diagonally across it, with a water-way of 20 feet on both sides. An examination revealed the fact that there is but little mud or ballast in her, and, instead of being stationary, she swings and careens with the tide. When first visited she was at least 20 feet from the first line of piles, careened into the direction of the tide. When I returned four or five hours afterwards she was in the same place, but careened in the opposite direction. When visited the second time her stern had drifted against the piles, partly removing several. From these circumstances I conclude that little difficulty will be experienced in removing her entirely from the cut.

The piles, thirty-three in number, of squared timber, are on the farther side of the vessel, arranged in three rows, so as to completely close the channel, but from the softness of the soil into which they are driven they can be removed quickly and easily by attaching an anchor chain to each, hitching to a tug-boat, and running her at full speed from it.

All the islands between New and Savannah Rivers are low salt marshes, subject to overflow at full flood tide aided by strong winds, and are impracticable for the transportation of troops or stores. Long Island and all the other islands in the Savannah below Fort Jackson are of the same character.

Wright River, although navigable for some distance, has no other practicable communication with the Savannah than those described above. It runs throughout its entire course through the marsh and finally becomes lost.

I am, sir, very respectfully, your obedient servant,

J. H. WILSON,
First Lieutenant Topo. Engrs., and Chief Top. Engr. E. C.

HEADQUARTERS EXPEDITIONARY CORPS,
Port Royal, S. C., January 4, 1862.

General LORENZO THOMAS,
Adjutant-General U. S. Army, Washington, D. C.:

SIR: Reconnaissances are being made on both sides the Savannah River to ascertain the practicability of getting gunboats into it from either or both sides and establishing batteries on the islands between Fort Pulaski and Savannah, and thus cutting off Pulaski and reducing it without the slow and expensive mode of bombarding it from Tybee. I have already had the creeks and inlets on this side examined, and the result of the examination is this: 1st. Steamers of light draught can get into the Savannah River from this side, entering it by the south end of Jones Island, about 2 miles above Fort Pulaski, provided it may be found practicable to remove the obstruction placed across Wall's Cut, which consists of a brig 90 feet in length sunk across it and secured by three rows of piles. 2d. That Jones Island and Long Island are entirely marsh, and that it is hardly practicable to construct batteries upon them. It is believed, however, that batteries may be erected on Elba Island, above both the former, though our party did not examine it. Important information, moreover, has recently been received of a route possibly practicable for small gunboats from Warsaw Sound into the Savannah River, turning the forts now on Skidaway Island and Thunderbolt. Captain Gillmore leaves to-day to examine the Wilmington Narrows for this object. I am just sending off a party to attempt removing the hulk and piles in Wall's Cut.

I hope to be soon able to report some of our command in the Savannah River. I should at once seize upon all the country between here and Savannah River, including the south end of the railroad, if I had some cavalry and more light artillery.

Very respectfully, your obedient servant,

T. W. SHERMAN,
Brigadier-General, Commanding.

HEADQUARTERS EXPEDITIONARY CORPS,
Port Royal, S. C., January 7, 1862.

Hon. SIMON CAMERON,
Secretary of War, Washington, D. C.:

SIR: I have the honor to acknowledge the receipt of your letter of the 26th ultimo.

I feel thankful for the confidence still reposed in me, and trust that I may do nothing that will diminish it.

The intimation in my letter of a want of cavalry was made with a view of bringing your mind to the subject in case my previous letters to the Adjutant-General had not reached the attention of the Department. In my letter of the 15th of November I mentioned the subject. In my letter of the 27th November I asked for "not exceeding a regiment," and in a letter of December 14 repeated the request.

From the letters above referred to it may be seen that if we attack Savannah on both sides a very large force will be requisite. I think the force should be sent, so that we can not only meet any emergency and attack in the manner that circumstances will prove to be the best, but so that we can have a force large enough to follow up rapidly our success.

I am trying to open Wall's Cut, and, if successful, the Navy, I think, will be able to throw gunboats into Savannah River, and we to erect batteries on some of its islands, cut off Fort Pulaski, shell Fort Jackson, and afterwards the city, without the slow and expensive process of first bombarding Pulaski.

The north side of Savannah will also have to be looked to, and I propose taking possession of that district of country as soon as I can get some cavalry and more light artillery.

But should we be not successful in getting into Savannah River, the siege of Savannah will be imperative in order to take it. This will require extensive operations from Ossabaw Sound in addition to those north of Savannah River. I have made all the necessary estimates for the operation.

The actual force under my command is 14,768, rank and file, including about 600 in Saint Helena Sound, 3,000 on Port Royal Island, 200 at Fort Seward, 1,400 at Tybee, leaving about 9,500 on hand in Hilton Head. I calculate to have available for the field out of this force, say, 9,000 men. These troops are all infantry except one company of light artillery. Before a step can be taken towards the enemy's forces we should have a full regiment of good cavalry and at least another battery of light artillery.

The number of additional troops we need I would estimate at 10,000 infantry, 1,000 cavalry, one regiment of regular heavy artillery, and one or two light batteries; but, whatever number of infantry, the cavalry is indispensable.

I have just received the latest news from Savannah, which confirms that received the other day, that there are about 20,000 men in and around the city, among which some two or three regiments of cavalry and four batteries of light artillery. Besides the works on Skidaway Island at Thunderbolt and Green Island, and the masonry work of Fort Jackson, the city is being covered with a line of intrenchments.

The force in our immediate front is estimated at about 9,000 men, stationed on the railroad between Savannah River and Pocotaligo, among which are said to be about two regiments of cavalry and two batteries of light artillery, besides some earthworks at various points.

I have the honor to remain, with the highest respect,

T. W. SHERMAN,
Brigadier-General, Commanding.

GENERAL ORDERS, No. 3. } HDQRS. OF THE ARMY, A. G. O., *Washington, January* 11, 1862.

I. A new military department, to be known as the Department of Key West, is hereby constituted, with the following bounds: Key West, the Tortugas, and the main-land on the west coast as far as Apalachicola and to Cape Canaveral on the east coast.

Brig. Gen. J. M. Brannan, U. S. volunteers, is assigned to the command.

* * * * * * *

By command of Major-General McClellan:

L. THOMAS,
Adjutant-General.

ADJUTANT-GENERAL'S OFFICE,
Washington, January 13, 1862.

Major-General DIX, *Baltimore:*

Send to General Wool, at Fort Monroe, by this evening's boat, the following order:

On the arrival of the steamer Constitution from Boston, send her to Port Royal, with her troops, to re-enforce General Sherman.

L. THOMAS,
Adjutant-General.

HEADQUARTERS EXPEDITIONARY CORPS,
Port Royal, S. C., January 15, 1862.

To the ADJUTANT-GENERAL U. S. ARMY,
Washington, D. C.:

SIR: I have the honor to ask the attention of the War Department to a subject upon which I have before hinted, but which is of so much importance, that I cannot refrain from again intruding it upon its notice. Of the large numbers of negroes on the islands in our possession some have come into the camps and obtained work, bringing with them their families. These are, therefore, cared for, and the work of the able-bodied men, numbering probably one out of five or six of a family, will be sufficient, with the rations issued, to support them. Those still remaining on the plantations are now living on the corn and potatoes left there, and when these are all consumed the negroes will be in a suffering condition or thrown upon the commissariat of the Army for support.

For the future maintenance of these people some system must be established, and one which will permit them to sustain themselves; but before they can be left entirely to their own government they must be trained and instructed into a knowledge of personal and moral responsibility—which will be a matter of time. I have, therefore, the honor to recommend that suitable instructors be sent to them, to teach them all the necessary rudiments of civilization, and secondly, and in the mean time, that agents, properly qualified, be employed and sent here to take charge of the plantations and superintend the work of the blacks until they are sufficiently enlightened to think and provide for themselves. They should receive wages, and the profits of the plantations, after all expenses are paid, should go to the Government. I can see no other way to lay a groundwork for future usefulness with this unfortunate class of people.

I would also suggest that a quantity of negro clothing be sent out here as soon as practicable, and this should include stuff for women's and children's wear.

Very respectfully, your obedient servant,

T. W. SHERMAN,
Brigadier-General, Commanding.

OFFICE CHIEF TOPOGRAPHICAL ENGINEER E. C.,
Hilton Head, S. C., January 18, 1862.

Capt. LOUIS H. PELOUZE,
Fifteenth U. S. Infantry, A. A. A. G., Headquarters E. C., Hilton Head, S. C.:

SIR: In accordance with the verbal instructions of the general commanding, I accompanied Capt. John Rodgers, U. S. Navy, in a boat reconnaissance of the channel from Tybee Roads, by Bloody Point, through Bull River, Wall's Cut, and Wright River to the Savannah, and have the honor to state that the opinions expressed in my report of January 2 are confirmed in all essential particulars, and that there is no longer any doubt in my mind concerning the practicability of passing our gunboats and lighter transports at high tide into the Savannah 2 miles above Fort Pulaski and entirely beyond the effective fire of that work. The channel leading from Wright River into the Savannah gives, according to the soundings made during the reconnaissance under the direction of Lieutenant Barnes, U. S. Navy, at least 5 (7) feet of water at mean low tide, which, added to the mean rise of the tides, would give a draught of 12 (14) feet for navigation under the most unfavorable circumstances.

The only point upon which there is any doubt is the width of the channel. On this my mind is convinced, and the pilot, Mr. Godfrey, says he has no fears whatever of being able to take through any gunboat drawing 12 feet of water.

Herewith I inclose a sketch, taken from the Coast Survey charts, showing the additional soundings made by Lieutenant Barnes.

I am, sir, very respectfully, your obedient servant,

J. H. WILSON,
First Lieutenant, Top. Engrs., and Chief Top. Engr. E. C.

HEADQUARTERS EXPEDITIONARY CORPS,
Port Royal, S. C., January 20, 1862.

ADJUTANT-GENERAL U. S. ARMY,
Washington, D. C.:

GENERAL: Reconnaissances of Savannah River had led me to the belief that Savannah might be taken by a combined operation of the Army and Navy by operating in the river itself, which would save the slow and expensive process of bombarding Pulaski by cutting it from Savannah, and also the slow process of besieging Savannah from the south, as recommended in my letter of the 14th December. Could Savannah have thus been taken at once, any future obstructions and defenses in the vicinity of Savannah by the river would have been prevented.

A combined reconnaissance, however, made by Commodore Rodgers, of the Navy, and Lieutenant Wilson, of the Topographical Engineers, subsequently, has led to a report from the former officer that the navigation of some portions of the Savannah River is too hazardous to attempt the running of gunboats and transports up the river without further examination.

It has therefore been agreed upon by Commodore DuPont and myself to at once commence this examination in force. This movement is particularly calculated to the cutting off of Fort Pulaski, and will do it, I believe, effectually.

In the mean while any operations by land on the north of Savannah River will be out of the question, because of the want of boats, wagons, and light artillery, none of which expected have yet arrived.

In case we find it practicable to effect a landing at or near Savannah by this route, I think it would be judicious and even necessary to send the force heretofore asked for as promptly as possible. As the process is a slow one, the enemy will have an opportunity to accumulate immense forces at that point, and we should be strong enough to make the thing sure.

The Atlantic I am keeping waiting, and must therefore close in haste.

Very respectfully,

T. W. SHERMAN,
Brigadier-General, Commanding

HEADQUARTERS THIRD BRIGADE, EXPED'Y CORPS,
Hilton Head, S. C., January 31, 1862.

General THOMAS W. SHERMAN, *&c.:*

GENERAL: I inclose for your consideration a brief draught of proposed operations with the forces under my command. It is drawn up from my recollection of the place, and may need modification after consultation of the map of the locality, a copy of which I asked for in my communication of this morning. If I am not much mistaken in my recollections of the locality, the whole plan is feasible, though for its full success more troops would be desirable in case the enemy is in large force. I feel confident, however, that a part, and perhaps the whole, may be carried out with the present force.

Very respectfully, your obedient servant,

H. G. WRIGHT,
Brigadier-General, Commanding.

[Inclosure.]

I propose landing on the shore of Amelia Island, to engage and cut off, if possible, the retreat of the rebel force—the landing to be beyond the reach of his batteries; the town of Fernandina to be taken possession of as soon as possible, as well as the railroad beyond. A floating force (naval) should be pushed as rapidly as possible up the Amelia River past Fernandina, to intercept the retreat of the rebels, to prevent the destruction of the railroad bridge, and to save any rolling stock of the road that may be at Fernandina. A portion of the land force may be pushed into the interior by the railroad, if thought desirable; and another portion, taken on board the gunboats, may be sent up Cumberland Sound, to intercept the retreat of the garrison on Cumberland Island. Our reliance is on the squadron for boats for landing the troops and for cover in landing.

It is of the highest importance to the full success of our operations that the wharves at Fernandina, which the enemy will no doubt attempt to destroy, should be preserved. They will afford the means of putting troops on board the transports or gunboats for the further operations with great rapidity, and facilitate the landing of stores, &c.

H. G. WRIGHT,
Brigadier-General.

HILTON HEAD, *January* 31, 1862.

HEADQUARTERS THIRD BRIGADE, EXPED'Y CORPS,
Steamer Empire City, Warsaw Sound, Ga., February 3, 1862.

General THOMAS W. SHERMAN, *&c.:*

GENERAL: I have the honor to report that we succeeded in getting into this harbor yesterday with the two vessels in tow of the Empire City without any important damage.

Yesterday the weather was too stormy for vessels to lay alongside each other, and hence nothing could be done toward coaling, watering, &c. To-day, however, the weather is moderating, and work is going on with all dispatch.

The men are so crowded on board the Cosmopolitan and Boston that I shall be compelled to transfer some from each to the Marion, and take the latter on the expedition, according to the understanding I had with the chief quartermaster, Captain Saxton. Part of the medicines to have been forwarded by the medical director have not come to hand, according to the report of the brigade surgeon.

I shall use every endeavor to have the transports ready by the time the naval force shall be ready to move.

Very respectfully, your obedient servant,

H. G. WRIGHT,
Brigadier-General, Commanding.

HEADQUARTERS EXPEDITIONARY CORPS,
Port Royal, S. C., February 5, 1862.

General M. C. MEIGS,
Washington, D. C.:

DEAR GENERAL: The light-draught steamers, which we understand left New York for this place a long time ago, have not arrived, neither the boats, wagons, &c., which Saxton has been so long expecting.

I fear now, as the season has so far advanced, we shall do little but simply garrison the coast. I am not my own master. My master thus far have been the exigencies created by want of means and facilities for operating in a way desirable to both ourselves and the country at large. Savannah should have been in our possession by this time, not in the way expected by the anxious public on our arrival here; for of all the visionary and impracticable ideas that could have been invented, nothing could have equaled that of marching on Savannah on landing here; but by a distinct process, in combination with the Navy, either in besieging it by Montgomery, or taking it by the horns by boldly ascending the Savannah River under cover of the gunboats. For the former mode our siege material has never arrived. For the latter mode the opportunity has now unfortunately passed, and if we can, after such delay (which is no fault of the Army), succeed in cutting off Pulaski's communications, we'll do well. My firm conviction is that if the gunboats could have been induced to enter the river as early as the 17th or 18th of last month, when Wall's Cut was then opened, and the enemy had no guns mounted at Savannah but those on Fort Jackson, Savannah would have fallen without a resistance of five hours duration, but it could not have been taken by the land force alone in that way.

As Savannah seems out of our grasp for the present, we shall go down to Fernandina as soon as the Navy is ready.

Very truly, yours,

T. W. SHERMAN.

HEADQUARTERS EXPEDITIONARY CORPS,
Port Royal, S. C., February 9, 1862.

To the ADJUTANT-GENERAL U. S. A.,
Washington, D. C.:

SIR: The imperative necessity of putting the blacks in the way of avoiding starvation before the planting season expires without a draw on the commissariat to an extent that would cripple the service, and for other reasons suggested in the general order which I herewith inclose, has induced me to the measures mentioned therein.

I would respectfully ask for a speedy reply to this communication, and should the plan be generally approved, then how far I shall be authorized to hire instructors. This is a point whereon I have entertained some doubts. I firmly believe, however, that the general agent of instruction should be employed by the Government, if not all the instructors; but the latter, the district or sub-instructors, may possibly be provided by the public charities.

This step which I have taken is of vital importance, and to be beneficial for the present year must go into operation at once. The present condition of the blacks, daily increasing in numbers and daily diminishing in their resources, must be alleviated both for their own welfare and the great cause itself.

No correct census has yet been taken, but I estimate the number of blacks now on land in possession of our forces to be at least 9,000, which is probably a low estimate.

Very respectfully, your obedient servant,

T. W. SHERMAN,
Brigadier-General, Commanding.

[Inclosure.]

GENERAL ORDERS, No. 9. } HEADQUARTERS EXPEDITIONARY CORPS,
Hilton Head, S. C., February 6, 1862.

The helpless condition of the blacks inhabiting the vast area in the occupation of the forces of this command calls for immediate action on the part of a highly-favored and philanthropic people.

The occupation of a large portion of this area of country on the 7th of November last led to an address to the people of South Carolina, briefly setting forth the causes which led to it, its objects and purposes, and inviting all persons to the reoccupation in a loyal spirit of their lands and tenements and to a continuance of their avocations under the auspices of their legitimate Government and the protection of the Constitution of the United States.

The conciliatory and beneficent purposes of that proclamation, except in a few instances, have not only been disregarded, but hordes of totally uneducated, ignorant, and improvident blacks have been abandoned by their constitutional guardians, not only to all the future chances of anarchy and starvation, but in such a state of abject ignorance and mental stolidity as to perclude all possibility of self-government and self-maintenance in their present condition.

Adequate provision for the pressing necessities of this unfortunate and now interesting class of people being therefore imperatively demanded even by the dictates of humanity alone, an additional duty, next only in importance to that of the preservation of a world-revered Constitution and Union, is now forced upon us by an unnatural and wicked rebellion.

To relieve the Government of a burden that may hereafter become insupportable, and to enable the blacks to support and govern themselves in the absence and abandonment of their disloyal guardians, a suitable system of culture and instruction must be combined with one providing for their physical wants. Therefore, until proper legislation on the subject or until orders from higher authority, the country in occupation of the forces of this command will be divided off into districts of convenient size for proper superintendence. For each of these districts a suitable agent will be appointed, to superintend the management of the plantations by the blacks; to enroll and organize the willing blacks into working parties; to see that they are well fed, clad, and paid a proper remuneration for their labor; to take charge of all property on the plantation, whether found there, provided by the Government, or raised from the soil, and to perform all other administrative duties connected with the plantations that may be required by the Government.

A code of regulations on this subject, as well as a proper division of districts, will be furnished in due time. In the mean while, and until the blacks become capable themselves of thinking and acting judiciously, the services of competent instructors will be received, one or more for each district, whose duties will consist in teaching them, both young and old, the rudiments of civilization and Christianity, their amenability to the laws of both God and man, their relations to each other as social beings, and all that is necessary to render them competent to sustain themselves in social and business pursuits.

For an efficient and complete organization of this system there will be appointed two general agents, one to have a general superintendence over the administrative or agricultural agents and the other over the educational department.

II. The above system is not intended in any respect to interfere with the existing orders respecting the employment of contrabands by the staff department of the Army and by the cotton agents.

III. As the blacks are now in great need of suitable clothing, if not other necessaries of life, which necessity will probably continue and even increase until the above system gets into working order, the benevolent and philanthropic of the land are most earnestly appealed to for assistance in relieving their immediate wants.

Never was there a nobler or more fitting opportunity for the operation of that considerate and practical benevolence for which the Northern people have ever been distinguished.

By order of Brig. Gen. T. W. Sherman:

L. H. PELOUZE,
Captain, Fifteenth Infantry, Actg. Asst. Adjt. General.

HEADQUARTERS THIRD BRIGADE, EXPED'Y CORPS,
Steamer Empire City, Warsaw Sound, Ga., February 10, 1862.

General THOMAS W. SHERMAN:

GENERAL: I send the steamer Marion to Hilton Head to-day to procure certain articles of property, officers' supplies, &c., left behind, which have become essential to the health and comfort of the command, with orders to the captain to return as soon as the objects of the trip are attained, or sooner if the remainder of the expedition should be sooner ready.

The troops have been landed and are in camp on Warsaw Island, but the debarkation has been made under unfavorable circumstances on account of the weather, and I fear the health of the command may suffer in consequence. So far the health of the men has been good, notwithstanding the confinement; much better than at Hilton Head.

A good deal of activity is exhibited by the rebels in their works at the Skidaway battery.

Very respectfully, your obedient servant,

H. G. WRIGHT,
Brigadier-General, Commanding Expedition.

HEADQUARTERS OF THE ARMY, A. G. O.,
Washington, February 12, 1862.

Brig. Gen. THOMAS W. SHERMAN, U. S. A.,
Commanding, &c., Port Royal, S. C.:

SIR: The General-in-Chief directs that you send about 300 or 400 contrabands to Key West, to be employed on the public works there.

I am, &c.,

L. THOMAS,
Adjutant-General.

HEADQUARTERS OF THE ARMY,
Washington, February 12, 1862.

Brig. Gen. THOMAS W. SHERMAN,
Commanding, Port Royal:

GENERAL: You will learn by the mail that brings you this of our success in the West and East. The line of the Tennessee is open to us. Our gunboats have reached Florence, Ala., after taking Fort Henry, on the line between Tennessee and Kentucky, and we hope to hear to-day that Fort Donelson, on the Cumberland, has also been taken.

Burnside has most gallantly carried Roanoke Island, with some loss, but inflicting terrible destruction upon the enemy. All their positions are taken, their fleet of gunboats captured or destroyed. Our raw troops, according to the rebel accounts, behaved most gallantly.

General Meigs has just informed me that he has ordered a large number of small boats. He is not yet informed of their leaving port. I have to-day a dispatch from Philadelphia in regard to shipping forty-eight surf-boats ready there to go to Port Royal. They will go forward at once.

I have been daily expecting to hear more definite accounts of what can be done in the Savannah River and of the possibility of starving out Fort Pulaski. While awaiting further re-enforcements, and while the rebels are pushed so much in other quarters, I would suggest for your consideration whether, by reducing your garrisons to the minimum, a successful combined attack cannot be made on Savannah so soon as Pulaski has fallen.

In great haste, I am, general, very truly, yours,

GEO. B. McCLELLAN,
Major-General, U. S. Army, Commanding.

HEADQUARTERS OF THE ARMY,
Washington, February 14, 1862.

Brig. Gen. THOMAS W. SHERMAN,
Commanding at Port Royal, &c.:

GENERAL: Your dispatches in regard to the occupation of Daufuskie Island, &c., were received to-day. I saw also to-day for the first time your requisition for a siege train for Savannah.

After giving the subject all the consideration in my power, I am forced to the conclusion that under present circumstances the siege and capture of Savannah do not promise results commensurate with the sacrifices necessary. When I learned that it was possible for the gun-boats to reach the Savannah River above Fort Pulaski, two operations suggested themselves to my mind as its immediate results:

First. The capture of Savannah by a *coup de main*—the result of an instantaneous advance and attack by the Army and Navy.

The time for this has passed, and your letter indicates that you are not accountable for the failure to seize the propitious moment, but that, on the contrary, you perceived its advantages.

Second. To isolate Fort Pulaski, cut off its supplies, and at least facilitate its reduction by a bombardment.

Although we have a long delay to deplore, the second course still remains open to us; and I strongly advise the close blockade of Pulaski and its bombardment as soon as the 13-inch mortars and heavy guns reach you. I am confident you can thus reduce it. With Pulaski you gain all that is really essential; you obtain complete control of the harbor; you relieve the blockading fleet, and render the main body of your force disposable for other operations.

I do not consider the possession of Savannah worth a siege after Pulaski is in our hands. But the possession of Pulaski is of the first importance. The expedition to Fernandina is well, and I shall be glad to learn that it is ours.

But, after all, the greatest moral effect would be produced by the reduction of Charleston and its defenses. There the rebellion had its birth; there the unnatural hatred of our Government is most intense; there is the center of the boasted power and courage of the rebels.

To gain Fort Sumter and hold Charleston is a task well worthy of our greatest efforts and considerable sacrifices. That is the problem I would be glad to have you study. Some time must elapse before we can be in all respects ready to accomplish that purpose. Fleets are *en route* and armies in motion which have certain preliminary objects to accomplish before we are ready to take Charleston in hand, but the time will before long arrive when I shall be prepared to make that movement. In the mean time it is my advice and wish that no attempt be made upon Savannah, unless it can be carried with certainty by a *coup de main*.

Please concentrate your attention and forces upon Pulaski and Fernandina. Saint Augustine might as well be taken by way of an interlude, while awaiting the preparations for Charleston. Success attends us everywhere at present.

Very truly, yours,

GEO. B. McCLELLAN,
Major-General, Commanding U. S. Army.

HEADQUARTERS EXPEDITIONARY CORPS,
Port Royal, S. C., February 15, 1862.

The ADJUTANT-GENERAL U. S. ARMY,
Washington, D. C.:

SIR: As I informed you on the 8th instant, General Viele had orders to erect his battery on the Savannah River, whether the Navy could assist him or not. Accordingly a battery of six siege guns was erected at Venus Point, on Jones Island, on the night of the 11th instant, and fortunately without molestation from the enemy.

In order to render the blockade of the river complete, a similar battery is to be erected at the head of Long Island. The preparations for this have, like the other, been ready ever since the day of the reconnaissance, the 28th of January.

As the naval gunboats cannot be prevailed upon to enter the river, I have given General Viele orders to likewise erect this battery without them, which I think will be done without much hazard, now that the Venus Point battery is up.

Commodore DuPont will leave two or three light-draught gunboats in Mud River, which will probably tend to cover our batteries from gunboats of the enemy coming down the Savannah and attempting to take us in rear by way of Mud River.

I have sent a 10-inch columbiad down there, which will now be necessary without the aid of the gunboats.

General Wright's troops are yet in Warsaw Sound, waiting for the Navy.

Our delays since the middle of January have grieved me to almost a state of mortification. The season is rapidly passing; we can work six weeks longer, and probably twelve. Now, if anything serious is to be done in that time over and beyond the expedition that is about to start, I will state candidly and explicitly what will be required at once: All the means of transportation that have been asked for (which I believe have been ordered but which have never got here); the mortars and siege equipage (which are gradually arriving, though none of the 13-inch are here yet), and 10,000 infantry troops.

The great extent of coast we have had to garrison and guard has absorbed a good portion of our troops.

The mortar battery against Pulaski will go up as soon as the mortars arrive.

Savannah is out of the question with our present force, particularly after the detachments to Fernandina and Edisto Island, which I did not desire to make at present; but, in order to do something in the absence of our ability to get on the main for want of transportation, was compelled to do so.

Very respectfully, your obedient servant,

T. W. SHERMAN,
Brigadier-General, Commanding.

[Indorsement.]

The 10,000 infantry asked for are not at present available. Recommend to General Sherman to reduce Fort Pulaski in preference to attempting Savannah.

GEO. B. McCLELLAN,
Major-General.

WAR DEPARTMENT, *February* 18, 1862.

Col. DANIEL D. TOMPKINS,
Assistant Quartermaster-General, New York City:

COLONEL: You are hereby directed to furnish transportation by sea from New York City to Port Royal, S. C., to all persons who may present to you written permits, issued under the authority of the Secretary of the Treasury, and setting forth that such persons are proceeding to Port Royal, under the sanction of the Government, upon business relating to the collection, safe-keeping, and disposition of cotton, rice, and other property abandoned by persons inhabiting any district within the late territorial limits of States declared by proclamation to be in insurrection, and to the condition and employment of persons of color, there or in the vicinity, lately held to service or labor by enemies of the United States, and now within the occupying lines and under the military protection of the Army. Said permits will specify whether the transportation shall be cabin or steerage, and will cover all baggage, agricultural instruments, and other articles mentioned therein.

You will also make suitable provisions for supplying said passengers with food during the voyage. Permits signed by the collector of the customs at New York City will be regarded by you as emanating from the Treasury Department.

EDWIN M. STANTON,
Secretary of War.

WAR DEPARTMENT, *February* 18, 1862.

Brig. Gen. THOMAS W. SHERMAN,
Commanding at Port Royal, S. C.:

GENERAL: You are hereby directed to afford protection, subsistence, and facilities, so far as may be consistent with the interests of the service and the duties and the objects of your command, to all persons who may present to you written permits, issued to them under the authority of the Secretary of the Treasury, setting forth that said persons have proceeded to Port Royal under the sanction of the Government, for the collection, safe-keeping, and disposition of cotton, rice, and other property abandoned by the late possessors within your military department, and for the regulation and employment of persons of color lately held to service or labor by enemies of the United States, and now within the occupying lines and under the military protection of the Army.

Such permits, signed by the collector of the customs at New York City, will be considered by you as emanating from the Treasury Department.

Under the head of subsistence will be included rations to such persons as may be employed under the direction of the Treasury Department in the temporary charge of abandoned plantations, or, with its sanction, in labors for the instruction and improvement of the laboring population.

EDWIN M. STANTON,
Secretary of War.

ENGINEER OFFICE, *February* 21, 1862.

[Maj. Gen. GEORGE B. McCLELLAN]:

DEAR GENERAL: The inclosed pages were drawn up by Colonel Woodbury at my request. I do not suppose you will have time to read them; but you may skim over them to get the main points, and the information may be useful in directing future operations. It is hardly likely you would care just now to get up an expedition of the magnitude required to take Charleston (it appears to be the most difficult point of the whole coast; I mean its forts), but you might hereafter find occasion to attack. Fort Pulaski taken—and that ought to be taken speedily—perhaps Sherman's and Burnside's army might unite upon Charleston. Woodbury thinks that Burnside can take Forts Macon and Caswell; if so, it may be a question whether he had not better take these than go to Goldsborough. But all these things are conjectural, and I give you the data, as much as I can, to post you for whatever may turn up.

If those Tennessee prisoners are really disposed to take the oath of allegiance, would it not be a wise policy to let them go home? We want to raise the State in our favor as speedily as possible.

You had better return me these notes as soon as you have glanced at them, as they will be of more use in my hands than yours just now.

Yours, respectfully,

J. G. BARNARD.

[Inclosure.]

CHARLESTON HARBOR.—NOTES RELATIVE TO AN ATTACK.

We may assume that we have not now the means required to carry the formidable works of Charleston Harbor by a *coup de main*. History furnishes no precedent of the success of such an undertaking, but does furnish many examples of failure. In the war of the Revolution a pretty formidable British fleet failed in a contest with old Fort Moultrie. Since that period the power of fleets has been greatly increased by the use of steam and of iron-plated vessels of war; but the fortifications of Charleston Harbor have gained power perhaps in equal ratio. It is quite possible that a few iron-clad steamers, assisted by other vessels, might silence Fort Moultrie, and batter down the walls of Fort Sumter in a very few days, and that the same fleet might take in succession all the other fortifications now in possession of the revolutionists But we have no such fleet, and cannot have for many months. We are compelled, therefore, to resort to the old methods. I regard, however, as essential to success at least two iron-plated steamers of great power; four such steamers, I believe, would insure success; six, easy success. The attack would comprise, I think, the following operations, the three first to be nearly simultaneous:

1st. Landing on Sullivan's Island and promptly investing Fort Moultrie.

2d. Landing on Morris Island with artillery to reduce Fort Sumter, including some twenty rifle cannon of large caliber.

3d. Two or more iron-clad war steamers must run in, under cover of partial darkness or of a fog, and take a position in Rebellion Roads, to keep off re-enforcements from Sumter and Moultrie.

4th. The erection of gun and mortar batteries against the forts, cannonade, bombardment, breaching, and finally assault, if necessary.

5th. Sumter and Moultrie taken, Castle Pinckney to be reduced by continued cannonade and bombardment from the iron-clad and other vessels. Some of these vessels may probably be able to take a position behind the fort.

6th. As soon as Sumter and Moultrie are taken the city of Charleston will be virtually in our hands, unless the Confederates have powerful batteries on both Cooper and Ashley Rivers; for the iron steamers at least may pass by Castle Pinckney without much damage. Still, to possess the harbor, it would be necessary to take that work, and it would be easy to do so by an attack on all sides after the capture of the works above mentioned. Fort Johnson and the other works around Charleston would, I think, be abandoned by the enemy.

I will now briefly discuss the *modus operandi* and the details, premising that all our knowledge of the channels and of the adjacent harbors is derived from the charts and notes of the Coast Survey and from the excellent map of Col. Hartman Bache, of the Topographical Engineers, published in 1825. I have myself, as light-house inspector, been somewhat familiar with Charleston Harbor, and have passed through the inner channel from that harbor to Bull's Bay.

BASE OF OPERATIONS—ADJACENT HARBORS.

Bull's Bay, 21 miles east of Fort Moultrie, is an excellent harbor, of easy entrance, with 13 feet on the bar at low water and 18 feet at high water. This place is said to be fortified. There are sand hills immediately behind the light-house, some 50 feet above the water, with a counter-slope and ravines affording excellent cover for infantry.

If the fortifications have been placed on these hills, which are, according to my recollection, about one-fourth mile from the beach, it will be necessary, probably, in order to seize them, to assail by land as well as by water. Troops may be landed from boats on the beach, as Professor Bache states, about 3 miles from the northeast bluff. I am disposed to think the enemy would abandon this place, if they have not already done so, as soon as they perceived that an attack was to be made in force. If they make a stand, the entire garrison ought to be captured. With one or more iron-clad vessels and some vessels of small draught and armed barges we can, I think, take possession of the entire channel around Bull Island. Escape by water would be impossible. Escape by land could only be made at low water through the marshes at the divide, and this I think would be very difficult. The next inlet of any importance, proceeding towards Charleston, is

Dewees' Inlet, 9 miles from Fort Moultrie, with 7 feet on the bar at low water and 12 feet at high water, and a good anchorage inside.

Breach Inlet, at the eastern end of Sullivan's Island, about 3 miles from Fort Moultrie, can be entered by boats and barges at high water. Passing by Charleston Harbor, the first inlet west is

Light-House Inlet, 4½ miles west of Fort Sumter and less than 1 mile from Charleston light. Boats entering here can pass through interior channels to Stono River and to Charleston.

Stono Inlet, about 8 miles westerly from Charleston main bar, has about 8 feet at low water and probably 13 feet at high water. It is said to be fortified.

North Edisto Inlet, 18 miles southwesterly from Charleston Bar, has 13 feet at low water and 19 feet at high water. It is, or has recently been, in our possession.

CHANNELS OF CHARLESTON HARBOR.

Sullivan's Island Channel, recently obstructed by "stone ships," has 11 feet at low water, 16 or 17 feet at high water.

North Channel, still open, 8 feet at low water, 13 or 14 feet at high water.

Swash Channel, still open, 9 feet at low water, 14 feet at high water.

Main Ship Channel, obstructed, 13 feet at low water, 18 or 19 feet at high water.

Lawford's Channel, open, 7 feet at low water, 12 feet at high water.

TIME, PLACE, AND MANNER OF LANDING.

Our southern Atlantic beach is alway rough on the flood tide whatever be the wind. It is always rough on the ebb tide with any considerable onshore wind. But an ebb tide with no wind, or a slight onshore wind, or any kind of offshore wind, secures a good landing. As these conditions are not fulfilled every day, or indeed every week, and as they cannot be predicted many hours ahead, it is necessary to have a rendezvous at hand—the nearer the better. I am disposed to think there should be two such places: Bull's Bay for the Moultrie party, North Edisto for Sumter. The interior channels from each of these places to Charleston Harbor may perhaps be used as auxiliary directions of attack. The inside channel from Bull's Bay enters Charleston Harbor at the point of Sullivan's Island, three-fourths of a mile from Fort Moultrie. It has of course a divide between each two inlets, and these divides, beingn early or quite bare at low water, will pass boats or vessels drawing 4 or 5 feet at high water. As the high water occurs on all these divides at the same time, it would generally be necessary for vessels drawing 4 or 5 feet to use several tides in going through. Moreover, the channel passes occasionally near the Banks, or narrow islands, which skirt the beach, and at these points a few field pieces would make the navigation difficult.

Enough has been said to show that we could not safely use this inside channel without first taking possession of the Banks. It is quite possible, however, that at the moment of landing on the beach of Sullivan's Island a few armed barges, having entered at Breach Inlet or Dewees' Inlet, might make a useful diversion in the rear.

LANDING ON SULLIVAN'S ISLAND.

The island generally is about one-fourth of a mile wide. Along the central part, about 1½ miles from Fort Moultrie and 2½ miles from Fort Sumter, along a reach more than one-half mile long at high water and during two or three hours after high water, gunboats of 10 feet draught can lie or maneuver within 300 yards of the beach. Under cover of their fire, and particularly of their cross-fire, good infantry, I think, could land and effect a footing. Once in possession of a strip of the island extending back to the marsh, they could face right and left, and, with the continued aid of the gunboats, first take possession of the eastern end of the island, then advance upon Fort Moultrie within range of its guns, and commence the operations of a siege.

But the preliminary operation in this case is not without its difficulties and its doubts. If the enemy has notice of the attack and suspects the point of attack; if he has strong inclosed batteries at that point, with large bodies of infantry behind the sand hills supporting those batteries, the undertaking would seem to be too hazardous.

There is another mode of attack which ought to be undertaken at the same time. The success of either will be sufficient. I allude to an attack upon the eastern end of Sullivan's Island. Small craft, drawing not more than 3 feet, made proof against musketry and field artillery, armed with musketry and boat howitzers, can be brought up in any number from Dewees' Harbor, only 6 or 7 miles off, and make an attack which it would be very hard to resist. Once landed in force, aided by the gunboats on one flank and perhaps by the same small craft on the other, our troops could, I am confident, without serious difficulty, drive the enemy down to Fort Moultrie, whatever batteries he may have along the beach. If we can obtain these small vessels of the right kind and in sufficient number I should think this last attack the most promising of the two. Preparations for the other, however, should by no means be omitted. There is in common use in North Carolina a small craft called a flat, drawing, when not loaded, about 15 inches, carrying from 10 to 20 tons, with a center-board, schooner-rigged, strong, easily managed by two men, fast-sailing, open, but seaworthy, as I know by experience, capable of carrying the timbers or bales of wet cotton necessary to make them shot-proof. They would answer the purpose in hand, I think, admirably.

LANDING ON MORRIS ISLAND.

I should recommend here the same preparation for a real or pretended attack on the beach and a simultaneous attack by small craft on the west end of Morris Island. Whether it will be best to make these attacks on Morris Island simultaneously with similar attacks on Sullivan's Island or to let the one follow the other at the interval of a day or two, I will not pretend to say. It must depend on the means at hand. Simultaneous attacks are certainly desirable.

Preliminary to the attack by small craft on the west end of Morris Island it may be necessary to take possession of Stono Inlet and Folly Island. Vessels of 12 feet draught entering at Stono Inlet can be taken along the channel immediately behind Folly Island to the divide, 2 miles from Light-House Inlet. This divide, according to Hartman Bache, has 1 foot at low water; 5 or 6 therefore at high water. There are several other channels from Stono to Light-House Inlet. The character of the country is such as to make it improbable that the enemy should make a stand around Folly Island. Once landed on Morris Island, our troops would, I think, aided by the gunboats, easily drive the enemy down that narrow strip of land, and probably capture those who had not the means of immediate escape.

As soon as possible after landing on the two islands two or more iron-plated vessels should take a position in Rebellion Roads.

OPERATION III—TO PREVENT RE-ENFORCEMENTS.

The extent of the harbor is such that the vessels may lie at anchor or maneuver 1¼ miles from Fort Sumter and Castle Pinckney, and as near Fort Johnson on the south and Haddrell's beacon on the north as it may be safe to go. These vessels could make it difficult for anything but small boats to pass from the city to the forts, and at the proper time, by a reverse fire, they could greatly assist in the reduction of the forts.

OPERATIONS AGAINST FORT MOULTRIE.

This is an irregular open barbette work, covering about 2½ acres of ground. It has three land fronts and three water fronts. The steamboat landing at the point of the island and the road therefrom to the fort are seen and commanded by a half bastion front 213 feet long, with nine guns, of which two are on the flank. The next land front facing the cove north of the fort is a regular bastion 405 feet long, with one gun on each face and two on each flank and room for more. The next front, directly opposed to our approaches, is a bastion front 244 feet long, with two guns on each flank, one on one face, two on the curtain, and room for three more.

Next a water front 121 feet long, with five guns.

Next a water front 251 feet long, with twelve guns.

Next a water front 173 feet long, with nine guns.

The guns are stated in accordance with the intended armament of the fort. The guns actually furnished by the United States before the fort was seized by the Confederates were as follows: Four 24-pounder howitzers; ten 8 inch columbiads; five 8-inch sea-coast howitzers; fourteen 32-pounders; sixteen 24-pounders.

The fort had been supplied with its full armament, and the Confederates have probably added all they found room for. In 1860-'61 Captain (now General) Foster made some repairs and additions, which are thus described by him:

A wet ditch, 15 feet wide all around the fort, of small depth, in consequence of quicksand, the latter readily yielding to pressure, is a good obstacle in itself. A picket fence all around the fort, bordering the ditch, and protected from fire by a small glacis; a bastionette for musketry at the northwest angle; a temporary machicoulis gallery at the southeast angle; two caponieres of bricks to flank the three water fronts; merlons on the whole of the east front.

The Confederates have added merlons on the water fronts, and it is probable that most of the guns may now be fired from embrasures. The guns are all in barbette, unless some casemate guns (howitzers) have been placed in the caponieres added by Captain Foster. The entrance is through the middle of the longest bastion front. This is or was the sally-port through the curtain of the other bastion front. Our approaches along the island will be opposed by a very short bastion front and by one flank of the other bastion front, mounting ten guns in all. The longest front, which contains the main entrance, will be enfiladed.

There can be no difficulty in breaching the work and dismounting its guns, provided we can advance along the narrow strip of land in places not more than 250 yards between water lines and cut off re-enforcements. If the enemy can carry off his wounded, renew his men and means at will, it will be difficult to obtain any advantage over him. His base of operations is close at hand, and he can build batteries in the sand as well as we can; moreover, he has every motive for fighting at this point desperately. Hence the necessity, already urged, of isolating the place, and the necessity of using inside some gunboats of light draught to assist others of heavier draught outside and the land forces in drawing the enemy into the fort. He cannot carry on a very long contest in the fort.

I don't think we need apprehend any very serious annoyance from Fort Sumter. It will be a mile and a quarter from the nearest part of the theater of operations. A drawing attached hereto* shows the situation of the work, its profile, magazines, barracks, officers' quarters, &c. I find no drawing at the Engineer Bureau illustrating the recent repairs and additions made by Captain Foster. The two brick caponieres on the water fronts are supposed to be entered from the terre-plein above. The masonry scarp stands about 14 feet above high water. The bottom of the ditch is probably 2 or 3 feet below high water. The merlons added by the Confederates increase still more the proper height of the scarp, except at the embrasures. The parapet is about 11 feet thick. The scarp wall is made of bricks, and is 7 feet thick at bottom and 3½

*Not found.

feet at top. There were no casemates in the original work, but little bomb-proofs. What bomb-proofs the Confederates may have added we do not know. The scarp is probably exposed to the view of distant batteries; but on this we ought not to count, as it is exceedingly easy to throw up a protecting barrier of sand. The small elevation of this work —its guns are only 15 feet above high water—exposes it greatly to the action of vessels afloat at the moment of assault. With four iron-plated men-of-war I am inclined to think the work could be carried by assault without waiting for the operations of a siege.

OPERATIONS AGAINST FORT SUMTER.

This is a strong casemated work, covering about 3½ acres of ground, rising from an artificial island three-quarters of a mile from the nearest land, armed, or capable of being armed, with 53 barbette guns, in a plane 50 feet above low water; 41 guns in casemates 27 feet above low water, and 41 casemate guns 15 feet above low water. There are no casemate guns on the gorge; light howitzers might, however, be mounted there. The wooden floors which have been placed in the gorge were not intended to bear heavy guns. Still it must be borne in mind that the Confederates may have propped up some of these floors, cut embrasures, and mounted cannon of large caliber in some of the casemates of the gorge. The guns bearing on Cummings Point are: 20 barbette guns at an angle of about 45° with the parapets; 3 barbette guns on the *pan-coupé* nearly direct; 4 casemate guns on the *pan-coupé* nearly direct; 27 in all. The Confederates may, however, add to the casemate guns by building oblique embrasures in the scarp.

The guns bearing on Fort Moultrie are: 10 barbette guns, nearly direct; 2 barbette guns, slightly oblique; 18 casemate guns, nearly direct; 4 casemate guns, oblique; 34 in all. The approaches to Fort Moultrie from the east are seen by these 34 guns belonging to the right face; and Sullivan's Island, northwest of Fort Moultrie, is exposed to an equal number of guns on the left face—some parts of it to nearly all the guns of both faces. Rebellion Roads are exposed to 30 guns in the left face, or 27 guns in the left flank, or all together, according to the situation. I have spoken above of all the guns that can be mounted in Fort Sumter. The guns actually supplied by the United States were, ten 42-pounders; forty-one 32-pounders; three 10-inch columbiads; ten 8-inch columbiads; eight 8-inch sea-coast howitzers; six 24-pounders; 78 in all, leaving 57 wanting.

A drawing of Fort Sumter, in connection with the chart of Charleston Harbor, will illustrate the strength and situation of the work. The principal question is, Can a practicable breach be made in Fort Sumter by batteries located on Cummings Point? I believe there can be. Captain Foster, in his journal of the bombardment of Fort Sumter in May last, reports as follows the breaching batteries on Morris Island or Cummings Point:

Breaching battery No. 1, two 42-pounders; one 12-pounder rifle gun=3.

Breaching battery No. 2, iron-clad, three 8-inch columbiads=3; 6 in all.

The fire commenced at daybreak on the 13th, and was discontinued at Cummings Point about 1 p. m. on the 14th. The two 8-inch columbiads and the rifle gun were the only ones that were used in the effort to make a breach. The latter was fired with great accuracy. All three missiles made the same penetration—11 inches in the brick masonry. They continued firing about twenty hours, and knocked off the face of the wall around one embrasure of the *pan-coupé* to the depth of 22 inches. Instead of one 12-pounder rifle gun, suppose we have twenty of large caliber, and instead of two 8-inch columbiads, some 12, 10, or 11 inch guns, there is little doubt of our ability to make a breach of any desired magnitude in a week or ten days. If we cut away the masonry between three or four of the lower embrasures to the depth of 3 feet, I believe the scarp opposite and above these cuts will fall over in a body, pressed as it always is by the thrust of the communicating arches. If we cut away the 5 by 7 inch pier between any two casemate arches, all the casemate arches on that front of the work will, I think, fall down, for the piers are far from being abutment piers. Should any such accident occur to the right flank—a matter simply of time—I think the work could not much longer hold out. An assault would hardly be necessary.

Vessels drawing about 9 feet can be taken around the south side of Fort Sumter and placed opposite the gorge, 150 feet from the work, below the range of the barbette guns. The two casemates of each story, at each end of the gorge, are occupied as powder magazines.

Fort Sumter can be taken the more easily if Fort Moultrie is taken first. From the latter place and its vicinity all the barbette guns which bear upon Cummings Point can be enfiladed or taken in reverse. There is a platform 10 feet in width around Fort Sumter, about 5 feet below the lower embrasures. The outer slopes of this platform are composed of rough granite, a part of the original artificial island. Landing from boats on this platform would be very difficult.

OPERATIONS AGAINST CASTLE PINCKNEY.

This small work could not make much resistance after the capture of Moultrie and Sumter, provided we have the two iron-plated vessels considered essential to success in the general attack. These vessels may take a position north of the work at the distance of about 500 yards, where only two guns can bear upon them, unless batteries have been built outside of the fort. Castle Pinckney, to vessels approaching Charleston by the main channel, presents a semi-circle 168 feet in diameter, with eight casemate and ten barbette guns; two other barbette guns look north. The interior crest stands about 25 feet above the foot of the scarp and probably about 35 feet above low water. The exterior pavement is 4 or 5 feet below the embrasures, and nearly on the level of the parade. The details may be learned from the drawing.

Castle Pinckney was supplied by the United States with the following armament: For casemates, four 42-pounders, four 24-pounders; for barbette, four 8-inch sea-coast howitzers, ten 24-pounders = 22; two more, apparently, than can be mounted in the work.

ESTIMATE OF THE MEANS REQUIRED FOR THE GENERAL ATTACK UPON CHARLESTON HARBOR.

Troops, including enough to hold some adjacent islands, 15,000; transports sufficient to carry the troops; fleet as large as the one which captured the works at Port Royal.

Iron-plated vessels required, 2.

Flats or small craft drawing 3 or 4 feet, and capable of carrying 100 men each, proof against musketry and field artillery, armed with boat howitzers, 30.

Siege train.—Twenty rifle cannon of large caliber, each with 1,000 rounds of ammunition, twelve 10 or 11 inch guns, twenty mortars, &c.

D. P. WOODBURY,
Lieutenant-Colonel, Aide-de-Camp.

[Indorsement.]

FEBRUARY 18, 1862.—Prepared for General J. G. Barnard, chief engineer Army of the Potomac, Washington, D. C.

HEADQUARTERS EXPEDITIONARY CORPS,
Port Royal, S. C., February 23, 1862.

Maj. Gen. GEORGE B. MCCLELLAN,
Commanding U. S. Army:

GENERAL: Yours of the 12th instant was received to-day by the Harriet Lane. We are all very much elated with your brilliant victories in North Carolina and Tennessee, and hope that they will extend farther South and strike a stunning blow to this rebellion.

We have now two batteries on Savannah River of six guns each; one on Jones Island at Venus Point, and the other on the upper end of Bird Island. The river is effectually blocked, but never were batteries put up and maintained under precisely the same circumstances before. The guns were hauled by hand over the soft marsh of Jones Island with the greatest labor the distance of a mile, the marsh knee-deep and covered with water at high tide; indeed, both batteries are actually in the river.

We have taken since yesterday morning some two or three citizens of Savannah endeavoring to get a mail down to Pulaski through a by-creek not far from Tybee. They say that Savannah could very easily have been taken thirty days ago had we gone straight up the river at that time, which fully confirms my opinion, which I endeavored to carry out, but failed in consequence of the unwillingness of the Navy to do it, though they at first agreed to.

The Navy have not yet been ready for Fernandina, but if the weather will suit we shall probably start to-morrow morning. Whilst this expedition is carried out our siege artillery will be arriving and our mortar and columbiad battery erecting on Tybee, when it is hoped that I shall be able to commence operations on Savannah.

The prisoners from Savannah bring word that the news of the fall of Fort Donelson had reached Savannah; that the victory was complete, and 5,000 prisoners taken. We hope it is true and believe that it is.

Very truly, yours,
T. W. SHERMAN,
Brigadier-General, Commanding.

Pulaski is reported to have from six to ten months' provisions for its garrison, about 500 men, but the prisoners say that they have only ammunition enough for two days' fighting.

HEADQUARTERS EXPEDITIONARY CORPS,
Off Tybee, Ga., February 27, 1862.

The ADJUTANT-GENERAL U. S. ARMY,
Washington, D. C.:

SIR: It was my intention to accompany the expedition for Fernandina, and while waiting in Warsaw Sound for the naval force to join us from Hilton Head I received the important information that Brunswick and the forts at Saint Simon's have been evacuated since the 15th instant. This news was brought by a refugee from Savannah, and is corroborated by the Charleston papers of the 18th instant. Our threat upon Savannah has therefore already reduced the strongest hold of the enemy south of us, and the fall of the city would undoubtedly produce the fall of all forts on the coast between here and Saint Augustine, as predicted in my letter of the 14th of December last. But as this expedition, planned upwards of a month ago, in order to economize and make the most of a short period of time, in which nothing else could be done with the troops engaged in it, has been waiting at the expense of many transports lying idle and some sacrifice of life, I think it should proceed, particularly as the Navy are anxious to complete it, notwithstanding the period of time in which it was to be accomplished has long since run out. But as the enemy are discovered to be concentrating most of their forces on Savannah, and guns too (as upwards of twenty pieces of heavy caliber are known to have recently been brought from Brunswick and planted about Savannah), I consider the coast now but a cobweb, to be penetrated with ease, and am therefore on my return to Port Royal, to continue the charge of affairs in that quarter, leaving the expedition with Brigadier-General Wright. This division of force at this particular juncture may be regarded as a fault, but the reason for it can be seen from what I have stated, and, besides, Fernandina and Brunswick are points of some importance.

The Savannah River is closed as tight as a bottle between Savannah and Pulaski, and we are pushing preparations at Tybee for bombardment as rapidly as the weather will allow.

Very respectfully, your obedient servant,

T. W. SHERMAN,
Brigadier-General, Commanding.

HEADQUARTERS EXPEDITIONARY CORPS,
Port Royal, S. C., February 28, 1862.

Maj. Gen. GEORGE B. MCCLELLAN:

GENERAL: The deserters just in from Savannah say there are about 65,000 troops in and about the city, which is well fortified both on the land and river sides. They are moving heaven and earth for a secure defense. So far as I can ascertain some of the smaller forts on the coast are being stripped of artillery with which to protect Savannah. The abandonment of Brunswick is an evidence of it. I hope to soon get under way at Tybee, though the rough stormy weather makes it very slow in getting the ordnance landed. We must get entirely ready before we open. The Massachusetts regiment has arrived, and we hope more will follow soon. I rather think we shall have to take Savannah by way of Vernon River. If the Navy could not assist us last month, when no guns had been put up on the river except those at Fort Jackson, it certainly cannot now, when the enemy have completed so many of them.

Our siege artillery is arriving. The news I have through Savannah papers (found with the prisoners) gives the most cheering and welcome accounts of your successes, and, general, I most sincerely congratulate you on your plans being carried out with such brilliant successes. My opinion is that you have about crushed this rebellion already. The Savannah and Charleston papers show a deeply saddened spirit among the people, though yet an apparently determined one; but I know the people of the South are unable to stand this state of things long. They are quick to fight when occasion offers, but as quick to fall when misfortune occurs.

Yours, very truly,

T. W. SHERMAN,
Brigadier-General.

Abstract from return of the Expeditionary Corps, commanded by Brig. Gen. Thomas W. Sherman, U. S. Army, for February, 1862.

Stations.	Present. Officers. For duty.	Officers. Total.	Men. For duty.	Men. Total.	Aggregate present and absent.	Remarks.
Beaufort, S. C	121	138	2,895	3,373	3,737	The 2d Brigade and Rockwell's (Connecticut) battery.
Daufuskie Island, S. C	34	37	790	852	906	Headquarters 1st Brigade and 48th New York.
Edisto Island, S. C	21	22	538	572	613	47th New York.
Fort Welles, S. C	61	65	1,310	1,570	1,705	76th Pennsylvania and 3d Rhode Island.
Hilton Head, S. C	188	201	4,657	5,034	5,568	8th Maine, 28th Massachusetts, 1st Massachusetts Cavalry, 3d New Hampshire, 1st New York Engineers, and 55th Pennsylvania.
Otter Island	33	33	772	856	935	45th Pennsylvania.
Savannah River	2	2	60	63	146	3d U. S. Artillery, Battery E.
Tybee Island, Ga	59	66	1,316	1,546	1,655	7th Connecticut and 46th New York.
Warsaw Sound, Ga	129	131	3,006	3,267	3,708	Headquarters 3d Brigade, 6th Connecticut, 9th Maine, 4th New Hampshire, and 97th Pennsylvania.
Division headquarters	28	28	26	26	55	Headquarters staff, &c.
Total	676	723	15,370	17,159	19,028	

ORGANIZATION OF THE EXPEDITIONARY CORPS, FEBRUARY 28, 1862.

First Brigade.

Brig. Gen. EGBERT L. VIELE.

8th Maine, Col. John D. Rust.
3d New Hampshire, Col. E. Q. Fellows.
46th New York, Col. Rudolph Rosa.
47th New York, Col. Henry Moore.
48th New York, Col. James H. Perry.
55th Pennsylvania, Col. Richard White.

Second Brigade.

Brig. Gen. ISAAC I. STEVENS.

8th Michigan, Col. Wm. M. Fenton.
79th New York, Col. Addison Farnsworth.
50th Pennsylvania, Col. B. C. Christ.
100th Pennsylvania, Col. Daniel Leasure.

Third Brigade.

Brig. Gen. HORATIO G. WRIGHT.

6th Connecticut, Col. John L. Chatfield.
7th Connecticut, Col. Alfred H. Terry.
9th Maine, Col. Rishworth Rich.
4th New Hampshire, Col. Thomas J. Whipple.
97th Pennsylvania, Col. Henry R. Guss.

Troops not brigaded.

28th Massachusetts, Col. Wm. Montieth.
1st New York Engineers, Col. E. W. Serrell.
45th Pennsylvania, Col. Thomas Welsh.
76th Pennsylvania, Col. John M. Power.
3d Rhode Island, Col. Nathaniel W. Brown.
1st Massachusetts Cavalry, Col. Robert Williams.
1st Connecticut Battery, Capt. A. P. Rockwell.
3d U. S. Artillery, Battery E, Capt. John Hamilton.

HEADQUARTERS THIRD BRIGADE, EXPED'Y CORPS,
Saint Andrew's Sound, Ga., March 2, 1862.

Col. H. R. GUSS,
Commanding Ninety-seventh Pennsylvania Regiment:

COLONEL: Intelligence, deemed reliable, has been received to the effect that the enemy has abandoned Fernandina and its vicinity, removing the guns and property at that point. It has therefore been decided that, instead of proceeding according to the original project, a portion of the light-draught gunboats, with a part of the land force, shall proceed at once by the inland passage, while the remainder of the fleet will go outside. Your regiment, or rather the eight companies on board the Boston, will accompany the gunboats by the inland passage, and the transport will at once move up the sound to join them.

On your arrival at Fernandina you will co-operate with the naval force under the command of Capt. P. Drayton, of the Pawnee, by landing your troops, taking possessionof the town and of the railroad and its crossing over the marsh and the river.

The possession of this road in a serviceable condition may be of the utmost importance to our further operations, and you will consequently use every exertion to prevent its destruction by the enemy.

Should any of the enemy be still upon Amelia Island, you will effect their capture, if possible.

Preserve all public property left behind, and afford every protection to private property, not permitting the appropriation of the smallest article by the troops of your command.

Wishing you every success, I am, very respectfully,

H. G. WRIGHT,
Brigadier-General, Commanding.

MARCH 6, 1862.

General SHERMAN,
Port Royal:

If it will not interfere with any operation of greater importance that you may now have on hand, the General-in-Chief hopes that you will be able to arrange with Commodore DuPont for the prompt occupation of Fernandina, in accordance with the original plan of the expedition. It is supposed that this operation will not interfere with the reduction of Fort Pulaski, which is regarded as a matter of very great importance.

The general would also be glad to have your views in regard to the best disposition to be made of your troops during the approaching unhealthy season, and whether any peculiar arrangements should be made to secure their health during the summer in regard to barracks, diet, &c.

Will General Thomas please write about the substance of the above and send it to the Navy Department before 1 o'clock to day, together with the private letter accompanying it?*

Very truly,

GEO. B. McCLELLAN,
Major-General.

---

*The letter based upon this, and acknowledged by Sherman (p. 253) March 26, is not found.

HEADQUARTERS THIRD BRIGADE, EXPED'Y CORPS,
Fernandina, Fla., March 7, 1862.

General THOMAS W. SHERMAN,
Commanding Expeditionary Corps, Hilton Head, S. C.:

GENERAL: After consultation with the flag-officer, it has been determined to send an expedition to the Saint John's River, to consist of several gunboats and a portion of the land force, and it is directed to start to-morrow morning. The troops will consist of eight companies of the Fourth New Hampshire Regiment, under the command of Col. T. J. Whipple.

From all that can be gathered in the way of information, it is believed that a portion, at any rate, of the guns removed from this place previous to our arrival have been taken to Jacksonville, or some point below on the river; that the enemy has a battery at the mouth of the river, another at Saint John's Bluff, and that a third has been commenced at Dame's Point. To destroy these batteries, take possession of the guns, and capture Jacksonville are the objects of the expedition.

It is agreed by Flag-Officer DuPont and myself that the permanent occupation of Jacksonville at this time would not be judicious, nor do I think it in accordance with the spirit of your instructions of the 27th ultimo. It has therefore been determined that, while it may be desirable to land and occupy Jacksonville or other points for a few hours for purposes of reconnaissance or other necessary service, the troops shall be withdrawn and return with the gunboats when this shall have been accomplished.

The McClellan, which did not reach this place till yesterday, will go back to Hilton Head to-morrow, with orders to report to you. The marines, at the request of the flag-officer, return in her. The Star of the South will also probably start for Hilton Head to-morrow.

Very respectfully, your obedient servant,

H. G. WRIGHT,
Brigadier-General, Commanding.

HEADQUARTERS THIRD BRIGADE, EXPED'Y CORPS,
Fernandina, Fla., March 7, 1862.

Col. THOMAS J. WHIPPLE,
Cammanding Fourth New Hampshire Regiment:

COLONEL: After having embarked the eight companies of your regiment on board the steamer Boston, in pursuance of the verbal instructions given you this evening, you will proceed with the gunboat expedition to the Saint John's River, under the command of Commander J. R. Goldsborough, and co-operate with that officer in the objects of the expedition.

It is understood between the flag-officer commanding the naval forces and myself that neither Jacksonville nor any point upon the river below is to be permanently occupied by our forces; but it may be desirable to land at one or more of these points, for the purpose of reconnaissance or other desirable services, and occupy them for a few hours only, returning, of course, with the gunboats to this place when this shall have been accomplished.

You will place yourself in official relation with Captain Goldsborough, commanding the naval force, who is now off the Saint John's entrance, on your arrival there, and arrange with him in regard to the operations in which the services of your command may be required.

Wishing you every success, I am, very respectfully, your obedient servant,

H. G. WRIGHT,
Brigadier-General, Commanding.

HEADQUARTERS EXPEDITIONARY CORPS,
Port Royal, S. C., March 8, 1862.

To the ADJUTANT-GENERAL U. S. ARMY,
Washington, D. C.:

SIR: I have the honor to acknowledge the receipt of your instructions of the 12th ultimo.

I find it impracticable to conform to those instructions with that promptitude which may perhaps be expected without incurring a strong liability to produce a misconception on the part of the blacks as to what the Government intends to do with them. There is much danger of producing a panic among them by too sudden a movement. Many of them surmise that they will ultimately be sent to Cuba and sold, and to permit a stir among them of this sort would be attended with unfortunate results.

I think, however, that from 400 to 500 will be induced to accept the offer made to them, viz, to accept their services for a limited period, with a promise that they shall return to their homes after their services are performed; and as soon as I hear from Edisto, if the result of the inquiry is as favorable as from other points, they shall be shipped by the first convenience.

Very respectfully, your obedient servant,

T. W. SHERMAN,
Brigadier-General, Commanding.

HEADQUARTERS EXPEDITIONARY CORPS,
Port Royal, S. C., March 8, 1862.

Maj. Gen. GEORGE B. MCCLELLAN,
Commanding U. S. Army:

GENERAL: Yours of February 14 was received on the 3d instant. Pulaski is thoroughly cut off, and the batteries are being erected on Tybee as rapidly as the rough weather for landing the ordnance will permit.

Agreeably to your instruction no further preparations will be made for the attack of Savannah.

Before the expedition sailed for Fernandina I ascertained that Brunswick and its dependencies had been evacuated for the re-enforcement in men and guns of Savannah, and though I have not yet received any positive information from Fernandina, there is but little doubt but it was occupied without the firing of a gun.

From information we have gathered since I wrote you on the subject of Charleston, I have arrived at the conclusion that that city and its defenses can be carried with much more ease than I anticipated in that letter. Our occupation of Edisto Island and some reconnaissances made by the Navy convince me that Charleston can be beleaguered in a very happy manner without having to carry the forts near the mouth of the Stono, and indeed by turning them. Gunboats can ascend the North Edisto and Wadmalaw Rivers, and possibly into the Stono itself, which would bring them within 5 miles of the city. There is a good road all the way from North Edisto River to Charleston, and so situated that a land force can co-operate with the gunboats and be at hand to assist removing any obstructions found in the river or reducing any works that may be found in approaching the city. To ascertain precisely where these obstructions and works are situated will require a reconnaissance in force preliminary to any grand movement. It is much more practicable a route than the one to Savannah. The route proposed will in a great measure turn all the defenses of the enemy on James Island and effectually cut off all approaches to the city by land from that quarter. The demonstration, if successful, will produce the evacuation of Charleston, or, should it not, the city can be shelled at leisure from the right bank of the Ashley. The forts in the harbor would probably fall of themselves, but, if not, Sumter can be shelled and possibly reached from James and Morris Islands. To make matters still more sure, a demonstration and indeed a real attack on Point Pleasant from Bull's Bay would probably produce the fall of Moultrie. Indeed I think Moultrie could be easily carried by a *coup de main*, if thought necessary.

I will endeavor to give this subject a very early attention and promptly inform you of all I can gather. In the mean while, general, please furnish me with your general idea of what harbors South should be garrisoned. I have no doubt but all down to Augustine will be at once at our disposal (including Saint John's River). Fernandina and Brunswick are harbors of importance, but are Augustine, Jacksonville, Darien, &c., sufficiently so to absorb our forces?

Very respectfully and truly, yours,

T. W. SHERMAN,
Brigadier-General, Commanding.

HEADQUARTERS THIRD BRIGADE, EXPED'Y CORPS,
Fernandina, Fla., March 8, 1862.

General THOMAS W. SHERMAN,
Hilton Head:

GENERAL: By the steamer McClellan, which left for Hilton Head this morning, I informed you of the expedition fitted out for the Saint John's River. It started about 11.30 a. m. to-day.

No very reliable information in regard to the whereabouts of the rebel force which left this place has yet been procured, though am induced to believe that a part, perhaps the whole, have stopped at Baldwin, the junction of Florida and Cedar Keys and the Jacksonville and Tallahassee Railroads, 47 miles from this place. The enemy, in his retreat, burned the bridges of the railroad, making the approach from this island to the main quite difficult; and I have not therefore considered it judicious, or indeed important as yet, to send any reconnaissance in that direction, as I am not in condition to move in force to any distance inland.

Bearing in mind your instructions to return as soon as practicable to Hilton Head any portion of the force not indispensable for the defense of this place, I have given much consideration to the question of the minimum garrison which would render the position secure, and have concluded that two regiments ought to be ample, provided a naval force of two vessels remains in the harbor. After a short time this force might, I believe, be still reduced, but for the present I cannot think it advisable.

I shall therefore, unless instructed to the contrary, send one regiment back to Hilton Head as soon as the Saint John's expedition returns, and other projects, if determined upon, shall be accomplished, remaining here myself till I hear from you that my services are needed elsewhere.

The people still remaining generally express their gratitude for the unexpected good treatment they experience at our hands and for the protection extended to their property, and profess a desire to have friends return to their homes.

Perhaps a liberal course toward these people may have a happy effect in the State at large, in proving to the inhabitants that we do not come amongst them with the designs against their persons and property which their leaders and their public journals have so falsely charged against us.

In pursuing this course I shall be careful to omit no precaution necessary to the full security of the command against any acts of the people by which intelligence can be conveyed to the enemy to our injury.

I desire to be distinctly understood that, while I propose to remain here in command till I receive your orders, I shall be much disappointed if I am kept here while active operations are being prosecuted elsewhere. Forty-eight hours will suffice to bring me to Hilton Head, or any intermediate point, after your orders are issued.

I inclose a copy of a report from Lieutenant Tardy* in regard to the condition of Fort Clinch, which agrees perfectly with the results of my own hasty examination of the work. I will call upon him for estimates for its improvement to the extent he suggests. The batteries on the seaward side of the fort, containing places for ten guns, need not be occupied by us.

I also send a copy of the report of a reconnaissance made by Captain Sears* of the enemy's defenses on the southern end of Cumberland Island. I have not had time to give them a personal examination.

I propose sending back one section of Captain Ransom's battery, perhaps both.

Very respectfully, your obedient servant,

H. G. WRIGHT,
Brigadier-General, Commanding.

HEADQUARTERS EXPEDITIONARY CORPS,
Port Royal, S. C., March 9, 1862.

To the ADJUTANT-GENERAL U. S. ARMY,
Washington, D. C.:

SIR: From the reports of Brigadier-General Wright, copies of which I herewith inclose,† you will perceive that Amelia Island has been occupied by our forces without resistance.

It is my desire to carry out the views of the Government as to the occupation of this coast in the most judicious manner.

With the force now at my disposal, and without any plan of operations into the interior, I propose to occupy only some of the most important harbor outlets, to the end only, at this time, of preventing the

---

* Not found. †See report of March 5, p. 96, and letter of March 7, p. 239.

running of the blockade. Saint Simon's, Fernandina, the mouth of the Saint John's, and possibly Saint Augustine, would, I think, be sufficient. Other places of some little importance could be blockaded by the Navy.

The occupation of the towns on the main, such as Jacksonville, Saint Mary's, Darien, Brunswick, would be injudicious with our present force, unless we are sure of being supported by a strong party of Unionists, and it is important to first ascertain whether such a party exists to much extent. The desertion of Fernandina and Saint Mary's does not look very favorable.

I shall endeavor to rally the Union men to the support of their flag.

Very respectfully, your obedient servant,

T. W. SHERMAN,
Brigadier-General, Commanding.

HEADQUARTERS THIRD BRIGADE, EXPED'Y CORPS,
Fernandina, Fla., March 9, 1862.

Col. THOMAS J. WHIPPLE,
Commanding Fourth New Hampshire Regiment:

COLONEL: Flag-Officer DuPont proceeds to-day to the Saint John's River, and, after the contemplated operations in that vicinity shall have been finished, will probably continue down the coast with the naval force to Saint Augustine, in which case you will still remain with the Navy and co-operate with it.

Should Saint Augustine be taken possession of, and it should be considered by the flag-officer important to occupy it, you are authorized to leave, say, two companies in Fort Marion as a garrison, with at least ten days' provisions, a trusty captain being placed in command. The remainder of your force will then return to its place in the Boston.

Very respectfully, your obedient servant,

H. G. WRIGHT,
Brigadier-General, Commanding.

HEADQUARTERS OF THE ARMY, A. G. O.,
Washington, March 10, 1862.

Brig. Gen. THOMAS W. SHERMAN, U. S. A.,
Commanding, &c., Port Royal, S. C.:

GENERAL: I am instructed to inform you that, in consequence of information just received that the enemy is abandoning his position at Centreville and towards Manassas, a forward movement of the Army of the Potomac has been ordered this day, to seize upon any advantage that may offer.

I am, sir, &c.,

L. THOMAS,
Adjutant-General.

HEADQUARTERS THIRD BRIGADE, EXPED'Y CORPS,
Fernandina, Fla., March 10, 1862.

Capt. LOUIS H. PELOUZE,
Acting Assistant Adjutant-General:

CAPTAIN: The inhabitants left behind in the evacuation of this place by the rebels are mainly of the poorer classes of whites and free blacks, with a few slaves, many of whom represent themselves as destitute of the means of living, and generally as without money, except the worthless paper in circulation before our occupation. Thus far it has not been necessary to assist them to any considerable extent, but it probably soon will be, unless some means can be devised to aid them in procuring their subsistence.

The army departments here need little, if any, hired labor, and there is no private business carried on to afford them employment. The question therefore presents itself, what is to be done with these people, who cannot be permitted to starve if they are ready to earn their subsistence, and only ask employment to take care of themselves? Instructions in regard to the course to be pursued in this matter are respectfully requested.

The contraband question also presents itself, and will soon require to be decided by the military authority, as regards their support. Some of these people were left behind, and others are presenting themselves daily, coming in from different directions. At Saint Mary's, where I was to-day on a reconnaissance in company with Captain Drayton, commanding the naval forces here, there are a great many negroes still remaining, some of whom have already followed us to Fernandina. As before remarked, we do not need their services at present, and I cannot conceive we shall, unless it be in building up Fort Clinch. At this work most of the men might be employed if there was any fund for the payment for their services, but unless the Quartermaster's Department can supply the money there is none available for the purpose. In this matter, too, I would request instructions. The suggestion just made for the employment of the contrabands might be extended to the free blacks and to the whites. None other presents itself to me in regard to either of the classes thrown upon our hands.

The Ben DeFord arrived this morning, bringing quartermasters' and commissary stores. She will be discharged and sent back without delay.

The five days' supply on hand, with that now received, will provide provisions for the present force for the next forty days, not including, however, what it may be necessary to issue to citizens and contrabands to keep them from starvation.

I have directed that the Boston be sent back to Hilton Head to report to the chief quartermaster. This will leave here, in the way of transports, the Empire City, the Belvidere, and the George's Creek, all of which will be needed for the return to Hilton Head of the force which I have proposed soon to send back.

Very respectfully, your obedient servant,

H. G. WRIGHT,
Brigadier-General, Commanding.

HEADQUARTERS THIRD BRIGADE, EXPED'Y CORPS,
Fernandina, Fla., March 13, 1862.

Capt. LOUIS H. PELOUZE,
Acting Assistant Adjutant-General:

CAPTAIN: I have to report, in regard to the slaves found here and those who have since come in, that I have not attempted to interfere with the rights of the owner so long as he remained within our lines and conducted himself in a quiet and orderly manner, but that I have refused permission to remove any slave from the limits of the command on any plea whatever.

I have conceived that the property of citizens in slaves should be protected to the extent referred to, and shall continue the same policy in regard to them unless I receive instructions to the contrary.

Very respectfully, your obedient servant,

H. G. WRIGHT,
Brigadier-General, Commanding.

[Indorsement.]

Approved, by order of Brigadier-General Sherman:

L. H. PELOUZE,
Acting Assistant Adjutant-General.

MARCH 15, 1862.

HEADQUARTERS EXPEDITIONARY CORPS,
Hilton Head, S. C., March 13, 1862.

General EGBERT L. VIELE,
Commanding Forces, Daufuskie Island, S. C.:

GENERAL: The general commanding directs me to inform you that he is forced to the conclusion, on his late inspection of the works in Savannah River, that not all the measures are taken to avoid disagreeable things that should be. Of the two light-draught steamers, the Petitt lays at Venus Point, and, if he understood you, does not move from there, and the Mayflower does very little at best.

It appears to him that these two boats should move rapidly about from place to place; for instance, the Petitt should be active enough to cover your rear from any assaults by way of New River, and at the same time be prepared to assist in the Savannah River in case of high tides or other emergencies. By taking advantage of the tides, a great deal might be done by these two steamers. They should be so handled as to be seen by the enemy at unexpected points and at unexpected times.

He does not think that, considering the amount of force at your disposal and the time occupied, the Venus Point battery is in that advanced state that it should be. As to the 10-inch columbiad, it should have been up ten days ago. It was sent from here a month ago.

The Bird Island battery seems to be everything that is desired, and great credit is due to Major Beard and his officers and men for their energy and industry.

I am also directed to communicate that the New Hampshire Battalion, under Lieutenant-Colonel Jackson, was sent to you with three days' provisions, for a particular purpose. That purpose should have been accomplished, if accomplished at all, in three days, and that he is dissatisfied with the delay that has attended all its movements.

I am further directed to remind you of the necessity of the chief of artillery and your engineer officer joining him the moment they can be spared.

Very respectfully, your obedient servant,

[L. H. PELOUZE,]
Captain, Fifteenth Infantry, Actg. Asst. Adjt. General.

WILLARD'S HOTEL,
Washington, D. C., March 14, 1862.

Hon. E. M. STANTON,
Secretary of War:

SIR: I have the honor to acknowledge the receipt of your note of this morning, ordering me to report without delay upon the military operations that have been executed or are in progress, or in contemplation, against Savannah and Fort Pulaski, to include everything that in my judgment "the Department should know, or that would be useful to the Government or the forces there, and generally as to the means proposed or wanted for a speedy and successful result."

In obedience to this order, I have the honor respectfully to state that, apparently with a view to forming a basis of operations, a considerable area has been fortified at Hilton Head by means of a line of earthworks, a block-house, beach batteries, flooding the marshes, &c., and the construction of piers, one of great length and to deep water (21 feet low tide).

This area is sufficient to encamp from 25,000 to 30,000 men, crowded; is now defended by the guns of Fort Welles, two guns in the beach battery on our right, and twenty-two guns in the works in the advance. The guns are not up in the beach battery on our left.

From this point detachments have been sent forward.

Early in January last, obstructions placed by the rebels in Wall's Cut, consisting of piles and an old ship, were taken away by our forces. Subsequently a battery of six guns was built by us on Jones Island, at Venus Point, in the Savannah River, and recently another on Bird Island, still nearer to Savannah, which by this time mounts three or four guns.

At Tybee Island mortars are being landed and mortar beds and platforms are being erected. A battery of three guns was placed on Goat's Point, but it was understood when I left that it was to be abandoned, and a sap worked up from near the Martello Tower (which has been repaired), and the mortars placed in position against Pulaski as far up the beach as possible. Thirteen mortars had been landed up to 8th instant, two of them 13-inch.

I learned from an officer of the Navy, on the way to New York, that an old hulk had just been placed by our forces in Lazaretto Creek, about one and a quarter miles from Fort Pulaski.

Fort Pulaski is said by a rebel deserter to contain 427 men, nine months' provisions, and six months' water.

The old rebel battery at the point of Great Warsaw Island is in our possession.

The Skidaway battery opposite Koming marsh, at the mouth of the Wilmington River, had not been reduced up to the 8th instant. It is said to be very strong.

The rebels are also camped near Bonaventura, and between there and Fort Jackson, on the Thunderbolt road. Rumor had it that about 30,000 to 35,000 rebels were in and about Savannah, but of the truth of these suppositions I have my doubts.

A large siege train is being put together at Hilton Head, but progresses very slowly; eight or nine guns were ready last Saturday. I was informed the ammunition was not yet prepared.

As to what is contemplated against Savannah I am entirely ignorant. Against Fort Pulaski, I know that orders have been given to prepare to reduce it.

It was for several weeks supposed that a passage for gunboats existed from Port Royal Sound into the Savannah River above Fort Pulaski when the obstructions in Wall's Cut were removed, but it is now found otherwise, at least for a draught of more than 7 feet of water at high tide, except within range of the guns of the fort.

A reconnaissance has been made up the north side of the Savannah River from Jones Island to above the Union Causeway, about a mile and a quarter from the City of Savannah, by which it has been ascertained that if troops could be landed above Elba Island they could march to a point directly opposite the city.

In reply to that part of your order requiring my judgment of the means wanted "to produce a successful and speedy result," I have the honor to state:

1st. That in my opinion the most essential requisite is an intelligent, vigorous, energetic general, in whom the Army would have entire confidence, who would counsel with his principal officers, and act promptly upon any decision he might form, and who, having orders, would concentrate his efforts on some particular object and accomplish it.

2d. That there should be harmonious action between the land and naval forces.

3d. The forces should either be greatly augmented or concentrated, instead of being scattered up and down the coast from North Edisto to Fernandina, a distance of 130 or 140 miles.

4th. That fire should not be opened upon Pulaski until at least all the mortars now landed on Tybee are in position, and then that the Navy would co-operate as well as they may, while, by having four or five reliefs of men at the mortars, shell should be poured into the fort day and night incessantly, without allowing any time for the rebels to eat, drink, or sleep in security until they surrendered. This will require of the land forces 1,400 or 1,500 men.

5th. That there should be two more ordnance officers sent there immediately, as there is now only one thoroughly efficient officer of that corps on the ground.

6th. That rafts of light pine and palmetto should be made to transport the siege train on the creeks and up the Savannah River, and that while this is being done the Navy should engage the batteries at Skidaway, and, if possible, silence and capture them, the siege of Pulaski being at the same time continued.

7th. Rafts and boats can be taken into the Savannah River above Jones Island, and might with proper management be forced up the river to Saint Augustine Creek, where there is firm ground. The siege train can be carried in the same way, and opposition at landing met at the point of the bayonet. One hundred additional ship boats would greatly facilitate such a movement. Having reached the firm ground anywhere near the Thunderbolt road, either through the Savannah or Tybee Rivers, the way is open to the city in the rear of Fort Jackson.

It might be well, if forces could be spared, to destroy the railroad bridge at Coosawhatchie, to cut off supplies from Charleston, but this is not worth much, as other channels are open by the Augusta and Savannah and South Carolina Railroads. The only materials required, in my judgment, are a few more boats and one or two more light-draught steamers.

Sufficient intelligence and energy to use what is now in that army can produce whatever else may be required.

Very respectfully, your obedient servant,

EDWARD W. SERRELL,
Colonel, Volunteer Engineers.

HEADQUARTERS EXPEDITIONARY CORPS,
Port Royal, S. C., March 15, 1862.

Major-General MCCLELLAN,
Commander-in-Chief, U. S. Army:

GENERAL: From information just received from our forces at North Edisto it is probable that gunboats, except such very small ones as would be of little use, cannot get into the Stono River by the way of the Wadmalaw, as there will be an obstruction found at New Cut, from the fact that even at high water this cut has not over 5 feet of water. There is a battery of six pieces at Church Flats and vessels sunk in the river at that point. Quite a large force is also at this point, and somewhere near the junction of the Wadmalaw and Stono Rivers is another battery. The rebels are evidently pretty strong in defenses at this point and along the whole line of the Stono. This district is too far off to get very specific information, and what we have thus far gathered is from prisoners and short reconnaissances made by the Army and Navy. The rebel force is too strong in that vicinity to risk the small force we have up there very far from the Edisto. When the gunboats return from the south it is contemplated by Commodore DuPont to make a reconnaissance in that direction, and, if our affairs justify it, I propose sending a force with him.

From last accounts from Fernandina the gunboats had not yet got into the Saint John's. I hope to send a small force, say one or two regiments, and probably a section of light artillery, across from Picolata to Saint Augustine, and take the place in reverse. For this purpose all the troops sent down with General Wright are left there, one regiment, General Wright informs me, being with the gunboats off the mouth of the Saint John's.

I am very anxious to raise our flag over Fort Marion and Saint Augustine Barracks, and, if the Navy are not too long in sounding out the channel, expect to do it without much resistance.

Very respectfully and truly, your obedient servant,

T. W. SHERMAN,
Brigadier-General, Commanding.

P. S.—I send the Atlantic back to hurry on the ordnance stores for Tybee.

GENERAL ORDERS, No. 26. } WAR DEPARTMENT, A. G. O.,
Washington, March 15, 1862.

The States of South Carolina, Georgia, and Florida, with the expedition and forces now under Brig. Gen. T. W. Sherman, will constitute a military department, to be called the Department of the South, to be commanded by Major-General Hunter.

By order of the Secretary of War:

L. THOMAS,
Adjutant-General.

HEADQUARTERS EXPEDITIONARY CORPS,
Port Royal, S. C., March 16, 1862.

The ADJUTANT-GENERAL U. S. ARMY,
Washington:

SIR: I have the honor to report that after Brigadier-General Wright had taken possession of Amelia Island I directed him to send one or two regiments, as circumstances would require, to Picolata, on the Saint John's River, and march upon the rear of Fort Marion and Saint Augustine.

I have just learned (unofficially) from private sources that General Wright is in quiet possession of Jacksonville; that some of the gunboats are in Saint Augustine Harbor, and that Fort Marion has surrendered to the Navy. Whether any of General Wright's force are yet there I have not heard.

Very respectfully, your obedient servant,

T. W. SHERMAN,
Brigadier-General, Commanding.

HEADQUARTERS EXPEDITIONARY CORPS,
U. S. Steamer Cahawba, Fernandina, Fla., March 21, 1862.

Brig. Gen. HORATIO G. WRIGHT,
Comdg. Third Brigade, Exped'y Corps, Fernandina, Fla.:

GENERAL: I am directed by the commanding general to communicate to you that you are authorized to concentrate any of the troops of the three posts, Saint Augustine, Fernandina, and Jacksonville, on any emergency that may arise that will not admit of time to communicate with these headquarters. Any such change will be at once reported.

I am further directed to instruct that all public property which may fall into your hands from the enemy at the posts referred to be inventoried and reported according to the regulations.

Very respectfully, your obedient servant,

[L. H. PELOUZE,]
Captain, Fifteenth Infantry, Actg. Asst. Adjt. General.

TREASURY DEPARTMENT, *March* 22, 1862.

Hon. E. M. STANTON,
Secretary of War:

SIR: Mr. Pierce, special agent of this Department at Port Royal, reports that the plantations have been deprived so generally of horses and mules that their cultivation is greatly hindered and in some cases almost entirely prevented. As these animals have been taken for the use of the Army, it seems but just that they should be restored through the agency of the War Department. If you concur with me, will you be good enough to give an order for sending 90 mules and 10 horses to Port Royal immediately, to be placed at the disposal of the special agent?

I suggest the expediency of an order directing the commanders to respect private property on plantations, so as to prevent the recurrence of such evils as those referred to.

Yours, truly,

S. P. CHASE,
Secretary of the Treasury.

WAR DEPARTMENT,
Washington, D. C., March 25, 1862.

Hon. SALMON P. CHASE,
Secretary of the Treasury:

SIR: The Secretary of War directs me to acknowledge the receipt of your communication of the 22d instant, requesting him to give an order for sending horses and mules to Port Royal to replace those which have been taken from the plantations in the neighborhood for the use of the Army.

He does not think that he has any authority to furnish horses and mules for the purposes mentioned, but would suggest whether the Treasury Department could not furnish them properly out of the proceeds of the cotton received from Port Royal.

I have the honor to be, your obedient servant,

P. H. WATSON,
Assistant Secretary of War.

HEADQUARTERS EXPEDITIONARY CORPS,
Port Royal, S. C., March 25, 1862.

To the ADJUTANT-GENERAL U. S. ARMY,
Washington, D. C.:

SIR: Since my letter of the 9th instant, on learning that General Wright, in conformity to my previous instructions, had detached a regiment from Fernandina to accompany the gunboats to the Saint John's River, and hearing in the mean time of the happy political sentiments prevailing at Saint Augustine, I sent him a dispatch, urgently recommending him to land that force at Picolata, and with it, and as much additional force as he might think it necessary to take, to march upon the rear of that city and take possession of Fort Marion and Saint Augustine Barracks.

It has since appeared, however, that whilst this force was entering the Saint John's and occupying Jacksonville a few gunboats were sent around to the front of Saint Augustine with one company of General Wright's command, and that on the appearance of this force Saint Augustine struck the rebel flag and gave up the place to Commodore DuPont.

As the force sent from Fernandina was landed at Jacksonville, contrary to the tenor of my instructions to General Wright, I felt so anxious about how far such a measure would commit me to any operation by land for which I might not be prepared, that I proceeded thither, to obtain a thorough understanding of the matter.

After thoroughly understanding the political situation of affairs there, and the reign of terror to which the Union men are still subjected, I not only confirmed General Wright's acts, but have increased the force at Jacksonville one regiment. The best information I can give the Department of the situation of affairs in East Florida is the forwarding herewith of a copy of the proceedings of a town meeting held in Jacksonville on the 20th instant and a copy of my proclamation to the people of East Florida on the same date. I have the sanguine hope that Florida will soon be regenerated. The force I have in Florida is three companies of infantry at Fort Marion and Saint Augustine Barracks (the Navy have some marines there also), sixteen companies of infantry at Jacksonville, one company of infantry in charge of a battery at the mouth of the Saint John's, one regiment of infantry and two sections of light artillery at Fernandina.

The force at Jacksonville was made sufficiently strong to resist any force of the enemy now occupying the railroad to Tallahassee that might be brought against it. It is probable that the artillery at Fernandina, or a portion of it, will be sent there also. Besides, there are three gunboats in the Saint John's River and I believe one or two in Saint Augustine Harbor.

Very respectfully, your obedient servant,

T. W. SHERMAN,
Brigadier-General, Commanding.

[Inclosures.]

HEADQUARTERS EXPEDITIONARY CORPS,
Jacksonville, Fla., March 20, 1862.

To the People of East Florida:

The troops of the United States have come amongst you to protect loyal citizens and their property from further molestation by the creatures of a rebel and usurped authority, and to enable you to resuscitate a Government which they have ruthlessly endeavored to destroy.

All loyal people who return to or remain at their homes in the quiet pursuit of their lawful avocations shall be protected in all their rights within the meaning and spirit of the Constitution of the United States. The sole desire and intention of the Government is to maintain the integrity of the Constitution and the laws and reclaim States which have revolted from their national allegiance to their former prosperous and happy condition.

There is great satisfaction in the fact, now become patent to all, that a large portion of you still cling in your hearts to that mother who first liberated you from the thraldom of a despotic government; who next rescued you from the deathly grasp of the wily savage at a frightful cost of life and treasure, and who afterwards elevated you from the condition of territorial dependence to that of a proud and independent State.

I earnestly recommend that in every city, town, and precinct you assemble in your primary and sovereign capacity; that you there throw off that sham government which has been forced upon you; swear true fidelity and allegiance to the Constitution of the United States, and organize your government and elect your officers in the good old way of the past. When this is done, then will you see the return of prosperous and happy days, in the enjoyment of that trade and industry to which your extensive coast is so well adapted, and in the immunity from that want and suffering to which you have been so wickedly subjected by the traitorous acts of a few ambitious and unprincipled men; then will you enjoy the fruits of your honest labor, the sweets of happy homes, and the consolation of living under those wise and salutary laws that are due only to an industrious and law-abiding people.

T. W. SHERMAN,
Brigadier-General, Commanding.

At a meeting of the loyal citizens of the "United States of America," held at Jacksonville, East Florida, March 20, A. D. 1862, at 10.30 a. m., C. L. Robinson, chairman; O. L. Keene, secretary; Col. John S. Sannius, S. F. Halliday, Paran Moody, John W. Price, and Philip Fraser, esqs., were appointed a committee to draught resolutions to lay before said meeting. The following is a true copy of said resolutions, which were received and adopted unanimously:

We, the people of the city of Jacksonville and its vicinity, in the county of Duval, and the State of Florida, embraced within the territory and jurisdiction of the United States of America, do hereby set forth our declaration of rights and our solemn protest against the abrogation of the same by any pretended State or other authority.

First. We hold that government is a contract, in which protection is the price of allegiance; that when protection is denied, through weakness or design, allegiance is no longer due.

Second. We hold that an established form of government cannot be changed or abrogated except by the will of the people, intelligently and willingly expressed and fairly ratified.

Third. We hold that no State of the United States has any legal or constitutional right to separate itself from the government and jurisdiction of the United States.

Fourth. We hold that the act of the Convention of the State of Florida commonly known as the ordinance of secession, is void, being in direct conflict with the Constitution of the United States, in never having been submitted to the people for ratification.

Fifth. We hold that the State of Florida is an integral part of the United States, subject to the constitutional jurisdiction of the same, and we have reason to believe that thousands of her citizens would hail with joy the restoration of the Government, bringing deliverance from the terrors of unrestrained popular and military despotism. We solemnly protest against all the acts and ordinances of the Convention of the State of Florida, which were designed to deprive us of our rights as citizens of the United States. We protest against the despotism fostered by the State and other authorities claiming jurisdiction over us, which has denied us the rights most dear to freemen—freedom of speech and a free press. We protest against the exactions which have been imposed upon us—forced contributions of money, property, and labor; enlistments for military service procured by threats and misrepresentations. We protest against the tyranny which demands of us as a measure of revolutionary policy abandonment of our homes and property and exposure of our wives and children to sickness, destitution, gaunt famine, innumerable and untold miseries and sorrows. We protest against that mad and barbarous policy which has punished us for remaining in our own homes by sending a brutal and unrestrained soldiery to pillage and burn our property, threaten and destroy our lives. We protest against the denunciation of the governor, who threatens to hang us because we do not tamely submit to such indignities and "lick the hand just raised to shed our blood." From such a despotism and from such dangers and indignities we have been released by the restoration of the Government of the United States, with the benign principles of the Constitution. The reign of terror is past. Law and order prevails in our midst.

It belongs now to the citizens of the State who hold to their allegiance to the United States to raise up a State government according to those provisions of the State which are not in conflict with or repugnant to the provisions of the United States:

Be it therefore resolved, That we adopt the foregoing protest and declaration of rights, and recommend that a convention of all loyal citizens be called forthwith, for the purpose of organizing a State government of the State of Florida.

Be it further resolved, That the chief of the military department of the United States be requested to retain at this place a sufficient force to maintain order and protect the people in their persons and property.

All of which is respectfully submitted.

PHILIP FRASER,
Chairman.

A true copy of the resolutions as passed at said meeting and adopted as their own act.

C. L. ROBINSON,
Chairman.

O. L. KEENE,
Secretary.

HEADQUARTERS,
Jacksonville, Fla., March 25, 1862.

Capt. LOUIS H. PELOUZE,
Acting Assistant Adjutant-General:

CAPTAIN: I have the honor to report, for the information of the general commanding, that I left Fernandina yesterday morning with the Ninety-seventh Regiment Pennsylvania Volunteers in the Cosmopolitan, and arrived here and landed the troops last evening. Having struck upon the Saint John's Bar, we were obliged to cast off the schooner in tow, laden with camp and garrison equipage and stores; and, as the tide was rapidly falling and the wind high, we were forced to leave her at anchor. The troops consequently had to be quartered in vacant buildings on shore, instead of going into camp, as I had designed.

Last night, or rather this morning, at about 3 o'clock, a party of the enemy, numbering some 50 perhaps, made an attack upon one of our picket stations, and, out of the 7 men composing it, killed 1; severely, and it is feared mortally, wounded another, and captured 3 more. The remaining two escaped. So far as I can learn from the reports and an investigation of the case, the picket was guilty of gross carelessness and suffered itself to be completely surprised.

Yesterday morning it seems that two members of another picket station went out beyond the lines, and have no doubt been captured. Indeed, it is so reported by a deserter from the enemy who has since come in. These occurrences will no doubt have the effect to make the guards more watchful, by proving to them the [consequences] to themselves of any neglect of vigilance in an enemy's country.

I have to-day looked carefully over the ground in advance of the town, and find it much more difficult to defend and to picket than I had imagined from the map. Two companies will be necessary for a proper picket guard; and this daily detail, with the number necessary for camp and provost guards, will bear heavily on the command. Some re-enforcement would be desirable if any troops can be spared.

Considerable fatigue work will be necessary also in cutting down the scrub and timber on the outskirts of the town, which now afford cover to parties approaching the pickets. This labor will be undertaken the moment the vessel referred to as having camp and garrison equipage, &c., arrives.

Very respectfully, your obedient servant,

H. G. WRIGHT,
Brigadier-General, Commanding.

HEADQUARTERS EXPEDITIONARY CORPS,
Port Royal, S. C., March 26, 1862.

Brig. Gen. LORENZO THOMAS,
Adjutant-General U. S. Army, Washington, D. C.:

GENERAL: Your letter of the 6th instant* was not received until the 21st instant, and then through the hands of Flag-Officer DuPont.

I had already been directed by Major-General McClellan to abstain from my preparations for the siege of Savannah and confine myself to Fernandina and the siege of Fort Pulaski. Your letter of the 6th recommends me to reduce Fort Pulaski in preference to attempting Savannah. In my letter of the 14th December last the Department will perceive that my plan was to carry on both at once. The essential

* See McClellan to Sherman, March 6, p. 238.

features of that plan I had not departed from, and have been very desirous of carrying out, particularly after the opportunity we discovered for taking Savannah by a *coup de main* failed for want of co-operation of the Navy, the particulars of which the Department has already been apprised of.

I humbly bow to the decisions of my superiors in Washington, but still, general, from the point here to view the subject, I cannot but regret that my plan could not have been carried out. I had every confidence in it, and believe it would have been executed with not so much sacrifice as the general seemed to imagine.

However, the preparations for the bombardment of Pulaski are being made as fast as the material arrives. The mortar and columbiad batteries are all constructed, mortars mounted, and all the shot and shell yet arrived in position. We are still waiting for the columbiad carriages and a considerable portion of the shot and shell. The work is of such a character, you are well aware, that we must be in a state of perfect preparation before opening fire.

It is hoped that we shall be permitted to get through this job early enough in the season to afford a pretty large force in the direction of Charleston, a nucleus from which, in the shape of two regiments, I have already forwarded on the North Edisto River.

The batteries on the mud flats of the Savannah River work like a charm, and, what is remarkable, our men there are in perfect health.

Very respectfully, your obedient servant,

T. W. SHERMAN,
Brigadier-General, Commanding.

ON BOARD THE ADELAIDE,
En route to Fortress Monroe, Baltimore, March 27, 1862.

Hon. E. M. STANTON,
Secretary of War, Washington, D. C.:

SIR: I have to state that my continued reflection convinces me that for efficient action it is indispensable that more troops should be sent immediately to South Carolina. I know as well now as I can possibly know when I shall have reached there that from 20,000 to 25,000 additional troops should be sent.

If you could send me General Sedgwick's division, which I suppose to be now with our rear *corps d'armée*, I should be very glad; and, even with these alone, would almost guarantee to have our flag waving over Fort Sumter by the anniversary of its capture.

I have the honor most respectfully and earnestly to solicit your early attention to this request, and that you will be kind enough to advise me of your decision by telegraph, addressed to Fort Monroe.

Very respectfully, your most obedient servant,

DAVID HUNTER,
Major-General.

HEADQUARTERS EXPEDITIONARY CORPS,
Port Royal, S. C., March 27, 1862.

To Hon. SECRETARY OF WAR,
Washington, D. C.:

SIR: I have just received the President's War Order, No. 3, which directs reports to be made direct to the Secretary of War.

My recent letters to the Adjutant-General will show the general status of affairs in this expedition. We hold the whole coast from North Edisto, S. C., to Saint Augustine, Fla. Rapid preparations are being made for the reduction of Fort Pulaski, Ga., and the Savannah River is occupied with a sufficient force to cut off all communications and supplies from Savannah.

The attack of Savannah, for which we have been making preparations, has been given up, by direction of Major-General McClellan.

The fire will be opened on Pulaski as soon as all the material has arrived from the North.

I have left Brigadier-General Wright, with three regiments and two sections of light artillery, in the occupation of Fernandina, Jacksonville, and Saint Augustine, with the hope and expectation that by judicious management East Florida will soon be regenerated.

No operations can be made on the main of South Carolina and Georgia for the want of proper means of transportation—viz, light-draught steamers, boats, and wagons—which have all failed to reach here, notwithstanding early and repeated requisitions for them. Now, indeed, that our forces have become so much scattered in the occupation of so extensive a coast, more troops will be required for any extensive inland operations.

Very respectfully, your obedient servant,

T. W. SHERMAN,
Brigadier-General, Commanding.

HEADQUARTERS,
Jacksonville, Fla., March 27, 1862.

Lieut. Col. LOUIS BELL,
Saint Augustine:

COLONEL: I have to acknowledge the receipt this evening of your two letters of the 26th and 27th instant, respectively; also yours of the 23d, forwarded by the dispatch schooner Azalea.*

I much regret that at present I do not see how any of the force at this post or at Fernandina can be spared to re enforce your command. Here our force is not too great for our own security against the force the enemy could readily bring if he were disposed to attack us, unprovided as we are with defenses of any kind and with a long line, which we must picket for our own safety. Neither is the force at Fernandina too large, seeing that the fort at that point is of little moment.

I look upon your position as the most secure by far of either of the three posts, even with your present small force, in view of the defensible condition of Fort Marion, now that you have so successfully established the heavy ordnance on the work.

It is no doubt true that you cannot with your present strength successfully defend the town from any attempt in force against it; and I should therefore advise that you confine your undertakings mainly to the fort and its surroundings, leaving the defense of the place, to some extent at least, to the inhabitants. Give the people to understand that they are to help themselves, and that you will then aid them. This, at any time, is all they could demand. In their present attitude, judging from your views as to their want of loyalty, it is more than they have a right to expect.

*None of these found.

Desirous, however, of strengthening you as soon as possible, I shall send to General Sherman a copy of your letter of the 26th instant, and ask that more troops be furnished, if they have them to spare.

Very respectfully, your obedient servant,

H. G. WRIGHT,
Brigadier-General, Commanding.

HEADQUARTERS,
Jacksonville, Fla., March 28, 1862.

Capt. LOUIS H. PELOUZE:

CAPTAIN: I have the honor to report that nothing of importance has occurred at this place since the date of my last letter.

Last night the pickets fired upon a party approaching them in what they conceived to be a suspicious manner, and of the two in advance killed one and wounded the other. They proved, upon examination, to be a party of negroes, who had escaped from their masters at Lake City.

Information in regard to the positions and strength of the rebel forces is somewhat indefinite. From the best I can gather there are still several companies—six or seven perhaps—in the neighborhood of McGist's Creek, about 12 miles from here, and an additional force at Baldwin and at Sanderson, still farther off on the railroad. The last are of Colonel Hopkins' regiment, the Fourth Florida; those at McGist's Creek are of the Third Florida Regiment, commanded by Colonel Dilworth. An attack upon a portion of this force may be expedient, but at this moment I have not the information to warrant the movement.

Lieutenant-Colonel Bell, Fourth New Hampshire Regiment, commander at Saint Augustine, applies pressingly for re-enforcements, as the marines sent by the flag-officer to that post have been withdrawn. I have replied in effect that the condition of affairs here and at Fernandina does not permit me to increase his garrison from my command, and that while he should afford such protection as is in his power to persons and property in town, he should not by so doing compromise the safety of his command. I have further advised him that Fort Marion, with the armament he has put in place, will enable him to resist any attack likely to be brought against him, and that he should therefore direct his attention mainly to that point.

He represents, as will be seen by his letter, that the loyalty of the people generally is doubtful, thus affording an additional reason for not exposing his force unnecessarily to protect a people who are not disposed to take active steps for their own defense. I think, however, with Lieutenant-Colonel Bell, that two additional companies to his garrison would be desirable, if they can be spared. With my present force I cannot spare them.

I would also suggest that the two sections of the light battery at Fernandina, under the command of Captain Ransom, would be of more service here than where they are. With that additional force I could operate against the enemy with much more prospect of success. I do not feel authorized, under existing orders, to bring them here for such a purpose without the sanction of the general commanding.

Very respectfully, your obedient servant,

H. G. WRIGHT,
Brigadier-General, Commanding.

HEADQUARTERS,
Jacksonville, Fla., March 28, 1862.

Capt. LOUIS H. PELOUZE:

CAPTAIN: From intelligence received this evening from a deserter I learn that the enemy has an attack upon this place in contemplation so soon as his force, now somewhat scattered, can be concentrated.

The force he is reported to have at command for such an enterprise is such as to make an addition to our strength here very desirable, and I have therefore decided to bring here the two sections of Hamilton's battery, now at Fernandina. The Cosmopolitan will leave here for the purpose to-morrow morning. The enemy is represented to have along the line of the railroad, or soon expected upon it, (1) the Third Florida Regiment; (2) the Fourth Florida Regiment; (3) a regiment of cavalry; (4) a company with six or seven pieces of artillery.

Very respectfully, your obedient servant,

H. G. WRIGHT,
Brigadier-General, Commanding.

PORT ROYAL, S. C., *March* 31, 1862.

Maj. Gen. D. HUNTER,
Commanding Department of the South:

GENERAL: On being relieved from this command it is proper that I should report the condition of affairs here at the present time.

We have been for some time making preparation for the reduction of Fort Pulaski, and are now only waiting to open our fire for the material brought in the Atlantic to be got out and landed at Tybee. The armament set up for the operations consists of twelve 13-inch sea-coast mortars, four 10-inch siege mortars, five 10-inch columbiads, three 8-inch columbiads, and five large rifled guns. In the mean time, and since the 11th of February last, all communication has been cut off from Savannah by batteries erected on the marshes of Jones and Bird Islands. I have no doubt but the place will fall in a short time.

Extensive preparations have also been made for the taking of Savannah, but I have been directed by the General-in-Chief to suspend all operations for the capture of that city.

A plan that was laid by me to take the city by a *coup de main* with a combined land and naval force about the 20th January last failed for want of the promised co-operation on the part of the Navy. Since that time the defenses constructed are of such a nature as to render it impossible to take it but by a siege entirely by land.

Preparations are making also on Port Royal Island for the occupation of the country up to the Charleston and Savannah Railroad, which we expected to accomplish in about a week or ten days hence.

After the fall of Pulaski, and a proper occupation of all important places on the coast in our possession, it was my calculation to have 900 men disposable for any operation upwards from North Edisto.

Very respectfully, your obedient servant,

T. W. SHERMAN,
Brigadier-General, Commanding Expeditionary Corps.

GENERAL ORDERS, } HDQRS. DEPARTMENT OF THE SOUTH,
No. 1. } *Port Royal, S. C., March* 31, 1862.

I. Maj. Gen. David Hunter, having arrived at this post, hereby assumes, in accordance with the order of the War Department, the command of the Department of the South, consisting of the States of South Carolina, Georgia, and Florida.

II. For the convenience of military operations and the administration of department affairs this department is divided into three districts, to be constituted as follows:

1st. The first, to be called the Northern District, will comprise the States of South Carolina, Georgia, and all that part of Florida north and east of a line extending from Cape Canaveral northwest to the Gulf coast, just north of Cedar Keys, and its dependencies, and thence north to the Georgia line. The headquarters of this district will be at Port Royal, S. C., and Brig. Gen. H. W. Benham (who will relieve Brigadier-General Sherman) is appointed to command this district and the troops therein, which troops will constitute a division, to be called the First Division of the Department of the South. General Benham will receive from General Sherman all charts, maps, plans, reports, moneys, &c., with all official records, returns, &c., appertaining to the expeditionary command in this district.

2d. The second, to be called the Southern District, will comprise all of Florida and the islands adjacent south of the said line from Cape Canaveral, extending northwest to the Gulf coast, just north of Cedar Keys. The headquarters of this district and the troops will remain, as at present, under command of Brig. Gen. J. M. Brannan.

3d. The third, to be called the Western District, will comprise that part of Florida west of the line before described as running north from Cedar Keys to the Georgia line. The headquarters of this district will remain at Fort Pickens, as at present, with Brig. Gen. L. G. Arnold commanding.

* * * * * * *

IV. The staff of the major-general commanding the department will consist of the following-named officers:

Maj. Charles G. Halpine, assistant adjutant-general; Lieut. E. W. Smith, acting assistant adjutant-general; Col. J. W. Shaffer, chief quartermaster; Capt. J. W. Turner, chief commissary of subsistence.

Maj. R. M. Hough, Maj. Edward Wright, Capt. R. W. Thompson, Capt. W. R. Dole, Lieut. S. W. Stockton, Lieut. Charles E. Hay, Lieut. A. M. Kinzie, Lieut. A. O. Doolittle, aides-de-camp.

D. HUNTER,
Major-General, Commanding.

GENERAL ORDERS, No. 2. } HDQRS. DEPARTMENT OF THE SOUTH,
Port Royal, S. C., March 31, 1862.

In relieving Brig. Gen. T. W. Sherman from duty in this department, pursuant to orders of the War Department, dated A. G. O., Washington, March 15, 1862, the major-general commanding desires to express to Brigadier-General Sherman his full appreciation of the amount and importance of the services rendered by the expedition under General Sherman's command, and his thanks for the full, reliable, and valuable information as to the condition of the troops, defenses, &c., in this portion of the Department of the South, which General Sherman has furnished.

By command of Maj. Gen. D. Hunter:

CHAS. G. HALPINE,
Assistant Adjutant-General.

HDQRS. NORTHERN DISTRICT, DEPT. OF THE SOUTH,
Hilton Head, S. C., April 1, 1862.

Brigadier-General VIELE:

MY DEAR GENERAL: I inclose you a copy of Major-General Hunter's order assigning me to the late command of General Sherman.

I regret much that different delays prevented my meeting you in person yesterday, and I missed communicating with your boat by supposing it was to have been off Stoddard's place, for which we were running, when we saw it where the pilot feared to go with our boat.

My principal desire was to consult you with reference to your means and opportunities of erecting mortar batteries at least, to take in reverse the south and southeast faces of Fort Pulaski and perhaps the northeast face, for by this means your forces can the more efficiently aid in the reduction of that work. I would be glad to have this subject receive your utmost attention. Now it occurs to me as possible to erect such a battery at the lower point of Long Island, with possibly one for direct fire on the faces next you, and I should wish a reconnaissance made there at once with this object.

General Gillmore has a project for preparing a large scow (such as could be brought to you through Wall's Cut) for the basis of a battery, and floating it to the required position, then to complete it as a land battery. It is very possible that this may be the best expedient for yourself. I shall, however, be happy to receive from you any suggestions or plans that may accomplish best the object to be attained—the most efficient aid from your force in the reduction of this stronghold.

I have in view, unless other circumstances or probabilities of what I am not now fully advised should prevent it, the restoration to you of a part, at least, of the excellent troops of your brigade.

Very respectfully, your obedient servant,

H. W. BENHAM,
Brigadier-General, Commanding.

HDQRS. EXPEDITIONARY CORPS, DEPT. OF THE SOUTH,
Hilton Head, S. C., April 1, 1862.

Brig. Gen. Q. A. GILLMORE,
Commanding U. S. Forces, Tybee Island, Ga.:

MY DEAR GENERAL: Upon reflecting upon your proposition to prepare a scow as the basis of another battery above the mouth of Lazaretto Creek, and, looking upon your sketch map, I would suggest if it would not be best to take it up that creek and prepare the battery there, as it appears that it might be at nearly the end of the first angle to the north and on the prolongation of the gorge wall of the fort. This last line I would by all means select as the line of fire, if the battery can be placed as well or nearly as well in that position, as it cuts off the cover the gorge might afford, gives more complete reverse fire on the north face, and nearly as well a sufficient reverse fire on the northeast face. If you can as securely, and with as much concealment, which would appear to me doubtful, place this battery on the south channel, which, however, appears but a short distance nearer, say 200 yards, it will perhaps be best.

I would like the sketch of your proposed arrangement, with the guns, &c., of the scow, as I would desire, if found feasible, that General Viele, if no better means offers, should prepare one or two batteries of the same kind to take the faces next you or reverse. Please have every means continued to cut off communication and another field piece sent up to the upper batteries.

I expect we shall re-enforce you before the actual commencement of the fire, but rest assured that, even if a senior should necessarily be sent with such troops (General Wright), General Hunter and myself will see (as he said to me) the fullest justice done to your labors and efforts.

Very respectfully, your obedient servant,

H. W. BENHAM,
Brigadier-General, Commanding.

HDQRS. NORTHERN DISTRICT, DEPT. OF THE SOUTH,
Hilton Head, S. C., April 2, 1862.

Brig. Gen. EGBERT L. VIELE,
Commanding U. S. Forces, Daufuskie Island, S. C.:

GENERAL: The general commanding the district (Benham) has learned from General Sherman that there is at Turtle Island, nearly opposite and above Bloody Point, a small dry ridge, upon which there is a probability that a mortar battery could be placed to act effectively against Fort Pulaski at a distance probably of not more than 2 miles, and which would of course take in reverse the faces exposed to the direct fire from Tybee.

All those large mortars are already landed at Tybee for service there, but there are at this place two of 10-inch and two of the 8-inch columbiads, which it is believed can be effectively used as mortars for the purpose indicated, and that those guns, with such other materials as you may require, can be sent to you at Daufuskie Island—for the latter part of the distance at night, if necessary.

Will you please to give your early attention to this matter, reporting as early as possible your opinion of its feasibility, and, if favorable, what material you will require, as it is now of the utmost importance to our plans that this work, if undertaken, should be completed at the earliest possible moment; your estimate of which time you will please report in your reply.

Very respectfully, your obedient servant,

A. B. ELY,
Acting Assistant Adjutant-General.

HDQRS. NORTHERN DISTRICT, DEPT. OF THE SOUTH,
Hilton Head, S. C., April 3, 1862.

Brig. Gen. EGBERT L. VIELE,
Commanding U. S. Forces, Daufuskie Island, S. C.:

DEAR GENERAL: I shall hope to have your report about the feasibility of a columbiad battery this morning.

The capture of 17 of Gillmore's men will, I fear, inform the rebels of our preparations, and we may be obliged to open fire from Tybee prematurely or earlier than we would wish.

Please take every precaution to seal the communication between the fort and city hermetically, if possible; even passing your men over at night to the south side of south channel, if you have the means.

Very truly, yours,

H. W. BENHAM,
Brigadier-General.

HEADQUARTERS U. S. FORCES,
Savannah River, April 3, 1862.

General H. W. BENHAM,
Commanding First Division Department of the South:

DEAR GENERAL: Your dispatch is just received, and as I have also just received the reports of the two officers whom I requested to make reconnaissances, I hasten to forward them, merely adding my own rapid conclusions that two flat-boats, properly arranged, one with two mortars and another with two rifled guns and one 8-inch howitzer, can be made very effective at the lower end of Long Island. I agree with Lieutenant Wilson in regard to Turtle Beach, more especially as the time that it would require to place columbiads in position (a week or ten days at least) would render our efforts at that point inoperative under the circumstances.

If you will let me know your views by the courier in the morning I will at once arrange to put them into immediate execution.

Very respectfully, your obedient servant,

EGBERT L. VIELE,
Brigadier-General, Commanding.

[Inclosures.]

BATTERY HAMILTON, GA.,
April 2, 1862.

Brig. Gen. EGBERT L. VIELE,
Commanding, Savannah River:

GENERAL: I have the honor to report that, as directed by you, I this day and night made a reconnaissance of Long Island, and I sketch the result on the next page.

The lower end of the island is detached at high tide. But, as I have viewed it, I cannot make the form of detachment and the maps agree. I sketch it as it looks to me. This afternoon, after examining the McQueen side of Long Island, I passed around its head and went to a point marked B, being in sight of Pulaski all the time. At this point, I was honored with a very wild shot. I then returned, and to-night proceeded as far as the point marked A.

A is the best point for a battery, but guns cannot be landed there unobserved. At B guns can be landed in the night without attracting notice. A clump of tall cane, covering an area 600 feet in length and about 150 feet in width, would cover work. The ground is sufficiently firm, and sand can be procured from the shore of the island 300 or 400 feet from the spot. But any battery placed anywhere on the lower end of Long Island except at A must necessarily be small, the ground capable of sustaining a battery being a strip parallel with the river and not over 30 yards wide at any point. This would be the maximum battery face procurable. At A both shore and soil are favorable, if observation could be avoided in landing guns. I do not think, however, that it would be possible to erect a battery anywhere below the point marked B, owing to the fact that there is scarce any growth of either weed, brush, or cane below that point. I should judge B to be about 1¼ to 1½ miles from the fort.

Very respectfully, your obedient servant,

O. T. BEARD,
Major, Commanding.

TURTLE ISLAND, GA., *April* 3, 1862.

Capt. J. H. LIEBENAU,
Asst. Adjt. Gen., First Brigade, U. S. Forces of the South:

CAPTAIN: In reply to your letter of this date, requesting a report of my reconnaissance of Turtle Island, with a view to its occupation by a battery to aid in the reduction of Fort Pulaski, I have the honor to report as follows:

I have twice visited and carefully examined that side of the island lying next to the fort, and am convinced that it is possible to erect batteries thereon, taking advantage of high tides for landing guns and material. But the labor would be exceedingly heavy, and the difficulties to be overcome in transporting the guns from the landing place over the marsh, a distance of about 500 yards, would be greater than any yet encountered in erecting batteries on the Savannah.

Considering the fact that the nearest point of fast land in Turtle Island is 2⅛ miles from Fort Pulaski, the battery, although mounting the heaviest guns, would necessarily be inefficient. The inclosed sketch, taken from the Coast Survey charts, shows the topography of the island.

The only point at which guns can be landed and removed to ground hard enough to support them is near the mouth of Wright River, marked A. From there to the head of the woods, the nearest point to the fort and the only one where cover can be obtained, is about 500 yards. The ground is comparatively hard, and by the use of corduroy road would allow the passage of the heaviest guns.

I am, sir, very respectfully, your obedient servant,

J. H. WILSON,
First Lieutenant, Topographical Engineers.

HDQRS. NORTHERN DISTRICT, DEPT. OF THE SOUTH,
Hilton Head, S. C., April 3, 1862.

Flag-Officer S. F. DUPONT,
Commanding U. S. South Atlantic Squadron:

SIR: By reports received this morning from Tybee Island we learn that some 17 of our men and a field piece, in a plantation canoe, have just been captured by the enemy at or near Wilmington Island, as we fear, through some mismanagement of the lieutenant in command.

Acting Brigadier-General Gillmore at once applied to the commanding officer of the gunboat near to aid him in protecting the Augustine Creek Channel, which he has kindly consented to do, by sending a boat there for the present, awaiting, however, your further orders or sanction in the matter,

As it will now be of the utmost importance to cut off the communication of Fort Pulaski with the city, it being rumored and learned that $12,000 has been offered there for bringing off the garrison, and, as I immediately after my visit to Tybee directed every precaution possible to be taken on our part, I will trust that you may be able to aid us in this matter, and would respectfully request that you would sanction the movement of your commanding officer there, and aid us in this effort by such further means as are in your power from this place; for, with the information which we fear the enemy may obtain from our men (if prisoners, as we expect), we may find it expedient to open our batteries somewhat prematurely or before we had intended.

I would mention that the Boston is now coaling, and as soon as she returns I propose to send her to Edisto, with a battery of artillery, and if you have been able to obtain a proper pilot, which my own inquiries have not enabled me to possess as yet, I should be happy to meet your wishes in having him accompany her, and tow the Dale out from Otter Island. Will you please let me know immediately if you have a pilot?

Very respectfully, your obedient servant,

H. W. BENHAM,
Brigadier-General.

HEADQUARTERS DEPARTMENT OF THE SOUTH,
Hilton Head, Port Royal, S. C., April 3, 1862.

Hon. E. M. STANTON,
Secretary of War:

SIR: I have the honor to report my arrival here on the 30th ultimo. I address you by the first opportunity since my arrival.

I find about 17,000 troops scattered along the coast from Saint Augustine, Fla., to North Edisto Inlet, South Carolina, distributed as follows:

At Saint Augustine, Fla	200
At Jacksonville, Fla	1,400
At mouth of Saint John's River, Fla	70
At Fernandina, Fla	900
At Tybee Island, Ga	2,200
At Daufuskie Island, S. C	1,600
At Bird Island, S. C	300
At Jones Island, S. C	300
At Hilton Head, S. C	4,500
At Bay Point, S. C	80
At Beaufort, S. C	3,600
At Otter Island, S. C	450
At North Edisto River, S. C	1,400
	17,000

It is my opinion that this force is entirely too much scattered and is subject to be cut off in detail.

I shall order an abandonment of Jacksonville, Fla., and the re-enforcement of Forts Marion and Clinch. From later accounts I may add the Union feeling in Florida is not so strong as we were first induced to believe.

The batteries for opening on Fort Pulaski have been retarded by the non-arrival of the necessary guns, ammunition, &c. But Captain Gillmore, who deserves great credit for his untiring and scientific exertions, is now nearly ready, and by the next steamer I hope to be able to announce to you the fall of Pulaski. We then shall be able to hold the Savannah River with a small force and to concentrate on Charleston.

General Sherman made a requisition in December for five steamers drawing not more than 6 feet each. He informs me that they were purchased for him and sent from New York, but put into Hatteras in a storm, and are there detained by General Burnside. We are still very much in want of these light-draught boats, and, as we have but three wagons to a regiment, they are absolutely essential.

On my leaving Washington you had the kindness to promise me whatever force I might ask. We shall do all that men can do with the small force we have; but it distresses me to be in such a beautiful situation for striking strong blows without the arms to strike. I beg that you will send us at once as many men as you think we can use to advantage, as all the officers in command report the re-enforcement of the enemy on their respective fronts.

I most earnestly request that 50,000 muskets, with all the necessary accouterments, and 200 rounds for each piece, may be sent to me at once, with authority to arm such loyal men as I can find in the country, whenever, in my opinion, they can be used advantageously against the enemy.

It is important that I should be able to know and distinguish these men at once, and for this purpose I respectfully request that 50,000 pairs of scarlet pantaloons may be sent me; and this is all the clothing I shall require for these people.

I believe the rebel regiments as they retreat from the Army of the Potomac come directly to their respective States, and that in this way the force opposed to us here is becoming considerably augmented.

I have the honor to be, sir, very respectfully, your obedient servant,

D. HUNTER,
Major-General, Commanding.

GENERAL ORDERS, No. 3. } HDQRS. DEPARTMENT OF THE SOUTH,
Port Royal, S. C., April 3, 1862.

The following-named officers are hereby announced as additional members of the staff of the major-general commanding Department of the South, and will report accordingly:

Surg. George E. Cooper (Medical Department, U. S. Army), medical director; Capt. Louis H. Pelouze (Fifteenth Infantry, U. S. Army), acting inspector-general; First Lieut. Francis J. Shunk (Ordnance Department, U. S. Army), chief of ordnance; First Lieut. James H. Wilson, (Topographical Engineers, U. S. Army), chief topographical engineer; First Lieut. E. J. Keenan (Eleventh Pennsylvania Volunteers), chief signal officer.

By command of Maj. Gen. D. Hunter:

CHAS. G. HALPINE,
Major and Assistant Adjutant-General.

HDQRS. NORTHERN DISTRICT, DEPT. OF THE SOUTH,
Hilton Head, S. C., April 4, 1862.

Brig. Gen. EGBERT L. VIELE,
Commanding U. S. Forces, Daufuskie Island, S. C.:

GENERAL: Your letters reporting your reconnaissance were received late in the night, and the conclusion I come to is that the point you have marked B on Long Island should be selected for a battery; the ridge has width enough by your description for all the guns. I propose four in all that we have available, for which 30 yards will suffice, as little traverse is required; and, if more were needed and were available, I can see no objection to placing a second battery in rear of the first, the latter to be vacated by the men at the actual time of firing the rear battery. I would hope it might be possible to prepare a battery of four guns in less time than eight or ten days. I think it will be best to make your arrangements for the construction of such a battery—not for direct fire, of course, at that distance—and, besides, we cannot conveniently arrange pintle centers, &c. This you will recollect is for two 10-inch and two 8-inch columbiads, and, if I can procure a proper scow, I will also arrange for a battery for rifled pieces for direct fire.

I will communicate with you again by this afternoon's courier or in the morning.

Very respectfully, your obediant servant,

H. W. BENHAM,
Brigadier-General, Commanding.

HEADQUARTERS U. S. FORCES,
Savannah River, April 4, 1862.

General H. W. BENHAM,
Commanding First Division, Department of the South:

GENERAL: In my communication of yesterday I referred to the time it would take to put guns on Turtle Island, which, on account of the peculiar topography of that island, would be attended with delay and difficulty. But the guns on Long Island can be put in position at once. I have one 8-inch and one 10-inch mortar which I can use. The rebels were busy all night last night moving troops towards Wilmington Island. They have evidently something on the *tapis*.

Very respectfully, your obedient servant,

EGBERT L. VIELE,
Commanding General.

HDQRS. NORTHERN DISTRICT, DEPT. OF THE SOUTH,
Hilton Head, S. C., April 5, 1862.

Flag-Officer S. F. DUPONT,
Commanding South Atlantic Blockading Squadron,
Port Royal Harbor, S. C.:

COMMODORE: I trust your dispatches for Warsaw have arrived in time to go by my courier, whom I have sent to recall, if possible, if not, I will have them at Tybee this afternoon, and if my engineers can contrive a means of obstructing Wilmington River, I will have it done, though I much fear now the force of the enemy, believed to have been increased lately in that vicinity, may render this more difficult than at a previous day, if not impossible even.

The reports from General Viele from Daufuskie last night lead us to fear that the rebels are concentrating troops near Wilmington Island, probably for an effort to relieve or re-enforce the garrison of Fort Pulaski, as it appears impossible for a land force to act efficiently in those marshes, and we have scarcely any means for effective action by water. General Hunter and myself were last evening most earnest in wishing that you had the means of increasing your own power to an important extent just now on the Wilmington Narrows and on the Tybee River.

Very respectfully, your obedient servant,

H. W. BENHAM,
Brigadier-General, Commanding.

HDQRS. NORTHERN DISTRICT, DEPT. OF THE SOUTH,
Hilton Head, S. C., April 8, 1862.

Col. ENOCH Q. FELLOWS,
Commanding U. S. Forces, Edisto Island, S. C.:

COLONEL: The general commanding desires that you would take every opportunity that offers, either by negroes who come from the rebels, by scouts, or other means, of acquiring and transmitting to him all information, with sketch, plans, and descriptions, when practicable, of the best routes of approaching Charleston or James Island, either by land or water. If the rebels come down in force to occupy or remain at Jehossee Island, and you feel sure that you have strength enough, with the aid from Otter Island, to make a dash at them and to rout them from there, you are authorized to do this; or, on learning from you that more force would be requisite, he would, if such force were available from this vicinity, either send or take it to you for this purpose.

It does not appear desirable to occupy the island farther inland, than Edisto, except such small portions of adjacent shores as may be necessary for the security of our pickets on that island, and the main body of your troops will habitually be kept in such position that they can easily be concentrated for resistance to an attack. An especial vigilance is urged upon you at this time, when other important efforts are being made here, as there may be attempts at diversion in your direction, and a full security for your forces would be preferable to attacks upon the enemy, if they even appear to be open to it, at this juncture.

Respectfully, your obedient servant,

A. B. ELY,
Acting Assistant Adjutant-General.

HEADQUARTERS DEPARTMENT OF THE SOUTH,
Hilton Head, Port Royal, S. C., April 8, 1862.

Flag-Officer SAMUEL F. DUPONT,
Commanding South Atlantic Blockading Squadron,
On Board U. S. S. Wabash:

COMMODORE: I contemplate opening the attack on Fort Pulaski by sunrise to-morrow morning, and have to ask of you all the co-operation and assistance in your power. A few days' further delay would place our batteries on Tybee Island in a perfect condition perhaps, but I am satisfied that such delay would be of more service to the enemy than to ourselves.

I have the honor to be, commodore, very respectfully, your obedient servant,

D. HUNTER,
Major-General, Commanding.

HEADQUARTERS U. S. FORCES,
North Edisto, S. C., April 9, 1862.

Lieut. A. B. ELY,
A. A. A. G., Hdqrs. Northern Dist., Dept. of the South:

I have the honor to acknowledge the receipt of your communication of the 8th instant. I will make every endeavor, through spies, intelligent contrabands, &c., to get the required information as regards the best approaches to Charleston, and will forward immediately to the commanding general whatever information I may get.

I visited the outposts of my command yesterday and find everything in an admirable condition; the pickets are well posted, and the whole force, consisting of two regiments of infantry and four pieces of artillery, can be quickly concentrated at any point. I do not think the rebels are in large force on Jehossee Island; their pickets are stationed and can be seen at Watt's Cut.

I do not think it advisable to make any advance on Jehossee Island at present with the force I have, as it could only be held with the assistance of a gunboat.

A field officer of the day was seen visiting the rebel pickets on the 7th instant, which indicates that there is more than one regiment in the vicinity. I am making every effort to ascertain the strength of the enemy's forces in that vicinity, and will report when I get the desired information.

I shall make a reconnaissance on the Pocahontas soon towards White Point and on the Dawho River. I would request, if it can be conveniently spared, a gunboat drawing not over 7 feet of water. The sloop-of-war Dale has not yet arrived at this port. The Pocahontas draws too much water to run in the South Edisto River. The contrabands will be forwarded immediately by the Mayflower.

I am, very respectfully, your obedient servant,

E. Q. FELLOWS,
Colonel Third New Hampshire Infantry.

CONFEDERATE CORRESPONDENCE, ETC.

SPECIAL ORDERS, No. 130. } ADJUTANT AND INSPECTOR GEN.'S OFFICE, *Richmond, August 21, 1861.*

* * * * * * *

XII. The undermentioned brigadier-generals of the Provisional Army of the Confederate States are assigned to duty as follows, viz:

* * * * * * *

2d. Brig. Gen. Roswell S. Ripley will assume command of the Department of South Carolina and the coast defenses of that State.

* * * * * * *

5th. Brig. Gen. John B. Grayson will proceed to Florida, and assume command of the Department of Middle and Eastern Florida, and the coast defenses of the same.

* * * * * * *

By command of the Secretary of War:

JNO. WITHERS,
Assistant Adjutant-General.

CHARLESTON, *August 31, 1861.*

General S. COOPER,
Adjutant-General:

Two transports with troops off bar yesterday; to-day off Bull Island. Probably enemy from Hatteras, after destroying batteries. Have re-enforced Stono heavily. Have ordered Orr's regiment to Summerville to reserve. Have called on governor for another, besides holding Charleston volunteers in readiness to move until our batteries are in order. Must have force to prevent enemy's landing, if possible. Hope, if uninterrupted, to dispense with extra force in fifteen days. If from one to four officers, having knowledge of ordnance or artillery duty, can be sent here, will assist greatly.

R. S. RIPLEY,
Brigadier-General.

HEADQUARTERS SOUTH CAROLINA,
September 1, 1861.

Hon. L. P. WALKER,
Secretary of War:

SIR: Colonel Gregg has two companies here, and desires that they may be received for the war into his regiment. As the law only admits of ten companies to a regiment, I refer the matter to you, and request an immediate decision, as I desire orders extended to these two companies. If agreeable to you I should most cordially assign these companies to his regiment, as he is a colonel of great experience and of the most distinguished standing. If there is any officer to whom twelve companies could be intrusted, then I should urge most respectfully the permission for Colonel Gregg. I shall not be able to arm them, as we have not a single arm to spare out of this State, and I am now remodeling the old arms picked up in the country, so as to try and be able to get arms for the forty-two companies now in camp under your requisition. You recollect you directed them to be formed into regiments and to elect their field officers. One of these regiments has done so, and the others will in a few days.

The President has telegraphed me to retain Colonel Orr's regiment for our coast defense. The exposed coast of North Carolina will now be in possession of the enemy, and it endangers our whole defenses.

Under these circumstances I would respectfully urge that Colonel Gregg's regiment be ordered to our coast, for the season is just approaching when an invasion may be anticipated, particularly after our recent disasters on the defenseless coast of North Carolina. If you were to order Colonel Gregg's regiment into this State I presume his commission given by the President would be of older date than any volunteer regiment in the State, and, if so, it would make him the ranking colonel, and his experience would thus give confidence to the country.

I shall also place Colonel Dunovant and his regiment, recently organized under your requisition for the 3,000, under orders for our sea-coast. I can arm and equip his regiment. Colonel Orr's I have already armed and equipped, and I will go on to arm the others as fast as I can, and if you inform me immediately that Colonel Gregg's regiment will be stationed in South Carolina, I will try and arm these two companies now here for his regiment, if you decide to receive them. Please inform me by telegram. With Orr's, Dunovant's, and Gregg's regiments I would feel safe, as I have a stationary force organized in the city of Charleston of 3,000 well armed and trained men, ready to act, besides Colonel Heyward's State regiment, now in actual service on the Beaufort coast and at the batteries recently erected.

I have also Colonel Manigault's State regiment on the coast of Georgetown, above Charleston, and in the batteries. I have ordered another State regiment of well-trained men, under Colonel Hagood, into the forts at Cole's Island, on the Stono, 25 miles from Charleston. These three colonels are thorough military men and of the highest standing and military education. I have also six companies of infantry (regulars) on Sullivan's Island, and four of the battalion of regular artillery in Fort Sumter and Fort Moultrie. I have ordered five months' supplies into the former, to stand a siege, if necessary, and am raising two new artillery companies to put into it, but in the mean time will order other companies into it for the present. Besides Colonel Hagood's regiment, now in the forts on Stono, I have there three regular companies of infantry and the battalion of regular dragoons, mustered in as infantry, under Major Lucas, so that I have in the forts and islands around

Charleston about 1,800 men, all well drilled, and a reserve in the city of about 3,000. This, with the State regiments under Colonels Heyward and Manigault, constitute about 7,500 men, and the additional regiments of Colonels Orr, Dunovant, and Gregg would make good 10,000 men. With this force, and ten cavalry companies I have on the coast and the reserves of about 3,000 men at the two camps of instruction, I think I could feel safe for the present. I am thus particular in details that you may understand our position and let the President know it. All I beg is an answer as soon as possible, so that I may act as soon as possible.

I also earnestly beg, if possible, that you will order me, if you have it at Norfolk, 40,000 pounds of cannon powder. I loaned the governor of North Carolina 25,000 pounds, and also the governor of Florida, for Fernandina and Saint Augustine, 5,000 pounds, besides what I sent to Memphis, Tenn. If I could be sure of getting 40,000 pounds as a reserve for Charleston, I would immediately order a full supply of cannon powder for about 100 guns I have now on our coast below Charleston. As it is, I fear to drain Charleston entirely. I bought for the State last December and January about 300,000 pounds from Hazard's Mills, in Connecticut, but I have distributed all of it but about 40,000 pounds, and used a great deal in our batteries in the harbor of Charleston. Please let me know immediately as to this point.

I now desire to get from you permission to raise for the war another regiment of rifles, and I think, if you give me the power, I can get it up with men who will arm themselves from our private rifles and arms in their own hands. I think I could make a choice regiment, and with little or no expense as to arms, and selected from men who would incur the necessary expenses, and, if you will give me the power to do so, and for me to appoint the field officers, and even the company officers, I could select men who were graduates of our State military institutions and of West Point, and I could select officers who are now in our regular State forces, and in the first volunteer regiments now in Virginia, to put in position. I would do so, because our regular forces and our forces in Virginia are only for one year, and most of their terms will expire in January and February next, and I desire to secure, in advance, the services of their officers "for the war," as many of them have been in the late United States Army, and all of our regular forces have military education. I know them, and could make selections of officers for companies that would advance the public service greatly.

Please let me know on this point as soon as you can, and I will then proceed, in a quiet way, to raise a rifle regiment for the war, with officers all selected with an eye single to secure military education and qualifications. I would also desire to raise two full companies of cavalry, to be attached to it, of men who would arm themselves.

I have the honor to be, very respectfully,

F. W. PICKENS.

HDQRS. PROVISIONAL FORCES, DEPT. OF S. C.,
Charleston, September 1, 1861.

GENERAL: I have the honor to request that authority may be given me to provide the force necessary for the defense of the batteries now being finished at different points of the coast. For this I think the following will be necessary.

1st. Authority to muster into service for the war, for special duty on the coast, a force not exceeding 1,500 men.

2d. Authority to establish a recruiting service for the enlisted troops now on duty, viz, the regiment of South Carolina infantry and the battalion of South Carolina artillery, that the former may be recruited and filled up to ten full companies, and the latter increased to a regiment, with its proper complement of field officers. This will, of course, require the co-operation of the governor of the State.

3d. Authority to procure, as speedily as may be, such means of transport, armed if necessary, as will insure a speedy communication and transport, by the inland routes, between the different points of the coast, as well as such facilities for guard service as may be necessary.

4th. To enable these things to be done as speedily as possible, and to provide such material as may be required by the chief engineer in charge of the coast defenses and by the ordnance officer on duty here, that means to the following amounts may be placed to the credit of the following officers, subject to draft for no other purpose than the defenses of the coast, unless by order of the Secretary of War: To the chief engineer, Major Trapier, $50,000; ordnance officer, Captain Childs, $25,000; quartermaster, Captain Lee, $100,000; total, $175,000.

The reasons for the above are as follows: For the first, that many men will be willing to muster into service for a particular locality who would not engage to go beyond the limits of the State or the coasts adjacent. It would also be bad policy to take too many men from the vicinity of these plantations, drawn from localities thickly settled with black population.

For the second, is the manifest importance of keeping up the strength of the small force enlisted in the department, being more reliable for the continued service of guarding the forts and batteries than men of a different class.

For the third, that our only means of communication are by the inland routes, which are tortuous and shallow, and only available for certain classes of vessels. If we have these vessels and speedy communication the inland navigation is a great element of strength, but without it it is one of weakness, enabling the enemy, by means of his barges, to overpower weak batteries, cut the communication, and lay waste whole sections of country containing valuable property. The guard service is required to enable us to watch the enemy's fleet, to assist vessels which may be endeavoring to run the blockade, and give timely notice of an attack in force. It is within my knowledge that one or two vessels at least have been warned off the harbor or captured which might have successfully run the blockade had there been a guard steamer to succor them. The brig West Indian, which ran the blockade this morning with 1,500 bags of coffee, came very near being lost by the wind failing when within 2 miles of the range of the forts and batteries. Had the calm lasted half an hour, chased as she was by the steam frigate and sloop of war now blockading here, she must have been captured by the boats of the squadron. A steam guard boat would have secured her from any hazard.

The reason for the fourth is, that while the War Department at Richmond is occupied with business of such gigantic importance as it now has in hand, many requisitions of vital importance lay by for their turn for consideration and action. Meantime master workmen and mechanics, many of them having their capital exhausted or in accounts against the Government, are in the present state of the money market often unable to pay their workmen, and delay ensues in important business. Funds provided for general service in the Quartermaster's Department often are expended by requisition from abroad. Of the three requisitions which have been made by the staff officers, attended to by my order, and which I have the honor to inclose, that most readily dispensed with is that of the Ordnance Department. Most of the material can be provided for by the guard service, but for various articles it would be well to have a fund for special purposes of coast defenses.

The estimate for the Quartermaster's Department will be wanted especially to carry out the purposes mentioned in the third paragraph.

I have to request that the inclosed special requisitions be submitted with this communication for such action as may be deemed most proper by the Department.

I am, very respectfully, your obedient servant,

R. S. RIPLEY,
Brigadier-General.

[Indorsement.]

SEPTEMBER 5, 1861.

The original letter of General Ripley, of which this is a copy, has not yet been received at this office. The subject is, however, of such importance as to require immediate action, and hence this paper is respectfully submitted to the Secretary of War.

S. COOPER,
Adjutant-General.

HEADQUARTERS, S. C., *September* 2, 1861.

Hon. L. P. WALKER,
Secretary of War:

DEAR SIR: In my letter of yesterday I urged you to send back Colonel Gregg's regiment to this State for the coast. Upon further reflection I withdraw any request of the kind, and leave it entirely to your own judgment as to the whole matter. You know the general plans and our resources, and I do not. I desire, therefore, now to leave the matter as to the disposition of Colonel Gregg's regiment entirely to your own judgment, and hereby withdraw any request of mine on that point. If you will immediately authorize me I can raise many more companies for the war, and put them at the two camps of instruction, and perhaps it would be better for the President to appoint all field officers, or, if he will leave the appointments to me, I will make them from graduates of West Point or our own military academies, or from officers who have shown merit in the regiments now in Virginia whose terms of service will begin to expire in January and February next. I could also take officers from the regular forces now in this State whose terms will expire about February next, and thus save all our best officers by their appointment in forces for and during the war. If I can have discretion of this kind, I can then at these camps increase our forces greatly for the war, and as our twelve-months' volunteers return from Virginia, I can catch nearly all of them immediately and save the best of their officers. Please give me an early answer on this point. The four regiments at the camps at present are electing, as you have, in yours of the 15th of July last, directed that they should do.

But all to be received after this, I desire field officers to be appointed either by the President or named by me and confirmed by the President or in any way the President thinks proper.

I have four very fine cavalry companies in camp, and would be glad if you would allow me to name a major to command them.

I desire you to give permission for me to raise two full regiments of cavalry besides, for and during the war, and if you can give me any assurance as to pistols and holsters, I think that I can do it. Let the President appoint their field officers, and let them elect their company officers, and when the number is full order them to the camp for Confederate service. If it is not your policy to raise two more regiments, then perhaps you might allow one.

The present four companies are by express telegraph from President Davis. I have three regiments and four companies of cavalry at one camp, and if you will permit I will appoint a very scientific officer, Major Stevens, the head of our military academy, to command them, and take charge of the camp for temporary purposes. Perhaps I could get Col. Thomas F. Drayton, who is a graduate of West Point, and a perfect and high-bred gentleman.

Very respectfully,

F. W. PICKENS.

P. S.—I most respectfully urge you will receive no more troops for any period except for and during the war, and let it be known.

COLUMBIA, *September* 2, 1861.

Hon. Mr. WALKER,
Secretary of War:

Will you allow me eight more companies for the war and formation of another regiment—the President to appoint, as he desires—Colonel Drayton to command? Please let me know.

F. W. PICKENS.

HEADQUARTERS MILITARY DISTRICT,
Savannah, *September* 3, 1861.

Hon. L. P. WALKER,
Secretary of War, *Richmond*, *Va.:*

SIR: I beg to call your attention to the pressing necessity for additional troops on this coast at the earliest possible moment. I have received and mustered into service enough to replace the two regiments suddenly ordered to Virginia (Semmes' and Williams' regiments), and these are but enough to man the batteries on the coast, leaving us no protection on the main-land in case of trouble. Nearly all the companies I have at this moment are entirely raw and undisciplined.

The large calls upon the State of Georgia have taken away nearly every trained company and all the arms, except such as may be found in private hands. I am now endeavoring to organize all such as can furnish their own arms and muster them into service. In this way only can I secure a force that will give any protection to this coast. May I ask the favor of you to say at once, by telegraph, that I may continue to organize new regiments and battalions on and near this coast? I wish to quiet the apprehensions of the people, by assuring them that I have full authority to organize and muster in until we have a sufficient force.

If the Department is willing to make appointments of colonels of these regiments, I recommend that Duncan L. Clinch (son of the late General Clinch) be forthwith appointed colonel, with authority to raise a regiment for this coast. In any event please send me the telegraphic dispatch which I have above requested.

Very respectfully, your obedient servant,

A. R. LAWTON,
Brigadier-General, Commanding.

HEADQUARTERS SOUTH CAROLINA,
Columbia, September 4, 1861.

Hon. L. P. WALKER,
Secretary of War, Richmond, Va.:

SIR: In reply to your communication of the 9th of August last to the governor of South Carolina, in relation to the First Regiment of South Carolina Volunteers, Lieutenant-Colonel Glover, I have the honor to state that in consideration of the large number of State troops already in Virginia, and the recent requisitions of your Department for five additional regiments (which regiments are now nearly ready to take up the line of march), and in view of the anticipated invasion on our coast this coming winter, as evidenced by the Northern press and the Hatteras affair, the State authorities deem it inexpedient to permit the First Regiment South Carolina Volunteers (State troops) to leave the State for their unexpired term of service. The regiment is now guarding an exposed portion of our coast. His excellency the governor and the State authorities feel assured that you will not accept the services of any independent troops without they present the consent of the governor.

I have the honor to be, very respectfully, your obedient servant,

S. R. GIST,
Adjutant and Inspector General of South Carolina.

HEADQUARTERS MILITARY DISTRICT,
Savannah, September 4, 1861.

Hon. L. P. WALKER,
Secretary of War:

SIR: In addition to what I said in my letter of yesterday in reference to the urgent necessity for a large addition to the military force on this coast and a recommendation that Duncan L. Clinch, esq., be authorized to raise a regiment for local defense, I take leave respectfully to suggest that the elections for field officers of regiments within my observation have proved very disastrous to discipline and efficiency. If consistent with the views of the War Department I would be truly pleased to see all such appointments here made by the President, and I will suggest names, if desired.

Very respectfully, your obedient servant,

A. R. LAWTON,
Brigadier-General, Commanding.

WAR DEPARTMENT, C. S. A.,
Richmond, September 6, 1861.

Brigadier-General RIPLEY,
Commanding Charleston, S. C.:

SIR: A copy of your letter of September 1 to Adjutant-General Cooper has been submitted to this Department. In view of its importance I take the earliest opportunity to reply.

The authority for which you ask, "to muster into service for the war, for special duty on the coast, a force not exceeding 1,500 men," is granted, but at the same time I take occasion to say that, as Governor Pickens is already organizing a force for home defense, it will be proper for you, so far as practicable, to act in concert with him, to avoid both unpleasant complications and unnecessary expenses.

2d. The authority asked for "to establish a recruiting service for the enlisted troops now on duty," &c., as proposed, is also granted.

3d. With regard to the proposal "to provide means of transport, armed, if necessary," &c., this Department must be, to a great extent, guided by your own view of the actual necessity of your position. The Department is, therefore, unwilling to refuse any means of defense which you recommend as necessary, and such armed transports as you propose will be allowed within the limits of as reasonable expenditure as may be rendered necessary. All requisitions made in consequence of this expenditure within the limit of necessary defense will be granted promptly, and the difficulties which you suggest as likely to arise in the execution of these plans, and in view of which you ask a departure from the usual rule, may, it is hoped, be without necessity of such departure, easily and satisfactorily obviated, without the necessity of such arrangements as you propose.

The requisitions inclosed by you have been sent to the proper bureaus, and will doubtless receive prompt attention.

Respectfully, your obedient servant,

L. P. WALKER,
Secretary of War.

SAVANNAH, *September* 8, 1861.

Hon. L. P. WALKER:

There is much alarm here about the coast. Stronger force and vigorous action absolutely necessary. Will you increase the force and quicken the energy, or will you furnish funds to support troops and approbate prompt State action for that purpose? I wish to avoid all conflict of authority, but prompt action is indispensable. Please answer immediately.

JOSEPH E. BROWN.

RICHMOND, *September* 9, 1861.

Governor BROWN,
Savannah, Ga.:

In a letter to General Lawton I have ordered him to increase his force as he may deem necessary. All legitimate expenditures for this purpose within the line of his approval will be paid by the Government.

L. P. WALKER,

RICHMOND, *September* 9, 1861.

General A. R. LAWTON,
Savannah, Ga.:

You are authorized to organize such military force as is in your opinion necessary for the defense of the coast of Georgia.

JOHN TYLER, JR.,
Acting Chief of Bureau of War.

WAR DEPARTMENT, C. S. A.,
Richmond, September 10, 1861.

His Excellency FRANCIS W. PICKENS,
Governor of South Carolina:

SIR: It affords me very great pleasure to acknowledge your very interesting communication to this Department of the 1st and 2d of the present month, and to congratulate you upon the evidence they furnish of the ceaseless energies put forth by the governor of South Carolina during your administration. Where such faithful manifestations of public concern exist, guided and controlled by such admirable wisdom and policy, it is profoundly to be regretted that this Department is so circumscribed by law as not always to have it in its power to second your suggestions. Under the law a regiment is limited to ten companies, and therefore your proposition to incorporate two additional companies into Colonel Gregg's regiment, although based on sound reasoning and solid facts, cannot be granted. Colonel Gregg has been informed more at large of the manner in which the action of this Department is circumscribed in the premises, and will doubtless communicate with you on the subject. Nor does there exist any authority by which I can authorize you to appoint company officers. They are invariably elected, according to the laws regulating the militia of the States respectively, and this is the case where vacancies occur after troops have been received and mustered into the Confederate service. To enable the Government even to appoint field officers troops must come to it direct, without State intervention, under the amended acts of Congress passed at the second session. Then they must come solely by companies, and be mustered into the service as such. Thus your excellency will perceive how utterly impossible it is for this Department to entertain your proposition in these respects. Neither can I gratify you by accepting the two unarmed cavalry regiments you generously offer. The service does not absolutely require them, and our present resources do not admit of their acceptance. But the two cavalry companies to which you allude will be received, if armed and equipped; and where there is necessarily so much negation of your wishes, I am happy to say that the rifle regiment you propose to raise for the war and to arm will be taken into service.

This Department, through an anxious desire to oblige you, will also receive ten companies, to be offered by companies, and to be organized by its authority into a regiment, thus reserving to itself the right to appoint the field officers; but if your excellency can possibly arm these companies, it is sincerely hoped you will arm them, though it be only with the flint musket, country rifle, or heavy shot-gun.

The cannon powder that you ask for cannot be spared by the Ordnance Office unless there be an absolute existing necessity for it, under the pressure of demand in other quarters, where it is indispensable. It is preferred that your excellency will retain your patience upon the subject for the present.

I entirely concur with your excellency in the policy of not accepting any more troops except for the war, and have endeavored ever since the Congress invested this Department with the discretionary power of thus receiving military tenders to limit its favor by this policy; but as our arms have not been abundant, it has been and still is a matter of pure necessity to accept tenders coming to us armed for a less period.

With renewed congratulations upon the martial force of your State and considerations of high personal regard, I remain, your excellency's obedient servant,

L. P. WALKER,
Secretary of War.

HDQRS. MIL. DEPT. MIDDLE AND EAST FLORIDA,
Fernandina, September 13, 1861.

Hon. L. P. WALKER,
Secretary of War, C. S., Richmond:

SIR: The whole population of Florida may well unite with me, as they do, in deploring the condition of the State. I have been in the State nine days and have been at this place for five days. I have pulled down much of the battery and magazine, and when completed (I hope in two weeks) the harbor will be guarded and protected. An alarm existed a few days since, and the governor promptly called out a large force of volunteers, and a strong resistance could have been made, but without aid from Fort Clinch and the battery it would have been useless to expect it. As sure as the sun rises, unless cannon, powder, &c., be sent to Florida in the next thirty days, she will fall into the hands of the North. Nothing human can prevent it. There are not 4,000 pounds of powder at every post combined. The batteries are incorrectly put up and not finished. The enemy can land where they please. Guns and chassis are lying on the beach, though that I have remedied. There is not an officer to put up the guns or an officer to superintend their instruction when put up. There is not an officer to receive the supplies when they arrive. I have no assistant adjutant-general, nor an assistant commissary, nor an assistant quartermaster, nor an aide-de-camp. Mr. Wood, if appointed a lieutenant, was applied for as aide, Mr. I'Anson as assistant quartermaster. Captain Gott was applied for, and received orders, which were revoked; I applied for no one else, as I knew no one to apply for. I applied to General Cooper for Lieutenant Thomas, adjutant of Colonel Ward's regiment Florida volunteers, who was dissatisfied with his position. Colonel Ward, Lieutenant Thomas informs me, will object to the transfer. I trust, Mr. Secretary, that you will take this communication under your immediate notice, and have the ordnance stores and the various officers sent at once. I send a list of guns and ammunition wanted forthwith. Florida will become a Yankee province unless measures for her relief are promptly made. I leave to-morrow for Tallahassee, and shall, with all dispatch, visit Saint Mark's, Apalachicola, Cedar Keys, and Tampa. I will communicate my movements from time to time. I send a copy of my requisition for ordnance; also a circular found, with many others, posted about this city.

Very respectfully, your most obedient servant,

JOHN B. GRAYSON,
Brigadier-General, C. A., Comdg. Middle and East Florida.

[Inclosures.]

Requisition for ordnance and ordnance stores required to be filled at the earliest moment for the Military Department of Middle and East Florida, and to be consigned to Capt. William Hickman, assistant quartermaster, Fernandina, East Florida:

14 32-pounder cannon; six to be rifled, if possible.

4 42-pounders, if possible, and rifled, with chassis. The chassis for the 32-pounders are promised from Charleston.

23,000 pounds of cannon powder for 29 cannon.
12,000 musket cartridges; few or none on hand.
300 shells for three 12-pounder howitzers at Saint Augustine. The fixtures for the 32-pounders are promised from Charleston.
12 12-pounders, with chassis and fixtures complete; the 32-pounders to be the army pattern.

JOHN B. GRAYSON,
Brigadier-General, C. A., Comdg. Middle and East Florida.

TALLAHASSEE, FLA., *September* 14, 1861.

Notice.

All loyal citizens of the United States are hereby notified that the Federal troops will take possession of the island of Amelia in a few days, and if they desire to escape the vengeance of an outraged Government they must assemble on the south end of the island. All those found at that point, except the military, will be regarded as good citizens of the United States.

Assemble on the right.

FORT PULASKI, *September* 15, 1861.

Capt. R. M. CUYLER,
Chief of Ordnance, Military District of Savannah:

CAPTAIN: I am in receipt of yours of the 14th. In compliance with your request I inclose herewith a statement of the companies stationed at this post, with number of men, number and description of arms, and amount of ammunition, as given me by the captains of companies.* Seven thousand of the 8,000 cartridges sent here, subject to the order of Colonel Mercer, have been sent to Tybee. Out of the 1,000 left the guard are being supplied.

The 4,000 cartridges in the ordnance store-room, to which you refer, were made by the Irish Jasper Greens, and are ball, without buck-shot. They will answer, perhaps, for the Washington Volunteers, but Captain McMahon prefers the cartridges with buck-shot. There are no caps with them.

We have not made any fuses yet, having no fuse die that we can use. As soon as we can obtain fuse dies we will commence making fuses. We can easily work three or four dies if we have them. We have ours made at the Central Railroad workshops, which is imperfect. I send it up by this boat. If you will send it to Mr. Burns, at the Central Railroad, I have no doubt but that he will have the mistake corrected. If you will examine it you will see around that some of the forms for the fuses are very irregular; the taper does not extend to the small end, and if it did it would make the fuse too large at that end.

We want about a dozen small copper funnels (perhaps tin would answer) for filling shells; there are but two here. We also want a few fuse reamers.

Will you permit me to suggest the propriety of holding a survey upon the carriages of the barbette guns? I very much fear that they are not calculated to withstand the shock of repeated firing. Would it not be well to attend to this at once, and, if it is decided that the pine is not

---

* Not found.

suitable, have oak procured and carriages made without delay? I am informed that seasoned oak enough to replace all the barbette carriages can be had at Darien.

Permit me also to bring to your notice the small supply of cannon powder now in our magazines, it being but about 45,000 pounds. The Navy holds an order on the fort for 1,700 or 1,800, which, if delivered, will reduce the quantity of shot made.

Why cannot Captain Echols and yourself visit the fort some day this week and assist us with your advice?

I am, very respectfully, your obedient servant,

JOS. S. CLAGHORN,
Captain, Commanding Post.

WAR DEPARTMENT, C. S. A., ENGINEER BUREAU,
Richmond, Va., September 21, 1861.

Hon. SECRETARY OF WAR:

SIR: The project of auxiliary coast defense herewith, as submitted by Col. A. J. Gonzales, though not thought to be everywhere applicable, is believed to be of great value under special circumstances. In the example assumed at Edisto Island, where the movable batteries rest on defensive works and are themselves scarcely exposed to surprise and capture, a rifled 24-pounder, with two small guns, rallying and reconnoitering from each of the fixed batteries, would prove invaluable. A lighter gun than the 24-pounder, and quite as efficient, might be devised for such service, but this is probably the best now available. Colonel Gonzales' proposed arrangements for re-enforcing certain exposed and threatened maritime posts seem to be judicious and to merit attention.

Very respectfully,

D. LEADBETTER,
Major, Engineers.

[Indorsement.]

SEPTEMBER 23, 1861.

Respectfully submitted to the Secretary of War.

S. COOPER,
Adjutant and Inspector General.

[Inclosure.]

RICHMOND, VA., *September* 14, 1861.

His Excellency JEFFERSON DAVIS,
President C. S. A.:

SIR: I have the honor to place before you the outline of a system of coast defense which, if adopted, will, I believe, very much increase the security of our Atlantic and Gulf States, and render a lesser force than otherwise would be required sufficient for the protection of our coast. I have not been bold to submit it to you for adoption without having first lied it before scientific officers of our Army and other gentlemen of military experience, who have highly commended it for practicability and efficiency. As acting inspector-general on Morris Island, and since up to this day as inspector of the troops and defenses on the coast of South Carolina by Governor Pickens, I have probably had opportunities for studying our coast and the way of protecting it not enjoyed by others. Taking the coast of South Carolina as a representation, with but few exceptions, of our Southern coast, and taking the island of Edisto as a representation of the nature of its seaboard, we have as roughly marked in the sketch on opposite page:

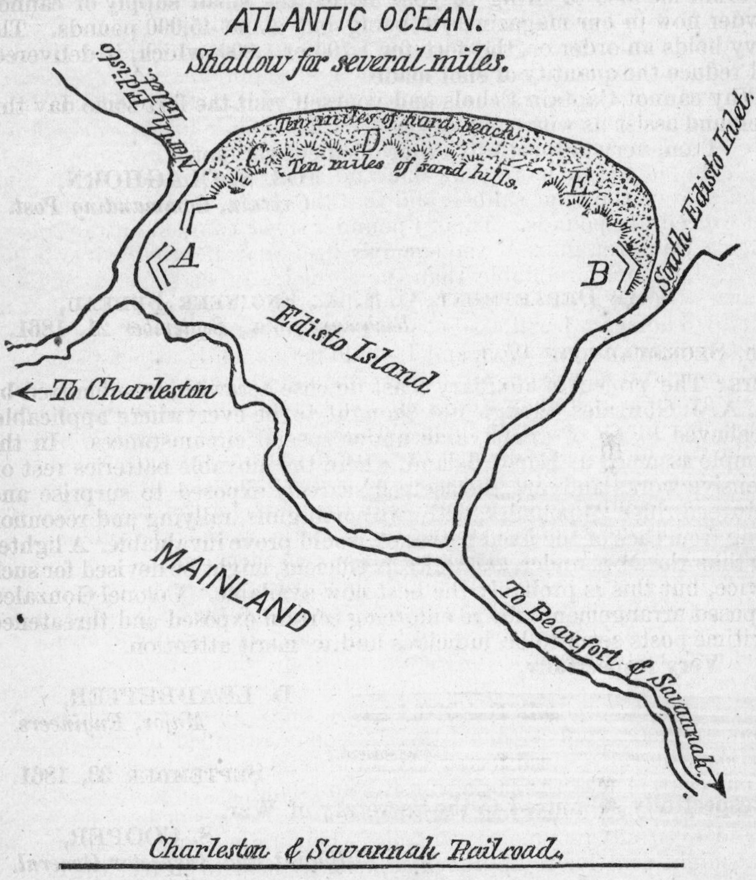

We have one of our most valuable agricultural regions, with a population of about 5,000 negroes and one hundred and odd voters, with one sand open work (A) on North Edisto entrance, mounting six guns, and another (B) on South Edisto entrance, mounting two guns. On this island, as on the whole of our coast, there is a hard practicable sand beach, and immediately behind it a line of sand hills, forming almost a continuous fort of nature's own making. The shallowness of the water opposite the coast, extending for several miles, would prevent any but the lightest vessels from approaching it. Hence the enemy's large steam frigates, except through their tenders and barges, can inflict no injury upon us. By means of these barges, however, a force can be landed, if unresisted, anywhere upon the beach, and the works at the inlets taken in the rear. Through these inlets the batteries can be engaged by third-class steamers and by gunboats. Supposing the armament at these inlets to be so increased (which should be done) as to prevent ingress of ships, and consequently of heavy artillery (for the latter cannot be landed in boats upon the beach), in the absence of an overwhelming land force lining the whole extent of our coast we should have upon the latter artillery of the greatest range, in order that it may engage small steamers lying off, sink approaching barges, and should the latter effect a landing with howitzers and men, crush them by the superiority of their metal and the advantages of range, and at the same time so portable that it can easily be used upon the coast, and even in emergencies upon the sandy roads on the island or the main-land. In the rifled 24-pounder on seige carriage we have the gun required.

Experience has shown that a rifled 24-pounder, not banded, can throw an elongated percussion shell, the most formidable to ships, much over 3 miles. The conditions necessary for the safety to the gun are, that the shell do not weigh more than one and a half the weight of the round solid shot of the same caliber, and that the charge for the 24-pounder do not exceed five pounds. This 24-pounder rifled cannon, outranging the largest Dahlgren guns of the enemy's fleet, and, if provided with good shells, far more formidable than the former, can, on siege carriages, be drawn with the greatest ease up and down the beach at half and at low tide by 6 horses. I will assign, however, 10 horses to each gun and 10 to each ammunition wagon, and I would permanently attach to each gun and ammunition wagon, for protection and support, for assistance in drawing them at high water or on heavy roads on extraordinary occasions, and for co-operation in action against infantry, a body of cavalry, at the rate of 10 mounted men to each gun and ammunition wagon. For such guns, stationed on the coast, no more carriages and no forges, &c., would be required to be moved with the guns, for the reason that this artillery has for its object to link the batteries at the inlets, to close and watch the space which intervenes between them, and to prevent their being taken in reverse. At night they are expected to unite in some central post upon the coast, or to fall back upon the forts which constitute their base. These forts they would flank against a land attack, and re-enforce materially in a contest against ships. For this purpose, at each fort or battery there should be constructed a suitable work, with magazine and stored ammunition, ready to receive these guns whenever recalled. Thus, if there were stationed three 24-pounder rifled cannon on siege carriages on the natural fortress of sand hills (a most important feature of our coast) back of the beach on Edisto Island, at the points marked C, D, and E, they would cross their fire against barges or land forces, and would even advantageously engage, when united, any small steamers that might contrive to approach sufficiently near to protect the enemy's landing.

To carry out beyond peradventure the operation of moving behind the sand hills, where the road is heavy, to move at high water in great emergencies along the beach, to cross with the sea-coast flying artillery a belt of country in order to intercept the enemy or to take a strategic position, a strong rope, with ten straps permanently affixed to it along its length, is to be connected to the chain the draught horses are pulling by. Each of these straps is hooked on temporarily to the breast-band of the saddle of each cavalry soldier assigned to each gun and ammunition wagon, and thus 20 horses will be the draught to each gun in any difficult traveling. In an emergency, to place the guns in position at the shortest notice and in the most difficult localities, the horses and horsemen belonging to the ammunition wagon can be attached temporarily to the gun, and thus 40 horses are at once available to extricate it even from a morass. This duty performed they can return, and still more easily remove the ammunition wagon. In case of an attempt of the enemy to land, the infantry at the two forts, A and B, could, unseen behind the hills, come to the support of cavalry and artillery. I would arm the cavalry with sabers and double-barreled guns. Behind sand hills, in defense of a battery from an enemy landing on the beach, where the space to be traversed by him is very short and open, I would prefer the double-barreled gun to any other arm, especially as in landing from the boats the enemy must be crowded. Two volleys of large buck-shot and the saber, even on foot, would do quick work. Our men are all used to the double-barreled gun, and they would fire it promptly and confidently. Besides, that weapon can now be furnished to the troops when rifles could not be had. Moreover, if the enemy is in motion, or the horsemen, or if both, he is far more likely to be hit at short ranges with the double-barreled gun than with a rifle. To the uses of a support as infantry the cavalry could add the services peculiar to itself of charging a disorganized or surprised enemy, vedette and patrol duty, and the transmission of intelligence and of dispatches. On the shells for these guns I would have two fuses—the percussion at the apex, to be used against ships, and the Bormann fuse on the side, to be punched when fired upon infantry, barges, or at sharpshooters on the tops of ships while in close action.

Nothing that the enemy can bring can neutralize this system. The inlets being closed, he can land no heavy artillery. These guns would help to close the inlets, and would prevent even the landing of small guns. These, if landed, would be crushed by our artillery, and so would their small ships, if after passing the inlets they should venture into the narrow and tortuous creeks beyond. In connection with these guns nothing prevents the use of howitzers. The former would always remain guns of position, superior in range and accuracy to the Dahlgren, as well as in destructiveness to ships.

To fully complete this system, however, in addition to the above means of defense permanently and immediately upon the coast, I would have at each State center of operations—at Charleston, for instance, for the defense of South Carolina—a central battery of sea-coast flying artillery of twelve rifled 24-pounders, organized on the same principle as those hereinbefore mentioned, with forges, sling-carts, extra ammunition-wagons, &c., superadded, as they would have to dart off much farther than the former from their magazines. For this central battery of rifled cannon the *personnel* of two companies of artillery and two squadrons of cavalry might be sufficient. Adding to these a regiment of rifles or light infantry, a compact, formidable flying column would be at hand—a fortress in itself on reaching any part of our coast where nature has provided suitable sandworks. Upon the receipt of intelligence of the proximate attack of any point upon the coast—North Edisto, for instance, in the above sketch—the whole of this armament, with provisions for a week, could be towed in two flats or lighters (such as Ferguson's, in Charleston) in the space of six hours by one or two small steamers. At each of our forts upon the coast a temporary work should be constructed to receive these guns, as well as those upon the beach, as soon as they are called in.

Let us suppose North Edisto fort, when the enemy's fleet appears off it, to have but the six guns it has at present. The three 24-pounders, rifled, on the beach, as soon as in battery, would increase its armament to 9. The arrival of the central battery would in six hours increase it to 21, of which at least 15 are rifled. Should the fleet move to attack another point upon the coast, the battery and its support would also move inland in the creeks on a line parallel to it, to meet it wherever its services are required, the fleet all the time unconscious that a fort is closely following it. Nothing but a few light-draught steamers and large flats always at hand is required for this most important service. Let us roughly estimate the value of the succor brought in this way at the beginning or in the progress of an engagement at North Edisto:

Guns from the beach	3
Guns from Charleston	12
Total	15
Artillerists from the beach, say	50
Cavalry from the beach, say	60
Artillerists from Charleston, say	190
Cavalry from Charleston	240
Regiment of rifles	700
Total	1,240

Fifteen pieces of formidable ordnance and 1,240 men, which, added to the force of even so small a post as it is at present, would give us 21 guns and 1,500 men.

Of course this infantry support from Charleston is what should at all times be ready to leave at a moment's warning. Other regiments could immediately follow—at any rate, within twelve hours. With suitable bomb-proofs at the fort and proper discretion on the part of the commanding officer the enemy could be held in check until the arrival of re-enforcements sufficient to discomfit them. Depots for ammunition for these guns should be kept at each post expressly for them, and all ammunition for them should be uniform.

Supposing Georgia to have a similar provision made for her defense, and Savannah to possess, too, her central battery and flying column in the same time—in somewhat more time than it would take to dispatch the Charleston flying column if Edisto is the point attacked, but in much less time if it be the important port of Port Royal Harbor—24 rifled guns can at once be sent to the scene of action from both cities, and together with them over 2,000 men. In a few hours more 5,000 men from the two States, uniting at Savannah by means of the railroad, would at Hilton Head fort defy the power of any assailant. The first point is to prevent surprise. This the sea-shore guns will do. The second is to prevent the enemy from seizing any inlet in less than a day's fight. This the flying column and central battery should do. The third is that he shall not move inland, and this the succors which can and should be sent in support of the flying column should be able to do. With more guns and of heavier metal at every inlet and strong garrisons at our isolated posts our coast would be secure, and the necessity of a large force up the country, where it can do no service except in re-enforcing Charleston, would not exist. Because the coast is weak, its support should not be more than a few hours removed; because Charleston is strong, its support might be at Aiken or Columbia. Much can be done in uniting the means of Georgia and South Carolina, and even of North Carolina, in defense of either of the three States against an invasion of the enemy.

At all the centers of operations, as, for instance, Wilmington, Charleston, and Savannah for our Atlantic coast, there should be one regiment assigned to the special duty of forming part of the flying column at a moment's warning during the said week. Everything needful for the transportation and for the subsistence of this column for one week should be stored up and kept in readiness to be carried off at a moment's warning. The quartermaster and the commissary of each regiment would upon their regiment entering on duty every week look into the quality and quantity of provisions, equipments, &c., designed for their regiment when put in motion. The advantages are obvious of having one regiment assigned each week from the militia of Charleston and other cities for this special duty. The balance are at rest, and the one on duty when called out is not flurried in its arrangements. Should the enemy have forced an entrance into one of our inlets, the central battery at Charleston, as well as the one at Savannah, starting by the railroad, marked upon the sketch, would meet him upon any of the bluffs on the main-land, under which he must necessarily pass in his progress through narrow and tortuous creeks. From these bluffs and within pistol shot the almost vertical fire of rifled guns would be destructive even to iron-clad boats, and if the enemy should effect a landing before the arrival of the battery, it is easy to perceive of what advantage it would be in enabling a flying column at the head of a bridge or in a debouch to arrest his progress, or even discomfiting him, before the arrival (necessarily more tardy) of an army. For carrying out such a plan sea-rangers in boats and small steamers on the lookout, telegraphs, a good system of signals, facilities of transportation in lighters and steamers, pre-arranged railroad facilities, and the co-operation of our Navy are a matter of course.

We have in South Carolina very nearly the number of 24-pounders on siege carriages required for the establishment of this system. I understand that there are twelve guns of this description lying idle at the Pensacola navy-yard, which I would recommend our authorities to obtain. By working day and night all these guns can be rifled in two or three weeks. Should there be serious difficulty in procuring horses for these guns, the loan of all the mules required could be obtained, I should think, from our planters for the matter of their own defense. They could be furnished already harnessed by the planters, the Confederate Government reimbursing them their value should they be lost or injured in the service. Cavalry of the very best description exists throughout the seaboard, and is anxious for employment. There is no reason, then, why, in as little time as it will take the Lincoln Government to fit out a squadron, we should not contrive to have an omnipresent fort along the whole extent of our seaboard.

All of which I have the honor to submit, with assurances of my respect and regard.

AMBROSIO JOSÉ GONZALES.

RICHMOND, *September* 25, 1861.

Brigadier-General LAWTON,
Savannah, Ga.:

Intelligence that I believe reliable indicates that the enemy's expedition is intended for Brunswick. Inform Governor Brown. Can I do anything to help you? Have ordered the Bartow Artillery company to Savannah.

J. P. BENJAMIN,
Acting Secretary of War.

SAVANNAH, *September* 25, 1861.

Hon. J. P. BENJAMIN,
Secretary of War:

I can do nothing, for want of arms, unless I hold those now landing from steamer Bermuda. I sent to-day a special agent to Richmond on this subject. Georgia is stripped of arms. Men in abundance, if a few days are allowed.

A. R. LAWTON,
Brigadier-General.

ATLANTA, GA., *September* 25, 1861.

J. P. BENJAMIN,
Secretary of War:

Colonel Stovall, whose battalion is at Lynchburg, is here. Cannot send another gun out of the State. I ask that you order his battalion back to Brunswick on the coast, and I will fill it up to a regiment in the State. I also request that five other armed companies of Georgia troops be ordered back to the coast without delay, as an invasion of the coast is looked for daily, and you have nearly all the State guns in the Confederate service. Please answer both requests immediately. Colonel Stovall will wait here till I hear from you.

JOSEPH E. BROWN.

RICHMOND, *September* 25, 1861.

Governor BROWN,
Atlanta, Ga.:

Have sent orders to Major Shackleford, as requested. Have ordered Bartow Artillery Company to Savannah to report to General Lawton. Am reliably informed that the enemy will attack Brunswick. Be prepared.

J. P. BENJAMIN,
Acting Secretary of War.

ATLANTA, GA., *September* 26, 1861.

Hon. J. P. BENJAMIN,
Secretary of War:

Thank you for the order for the 1,000 guns to General Lawton. Let me beg of you to order Colonel Stovall's battalion back from Lynchburg and let me fill it up to regiment for the coast.

JOSEPH E. BROWN.

RICHMOND, *September* 26, 1861.

Gov. JOSEPH E. BROWN,
Atlanta, Ga.:

Your dispatch received. I cannot order back to Georgia any armed troops, for reasons which I will explain by letter. Instead of sending you a thousand men, I have ordered 1,000 of the rifles at Savannah, with the proper quantity of ammunition, to be turned over to General Lawton for arming that number of your men, as I understand you have plenty of men.

J. P. BENJAMIN,
Acting Secretary of War.

RICHMOND, *September* 27, 1861.

GOV. JOSEPH E. BROWN,
Atlanta, Ga.:

The thousand rifles were ordered to be given you instead of sending back the battalion from Lynchburg. Grave reasons of policy forbid sending back any troops from Virginia.

J. P. BENJAMIN,
Acting Secretary of War.

RICHMOND, *September* 30, 1861.

E. P. LAWTON,
Assistant Adjutant-General, Savannah:

One thousand small-arms and one rifled 12-pounder were assigned by order issued to the proper ordnance officer for the service of Georgia.

J. P. BENJAMIN,
Acting Secretary of War.

Abstract from report of the Provisional Forces, Department of South Carolina, Brig. Gen. R. S. Ripley, commanding, for September, 1861.

Stations.	Present for duty.		Aggregate present.	Aggregate present and absent.
	Officers.	Men.		
Sullivan's Island (Colonel Orr)	69	1,244	1,521	1,603
Stono forts (Colonel Hagood)	54	904	1,115	1,274
North and South Edisto (Colonel Dunovant)	15	293	367	382
Near Georgetown (Colonel Manigault)	26	397	538	567
Near Aiken (Colonel Jones)	38	629	739	898
Field's Point	4	73	106	112
Port Royal Harbor	4	185	227	239
Fort Walker	9	195	224	256
Sam's Point	6	56	69	76
Braddock's Point	4	53	57	69
Camp Lookout	3	48	75	96
Near Columbia (cavalry)	11	162	173	194
Lightwood Knot Spring (cavalry)	3	52	62	64
Charleston Arsenal (artillery)	3	45	68	69
12th 13th and 15th Regiments S. C. Volunteers*	....	....	....	2,372
Total	249	4,336	5,341	8,271

*Stations not given.

Abstract from monthly return of the Military District of Savannah, Ga., commanded by Brig. Gen. A. R. Lawton, for September, 1861.

Stations.	Present for duty.		Aggregate present.	Aggregate present and absent.	Artillery.	
	Officers.	Men.			Heavy.	Field.
Little Cumberland Island	3	48	63	71	5	.....
Sunbury, Ga	3	54	57	59		
Sapello Island	6	177	200	208	5	.....
Great Warsaw	3	70	75	79	5	.....
Isle of Hope	2	42	44	60		6
Fort Pulaski	10	204	250	273	36	.....
Thunderbolt battery	4	94	110	115	4	.....
Genesis Point	2	56	72	76	4	.....
Oglethorpe Barracks	4	49	79	80	.....	6
Fort Screven	6	159	170	181	8	.....
Saint Catharine's Island	2	67	72	91	2	.....
Camp Lawton, Savannah	16	242	273	305	.....	.....
Brunswick, Ga	32	477	578	587	2	5
Tybee Island	40	856	973	1,056	2	.....
South end Big Cumberland Island	2	53	65	74	4	.....
Blackbird Island	3	90	105	112	5	.....
Grand total	138	2,738	3,186	3,427	82	17

APALACHICOLA, *October* 1, 1861.

HON. SECRETARY OF WAR,
Richmond, Va.:

SIR: The citizens of Apalachicola, under a deep sense of their present insecurity and anxiety for the safety and protection of their families and property, deem it their duty to address you on the subject of the defenses of their city. About the 1st June last, upon application, the executive of our State ordered two 32-pounders (old guns) to be delivered to us, and these, at the expense of the citizens, were brought here and placed in battery in the most eligible position to command the several approaches to the town. At a later period a messenger was dispatched to Richmond, who succeeded in obtaining an additional number of guns, and it was deemed advisable that these should be placed in battery at Saint Vincent's Island, to command the entrance (West Pass) to our harbor, and the work was commenced and prosecuted with all the means and men that the city could command.

More recently a regiment in the Confederate service has been organized, five companies of which have been detailed to this point, and are now under command of Colonel Hopkins, who has established his headquarters at Saint Vincent's Island, removed all the troops to that point, dismantled the battery here, and issued a peremptory order for two rifled cannon, daily expected, and ordered siege guns, mounted for the use of the city, to be sent to him on arrival, thus monopolizing for that station every available means of defense, leaving to our company of volunteer artillery and two companies of undrilled infantry, with less than 100 invalids and exempts, the entire and sole protection of the city, and 1,500 women and children, whose natural protectors are most of them enlisted in the service, and without the means to remove their families to places of greater security. The only means of communication is with boats, not only requiring a heavy expenditure in their employ, but they are subject to capture at any moment, as they may easily be intercepted in their trips to and from the city to the island through a wide and deep channel across Saint George's Island between the two points, and entirely beyond the reach of any guns that can be put in battery at Saint Vincent. The approaches to our town by land, as also from the East Pass, are entirely unguarded, and it would not require a large number of such boats as are now being constructed by the enemy to capture the city before any intelligence of an attack could reach Saint Vincent or assistance be rendered by the forces there. The capture of the city would invest Saint Vincent on the main-land side, their supplies would be cut off, and their entire force easily reduced to the alternatives of death or capture without even a show of defense, as no possible outlet of escape would be open to them. The armament at Saint Vincent consists of four ship-mounted and two long 32-pounders, and recent events at Hatteras have demonstrated the insufficiency of such ordnance against the heavy and long-range guns of the enemy. It is believed by military and scientific men that an abandonment of that position would not leave the city exposed to large vessels, and that by removal of the guns and troops, erecting batteries with long-range guns to command approaches by water, causing earthworks to be thrown up at assailable points around the city, with a battery of light artillery to furnish our present company, our town would be more secure than it could possibly be made in any other manner.

Lieutenant McLaughlin, of the Navy, left here a few days since for Richmond, and to him, as an officer qualified by experience and examination of our position, we refer to present these matters more fully before you.

Insecurity and apprehension are predominant feelings now, yet these will in nowise lessen the determination of our people to perish beneath the ruins of their city rather than ignobly desert or suffer it to become the prey of the vandal hordes who threaten to assail it. We would speak modestly and respectfully of the officers who have been furnished by the Confederate Government to conduct military operations in our State, and the announcement of General Grayson's appointment, from his long-tried and acknowledged capability, gave general satisfaction, but a recent visit from him has exhibited in him such an enfeebled state of health and constitution as almost to forbid hope of amendment, and we must necessarily be deprived, if not altogether, to a great extent, of his valuable aid and counsel in our necessity.

We have the honor to be, very respectfully, your obedient servants,

H. R. TAYLOR *et al.*

MARIANNA, *October* 2, 1861.

Hon. S. R. MALLORY:

DEAR SIR: I returned from Tallahassee on yesterday and received yours of the 15th ultimo. I expected to have received a letter from you at Tallahassee, but was disappointed. Having heard that Governor Perry had received one from you informing him that two rifled cannon, &c., had been ordered to Apalachicola, I inquired of him if it were true. He said it was, and read the part of the letter only which referred to the rifled cannon and powder being sent. I regret that Lieutenant McLaughlin was ordered back to Richmond by Colonel Hopkins and the consequent excitement among the citizens, but I know nothing of the particulars. The fact is, our State is in a most deplorable condition. The regiment at Fernandina is said to be demoralized by habitual intemperance of the colonel and lieutenant-colonel, and I am informed even the cannon have not been mounted, and dissipation and disorder prevail. There are but eight companies, and never have been more in Hopkins' regiment—three companies at Apalachicola, two near Saint Mark's, one at Tampa, and two at Cedar Keys. You will perceive the useless expense of field officers by the arrangement. Would it not be advisable to concentrate the regiment—if, indeed, eight companies be a regiment—and transfer them to General Bragg's command at Pensacola, and order the Magnolia Regiment, commanded by Colonel Anderson, at Pensacola, to the defense of Apalachicola? Under General Bragg's command Hopkins' regiment would be drilled and made useful, and Colonel Anderson's regiment, with the aid of State troops convenient to Apalachicola, could successfully defend the place with the aid of Lieutenant McLaughlin and a few experienced artillerists.

Suggest the proposed change to the President and Secretary of War. Several companies are organized and ready to tender their services to the Confederate States for twelve months, and consequently there would be no difficulty in supplying the places of the companies of Hopkins' regiment, now at Fort Williams, near Saint Mark's, Tampa, and Cedar Keys, by more efficient companies under suitable commanders. The officers of the regiments mustered into the Confederate service in the State imagine that they are entirely independent of State authority, and if it is proper I wish you would request the Secretary of War to issue a suitable general order upon the subject, especially in this State. I anticipate no difficulty whatever with General Bragg or General Grayson, or any gentleman of military education. We can co-operate harmoniously. By the by, General Grayson and myself are old personal acquaintances and friends, though twenty years have elapsed since we parted, and met a day or two ago in Tallahassee. General Grayson's health is very bad. He is nearly spent with consumption. I thought he would die last Wednesday night, and I fear will not have physical strength to discharge necessary duties in Florida.

I think there would have been no difficulty in forming the Fifth Regiment, but Governor Perry has organized five of the companies intended for the Fifth Regiment with an artillery battalion, and appointed D. P. Holland, esq., lieutenant-colonel to command it for Confederate service. The governor acted, if by any authority, by such as is unknown to me. In the present deranged state of affairs I shall be inaugurated and enter upon the duties of governor on next Monday with a heavy heart and a fearful apprehension of my inability to perform the duties of the office creditably and very usefully; but to the best of my judgment I will encounter surrounding difficulties, resolved to place the State upon the best war footing, and rely upon the Army Regulations and the laws of the State and the efficient aid of the officers sent here by the President to correct existing evils. From recent indications I think a scheme of systematic opposition to you is designed by some men in our State, and permit me to say to you that under all circumstances you may rely upon my friendship promptly to meet, and, if need be with personal responsibility, the most prominent assailants.

In haste, yours, &c.,

JOHN MILTON.

SPECIAL ORDERS, No. 176. } ADJUTANT AND INSPECTOR GEN.'S OFFICE, *Richmond, October* 10, 1861.

* * * * * * *

X. Brig. Gen. E. K. Smith is assigned to the command of the Department of Middle and Eastern Florida, and will relieve Brig. Gen. J. B.

Grayson, whose state of health is such as to prevent him from discharging the active duties of that command.*

* * * * * * *

By command of the Secretary of War:

JNO. WITHERS,
Assistant Adjutant-General.

HDQRS. THIRD REGIMENT FLORIDA VOLUNTEERS,
Fort Clinch, Fernandina, Fla., October 14, 1861.

To the SECRETARY OF WAR,
Confederate States of America, Richmond, Va.:

SIR: I have the honor to request that you order me to order one of my officers to muster in for twelve-months' service Lieutenant Colonel Holland's battalion of artillery. This battalion is absolutely necessary here. They are now in service under the order of the brigadier-general, and have been under my command and now are. The field officers, Lieutenant-Colonel Holland and Maj. Charles F. Hopkins, are fine officers. They are good artillerists, and thoroughly understand their profession. They were appointed by Governor Perry, and are the unanimous choice of the whole battalion. They are the most important aid that could be given me. I would respectfully request that the Department authorize me to have them mustered in without delay, and that they may muster with six companies. They are now erecting batteries, signal stations, establishing points for the ranges of the guns, and have been for some time. They are in the Confederate service, but not yet mustered in, and Captain Stockton has other companies to attend to, and cannot muster the troops as speedily as their efficiency requires. I have the honor to refer the Department to the accompanying copies of orders and letters for information as to the condition of this force and what it is doing.†

Owing to the illness of Brigadier-General Grayson, I cannot ascertain when the guns and ordnance stores for here will arrive. I have to specially request that the ordnance officer be required to send me without delay a supply of ammunition. I have only 2,000 caps and about fifteen rounds of musket cartridges, and the artillery battalion have four 6-pounders and only about five rounds of musket cartridges. I trust the Department will send me at once the necessary ammunition for musketry which can be spared for this point. I would urge the speedy forwarding of the guns and requisition made by Brigadier-General Grayson. His ill-health has caused me to make this statement and request. The general has done everything that man could. His command have perfect confidence in him, and I trust the officious meddling of scared politicians, who have never raised voice or hand for our independence, will receive that merited rebuke from headquarters it deserves for meddling with the acts of better men. Neither the troops nor the people have confidence in them. We are satisfied, and all we want is ammunition.

I have the honor to be, very respectfully, your obedient servant,

W. S. DILWORTH,
Colonel, Commanding.

---

*Revoked October 22, and Brig. Gen. James H. Trapier assigned.
†Not found.

EXECUTIVE DEPARTMENT,
Tallahassee, Fla., October 18, 1861.

His Excellency JEFFERSON DAVIS,
President of the Confederate States:

SIR: I feel it my duty to present for your consideration the following facts:

First. That for the defense of Florida cavalry is, perhaps, less efficient than for the defense of any other State. At the most important points we should have batteries with guns of heavy caliber. To guard between important points, boats of light draught, with signals, at proper distances, and convenient to those guarding distant and exposed positions a few good horses, to be used by expressmen to give notice of any imposing approach of the enemy. Not many troops are required in the Confederate service, if those in service shall be commanded at important points by brave and skillful officers. There is much derangement of military affairs in this State, owing chiefly to the desire to enter the Confederate service for short periods and certain pay; but if the War and Navy Departments will respect my opinions I hope to establish such military organizations as will in the end be least expensive and most useful. Our chief reliance in connection with the coast defense should be infantry and light artillery, not in service, but ready to be at a moment's warning, and to be concentrated where needed to support those in the Confederate service.

The recent authority to W. G. M. Davis, esq., to raise a cavalry regiment has excited a perfect furore upon the subject. The large majority of those who were willing to serve as soldiers of infantry are now in favor of riding into service, and I assure you, sir, a battle will never be fought in Florida by cavalry, unless the want of proper coast defenses, artillery, and infantry, shall induce an invasion, and will then be fought at great disadvantage. I entertain no feeling or thought personally unkind to Mr. Davis. He is a gentleman of fine legal abilities. But I do regret that the material for the judicious defense of the State has been so much interfered with by the disposition excited in favor of cavalry service. Independent of the companies raised for Colonel Davis' regiment I have refused commissions to ten associations for cavalry companies within the last two days. Almost every man that has a pony wishes to mount him at the expense of the Confederate Government, and I would most respectfully urge the necessity of the appointment of an honest, prudent, and experienced officer to visit Florida immediately, and inquire into and report the expenses being incurred. Let him first go to Apalachicola, and ascertain the nature and necessity of the expenditures there in the employment of boats, &c., and report immediately to the proper Departments; thence to other positions, and examine and report. It will afford me pleasure to aid in the investigation, and if the officer will come to Tallahassee I will, to the best of my ability, direct the course of inquiry. I am fully persuaded that one-half the amount that will be expended, if there shall be no immediate check to expenditures, wisely appropriated, will secure the defense of Florida, and by means that will be useful in a future emergency. The unnecessary expense for cavalry would supply the means for the proper coast defenses; would enable me to equip companies of light artillery and infantry, which equipments might be preserved to protect the peace which we hope to obtain by the present war. But the hundreds of horses which are now being withdrawn from agricultural industry will be of little avail in war, and leave the State without the means of agriculture, which will be difficult to supply.

General Grayson is in a dying condition. General E. K. Smith, I am informed, has been appointed to succeed him, and permit me to suggest that his command shall extend west, so as to embrace Apalachicola and Saint Andrew's Bay, and to express the hope that his staff will be composed of gentlemen of military education and experience. This suggestion is made because Colonel Hopkins entertains the opinion, if I am correctly informed, that General Grayson's command does not embrace Apalachicola, and I regret to say that Colonel Hopkins' military ability is much doubted by many worthy citizens, and unpleasant circumstances have consequently occurred, which I apprehend will result unhappily.

From a misapprehension of facts, the Fourth Regiment was tendered by my worthy predecessor without a full complement of companies. Colonel Hopkins has three of these companies at Apalachicola; there are two at Saint Mark's, two at Cedar Keys, and one or two in the neighborhood of Tampa. Thus scattered, it is impossible for them to act as a regiment without previous instructions and competent officers.

I would respectfully suggest that Colonel Hopkins be ordered with his three companies to Saint Mark's, to protect that place and the coast between the Ocella and Crooked Rivers, and if the Departments will furnish me with two good engineers and two good drill officers of artillery I will defend Apalachicola with State troops, and such troops as I may be able to raise and place in a camp of instruction for the army of reserve. If such an order should be deemed advisable, I would be pleased to be informed of it three or four days before Colonel Hopkins shall leave there, and I will visit the place and put the troops in proper positions of defense.

There is another matter to which I would respectfully invite attention. By letter from the War Department, dated June 30, 1861, the governor of this State was required to furnish 1,000 men as the quota of the State in the army of reserve, and to place them in a camp of instruction. For this purpose four companies were raised under special commission, and only four, and these were assembled at Fernandina, called a battalion of artillery, and put into the Confederate service, under command of Mr. D. P. Holland as lieutenant-colonel, with Mr. Charles F. Hopkins as major. I am not apprised that such a battalion, if any, was called for or authorized by the Secretary of War, and the appointment of the officers by the governor was, in my judgment, without authority, and contrary to the ordinances of the Convention, the Constitution, and the laws of the State, and that, if in the course of events, any court-martial shall be ordered, the matter will be inquired into by the civil authority, the commissions declared void, and the so-called battalion will be disorganized and demoralized.

I have felt it my duty thus candidly to submit to you my opinion, and invoke your judgment upon the matters submitted for your consideration. It has been said that perhaps General Smith would not accept the command in Florida, in which event I hope the regiments and companies which have been or may be accepted for service in this State by a general order of the War Department, not interfering with General Bragg's command, may be made subject to my orders, and the defense of the State shall be successful, and at the least possible expense.

I am, sir, very respectfully,

JOHN MILTON,
Governor of Florida.

OCTOBER 21, 1861.

Hon. J. P. BENJAMIN,
Secretary of War.

MY DEAR SIR: The following are the only points that occur to me to suggest:

1. That the special attention of General Trapier be directed to such points in his department as the governor may consider to be of chief military importance.

2. That he should be instructed to arrange with the governor for obtaining the ten companies in the speediest manner possible, and, in order to avoid delay in bringing the post at Fernandina under better command, he should be authorized to appoint a colonel to take command of the companies as they are mustered, unless the Department is prepared to designate one at once for the command.

3. That he should be authorized to make such alterations in the number and organization of the forces employed in Florida as may in his judgment be advisable; for which purpose he might be authorized to muster or discharge troops according to exigency, keeping the Department advised of his acts.

4. It would also be well to authorize him, if he deems it advisable, to arrange with the Cuban Telegraph Company for the surrender of the line between Savannah and Florida to the Confederate States during the war.

5. If it requires special authority to enable him to do so, he might be authorized to employ and attach to each post a capable drill officer.

Respectfully, yours,

D. L. YULEE.

COLUMBIA, *October* 22, 1861.

Hon. Mr. BENJAMIN,
Secretary of War:

I have been informed another large vessel has arrived at Saint Mary's with arms, &c. From your last letter I am in hopes you will send 2,000 rifles for our flanking companies and 300 cavalry pistols for the men just mustered in. It is essential to our service, as I have put out 4,000 of arms in a few days past, which entirely exhausted our supply.

F. W. PICKENS.

WAR DEPARTMENT, C. S. A.,
Richmond, October 22, 1861.

Brig. Gen. J. H. TRAPIER:

SIR: The President has, as you will perceive from the inclosed papers, accepted your tender of service, has appointed you brigadier-general, and assigned you to the Department of Eastern and Middle Florida. Your instructions are brief and simple. Do everything that your means and energies will permit to place the coast of Florida in a state of defense. You will first proceed to Fernandina, as the point most important and most likely to attract the attention of the enemy; but you are left to your own discretion as to the proper location of your headquarters.

Your staff will be appointed and commissioned in accordance with your recommendation, unless some special objection should exist. Upon one point you may require the aid of this Department. You will find, as I am informed, that troops have been mustered into the service of the Confederacy in such manner as to render their services almost valueless, either by reason of the incompetency and inefficiency of their officers, or because mustered for cavalry or artillery where such arms are not required or cannot be procured, or for other like reasons. In a word, I am informed that a radical reform on this subject is required in Florida. Under these circumstances you may be at a loss how to proceed, and I would therefore suggest that on your application the Department would not hesitate to muster out of service all such organizations as would come within the class above described, and then muster the men afresh by companies, so as to leave it in our power to organize the regiments and appoint the field officers, instead of leaving them to be elected by the men. We might thus hope to obtain efficient and competent officers; and for your guidance I inclose you a circular letter, prepared in answer to the constant inquiries addressed to this Department, and which will inform you of the policy on which we act in receiving tenders of troops. I send you likewise a set of the laws, so far as passed, which you will require for your guidance in many cases that must arise.

I am informed by Mr. Yulee that the Cuban Telegraph Company would place its line at the service of the Government at little or no cost, with the view of having it kept in order until the return of peace shall make it profitable. If this be so, you are authorized to make arrangements with them for that purpose, as the keeping up of your communications with Savannah cannot but be very useful in your operations.

You will be sustained by this Department as far as possible in your efforts to discharge the duties confided to you, but our resources in small-arms, in ordnance, and ammunition are very limited when compared with the enormous coast line we have to defend, and we cannot therefore supply, as we would wish, the several points where defenses are necessary. We must concentrate our means as promptly as possible at the different assailable points after the attack, not having enough to furnish any but the most important in advance.

Wishing you success and distinction in your new command, I am, your obedient servant,

J. P. BENJAMIN,
Acting Secretary of War.

[Inclosure.]

SPECIAL ORDERS, No. 186. } ADJUTANT AND INSPECTOR GEN.'S OFFICE,
Richmond, October 22, 1861.

* * * * * *

X. Paragraph X, Special Orders, No. 176, Adjutant and Inspector General's Office, of October 10, 1861, is revoked.

Brig. Gen. James H. Trapier, Provisional Army, is assigned to the command of the Department of Eastern and Middle Florida, and will proceed at once to Fernandina, under such special instructions as may be given him by the Secretary of War.

By command of the Secretary of War:

JNO. WITHERS,
Assistant Adjutant-General.

HDQRS. MIL. DEP'T, MIDDLE AND EAST FLORIDA,
Tallahassee, October 23, 1861.

Hon. SECRETARY OF WAR,
Richmond, Va:

SIR: I have the honor to inclose a copy of the report of Maj. W. L. L. Bowen, announcing the capture of two sloops and their crews. I have submitted a like copy to Col. W. S. Dilworth, Third Regiment Florida Volunteers, at Fernandina, who succeeded to the command upon General Grayson's death.

The vessels you notice sail under the "American colors, with papers from Key West, with license to engage in the fishery on the Florida coast, and supply the Key West market with the same." There is a feature in this case that induces me to inform the Department, after a consultation with his excellency the governor of Florida. It seems the smacks belong to a firm in Key West, known as William H. Wall & Co., who I learn from a refugee here from the island are men good to the Southern cause. One of the firm, though a signer of the ordinance of secession, has taken the oath to the Federal side, but says it was done under duress. The refugee states he was a book-keeper for several years in the house of the Messrs. Wall & Co., the alleged owners of the smacks, and says, in addition, that he is sure the firm has not only wished for the success of our struggle, but that they have aided with money. It has not been made known to any one here that they (the vessels) are true to the Confederacy; so, in the absence of Colonel Dilworth at his post near Fernandina, I, acting as assistant adjutant-general during Lieutenant Wood's absence, most respectfully write the Department, that a delay of several days may not occur in this case, where doubts exist as to whether the smacks are prizes or not, it being said they belong to friends, yet sail under our enemy's flag. In the mean time I have written to Major Bowen, and said it would be well to keep his prisoners under guard until he can hear from higher authority. His excellency Governor Milton informs me that the crews are for the most part Spaniards, and may claim protection of that flag, and also that at Key West the Federal authorities force all persons, regardless of nationality, to take the oath of allegiance to the United States.

I respectfully inform you that in my letter to Colonel Dilworth I mentioned my intention of addressing you, to avoid delay.

I have the honor to be, sir, most respectfully, your obedient servant,

GEORGE UPSHUR MAYO,
First Lieutenant, C. S. Army.

[Inclosure.]

HEADQUARTERS, FORT BROOKE,
Tampa, Fla., October 16, 1861.

Brig. Gen. JOHN B. GRAYSON,
Commanding Middle and East Florida:

DEAR SIR: After my complimentary regards, permit me to report for your orders 13 prisoners of war, captured under my command on the 10th and 11th of this month, being the crew of the sloops William Batty and Lyman Dudley, sailing under the American colors (Stars and Stripes), with papers from Key West, with license to engage in the fishery on the Florida coast, and supply the Key West market with the same. The sloops are of the first class, well rigged, and in good order. One measures $65\frac{16}{95}$ tons, the other $56\frac{80}{95}$ tons.

The sloops have been duly turned over to the prize commissioner as legal prizes to the Confederate States, and the prisoners are detained in safe custody for your disposal; and, in consequence of the inconvenience and difficulty of subsisting troops at this post, I hope you will order the prisoners to be sent to some other place, or disposed of in some other manner as soon as practicable.

With a deep regret for your ill-health, and with due regard to your orders, I am, sir, most respectfully, yours, &c.,

W. L. L. BOWEN,
Major, Commanding Military Forces, Tampa Bay.

The sloops William Batty and Lyman Dudley are, to the best of my knowledge and belief, the property of William H. Wall & Co., of Key West. They have been seized at Tampa Bay by the military for sailing under the Federal colors and with papers from Key West. Having been in the employment of Messrs. William H. Wall & Co. for several years, I know them to be true Southern men, and have largely aided the Confederate cause.

William Pinkney, one of the firm, has taken the United States oath under duress on the island, but signed the ordinance of secession. The permission for their vessels to sail under the Federal flag is only to keep him from seizure and imprisonment.

CHAS. ANTONIO.

RICHMOND, *October* 23, 1861.

GOV. JOHN MILTON,
Tallahassee, Fla.:

General Kirby Smith has been assigned to duty with Army of the Potomac. General Trapier, of South Carolina, has been assigned to your State, and Mr. Yulee leaves to-morrow morning with his instructions. General Trapier will go first to Fernandina, and you can address him there.

J. P. BENJAMIN,
Acting Secretary of War.

EXECUTIVE DEPARTMENT,
Tallahassee, October 24, 1861.

Hon. J. P. BENJAMIN,
Secretary of War:

Well pleased that General Trapier has been assigned to the Military Department of Middle and East Florida. Would respectfully suggest that the Military Department of the State be so arranged as to embrace the State, distinguishing the departments to which General Bragg and General Trapier have been assigned. The reason of the suggestion is that Apalachicola and Saint Andrew's, two important points, are not embraced in a general order. We have at Saint Mark's howitzers and empty shells. No powder or fuse to prepare them. We need guns of large caliber and ammunition.

Respectfully,

JOHN MILTON,
Governor of Florida.

SPECIAL ORDERS, No. 300. } HDQRS. MIL. DIST., SAVANNAH, GA., *October* 25, 1861.

* * * * * * *

2. By direction of the Secretary of War all unarmed troops in camps of instruction, who have been mustered in for the war, will hold themselves in readiness to proceed forthwith to Richmond, Va. Commanding officers, quartermasters, and commissaries of such troops will make the necessary arrangements for an immediate move, and report, by letter, to these headquarters.

By order of Brig. Gen. A. R. Lawton:

THOS. J. BERRY,
Aide-de-Camp, Acting Assistant Adjutant-General.

WAR DEPARTMENT, C. S. A.,
Richmond, October 26, 1861.

Col. W. S. DILWORTH,
Comdg. Third Regt. Fla. Vols., Hdqrs. Fort Clinch, Fla.:

SIR: I am in receipt of your letter of the 14th October, with its several inclosures, submitted to this Department by Capt. Thomas E. Buckman, who came to Richmond by your orders. Captain Buckman's company having been accepted as a "company of infantry, armed with double barreled shot-guns, for twelve months," I have directed Brigadier General Trapier to have the company mustered in on those terms whenever the required conditions are fulfilled.

With regard to your request that Lieutenant-Colonel Holland's battalion of artillery be mustered in as organized, with six companies, for twelve months, I have to say that this battalion has never been accepted by this Department, nor can we accept artillery companies in battalions, but only by independent companies or batteries, leaving the question of any further organization to rest with the proper authority. Neither do we furnish any batteries to companies of artillery offered for twelve months only. It appears, however, that this battalion possesses but a single battery, sufficient only, and barely sufficient, for a single company. I have therefore directed Brigadier-General Trapier to accept, and muster in a single company, if offered, furnished with this battery for twelve months, but not to accept any other company of artillery for twelve months not armed with batteries, except such as he may deem necessary for working heavy guns in battery, and those only by independent companies. Lieutenant-Colonel Holland has been informed that his battalion cannot be accepted as at present organized, and therefore that his commission cannot be confirmed. However able he may be as an officer, and however valuable his services may be to you as an artillerist, of which I have read with great pleasure your flattering testimonials, this course is dictated necessarily by a regard for the interests of the service and for the general policy of this Department, a brief view of which, so far as concerns the accepting and organization of troops, &c., you will find stated in the accompanying circular, which I respectfully inclose. It is now, of course, needless for me to add that the additional field pieces which you ask for on behalf of this battalion cannot be furnished.

An artillery company furnishing its own battery will be equipped for the field when mustered into service, but no person other than the proper officer of the Government can be authorized to purchase horses or any other equipments or supplies for the battery or for the company, and such as may be furnished will be accepted only at a fair valuation.

The remaining topics of your letter shall receive due consideration, and your requisitions for ammunition, &c., are referred to the attention, of the Chief of Ordnance.

Very respectfully,

J. P. BENJAMIN,
Acting Secretary of War.

NORFOLK, *October* 26, 1861.

Hon. J. P. BENJAMIN:

A Federal soldier's hat was picked up to-day at Colonel Taylor's farm, near Willoughby's Point, 3½ miles from Old Point. It contained two Boston papers, one of the 19th and one of the 21st. They contain important developments as to the destination of the great expedition. The gunboats are to concentrate in Hampton Roads, and the transports are to repair to Annapolis, and there embark a force of 25,000 men, under General Sherman. Several of the larger steamers are loaded with surf-boats. The papers state that the expedition is intended for Charleston and other places on our coast. At sundown the lookout reports over 100 sail of vessels in the Roads. They are arriving and departing continually. The main part of the expedition is still at the Roads, and great activity prevails in the fleet. Will send papers by Monday's mail.

JAS. F. MILLIGAN,
Captain, Signal Officer, Department of Norfolk.

SPECIAL ORDERS, } No. 190. } ADJUTANT AND INSPECTOR GEN.'S OFFICE,
Richmond, October 26, 1861.

* * * * * * *

XIII. The State of Georgia will hereafter constitute a separate department, to be designated the Department of Georgia, the command of which is assigned to Brigadier-General Lawton, headquarters Savannah, Ga.

XIV. The Department of Middle and Eastern Florida, announced in paragraph XII, Special Orders, No. 130, Adjutant and Inspector-General's Office, of August 21, 1861, will extend west to Choctawhatchee River.

* * * * * * *

By command of Secretary of War:

JNO. WITHERS,
Assistant Adjutant-General.

EXECUTIVE DEPARTMENT,
Tallahassee, October 28, 1861.

Hon. J. P. BENJAMIN,
Secretary of War:

SIR: The special order by which the Chattahoochee River is established as the line between the two military departments of Florida excludes Apalachicola and Saint Andrew's Bay from the department to which General Trapier has been assigned, both places being west of the river, and therefore in West Florida. It may be best that these places should be in General Bragg's department, for the following reasons, viz:

First. For necessary supplies Apalachicola and Saint Andrew's are more conveniently connected with Pensacola than with any important position in Middle or East Florida.

Second. The means of communication by telegraph and mail facilities are more speedy and less expensive; also for transportation of troops, guns, ammunition, &c.

Third. The military department east of the Chattahoochee River, in the present deranged state of affairs, is more than sufficient to command the utmost energies of any general to make a successful defense of the various important positions subject to and threatened with attack.

You may inquire, then, why I suggested by telegram that Apalachicola and Saint Andrew's Bay should be embraced in General Trapier's command. At the time the suggestion was made these places were not, by any general orders emanating from or authorized by the War Department known to me, embraced in any military department. From a misapprehension of the locality of Apalachicola General Grayson had assigned Colonel Hopkins to the command of the fort at Apalachicola, meaning, I suppose, the fort at Saint Vincent's Island, 12 miles distant from Apalachicola. The public interest and the proper defense of the place required the immediate attention of an experienced and competent officer. Very heavy, and in my judgment, upon the information received, very unnecessary, expenses were being incurred. As to expense, one item of $130 per diem for a steamboat, for which there was neither urgent nor reasonable necessity. As to defenses, one item: a ditch was commenced, to be 3 feet deep, 3 feet wide, and about 3 miles long, to be depended upon to enable not exceeding 500 men to defend the city from an attack by land.

Moreover, unpleasant differences had arisen between Colonel Hopkins and Captain Dunham, of the State troops, which excited and alarmed the citizens and threatened most serious and disreputable consequences, the official orders relative to which by General Grayson and myself will be made known to you by certified copies inclosed by next mail. I did not suppose that General Bragg could give his immediate personal attention at Apalachicola, or that I could confer as promptly with him as with General Trapier, to remedy existing evils. Colonel Hopkins is a gentleman, but perhaps a little too excitable, and may not be possessed of, in an eminent degree, the knowledge of men and science of war requisite in a military commander.

In a letter bearing date 30th June the Secretary of War notifies the governor of this State that "the President deems it prudent, if not essential to the public safety, to form and organize a reserve army corps of 30,000 men, and apportion to Florida the quota of 1,000 men. Your excellency will therefore receive for the war 1,000 men by independent companies," &c.

When I came into office not a company had been raised, and the opinion, I think, was entertained by my worthy predecessor that the requisition could not be even partially complied with. I entertain a different opinion, and hope to be able in a few weeks to report to you 1,000 men in camps ready for instruction. For one battalion I shall establish a camp near Apalachicola, to be known as Camp Benjamin, in honor of the Acting Secretary of War, when, if necessary, the companies can be used in defense of the place. I have not yet decided where the other camp will be established, desiring, after an interview with General Trapier, to place it where it can be sustained at least expense and the companies that compose it made most useful; but permit me, with due deference, to protest against any authority in future to individuals to raise a company or companies of any kind in this State. It brings their influence to accomplish the objects they have in view in conflict with State authority, and has prevented, and will continue to prevent, if not checked, the executive of the State from being able to comply with the requisitions of the President through the War Department.

Your attention, and through you that of the President, is respectfully invited to the following extract of a letter addressed to me officially by Col. J. P. Anderson, commanding near Pensacola the First Florida Regiment, viz:

You will have heard of the affair on Santa Rosa Island, on the morning of the 9th instant. The object of the expedition was fully and completely accomplished, though the loss of such men as Captain Bradford, of Florida; Lieutenant Nelms, of Georgia; Sergeant Routh, of Tallahassee; Private Tillinghast, &c., would not be compensated for, in my opinion, by the total annihilation of Billy Wilson and his whole band of thieves and cut-throats. The Florida Regiment only had 100 men in the expedition out of 1,060, and lost 6 killed, 8 wounded, and 12 prisoners, as follows, viz: Killed, Captain Bradford, Sergeant Routh, Privates Tillinghast, Hale, Thompson of Apalachicola, and Smith. Wounded, Corporal Lanier, Privates Echols, McCorkle, Sims, William Denham, Hicks, Sharrit, and O'Neal (Peter, of Pensacola). These are doing well and will recover; some are only slightly wounded. Prisoners: R. Hale, Company A, and Bond, Company A; Mahoney, Company B, and Nichols, Company B; Bev. Parker and Finley, Company E; Holliman, Godlie, John Jarvis, M. Mosely, and Patterson, of Company F; also Lieutenant Farley, Company E. I deeply regret that such men as Lieutenant Farley, Parker, and Finley should have fallen into the enemy's hands. However, they write to us that they are well treated, but destiny unknown. By any civilized nation in the world most of these prisoners would be promptly delivered up, for they were taken while standing as a safeguard over the enemy's hospital, to prevent it from sharing the fate of the balance of the camp. They protected it from flame and sword most scrupulously, but failing to hear the signal for us to retire, only remained too faithful to their trust, and have fallen into the hands of the enemy by so doing. Their names should illustrate one of the brightest pages of Florida's history.

In a few days I will present to your consideration my views in regard to the defenses of Florida and the organization of a military department embracing parts of Georgia and Alabama adjacent to the Chattahoochee River, the importance and advantage of which will be readily understood.

I have the honor to be, very respectfully, your obedient servant,

JOHN MILTON,
Governor of Florida.

RICHMOND, *October* 29, 1861.

General LAWTON,
Savannah:

Colonel Mercer was appointed brigadier-general to-day. The enemy's fleet sailed South this morning; destination unknown.

J. P. BENJAMIN,
Acting Secretary of War.

TALLAHASSEE, *October* 29, 1861.

Hon. J. P. BENJAMIN:

Florida wants arms. She has never received a musket from the Confederate States. The Gordon brings sabers and pistols. Can I get some?

Respectfully,

JOHN MILTON,
Governor of Florida.

EXECUTIVE DEPARTMENT,
Tallahassee, Fla., October 29, 1861.

His Excellency JEFFERSON DAVIS,
President C. S. A.:

SIR: On the 28th instant I addressed a letter to the Hon. J. P. Benjamin, Secretary of War, in which I invited his attention and requested him to call the attention of your excellency to the extract made from a letter of Col. J. Patton Anderson, First Florida Regiment, relative to members of his regiment being made prisoners "while standing as a safeguard over the enemy's hospital to prevent it from sharing the fate of the balance of the camp."

Permit me, sir, with all due respect, to invite such demand on the part of your excellency as the laws of nations will sustain for the honorable release of all the prisoners, and especially those from Florida, captured under these circumstances; but, should the enemy be insensible to such demand, then, that in any exchange of prisoners which may be made, the prisoners thus taken may be among the first exchanged.

October 30.—I had the honor to receive your highly-esteemed favor of the 25th,* and avail myself of the courteous invitation to a free correspondence.

The extent of our coast and its character are easily ascertained by maps and coast surveys, but a personal acquaintance with the localities, settled portions of the State, and mixed character of the population would be requisite to a just appreciation of our exposed position in the present war. My opinion has been and is yet, that if General Scott, as the Commander-in-Chief of the United States troops, with full powers to direct their movements, really desired the subjugation of the South, of which I have no doubt, and had possessed the distinguished qualities of a soldier which have been ascribed to him, with the least intelligence as a statesman as to causes and effects, the conquest of Florida would have been promptly made. Virginia would not have been disturbed. The conquest of Florida, as one of the seven States, would have had a powerful influence upon foreign nations, an inspiring effect upon the minds of his troops and of the citizens and Government of the United States, and formed a basis for future operations which would have checked Virginia and other States that have not seceded, and dispirited many in the seceded States who apprehended with fear and trembling the consequences of a change of government. The fate of the South would have been hair-hung. But, as if God in mercy permitted General Scott's madness and folly, every movement he made but gave strength and vigor to our cause. As it is, unable to conquer any other State, may not Florida claim their attention? With our feebleness they are well acquainted through traitors, some of whom yet remain among us.

Independent of the force at and about Pensacola there are no troops by proper authority in Confederate service except the Third and what is termed the Fourth Regiments, and such companies of cavalry as have been received. The Third Regiment, commanded by Col. W. S. Dilworth, a civilian, is scattered from Fernandina to the mouth of the Saint John's River and Saint Augustine, and, if I am correctly informed, is in a deplorable condition. I presume there is not a field officer attached to it, unless it may be Major Church, at Saint Augustine, of

*Not found.

strict sobriety; but the colonel, W. S. Dilworth, is improving, and will, I think, make an efficient officer.

With regard to what is called the Fourth Regiment, commanded by Col. Edward Hopkins, there were but eight imperfect companies when he was elected, and I shall not consent that another may be added to it, for reasons you will appreciate. Of two companies ordered to vote, one was never attached to it, but was under the command of General Bragg, and did not vote. The other was in State service for six months, commanded by a nephew of Colonel Hopkins, voted for him for colonel, was in three weeks afterwards mustered out of service, and has never had a moment's connection with the regiment. The time of election was only known a day or two before it occurred, and was intended to secure the command to D. P. Holland, who happened to be a pet of Governor Perry, and whose character was so odious that he was beaten by Hopkins—the only man, perhaps, in the State that, if the election had been properly advertised, Hopkins could have defeated; and the reason assigned by Governor Perry to the attorney-general of the State, to myself, and perhaps others, why he commissioned Hopkins, was that he apprehended that if he refused to do so he would be charged with having refused because he defeated Holland. For the character of Mr. Holland I refer you to Mr. Mallory, Judge Hawkins, or any other gentleman in West or Middle Florida, where he is known. In East Florida, where his true character is not yet ascertained, he is figuring in command of four companies, by the illegal appointment of Governor Perry as lieutenant-colonel of an artillery battalion, to which I have, in a previous letter, invited your attention.

Governor Perry is, I reckon, as you have perceived, a man of strong prejudices, without very extraordinary intellectual abilities.

The eight companies said to compose the Fourth Regiment are some of them in a deplorable condition, and scattered as follows: Three of the companies are on Saint Vincent's Island, 12 miles from Apalachicola, relative to which you will find papers inclosed; one company at Saint Mark's, commanded by Captain Dial, an efficient officer; one at the light-house, 12 miles off, commanded by Captain Law, a well disposed but ignorant man, and his men, that would have made fine soldiers if properly commanded, are much demoralized; one company is at Tampa, and an effort making there to get another, commanded by a major of no military education, and, if I am informed rightly, on an accidental visit to Florida; the other two companies at Cedar Keys, commanded by Lieut. Col. M. Whit. Smith, who is said to drink to great excess.

Hopkins, whom I now believe most honestly to be too irritable, involved himself in difficulties at Apalachicola, and was ordered by General Grayson to remain on Saint Vincent's Island, with his three companies, but left without permission and came to Tallahassee. General Grayson was very sick and would not see him, but I have reason to believe if he had lived he would have had him dismissed from the service.

General Grayson requested me to direct all military movements. We were personal acquaintances thirty years ago. To discourage young officers from coming in conflict with officers claiming to be in Confederate service, I ordered Lieutenant-Colonel James, in command of State troops at Apalachicola, to report to and obey the orders of Colonel Hopkins, and for a few days intrusted the defense of the place to him; but his conduct has been so extraordinary that I have revoked the order, and thrown him back upon General Grayson's order—to confine himself to Saint Vincent's Island and its defenses.

As a matter of economy and public safety I would respectfully suggest that, inasmuch as the regiment has never been completed according to the terms upon which it was understood to have been accepted, the field officers be retired from the service, and the companies be retained, for the present, under the command of their respective captains, subject to the orders of General Trapier or the governor of the State; that the pretended battalion of artillery be refused, and thrown back for the present upon the State. There was but one order relative to it obtained from General Grayson, a copy of which is inclosed, and under circumstances a knowledge of which you can obtain from Dr. Sabal, the medical director of General Grayson, now on his way to Richmond.

Then, sir, if you will accept of twenty companies for twelve months, and reserve to yourself the appointment of field officers, and appoint such as are known to you, or such as I may recommend, I can have the companies ready, I think, in a fortnight, embracing the eight companies now under Hopkins' command. Freed of him, I will add two fine companies, and the regiment will be complete and equipped. Then, by adding six companies to the four now commanded by Lieutenant-Colonel Holland, another regiment of infantry may be formed, with an artillery company attached, equipped with the guns, &c., now used by Holland's battalion, the entire equipment being not more than sufficient for one company, allowing, meanwhile, Holland's four companies to remain on duty where they now are until the regiment is completed.

The State troops at Apalachicola are under command of my aide-de-camp, Col. Richard F. Floyd—an accomplished gentleman and competent officer—and a copy of his orders is inclosed. By letter he is ordered to defend the place, if attacked, to the last extremity.

Now, permit me to say that Georgia and Alabama are as much, if not more, interested in the defense of Apalachicola, so far as commerce is concerned, as Florida; therefore, in view of our extended coast, and the almost insurmountable obstacles to its successful defense, I would recommend, most respectfully and earnestly, that a military department be composed of the counties contiguous on both sides of the Chattahoochee River, so as to embrace Columbus, Ga. Look at the map and the relative positions of the counties in Georgia, Alabama, and Florida. Such a military department, under a brigadier-general of military education, experience, and sobriety, would contribute greatly to Southern defense.

The military department proposed, most respectfully, may be composed of the following-named counties in Georgia, Alabama, and Florida, viz: In Georgia, the counties of Decatur, Thomas, Miller, Early, Baker, Clay, Calhoun, Randolph, Quitman, Stewart, Muscogee; in Alabama, the counties of Henry, Dale, Barbour, and Russell; in Florida, the counties of Leon, Gadsden, Wakulla, Jefferson, Madison, Liberty, Washington, Calhoun, Jackson, and Franklin.

The proposed military department has been submitted to the consideration of the governors of Georgia and Alabama. The remaining counties of Middle, East, and South Florida will form a military department sufficient in itself to command the utmost vigilance of an experienced and able officer.

I have the honor to be, very respectfully,

JOHN MILTON.

ADJUTANT AND INSPECTOR GENERAL'S OFFICE,
Tallahassee, Fla., October 30, 1861.

His Excellency JOHN MILTON,
Governor of Florida:

SIR: In obedience to your instructions of the 16th instant, requiring me to visit Fernandina and report to you the condition of the defenses at that place, I have the honor to submit the following, viz:

The defenses consist of a sand and palmetto-log battery of eight guns, all mounted, to wit: Five 32-pounders, two 24-pounders (smooth bore), and one rifled 6-inch gun on a ship carriage. This battery I conceive to be very injudiciously arranged, having 24-pounders, 32-pounders, and rifled guns all in the same battery in barbette, except that two of the 32-pounders are partially masked by slight traverses on the parapet. These traverses confine the field of fire seaward to about 15°. These guns are all placed on a straight line, except the rifled gun, which is placed just in rear of the left gun, and when fired its direction will be obliquely over the short-range guns, thereby endangering the men at these guns, and at the same time drawing the fire of the enemy on the whole battery long before they come within the reach of the 24-pounders and 32-pounders. There is also one 24-pounder and two 32-pounders unmounted at Fort Clinch, and one 8-inch columbiad landed at the wharf at Fernandina on the 27th instant.

The weather during my visit was so stormy as to render it impossible for me to visit Colonel Holland's camp at the south end of the island, 18 miles distant; neither did I witness the drill of the troops in the immediate vicinity of Fernandina for the same reason; but the idea formed by seeing the men and officers about the streets was anything but favorable to their discipline, having seen several staggering through the streets on the Sabbath day. They are sadly in want of an efficient commander and a good drill-master for both artillery and infantry. I learned that Colonel Holland had not yet located his permanent camp at the south end of the island; neither had any breastworks been thrown up, he having but a few days before moved to that point. His command consists of four companies of artillery, with four brass 6-pounders, 500 6-pound balls, and 75 grape and canister, and 500 cannon friction tubes—his men are armed with muskets and carbines—4,000 caps, and a lot of balls. Of ammunition, as far as I could learn, there are 300 32-pounder caps, 500 cannon friction tubes, 770 32-pound balls, 80 32-pound shells, 100 rounds of shell and fixed ammunition for the 32-pounder rifled gun, 90 24-pound balls, 12,000 ball and buck-shot cartridges, 2,000 caps (the latter—balls and caps—delivered to the officer in command of the fort), 7,000 caps still in possession of General Finegan. The above constitutes, as far as I could learn, all the ammunition on the island.

There are at this time seven companies on the island, one of which is a cavalry company and the others are infantry. These are exclusive of the four companies belonging to Colonel Holland's battalion of artillery. This battalion has never been mustered into either State or Confederate service, but an order for them to be furnished with the requisite arms and equipments issued by General Grayson has been forwarded to Richmond, showing the amount necessary to place this battalion in condition for active and efficient service.

Respectfully, your obedient servant,

F. L. DANCY,
Adjutant and Inspector General.

TALLAHASSEE, *October* 31, 1861.

HON. J. P. BENJAMIN:

Have not seen or heard from General Trapier. Full investigation satisfies me that troops, guns, &c., should be removed promptly from Saint Vincent's Island to Apalachicola. Shall I order the movement? A messenger here waiting for the order.

JOHN MILTON,
Governor of Florida.

RICHMOND, *October* 31, 1861.

GOV. JOHN MILTON,
Tallahassee, Fla.:

You are authorized to remove the guns and other munitions of war from Saint Vincent's Island to Apalachicola. General Trapier will be in Fernandina in two or three days.

J. P. BENJAMIN,
Acting Secretary of War.

EXECUTIVE DEPARTMENT,
Tallahassee, Fla., October 31, 1861.

His Excellency JOSEPH E. BROWN,
Governor of Georgia:

SIR: I have this day recommended to the President and Secretary of War the establishment of a military department, to be composed of the following counties in Georgia, Alabama, and Florida, lying on or near the Chattahoochee River, viz:

In Georgia: Decatur, Thomas, Miller, Early, Baker, Clay, Calhoun, Randolph, Quitman, Stewart, and Muscogee. In Alabama: Henry, Dale, Barbour, and Russell. In Florida: Leon, Gadsden, Wakulla, Jefferson, Madison, Liberty, Washington, Jackson, Calhoun, and Franklin.

I respectfully invite your consideration and approval of the measure proposed. Georgia and Alabama derive even more commercial advantages from Apalachicola than Florida herself, and both those States are deeply interested in its defense.

I am, sir, very respectfully,

JOHN MILTON.

Abstract from monthly return of the Department of Georgia, commanded by Brig. Gen. A. R. Lawton, for October, 1861.

Stations.	Present for duty.		Aggregate present.	Aggregate present and absent.	Artillery.	
	Officers.	Men.			Heavy.	Field.
South end Big Cumberland Island	6	116	142	150	4	....
Fort Pulaski	17	290	352	379	36	....
Brunswick, Ga	9	129	140	154	....	5
Oglethorpe Barracks	1	68	87	99	....	6
Genesis Point	2	39	70	76	5	....
Great Warsaw battery	6	120	140	171	5	....

Abstract from monthly return of the Department of Georgia, &c.—Continued.

Stations.	Present for duty.		Aggregate present.	Aggregate present and absent.	Artillery.	
	Officers.	Men.			Heavy.	Field.
Thunderbolt battery	3	100	109	116	4	....
Saint Simon's Island	39	697	855	919	8	....
Sapello Island	11	268	321	364	5	....
Isle of Hope	2	50	55	70	....	6
Jekyl Island	23	359	499	563	6	....
Sunbury, Ga	3	43	49	71	....	....
South Newport	4	67	73	73	....	....
Near Darien	4	68	74	75	....	....
Carteret's Point	3	53	56	64	....	....
Camp Lawton (Savannah)	21	396	421	432	....	....
Camp Cumming (Savannah)	6	63	86	101	....	....
Skidaway Island	28	498	636	658	....	....
Tybee Island	54	896	1,086	1,183	2	....
Camp Wayne, Waynesville	7	165	175	190	8	....
Other points	4	67	71	74	....	....
Grand total	253	4,552	5,497	5,982	83	17

HEADQUARTERS DEPARTMENT OF GEORGIA,
Savannah, November 1, 1861.

Hon. J. P. BENJAMIN,
Acting Secretary of War, Richmond, Va.:

SIR: I have the honor to inclose to you a communication received to-day from Col. T. J. Warthen, commanding a regiment at one of the camps of instruction recently placed under my authority, and by your directions ordered to Richmond. These camps having been established by the governor, under some sort of authority from the late Secretary of War, he (the governor) attempts such control over them as may delay their preparations for departure. Of course no attention will be paid by me to this notice of "protest," and I only inclose the letter to explain the precise state of things at the time I assume command of these camps.

Very respectfully, your obedient servant,

A. R. LAWTON,
Brigadier-General, Commanding.

[Inclosure.]

HEADQUARTERS CAMP STEPHENS,
October 30, 1861.

General A. R. LAWTON:

But a few hours since I received a communication from his excellency the governor, stating that he had not been advised by the Secretary of War of the action of the Department in ordering this regiment to Virginia, and, moreover, stating that he had just written to the Department protesting, in the name of the State, against this and other regiments being removed from the State. I thought it due to you that you should be notified of the same.

Again signifying to you that I shall obey with pleasure any order emanating from you, I subscribe myself, your obedient servant,

THOMAS J. WARTHEN,
Colonel, Commanding Twentieth Regiment Georgia Volunteers.

RICHMOND, *November* 1, 1861.

GOV. FRANCIS W. PICKENS,
Columbia, S. C.:

I have just received information, which I consider entirely reliable, that the enemy's expedition is intended for Port Royal.

J. P. BENJAMIN,
Acting Secretary of War.

(Same to Generals Drayton and Ripley.)

COLUMBIA, *November* 1, 1861.

Hon. Mr. BENJAMIN:

Telegraph received. Please telegraph General Anderson, at Wilmington, and General Lawton, Savannah, to send what forces they can spare, as the difficulty with us is as to arms. I have telegraphed them both.

F. W. PICKENS.

CHARLESTON, *November* 1, 1861.

To SECRETARY OF WAR:

Dispatch received. Will act at once. A fine strong southeast gale blowing, which will keep him off for a day or so. Will advise.

R. S. RIPLEY.

HEADQUARTERS DEPARTMENT OF GEORGIA,
Savannah, November 1, 1861.

Hon. J. P. BENJAMIN,
Acting Secretary of War, Richmond, Va.:

SIR: It is now generally understood that the governor of this State is preparing to call out a large force of State troops, to be thrown on the coast of Georgia. A brigade has already been organized and a brigadier-general appointed by the governor. This may not be at all embarrassing, but I am now informed that the governor proposes to organize a division forthwith, and to commission a major-general and send him to the coast, under an act passed at the last session of the legislature of Georgia. This may lead to serious embarrassment, and both General Mercer and myself see cause for uneasiness in the contemplated action of the governor. As all the arrangements for defense on this coast have been made without reference to State authority, I desire instructions from the Department as to the course which must be adopted, if an officer, commissioned by the governor of Georgia, of a higher grade than the Confederate general now on duty here, shall claim the command. I desire the views of the Department, that I may act with promptness and feel assured that my action will be approved.

Very respectfully, your obedient servant,

A. R. LAWTON,
Brigadier-General, Commanding.

SAVANNAH, *November* 1, 1861.

Hon. J. P. BENJAMIN,
Acting Secretary of War, Richmond, Va.:

DEAR SIR: I have to-day written you an official letter in reference to the prospect of a major-general of the State of Georgia being ordered by the governor to this coast. Pardon me for using the vehicle of a private note to convey some facts which I did not wish to communicate more formally. Governor Brown has suddenly shown a disposition to exercise a good deal of authority over, and claim much credit for, the coast defense, and his desire now is to make such appointments as will secure the control to him in case of an attack. He was anxious to appoint Colonel Mercer major-general, so as to secure it through him; but Colonel Mercer would not lend himself to the arrangement. Hence my urgent dispatch in reference to his appointment in the Confederate service, and I was much gratified to find by your reply that the appointment was made. It is now well understood that Governor Brown will at once appoint General W. H. T. Walker a major-general, and his commission will no doubt bear date before the time that this note will reach you. General Walker is an old friend of mine, and under other circumstances I could have no objections whatever to serving under him, as he is several years my senior, but I fear that the feelings with which he has now left the Confederate service, fomented by the temper which Governor Brown has (in the past at least) exhibited towards the War Department, might cause great embarrassment here, if he is permitted to assume command under State authority. Besides, after passing through the labor, the anxiety, the alarms, and complaints of the people on the coast, I would regret to see the results pass from my control, when we are comparatively in a condition to receive the enemy. If it must pass into other hands, I would gladly receive an order for service in some other department.

Very respectfully, your obedient servant,

A. R. LAWTON.

CHARLESTON, *November* 1, 1861.

His Excellency Governor MILTON,

Tallahassee, Fla.:

SIR: You have, I presume, been officially informed from the War Department of my appointment to the command of the Military Department of East and Middle Florida. I accordingly write to put myself in correspondence with your excellency, and to advise the adoption of such preliminary measures for the defense of that portion of the State as may very well be commenced in anticipation of my arrival to take command in person. I am not accurately informed as to the number of troops now in the field in that portion of Florida. The force which, in my judgment, with the lights now before me, will be required cannot fall short of 7,000 men, of all arms, and I would respectfully suggest the propriety of at once calling for a sufficient number of regiments to make up that force.

Fernandina (or Amelia Island) is obviously the point most likely to become the object of the enemy's first attack, and I have accordingly already taken steps for its better protection. An engineer officer of the corps of this State, a gentleman of skill and experience, kindly put at my service by Governor Pickens, is now under orders for that place and on his way there, with instructions from me for his guidance, and authority to make such alterations and additions to the batteries already erected there as may seem to be immediately called for for their greater strength and security.

I am organizing my staff, and hope to be able to proceed to Florida by the 10th of this month. Meanwhile I shall be glad to hear from your excellency, and to receive any suggestions you may have to make at this city.

I am, very respectfully, your obedient servant,

J. H. TRAPIER,
Brigadier-General.

[Indorsement.]

EXECUTIVE DEPARTMENT,
Tallahassee, Fla., November 5, 1861.

To the SECRETARY OF WAR:

Will the President receive two more infantry regiments in this State, for twelve months' service, under command of General Trapier, the companies to be raised by me, and when reported ready the President to appoint the field officers? I do not think it possible to raise immediately more than two regiments in this State. If other forces are needed, therefore the necessity of the new military department recently suggested by me.

Very respectfully,

JOHN MILTON,
Governor of Florida.

RICHMOND, *November* 2, 1861.

Governor PICKENS,
Columbia, S. C.:

Will send dispatches and give you re-enforcements with speed as soon as I know that your coast is actually the point of attack.

J. P. BENJAMIN,
Acting Secretary of War.

EXECUTIVE DEPARTMENT,
Tallahassee, October 31 (*via Columbus, November* 2), 1861.

Hon. J. P. BENJAMIN,
Secretary of War:

The steamer Salvor, owned and commanded by James McKay, of Tampa, has been captured by the enemy on the quicksand between Tortugas and Key West. Cargo, 21,000 stand of arms, 100 boxes of revolvers, 6 rifled cannon, and ammunition.

JOHN MILTON,
Governor.

WILMINGTON, *November* 2, 1861.

Hon. J. P. BENJAMIN:

I promised Governor Pickens if he would help me to return the favor in case South Carolina was attacked. He says the fleet will attack Port Royal. In that event will you justify me in sending one or two regiments and a field battery?

J. R. ANDERSON,
Brigadier-General, Commanding.

RICHMOND, *November* 4, 1861.

General JOSEPH R. ANDERSON,
Wilmington, N. C.:

As soon as Governor Pickens informs you that South Carolina is attacked, you may send him all the aid that you can possibly spare.

J. P. BENJAMIN,
Acting Secretary of War.

SAVANNAH, *November* 4, 1861.

J. P. BENJAMIN,
Acting Secretary of War:

The enemy's fleet concentrating between Savannah River and Port Royal. Point of attack still doubtful. More than twenty vessels in sight.

A. R. LAWTON,
Brigadier-General.

CHARLESTON, *November* 4, 1861.

General COOPER,
Adjutant-General:

Enemy's fleet concentrating between Tybee and Port Royal. Have started re-enforcements to General Drayton. Am occupying the country inland with cavalry, and concentrating the force here to re-enforce either Drayton or Lawton. Desire authority for General Anderson to re-enforce me. Not much fear of any landing north of Edisto.

R. S. RIPLEY.

CHARLESTON, *November* 5, 1861.

General S. COOPER:

Forty-one vessels reported off Beaufort. Attack imminent. Have requested General Lawton to re-enforce Hilton Head with from 500 to 1,000 men, and have requested General Anderson to send me two regiments and a field battery. Will you confirm the requests? Shall start in person as soon as reserve is organized, and attack as soon after they land as I can reach them.

R. S. RIPLEY.

SPECIAL ORDERS, No. 206. } ADJUTANT AND INSPECTOR GEN.'S OFFICE,
Richmond, November 5, 1861.

* * * * * * *

XII. The coasts of South Carolina, Georgia, and East Florida are constituted a military department, and General R. E. Lee, C. S. Army, is assigned to its command.

By command of the Secretary of War:

JNO. WITHERS,
Assistant Adjutant-General.

GOLDSBOROUGH, *November* 6, 1861.

General S. COOPER:

The following letter has just reached me, having been picked up near the wreck of the steamer Union, addressed by Louis H. Pelouze, acting assistant adjutant-general, to the captain of that steamer:

In the event of your transport being separated from the fleet, you will proceed to Port Royal, S. C., and report to the quartermaster of that port.

R. C. GATLIN,
Brigadier-General.

COLUMBIA, *November* 6, 1861.

Hon. Mr. BENJAMIN,
Secretary of War:

As I anticipated, they have passed the batteries, and will take Beaufort. My difficulty is in want of arms. I gave out the last to arm the 4,000 recently mustered in. I cannot rely on half-armed men ordered out, except to defend the railroad. If I cannot get arms, can you not spare Gregg's regiment from Suffolk, and order it immediately to Pocotaligo, or near there? See if any troops there at present. All to report to General Lee.

F. W. PICKENS.

CHARLESTON, *November* 6, 1861.

S. COOPER,
Adjutant-General:

General Drayton telegraphs from Fort Walker at 11 p. m. yesterday: "No one wounded here; only 3 slightly at Bay Point. Enemy threatened another attack this afternoon, but withdrew on firing four or five shots at them. Now about fifty sail within 4 or 5 miles, several brigs, large transports." De Saussure's regiment I trust reached Drayton this morning, and hope that General Lawton has re-enforced him with 1,000 men from Savannah. One regiment from Wilmington expected to arrive momentarily here. Have arranged transportation by Savannah Railroad, and hope to have steamers to transport a large force to attack speedily, should he effect a landing.

R. S. RIPLEY.

EXECUTIVE DEPARTMENT,
Milledgeville, Ga., November 7, 1861.

Hon. J. P. BENJAMIN,
Acting Secretary of War, Richmond, Va.:

SIR: I herewith transmit to your Department copy of letter received by me from his excellency the governor of Florida, informing me that he has "recommended to the President and Secretary of War the establishment of a military department, to be composed of" certain counties of Georgia, Alabama, and Florida.*

While I am not fully convinced of the necessity of establishing the new military department proposed by the able and patriotic executive of Florida, I have no objection to its establishment should the President

---

* See Milton to Brown, October 31, p. 304.

and War Department deem it advisable to carry out the recommendation of Governor Milton.

Very respectfully, &c.,

JOSEPH E. BROWN.

WILMINGTON, *November* 7, 1861.

Hon. J. P. BENJAMIN,
Secretary of War:

I have sent one regiment and one field battery to Charleston, and await such certain information of attack as will justify me in sending more troops under your instructions.

J. R. ANDERSON,
Brigadier-General, Commanding.

SAVANNAH, *November* 8, 1861.

J. P. BENJAMIN:

The enemy has taken complete possession of Port Royal entrance and now controls the inland navigation at that point. I sent 1,000 men to re-enforce General Drayton on Hilton Head. They have returned to me with but few casualties, having been in the hottest of the fight.

A. R. LAWTON,
Brigadier-General.

COLUMBIA, *November* 8, 1861.

Hon. Mr. BENJAMIN,
Secretary of War:

I telegraphed you this morning to ask for Gregg's regiment to report at Pocotaligo, but have no reply. Ripley is absent from Charleston. Telegraph me for Captain McCord's company to report. It is ready. A fine company just received for Hampton's Legion, but I armed it to-day to send to Beaufort. Do give me an order for Coit's company also. All our regiments are safe from Hilton Head and Bay Point. We must defend Charleston, and I have no arms for any more men, but have ordered out a large reserve to meet at Gillisonville or Pocotaligo. Let me know if Lee is in command, so I may order troops to him.

F. W. PICKENS.

COOSAWHATCHIE,
November 8, 1861 (*via Pocotaligo*).

General COOPER,
Adjutant-General:

Enemy attacked forts in Port Royal yesterday morning. After a hard cannonade silenced Fort Walker. General Drayton withdrew his troops last night to main line. No positive news from Bay Point, but the enemy have passed in and have possession of Port Royal. General Lee arrived.

R. S. RIPLEY.

GENERAL ORDERS, No. 1.
HEADQUARTERS, *Coosawhatchie, S. C., November* 8, 1861.

I. In pursuance of instructions from the War Department, General R. E. Lee, C. S. Army, assumes command of the military department composed of the coasts of South Carolina, Georgia, and East Florida.

II. Capt. T. A. Washington, C. S. Army, is announced as adjutant-general of the department; Capt. Walter H. Taylor, Provisional Army, as assistant adjutant-general; Capt. Joseph C. Ives, C. S. Army, as chief engineer; Lieut. Col. William G. Gill, Provisional Army, as ordnance officer, and Mr. Joseph Manigault as volunteer aide-de-camp to the commanding general.

* * * * * * *

By order of General Lee:

T. A. WASHINGTON,
Captain, and Assistant Adjutant-General, C. S. Army.

HEADQUARTERS, *Coosawhatchie, November* 9, 1861.

Hon. J. P. BENJAMIN,
Secretary of War:

SIR: On the evening of the 7th, on my way to the entrance of Port Royal Harbor, I met General Ripley, returning from the battery at the north end of Hilton Head, called Fort Walker. He reported that the enemy's fleet had passed the batteries and entered the harbor. Nothing could then be done but to make arrangements to withdraw the troops from the batteries to prevent their capture and save the public property. The troops were got over during the night, but their tents, clothing, and provisions were mostly lost, and all the guns left in the batteries. General Drayton's command was transferred from Fort Walker to Bluffton; Colonel Dunovant's from Bay Point to Saint Helena Island and thence to Beaufort. There are neither batteries nor guns for the defense of Beaufort, and Colonel Dunovant crossed Port Royal Ferry yesterday, and was halted at Garden's Corner. General Drayton reports he has but 955 men with him, and no field battery, the troops from Georgia that were on the island having returned to Savannah without orders. Colonel Dunovant's regiment is in as destitute a condition as General Drayton's command, as they were obliged to leave everything behind, and number between 600 and 700 men. I wrote to General Lawton to endeavor to withdraw the guns from the battery at the south end of Hilton Head. I have received as yet no report from him nor any official account from the commanders of the batteries. I fear every gun has been lost. At present I am endeavoring to collect troops to defend the line of the railroad and to push forward the defenses of Charleston and Savannah.

Colonel Clingman's regiment of North Carolina volunteers, six companies of Colonel Edwards' regiment of South Carolina volunteers, and Colonel Martin's South Carolina cavalry compose the force now here. The enemy, having complete possession of the water and inland navigation, commands all the islands on this coast, and threatens both Savannah and Charleston, and can come in his boats within 4 miles of this place. His sloops of war and large steamers can come up Broad River to Mackay's Point, the mouth of the Pocotaligo, and his gunboats can ascend some distance up the Coosawhatchie and Tulifiny. We have no guns that can resist their batteries, and have no resource but to prepare to meet them in the field. They have landed on Hilton Head. Their fleet is in Port Royal Harbor. Four of their gunboats are reported to be approaching Beaufort. I fear there are but few State troops ready for the field. The garrisons of the forts at Charleston and Savannah and on the coast cannot be removed from the batteries while ignorant of the designs of the enemy. I am endeavoring to bring into the field such light batteries as can be prepared.

I have the honor to be, your obedient servant,

R. E. LEE,
General, Commanding.

RICHMOND, *November* 9, 1861.

Governor PICKENS,
Columbia, S. C.:

General Lee is in command of the department embracing South Carolina and Georgia, as well as Eastern Florida. This was done in order to enable him to concentrate all our forces at any point that might be attacked. It is not necessary to send you regiments from this distance, but we will order more troops to your aid from North Carolina. You may retain all armed troops in South Carolina and all unarmed troops that can be made useful in batteries. General Lee has full power to act, and it would be well to send him a copy of this dispatch, that he may not scruple in using all the means of the Government within his reach for your defense.

J. P. BENJAMIN,
Acting Secretary of War.

CHARLESTON, *November* 10, 1861.

SECRETARY OF WAR:

Circumstances may soon arise to make it necessary that martial law should be proclaimed in this city. I ask for authority to take the step.

J. H. TRAPIER.

HEADQUARTERS DEPARTMENT OF GEORGIA,
Savannah, November 10, 1861.

General R. E. LEE,
Coosawhatchie, S. C.:

GENERAL: I had the honor to receive yesterday your letter of the 8th instant,* covering extract of Special Orders, No. 206, from headquarters of the Army [A. and I. G. O., November 5, 1861].

Permit me to express my extreme gratification at the contents of this extract, which assures me that I am to have the benefit of your military skill and experience in the present emergency; no one can appreciate the necessity for such assistance more than I do. I earnestly desire a personal interview with you at the earliest practicable moment, and trust that it may be in your power to visit Savannah, if only to remain here one night and return to Carolina the next morning. The present arrangements of the railway trains will make it very convenient for you to accomplish such a visit. It would afford me great pleasure to call on you at your present headquarters and there confer fully with you, but scarcely feel justified in absenting myself from my command at this

* Not found.

critical juncture, even for the space of twelve hours, unless you attach much importance to it, and cannot visit Savannah.

The number of troops recently received by me in a comparatively unorganized condition, and the changes now suddenly made in the posting and disposition of them to meet the movements of the enemy, together with the great pressure at this moment on each department of the staff, will necessarily cause delay in furnishing you with an accurate and forward statement of the troops, guns, ammunition, &c., under my command. In the mean time I have the pleasure to state, for your information, that my command consists of about 5,500 men, mustered into the service of the Confederate States, and distributed along the coast. About 2,000, under command of Brigadier-General Mercer, are stationed at and near Brunswick. The remainder, say 3,500 men, are on this side of the Altamaha River, and all but 500 of this number within 20 miles of Savannah.

Having to-day ordered up all the troops from Tybee Island (about 1,000), I will have about 2,800 men near the city that can move promptly, exclusive of 450 at Fort Pulaski and 200 at Green Island battery, on Vernon River, protecting an important landing about 12 miles in rear of Savannah.

Of the 5,500 troops under my command, about 500 are cavalry and the rest infantry, with the exception of three field batteries (two of these pieces were sent to Hilton, with the re-enforcements to General Drayton, and lost).

The cavalry are very well mounted and armed; the light batteries have a limited supply of horses, and but moderately well drilled. The infantry are made up chiefly of raw troops, though all substantially armed; about 2,000 of them are very well drilled and disciplined.

As all the volunteer corps in and about Savannah have been mustered into service, they are included in the 5,500; but there are about 3,000 men, armed after a fashion, under State organization, now in camp on the line of railway, and can be called to Savannah in a few hours. With the assistance of the naval officers we are now blocking up the channel in several places, and hope for good results.

I am, very respectfully, your obedient servant,

A. R. LAWTON,
Brigadier-General, Commanding.

COOSAWHATCHIE, *November* 10, 1861.

Hon. SECRETARY OF WAR:

Dispatch from Governor Pickens received. Am I at liberty to employ troops in South Carolina and Georgia passing through the States to Virginia?

R. E. LEE.

RICHMOND, *November* 11, 1861.

General R. E. LEE,
Coosawhatchie (via Pocotaligo):

You are authorized to use the entire resources of South Carolina and Georgia that are under control of the Confederate Government for your defense, whether troops, munitions of war, or supplies of every kind.

J. P. BENJAMIN,
Acting Secretary of War.

MILLEDGEVILLE, *November* 11, 1861.

J. P. BENJAMIN,
Secretary of War:

The city of Savannah is menaced by the enemy, and we are in great need of arms. You have nearly all our guns. I request that you send to Savannah immediately the brigade of State troops trained here under command of General W. Phillips, now known in the Confederate service as the Phillips Legion, Colonels Wofford and Boyd's regiments, and Stovall's battalion; also regiment of Georgia regulars. All these troops were trained at the State's expense and thoroughly armed by her, and her safety now requires their services with their arms. Please answer immediately.

JOSEPH E. BROWN.

COLUMBIA, *November* 11, 1861.

Hon. Mr. BENJAMIN,
Secretary of War:

There are 910 Enfield rifles in Charleston not paid for by Colonel Cunningham. If I can get them for troops mustered into the Confederate service can I do so? I would like to know the number of armed men I can rely on to be sent me. I have no arms; if I had I would ask for none. The great battle will be near Stono, but cannot take place until they are largely re-enforced, some weeks hence. I could raise 20,000 men if I only had the arms. Mr. Lee has been acting commissary here, but has no direct authority, and cannot act without constant permission. There is a necessity for an assistant commissary.

F. W. PICKENS.

HDQRS. MIL. DEPT. MIDDLE AND EAST FLORIDA,
Fort Clinch, Amelia Island, Fla., November 12, 1861.

Hon. J. P. BENJAMIN,
Acting Secretary of War, C. S. A., Richmond, Va.:

SIR: I had the honor to receive yours of the 26th ultimo by the hands of Captain Buckman, and strictly adhered to the instructions therein contained until the present emergency arose, which has thrown on me a heavy responsibility, as unexpected as it has been onerous and disagreeable. A full report of my acts and doings I ask to submit to you, and which I trust, under the circumstances, you will indorse and sanction. Let me premise by stating that General Trapier has not yet assumed command of this department, and consequently I am in command of this department. I cannot now state when General Trapier will be here, as I cannot calculate how the disaster at Port Royal may influence the movements of our Government. But to the point. In my last communication I addressed you on the subject of the battalion of artillery, Lieutenant-Colonel Holland in command and Major Hopkins second in command. They were presented in this shape by Governor Perry, and received by Brigadier-General Grayson, deceased, then in command of this department.

On the 28th day of September, A. D. 1861 (see copy of order of Brigadier-General Grayson), Brigadier-General Grayson also ordered them supplied by the quartermaster and commissary departments at this place. Four companies were received in this way, and, stating that the mustering officers would soon muster them into the service formally, under this order they have continued in service. Last week, however, an order arrived from Governor Milton to disband them, they—the battalion—regarding that they were not in the State service but in the Confederate service. In the mean time the Port Royal affair occurred on Thursday last. The United States war vessels are in sight every day, though not more than one at a time, evidently reconnoitering our coast and condition. This battalion of four companies on Saturday offered to go in the service in any shape I might name, but if not mustered at once they would leave the island or accept a proposition which had been made by an officer in Georgia to receive them there into service in Georgia. It is only one mile and a quarter from this (Amelia Island) to Cumberland, in Georgia. The four companies composing this battalion—Captain Buckman's, Richards', Brink's, and Kendrick's—are well drilled. They are armed with muskets, and I supplied them with five field pieces, and since have received from our Government two beautiful 6-pounders, rifled-bore field pieces, carrying some 12 or 14 pounds elongated shot and shell. Placed in this situation, in imminent peril, with only, in the aggregate of the Third Regiment at this post, 659 men, no soldiers that I could call from other posts, I have mustered these companies into the Confederate States service as light infantry, and will accept two companies more, making in all six companies in the battalion for twelve months from the 28th day of September last, the day on which four of the companies were received by General Grayson.

I have also notified proper parties that horses will be received on the same terms as in the cavalry service for the purpose of working the field artillery. I am fully aware that it is irregular to use infantry as field artillery; still, the regiments which I have the honor to command were mustered into the service as light infantry, and now they are converted into heavy artillery in part. I would ask that this battalion be increased into a regiment. We want them; we really need them. This island is 20 miles long on the sea-shore. I have, exclusive of the battalion, only 659 soldiers to defend it. When in surf-boats a landing can be effected anywhere, and small gunboats can come in in the rear from Georgia or from the south end, there should be here at least 2,000 troops, stationed here permanently. Allow me also to state that I do not believe it possible to raise ten men in this State who will enlist for the term of three years or during the war. This was a strong reason why I ordered this battalion to be mustered into the service. I find, sir, that it will not do to rely on State troops to defend our country. There should be but one system of defense, and that should be originated and organized and systematized by the Confederate States Army. I hope, sir, that my course will receive the sanction of the Government which I have the honor to serve, and I assure you nothing was ever more painful to me in my life than this of being so situated when I felt compelled to act without having the proper authority; and I beg leave to refer you to Messrs. Ward, Morton, and Owens—our Delegates in Congress—who know my character, and that it is not my disposition or nature to assume unauthorized and undelegated power. Should the Government sustain my acts in this matter it will be a source of pleasure and gratification, but if condemned, then my mortification will be most acute. Still, I will have the consolation of knowing that I was actuated by the purest and most patriotic motives. Ex-Senator Yulee and every man with whom I have had any conversation say that my course was dictated by necessity; still I hope soon to have your approval.

My adjutant, Lieut. J. O. A. Gerry, will inform you particularly as to our defenses, ammunition, &c. We have at this point, the northeast end of Amelia Island, at and near Fort Clinch, eight 32-pounders; two 24 and one 32 pounder rifle, mounted; one 10-inch rifle and three 8-inch columbiads, nearly mounted. We are hard at work placing these last in position, and we hope by the end of this week to have them in fighting trim. We have about 100 rounds for each gun. So soon as these guns are up I have little fear that the enemy can come in through the main channel; at least I shall not believe it until I have a practical demonstration of the fact. With proper batteries at the south end of the island—say one 8-inch columbiad and four 32 or 24 pounders, and infantry enough, say 2,000 in all—I do not think the enemy could even land, or if they did land, we could make them embark. We need particularly field artillery, which could be carried with great rapidity from point to point over the island or along the beach; and nature has done much in making breastworks all along the beach in the shape of sand hills, behind which not only field artillery could be maneuvered to great advantage, but also musketry, though in this respect our muskets are the old United States musket, and not an efficient weapon by any means.

For the port of Saint Augustine I need everything in the way of defense except the guns. However, I shall write you or the proper officer fully on this topic in the event General Trapier should not arrive soon. We heard distinctly the firing at Port Royal at this place on last Thursday for about five hours, and the news of its occupancy has saddened us, but at the same time determined us to stand more firmly at our post, as we regard an attack here as imminent. On Friday a war steamer appeared in the offing, three-masted. On Saturday another, and on Sunday and Monday a sloop of war. To-day none have come in sight. They come near the west end, run south, and usually go as near the shore as 3 miles at the south end, showing that they are reconnoitering and making a critical examination of our defenses, &c. They have now cut off all water communication with Charleston, and their next object, I apprehend, will be to break up the inland navigation between this and Savannah, the benefits of which to us are incalculable. I hope our Government will adopt some more speedy means of raising troops for the Confederate States. I could raise all the troops necessary for our defense in one week from this time if they could go immediately into the Confederate States service for twelve months; but when raised by the State the whole military body has been attempted to be painted with the political hues of the poor politicians, and our citizens are very averse to going through the chrysalis condition of State service, and after being pulled, hauled, and packed, as a gambler would his cards, for two or three months, then turned over to the Confederacy, unarmed, undisciplined, and undrilled, their time wasted and their country unbenefited. There has been in Florida East too much politics mixed with the military in organizing the regiments.

Again expressing my most sincere and deep regret that circumstances have compelled me to act without the proper authority, and which necessity alone could or should justify, and hoping soon to have the sanction of my country to the course I have pursued, I leave the matter in your hands. I fear I have already tried your patience, but your name is so familiar, though not acquainted personally with you, I feel that I am addressing a friend to every man who is true to his country, and I ask you to mete out to me in this matter that same measure you would have meted to you under similar circumstances. God knows I have worked harder here than I ever did in my life, and that my only motive has been to serve my country. I volunteered and was a private in the ranks until this (the Third) regiment was formed, when I was elected a colonel, and to-day would have been a private, had I not been elected to the colonelcy of the regiment.

Trusting that our country may soon be delivered from its present troubles, I subscribe myself, your obedient servant,

W. S. DILWORTH,
Colonel, Commanding Department.

RICHMOND, *November* 12, 1861.

GOV. JOSEPH E. BROWN,
Milledgeville, Ga.:

There are reasons of public policy which would make it suicidal to comply with your request to withdraw Georgia troops from the enemy's front at this moment. This Government will co-operate with all its power for the defense of your State, but it must do so in the manner it deems most certain to produce the desired effect of repulsing the enemy at all points, and cannot scatter its armies into fragments at the request of each governor who may be alarmed for the safety of his people. Be assured that no effort will be spared to aid you, and be good enough to communicate your confidence in this assurance to your people, thus allaying all needless panic.

J. P. BENJAMIN,
Acting Secretary of War.

RICHMOND, *November* 12, 1861.

General J. H. TRAPIER,
Charleston, S. C.:

General Lee has now command of the whole coast of Carolina and Georgia. I cannot authorize you to proclaim martial law. Let the governor take that responsibility, if found necessary. If the enemy advance to attack the city, of course the city will then become a camp under military law, if the necessities of its defense so require.

J. P. BENJAMIN,
Acting Secretary of War.

COLUMBIA, *November* 13, 1861.

President DAVIS:

Steel-clad steamer Fingal, cargo arms, &c., just run the blockade, and safe at Savannah. Now please send me an order for arms, as it is necessary. I am just off for Charleston. Arm us, and we are safe.

F. W. PICKENS.

SAVANNAH, *November* 13, 1861.

Hon. J. P. BENJAMIN,
Secretary of War:

Your dispatch refusing to send back any of Georgia's guns with her troops is forwarded to me here. You said a few days since in your dispatch that you would send us armed troops if attacked. A kind Providence has enabled Major Anderson to land here to-day with over 10,000 Enfield rifles belonging to the Confederacy. I now ask, not for men, but guns. Let us have 5,000 of these in place of 5,000 of the State's guns now in your service. Please answer immediately.

JOSEPH E. BROWN.

RICHMOND, *November* 13, 1861.

Gov. JOSEPH E. BROWN, *Savannah:*

As soon as I know what arms I have received I will give to Georgia troops all that I can possibly spare for her defense. I beg you to remember that ten other governors are making just such demands as yourself, and that it is not reasonable to complain that other exposed points should also be provided for. I will do my best, if not prevented by exaggerated demands which I have no means of satisfying.

J. P. BENJAMIN,
Acting Secretary of War.

RICHMOND, *November* 13, 1861.

General LAWTON, *Savannah:*

Order to Savannah all the unarmed troops offered for the war that are or can be mustered into our service, so that I may arm them with rifles from the Fingal as far as I can possibly spare them. I cannot consent to put these arms into the hands of any troops mustered for a less term than the war.

J. P. BENJAMIN,
Acting Secretary of War.

RICHMOND, *November* 13, 1861.

Governor PICKENS, *Columbia, S. C.:*

Have you got the rifles from Fraser & Co.? As soon as I know what number of arms I have received by the Fingal, I will arm your troops with every musket or rifle that I can possibly spare.

J. P. BENJAMIN,
Acting Secretary of War.

TALLAHASSEE, *November* 14, 1861.

Hon. J. P. BENJAMIN:

General Trapier has not arrived. The troops and munitions of war removed from Saint Vincent's Island and works destroyed. An attack threatened at Apalachicola. We need arms and munitions of war. With them we can hold the place. A vessel has arrived at Savannah with arms, &c. Authorize me by telegraph to send an agent to get one or two good cannon and equipments and small-arms, and I will defend Apalachicola successfully. Please answer immediately.

JOHN MILTON.

WAR DEPARTMENT, C. S. A.,
Richmond, November 14, 1861.

General R. E. LEE,
Commanding Department of South Carolina, &c.:

SIR: I have the honor to acknowledge receipt of your report of the 9th instant, not very encouraging in its contents, but evidently written before you had been enabled to gather in all the information necessary to enable you fully to judge of the condition of your department.

The arrival of the steamer Fingal at this critical moment is very opportune, and although the number of small-arms received is smaller than I had at first hoped, it is no contemptible addition to our means of defense.

Misled by a telegram which reported you to be at Savannah, I sent to you yesterday at that point the following dispatch, which I hope was forwarded to you:

> Of the 9,000 Enfield rifles received by the Government on the Fingal, 4,500 are assigned to your command, to be placed by you in the hands of Georgia and South Carolina troops in our service for the war. Order 4,500 to be sent immediately to General Albert S. Johnston at Nashville, and a few hundred will remain, which please send here. Put none of these arms in the hands of troops not enlisted for the war. The governor of Georgia has received 1,100 rifles by the same steamer, so that you will have 5,600 for service within your department.

As soon as I hear what further supplies we have on the Fingal in the way of cannon, &c., I will appropriate to you as full a share as I possibly can of whatever you may desire to aid your defense. I ordered Col. A. R. Wright, by dispatch yesterday, to proceed at once to Savannah for aiding the coast defense, and, as this is a full regiment, for the war, I doubt not you will find it expedient to arm it with the new weapons. The 10,000 blankets on the Fingal have been ordered here, where our troops need them much more than in more southern latitudes. It is the President's wish that you scruple not in employing every governmental resource within your reach, even troops in transit. You will, however, scarcely need this, for most of these troops are without arms, and have been ordered here to receive arms collected by the Potomac Army from various sources. I have a long letter from an inhabitant of Charleston, signing himself John H. Robertson, informing me that the forts in the harbor are in very incompetent hands. The writer speaks highly of Captain Rhett as a gentleman, but says he is totally without the experience necessary for so important a post. Of Captain Wagner he speaks in very different terms, representing him to be not only incompetent, but neglectful and dissipated, never spending the night in his fort, but coming to town to indulge in excesses with the common prostitutes. Of course this is for your private information, and the writer, who seems to be actuated by the best of motives, ought not to be exposed to the hostility of these officers. I know, however, your habitual vigilance, and this communication was perhaps needless.

Don't fail to keep us constantly advised, especially of your wants, and rely on my very best efforts to support you with the whole means of the Government that can with prudence be diverted from other exposed points.

I am, your obedient servant,

J. P. BENJAMIN,
Acting Secretary of War.

SAVANNAH, *November* 14, 1861.

J. P. BENJAMIN,
Secretary of War:

I trust you will let us have as many of the guns as possible. They landed here, and cannot be needed worse elsewhere. There are four rifled cannon. Do let us have two of them for fort, which lacks heavy guns. Answer at Milledgeville.

JOSEPH E. BROWN.

RICHMOND, *November* 14, 1861.

GOV. JOSEPH E. BROWN,
Milledgeville:

Out of about 9,000 rifles, I have assigned half to General Lee's command and the other half to General A. S. Johnston's command. General Lee will therefore have 4,500, which, when added to the 1,100 brought in for Georgia, makes 5,600 arms for the defense of Charleston and Savannah. As soon as I get the account of the cannon on board I will appropriate to the same purpose every piece that I can fairly assign to your coast. I shall know in a day or two what is possible.

J. P. BENJAMIN,
Acting Secretary of War.

CHARLESTON, *November* 14, 1861.

J. P. BENJAMIN:

I have just learned that the small-arms, &c., on the Fingal are the property of the Confederate Government. General Lee is now here, and has made requisition on me for five regiments. I have the men ready, but no arms. Will you send me an order for them? You know their situation, and will surely help us in ammunition.

F. W. PICKENS.

RICHMOND, *November* 14, 1861.

Governor PICKENS,
Charleston, S. C.:

I have assigned to General Lee 4,500 of the arms received by the Fingal, being half of all that are for us. The State of Georgia has also 1,100 on board, so that General Lee will have 5,600 for arming his department.

J. P. BENJAMIN,
Acting Secretary of War.

HDQRS. FIRST MILITARY DISTRICT, DEPT. OF S. C.,
Georgetown, November 15, 1861.

Maj. Gen. R. E. LEE:

GENERAL: There are two redoubts near the mouth of Winyaw Bay, on Cat and South Islands.

The first has mounted two 32-pounders, 50 rounds each; one rifled 12-pounder, 50 rounds, and two 24-pounders, 150 rounds each; three principal faces nearly completed; two bastions in rear, and curtain entirely unfinished; no bomb-proof. South Island redoubt, four 24-pounders, 125 rounds each; one rifle 6-pounder, 50 rounds; one 18-pounder, 125 rounds; three faces finished, still open in rear; bomb proof will be completed in ten days; garrisoned by 320 men of Tenth Regiment. There are near Georgetown, of Tenth Regiment, 565 men; three companies cavalry are on South Island, two near Georgetown, 135 men; one company rifles attached to Tenth Regiment, for local duty near Georgetown, 50 men; one section light artillery on Waccamaw Neck, 40 men—1,110 men. I have called on General Harllee, local volunteers, for 800; 280 have reported for duty; 200 more to arrive to-morrow; 480—1,590; the remainder, 320 cannot be here under a week. The 1,110 men are well armed, drilled, and equipped, and have about 100 rounds of ammunition to each man. The 480 are badly armed, mostly with shot-guns, are undrilled, fully supplied with ammunition, but are scarcely fit for service yet.

I will do the best I can, should the enemy appear.

There is also at the mouth of the North Santee River a redoubt mounting three guns, 12-pounders, not yet completed and not garrisoned; ammunition there sufficient. We have a full supply of powder and sufficient 24, 18, and 12 pounder round shot. You will perceive that the other guns are short of the proper number of balls.

Your obedient servant,

A. M. MANIGAULT,
Colonel Tenth Regiment, &c.

CHARLESTON, *November* 15, 1861.

Hon. Mr. BENJAMIN,
Secretary of War:

I understand the Fingal has powder as well as arms. Be so kind as to set aside, if possible, 30,000 pounds of cannon powder as essential for a supply of our forts if we are to fight such a fight as at Hilton Head. I believe we can have musket and rifle powder, but I would be glad if some musket were allowed also. If they are re-enforced by 30,000 men, we will use at least 15,000 men on James Island. I am deeply obliged for the arms divided between us and Georgia. We only want more. Can we get another regiment from North Carolina? We only have two.

F. W. PICKENS.

SPECIAL ORDERS, No. 1. } HEADQUARTERS, *Charleston, S. C., November* 16, 1861.

I. Commodore Ingraham, C. S. Navy, is assigned to duty in Charleston Harbor. He will superintend the preparation and armament of the batteries for its defense; assign to duty the naval officers at his disposal as ordnance officers at the batteries, and execute such other orders relative to the naval operations in the harbor as he may receive from Flag-Officer Tatnall, Provisional Army.

II. Lieut. Col. John S. Preston, assistant adjutant-general, C. S. Army, is hereby ordered to inspect and muster into the service of the Confederate States for the war such troops of the State of South Carolina as may be transferred by the governor of the State. These regiments must be armed and equipped by the State, except three regiments, or 2,500 men, who will be armed by the Government with the Enfield rifle. Upon the assembling of these troops at such places of rendezvous as may be selected by the governor, the mustering and inspecting officer will make requisitions upon the proper Departments for arms, transportation, and such other munitions as may be necessary, and report his operations from time to time to the general commanding.

By order of General Lee:

T. A. WASHINGTON,
Captain, Assistant Adjutant-General.

RICHMOND, *November* 17, 1861.

Gov. FRANCIS W. PICKENS,
Charleston, S. C.:

As soon as I can learn what ammunition is on board the Fingal you shall have your full share of everything. Be assured my solicitude for your defense is as great as your own, and nothing shall be refused that we can possibly give.

J. P. BENJAMIN,
Acting Secretary of War.

SPECIAL ORDERS, } No. 2. }

HEADQUARTERS,
Coosawhatchie, S. C., November 17, 1861.

I. Brig. Gen. R. S. Ripley, Provisional Army, will proceed to Charleston, S. C., and relieve Brig. Gen. J. H. Trapier in his command at that place. The latter, on being relieved, will proceed to Fernandina, Fla., and take command, pursuant to existing orders from the War Department. General Ripley will prosecute vigorously the completion of the water and land defenses of Charleston, and General Trapier will make use of all means in his power for the defense of Cumberland Sound.

II. The following disposition of troops will be carried into effect as soon as practicable, viz: Heyward's and De Saussure's regiments, South Carolina volunteers, under the immediate command of General Drayton; Clingman's and Radcliffe's North Carolina volunteers will continue near Grahamville, and Dunovant's and Edwards' South Carolina volunteers at their present positions.

* * * * * * *

By order of General Lee:

T. A. WASHINGTON,
Captain, and Assistant Adjutant-General, C. S. Army.

HEADQUARTERS PROVISIONAL FORCES,
Coosawhatchie, November 18, 1861.

Capt. T. A. WASHINGTON,
Assistant Adjutant-General:

CAPTAIN: Being about to repair to Charleston, in obedience to the orders of the general commanding, I have the honor to submit the following information concerning the troops in this vicinity:

Bluffton is held by Lieutenant-Colonel Colcock's cavalry, in observation only. It has been reported to me that there are two companies of infantry of Heyward's Ninth [Eleventh] regiment remaining there, but I have nothing definite. This section of country is under charge of General Drayton's command, which it is intended to move forward as soon as possible to occupy positions to cover Bluffton and the roads to Hardeeville. General Drayton's command is composed of Heyward's and De Saussure's regiments, Ninth [Eleventh] and Fifteenth South Carolina Volunteers, Lieutenant-Colonel Colcock's cavalry. Colonel Clingman's regiment of North Carolina volunteers (Twenty-fifth), occupies a point on the Honeywood road in advance of Grahamville, intended to be a guard for that town and to cover the roads leading from Tenny's or Boyd's Landing. His quartermaster and commissary are directed to establish depots and obtain supplies of subsistence at Grahamville, as far as possible; whether they will be successful remains to be seen, and the regiment will have to be looked after in the general depots.

Captain Trezevant's company of cavalry is in advance of Colonel Clingman, in observation of Boyd's and Tenny's Landings. General Drayton's command is supplied from his own depots at Hardeeville.

At the estate's landing, near Huguenin's plantation, are stationed the 8-inch howitzer battery, under General Gonzales, as volunteer aide-de-camp to myself. The howitzer battery is manned by the Palmetto Guard (State troops), and has attached to the command the Charleston Light Dragoons and Rutledge Mounted Rifles; the last are, however, in observation near Pocotaligo and Port Royal Ferries.

Colonel Radcliffe's Eighth North Carolina Volunteers is on the right of Gonzales' command, in position to support the battery or to defend the roads from Eutaw Church or to move forward to support Clingman. He is supplied partly by purchase and partly from the depot here.

A force of negroes, under the supervision of General Gonzales, is engaged in obstructing the Coosawhatchie below the landing; and, this being done, the steamer John A. Moore and several flats, sent from Charleston, are available for transportation from the railroad to the landing by water. Mr. Gregory is engaged with his negroes in obstructing the Tulifiny.

At Coosawhatchie is Colonel Edwards' full regiment and Captain Moore's light artillery, both waiting orders, &c.

Six companies of Dunovant's Twelfth South Carolina Volunteers are at Pocotaligo Corners, the remaining four being at Hardeeville. It is supposed that it was intended to order them to rejoin their regiment, but the order may be delayed until the arrival of the general.

Colonel Jones' Fourteenth South Carolina Volunteers holds Garden's Corner, and is stretched in observation towards Combahee Ferry, in advance towards Port Royal Ferry. This is guarded by Fripp's cavalry. Another force of Colonel Martin's regiment, which has its headquarters at Pocotaligo (it may be well to add that Lieutenant-Colonel Colcock's regiment is a portion of Colonel Martin's regiment, with one or two [companies] under Major Farr, a force of Martin's regiment), is also guarding the district of country about Combahee, Ashepoo, and Paw Paw.

Capt. Leo. D. Walker, assistant adjutant-general, with Messrs. Walter Blake, Rawlins Lowndes, and Paul, volunteer aides-de-camp, are now engaged in endeavoring to block the rivers at some point below the railroad bridges. They are to be assisted by Mr. Nolan, who has been sent out by the superintendent of the railroad for the purpose.

The general idea of the disposition of the troops has been to cover the railroad bridges in the direction of Savannah and have them not too far from the railroad, that they might move in either direction, in case of an attack on the road or on Savannah or Charleston.

If everything were in order, and the troops well disciplined, there would be no great difficulty in accomplishing the ends of the disposition, but General Drayton's command has not moved from Hardeeville, and our troops are very raw; they require severe discipline and constant watching; it will take some time of this to make them efficient.

I am, very respectfully, your obedient servant,

R. S. RIPLEY,
Brigadier-General.

EXECUTIVE DEPARTMENT,
Tallahassee, Fla., November 19, 1861.

His Excellency JEFFERSON DAVIS,
President of the Confederate States of America:

DEAR SIR: The presence of General Grayson, although unable to render service, the expectation of General Smith for two weeks, and of General Trapier for the last three weeks, have prevented me from adopting and enforcing with energy measures necessary to the defense of the State. At all important points we are threatened with attack; nowhere prepared to meet the enemy; and when, as governor of the State, I have applied for arms and munitions of war, I have been answered a requisition should be made by the officer in command of the military department, yet none is in command. It would have been almost as reasonable under the circumstances to have referred me to the Emperor of China. We need troops and munitions of war, and officers of military education, experience, and ability, and, if not promptly aided, Florida may be lost to the Southern Confederacy. Her citizens have almost despaired of protection from the Confederate Government—will lose confidence in it; but being one of the first States to withdraw from the United States, and to resolve to maintain her independence, her gallant sons and daughters would rather perish bravely, sword in hand, vindicating their rights, than yield submissively to or entertain a moment's thought of ever living under the same Government with the people of the North. If General Trapier will not accept the command (and I presume he will not while the enemy holds or threatens an inch of South Carolina), let us have arms and munitions of war, and have an order issued immediately, placing the troops in this State which have been mustered into the Confederate service, not embracing any in General Bragg's department, under my command, and subject to my orders as governor and commander in-chief of Florida, and if I cannot hold positions exposed to the naval armament of the enemy, I will prevent the enemy from holding the positions and defend the State against invasion. From every portion of the State I have been appealed to by the citizens to assume the command in person, and have been prevented by a desire to avoid coming in conflict with the authority and policy of the Confederate Government. Since the death of General Grayson I have corrected the evils arising from intemperance among the Confederate as well as the State troops. It is highly important that some one should be in command having the experience and common sense necessary to avoid useless expenditures and to enforce discipline among the troops, and make them available for the defense of the State.

These views are respectfully suggested for your consideration, with the sincere avowal that I would rather co-operate with General Trapier in this military department, if he will accept the command and repair here immediately.*

I have the honor to be, very respectfully, sir,

JOHN MILTON.

P. S.—I am informed that upon the steamer which has just arrived at Savannah rifled cannon and Enfield rifles have been received, and respectfully ask your excellency to place at my disposal 1,000 Enfield rifles and two rifled cannon, with equipments complete, and send them by Captain Noyes, the bearer, and I will successfully defend Apalachicola and Saint Mark's. Also, let Florida have 1,000 sabers, 1,000 pis-

* Some personal matters here omitted.

tols for cavalry, and equipments, and a few hundred bags of buck-shot. If General Trapier should decline the command here, and your excellency would prefer to have the military department under the command of an officer appointed by yourself rather than the governor of Florida, then I respectfully recommend Col. Richard F. Floyd, a citizen of this State, a native of Georgia, and now in command at Apalachicola by my appointment. He is about fifty years old; a soldier and a gentleman of strict sobriety and integrity; a good disciplinarian, and a gentleman of excellent sense and unquestionable courage.

Respectfully,

JOHN MILTON.

STATE OF SOUTH CAROLINA,
Headquarters, November 19, 1861.

General LEE,
Commanding:

SIR: As you have recently arrived to take command, I think, perhaps, it may be useful to you to have a general and authentic statement of the forces now in actual service from Georgetown to Hardeeville. I therefore inclose the within statement, that you may know what troops you can use for any immediate emergency.

I am not yet prepared to state exactly what regiments can be raised immediately or mustered in. I suppose you will have about 2,500 of the arms recently arrived to put in their hands and I think I can have 1,000; that is, in all 3,500. If the regiments are mustered in and get those arms, which no doubt will be the case, it will give about 20,000 men, who can be relied on, with arms. As to what you can get in an emergency from General Lawton and General Anderson, I can know nothing certain.

With very great respect, your obedient servant,

F. W. PICKENS.

[Inclosure.]

Commands.	Stations.	Strength.
Boyce's artillery		124
Citadel Cadets		126
Claremont troops		65
Clingman's regiment	Grahamville	1,100
Coit's artillery		132
College Cadets		60
De Saussure's brigade	Charleston	2,750
De Saussure's regiment	Hardeeville	800
Dunovant's regiment	Pocotaligo and Hardeeville	800
Edwards' regiment	Coosawhatchie	600
Gonzales' siege train (four guns)	Huguenin's Neck	80
Hagood's regiment	Cole's Island	750
Hatch's battalion	James Island and Bull's Bay	500
Heyward's regiment	Hardeeville	1,000
Jones' regiment	Garden's Corner	800
Lafayette Artillery	Fort Pickens (Stono)	60
Lamar's artillery	Fort Johnson	131
Lucas' battalion	Fort Pickens (Stono)	70
Martin's regiment (mounted)		650
McCord's Zouaves		92
Moore's artillery (6 guns)	Grahamville	110
Radcliffe's regiment	Huguenin's Neck	1,000
Regular artillery	Fort Sumter	560
Regular infantry	To be kept in Fort Moultrie	420
Vigilant Rifles	Fort Palmetto (Stono)	80
White's battalion		240
Total		13,100

RICHMOND, *November* 19, 1861.

General R. E. LEE,
Charleston:

I desire the cartridges for Enfield rifles divided between you and General Johnston in proper proportion, reserving for me such portion of the cartridges as is proper for the rifles that remain after dividing 9,000 between you and General Johnston. Divide the accouterments equally between yourself and General Johnston. Send to him the 500 sabers that are aboard. Keep the 10,000 pounds of the cannon powder, and send me the remaining 7,000 pounds belonging to the War Department. Send me all the rifle powder, as you have plenty at Augusta Arsenal.

J. P. BENJAMIN,
Acting Secretary of War.

SAVANNAH, *November* 21, 1861.

General S. COOPER,
Adjutant and Inspector General, Richmond, Va.:

GENERAL: I have the honor to report, for the information of the Secretary of War, that I have just returned to this city after having inspected the batteries and posts along the coast from Charleston to Fernandina, Fla.

The guns from the less important points have been removed, and are employed in strengthening those considered of greater consequence. The entrance to Cumberland Sound and Brunswick and the water approaches to Savannah and Charleston are the only points which it is proposed to defend. At all of these places there is much yet to be done, but every effort is being made to render them as strong as the nature of the positions and the means at hand will permit. They ought, after their completion, to make a good defense against any batteries that are likely to be brought against them. More guns could be usefully employed if available for this service; those at hand have been placed in the best positions and the troops distributed so as to work them to advantage. The batteries are tolerably supplied with ammunition, having about 50 rounds to the gun. This amount it would be well to have increased to 100 rounds.

The greatest difficulty to be contended with is the want of artillerists and proper officers as instructors. The naval officers directed to report to me have been assigned to duty at the batteries in Charleston Harbor as ordnance and artillery officers, with the exception of Captains Buchanan and Sinclair, whom I have directed to return, having, while uncertain as to any attack being in contemplation, no appropriate duties for them to perform, and believing their services were important at their former stations.

I have been able to learn nothing of any movements of the enemy's fleet along the coast of Georgia or Florida, and am inclined to believe that they have not yet made any further demonstrations of attack.

Very respectfully, your obedient servant,

R. E. LEE,
General, Commanding.

GENERAL ORDERS, } No. 2. }

HEADQUARTERS,
Coosawhatchie, S. C., November 21, 1861.

I. In consequence of the general scarcity of ammunition, the general commanding desires to impress upon the commanders of regiments and corps the absolute necessity of economizing the supplies they have on hand to the utmost extent. To this end the guards will not be allowed to load their pieces unless in the actual presence of the enemy or in danger of surprise, and all hunting parties will be strictly forbidden to use the public ammunition. Each soldier will be held strictly accountable for the number of rounds issued to him, and company officers are directed to make constant inspections of the cartridge-boxes and their magazines, in order to assure themselves that there is no improper wastage.

II. The commanding general has also learned that the arms issued to some of the regiments are not of uniform caliber, and, consequently, there has been some disproportion in the corresponding ammunition. As this might not improbably prove a fatal error, it is strictly enjoined upon all commanders to give a careful personal examination of all requisitions for ammunition, and also to superintend the distribution of the same to the men.

III. The attention of the troops in this department is called to the evil practice of tearing down fences and other private property for fire-wood and other purposes. All interference with the rights of citizens is highly injurious in its tendency, and is strictly forbidden. The general hopes that it will only be necessary to remind the troops that they are citizens as well as soldiers, and that, as they take up arms to repel the enemy from our soil, they should still be more careful to preserve it sacred from their own depredations. Prompt and severe punishment will follow all irregularities of this nature in future, and it is strictly enjoined upon all officers to see to the literal execution of this order.

By order of General Lee:

T. A. WASHINGTON,
Captain, and Assistant Adjutant-General.

RICHMOND, *November* 22, 1861.

Governor MILTON,
Tallahassee:

We shall not recognize any action of Colonel Dilworth in contravention of instructions sent to him. General Trapier has gone to Fernandina and will assume command at once, and thus bring matters into proper order. His command extends to the Choctawhatchee, and not to the Chattahoochee, as you supposed.

J. P. BENJAMIN,
Secretary of War.

COLUMBIA, *November* 26, 1861.

Hon. J. P. BENJAMIN,
Secretary of War:

You telegraphed me that instead of sending me Gregg's regiment or others you would send some North Carolina regiments to us. If you could send another it would be of great service, particularly if armed. You must judge if an attack on Charleston is intended, for if it is we will want at least six more armed regiments there, the line is so long.

F. W. PICKENS.

HEADQUARTERS PROVISIONAL FORCES,
Charleston, November 26, 1861.

Capt. T. A. WASHINGTON,
Assistant Adjutant-General, Coosawhatchie:

CAPTAIN: I have received a dispatch from Lieutenant-Colonel Black that he has received reliable information that the enemy has landed at Otter Island and Fenwick's Island. The abandonment of the ports of course leaves the streams Ashepoo and Paw Paw open, as, from what I learn from Captain Walker, they cannot be immediately obstructed. Forces are required for each river. I have none at my disposal. I shall, however, in addition to the movement of the Rifle Regiment, South Carolina Militia, send two companies of Orr's regiment, to act with Lieutenant-Colonel Black on the main, and annoy, if not stop, the enemy if he attempts to pass through Dobson Creek.

Meantime the work of fortifying and arming progresses slowly, but, as there is but little more powder to be had, the number of our guns will not assist us very materially. I beg to represent the want to the general commanding, that it may be supplied, if possible.

I am, very respectfully, your obedient servant,

R. S. RIPLEY,
Brigadier-General, Commanding.

HEADQUARTERS,
Coosawhatchie, November 26, 1861.

General R. S. RIPLEY, P. A.,
Charleston, S. C.:

SIR: The commanding general directs me to say that the enemy can land on all the islands he can approach with his armed vessels, but he will hardly find it to his advantage to hold them after they have been pillaged. Urge forward, therefore, the obstructions to the Ashepoo and Edisto, and see if laborers cannot be obtained on the line of rivers to be obstructed.

The deficiency in powder is a serious calamity, and the general desires you to furnish these headquarters with a statement of what is at your disposal on account of the Confederate States. The State has in addition 14,175 pounds of cannon powder, which it will no doubt distribute for the defense of Charleston.

Col. William V. Mallard is reported to be at Jacksonborough, on the Edisto, with two companies of infantry. As he is not mentioned in your report of troops furnished this office on your departure, you will please inform these headquarters in what service he belongs.

Very respectfully, your obedient servant,

T. A. WASHINGTON,
Captain, and Assistant Adjutant-General.

HEADQUARTERS THIRD MILITARY DISTRICT,
Hardeeville, November 26, 1861.

Capt. T. A. WASHINGTON,
Assistant Adjutant-General, Coosawhatchie, S. C.:

SIR: I inclose you a copy of a communication from Lieutenant-Colonel Colcock, and although I have indorsed my approval of his application for howitzers, I nevertheless need some guns at Red Bluff and New River Bridge at once, if in your reach.

The enemy are evidently sounding and examining our rivers with reference to Savannah, and to retard their approach towards it via New River would be only secondary to doing so via Tybee and Pulaski. I am desirous of taking the offensive, but, without artillery, any display with my small infantry and cavalry force would prove of little avail against any expedition of respectable numbers.

I feel assured of an onward movement towards Red Bluff whenever our enemy gets a hint of its strategic importance.

It is not only difficult to get the pile-driver, as proposed at our last interview, but mechanics also. I am now endeavoring to procure chains and anchors from Savannah, and, by the aid of the rafts as supports to the chain cables, present a very strong resistance to any advancing boats. When I get the pile-driver I will sink piles and flats likewise.

I have an expedition out to-night, and hope to produce such an impression upon the marauders as will make them less venturesome, for some few days at least, and afford me better opportunity of carrying on my defenses on New River.

Respectfully, yours,

THOS. F. DRAYTON,
Brigadier-General, Commanding.

[Inclosure.]

HDQRS. LOWER SQUADRON MOUNTED REGIMENT,
Bluffton, November 26, 1861.

Brigadier-General DRAYTON,
Hardeeville:

GENERAL: I sent out a guard boat last night, under command of Sergeant Mikell; he returned this morning with a boat load of negroes and plunder, whom he captured while making their way to Bull Island.

About three nights ago Baynard's man Cyrus sent two negroes (William and Paddy, supposed to be trustworthy) to Bull Island to reconnoiter, with instructions to return the same night. They remained on the island two days, and then returned stealthily during Cyrus' absence and enticed off portions of their families. Last night William attempted to repeat the operation, but was caught and brought over to me. I have had him tied, and, together with the negroes captured by Mikler, placed under a guard and sent off to Hardeeville, with instructions to report to you. Some of them belong to the Baynards, who I believe are at Hardeeville, to whom they can be delivered there. Most of them belong to Mr. James Pope, who I am told is at Robertsville. You will please communicate to him the fact of their arrest. Mr. Farr will inform you what disposition he wishes made of his boy. I thought it necessary, both for the example to the other negroes and to save so much property, that these negroes should be placed inside of our lines and in a place of safety.

Our vedettes who have come in so far report all quiet this morning. I have omitted to mention that a barge of considerable size, and filled with men, approached Hunting Island Landing yesterday morning. On the reception of the intelligence I ordered out a detachment of infantry and one of cavalry and hurried down in person to reconnoiter, but the enemy was in full retreat, having probably heard our drum and retired without attempting to land. These boats are getting rather impertinent, and we want one or two howitzers down here. I wish you would telegraph to General Lee, requesting him to send me down two howitzers in addition to the cavalry which he wrote me this morning he was trying to get to me.

I inclose a list of the names of the negroes sent, with the names of their owners.

Respectfully, your obedient servant,

C. J. COLCOCK,
Lieutenant-Colonel Mounted Regiment.

HEADQUARTERS CAMP MARION,
November 27, 1861—7 a. m.

[Brig. Gen. THOMAS F. DRAYTON:]

GENERAL: The expedition to Bull Island, about which I wrote you, left here last night about 10.30 o'clock, consisting of a detail of about 40 men from Major Smith's command, under command of Capt. Manning J. Kirk. It was conducted by him with great prudence and ability and proved a complete success, resulting in the capture of 38 negroes, most of them belonging to Joseph Baynard. By my directions, after the party were embarked, fire was applied to the fodder and corn houses, which were completely destroyed. From what I can learn from the negroes there were no Yankees on the island last night. My impression is that they only come over in the day-time for foraging purposes and leave at night. As some of our wagons are going to Hardeeville for stores, I have ordered the prisoners sent up to Hardeeville, under a proper guard. Please have them delivered to their owner, Mr. Baynard, who, not being in the village, I suppose must have returned last night to Hardeeville.

Please telegraph this information to General Lee, from whom I received a letter yesterday, saying he was making an effort to send me down a re-enforcement of cavalry, and request him to hasten them forward, as I have but little doubt that the enemy will attack us soon in retaliation for our Bull Island expedition. I wish you would send down a regiment of infantry as soon as possible.

Respectfully, your obedient servant,

C. J. COLCOCK,
Lieutenant-Colonel, Comdg. Lower Squadron Mounted Infantry.

P. S.—I neglected to inform you that Baynard's fellow (Pompey) had to be killed to prevent his escape. Captain Young and his party arrived late last night and shall have every assistance I can render.

[Indorsement.]

General Drayton takes pleasure in forwarding the inclosed letter to General Lee, and trusts the next one may result in the capture of some of the Lincolnites. Cavalry, artillery, and transportation are our great wants.

THOS. F. DRAYTON,
Brigadier-General, Commanding.

SAVANNAH, GA., *November* 27, 1861.

Capt. T. A. WASHINGTON,
Assistant Adjutant-General:

SIR: As directed in Special Orders, No. 2, Headquarters, Coosawhatchie, November 17, 1861, I proceeded to Fernandina and to the batteries along the coast to examine the condition of their armament, and have the honor to make the following report:

1st. The batteries on Amelia Island are not yet completed; some of the guns are to be changed, and others have yet to be mounted. These are, one 10-inch rifle gun; one 32-pounder rifle gun; three 8-inch columbiads; four army and four navy pattern 32-pounder guns; two 24-pounder guns; and of field guns, two 3-inch rifle guns; four 6-pounder bronze guns; one 6-pounder iron gun.

The guns in position (barbette) are well mounted, except an 8-inch columbiad, which has an unequal bearing on the platform. It is being remedied by letting the pintle bolster deeper into the pintle cross. In the columbiad carriages yellow pine is substituted for oak, and I directed an additional iron strap, to secure the braces, to be added to each brace. I may add that all the columbiad carriages on the coast are made of yellow pine, and are additionally strengthened in the same way.

The guns are all supplied with the necessary equipments; have all the implements for firing hot shot and for preparing and firing shells, and are provided with shot, shells, fuses, and ammunition for 70 rounds each.

I have directed a few articles to be sent to Colonel Dilworth. He asked for 45 sabers and 1,000 Enfield rifles.

2d. The battery on the south end of Cumberland has four 32-pounder naval guns *en barbette.* The carriages, platforms, and guns are in excellent order, but the battery is almost deficient in implements. There are no shells; 50 rounds of powder and shot for each gun. Orders have been given for its supply at once, and until furnished spare implements and shells have been sent from Amelia Island.

3d. The battery on Jekyl Island has one 42-pounder gun *en barbette;* four 32-pounder navy guns *en barbette.* They appear to work well, and have each about 60 rounds shot and shell; not a sufficient number of the latter. This battery is scantily furnished with implements. I have arranged to send them, through Lieutenant Harden, acting ordnance officer at Brunswick, all that will be required.

4th. Saint Simon's batteries have one 10-inch columbiad; one 8-inch columbiad (in process of mounting); two 42-pounder guns; five 32-pounder guns. The guns and carriages work well, except the 10-inch columbiad, which bears too heavily on the pintle bolster. This was directed to be remedied by cutting away a small part of the chassis. The battery is supplied with implements; each gun has about 75 rounds of shot and shell, with the ammunition. But as the guns are to be distributed in several batteries, I conceived it proper to order additional stores. (See requisition for depot at Brunswick.)

5th. Fort Pulaski has five 10-inch columbiads *en barbette;* six 8-inch columbiads *en barbette;* two 10-inch mortars *en barbette;* three 8-inch columbiads in casemate; two 42-pounder guns in casemate; twenty 32-pounder guns in casemate; one 24-pounder gun, plank casemate. The guns and carriages are in excellent condition; have an abundance of all kinds of implements, fuses, &c. Each gun has about 120 rounds of shot and shell. Some of the fuses are imperfect; these I am renewing with new ones from the Augusta Arsenal.

The fuses in a number of instances are imperfect in several batteries; as fast as they can be made others are supplied. The two mortars have but 70 shells between them. I have ordered an additional supply to the fort, and have recommended two 12-pounder field howitzers to be placed so as to flank the ditch.

6th. Fort Jackson [Ga.] has one 32-pounder navy gun (rifled); five 32-pounder navy guns; three 18-pounder guns. They are in good order, and are supplied, or being supplied, with the necessary implements, &c. Each gun has about 60 rounds.

7th. Battery on Green Island has one 10-inch rifled gun (caliber 6.4); one 10-inch columbiad; two 8-inch columbiads; two 42-pounder guns; four 32-pounder guns. The rifle gun has just been mounted. I fired from it, and with $9\frac{1}{2}°$ elevation attained a range of about $1\frac{3}{4}$ miles. The guns and carriages work extremely well; they have everything to make their fire effective. The battery is supplied with about 60 rounds to a gun; has a portable shot-furnace, which I think too small for this point.

8th. Thunderbolt battery has one 8-inch gun (columbiad); three 18-pounder guns. The battery is in good order, and has about 50 rounds to a gun.

The batteries in the neighborhood of Savannah are well served, and with the allowance of ammunition will do very effective service.

I have advised in every case the adoption of ricochet firing. This, if the guns are not fired too rapidly, will, in my opinion, enable all the batteries to make a good defense against shipping. To make the men more deliberate, particularly in the commencement of an action, the gunners should not be permitted to fire but a certain number of rounds in an hour, and the loading be by "detail."

There has been some trouble in firing shell from several of the batteries; the fuses in some instances were imperfect, and the fuse plugs improperly driven in others. I have made arrangements for a new supply of fuses as rapidly as they can be supplied at the Augusta Arsenal, and have given instructions so as to insure the proper loading of shells, &c.

Some of the regiments on the coast are armed with shot-guns and sporting rifles. They have little or no ammunition. I propose to put up for the shot-guns a blank cartridge, to fire a small linen bag containing twelve buck-shot.

I requested the State Ordnance Officer to give me the calibers of the rifles, to make fixed ammunition for them. I will furnish each regiment with a caliber gauge, and it will enable them to furnish me with the kind and quantity of cartridges required.

Fire and light balls, rockets, fuses, port-fires, fixed ammunition and cannon powder, implements and gun carriages, are required most at present. These I have been engaged on at the Augusta Arsenal, and I will repair thither and push the force employed there as much as possible in supplying the above deficiency. I find it necessary to be there to superintend the works in construction, as there is no one there of sufficient experience in artillery or ordnance duties to direct matters.

In an order from the Ordnance Officer, received in October, I was directed to obtain reports from all the batteries along the coast of Georgia and Florida as far as Apalachicola, with the view of furnishing those batteries with ordnance and ordnance stores. Some of these reports have been received, and I will prepare the arsenal to supply their wants.

In conclusion, I will state that the powder mills at the arsenal have been delayed in their work. On my return there I will work them at once night and day, and expect to turn out from 300 to 500 pounds of cannon per day. If possible, this amount shall be increased.

I have the honor to be, very respectfully, your obedient servant,

W. G. GILL,
Lieutenant-Colonel, Ordnance Officer.

RICHMOND, VA., *November* 29, 1861.

His Excellency FRANCIS W. PICKENS,
Columbia, S. C.:

MY DEAR SIR: I have received your letter of the 24th instant,* and thank you for writing so freely.

Generals Evans and Pemberton will be sent to General Lee immediately.

The deficiencies of which you speak in the character of your brigadier-generals will, I hope, be compensated for by the presence of General Lee and the addition of General Pemberton.

More than half the amount of powder received was ordered to be furnished to General Lee. The whole amount was less than that asked for by you.

In regard to arms, I wish indeed that I had more to give you. Governor Letcher has now 500 for you in addition to the 500 previously furnished. This is but a small supply, but will be increased as fast as our means will admit.

Very respectfully and truly,

JEFFERSON DAVIS.

WAR DEPARTMENT, C. S. A.,
Richmond, November 29, 1861.

His Excellency Governor MILTON,
Tallahassee, Fla.:

SIR: The President has received your letter of the 19th instant in regard to the condition of things in Florida, &c., and has referred it to me for reply.

Since the date of your letter the arrival of General Trapier and the organization of the military district under his command have doubtless put an end to the apprehensions you suggest, and render it, therefore, unnecessary for the President to avail himself of your proffered services. We rely, nevertheless, with confidence upon your vigilant and zealous co-operation in all our efforts for the defense of Florida against the common enemy. Your excellency may rest assured, and you may assure the patriotic people of your State, that you shall not be overlooked in our efforts for the common defense. Of this the arrival, I hope by this time, of the munitions, &c., requested by Judge Baker and the measures of preparation organized by General Trapier have already given you some assurance. No effort shall be intermitted by the Confederate Government to insure the safety of your State, either now or hereafter.

Respectfully, your obedient servant,

J. P. BENJAMIN,
Secretary of War.

---

* Not found.

HEADQUARTERS,
Coosawhatchie, S. C., December 3, 1861.

Hon. J. P. BENJAMIN,
Secretary of War, Richmond, Va.:

SIR: In a letter received to-day from Col. John S. Preston, whom I had assigned to the duty of mustering into the service of the Confederate States such troops as might offer themselves for the war from the State of South Carolina or be transferred by the governor, it is stated that the only transfers made up to this time are four companies for twelve-months' service. Even for twelve months the recruiting is very languid; for the war not one company has yet offered, and not one new regiment will be organized in three months. The entire levy will be for terms less than the war, and generally for twelve months, for local defense and special service. I fear that there will be great delay in organizing even such a force as can be armed, unless some measures can be resorted to to procure men.

I have received an application from J. C. B. Mitchell, Montgomery, Ala., to furnish arms to a regiment of that State on my own terms, and have also been informed that Col. Charles C. Lee, Thirty-seventh Regiment North Carolina Volunteers, has written to Governor Clark to know if his regiment could not be transferred to this State and armed. I consider that the arms at my disposal are for the troops of Georgia and South Carolina.

I yesterday visited Port Royal Sound, with the view of organizing a light force to cut off, if possible, the enemy's marauding parties on the islands. No attempts have yet been made on the main-land, nor could I discover any indication of any movement. The fleet in large force lay extended across the sound from Hilton Head to Bay Point, perfectly quiescent, and no troops were visible except a picket at Hilton Head Ferry.

General Lawton reports that the enemy has evacuated Tybee Island.

I have the honor to be, very respectfully, your obedient servant,

R. E. LEE,
General, Commanding.

HEADQUARTERS,
Coosawhatchie, December 4, 1861.

General R. S. RIPLEY,
Commanding, &c., Charleston, S. C.:

GENERAL: Will you please inform me whether the Marion Artillery mentioned in your letter of the 4th,* now preparing for field service, is the battery referred to in General Gist's communication, of which you were notified, and whether the Washington Artillery is intended by the governor to be attached permanently to Stevens' Legion, or for general service in the field?

Your plan of occupying the country between the Edisto and Combahee and occupying Edisto Island would be advantageous, if you had sufficient troops and guns to retain such an extent of country; but unless you can make the line sufficiently strong, or at least have the means of withdrawing the troops, it will, I fear, expose them to be taken in detail. If all the force was concentrated at advantageous points, I think the defense of the approaches would be more effective. I do not know

---

*Not found.

whether you intend the forts at Tar Bluff, Rhett's Bluff, Edisto Inlet, &c., to be temporary and for the protection of the property in their vicinity, or permanent.

R. E. LEE,
General, Commanding.

HEADQUARTERS DEPARTMENT OF SOUTH CAROLINA,
Charleston, December 5, 1861.

Capt. T. A. WASHINGTON,
Coosawhatchie:

CAPTAIN: I have the honor to acknowledge the receipt of a letter from the commanding general of the 4th, and one from yourself of the same date. I telegraphed to General Gist to ask him what battery was intended by him, and received the answer as follows:

De Saussure said the Marion Light Artillery and the Germans would be ready by to-day. Call upon the commanding officer Fourth Brigade South Carolina Militia.

From information here neither the Marion nor the German sections will be ready for two or three days, nor do I believe they will be ready for a week. The Washington Artillery commenced its preparation some time ago by my direction, and was called out. Meantime, while absent, it was intended to attach it to the Stevens Legion, and the governor had an idea of also attaching Boyce's company of so-called light artillery. The Washington Artillery, however, have not mustered into Confederate service, and I doubt whether they will, and they stand now as a company of State troops temporarily in Confederate service, with State guns (six pieces, three caissons, battery wagon, and forge), and horsed partly by State and partly by Confederate horses. Their preference is to a regiment of militia artillery of South Carolina; but I should have no hesitation in making them perform any duty they are capable of.

With regard to the intention, if more troops can be got, to hold in advance and reoccupy Edisto, it seems to me as far forward as we can go with safety from Charleston the better we are for its defense. Now, occupying positions to defend the rivers Ashepoo, Paw Paw, and Combahee involves taking position on the main only. The rivers will be obstructed above the batteries. Paw Paw will be defended by two 24-pounders recovered by Lieutenant-Colonel Black, and two light 4-pounders. The other rivers I had intended to defend with two 12s each, and to let a section of light artillery be with each battery, and to have such a supporting force of infantry and cavalry to support them as it may be possible to give or the necessity demands, the defense to be made either permanent or temporary, as circumstances might dictate, and to have for its object the protection of that section of country from which most of our subsistence must be drawn. As it stands now, the enemy can run up to the railroad at any moment and cut our communication at once in his barges, ravage the plantations on either side, and return. The obstructions will detain his vessels, it is true, but, unguarded, will be removed speedily, and his barges can come at any time. There is not even the show of a force to render him cautious, and it has been reported to me by Lieutenant-Colonel Black that the enemy's officers have made several pertinent inquiries from negroes with whom they have had intercourse with regard to our armament on the rivers. Each of the positions being on the main, retreat to the railroad is easy, over a low, flat country, impracticable in many places except by the roads, and these tolerably secure so long as the defenders have a force of light artillery. The infantry force, unless a large quantity [is] at our disposal, need be no larger than to support the artillery against a sudden attack and give confidence to the population. Moreover, with a small force in position, the enemy, it appears to me, will be obliged to take time if he wishes to cut our communication and land in strength.

With regard to Edisto, with the three rivers held as proposed, our inland navigation south of Jehossee being gone, we can block Dawho on both sides of the Edisto Ferry, or one to be established at Pineberry or vicinity. The obstructions there can be defended by riflemen, assisted by light guns from Willstown Bluff, the place of obstruction on Paw Paw. If it be possible to place another battery on Edisto or Seabrook's Island, if an enemy passes he cannot cut off the troops on Edisto, who can gain the main before he can remove the obstructions. Not many are wanted there, if they can, under a proper officer, be made moveable and vigilant to protect property and to retire.

The troops on John's Island, should the enemy attempt to run by and force Church Flats battery, can fall back through Wadmalaw to a church, which is a fine position for a battle on a small scale, and where the main fight should be on John's Island. If Church Flats are forced, they can cross the Stono by Legareville, between Stono and Battery Island; or, should the enemy land on the main south of Church Flats, the communication is direct to the lines on James Island or the city. As a defense for Charleston it seems to me that the farther out our posts are, so long as our force is not too small here, the longer the enemy will take to make his attack.

I have written at length, as I shall not probably have an opportunity of seeing the commanding general on the subject soon. But we want two or four more regiments to fulfill these objects, and I regret to state that under present arrangements they are coming slowly.

My commission as brigadier-general dates August 15.

I am, very respectfully, your obedient servant,

R. S. RIPLEY,
Brigadier-General, Commanding.

HDQRS. FIRST MIL. DIST., DEP'T OF SOUTH CAROLINA,
Georgetown, December 6, 1861.

Maj. T. A. WASHINGTON,
Department Adjutant-General:

MAJOR: Yours of the 3d received* this morning. The additional 150 32 round shot was received yesterday.

Not having had any authority over the engineers in charge of works here until within the past week, although for two months in charge of the district, I have been unable, until authorized as above, to carry out any of my own views in regard to the defenses of coast in this district. I had already directed the abandonment of the work at North Santee and ordered the guns there removed. They will be temporarily placed on the work at Cat Island. Should I make any other disposition of the guns, I will inform you of it. I would place them higher up the river, but there is no position for them without incurring heavy expense in piling, &c., the land being all swamp or rice land and below the level of

*Not found.

the daily tides. The first point would be 10 miles above the present position, leaving many plantations below it entirely exposed.

I can use these guns to greater advantage on the main than at any point on the banks of the Santee. At present my entire available force is employed in the completion of the south and Cat Island redoubt.

I desire to call the attention of the general commanding to a matter, and in the absence of any instructions on the subject it is proper, I believe, that I should inform him that I have directed the officers under me commanding at the different posts in this district immediately on the coast that, should it be apparent that the enemy intend to make an effort in force to occupy any portion of this coast and it be evident that they will succeed in establishing themselves or actually succeed in doing so, they direct the rice planters to destroy all the rice and provision crops on their plantations; and, in the event of their failing so to do, to cause it to be destroyed themselves as a military necessity; the negroes to be removed also by force, if necessary.

With a view to this, I sent to each rice planter on the adjacent rivers some three weeks since a circular recommending that provision be made with as little delay as possible for the probable removal of their negroes, with subsistence for one year, to different points inland, not less than 15 or 20 miles from the coast, the plantation flats and boats with which each planter is supplied readily furnishing the transportation by the rivers, beyond the reach of their gunboats and vessels; also informing them that I would endeavor to make such arrangements that, on their requiring it, a military force would be furnished them to insist on obedience on the part of the slaves to their masters' orders.

In many instances these suggestions have been complied with, and such arrangements are being generally made. Over two-thirds of the rice crop of the State is made in this neighborhood, and as the entire crops are in the different barn-yards, it would be disastrous in many ways should our enemies ever succeed in possessing themselves of so large an amount of provisions, particularly valuable to them for reasons too numerous to mention here.

So satisfied am I that our true policy is to destroy all we cannot remove or hold, that unless otherwise directed I shall carry out the instructions that I previously mention having given. I do not, however, intend that they shall take possession quietly or without a struggle while I have the means of opposing them.

Respectfully, your obedient servant,

A. M. MANIGAULT,

Colonel Tenth Regiment, Commanding First Military District.

RICHMOND, *December* 7, 1861.

Governor PICKENS,

Columbia:

I have ordered three regiments—two of Tennesseeans and one of Virginians—to your State. Several more will follow. Two batteries of flying artillery have been sent and one more will follow, and one regiment of Mississippians have been ordered to Savannah. You are kept in constant remembrance.

J. P. BENJAMIN,

Secretary of War.

HEADQUARTERS,
Coosawhatchie, December 7, 1861.

General R. S. RIPLEY,
Commanding, &c., Charleston:

GENERAL: I have read with attention your letter of the 5th instant. I regret to learn that the Marion Light Artillery is not yet prepared for the field. When it is ready please inform me whether it will be required in the vicinity of Charleston.

Unless more field artillery can be obtained, it will be almost impossible to make head against the enemy, should he land in any force. I understand from your letter that the Washington Artillery is only temporarily in Confederate States' service, and suppose, therefore, cannot be calculated upon for general service. Being partly equipped by the State and partly by the Confederate States causes embarrassment in supplying it with necessary articles. It is very desirable that the battery should enter the Confederate service so soon as to be rendered as efficient as possible.

The defense of the rivers Ashepoo, Paw Paw, and Combahee, for the protection of the railroad, is of the greatest importance, and I trust may be speedily accomplished.

As the positions occupied will be on the main, the withdrawal of the troops, in case of necessity, can be easily effected. Moreover, the protection of that section of the country, upon [which] you rely for subsistence, is very desirable. The only difficulty I see to the measure is the want of troops to insure successful resistance should the enemy land in force. The three rivers being defended as proposed, the passage through Dawho and at Church Flats being obstructed, preclude the enemy's approach to the railroad. It would be also desirable to prevent his occupation of Edisto, but whether fixed batteries can now be erected of sufficient strength I think is doubtful. It will also, I fear, be impossible to obtain the regiments which you think necessary for the purpose. I can learn of no regiments in South Carolina entering the service. Several have been offered to me from other States, but they are all unarmed, and I have none for them.

Very respectfully,

R. E. LEE,
General, Commanding.

GENERAL ORDERS, No. 4.

HEADQUARTERS,
Coosawhatchie, S. C., December 7, 1861.

I. The recent inspection by the medical director of the department discloses the existence of much sickness among the troops. No special means can be devised for banishing measles, but catarrhal affections, pneumonia, and rheumatic complaints are produced, in many instances, by bad selection of sites for camps. They should always be located on high and dry ground, exposed to the healthful influences of the sun. It is believed that typhoid disease is developed by the close air of tents, the want of personal cleanliness, the neglect of proper police, and the prolonged occupation of the same ground of encampment. Commanding officers are particularly desired to establish proper sinks, remote from the tents, and to cause the daily removal of all garbage and offal. The tents must be frequently emptied and ventilated and the bedding thoroughly aired and cleansed. A proper attention to these measures on the part of commanding and medical officers will do much to mitigate disease and promote the health and efficiency of the men.

II. The commanding general finds it necessary to urge upon the officers in every department the practice of strict economy in all purchases and expenditures. Commanding officers will see that the regulations in this respect are rigidly observed, and that the supplies for the Army are properly cared for and used. The good of the service and the comfort of the troops demand strict attention to this subject.

By order of General Lee:

W. H. TAYLOR,
Assistant Adjutant-General.

COLUMBIA, *December* 8, 1861.

Hon. Mr. BENJAMIN,
Secretary of War:

I am greatly obliged to you for the regiments promised and the flying artillery companies. I began to fear you had forgotten us. I start twenty companies with our State arms in the morning and more coming in. The fleet at Saint Helena cannot be counted. Please push on your troops, for by Thursday we will begin to feel the enemy.

F. W. PICKENS.

WAR DEPARTMENT, C. S. A.,
Richmond, December 8, 1861.

Maj. Gen. R. E. LEE,
Coosawhatchie, S. C.:

SIR: Your letter of 3d instant was received on the 7th. Since its reception I have telegraphed, announcing that measures had been taken to re-enforce you with three batteries of field artillery and three regiments of infantry, and that several other regiments would be sent. The three on the way to you are Donelson's brigade, of two Tennessee regiments, and Starke's regiment. They were all ordered to re-enforce General Floyd, but did not reach him in time to prevent his retreat. His whole force has now been withdrawn from Western Virginia, and I expect further to send you Russell's Mississippi regiment, Phillips' Georgia regiment, Waddill's Louisiana battalion, and perhaps some others. Floyd's army is now on railroad near Wytheville, and as soon as it has been inspected and furnished with its necessary supplies of tents, camp equipage, &c., say in about five or six days, the additional troops just mentioned will be sent you, unless some unforeseen exigency shall render it impossible. I am firm in my purpose not to give a musket to a man enlisted for less than the war (or three years, which is the same thing), and therefore I beg that you will inform Governors Pickens and Brown that if they have no "war" troops ready to receive the arms you still retain in your hands, you will at once arm the other regiments mentioned in your letter, and if they are unable to promise the troops immediately, you will please write Colonel Mitchell that you are authorized by this Department to arm his regiment, and to order it to Savannah or Charleston for that purpose. I had nearly forgotten to say Colonel Dowd's regiment of Mississippians, unarmed, has been ordered to Savannah to receive arms from you if Georgia has no "war" troops to receive them, and must therefore be armed before Colonel Mitchell's regiment. Keep me advised of your wants, that I may send you everything our means will permit.

Your obedient servant,

J. P. BENJAMIN,
Secretary of War.

GARDEN'S CORNER, *December* 8, 1861—11.30 p. m.

Capt. T. A. WASHINGTON,
Assistant Adjutant-General, Coosawhatchie, S. C.:

CAPTAIN: Half an hour ago I received information from Captain Maffit that a small force of the enemy were landing at Cunningham Point; that with my company from Page's Point he would attack them. Just now I have by a courier further information from Captain Maffit that the enemy are landing in force at Cunningham Point, landing continuously from boats and flats. Upon conference with Colonel Dunovant, who is now in my quarters, he will take his command to the junction of the road from Cunningham Point with the main road from Pocotaligo to this point. We will await further orders. Shall we move on to the attack provided the enemy does not advance to the road occupied by Colonel Dunovant? Colonel Dunovant is senior colonel.

Very respectfully, your obedient servant,

JAMES JONES,
Colonel Fourteenth Regiment South Carolina Volunteers.

RICHMOND, *December* 9, 1861.

Col. GEORGE DEAS,
Dublin Station, Va.:

Hasten forward Donelson's Tennessee brigade and Starke's regiment to Charleston, S. C., as already ordered. Answer by telegraph.

S. COOPER,
Adjutant and Inspector General.

EXECUTIVE DEPARTMENT,
Tallahassee, December 9, 1861.

Hon. JEFFERSON DAVIS,
President of the Confederate States of America:

SIR: For some time before his death General Grayson was rendered *non compos mentis* by disease, and acted upon suggestions. Satisfied of this fact, and with the view so far as was possible of protecting him from imposition, I requested his attendants to invite my attention whenever he should be called upon to discharge any official duty. This, however, was not at all times practicable, nor perhaps possible. As an illustration, upon one occasion I was called upon at night by one William J. Turner, of the vicinity of Tampa Bay, and requested to commission him and others as officers of a cavalry company. I refused to do so. This was about 10 o'clock at night. In half an hour after a dispatch came, addressed to General Grayson and myself, bringing information that the enemy were landing near Saint Mark's. General Grayson was confined to his bed (which he never left alive), and before 2 o'clock I left the capital by railroad, with a company of light artillery and one of infantry, with the aid of other troops near the place, to repel the invasion. The enemy, however, not landing, I returned to the capital, and learned that Turner had departed with orders from General Grayson under which his company has since been mustered into the Confederate service. I am now informed, by men of high respectability and undoubted veracity and standing in the country, that Turner has 116 men mustered into the service, and many of them upon horses which could not stand a day's march. This company is in the vicinity of Tampa Bay, a region of country where cavalry cannot possibly be of any use. That point (and indeed all others in Florida), if it can be defended from invasion, will be by artillery and infantry. Also that the quartermaster (McKay), in the purchase of supplies for said company, is paying from $1.50 to $2 per bushel for corn, and is hauling it from 20 to 60 miles, in wagons (with the teams) hired at $7 per day. One of the gentlemen who gave me this information also informed me that his own wagon and team are hired at that price. This company is not one of those recently raised by W. G. M. Davis, but is an additional company, authorized by the order of General Grayson, obtained at a time when he could not have been responsible for any act that he might have done.

This is but one fact in relation to the abuse which cannot but grow out of the presence in this State of such troops in the Confederate service. Doubtless the same facts, though perhaps not to the same extent, exist in the supply of every other company of cavalry recently raised for the Confederate service, and every reflecting man in the country is becoming alarmed at the uncalled-for waste of the substance of the land at the very time when it should be husbanded; and throughout the State the people are becoming indignant that such bodies of unarmed men and idle horses should be reared up among them, with no prospect but to consume the means of support for the women and children, cripple the usefulness of the armed troops for defense against the enemy, and bring ruin upon the people and disgrace upon the Confederate Government.

These troops have been raised by authority of the War Department in disrespect to State authority and in disregard of State rights; and, in addition to the fact of vital ruin they are bringing upon the country, against which it is my duty to and I do most solemnly protest, the tendency of the assumption and exercise of such power by the Confederate Government is to sap the very foundation of the rights of the States and is to consolidation. The worst feature of Black Republicanism was that which threatened to ignore State boundaries and the rights of States as free, sovereign, and independent parties to the compact known as the Constitution of the United States of America. The sinuosities of the policy of that party were not seen or comprehended, and the great body of the people, in their devotion to the Union, were blind to the fact that inroads were constantly but quietly being made upon the guarantees secured by the Constitution. Had the effort been made by act of Congress to elect the President, Representatives in Congress, and Federal officers generally by the people, regardless of State political organization, the attempt would have been so open and glaring, that every man of intelligence and patriotism throughout the country would have declared it a usurpation of power and a violation of constitutional authority. That would have been so palpable as not to have escaped any intelligent mind. Yet the effect would not have been half so ruinous as is the policy pursued by the War Department in assuming to raise up armed bodies of men within the limits of a State in disregard of the constituted authorities of the State. And why? The answer is, that the first, being seen and comprehended as a flagrant invasion and usurpation, would have roused the people in resistance throughout the length and breadth of the land; the last is so insinuating as not to have alarmed any one, and hence good and true men are found advocating it, without thought, as a right. Well, admit and exercise it as a right, and let it be continued, and before the lapse of a century such bodies of men will be reared up within the limits of the States by some able and ambitious Executive of the Confederate Government as to enable him to override the constituted authority of the States and destroy the last vestige of human liberty. Is this an unreasonable conclusion? Is it half so unreasonable as the facts which now exist in the United States? "When we see a President making war without the assent of Congress; when we behold judges threatened because they maintain the writ of habeas corpus, so sacred to freemen; when we see justice and law trampled under the armed heel of military authority, and upright men and innocent women dragged to distant dungeons upon the mere edict of a despot; when we find all this tolerated and applauded by a people who had been in the full enjoyment of freedom but a few months ago," we may be admonished that there may, in time, be danger to us, unless we meet with our opposition at the very threshold every invasion of the rights of the States, whether that invasion be intentional or not. I have no thought that a man could be found who would say that the course pursued by the War Department is intended as a usurpation or in derogation of the rights of the States. But we must forget the teachings of history to suppose that men will not be what men have been. Look again at the people of the United States. Once, who more firm in the maintenance of chartered guarantees than they? Who more watchful of their rights or more quick to resist aggression than they? So devoted were they to the sacred cause of freedom, that a temple in one of their chief cities has been denominated the "Cradle of Liberty." And yet where are they now? Their Constitution openly violated; their laws trampled under foot; their press muzzled; the freedom of speech a thing of the past and they applauding. Would they have believed this if they had been told it fifty years ago? Had they been as watchful in this as in former ages, and had checked aggression at its incipiency, they would not now have been as they are; and unless we shall be watchful of our rights, we may in an age to come be as they are. What has been may again be, if we neglect that maxim of patriotism, "Eternal vigilance is the price of liberty."

I have the honor to be, sir, very respectfully,

JOHN MILTON.

HEADQUARTERS,
Coosawhatchie, December 9, 1861.

Col. R. G. M. DUNOVANT,
Commanding, &c.:

COLONEL: The Thirteenth Regiment South Carolina Volunteers, Col. O. E. Edwards, has been ordered to take the road towards Garden's Corner and to halt at the first convenient spot beyond Pocotaligo. This is intended as a precautionary movement, and should you need support, you will call upon Colonel Edwards to join you. In the event of not being required, Colonel Edwards is ordered to return to his camp this evening. You are desired to use all the force under your command in driving the enemy from the main whenever he may land within your reach.

I have the honor to be,

R. E. LEE,
General, Commanding.

HEADQUARTERS,
Coosawhatchie, December 9, 1861.

Colonel [R. G. M.] DUNOVANT,
Commanding, &c.:

COLONEL: A dispatch has just been received from Colonel Jones, stating that the enemy was landing at Cunningham Point, and asking whether you should move to the attack, provided the enemy does not advance to the road now occupied by you.

The general commanding directs me to say that if the enemy attempts to effect a landing on this side you will attack him and drive him back.

W. H. TAYLOR,
Assistant Adjutant-General.

HEADQUARTERS,
Coosawhatchie, December 10, 1861.

General J. C. PEMBERTON,
Commanding Fourth Military District, South Carolina:

GENERAL: Captain Ives reports that the obstruction placed in the Combahee River, even should it stop the advance of an enemy, would arrest him within 2½ miles of the railroad, and unless prevented by a strong force he could easily reach it by land. There is no defense of this corner projected, nor could one be advantageously arranged. The work, however, is partially completed, and is therefore of some benefit. Two 12-pounders are placed at Tar Bluff, with a view of opposing the ascent of the river. They can make but slight resistance, especially as they are unprotected by defensive works, and being within 1½ miles of Field's Point, a good landing place for the enemy, they can easily be captured.

If an obstruction can be placed in the Combahee below the bluff it would give more stability to the battery, and perhaps prevent the enemy from attempting the ascent of the river. The width is about 200 yards and the depth at least 40 feet. It would therefore require great labor to obstruct it. I understand, however, that the planters interested in the project are willing to furnish labor and material, and the matter is left to your discretion.

Very respectfully,

R. E. LEE,
General, Commanding.

SPECIAL ORDERS, No. 17. } HEADQUARTERS,
Coosawhatchie, S. C., December 10, 1861.

I. The coast of South Carolina will be divided into five military districts:

The First, or Eastern District, will extend from Little River Inlet to the South Santee River, under the command of Col. A. M. Manigault, headquarters at Georgetown.

The Second, beginning at the South Santee, will extend to the Stono River and up Rantowles Creek, under the command of Brig. Gen. R. S. Ripley, headquarters at Charleston.

The Third will comprise the country between the Stono and Ashepoo Rivers, under the command of ———, headquarters at Adams Run.

The Fourth will extend from the Ashepoo to the Port Royal entrance, thence through the Colleton River and Ocella Creek to Ferebeeville, under the command of Brig. Gen. J. C. Pemberton, headquarters at Coosawhatchie.

The Fifth will embrace the country between the last-named boundary and the Savannah River, under the command of Brig. Gen. T. F. Drayton, headquarters at Hardeeville.

* * * * * * *

V. The Third Military District, as organized in Paragraph I, is for the present attached to the Second.

By order of General Lee:

W. H. TAYLOR,
Assistant Adjutant-General.

STATE OF SOUTH CAROLINA, A. AND I. G. O.,
Columbia, S. C., December 12, 1861.

General R. E. LEE,
Commanding Southern Department, Coosawhatchie:

GENERAL: Having understood from unofficial sources that you feel somewhat embarrassed as to the control and disposition of the State troops in service, in consequence of conflict of orders, I have the honor to state that no orders have been issued at any time from this office which can in the slightest degree conflict with your implied or expressed wishes. In fact, I know of no orders but those requiring troops of the State to report to you or your subalterns for duty upon requisitions made. The troops of the State are entirely without any reservation under your control, and the only irregularity attending the matter, as far as this office is concerned, is that requisitions for troops are often made by subalterns instead of coming through the department office.

I would assure you again of the most hearty and sincere co-operation of the State authorities in all possible matters; of their earnest desire to carry out your designs and wishes when made known to them, and their readiness to respond to any call you may make upon them to the utmost extent of their ability. Permit me to add that they do this the more cheerfully, as you possess their entire confidence.

I have just read this letter to the governor, and he approves and indorses my expressions of confidence and support.

I have the honor to inclose a copy of my orders* under act of the general assembly of the State, and as soon as the militia organizations can be relieved and their places supplied by volunteer troops I shall no longer have any distinct State troops in the field, but all will have taken Confederate service.

Allow me to say that the troops now being sent forward are sent in accordance with the instructions of Lieutenant-Colonel Preston, assistant adjutant-general. I have given orders for the fitting up of two additional batteries of light artillery, making five State batteries in all, and have written to ask for the guns of our battery in Virginia, as the term of service of the men who are with it expires in January next.

Let me ask of you to inform me at once of any irregularity that can be remedied by State authority, and it will be promptly attended to.

With great respect, I am, your obedient servant,

S. R. GIST,
Adjutant and Inspector General of South Carolina.

---

*Not found.

HEADQUARTERS,
Charleston, S. C., December 13, 1861.

General D. S. DONELSON,
Commanding Third Brigade Tenn. Vols., Charleston, S. C.:

GENERAL: The general commanding directs that you should proceed with your brigade to Coosawhatchie, S. C., as soon as the quartermaster at this place (Maj. H. Lee) can furnish you with the necessary transportation. Directions have already been given to him to that effect.

Very respectfully, &c.,

T. A. WASHINGTON,
Assistant Adjutant General.

CHARLESTON, S. C., *December* 16, 1861.

Hon. J. P. BENJAMIN,
Secretary of War, Richmond, Va.:

SIR: Your letter of the 8th instant, forwarded from Coosawhatchie, has just been received. Two of the batteries (Thornton's and Leake's) and two of the regiments (Fulton's and Savage's) mentioned in your letter have arrived. I hope the others named will be dispatched without delay.

I have notified Governors Pickens and Brown that unless they had troops from their States "for the war" ready to receive the arms at my disposal, I should issue them to regiments from other States that have offered themselves for service in this department. On being informed by General Lawton that he had been advised by Governor Brown that he had none from Georgia, I directed him to arm the Mississippi regiment (Colonel Dowd). On the application of General Trapier for re-enforcements, having no other regiment available, I have directed General Lawton to send the Mississippi regiment to Fernandina, where they have only 1,300 men.

The Mississippi regiment, with some Georgia companies that have been mustered into the Confederate States service for the war, will absorb all the arms intended for Georgia troops. There are several companies in this State organized for the war, recently raised, and unarmed, attached to Colonels Orr's and Dunovant's regiments, that will require so many arms, as not to leave more than sufficient for one regiment. If a regiment is not furnished by South Carolina, I will receive either Colonel Mitchell's or Col. C. C. Lee's regiment from North Carolina. The latter officer is a graduate of the West Point Academy, and I believe before his recent resignation was in the Ordnance Corps. He served in Virginia as lieutenant-colonel of Colonel Hill's regiment, North Carolina Volunteers.

Could more arms be had for the troops for the war, as I believe, there would be no difficulty in procuring men. There is great need of more heavy guns, but knowing the constant demand in every section of the country for arms and ammunition, hesitate to make requisitions. If, however, twenty could be spared for this department they would be of great benefit—8 or 10 inch guns, 42 and 32 pounders, for water defense, and 8-inch howitzers, 24-pounders or less, for land defense.

The land defenses around the city, commencing on the coast side of James Island, extending to Wappoo Creek, thence to Ashley River, across the neck between Ashley and Cooper, and from the branch through Christ Church Parish to the sound, are in good state of progress, and will now give steadiness and security to our troops in any advance of the enemy from any of those quarters, and afford time to move troops to meet them. The works have been mostly constructed by labor furnished by the planters. I hope they will be completed this week. The batteries in the harbor are in good condition, and if properly served should arrest the approach by the channel. Wappoo Creek is also provided with batteries in addition to those previously constructed at the mouth of the Stono, which should stop vessels by that direction. They form part of the lines of land defense and points of support where they touch the creek.

I have the honor to be, your obedient servant,

R. E. LEE,
General, Commanding.

CHARLESTON, *December* 16, 1861.

Hon. J. P. BENJAMIN:

Tennessee regiments arrived. Want what can be spared from other points. Require heavy guns, if available. Land defenses around Charleston progressing. If batteries are well fought, enemy ought not to succeed by water approaches. Eighty vessels of enemy counted at Port Royal on the 12th.

R. E. LEE.

RICHMOND, *December* 16, 1861.

General R. E. LEE,
Charleston:

I send you six 32-pounders, with barbette carriages. They will leave here on Wednesday. Have sent you Waddill's Louisiana battalion and Ector's Georgia regiment. Will send you Russell's Mississippi regiment and Phillips' Georgia Legion in a day or two. Will you want any more heavy guns?

J. P. BENJAMIN,
Secretary of War.

COOSAWHATCHIE, *December* 17, 1861.

Hon. J. P. BENJAMIN:

In addition to the six 32-pounders, require guns and howitzers on traveling carriages for land defense. Understand they can be had at Norfolk. Have written on the subject.

R. E. LEE.

SPECIAL ORDERS, No. 22. } HEADQUARTERS,
Coosawhatchie, S. C., December 18, 1861.

Brig. Gen. N. G. Evans, C. S. Provisional Army, having reported at these headquarters, pursuant to instructions from the Secretary of War, is hereby assigned to the command of the Third Military District of South Carolina, as set forth in Paragraph I, Special Orders, No. 17, current series, from these headquarters.

T. A. WASHINGTON,
Assistant Adjutant-General, C. S. Army.

HEADQUARTERS,
Coosawhatchie, S. C., December 20, 1861.

Hon. J. P. BENJAMIN,
Secretary of War, Richmond, Va.:

SIR: I am much in need of guns for land defense and the protection of the rivers extending into the country. I have understood that there are carronades at the Norfolk navy-yard unemployed. Please, if practicable, send me eight 42-pounder corronades on chassis carriages, with a supply of shot, grape, shell, and primers, implements, &c., complete, with as little delay as possible.

I have the honor to be, very respectfully, your obedient servant,

R. E. LEE,
General, Commanding.

[Indorsement.]

Lieutenant-Colonel Gorgas, for immediate attention.

J. P. B.

On the 17th December three 32-pounder heavy guns. On the 21st December two 8-inch columbiads were sent to General Lee, and to-morrow one 8-inch columbiad and one 24-pounder siege gun will be sent.

Very respectfully,

L. GIBBON, *Captain.*

DECEMBER 30, 1861.

Eight 42-pounder carronades were sent from Norfolk navy-yard to General Lee December 27, as per invoice received from Commodore Fairfax. The ammunition will be sent from here to-day.

J. GORGAS,
Lieutenant-Colonel, Chief of Ordnance.

RICHMOND, *December* 20, 1861.

General R. E. LEE,
Charleston:

I have no objections to your giving arms to any companies mustered for the war, as requested by Governor Pickens. It is not necessary to reserve them for an organized regiment unless you prefer to do so.

J. P. BENJAMIN,
Secretary of War.

SPECIAL ORDERS, No. 23.

HEADQUARTERS,
Coosawhatchie, December 20, 1861.

* * * * * * *

III. The following regiments and battalion of South Carolina volunteers, recently mustered into the service of the Confederate States, are assigned to the command of Brig. Gen. N. G. Evans, and will immediately proceed to such destinations as that officer may designate, viz: Sixteenth South Carolina Volunteers, Col. C. J. Elford; Seventeenth South Carolina Volunteers, Col. J. H. Means; Laurens battalion, Maj. G. S. James.

* * * * * * *

By order of General Lee:

T. A. WASHINGTON,
Assistant Adjutant-General.

COOSAWHATCHIE, *December* 21, 1861.

Hon. J. P. BENJAMIN:

Have already stated, after arming organized corps would arm companies for the war if arms remained.

R. E. LEE.

HEADQUARTERS,
Coosawhatchie, December 23, 1861.

General R. S. RIPLEY,
Commanding, &c., Charleston, S. C.:

GENERAL: I am gratified to learn by your letter of the 21st instant that the battery at Church Flats is ready for action and the obstruction prepared for closing the channel. The troops that you have advanced from Charleston into the Third Military District must remain for the present under the command of General Evans. I hope by this time that the Sixteenth and Seventeenth Regiments and Laurens battalion of South Carolina Volunteers have reached him. As soon as he can be properly re-enforced, the regiments that it may be desirable to have around Charleston can be recalled into your district. In the mean time I request that you will furnish the necessary supplies to the troops, upon proper requisitions, and aid General Evans in every way in your power in the organization of his district and by furnishing him all needful information and facilities that he may require.

I wish as soon as possible that you would inform me of the number, &c., of troops present in the Third Military District, as it may be some time before General Evans can furnish me with an official return.

I agree with you as to the importance of holding John's Island and the post at Church Flats, and beg that you will re-enforce General Evans, if necessary, to enable him to do so.

I have the honor, &c.,

R. E. LEE.

SPECIAL ORDERS, } No. 24. }

HEADQUARTERS,
Coosawhatchie, S. C., December 23, 1861.

I. Brig. Gen. Maxcy Gregg, C. S. Provisional Army, having reported at these headquarters, in compliance with instructions from the War Department, will report to Brig. Gen. J. C. Pemberton for duty with the South Carolina troops serving in the Fourth Military District.

II. Brig. Gen. D. S. Donelson, commanding Tennessee Brigade, and Col. W. E. Starke, commanding Sixtieth Virginia Volunteers, will report their commands to Brigadier-General Pemberton for duty in the Fourth Military District of South Carolina.

* * * * * * *

By order of General Lee:

T. A. WASHINGTON,
Assistant Adjutant-General, C. S. Army.

COOSAWHATCHIE, *December* 24, 1861.

[MAGRATH]:

MY DEAR SIR: I have just received your note announcing the meeting of the Convention about to take place at Columbia. The exposed condition of the State and the presence of a powerful enemy on her shores will naturally occupy the earnest consideration of that enlightened body. I do not think that any suggestion from me will be necessary or even useful, as I feel certain that every measure requisite for the protection of the State or her citizens will be adopted. In compliance, therefore, with your kind request to make to you any suggestions that may seem to me required by present circumstances, I think it only necessary to repeat more emphatically than perhaps I have been able to do in person the urgent necessity of bringing out the military strength of the State and putting it under the best and most permanent organization. The troops, in my opinion, should be organized for the war. We cannot stop short of its termination, be it long or short. No one, I presume, would desire to do so; no one, therefore, will continue in service longer than the war requires. The disbanding and reorganization of troops in time of peace is attended with loss and expense; what must it be in time of war, when it may occur at periods that might otherwise prove highly disastrous?

I tremble to think of the consequences that may befall us next spring when all our twelve-months' men may claim their discharge. At the opening of the campaign, when our enemies will take the field fresh and vigorous, after a year's preparation and winter's repose, we shall be in all the anxiety, excitement, and organization of new armies. In what different condition will be the opposing armies on the plains of Manassas at the resumption of active operations! I have thought that General McClellan was waiting to seize the advantage he would then possess.

I beg you will put a stop to this lamentable state of affairs. The Confederate States have now but one great object in view, the successful issue of their war of independence. Everything worth their possessing depends on that. Everything should yield to its accomplishment.

There is another point to which I would invite your attention. The best troops are ineffectual without good officers. Our volunteers, more than any others, require officers whom they can respect and trust. The best men for that position should be selected, and it is important to consider how it can be effected. It would be safe to trust men of the intelligence and character of our volunteers to elect their officers, could they at the time of election realize their dependent condition in the day of battle. But this they cannot do, and I have known them in the hour of danger repudiate and disown officers of their choice and beg for others. Is it right, then, for a State to throw upon its citizens a responsibility which they do not feel and cannot properly exercise? The colonel of a regiment has an important trust, and is a guardian of the honor of the State as well as of the lives of the citizens. I think it better for the field officers of the regiment in the State service to be appointed by the governor, with the advice and consent of its legislature, and those in the Confederate service by the President and Congress. It would also, in my opinion, add to the simplicity and economy of our military establishment to conform to the same principle of organization. That adopted by Congress is formed by the united wisdom of the State representatives, and is followed in its army. It would be well for the State governments to adopt it, as far as circumstances will permit. Special corps and separate commands are frequent causes of embarrassment.

It is useless for me to suggest that measures be taken to develop the military resources of the State; to advance the fabrication of powder, arms, and all the necessaries of war, as well as the production of bountiful supplies for her troops and citizens. The strictest economy should be enforced in every department and the most rigid accountability required of its officers. I have not been able to get an accurate report of the troops under my command in the State. I hope it may be as large as you state, but I am sure those for duty fall far short of it. For instance, De Saussure's brigade is put down at 3,420 men. When last in Charleston (the day inquired) I was informed that in one regiment there were 110 men for duty in camp on the Race-Course and in the other about 200. Colonel Branch, I am told, had only about 200 men with him at Rockville, though I have had no official report of his retreat from there.

The companies of mounted men in the service are very much reduced. The Charleston Light Dragoons and the Rutledge Mounted Rifles have about 45 men each. The companies of Colonel Martin's regiment are very small. One of them—Captain Fripp's—reports 4 commissioned officers, 9 non-commissioned officers, and 19 privates. It is very expensive to retain in service companies of such strength, and I think all had better be reorganized.

I have only on this line for field operations Heyward's, De Saussure's, Dunovant's, Jones', and Edwards' regiments from South Carolina and Martin's cavalry. General Ripley writes that Elford's and Means' regiments are poorly armed and equipped and at present ineffective, and that the organization of the troops thrown forward on James Island is so brittle that he fears it will break. The garrisons at Moultrie, Sumter, Johnson, and the fixed batteries—the best and most stable of our forces—cannot be removed from them; neither can those at Georgetown, and should not be counted among those for operations in the field.

You must not understand that this is written in a complaining spirit. I know the difficulties in the way, and wish you to understand them, explain them to the governor, and, if possible, remove them. Our enemy increases in strength faster than we do and is more enormous. Where he will strike I do not know, but the blow when it does fall will be hard.

I am, &c.,

R. E. LEE.

HEADQUARTERS,
Coosawhatchie, December 24, 1861.

General A. R. LAWTON,
Savannah, Ga.:

GENERAL: Your communication of 23d instant* has been received. The general commanding is glad to learn that instructions have been given to officers commanding batteries to withhold their fire till the enemy's vessels are within effective range of the guns, and trusts that this practice will in all cases be strictly adhered to. The general hopes that the threatening approach of the enemy's boats will stimulate the officers and the troops of your district to press forward the projected earthworks and defenses to a speedy completion. As no further re-enforcements can be spared to send to you, it will be necessary, should your command require strengthening, to call upon the governor of the State of Georgia.

The general has been informed that three 32-pounders are on their way from New Orleans, and as they will probably be sent by Augusta, he is desirous that you should make arrangements to have them forwarded from that place to Savannah. Two of them will be sent to Gen-

---

* Not found.

eral Trapier at Fernandina, and the third placed at such point as may be, in your judgment, most necessary. Should the guns be unprovided with carriages, Colonel Gill has been directed to supply them.

The guns for General Trapier the latter has made a requisition for, and desires to have forwarded to him without delay.

Very respectfully,

W. H. TAYLOR,
Assistant Adjutant-General.

RICHMOND, *December* 25, 1861.

General R. E. LEE,
Coosawhatchie:

Yours of 20th received. On the 17th sent you three 32-pounders from here, and ordered three more sent to you from New Orleans. On the 21st sent you two 8-inch columbiads. Will send you to-morrow one more 8-inch columbiad and one 24-pounder siege gun.

J. P. BENJAMIN,
Secretary of War.

HDQRS. FIRST MILITARY DISTRICT, DEPT. OF S. C.,
Georgetown, December 25, 1861.

T. A. WASHINGTON,
Assistant Adjutant-General:

MAJOR: The schooner Prince of Wales, from Nassau, loaded with salt, fruit, &c., having been chased by a steamer and bark of the Federal Navy, ran into North Inlet, one of the harbors of this district, the enemy's vessels not being able to follow her, and she getting aground when inside, and having been hulled several times by their shot, boats were sent in to take her, when the captain fired the vessel and escaped with his crew. The enemy proceeded to tow her out, when a mounted detachment of Captain Tucker's company arrived, opened fire from the north side of the inlet upon the boats, and forced them to abandon their prize and return to their ships.

About 4 o'clock in the afternoon five boats filled with men put off again from the vessel, to come in either to land on North Island or again take possession. Lieutenant Harllee, with 6 men (picket guard), Company D, Tenth Regiment, as soon as they came within reach, fired upon them and continued to do so, eventually driving them back to their vessels. The boats' crews in both instances returned the fire of our men. No one hurt on our side. Detachments sent to support the picket guards did not arrive in time to take any part in the affair. I regret to state that the vessel has since burned to the water's line, and is, with her cargo, a total loss. She was owned, I believe, by the house of John Fraser & Co., Charleston.

I remain, respectfully,

A. M. MANIGAULT,
Colonel, Commanding First Military District.

HEADQUARTERS SECOND DISTRICT SOUTH CAROLINA,
Charleston, December 25, 1861.

CAPTAIN: I have the honor to acknowledge the receipt of a letter from General Lee, of the 23d instant, and inclose herewith a memorandum of the troops in General Evans' district.* I shall do everything in my power to furnish his troops and give him every information and facility. The Laurens battalion moved yesterday, but I fear that the Sixteenth and Seventeenth Regiments will not be ready for service for some days.

Referring to a letter of former date from General Lee, in which I am directed to give my attention to extended operations to meet the predatory excursions of the enemy (supposing the Stono fleet to have demonstrated his abandonment of an attack on Charleston), I beg to say that I shall do so to the utmost of my ability. The enemy will hardly attempt any such incursions between Charleston and Stono, the limit of my command, and, if he does, the locality is pretty well guarded. Northward there is but little to attract for plunder until he gets to Bull's Bay; thence to the limits north, the Santee country, it is very difficult of approach on account of the intricate navigation; it is rich, however, and invites attack on that account. I have there only the newly-raised command of Maj. Edward Manigault. I intend to re-enforce it by Lieutenant-Colonel Moore's battalion (made up of the extra companies of Orr's regiment) as soon as it is armed completely; Lieutenant-Colonel Moore is endeavoring to raise his battalion to a regiment, in which I hope he will succeed.

I also inclose a memorandum of the troops in the Second Military District.* The force is nominally large, and would allow re-enforcement of other points, but from the peculiar position, and the character of the country, which does not admit of celerity of movement without an almost unprecedented amount of land and water transportation. These facilities I shall of course endeavor to improve, but with the crippled mechanical resources of this city it may take some time. Brigadier-General Evans wrote to me day before yesterday requesting that I would place a steamer at his disposal for the ferry at John's Island; I have done so. Meantime I have been informed that there is a steam-flat nearly completed, which will cost about $4,500. I have ordered her inspected, and were John's Island in my command should have her employed as a ferry-boat. The ferry is in bad order, and it will be difficult to make a rope ferry of it on account of the diagonal position of the landings.

The State Troops Rifle and Seventeenth Regiment South Carolina we will probably break up as soon as they are called in, and we shall probably get one respectable well-armed regiment from them. It would facilitate its formation if those troops could be relieved as soon as possible after the Sixteenth and Seventeenth South Carolina Volunteers take the field.

The lines on James Island, were the troops in readiness to occupy them, might be considered finished. As they are not, 50 or 100 hands for three or four days will be necessary to put the works in a little permancy. The lines on Christ Church will be done in the course of three days, and will be quite strong; Lieutenant Blake has carried them quite down to the inland navigation, covering the landing. One company of Hatch's regiment has been ordered to take post as a lookout on the islands to the northward of the city, to give notice of the approach of an enemy and protect, as far as possible thereby, the rice-boats coming from Santee. It seems to me important to get as much of rice to market as may be, should our communication be in danger of being interrupted.

The lines on the Neck are progressing but slowly, for want of the

* Not found.

hands. I trust, however, as a law has been passed authorizing impressment of negro labor, that as soon as Christmas is over we shall have a considerable force, without the necessity of making use of the law.

It seems that there will be a good deal of difficulty in arming and equipping the companies of light artillery in Major White's battalion and of Captain Boyce. Major White is still garrisoning the batteries at Wappoo, which I shall endeavor to increase in armament with the two 12-pounder ship guns from the Theodora. The 24-pounder I think of placing on Castle Pinckney. The one-gun battery on the right of the James Island line is constructed, and will be armed and garrisoned with one of White's companies speedily; but for guns, caissons, or harness for them I am utterly at a loss.

From such observation as has been lately made the sunken fleet is gradually disappearing.

I have omitted to mention that the Marion Artillery will be ready for the field, with four pieces, within a day or so; they are State troops.

I am, very respectfully, your obedient servant,

R. S. RIPLEY,
Brigadier-General, Commanding.

HEADQUARTERS THIRD MILITARY DISTRICT,
Adams Run, December 26, 1861.

GENERAL: I have the honor to report, for your information, that my express has just arrived, with the intelligence that the enemy, with a force of ten vessels, are advancing up Wadmalaw Sound, firing, as they advance, both upon Edisto Ferry and White Point. These points, it is understood, are being occupied by the enemy. Please send me re-enforcements; my force is only 250 strong.

Truly, yours,

N. G. EVANS,
Brigadier-General, C. S. A.

MARIANNA, *December* 26, 1861.

Hon. J. P. BENJAMIN,
Secretary of War:

SIR: Inclosed is a report from General Floyd, who is in command at Apalachicola; also a copy of a report made by Lieut. B. Mickle, who, at my request, was sent by General Bragg upon an application for a skillful engineer and artillerist.

Much has been accomplished by the forces in service by State authority since Colonel Hopkins was ordered from and left there, who is in Confederate service; and immense expense has been saved, which was being, to say the least, uselessly incurred.

If the Confederate Government will become definitely responsible for the defense of Apalachicola by State authority, the expense will be less and its defense more certain. The forces in State service at Apalachicola have been well equipped and well drilled, and are generally substantial men and men of intelligence, and this body of gallant men cannot enter the Confederate service without breaking up the most efficient organization of State troops unless they will be received in their present organizations. It is extremely difficult to associate forces in the service of the Confederate Government and those serving by State authority harmoniously. If it can be done, no officer is better qualified to accomplish it than General Floyd. Thrice the expense has been incurred and thrice the force assembled for the defense of Fernandina, and yet Apalachicola is decidedly the most important commercial city, and, in a strategic point of view, in the hands of the enemy would afford greater facilities for injury to the South. Both places are worthy of the means necessary to a successful defense.

These matters are respectfully submitted to the consideration of the Secretary of War and President, provided the proposition submitted to establish a military department in parts of Georgia, Florida, and Alabama shall not meet with a favorable consideration. I am now engaged in raising a regiment of infantry in West Florida for service twelve months—Confederate service—to be armed and equipped by the State and for the defense of Apalachicola. There should be at least one artillery company at Saint Andrew's Bay, the entrance to which can be successfully defended by two cannon, 42-pounders, with equipments.

The cavalry companies in State service at Apalachicola I propose to retire from the service. By an order issued by General Grayson, if I was informed correctly, the State troops have been supplied.

I shall return to the capital to-morrow, when I shall be pleased to hear from you.

Very respectfully,

JOHN MILTON.

[Inclosures.]

BRIGADIER-GENERAL'S OFFICE,
Apalachicola, December 18, 1861.

His Excellency Governor MILTON,
Tallahassee, Fla.:

SIR: I have the honor to state to you that there are under my immediate command at this post but 612 men, rank and file, including the two dragoon companies. The additional troops to be sent here, as mentioned by your excellency, have not arrived, nor do I know where they are. If these troops are to come, I would respectfully suggest that it should be at an early day, in order that they may have the all-important advantages of drill to prepare them for battle when it should come. The troops here are improving rapidly under regular drill and discipline and are already quite efficient.

From reports I received I deemed it prudent to remove from Saint Vincent's Island to this place and detain them one white man and two negroes who had been kept there to butcher for this market. From certain indications since I am convinced that the measure was correct, and precludes any possibility of intercourse between them and the United States blockaders. There is no *proof* that such intercourse had existed, but some strong suspicions.

I think it important to request your excellency to appoint a chaplain to this regiment. There will then be no excuse for any of the men leaving camp on the Sabbath to attend church in the city. The restrictions I have necessarily placed upon them in this respect and in the absence of a regular chaplain produce dissatisfaction, although no disobedience.

I am informed by Second Lieutenant Mickle, who was sent to me by General Bragg recently as an engineer, that there are two 42-pounders at Pensacola not in use, and that it is probable they might be, by proper application, easily procured for this place. He also informed me that they can be readily rifled at Mobile. My largest guns here are 32s. If your excellency sanctions it, will it not be advisable to procure these guns at once, have them rifled at Mobile, and forwarded to this post, with about 100 rounds (or less) of balls for each? We could then hold the enemy in check at long range.

I beg to call the above particularly to the notice of your excellency, and trust my suggestion will meet your approval.

The batteries here are all so forward towards completion and their construction approved by Lieutenant Mickle (whose report upon them I have the honor to transmit herewith), that I send him back to Pensacola, having no further occasion for his services. He is not acquainted with artillery drill, else I would have retained him here.

I have the honor to be, your excellency's very obedient servant,

R. F. FLOYD,
Brigadier-General, Commanding.

APALACHICOLA, FLA., *December* 14, 1861.

General RICHARD F. FLOYD,
Commanding Troops at Apalachicola:

GENERAL: In company with Mr. Benezet, who has the supervison of the works, and to whom, by the way, I am indebted for his kindness in showing me the batteries and their bearings on the approaches to the city, I to-day visited the defenses of Apalachicola.

Presuming that I have but little experience in military engineering, I proceed without further apology to give you, in compliance with your request, a brief report as to the efficiency of your batteries.

To my astonishment I found that, though built by men of little or no experience, they differ but little from those around the harbor of Pensacola, and that, too, on points involving mere convenience, or which from surrounding circumstances require a difference. Your magazines are built farther from the guns than those in the batteries at Pensacola, and are therefore not so convenient; and the parapets are not so high in your batteries as in those at Pensacola, but from the nature of the approaches that is to a great extent necessary.

Except a suggestion to young gunners to practice at a target placed where the attacking force would probably be stationed, I know of no other that I can make which would be practicable.

From my limited knowledge of your harbor and the enemy's fleet, I am unable to form an opinion as to the armament he may bring against you, but think I hazard nothing in saying it must be sufficiently heavy to destroy your city at the distance of 2 miles or he must adopt another plan of attack.

I have the honor to be, very respectfully, your obedient servant,

B. MICKLE,
Second Lieutenant, C. S. A.

HEADQUARTERS,
Coosawhatchie, December 27, 1861.

His Excellency FRANCIS W. PICKENS,
Governor of South Carolina, Columbia:

GOVERNOR: I had the honor to receive your letter of the 20th inst.* In a previous [letter] I endeavored to express to your excellency my

*Not found.

entire willingness to arm certain companies of regiments already in the service named by you, provided any arms remained after arming the regiments being organized for the war, but I cannot issue the arms before the arming of the regiments is completed.

If the companies of Captain Blair, McCord, and Rives, which I understand are for the war, and attached by you to Stevens' Legion, were assigned to the battalion commanded by Lieutenant-Colonel Moore, which embraces the six companies attached to Orr's regiment, this battalion would only require one more company for the formation of a regiment, and might then be armed with Enfield rifles. My object is to make the arms available for the defense of the State as soon as possible, and I hope your excellency will aid me in this.

Major James' battalion has been ordered to report to General Evans, who is in great need of troops. General Ripley informs me that Colonels Elford's and Means' regiments will not be able to take the field for some days. In the mean time he has sent forward Colonel Stevens' Legion to re-enforce General Evans.

The enemy is making demonstrations against Wadmalaw Island, and our force there is not strong enough to resist him. Since your letter authorizing me to take command of the State troops in the field, I have felt no hesitation in doing so. Previously, although aware that certain forces were called into service and placed under the command of General Ripley, I did not know when or how it was designed to use them. According to the last returns received the number of troops mustered in Confederate service from South Carolina within the department present for duty is 10,036, including officers, non-commissioned officers, and privates. The strength of the Fourth Brigade South Carolina Militia (De Saussure's), present for duty, including officers, non-commissioned officers, and privates, is reported to be 1,531. Its total strength present and absent is 2,021, and differs from the number stated in your excellency's letter, which is 3,420.

The strength of Colonel Martin's regiment in the field, by the last returns, is 628; the number reported for duty, including officers, non-commissioned officers, and privates, is 567. The number of troops in Confederate States service, as stated above, 10,036, does not include the regiments of Colonels Elford and Means, the Laurens battalion, and the other companies mentioned in your letter, which have arrived since the returns were made. In addition to this force there are two regiments from North Carolina, two from Tennessee, and one from Virginia, and four field batteries.

My object is to inform your excellency of the amount of the force for actual service in the State. You must, however, bear in mind that the garrisons for the forts at Georgetown, of Fort Moultrie, Forts Sumter, Johnson, Castle Pinckney, and the field works for the defense of the approaches through Stono, Wappoo, &c., which embrace the best and steadiest of our troops, cannot be removed from their posts, and must not therefore be included in the force for operations in the field.

The strength of the enemy, as far as I am able to judge, exceeds the whole force that we have in the State. It can be thrown with great celerity against any point, and far outnumbers any force we can bring against it in the field.

I am, &c.,

R. E. LEE,
General, Commanding.

HEADQUARTERS,
Coosawhatchie, December 27, 1861.

General R. S. RIPLEY,
Commanding, &c., Charleston:

GENERAL: I have had the honor to receive your letter of the 25th instant, inclosing a memorandum of the troops under General Evans, and desire to express my gratification at the steps taken to re-enforce and support that officer.

Should you find that the enemy intends a movement against Charleston through the Stono approaches, I desire that you will resist him with all your available force and support General Evans should he be compelled to retire upon you. In the event of the two commands uniting on duty, as the senior officer of course you will direct the operations of the whole. General Evans has been directed in case of necessity to close the avenue through Church Flats; I request you to afford him every facility in completely obstructing it at the proper time.

Please inform me whether Maj. Edward Manigault's battalion has entered the Confederate service for twelve months or for the war. If for the latter period, it might be united to Lieutenant-Colonel Moore's battalion, and, by the addition of the two companies reported by Colonel Preston to have been mustered in for the war by him, would form a regiment for the war. In that event I should apply to the President for the appointment of a colonel for the regiment. Should Manigault's battalion be not enlisted for the war, could you not attach companies raised for the war, which I learn from the governor have been sent to Stevens' Legion, so as to form a regiment? All the companies could then be armed with the Enfield rifles by Colonel Preston, and placed under the command of Col. Carter L. Stevenson (formerly of the old service), or such other officer as the President might think proper. Should detached companies be sent to you by Colonel Preston, mustered into the Confederate service either for twelve months or for the war, I desire you to collect them into battalions and regiments according to their period of service, and place them under the command of such field officers as are at your disposal until their regular field officers are appointed. According to my understanding of the act of the legislature of South Carolina of December 7, 1861, the First Regiment Rifles South Carolina Militia, Colonel Branch, and the Seventeenth Regiment South Carolina Militia, Colonel De Treville, being part of the Fourth Brigade, will not be disbanded on being relieved from service. I do not see, therefore, how the formation of a regiment can be facilitated by relieving them, as you propose, after the Sixteenth and Seventeenth South Carolina Volunteers take the field. As the aggregate strength of the two regiments as reported by you will only make one regiment, namely, 854, should you be able to unite them you are authorized to relieve them from duty for that purpose when their services can be spared.

The measures taken by you to secure the delivery of the rice crops are judicious, and I hope you will do the same to insure supplies of other provisions, corn, provender, &c.

I beg you to use every exertion to complete the line of defenses around the city, and hope you will get a sufficiency of hands as soon as the Christmas holidays are over, and desire that you will take the necessary steps for this purpose.

I will write to the Ordnance Department to see if nothing can be done in supplying Major White's battalion with artillery. As soon as the

Marion Artillery can be got ready for the field, assign it to such station as you think fit.

I am, &c.,

R. E. LEE,
General, Commanding.

HEADQUARTERS THIRD MILITARY DISTRICT,
Adams Run, December 27, 1861.

Capt. T. A. WASHINGTON,
Assistant Adjutant-General, Coosawhatchie, S. C.:

CAPTAIN: I have the honor to report that the enemy commenced firing on my pickets at White Point yesterday at about 12 o'clock. He then proceeded up the Wadmalaw Sound as far as the mouth of the Tugaloo Creek, and shelled the house of Mr. James King for four hours, throwing 10-inch shells, but without effect.

The enemy at the same time made a demonstration at Edisto Ferry on land, though but few were seen. Their drums were distinctly heard by my vedettes at the ferry.

The gunboat that proceeded up the sound was accompanied by a number of row-boats and a barge. From an elevated point I could distinguish the troops aboard. They seemed about 500 on the gunboat to White Point. The enemy sent a few men ashore, and burnt the summer house of Col. James Lezau, which was situated immediately on the water.

As soon as I learned the enemy would attempt to land I ordered Major James' battalion, of 250 strong, and a cavalry force of 30 men to take a concealed position on Slann's Island. I also ordered Captain Walter to bring his battery to these headquarters as soon as possible, whence I detached a section to the support of Major James. They arrived in their position about 4 o'clock. The enemy retired about sundown towards their large vessels now in Edisto Inlet. As it was now probable he would land, and my only available force being the above-mentioned troops, I wrote to Brigadier-General Ripley for re-enforcements, which he readily granted.

I will here report that, having heard the enemy was seen some two or three days since near Rockville, I ordered Colonel De Treville to cross over to John's Island with his battalion and a cavalry force and reconnoiter the enemy, and attack him should he find himself able to make a successful stand. I have made arrangements for the return of this force at Church Flats by a bridge of boats.

Colonels Means and Elford have reported in person, and report their regiments as not yet armed or equipped. They are now encamped near Charleston.

Very respectfully, your obedient servant,

N. G. EVANS,
Brigadier-General, Commanding Third Military District.

HDQRS. FIRST MILITARY DIST., DEPT. OF S. C.,
Georgetown, December 27, 1861.

T. A. WASHINGTON,
Assistant Adjutant-General, Coosawhatchie:

MAJOR: I have never seen or received General Order, No. 1, from General Lee's headquarters, although I have written for said missing number. I have since heard, however, that my reports, returns, &c., are to be made to yourself. This will account for my seeming negligence, as I have been reporting regularly to the headquarters of General Ripley, in Charleston. It is proper (not having [been] informed of any general officer having been appointed to the command of this district), being responsible for this section of country, that I should inform you that a great portion of my force here, consisting of 650 men of Harllee's Legion, will, under the late act of the legislature, be disbanded within a week. Also that Captain Walker's company of horse, Black's battalion, under orders from General Lee's headquarters, has been ordered to report to Colonel Black, and is now on the road to join him. This will leave me with but my own regiment (the Tenth) not more than 800 strong, as the measles and mumps have broken out amongst them; two small companies of State cavalry (volunteers), together numbering 70 men; one section of artillery, 30 men, badly horsed, and 20 mounted riflemen.

With the long line of coast to be watched and guarded, the force that will be left me on the 1st January will scarcely be adequate. I am aware that there are other more exposed and more important districts, requiring all the available force for its defense, and it may not be possible to re-enforce me. I do, however, desire it known of what my means of defense consist, so that more may not be expected of me than my force would warrant. It would be well if I could get another company of cavalry; a battery of artillery also. There is a State battery here, four iron 6-pounders, old carriages, but in good order, with harness and ammunition. Were I furnished with horses I could make good use of them.

Effective force of First Military District after the disbandment of Harllee's Legion.

10th Regiment	800
Two companies cavalry	70
One section artillery	35
Detachment Mounted Rifles	20
	925

Respectfully, your obedient servant,

A. M. MANIGAULT,
Colonel, Commanding First Military Dist., Dept. of S. C.

HDQRS. SECOND DISTRICT OF SOUTH CAROLINA,
Charleston, December 27, 1861.

Capt. T. A. WASHINGTON,
Coosawhatchie:

CAPTAIN: I have the honor to acknowledge the receipt of a letter from General Lee of the date of December 24*. In answer to the inquiries concerning Elford's and Means' regiments, I have the honor to inclose letters from both of those colonels, showing the state of those regiments. Other information respecting them, as well as any knowledge of their or other troops reporting here, I generally get from inquiry after their arrival.

I duly received the dispatch from General Lee concerning General Evans. Previously General Evans had sent to me, and I ordered the Holcombe Legion, about 650 strong, and the best of the new troops, to

*Not found.

move at once. It is at Adams Run before this. I also directed Elford's to be in readiness to move this morning, but received the report inclosed. This and Colonel Means' letter show it to be impossible to depend on either for any support to General Evans for a week at least.

By a reference to the memorandum inclosed yesterday it will be seen that the only disposable troops would be the remainder of Orr's regiment, and that would leave Sullivan's Island with only Dunovant's regiment, acting as artillery, for the defense of that point. It would, I think, be manifestly improper to take a man from Stono, as the enemy are in front of it sounding and making other demonstrations; I do not think with a view to attack, unless they should find the point undefended. I shall, however, do the best I can, and if General Evans calls upon me, shall support him with as efficient a force as I can muster, even at the hazard of weakening the garrisons in the harbor. It appears to me that the importance of defeating our enemy once well on this coast is worth a great deal of risk.

I have directed a telegraph station to be put in operation at Adams Run, which will save General Evans' cavalry and afford information on both points.

Upon Colonel Preston's requisition I have ordered Mr. Lowndes, volunteer aide-de-camp, to proceed to Mars Bluff, and muster in the Pedee Legion. Authority to employ volunteer aides-de-camp on this service was given by General Cooper, and thus far has not been revoked. Mr. Lowndes has already mustered in several corps.

At Stono yesterday a gunboat, reconnoitering, threw a shell at the light-draught steamer supplying the post. The batteries returned it, contrary to instructions, at long range, and the two continued to waste shots for half an hour. I have sent to forbid any more practice of that kind.

It would materially assist in the continuance of our works if Captain Ives could be spared for a few days, as his office is, I learn, now in funds.

I am, very respectfully, your obedient servant,

R. S. RIPLEY,
Brigadier-General, Commanding.

[Inclosures.]

CAMP MOORE,
Charleston, S. C., December 26, 1861.

Brig. Gen. R. S. RIPLEY, C. S. A.:

GENERAL: I have the honor to report that my regiment is not in a position to move with efficiency immediately. One of our companies is unarmed. Of the remaining arms, about 100 have proved defective and are in the hands of the armorer for repair. We have not a bayonet-belt, or scabbard, or cartridge-box in the regiment. Major Eason, the ordnance officer, informed me to-day that these could be procured in eight or ten days. We have about three rounds of cartridges and caps, but I understand that ammunition can be obtained. I have been pressing our requisition for accouterments continually since we have been here, but hitherto without success. So soon as we can procure these we are ready and anxious to march to the point of duty.

Respectfully,

C. J. ELFORD,
Colonel Sixteenth Regiment South Carolina Volunteers.

CAMP LEE, *December* 26, 1861.

Brigadier-General RIPLEY:

GENERAL: In obedience to verbal orders received through your aide, I have the honor to report my regiment as organized but not full. Seven companies are here encamped, comprising in the aggregate 547 officers and men. I have 75 good muskets (percussion) and 415 flint-and-steel muskets utterly unfit for service; no transportation, but have been authorized by the quartermaster to purchase it, and will send agents to-morrow to do so. No knapsacks; 75 cartridge-boxes and bayonet scabbards; no ammunition. I hope to have my regiment full in the course of a week or ten days. I am under orders for General Evans to march as soon as ready to Adams Run.

Very respectfully, your obedient servant,

J. H. MEANS,

Colonel Seventeenth Regiment South Carolina Volunteers.

HEADQUARTERS OF STATE FORCES,

Savannah, Ga., December 28, 1861.

General R. E. LEE,

Commander-in-Chief:

GENERAL: I have assumed command of a division of State troops actually in the field. This, for reasons personal to myself, I had refrained from doing until a question as to their willingness to be transferred to the Confederate service, submitted to them by act of the legislature, had been decided. It is hardly necessary to say that, although in the immediate service of the State for State defense, I hold myself subject to your directions in all military operations looking to that end, and will make such reports, at such times, and to such quarters as you may be pleased to designate.

From conversations with my friend General Lawton I learn that the necessity of this auxiliary force, in the character of a reserve, is fully recognized. I shall labor to render it efficient.

I am happy to add that my personal relations with General Lawton are of such a character as to insure between us the most cordial of feelings and a perfect harmony of action.

I am, general, very respectfully, your obedient servant,

H. R. JACKSON,

Major-General, Commanding State Forces.

DEPARTMENT OF GEORGIA, C. S. A.,

Ordnance Office, Sec'd Mil. Dist., Brunswick, Dec. 30, 1861.

Capt. R. M. CUYLER,

Ordnance Office, Savannah:

DEAR SIR: By General Mercer's direction I write to urge upon you the necessity of sending us more powder. It is his belief, in which all who have seen the batteries concur, that we can whip off the fleet upon the first attack; but that if it is renewed the next day, as in all probability it would be, our powder would be exhausted, and they could pass us without our being able to fire a gun. Officers and men are all confident of success and anxious to redeem the Port Royal disgrace, for so they all consider it, and I think they will if the powder does not give out. You must be able to afford us some by this time, and we will put it to good use and see that none is wasted. I want 20 barrels large grain and 30 barrels fine grain, in all 5,000 pounds, cannon powder. I know you will do all you can.

Very respectfully, your obedient servant,

WM. D. HARDEN,
Ordnance Officer.

General Mercer requests me to add that Fernandina is vastly better supplied with guns and ammunition than we are.

STATE OF SOUTH CAROLINA,
Headquarters, December 31, 1861.

General LEE,
Commanding:

SIR: I have received yours of the 27th and 29th instant.* In the former you make the number of troops mustered into Confederate service from this State under your command 10,036. I inclose with this a correct copy † of the exact number mustered in whose rolls are in the adjutant-general's office, which is correct from the record. You say in yours you do not include the regiments of Colonels Means and Elford nor the companies mentioned in mine. From your remark in relation to the garrisons at Cole's Island and Sumter and Moultrie not being considered troops for field service, I suppose you exclude them also, and perhaps the troops at or near Georgetown. If I am right in this construction of your letter, then the estimates, according to the rolls in the adjutant-general's office, making 17,000, vary but little from yours of 10,036, but if these are added it would make about the same. If this is not the case, and I do not understand you right, then the officers in command of your different districts have not sent you in a full report of the troops mustered in.

As to the suggestion you make in relation to a cavalry regiment, I will cordially unite with you to raise the other four companies, and we have a company now which General Gist is trying to get in for the war unconditionally. There are many offering, and we will try to get enough for the regiment and report to you, so that the President may send an officer to command them.

I regret to hear and to know of the unpleasant feeling amongst the officers under General Ripley, particularly of the junior officer in the artillery. Appointments cannot be made to please all, and none have been made but with an eye single to the strength of the service. Ferguson and Beauregard were appointed supposing they had a company ready to bring right into the battalion of artillery, and their commissions are not to be presented unless this is done first. There is great difficulty in enlisting regulars now, and as a large portion of a company was already enlisted for young Beauregard in New Orleans, I thought it was well to secure a company for our service, and besides I thought it would be very agreeable to all to appoint a son of General Beauregard. The appointment of Kemper as second lieutenant was because he was a brother of the gallant commander of the battery from Alexandria, who was with one of our regiments in service, and because this Mr. Kemper whom I appointed had settled in Beaufort and was ruined by the inva-

* Of 29th not found. † Not found.

sion there. Why these appointments should create such excitement among the junior officers in Fort Sumter I am at a loss to understand.

With great respect and esteem, your obedient servant,

F. W. PICKENS.

HEADQUARTERS,
Coosawhatchie, December 31, 1861.

General S. R. GIST,
Adjutant and Inspector General South Carolina:

GENERAL: General Ripley, commanding in Charleston, reports that the line of intrenchments for the defense of that city may be considered as completed except those between the Cooper and Ashley Rivers. He also reports that he is entirely without troops to defend them, those not required at the forts and batteries being advanced on James Island and beyond the Stono to check the approach and marauding parties of the enemy.

The Sixteenth and Seventeenth Regiments South Carolina Volunteers, as soon as equipped for the field, will be sent to General Evans for similar service. Will you be kind enough to inform me when you can place in the field the other regiments of the State you have called into service?

It will give me pleasure to meet you in Charleston, as proposed in your dispatch of yesterday, after my return from Savannah, where I shall go to-day.

R. E. LEE.

Abstract from monthly report of the Department of Middle and East Florida, commanded by Brig. Gen. James H. Trapier, for December, 1861.

Troops.	Present for duty. Officers.	Present for duty. Men.	Aggregate present.	Aggregate present and absent.
1st Florida Special Battalion Infantry	23	386	455	511
3rd Regiment Florida Volunteers	44	800	889	950
4th Regiment Florida Volunteers	39	664	823	881
24th Regiment Mississippi Volunteers	40	409	614	932
Coast-guard on board steamer General Grayson			45	45
Battalion of cavalry	28	628	674	701
Hopkins' independent troop	4	61	68	80
Owens' independent troop	3	93	105	116
Pickett's independent troop	3	70	73	74
Turner's independent troop	4	90	95	95
Baya's company of artillery	4	62	66	66
Martin's light battery	3	60	65	76
Grand total	195	3,323	3,972	4,527

HEADQUARTERS,
Coosawhatchie, S. C., January 2, 1862.

Brig. Gen. J. H. TRAPIER,
Commanding, &c., Fernandina:

GENERAL: I have not yet been informed whether you have determined to remove the guns from the south end of Cumberland Island. The battery at that point, in conjunction with the fire of Fort Clinch, would add greatly in my opinion to the defense of the harbor. Its fire would reach a ship after it had passed beyond the range of the guns of the fort, and the position, if not occupied, might be used by the enemy. I hope, therefore, you will be able to make arrangements to get sufficient troops from the State of Florida to support the battery; and, if I recollect aright, works could be easily thrown up to defend its rear.

Respectfully, &c.,

R. E. LEE,
General, Commanding.

HEADQUARTERS,
Coosawhatchie, S. C., January 2, 1862.

His Excellency FRANCIS W. PICKENS,
Governor of South Carolina, Columbia:

GOVERNOR: I have had the honor to receive your communication of the 29th ultimo,* inclosing a copy of the resolution adopted by the general assembly at its recent meeting relative to the employment of slaves on works for military defense. I have given instructions to General Ripley to make with your excellency the necessary arrangements and to urge forward the works around Charleston as rapidly as possible. I hope that your excellency will see that his wants in the matter of laborers are complied with.

I beg leave again to submit to your excellency the great need of troops to defend this line, and would respectfully ask that you urge forward their organization with all possible dispatch.

I am, &c.,

R. E. LEE,
General, Commanding.

HEADQUARTERS,
Coosawhatchie, January 3, 1862.

Maj. Gen. H. R. JACKSON,
Commanding First Division Georgia Troops, Savannah:

GENERAL: I have had the honor to receive your letters of the 28th ultimo and 2d instant.† I am much gratified to learn that the division under your command is ready for the defense of the State of Georgia and is placed at my disposal for that purpose. The troops in the Confederate service under General Lawton have already been distributed with a view to the protection of the most exposed points, and particularly to guard the approaches to Savannah. There is no point at which re-enforcements may not be required. I will direct General Lawton to indicate to you where your troops can be of most service, and to designate such points as you may take under your exclusive charge. At present, or until called upon by General Lawton, I beg that you will see that the preparation of your command for service in the field be perfected as far as possible. The camp and garrison equipage and baggage of every sort should be curtailed to the regulation allowance. Transportation ought to be provided and a supply of ammunition for field service. I need not suggest to you the necessity for instituting discipline and a regular and thorough course of instruction for officers and men; your own experience will show you its propriety and benefit.

---

*Not found. †Of 2d instant not found.

I shall be glad to receive from you a return of the strength of your troops and a report of the condition of their arms, equipments, &c.

I am, &c.,

R. E. LEE,
General, Commanding.

STATE OF SOUTH CAROLINA,
Headquarters, Columbia, January 7, 1862.

President DAVIS:

MY DEAR SIR: I have been informed from pretty high authority that the telegraph operator at Wilmington, N. C., and perhaps at Petersburg, Va., were not true to us, and perhaps they use their position to suppress or delay matters of importance. I mention this, and would most respectfully suggest that a secret detective be appointed to ascertain the facts, not only there, but anywhere else that there may be suspicion about.

I do not know if it prevails elsewhere in the Army, but I take the liberty to inform you that I fear the feeling of General Ripley towards General Lee may do injury to the public service. His habit is to say extreme things even before junior officers, and this is well calculated to do great injury to General Lee's command. I do not think General Ripley means half what he says in his energetic way, but others construe it differently.

From a copy of the report of forces sent to General Lee by General Ripley, up to December 1, I find many very important omissions. I suppose it must be from inadvertence, for I do not think Ripley at all exact in relation to infantry. I have sent General Lee a correct return. General Lee is a perfect head, quiet and retiring. His reserve is construed disadvantageously. I find him all that a gentleman should be, and all that ought be expected of a thorough and scientific officer. The two are in contrast.

I have sent forward lately from this camp five new regiments, not yet reported to Lee by Ripley.

The enemy are only feeling the different points at present. It will be difficult to approach Charleston with less than 50,000 men; and that will be through North Edisto, over John's Island or Stono and over James' Island. They will endeavor to reach the Ashley about 1 mile above Fort Johnson.

If the strength of the forces under General Pemberton were nearer Adams Run it would be safer for Charleston, for if they should happen to cut off the railroad at Pocotaligo, it would cut off 10,000 of our most efficient forces so they could not approach to defend the city. My private opinion is that they will hardly attack Charleston, at least until towards spring. Savannah may be attacked sooner, but they will have to increase their forces first before any serious move can be made against either place.

It will be more difficult to re-enforce with the feeling rising in the North as to the danger of collision with Great Britain. If I could be certain of 3,000 arms from any quarter, I could send forward 3,000 more troops. I have given out State arms in the last two weeks to 4,900 men. These arms I got from disbanded companies in the State, with 1,000 sent from Virginia.

With great respect, and very truly, your obedient servant,

F. W. PICKENS.

SAVANNAH, *January* 8, 1862.

General S. COOPER,

Adjutant and Inspector General, Richmond, Va.:

GENERAL: From a paragraph in the Charleston and Savannah journals, to which my attention has been called, I fear I may have inadvertently misled the Department as to my opinion of the strength of the defenses of those cities and of my ability to prevent the enemy from penetrating into the interior of the country. In my letters describing the works and batteries in progress of construction, to which I cannot now refer, I intended to express the hope rather than the confident assurance that when completed, armed, and manned, if properly fought, the enemy's approach ought to be successfully resisted. I am aware that we must fight against great odds, and I always trust that the spirit of our soldiers will be an overmatch to the numbers of our opponents.

Our works are not yet finished; their progress is slow; guns are required for their armament, and I have not received as many troops from South Carolina and Georgia as I at first expected. The forces of the enemy are accumulating, and apparently increase faster than ours. I have feared, if handled with proportionate ability with his means of speedy transportation and concentration, it would be impossible to gather troops necessarily posted over a long line in sufficient strength to oppose sudden movements.

Wherever his fleet can be brought no opposition to his landing can be made except within range of our fixed batteries. We have nothing to oppose to its heavy guns, which sweep over the low banks of this country with irresistible force. The farther he can be withdrawn from his floating batteries the weaker he will become, and lines of defense, covering objects of attack, have been selected with this view.

I have thought his purpose would be to seize upon the Charleston and Savannah Railroad near the head of Broad River, sever the line of communication between those cities with one of his columns of land troops, and with his other two and his fleet by water envelop alternately each of those cities. This would be a difficult combination for us successfully to resist. I have been preparing to meet it with all the means in my power, and shall continue to the end. Any troops or guns that can be withdrawn from other points will greatly aid in this result.

I have the honor to be, your obedient servant,

R. E. LEE,

General, Commanding.

SAVANNAH, GA., *January* 15, 1862.

Lieut. Col. J. GORGAS,

Chief of Ordnance, Richmond, Va.:

COLONEL: During my recent visit to Fernandina I learned from Captain McBlair, C. S. Navy, that two 8-inch columbiads were *en route* for that place in addition to the two that reached there on the 11th. Captain Cuyler, ordnance officer at this place, informs me by a dispatch from your office he is informed that four 8-inch columbiads are on the way to Fernandina, for which he is preparing carriages.

I am glad to find that you can supply these guns, for they will aid materially in the defense of Cumberland Harbor, and I hope that you may be able to furnish others for this point. If you could send one or two columbiads to Savannah and give me six guns, 24-pounders, 32-pounders, or heavier, for Brunswick, I should feel much better satisfied of the strength of this coast. I also request that you will inform me when you send guns or munitions upon the requisitions of others within this department, that I may know their destination and application. I had not been informed of your intention to send the six columbiads to Fernandina.

I have the honor, &c.,

R. E. LEE,
General, Commanding.

P. S.—There is a want of cannon powder at Fernandina. Captain Cuyler will send 2,000 pounds, received from Augusta, for immediate use.

SAVANNAH, GA., *January* 15, 1862.

COMMANDING OFFICER, *Fernandina, Fla.:*

SIR: In reference to the deficiency of accouterments for the troops on Amelia Island, to which my attention was called during my recent visit, I find that, in compliance with my previous orders, 500 sets, on the 21st ultimo, were sent by Captain Cuyler, of the ordnance, to Maj. John G. Barnwell, Fernandina; 500 sets Enfield accouterments, on the 28th ultimo, by Lieutenant Harden, from Brunswick, to Major Barnwell; that on the 31st ultimo Lieutenant-Colonel Gill wrote from Augusta that he would send "300 infantry accouterments to Major Barnwell, Fernandina, in charge of a special messenger."

If these accouterments have been received there is no reason for the deficiency complained of, and I request you will report the fact to my headquarters.

I have directed 300 pairs of shoes to be sent from this place to the brigade quartermaster at Fernandina and some clothing from Columbus, which I understand is at that place. Captain Cuyler will send some cannon powder from here to Captain McBlair (2,000 pounds), which will increase his supply for the 8-inch guns. I also directed when at Brunswick 500 pounds of lead to be sent to Fernandina, to enable the colonel of the Mississippi regiment to make additional cartridges for his regiment. I understood he had powder.

By a dispatch from Richmond I learn that four 8-inch guns are on their way to Fernandina. Carriages have been ordered for them here, but only one is now completed. I understand that these are in addition to the two which reached Fernandina on the 11th instant. Should this be the case, I think one or two of them had better be mounted on the south end of Cumberland Island.

I request this letter to be forwarded to General Trapier.

I have the honor, &c.

R. E. LEE,
General, Commanding.

SAVANNAH, *January* 17, 1862.

General S. COOPER,
Richmond, Va.:

GENERAL: By a communication from the commandant of Saint Simon's Island I am informed that the port of Brunswick is continually blockaded by a heavy side-wheel steamer, and that the enemy's gunboats have been cruising inside of Sapello and the adjacent inlets.

I apprise you of the fact in view of the shipments expected over from Nassau, some of which may perhaps have been ordered to seek access into the ports named.

My letter to the Department of the 15th December reported the coast clear at those points; since then the Federals seem to be on the alert.

The entrance to Warsaw is effectually sealed; a vessel is permanently anchored inside.

Very respectfully,

ED. C. ANDERSON,
Major, Artillery.

HEADQUARTERS,
Coosawhatchie, January 17, 1862.

Hon. C. M. FURMAN,
Commissioner, &c., City of Charleston:

SIR: I have had the honor to receive your letter of the 16th instant* in reference to an ordinance of the State Convention to provide for the removal of property from portions of the State which may be invaded by the enemy and to certain resolutions intended to carry its provisions into effect. Copies of the ordinance and resolutions have been furnished me, and I shall take great pleasure in doing all in my power to aid the commissioners in the performance of the duties required of them.

As regards the probability of the occurrence of the contingencies in which you will be called to act, and of which you ask my opinion, I can only say that, seeing no reason now for apprehension, I think it an act of prudence to make provision in time of security for what would be required in time of danger, and that steps should be taken for the formation of depots, &c. Every arrangement made in anticipation of events which, should they happen, would mitigate their evil consequences.

As regards the information which you may require from time to time to govern your action in relation to the city of Charleston, I suggest that you apply to the Confederate officer commanding in the city, should it not be convenient to refer to the commanding general of the department, as by so doing valuable time may be saved. I shall certainly apprise you of any danger I can foresee.

With great respect,

R. E. LEE,
General, Commanding.

HEADQUARTERS,
Coosawhatchie, S. C., January 17, 1862.

General R. S. RIPLEY,
Commanding Second Military District S. C., Charleston:

GENERAL: In reply to your letter of this date,* relative to the proposed operations against the enemy at North Edisto, I wish to state that when my approval to Captain Ives was given to make the attempt, I did not sufficiently understand the plan to be able to form an opinion as to the practicability of its accomplishing the object. Of this you must judge and of the means to effect it.

General Evans has been apprised of the projected expedition, and

*Not found.

wishes to be informed of the time, place, &c., so as to prevent any collision of our troops.

In a conversation had with General Evans to-day he fears from demonstrations of the enemy that he may be preparing to land on Bohicket Creek, near West Seabrook's, and push forward to the Stono, east of Rantowles Creek, or to Legareville. His troops only extend to Dr. Whitridge's, on the west bank of Bohicket Creek. In the former case they would turn left, and your right. In the latter, with the assistance of his floating batteries, he would endeavor to silence your batteries on Cole's and Battery Islands, and thus ascend the Stono. The paucity of troops in General Evans' district prevents his guarding this route. Can you not forward from the regiments ordered to him, or others that may have reported since, a sufficient detachment for this purpose? Should this not be practicable, I suggest that you hold Orr's regiment in readiness, or advance it to some convenient point, to move at a moment's notice.

I have the honor, &c.,

R. E. LEE,
General, Commanding.

COOSAWHATCHIE, S. C.,
January 17, 1862.

General J. H. TRAPIER,
Commanding in Florida:

GENERAL: Arrangements have been made for running into Musquito Inlet, on the east coast of Florida, arms and ammunition, by means of small fast steamers. The department considers it necessary that at least two moderate sized guns be placed at New Smyrna, to protect the landing in the event of our steamers being chased by the enemy's gunboats. You are therefore desired to send temporarily to New Smyrna some defense of this kind as soon as possible. The cargoes of the steamers are so valuable and so vitally important, that no precaution should be omitted. It will also be necessary to act very promptly, as it is hoped the steamers (two) will arrive within ten or fifteen days.

There are two Parrott guns at Fernandina, if nothing better and more available are at hand, that could be sent to the waters of the Saint John's, and thence as near the desired point as practicable, with ammunition, &c., under an active officer, with their complement of men, &c. But the guns, way, and means are left to your better knowledge and judgment.

I have the honor, &c.,

R. E. LEE,
General, Commanding.

HEADQUARTERS,
Charleston, January 22, 1862.

Brig. Gen. R. S. RIPLEY,
Commanding Second Military District, &c., Charleston, S. C.:

GENERAL: The general commanding directs me to inform you that he has just received a dispatch containing an extract from a letter dated the 19th instant, stating that an officer of the Confederate service, who had been a prisoner at Boston, had reached Norfolk and said that it was understood at the North that two persons, prompted by heavy bribes, had left there to burn the principal bridges on the Wilmington and Charleston Railroad; that the Burnside expedition is to take that road, and that the other fleet, acting in concert, will take the road from Charleston to Savannah, thus isolating Charleston.

The general is of opinion that this may be reliable, and desires that you take such precautionary measures as may be in your power to insure the safety of the railroad from any incendiary attempts within the limits of your district.

Respectfully, &c.,

T. A. WASHINGTON,
Assistant Adjutant-General.

RICHMOND, *January* 30, 1862.

General R. E. LEE,
Savannah:

I send you to-morrow three heavy guns, two of them 10-inch and one 8-inch, equipped complete. Will send three more in three or four days. They are all we can give you. We have no iron carriages, and send wooden carriages.

J. P. BENJAMIN,
Secretary of War.

Abstract from monthly report of the Department of Middle and East Florida, commanded by Brig. Gen. J. H. Trapier, for January, 1862.

Troops.	Present for duty.						Aggregate present.	Aggregate present and absent.
	Infantry.		Cavalry.		Artillery.			
	Officers.	Men.	Officers.	Men.	Officers.	Men.		
4th Regiment Florida Volunteers	37	474					721	777
3d Regiment Georgia Volunteers	28	551					655	823
24th Regiment Mississippi Volunteers	39	443					787	895
Bailey's company of infantry	4	74					78	78
Evans' company of infantry	3	80					83	84
Simmons' coast-guard	4	41					45	45
1st Florida Special Battalion	18	331					502	577
1st Florida Cavalry			35	761			827	867
Hopkins' independent troop			3	76			81	82
Owens' independent troop			2	75			99	120
Pickett's independent troop			2	68			74	74
Turner's independent troop			4	100			115	115
Baya's company of artillery					3	29	34	67
Martin's light battery					3	60	65	76
Grand total	133	1,994	46	1,080	6	89	4,166	4,680

[FEBRUARY 2, 1862.—Requisitions made by the Confederate Government for two and a half war regiments from Florida, twelve from Georgia, and five from South Carolina.*]

* Requisition will be found in Series IV, Vol. I.

STATE OF SOUTH CAROLINA,
Headquarters, February 3, 1862.

President DAVIS:

MY DEAR SIR: My aide, Colonel Duryea, has just returned, and I regret that you should have thought anything of my sending on to claim the arms that belonged to our regiments, if out of use. I said that they belonged to the State, with the equipments, for I sent on all our regiments without charging for them.

I had been informed by the Ordnance Officer of North Carolina that that State had a claim of $2,000,000 for what she had sent on, and inquired of me what course I intended to pursue. I wrote back I had made no such charges at all. Of course I calculated, when the regiments had served their time out and were discharged, they would bring back their arms, for their field officers have all given bonds to the State for their return or to be accounted for. If the war were to end, of course I take it for granted the arms would be ours. The arms received from the old United States arsenal were accounted for by General Jamison at Montgomery, and settled in the transfer he then made of everything taken by us as a State before any other State had acted and before any Confederate Union had been formed at all.

I did not mean to make any unusual claim as long as the arms were in actual service, but only if they were not in use, and I only wanted to state the general principle upon which our claims to the arms rest.

When Colonel Gregg's regiment was discharged his arms were, under my orders, brought to Richmond, to be brought home, and he asked the privilege to reorganize his regiment in Virginia, and asked to retain his arms there and to receive companies commissioned by you, &c. I refused, because I could not do so in good faith to the State. We had companies of our own citizens who were eager to go into service, and as the arms were public property, I had no right to assign them to companies from other States, and if I did so, it would produce great excitement and discouragement amongst our own people.

Mr. Memminger then interceded, and also the then Secretary of War, and joined in an urgent appeal to me to allow Gregg to retain the arms in Virginia, and then Gregg pledged himself to give them alone to companies from our own State. Upon this I agreed to their wishes, but a claim that the arms did not belong to the State I never heard of or imagined at that time.

So, too, with our six pieces of flying artillery, sent on with Company A, under Calhoun, with the harness, caissons, &c. I wrote the Secretary of War to send them back, if possible to spare them, as we needed them much on our own coast, and as the company had not been re-enlisted. He declined, because it would produce a bad effect for South Carolina troops to be sent back at that time from the Potomac line. I acquiesced in it, because, upon reflection, I thought the reason was sound and wise, but I never heard of any claim made that the guns, &c., were not ours. I hope now that I am mistaken in the impression that any claim of that kind is to be set up. But I am informed by Colonel Duryea that the Secretary of War told him that my true way was to charge the Confederate Government for the arms and equipments sent on with our troops, and that this would be the proper course, and that it would be recognized, and the arms, &c., would then be considered as belonging to the Confederate Government and not to the States.

I was not aware that the States had taken this course, but I would be very glad to be informed if Colonel Duryea has understood the Secretary aright, and if so, I will be most happy to try and conform to what has been done by other States and to what is most agreeable to the Confederate Government in the general policy you may direct.

I have no object but to do justice to the State, and surely should never have made any demand at all for the arms until the war was closed if our own State had not been invaded and our arms absolutely needed to put into the hands of regiments now actually mustered into Confederate service. Having been informed that we had arms out of use now, I thought it nothing but right to send for them.

Be so good as to let me know if I am right as to the general information I have received through Colonel Duryea.

I have the honor to be, with great respect, yours, truly,

F. W. PICKENS.

HEADQUARTERS FIFTH MILITARY DISTRICT,
Hardeeville, February 3, 1862.

Capt. W. H. TAYLOR,
Assistant Adjutant-General, Headquarters, Savannah, Ga.:

SIR: I have the honor of acknowledging the receipt of your letter of the 31st ultimo, asking the cause of the "withdrawal of the guns and forces from Red Bluff."

I evacuated Red Bluff, as already communicated to headquarters at Coosawhatchie, on the 1st instant,* because I regarded it as indefensible against gunboats armed with heavy pieces.

With the two 24-pounders and the two short howitzers, aided by the obstructions I had placed 1,000 feet below the fort, any attack from open boats could probably have been repulsed.

As long as I was in expectation of receiving a large gun for the single gun battery marked D on sketch*, I felt disposed to risk keeping the troops at Red Bluff; but when the general of the department told me in the cars the other day that the cannon he had intended for me must under the threatened attack upon Savannah be sent there, I concluded to fall back with the whole command to such a point about 4 miles distant as would not only permit a prompt resumption of the post whenever an 8-inch howitzer or columbiad could be obtained, but at the same time occupy a position near Savannah [and] adjacent plantations as would overcome the negroes, who had just given some evidence of insubordination.

By reference to the sketch accompanying this, the commanding general will observe a sector of fire, A, B, 1,000 yards off from the fort, from whence the gunboats might fire into the embrasures without receiving a single shot in return. The two batteries are connected by a covered way. While I now write, four steamers and gunboats are close up to the chain obstruction below the fort, throwing shells into it. The guns, ammunition, and public property of all kinds have been removed to a place of safety and are now with Captain Elliott's command at Hardee's, in which direction I am now going.

Very respectfully, your obedient servant,

THOS. F. DRAYTON,
Brigadier-General, Commanding.

---

* Not found.

HARDEEVILLE, *February* 3, 1862.

Capt. W. H. TAYLOR,
Assistant Adjutant-General:

The enemy have shelled and burnt Box's and Lawton's houses, on New River. The obstruction near Red Bluff removed, and the sailors are sounding above it. No soldiers on board gunboats. One company cavalry and three of infantry close by, watching them, ready to attack in case they leave edge of water. The shells from guns of steamers picked up 3 miles off.

THOS. F. DRAYTON,
Brigadier-General.

HEADQUARTERS DEPARTMENT OF SOUTH CAROLINA,
February 4, 1862.

General THOMAS F. DRAYTON,
Commanding, &c., Hardeeville, S. C.:

GENERAL: Mr. T. A. Reynolds, overseer of Capt. John Screven, reports that on last Saturday night a party of Federal troops visited Captain Screven's Proctor plantation, and that on Sunday they made their appearance with negroes. After taking a view of Fort Jackson, &c., they retired, without disturbing anything on the plantation. They reached Proctor's by the way of Wright's Cut, which leads through the marsh from Savannah River to Wright River. This information is derived from the watchman (negro) on the plantation, and is believed by Mr. Reynolds.

You are desired to advance a company, mounted or on foot, convenient to throw out pickets to observe the approaches to the Savannah River, and to endeavor to catch or intercept reconnoitering parties of the enemy. I would suggest that they keep themselves concealed by day and take positions by night to accomplish their object effectually. Select a bold and intelligent officer for the service.

I am, &c.,

R. E. LEE,
General, Commanding.

HDQRS. DEPARTMENT OF SOUTH CAROLINA, &C.,
Savannah, Ga., February 4, 1862.

Brig. Gen. THOMAS F. DRAYTON,
Commanding, &c., Hardeeville, S. C.:

GENERAL: Your letter of the 3d instant has been received, and your withdrawal of the guns from Red Bluff is approved. It will be necessary for you to take a line removed from New River, so as to prevent the advance of a land force of the enemy, should one be attempted from New River to Savannah River, sufficiently distant from the former not to be affected by the enemy's gunboats.

You will strengthen this line by artificial defenses, breastworks, abattis, &c., as you best can, and have a sufficient force at hand to attack and drive back an advancing foe. Should this be impracticable, you will hang upon his flank and rear to retard his progress until re-enforcements can reach you. Should a force be landed with which you may consider yourself unable to cope, you will notify General Pemberton, who is ordered to march to your relief. Should you require additional artillery, I can send you two 42-pounder carronades on siege carriages, but have neither harness nor horses for them. These you must endeavor to procure, if wanted.

R. E. LEE,
General, Commanding.

HDQRS. DEPARTMENT OF SOUTH CAROLINA, &c.,
Savannah, Ga., February 4, 1862.

Brig. Gen. J. C. PEMBERTON,
Commanding, &c., Pocotaligo, S. C.:

GENERAL: It has been reported to me by General Drayton that two of the enemy's gunboats, accompanied by two steamers, ascended New River yesterday, and burnt the houses of Mr. Box and Mr. Lawton. The obstruction near Red [Bluff?] was removed, and I have learned that one of the enemy's steamers has passed above it. The guns had been previously removed from the battery at that place. I have also heard that a party of the enemy visited Captain Screven's Proctor plantation, on the Savannah River, and that three appeared there on Sunday, accompanied by negroes, who, after viewing Fort Jackson, &c., retired. The party of the enemy came by Wright's Cut, which leads through the marshes from Savannah River to Wright River.

It seems probable that the enemy is meditating an advance from New River to the banks of the Savannah, and General Drayton has been directed to take up a line removed beyond the reach [of] the gunboats on New River to intercept him; should the enemy land too large a force for him to cope with, he has been directed to notify you. In that event you are desired to send to his support such of your available force as may be necessary, and to march with it, should you deem it requisite, and to take command of the whole operation. With this view it is suggested that you repair to Hardeeville, visit the field of operation, and concert with him a plan of operations. Should you not be able to drive him back under cover of his boats, you will attack him in his flank and rear, so as to prevent his approach to the Savannah River.

I am, &c.,

R. E. LEE,
General, Commanding.

HDQRS. DEPARTMENT OF SOUTH CAROLINA, &c.,
Savannah, Ga., February 5, 1862.

Lieut. Col. J. GORGAS,
Chief of Ordnance Department, Richmond, Va.:

COLONEL: I have just received your letter of the 30th ultimo, advising me that two 10-inch and one 8-inch columbiads would be forwarded to me the next day. I hope that the others required are also on their way, and if it would be any relief to the department, as it will avoid the cost of transportation, the shot and shell can be procured here. I therefore desire to be informed of the caliber of the guns, that I may provide them. Please send an agent with the guns to hasten their transportation, and it has occurred to me that this might be expedited by sending them through Charlotte to Augusta, as the connection of the roads at Augusta is better than at Charleston, and much time will therefore be saved. I require nine heavy guns in addition to the three sent.

Captain Cuyler, ordnance officer at this post, has just stated to me that O. G. Parsley & Co., of Wilmington, N. C., have bought the whole stock of iron of Weed, Connell & Co., the principal importers and holders of iron in this city, at the market price at which it has been sold to the Government. He has left the iron here, with directions that it be sold at double the former price, 12 and 16 cents per pound. I have directed that all iron required by the Government should be taken and paid for at the original price. This seemed to be such a palpable act of speculation, that it ought to be stopped.

I report the facts, that you may bring the matter to the notice of the Secretary of War, as the practice may be extended to other points.

I am, &c,

R. E. LEE,
General, Commanding.

HEADQUARTERS DEPARTMENT, &c.,
Savannah, Ga., February 6, 1862.

Hon. J. P. BENJAMIN,
Secretary of War, Richmond:

SIR: The replacing the troops in the Confederate service in this State is a matter of serious consideration. The period of service of several companies serving the batteries for the defense of the city of Savannah is about to expire. One that was mustered out of service a few days since at Fort Pulaski declines to re-enter the service, and it is supposed that others will be equally averse. The loss of these companies at this time will be a serious injury to the defense of the city, as artillerists cannot be made on the eve of a battle. But the prospective injury to the service, I fear, will be equally great, as neither the sentiment of the people nor the policy of the State seems to favor the organization of troops for Confederate service. I have thought it probable that the influence of the Department might be able to avert the evil I apprehend.

I have been very anxious to assign another general officer to duty with the troops in the State of Georgia. At the time the officers of that grade reported to me an attack on the Carolina coast seemed so imminent and it was so unprovided that all re-enforcements were assigned to its defense and every effort made to prepare the troops for their duty. The movements of the enemy for the last week indicate Savannah as the threatened point of attack, but I do not think it safe to withdraw troops from Carolina. I have no one to place in charge of the body of troops guarding the approaches from the Ogeechee to Savannah. The troops are fresh, officers new in the service, and all require instruction. If some instructed officer could be spared me I should be greatly relieved. I have already mentioned General Heth and Colonel Stevenson, but have been informed they were wanted elsewhere, and I can name no one not disposed of. I therefore leave the matter to the Department.

I have the honor to be, very respectfully, your obedient servant.

R. E. LEE,
General, Commanding.

RICHMOND, *February* 7, 1862.

General BRAXTON BRAGG,
Pensacola:

General Lee says he understands there are twenty heavy guns at Pensacola that could be spared. If this is true, send him any you can spare to Savannah.

J. P. BENJAMIN,
Secretary of War.

MOBILE, ALA., *February* 8, 1862.

Hon. J. P. BENJAMIN,
Secretary of War:

Not a gun to spare here or at Pensacola, and we need eight or ten heavy shell guns here now. See my requisition on Ordnance Office.

BRAXTON BRAGG.

EXECUTIVE DEPARTMENT,
Milledgeville, February 8, 1862.

General R. E. LEE:

GENERAL: I have learned from General Wayne the substance of the conversation in your interview with him relative to the removal of the troops from Brunswick to Savannah. I have a great desire to see Brunswick remain in the possession of our troops, and should be very reluctant to see it abandoned to the enemy. If, however, it is not reasonably certain that you can with the force at your command, including the State troops, hold both Brunswick and Savannah, I do not hesitate to say that it is important that the whole force be at once concentrated at Savannah. It is the key to the State, and if it falls into the hands of the enemy Brunswick and the balance of the coast must of course be under their control.

All the indications are that Savannah is to be the point of attack, and we must repel the attack at any cost and at every hazard. If my home were in the city I would fight for it as long as possible, and if driven from it by overpowering force, I would never permit its roof to shelter the enemy, but would leave it in smoking ruins when driven from it.

The troops at Brunswick are under your command, and you are the best judge of the military necessities by which we are surrounded. Exercise your own judgment, in which I have the highest confidence, and I shall be content with and shall do all in my power to sustain your action, as I have no doubt you will so act as will best promote the highest interest of the people of the whole State.

Should you determine to withdraw the troops from Brunswick, I wish all the assistance afforded the inhabitants which is in your power for the removal of such property as they wish to carry into the interior; to this end you are at liberty to use the Brunswick Railroad, now in the military possession of the State. When all is removed that can be, let the engines and cars be brought to the junction of that road with the Savannah, Albany and Gulf road. I have directed General Jackson to call out such of the militia force of Savannah as he can arm for immediate service in addition to the State troops now in the field, and hope the order will meet your approval.

Very respectfully,

JOSEPH E. BROWN.

RICHMOND, *February* 9, 1862.

General R. E. LEE,
Savannah:

General Bragg says he has not a gun to spare. I will send you this week five 8-inch columbiads and one 24-pounder howitzer. I have ordered 1,000 Enfield rifles sent to you and 20,000 pounds of cannon powder, besides the fixed ammunition for the rifles.

J. P. BENJAMIN,
Secretary of War.

RICHMOND, *February* 9, 1862.

General LEE,
Savannah:

Send 10,000 pounds cannon powder to Norfolk immediately, and you will receive 20,000 pounds of the powder just received by the Kate. Send it from Charleston, if possible. Urgent.

J. P. BENJAMIN,
Secretary of War.

APALACHICOLA, FLA., *February* 10, 1862.

Hon. J. P. BENJAMIN,
Secretary of War:

SIR: The foregoing [following] copy of a letter addressed to me by General Floyd, commanding post, is respectfully commended to your consideration.

I have the honor to be, sir, your obedient servant,

JOHN MILTON,
Governor of Florida.

[Inclosure.]

BRIGADE HEADQUARTERS,
Apalachicola, February 9, 1862.

His Excellency Governor MILTON,
Commander-in-Chief, at Apalachicola, Fla.:

SIR: Your suggestion this morning, that I should freely express my views to you respecting the future action to be taken for the defense of this place, I beg here respectfully to submit them.

If, in accordance with a decree of the late Convention, the State troops here are to be disbanded by the 10th of March ensuing, unless in the mean time they should enlist in the Confederate service, the defense of this place seems at present to rest entirely upon that contingency.

My opinion is that the companies will not enlist in the Confederate service until they shall have been discharged in March, and even if they will then do so, an entirely new organization will have to be effected. This, in my opinion, will not be done until they have enjoyed the privilege of going home, which seems to have been accorded; and even though they should enlist before doing so, they will still consider a thirty-days' furlough as their right. Unless in the mean time other troops are sent here to fill their place, the absence of even half of the present force would leave the place comparatively defenseless.

Supposing that the 10th of March arrives, and that other troops are not sent here to supply the place of those who will be mustered out of service on that day, it would be highly improper to leave the cannon and ordnance stores here at the disposal of any gunboat and crew which the enemy might send here to capture them.

If such a state of things as I have supposed should occur, in the absence of orders relating to them I should feel it incumbent upon me to dismantle the batteries and remove the guns and ordnance stores to a place of security up the river before the men were disbanded or by that time, as I think it questionable, under the circumstances, whether I could detain them after that date.

Taking the above view of this matter, I would respectfully suggest to your excellency, that every effort be made to get a force here for the defense of the place before the 10th of March, and not to depend upon a reorganization of the force now here until after that time.

It would seem that General Trapier, upon an application to him, would send a regiment of Confederate troops perhaps from Fernandina; or the Secretary of War might be induced to do so in case General Trapier does not possess the authority; that at least the property of the Confederate Government might be protected, obviating the necessity of removing it from this post.

From all I can discover, it is my firm impression that but comparatively few of the troops now here will enlist in the service of the Confederacy; and even though the majority of them were disposed to do so, I fear there would be much confusion in their reorganization into companies, owing to the ambition of officers to get higher rank than they now enjoy.

I know of nothing more that I could now say on this subject, and have the honor to remain, your very obedient servant,

R. F. FLOYD,
Brigadier-General, Commanding.

HDQRS. DEPARTMENT OF SOUTH CAROLINA, &C.,
Savannah, Ga., February 10, 1862.

Hon. JOSEPH E. BROWN,
Governor of Georgia, Milledgeville, Ga.:

SIR: I have had the honor to receive your letter of the 8th instant in reference to the withdrawal of the batteries from Saint Simon's and Jekyl Islands. No one can regret the apparent necessity of such a measure more than I do, and so great is my repugnance to yield any point of our territory to our enemies, that I have endeavored from the time of my arrival to give strength to the defenses of Brunswick. I find it impossible to obtain guns to secure it as I desire, and now everything is required to fortify this city. I have therefore given General Mercer discretionary authority to withdraw the troops and guns from the islands to the main [land], should he, upon a reconsideration of the subject, hold to his opinion as to the inability of the batteries to contend with the enemy's fleet.

I have sent Maj. Edward C. Anderson to assist in removing the guns, &c., and as soon as I know his determination will inform you. With the exception of the fact of opening another harbor on the coast to the enemy and receding from a point we have occupied, I do not know that any material interest is sacrificed. As the inhabitants of the islands and of Brunswick have removed their families and property, there is no trade or commerce with Brunswick, and no immediate back country to be injuriously affected.

I am, &c.,

R. E. LEE,
General, Commanding.

HDQRS. DEPARTMENT OF SOUTH CAROLINA, &C.,
Savannah, Ga., February 10, 1862.

Hon. J. P. BENJAMIN,
Secretary of War, Richmond, Va.:

SIR: From the reports of General Mercer as to the inability of the batteries on Saint Simon's and Jekyl Islands to withstand the attack of the enemy's fleet, the isolated condition of those islands, and the impossibility of my re-enforcing him with guns or men, I have given him authority, should he retain that opinion upon a calm review of the whole subject, to act according to his discretion; and, if deemed advisable by him, to withdraw to the main-land, and take there a defensible position for the protection of the country. Should he adopt this course, the heavy guns at those batteries will be sent here for the defense of Savannah River, where they are much needed and cannot otherwise be obtained. The channel between Saint Simon's and Jekyl Islands leads into Brunswick Harbor.

Brunswick is a summer resort for certain planters, and is the terminus of a railroad extending about 60 miles into the interior, where it intersects the Savannah, Albany and Gulf Railroad. There are no inhabitants now in Brunswick, and the planters on the islands have removed their property to the interior; nor is there any population in the vicinity of Brunswick that would seem to warrant jeopardizing the men and guns necessary elsewhere. I would not, therefore, originally have occupied Saint Simon's or Jekyl, but the batteries, though small, are well placed, and the guns well distributed, and I think would defend the channel against ordinary attacks, and I exceedingly dislike to yield an inch of territory to our enemies. They are, however, able to bring such large and powerful batteries to whatever point they please, that it becomes necessary for us to concentrate our strength. As this point may be selected by some of our forward-bound vessels to run the blockade, I think proper to give you the earliest information of its probable relinquishment.

I am, &c.,

R. E. LEE,
General, Commanding.

RICHMOND, VA., *February* 13, 1862.

General R. E. LEE,
Savannah:

The order of Colonel Myers was only meant to hurry on the cannon powder without waiting for anything else. Twenty thousand pounds of it are to be retained by you, and remainder sent here as quickly as possible.

J. P. BENJAMIN,
Secretary of War.

HDQRS. DEPARTMENT OF SOUTH CAROLINA, &C.,
Savannah, Ga., February 14, 1862.

Brig. Gen. J. H. TRAPIER,
Commanding, &c., Tallahassee, Fla.:

GENERAL: In reply to your letter of the 5th instant, in relation to the defenses of Saint John's River, I am directed by the commanding general to say that he has directed four 32-pounders to be sent to you at Fernandina, if practicable, to strengthen that point, unless you think it more advisable to place them elsewhere. He has been obliged to withdraw the troops from Saint Simon's and Jekyl Islands to obtain means for defense of this city, and he deems it advisable to strengthen Fernandina as far as in his power. He also desires you to relieve as soon as possible Captain Blain's company at Cumberland Island, and to order it to rejoin its regiment.

As regards the defense of the Saint John's, he suggests to you, if possible, to place the guns that may be available for that purpose at one point rather than at two, distant or out of support of each other, as united they might withstand the attack of the enemy, which, [while?] if distant, each might be suppressed separately. Not knowing the ground, he leaves the matter to your better judgment.

I am, &c.,

[W. H. TAYLOR,]
A. A. G.

STATE OF GEORGIA, ADJT. AND INSP. GEN.'S OFFICE,
Milledgeville, Ga., February 14, 1862.

General R. E. LEE, C. S. A.,
Commanding Southern Military District, Savannah:

GENERAL: By direction of the governor I send you herewith two communications relative to the defenseless condition of the city of Augusta, in this State—one written by the mayor of that city, the other by a highly respectable citizen of it, and holding the commission of colonel in the militia of the State. These letters express fully the weakness of the city and the interests there to be protected, and entering heartily into the views of the writers, the governor directs me to commend them to your earnest consideration.

Very respectfully, your obedient servant,

HENRY C. WAYNE,
Adjutant and Inspector General.

[Inclosure No. 1.]

MAYOR'S OFFICE,
Augusta, February 11, 1862.

His Excellency JOSEPH E. BROWN,
Governor, &c.:

DEAR SIR: I desire to call your attention to the fact that there now exists among a portion of our citizens considerable apprehension that an attempt may be made before long by the Federal forces near Savannah to ascend the Savannah River to Augusta. Whether this apprehension is well grounded or not, there can be no doubt that if the enemy are placed in a position to enable them to do so, great exertion will be made to reach Augusta, as it must be generally known that we have a large quantity of cotton stored and that manufactories of arms and powder are being erected near our city. It is suggested that it may become necessary to obstruct the Savannah River. I address your excellency for the purpose of bringing the matter to your notice, and thus enabling you to give such directions as you may think required by the circumstances. Should it be deemed important to obstruct the river, and you have no engineer whom you can direct to the duty, I will cheerfully undertake any service connected with the matter which you may think proper to designate.

With sentiments of highest esteem, I am, very respectfully, your obedient servant,

ROBT. H. MAY,
Mayor of City of Augusta.

[Inclosure No. 2.]

AUGUSTA, *February* 11, 1862.

His Excellency JOSEPH E. BROWN,
Governor State of Georgia:

SIR: Some apprehension is felt in this city that the enemy will endeavor to take it, provided they succeed at Savannah. In the event of their success there (which Heaven forbid), and they make the attempt, we are entirely at their mercy, for we have neither artillery nor arms for infantry; in fact, the city is for effective service totally defenseless, and no matter how willing we all might be to fight to the last, we could do no good unless we have arms.

It has been suggested to me to write to you on this subject. There is now 82,000 bales of cotton here, besides the powder-mills, factories, &c., which should be protected. I would respectfully suggest that an efficient battery of twelve or fifteen guns of suitable caliber should be at once placed at Silver Bluff, on the Carolina side, about 2 to 5 miles below the city, and also that rafts or old boats and other material suitable for the purpose should be used to barricade the river, which could be effectually done at Matthew's Bluff, about 90 miles below the city. It is the opinion of well-informed men as well as myself that this should be done immediately.

I hope your excellency will excuse me for mentioning this important matter to you, and I hope it will meet with a favorable consideration. And, further, let me assure you that any service I can do you and my State in this war [illegible] or any other business will be cheerfully done to the best of my ability, without fear or reward.

Very respectfully, your obedient servant,

W. B. GRIFFIN,

Colonel, Commanding Tenth Regiment Georgia Militia.

HDQRS. DEPARTMENT OF SOUTH CAROLINA, &C.,

Savannah, Ga., February 14, 1862.

Brig. Gen. R. S. RIPLEY,

Commanding, &c., Charleston:

GENERAL: I am directed by the general commanding to say that General Evans has reported that the enemy have landed in considerable force on Edisto and driven his pickets from Jehossee, and has requested that his force be increased as soon as possible. He therefore desires you to send as soon as possible the four companies intended for the battalion under Messrs. Nelson and Aiken, and to request General Gist to hasten the organization of the two regiments lately withdrawn from the Third Military District South Carolina. In the mean time, should there be one of the new regiments ready to take the field, he desires you to order it to report to General Evans and to notify him accordingly.

I am, &c.,

[W. H. TAYLOR,]

A. A. G.

HEADQUARTERS THIRD MILITARY DISTRICT,

Adams Run, February 15, 1862.

Capt. W. H. TAYLOR,

Assistant Adjutant-General, Savannah, Ga.:

CAPTAIN: Inclosed please find charges and specifications against Capt. J. H. Rion, Lieutenants Harrison, Kennedy, and Isbell, of the Lyles Rifles. These officers have positively refused to obey my order. I have arrested them, and placed an officer of another company in command of the Lyles Rifles.

I would respectfully request that a court-martial be ordered as soon as possible for their trial, and that the court consist of as many officers of experience as the good of the service will admit.

I beg leave to report, for the information of the general commanding, that I have now but 1,305 men for duty on the main-land, at least half of whom are raw militia, composed of the new companies joining battalions and men returned from sick furloughs. The troops I have distributed as follows:

The Holcombe Legion, Colonel Stevens, 492 strong, between Togodo and Willstown, opposite Jehossee Island; Laurens battalion, Major James, 281 strong, in rear of the intrenchments at Slann's Island Causeway; a section of light artillery is also stationed here; Colonel Elford, Sixteenth Regiment South Carolina Volunteers, is stationed at a central position on the Willstown road, between this place and Church Flats, guarding the approach of the enemy up the Wadmalaw. The enemy have occupied Edisto Island in considerable force and have thrown pickets as far out as Jehossee Island, and from observation I am convinced are making preparation for an early attack.

With my present forces I find myself entirely unable to strengthen my position in front of Jehossee Island, as the forces on John's and Wadmalaw Islands, now not adequate to their positions, could not be withdrawn without exposing an open way to the railroad for the enemy. With reference to the disposition of the troops on the islands, please see letter inclosed from Colonel De Treville, commanding. It will then be readily perceived by the general commanding that should the enemy occupy Jehossee Island (which he can whenever he pleases) and erect batteries on the island out of range of our guns (24-pounders), he could, with the assistance of his gunboats, take our batteries, overpower my small force, and make his way to the railroad. I would therefore request, if possible, an additional force be sent to this district.

Very respectfully, your obedient servant,

N. G. EVANS,
Brigadier-General, Commanding.

[Inclosure.]

WADMALAW ISLAND, *February* 6, 1862.

Brigadier-General EVANS,
Adams Run:

DEAR GENERAL: In accordance with your orders we will leave today for Charleston.

Colonel Moore's battalion, with the exception of three detached companies, moved to Bear's Bluff yesterday. Colonel Means' regiment will move to our camping ground as soon as we move. The two pieces of light artillery from Bear's Bluff I have stationed near Rockville.

Though this ends my connection with the military, perhaps forever, I cannot but remark again upon the undefended condition of these islands. There is now no guard at Church Bridge and nothing on the road from the Haulover to Legareville but two companies from Colonel Moore's battalion and Nesbitt's cavalry. If the enemy intend, as the Herald says they intend to do and as I think very probable, to make North Edisto their base of operations against Charleston, they can with perfect impunity land any number of troops on that island and at any moment transport them to Haulover, Rockville, and Bear's Bluff, and advance in these directions to the ferry or to Legareville. We are totally unprepared to meet them, but of this your own personal observation has made you fully aware. With less than three more good regiments, well drilled, if the duty of defending these islands is still on you, you ought not to be content.

I forgot to mention that General Ripley has relieved Captain Pinckney's company at the ferry by one of the regulars of Colonel Dunovant's regiment; so there is now no picket on the John's Island side of the ferry. The ship went reconnoitering on Tuesday morning towards Bear's Bluff, and approached, as we thought, within the range of your guns at White Point. We expected you to fire on the enemy before they fired on our pickets and damaged some of the houses at Rockville.

Wishing you a prosperous and brilliant campaign and that you may add to your Leesburg laurels, I remain, dear general, yours, truly,

RICHARD DE TREVILLE.

HDQRS. SECOND MILITARY DISTRICT SOUTH CAROLINA,
Charleston, February 15, 1862.

Capt. W. H. TAYLOR,
Assistant Adjutant-General, Savannah, Ga.:

CAPTAIN: I have the honor to acknowledge the receipt of order concerning mechanics, &c. I have taken the necessary steps for obtaining the reports required.

General Evans telegraphs, date of 15th:

> Enemy landed one regiment on Edisto yesterday. A spy taken this morning says he will ascend the Wadmalaw and land at Simon's Landing. Please send me two heavy guns; if none other, 8-inch howitzers.

I have not a gun to send him, the number of guns here belonging to the State being held for our lines. Am preparing to support him with infantry, but regret to add that the regiments are not what I could wish. Moragné's and Gadberry's are still down with measles, and Keitt's not armed yet.

Although I think the movement here is rather demonstrative than positive, so long as the enemy threatens Savannah so seriously there is no doubt that Simon's Landing is a very important point, and if possible would like to arm and hold it. I do not see how I can assist General Evans, except by infantry such as I have.

The store of powder in Fort Sumter has been very much diminished, and I should like much to have it replaced as soon as possible. The further supplies for the lines, I suppose, will have to come from that fort, and it would be well to keep it in full condition.

I am, very respectfully, your obedient servant,

R. S. RIPLEY,
Brigadier-General.

HDQRS. DEPARTMENT OF SOUTH CAROLINA, &C.,
Savannah, February 15, 1862.

Lieutenant-Colonel GILL,
Commanding Arsenal at Augusta:

COLONEL: I wrote yesterday to Major Rains in reference to the advisability of obstructing the navigation of the Savannah River below Augusta, for which he had suggested a plan. As he informed me he should be absent on official business for some time, I find it necessary to apply to you for information. I desire to know whether any examination of the river has been made with a view to the selection of the most eligible point, and whether any guns can be had to arm a battery for the protection of the river obstructions. In that event the point selected, besides being favorable to the work, should be contiguous to a position where a battery could be placed to prevent its removal. If no guns can be procured, then rifle-pits should be dug, where good marksmen could drive off working parties of the enemy. The position of the obstruction should be below the bluff, from which it could be protected. If no examination has been made and you are not able to do so yourself, could you select a person for the service and make arrangements for the conduct of the work, should Major Rains not return in time? The navigation of the river should be retained until it becomes necessary to close it, and for this purpose an outlet for the boats should be left.

The work, in my opinion, should be undertaken at once as a purely prudential measure, and as soon as the plan is matured should be pushed forward with vigor.

From the tenor of Major Rains' letter, I inferred that the citizens of Augusta would provide the necessary labor, &c., and that Col. Henry Cummings would superintend the work.

I am, &c.,

R. E. LEE,
General, Commanding.

HDQRS. DEPARTMENT OF SOUTH CAROLINA, &C.,
Savannah, Ga., February 15, 1862.

General HENRY C. WAYNE,
Adjutant and Inspector General State of Georgia:

GENERAL: I have had the honor to receive your letter of the 14th instant, inclosing communications from the mayor of Augusta and Colonel Griffin to his excellency Governor Brown, in reference to the propriety of obstructing the navigation of the Savannah River.

This subject had already attracted my attention, and, in addition to measures contemplated for closing the river above this city, I have authorized the adoption of a plan, suggested by Major Rains, for arresting its navigation below Augusta. To prevent the removal of obstacles, however, placed in the bed of the stream, there should be a battery contiguous. For this I have no guns, and cannot possibly obtain more than necessary for the defenses of Savannah. I was, therefore, on the point of requesting the Governor to permit me to apply any belonging to the State to the defense of the upper river, and am glad that the subject has been brought to his notice. May I ask you to inform me whether there are any State guns available for this purpose, whether they can be procured, their caliber, &c.?

I am, &c.,

R. E. LEE,
General, Commanding.

HDQRS. DEPARTMENT OF SOUTH CAROLINA, &C.,
Savannah Ga., February 15, 1862.

Brig. Gen. R. S. RIPLEY,
Commanding, &c., Charleston:

GENERAL: There are abundant indications of the presence of the enemy in force, both on land and water, in this vicinity; but as far as I can judge from the character of the vessels and the position of their troops, I see no indications of an immediate attack. They may be waiting for re-enforcements, or intend to deceive by demonstrations here while preparing for an attack on the coast elsewhere. I desire to know whether you can detect any indication of a movement against Charleston, and whether, should the attack be made against this city, you could detach two or more good artillery companies, skilled in the management of heavy guns, for service in the open batteries on Savannah River. These companies of course are only intended for temporary service and to provide against the impracticability of obtaining good artillerists from the new troops in this State.

I am, &c.,

R. E. LEE,
General, Commanding.

HDQRS. DEPARTMENT OF SOUTH CAROLINA, &C.,
Savannah, Ga., February 15, 1862.

Brig. Gen. N. G. EVANS,
Commanding, &c., Adams Run:

GENERAL: I have had the honor to receive your letter of this day's date, and have directed that a court-martial be convened at Adams Run for the trial of the officers of the Lyles Rifles.

As regards the re-enforcements that you request, I wrote you yesterday on the subject, which is all, under the circumstances, that can be done. It will be impossible to find sufficient troops to garrison the whole line of the coast, and all that can be done is to ascertain the points of attack, concentrate the troops in the district to meet the advance of the enemy, and, if unable to drive him, to hold him in check until re-enforcements can be forwarded from other districts.

I am, &c.,

R. E. LEE,
General, Commanding.

HDQRS. MILITARY DISTRICT, DEPT. OF GEORGIA,
Brunswick, February 16, 1862.

Capt. T. A. WASHINGTON,
Assistant Adjutant-General:

CAPTAIN: I have the honor to report, for the information of General Lee, that the guns have all been removed from the islands and brought to this place, with the exception of one 32-pounder, which I expect up in the course of the day. One 42-pounder and eight 32-pounders have been shipped to Savannah by rail, and I hope to get off to-day and to-morrow the columbiads and the remaining 32s, reserving four 32s to be sent to Fernandina. Lieutenant-Colonel Lamar's battalion is now encamped at this place, and Colonel Styles' command, it is hoped, will all be withdrawn before to-morrow night, though the weather is now very unfavorable, especially for the removal of his horse company and light artillery.

Before finally evacuating this position I beg to bring to the consideration of the general the question of burning the town of Brunswick. For the moral effect it would produce upon the enemy, as evidencing our determination to continue the present contest with unconquerable determination and at every sacrifice, and for other obvious reasons, which you will think it needless for me to recite, I would respectfully urge that I be furnished with precise orders to destroy all the buildings that can afford shelter and comfort to the enemy. I desire also again to request of the general that I may be allowed to bring back Blain's company from Cumberland. The captain and colonel are both anxious that this company should not be withdrawn from my command, and its anomalous position will be fruitful of embarrassments, without, as it appears to me, any corresponding benefit. In this connection I would respectfully submit that General Trapier is much better able to supply a garrison for Cumberland than I am to spare a good company from this military district.

I am, captain, very respectfully, your obedient servant,

H. W. MERCER,

Brigadier-General, Commanding.

HDQRS. SECOND MILITARY DISTRICT SOUTH CAROLINA,

Charleston, February 16, 1862.

Capt. W. H. TAYLOR,

Assistant Adjutant-General, Savannah, Ga.:

CAPTAIN: I have the honor to acknowledge the receipt of your communication of the 14th, relating to the re-enforcement of General Evans. I have taken steps to re-enforce him with all I can muster on short notice. Nelson's battalion will be sent out as soon as possible, but I regret to state that Captain De Russ' or De Pass' company has not yet filled, and that the rest are suffering from disease.

On the other hand, Gadberry's and Moragné's and Keitt's people are rapidly recovering. Keitt received arms yesterday. Clement Stevens' regiment is filling up, and General Gist is using every exertion to reorganize the troops of the city. He has three companies of cavalry here, which I shall endeavor to have equipped and make use of. Two companies of Black's cavalry have also reported lately, which will join the headquarters of the regiment as soon as they can be equipped.

I have respectfully to request that Captain Childs may be authorized to issue or purchase arms for the troops for the war upon my requisition. There may be one or two more cavalry corps offering for the war, and there are a good quantity of Colt's pistols and rifles still for sale in different hands. Capt. Ap C. Jones, of Black's regiment, has found about 20 army revolvers and some 10 Enfield rifles, which have been in the hands of merchants and gun-dealers for some time. He has purchased them, trusting to have his purchase authorized.

I yesterday sent Captain Walker, assistant adjutant-general, to confer with General Evans. He brought back with him the man reported as a spy. I inclose his statement, and although by no means a man of unimpeachable veracity, I think he told nearly all he knew. As he is not entirely reliable, however, and it has occurred to General Evans that he may have been set at liberty in order to act as a spy and gain information for the enemy, I have to request instructions as to whether I shall hold him confined or release him. The works on the lines are nearly completed, but require dressing.

I am employing a force on the inundation in Saint Andrew's, which will be done in a few days. Have also started to place a fixed battery on the middle ground between Castle Pinckney and Fort Johnson. The water is but about 8 feet deep, and the timber caissons can be ballasted with the rubbish of the late fire. The idea was suggested by the necessity of putting more traverses in Fort Moultrie if that place is to be bombarded. Not wishing to lose the fire of the guns and having no place for them on the forts, it seemed to me that if it can be done in time it will be a strong additional defense to the city. Before removing the guns, however, will see that it is not going to take too long.

I inclose copy of the pass given by Captain Ammen, of the Seneca gunboat, to Black, the party alluded to in a former paragraph.

I am, very respectfully, your obedient servant,

R. S. RIPLEY,
Brigadier-General.

[Inclosure.]

Statement of Thomas Black.

Black left Charleston on the 16th December, with a flat and two hands, for Edisto Island, to obtain his own and Major Whaley's furniture, having first obtained a pass from the mayor. Arrived on Edisto on the 19th. On the night of his arrival his flat was stolen by negroes. Whilst hunting for his flat the next day he was taken by negroes, who were armed with guns and pistols and bayonets on sticks; there were between 30 and 50 negroes; drew their weapons and threatened to shoot him if he offered resistance. Black was carried on board gunboat Penguin, where he was kept two weeks, and then transferred to the Seneca, and sent to Hilton Head, and then transferred to the Wabash.

He was kept on board for a week, and sent back by the Seneca to North Edisto. Flag-Officer DuPont, upon reading the letter of the captain of the Penguin, said he did not consider Black a prisoner of war, as he was taken by negroes, and was sorry the captain gave him the trouble of being sent to Hilton Head. Whilst on Hilton Head he heard that there were about 8,000 troops on the island. Heard them speak of attacking Savannah and Charleston, but most of attacking Charleston. From what he heard, thought they were going to attack Charleston by way of Wadmalaw Island and Simon's Bluff. They spoke of burning Rockville yesterday.

He heard the steward of the Ben DeFord say that he had heard the officers say that a portion of the Burnside fleet would be in North Edisto soon. Heard the provost-marshal of Hilton Head say that he had been in Savannah about two weeks since.

Was sent back, after first having been returned to North Edisto by Flag-Officer DuPont to Hilton Head, and at the instance of Mr. Boutelle was sent back again to North Edisto in the Ben DeFord.

One regiment of troops, about 600 strong, landed at Edisto; they had two transportation wagons and mules; had commenced to remove everything that was valuable in the way of furniture from the island.

Heard Boutelle say that he had received a Charleston paper of the 10th on the 11th. Was landed at White Point by Mr. Boutelle, under a flag of truce. The flag was not received by any one, and Black walked on until he met the pickets.

The negroes go up from Edisto to White Point continually, and Black thinks they get information by communicating with the negroes on the main.

Thinks they have given up the attack on Savannah, as we have too many troops there. They have a machine for cutting off pile obstructions close to the bottom, &c.

P. S.—Captain Rogers, of General Evans' staff, saw the boat with the flag when it was coming ashore.

HEADQUARTERS DEPARTMENT OF SOUTH CAROLINA, &c.,
Savannah, Ga., February 17, 1862.

Col. C. H. OLMSTEAD,
Commanding, &c., Fort Pulaski:

COLONEL: From the position the enemy has taken in the Savannah River, it becomes necessary that you look to your defense in that direction. I therefore recommend that, if necessary for that purpose, you shift some of your barbette guns to the gorge of the work, and the casemates in the northwest angle, which bear up the river, be provided with guns. I would also recommend that the parapets of the mortar batteries be carried all around, so that the mortars can be protected from the fire up the river as well as from Tybee Island, and that everything be done to strengthen the defenses of your work in the rear. As far as it is possible your safety will be anxiously cared for, and for the present your communication with the city will have to be by light boats over the marsh and through Wilmington Narrows to Causton's Bluff, or by any other mode by which you can better accomplish it.

I am, sir,

R. E. LEE,
General, Commanding.

HEADQUARTERS SECOND MILITARY DISTRICT,
Charleston, February 17, 1862.

Capt. W. H. TAYLOR,
Assistant Adjutant-General, Savannah, Ga.:

SIR: I have the honor to acknowledge the receipt of the letter of General Lee of the 15th.

The only indications of an attack on Charleston are those reported by General Evans and such information as was derived from Mr. Black, the prisoner who was at Hilton Head. I consider these vague, and were it not for the bitter animosity against this city by the enemy should not be much alarmed. As for the artillery companies, General Lee will agree with me that properly they cannot be spared, but I think a certain number might be sent with a comparatively small risk. I should send them from Lamar's and White's battalions, which, although not by any means perfect, have had some little practice.

Fort Sumter has now but four well-instructed companies in garrison, the others being recruits. Castle Pinckney is garrisoned by one company, which relieved the State volunteer company under Captain Chichester. Colonel Hagood requires an additional force of artillery-men at Stono, and General Evans calls on me for guns and men, which I have been unable to furnish.

The troops are holding themselves in readiness to march at a moment's notice, but are suffering from disease, as I have informed you.

If the general thinks the necessity absolute, I will endeavor to send the troops required with as little risk as possible. Meanwhile the people here are under a little excitement and fear an attack. I am not going to allay it, hoping they may volunteer at once.

Very respectfully, your obedient servant,

R. S. RIPLEY,
Brigadier-General, Commanding.

RICHMOND, VA., *February* 18, 1862.

General R. E. LEE,
Savannah:

Order the cavalry regiment of Colonel Davis from Florida to Chattanooga immediately, to report to General A. S. Johnston. Withdraw all forces from the islands in your department to the main-land, taking proper measures to save the artillery and munitions of war.

J. P. BENJAMIN,
Secretary of War.

SAVANNAH, GA., *February* 18, 1862.

General S. COOPER,
Adjutant and Inspector-General, Richmond, Va.:

GENERAL: I have the honor to report, for the information of the honorable Secretary of War, that the guns have been withdrawn from the batteries on Saint Simon's and Jekyl's Islands and the troops removed to Brunswick. The former are now in progress of transportation to this place, to be used in the defense of the city of Savannah, and the latter directed to occupy a position, to command the railroad and protect the back country. The nature of the ground prevents the possibility of holding the town of Brunswick, as the gunboats of the enemy can unmolested ascend the river within 4 miles of the railroad at Waynesville and about 25 miles in the rear of Brunswick. Brunswick would prove a convenient and healthy position, if occupied by the enemy, affording shelter and comfortable quarters for the troops and hospitals for the sick. It is used as a summer resort, and at this time mostly uninhabited. Should it fall into the possession of the enemy, its convenient harbor, salubrious climate, and comfortable buildings might tempt him to hold it for the continuance of the war, and, rather than it should fall into his hands, I propose to destroy it.

Before issuing orders to this effect, I desire that my views be known to the Secretary, so that if not approved by him I may be informed.

Very respectfully, your obedient servant,

R. E. LEE,
General, Commanding.

SAVANNAH, *February* 18, 1862.

Brig. Gen. R. S. RIPLEY,
Commanding, Charleston:

GENERAL: I am directed by the commanding general [Lee] to acknowledge the receipt of your letter of the 16th instant to-day; that he hopes you will use every effort to organize the Carolina troops and to get them into the field. The three cavalry companies that you are equipping can be retained for service in your district if you desire it. Captain Childs will be authorized to issue arms to the cavalry companies mustered into the Confederate service for the war upon your requisition, but the Enfield rifles must be reserved for the infantry. As regards Thomas Black, who has been released by the enemy, you must judge from his character and antecedents whether he can be trusted at large; if you feel satisfied, you can release him and keep him under surveillance. If not, he had better be sent to Colonel Preston, at Columbia, to be retained in close custody or within prescribed limits on parole.

In reference to the fixed battery you propose on the middle ground, if adopted he would recommend that it be casemated, using heavy timber and railroad iron for the purpose. Similar protection should be given to our other water batteries, where practicable, if time permits, and, indeed, every preparation made to shelter the men from the bombardment of the enemy's fleet.

I am, &c.,

——— ———.

SAVANNAH, *February* 18, 1862.

His Excellency JOSEPH E. BROWN,
Governor of Georgia, Milledgeville:

GOVERNOR: I have the honor to report for the information of your excellency that the guns have been removed from the islands of Saint Simon's and Jekyl, and the troops withdrawn to the main-land; the former are in process of transportation to this city, and the latter ordered to take a position to command the railroad and to protect the back country.

In giving final orders for the defense of that portion of the State, I wish to give directions in reference to the town of Brunswick, provided the enemy attempt to possess. Besides the moral effect of showing our determination to defend the country at any sacrifice, its destruction would deprive the enemy of comfortable quarters in a healthy position, which they might otherwise be tempted to occupy during the continuance of the war, the present buildings saving them much labor and expense, and the hotel serving as a hospital for their sick. As there are other considerations besides those, purely military, involved in this question, I am unwilling to order the destruction of the town without the knowledge and approbation of your excellency.

I am, &c.,

R. E. LEE,
General, Commanding.

HDQRS. SECOND MILITARY DISTRICT SOUTH CAROLINA,
Charleston, February 18, 1862.

Capt. W. H. TAYLOR,
Assistant Adjutant-General, Savannah, Ga.:

CAPTAIN: In view of the reported recent successes of the enemy at Fort Donelson, which, although not entirely reliable, will probably lead to renewed activity on the part of the enemy, I beg leave respectfully to suggest the following for the consideration of the commanding general. We may, I opine, consider it as certain that the enemy will soon attack Savannah or Charleston, directly or by the shortest land approach, especially if their generals have a proper appreciation of a moral effect of a victory.

With this letter I have the honor to inclose a copy of the weekly return of the troops in this district. It will be seen that the aggregate "present and absent" is 7,754, while the number of effectives, sabers and bayonets and artillery-men, is but 4,569, including sergeants and corporals.

General Evans has nominally from 2,800 to 3,000, probably 1,500, effectives.

The commands to the south and west are, I doubt not, proportionally weak, according to the extent of their lines.

I do not know the force in Savannah, but, with over 200 miles from the North Carolina to the Georgia line, it seems to me that we have not more than 20,000 effectives, and probably that estimate is too large. The greater portion of this force is between this point and Savannah, guarding our line of communications between the two cities, and from circumstances of topography it is weak and liable to be cut.

Free communication between the cities is of great importance, and so long as there were any hopes of a speedy termination of the war the defense of the rich plantations on Paw Paw, Ashepoo, and Combahee of little less. But if the news of our disaster in Tennessee be correct, the war may last long indeed. The Santee, Pedee, and Waccamaw countries are comparatively undefended, except by nature, which has provided a strong defense in the shoals and bars at the mouths of the rivers. Nevertheless, should the enemy be successful in an attack upon either of our cities, we must expect to be attacked there. If, however, we hold the cities and the Santee and Georgetown districts, the Ashley and Cooper being within the limits of Charleston, with the resources of the interior at command, we shall have the principal part of the grain country within our hands. I take it for granted that it will be out of the question to get a crop from either Combahee, Ashepoo, or Paw Paw.

Our weakest points between this city and Savannah are this side Paw Paw, and near Charleston. North Edisto affords a safe harbor for vessels of from 14 to 16 feet of water, and thence they can come to White Point or Simon's Landing in force. They are from 5 to 8 miles of the railroad, a short half day's march.

General Evans' force, it must be remembered, is divided, a considerable portion being on John's Island. I shall certainly support him with all the means at my disposal, but out of my effectives it would be hard to get 1,500 movable troops. This would hardly suffice to make a successful stand.

Now, if a disposition is made which would strengthen the points near to Charleston by drawing troops from the vicinity of Pocotaligo, this side of Paw Paw, strong guards being at or in advance of the railroad bridges on Ashepoo and Combahee, while the obstructions in the Coosawhatchie is held as a strong advanced post by the troops defending the Carolina shore of the Savannah, General Evans' force closing in on the landings on the Wadmalaw and Stono, the approach to Charleston from that vicinity would be comparatively secure. Troops here and to be raised could be thrown in readiness to support the advance as soon as they convalesced, and any surplus we may have can be placed northward to defend the country in that direction.

This it may be said would leave a very rich section of the country undefended. But no crop comes from that country this year if the war continues, and it is well-nigh exhausted now of those necessaries which, in my opinion, first rendered it advisable to hold it in force. Our weak point on the Charleston and Savannah road would be about Ashepoo and Combahee. The weak point now is close to Charleston. Should the forces of the enemy make a dash, they have comparatively no distance to march to cut the rail.

In the case supposed, they would at any point have twice or thrice the distance to march, or take a narrow and tortuous route of from 30 to 50 miles up tidal rivers; moreover, neither we nor the enemy can hold the line of the railroad about Coosawhatchie or Pocotaligo or at Salkehatchie or Ashepoo Ferry more than six or seven weeks longer. We shall have to take the healthy regions about Adams Run, and the sandy sea islands in the vicinity of Charleston and to the north of Grahamville would be one good location for the troops south of Broad River.

In the vicinity of Charleston we have Long, Sullivan, and Morris Islands, besides Folly, and perhaps Kiawah and Summerville, 20 miles up the South Carolina road, for a reserve.

Communication with Savannah could be kept up by the rail until it was cut, and if it should so happen, the rolling stock could be transferred to the South Carolina and Georgia Central for transportation by way of Augusta.

The various arguments on the subject it would be hard to embody in a single letter, but the general idea is that in the present state of affairs, while a considerable portion of our troops are guarding a long line of railroad through a country which we must soon leave and now nearly exhausted, our weakest point is close to, perhaps, our most important city, and that city has not men enough to defend it in case of attack.

If the enemy dashes at General Evans, and the rail is cut, the danger would be imminent, and should either or both Charleston or Savannah fall, we shall be forced to hold unhealthy positions in an exhausted country, or to retire into the interior and give up the seaboard, with its advantages of grain crops and communications. My opinion upon these matters has not been asked, but, charged as I am with the defense of this military district, I have felt it my duty to submit the considerations to the commanding general. I regret that I could not state them more forcibly and in fewer words.

I am, very respectfully, your obedient servant,

R. S. RIPLEY,
Brigadier-General, Commanding.

SAVANNAH, GA., *February* 19, 1862.

His Excellency JOHN MILTON,
Governor of Florida, Tallahassee:

GOVERNOR: I have had the honor to receive the letter of the 9th instant, from Brig. Gen. R. F. Floyd to your excellency, referred to me. From his statement, the necessity for additional troops at that point is apparent, and as I have none under my command to send, I have to request that your excellency will transfer into the service of the Confederate States a regiment for the war, if possible, and order it to report to Brigadier-General Trapier. I have already written to General Trapier on the subject. Unless troops can be organized in Florida for its defense, I know not whose they can obtain.

I am, &c.,

R. E. LEE,
General, Commanding.

SAVANNAH, GA., *February* 19, 1862.

General J. H. TRAPIER,
Commanding District Florida, Tallahassee:

GENERAL: In looking at the whole defense of Florida, it becomes important to ascertain what points can probably be held and what points had better be relinquished. The force that the enemy can bring against any position where he can concentrate his floating batteries renders it prudent and proper to withdraw from the islands to the main-land and to prepare to contest his advance into the interior. Where an island offers the best point of defense, and is so connected with the main that its communication cannot be cut off, it may be retained. Otherwise it should be abandoned.

A dispatch was sent to you this morning on this subject, and I now wish you, in reviewing the defensive positions in your district, to see what changes and improvements can be made in the number and strength of the points occupied. I fear but little aid can be offered you from without the State of Florida. You must therefore use every exertion to make available the resources in it, and apply the means at your disposal to the best advantage. Whatever can be given from the means under my control will be cheerfully accorded. You must, however, prepare to concentrate your forces at the point liable to be attacked, and make every arrangement to secure the troops, guns, and munitions of war at such points as you may deem proper to relinquish.

I am, &c.,

R. E. LEE,
General, Commanding.

SAVANNAH, GA., *February* 19, 1862.

Brig. Gen. R. S. RIPLEY,
Commanding, &c., Charleston:

GENERAL: From the progress of the war, it seems plain that the enemy, when ready to move against Charleston, should he select it as a point of attack, will advance in great force. We should therefore be prepared to concentrate rapidly in his front, on the lines that can be best defended, so as to be able to contend to the utmost of our strength. Beyond these lines every preparation should be made to withdraw guns and munitions of war when it becomes necessary or when the route of the enemy renders them valueless in the positions occupied. My object is to ascertain your opinion, whether, without weakening the plan of defense, our lines could be contracted, and exposed or distant points abandoned.

The batteries at Cole's Island, for instance, would not be available, provided the enemy should advance by the Edisto, and, unless arrangements are made to withdraw them, would be lost. If they can be reached in great force by the enemy's gunboats they might be suppressed, and the Stono seized as an avenue of approach. If it is necessary to maintain these batteries, they should be made as strong as possible and their communications rendered practicable in case of a reverse. So at other exposed points.

I am in favor of abandoning all exposed points as far as possible within reach of the enemy's fleet of gunboats and of taking interior positions, where we can meet on more equal terms. All our resources should be applied to those positions. I wish you therefore to review the whole subject, and see what changes or improvements can be made, both as to the importance and strength of the positions retained.

I am, &c.,

R. E. LEE,
General, Commanding.

SAVANNAH, GA., *February* 20, 1862.

Brig. Gen. N. G. EVANS,
Commanding, &c., Adams Run:

GENERAL: If I have correctly gathered your opinion, you seem to think it probable that the enemy, in his advance upon the railroad or in attack upon Charleston, would ascend the North Edisto Island either at White Point or Simon's Landing. I hope you have this point well watched, and your forces prepared to throw them in advance of the enemy to cut them off from the railroad, and if forced to retire to place your troops so as to defend the route to Charleston. Should you discover a movement of the enemy in this direction, I desire you to notify General Pemberton as well as General Ripley, the former of whom can by a flank movement press upon the rear of the enemy, while the latter can move directly to your support. In this connection I deem it proper that you should hold your troops as concentrated as possible, and watch your exposed points by strong guards. If necessary to retain troops on Wadmalaw and John's Islands, they should be light, not encumbered with baggage, with communications free to retire to the main and join your main body. I take it for granted that everything that can be removed from these islands, and indeed from your front, has already been brought off by the inhabitants, and that no crops can be raised there the ensuing year. The country therefore does not require troops for protection, but merely to watch the enemy and guard the avenues of approach.

I am, &c.,

R. E. LEE,
General, Commanding.

SAVANNAH GA., *February* 20, 1862.

Maj. Gen. J. C. PEMBERTON,
Commanding, &c., Pocotaligo, S. C.:

GENERAL: The observations of Generals Ripley and Evans lead them to believe that the enemy in his attack upon Charleston will ascend the North Edisto as high as White Point and Simon's Landing, and make a dash at the railroad, of which he will be within 7 miles, so as to cut our communications. It will be apparent to you that this is one of our weak points, and is as likely to be seized upon by the enemy as any other. General Evans has been requested to give it careful attention, and in the event of the movement apprehended to give you notice. I wish you to be prepared, therefore, by a flank movement to intercept him, and, if possible, place yourself in his front, so if he is not driven back that we can fall upon him with our whole force in his movement against Charleston. I have always thought it probable that preparatory to an attack upon Charleston or Savannah the enemy would attempt to seize the line of the railroad both east and west of the waters of the Broad River, so as to isolate your force, the strength of which is probably known to them, as well as the cities themselves.

I wish you to be prepared against such a movement, and have your forces well in hand to move to any threatened point and take direction of the operations. I take it for granted that all property of value has been removed from your front, and that no crops can be raised in the country of the Broad, Combahee, and Ashepoo Rivers, and that the resources in this vicinity are nigh exhausted. The disposition of the troops, therefore, should look rather to their concentration to resist the enemy than to hold the country.

I am, &c.,

R. E. LEE,
General, Commanding.

EXECUTIVE DEPARTMENT,
Milledgeville, February 21, 1862.

R. E. LEE,
General, Commanding:

GENERAL: I have to acknowledge the receipt of your favor of the 18th instant. I am happy to learn that you have removed the troops from the islands and that you now have the guns at Savannah. God grant that they may enable you to drive the enemy's gunboats from the river when the attack comes.

In reference to the other point in your letter, I have to say that if my own house were in Brunswick I would certainly set fire to it, when driven from it by the enemy, rather than see it used by them as a shelter. We should destroy whatever the military necessities require. I am therefore prepared to sustain any order which in your opinion it is necessary to have executed. Private property and private rights must yield to the great public interests now at stake. The question of compensation will be one which will address itself to the State. When the war is over, justice to sufferers will no doubt be done.

Very respectfully, &c.,

JOSEPH E. BROWN.

AUGUSTA, GA., *February* 22, 1862.

General R. E. LEE, C. S. A.,
Commanding:

GENERAL: I have sent the bearer, Mr. N. B. Grant, a civil engineer in my employment, to ascertain if a small steamboat can be procured in Savannah for aiding in placing obstructions in the river.

I made a reconnaissance for about 70 miles down the river yesterday and the day before, and decided to place the proposed obstructions at that part of its course called Shell Bluff, about 45 miles from this city by water and 6 miles to the nearest point of the railroad. The stream at this place is 300 feet in width, impinging against the shell formation, which is surmounted by a ridge some 100 feet in height parallel to the course of the river, with a spur, affording direct fire at the point selected, at right angles to the stream and 100 yards distant.

There is also a small plateau about 30 feet perpendicular above the river at its highest stage, affording room for a battery or intrenchment of limited dimensions immediately on the river and at the foot of the ridge. This is the point I have selected to place the proposed obstructions, and offers excellent advantages for such purpose. The depth of the channel is about 30 feet at high water.

The river has many sudden and sharp turns in the part examined, with side currents of much force passing over the intervening inundated lands, thus rendering the navigation slow and difficult for a screw steamer at a high stage of the water, and I understand the shallowness of the bars and numerous projecting stumps of trees render its navigation dangerous for boats drawing 6 feet or over of water at a medium stage of the river, and impracticable at low water to this place.

Thus a high stage of the water is probably the only period at which gunboats would make the attempt, and from the numerous high bluffs bordering the right bank of the river and commanding its channel at more than 200 yards distant, I think its navigation could be, in the general case, rendered dangerous to the enemy, if not absolutely stopped, by small-arms alone.

We would want a steamboat about two weeks probably. One could be procured here, but of larger size than is necessary or desirable, and at a corresponding increased rate of charter; hence I have thought it proper to send Mr. Grant to obtain one of the small boats which I understand is now at Savannah in Government employ, if practicable. The work of procuring the timber, iron, &c., has already commenced, and matters will be pushed forward with all the celerity possible.

Respectfully, general, your obedient servant,

GEO. W. RAINS,
Major, Artillery and Ordnance, &c.

SAVANNAH, GA., *February* 22, 1862.

His Excellency JOSEPH E. BROWN,
Governor of Georgia, Milledgeville:

GOVERNOR: In the present condition of affairs the connection between the cities of Charleston and Savannah by the Charleston and Savannah Railroad is very precarious. Should the force now on this coast be re-enforced, an attempt will be made in all probability to cut the road between the two cities, and, in view of this contingency, I have the honor to call your attention to the importance to the defense of the cities of Charleston, Augusta, and Savannah, as well as to the States of Georgia and South Carolina, of connecting the Augusta and Savannah Railroad with the Georgia or South Carolina Railroad at Augusta. I am informed that the Augusta and Savannah Railroad Company is willing to build the connection at its own expense, provided they be allowed to take the route which they would prefer, and which the president of the road (Dr. Willis) informs, me is but one-fourth of a mile in distance, and if permission were given at once, the connection could be completed in one week. I am moreover informed by Dr. Willis that the railroad company will make the connection, taking the route selected by the city council of Augusta—more than twice the distance, however—if the State of Georgia will direct it and assume the expense. In the latter case, no doubt the State would be reimbursed by the Confederate Government, but all considerations of time and expense would seem to recommend that the former plan be adopted, and I earnestly request that, if there is no insurmountable objection to its being carried out, your excellency lend your aid and influence to have it done immediately.

I am, &c.,

R. E. LEE,
General, Commanding.

HDQRS. DEPARTMENT OF SOUTH CAROLINA, &C.,
February 23, 1862.

Maj. GEORGE W. RAINS,
Augusta, Ga.:

MAJOR: I am glad to learn by your letter of the 22d instant that your examination of the Savannah River has been successful, and that you have selected a point suitable for obstructing its navigation. I request that you will commence immediately the construction of the work, push it forward with vigor, and at the same time erect such batteries, intrenchments, and rifle pits as in your judgment will best defend it, and which we may have the means of arming and manning.

The position you have selected seems to possess excellent advantages for this purpose, and I trust by your skill and energy will be made impregnable. It should be provided with bomb-proofs to shelter the men from shells, &c., provided the guns cannot themselves be protected from these missiles. I have written to the governor, who has no guns which can be applied to your position, and I cannot say now whether any can be sent from here. Please inform me of your progress, and whether I can give any aid to the work.

Mr. Grant has gone to inquire about a suitable boat. The two most convenient for your purpose, Talemino and Habersham, are in constant use, and I do not suppose can be spared. In that event you must impress a boat and pay the rates given here.

I am, &c.,

R. E. LEE,
General, Commanding.

WAR DEPARTMENT, C. S. A.,
Richmond, Va., February 24, 1862.

General R. E. LEE,
Savannah, Ga.:

SIR. The recent disaster to our arms in Tennessee forces the Government to the stern necessity of withdrawing its lines within more defensible limits, so as to enable us to meet with some equality the overpowering numbers of the enemy. The railroad line from Memphis to Richmond must be defended at all hazards. We can only do this by withdrawing troops from the seaboard. You are therefore requested to withdraw all such forces as are now employed in the defense of the seaboard of Florida, taking proper steps to secure the guns and munitions of war, and to send forward the troops to Tennessee, to report to General A. S. Johnston, by the most expeditious route.

The only troops to be retained in Florida are such as may be necessary to defend the Apalachicola River, as the enemy could by that river at high water send his gunboats into the very middle of the State of Georgia. Let General Trapier put that river and harbor in a satisfactory state of defense, and then further orders can be given to him; but I beg that there be no delay that you can possibly avoid in forwarding to Tennessee the troops now at Fernandina and on the eastern coast.

I am, your obedient servant,

J. P. BENJAMIN,
Secretary of War.

SAVANNAH, GA., *February* 24, 1862.

Brig. Gen. J. H. TRAPIER,
Commanding, &c., Tallahassee:

GENERAL: I have the honor to acknowledge the receipt of your letter of February —, from Fernandina, relative to the indefensibility of the position on Amelia Island. The withdrawal of the troops from Saint Simon's and Jekyl Islands can only affect the inland communication between Brunswick and Cumberland Sound, rendering it less secure and certain. The batteries commanding the principal entrance into Cumberland Sound can be as easily turned through Saint Andrew's Sound as Saint Simon's, which is nearer and as accessible as the latter. I had hoped that guns could be obtained in time to defend these rear approaches, but as I now see no possibility of doing so, and as the means on the island are incompetent in your opinion for its defense, you are authorized to retire both from Cumberland and Amelia Islands to the main-land, taking such positions as will best defend the interests of the State, and using the guns and troops for that purpose. Captain Blain's company must be sent as soon as possible to this city, to report to General Lawton.

The withdrawal of the troops and guns will have to be done with extreme caution, and your arrangements for that purpose must be done so quietly and executed so speedily as not to attract the attention of the enemy.

The guns from Cumberland should first be removed and transported across at night; logs in imitation of guns should be mounted in their place as the guns are removed. The same precaution should be taken in dismantling the batteries at Amelia Island; the platforms, ammunition, and munitions of all sorts secured. It is hoped that the guns and ammunition derived from these points will enable you to secure other important points in the State of Florida, for supplying which I see no other means.

I am, &c.,

R. E. LEE,
General, Commanding.

SAVANNAH, GA., *February* 24, 1862.

Col. J. GORGAS,
Chief of Ordnance, &c., Richmond, Va.:

COLONEL: I am in receipt to-day of a letter from Brigadier-General Trapier, commanding, &c., Florida, requesting most earnestly to be at least supplied with 1,000 muskets for the arming of the new troops under his command. One company, which was mustered in the service on 11th December last for the war, has not as yet, he informs me, received a single arm. I have not any at my disposal to give him, those allotted to my department having already been devoted to the arming of troops mustered into service from Georgia and South Carolina. I see by the disposition that has been made of the arms that 900 are to be sent to Richmond; if those are not wanted there I would recommend that they be applied to the arming of the troops now mustering for the war in this department. General Trapier also applies for some blankets and powder, if they can be spared. Similar applications have been made to me by the governor of Florida.

I am, &c.,

R. E. LEE,
General, Commanding.

SAVANNAH, GA., *February* 24, 1862.

His Excellency JOHN MILTON,
Governor of Florida, Tallahassee:

GOVERNOR: I have had the honor to receive your letter of the 21st instant,* handed to me by Col. J. J. Williams, of Florida.

I regret very much to learn that the means for the defense of the capital of the State are so deficient. Not finding it possible to defend

---

*Not found.

all the important points in the State, or to obtain guns to place Cumberland Harbor out of the reach of capture, I had previously authorized General Trapier to withdraw the troops and guns from that point, and to apply them to other vital portions of the State. This is the only course now left to supply means for defending it. I have also authorized him to withdraw generally from the islands to the main; the only way, in my opinion, successfully to resist the large force that can be brought against us by the enemy, and to deprive him of the benefit derived from his fleet and heavy floating batteries.

In reference to the cargo landing from the steamer Carolina, its disposition has been made by the War Department at Richmond, which will go but a little way in supplying the urgent demands of the service. It is now impossible to arm troops entering the service for the war. I consider it therefore useless for troops entering the service for a less period to expect arms from the Government. If regiments can be raised in Florida for the war (the only period, in my opinion, for which they ought to be accepted), I will endeavor to procure arms for them.

It will be necessary for the citizens of Florida to turn out to a man to defend their homes, and the sooner your excellency can impress upon them this fact, the easier will be its accomplishment. Troops cannot now be drawn from other States for this purpose. Every State is looking to the protection of her own borders and providing the regiments called for by the Secretary of War. The governor of Georgia has been obliged to refuse my recent application to him for two regiments, to be placed under the command of General Trapier, for the purpose of preventing an advance of the enemy through Florida into the southwest portion of Georgia.

I am, &c.,

R. E. LEE,
General, Commanding.

HEADQUARTERS, *Savannah, Ga., March* 1, 1862.

Hon. J. P. BENJAMIN,
Secretary of War, Richmond, Va.:

SIR: I have had the honor to receive your letter of the 24th February, in reference to withdrawing the forces from the sea-coast of Florida, and have directed General Trapier accordingly. By telegraph he has been directed to send Colonel Dowd's Twenty-third Mississippi Regiment immediately to Tennessee, to report to General A. S. Johnston. On the 19th ultimo he was directed by telegraph to send Colonel Davis' regiment of cavalry from Florida to Chattanooga, to report to General A. S. Johnston. As soon as Amelia Island has been evacuated, the public property secured from there and other points along the seaboard, troops not necessary to prevent the enemy from penetrating into the interior will be forwarded to General Johnston.

I have the honor to be, your obedient servant,

R. E. LEE,
General, Commanding.

RICHMOND, VA., *March* 2, 1862.

General R. E. LEE,
Savannah:

If circumstances will, in your judgment, warrant your leaving, I wish to see you here with the least delay.

JEFFERSON DAVIS.

HDQRS. DEPARTMENT OF SOUTH CAROLINA, &c.,
March 3, 1862.

General A. R. LAWTON,
Commanding District of Georgia:

GENERAL: I shall be compelled to leave Savannah this evening on duty. Major Long, Captain Ives, and Captain Tatnall, members of my staff, will remain here for the present on the duties on which they are now engaged, the former in preparing and arming the new batteries in the vicinity of Fort Jackson; the second in superintending the batteries and obstructions on and near Saint Augustine Creek, and the latter in getting up certain boats for operations on the water. I need not press upon you the necessity of urging forward all these operations with the utmost expedition. It is my wish that as soon as the batteries are in fighting condition the work of protecting the guns from the enemy's missiles be vigorously pushed on, a commencement of which has been made at Thunderbolt and the battery at Fort Jackson under Captain Ives and Captain Echols. As it is a subject attended with difficulty, I beg you will give attention to it and adopt the plan that promises the best success.

The three-gun battery located on the right bank of the river to unite with the battery on Hutchinson Island should be commenced at once, and the bomb-proof arrangement be carried on with its construction. The raft must be put in position below Fort Jackson, and strengthened as far as time and opportunity allow. I have proposed a casemated battery of one or two guns, if they could be obtained, situated on the right bank of the Savannah, with embrasures and loop-holes for riflemen, looking across the river, to fire on boats reaching the raft. The battery will be located at the end of the raft, and have no opening down the river by which the raft or guns could be harmed by the shot of the enemy from that direction. If no better arrangement can be made, the 18-pounders from Fort Jackson, replaced by the 32-pounders, could be used for this battery. The batteries now under construction are so far advanced that a portion of the hands could be diverted to these last-named batteries.

I beg now to refer to a matter that must claim your earnest and close attention—the probable route of the approach of the enemy. It looks now as if he would take the Savannah River. In that event, the batteries of Skidaway and Green Island would be out of the line of approach, and if the guns can be applied to the defense of the Savannah, should be so used. They can be removed from these batteries in any event, should you determine it best to withdraw to the main. Thunderbolt battery must then be re-enforced and some 32-pounders mounted at the battery at Beulah, reserving the heavy guns for the Savannah. You are aware that arrangements are made for obstructing the navigation of the river at Shell Bluff, 35 miles below Augusta. This matter has been intrusted to Lieutenant-Colonel Gill and Major Rains, C. S. Army, and any aid they may require and you can give I desire you to afford.

Examinations have also been made with a view of obstructing the river above Savannah. Captain Walker, of my staff, has been on this duty, and will continue for the present. He recommends a battery at Mulberry Grove, and that the main and minor channels be obstructed. I wish these subjects attended to. No precise instructions can now be given, but they are left to your judgment. An obstruction on the Ogeechee has been proposed, and the planters on the river have offered to furnish the necessary labor. You are referred to Captain Hartridge's letter on the subject, and requested to forward the matter as much as possible.

Every effort must be made to retard, if not prevent, the further progress of the enemy up the river. If he attempts to advance by batteries on the marshes or islands, he must be driven back, if possible. Bold scouts must be established on Elba, and the right and left banks of the river closely watched, so as to discover his first lodgment, when they can be broken up. With this view I invite your attention to the propriety of establishing a battery at Mackay's Point, to drive him from Elba. There are three 32-pounders that could be used for that purpose, if a battery there is deemed advisable. It could not be maintained against his gunboats should they enter the river in force, but might with the aid of boat attacks, prevent the establishment of batteries on Elba.

It is of the utmost importance that the work at every point should be pushed forward with the utmost vigor and the closest attention given to the whole subject of the defense of the city.

I am, &c.,

R. E. LEE,
General, Commanding.

GENERAL ORDERS, No. 6. } HDQRS. DEPT. SOUTH CAROLINA, &c.,
Pocotaligo, S. C., March 4, 1862.

During the absence of General R. E. Lee, and in compliance with his instructions,* the undersigned assumes command of the Department of South Carolina, &c.

The headquarters of the department will be for the present at Pocotaligo Station, S. C., and all official communications intended for department headquarters will be addressed to Maj. T. A. Washington, assistant adjutant-general.

J. C. PEMBERTON,
Major-General, Commanding.

STATE OF FLORIDA, EXECUTIVE DEPARTMENT,
Tallahassee, March 5, 1862.

Hon. J. P. BENJAMIN,
Secretary of War:

SIR: Permit me to present to your acquaintance the Hon. David S. Walker, who visits you with a copy of an order recently issued by General R. E. Lee to General J. H. Trapier.

The effect of the order is to abandon Middle, East, and South Florida to the mercy or abuse of the Lincoln Government. It cannot be possible that the order was intended to have such an effect. If strictly obeyed, the forces at Saint Augustine, on the Saint John's River, at Tampa, and at this place, have to be ordered to the defenses of the Chattahoochee River or to Tennessee. I cannot and will not believe that an order to have that effect would have been issued without previous notice to the executive of the State, that proper measures might have been advised for the protection of the lives, liberty, and property of the citizens of Middle, East, and South Florida. Moreover, the order, if executed, would not, with the forces now in Florida, secure the defenses upon the Chattahoochee, for, if the enemy were in possession of

* Special Orders, No. 34, of March 3.

Tallahassee and Saint Andrew's or Saint Joseph's Bays, they can attack in the rear all batteries which may be constructed on either side of the river.

But, sir, if the sacrifice of Florida is necessary to secure the sacred rights claimed by the people of the Confederate States, there is not a man, woman, or child, true to the cause of liberty in Florida, but what will say amen, and in the midst of desolation, however fearful, advocate and cheer the progress of freedom to the South.

But, sir, we do not wish to give up our personal rights without striking a blow in their defense, and we are destitute of arms and the munitions of war, while in the State is a large quantity of arms and ammunition belonging to the Confederate Government not only liable but in danger of being captured by the enemy. I allude to the arms and ammunition at Smyrna. Moreover, when brought from Smyrna to Madison (the railroad depot), for the want of ready and sufficient means of transportation, they are subject to be seized and used by slaves against the lives of our citizens. I propose to order these arms and munitions of war to be sent to this place for safe-keeping, and, if necessary, for use by the forces now being mustered in for Confederate service during the war. To get them from Smyrna, I shall probably order some companies to that place to take the arms and march with them to protect the wagons of transportation. If here, they will be subject to your order or forwarded without it as soon as possible. If the enemy should get command of the Saint John's River, it will not be possible to get the arms from Smyrna without a long and tedious march, where subsistence for the forces cannot be easily obtained. Say to me to arm and equip 2,500 men in Florida for Confederate service for the year, or for the war, if it is to the end of time, and the 2,500, upon the terms, will be armed and equipped, and the balance of the arms and equipments will be protected from the enemy and slaves, and forwarded in one-third of the time which will be otherwise consumed in their transportation, even if not interrupted.

In conclusion permit me to invite your attention to the inclosed copy of a resolution of the so-styled executive council. My views with regard to this regiment have been too freely avowed to justify my saying more on the subject.

I have the honor to be, very respectfully,

JOHN MILTON.

[Inclosure No. 1.]

SAVANNAH, GA., *March* 1, 1862.

Brig. Gen. J. H. TRAPIER,
Commanding, at Tallahassee:

GENERAL: In pursuance of instructions from the War Department, you are directed to send the Mississippi regiment, Colonel Dowd commanding, to Tennessee, by the most expeditious route, to report to General A. S. Johnston. He is reported to be at Murfreesborough, and it is presumed that the route by Chattanooga will be the most direct. I desire that no delay that you can possibly avoid will take place in forwarding these troops, as there is an immediate necessity for defending the road from Memphis to Richmond. The recent disasters to our arms in Tennessee forces the Government to withdraw forces employed in the defense of the seaboard. The only troops to be retained in Florida are such as may be necessary to defend Apalachicola River, by which the enemy's gunboats may penetrate far into the State of Georgia. You are therefore desired to put that river and harbor in a satisfactory state of defense, and forward all troops not necessary for that purpose to report to General A. S. Johnston. All the guns and munitions of war must be secured. Let me know what arrangements you can make, and whether all of the guns will be needed for local defense.

I am, very respectfully, your obedient servant,

R. E. LEE,
General, Commanding.

[Inclosure No. 2.]

STATE OF FLORIDA, EXECUTIVE DEPARTMENT,
Tallahassee, March 5, 1862.

Hon. J. P. BENJAMIN,
Secretary of War:

RESPECTED SIR: The following is a copy of resolutions of the executive council of the State, passed the 3d instant, in regard to the cavalry regiment commanded by Col. W. G. M. Davis, in this State:

Resolved, That the governor be requested to correspond with his excellency Jefferson Davis, the Secretary of War, General R. E. Lee, and the officers of Colonel Davis' regiment, as to the necessity of the regiment being converted into an infantry regiment and remain in the State for its defense.

Adopted.

True copy.

E. BERNARD,
Private Secretary to his Excellency.

JOHN MILTON,
Governor of Florida.

STATE OF SOUTH CAROLINA,
DEPARTMENT OF THE MILITARY,
Columbia, S. C., March 7, 1862.

Hon. J. P. BENJAMIN:

SIR: I have the honor to inclose, for your information, a statement from the adjutant and inspector general's office of the State, showing number of troops sent by this State into Confederate service. It embraces a period up to 20th February last. Since that time 2,000 men have been added.

With great respect, your obedient servant,

JAS. CHESNUT, JR.,
Chief, &c.

[Inclosure 1.]

STATE OF SOUTH CAROLINA, A. AND I. GEN.'S OFFICE,
Columbia, February 20, 1862.

Hon. JAMES CHESNUT, JR.,
Chief of Military Department of
Executive Council of South Carolina:

SIR: In accordance with your request and instructions, received from Brig. Gen. S. R. Gist, adjutant and inspector general of South Carolina, I have the honor herewith to submit a statement of the number of South Carolina volunteer troops now in Confederate service. I would respectfully state that the report shows the original strength (except in the case of the regular force, where enlistments are still progressing) will reach 1,500, the troops passing entirely out of the State departments after their muster into Confederate service, except as to simple matters of organization.

The statement is classified as follows:

First. Those in service beyond the State.

Second. Those in service within the State.

Third. Those for and during the present war.
Fourth. Those for shorter terms of service.
With much respect, your most obedient servant,

G. A. FOLLEN,
Clerk Adjutant-General's Department.

[Inclosure 2.]

Recapitulation.

1. Those in service beyond the State	9,636
2. Those in service within the State	21,271
	30,907
3. Those for and during the war	8,153
4. Those for shorter terms of service	22,754
	30,907

STATE OF SOUTH CAROLINA, A. AND I. GEN.'S OFFICE,
Columbia, March , 1862.

Hon. J. P. BENJAMIN,
Secretary of War, Richmond, Va.:

SIR: In compliance with the requisition of your Department for five regiments of infantry to serve for and during the present war, I have the honor to inform you that a proclamation and orders for the rendezvousing said regiments have been issued by the State authorities and that the troops will soon begin to report in camp. The present camp of rendezvous selected will be at the Lightwood Knot Springs, near Columbia, on the Columbia and Charlotte Railroad.

You say "these troops will be clothed, supplied, and armed on Confederate expense," and "each soldier will receive a bounty of $50," &c. I have to request that you will at once cause the necessary arrangements to be made for the reception of the troops at the camp of rendezvous and for the compliance with the above-quoted stipulations, and to tender you the assistance of this office in the premises.

I have the honor to be, very respectfully, your obedient servant,

S. R. GIST,
Adjutant and Inspector General of South Carolina.

HDQRS. DEPARTMENT OF SOUTH CAROLINA,
Charleston, March 9, 1862.

Hon. ISAAC W. HAYNE,
Chief Police and Justice:

SIR: After an examination of the land defenses on James Island, I desired Brigadier-General Ripley, commanding Second Military District, to strengthen them in part, and to construct certain other works on the island, and also in the direction of Rantowles Bridge. General Ripley, though appreciating the importance of the work to be done, informs me that it is impossible with the hands now at his disposal to undertake it, and that the difficulty of obtaining a sufficient number will delay it indefinitely.

Regarding the proposed addition as essential to the safety of the city, should the enemy attack in large force, I deem it my duty to ask your co-operation, or, if necessary, that of the executive and council, to enforce the supply of labor which General Ripley may require.

I am, &c.,

J. C. PEMBERTON,
Major-General, Commanding.

RICHMOND, VA., *March* 13, 1862.

Brig. Gen. J. H. TRAPIER,
Commanding, &c., Tallahassee:

GENERAL: In my letter to you of the 1st instant, from Savannah, it was my purpose, under the instructions that I had received from the Secretary of War, to indicate to you the measures that would necessarily be adopted under the emergency of the occasion. Colonel Dowd's Mississippi regiment was to be sent with the least practical delay to report to General A. S. Johnston. Colonel Davis' regiment had been previously directed to do so. Both orders, I hope, have been executed. The Secretary, in his instructions, directed that the only troops to be retained in Florida were those employed in the defense of the Apalachicola, and I wished you to understand that our necessities might limit us to the defense of that avenue through Florida into Georgia. But I did not intend that you should send from your department immediately any troops but Dowd's and Davis' regiments, retaining the rest to secure the public property, guns, &c., until you saw what arrangements you could make for the defense of the State generally, after withdrawing from those points of the seaboard which in your judgment could not be maintained. It was with this view that I asked to be informed what arrangements you could make for local defense. It was then to be determined, under the instructions from the War Department, what other forces could be spared to reinstate our operations in the West. My own opinion and desire is to hold the interior of the State, if your force will be adequate, the Saint John's River, as well as the Apalachicola. I do not think you will be able to hold Tampa Bay, and the small force posted at Saint Augustine serves only as an invitation to attack; but on these points you must judge, and I desire your opinion.

I am, &c.,

R. E. LEE,
General, Commanding.

RICHMOND, VA., *March* 14, 1862.

Maj. Gen. J. C. PEMBERTON,
Commanding, &c., Pocotaligo, S. C.:

GENERAL: You will receive from the Adjutant and Inspector General's Office an order placing you in command of the military department composed of the States of South Carolina and Georgia. General Trapier will command the Department of Florida.

Being assigned to duty at the seat of government, I shall require certain members of my staff left at my headquarters at Coosawhatchie. I desire you to send to me at once Maj. T. A. Washington, assistant adjutant-general, with such official books and papers not appertaining to the Department of South Carolina, &c. Captain Memminger may continue on duty with you, as you will require additional assistance in your office. Major Long and Captain Ives, having in charge certain operations in the vicinity of Savannah at the time of my leaving the department, I am unwilling to withdraw them until I learn that their services can be dispensed with; they will therefore continue with you for the present. I take pleasure in commending to you my volunteer aide-de-camp, Capt. J. Manigault, who, from his local knowledge and other considerations, I presume would prefer serving in South Carolina, and hope that you may give him some position in which his services may be secured to his native State. I also left in Savannah Capt. J. R. F. Tattnall, C. S. Marine Corps, volunteer aide-de-camp, in charge of certain operations, in which it may be desirable for you to continue him. He is also commended to your attention, as I believe that you will require the aid of every good citizen of your department to contribute to its defense.

I am, &c.,

R. E. LEE,
General, Commanding.

[Inclosure.]

SPECIAL ORDERS, No. 59. } ADJT. AND INSP. GENERAL'S OFFICE,
Richmond, March 14, 1862.

* * * * * * *

XXII. Maj. Gen. John C. Pemberton is assigned to the command of the Department of South Carolina and Georgia.

XXIII. Brig. Gen. J. H. Trapier is assigned to the command of the Department of Middle and Eastern Florida. The western boundary of this department will be the Choctawhatchie River.

* * * * * * *

By command of the Secretary of War:

——— ———,
Assistant Adjutant-General.

HDQRS. DEPT. OF SOUTH CAROLINA AND GEORGIA,
Pocotaligo, March 18, 1862.

Hon. ISAAC W. HAYNE,
Of Executive Council:

DEAR SIR: I have just returned from an official visit to Florida, which I hope will excuse the tardy acknowledgment of your favor of the 9th instant. I have to express my thanks for the prompt attention given by the executive council to my application in reference to negro labor. The resolution of the council will no doubt be sufficient to accomplish all that is desired. It is, in my opinion, a matter of great public interest that the connection between the South Carolina Railroad and Charleston and Savannah Railroad be made as soon as practicable. Any assistance in my power will be most cheerfully given. The connection is emphatically a military necessity. Be pleased to inform me in what manner I can best aid in the work.

Very respectfully,

J. C. PEMBERTON,
Major-General, Commanding.

HDQRS. DEPARTMENT OF SOUTH CAROLINA,
Pocotaligo, March 18, 1862.

General S. COOPER,
Adjutant and Inspector General:

GENERAL: I have the honor to report my return from an official visit, via Chattahoochee River, to the cities of Apalachicola and Tallahassee,

Fla. On my arrival at Apalachicola, I found the batteries dismantled and the guns, carriages, ammunition, &c., already on board the steamboat Marianna and about leaving for Ricco's Bluff, a point on the river which would no doubt admit of a good defense, but which, after a personal examination of its advantages, seemed to me to be inferior in that respect to a position some miles lower, and known as Fort Gadsden. In a personal interview with Brigadier-General Trapier it was decided to establish the batteries at the latter place, against which an attack by land ought easily to be repulsed, by reason of the almost impassable country through which an enemy must necessarily advance.

I ascertained during my brief stay in Apalachicola that very many of the citizens—probably a majority—prefer to remain there. A large class of the population is compelled to do so, having no means of subsistence elsewhere. Many, however, are abandoning everything and going into the interior. All public property had been removed before my departure. All river pilots were required to leave the city with the troops. The telegraph office was closed, and the instruments for the present transferred to Chattahoochee.

It is proposed to occupy Fort Gadsden with from 600 to 800 infantry, a battery of six field pieces (not yet equipped), and, in connection with the position, two or three companies of cavalry, to be used as advanced pickets for courier service. Under present instructions from the War Department these are the only troops to be retained in Florida (being considered sufficient for the defense of the Apalachicola River), unless it is deemed advisable to continue a competent guard in the direction of New Smyrna and the Saint John's River, for such arms, ammunition, and other public stores as may be hereafter landed at New Smyrna. This guard I have directed to be retained for the present. It is the more necessary in view of the fact that the enemy, being in possession of Jacksonville, may intercept the stores sent to Baldwin, only 20 miles distant, for transportation by rail. Their safety, therefore, may require a further wagoning to Lake City.

I regret to report a very unsatisfactory condition of affairs in East and Middle Florida. The Mississippi regiment, some time under orders to repair to Tennessee, has not yet moved, for the want of the necessary transportation, as stated by General Trapier. Davis' regiment, also under orders for General A. S. Johnston's army, is in a state of mutiny, positively refusing, as I am informed, to move until the arrearages of pay due are received and until satisfied that a sufficient army is left in Florida for the protection of their families. A paper to this effect was shown me by General Trapier a few moments before my leaving Tallahassee, which was signed by several captains, lieutenants, and apparently by some of the rank and file of the regiment. General Trapier desiring to consult with me on the subject, I gave him my views, which will be carried out, *i. e.*, to arrest and bring to trial the captains whose signatures were attached; that the articles of war (7 and 8) bearing upon mutiny be read before the regiment, and the order for the movement immediately reiterated. A personal interview of a few moments with Colonel Davis, commanding this regiment, whom I met with yesterday, on his way to rejoin his command, leads me to hope that this mutinous spirit may be quelled without resorting to stronger measures, and the orders of the Department be carried into execution without further delay.

I find the citizens of Tallahassee much excited on the subject of the withdrawal of the troops, and am informed by Governor Milton and others that the feeling in many cases amounts almost to disaffection.

I observe also a disposition to plant cotton the coming season. Several thousand bales are still in the vicinity, which I have directed General Trapier to notify the people must be destroyed rather than permitted to fall into the hands of the enemy. The four pieces of siege artillery now at Saint Mark's I have directed to be withdrawn, as no troops are to be retained there. They will be forwarded to Fort Gadsden.

I respectfully renew the request that General Trapier be authorized to retain a sufficient number of arms from those landed at New Smyrna to equip the unarmed troops mustered into the Confederate service for the war. It is represented to me by Governor Milton that if arms could be issued to troops called out by the State, there would be no desire to retain Confederate forces, and that a feeling of security would be engendered which does not now exist.

In bringing this subject to the consideration of the Department I would add, that if a system of guerrilla warfare should be instituted in a country so sparsely settled as is Florida, it would probably result in great suffering to many unprotected families. Unless, therefore, the district of country liable to incursions of the enemy be entirely abandoned by the people, I have advised the governor to discountenance such mode of warfare.

I have the honor to transmit herewith a copy of a communication addressed to myself by General Trapier, showing the regiments and separate corps to be transferred, as also those to remain in the State, under the present instructions of the War Department.

Very respectfully, your obedient servant,

J. C. PEMBERTON,
Major-General, Commanding.

[Inclosure.]

HDQRS. PROV. FORCES, DEPT. EAST AND MIDDLE FLA.,
Tallahassee, March 16, 1862.

Maj. Gen. J. C. PEMBERTON, P. A. C. S.,
Comdg. Dept. of S. C., Ga., and Middle and East Fla.:

GENERAL: I have the honor very respectfully to inform you that, in obedience to instructions from General R. E. Lee, the Twenty-fourth Mississippi Regiment, Colonel Dowd, and the First Regiment Florida Cavalry, Colonel Davis, are now under orders to proceed to Tennessee, and will leave as soon as transportation can be furnished.

The remaining troops in this district to proceed hereafter to Tennessee under the same instructions will be—

(Twelve-months:) Third Regiment Florida Volunteers, Colonel Dilworth, now at Baldwin.

(Twelve-months:) Fourth Regiment Florida Volunteers, Colonel Hopkins, now at Sanderson.

Fifth Regiment Florida Volunteers (for the war), in camp of instructions; not yet fully organized.

Martin's light battery, six pieces.

Gamble's battery, three pieces, not equipped.

The troops to remain [in] Florida, by your direction, for service on the Apalachicola River, and for scouts, couriers, &c., are the First Florida Special Battalion, six companies, Major Hopkins.

Baya's company of artillery (independent).

Dunham's light battery.

Owens' troop.

Brokaw's troop.

Capt. C. Smith's company of cavalry.
Captain Partridge's company of cavalry.
Captain Thigpen's company of cavalry.
Captain Smith's company of cavalry.
Captain Turner's company of cavalry (to be disbanded).

I am, sir, very respectfully, your obedient servant,

J. H. TRAPIER,
Brigadier-General, Commanding.

HDQRS. DEPARTMENT OF SOUTH CAROLINA, &c.,
Pocotaligo, March 18, 1862.

General J. H. TRAPIER,
Comdg. Dept. of East and Middle Fla., Tallahassee, Fla.:

GENERAL: The general commanding the department directs me to in form you that he considers it of great moment that all the cotton that has been accumulated at Tallahassee and vicinity should be removed as speedily as possible to some secure place or places in the interior, where there would be no chances of capture by the enemy in case of their getting possession of the city. To this end you will give the necessary notice to the citizens and owners, and in case such an emergency as the probable loss of it should ensue, you should be prepared to burn or otherwise destroy it rather than that it should fall into the enemy's hands.

I am, general, very respectfully, your obedient servant,

T. A. WASHINGTON,
Major, and Assistant Adjutant-General.

HDQRS. DEPARTMENT OF SOUTH CAROLINA, &c.,
Pocotaligo, March 18, 1862.

General HENRY C. WAYNE,
Adjutant and Inspector General Georgia:

GENERAL: I have the honor to acknowledge the receipt of your letter of March 8, 1862,* and in answer am instructed to state that he [General Pemberton] approves of your idea of ordering out the militia in that part of your State invaded by the enemy; but before inaugurating a system of guerrilla warfare he would recommend that all women and children be removed before such operations are commenced on our part

I am, &c.,

[T. A. WASHINGTON.]

HDQRS. PROV. FORCES DIST. MIDDLE AND EAST FLA.,
Tallahassee, March 19, 1862.

Maj. T. A. WASHINGTON,
Assistant Adjutant-General, Pocotaligo, S. C.:

MAJOR: I have the honor to forward herewith a copy of a letter received yesterday from General Lee† for the information of the major-general commanding. Under these instructions it becomes my duty to suspend the movement of all troops except that of Dowd's and Davis' regiments and the battalion which is to garrison the works on the Apalachicola River. Want of transportation on the Apalachicola River

---

* Not found.

† See Lee to Trapier, March 13, p. 406.

has prevented my visiting and deciding upon the proper position for a defense of that river up to this time. I leave here to-morrow morning for that purpose. I learn, however, from General Floyd that all the guns were landed at Ricco's Bluff, and that they were being put in battery. Unless, therefore, I find the advantages of the lower position (old Fort Gadsden) greatly superior to those of Ricco's Bluff, I shall decide to allow the guns to remain at the latter place.

I am, major, very respectfully, your obedient servant,

J. H. TRAPIER,
Brigadier-General, Commanding.

HDQRS. PROV. FORCES, DEPT. EAST AND MIDDLE FLA.,
Tallahassee, March 19, 1862.

Capt. W. H. TAYLOR,
Assistant Adjutant-General, Richmond, Va.:

CAPTAIN: I have the honor to acknowledge the receipt of the letter of the commanding general, dated Richmond, March 13, 1862.

The regiments of Colonels Dowd and Davis were put under orders for Tennessee immediately upon the receipt of the general's instructions to that effect. I regret to say that owing to the limited means of transportation in this military district neither of them has as yet left the State. Their arrangements, however, are now nearly complete, and Colonel Dowd will take up the line of march to-morrow from Madison, on the Tallahassee Railroad, for Quitman, on the Savannah road. Colonel Davis will follow by another route in a couple of days, I hope.

I regret very much my misapprehension of the spirit and intention of the general's letter of instructions of the 1st March. The language used was explicit, and did not seem to leave any discretion with me. I was told "the only troops to be retained in Florida are such as may be necessary to defend the Apalachicola River," and, further, to "send forward all troops not necessary for that purpose, to report to General A. S. Johnston."

With the purpose of carrying out this order, I was assembling the troops in the interior of the State, where it was my intention to have held them till "all the guns and munitions of war" had been secured, if possible; sending forward, however, to the Apalachicola River the forces intended for its defense.

Major-General Pemberton visited this military district a few days since, and had ordered immediate preparations made for the movement of the troops to Tennessee, excepting the guard for the protection of the arms that had been landed at Smyrna, a regiment which was to remain temporarily in observation before Jacksonville, and the independent companies of cavalry, all of which he directed should be retained in the State.

Carrying out my instructions, I had withdrawn from the Saint John's River, which river is now in the possession of the enemy.

I concur entirely in opinion with the general that we should "hold the interior of the State," if practicable, and to this end I recommend the raising and thoroughly arming and equipping bands of guerrillas. The forces at my command are utterly inadequate to the defense of the State generally by heavy bodies of troops, except it be the capital of the State. In front of this place masses of troops may operate, and I strongly advise the concentration here of an army of at least 3,000 men.

I have ordered the troops to withdraw from Saint Augustine, and shall not countermand the order, for I agree with the general that the place is not tenable. Tampa I think we may hold, and I shall countermand the order for its evacuation, since the general leaves it discretionary with me to do so.

I am, captain, very respectfully, your obedient servant,

J. H. TRAPIER,
Brigadier-General, Commanding.

EXECUTIVE DEPARTMENT,
Tallahassee, March 19, 1862.

Hon. J. P. BENJAMIN,
Secretary of War:

SIR: The inclosed copy of [letter of] General Richard F. Floyd is respectfully submitted to your consideration.

I am informed that General Trapier desires to be relieved from service in this military department, and respectfully recommend General Floyd to be appointed brigadier-general and assigned to duty here.

Nearly all our guns have been lost at Fernandina and on the Saint John's River, and an immediate and rigid inquiry into the causes is alike due to the public interests and the character of officers.

The prejudices excited against General Trapier, whether just or unjust, prevent his being an efficient officer in this department. I regret it very much, and entertain for him the kindest regard, but an immediate change, in my opinion, is necessary to the defenses of the State. If agreeable to you, submit this letter to the consideration of his excellency President Davis, and moreover whether it will be agreeable to him and the War Department for me, as the governor and commander-in-chief of the State, to command the Confederate forces a few weeks for the defense of the State.

I have the honor to be, respectfully,

JOHN MILTON.

[Inclosure.]

BRIGADIER-GENERAL'S OFFICE,
Tallahassee, Fla., March 17, 1862.

His Excellency Governor MILTON,
Tallahassee, Fla.:

SIR: I have the honor to report to you that as the State troops were to go out of service on the 10th instant, and as others were not forthcoming to replace them at Apalachicola, I deemed it proper to remove the guns, ordnance stores, and other public property from that post to one of greater security. I therefore commenced to take the cannon from the batteries on the 10th. The State troops were held for this purpose by their own voluntary action. After many days and nights of constant labor I got the cannon, with all their appliances, ammunition for small-arms also, on board steamers, and removed them to Ricco's Bluff, on the east side of the Apalachicola River. At this point the cannon (thirteen in number, being all I had at Apalachicola) were being placed in position for immediate use, if necessary, and orders have been issued to Lieutenant-Colonel James, in command there for the present, to erect batteries with all dispatch. The brass field pieces of the Milton Artillery, together with all things pertaining to them, I brought to Chattahoochie Arsenal, at which place they are now, in charge of Second Lieutenant Bull, of the Milton Artillery.

Your instructions that Lieutenant-Colonel James and Major Richardson should continue for the present in their respective commands have been made known to those officers, and they have cheerfully complied with your wishes. Lieutenant-Colonel James has been very efficient and energetic in his duties, almost everything having devolved upon him in the absence of Major Richardson upon recruiting service.

The companies of Captains Grace and Attaway, for Confederate service, now full, and Captain Gregory's, not yet full, constitute the force now at Ricco's Bluff. All other troops have returned to their homes. Subsistence for the troops at Ricco's Bluff has been sent from Apalachicola to that point.

The balance of Captain Dunham's company, the Milton Artillery, have orders to be at Chattahoochie to-day. I deemed it prudent to leave him with the remainder of his company at Apalachicola for a few days, to keep order there and prevent communications being sent to the enemy's vessels and to protect the balance of the women and children desiring to leave that place immediately. Captain Thigpen's company of dragoons was not reorganized in full.

I had the telegraph office at Apalachicola closed, and apparatus removed on the day of my departure. Some river pilots have been arrested and brought to Chattahoochie. This was done as a measure of prudence, and not because their loyalty was suspected.

In descending the river I examined all the available positions with a view to the erection of batteries on the east bank. I beg to submit to you my opinion of these. Fort Gadsden is too much exposed; a long and wide reach of the river would enable the enemy to take distant positions, and with their heavy guns play upon batteries erected there. The only advantage this place has is that there is a thick swamp below it. Ricco's Bluff also possesses this advantage, besides many others. The sharp bend of the river compels vessels to approach within very short range of our guns in coming up and they must come immediately under them in turning the point, and again be in short range if they succeed in passing the point. Fort Gadsden is also represented by old settlers to be extremely unhealthy, while Ricco's Bluff is reported to be a healthy location.

I examined other points, and regard them all as possessing but few advantages by comparison with Ricco's Bluff. Re-enforcements are much required to expedite the works now progressing at that point, and I earnestly recommend that they should be sent there as early as practicable.

I have the honor to be, your excellency's very obedient servant,

R. F. FLOYD,
Brigadier-General.

SPECIAL ORDERS, No. 63. } ADJT. AND INSP. GENERAL'S OFFICE, *Richmond, March* 19, 1862.

* * * * * *

XXIX. Brig. Gen. J. H. Trapier is relieved from the command of the Department of Florida, and will proceed without delay to Decatur, Ala., and report for duty to General A. S. Johnston, commanding. Col. W. S. Dilworth is assigned to the temporary command of the Department of Florida.

* * * * * *

By command of the Secretary of War:

JNO. WITHERS,
Assistant Adjutant-General.

GENERAL ORDERS, No. 1. } HDQRS. DEPARTMENT S. C. AND GA., *Pocotaligo, S. C., March* 19, 1862.

I. By direction of the War Department the undersigned assumes command of the Departments of South Carolina and Georgia.

II. The following-named officers are announced as composing the department staff, viz:

Capt. J. R. Waddy, adjutant-general of the department.
Capt. R. W. Memminger, assistant adjutant-general.
Col. W. S. Walker, acting inspector-general.
Maj. A. L. Long, chief of ordnance.
Capt. W. W. McCreery, assistant to chief of ordnance.
Capt. J. C. Ives, chief engineer.
First Lieut. J. H. Morrison, P. A. C. S., aide-de-camp.

III. The headquarters of the department are for the present established at Pocotaligo, S. C.

[J. C. PEMBERTON.]

SPECIAL ORDERS, No. 44. } HDQRS. DEPARTMENT OF S. C., &C., *Pocotaligo, S. C., March* 19, 1862.

* * * * * * *

IV. Special Orders, No. 17, dated Headquarters Department South Carolina, &c., December 10, 1861, are so far amended as to cause the Fourth Military District to embrace that part of the coast between the Ashepoo and east bank of the Pocotaligo River, to be commanded by Brig. Gen. Maxcy Gregg, P. A. C. S.

The Fifth Military District will embrace that part of the coast of South Carolina between the west bank of the Pocotaligo River and Ocella Creek to Ferebeeville, under the command of Brigadier-General Donelson, P. A. C. S.

V. The district heretofore known as the Fifth Military District will hereafter be known as the Sixth Military District, the limits of said district remaining the same, and commanded by Brigadier-General Drayton, P. A. C. S.

VI. The brigadier-generals commanding the Fourth and Fifth Military Districts will have control of the quartermaster and commissary departments within the limits of their respective districts.

* * * * * * *

By order of Major-General Pemberton:

J. R. WADDY,
Assistant Adjutant-General.

HDQRS. PROV. FORCES, DEPT. EAST AND MIDDLE FLA.,
Tallahassee, Fla., March 20, 1862.

Maj. T. A. WASHINGTON,
Assistant Adjutant-General, Pocotaligo, S. C.:

MAJOR: Through inadvertency I have neglected, until the present time, to report, for the information of the commanding general, that by my order eight steam saw-mills, near Jacksonville, in this State, had been burned, to prevent their falling into the hands of the enemy, together with a large quantity of sawed lumber lying near them. I caused also to be burned an iron foundery and work-shops, the property of a Mr.

Mooney, in the same place; also the gunboat which was building near Jacksonville for the Government.

I am, major, very respectfully, your obedient servant,

J. H. TRAPIER.
Brigadier-General, Commanding.

RICHMOND, VA., *March* 21, 1862.

General HENRY C. WAYNE,
Milledgeville:

I have ordered 2,400 Enfield rifles, with a like number of infantry accouterments and a proper supply of cartridges, sent to Pocotaligo for your three regiments. Send to us at Goldsborough, N. C., three or four of your new regiments as promptly as possible, and they will be armed in like manner. The necessity for troops is most urgent, and not an hour should be lost. Advise me when you send them.

J. P. BENJAMIN,
Secretary of War.

HDQRS. DEPT. OF SOUTH CAROLINA AND GEORGIA,
Pocotaligo, March 21, 1862.

General R. S. RIPLEY,
Commanding Second Military District South Carolina:

GENERAL: I have received your communication of to-day's date, marked "confidential."* General Evans writes, March 21:

Yesterday the enemy were seen making preparations to cross Watt's Cut, and are evidently making arrangements either to make a feint from Jehossee or land on the mainland, &c.

Of course you keep in communication with General Evans. You are aware that three regiments have been removed from what was the Fourth Military District out of the State. No other troops have as yet arrived to replace them. I look for them, however, on Monday or Tuesday next. You will of course keep securely the prisoners sent by General Evans. I shall write immediately for instructions with reference to them to War Department.

I wish you to assist in any way you can to provide transportation for rice to points where it will be available.

How do your fortifications progress? I shall endeavor to see you in a few days.

Very respectfully, your obedient servant,

J. C. PEMBERTON,
Major-General, Commanding.

HDQRS. DEPT. SOUTH CAROLINA AND GEORGIA,
Pocotaligo, March 22, 1862.

Hon. ISAAC W. HAYNE,
Chief Justice and Police:

DEAR SIR: Yours of the 21st* is just received, and I regret to learn that in your opinion the governor and council have in terms conferred

---

*Not found.

greater powers upon me than they intended in the matter of the impressment of slaves for labor on fortifications. No new fortifications have been directed by me since the receipt of the resolution, nor do I at present contemplate any. Up to this date all my requisitions for labor have been for work previously under way. Lines of defense which I consider important had been suspended in their progress to completion for want of hands; the engineer in charge in this military district informing me that all but nine negroes had been withdrawn by their owners. As to voluntary labor being furnished, experience has taught me that it is not to be relied on at all, each owner of slaves judging apparently of the value of the work by what amount of protection his individual interest may seem to derive from it.

Where emergencies do not exist, I am of opinion that in a country where slave labor ought to be so abundant the soldiers can be more appropriately and profitably employed in attaining proficiency in drill, &c. You may rest assured, sir, that I will not call for labor under the authority of the resolution which in my opinion can be safely dispensed with.

Very respectfully,

J. C. PEMBERTON,
Major-General, Commanding.

HDQRS. DEPT. OF SOUTH CAROLINA AND GEORGIA,
Pocotaligo, S. C., March 23, 1862.

Col. W. S. WALKER,
Provisional Army, Adjutant and Inspector General:

COLONEL: The following telegraphic dispatch was received last night, and its tenor telegraphed to you at Camp McDonald. You are directed to proceed to Columbus, Ga., and impress the powder referred to. Take immediate measures to have it tested under your own supervision; report its quality to me, also to the Secretary of War direct, stating likewise the proportion of cannon powder. Report as promptly as possible:

RICHMOND, *March* 22, 1862.

To Major-General PEMBERTON:

The steamer Florida brought 64,000 pounds of powder, which the parties want to buy [sell] at $2 per pound, deliverable at Marianna, Fla., and the Government to take the risk of forwarding it to Columbus. This I have refused.

I have answered that I would pay the price for it when delivered at Columbus, if found to be of good quality. You are required to impress the powder, and have it tested by a competent officer, and report as promptly as possible of its quality. Let me know also what proportion of it is cannon powder. The arms on board are for the State of Louisiana, and cannot be impressed.

J. P. BENJAMIN,
Acting Secretary of War.

Very respectfully,

J. C. PEMBERTON,
Major-General, Commanding.

HDQRS. DEPT. OF SOUTH CAROLINA AND GEORGIA,
Pocotaligo, S. C., March 24, 1862.

General S. COOPER,
Adjutant and Inspector General:

GENERAL: I have the honor to report that I have taken the necessary steps to impress the 64,000 pounds of powder brought by the steamer

Florida immediately upon its arrival in Columbus, Ga. It will be thoroughly tested, under the supervision of Maj. A. L. Long, chief of ordnance and artillery in this department, and if of good quality 20,000 pounds will be at once forwarded to Maj. Gen. Sam. Jones, at Mobile, and the remainder to Major-General Lovell, at New Orleans. I have sent an agent—Mr. J. Manigault—to Marianna, Fla., to keep an eye upon the powder, which is there and in transit.

Very respectfully, your obedient servant,

J. C. PEMBERTON,
Major-General, Commanding.

HDQRS. PROV. FORCES DEPT. EAST AND MIDDLE FLA.,
Tallahassee, March 25, 1862.

Maj. T. A. WASHINGTON,
Assistant Adjutant-General, Pocotaligo, S. C.:

MAJOR: I have the honor to report, for information of the commanding general, that having received intelligence which leads me to doubt the accuracy of the report as to the enemy's forces in Jacksonville, which came to me yesterday, and having at the same time received orders relieving me from the command in this district, I am making my preparations for an early departure for the headquarters of General A. S. Johnston.

The forces in East Florida are reported so much weakened by sickness, that I have taken the responsibility of keeping Davis' regiment in that part of the State till the arms from Smyrna are in a place of safety. The colonel of the regiment has reported that it would not be prepared to march for some days, at any rate.

I am, major, very respectfully, your obedient servant,

J. H. TRAPIER,
Major-General, Commanding.

[Indorsement.]

HDQRS. DEPT. OF SOUTH CAROLINA AND GEORGIA,
Pocotaligo, S. C., April 2, 1862.

Having no control over Florida, this communication is respectfully forwarded for the information of the War Department.

J. C. PEMBERTON,
Major-General, Commanding.

HDQRS. DEPT. OF SOUTH CAROLINA AND GEORGIA,
Charleston, March 25, 1862.

Col. A. M. MANIGAULT,
Commanding First Military District South Carolina:

COLONEL: Having maturely considered the subject, I have determined to withdraw the forces from Georgetown, and therefore abandon the position.

You will accordingly take immediate measures to have the guns dismounted, taking care to have at hand heavy logs to place in position as each gun shall be dismounted. Do not allow more guns to be displaced at a time than you can immediately remove.

The heavy metal should be removed first, and the work should be done as far as practicable by night, and as rapidly as the means at your disposal will admit of. You will use the light-draught steamers for transportation to the railroad, and forward the guns and all munitions to Charleston. I earnestly impress upon you the necessity of promptness and caution in this movement.

You will, so soon as the batteries are dismantled and the material secured to a certainty against capture by the enemy, proceed with all the infantry force under your command (except troops for local defense) to this city and report to Brigadier-General Ripley.

The cavalry, field artillery, and local troops will for the present be continued as guard, and you will make such disposition of them for that purpose as your judgment and experience shall dictate.

If the field artillery is not equipped, it may be well also to remove it. You are requested to make immediate report on this point and upon any other connected with this movement which you may deem of interest.

Respectfully,

J. C. PEMBERTON,
Major-General, Commanding.

SPECIAL ORDERS, No. 118. } DEP'T EAST AND MIDDLE FLORIDA,
Tallahassee, March 25, 1862.

* * * * * * *

Col. William G. M. Davis, First Florida Cavalry, will proceed to Camp Langford, with his whole command, and relieve Colonel Dilworth, Third Regiment Florida Volunteers, in command of all the forces in that portion of the State, provided Colonel Hopkins' Fourth Regiment Florida Volunteers is not present.

As soon as the arms now *en route* for Lake City shall have arrived at that point Colonel Davis will, with his regiment, proceed immediately to Tennessee, and report for duty to General A. S. Johnston, C. S. Army.

* * * * * * *

By order of General Trapier:

R. H. ANDERSON,
Major, and Assistant Adjutant-General.

POCOTALIGO, S. C., *March* 26, 1862.

General A. R. LAWTON,
Savannah, Ga.:

GENERAL: I have just received the following telegraph. Answer me at once by telegraph, and report facts in full by letter:

RICHMOND, *March* 26, 1862.

Major-General PEMBERTON:

The governor of Georgia complains that arms imported in the Gladiator and landed at Savannah have been seized by the Confederate officers. If this be so, have them released.

GEO. W. RANDOLPH.

J. C. PEMBERTON,
Major-General, Commanding.

HDQRS. DEPT. OF SOUTH CAROLINA AND GEORGIA,
Pocotaligo, March 26, 1862.

Brig. Gen. THOMAS F. DRAYTON,
Commanding Sixth Military District South Carolina:

GENERAL: It is impossible at this time to send you permanent re-enforcements. The three Georgia regiments which have just reported are without arms or instruction. I expect, however, to have them armed immediately. One of these regiments is at Grahamville, and will, with the rest of General Donelson's brigade between Broad and New Rivers, be the principal assistance upon which you must depend for a movement against the enemy should he land east of New River. You have sufficient force now west of that stream, together with such aid as may be sent you from General Lawton's command, to effectually resist its passage or to meet the enemy should he approach from Red Bluff. The rest of your troops can be made disposable for any emergency in the south and west of New River.

I do not expect you to protect any possible landing place. Generally cavalry advanced guards are sufficient; the great object being to have information communicated rapidly, and to this end I desire you to keep your cavalry scouts in constant communication and in close proximity with General Donelson's, who will also be directed to establish them for that purpose at the head of Fording Island road. The only reason why the powder for torpedoes was not sent was because I found when in Charleston that the amount in hand was not sufficient to admit of it.

Very respectfully, your obedient servant,

J. C. PEMBERTON.

HDQRS. DEPT. OF SOUTH CAROLINA AND GEORGIA,
Pocotaligo, March 27, 1862.

General S. COOPER,
Adjutant and Inspector General:

GENERAL: I have the honor to acknowledge the receipt of a telegram from the Secretary of War, dated March 26, 1862, in relation to a complaint from the governor of Georgia that certain arms imported in the Gladiator and landed at Savannah had been seized by the Confederate officers. The Secretary directs, if this be so, the arms shall be released.

I have replied by telegraph of this date, on report from Brigadier-General Lawton, commanding at Savannah, this moment received, that—

> The arms were not seized, but came into the hands of the ordnance officer with Confederate arms and without any notice of the State's claim until they were shipped. Those arms cannot be recovered for the State, as they were shipped to Tennessee, Richmond, and other places, but they may be replaced by others to arrive from Florida.

Having had no notification of the disposition to be made of arms, &c., from the cargo of the Gladiator, I am not prepared to say at present how the arms were diverted from their proper destination. General Lawton will report in full by mail to-morrow. I respectfully request to be instructed by the Department as to the course to be pursued in replacing these arms from any future arrival.

I telegraphed to the Secretary of War this morning that certain parties in Atlanta, Ga., offered to dispose of about a ton of pig lead to the Government at 30 cents per pound. The highest price paid heretofore, as I am informed by Captain Cuyler, ordinance officer at Savannah, has been

16 cents. The lead is very necessary and becoming very scarce. I would suggest that general instructions be given me to impress for the use of the Confederate States in all cases where such gross extortion is attempted.

The 64,000 pounds of powder which I was directed to impress on its reaching Columbus, Ga., has not yet arrived there. Officers are in attendance to carry out the instructions of the Secretary.

Very respectfully, your obedient servant,

J. C. PEMBERTON,
Major-General, Commanding.

HDQRS. DEPT. OF SOUTH CAROLINA AND GEORGIA,
Pocotaligo, March 27, 1862.

General S. COOPER,
Adjutant and Inspector General:

GENERAL: I have the honor to report that Brigadier-General Ripley has been directed to withdraw the guns from the batteries on Cole's Island, and to confine the defenses of the city of Charleston by that approach to James Island and the Stono River.

Col. A. M. Manigault, commanding at Georgetown, S. C., has also been instructed to remove the guns from the works at that place to Charleston, and to withdraw all troops except those raised for "local defense." These last, amounting in the aggregate, present and absent, to about 1,200 infantry and 400 cavalry, I propose to continue for the present as a sufficient guard against raids by the enemy.

Very respectfully, your obedient servant,

J. C. PEMBERTON,
Major-General, Commanding.

POCOTALIGO, *March* 27, 1862.

Hon. GEORGE W. RANDOLPH,
Secretary of War, Richmond, Va.:

General Lawton reports—

The arms were not seized, but came into the hands of ordnance officer with Confederate arms, and without notice of State's claim until they were shipped. Those arms cannot be recovered, as they were shipped to Tennessee, Richmond, and other places, but can be replaced by others to arrive from Florida.

Shall they be so replaced?

J. C. PEMBERTON,
Major-General, Commanding.

RICHMOND, VA., *March* 28, 1862.

General PEMBERTON,
Pocotaligo, S. C.:

Replace the arms belonging to Georgia when you receive others.

GEO. W. RANDOLPH,
Secretary of War.

RICHMOND, VA., *March* 28, 1862.

Governor BROWN,
Milledgeville, Ga.:

Your arms were taken by mistake and distributed to various points. They cannot be recovered, but I have ordered General Pemberton to replace them from others expected from Florida.

GEO. W. RANDOLPH,
Secretary of War.

HDQRS. DEPT. OF SOUTH CAROLINA AND GEORGIA,
Pocotaligo, March 28, 1862.

Brig. Gen. MAXCY GREGG,
Commanding Fourth Military District:

GENERAL: The major-general commanding wishes me to say to you that it would be well for you to notify the planters in the vicinity of Ashepoo River (Chapman's fort) that as spring approaches the troops in that section will be compelled to fall back to a more healthy region of the country, and the guns at Chapman's fort will be removed to some other point, as necessity may require.

I am, general, very respectfully,

J. R. WADDY,
Assistant Adjutant-General.

HDQRS. DEPT. OF SOUTH CAROLINA AND GEORGIA,
Pocotaligo, March 30, 1862.

General S. COOPER,
Adjutant and Inspector General:

GENERAL: I have the honor to transmit the two accompanying papers,* received through Brigadier-General Lawton, in relation to certain arms represented by his excellency the governor of Georgia to have been seized by Confederate officers in Savannah, the arms being the property of the State of Georgia.

The Secretary of War directs that if the arms were taken, as charged, that they be restored. It will be seen by General Lawton's letter, that, having been shipped to various and distant points, it is impracticable to recover them. I request further instructions on the subject.

Very respectfully, your obedient servant,

J. C. PEMBERTON,
Major-General, Commanding.

HDQRS. DEPT. OF SOUTH CAROLINA AND GEORGIA,
Savannah, March 31, 1862.

His Excellency JOSEPH E. BROWN,
Governor of Georgia:

SIR: It has recently been brought to my notice that there is at present a large amount of cotton stored in and near Augusta, and it has been suggested to me that an expression of the intention of the commander of the military department to have this cotton destroyed rather than allow it to fall into the hands of the enemy might have a beneficial effect

---

* Not found.

in inducing its removal. Should the enemy be successful in his attempt upon Savannah, Augusta will be seriously threatened, and if rapid in his movements it is probable that, in the confusion and panic which would be likely to ensue, much of the cotton would not be removed. I therefore refer to your excellency's serious consideration the propriety of the State authorities notifying the people of the intention of the military commander, in order that such preliminary arrangements may be made for the removal of the cotton should the unfortunate emergency arise, which would otherwise involve serious loss of property.

Very respectfully, your obedient servant,

J. C. PEMBERTON,
Major-General, Commanding.

Abstract from return of the Department of South Carolina and Georgia, Maj. Gen. John C. Pemberton commanding, for March, 1862.

Troops.	Present for duty. Officers.	Present for duty. Men.	Aggregate present.	Aggregate present and absent.
Infantry	1,347	23,146	29,043	34,505
Artillery	100	2,056	2,609	3,167
Cavalry	131	2,249	2,774	3,220
Total	1,578	27,451	34,426	40,892

HDQRS. DEPT. SOUTH CAROLINA AND GEORGIA,
Pocotaligo, April 1, 1862.

Brig. Gen. MAXCY GREGG,
Commanding Fourth Military District:

GENERAL: The general commanding wishes Colonel Dunovant's regiment advanced as skirmishers until they engage the enemy. You will make such disposition of Leake's battery as circumstances may require. He has ordered two 42-pounder carronades to the work at Stony Creek. The general wishes you to keep him constantly advised of the enemy's movements.

I am, general, very respectfully,

J. R. WADDY.

P. S.—Move the two Georgia regiments down as far as the work on Stony Creek.

By order Major-General Pemberton:

J. R. WADDY,
Assistant Adjutant-General.

Occupy the several causeways (intrenched) and all important positions from Stony Creek to Benton Causeway with one of the Georgia regiments. Keep Leake's battery in hand to occupy any work which may be threatened. Let the mounted troops keep the enemy always in view. If compelled to fall back from Hosper's Creek, burn the boats.

Respectfully,

J. C. PEMBERTON,
Major-General, Commanding.

HEADQUARTERS FOURTH MILITARY DISTRICT S. C.,
Jericho, April 1, 1862—11 a. m

Capt. J. R. WADDY,
Assistant Adjutant-General, Pocotaligo:

CAPTAIN: I learn that the enemy have retired to the other side at Port Royal Ferry. I send you a copy of a slip of paper left by them.*

The enemy landed this morning at Page's Point at a later hour than at Port Royal Ferry. They were burning some houses when last heard from. I have not yet been informed of any advance by them. Our advanced guards of infantry, at Garden's Corner and Camp Pemberton have not been approached. I am about proceeding down the road to ascertain the precise situation of affairs, taking the Twelfth Regiment South Carolina with me.

I am, captain, very respectfully, your obedient servant,

MAXCY GREGG,
Brigadier-General, Commanding Fourth Military District.

P. S.—While writing the above I have received your two notes, with General Pemberton's postscript to me.

In my dispositions to receive the enemy, made early this morning, I ordered Major Huger, with the artillery, from near Fishburn's Causeway to the east end of the Combahee Ferry Causeway, there to await further orders, supported by four companies of the Thirteenth South Carolina Volunteers (two more of which are on this side of the ferry). I had not intended to move the two Georgia regiments farther than Old Pocotaligo before being assured of the enemy's advance. In obedience to General Pemberton's instructions, I will now move them forward to the intrenchments.

MAXCY GREGG.

HDQRS. DEPT. OF SOUTH CAROLINA AND GEORGIA,
Pocotaligo, April 2, 1862.

Hon. GEORGE W. RANDOLPH,
Secretary of War:

Information just received by telegraph from Colonel Dilworth, commanding Department of East and Middle Florida, shows it necessary that immediate instructions be given him as to disposition of arms *en route* from Smyrna, Fla.†

J. C. PEMBERTON,
Major-General, Comdg. Dept. South Carolina and Georgia.

HEADQUARTERS, *Richmond, Va., April* 2, 1862.

Maj. Gen. J. C. PEMBERTON,
Comdg. Dept. South Carolina and Georgia, Pocotaligo, S. C.:

GENERAL: By direction of General Lee, commanding, &c., I have the honor to state that he has just received a telegram from Governor Pickens, who states that the abandonment of Cole's Island before the inner lines are prepared opens the approach to the city by Stono to the enemy, and requests that the guns may be retained there for the present. He further states that the sickly season is approaching, and that there is no place on James Island where troops can live.

---

*Not found.

†See report of affair March 23, at Smyrna, p. 111.

Governor Pickens has already been informed by telegraph that movements of this character can only be decided by the officer in command of the Department, although the matter is respectfully referred for your further consideration.

Very respectfully, your obedient servant,

T. A. WASHINGTON,
Major and Assistant Adjutant-General.

HEADQUARTERS,
Richmond, Va., April 3, 1862.

Brig. Gen. A. R. LAWTON,
Commanding, &c., Savannah, Ga.:

GENERAL: I am directed by General Lee to acknowledge the receipt of your letter of the 22d instant, and to say in reply that the State troops should by all means be retained in the service for the war by the Confederate Government, if possible, and, if not, by the State government. He agrees with you that, "if the entire State forces with their arms could at once be received into the Confederate service, it would add materially to our security." But at all events the troops should be retained, and for the war, and he has advised Governor Brown to this effect.

As regards the matter of the State's undertaking its own defense, he thinks the Confederate Government should do all in its power to protect the State and defend her interests; and if for any reasons it should appear advisable that the State alone and unaided undertake her defense, the proposition should come from her and not from him.

I am, very respectfully, your obedient servant,

W. H. TAYLOR,
Assistant Adjutant-General.

HDQRS. DEPT. OF SOUTH CAROLINA AND GEORGIA,
Pocotaligo, April 4, 1862.

Colonel DILWORTH,
Tallahassee, Fla.:

By direction of the Secretary of War, you will send at once 1,500 muskets or rifles to Col. T. M. Jones, at Pensacola, Fla., and report to the War Department by telegraph the number on hand.

J. R. WADDY,
Assistant Adjutant-General.

HEADQUARTERS,
Richmond, Va., April 4, 1862.

Maj. Gen. J. C. PEMBERTON,
Comdg. Dept. South Carolina and Georgia, Pocotaligo, S. C.:

GENERAL: General R. E. Lee, commanding, directs me to acknowledge the receipt of your letter of the 27th ultimo, in which you report that you have directed the withdrawal of the guns and troops from the batteries at Georgetown and on Cole's Island. Since the receipt of your letter a communication has been written by Governor Pickens, representing the exposed condition to which the inhabitants and much property must be subjected in the country about Georgetown, and also that the enemy's gunboats easily ascend the river to the railroad unless there be interposed sufficient guns and troops to prevent them.

In view of these facts, the general commanding suggests the propriety of complying with the governor's suggestions at least until such a time as would enable the planters, &c., to remove their property, and also to allow time to those who desire it to move away themselves.

In conclusion, it is respectfully submitted to your judgment whether, in order to preserve harmony between the State and Confederate authorities, it would not be better to notify the governor whenever you determine to abandon any position of your line of defenses, in order that he may give due notice to the inhabitants to look out for their security.

Very respectfully, your obedient servant,

T. A. WASHINGTON,
Major, and Assistant Adjutant-General.

RICHMOND, VA., *April* 5, 1862.

Governor BROWN,
Savannah:

SIR: I regret extremely the interference with your arms; will use every exertion to recover and restore them, or to return others of equal value. The arms sent to Richmond were many of them stopped at Raleigh and turned aside to Goldsborough, for the purpose of arming three Georgia regiments called for by General Lee. It may be that those were your arms.

I have instructed General Pemberton to call on you for an invoice or other description of the arms, and to return them out of the first parcel received. If they cannot be replaced, they can be paid for. I have cautioned Colonel Dilworth, at Tallahassee, against using any State arms, and will cause any officer to be punished who knowingly takes them.

GEO. W. RANDOLPH,
Secretary of War.

HDQRS. TENTH REGT. S. C. V., C. S. P. A.
Second Military District, Mount Pleasant, April 5, 1862.

Capt. J. R. WADDY,
Assistant Adjutant-General, Headquarters, Pocotaligo:

CAPTAIN: By permission of General Ripley, to whom I reported on my arrival here from Georgetown with my command, the Tenth Regiment, I have the honor to report that the instructions received from the general commanding have been executed. The redoubts in the First Military District have been abandoned; the guns, 20 in number, dismounted, and are now on their way by railroad to Charleston, with ammunition, ordnance stores, &c. Logs of wood resembling pieces of ordnance have been mounted in the place of each gun that has been removed, and three companies of cavalry and three of infantry are encamped near them; the positions have the appearance of being still occupied. The troops cannot be cut off by any but a land attack, against which only ordinary precaution will be necessary.

The works are uninjured, having received no orders to destroy them, and deeming it inexpedient to do so.

The command of the district I have turned over to Col. R. F. Graham, commanding Twenty-first Regiment South Carolina Volunteers, with the following-named force under him:

State defense: Twenty-first Regiment, R. F. Graham, commandant, ten companies, 700 men; battalion, R. Nesbit, commandant, seven companies, 500 men. Fourth Battalion Cavalry, Maj. J. C. Wilson, four companies, 240 men; Tucker's cavalry, one company, 115 men.

For the war unconditionally: Ward's light battery, six pieces, one company, 112 men.

The district in its present defenseless condition requires a considerable cavalry force as a coast guard and police force. The five companies left there are, I think, sufficient for that purpose. The infantry can be of but little use, and I think it would be better to place them on the line of railroad (Kingstree), from which point they could be easily moved in any direction in the State where their services may be needed. At Georgetown where they now are, it would be a three days' march to reach any point on the railroad, and requires by the ordinary mail route two days nearly to convey information to them. I arrived here on the 3d instant with Tenth Regiment, 903 strong, having left behind, sick and convalescents, 123 men, the greater portion of whom will rejoin me on Tuesday next, also 77 men on furlough at that time, 30 of whom are on thirty days' furlough. Aggregate strength, 1,103.

I have the honor to be, your obedient servant,

A. M. MANIGAULT,

Colonel Tenth Regiment South Carolina Volunteers.

STATE OF FLORIDA, EXECUTIVE DEPARTMENT,

Tallahassee, April 7, 1862.

His Excellency JEFFERSON DAVIS:

SIR: The retiring of forces from Fernandina and the Saint John's River was attended with the loss of nearly all our guns, &c. The transportation of the arms and munitions of war from Smyrna has also been so mismanaged as to cause heavy losses. The causes should be promptly and rigidly inquired into.

The troops have become demoralized, and the faith of many citizens in the integrity and ability of the Government impaired.

The enemy is in possession of all of Florida east of the Saint John's River, and doubtless intend to take this place and hold Saint Mark's and Apalachicola.

The forces which were in Fernandina and are now here, if properly commanded, are enough to drive the enemy from the State.

The militia have not yet been ordered into the field, first because of the difficulty of procuring subsistence and arms, secondly because, from the prejudices excited, it would be difficult to preserve harmony between them and those in Confederate service.

I have recommended General Richard F. Floyd to be appointed brigadier-general and assigned to this military department. He is brave and yet prudent, and commands the confidence not only of the citizens (militia), but of those in Confederate service. He was in command at Apalachicola until the troops were retired from that place, and if we could have gotten a regiment there in addition to the 500 men he had, would, with the preparation he had made, have defended the place. As it was, in the presence of the enemy he retired in order without the loss of a gun or any ammunition or military stores.

There is much confusion and disorder among those in Confederate service, and simply because a competent officer in command is necessary. When General Trapier was relieved of the command, I expressed to the Secretary of War a willingness to direct the military movements in the State a few weeks, until a suitable officer could be assigned to the duty, if he would order the officers in command of regiments to report to me, but he replied there was no law to authorize it.

As soon as an officer shall be assigned to the command, competent to the discharge of the duties, I shall proclaim martial law throughout the Military Department, because of the disposition manifested in several places to submit to the enemy, and in fact upon the first opportunity to rally to their standard. I would much rather be in the field than discharging the duties of civil life, and would like to be appointed to the command of a brigade, where active service will be required and the enemy can be met.

Agreeably to a requisition of General Lee, four cavalry companies have been mustered into Confederate service and are upon duty, to supply the place of the cavalry regiment commanded by Col. Wm. G. M. Davis, who was ordered to report to General Johnston. Col. Davis' regiment is still here, and your attention is respectfully invited to the inclosed correspondence.*

I have the honor to be, respectfully,

JOHN MILTON.

HDQRS. DEPT. OF SOUTH CAROLINA AND GEORGIA,
Pocotaligo, April 7, 1862.

Brig. Gen. R. S. RIPLEY,
Commanding Second Military District S. C.:

GENERAL: The remaining Charleston companies, referred to in our conversation of the 5th instant, can be mustered in for one year, to complete the organization of corps. I trust, however, that every effort will be made to bring all these troops in for the war. I believe it can be done, and such I heard is also the opinion of Adjutant-General Gist.

If the accounts we have just received from the West of the success of our Army be true, it seems to me very probable that, to counterbalance his defeat there, the enemy may make a prompt and serious attack upon some important point on this seaboard. I am very anxious, therefore, that every exertion should be made to get the works at Elliott's Cut into condition to receive the guns from Cole's Island. If you cannot obtain labor otherwise, you should impress it at once. You are so confident of being able to hold Cole's Island, that I will not insist on the removal of the guns from there until they can be fought at Elliott's Cut. Let me know by telegraph whether the work there is under way; if not, when it will be.

Very respectfully, &c.,

J. C. PEMBERTON,
Major-General, Commanding.

---

*Not found.

SPECIAL ORDERS, No. 79. } ADJT. AND INSP. GENERAL'S OFFICE, *Richmond, Va., April 7, 1862.*

* * * * * * *

X. Major-General Pemberton's command is extended so as to include Eastern and Middle Florida as far west as the Choctawhatchie River.

* * * * * * *

By command of the Secretary of War:

JNO. WITHERS,
Assistant Adjutant-General.

HDQRS. DEPT. OF SOUTH CAROLINA AND GEORGIA,
Pocotaligo, April 8, 1862.

Brig. Gen. THOMAS F. DRAYTON,
Commanding Sixth Military District South Carolina:

GENERAL: I desire you to proceed with as little delay as possible to the city of Augusta, Ga., and confer with the mayor, R. H. May, esq., in relation to the immediate connection through Augusta of the Waynesborough and Augusta and South Carolina Railroads. You will explain to the city authorities and to the presidents and directors of the railroad companies that this measure is a military necessity, which I trust those interested will acknowledge. It is only necessary to revert to the important fact that, should the enemy cut the Charleston and Savannah Railroad, there will be no direct communication between the cities of Charleston and Savannah by railroad unless this connection is made. I am informed by his excellency Gov. J. E. Brown, of Georgia, that the route through Augusta proposed by Dr. Willis, president of the Waynesborough and Augusta road, and which he is willing to construct at the expense of the company, is the shortest; and being, for military necessities, the proper route, you will therefore require the said connection to be made by this route, and as expeditiously as possible.

I am, very respectfuly, &c.,

J. C. PEMBERTON,
Major-General, Commanding.

HDQRS. DEPT. OF SOUTH CAROLINA AND GEORGIA,
Savannah, Ga., April 8, 1862.

Capt. N. C. TILTON,
Assistant Quartermaster, P. A. C. S.:

CAPTAIN: The major-general commanding department directs that you proceed at once to Tallahassee and other points in Florida, and collect such of the arms recently landed in Florida belonging to the Confederate States as may be in the possession of parties not authorized by the Government of the Confederate States to hold them. You will call on Governor Milton, of Florida, and the commanding officer at Tallahassee, for such assistance as you may require, in order to secure the arms referred to. After executing this order you will report immediately, first by telegraph and then by letter.

I am, respectfully, &c.,

J. R. WADDY,
Assistant Adjutant-General.

RICHMOND, VA., *April* 8, 1862.

Gov. JOHN MILTON,
Of Florida, Tallahassee, Fla.:

Before receipt of your dispatch of yesterday, Joseph Finegan had been appointed brigadier-general and assigned to command East and Middle Florida.

JEFFERSON DAVIS.

HEADQUARTERS,
Richmond, Va., April 8, 1862.

His Excellency JOHN MILTON,
Governor of Florida:

GOVERNOR: Your letter of the 19th March, to the Secretary of War, was submitted by that officer to the President, who has requested me to inform you of the action that has been taken with reference to the appointment of a brigadier-general for command in Florida.

When the desire of General Trapier to be relieved from his command in Florida became known, the President was advised by prominent citizens of that State to appoint General J. Patton Anderson as successor of General Trapier, if the former officer could be spared from his present command. Acting upon this advice, the President proceeded to ascertain whether the services of General Anderson could be had. Before, however, this information could be obtained, and when the posture of affairs in the department to which General Anderson is attached rendered it unlikely that the commanding general would be willing to detach General Anderson, an application was made to the President by the Florida delegation for the appointment of General Jos. Finegan as brigadier-general in the event that the services of General Anderson could not be obtained. The application for appointment of a commander in Florida being urgent, and the necessity for prompt action being fully appreciated by the President, he availed himself of the advice of the members of Congress from Florida, and nominated General Finegan to the position of brigadier-general, and that officer, if his nomination be confirmed, will be assigned to command in Florida.

The President has no doubt, from the statements made to him by all the Representatives from your State as to the qualifications of General Finegan, that, while he has not been able to follow the recommendation of your excellency in making the appointment, you will find that your object in making that recommendation has been fully attained by the action that has been taken.

I am, governor, very respectfully, your obedient servant,

R. E. LEE,
General, Commanding.

HDQRS. DEPT. OF SOUTH CAROLINA AND GEORGIA,
Pocotaligo, April 8, 1862.

Maj. T. A. WASHINGTON,
Assistant Adjutant-General:

MAJOR: I have the honor to acknowledge the receipt of your letter of the 4th instant. A portion of the guns from the batteries near Georgetown are already in Charleston, the remainder *en route*, and all secure. The aggregate of all arms left for the protection of the local interests is 1,555, in which are included two companies of cavalry and a field battery—four pieces equipped with horses, two without, but soon to be. These are all troops for local defense. Great stress has been laid by some who have objected to the removal of the guns from Georgetown on the asserted fact that but 8 feet can come over the bar. In reply I will only state that the Nashville, drawing 11 feet, passed in and out under a midshipman at less than half tide and without detention. Gunboats drawing over 12 feet might therefore readily engage our batteries, and to oppose them we had in position two 32-pounders, six 24-pounders, four 18-pounders, one 12-pounder rifled, one 6-pounder rifled, two 12-pounders rifled, two 12-pounder howitzers.

In my estimation such a battery was worse than useless, and if the destruction of the railroad bridge was an object, the capture of the guns would only have added a certain *éclat*. I will add further on this subject that almost two weeks before I issued the order in question I mentioned to General Gist, then adjutant and inspector general of the State, that I thought seriously of withdrawing the batteries from Georgetown, and he has since informed me that he stated to the governor and council that I contemplated so doing.

I will, however, in future be more particular in giving notice of any intended change, and have in fact done so to the planters interested in the Ashepoo. As to the probable speedy withdrawal of the battery from Chapman's fort, so far as I am aware, I beg to assure the general commanding that perfect harmony exists between the Confederate States authorities, as represented by myself, and the government of South Carolina, notwithstanding the difference of opinion on the subject in question. Of this I am assured, having had several interviews with his excellency Governor Pickens since the date of his letter to the general commanding.

As regards Cole's Island, the guns are still in position and will remain so until the works on Stono River are ready to receive them, which I trust will be in a very few days.

Very respectfully, your obedient servant,

J. C. PEMBERTON,
Major-General, Commanding.

SPECIAL ORDERS, No. 80. } ADJT. AND INSP. GENERAL'S OFFICE, *Richmond, Va., April 8, 1862.*

* * * * * * *

VI. Brig. Gen. Joseph Finegan will report to Major-General Pemberton, commanding, &c., for assignment to the command of the Department of Eastern and Middle Florida.

* * * * * * *

XXII. Brig. Gen. S. R. Gist will report for duty to Major-General Pemberton, commanding Department of South Carolina and Georgia.

* * * * * * *

By command of the Secretary of War.

JNO. WITHERS,
Assistant Adjutant-General.

HDQRS. DEPT. OF SOUTH CAROLINA, GEORGIA, &C.,
Pocotaligo, April 9, 1862.

General S. COOPER,
Adjutant and Inspector General:

GENERAL: I have the honor to transmit herewith a copy of a letter addressed by me to General H. C. Wayne, adjutant and inspector general of Georgia. In reply I received a printed copy of Gov. J. E. Brown's speech to the State troops at Savannah on the 15th instant, which General Wayne says "develops his (the governor's) policy with regard to their continuance in service," and adds, "if they do not re-volunteer within the week, as set forth in his speech, he will replace them by an equivalent force of new volunteers."

On the 7th instant I had a personal interview with Governor Brown, when the subject was discussed more at large. In conversation the governor authorized me to say that he did not think more than 3,500 of the State troops now in service could be counted upon at any one time within the next two or three months for the defense of Savannah. My own opinion is, after a great deal of inquiry, that even this number is an overestimate. I am convinced that there is a general indisposition to re-enter the State service, though the governor thinks differently.

I did not in any manner enter into the question of the comparative advantages or disadvantages of the organization of State troops for local defense; my object being entirely to ascertain how far I could rely on such forces to make up the requisite numerical strength for the protection of the city and State.

Allowing the estimate of Governor Brown to be correct, the effective force will be diminished by 4,000 at least for several months to come.

I do not consider the present strength as more than adequate to the defense, but the direct purpose I have in view is to bring to the notice of the department the fact that this strength is daily diminishing, and that, should the exigencies of the service elsewhere demand the withdrawal of troops from this department, it will become necessary to abandon at least a part of our line of defense and with it some of the approaches to the Charleston and Savannah Railroad. In view of the possibility of these exigencies, I am taking measures to secure an uninterrupted communication between the two cities, by requiring a connection to be made through Augusta of the Waynesborough, Augusta and South Carolina Railroad. I consider the connection referred to a military necessity, and I believe it to have been so regarded by General Lee, as I know that he desired it to be made. Some difficulties, however, as to the particular route intervened to prevent it, and, the general leaving the department about that time, no steps were taken to enforce it.

Very respectfully, your obedient servant,

J. C. PEMBERTON,
Major-General, Commanding.

[Inclosure.]

HDQRS. DEPT. OF SOUTH CAROLINA AND GEORGIA,
Pocotaligo, April 1, 1862.

General HENRY C. WAYNE,
Adjutant and Inspector General of Georgia:

SIR: As the term of service of the Georgia State troops is about to expire, I would be glad to know the views of his excellency the governor in regard to that force, now forming so large and important a part of the army intended for the defense of Savannah and Georgia.

If it is the intention of the State government to continue the present or an equivalent force in service, it may be unnecessary for the Confederate Government to furnish more regiments. It is very desirable that this matter be determined without delay, as the safety of the city may depend upon prompt action.

I shall defer communication with the War Department on the subject, awaiting his excellency's reply,

Very respectfully, your obedient servant,

J. C. PEMBERTON,
Major-General, Commanding.

GENERAL ORDERS, No. 5. } HDQRS. DEPT. OF S. C., GA., &C., *Pocotaligo, S. C., April* 9, 1862.

I. The undersigned having been officially notified from the Adjutant and Inspector General's Office, Richmond, that East and Middle Florida as far west as the Choctawhatchie River is included within his command, hereby assumes command thereof. All reports and returns will be made accordingly.

II. Maj. A. L. Long, P. A. C. S., in addition to his duties as chief of ordnance, is assigned to those of chief of artillery of the department.

By order of Major-General Pemberton:

J. R. WADDY,
Assistant Adjutant-General.

SPECIAL ORDERS, No. 81. } ADJT. AND INSP. GENERAL'S OFFICE, *Richmond, Va., April* 9, 1862.

* * * * * * *

XX. Eastern and Middle Florida will hereafter constitute a separate department, under the command of Brig. Gen. Joseph Finegan.

* * * * * * *

By command of the Secretary of War:

JNO. WITHERS,
Assistant Adjutant-General.

RICHMOND, *April* 10, 1862.

Major-General PEMBERTON:

Beauregard is pressed for troops. Send, if possible, Donelson's brigade of two regiments to Corinth. If Mississippi Valley is lost Atlantic States will be ruined.

Very respectfully,

R. E. LEE.

POCOTALIGO, S. C., *April* 10, 1862—6.30 p. m.

General R. E. LEE,
Richmond, Va.:

Your telegram just received. I consider it an order. Donelson's brigade—two Tennessee regiments, aggregate 1,572—will move to Corinth as soon as transportation can be got ready. The enemy opened fire at 8 o'clock this morning from his land batteries on Fort Pulaski. Firing continuous. The Georgia State troops are being fast discharged. I shall order down the rest of the troops from Georgetown, S. C.

J. C. PEMBERTON,
Major-General, Commanding.

COLUMBIA, *April* 10, 1862.

Major-General PEMBERTON:

The President telegraphs me to send immediately troops to Beauregard. I have none, but I telegraphed Ripley to send Colonel Dunovant's, Manigault's, and Marshall's, as best prepared, from Charleston. Please let me know. Let Ripley have your orders.

Very respectfully,

F. W. PICKENS.

POCOTALIGO, *April* 10, 1862.

Gov. JOSEPH E. BROWN,
Milledgeville, Ga.:

Two regiments have been ordered from here to Tennessee. I am not aware that they are to be replaced by Confederate troops.

J. C. PEMBERTON,
Major-General, Commanding.

SPECIAL ORDERS, No. 20. } HDQRS. DEPT. S. CAROLINA, GEORGIA, &c., *Pocotaligo, April* 10, 1862.

I. Brig. Gen. W. D. Smith, P. A. C. S., having reported at these headquarters, in obedience to orders from the War Department, is assigned to duty in the Military District of Georgia, and will report to Brigadier-General Lawton, commanding at Savannah, Ga.

* * * * * * *

III. Brig. Gen. D. S. Donelson, commanding Fifth Military District, with the Eighth and Sixteenth Regiments of Tennessee Volunteers, will proceed with as little delay as possible and report to General Beauregard at Corinth, Miss., for duty.

* * * * * * *

V. Col. P. H. Colquitt, commanding Forty-sixth Regiment Georgia Volunteers, is assigned to the temporary command of the Fifth Military District, which extends from Pocotaligo River to Ocella Creek.

* * * * * * *

X. Maj. Gen. Maxcy Gregg will take immediate measures to have Chapman's fort, on Ashepoo River, dismantled, dismounting the guns, having at hand heavy logs to place in position as each gun shall be dismounted, and taking care that no more guns be displaced at a time than can be immediately removed. You will forward the guns immediately to Green Pond, S. C., for transportation to Savannah.

Colonel Graham will take immediate measures to move all troops and public stores under his command from Georgetown to Charleston.

By order of Major-General Pemberton:

J. R. WADDY,
Assistant Adjutant-General.

HEADQUARTERS,
Richmond, Va., April 11, 1862.

Maj. Gen. J. C. PEMBERTON,
Commanding Department of South Carolina and Georgia:

GENERAL: General Lee, commanding, directs me to inform you that he has notified General Beauregard by telegraph that the Tennessee brigade, the two South Carolina regiments, and the two regiments of Georgia State troops would be sent from your department to re-enforce him temporarily, and that they must be returned to you as soon as their services can be dispensed with.

Very respectfully, your obedient servant,

T. A. WASHINGTON,
Major, and Assistant Adjutant-General.

COLUMBIA, *April* 11, 1862.

General PEMBERTON:

Telegraph received. Ripley has two raw regiments and also twelve new Charleston companies, just mustered in and well armed. I hope, therefore, it is not necessary to withdraw the troops from Georgetown, for it is the only protection they can have, even for domestic police. Colonel Manigault's Georgetown regiment is one of the —— to send to Corinth, together with the regulars.

Very respectfully,

F. W. PICKENS.

HEADQUARTERS DEPT. SOUTH CAROLINA, GEORGIA, &c.,
Pocotaligo, April 11, 1862.

General N. G. EVANS,
Commanding Third Military District:

GENERAL: I am instructed by the major-general commanding to say to you that he desires you to look rather to the approach of the enemy by the Willstown road than to the holding of the point of your line. You will therefore make such disposition of the troops of your district as will enable you to concentrate towards Rantowles Bridge, to resist the enemy should he approach in that direction. The general also suggests the immediate withdrawal of all batteries not absolutely necessary to the protection of Charleston. We need all the guns we can obtain for the defense of our extensive interior lines of intrenchments. Two regiments have been ordered to Tennessee from General Ripley's command and two from the Fifth Military District. It becomes therefore more necessary for you to have your forces in hand and aid General Ripley if called upon.

Very respectfully, &c.,

J. R. WADDY,
Assistant Adjutant-General.

HDQRS. DEPT. OF SOUTH CAROLINA, GEORGIA, &c.,
Pocotaligo, April 11, 1862.

Brig. Gen. MAXCY GREGG,
Commanding Fourth Military District:

GENERAL: I am instructed by Major-General Pemberton to say to you that you will immediately assume command of what is at this time and under existing order known as the Fourth and Fifth Military Districts, that is, the old Fourth Military District, recently commanded by himself.

The general goes to Savannah early in the morning and will remain for several days. The order assigning Colonel Colquitt will be at once countermanded.

I am, general, &c.,

J. R. WADDY,
Assistant Adjutant-General.

HDQRS. DEPT. OF SOUTH CAROLINA, GEORGIA, &C.,
Pocotaligo, April 11, 1862.

Brig. Gen. MAXCY GREGG,
Commanding Fourth Military District S. C.:

GENERAL: I am directed by the major-general commanding to inform you that your military district is extended as far west as the Coosawhatchie River, including the station at Coosawhatchie, from and below Coosawhatchie Station, bounded by the east bank of the Coosawhatchie River.

The major-general commanding would suggest that you send a company of cavalry under your command to take the place of the company of Tennessee volunteers about to be removed, and also that, as soon as the guns on the Ashepoo River are removed, the company of German artillery now at Chapman's fort be divided into three detachments, one to serve the guns at Combahee Ferry, the second to serve the carronades at Stony Creek work, and the third to man the heavy guns at Bee Creek battery, each detachment to be under the command of a commissioned officer; the captain to be stationed at such point as you in your judgment may designate.

Very respectfully, &c.,

R. W. MEMMINGER,
Assistant Adjutant-General.

RICHMOND, VA., *April 11, 1862.*

Governor PICKENS,
Columbia, S. C.:

Thank you for your prompt attention to my request. General Pemberton has sent two of your regiments and the two from Tennessee. I am not willing to tax you further.

JEFFERSON DAVIS.

CHAPTER XVI.

OPERATIONS IN WEST FLORIDA, SOUTHERN ALABAMA, SOUTHERN MISSISSIPPI, AND LOUISIANA.

September 1, 1861–May 12, 1862.

SUMMARY OF THE PRINCIPAL EVENTS.

Sept. 2, 1861.—Destruction of United States dry-dock at Pensacola, Fla.

14, 1861.—Descent on Pensacola navy-yard by boats from U. S. squadron.

Oct. 1, 1861.—The Department of New England constituted, under command of Maj. Gen. Benjamin F. Butler, U. S. A.*

7, 1861.—Maj. Gen. Braxton Bragg's command extended over the coast and State of Alabama.

9, 1861.—Action on Santa Rosa Island, Fla.

14, 1861.—The Department of Alabama and West Florida constituted, under command of Major-General Bragg, C. S. Army.

18, 1861.—Maj. Gen. Mansfield Lovell, C. S. Army, supersedes Maj. Gen. David E. Twiggs in command of Department No. 1.

Nov. 22-23, 1861.—Bombardment of the Confederate lines about Pensacola, Fla.

27, 1861.—The Ship Island Expedition sails from Hampton Roads, Va.

Dec. 3, 1861.—Ship Island, Miss., occupied by Union forces.

12, 1861.—The Department of Alabama and West Florida extended to embrace Pascagoula Bay and that portion of Mississippi east of the Pascagoula River.

Jan. 1, 1862.—Bombardment of Forts McRee and Barrancas, Pensacola Harbor.

20, 1862.—Contest over the British schooner Andracita on the coast of Alabama.

27, 1862.—Brig. Gen. Jones M. Withers, C. S. Army, assigned to command of the Army of Mobile.

Brig. Gen. Samuel Jones, C. S. Army, assigned to command of the Army of Pensacola.

Feb. 22, 1862.—Brig. Gen. Lewis G. Arnold, U. S. Army, supersedes Col. Harvey Brown, Fifth U. S. Artillery, in command of the Department of Florida.

23, 1862.—The Department of the Gulf constituted, under command of Maj. Gen. Benjamin F. Butler, U. S. Army.

---

*This department was created in connection with the organization of the Gulf Expedition and was discontinued February 20, 1862.

Feb. 28, 1862.—Brig. Gen. Samuel Jones, C. S. Army, supersedes Major-General Bragg in command of the Department of Alabama and West Florida.*

March 8, 1862.—Col. Thomas M. Jones, Twenty-seventh Mississippi Infantry, assigned to command at Pensacola.

15, 1862.—The Department of Florida merged into the Department of the South, Maj. Gen. David Hunter, U. S. Army, commanding.

20, 1862.—Maj. Gen. Benjamin F. Butler, U. S. Army, assumes command of the Department of the Gulf.

27-31, 1862.—Reconnaissance on Santa Rosa Island, Fla.

April 3- 4, 1862.—Expedition from Ship Island to Biloxi and Pass Christian, Miss.

7, 1862.—Affair at Saint Andrew's Bay, Fla.

18-28, 1862.—Bombardment and capture of Forts Jackson and Saint Philip, La.

25, 1862.—New Orleans, La., captured by the U. S. Navy.

27, 1862.—Fort Quitman, La., abandoned by the Confederate forces.

Forts Livingston, Pike, and Wood, La., recaptured by Union forces.

28, 1862.—Surrender of Forts Jackson and Saint Philip, La.

28, 1862.—Brig. Gen. John H. Forney, C. S. Army, assigned to command of the Department of Alabama and West Florida.

May 1, 1862.—New Orleans, La., occupied by the Union forces.

9-12, 1862.—Evacuation of Pensacola, Fla., by the Confederates, and its occupation by the Union forces.

SEPTEMBER 14, 1861.—Descent on Navy-Yard at Pensacola, Fla.

REPORTS.

No. 1.—Col. Harvey Brown, Fifth U. S. Artillery.
No. 2.—Brig. Gen. Braxton Bragg, C. S. Army.

No. 1.

Report of Col. Harvey Brown, Fifth U. S. Artillery.

HEADQUARTERS DEPARTMENT OF FLORIDA,
Fort Pickens, September 14, 1861.

COLONEL: A naval boat expedition, under command of Lieutenant [John H.] Russell, of the flag-ship Colorado, this morning, at 2 o'clock, burned the piratical schooner Judah and spiked the gun of the only battery in the navy-yard. The schooner was armed with five guns, and was lying in the slip in front of the battery, evidently awaiting an opportunity to go to sea. We lost three killed (one of them instantly, by one of our own party), four badly and three or four slightly wounded, among the latter Lieutenants Russell and [F. B.] Blake, [Capt. E. McD.] Reynolds, of the Marines, and a midshipman. The whole affair was well conceived, well managed, and entirely successful.

I took it for granted it would cause the opening of the rebel fire on this fort, but until the present time no demonstration has been made.

I am, very respectfully, your obedient servant,

HARVEY BROWN,
Colonel, Commanding.

Lieut. Col. E. D. TOWNSEND,
Assistant Adjutant-General.

---

*On March 4 Major-General Bragg, at Jackson, Tenn., issued an order resuming command of the Department of Alabama and West Florida, but that order appears to have been inoperative.

No. 2.

Report of Brig. Gen. Braxton Bragg, C. S. Army.

HEADQUARTERS TROOPS OF THE CONFEDERATE STATES,
Near Pensacola, Fla., September 16, 1861.

SIR: I have the honor to report, for the information of the Department, that a row-boat, with nine enlisted men of marines, sent on patrol duty on the night of the 8th instant in the harbor, failed to return. The crew has no doubt deserted to the enemy. It was a gross neglect on the part of the officer in charge of this service in not sending an officer in command on such a duty.

On the night of the 13th a boat expedition of three ships' launches, heavily armed, made an attack on a point at the navy-yard where the boats of our harbor police were moored, and succeeded in setting fire to and destroying a small armed vessel in our service. Our guards were not surprised, but by some strange neglect, which is now under investigation, permitted the success of this daring exploit, led, no doubt, by our deserters. I hope to fix the responsibility and make an example of the guilty parties.

I am, sir, very respectfully, your obedient servant,

BRAXTON BRAGG,
Brigadier-General, Commanding.

ADJUTANT-GENERAL C. S. ARMY,
Richmond, Va.

OCTOBER 9, 1861.—Action on Santa Rosa Island, Fla.

REPORTS, ETC.

No. 1.—Col. Harvey Brown, Fifth U. S. Artillery, commanding Department of Florida.
No. 2.—Maj. Zealous B. Tower, U. S. Corps of Engineers.
No. 3.—Maj. Lewis G. Arnold, First U. S. Artillery.
No. 4.—Col. William Wilson, Sixth New York Infantry.
No. 5.—Capt. John McL. Hildt, Third U. S. Infantry.
No. 6.—Lieut. Chauncey B. Reese, U. S. Corps of Engineers.
No. 7.—Capt. James M. Robertson, Second U. S. Artillery.
No. 8.—Capt. Richard C. Duryea, First U. S. Artillery.
No. 9.—Lieut. Alexander N. Shipley, Third U. S. Infantry.
No. 10.—Capt. Loomis L. Langdon, First U. S. Artillery.
No. 11.—Lieut. Francis W. Seeley, Fourth U. S. Artillery.
No. 12.—Lieut. Richard H. Jackson, First U. S. Artillery.
No. 13.—Congratulatory orders from Major-General McClellan, U. S. Army.
No. 14.—Maj. Gen. Braxton Bragg, C. S. Army, commanding at Pensacola, with congratulatory orders.
No. 15.—Brig. Gen. Richard H. Anderson, C. S. Army, commanding expedition.

No. 1.

Reports of Col. Harvey Brown, Fifth U. S. Artillery, commanding Department of Florida.

HEADQUARTERS DEPARTMENT OF FLORIDA,
Fort Pickens, October 9, 1861.

COLONEL: The enemy, 1,200 or 1,500 strong, landed on this island this morning, about 3 o'clock, some 3½ or 4 miles from the fort. They marched down the island in three columns, and attacked and partially burned the camp of the Sixth New York Volunteers. They were promptly met and driven by the regulars of the fort, and a small number of Zouaves, under Major Arnold, of the First Artillery, to their place of landing, and left the island under a well-directed and deliberate fire of our musketry, within good range, which must have done great execution, their boats being densely crowded. Their departure was hailed with three heavy cheers from our gallant soldiers, which were received with the most solemn silence. We have about a dozen of their dead; some 30 prisoners, including 5 officers. Our loss is, of regulars, 5 killed, about 15 wounded, and 8 missing, including 1 officer, Major Vogdes, who was taken prisoner early in the action; of the volunteers, 7 killed, 8 or 9 wounded, and 10 missing. I will make a detailed report so soon as I can receive those of Major Arnold and the officers engaged.

I am, colonel, very respectfully, your obedient servant,

HARVEY BROWN,
Colonel, Commanding.

Col. E. D. TOWNSEND,
Assistant Adjutant-General, Washington, D. C.

HEADQUARTERS DEPARTMENT OF FLORIDA,
Fort Pickens, October 11, 1861.

COLONEL: I briefly reported to you on the 9th instant that the rebels had landed on this island, partially destroyed the camp of the Sixth Regiment New York Volunteers, and been driven off by our troops. I now report in more detail the events of the attack.

For the better understanding of the several movements it may be well to state that the enemy landed about 4 miles from this fort, (the place may be recognized on the map by three ponds and a mound); that the island there is about three-quarters of a mile wide; that a short distance below it narrows to some 200 hundred yards, then widens again, and at the camp the distance across is about five-eighths of a mile; that a succession of three or four sand ridges run on the sea-side parallel to the coast along the island, and low, swampy ground, interspersed with sand hillocks, some bushes, and a few trees, extends along the harbor side, both shores being sandy beach. Wilson's camp is near the sea-coast and a short mile from the fort. The two batteries spoken of in his report, and to which he retreated, Batteries Lincoln and Totten, are, the first on the harbor, and the other on the Gulf side, about 400 yards from Fort Pickens.

About 2 o'clock on the morning of the 9th instant I was awakened by the officer of the day, who reported that a picket driven in had reported the landing of 60 men on the point. Having little confidence in the correctness of this report I directed that no alarm should be made, and shortly after he reported that the alarm was false. About 3.30 o'clock he again reported that volleys of musketry were heard at the camp of the Sixth New York Volunteers. I immediately ordered the roll to be beaten, Major Vogdes to take two companies and proceed to the spot, and Major Arnold to man the guns on the ramparts on that face. About half an hour after this time the firing was heavy and the light of the burning camp seen, and I sent a staff officer to communicate with Major Vogdes, who returned very soon, and said that he had fallen in with a large body of the enemy on the inside shore, and could not find the major. I immediately ordered Major Arnold to proceed to support Major Vogdes with two companies, and at the same time sent an order to Colonel Wilson to advance and attack the enemy. I also dispatched a staff officer, on board the steamer McClellan, with orders for him to take position opposite the landing place and open on the enemy; unfortunately at the same time directing him to go to the Potomac, lying near, and ask for some men to assist him in case landing was necessary. Captain Powell directed him to tow his ship to the scene of action, which so delayed him that he did not arrive until after the enemy had vacated. Captain Powell acted from the best motives, and under ordinary circumstances from correct principles, but the result was unfortunate, as the McClellan could have driven the rebel steamer away, and we must have made prisoners of most of the invaders.

At the request of Major Arnold, late in the morning I sent forward a light field gun, which, however, did not reach until the affair was over.

As I propose only briefly to allude to the volunteers, I respectfully refer you to the official report, marked A [No. 4], of the colonel of the regiment. The picket of this regiment and guards sustained its principal if not entire loss, and behaved well. Captain Dobie's company, on duty with the regulars, did good service, and the captain is spoken of by Major Arnold in terms of high approbation. He had 2 men killed. Captain Bailey's company was at a battery, and not called out. He was performing his appropriate duty during the fight. Major Vogdes, with Companies A, First Artillery, and E, Third Infantry, proceeded beyond the Spanish fort, about a mile from the fort, when from the obscurity of the night he found himself and command completely intermingled with the enemy. He was immediately recognized and made prisoner, the command devolving on Captain Hildt, of the Third Infantry, who disengaged his command from their perilous position, and opened a heavy fire on the enemy, and finally, with great gallantry, forced them to retreat (he being ably supported by Lieutenant Seeley, my assistant adjutant-general, who volunteered for the occasion), with a loss of 11 killed. Major Arnold at this moment came up and, the enemy retreating, followed on. During this time Major Tower and Lieutenant Jackson, who I had successively sent to push forward the Zouaves, succeeded in getting some collected, and Colonel Wilson also advanced, the enemy precipitately retreating. Major Arnold, with Captain Robertson's and Lieutenant Shipley's companies, promptly followed, and attacked as they were embarking, the other companies coming up successively. Captain Robertson opened a heavy fire at short musket range on the crowded masses, and Lieutenant Shipley some fifteen minutes later joined him, and their fire must have been very effective. This was continued as long as they were within range. When they had got beyond it the gallant major ordered them to cease firing and to give them three cheers, to which no response was made. During the time of this occurrence Major Tower came up with two small companies of Zouaves, and subsequently Colonel Wilson with a portion of his regiment. When it is considered that less than 200 regulars, with some 50 volunteers, pursued five times their number 4 miles and expelled them under a heavy fire from the island they had desecrated, it will, I trust, be considered an evidence of their having gallantly performed their duty. The plan of attack of the enemy was judicious, and, if executed with ordinary ability, might have been attended with serious loss; but he failed in all, save the burning one-half of the tents of the Sixth Regiment, which, being covered with brushes, was very combustible, and in rifling the trunks of the officers. He did not reach within 500 yards of either of the batteries the guns of which he was to spike, nor within a mile of the fort he was to enter pell-mell with the fugitives retreating before his victorious arms. I have now in my possession nine spikes, taken from the bodies of the dead, designed for our guns.

Our loss is, of regulars, 4 killed, 20 wounded (most very slightly), and 8 missing, among whom is Major Vogdes; of the Sixth Regiment New York Volunteers, 10 killed, 9 wounded, and 16 missing. The enemy lost, as known to us, 14 killed, including 1 captain; 7 wounded, including 1 lieutenant (2 since dead), and 5 officers and 22 enlisted men prisoners, and as he was known to have carried off some of his dead and probably most of his wounded, those in our hands being all severely so and unable to be removed, and as the heaviest loss is supposed to have been in the boats at the re-embarkation, it was probably three times as great in killed and wounded as I have named.

I close with the agreeable duty of naming to you the officers engaged who so faithfully performed their duty. I mention Major Vogdes first, who, unfortunately, was taken prisoner before a gun on our part was fired, to say that, as second in command and my executive officer, he has efficiently and industriously performed his duty during the whole time of my command, and his services have been very valuable.

Major Arnold, who succeeded to the command after the capture of his superior, conducted the affair with great gallantry, prudence, and ability. He speaks in the highest terms of Captains Robertson and Hildt and Lieutenants Shipley and Seeley, and indeed of all the others whose names I give: Major Tower and Lieutenant Reese, of the Engineers; Lieutenants Duryea, Langdon, Jackson, and Taylor, U. S. Artillery, and Captain Dobie, of the New York Volunteers; and it gives me great pleasure to append the names of non-commissioned officers and privates named by their company commanders for distinguished good conduct, and to recommend them to the favorable notice of the Government.

The following are the companies of Major Vogdes' and Arnold's command who participated in the battle, and (with a very few exceptions of individuals) to whom the greatest praise is due: Company A, First Artillery; H, Second Artillery, and Companies C and E, Third Infantry.

I estimate the force of the enemy at 1,200 or 1,500, having closely observed them through a fine telescope as they retreated. There were two large steamers and a barge of equal size and five or six launches all crowded with troops, and the almost unanimous estimate of the officers engaged is 1,500, from personal observation close by.

I am, colonel, very respectfully, your obedient servant,

HARVEY BROWN,
Colonel, Commanding.

Col. E. D. TOWNSEND,
Assistant Adjutant-General, Washington, D. C.

P. S.—I have just seen the Pensacola paper, which gives their loss as follows: Killed, 21; wounded, 38; prisoners, 22, which probably is not one-fourth of the actual loss. General Anderson is severely wounded.

[Inclosure.]

Table of distances from Fort Pickens to where the rebels landed on the morning of the 9th *of October*, 1861, *to the intermediate points, by actual measurement, made October* 23, 1861.

	Yards.
From Fort Pickens to Battery Cameron	580
Battery Lincoln	803
Spanish Fort	2,612

	Yards.
From the first place of fighting, where Major Vogdes was captured	3,331
The first pine trees	4,043
Long Point Beach	6,101
Where we first fired on the steamers	6,832
Where the rebels landed, and where they were attacked by Major Arnold, with Captain Robertson's and Lieutenant Shipley's companies	7,306

or 4 miles 266 yards.

HARVEY BROWN,
Colonel, Commanding.

—

HEADQUARTERS DEPARTMENT OF FLORIDA,
Fort Pickens, October 12, 1861.

GENERAL: In my official report of the affair of the 9th instant it will be perceived that I briefly notice the New York volunteers. I did so because the regiment did not behave well on the occasion, and because I think that, if properly officered, its conduct would have been different. I desired to spare it the stigma of cowardice, which I should have been compelled to inflict. The material of the rank and file is very good, and in the hands of even respectably intelligent officers might be made efficient; but as a body, and with very few exceptions, the officers are in every respect unfit for officers, and incapable of performing their appropriate duties, and the enlisted men consequently can have but little respect for or confidence in them. If it can legally be done, I would recommend the transfer to other regiments of the few efficient officers, the disbandment of the others, and the transfer of the enlisted men to the regular companies at this post. By so doing the regiment can in one month be made efficient, and I would with confidence lead them into battle, which I should now be very sorry to do.

I am, general, very respectfully, your obedient servant,

HARVEY BROWN,
Colonel, Commanding.

Brig. Gen. LORENZO THOMAS,
Adjutant-General, Washington City, D. C.

—

HEADQUARTERS DEPARTMENT OF FLORIDA,
Fort Pickens, October 17, 1861.

COLONEL: I had occasion yesterday to send Lieutenant Seeley, my assistant adjutant-general, with a flag to the other side. While there he saw a rebel newspaper, containing an article on the action of the 9th instant, in which was this paragraph:

> It is now certain that 175 in killed, wounded, and missing will more than cover our entire loss, while 250 will probably barely cover that of the Federalists.

This shows that in estimating in my official report their loss at three times the number left on the island, viz: 1 captain, 13 enlisted men killed, 1 lieutenant, 6 enlisted men wounded, and 5 officers and 22 enlisted men prisoners, I underestimated their actual loss according to their own acknowledgment, and we may safely infer from past experience that only half the truth is here told. Their loss, therefore, is nearly equal to the whole number of troops actually inflicting it, and this without attaining one single object proposed by the expedition, except the partial burning of the camp of the Sixth Regiment New York Volunteers and the robbing its officers. They did not destroy a single article of quartermaster's or commissary stores; they did not destroy one-half of the tents of the volunteers; they did not spike a single gun, nor do any other injury whatever, except the burning of 30 tents and the capture of some dozen muskets, and of which we have of theirs more than two for one. Our whole casualties are, as stated in my official report, 4 regulars and 9 volunteers killed, 20 regulars and 7 volunteers wounded, and 10 regulars and 11 volunteers missing, and it gives me very great pleasure to state that Surgeon Campbell reports all our wounded as doing well, and he thinks we will not lose a man. Their actual number on the island, by their own acknowledgment, was 1,500 men.

I am, colonel, very respectfully, your obedient servant,

HARVEY BROWN,
Colonel, Commanding.

Col. E. D. TOWNSEND,
Assistant Adjutant-General, Washington, D. C.

HEADQUARTERS DEPARTMENT OF FLORIDA,
Fort Pickens, October 22, 1861.

COLONEL: I desire to correct an omission in my official report. Capt. Henry L. Hoelzle, of the Sixth New York Regiment Volunteers, joined Major Arnold with 10 men of his company and behaved gallantly. Lieut. Moore Hanham, of the same regiment, commanded the picket guard, and behaved with courage and firmness under a heavy fire, in which most of his sentinels were killed or wounded.

I am, very respectfully, your obedient servant,

HARVEY BROWN,
Colonel, Commanding.

Col. E. D. TOWNSEND,
Assistant Adjutant-General, Washington, D. C.

No. 2.

Report of Maj. Zealous B. Tower, U. S. Corps of Engineers.

FORT PICKENS, FLA., *October* 15, 1861.

SIR: I have the honor to forward what information I can collect in reference to the forces opposite and their means of attack. The most reliable authority gives General Bragg's forces on the 11th October as 7,000 men. It is also stated that two regiments some weeks since were ordered North, but that General Bragg had refused to let them go, and had asked for re-enforcements. He has eighteen field pieces, six of which are rifled. A party at that time (October 11) were at Pensacola, who had come over to rifle guns.

Between twenty and thirty 10-inch columbiads have been brought by railroad to Pensacola. The person describing them (while looking at our pieces of the same caliber) said that they were straight at the muzzle and were heavier and shorter behind the trunnions, and that they were made at Richmond. He also informed me that as many as eight 10-inch sea-coast mortars had come by railroad to Pensacola.

You will perceive that the armament the enemy received, together with that found at the works, is heavier than ours. I have not heard of other guns, excepting one Dahlgren; but should any heavier guns be cast, the walls of this fort will hardly be able to stand them even at

2,300, 2,400, and 2,500 yards. Twenty 10-inch guns of the new pattern, firing at $1\frac{1}{2}$ miles, with solid shot, constantly at one part of this old work of very poor masonry, may possibly shake the walls. Our forces are small in number. It is absolutely necessary that naval steamers assist us here, otherwise the island may be seized at any time and the siege commenced. The enemy has large quantities of shells and mortars. Whether it will be his policy to besiege us or to try to crush us with curvated fire, and by heavy guns and rifled cannon to knock down a portion of our work, I cannot foresee. The serious obstacle to such means on his part will be the great expenditure of powder. Navy ships, with their large crews, of course would be a great security and assistance to us. Gunboats are wanted if the position opposite is to be attacked. The late unfortunate affair at the head of the Mississippi Passes will call away the Niagara and leave the Colorado here for the present.

I have given Captain Kurtz a description of the night attack made by the secession forces upon Wilson's camp on the night of the 8th and 9th October. I have no doubt that the enemy were much disappointed with the results. The Zouaves (excepting the pickets) proved of little account. They are badly commanded. If incorporated with the regulars they might be made effective. Contrary to the reports in the Southern papers, the enemy did not spike one gun or burn a storehouse. They destroyed about three-fourths of the tents of five companies of Zouaves and robbed some of the officers' trunks. They ought to have been more severely punished for coming with 1,000 men within a mile of our work, but in the confusion of a night attack matters do not always get on well.

Very respectfully, your obedient servant,

Z. B. TOWER,
Major of Engineers.

Bvt. Brig. Gen. JOSEPH G. TOTTEN,
Chief Engineer, Washington, D. C.

No. 3.

Reports of Maj. Lewis G. Arnold, First U. S. Artillery.

FORT PICKENS, FLA., *October* 10, 1861.

SIR: In accordance with the directions of the colonel commanding, I have the honor to report the operations of the troops under my command which yesterday aided in driving the rebel force of not less than 1,000 men, under command of Brig. Gen. Richard H. Anderson, discomfited and in confusion, from the island of Santa Rosa.

I was ordered by the colonel commanding, at 5 o'clock a. m., October 9, to take command of two companies of regulars, Captain Robertson, Company H, Second Artillery, and Lieutenant Shipley, commanding Company C, Third Infantry, and support Major Vogdes, First Artillery, in command of two companies of regulars; Captain Hildt, Company E, Third Infantry; Lieutenant Taylor and 30 men of Company A, First Artillery, and Captain Dobie, Company G, New York volunteers, who had preceded me along the north beach of the island about an hour, with the purpose of attacking in flank the rebels, who had made an attack on Camp Brown, three-quarters of a mile from the fort. Having formed my command very promptly, owing to the efficiency and zeal of the company commanders, I rapidly marched up the beach about 1½ miles, when I reached the scene of a sharp action between Major Vogdes' command and the rebels, in which 11 of the enemy were killed, and probably many more than that number wounded.

It is due to Captain Hildt, Third Infantry, to state that our troops here engaged were under his directions, as, from the statements of that officer and Lieutenants Seeley and Taylor, the only officers with Major Vogdes, he must have been taken prisoner before the fight commenced. After marching half a mile farther up the beach I discovered a large row-boat, about 1,200 yards off, filled with men, making for the navy-yard. I directed the men to fire at great elevation on this boat, which was well executed, with some effect. Soon after this, whilst advancing rapidly, I discovered, nearly 2 miles away, on a point or neck of land, a very large body of the enemy, which I judged to be ten times my strength. I shortly after left the beach, going behind the sand ridge which skirts it, and deployed my command, for the purpose of concealing its weakness and to attack them in flank and rear. I very soon met Captain Hildt, Third Infantry; Lieutenants Duryea, Langdon, Seeley, and Taylor, of the artillery, who informed me of the capture of Major Vogdes. I ordered Captain Hildt to join me with the remnant of his command, Lieutenant Duryea to act as my staff officer, in which capacity he made a bold reconnaissance, supported only by six men, bringing me the valuable information that the enemy were embarking in two steamboats 4 miles from the fort. I directed Lieutenant Langdon to report to the colonel commanding my relative position with that of the enemy, which he could well and quickly do, being mounted, and from his recent dangerous proximity to the enemy, and to request that a field gun and a supporting force be sent me. I ordered Captain Robertson, Second Artillery, to move with his company along the sand hills skirting the beach, and to attack the enemy if a favorable opportunity should offer, which he did in the most effective manner. I proceeded with the balance of the command, Lieutenant Shipley, with his company (C, Third Infantry), leading off, within supporting distance of Captain Robertson, which portion of the command was unfortunately delayed about fifteen [five] minutes by having to turn a swamp which intervened. Both divisions of the command displayed great zeal and coolness in coming into the action. The fire of the men was deliberate and well delivered into the crowded mass on board the steamboats and flats in tow, which must have punished the enemy severely—particularly the fire delivered by Captain Robertson's company for fifteen or twenty minutes, at short range, while the flat in tow of one of the steamers was aground. I am indebted to Major Tower, Engineer Corps, for his advice on the field and for ordering up the New York volunteers as a supporting column.

Captain Robertson, Second Artillery; Captain Hildt, Third Infantry; Lieutenants Shipley, Third Infantry; Langdon, Seeley, Jackson, and Taylor, First Artillery, and Captains Dobie and Hoelzle, Sixth Regiment New York Volunteers, who served under my command during the day, did their duty nobly. My special thanks are due to Capt. J. M. Robertson, Second Artillery, and First Lieut. A. N. Shipley, Third Infantry, the two officers of my original command, for their activity, energy, and coolness displayed and valuable services rendered by them and their commands.

I refer the colonel commanding to the reports of the commanders of companies and parties specially detached for individual instances of good conduct displayed; also a list of officers and enlisted men (regulars) killed, wounded, and missing, which reports, &c., I herewith inclose.

The enemy's loss in killed, wounded, and prisoners left in our hands (they carried off all those killed on the boats and many of those wounded on the shore), amounts to 1 captain and 15 enlisted men killed, and 1 lieutenant and 5 enlisted men wounded, and 6 commissioned officers and 27 enlisted men prisoners.

Respectfully submitted.

L. G. ARNOLD,
Major First Artillery, Commanding.

Lieut. F. W. SEELEY,
Acting Assistant Adjutant-General, Hdqrs. Dept. of Florida.

FORT PICKENS, FLA., *December* 24, 1861.

COLONEL: My attention has been called to an error as regards time in my report of the engagement of the troops under my command with the rebels on Santa Rosa Island, October 9, 1861, which error I perceive has been adopted in your published report of the same engagement. It is really not of much moment, but I consider it due to Lieutenant Shipley and his company (C, Third Infantry) and to truth to correct it. Quotation from my report:

> I proceeded with the balance of the command, Lieutenant Shipley, with his company (C, Third Infantry), leading off, within supporting distance of Captain Robertson, which portion of the command was unfortunately delayed about *fifteen minutes* by having to turn a swamp which intervened.

Instead of *fifteen minutes*, it should have been *five minutes*. Both companies behaved handsomely, firing on the enemy with great effect, and deserve much more credit than has been accorded to them.

I am, very respectfully, your obedient servant,

L. G. ARNOLD,
Major, First Artillery.

Col. HARVEY BROWN,
Commanding Department of Florida.

[Indorsement.]

HEADQUARTERS DEPARTMENT OF FLORIDA,
Fort Pickens, December 25, 1861.

Repectfully forwarded to the Adjutant-General, with a request that my report and that of Major Arnold may be altered so as to conform to the within statement.

I desire also to correct another error. *Captain Dobie* himself did good service on the night of the 9th October, but *his company* did nothing worthy of notice.

HARVEY BROWN,
Colonel, Commanding.

No. 4.

Reports of Col. William Wilson, Sixth New York Infantry.

CAMP BROWN, FORT PICKENS, FLA.,
Sixth Regt. N. Y. S. V., October 11, 1861.

SIR: I have the honor to report that on the morning of the 9th instant, at about 3.30 o'clock, the camp was alarmed by rapid discharges and volleys of musketry in the direction of the hospital. My command of five companies, numbering 250 men, was turned out, and formed on the drill ground fronting the hospital. Lieutenant Hanham came running in, and informing me that about 2,000 armed men in two columns were marching upon us; that the pickets were all attacked about the same time. I at once sent (no officer being near) an orderly to inform Colonel Brown. The orderly, when returning, was made prisoner. Skirmishers were thrown out in advance and on the left flank. I was on the left flank, preparing to wheel by companies to the left and then deploy, when volleys of musketry were fired into us from the direction of the camp. The two left companies wheeled to the left, deployed, and returned the fire. Immediately the tents were in a blaze, and the enemy could be seen in the center of the camp closed in mass, apparently 400 or 500 men. Other companies were in line on the ridge extending towards the old commissary store. Companies were seen moving across the ridges. My men, on seeing this, broke for the beach. I managed by the assistance of Lieutenants Hanham and Kraell to halt and form about 60 of them behind the first ridge from the drill ground. I then sent for Lieutenant-Colonel Creighton and the remainder of my command. The men returned, stating that they could not find him. Stragglers came in, informing me that Lieutenant-Colonel Creighton, Captain Hazeltine, Captains Hoelzle and Henberer, and Lieutenant Silloway, with the rest of the command, had marched towards the batteries. My men on hearing this could not be restrained, and moved towards the beach and then to Battery Totten, where we halted and rested a short time.

Up to this time I was ignorant of the whereabouts of my officers or men or the movements of troops from the fort. Major Tower came up and informed me that several companies of regulars were in pursuit of the enemy, and for me to advance, which I did as rapidly as the tired condition of the men would permit. About half a mile above the hospital I met the remainder of my command, under Lieutenant-Colonel Creighton. At Major Tower's request I sent forward two companies at double-quick time. I then moved on, endeavoring to overtake the enemy or render what assistance I could. I reached the place where the enemy embarked just as our men were returning. On my returning I deployed two companies across the island as skirmishers to pick up stragglers and the dead and wounded. I have to report the following losses: Killed, 9; wounded, 7; missing, 11.

I would respectfully add that I am pleased with the good-will and promptness of the officers and men in the performance of their duties.

Your obedient servant,

WM. WILSON,

Colonel, Commanding Sixth Regiment N. Y. S. Vols.

Col. HARVEY BROWN,

Commanding Department of Florida.

HDQRS. CAMP BROWN, DEPARTMENT OF FLORIDA,
October 14, 1861.

SIR: In accordance with instructions to report the manner of attack and conduct of officers and men in the late attack on the morning of the 9th instant, I respectfully report:

The sentinels of the picket guard were all attacked the same time by small bodies of the enemy, supported by three detachments of them, each about 600 strong, approaching upon them from the Gulf beach, center of island, and bay shore. Lieutenant Hanham was officer of the picket guard. He formed his relief in good order and retreated, firing upon the enemy, and rallied upon the battalion then on the parade ground.

Captain Hoelzle was officer of the day. He, on the first alarm, formed the main guard and marched towards the beach, where alarms were being given. He met a large body of the enemy, fired into them, and was fired into in return. Captain Hoelzle was knocked down and walked over. He arose quickly and shot a man who was taking aim at him. He then retreated to the front of the guard-house, and met Captain Hazeltine, who was in command of the skirmishers, then retreating before the enemy.

Captain Duffy, who had command of the skirmishers on the left, was cut off with four men, and had to remain in front of the camp until near daylight.

The sentinels all stood their ground manfully, firing while retreating. Corp. William Parsonage, of Company H (since dead), while supporting a sentinel and fighting manfully, was shot through the body in three places and bayoneted, but killed his opponent. Private P. McGrail, of Company F, posted at the Spanish Fort, was killed at his post after firing three shots at the enemy. Private William Scott, of Company C, on the approach of the enemy from the Gulf beach, waited until they approached to within 10 feet, and deliberately shot Captain Bradford, who was leading them on.

I must thank Lieutenant Hanham, Lieutenant Kraell, and Sergt. Maj. Robert Gill for the valuable assistance they rendered me in keeping my men in order, and for their good behavior while under the fire of the enemy.

Yours, respectfully,

WM. WILSON,
Colonel Sixth Regiment New York Volunteers.

Col. HARVEY BROWN,
Commanding Department of Florida, Fort Pickens.

No. 5.

Report of Capt. John McL. Hildt, Third U. S. Infantry.

FORT PICKENS, FLA., *October* 10, 1861.

SIR: I have the honor to make the following report of an engagement with the enemy on the morning of the 9th of October:

About 3.30 o'clock a. m., it having become evident from firing from the direction of Camp Brown that the enemy had made an attack on the companies of the Sixth New York Volunteers stationed at that point, Company E, Third Infantry, 62 rank and file, under command of Capt. J. McL. Hildt, Third Infantry, and 31 rank and file of Company A, First Artillery, under command of Second Lieut. F. E. Taylor, First Artillery, the whole commanded by Maj. I. Vogdes, First Artillery, left the fort to render any necessary assistance. The command proceeded through Batteries Cameron and Lincoln, being re-enforced at the latter by Company G, Sixth New York Volunteers, Captain Dobie. After proceeding a short distance up the north beach, Captain Dobie was directed to deploy his company as skirmishers on the right flank. The company became separated from the rest of the command, and I saw no more of it. We proceeded along the beach until some distance above Camp Brown. A large force appeared on our right flank and rear. Owing to the darkness it was impossible to tell whether this force was the enemy or New York volunteers. Major Vogdes, who was in front, immediately faced the command to the right and rode towards the right of the line. This was the last I saw of him. A moment afterwards an officer (of the enemy) stepped up to me, stating that our commanding officer was a prisoner, and requesting me to surrender the command. The first firing (two shots) was directed at this officer. I then moved the command to and formed as well as circumstances would permit behind some rising ground about 20 yards in front. First Lieut. F. W. Seeley, Fourth Artillery, who had volunteered and joined the advance guard during the march, here rendered valuable service in forming and encouraging the men.

After some very effective firing from this point it became necessary to move part of the command to the left, to oppose a threatened flank attack. The men became more exposed and the fire of the enemy very severe. Finding ourselves greatly outnumbered, and encumbered by the wounded, we fell back diagonally towards the opposite beach and the enemy's flank, halting behind the numerous sand-hills and delivering our fire. A party of 3 surgeons and guard of 8 men were at this time made prisoners. Several other prisoners had been previously taken. As soon as his front was clear the enemy proceeded along the north beach. His force, as given by the prisoners, was 1,010 men. Our actual force engaged, owing to the flankers being made prisoners previous to the action, did not exceed 80 men. We then proceeded to collect our remaining wounded until the arrival of Major Arnold's command. The men generally behaved well. Many could be mentioned who were conspicuous. Among them First Sergt. David Grier, Company E, Third Infantry, who, although with the flankers, succeeded in eluding the enemy and joining the command; Corp. Thomas G. Duncan, Privates James Clark, James Corcoran, John Moran, Michael Coleman, Company E, Third Infantry, and Privates James Connelly, Timothy Kelly, and Michael Lavelle, Company A, First Artillery. I desire to mention particularly Corp. Charles Schafer, Private William Dougherty, Company E, Third Infantry, and Lance Corp. Edward B. Fitzgibbons, Private Franklin Eastman, Company A, First Artillery. Lieutenants Seeley and Taylor throughout the affair acted with marked coolness and bravery, and by their exertions and examples contributed largely to the safety of the command.

Our loss was 4 killed, 20 wounded, and 1 officer and 8 men missing. The loss of the enemy, judging from the number of dead left on the ground, was much larger. A list of the killed, wounded, and missing I herewith inclose.

I am, sir, very respectfully, your obedient servant.

J. McL. HILDT,
Captain, Third Infantry.

Major L. G. ARNOLD,
First Artillery.

No. 6.

Report of Lieut. Chauncey B. Reese, U. S. Corps of Engineers.

FORT PICKENS, FLA., *October* 11, 1861.

SIR: In obedience to your instructions, I have the honor to transmit the following as connected with the operations against the enemy on the morning of the 9th instant:

At a little before daybreak I was directed by the colonel commanding to instruct Major Vogdes to pursue the enemy with his command, keeping his left flank upon the north beach. The colonel at the same time stated that Major Vogdes had gone up the north beach via Battery Lincoln. I started on horseback, and when about half a mile beyond Battery Lincoln came upon a body of troops about 75 strong, which I at first took for Major Vogdes' command, but which proved to be the enemy, who fired one shot at me as I turned to retreat. While returning I met Lieutenant Duryea at Battery Lincoln in seach of Major Vogdes' command. I intrusted the message to Lieutenant Duryea, and returned to report the position of the enemy. About fifteen minutes after my return I was directed by the commanding officer to proceed to "the Potomac, and ask Captain Powell to place a detachment on board the McClellan and direct Captain Gray to proceed along the island in order to shell the enemy." The commanding officer also directed me to go with Captain Gray. These instructions were afterwards modified so as "to request of Captain Powell as large a force as he could spare, with a view to landing it, if necessary." After being delayed something like half an hour in getting a boat, I went to the Potomac and delivered the substance of the message to Captain Powell, who stated that he would have Captain Gray take him in tow while the men were getting ready. (I will here state that four or five shots had been fired from Battery Lincoln, and Captain Powell asked me what I thought it was. I replied that it must be from our batteries upon the boats of the enemy retreating.)

I then went on board the McClellan. Captain Gray took the Potomac in tow, but had hardly started when the hawser parted. We had seen a steamer approach the north beach of the island. Upon going near the Potomac, preparatory to getting another hawser, Captain Gray asked Captain Powell if he did not think the steamer was trying to take the enemy off. I heard no reply. The Potomac was then towed in about 2 miles towards the hospital. Forty-four marines, including one officer, were put on board the McClellan, and Captain Powell asked if more were needed. It was thought best not to wait for more to be put on board, but Captain Powell said he would have enough ready to make 100, if we should want them.

I had noticed several parties of from 5 to 20 soldiers, whom I thought to be of Colonel Wilson's regiment, going along the beach towards the fort, and it was thought advisable to go ashore for information. I went ashore, and learned that the enemy had left the island and that the troops from the fort had returned. I stated this to Captain Gray, and it was agreed to go along the island some 15 miles to discover if any rebels had been cut off and retreated up the island. This was done, and no signs of the enemy were seen. The McClellan then returned, arriving at her anchorage at about 2 p. m.

I have the honor to be, very respectfully, your obedient servant,

C. B. REESE,
First Lieutenant of Engineers.

Col. HARVEY BROWN,
Fifth Artillery, Commanding Department of Florida.

No. 7.

Reports of Capt. James M. Robertson, Second U. S. Artillery.

BATTERY LINCOLN,
Santa Rosa Island, Fla., October 10, 1861.

SIR: I have the honor to report that about 3.30 o'clock a. m. yesterday I was awakened by the report of musketry on the island. I at once ran out and joined my company, which was just forming in rear of their bomb-proof. Almost immediately after I was joined by Company G, Sixth Regiment New York Volunteer Militia, under command of Capt. J. H. Dobie, assisted by Lieutenant Black. When the companies were properly formed I moved forward, with the exception of the detachments for the 12 pounder howitzers and rifled 42-pounder, to the cover of a sand hill near my camp, and ordered the men to lie down, at the same time sending out 5 men with a non-commissioned officer, with orders to take positions on the best grounds for observing the approach of an enemy from 100 to 300 yards in advance. After making these dispositions I waited for orders. About 4.30 a. m. Major Vogdes, First Artillery, passed with a detachment of regular troops from Fort Pickens and took with him Captain Dobie and his company. Soon after this I received orders from Colonel Brown to be ready and fire on any boat which should leave this island for the opposite shore. When you arrived at daybreak under your orders I left the first sergeant of my company (H, Second Artillery, to which I am assigned for temporary duty), and joined your column with the remainder—48 men.

From this time till I was detached from your column with my company you are aware of what transpired. After leaving you I threw forward a portion of my company as skirmishers and advanced up the island about 1 mile, diminishing and extending my front according to the nature of the ground, when I discovered three steamers, each having in tow a large scow or flat boat densely packed with armed men. I at once put my company into a double-quick, advanced about half a mile in that manner, and took shelter behind a ridge of sand from 200 to 250 yards from the largest steamer (Time) and the flat she had in tow, and which at that time was aground, and remained so for full fifteen minutes. I at once opened fire, cautioning the men to take cool and deliberate aim. Never was an order better obeyed. The men delivered their fire, lay down and loaded, then rose, took aim, and fired with as much coolness as on an ordinary drill of the company. For the fifteen minutes that the flat was aground, and nearly up to the time that you arrived with the remainder of your column, the enemy returned our fire very briskly, but owing to the almost perfect cover behind which my men were placed I have no casualties to report. During the whole fire my attention was particularly attracted to one man, Private Michael M. O'Doud, of Company H. First placing himself behind a small pine tree, turning his side to load, he would then step out, rest his piece against the side of the tree, take deliberate aim, and fire, almost every time remarking that "There goes another of them down." While loading he would frequently remark "Well, my tree saved me that time." He afterwards informed me that he fired sixteen rounds. After the action was over I examined the tree behind which O'Doud stood, and found seven musket-balls buried in it in front of where his body was. When all the men behaved as well as the men of Company H did the whole time while under fire, it is hard to particularize. I cannot, however, pass this occasion to give special thanks to Sergt. Charles Wendall, and

John Keegan, for the efficient manner in which they assisted me during the whole morning by their cool and steady bearing and prompt action.

I cannot close this communication without paying a well-deserved compliment to Capt. J. H. Dobie, Sixth Regiment of Volunteers, and tendering him my most sincere thanks for his most able assistance. Captain Dobie, having been separated from his company before daylight, joined me as a volunteer, and was with me until after the close of the action, and was of the greatest assistance in restraining the men while on the march and encouraging them by his cool manner and voice while under fire. From my observation, the cool manner of my men, the length of time and distance of fire, the loss of the enemy must have been very considerable both on the steamer and flat-boat.

Respectfully submitted.

J. M. ROBERTSON,
Captain, Second Artillery, Commanding Company H.

Maj. LEWIS G. ARNOLD,
Commanding Column on morning October 9, 1861.

BATTERY LINCOLN, SANTA ROSA ISLAND,
October 26, 1861.

SIR: I have to request that in my report of the affairs of the morning of the 9th instant the name of Private Michael M. O'Doud, of Company H, Second Artillery, be erased, and that of Private John Gannon (same company) inserted in its place. At the time of the affair spoken of I had been but a few days (since the 1st instant) with the company, and knew none of the men. When writing my report I directed the first sergeant to bring me the name of the man referred to, which he did as O'Doud, and I have supposed him to be the man till yesterday, when Gannon informed me of my error, and I at once recognized him as the man I had noticed. Since then I have made further inquiries, and find from the statements of my non-commissioned officers and others that O'Doud was behind another tree and did good service. Should a copy of my report have been forwarded to Headquarters of the Army before the receipt of this, I respectfully request that a copy of this note may also be forwarded, to be placed on file with it.

I am, very respectfully, your obedient servant,

J. M. ROBERTSON,
Captain, Second Artillery, Commanding Company H.

Lieut. F. W. SEELEY,
Adjutant, Fort Pickens, Fla.

No. 8.

Report of Capt. Richard C. Duryea, First U. S. Artillery.

FORT PICKENS, FLA., *October* 10, 1861.

SIR: In obedience to your instructions, I have the honor to make the following report of the attack and repulse of the rebel troops yesterday morning:

A detachment of Company A, First Artillery, consisting of 30 men and 1 corporal, under Lieutenant Taylor, formed on the parade ground.

The main part of my company being at the guns on the ramparts, was ordered by Major Vogdes, without my being informed of the fact, to join Company E, Third Infantry, and proceed to the assistance of Colonel Wilson. As soon as I was informed of the detachment leaving I immediately left the fort and proceeded to join it. On my way meeting Lieutenant Reese, who had been sent with orders from Colonel Brown to the major, I received his orders and pushed on to communicate them. I arrived at the scene of action when the firing first commenced, and found the enemy drawn up between our command and myself and the fort. Making a short detour, I again came upon the enemy. The action had been sharp and of short duration, and at this time the enemy were retiring up the beach. I was then joined by Lieutenant Langdon, and picking up 8 or 10 men who had been cut off from the command, we followed the enemy to the first boat, the men firing upon them while embarking; it is of course impossible to say with what effect. Your column soon after coming up, I joined it.

Very respectfully, your obedient servant,

R. C. DURYEA,
First Lieutenant, First Artillery.

Maj. LEWIS G. ARNOLD,
First Regiment Artillery.

No. 9.

Report of Lieut. Alexander N. Shipley, Third U. S. Infantry.

FORT PICKENS, FLA., *October* 10, 1861.

SIR: I have the honor to state that, in obedience to orders, I left this fort at daybreak on the morning of the 9th instant with Company C, Third Infantry, consisting of 3 sergeants, 3 corporals, and 51 privates. Attached to my company were 4 privates of Company A, First Infantry, also 3 unassigned recruits, making a total of 64 enlisted men. We proceeded up the island by way of Batteries Cameron and Lincoln. At the latter battery I was joined by Captain Robertson, with a portion of his company (H, Second Artillery), from which point we marched as rapidly as possible to near a place known as the Four Mile Point, where we were halted, and ordered to open fire upon a small barge which had left our shore and distant probably 1,200 yards. My company fired two volleys at the barge. Many of the shots must have taken effect. I saw the ricocheting of many of the balls on the water in front and close to the barge.

From this place I was ordered up the beach at a double-quick after a large body of rebels seen at a distance of at least 1 mile. On arriving near the place where they were seen I deployed my company, as directed, and moved rapidly up the island to a point opposite where the rebels had embarked. On seeing them I immediately ordered my company at double-quick in the direction of the steamers and scows. The latter were being towed by a large steamer and distant from the beach about 500 yards. I formed my men under shelter of the sand hills immediately on the beach and opened fire upon the rebels. An incessant fire was kept up for some twenty minutes, when the vessels got out of range of my guns and the firing ceased for a few minutes, when a small boat was seen off to our right and distant some 1,200 yards. I ordered my company to fire upon it. They fired two well-directed volleys. The firing upon the rebels on leaving our shore was very effective, throwing them, in their crowded state, into great confusion. I was then ordered to proceed with my company to the fort, deploying them so as to scout the island from the south beach to near its center. On my way down I found 2 dead bodies and 1 wounded man, all rebels. The dead bodies I had carried to the south beach (the dead were to be collected on that beach). The wounded man—Private Furguson, Seventh Alabama Regiment—was sent in a cart to the upper hospital. I also captured Lieutenant Farley, of the Florida volunteers, and 2 privates—viz, Moore, Seventh Alabama Regiment, and Goodley, of the Seventh Florida Regiment Volunteers—whom I brought into this fort and turned over to the guard.

It is perhaps unnecessary for me to testify to the good conduct and coolness of the non-commissioned officers and privates of my company, as well as those attached, as from the time of leaving the fort to the time the firing ceased they were under your personal observation.

I have the honor to be, very respectfully, your obedient servant,

A. N. SHIPLEY,
First Lieutenant, Third Infantry, Commanding Company C.

Maj. LEWIS G. ARNOLD,
First U. S. Artillery, Commanding Column.

No. 10.

Report of Capt. Loomis L. Langdon, First U. S. Artillery.

FORT PICKENS, FLA., *October* 10, 1861.

SIR: Pursuant to instructions, I have the honor to report my action in the engagement yesterday morning between the Federal troops and the rebels near the camp of the Sixth Regiment New York Volunteers.

About an hour before daybreak I was ordered by Colonel Brown to go up the island, find Colonel Wilson, and give him the order to follow the rebels, then believed to be retreating, and attack, and, if compelled to himself fall back, to do so slowly and in good order. After passing through a number of volunteers gathered at the fork of the two tramways about musket-shot from the fort (and whom I now understand to have been Wilson's command that I was searching for), I arrived at the commissary store, which was burning. The camp was in flames and the tents of four companies almost consumed. Two or three corpses lay in the camp, but the place was utterly deserted. I then hastened on to the hospital, where I found and got 8 of them from Dr. Sutherland to put out the fire in the commissary store-shed. Returning, I passed through the camp, and found about 6 volunteers with muskets, apparently guarding 2 officers' tents. I added them to my 8, and put them to work extinguishing the fire and saving the stores, which was soon done. I then crossed the island, still searching for Colonel Wilson, whom, it seems, I had passed before. I had a mounted man out also looking for him.

On arriving on the north side of the island I met Lieutenant Duryea, of the First Regiment Artillery, who was carrying orders from Colonel Brown to Major Vogdes. We heard a smart firing about 200 yards up the beach, and supposing that the major and Captain Hildt were there engaged we hurried up, but soon finding a soldier who, when questioned, answered "Second Alabama," and ascertaining that the men in front and very near us were enemies, we came back a little and made a detour to reach our friends, who had the enemy between them and the fort. Proceeding slowly, we saw the rebels slowly retreating from the sand hills and up the beach. We here gathered about 8 stragglers from the regulars, who were in advance, and with them we pushed on, and, deploying the men, soon found ourselves before the enemy in force. They fired on us and commenced shoving off a small boat. We returned the fire on the boat, but, a large force preparing to cut us off, we came back slowly for about half a mile, where we met Major Arnold's command. Informing him of the position of the enemy and asking for orders, I was sent to the fort to report and bring up a field piece.

Returning to the field, I overtook a battalion of volunteers acting as a reserve, but at too great a distance to be of any service. I advised the officer in command to get closer to the advance, which he was subsequently doing when there was no occasion for his services, Lieutenant Jackson having brought him the order to move on, which was obeyed. Then I joined Lieutenant Jackson, who had gathered about 80 volunteers from Colonel Wilson's camp and including 2 or 3 regulars, the latter being taken from the guard. I assisted Lieutenant Jackson in deploying his men. Here we got ahead of the reserve and were going on, when we met Major Arnold returning, the enemy's steamboats having taken the boats in tow, and, after suffering a fire from Captain Robertson's immediate command, retreated to the other side. The command was then rested and ordered into the fort.

Lieutenant Duryea and myself took prisoner a wounded marine officer and had him conveyed to the hospital. I sent 2 wounded rebels also to the hospital, and spent the rest of the forenoon collecting the dead and wounded and conveying them to the hospital and fort. It may be well to mention that so much time was lost in fitting harness to the mules for the field piece, that by the time it arrived within 2 miles of the place of embarkation the enemy were gone, the horses for the gun being in use for the officers.

I am, sir, very respectfully, your obedient servant,

LOOMIS L. LANGDON,
First Lieutenant, Fifth Artillery, A. A. Q. M.

Maj. LEWIS G. ARNOLD,
First Artillery, U. S. Army.

No. 11.

Report of Lieut. Francis W. Seeley, Fourth U. S. Artillery.

FORT PICKENS, FLA., *October* 11, 1861.

MAJOR: In obedience to your directions, I have the honor to report that about 3.30 o'clock on the morning of the 9th of October, soon after the firing was heard at Camp Brown, I was sent by the colonel commanding to give some orders to Captain Robertson, commanding Batteries Lincoln and Cameron. On my return I met Major Vogdes and his command. The major requested me to take command of his advance guard, consisting of about 20 men, and to keep along the north beach about 15 rods in advance of the main body. With this request I complied, and marched quietly along the beach, keeping a sharp lookout in advance and on my right flank. After advancing about 1½ miles from the fort I saw a squad of men in front of my party. I immediately pushed my guard forward at double-quick, and succeeded in capturing 2 of them. They proved to be a party of stragglers from the main body of the enemy. No sooner were my prisoners secured than I heard sharp firing in rear, showing that our command was engaged with the enemy. I immediately fell back with my party and joined our main body, which I found under command of Captain Hildt, Third Infantry, Major Vogdes having been taken prisoner by the enemy, whose whole force was posted about 25 or 30 yards in front of our command. By direction of Captain Hildt I then took command of our right, and, ably assisted by Lieutenant Taylor, First Artillery, posted our men as advantageously as the ground would permit. The enemy then opened a pretty sharp fire on us, which our men returned with spirit.

Our force actually engaged at this time was about 75 or 80 men, while that of the enemy was about 1,000, as we have since ascertained. Notwithstanding this disparity of numbers, our men, under the able command of Captain Hildt, bravely held their ground until the enemy made a movement evidently with the intention of attacking our left flank, when Captain Hildt gave orders to fall back gradually towards the south beach, which our men executed in good style, carrying off our wounded, facing about occasionally and delivering their fire. Soon after we took 3 army surgeons and 8 enlisted men belonging to the enemy prisoners, and Captain Hildt sent them under proper guard to the fort. As soon as the enemy found his front clear he continued his retreat up the island. We remained, collecting and caring for our wounded, until your command came up. We had 4 men killed, 20 wounded, and 1 officer (Major Vogdes) and 8 men missing. During the whole action our men behaved admirably, loading and firing with perfect coolness. Of those who were particularly distinguished for their coolness and bravery mention has, I believe, been made by Captain Hildt in his official report of the affair.

I am, major, very respectfully, your obedient servant,

F. W. SEELEY,
First Lieutenant, Fourth Artillery.

Maj. LEWIS G. ARNOLD,
First Artillery, U. S. Army.

No. 12.

Report of Lieutenant Richard H. Jackson, First U. S. Artillery.

FORT PICKENS, FLA., *October* 10, 1861.

SIR: In accordance with your directions I have the honor to report that a little after daybreak yesterday morning I was ordered by Colonel Brown to follow your command and take any men that I could find who in the darkness of the night might have become separated from Major Vogdes' command, as well as any of Colonel Wilson's men who could be picked up, and with them proceed to join your command, and to give instructions to the officers commanding detachments who might be in your rear to follow promptly to your support. I proceeded at once to Colonel Wilson's encampment and collected about 80 men of his regiment and 3 officers. I immediately formed them and proceeded at their head to join you. After marching at double-quick for about a mile, I heard heavy firing on the beach, and seeing a swamp in front of me, I galloped ahead of my detachment in order to select the shortest route to the scene of action. About 300 yards in front of my command I fell in with and captured two of the rebels, who were guarding 3 men of Colonel Wilson's regiment, who had been made prisoners a short time before. I disarmed them, and sent them under guard to the fort. After proceeding a short distance I came up with about 150 men of the New York regiment, under Lieutenant-Colonel Creighton. They were halted. I ordered him to advance at once to your support. He accordingly did so. I went in advance of him at the double-quick and soon came on the beach. I then saw that the rebels had taken to their boats. I heard heavy firing from our troops in advance of me on the beach, and saw a great many of the enemy fall on one of their large flat-boats. They, however, succeeded in getting off before I could get close enough to fire on them. I in a few minutes afterwards joined your command.

I am sorry to have to state that on my arrival at Colonel Wilson's camp I was greatly surprised to see so many men wandering around, some of them without arms (although there were plenty to be had), and to find in camp with them 3 or 4 officers, who did not even attempt to organize the men or move forward with them. A great many of the men said that they would have been glad to have gone forward before my arrival if they had had any person to organize and lead them.

I am, sir, very respectfully, your obedient servant,

R. H. JACKSON,
First Lieutenant, First Artillery.

Maj. LEWIS G. ARNOLD,
Major, First Artillery, U. S. Army.

No. 13.

Congratulatory orders from Major-General McClellan, U. S. Army.

GENERAL ORDERS, No. 109. } HDQRS. OF THE ARMY, A. G. O., *Washington, December 21, 1861.*

The Commanding General has the satisfaction of announcing to the Army another instance of skill and good conduct on the part of the beleaguered garrison of Fort Pickens, harbor of Pensacola, under the command of Col. Harvey Brown, Fifth Regiment U. S. Artillery.

On the night of October 9 an attempt was made by a large body of rebels to burn the camp of Wilson's Zouaves, spike the guns of the outer batteries, and take Fort Pickens by assault. The enemy were signally repulsed from Santa Rosa Island, with heavy loss on their side, after firing a few of our tents.

A subsequent attempt to make a lodgment on the island was defeated by well-delivered fire from one of our ships of war.

To put a stop to such aggressions a combined fire was opened upon the enemy's batteries from Fort Pickens and the ships of our squadron in Pensacola Harbor, which was kept up throughout the 22d and 23d of November. On the first day Fort McRee and several guns in the other hostile batteries were silenced; and this was followed by the destruction, under our heavy cannonade, of nearly two-thirds of the towns of Warrington and Woolsey, adjoining the navy-yard, and by very serious damage to the navy-yard and its buildings. Fortunately but little loss was sustained by us in men or in the condition of our works.

It is with pride and gratification that the Commanding General finds in the official reports the most honorable mention of each and every officer, as well as of the enlisted men, engaged on these occasions.

By command of Major-General McClellan:

L. THOMAS,
Adjutant-General.

No. 14.

Reports of Maj. Gen. Braxton Bragg, C. S. Army, commanding at Pensacola, with congratulatory orders.

BARRANCAS, *October* 9, 1861.

We chastised the enemy on Santa Rosa last night for his annoyances; drove him from his camps, burned his tents and many stores, spiked some of his guns, and retired in good order. Our loss was 30 or 40 killed and wounded. The enemy's supposed to be larger, as he was completely surprised. General Anderson commanded and was disabled. Can I retain General Ruggles a few days? It may be very important. Major Vogdes is our prisoner, with several others. Am I authorized to exchange?

BRAXTON BRAGG,
Major-General.

General S. COOPER.

HDQRS. TROOPS OF THE CONFEDERATE STATES,
Near Pensacola, Fla., October 10, 1861.

SIR: Satisfied from information received that the enemy contemplated opening fire upon us very soon, and desirous of avenging the annoyances he had recently caused my command, an expedition was projected against his outposts on Santa Rosa Island. It was executed on Tuesday night, by 1,000 men, under Brig. Gen. R. H. Anderson, in a very handsome manner. We attacked and drove in his pickets and outposts, routed a regiment of New York volunteers, Col. Billy Wilson; burned the camp and stores in the vicinity, including a large quantity of stores and provisions; inflicted a loss of about 50 killed, including a number of officers, from the best information we can get; wounded a number unknown; made some 20 prisoners, Major I. Vogdes, First Artillery, with them, and retired within our lines.

Our loss is more severe than at first reported. The men became much exhausted from the long and fatiguing march through the deep sand of the island, and no doubt a considerable portion of the loss was from this cause. We might have easily defended ourselves against the troops on the island, but it was necessary to leave before the enemy's shipping should open and destroy our transportation, and our means would not enable us to keep them off. Thus far I hear of about 20 killed on our side, including 3 officers. Many of them have undoubtedly been massacred after being captured, from the appearance of their bodies which were delivered to us. The enemy also have about 40 of our party prisoners, several of them wounded.

The exact state of affairs will be communicated more in detail as soon as the reports of subordinates are received, when I will take occasion to do full justice to individuals for special acts of gallantry. Each State and corps represented in the army participated in the affair, and the gallantry and good conduct of the troops were conspicuous. Brig. Gen.

R. H. Anderson conducted the expedition with a zeal and gallantry worthy of high commendation. At the close he received a painful wound in the left elbow, temporarily disabling him; but it is trusted we shall not long be deprived of his valuable services.

I am, sir, very respectfully, your obedient servant,

BRAXTON BRAGG,
Major-General, Commanding.

ADJUTANT-GENERAL C. S. ARMY,
Richmond, Va.

HEADQUARTERS ARMY OF PENSACOLA,
Near Pensacola, Fla., October 29, 1861.

SIR: Owing to the disability of Brigadier-General Anderson from his wound I have been unable to procure earlier a detailed report of the affair with the enemy on Santa Rosa Island on the night of the 8th and 9th instant, with a tabular statement of killed, wounded, and prisoners. It is herewith inclosed. [No. 15.] The circumstances attending this little expedition rendered it a most daring and successful feat of arms.

Landing from steamers and flats on the enemy's shore within sight of his fleet, marching some 3 or 4 miles in the darkness of night over an unknown and almost impassable ground under his guns, killing his pickets, storming his intrenched camp of 600 or 700 men, driving the enemy off in utter confusion and dismay, and burning every vestige of clothing, equipage, and provisions, leaving them individually in a state of destitution, and this under the close range of the guns of his stronghold, Fort Pickens, without his discovering our object or firing a gun, is an achievement worthy of the gallant men who executed it. Our loss was almost entirely the result of exhaustion from the fatigue of the march and from the over-zeal of the hospital guard left to protect the enemy's sick when they were captured.

From the nature of the service and the necessity of rapidly retiring with our small force before the enemy could rally from his surprise some of our wounded were left on the field, and, I regret to say, indications show they were brutally murdered by the enemy. Of 13 dead bodies recovered 11 were shot through the head, having at the same time disabling wounds in the body. This fact admits of but one inference.

Brigadier-General Anderson commends in very just terms the gallantry of his little band, who have fully justified the high estimate I had formed of this excellent little army. They have shown it is only necessary to order and they will promptly execute, however desperate the undertaking. The general modestly omits to mention that at the close of the affair he received a painful wound in the left arm from a musket-ball, which will disable him for several weeks.

In commending the troops generally for their good conduct I cannot omit to mention the separate commanders of the three small columns—Col. J. Patton Anderson, First Florida Volunteers; Col. J. K. Jackson, Fifth Georgia Volunteers, and Col. J. R. Chalmers, Ninth Mississippi Volunteers. The darkness and nature of the service rendered it necessary for each one to act an independent part. They proved themselves not only gallant leaders, but competent commanders.

To Capt. W. R. Boggs, engineer, C. S. Army, and First Lieut. J. E. Slaughter, C. S. Artillery, acting inspector-general, I am indebted for the perfect knowledge of the enemy's pickets and positions, obtained by close reconnaissances, on which the expedition was based, and for the secret and complete organization which insured its success.

I am, sir, very respectfully, your obedient servant,

BRAXTON BRAGG,
Major-General, Commanding.

ADJUTANT-GENERAL C. S. ARMY,
Richmond, Va.

GENERAL ORDERS, No. 108. } HEADQUARTERS TROOPS C. S.,
Near Pensacola, Fla., October 10, 1861.

I. Brig. Gen. R. H. Anderson and the officers and men of his command will accept the thanks of the major-general commanding for their gallant expedition of Tuesday night. The object was attained, and the enemy taught a severe lesson for his marauding parties, which have recently annoyed us. The sacrifice which must be made in such exploits was not unexpected, and we can only mourn the loss of our gallant comrades, whilst we prepare to meet their fate and deserve their honors.

II. The circumstances attending this affair should teach us the necessity of vigilance, our success being greatly aided by the want of it on the part of the enemy, and especially as an attempt at retaliation may be expected.

By command of Major-General Bragg:

GEO. G. GARNER,
Assistant Adjutant-General.

No. 15.

Report of Brig. Gen. Richard H. Anderson, C. S. Army, commanding expedition.

PENSACOLA, FLA., *October* 23, 1861.

SIR: I have the honor to submit the following report of the affair on Santa Rosa Island on the night of the 8th and morning of the 9th of October:

The detachments which had been ordered to assemble at the navy-yard arrived at the hour appointed, and were embarked in good order on the steamer Time. Whilst proceeding from the navy-yard to Pensacola the troops were divided into battalions, as follows:

The First Battalion, 350 strong, to the command of which Col. James R. Chalmers, Ninth Mississippi Regiment, was assigned, was composed of detachments from the Ninth and Tenth Mississippi and First Alabama Regiments. Three companies of the Seventh Regiment Alabama Volunteers, two companies of Louisiana infantry, and two companies of the First Regiment of Florida Volunteers, composed the Second Battalion, 400 strong, to the command of which Col. J. Patton Anderson, First Regiment Florida Volunteers, was assigned. The Third Battalion, 260 strong, under command of Col. John K. Jackson, Fifth Regiment Georgia Volunteers, was composed of detachments from the Fifth Georgia Regiment and the Georgia Battalion. An independent company of 53 men, selected from the Fifth Georgia Regiment, and Captain Homer's company of artillery, lightly armed with pistols and knives, carrying materials for spiking cannon, burning and destroying buildings, gun-carriages, &c., were placed under command of Lieutenant Hallonquist, acting ordnance officer. Lieutenant Nelms, adjutant Fifth Georgia Regiment, was attached to this command.

The medical officers who accompanied the expedition were: Dr. Micks, of the Louisiana infantry; Dr. Tompkins, of the Fifth Georgia Regiment; Dr. Gholson, of the Ninth Mississippi Regiment; Dr. Lipscomb, of the Tenth Mississippi Regiment, and Dr. Gamble, of the First Florida Regiment, and a detail of 20 men was made to attend on and assist them.

Arriving at Pensacola at about 10 o'clock p. m., the transfer of the troops to the steamer Ewing and the barges and flats which had been provided was pushed on as rapidly as possible, but not without some unavoidable delay. It was found absolutely necessary to employ the Neaffie to assist in towing, and at length, all preparations having been completed, the boats departed from Pensacola at a little after 12 o'clock, crossed the bay, and effected a landing at the point which had been indicated by instructions. Disembarkation was rapidly executed in good order and silence, and the battalions were formed upon the beach at a little after 2 o'clock a. m.

To effectually accomplish the object of the expedition Colonel Chalmers was directed to advance rapidly along the north beach, Colonel Anderson along the south beach, and Colonel Jackson, following a few hundred yards in rear of Colonel Chalmers, was to push his command to the middle of the island, and deploy it as soon as he should hear firing from either of the other battalions or should perceive from any other indications that the enemy's camp was approached or assailed by the other columns. Colonels Chalmers and Anderson had been further directed to endeavor to restrain their men from firing, to capture guards and sentinels, and to place their commands, if possible, between Fort Pickens and the camp of the enemy. Lieutenant Hallonquist followed in rear of Colonel Jackson's battalion, with orders to do whatever damage he could to the batteries, buildings, and camps from which the enemy might be driven.

After a march of 3 or 4 miles, rendered toilsome and fatiguing by the nature of the ground, the head of Colonel Chalmers' column came suddenly upon a sentinel, who fired ineffectually at our troops, and was himself instantly shot down. The alarm having been thus given, and it becoming impossible to conceal our further advance from the enemy, I ordered Colonel Jackson to push his way through the thickets to the middle of the island, and advance as rapidly as possible. The guards and outposts of the Zouaves were now rapidly driven in or shot down, and the progress of a few hundred yards, quickly accomplished by Colonel Jackson, brought him upon the camp of the enemy in advance of either of the other battalions. Without a moment's delay he charged it with the bayonet, but met with no resistance. The camp was almost entirely deserted, and our troops speedily applied the torch to the tents, store-houses, and sheds of Wilson's Zouaves.

In the mean time Colonels Chalmers and Anderson, advancing along the shores of the island, encountered pickets and outposts, with which they had some sharp skirmishing, but quickly beat them off, and joined in the work of destroying the camp. This having been most thoroughly executed, the troops were reassembled, with a view to proceeding against and destroying the batteries which lay between the camp and Fort Pickens; but daylight appearing, and there being no longer a possibility of a surprise of the batteries, I directed the signal for retiring to be sounded and the troops to be put in march for the boats.

At about half way between the Zouave camp and the point of disembarkation of our troops we encountered two companies of United States regulars, which had passed us under cover of the darkness, and posted themselves behind a dense thicket to intercept our retiring column, and a very sharp but short skirmish ensued. The enemy was speedily driven off, and our troops resumed their march. The re-embarkation was successfully accomplished, and the order given to the steamers to steer for Pensacola, when it was discovered that a hawser had become entangled in the propeller of the Neaffie, and that she could not move.

After some delay, from ineffectual attempts to extricate the propeller, she and the large flat which she had in tow were made fast to the Ewing. It was soon found, however, that with this incumbrance the Ewing would not obey her helm, and that a change in the manner of towing the Neaffie was necessary. While attempting to make this change the flats and barges which the Ewing had in tow became detached from her, and still further delay was occasioned in recovering them. By the time this had been done the hawser was cut away from the propeller, and the Neaffie proceeded on her way. The enemy, taking advantage of these circumstances, appeared among the sand hills near the beach, and opened a fire upon the masses of our troops densely crowded upon our transports, but without doing much execution, and we were soon out of range of their rifles. The necessity of using the Neaffie as a tug and the accident which for some time disabled her prevented her guns from being brought into play, otherwise she might have rendered effectual service in driving back the enemy who harassed us from the beach.

Our loss in this affair was as follows: Killed, 2 commissioned officers, 4 non-commissioned officers, 11 privates, and 1 citizen volunteer; wounded, 2 commissioned officers, 5 non-commissioned officers, and 32 privates; taken prisoners, 5 commissioned officers, 2 non-commissioned officers, and 23 privates. The larger portion of the officers, non-commissioned officers, and privates captured by the enemy were the guard left for the protection of their hospital and sick and the medical officers who had remained in the building to attend to such of our wounded as might be carried there. Notwithstanding that I caused the signal for retiring to be repeatedly sounded during the return of the troops it was not heard at the hospital, and the guard and medical officers were cut off and taken prisoners.

The loss of the enemy in killed and wounded has not been precisely ascertained, but is certainly known to have much exceeded our own. From such imperfect observation as I made in passing over parts of the ground I will estimate his loss at 50 or 60 killed and 100 wounded. Twenty prisoners were taken, among them Maj. Israel Vogdes, of the United States artillery.

The destruction of property in the conflagration was very great. Large stores of provisions, supplies of clothing, camp and garrison equipage, arms, and ammunition were entirely consumed. Some arms were brought away by our men, and in a few instances money and clothing, as will be seen by the report of Colonel Jackson, and I would respectfully recommend that the captors be permitted to retain whatever private property they have taken.

It is with pride and pleasure that I bear testimony to and call to the notice of the general commanding the admirable conduct of the troops throughout the expedition and conflict. The alacrity, courage, and discipline exhibited by them merit the highest commendation, and give assurance of success in any future encounters which they may have with the enemies of our country.

I beg leave to refer you to the accompanying reports of commanders of battalions and of Lieutenant Hallonquist for particulars concerning casualties, incidents, and individual instances of meritorious conduct. I inclose the report of Captain Brent, C. S. Navy, who was charged with the entire arrangements for the transportation of my command, under whose direction this important matter was very successfully managed.*

The report of Major Lovell, C. S. Army, chief of harbor police, and in command of the steamer Neaffie, is also submitted.* The members of my staff, Capt. T. S. Mills, assistant adjutant-general, and Capt. Hugh M. King, Fifth Regiment Georgia Volunteers; Lieuts. Calvin L. Sayre and Wilber Johnson, C. S. Marines, who volunteered their services and acted as my aides, rendered me active and efficient assistance throughout the whole of the operations. Captain Mills, who was with Colonel Anderson's battalion in its first encounter with the enemy, received a severe contusion in the chest from a partially-spent ball, but nevertheless continued energetically to perform his duties, and Lieutenant Sayre, while fearlessly using his revolver with effect, had his thigh bone shattered just above the right knee by a musket-ball, and, being left upon the ground, fell into the hands of the enemy. Capt. Hugh M. King, in conveying orders and superintending the destruction of the camp, displayed commendable zeal and activity, and the ardor and intrepidity of Lieutenant Johnson, while deserving especial notice, give promise of this young officer's future success and distinction.

The officers of the medical staff rendered to the wounded every service which under the circumstances was possible.

Colonels Anderson and Jackson pay graceful tribute to the memory of Captain Bradford and Lieutenant Nelms, of their regiments, to which I desire to add my respectful admiration for them and for every brave patriot who fell with them in defense of their country's liberties.

I am, very respectfully, your most obedient servant,

R. H. ANDERSON,
Brigadier-General, Provisional Army.

Maj. G. G. GARNER,
Asst. Adjt. Gen., C. A., Hdqrs. Army of Pensacola.

DECEMBER 3, 1861.—Occupation of Ship Island, Miss.

REPORTS.

No. 1.—Maj. Gen. Benjamin F. Butler, of the departure of the expedition.
No. 2.—Maj. Gen. Benjamin F. Butler, of the arrival of the expedition at Ship Island.
No. 3.—Brig. Gen. J. W. Phelps, commanding.

No. 1.

Reports of Maj. Gen. Benjamin F. Butler of the departure of the expedition.

HEADQUARTERS DEPARTMENT OF NEW ENGLAND,
Boston, December 2, 1861.

GENERAL: I beg leave to report that the steamship Constitution sailed from Boston to Portland, in the State of Maine, upon Thursday, the 21st ultimo, with two regiments of infantry—the Ninth Connecticut and the

---

* None of these subordinate reports have been found.

Twenty-sixth Regiment of Massachusetts Volunteers—together with the Fifth Massachusetts Light Battery, in all numbering about 1,900 men. One company of the Ninth Connecticut was allowed to remain at Camp Chase, in Lowell, to recruit for the regiment, where it is now stationed. Subsistence stores for thirty days for 300 men were taken on board at Boston. It was my intention to have placed on board this ship at Portland the Twelfth Maine Regiment, this coming within the chartered capacity of the vessel, but upon arriving at that place the captain became uneasy and doubtful of the capacity of the ship, entered a written protest against taking it on board, and upon the 23d ultimo sailed from that port with the freight taken at Boston. I have since had the Twelfth Maine Regiment brought to this State and encamped at Camp Chase, where it now remains, waiting the remainder of vessels to carry it on, and undergoing instruction.

By the action of the captain of the Constitution he made forfeit his charter-party and leaves the claim of the owners to be adjusted upon the principles of equity.

On the 26th ultimo I forwarded the bark Kingfisher, of Boston, for the same destination from Boston, with extra clothing for three regiments and other quartermaster's stores, including parts of a floating bridge half a mile long, lumber, &c., for building wharf, &c., carriages for field battery, subsistence and sutler stores, and 130 horses and forage, details of which bill of lading are in Schedule A.

I have the George Green, Idaho, and Black Prince now loading, all from 1,000 to 1,400 tons register, all sailing vessels. The George Green is loading with lumber, subsistence stores, and horses, and will be ready to sail about the 10th instant. The Idaho and Black Prince will take on board the Twelfth Maine Regiment, with subsistence stores, lumber, horses, and forage. They will be ready to sail about the 10th instant. I am loading the bark with lumber, cement, horses and forage, and surf-boats. It will be ready to sail about the 10th instant. I have chartered the steam-tug Saxon, to take out a company of artillery, with their guns and subsistence stores, and intend that it shall sail as convoy and tug to the above vessels.

The Constitution touched at Fortress Monroe, and on the 27th ultimo, having taken on board Brigadier-General Phelps, sailed for Ship Island, where it becomes due upon the 3d instant. If it succeeds in unloading to leave there on the 7th, it will be due here, in ordinary course, upon the 15th instant, ready for further service.

I have been obliged to use sailing ships for transporting the men because of the impossibility of getting steamers, being informed by those in whose judgment confidence may be placed that they are equally safe.

I have in process of recruitment—more of which will be ready by the time of the return of the Constitution than can be taken on board of her—two regiments in Massachusetts, one regiment in Vermont, and one regiment in Connecticut, a squadron of mounted men, and three batteries, of full complement. I have secured and in process of being ready arms, ammunition, uniforms, and equipments for all of these. I have in my report of the 2d instant given a complete list of ordnance and ordnance stores which can be obtained for the objects of the expedition. I do not send herewith lists of commissary stores purchased, but these may be stated generally to be sufficient for 5,000 men for three months, besides the fresh provisions for the voyage. I have also such stores and provision of materials as may be necessary to a post fortified on Ship Island in a reasonable state of defense.

Schedule B contains the list of quartermaster's stores shipped on board the Constitution.

I have the honor to remain, very respectfully, your obedient servant,

BENJ. F. BUTLER,
Major-General, Commanding.

To the ADJUTANT GENERAL U. S. ARMY.

No. 2.

Report of Maj. Gen. Benjamin F. Butler of the arrival of the expedition at Ship Island.

WASHINGTON, *December* 19, 1861.

I have the honor to forward to the Commanding General a copy of the report of Brigadier-General Phelps of the landing of a portion of my division upon Ship Island, together with details of the state of the island and its needs for a defensive position.

I have not received from General Phelps any official copy of the proclamation to which he refers, but from other sources have such information as renders it certain that the printed copies are substantially correct. I need hardly say that the issuing of any proclamation upon such occasion was neither suggested nor authorized by me, and most certainly not such a one. With that important exception I commend the report, and ask attention to its clear and business-like statements.

I have the honor to be, your most obedient servant,

BENJ. F. BUTLER,
Major-General, Commanding.

To the ADJUTANT-GENERAL U. S. ARMY.

No. 3.

Report of Brig. Gen. J. W. Phelps, commanding.

SHIP ISLAND, MISSISSIPPI SOUND,
December 5, 1861.

SIR: A part of the Middlesex brigade, consisting of the Massachusetts Twenty-sixth and Connecticut Ninth Infantry Volunteers, with Captain Manning's battery of artillery (volunteers), numbering in all (servants included) 1,908, arrived off Fort Monroe, Va., on board steam-transport Constitution, on the 26th November. In compliance with previous orders and instructions I relieved Colonel Jones, of the Massachusetts Twenty-sixth, in command, and we stood out to sea on the afternoon of the 27th. After a pleasant passage we reached Ship Island Harbor, Mississippi Sound, on the evening of the 3d December. Dispatches for Flag-Officer McKean, with which I was intrusted were sent by Lieutenant Winslow, of the R. R. Cuyler, the same evening, to Pensacola Station, where the flag-officer then was, and to whom I made known my arrival.

Captain Smith, of the Massachusetts, offered us all the means within his power to facilitate our landing—an operation which we have not yet completed, and which we should have found very difficult, if not impossible, were it not for the zealous assistance rendered by Lieutenant Buchanan and other officers of his command, aided by two high-pressure steamers which the Navy had recently captured. We found in the harbor on our arrival the United States war vessel Massachusetts and the R. R. Cuyler, besides several prizes; and not long afterwards the steam gunboat New London and an armed schooner, a part of the Gulf Blockading Squadron, came in.

Some six or more steam gunboats, if not drawing more than 6 or 7 feet, could be well employed here in stopping a considerable trade and in otherwise annoying the enemy. Without them the enemy's light-draught boats can pass in view between New Orleans and Mobile with impunity. On no part of our coast could gunboats be better at this time employed. Upon the west end of the island a partially-finished fort is occupied by about 170 sailors and marines, commanded by Lieutenant Buchanan, of the Navy, who has several Dahlgren large-caliber guns in position on navy carriages. The rebels, by whom the island was held several months, abandoned it in September last, and destroyed nearly everything which they could not carry off. The fort and light-house, with keeper's lodgings, remain, the former unfinished and the latter injured to some extent by fire. The walls of the fort have been carried up to a sufficient height by the rebels to form nearly a tier of casemates, and partly covered over with some considerable mason work; and with material now on the ground, except lime, it might receive some twenty guns on casemate carriages. I would recommend that number, one-half or part Sawyer's 24-pounder rifles, the other half 8 or 10 inch columbiads. Traverse circles, traverse blocks of stone or wood, and iron pintles to hold the tongue of the chassis, would be necessary. A magazine would have to be constructed, for which more brick would be needed. For immediate use a large number of sand bags might not be out of place. For the purpose of landing guns, coal for the Navy, and other heavy materials, a large convenient wharf will be necessary, with some quarter or a half mile of railway, the iron for which, and perhaps the lumber, would have to be brought from the North, together with a pile-driver and other tools for construction; though perhaps timber partly enough might be found here.

The island is a long, narrow strip of land running north of east. Some 6 or 7 miles towards the west end, where the harbor lies, and where we are encamped, it consists of sand hummocks of pure white sand, interspersed with sedgy spots of water. It bears evidence of having been overflowed in some extraordinary storms, large trunks of trees having drifted on some of its higher hummocks. The east end widens out in a triangular shape, embracing about 1 square mile, and is covered with pine trees. I made an unsuccessful effort to have it examined on the day of our arrival, and regret having been too much occupied since to repeat it. From appearances, it would be well to have the camp there, with a wharf, and a small steamer to ply between the two points. For the present, and to expedite the return of the Constitution, I concluded to land here, where I can place, though indifferently well, one or two more regiments. The land is in no respects suitable for a camp, especially in view of such instructions as one of the regiments present particularly needs. Should the stay here be of long continuance, huts with floors will be necessary.

While writing this report I learn, much to my regret, that in transferring the baggage from the Constitution to the lighter one of Captain Manning's 6-pounder rifled guns has been lost overboard in 4 fathoms of water. How such an unpleasant accident could have happened I have not yet been informed.

Deeming it proper to make known to the people of this region the remoter objects of this expedition, I have prepared a proclamation, which I shall endeavor to have disseminated as early and widely as possible, consistent with the more pressing demands of the servce.*

December 6.—The work upon the fort would require the superintendence of a military engineer. For present purposes the walls now standing, though built of brick, may answer, but for future use a granite work of solid foundation and three tiers of guns might be necessary. It might be well for the present to have three Sawyer's mounted outside the work, on entire traverse circles, to be covered by sand bags. For this purpose suitable platforms will be needed. I have to-day, in accordance with my instructions, held an interview with Captain Smith, of the Massachusetts, Flag-Officer McKean not having yet arrived. Captain Smith thinks that there is water enough on the island and in the vicinity to supply gunboats and other vessels of the station, although procuring it will be slow and difficult. He says that the flag-officer has ordered more guns for the fort, and that they are daily expected. He suggests that there should be a coal depot established here on the island, and that a regular steam packet should ply between the island and Fort Monroe, Va., or some other Northern port. He also proposes the occupation of other points upon the islands along the sound, with a view to the more complete cutting off of communication between New Orleans and Mobile, which has been to a great extent unimpeded from the want of proper gunboats and sufficient force. He, moreover, suggests a plan of driving piles across several of the mouths of the Mississippi, leaving but one open.

The discharging of the cargo of the Constitution is still going on by means of the two steamers before mentioned and a temporary wharf. The wind since our arrival has prevailed from north of east, and the water last night rose to such a height that a considerable portion of the island between the fort and light-house was overflowed, leaving a thin sheet of water there; an event which I am informed is not unfrequent. The narrow strip of sand, about a quarter or third of a mile in width, which forms the western extremity of the island, is but ill-suited for a camp, either regulars or volunteers.

The Connecticut regiment (the Ninth) has never yet received its arms, nor is it supplied with a proper allowance of tents. It is new, and requires a great deal of instruction. Of quartermaster's stores, such as spades, shovels, axes, camp hatchets, carpenters' and masons' tools, a large supply, I understand from Captain Butler, has been ordered, and they will probably be needed.

This afternoon a dispatch from Flag-Officer McKean has arrived by the De Soto, by which I learn that he will soon be here, and make this point his headquarters.

On board the New London, Captain Reed, I have visited the eastern extremity of the island; the part that lies beyond the lagoon. There is space sufficient there for 5,000 men, but the land is so interspersed with marshes that I consider a camp there for that number to be out of the question. The water along the northern shore for some distance is so shallow that our row-boats dragged bottom. The beach is lined by a ridge of sand hummocks some 10 feet in height, but beyond these the land is generally low, and covered with pines, scrub oak, scrub palmetto, and marsh grass in patches. Mosquitoes would be troublesome there at all seasons, and in rainy weather much of the ground would be under

* Proclamation not found.

water. The process of reclamation seems still to be going on with an activity as if it had but just begun, though the island is probably as old as the main-land. The animals seen are snakes, toads, birds, raccoons, pigs, and, it is said, alligators.

The New London, with four long 32s and one rifle, appears to be, under her present commander, a very effective, well-managed craft. Since her arrival here, some fifteen days ago, she has captured over five prizes and given the enemy great annoyance. The enemy's gunboats are of light draught, and are armed with rifles, and it is folly in us to allow them such an unnecessary advantage. With such an advantage on our side we could make ourselves felt in this quarter in a way calculated to produce an effect.

December 7.—The land on this side of the lagoon has been examined by several persons, and it represented as better fitted for a camp than the part beyond the lagoon, being higher and drier, but the water is so shallow that a long wharf would have to be built, and even then the space would hardly be suitable for a camp of 5,000 men. Nor are the islands in the neighborhood apparently much better. I shall endeavor to make the most of our position for the public service.

2 o'clock p. m.—The Constitution has been completely discharged, and will sail before dark. While reperusing this report, the De Soto and New London have been engaging the enemy's boats in the direction of New Orleans.

I have the honor to be, very respectfully, your obedient servant,

J. W. PHELPS,
Brigadier-General, Commanding.

Maj. Gen. BENJAMIN F. BUTLER,
Commanding Department New England, Boston, Mass.

NOVEMBER 22-23, 1861.—Bombardment of the Confederate lines about Pensacola, Fla.

REPORTS, ETC.

No. 1.—Col. Harvey Brown, Fifth U. S. Artillery, commanding Department of Florida.
No. 2.—Maj. Lewis G. Arnold, First U. S. Artillery, commanding batteries.
No. 3.—Capt. Richard C. Duryea, First U. S. Artillery.
No. 4.—Lieut. Richard H. Jackson, First U. S. Artillery.
No. 5.—Capt. James M. Robertson, Second U. S. Artillery.
No. 6.—Capt. Harvey A. Allen, Second U. S. Artillery.
No. 7.—Lieut. A. C. M. Pennington, Second U. S. Artillery.
No. 8.—Lieut. Francis W. Seeley, Fourth U. S. Artillery.
No. 9.—Capt. Samuel F. Chalfin, Fifth U. S. Artillery.
No. 10.—Capt. Loomis L. Langdon, First U. S. Artillery.
No. 11.—Capt. John McL. Hildt, Third U. S. Infantry.
No. 12.—Lieut. Alexander N. Shipley, Third U. S. Infantry.
No. 13.—Capt. Matthew M. Blunt, Twelfth U. S. Infantry.
No. 14.—Lieut. Walter McFarland, U. S. Corps of Engineers.
No. 15.—Maj. Gen. Braxton Bragg, C. S. Army, commanding Army of Pensacola, with congratulatory orders.
No. 16.—Brig. Gen. Richard H. Anderson, C. S. Army.

No. 1.

Reports of Col. Harvey Brown, Fifth U. S. Artillery, Commanding Department of Florida.

HEADQUARTERS DEPARTMENT OF FLORIDA,
Fort Pickens, November 25, 1861.

GENERAL: That Fort Pickens has been beleaguered by the rebels for the last nine months, and that it was daily threatened by the boasting rebels with the fate of Sumter, is a fact notorious to the whole world. Since its occupancy by Lieutenant Slemmer the rebels have been surrounding it with batteries and daily arming them with the heaviest and most efficient guns known to our service—guns stolen from us—until they considered this fort as virtually their own, its occupancy being only a question of time. I have been in command since the 16th of April, and during the whole of that time their force has averaged, so far as I can learn, from eight to ten times the number of mine. The position in which I have thus been placed has been sufficiently trying, and I have at three separate times intended to free myself from it by opening my batteries on them; but imperious circumstances, over which I had no control, have unexpectedly in each instance prevented.

Affairs were in this state on the morning of the 9th of October, when the enemy, 1,500 strong, attacked by surprise a portion of my command on an intensely dark night. They were defeated and driven from the island with great loss by less than 200 regulars and 50 volunteers, all the efficient force I had disposable for the purpose. An insult so gross to the flag of my country could not by me be passed unnoticed, and I designed immediately to take appropriate notice of it, but, as I said before, circumstances over which I had no control prevented. I make these prefatory remarks to explain why I have now opened my batteries on the enemy, when from the smallness of my forces—about one-sixth of his, 1,300 to 8,000—I have not the means of producing any decisive results, and as evidence of my having accomplished what I designed—the punishing the perpetrators of an insult on my country's flag.

Having invited Flag-Officer McKean to co-operate with me in attacking the rebels, and to which he gave a ready and cordial assent, I on the morning of the 22d opened my batteries on the enemy, to which in the course of half an hour he responded from his numerous forts and batteries, extending from the navy-yard to Fort McRee, a distance of about 4 miles, the whole nearly equidistant from this fort, and on which line he has two forts, McRee and Barrancas, and fourteen separate batteries, containing from one to four guns, many of them being 10-inch columbiads and some 12 and 13 inch sea-coast mortars, the distance varying from 2,100 to 2,900 yards from this fort. At the same time of my opening Flag-Officer McKean, in the Niagara, and Captain Ellison, in the Richmond, took position as near to Fort McRee as the depth of water would permit, but which, unfortunately, was not sufficiently deep to give full effect to their powerful batteries. They, however, kept up a spirited fire on the fort and adjacent batteries during the whole day. My fire was incessant from the time of opening until it was too dark to see, at the rate of a shot for each gun every fifteen or twenty minutes, the fire of the enemy being somewhat slower. By noon the guns of Fort McRee were all silenced but one, and three hours before sunset this fort and the adjoining battery ceased to fire. I directed the guns of Batteries Lincoln, Cameron, and Totten principally on the batteries adjacent to the navy-yard, those of Battery Scott to Fort McRee and the light-house batteries, and those of the fort to all. We reduced very perceptibly the fire of Barrancas, entirely silenced that in the navy-yard and in one or two of the other batteries, the efficiency of our fire at the close of the day not being the least impaired.

The next morning I again opened about the same hour, the Navy, unfortunately (owing to a reduction in the depth of water, caused by a change of wind), not being able to get so near as yesterday, consequently the distance was too great to be effectual. My fire this day was less rapid and, I think, more efficient than that of yesterday. Fort McRee, so effectually silenced yesterday, did not fire again to-day. We silenced entirely one or two guns, and had one of ours disabled by a shot coming through the embrasure. About 3 o'clock fire was communicated to one of the houses in Warrington, and shortly after to the church steeple. The church and the whole village being immediately in rear of some of the rebel batteries (they apparently having placed them purposely directly in front of the largest and most valuable buildings), the fire rapidly communicated to other buildings along the street, until probably two-thirds of it was consumed, and about the same time fire was discovered issuing from the back part of the navy-yard, probably in Woolsey, a village to the north and immediately adjoining the yard, as Warrington does on the west. Finally it penetrated to the yard, and, as it continued to burn brightly all night, I concluded that either in it or in Woolsey many buildings were destroyed. Very heavy damage was also done to the buildings of the yard by the avalanche of shot, shell, and splinters showered unceasingly on them for two days, and as they were nearly fire-proof (being built of brick and covered with slate), I could not succeed in firing them, neither my hot shot nor shells having any power of igniting them. The steamer Time, which was at the wharf at the time, was abandoned on the first day and exposed to our fire, which probably entirely disabled her.

The fire was again continued until dark, and with mortars occasionally, until 2 o'clock the next morning, when the combat ceased. This fort at its conclusion, though it has received a great many shot and shell, is in every respect, save the disabling of one gun-carriage and the loss of service of 6 men, as efficient as it was at the commencement of the combat, but the ends I proposed in commencing having been attained, except one, which I find to be impracticable with my present means, I do not deem it advisable further to continue it, unless the enemy thinks proper to do so, when I shall meet him with alacrity. The attack on "Billy Wilson's" camp, the attempted attack on my batteries, and the insult to our glorious flag have been fully and fearfully avenged. I have no means of knowing the loss of the enemy, and have no disposition to guess at it. The firing on his batteries was very heavy, well-directed, and continuous for two days, and could hardly fail of having had important results. Our losses would have been heavy but for the foresight which, with great labor, caused us to erect elaborate means of protection, and which saved many lives. I lost 1 private killed, 1 sergeant, 1 corporal, and 4 privates wounded, only 1 severely. My officers, non-commissioned officers, and privates were everything I could desire. They one and all performed their duty with the greatest cheerfulness and in the most able and efficient manner.

I am much indebted to Major Arnold, my executive officer, for his valuable assistance. His whole conduct was admirable, and Captains Allen, Chalfin, Blunt, Robertson, Hildt, and Duryea, and Lieutenants

McFarland, Langdon, Closson, Shipley, Jackson, Pennington, Seeley, and Taylor, merit my warmest encomiums for the coolness and deliberation with which they performed, without one exception, their duty under a heavy and continuous shower of shot, shells, and splinters for two successive days. Lieutenant Todd, ordnance officer, had full supplies of all required articles which were on hand at the post, and his department was conducted with system and efficiency. Major Tower, Surgeon Campbell, and Assistant Surgeon Sutherland, in their respective duties, sustained their high reputations. Captains Robertson, Duryea, and Blunt, and Lieutenants Pennington and Seeley, respectively, commanded Batteries Lincoln, Scott, Totten, and Cameron, and a small battery at Spanish Fort, and the other officers batteries in the fort, with distinguished ability. Captains Dobie's and Bailey's companies were with the batteries at Lincoln and Cameron, and did their duties faithfully and efficiently. The companies of Captains Henberer and Duffy, of the Sixth Regiment New York Volunteers, were successively on duty at the fort, and rendered cheerfully important assistance to me. The regular companies engaged at the batteries, all of whom performed their duty so efficiently as to preclude my making a distinction, are Companies A, F, and L, First Artillery; C, H, and K, Second Artillery; C and E, Third Infantry, and Companies G and I, Sixth Regiment New York Volunteers.

In closing, I tender to Flag-Officer McKean and Captain Ellison, of the Navy, and to their officers and crews, my best thanks for their able co-operation, which would have had the happiest results but for the unfortunate fact that the great draught of water prevented their sufficiently near approach to the works of the rebels.

I am, general, very respectfully, your obedient servant,

HARVEY BROWN,
Colonel, Commanding.

Brig. Gen. LORENZO THOMAS,
Adjutant-General U. S. Army, Washington, D. C.

HEADQUARTERS DEPARTMENT OF FLORIDA,
Fort Pickens, December 3, 1861.

GENERAL: I intended to have made out a list of meritorious non-commissioned officers and privates on the 22d and 23d, but on looking over the sub-reports of the officers I find some are not noticed by name who under my own personal observation behaved with great gallantry and coolness. Indeed, I think where all really showed such cool, deliberate courage that distinction can hardly be made without doing injustice. I heartily indorse the recommendations of Major Arnold and the officers, and extend my approbation to every one engaged. I would respectfully suggest that by submitting these reports to the Ordnance Department it might give information which, if acted on, would very much benefit the service, particularly those parts relating to shells and rifled projectiles, and to the fuses, which were detestable.

I am, general, very respectfully, your obedient servant,

HARVEY BROWN,
Colonel, Commanding.

Brig. Gen. LORENZO THOMAS,
Adjutant-General U. S. Army, Washington, D. C.

HEADQUARTERS DEPARTMENT OF FLORIDA,
Fort Pickens, December 2, 1861.

GENERAL: I herewith forward you the report of Maj. Lewis G. Arnold of the bombardment on the 22d and 23d ultimo, with the sub-reports of the officers commanding batteries, and which could not be prepared so as to be forwarded with my own. The bombardment having discovered to us the position and number of the enemy's batteries and of the number and caliber of the guns, and which we find to be more and heavier than we supposed, and one or two of them so placed as to take us in rear in case of a night attack in front, I have, by the unanimous opinion of my officers, though, I acknowledge, not entirely in accordance with my own, in consideration of the reduced number and our receiving no re-enforcements, decided very considerably to contract my lines of defense. The safety of the fort being paramount to every other consideration, I have brought the Sixth Regiment near the fort, partially abandoned Batteries Lincoln, Cameron, and Totten, and greatly strengthened the fort and Battery Scott. When the proposed change now being made is effected, the fort will be entirely secure under any and every contingency. I must, however, repeat that my present force is entirely inadequate to the defense of the island, and that I cannot prevent a landing of the enemy at some distance and his erecting batteries against the ships, and, doing so, with one rifled gun he could drive them all away.

The enemy have two regiments at Deer (City) Point and are erecting batteries there, which, in case of our taking the offensive and occupying the harbor, will give us great annoyance. Two contrabands came in this morning. They state the loss of the enemy in killed at 40; wounded not known. Colonel Villepigue severely wounded by a splinter at Fort McRee. About two-thirds of Warrington and of Woolsey are burned, and the navy-yard buildings with a great many holes in them. If I had had carcasses and rock-fire, which I have been vainly trying to get ever since my first arrival here, I think I could have destroyed many, if not the most, of the buildings. I tried them with hot shot and with shells having pieces of port-fire in them, but could not succeed in firing them.

I forward a list of the casualties on the 22d and 23d November.* Two of the men wounded by the unfortunate accident of the 25th have died, and I fear one more will die.

I am, general, very respectfully, your most obedient servant,

HARVEY BROWN,
Colonel, Commanding.

Brig. Gen. LORENZO THOMAS,
Adjutant-General U. S. Army.

No. 2.

Report of Maj. Lewis G. Arnold, First U. S. Artillery, Commanding Batteries.

FORT PICKENS, FLA., *November* 25, 1861.

COLONEL: In obedience to your instructions I have the honor to report the service of the batteries in the fort proper, and of Batteries

* The list shows 1 killed and 7 wounded.

Scott, Lincoln, Cameron, Totten, and the battery at the old Spanish Fort, and the operations of the troops engaged in the bombardment of the 22d and 23d of November, 1861, specially under my command, per Special Orders, No. 208, headquarters Fort Pickens, Fla. The guns in the fort proper were divided into seven distinct batteries, each battery having a separate commander. A one-gun battery in the covered way, 10-inch columbiad *en barbette*, manned by a detachment from Company C, Second Artillery, commanded by Lieutenant McFarland, Engineer Corps; the battery manned by Company A, First Artillery, commanded by Captain Chalfin, Fifth Artillery, assisted by Lieutenant Taylor, First Artillery, consisted of one 10-inch columbiad, one 42-pounder rifled gun and seven 32-pounders *en barbette*, and one 42-pounder rifled gun and two 8-inch columbiads in casemates; the battery manned by Company L, First Artillery, commanded by Lieutenant Jackson, First Artillery, consisted of one 10-inch columbiad and five 32-pounders *en barbette*, one 42-pounder rifled gun, one 8-inch columbiad (unchambered), and two 42-pounders (smooth bore) in casemates; the battery manned by Company K, Second Artillery, commanded by Captain Allen, Second Artillery, consisted of 10-inch columbiad *en barbette* and three 42-pounder rifled guns in casemates; the battery manned by Company E, Third Infantry, commanded by Captain Hildt, Third Infantry, consisted of one 10 inch columbiad and one 42-pounder rifled gun *en barbette* and two 8-inch columbiads (one chambered and one unchambered) in casemates; the battery manned by Company C, Third Infantry, commanded by Lieutenant Shipley, Third Infantry, consisted of one 10-inch columbiad *en barbette* and two 42-pounder rifled guns and one 8-inch columbiad (unchambered) in casemates; the mortar battery in the ditch, curtain A to B, manned by detachments from the command commanded by Lieutenant Langdon, Fifth Artillery, consisted of four 10-inch sea-coast mortars; Battery Scott, manned by Company F, First Artillery, commanded by Captain Duryea, First Artillery, assisted by Lieutenant Closson, First Artillery, consisted of two 10-inch columbiads and one 42-pounder rifled gun *en barbette* and two 10-inch sea-coast mortars; Battery Lincoln, manned by Company H, Second Artillery, commanded by Captain Robertson, Second Artillery, consisted of four 8-inch sea-coast howitzers and one 42-pounder rifled gun *en barbette* and two 10-inch sea-coast mortars; Battery Totten, manned by Company C, Second Artillery, commanded by Captain Blunt, Twelfth Infantry, consisted of one 13-inch and one 12-inch sea-coast mortars; Battery Cameron, manned by Company I, Sixth Regiment New York Volunteers, the gunners and purveyors from Company H, Second Artillery, commanded by Lieutenant Pennington, Second Artillery, consisted of two 10-inch columbiads *en barbette* and one 10-pounder Parrott rifled gun (the second day); the battery at the old Spanish Fort, manned by a detachment detailed from the command commanded by Lieutenant Seeley, consisted of one 10-pounder Parrott rifled gun (the first day). The guns fired from the fort and the batteries outside against the enemy's line of forts and batteries, including the town of Warrington and the navy-yard, were ten 10-inch columbiads, six 8-inch columbiads, eleven 42-pounder James rifled guns, and two 42-pounder smooth bore, four 8-inch sea-coast howitzers, eight 10-inch sea-coast mortars, one 13-inch and one 12-inch sea-coast mortars, and twelve 32-pounders *en barbette.*

The bombardment opened at 10 o'clock a. m., November 22, 1861, when a signal gun at the flag-staff was fired under your personal direction. I ordered those guns that could conveniently be brought to bear to fire on two rebel steamboats lying at the navy-yard wharf and a 10-inch columbiad sand battery established on the same wharf. The effect of the firing was apparent, by driving the rebels from the sand battery on the wharf, disabling the steamboat Time, and injuring the iron steam-tug Neaffie, which escaped by steaming off and being a small boat. After firing for a short time I directed the most of these guns to fire on the enemy's forts and batteries, particularly Forts McRee and Barrancas, the light-house batteries, Wheat's and the church batteries, which soon attracted attention by their superior armament (10-inch columbiads) and superior firing, having the range and time of flight very accurately from previous practice with the same guns at the same distance. Our fire from 10-inch columbiads on these batteries, &c., was well directed and effective, but our fire from James rifled guns in casemate was not effective, owing to the long range and probably inherent defect in the principle by which a rotary motion is given to these shot and shell, for I observed that the firing from these guns was very irregular and uncertain for ranges over 2,000 yards.

I ordered Captain Duryea, First Artillery, commanding Battery Scott, ably assisted as he was by Lieutenant Closson, of the same regiment, to direct the fire of his powerful battery, consisting of two 10-inch columbiads, one 42-pounder rifled gun, and two 10-inch sea-coast mortars, to fire on Fort McRee and sand battery south of it. I at the same time ordered the four 10-inch sea-coast mortars in the ditch, commanded by Lieutenant Langdon, and one 13-inch and one 12-inch sea-coast mortars, Battery Totten, commanded by Captain Blunt, and one 8-inch columbiad and two 42-pounders in casemate, of Lieutenant Jackson's battery, to fire on Fort McRee and sand battery south of it, for the purpose of co-operating with the Navy in endeavoring to take and destroy that important fort and its outworks, which guard the enemy's right flank and the entrance to the harbor of Pensacola. The direct fire of these guns was excellent, and, together with the heavy firing from United States steamships Niagara and Richmond, produced a marked impression on this stronghold of the enemy, by silencing the guns of the fort and by driving the detachments from the guns in the sand battery, which would no doubt have decided the fate of Fort McRee, by enabling the command from the Navy to take the fort, but for the opening of an unexpected and concealed battery, armed with rifled cannon of large caliber or possibly a 10-inch columbiad, which was served with effect, on the Richmond.

I will conclude my report of the first day's firing on our part by remarking that in the afternoon it was good and effective, both from the batteries inside the fort as also those outside, and reflected great credit on the skill and coolness of the officers commanding the several batteries and their assistants and the enlisted men serving the guns. I will add, the firing from our batteries was kept up till dark, when it ceased by my orders, in accordance with those of the colonel commanding, to enable the magazines of the batteries outside of the fort as well as the service magazines of those inside to be replenished with powder, shot, and shell.

Our batteries opened fire on the enemy the second day about the same hour as the day previous, the ten 10-inch columbiads each firing a shell every fifteen minutes and the rifled 42-pounders a solid shot at the same rate. The 10-inch columbiad *en barbette*, bastion C, was under the command of Lieutenant Seeley, Fourth Artillery, who was assigned to it at his own request. The mortars were fired every half hour. Our firing the second day was better than that of the first. We succeeded in silencing for two hours Wheat's and the church batteries, Fort Barrancas, and all the guns on the front line of the enemy excepting one gun at the Fort McRee sand battery and the famous battery on the height between Fort Barrancas and the light-house battery. The flag-staffs at Forts McRee and Barrancas were shot away. The fire continued till dark, more than an hour after the Niagara had ceased firing. The effect of our fire on the 23d was destructive; a portion of Warrington and the navy-yard was burned, either ignited from the hot shot fired from 32-pounders or the shells from 10-inch columbiads. The navy-yard was much damaged by the fire of our 10-inch, 12-inch, and 13-inch sea-coast mortars.

Our loss during the bombardment was small, owing, doubtless, to the defensive arrangements of your chief engineer, Major Tower, in erecting the traverses to protect the guns *en barbette*, the shell-proofs, or covers for the men, &c.

Private Cooper, Company H, Sixth Regiment New York Volunteers, detailed to carry ammunition for the batteries, was mortally wounded, on the 22d, while standing in one of the casemates, by a fragment of a shell, which exploded about the center of the fort. Corporal Beeler, Company L, First Artillery, was severely wounded by a fragment of shell whilst serving a 10-inch columbiad *en barbette;* his fore-arm has been amputated. Sergeant Massey, Privates Fitzsimmins and White were wounded slightly, and Corporal Moran and Privates Galbreth and Purcell severely—all of Company E, Third Infantry. Those men were wounded whilst serving an 8-inch columbiad in casemate by a 10-inch shell penetrating the embrasure, which disabled the carriage.

The fire from the enemy's batteries was heavy and well directed. There were many marvelous escapes from wounds. Among the most notable was that of Lieutenant Shipley, Third Infantry, and the detachment serving the 10-inch columbiad *en barbette* of his battery. A 10-inch shell struck the shell-proof and burst among his men and himself without wounding any one, although the sand and sand bags were knocked down over and around them. I will remark in this connection that I observed with admiration the gallant and efficient manner that Lieutenant Shipley commanded his battery the two days of the bombardment. My thanks are especially due to the officers serving with the batteries for the valuable services rendered by them and the cool and efficient manner they commanded their guns. They were as follows: Lieutenant McFarland, Engineer Corps; Captain Duryea and Lieutenants Closson, Jackson, and Taylor, First Artillery; Captains Allen, Robertson, and Lieutenant Pennington, Second Artillery; Lieutenant Seeley, Fourth Artillery; Captain Chalfin and Lieutenant Langdon, Fifth Artillery; Captain Hildt and Lieutenant Shipley, Third Infantry, and Captain Blunt, Twelfth Infantry. I take pleasure in stating that Major Tower, Engineer Corps, and Lieutenant Todd, Ordnance, performed the duties of their departments with ability.

I respectfully refer the colonel commanding to the report of commanders of batteries, herewith inclosed, for individual instances of good conduct and valuable services rendered by the enlisted men. As Private John D. Hickey, of Company C, Second Artillery, was detached from his company, acting as my orderly, I take this occasion to recommend him to notice for signal courage displayed during the bombardment. I am under obligations to Captain Henberer, Company H, and Captain Duffy's company (D), Sixth Regiment New York Volunteers, for valuable services in purveying shot, shell, and powder, and for performing guard duty the two days of the bombardment.

Respectfully submitted.

L. G. ARNOLD,
Major, U. S. Army, Commanding Batteries.

Col. HARVEY BROWN,
Commanding Fort Pickens, &c.

No. 3.

Report of Capt. Richard C. Duryea, First U. S. Artillery.

FORT PICKENS, FLA., *November* 25, 1861.

SIR: In obedience to the instructions of the colonel commanding I have the honor to make the following report of the part taken in the bombardment of the 22d and 23d instant by Battery Scott, consisting of one rifled 42-pounder, two 10-inch columbiads, two 10-inch sea-coast mortars, and one 10-inch siege mortar, manned by Company F, First Regiment of Artillery.

Throughout the entire day (the 22d) the fire from all these pieces except the siege mortar (the range of this not being sufficiently great) was directed upon Fort McRee and the batteries in its immediate vicinity. The return fire from Fort McRee continued throughout the day, but much slackened towards night, and on the following day it did not return our fire. The sand battery near McRee ceased firing about 3 p. m. on the first day, but reopened on the second and continued until nearly night.

From my own observation and from others who had opportunities of observing I should judge the fire from our battery (particularly of the columbiads) was quite effective, but what damage was done besides the mere driving of the enemy from their guns I cannot say.

The following is the practical results of the firing: With the rifled gun, distance 2,060 yards, elevation $5\frac{1}{2}^{\circ}$, the fire was effective; beyond that range, uncertain. With columbiads, distance 2,060 yards, charge 12 pounds, elevation $7\frac{1}{2}^{\circ}$ to 8°, fuse 8 seconds, very effective. From the mortars, on account of the inequality of powder, several shells were thrown away. The most satisfactory results are as follows: For a distance of 2,060 yards, a charge of 3 pounds 6 ounces, and fuse 21 to 22 seconds; for distance of 2,560 yards, a charge of 4 pounds 12 ounces, and fuse 24 to 25 seconds.

In conclusion, I cannot too highly speak of the invaluable assistance rendered me by Lieutenant Closson. The gunners—Sergeants Morgan, Mahon, Chilcutt, and Grimes; Corporals Burdell, Cronin, Harris, Capron; and Musician Walker, Artificers Gilbert and Connerty, and Privates Lavery, McCormick, Mack, and Moore—behaved with admirable coolness, while all others in their less responsible positions did well their duty.

I am, sir, very respectfully, your obedient servant,

R. C. DURYEA,
Captain, First Artillery, Comdg. Co. F and Battery Scott.

Maj. LEWIS G. ARNOLD,
First Regiment of Artillery.

No. 4.

Report of Lieut. Richard H. Jackson, First U. S. Artillery.

FORT PICKENS, FLA., *November* 25, 1861.

SIR: In accordance with your instructions I have the honor to submit the following report of the operations of the battery under my command during the bombardment of the 22d and 23d November, 1861:

The battery consisted of one 10-inch columbiad and four 32-pounders *en barbette* in the flag-staff bastion (A), one 8-inch unchambered columbiad and two 42-pounders in casemate, curtain B C, and one 42-pounder rifled gun in casemate in bastion C. The guns were served by Company L, First Artillery.

At 10 o'clock a. m. on the 22d I was directed by the colonel commanding to open the bombardment, and in obedience thereto I pointed and fired the 10-inch columbiad at the rebel steamer Time, then lying at the navy-yard wharf. The shell exploded directly over the steamer. All of the guns from the fort and batteries immediately opened on the enemy's position, and the steamer and navy-yard were quickly abandoned by the rebels. The fire from the 10-inch columbiad and 32-pounders was, during the bombardment, principally directed at the navy-yard and the wharf and church batteries. It was very effective. Two of the shells from the columbiad exploded in the wharf battery, the remainder in the buildings in the navy-yard. The fire from the casemate guns in curtain B and C was directed against Fort McRee and the sand battery westward of it. The shells from the 8-inch columbiad were seen to explode over Fort McRee, and when directed at the sand battery were very accurate, one of them exploding within the embrasure. The firing from the 42-pounders was effective. The rifled gun in bastion C was in position against the light-house battery. The James projectile was used. The firing from this gun was very inaccurate, particularly when shells were used, nearly all of them either falling short of or passing over the enemy's battery. The lateral deviation was considerable. On the second day solid shot were projected from this gun, a few of which struck the battery and light-house. The range was about 2,855 yards. I attribute the inaccuracy of fire with this projectile to the stripping of the lead and canvas packing or wrappers on the cylindrical portion of it during its flight.

I respectfully ask to call particular attention to Sergeant Conroy for his coolness and zeal in the discharge of his duty; Sergeant Newton, who distinguished himself as an efficient practical artillerist; Corporal Beeler, for his coolness (he was wounded while serving his gun and has since had his arm amputated); First Sergt. Lewis Keller, Sergeant Becker, Corporals Wicks and Spangler, and Privates Jackel and Hanney. To mention other names would be invidious, for all the enlisted men behaved well.

I am, sir, very respectfully, your obedient servant,

R. H. JACKSON,
First Lieutenant, Comdg. Co. L, First Artillery.

Maj. LEWIS G. ARNOLD,
First Artillery, U. S. Army, Commanding Batteries.

No. 5.

Report of Capt. James M. Robertson, Second U. S. Artillery.

BATTERY LINCOLN, SANTA ROSA ISLAND, FLA.,
November 25, 1861.

SIR: In obedience to your instructions of this date I have the honor to make the following report of the service of my battery (Lincoln) during the bombardment on the 22d and 23d of November, 1861:

The battery consists of the following guns, viz: One 42-pounder gun (rifled), four 8-inch sea-coast howitzers, and two 10-inch sea-coast mortars. At the firing of the signal gun from Fort Pickens, about 9.30 o'clock a. m. on the 22d, I opened fire with my entire battery upon the rebel steamer Time, then lying at the Warrington navy-yard, and kept it up briskly for about two hours. About 11.30 a. m., by your order, I directed the fire from my mortars upon Fort Barrancas and the howitzers on the navy-yard, and kept up a steady fire, as directed, till about an hour before sunset, when by your order I again concentrated all my fire on the steamer and continued till ordered to cease firing at dark. During the day I saw several shots strike the steamer, but owing to her hull (except a very small portion) being covered by a projecting pier, I think very little material damage was done. During the entire day the firing from my 42-pounder was very unsatisfactory. With the same charge, same elevation, and pointed with the greatest care, one shot would fall far short, and others would go wild and entirely over the mark. During the day forty-five shots were fired from this gun.

On the firing of the signal gun from Fort Pickens, about 10.30 a. m. on the 23d (the rebel steamer having been removed during the night of the 22d), I opened fire, as directed, with the rifled gun on the one-gun sand battery on the head of the navy-yard pier, firing one shot every fifteen minutes with the howitzers and mortars on the navy-yard, firing each of the first once in forty and the latter once in thirty minutes. During this day's and night's firing my mortar shells were loaded with 1½ pounds of port-fire in addition to the ordinary charge of powder. During the day I saw many shell strike and explode in the navy-yard, but no perceptible impression was made upon it. At 2.30 o'clock p. m. a fire was lighted in a wooden building in the southwest portion of the town of Warrington, either by a gun from the fort or Battery Cameron. I then directed my mortars on the northeast part of the town, near the navy-yard. Soon after that portion of the town was also on fire, and I again directed my mortars to the navy-yard.

At dark, firing having ceased, except from mortars, I left to go to Fort Pickens. After I left, Sergeant Roder, of Company H, Second Artillery, fired two shots, when you ordered the firing to cease for the night. On my way to the fort I stopped at Battery Cameron to inspect. After being there about fifteen minutes I discovered a fire had broken out in the navy-yard, and men were distinctly seen endeavoring to put it out. I ordered Lieutenant Pennington to load and fire one of his columbiads, which he did with such good effect that the rebels instantly left, and the building was soon in a bright blaze.

At 7 o'clock p. m., by your order, I again opened with one of my mortars, dropping a shell into the navy-yard every fifteen minutes. At 8.30 p. m. a large fire was started near the north gate of the yard, which burned furiously till after midnight. At 11.30 p. m. another fire, still larger than the first, broke out about one-fourth of a mile to the east of the first and was still raging at 2 o'clock a. m. the 24th. At 1 a. m. the 24th a third fire was started between the two first, but it burned only a short time. At 2 o'clock a. m. the 24th, by your order, I stopped firing. Whether the fires on the night of the 23d and 24th were in the northern portion of the navy-yard or in the town of Woolsey I am unable to say, but from the size of the fires several large buildings must have been burned. During the night I had good opportunity of observing the falling of my shell, and found the practice admirable; every shell either burst just above or within one second after striking the ground, and scattered the pieces of port-fire in every direction. In many instances pieces of port-fire were seen to light on the roof of the buildings and burn as long as five seconds, but, the roofs being entirely of slate, it was impossible to ignite the buildings, unless when a shell, after passing through the roof, burst inside. The firing from my 42-pounder rifle on the 23d was much more satisfactory than the previous day. Five shots were seen to strike the battery, but with what effect I am unable (owing to the great distance) to say. During the first day's firing many of the rebel shell burst near my battery and several splinters came inside. Several round shot and unexploded shell from the direction of Fort McRee, after passing over Pickens, came into the left of my battery, and passed down the whole line, but without doing the slightest damage.

During the second day only a few shell burst near me. After night on the 23d no fire was returned from the rebels, except from the one-gun battery on the pier-head, and that only once an hour. This fire was apparently directed on Fort Pickens, but every shell burst far short. During the whole bombardment all the non-commissioned officers and men of my command (Company H, Second Artillery) and Captain Dobie's company (G, Sixth Regiment New York Volunteers) worked and behaved in that cool, cheerful, and deliberate manner which makes it impossible for me to mention any one in particular. All deserve, and I take this occasion to give them, my most sincere thanks. I have no casualties or damage to my battery to report, either from carelessness on the part of my own men or from the fire of the rebels. I have made no mention of the operations of Battery Cameron except in the one instance, as Lieutenant Pennington was in immediate charge, and will, I presume, make a special report.

Respectfully submitted.

J. M. ROBERTSON,
Capt. Second Art., Comdg. Batteries Lincoln and Cameron.

Maj. LEWIS G. ARNOLD,
First Art., Comdg. Batteries Fort Pickens and Santa Rosa Island.

No. 6.

Report of Capt. Harvey A. Allen, Second U. S. Artillery.

FORT PICKENS, FLA., *November* 25, 1861.

SIR: I have the honor to report the duties of Company K, Second Artillery, which I commanded during the bombardment on the 22d and 23d of the present month. Eight men were detached, 7 serving a mortar under Lieutenant Langdon, and 1 on the first day with Lieutenant Seeley's rifled gun at the old Spanish Fort. The columbiad in bastion

C, barbette, was served by 14 men, two detachments, relieved every two hours, and the three rifled guns in bastion D, casemate, by the remainder of the company; the columbiad firing every fifteen minutes and each rifled gun at the same rate a greater portion of the time and every half hour the remainder. The columbiad was pointed first on the navy-yard, but on account of the smoke, which concealed it entirely, an opening was made in the epaulement, and the gun turned on Fort Barrancas, where it continued to fire the first day. On the second day Lieutenant Seeley had charge of it, with the same detachments. The rifled guns were fired at two batteries near the light-house with the same charges and elevations. Shot were observed to fall in the water, to strike the battery, and sometimes, not being seen, were believed to pass over the object. The guns or shot appear to be defective, and not to be relied on. Great care was taken in pointing, and every shot watched by men on the parapet as well as below. The whole company were zealous and active, and gave entire satisfaction.

I am, sir, very respectfully, your obedient servant,

H. A. ALLEN,
Captain, Second Artillery.

Major ARNOLD,
First Artillery, Commanding Batteries.

No. 7.

Report of Lieut. A. C. M. Pennington, Second U. S. Artillery.

FORT PICKENS, FLA., *November* 25, 1861.

Pursuant to your instructions I have the honor to submit the following report of the service done by Battery Cameron, which I commanded during the bombardment of Fort Pickens on the 22d and 23d of November. My battery consisted of two 10 inch columbiads on the first day, and of the same, with the addition of a 10-pounder Parrott rifled gun, on the second day. With one of my columbiads I had a lateral field of fire from the eastern extremity of the navy-yard to a point a short distance west of a battery known as the church battery (a haxo-casemate, containing a heavy shell gun). With the other I had a field of fire from a point above the Marine Barracks, at the west end of the navy yard, to a short distance below a battery, consisting of three guns, known as Wheat's battery.

The steamer Time making her appearance at the navy-yard about 9.30 o'clock a. m., I pointed my right-hand gun at it, and my other I directed at the church battery. At the signal gun from the fort I opened the fire from my battery, but from the great number of shot fired I could not determine the effect of my fire. I kept up my fire with one gun on the steamer for some time, and I think with good effect, as several shells burst near her smoke-stacks, and others, I think, struck and burst near her bow. As Battery Lincoln was keeping up a fire upon her with rifled shell I turned this gun upon the church battery and the other I directed upon the Wheat battery, not, however, till it had done good service in doing considerable damage to the church battery while the other was firing on the steamer. Until late in the afternoon I kept the two guns on these batteries, keeping up a well-directed and very effective fire upon them. About an hour before sundown I again directed my right-hand gun upon the steamer, one shot striking in her stern. Whether any serious damage was done to the guns in the batteries or the men serving them I am unable to state, owing to the great distance from my battery.

On the second day my guns were directed on the same batteries as the day previous almost uninterruptedly till late in the afternoon, when I fired with one gun upon the battery at the end of the wharf, near the shears, with some effect. I fired with the 10-pounder rifled gun upon the two batteries alternately, nearly every shot striking in and around the battery at which it was directed as near as I could determine.

I had no casualties at the battery, which was ably and zealously served by Company I, Sixth Regiment New York Volunteers. All the men behaved with great coolness and did good service at the guns. My thanks are due to Captain Bailey and Lieutenants Kaufman and Spence, of Company I, Sixth New York Volunteers, for their efficient co-operation during the two days' firing. Lieutenant Kaufman had charge of one of the columbiads and made very effective shots. I had two privates and a corporal of Company H, Second U. S. Artillery, to attend to the service at the magazines, which duty they performed admirably. The corporal (Corporal Nolan) acted as gunner of one of the guns, directing his gun with great care and making effective shots.

I am, sir, very respectfully, your obedient servant,

A. C. M. PENNINGTON,

First Lieutenant, Second Artillery, Comdg. Battery Cameron.

Maj. LEWIS G. ARNOLD,

First Regiment Artillery, U. S. Army, Comdg. Batteries.

No. 8.

Report of Lieut. Francis W. Seeley, Fourth U. S. Artillery.

FORT PICKENS, FLA., *November* 25, 1861.

MAJOR: Pursuant to your instructions I have the honor to submit the following report of the participation of the guns which I commanded in the bombardment of the enemy's position on the 22d and 23d of November, 1861:

On the morning of the 22d, pursuant to orders received from you, I took up my position with a Parrott 10-pounder rifled gun, a detachment of 11 artillery-men, and one company of New York volunteers, commanded by First Lieut. Jacob Silloway, as a supporting force, at the old Spanish Fort opposite the navy-yard. At 8 o'clock a. m., on hearing the first gun from the fort, I opened fire on the steamer Time, then lying at the navy-yard, as were also the Neaffie and another armed tug-boat. I fired about fifteen shells in rapid succession, putting nearly every one of them into the steamer Time. Several shots from the fort also struck her, by which time she seemed completely disabled. One of my shots must have penetrated her boilers, as immediately after it was delivered the steam was seen escaping in dense clouds from under her guards. I also put a shell through each of her wheels. Two of the steamers (the Time and one of the tugs) were then abandoned by the enemy, but the Neaffie succeeded in making her escape up the bay towards Pensacola, although I think she must have been seriously injured, as she moved very slowly and I distinctly saw two shots strike her.

The enemy by that time appeared to have abandoned the navy-yard, and I contented myself with firing one shot every fifteen minutes, nearly every one of which took effect either on the buildings or steamers. At about 12 o'clock m. the enemy opened fire from the 10-inch columbiad stationed in battery on the large stone wharf of the navy-yard, and succeeded in firing two shots. I immediately fired three percussion shells in quick succession. Each one exploded inside of the battery and effectually silenced it for the remainder of that day. I continued firing until sunset, having fired during the day sixty-two shells into the steamers, the buildings, and the battery.

My men deserve great credit for their coolness and soldierly bearing during the whole day, especially Sergt. John J. Driscoll, of Company A, First Artillery, who about 2 p. m. was injured by a fall from his horse when riding through the shower of shot and shell then falling about the fort, where I had sent him with a message to the colonel commanding; also Private George W. Doyle, of Company H, Second Artillery, who was gunner of my piece, and by his skill as an artillerist and his coolness greatly contributed to render our fire effective.

It may not be amiss here to state that from my experience with the Parrott rifled gun I consider it to be the most perfect rifled cannon that we have in our service, *i. e.*, when the percussion shell (Reed's) is used, which explodes on striking the object fired at. Shells fired from this gun with time fuses seldom explode. The reason of this is, as near as I can ascertain, that when fired, from the sudden expansion of the rim attached to the ball, there is not sufficient windage left to permit the flame to communicate with and ignite the fuse. Under these circumstances, therefore, the shells are no better than solid shot.

On the 23d November I was assigned to the command of the 10-inch columbiad in bastion C, with a detachment, consisting of a sergeant, corporal, and 14 privates, from Company K, Second Artillery. At 11 o'clock, on the signal being made to open fire from our batteries, I directed my piece on Fort Barrancas, and fired, as directed, one shot every fifteen minutes, exploding a great number of shells immediately in and about the work. About 12 m. the flag on Fort Barrancas was shot away, whether by one of my own shots or not I cannot say, as several guns besides mine were also firing on the fort at the time. About 1 o'clock p. m., Fort Barrancas having ceased to reply, only at long intervals, to the fire of our guns, I directed my fire on the battery stationed on the rising ground to the right of Fort Barrancas, and which had by the accuracy of its fire annoyed us considerably. After the first fire I succeeded in getting the range of that battery completely, and during the remainder of the day exploded nearly every shell that I fired inside of the work, and before I ceased firing at night had nearly succeeded in silencing its fire, as it only replied at long intervals and without much accuracy. There were one or two guns from the fort besides my own firing on this battery during the afternoon. I ceased firing by your order about 6 o'clock p. m.

My men all behaved well, especially Sergeant Jones, of Company K, Second Artillery, who, notwithstanding that the shot and shells from the enemy's guns were flying in every direction, many of them exploding immediately in our bastion, maintained his position on the parapet during the whole time that he was on duty, watching the effect of our shot on the enemy's batteries. I have no casualties to report.

I am, sir, very respectfully, your obedient servant,

F. W. SEELEY,

First Lieutenant, Fourth Artillery.

Maj. LEWIS G. ARNOLD,

First Artillery, U. S. Army, Commanding Batteries.

No. 9.

Report of Capt. Samuel F. Chalfin, Fifth U. S. Artillery.

FORT PICKENS, FLA., *November* 25, 1861.

MAJOR: In obedience to instructions from the colonel commanding I have the honor to submit the following report of the operations of the two batteries under my direction during the bombardment of the 22d and 23d instant:

One battery is in barbette, the other in casemate. The barbette battery consists of one 10-inch columbiad along the capital, one 42-pounder rifled gun and two 32-pounders on the north flank of bastion E, and of seven 32-pounders on curtain D E. The casemate battery comprised two 8-inch columbiads, one unchambered and one 42-pounder rifled gun. Both these batteries were served by Company A, First Regiment of Artillery. After the signal gun was fired, at 10 o'clock a. m. on the morning of the 22d, all the guns of the barbette battery except the rifle were opened on the navy-yard and the enemy's boats lying at the wharves. Owing to the dense smoke which arose after the first discharge, and to the great distance (1¾ miles), it was almost impossible to observe with any certainty the effect of the 32-pounders. Before the firing commenced with these guns the elevating screws and their beds had been removed and quoins substituted, by means of which an elevation of 12° and 13° could be obtained. From an occasional observation it could be seen that the shots were not falling short. After about two hours' firing with the 32-pounders the cannoneers were taken away from them and placed at the casemate guns and barbette rifle. The 10-inch columbiad, under charge of Second Lieut. F. E. Taylor, First Artillery, maintained a steady and effective fire throughout the day. The barbette rifle opened on Fort Barrancas about 12 m., and did good execution. The casemate guns opened about the same time, the rifle on Fort Barrancas and the columbiads on the enemy's batteries near the Marine Hospital. The firing from these guns was generally very effective, and kept up steadily at the prescribed intervals until ordered to cease.

About 4 o'clock p. m. a shell from one of the enemy's batteries lodged and exploded in the parapet immediately in front of the 10-inch columbiads, by which one of the cannoneers, Private Theodore Shauer, was slightly wounded on the head.

On the morning of the 23d the barbette rifle and 10-inch columbiad opened when the signal was given, the first on the barbette gun on the east face of Barrancas, the second on the Haxo, Boggs', or Church battery (for it has been called by all these names). The fire from this latter gun was steady and effectively kept up throughout the day. The fire from the rifle was maintained steadily, but many of the shots fell short, and towards evening became decidedly uncertain, owing in a great measure, doubtless, to the giving way of the stone work under the traverse circle. After the fire opened in the morning six of the 32-pounders were used for throwing hot shot at the buildings in Warrington and the vicinity. About 12.30 o'clock the cannoneers were taken from five of these guns and put at the casemate guns, which they continued to serve regularly until night. About 3 o'clock p. m. the 32-pounder, still used for hot shot, burst the chase, throwing the fragments into bastions D and E, as well as amongst its own cannoneers, without, however, doing any injury.

About 4 o'clock a building in rear of the church battery was observed to be on fire, and soon after the steeple of the church was seen in flames.

From these the fire spread rapidly towards the navy-yard, and some buildings in its immediate vicinity are known to be burned. The firing from the casemate columbiads was steadily kept up with good effect on the same battery as the day before. The unchambered gun was used for throwing solid shot. The casemate rifle was admirably served by First Sergt. Edward O'Brien, of Company A, First Artillery, and did good execution.

In conclusion, I take great pleasure in calling the attention of the colonel commanding to the zealous and efficient manner in which Second Lieut. F. E. Taylor, First Artillery, performed his duties throughout the bombardment. He was placed in charge of the 10-inch columbiad and the barbette rifle, where he displayed great coolness and remained constantly at his post. I have also the pleasure of directing the colonel's attention to the good conduct, coolness, and excellent services of First Sergt. Edward O'Brien and of Corporals John Feeney and John Clancy, of Company A, First Artillery. All of the men of the company behaved so well that it would be invidious to make a distinction between them.

I am, major, very respectfully, your obedient servant,

S. F. CHALFIN,

Captain, Fifth Artillery, Comdg. Company A, First Artillery.

Maj. LEWIS G. ARNOLD,

First Artillery, Commanding Batteries, Fort Pickens, Fla.

No. 10.

Report of Capt. Loomis L. Langdon, First U. S. Artillery.

FORT PICKENS, FLA., *November* 25, 1861.

SIR: Pursuant to instructions from the colonel commanding, I have the honor to report as correctly as I can the service rendered by the battery under my command during the bombardment of the 22d and 23d of November.

This battery, consisting of four 10-inch sea-coast mortars, was directed at the opening of the firing on the steamers lying at the navy-yard wharf. One or two effective shots were made, but the result of the firing being unsatisfactory, the mortars were directed to Fort Barrancas and the sand battery to the left of Fort McRee. The firing at the latter was the best. So many shots were being thrown at Fort Barrancas from other guns that I was unable to mark the effect of mine. In the afternoon the mortars were fired more slowly and greater care taken to distinguish the shots. A marked improvement in the firing was observed. The last shots were fired after dark, during the rain-storm, and were thrown at Fort Barrancas.

On the second day (the 23d) I had a table of fire carefully kept, and the range, charge, length of fuse, and effect of each shot accurately noted. The navy-yard and sand battery near Fort McRee received all my attention, two mortars being directed at each point the whole day, and the firing slow and regular. The effect was very satisfactory, and after the signal was hoisted on the Niagara "*Too great a range*," I succeeded in placing the shells with good effect.

The men behaved admirably, exposed as they were without a splinter-proof and to the falling bricks and earth from the parapet above. The fragments of bursting shells frequently came among them, and a shell fell in their midst, but burst without injuring any one. The most exposed man was Private Arthur R. Kermer, of Company C, Third Infantry, quartermaster's clerk, who, assisted by Corporal Schonborn, of Company K, Second Artillery, remained on the parapet the whole of the second day recording the shots, and they both rendered good service. Corporal Mulvihill, of Company C, Third Infantry; Corporal Baby, Company L, First Artillery; Sergeant Magnitzky, Company C, Second Artillery, and Privates De Bleeckere and De Meyers, of Company A, First Artillery, I would mention for their care, attention, and coolness. The non-commissioned officers bore the fatigue without being relieved during the whole time, and deserve much credit.

I am, sir, your obedient servant,

LOOMIS L. LANGDON,
First Lieutenant, Fifth Artillery, Commanding Battery.

Maj. LEWIS G. ARNOLD,
First Artillery, U. S. Army, Commanding Batteries.

No. 11.

Report of Capt. John McL. Hildt, Third U. S. Infantry.

FORT PICKENS, FLA., *November* 25, 1861.

SIR: In obedience to instructions, I have the honor to submit the following report of the service of the guns under my charge on the 22d and 23d of November:

These guns, viz, one 10-inch columbiad *en barbette*, bastion B; one 42-pounder rifled gun *en barbette*, bastion D, and two 8-inch columbiads (one new and one old pattern) in casemate, curtain C D, opened fire about 9.30 on the morning of the 22d. The rifled gun and 8-inch columbiads were directed exclusively at the light-house and adjacent batteries. The 10-inch columbiad, after firing a few shells at the steamer Time, was directed at Fort Barrancas, and so continued almost the entire time. The most accurate firing was made by and probably the best results obtained from the 10-inch columbiads. Many good shots were made, the shell exploding immediately over and near the barbette guns of Fort Barrancas. Any statement of results must, however, be mere speculation. I regret being obliged to report 6 men wounded, caused by a 10-inch shell entering the embrasure of the casemate battery. The shell knocked off a considerable quantity of brick from each side of the embrasure, and wedged between the carriage and chassis of the 8-inch chambered columbiads, destroying the carriage. The shell, fortunately, did not explode, the wounds being inflicted by brick. My men, non-commissioned officers and privates, performed their appropriate duty cheerfully and well. Being the only officer with the company, and my batteries being widely separated, the duties devolving on First Sergt. David Grier were necessarily such as usually fall to a commissioned officer. He performed them intelligently, and the ability displayed by him on this and other occasions merits advancement.

I am, sir, very respectfully, your obedient servant,

J. McL. HILDT,
Captain, Third Infantry, Commanding Company E.

Major LEWIS G. ARNOLD,
First Artillery, U. S. Army.

No. 12.

Report of Lieut. Alexander N. Shipley, Third U. S. Infantry.

FORT PICKENS, FLA., *November* 26, 1861.

SIR: I have the honor to report the services rendered by the batteries under my command during the bombardment of the 22d and 23d instant.

I had charge of one 10-inch columbiad in bastion D, barbette; two rifled guns, 42-pounders, James projectiles, in casemate in curtain D E, also one 8-inch columbiad, old pattern, in same curtain. The signal gun was fired at about 10 o'clock a. m. of the 22d, and, in obedience to instructions, the fire from the rifled-gun battery was directed on the rebel steamers lying at the navy-yard wharf. I used shells at an elevation of 6° 30′; charge of powder, 8½ pounds; range, 3,220 yards; fire inefficient; increased elevation to 8°, and subsequently to 9° and 9½°, before the steamers could be reached, it being necessary to break the arch of the embrasures to procure this last elevation. With these last data, so far as I could judge, the fire was effective. The firing from the rifled-gun battery was directed during the remainder of the first day and all of the second at the rebel batteries on the beach betwixt Barrancas Barracks and the navy-yard; the charge of powder same as before; range, from 2,235 yards to 3,220 yards; elevation, 6½° to 9½°. Projectiles during the first day were shells, and during the second solid shot, except an occasional shell. The firing generally, I think, was effective.

The 8-inch columbiad was directed on the same batteries both days; charge, 8 pounds; range as above; projectiles, shells; fuses varying from 10″ to 14″. The firing from this gun was much more accurate than that of the rifled battery. My 10-inch columbiad *en barbette*, bastion D, was directed on Fort Barrancas for the greater portion of the first day; range, 2,654 yards; charge, 12 pounds; projectiles, shells; fuse 13″, and the firing satisfactory. During the rest of the first day and all of the second I directed its fire on the rebel batteries adjacent to Fort Barrancas; range nearly the same; charge the same; fuse varying from 12″ to 15″, and firing satisfactory.

I wish to speak well of the conduct of all my men, particularly my first sergeant, Francis C. Choate, and Sergts. William McClenzey and John Morris, and Corporals Theodore Kutcher and Nicholas Harper. I am glad to notice the coolness under a very heavy fire of the cannoneers of the columbiad *en barbette* and the alacrity and skill with which they discharged their duties. One of the rebel shells fell beside the gun, but fortunately failed to explode. A second buried itself in the magazine cover and exploded, setting fire to the sand bags and canvas cover. A third came through the splinter-proof erected for the shelter of the men, and, exploding, destroyed it, fortunately doing no serious injury to myself or the men beneath it. The firing of the casement guns I left principally in charge of Sergeants McClenzey and Morris. The magazine duties of the barbette gun I intrusted to my first sergeant, Choate.

I am, major, very respectfully, your obedient servant,

A. N. SHIPLEY,
First Lieutenant, Third Infantry, Commanding Company C.

Maj. LEWIS G. ARNOLD,
First U. S. Artillery, Commanding Batteries.

No. 13.

Report of Capt. Matthew M. Blunt, Twelfth U. S. Infantry.

FORT PICKENS, FLA., *November* 25, 1861.

MAJOR: In compliance with orders from the colonel commanding I have the honor to submit to you the following report of the service of the battery under my charge during the 22d and 23d of this month:

The battery consists of one 13-inch and one 12-inch sea-coast mortar. Both mortars were ready on the morning of the 22d, and at the signal gun opened fire on the steamboat at the navy-yard, at which a rapid fire was kept up for about three-quarters of an hour, each mortar being discharged as soon as loaded. The majority of the shells then thrown went into the navy-yard, but on account of the very heavy fire in that direction (a large number of our guns and mortars firing at the steamboat at that time) I could not tell the effect of the shells thrown, but am confident that very few were lost by falling into the water. After firing at the steamboat for about three-quarters of an hour, my fire was directed, according to your orders, on Fort McRee, and was continued during the day at intervals of twenty minutes. Several shells went inside the fort and others near the batteries on either side of it. This fire was continued until sundown, when a sudden thunder-storm put a stop to all firing. Early in the day the elevating screws began to bend, and by means of blocks and quoins the 13-inch mortar was kept at an elevation of about 40°, and was fired at that elevation during the afternoon, when the screw broke off entirely.

About 3 p. m. the elevating screw of the 12-inch mortar broke off, and the mortar rested on the bolster, and was not used for the rest of the day. At 5 a. m. on the 23d a party was set to work to arrange means for elevating the mortars, and by 7 a. m. everything was ready for action. During the 23d our fire was directed entirely on the navy-yard, and, with the exception of the first shell, which bursted at the edge of the water, all the others lodged within the yard, and several were observed to strike and enter the buildings in it. The fire was at an interval of half an hour and was continued until after sunset, and, having ceased for about an hour and a half, was renewed by your order, to prevent the enemy from putting out the fire, which, commencing in the village of Warrington, had then reached the vicinity of the yard. Our firing was continued until 11.30 p. m., when, the fire being well under way, I thought it useless to throw any more shells.

With respect to the conduct of the enlisted men under my command I can only speak well of all, as all did their duties promptly and efficiently. The service was of such a nature as not to call out any acts of daring or bravery, for though the enemy directed at least two mortars at us during the greater part of both days, the majority of the shells fell short or went to our right. Many of the columbiad shells intended for our fort passed over it and burst in our vicinity.

I am, major, very respectfully, your obedient servant,

M. M. BLUNT,
Captain, Twelfth Infantry.

Maj. LEWIS G. ARNOLD,
First Artillery, U. S. Army, Commanding Batteries.

No. 14.

Report of Lieut. Walter McFarland, U. S. Corps of Engineers.

FORT PICKENS, FLA., *November* 25, 1861.

SIR: I have the honor to report as follows concerning the operations of the 10-inch columbiad in the salient of the covered way under my command during the bombardment of the 22d and 23d of November:

Firing was commenced about 10 o'clock a. m. on the 22d, directed upon the steamer Time, lying at the navy-yard wharf, 3,200 yards distant, and was continued for about two hours, with what effect I could not ascertain, other than that the steamer was several times hit. The piece was then directed upon Wheat's battery, a little to the east of the Marine Hospital, and fired upon it uninterruptedly during the remainder of the day, making for that range (2,200 yards) some very excellent firing, but whether or not to the serious detriment of the enemy it was impossible for me to determine. Firing ceased at dark, after we had thrown 59 shell, 50 of which were navy shell, the remainder 10-inch columbiad shell.

Firing was resumed the next morning at about the same hour, directed upon the same point (Wheat's battery), limited by order to one round in fifteen minutes, and was continued with similar results until nightfall, when we stopped, having fired 31 rounds.

The conduct of the men was excellent, and though subjected to a heavy direct fire from six 10-inch guns, seven or eight guns of smaller caliber, and three or four heavy mortars, as well as a reversed fire from Fort McRee and the batteries adjoining, I have no casualties to report. Sergeant Ohlenroth, of Company C, Second Artillery, acted as gunner during the entire bombardment, and the excellent firing of the piece is chiefly due to his exertions.

I beg leave to call your attention to the fact that neither the columbiad shells nor the fuses furnished were of the proper quality; the shells breaking so uniformly in the piece that I was compelled to reduce the charge 1 pound, making it 11 pounds, and the fuses, in perhaps a majority of cases, failing to ignite, though treated with the utmost care.

Very respectfully, your obedient servant,

WALTER McFARLAND,
First Lieutenant, Engineers, Comdg. Battery in covered way.

Maj. LEWIS G. ARNOLD,
First Artillery, Commanding Batteries.

No. 15.

Reports of Maj. Gen. Braxton Bragg, C. S. Army, Commanding Army of Pensacola.

HEADQUARTERS ARMY OF PENSACOLA,
Near Pensacola, Fla., November 25, 1861.

SIR: As you were advised by telegraph at 9.30 a. m., on the 22d the enemy opened fire on our lines, without notice, from Fort Pickens and his sand batteries. Shortly thereafter his two large naval steamers off our harbor took up position and joined in the conflict. We responded from such of our guns as were best calculated to damage him in a contest at long range. His fire was first directed on the navy-yard, where our transportation steamer had just arrived heavily loaded, but in a short time our whole line was enveloped in a terrific fire, which was kept up without intermission until darkness put an end to it. Fort McRee seemed to be the main point of attack, the ships, the heaviest out-batteries, and a large portion of Fort Pickens devoting their entire time to it. Knowing the condition of it, I felt great apprehension, but was strengthened in my hope by the confidence I had in its noble commander, Colonel Villepigue, and his brave garrison of Georgians and Mississippians.

Our casualties for the day, thanks to the enemy's wild firing, were only 9 wounded, 2 mortally, 2 severely, and 5 slightly, Colonel Villepigue among the latter. Five valuable lives were lost in addition near Fort McRee by an unfortunate accident.

The conflict was renewed at 10 a. m. the next day, and continued on our part until dark, by the enemy until 12 at night, a few random shots only being fired after that until 4 a. m., when a single 10-inch shell from our side announced our wakefulness, but respect for the Sabbath and quiet reigned. The firing was steady and regular for the whole day, only one ship being engaged, the other apparently crippled. Thanks to the prudent care of their officers, the wild firing of the enemy, and, above all, to the visible and acknowledged preservation of a merciful Providence, not a casualty occurred for the whole day.

Yesterday and to-day the enemy has not renewed the contest, and, for reasons which the Department will appreciate, it is not my policy to do so. Their ships, both crippled, are withdrawn to their former anchorage, a miserable failure being their reward for commencing an engagement without notice, by firing into houses they knew to be occupied by women and children, and closing it by disgracefully violating the hospital flag, in accordance with a former barbarous threat.

When the more circumstantial reports of subordinates are received the Department shall have a detailed account of the whole, when I will endeavor to do justice to individuals and corps. It will suffice to say now that the conduct of my gallant little army fully equaled the high expectation I had formed of it. To Brig. Gens. R. H. Anderson and A. H. Gladden I am indebted for able support and prudent counsel during the whole time, and the army will pardon the single exception I make in giving credit at this time to Col. John B. Villepigue and his Georgians and Mississippians, for their heroic defense of Fort McRee.

I am, sir, very respectfully, your obedient servant,

BRAXTON BRAGG,
Major-General, Commanding.

ADJUTANT-GENERAL C. S. ARMY,
Richmond, Va.

HEADQUARTERS ARMY OF PENSACOLA,
Near Pensacola, Fla., December 4, 1861.

SIR: The reports of subordinate commanders having been mostly received,* I am enabled to give you a more detailed account of our recent passage at arms with the enemy:

On the morning of the 22d of November, about 9.30 o'clock, he opened fire from Fort Pickens and all his outer batteries without the slightest

*That of Brigadier-General Anderson the only one found.

warning. His first shot were directed principally upon the navy-yard and Fort McRee, the former known to be occupied by women and children and non-combatants, and used by us for defensive purposes only. In less than half an hour we were responding, and the enemy distributed his fire on our whole line.

Soon after Fort Pickens opened two large naval steamers, supposed to be the Niagara and Hartford [Richmond], took position due west from Fort McRee and within good range, from whence they poured in broadsides of the heaviest metal throughout the day. From the defective structure of Fort McRee it was unable to return this terrific fire with any effect.

Assailed at the same time from the south by Fort Pickens and its outer batteries, the devoted garrison of this confined work, under the gallant Colonel Villepigue, Georgia and Mississippi regiments, seemed to be destined to destruction. Three times was the wood work of the fort on fire, threatening to expel its occupants, and as often extinguished.

The magazines were laid bare to the enemy's shells, which constantly exploded around them, and a wooden building to the windward, on the outside of the fort, taking fire, showers of live cinders were constantly driven through the broken doors of one magazine, threatening destruction to the whole garrison.

In the midst of this terrible ordeal the coolness and self-possession of the commander inspired all with confidence, and enabled him to hold a position which seemed to others utterly untenable.

Towards evening our sand batteries appeared to have crippled the Hartford [Richmond], and she drew off, and did not again join in the combat. Darkness closed the contest, which had lasted for more than eight hours without an intermission. For the number and caliber of guns and weight of metal brought into action it will rank with the heaviest bombardment in the world. It was grand and sublime. The houses in Pensacola, 10 miles off, trembled from the effect, and immense quantities of dead fish floated to the surface in the bay and lagoon, stunned by the concussion. Our troops behaved with the greatest coolness and gallantry, and surprised me by the regularity and accuracy of their firing, a result which would have been creditable to veterans.

A dark cloud, accompanied by rain and wind, at 6 o'clock so obscured the night as to enable us to withdraw in safety our transport steamers, which had been caught at the navy-yard. The gunboat Nelms, Lieutenant Manston, Louisiana infantry, commanding, was also at the yard when the firing commenced; but she was gallantly backed out, and proceeded to Pensacola unharmed. The fire of the enemy, though terrific in sound and fury, proved to have been only slightly damaging, except to McRee. From Fort Pickens and the sand batteries we sustained very little injury. From the shipping, which fired with much greater accuracy, the fort and garrison of McRee suffered more.

Our loss from the enemy's shot was 21 wounded—1 mortally, who died that night; 12 of the others so slightly as not to take them from duty. By an unfortunate accident—the caving in of a defective magazine, badly planned and constructed—we had 6 other gallant men smothered, who died calling on their comrades never to give up the fort. Our women and children escaped, through a shower of balls, without an accident.

The reports brought in during the night by my staff officers, dispatched to every point, were very satisfactory and encouraging, except from Fort McRee. Exposed in front, flank, and reverse, with half its armament disabled and magazines exposed, without the ability to return the enemy's fire, it was proposed to blow it up and abandon it. Upon mature reflection as to the effect this would have on the *morale* of my own troops as well as the enemy, I determined to hold it to the last extremity. An engineer officer and large working party were dispatched to Colonel Villepigue with this decision. Though suffering from a painful wound, he devoted the entire night to the necessary repairs. It was not our policy to keep up this unequal contest at long range, so we awaited the enemy's fire the next morning.

At about 10.30 he again opened, though much more slowly, and with only one ship. We responded, as before, with caution and deliberation. Their fire was so much slackened that our apprehension about McRee was greatly relieved, and our sand batteries played with a better prospect of success against the remaining ship. Towards evening the enemy, finding all his efforts foiled, that our guns were not silenced, and McRee not reduced, as he had predicted, turned upon the hospital, and put several shot into the empty building (the sick having all been removed in anticipation of this barbarous act). The evacuation, however, was not known to them. All the appearance of occupation was kept up; the yellow flag was still flying. After this he poured hot shot and shell into the empty dwellings of non-combatants in the villages of Warrington and Woolsey, by which considerable portions of each were burned. The navy-yard, too, received a large supply of these shot and a shower of mortar shells until past midnight, but only one unimportant building was fired, though many houses were struck and more or less damaged. Notwithstanding thousands of shot and shell fell in and around our positions, not a casualty occurred in the whole army for the day. Our fire ceased at dark, except an occasional shell, as a warning that we were on the alert, the last shot being ours, about 4 a. m., on the 24th.

We had fired about 1,000 shots, the enemy not less than 5,000. There are no means of knowing or conjecturing the loss or damage inflicted on them, but we believe it to have been very considerable. They certainly did not accomplish the object they had in view nor fulfill the expectations of their Government. The injury to our side was the loss in killed and wounded given above; a few hundred dollars' damage done the navy-yard; the burning of two churches surmounted by the Holy Cross—the first buildings fired—and some twenty humble habitations of poor laboring men and women, mostly emigrants from the North; and, finally, a violation of our hospital flag, in accordance with a previous threat. This last act stamps its author with infamy, and places him beyond the pale of civilized commanders.

As they did not renew the action, and drew off with their ships in a crippled condition, our fire was not reopened on Fort Pickens, to damage which is not our object. A fair challenge, however, was offered them on the 27th, when a small row-boat, attempting to enter the harbor, was fired on by us and abandoned by them. Several of our shots necessarily passed very near their works, but they declined our invitation.

The reports of the brigade and regimental commanders and the chief of artillery are inclosed, with a tabular statement of killed and wounded. I can cordially indorse all that is said by them in commendation of the troops generally, and specially of the individuals mentioned. My thanks are particularly due to Brig. Gens. R. H. Anderson and A. H. Gladden for the able support given me throughout the engagement. It fell to the lot of the latter to have much the largest number of guns engaged, and in consequence a greater sphere of usefulness. The efficiency of the batteries shows the labor and care which have been bestowed, and fully sustains their reputation as gallant veterans. Their reports specify the particular corps whose good fortune it was to be actively engaged. Col. H. D. Clayton, First Regiment of Alabama Volunteers (Gladden's brigade), whose entire regiment served both days at the batteries, has received the just commendation of the general. This gallant regiment has toiled for near ten months in the construction and garnishment of the works they almost despaired of using. Having been the first on the ground, much the largest portion of the labor fell to their lot. When least expected the opportunity has been offered to test their skill, and most nobly have they availed themselves of it.

A mere narrative of the events at Fort McRee and its sand battery (Gladden's brigade) expresses in eloquent simplicity the heroic conduct of Col. J. B. Villepigue, and his command of Georgians and Mississippians. An educated soldier, possessing in an eminent degree the love and confidence of his officers and men, he had been specially selected for this important and perilous post. The result fully vindicates the fortunate choice, and presents for our admiration, blended in perfect harmony, the modest but heroic soldier with the humble but confiding Christian.

Three companies of the regiment of Louisiana Infantry (Anderson's brigade), under Lieutenant-Colonel Jaquess, served as many batteries throughout the action most efficiently and gallantly, fully sustaining the high reputation that excellent regiment has achieved for discipline and instruction. Captain Van Benthuysen, with his company Confederate States Marines, served a battery, with one 10-inch columbiad, at the navy-yard, which was constructed by them, in a handsome and efficient manner. All these batteries were exposed to very heavy fire from the enemy during the whole bombardment, and bear marks of having been very often struck, but not a man in either was injured, owing in some measure, no doubt, to the admirable manner in which they have been protected by the labor of the officers and men occupying them. The members of my personal staff, who have so long and faithfully served in the discharge of the important but monotonous duties at this station, have placed me under renewed obligations, personal and official, and it is but justice their names should appear in this report. Maj. George G. Garner, assistant adjutant-general; First Lieut. J. E. Slaughter, acting inspector-general, Towson Ellis and Francis S. Parker, jr., aides-de-camp, and H. W. Walter, Mississippi volunteers, acting judge-advocate, were constantly with me throughout the engagement, and bore themselves most gallantly under the heaviest fire in carrying orders and making observations for my use. Majs. L. W. O'Bannon, assistant-quartermaster, and T. M. Jones, commissary of subsistence, and Capt. W. R. Boggs, Engineers, when not otherwise engaged in their several departments, were in attendance on the field, sharing its dangers and aiding its operations.

The Hon. A. E. Maxwell, of Florida, a volunteer aide, joined me on the field soon after the action commenced, and participated in all the duties of my staff up to the close. Capt. H. Oladowski, C. S. artillery, chief of ordnance, a veteran of many European campaigns, was temporarily absent on duties of his department, but the results of his valuable services were everywhere conspicuous. The admirable manner in which he had supplied the batteries and regulated the affairs of his department generally reflects great credit on his skill and industry.

To First Lieut. J. E. Slaughter, C. S. Army, acting inspector-general, an officer of fifteen years' unrequited service, I am more indebted, probably, than to any other in this command for the patient labor and unceasing vigil he has given in its organization and instruction.

At the commencement of the firing immediate steps were taken by Surg. A. J. Foard, medical director, in accordance with previous instructions, to remove his sick and stores to a place of security already prepared in anticipation of this outrage upon our hospital flag. By the activity and energy of this indefatigable officer every patient and every article of value had been transferred before any damage occurred. After superintending this important duty he joined me in the field. The high professional attainments of this admirable officer, united to his gentleness of manner, kindness of heart, and untiring zeal, peculiarly adapt him for the very important post he fills with so much credit to himself and satisfaction to this Army. To his labors have been entirely due the admirable arrangements by which the sufferings of our sick have been so greatly alleviated. To him and to the officers of his department generally, to Father Pont and our good Sisters of Charity, who have labored in our hospital without money and without price, the Army and the country owe a debt of gratitude.

At the close of the engagement on Saturday night Maj. Thomas M. Jones, commissary of subsistence, with my approbation, volunteered to go to the assistance of Colonel Villepigue at Fort McRee, who was well-nigh exhausted by his painful wounds, anxiety, and long-continued watchfulness. His services were of the utmost importance in restoring the fort to its defensive condition, and in constructing an additional outwork, which it is hoped will render it less assailable in future. Colonel Villepigue, in his report, pays a just tribute to this excellent officer, whose sense of duty rose far above all personal considerations.

This would seem not an improper occasion to place on record an expression of the admiration and gratitude I feel for the noble, self-sacrificing spirit which has ever pervaded the whole of this gallant little army. Called suddenly from home, without preparation, to serve an unorganized Government, in the midst of a country destitute of supplies, it has patiently, and without a murmur, submitted to privations and borne labors which never can be appreciated. Consigned by fate to inactivity when their brothers elsewhere, later in entering the service, were reaping a harvest of glory, they have still nobly sustained their commander, and maintained a well-deserved reputation for discipline rarely equaled, never surpassed. With a people capable of such sacrifices we may defy the world in arms.

But in giving this praise to human virtue let us not be unmindful of an invisible Power, which has ruled all things for our good. The hand of disease and death has been lightly laid upon us at a place and in a season when we had reason to expect much suffering and great mortality. And in the hour of our trial the missiles of death, showered upon us by an infuriated enemy, respecting neither women, children, nor the sick, have been so directed as to cause us to laugh at their impotent rage. Verily, "Except the Lord keep the city, the watchman waketh but in vain."

I am, sir, very respectfully, your obedient servant,

BRAXTON BRAGG,
Major-General, Commanding.

ADJUTANT-GENERAL,
Richmond, Va.

GENERAL ORDERS, No. 130. } HEADQUARTERS ARMY OF PENSACOLA, *Near Pensacola, Fla., November* 25, 1861.

The signal success which has crowned our forty hours' conflict with the arrogant and confident enemy, whose Government, it seems, is hourly looking for an announcement of his success in capturing our position, should fill our hearts with gratitude to a merciful Providence. This terrific bombardment, of more than a hundred guns of the heaviest caliber—causing the very earth to tremble around us—has, from the wild firing of the enemy, resulted in the loss of only 7 lives, with 8 wounded, but 2 of them seriously; 5 of the deaths from an accident, and but 2 from the enemy's shot.

We have crippled his ships and driven them off, and forced the garrison of Fort Pickens, in its impotent rage, to slake its revenge by firing into our hospital, and burning the habitations of our innocent women and children, who had been driven therefrom by an unannounced storm of shot and shell.

For the coolness, devotion, and conspicuous gallantry of the troops the general tenders his cordial thanks; but for the precision of their firing, in this their first practice, which would have done credit to veterans, he is unable to express his admiration. Their country and their enemy will both remember the 22d and 23d of November.

By command of Major-General Bragg:

GEO. G. GARNER,
Assistant Adjutant-General.

No. 16.

Report of Brig. Gen. Richard H. Anderson, C. S. Army.

HEADQUARTERS SECOND BRIGADE,
Camp near Warrington, Fla., November 28, 1861.

MAJOR: At 10 o'clock a. m. on the 22d instant the enemy opened fire upon the navy-yard and the batteries in the Second Brigade. This attack was made suddenly and with great fury.

Capt. J. T. Wheat, Louisiana infantry, commanding Battery No. 2, was the first to return the fire. Capt. S. S. Batchelor, Louisiana infantry, commanding Battery No. 1, and Lieut. G. W. Mader, of the same regiment, commanding one of the mortar batteries, followed a few moments after, and they all replied to the attack as hotly as it had been begun, until the orders of the general commanding, regulating the rate of fire, were communicated to them, and it was then more moderately continued until after dark, when it was suspended on both sides.

Capt. A. C. Van Benthuysen, C. S. Marine Corps, who commanded the battery on the stone wharf, misconstruing an order which had been given on the occasion of the Santa Rosa expedition, did not open until he received orders to do so. After firing two shots he was ordered to cease, on account of the damage which it was feared the steamer Time, lying at the wharf, would sustain, by provoking a continued fire in that quarter from the guns of the enemy. The steamer Time and the steam gunboat Nelms were both at the wharf when the attack began, and it seemed to be the design of the enemy to damage or destroy them, but the Nelms made her escape at once, and the Time, although struck by several balls, was not much injured, and effected her escape after dark.

The enemy reopened the fire at about 10 o'clock a. m. on the 23d, and was responded to until dark, when it again ceased, with the exception of an occasional shell from the other side, directed aginst the navy-yard, and a reply from Van Benthuysen's battery. Near daylight it was discontinued by both parties. The attack was not resumed on the following morning, and the batteries have consequently remained silent.

Agreeably with instructions previously given the troops not needed at the batteries retired from the navy-yard and its vicinity at the commencement of the attack and took a position outside the north wall. To be prepared for anything the enemy might attempt, Colonel Adams, commanding the Louisiana infantry, was ordered to post his regiment near the navy-yard. This order was executed with the utmost promptness, and the most commendable zeal was exhibited by the regiment, which remained on duty on the beach until near midnight.

The skill and enthusiastic spirit displayed by the officers and troops at the batteries is worthy of all praise, and I am happy to report that no casualty whatever occurred amongst them. While the troops withdrawn from the navy-yard were standing near the north wall, where they had been ordered to rendezvous, a shot penetrated the wall, and the fragments of brick wounded a soldier of Captain Cropp's company, of Florida Regiment Volunteers, and two of Captain Thom's company of Marines.

The batteries commanded by Captains Wheat, Batchelor, and Van Benthuysen were manned by the companies of these officers respectively. Lieutenant Mader's mortar battery was manned by a detachment from the Louisiana infantry.

A trunnion was knocked off one of the 8-inch guns in Wheat's battery, and slight damage was done to the carriage of Batchelor's 42-pounder. One of the mortars in Lieutenant Mader's battery was cracked and rendered useless after the seventeenth discharge. These comprise all the injuries sustained by the batteries of the Second Brigade. Very little damage has been done to the navy-yard. About fifty of the buildings in Warrington and Woolsey have been burnt.

The reports of Lieutenant-Colonel Jaquess, Louisiana infantry, and Captain Van Benthuysen, C. S. Marine Corps, are herewith submitted.*

I am, very respectfully, your obedient servant,

R. H. ANDERSON,

Brigadier-General, P. A., Commanding Second Brigade.

Maj. GEORGE G. GARNER, *A. A. G., C. A.*

JANUARY 1, 1862.—Bombardment of Forts McRee and Barrancas, Fla

REPORTS.

No. 1.—Col. Harvey Brown, Fifth U. S. Artillery, commanding Department of Florida.
No. 2.—Maj. Gen. Braxton Bragg, C. S. Army, commanding Army of Pensacola.

No. 1.

Report of Col. Harvey Brown, Fifth U. S. Artillery, commanding Department of Florida.

HEADQUARTERS DEPARTMENT OF FLORIDA,
Fort Pickens, January 2, 1862.

GENERAL: Yesterday afternoon, about 3 o'clock, a steamer came to the wharf at the navy-yard within range of our guns. The enemy

* Not found.

having, under similar circumstances, fired into a small yawl-boat (which, desirous of avoiding continuous desultory warfare, leading to no results, I did not notice, although four shots were fired), and this being the first instance of a boat of any kind coming to the navy-yard or within the range of my guns since the last bombardment, I could only view it as bravado, or as done with an intention of drawing my fire. I therefore ordered her to be fired into, which was done three times while she lay at the wharf and was leaving it. A gun was fired from a neighboring battery at ours, which was returned, it being directly in range of the departing steamer, and here, as I supposed, the affair would rest; but in about three-quarters of an hour the enemy opened on me from most of his batteries, which was promptly returned, and a regular bombardment ensued, and which continued in our front until too dark to see, when I ceased, except an occasional fire from two or three mortars, the enemy continuing until about 9 o'clock, at which hour a bright light became visible from the yard, and in an hour the whole firmament was illuminated, several of the largest buildings being on fire. The fire continued to burn until towards morning, and the mortar firing continued on our part until 2 and on that of the enemy until 4 o'clock this morning.

I used only my heaviest guns, and not all of them, with an occasional fire from an 8-inch columbiad and a 42-pounder rifled gun. Our firing was much slower than before, and was excellent. I have rarely or never seen better; the officers and men being cool and collected, and doing their duty manfully, such as Yankee soldiers should do. The enlisted men seemed to consider it a New Year's amusement.

Convinced by former experience of the great difficulty of harming or burning his buildings at so great a distance I took the affair very coolly and deliberately, firing seldom, but with great care, and using freely rock-fire and carcasses, with both of which I have been supplied since the last bombardment, and to which I attribute our present success in firing the navy-yard, and the failure of my doing so before to the want of them. The firing of the rebels was not so good as before, very few shot or shell having struck our walls or entered the fort, although the latter burst continuously all around us. He probably expended very considerably more ammunition than on either of the previous days, and with less effect.

I am impressed with the belief that General Bragg was not present, and that a less experienced and more hot-headed officer commanded. If he was, he certainly did not in this affair display his usual prudence and caution.

I had two men slightly injured—one a zouave, by a splinter hitting the calf of his leg, and the other a regular, by a contusion—both trifling; and the injury to the fort is of the most unimportant kind—a few shot on the scarp-wall and some few holes, made principally by the explosion of shells inside, neither of any consequence; and not a gun was disabled or injured, with the exception of one carriage, and, except the 2 named, not a man hurt.

I am more than satisfied with the result, as it has again clearly demonstrated that the immense batteries with which we are nearly surrounded (and to the number of which four have been added since the last bombardment) are unable to do us any serious injury.

We have burned several large buildings in the navy-yard, and must have seriously injured those which are fire-proof, giving the best possible evidence of the superiority of our fire.

I respectfully and earnestly recommend to the executive justice the brave men who have now three times so faithfully defended their country's flag, and who for their reward have in several instances had the mortification of seeing their juniors placed over their heads, and who have never heard the first cheering word of approval for their former gallant deeds. The conduct of all was so uniformly gallant and meritorious that I will make no discrimination in naming them, except to express my thanks to Major Arnold, my executive officer, for his able assistance. They are Surgeon Campbell; Major Tower, Engineers; Lieutenant Todd, Ordnance Department; Assistant Surgeon Sutherland; Lieutenant McFarland, Engineers; Captains Allen, Second Artillery; Chalfin, Fifth Artillery; Robertson, Second Artillery; Blunt, Twelfth Infantry; Hildt, Third Infantry; Duryea, Closson, and Langdon, First Artillery; First Lieutenants Shipley, Third Infantry; Jackson, First Artillery; Pennington, Second Artillery; Seeley, Fourth Artillery; and Taylor, First Artillery; and Second Lieutenants Heaton and Bradley, Second Artillery, and Duer, First Artillery, the three last named who now for the first time fleshed their maiden swords.

I also desire to express my decided approbation of the conduct of the non-commissioned officers and privates of my command. Every one did his duty manfully. I commend the former to the notice of the commanding general.

At the commencement of the bombardment the Sixth Regiment New York Volunteers took post at Camp Brown, and I ordered Colonel Dodge to march his regiment (the Seventy-fifth New York) beyond the range of fire. He moved 2 miles up, and guarded us from any attack the enemy might make during the night. This is a fine regiment, and will, I doubt not, do good service when they have the chance.

As I only fired on the steamer to drive her off, as the enemy had done with our boats, and as he opened his batteries on me, I have not deemed it advisable further to pursue the contest, and as he has not renewed it, I presume it for the present to be ended.

I am, general, very respectfully, your obedient servant,

HARVEY BROWN,
Colonel, Commanding.

Brig. Gen. LORENZO THOMAS,
Adjutant-General.

No. 2.

Report of Maj. Gen. Braxton Bragg, C. S. Army, commanding Army of Pensacola.

HEADQUARTERS ARMY OF PENSACOLA,
Near Pensacola, Fla., January 3, 1862.

SIR: On my way to this point from Mobile on the first instant I was privately advised by telegraph that firing was going on between our batteries and Fort Pickens. I hastened as rapidly as possible, and reached here at 4 a. m. the 2d. It appears a small private steamer had been imprudently allowed to run to the navy-yard, and was fired on by the enemy at Fort Pickens. This fire was returned by order of Brigadier-General Anderson, in temporary command, and a brisk canonnade was kept up on both sides until dark, when the enemy ceased. Ours was continued irregularly and apparently without effect or an object until stopped by my order. No casualty is reported on our side, and we can see no damage to the enemy. A large and valuable store-house, with considerable property, in the navy-yard, was burned by the enemy's shells

I regret exceedingly to add that the concurrent testimony of many officers of rank represent Brigadier-General Anderson as so much intoxicated as to be entirely unfit for duty, and that his conduct was very reprehensible. It is being investigated, and I fear that an arrest and prosecution will be necessary. Holding juniors to a rigid accountability, I shall not overlook a similar offense in a commanding general under such aggravating circumstances.

Not the least cause of regret was the large and criminal waste of means so necessary for our defense, and which we cannot replace.

I must again urge on the Department my request for a second in command here who could be intrusted with this army in my necessary absence. Mobile demands much of my time; indeed, the state of affairs there is alarming, but I am almost powerless for want of the proper officers for command. The material is here, but it cannot be used.

I am, sir, very respectfully, your obedient servant,

BRAXTON BRAGG,
Major-General, Commanding.

ADJUTANT-GENERAL C. S. ARMY, *Richmond.*

JANUARY 20, 1862.—Contest over the British schooner Andracita, on the coast of Alabama.

REPORTS.

No. 1.—Maj. Gen. Braxton Bragg, C. S. Army.
No. 2.—Col. W. L. Powell, C. S. Army.

No. 1.

Report of Maj. Gen. Braxton Bragg, C. S. Army.

HDQRS. DEPT. OF ALABAMA AND WEST FLORIDA,
Near Pensacola, Fla., February 1, 1862.

SIR: I inclose a copy of a report from Colonel Powell, Provisional Army, of a recent contest by a portion of his command with the enemy over a British schooner. The conduct of our troops was highly creditable, though they were unable to save the vessel from capture. Every facility has been extended to the British consul in prosecuting the case, and I hope he has succeeded, as he desired, in complicating affairs between the United States and Great Britain. A copy of an article from a Mobile paper, inclosed,* gives a very correct history of the vessel and her movements.

I am, sir, very respectfully, your obedient servant,

BRAXTON BRAGG,
Major-General, Commanding.

ADJUTANT-GENERAL, *Richmond, Va.*

No. 2.

Report of Col. W. L. Powell, C. S. Army.

CAMP BRAGG, *January* 21, 1862.

CAPTAIN: I avail myself of the boat from this point to-day to report that a sharp contest took place at the mouth of the lagoon yesterday

*Omitted.

between two of the enemy's steamers, with their boats, and Captain Cottrill's command, for the possession of the schooner Andracita, formerly J. W. Wilder, which had been run on shore at that place, with the hope of saving her cargo. All the particulars of the affair cannot be given at this time, as I have not a report as to the part taken in it by the force, consisting of two field pieces and two companies ordered up from Fort Morgan and Camp Bragg, and which were on the west side of the lagoon, under Acting Assistant Adjutant-General Jones.

Upon my getting on this side of the lagoon to put Captain Cottrill's company in action, that officer had already moved his available force across the lagoon to within a short distance of the schooner, and there he kept up so sharp and well-directed a fire upon the schooner and the boats of the steamers as to drive those of the enemy, who had previously reached her below and prevented the boats from getting to their assistance, while he sheltered his men so securely behind the sand hills as to maintain his position, though it was only about 100 yards from the beach and not more than 600 or 800 yards from the steamers, without losing a life.

Captain Cottrill and his command deserve great credit for the skillful and daring manner in which they performed their parts in a defense which, judging from the effect of their fire while continued, must have been successful, if it had not been the case that the schooner was run on shore at low tide, and that the enemy succeeded in making a hawser fast to her before he got his men into position, by which she was hauled out of range after the tide, in rising, had caused her to float.

What loss the enemy met with I will not pretend to state, as I was not fortunate enough to reach the scene of action; but it must have been considerable, as two of their boats, one of which is now reported as on the beach and in the possession of our men, were sunk or turned over, and another had every oarsman shot or driven off their seats, and was towed out of range by another sent to her assistance.

As I mentioned above, there was no loss of life from this command so far as heard from, and we have only to regret that of the schooner and cargo, which I am sorry to say the captain neglected to fire in his desire to save it. Upon returning to Fort Morgan I shall be able to furnish any further particulars which may be brought to my notice.

I am, captain, very respectfully, your obedient servant,

W. L. POWELL,
Colonel, Commanding Second Brigade.

Capt. D. E. HUGER,
Assistant Adjutant-General.

MARCH 27-31, 1862.—Reconnaissance on Santa Rosa Island, Fla.

REPORTS.

No. 1.—Brig. Gen. Lewis G. Arnold, U. S. Army.
No. 2.—Capt. Henry W. Closson, First U. S. Artillery.

No. 1.

Report of Brig. Gen. Lewis G. Arnold, U. S. Army.

HEADQUARTERS DEPARTMENT OF FLORIDA,
Fort Pickens, April 4, 1862.

I respectfully forward a report of Captain Closson, First Artillery, of an armed reconnaissance 40 miles up the island of Santa Rosa, made in obedience to my orders, for the purpose of ascertaining the character of the upper end of the island and to punish and take prisoners any rebels he might meet, I having received information that about 200 armed rebels were encamped near the Southeast Pass, where they had a few days previously killed 2 sailors and wounded 2 others belonging to the blockading schooner stationed there.

Respectfully submitted.

L. G. ARNOLD,
Brigadier-General, U. S. Volunteers, Commanding.

No. 2.

Report of Capt. Henry W. Closson, First U. S. Artillery.

FORT PICKENS, FLA., *April* 2, 1862.

SIR: On the 26th of last month I received your instructions from the general commanding to make an armed reconnaissance of Santa Rosa Island, my command to consist of Company L, First Artillery, and Company K, Sixth Regiment New York Volunteers, rationed to include the 31st, and a 10-pounder Parrott rifle.

On the night of the 27th I camped 12 miles from here, and at midnight received an express, directing me to wait until 3 p. m. the next day for the arrival of Lieutenant Shipley with further instructions. He not arriving at that hour, I went into camp that night 8 miles beyond, when I was overtaken by Lieutenant Jackson, acting assistant adjutant-general of the department, with Company D, Sixth Regiment New York Volunteers, and a guide—Mr. Woods, a rebel refugee. Lieutenant Jackson informed me that I was to move up towards the east end of the island and surprise and capture a rebel force in that vicinity on the main-land—boats to be furnished from the naval volunteer schooner Maria Wood, on blockade duty at the East Pass—one part of my command with the rifled gun to shell the rebel camp from the island, one portion to cross the sound and move up the main-land, and one portion to enter the pass and move down the sound. The latter part of the plan I abandoned, on account of the distance of the pass from the point of attack, some 10 miles. All the necessary material and arrangements had been provided and made with the schooner at Fort Pickens by Acting Assistant Quartermaster Shipley.

At noon on the 31st I went into camp about 36 miles from here and 4 from the supposed location of the rebel force, having communicated with the schooner, and requested that at dark she would put three surf-boats on the outside beach, where I should establish a signal fire. Lieutenant Jackson and Lieutenant Appleton made a thorough and close reconnaissance of the island and main-land at this point, selected where to put the gun and to cross the sound, giving 600 yards of boating.

At sunset, leaving animals, disabled men, and stores at camp, I moved with 170 men 2 miles up the beach to the crossing and lit the signal fire. At 11 o'clock two surf-boats arrived. I had them hauled about 800 yards over the sand hills to the inside beach, and directed Lieutenant Jackson to march the volunteer battalion there and wait my arrival with the regulars and the third surf-boat. At 1 o'clock in the morning the third surf-boat made its appearance. The unaccountable lateness of their arrival had now precluded all possibility of the surprise, and here I received a message by Lieutenant Gibbs from Lieutenant Jackson that two rebel spies had been in the vicinity of his command and a party had been detached for their capture—unsuccessfully. I directed the two boats to be returned to the outside beach, Company K, Sixth Regiment New York Volunteers, to proceed to my camp, while I took Company D, Sixth New York Volunteers, and the regulars, with the rifled gun, 2 miles farther up, crossed the island, and put the gun into position on the inside beach, directly opposite the rebel camp, and about 250 yards from it. I remained here until their huts could be seen in the dawn, and then directed Lieutenant Jackson to open fire. The shells burst right in their midst. Loud cries and yells were heard, and the rebels could be barely seen through the brush in their shirt-tails making rapidly into the back country. A scattering volley was fired from what I supposed to be their guard, who then disappeared also.

After shelling the vicinity thoroughly I returned to my camp. My supply of rations and forage was nearly exhausted, the mules nearly broken down by a very severe pull of 40 miles through the heavy sand on the beach. I therefore sent all my sick men (some 6) and all the bedding I could spare to the schooner, and started on my return. Late on Monday afternoon Lieutenant Appleton reported a schooner making its way up the sound. The rifled gun was taken over to the inside beach and Lieutenant Jackson directed to open fire. The range ran from 1,800 to 3,000 yards, but the firing was very satisfactory; the schooner was several times struck, her small boat hit, but after firing some twelve shots it became so dusky that she could be no longer distinguished.

On Tuesday afternoon I reached Fort Pickens.

I am, sir, very respectfully, your obedient servant,

HENRY W. CLOSSON,
Captain, First Artillery.

Lieut. R. H. JACKSON,
Acting Assistant Adjutant-General, Dept. of Florida.

The instructions given me by Lieutenant Jackson interfered somewhat with any very close observation. The island varied in width, so far as I had an opportunity to notice, from half a mile to 500 yards; is cut up by sand ridges, so as to make the passage of teams across very difficult and generally impossible; furnishes good water in pools or by digging in the depressions; but very little grass indeed, and that very coarse. The only practicable road for teams, in the direction of its length, is along the outside beach, and that generally is excessively heavy and quite narrow, and in many places at full tide impassable for any ordinary load. The condition of the horses and mules of my command furnishes some evidence of the character of this road. In many places the island is perfectly open, in others screened from the main-land by ridges of sand hills and fringes of forest. The sound is in width from 3 miles to 300 yards, I should judge. The narrowest point is about 40 miles from the fort. Here the rebel camp was located. It is nowhere fordable; navigable for its whole extent for vessels of 7 feet draught, the channel running generally close along the main-land.

These remarks are the result of my own observation and information of the guides, and a thorough examination might not substantiate them.

All of which is respectfully submitted.

HENRY W. CLOSSON,
Captain, First Artillery.

APRIL 3-4, 1862.—Affairs at Biloxi and Pass Christian, Miss.

Report of Maj. Gen. Mansfield Lovell, C. S. Army.

HEADQUARTERS DEPARTMENT NO. 1,
New Orleans, La., April 16, 1862.

SIR: I have the honor to report that on the 3d instant the enemy landed a force of 500 men at Biloxi, having three steamers off the town. We had seven companies of the Third Mississippi Regiment at Handsborough and three at Pass Christian. I arranged with Commodore Whittle that the steamers Carondelet, Pamlico, and Oregon should engage these vessels while we attacked their troops at daylight on the 4th, but their fleet was re-enforced by two vessels at night, which re-embarked their troops, and, having engaged our ships with superior forces, they proceeded to Pass Christian, landed 1,200 men, with several pieces of artillery, and drove away our three companies, burning their camp and destroying a portion of their clothing and stores.

Our men, finding themselves greatly overmatched and outflanked, retreated without loss of life to Gainesville. Colonel Deason proceeded with his seven companies of infantry, one of cavalry, and a battery of artillery to Biloxi, which he found abandoned by the enemy. I subsequently ordered the troops to rendezvous at Pass Christian, where they now remain, but on account of the difficulty of supplying them by water I shall probably bring them to this city.

Respectfully, your obedient servant,

M. LOVELL,
Major-General, Commanding.

General S. COOPER, *Adjutant and Inspector General.*

APRIL 7, 1862.—Affair at Saint Andrew's Bay, Florida.*

Report of Capt. R. S. Smith, Marianna Dragoons.

BLUE SPRING CAMP, *April* 16, 1862.

Brig. Gen. JOSEPH FINEGAN, *Commanding Department:*

SIR: In compliance with a telegraphic order (a copy of which is herewith inclosed) from Colonel Dilworth, then commanding, and received at my camp, 6 miles east of Marianna, at 12 o'clock m. on the 7th instant, I started at 3 p. m. of the same day with my command, and arrived at 3.02 p. m. the next day at Saint Andrew's Bay, having been in the saddle twenty-four hours, with only a rest of two hours to feed our horses. I found that the enemy had succeeded in getting the steamer Florida from her anchorage up North Bay, and was then opposite the town of Saint Andrew's. When about 3 miles from the town we heard a gun from the steamer, and, riding then at half speed, I met one of my advance guard just before reaching the town, who informed me that the enemy were landing from a small sloop about a mile from us. I then dismounted my command and advanced rapidly through the woods, hoping to capture them. But the enemy saw us when 200 yards off, and took to their boats. I then caused my command to open fire upon them. They were out of shot-gun reach, but a portion of my command, who were armed with Maynard rifles, killed or disabled four or five of the seven. Having only five cartridges to the rifle, our ammunition was soon exhausted. Had I had sufficient cartridges I am sure that I could have taken the

---

* Belongs properly to Chapter XV, but report found too late for insertion there.

sloop, and probably have retaken the steamer, or at least burned her. The enemy fired on us with a long-range gun, carrying round balls, which passed over our heads at a distance of half a mile. They also sent a few shell after us, but no one was hurt on our side. The steamer then left the bay, and, after remaining some days, I returned with my command to camp.

Yours, obediently,

R. S. SMITH,
Captain, Commanding Marianna Dragoons.

[Inclosure.]

HDQRS. PROV. FORCES, DEPT. E. AND M. FLA.,
Tallahassee, Fla., April 7, 1862.

Capt. R. S. SMITH, *Comdg. Marianna Dragoons, Marianna, Fla.:*

CAPTAIN: You will immediately proceed in the direction of Saint Andrew's Bay with your troops, and, if possible, recapture the steamer Florida, prevent all unnecessary communication with the enemy, and arrest any person which you may have found grounds to suspect of treason.

Respectfully, yours, &c.,

W. S. DILWORTH,
Colonel, Commanding District.

APRIL 18–MAY 1, 1862.—Bombardment and capture of Forts Jackson and Saint Philip, and occupation of New Orleans, La., by the Union forces.

REPORTS, ETC.

No. 1.—Maj. Gen. Benjamin F. Butler, U. S. Army, of co-operation with the naval forces, and occupation, May 1, of the city of New Orleans.

No. 2.—Brig. Gen. John W. Phelps, U. S. Army, of the occupation of Forts Jackson and Saint Philip.

No. 3.—Maj. Gen. Mansfield Lovell, C. S. Army.

No. 4.—Brig. Gen. Johnson K. Duncan, C. S. Army, of the bombardment and capture of Forts Jackson and Saint Philip.

No. 5.—Lieut. Col. Edward Higgins, C. S. Army, of the bombardment and capture of Forts Jackson and Saint Philip.

No. 6.—Capt. M. T. Squires, Louisiana Artillery, of the bombardment of Fort Saint Philip.

No. 7.—Brig. Gen. M. L. Smith, C. S. Army, of operations on the "Chalmette and McGehee Lines."

No. 8.—Proceedings of the Confederate Court of Inquiry upon the fall of New Orleans.

No. 9.—Message from the President of the Confederate States, transmitting correspondence with the Governor of Louisiana and General Lovell.

No. 1.

Reports of Maj. Gen. Benjamin F. Butler, U. S. Army, of co-operation with the naval forces, and occupation, May 1, of the city of New Orleans.

HEADQUARTERS DEPARTMENT OF THE GULF,
Forts Jackson and Saint Philip, April 29, 1862.

SIR: I have the honor to report that in obedience to my instructions I remained on the Mississippi River, with the troops named in my former dispatch, awaiting the action of the fleet engaged in the bombardment of Forts Jackson and Saint Philip. Failing to reduce them after six days of incessant fire, Flag-Officer Farragut determined to attempt their passage with his whole fleet, except that part thereof under the immediate command of Captain Porter, known as the Mortar Fleet.

On the morning of the 24th instant the fleet got under way, and twelve vessels, including the four sloops of war, ran the gauntlet of fire of the forts and were safely above. Of the gallantry, courage, and conduct of this heroic action, unprecedented in naval warfare, considering the character of the works and the river, too much cannot be said. Of its casualties and the details of its performance the flag-officer will give an account to the proper Department. I witnessed this daring exploit from a point about 800 yards from Fort Jackson and unwittingly under its fire, and the sublimity of the scene can never be exceeded. The fleet pressed on up the river to New Orleans, leaving two gunboats to protect the quarantine station, 5 miles above.

In case the forts were not reduced, and a portion of the fleet got by them, it had been arranged between the flag-officer and myself that I should make a landing from the Gulf side on the rear of the forts at the quarantine, and from thence attempt Fort Saint Philip by storm and assault, while the bombardment was continued by the fleet. I immediately went to Sable Island with my transports, 12 miles in the rear of Saint Philip, the nearest point at which a sufficient depth of water could be found for them.

Captain Porter put at my disposal the Miami, drawing 7½ feet, being the lightest-draught vessel in the fleet, to take the troops from the ship, as far as the water would allow. We were delayed twenty-four hours by her running ashore at Pass à l'Outre. The Twenty-sixth Regiment Massachusetts Volunteers, Colonel Jones, were then put on board her and carried within 6 miles of the fort, where she again grounded. Captain Everett, of the Sixth Massachusetts Battery, having very fully reconnoitered the waters and bayous in that vicinity, and foreseeing the necessity, I had collected and brought with me some 30 boats, into which the troops were again transshipped and conveyed, by a most fatiguing and laborious row, some 4½ miles farther, there being within 1 mile of the steamer only 2½ feet of water. A large portion of this passage was against a heavy current, through a bayou. At the entrance of Manuel's Canal, a mile and a half from the point of landing, rowing became impossible, as well from the narrowness of the canal as the strength of the current, which ran like a mill-race. Through this the boats could only be impelled by dragging them singly, with the men up to their waists in water. It is due to this fine regiment and to a portion of the Fourth Wisconsin Volunteers and Twenty-first Indiana, who landed under this hardship without a murmur, that their labors should be made known to the Department, as well as to account for the slowness of our operations. The enemy evidently considered this mode of attack impossible, as they had taken no measures to oppose it, which might very easily have been successfully done. We occupied at once both sides of the river, thus effectually cutting them off from all supplies, information, or succor while we made our dispositions for the assault.

Meantime Captain Porter had sent into the bayou in the rear of Fort Jackson two schooners of his mortar fleet to prevent the escape of the enemy from the fort in that direction. In the hurry and darkness of the passage of the forts the flag-officer had overlooked three of the enemy's gunboats and the iron-clad battery Louisiana, which were at anchor under the walls of the fort. Supposing that all the rebel boats had been destroyed (and a dozen or more had been) he passed on to the city, leaving these in his rear. The iron steam battery being very formidable, Captain Porter deemed it prudent to withdraw his mortar fleet some miles below, where he could have room to maneuver it if attacked by the iron monster, and the bombardment ceased.

I had got Brigadier-General Phelps in the river below with two regiments to make demonstrations in that direction if it became possible. In the night of the 27th, learning that the fleet had got the city under its guns, I left Brigadier-General Williams in charge of the landing of the troops and went up the river to the flagship to procure light-draught transportation. That night the larger portion (about 250) of the garrison of Fort Jackson mutinied, spiked the guns bearing up the river, came up and surrendered themselves to my pickets, declaring that as we had got in their rear resistance was useless, and they would not be sacrificed. No bomb had been thrown at them for three days nor had they fired a shot at us from either fort. They averred that they had been impressed and would fight no longer.*

On the 28th the officers of Forts Jackson and Saint Philip surrendered to Captain Porter, he having means of water transportation to them. While he was negotiating, however, with the officers of the forts under a white flag the rebel naval officers put all their munitions of war on the Louisiana, set her on fire and adrift upon the Harriet Lane, but when opposite Fort Saint Philip she blew up, killing one of their own men by the fragments which fell into that fort.

I have taken possession of the forts, and find them substantially as defensible as before the bombardment—Saint Philip precisely so, it being quite uninjured. They are fully provisioned, well supplied with ammunition, and the ravages of the shells have been defensibly repaired by the labors of the rebels. I will cause Lieutenant Weitzel, of the Engineers, to make a detailed report of their condition to the Department. I have left the Twenty-sixth Regiment Massachusetts Volunteers in garrison, and am now going up the river to occupy the city with my troops and make further demonstrations in the rear of the enemy, now at Corinth.

The rebels have abandoned all their defensive works in and around New Orleans, including Forts Pike and Wood, on Lake Pontchartrain, and Fort Livingston from Barataria Bay. They have retired in the direction of Corinth, beyond Manchac Pass, and abandoned everything up the river as far as Donaldsonville, some 70 miles beyond New Orleans. I propose to so far depart from the letter of my instructions as to endeavor to persuade the flag-officer to pass up the river as far as the mouth of Red River, if possible, so as to cut off their supplies, and make there a landing and a demonstration in their rear as a diversion in favor of General Buell if a decisive battle is not fought before such movement is possible.

Mobile is ours whenever we choose, and we can better wait.

I find the city under the dominion of the mob. They have insulted our flag—torn it down with indignity. This outrage will be punished in such manner as in my judgment will caution both the perpetrators and abettors of the act, so that they shall fear the stripes if they do not reverence the stars of our banner.

I send a marked copy of a New Orleans paper, containing an applauding account of the outrage.†

*See Butler to Stanton, June 1, 1862, in Chapter XXVII.

†Not found.

Trusting my action may meet the approbation of the Department, I am, most respectfully, your obedient servant,

BENJ. F. BUTLER,
Major-General, Commanding.

Hon. E. M. STANTON,
Secretary of War.

HEADQUARTERS DEPARTMENT OF THE GULF,
New Orleans, May 8, 1862.

SIR: I have the honor to report my further operations since my dispatch of the 29th ultimo.

I commenced the disembarkation of my men on May 1, when I took formal possession of New Orleans.

The Twenty-first Indiana was landed at Algiers, a small town on the right bank of the river, opposite New Orleans, at the inner terminus of the New Orleans and Opelousas Railroad. All the rolling stock of the road has been seized, and the road is now running under my direction, only for the purpose of bringing in provisions to the city. That regiment, under Colonel McMillan, on the 5th of May was sent to Brashear, 80 miles (the whole length of the railway), and Berwick Bay, and there captured two brass 6-pounder field guns, with ammunition for the same, some 1,500 pounds of powder, and some other ordnance stores, and dispersed a military organization there forming, captured and brought off two citizens who persisted in insulting our troops.

There are now no Confederate forces on the right or western bank of the Mississippi within possible reaching distance of which I have any intelligence.

The remainder of my troops which I had been able to take with me by means of any transportation which I had, to wit, Thirtieth and Thirty-first Massachusetts, Fourth Wisconsin and Sixth Michigan, Ninth and Twelfth Connecticut, with Manning's and Everett's Fifth and Sixth Massachusetts Batteries, and Holcomb's Second Vermont Battery, and two companies of cavalry, I landed in the city proper, posting and quartering them at the custom-house, city hall, mint, and Lafayette Square. I thought it necessary to make so large a display of force in the city. I found it very turbulent and unruly, completely under the control of the mob; no man on either side daring to act independently for fear of open violence and assassination. On landing we were saluted with cheers for "Jeff. Davis" and "Beauregard." This has been checked, and the last man that was heard to call for cheers for the rebel chief has been sentenced by the provost judge to three months' hard labor at Fort Jackson, which sentence is being executed. No assassinations have been made of any United States soldiers, with the exception of a soldier of the Ninth Connecticut, who had left his camp without orders in the night and was found dead the next morning in an obscure street, having probably been engaged in a drunken brawl.

My officers and myself now walk in any part of the city where occasion calls by day or night, without guard, obstruction, or annoyance. There is, however, here a violent, strong, and unruly mob, that can only be kept under by fear.

On the 5th instant I sent Brigadier-General Phelps, with the Ninth and Twelfth Connecticut and Manning's battery, to take possession of the rebel works on the north side of the city, which run from the river to the marshes of Lake Pontchartrain, about 7 miles above the city. I could make no earlier movement, because all the steamers captured and in repair were claimed by the Navy, and were used either in towing their supply ships or tugging off the Rhode Island, which had gone on shore and detained us all three days. This point, in the judgment of the engineers on both sides, is a most defensible one on the northerly side, had been fortified by the rebels with heavy earthworks, and can be maintained with a few regiments against any force, however large, that may be brought against it.

The sloop-of-war Portsmouth and the gunboat Iroquois are anchored so as to enfilade the front of the enbankments which were abandoned by the rebels. These can easily be put in defensible condition, although before the arrival of the army and after the evacuation by the enemy, who spiked the guns, a party from the advanced gunboats landed and burned the gun-carriages, which we must supply from those captured at the custom-house.

All the rolling stock of the Jackson Railroad was carried away by the retreating General Lovell, and he has cut the road 14 miles above the city. I am now taking measures to possess ourselves of the whole road to Manchac Pass. The fleet have gone up the river as far as Baton Rouge. The flag-officer started yesterday, and I have sent two regiments to accompany him and make any landing necessary.

The projected expedition from Vicksburg to Jackson, of which I spoke in my last dispatch, has become nugatory, because I am reliably informed from different sources that Beauregard has fallen back upon Jackson with his whole army, and is there concentrating his means of defense. My spies inform me that he is suffering greatly for want of food; that his army is daily becoming demoralized and leaving him.

As soon as all necessary points can be occupied here and my instructions carried out as regards Mobile, I will endeavour to march upon his rear with all the force I can spare consistently with reasonable safety of this point.

As in case of defeat he must retreat upon us, it will be perceived that I must be prepared to meet the *débris* of his army, or indeed, as he has ample rolling stock (the Telegraph says 13 miles of cars), he may precipitate any amount of force upon me at any moment; for which we will try to be ready. I have caused Forts Pike and Wood, the defenses of Lake Pontchartrain, to be occupied by detachments of the Seventh Vermont and Eighth New Hampshire Regiments. I have not yet occupied either the Chalmette, Tower Dupré, or Battery Bienvenue. Our boats hold the lake, and these are only defenses from exterior enemies; are in no need to occupy them at present. The same observation will apply to Fort Livingston.

I have the honor to inclose copies of a proclamation and the several general orders necessary in the administration of the affairs of so large a city.* The order most questionable is the one in regard to cotton and sugar, No. 22; but it has had a most salutary effect. Both cotton and sugar are now being sent for to be brought into this market, and the burning through the adjacent country has ceased.

My action in regard to provisions was made absolutely necessary by the starvation which was falling upon the "just and the unjust," and as the class of workmen and mechanics on whom it is pressing most heavily, I am persuaded, are well disposed to the Union, I may have to take other measures to feed these.

It will become necessary for me to use the utmost severity in rooting

---

* See "Correspondence, etc.," *post*.

out the various rebel secret associations here, which overawe the Union men, and give expression to the feelings of the mob by assassination and murder, and usurping the functions of government when a government was here pretended to. I propose to make some brilliant examples.

I take leave to suggest whether it might not be well to send to this point or Mobile a large force by which to operate on the rebel rear, so as to cut him off completely.

I send this dispatch by Colonel Deming, a gentleman known to you, who is possessed of my confidence, and will present to you some matters of interest more at length than could be done in this form of communication. I desire, however, to add urgently to anything he may say that there is an immediate necessity for a paymaster here. As well for the spirit, health, and comfort of the troops, I have established the strictest quarantine at the proper point (the quarantine grounds), and hope to preserve the present good health of my command. I hope my action will meet the approval of the President and the Department of War. Much of it has been done in the emergencies called for by a new and untried state of things, when promptness and movement were more desirable than deliberation. I await with anxiety instructions from the Department for my guidance in the future.

I have the honor to be, most respectfully, your obedient servant,

BENJ. F. BUTLER,
Major-General, Commanding.

The SECRETARY OF WAR.

No. 2.

Report of Brig. Gen. John W. Phelps, U. S. Army, of the occupation of Forts Jackson and Saint Philip.

TRANSPORT SHIP NORTH AMERICA,
Mississippi River, April 30, 1862.

SIR: In compliance with General Orders, April 24, 1862, from your headquarters, received at the mouth of the river, to take possession of Forts Saint Philip and Jackson, with the Thirtieth Massachusetts and Twelfth Connecticut, I proceeded up to the Head of the Passes on the 25th instant, and joined those two regiments. All the mortar boats, steamboats, and sail vessels below the forts had already gone or were going down towards the Southwest Pass, except a few gunboats, which anchored just ahead of us.

I informed Commander Porter on the 26th, who was then at the Head of the Passes, of my readiness to occupy the forts, and directed Lieutenant Hall, my aide, to offer him any assistance that I could render.

The commander returned to the forts on the 27th. On the morning of the 28th he sent word by Captain Baldwin, of the gunboat Clifton, that the forts were about to surrender. As the wind was then favorable, I directed the North America, with the Thirtieth Massachusetts, Read's cavalry, and Manning's battery, under Colonel Dudley, to set sail, Captain Baldwin assisting to tow her, and sent word to Colonel Deming, with the Twelfth Connecticut, on board the Farley, to follow us. Our progress with sail vessels against the current of the Mississippi, swollen to its fullest height, was, as may readily be conceived, not rapid. On our way we observed suddenly, in the direction of the forts, an immense column of smoke rising rapidly to the clouds, and after an interval heard an explosion. Transshipping three companies of the Thirtieth Massachusetts, one company cavalry, and part of Manning's battery, on board the Clifton, with Colonel Dudley, Major Whittemore, and my staff, we left the North America at anchor just below the forts, and joined the flotilla at about 3 o'clock p. m. At this moment the rebel flags of the forts were hauled down and the national colors run up; a part of the ceremony which was greeted by our men with nine hearty cheers.

Continuing on a short distance above the forts, towards some steamboats that were bows ashore, on the right bank, we took aboard from them about 200 prisoners of the rebel Navy and artillery, who had treacherously, and with that peculiar wantonness which characterizes the conspiracy from its origin, set fire to and blown up the iron-clad gunboat Louisiana, thus killing one of their own men in Fort Saint Philip and endangering the lives and property of their own people, as well as of the Government forces there present.

Landing with these prisoners at Fort Saint Philip, we proceeded to take possession of the forts and garrison them with about 200 men each, that of Fort Saint Philip, under Major Whittemore, of the Thirtieth Massachusetts, and that of Fort Jackson, under Captain Manning, of the Fourth Massachusetts Battery, the former relieving Lieutenant-Commander Nichols, and the latter Captain Renshaw, of the Navy. While thus employed the United States steam-frigate Mississippi, Capt. Melancton Smith, came down the river with Colonel Jones, of the Twenty-sixth Massachusetts, who reported that he had landed with his regiment at the quarantine from the outside, and had captured several hundred prisoners who were fleeing from the forts.

Commander Porter had alone accepted of the surrender of the forts, and had granted terms of capitulation to their defenders, allowing them to go at large on their parole, excepting those implicated in blowing up the Louisiana.

On the 29th I placed Colonel Deming in command of Fort Jackson, designing to garrison it with his regiment, and to occupy Fort Saint Philip with the Thirtieth Massachusetts, under Colonel Dudley. While thus occupied I received orders from the major-general commanding the department, in person, to withdraw my troops and proceed up the river, leaving the forts to be garrisoned by the Twenty-sixth Massachusetts. Accordingly the garrisons were withdrawn, excepting small guards to take charge of the prisoners and property, and we got under way at about sunset, the Farley preceding us by about half an hour.

I transmit herewith copies of the reports rendered by officers engaged in occupying the forts.* I may state, in conclusion, that the forts appeared to be abundantly provided with all the material, including commissary stores, necessary for a long defense. I had not time to effect a perfect enumeration of it, but in general terms I may say that the artillery and small-arms of Fort Saint Philip consisted of 43 guns *en barbette*, 1 13-inch mortar, 4 10-inch sea-coast mortars, 3 pieces of light artillery, 1 10-inch and 1 8-inch siege mortars; in all, 53 cannon, and about 45 stand of muskets, with equipments. Some of these latter were from Springfield, of the date of 1861.

One important rifle gun, bearing on the position of the mortar fleet, had been broken by its own discharge. Another gun had been broken short off a foot or two back from the muzzle by a shot which struck

* Not found.

squarely against it; another, and the 13-inch mortar, had been dismounted. In other respects not much harm was done either to the armament or Fort Saint Philip.

The armament of Fort Jackson consisted of 45 heavy guns *en barbette*, 20 in casemate, 2 pieces of light artillery, and 6 mortars; in all, 73 cannon, and 509 stand of small-arms, with equipments.

Fort Jackson had been very much injured by the bombardment. Of the some 7,000 13-inch shells which had been thrown at it, besides other large shots from our gunboats, many had either struck within it or burst over it. It was in a great state of disorder, the brick barracks inside being destroyed by fire, the parapets and terre-plein much pitted and torn by the shells, and the work partly flooded with water. The country generally is so flooded that a ferry-boat is necessary to reach the counterscarp of the works. Of the artillery *en barbette* several pieces had been dismounted. Three instances are reported where casemate arches had been broken through.

Some of the defenders of the forts whom I particularly noticed had been members of the garrison during a period of fourteen months, the forts having been seized by the conspirators as early as the 21st February, 1861; they seemed to be generally foreigners, heartily tired and disgusted with the thralldom under which they have so long labored, and well satisfied with their recovered liberty. The only question is whether they can maintain it now that it has been restored to them.

I am, very respectfully, your obedient servant,

J. W. PHELPS,
Brigadier-General, First Brigade, Department of the Gulf.

Maj. GEORGE C. STRONG,
Assistant Adjutant-General, Department of the Gulf.

No. 3.

Reports of Maj. Gen. Mansfield Lovell, C. S. Army.

HEADQUARTERS DEPARTMENT NO. 1,
Camp Moore, La., April 26, 1862.

SIR: The bombardment of Fort Jackson, which commenced Friday, the 18th instant, was continued day and night until about 3 a. m. on the 24th, when the whole of the enemy's fleet came up abreast the forts, and while a portion of them engaged our batteries and vessels the remainder passed under the fire, our men being greatly worn and exhausted with an incessant fight of six days. General Duncan and Colonel Higgins were in command of the troops.

I had just arrived in a river steamer and was about to disembark as the engagement commenced. When the enemy's fleet passed I was satisfied that New Orleans could not be held for more than twenty-four hours; I therefore started at once for the city, in order to remove as many of the troops and as large a quantity of stores as possible. I was well aware that my batteries of 32-pounders at the lower levees, manned by inexperienced troops, could not detain for any length of time the heavy ships of war of the enemy armed with 9 and 11 inch guns.

I will state that when the current and drift had carried away the obstructions in the river I became convinced that a portion at least of their fleet would pass whenever the attempt was made, and had already given orders to prepare for removal a large portion of the Government stores, directing cars and steamers to be held in readiness for that purpose. On my arrival at New Orleans I gave orders to the few regiments that I was organizing there to be ready to move, and had the larger portion of the Government property placed on the boats and cars and started north. In this manner a very inconsiderable portion of our stores was left behind. The guns on the levees about the city could not be removed for want of transportation. Moreover, as soon as it became known that the enemy had passed the forts, laborers refused to work, and the larger majority of persons declined to take any more Confederate notes for property bought.

On the morning of the 25th thirteen of the enemy's ships engaged our batteries 5 miles below the city, and after two hours' firing, during which time they drove the men from one battery and disabled the other, they passed up and anchored abreast the city. General Smith had a few companies of his brigade at these works. At 11 a. m. our last batteries were passed.

I immediately ordered the troops and stores to be sent off rapidly by rail towards Jackson, Miss.

At 3 p. m. Captain [Theodorus] Bailey and another officer of the Federal Navy came ashore and demanded the surrender of the city, and that the United States flag be put up on the principal public buildings.

I declined peremptorily to surrender, saying to Captain Bailey that while they were too strong for us on the water, I felt abundantly able to beat them on the land; but that, as I did not feel willing to subject to bombardment a city filled with the wives and children of absent soldiers, I should evacuate, with my command, and turn the city over to the mayor; that, if they were willing to consent to this proposition, I would quietly withdraw; if not, they might commence the bombardment at once.

He said he would report to his commander and at his request I sent two of my staff with them to their boat, to protect them from the people.

I then continued the removal of troops and stores, and left the city at 5 p. m. in the last train of cars. I have been unable to receive any report from Generals Duncan or Smith, so am unable to give any details further than above stated, but will communicate with the Department as soon as possible.

I shall probably fall back to Jackson, to prevent the enemy from going up to Vicksburg and coming in rear of Beauregard.

Respectfully, your obedient servant,

M. LOVELL,
Major-General, Commanding.

General S. COOPER,
Adjutant and Inspector General.

P. S.—SIR: I will add, as a postscript to my letter, that, as far as I could see, the river-defense boats, six in number, made a very poor show—want of discipline, system, and training. I had but a few regiments, apart from the miscellaneous and half-armed militia of the city, and think I shall endeavor to collect such men as I can from the various forts in the department and fall back to Jackson, to prevent the enemy, now in possession of the river, from getting in rear of Beauregard, by way of Vicksburg and Jackson Railroad. I write this in great haste and without any facilities or conveniences.

Respectfully,

M. L.

HEADQUARTERS DEPARTMENT NO. 1,
Jackson, Miss., May 27, 1862.

SIR: Herewith I have the honor to inclose my report of events attendant upon the fall of New Orleans; also the reports of Generals Smith and Duncan. Accompanying the latter is a diagram of Forts Jackson and Saint Philip, the reports of Lieutenant-Colonel Higgins and Captain Squires, and a report of the killed and wounded at these points.

Respectfully, your obedient servant,

M. LOVELL,
Major-General, Commanding.

General S. COOPER,
Adjutant and Inspector General, Richmond, Va.

[Inclosure.]

HEADQUARTERS DEPARTMENT NO. 1,
Vicksburg, Miss., May 22, 1862.

SIR: Herewith I have the honor to transmit the reports of Brigadier-Generals Duncan and Smith, with the accompanying documents, of the operations preceding and attendant upon the fall of New Orleans.

The Department is fully aware, from my official correspondence and telegraphic dispatches, of the exact nature of the defenses erected for the protection of that city, consisting, in general terms, of an exterior line of forts and earthworks, intended to prevent the entrance of the armed vessels of the enemy, and an interior line in the immediate vicinity of the city, which was constructed almost entirely with reference to repelling any attack made by land with infantry. Where this line crossed the river below the city it was intended to have a battery of twelve 32 and ten 42 pounders, which it was considered would enable us to drive back any small number of ships that might succeed in passing the obstructions at the forts under the fire of their guns; but whether sufficient or not, no more were to be had, and subsequently, at the earnest request of the naval authorities, I transferred the 42-pounders to the steamers Carondelet and Bienville for service on Lake Pontchartrain in connection with Forts Pike and Macomb.

Immediately after I assumed command of the department, finding that there were no guns of the heaviest caliber, I applied to Richmond, Pensacola, and other points for some 10-inch columbiads and sea-coast mortars, which I considered necessary to the defense of the lower river, but none could be spared, the general impression being that New Orleans would not be attacked by the river, and I was therefore compelled to make the best possible defense with the guns at my disposal. Twelve 42-pounders were sent to Forts Jackson and Saint Philip, together with a large additional quantity of powder, and being convinced that with the guns of inferior caliber mounted there we could not hinder steamers from passing unless they could be detained for some time under the fire of the works, I pushed forward rapidly the construction of a raft which offered a complete obstruction to the passage of vessels up the river, except through a small opening, and then only one at a time. The forts had seventy-five or eighty guns that could be brought successively to bear upon the river; were manned by garrisons of well-trained artillerists, affording a double relief to each gun, and commanded by officers who had no superiors in any service. Under these circumstances, although I feared that the high water in the spring, with the accompanying drift, would carry away the raft, yet every confidence was felt that the river would remain closed until such time as the iron-clad steamers Mississippi and Louisiana could be finished, which I was confidently informed would not be later than February 1.

The first raft constructed was not carried away by the high water and drift until the latter part of February; but with funds placed at my disposal by the citizens of New Orleans another was placed in position in March by the energetic labors of Colonel Higgins and others, and the position was again temporarily secure. No heavy guns had yet been received, although strenuous applications were made by me to get some from Pensacola when that place was abandoned. The general impression of all those to whom I applied was that the largest guns should be placed above New Orleans, not below (although I had notified the Department on March 22 that, in my judgment, the fleet only awaited the arrival of the mortar vessels to attempt to pass up the river from below). By means, however, of an energetic and persevering officer, Maj. W. P. Duncan, commissary of subsistence, three 10-inch columbiads and five mortars were finally procured and brought over just in time to be put up as the firing commenced.

Thinking that the enemy's troops at Isle Breton were intended to land at quarantine and act in the rear of Fort Saint Philip, I ordered Colonel Szymanski's regiment of ninety-days' men, armed with shot-guns, to that point as a protection. I had likewise organized two companies of sharpshooters and swamp-hunters, under Captains Mullen and Lartigue, which were sent down for operation upon the enemy's vessels from the banks of the river; but the high water, keeping the men day and night nearly waist deep in the water, soon compelled them to abandon their positions.

I will here state that every Confederate soldier in New Orleans, with the exception of one company, had been ordered to Corinth, to join General Beauregard in March, and the city was only garrisoned by about 3,000 ninety-day troops, called out by the governor at my request, of whom about 1,200 had muskets and the remainder shot-guns of an indifferent description.

The river rose rapidly in April and soon drove out Szymanski's regiment, which was removed to the west bank, about 6 miles above Fort Jackson. The whole country became one vast sheet of water, which rose in the forts and covered places heretofore safe from its encroachments.

Under the tremendous pressure of this current and a storm of wind and rain the second raft was broken away on the night of Friday, April 11, two days before the enemy first opened fire. The fourteen vessels of Montgomery's River Defense Expedition had been ordered by the Department, when completed, to be sent up to Memphis and Fort Pillow; but, believing the danger of attack to be greater from below, I detained six of them at New Orleans, of which change the Department was fully advised.

At my suggestion Governor Moore had also fitted up two steamers, which were sent to the forts below the city. A large number of fire rafts were also constructed and towed down, and two small steamers were employed for the special purpose of towing these rafts into position where they could be most effective, so as to leave the armed vessels free to operate against the enemy.

I telegraphed General Beauregard to send down the iron-clad ram Manassas, and when the Secretary of the Navy ordered the steamer Louisiana to be sent also up the river I protested through the War Department, being satisfied that we required more heavy guns below.

She was eventually permitted to go down the river on Sunday, April 20, but not in a condition to use her motive power with effect. It was hoped that, notwithstanding this, she would be able to assume a position below Fort Saint Philip, discovering the location of the mortar boats, and, being herself proof against direct fire, dislodge the enemy with her guns, which were of very heavy caliber. Knowing also that the incessant bombardment kept General Duncan closely confined to Fort Jackson, so that he could give no orders to the river defense steamers, I placed the whole under the control of Captain Mitchell—the armed steamers as well as the tugs intended to tow down the fire rafts.

I will here state that the river-defense fleet proved a failure for the very reasons set forth in my letter to the Department of April 15. Unable to govern themselves, and unwilling to be governed by others, their almost total want of system, vigilance, and discipline rendered them nearly useless and helpless when the enemy finally dashed upon them suddenly on a dark night. I regret very much that the Department did not think it advisable to grant my request to place some competent head in charge of these steamers.

Learning subsequently that the Louisiana was anchored above the forts and that the fire rafts were not sent down, I telegraphed Captain Mitchell, requesting him to attend to it, and afterwards called upon Commodore Whittle and entreated him to order the steamer to take the desired position below the forts. This he declined to do, but telegraphed Captain Mitchell, telling him to "strain a point to place the vessel there if in his judgment it was advisable." No change, however, was made, and on the night of April 23 I went down myself in a steamboat, to urge Captain Mitchell to have the Louisiana anchored in the position indicated, and also to ascertain why the fire rafts were not sent down. A few moments after I arrived the attack commenced, and the enemy succeeded in passing with fourteen ships, as described in General Duncan's report, and the battle of New Orleans, as against ships of war, was over.

I returned at once to the city, narrowly escaping capture, and, giving orders to General Smith, in command of the interior lines, to prepare to make all possible resistance to the enemy's fleet at the earthwork batteries below the city, instructed Colonel Lovell to have several steamers ready to remove, as far as possible, the commissary and ordnance stores, being satisfied that the low developments at Chalmette could offer no protracted resistance to a powerful fleet whose guns, owing to the high water, looked down upon the surface of the country and could sweep away any number of infantry by an enfilading fire. These lines, as before remarked, were intended mainly to repel a land attack, but in a high stage of water were utterly untenable by infantry against guns afloat. It having been reported to me that a sufficient number of desperately bold men could easily be got together to board the enemy's vessels and carry them by assault, I authorized Major James to seize such steamers as might be necessary for his purpose and to attempt it. He called for 1,000 men, by public advertisement, but being able to find but about 100 who would undertake it, he abandoned the project.

On the morning of the 25th the enemy's fleet advanced upon the batteries and opened fire, which was returned with spirit by the troops as long as their powder lasted, but with little apparent effect upon the enemy. The powder intended for this battery of 32-pounders had been transferred by me to the steamer Louisiana a few days before, under the supposition that it would render much better service from her heavy rifles and shell guns than with a battery of light 32-pounders.

For the operations at these works you are respectfully referred to General Smith's report.

The greater portion of the ordnance stores, provisions, and quartermaster's property were sent from the city by rail or steamer, and a portion of the volunteers also took the cars for Camp Moore, 78 miles distant, on the Jackson Railroad. The greater part of the ninety-day troops disbanded and returned to their homes. There were two or three regiments and smaller bodies of men raised for Confederate service in the city at the time, but being entirely without arms of any kind, they could be of no service, and were also ordered to Camp Moore.

I adopted this course, recognizing the perfect absurdity of confronting more than 100 guns afloat of the largest caliber, well manned and served, and looking down upon the city, with less than 3,000 militia, mostly armed with indifferent shot-guns. It would, in my judgment, have been a wanton and criminal waste of the blood of women and children, without the most remote possibility of any good result, for the enemy had only to anchor one of his ships at Kenner to command the Jackson Railroad, and he could have reduced the city to ashes at his leisure, without our being able to make any resistance whatever (or without firing a shot he could have starved the city into a surrender in less than three weeks, as there was not more than eighteen days' food on hand for the population, from which my troops were almost entirely drawn*). Why he did not occupy Kenner and cut off all exit from the city immediately I do not understand. Presuming that he would do so, as a matter of course, I had requested Captains Poindexter and Gwathmey, of the Navy, to have all the steamers ready in Lake Pontchartrain to carry the troops over to Madisonville, whence they could march to Camp Moore. A portion of them were taken over by this route.

Knowing that the enemy would at once seize the Opelousas Railroad, and thus cut off the troops occupying the works on the coast of West Louisiana, I sent orders to the different commanding officers at Forts Livingston, Guion, Quitman, Berwick, and Chène to destroy their guns, and, taking their small-arms, provisions, and ammunition, join me at Camp Moore.

Major Ivey brought away the troops at the two latter forts in a very creditable manner, but those at the other works became demoralized, disbanded, and returned to New Orleans. I gave verbal instructions to Colonel Fuller to have the garrisons of Forts Pike and Macomb, Batteries Bienvenue and Tower Dupré ready to move at a moment's notice, as their posts were dependent on the city for provisions and frequently for water. It was understood that the naval steamers, in connection with other vessels in the lake, should bring away these garrisons when called upon to do so, and after my arrival at Camp Moore orders were given, on the 26th, to go for them, as I had been informed that Forts Jackson and Saint Philip had been surrendered.

Finding that this report was untrue, I immediately countermanded the orders, giving instructions that they should be held until further notice; but before either order could reach Madisonville it was reported to me that the whole command was already at Covington. I advised Captain Poindexter to make his way to Mobile, with his armed steamers; but he concluded to destroy them. We, however, procured from them some of the guns and ordnance stores, which I ordered immediately to Vicksburg, to be put in position there.

* See General Lovell's letter of June 18, 1863, p. 518.

On the 25th Captain Bailey, of the Federal Navy, demanded the surrender of the city, and that the flags should be taken down, and the United States flag be put up over the mint, custom-house, and other public buildings.

To this demand I returned an unqualified refusal, declaring that I would not surrender the city or any portion of my command, but added that, feeling unwilling to subject the city to bombardment, and recognizing the utter impossibility of removing the women and children, I should withdraw my troops and turn it over to the civil authorities.

This I did in compliance with the openly-expressed opinion of all the prominent citizens around me, that it would be a useless waste of blood, without being productive of any beneficial results to the cause for the troops to remain.

Captain Bailey then returned to his ship, under escort through the city (at his own request) of two officers of my staff, Colonel Lovell and Major James, and I then advised the mayor not to surrender the city, nor to allow the flags to be taken down by any of our people, but to leave it to the enemy to take them down himself.

This advice was followed by the city authorities; but the idea being held out, in their subsequent correspondence with the Federal officers, that they were placed in a defenseless condition by the withdrawal of the troops, but for which a different course might be pursued, I promptly telegraphed to Major James, of my staff, then in the city, offering to return at once, with my command, if the citizens felt disposed to resist to the last extremity, and remain with them to the end.

I had deliberately made up my mind that, although such a step would be entirely indefensible in a military point of view, yet, if the people of New Orleans were desirous of signalizing their patriotism and devotion to the cause by the bombardment and burning of their city, I would return with my troops and not leave as long as one brick remained upon another. The only palliation for such an act would be that it would give unmistakable evidence to the world that our people were in deadly earnest.

This determination, plainly expressed in my dispatches to Major James (herewith transmitted, marked A), was read by him to the mayor and also to the city council in the presence of one or more prominent citizens. The opinion was generally and freely expressed by the mayor and others that the troops ought not to return. (See report of Major James, hereunto appended, marked B.)

I went to the city myself, however, on the night of April 28, and, in order that there might be no mistake, made the same proposition in person to the mayor. He said he did not think it advisable for the troops to return; that such a step would only be followed by a useless sacrifice of life without any corresponding benefit, and urged decidedly that it be not done.

I, however, addressed him a letter (herewith appended, marked C), declaring my willingness to return and share a bombardment with them, and waited until the night of the 29th for an answer; but, receiving none in writing, returned to Camp Moore. The same proposition was made by me in the course of the day to several prominent citizens, but was invariably discountenanced by them.

For a week after the withdrawal of the troops I had a number of officers in the city and kept trains running regularly, which brought out a large amount of Government property and stores, as well as those of the State of Louisiana. Nearly everything was brought away except the heavy guns and some property which persons in their flight had destroyed, and everything might have been saved had not persons refused to work for my officers, fearing that they might be subjected to punishment by the enemy. Many also refused to work for Confederate money, which occasioned some delay and difficulty in the removal of stores.

I feel gratified, however, in being able to state that we brought away all the troops that would leave, and, including the property of the State, a greater amount in value than belonged to the Government. What we failed to bring was from inability to get transportation.

In this duty I was mainly assisted by Colonel Lovell, Majors James and Bell, Captain Venable, and Lieutenant McDonald, to whom the Government is greatly indebted for the safety of much valuable property.

It was a source of great distress to me to see the result of months of toil and labor swept away in a few hours; but it was, in my opinion, mainly attributable to the following causes, which I could not by any possibility control:

1st. The want of sufficient number of guns of heavy caliber, which every exertion was made to procure without success.

2d. The unprecedented high water, which swept away the obstructions upon which I mainly relied, in connection with the forts, to prevent the passage of a steam fleet up the river; and

3d. The failure, through inefficiency and want of energy of those who had charge of the construction of the iron-clad steamers Louisiana and Mississippi to have them completed in the time specified so as to supply the place of obstructions; and, finally, the declension of the officers in charge of the Louisiana to allow her, though not entirely ready, to be placed as a battery in the position indicated by General Duncan and myself. On these last points I could only advise and suggest, as they appertained to a separate and independent department, over which I had no control whatever. (See letter of Major James, hereunto appended, marked D.)

Opened fire on April 13, which was kept up at intervals for five days, when the mortars opened, and from that time, with but a single intermission of a few hours, a bombardment was kept up for seven days and nights, which for great rapidity and wonderful accuracy of range has no parallel. More than 25,000 shells were thrown, of which not less than one-third fell within the limits of Fort Jackson; yet the garrisons held out, although wet, without change of clothing, and exhausted for want of rest and regular food, with a heroic endurance which is beyond all praise. That the enemy succeeded in passing a large portion of his fleet by the flats on a dark night, under a heavy fire, is due to no fault of the garrisons of the forts. They did their whole duty nobly and heroically, and had they been seconded as they should have been by the defenses afloat, we should not have had to record the fall of New Orleans.

To the officers of my staff, who underwent months of severe and arduous labor collecting supplies, creating resources, with the most limited means, and preparing all sorts of materials and munitions of war by ingenious make-shifts, I return my warmest thanks. Left in the city with a small force of badly-armed militia, all opportunity for distinction or glory was cut off, yet they never flagged in their zeal and devotion to the cause. When the country knows all that was done and in what disadvantage it was accomplished, I feel confident that its verdict will do ample justice to those who shared equally in the labors of preparation, while they were denied the glory of taking part in the defense.

The battle for the defense of New Orleans was fought and lost at Forts Jackson and Saint Philip.

The extraordinary and remarkable conduct of the garrisons of these forts, in breaking out in open mutiny after covering themselves with glory by their heroic defense, is one of those strange anomalies for which I do not pretend to account. The facts are recorded and speak for themselves. The causes will probably never be known in full.

For the detailed accounts of the bombardment of the forts and the engagements at the time of the passage of the fleets by them and the batteries at Chalmette, you are respectfully referred to the accompanying reports of Generals Duncan and Smith. There were no batteries except at these two points, for the reason that no guns could be procured to place in them.

I had frequent occasion to regret that it was found impossible to give me control of the defenses afloat as well as ashore. A single controlling head might have made all the resources more available and efficient in working out the desired results.

Very respectfully, your obedient servant,

M. LOVELL,
Major-General, Commanding.

General S. COOPER,
Adjutant and Inspector General C. S. Army, Richmond, Va.

RICHMOND, VA., *June* 18, 1863.

SIR: Observing several errors in the printed copy of my report of the evacuation of New Orleans, I compared it with the copy on file in your office and the latter with the original in my possession. I find an omission in the office copy, and have the honor to request that the proper alteration may be made, as without it the pertinency of the succeeding sentence is not apparent.

The following words were omitted after the word "whatever," on page 8, line 20, viz, "or without firing a shot he could have starved the city into a surrender in less than three weeks, as there was not more than eighteen days' food on hand for the population, from which my troops were almost entirely drawn."*

By giving this attention you will much oblige, respectfully, your obedient servant,

M. LOVELL,
Major-General, &c.

General S. COOPER,
Adjutant and Inspector General.

[Inclosure A.]

CAMP MOORE, LA., *April* 28, 1862.

If the people are willing to stand the result, I will bring 4,500 men down as soon as I can give them arms and powder, and stay as long as a brick remains. It is their interest I am endeavoring to consult, not the safety of my men. I have nothing but infantry and two batteries of field artillery, which would be of no use against ships. I will come down myself if they wish it, and bring the men along as fast as ready. They are newly-raised regiments, and are being now armed and equipped, as you know. Can begin to bring them down to-morrow if that is the

*Correction made in the text.

desire of the citizens. Shall I come down myself to-night? Will do so if I can be of any assistance, and leave General Smith to complete the organization, and bring down the five regiments when ready. The citizens must decide as to the consequences. I will come, if it is wished, cheerfully.

M. LOVELL,
Major-General, Commanding.

Major JAMES,
New Orleans, La.

CAMP MOORE, LA., *April* 28, 1862.

I shall start down myself, with an aide, now, and am perfectly ready, if it is the desire of the city, to hold it to the end. It is for them to say, not me.

M. LOVELL,
Major-General, Commanding.

Major JAMES,
New Orleans, La.

[Inclosure B.]

JACKSON, MISS., *May* 24, 1862.

SIR: I have the honor to report that while I was in the city of New Orleans, on April 27, executing your orders, to assist in removing the Government and State property, and while the negotiations were going on between the city authorities and the Federal officers for the surrender, I was informed that the nature of the replies to the naval commander was such as to throw some censure upon yourself for leaving them, as the mayor styled it, without military protection. I deemed it my duty to advise you of this immediately, the result of which was the inclosed dispatches from you, offering to return with your troops and afford them all the protection in your power, but that the responsibilty of any results that might ensue must rest upon the citizens themselves.

I read your dispatches to the city council, which was then in session, in the presence of Mr. Pierre Soulé, who happened to be there at the time. That gentleman, who seemed to speak for the mayor and council, most emphatically declared that you ought not to return with your troops, as did also the mayor and members of the council. Several of them, however, declared that they would be glad to have you return alone and see matters for yourself, to which effect I telegraphed you.

You came to the city that evening with a single aide-de-camp and went with me to the mayor's house, where you, in my presence, told him that the citizens of New Orleans should have no cause to say that they were obliged to submit for want of military protection; that you were ready and willing to bring your whole command into the city within twenty-four hours and undergo a bombardment with them if that was their desire; that you had withdrawn to enable the citizens to decide the matter for themselves, as it was they and not you who had their families and property at stake. In reply, the mayor earnestly declined your offer, stating that you had done all in your power, and that it would be a useless waste of life to bring the troops into the city. He also urged you by all means to retire from the city for your own safety, and subsequently asked me to persuade you to leave as soon as possible, as he would be hung if the United States authorities found you were at his house.

Very respectfully, general, your obedient servant,

S. L. JAMES,
Volunteer Aide-de-Camp.

General MANSFIELD LOVELL.

[Inclosure C.]

HEADQUARTERS DEPARTMENT NO. 1,
New Orleans, La., April 29, 1862.

SIR: When the enemy, having succeeded in passing our defenses on the river with his fleet, anchored abreast the city, it was apparent that the infantry troops under my command could offer no effectual resistance, and their presence would only serve as a pretext and a justification for them to open their guns upon a city crowded with women and children, whom it was impossible to remove.

Under these circumstances I determined at once to withdraw my troops and leave it to the citizens themselves to agree upon the course of action to be pursued in relation to the welfare of their families and property.

I now beg leave to say that, if it is the determination of the people of the city to hold it at any and all hazards, I will return with my troops and share the danger with them. That my return will be followed by bombardment, is in my opinion certain, but if that is the conclusion come to, I will afford all the protection in my power.

Very respectfully, your obedient servant,

M. LOVELL,
Major-General, Commanding.

Hon. JOHN T. MUNROE,
Mayor of New Orleans.

[Inclosure D.]

CAMP MOORE, LA., *April 30, 1862.*

GENERAL: At your request, upon my return from Forts Jackson and Saint Philip, I accompanied you to call upon Commodore [W. C.] Whittle, of the Navy, at his headquarters in New Orleans, for the purpose of getting that officer, if possible, to place the iron-clad gunboat Louisiana in a position below Forts Jackson and Saint Philip from which she could enfilade the position of the enemy's mortar fleet and drive them from it, thereby relieving the forts, for a time at least, from the heavy bombardment then going on, which would allow Brigadier-General Duncan to make such repairs as were necessary, and, what was equally necessary, give the garrisons some rest.

The position designated for the vessel to be placed in was in an eddy upon the Fort Saint Philip side of the river, and under the protection of the guns of both forts, and entirely out of the line of the bombardment, and it would require a change of position of the mortar fleet to enable them to strike the vessel with shell, if she could have been struck at all.

All these facts were fully explained by yourself to Commodore Whittle, and he was requested by you by all means to place the vessel in question in said position, even if she was lost, as the maintaining the position then held by your troops in the forts, without this assistance, was merely a question of time.

To this earnest appeal upon your part Commodore Whittle telegraphed to Commander [J. K.] Mitchell, of the fleet stationed just above the forts, to strain a point, if, in his judgment, it was necessary, to comply with your request, and place the Louisiana in the position before spoken of. As the result shows, the request of Commodore Whittle to Commander Mitchell was not complied with.

I make this statement voluntarily, in order that, if ever the question of the defenses of New Orleans should arise, you can have every evidence to show that it was not certainly the want of proper exertions on the part of the land forces which caused the fall of New Orleans.

Very respectfully, your obedient servant,

S. L. JAMES,
Volunteer Aide-de-Camp.

General MANSFIELD LOVELL,
Commanding Department No. 1.

No. 4.

Report of Brig. Gen. Johnson K. Duncan, C. S. Army, of the bombardment and surrender of Forts Jackson and Saint Philip.

NEW ORLEANS, LA., *April* 30, 1862.

MAJOR: I have the honor to submit the following report of the bombardment of Forts Jackson and Saint Philip, La., from April 16 to 24:

About March 27 I was informed by Lieut. Col. E. Higgins, commanding Forts Jackson and Saint Philip, composing a part of the coast defenses under my command, that the enemy's fleet was crossing the bars and entering the Mississippi River in force. In consequence I repaired at once to that post, to assume the general command of the threatened attack upon New Orleans, which I had always anticipated would be made from that quarter.

Upon my arrival I found that Fort Jackson was suffering severely from transpiration and backwater, occasioned by the excessive rise in the river and the continued prevalence of strong easterly winds. Notwithstanding every effort which could be made the water kept daily increasing upon us, partly owing to the sinking of the entire site and to the natural lowness of the country around it, until the parade plain and casemates were very generally submerged to a depth of from 3 to 18 inches. It was with the utmost difficulty, and only then by isolating the magazines and by pumping day and night, that the water could be kept out of them.

As the officers and men were all obliged to live in these open and submerged casemates, they were greatly exposed to discomfort and sickness, as their clothing and feet were always wet. The most of their clothing and blankets, besides, were lost by the fire hereinafter mentioned. Fort Saint Philip, from the same causes, was in a similar condition, but to a lesser extent.

No attention having been previously paid to the repeated requisitions for guns of heavy caliber for these forts, it became necessary, in their present condition, to bring in and mount and to build the platforms for the three 10-inch and three 8-inch columbiads, the rifled 42-pounder, and the five 10-inch sea-coast mortars recently obtained from Pensacola on the evacuation of that place, together with the two rifled 7-inch guns temporarily borrowed from the naval authorities in New Orleans. It was also found necessary to prepare the old water battery to the rear of and below Fort Jackson, which had never been completed, for the reception of a portion of these guns, as well as to construct mortar-proof magazines and shell rooms within the same.

In consequence also of the character of the expected attack by heavy mortars, it was deemed advisable to cover all the main magazines at both forts with sand bags to a considerable depth, to protect them against a vertical fire.

After great exertions, cheerfully made by both officers and men, and by working the garrisons by reliefs night and day, this work was all accomplished by April 13. No sooner had the two rifled 7-inch navy guns been placed in position, however, than orders arrived to dismount one of them immediately, and to send the same to the city at once, to be placed on board of the iron-clad steamer Louisiana. I strongly remonstrated against this removal by telegraph, but was informed, in reply, that the orders were imperative, and that the gun must be sent without fail. It was accordingly sent, but with great difficulty, owing to the overflow and the other causes stated.

The garrisons of both forts were greatly fatigued and worn-out by these labors, performed as they were under pressure and within sight of the enemy and owing to the many discomforts and disadvantages we were laboring under in consequence of high water.

In the mean time I had called upon the general commanding the department for two regiments, to be stationed at the quarantine buildings, 6 miles above the forts, to act as a reserve force and to co-operate with the forts in case of a combined land and water attack. I also asked for Capt. W. G. Mullen's company of scouts and sharpshooters, to be stationed in the woods below Fort Jackson, on the right bank of the river, for the purpose of picking off the officers and men from the enemy's vessels when assuming their several positions of attack.

Captain Mullen's company, of about 125 men, was sent down as requested, and stationed in part in the point of woods below Fort Jackson, and the remainder on the Fort Saint Philip side, opposite the raft obstructing the river.

The Chalmette Regiment, consisting of about 500 men, Colonel Szymanski commanding, was sent to the quarantine. A part of it was stationed there, and company detachments were placed at the heads of the several canals leading from the river into the bays back of the same, to guard against a land force being thrown in launches above us.

Four steamers of the river fleet protected, and to a certain extent made shot-proof, with cotton bulkheads, and prepared with iron prows, to act as rams, viz, the Warrior, Stonewall Jackson, Defiance, and Resolute, commanded by Captains Stephenson, Philips, McCoy, and Hooper, respectively, were sent down to report to and co-operate with me. The steamers Governor Moore and General Quitman, prepared as those before mentioned, and commanded by Capt. B. Kennon and A. Grant, were sent down in a like manner, to co-operate with the forts and ram such vessels of the enemy as might succeed in passing.

The naval authorities also sent down the Confederate States steam ram Manassas, Captain [A. F.] Warley, C. S. Navy, commanding. She was stationed a short distance above Fort Jackson, with her steam up constantly, to act against the enemy as the occasion might offer.

Subsequently, also, Capt. F. B. Renshaw, C. S. Navy, arrived, in command of the Confederate States steamer Jackson.

The raft of logs and chains which had formerly been placed across the river having proven a failure upon the rise in the stream and consequent increase of the velocity of the drift-bearing current, a new obstruction had been placed across the river, opposite Fort Jackson, by Lieut. Col. E. Higgins prior to his assumption of the command of the forts. This consisted of a line of schooners anchored at intervals, with bows up stream, and thoroughly chained together amidships, as well as stem and stern. The rigging, ratlins, and cables were left to trail astern of these schooners, as an additional impediment, to tangle in the propeller wheels of the enemy.

The schooner raft was seriously damaged by the wind-storm on April 10 and 11, which parted the chains, scattered the schooners, and materially affected its character and effectiveness as an obstruction. In addition to the wind, the raft was also much damaged by allowing some of the fire barges to get loose and drift against it, through the carelessness of those having them in charge. A large number of these fire barges were tied to the banks above both forts, ready at all times to be towed into the current and against the enemy, for the double purpose of firing his ships and to light up the river by night to insure the accuracy of our fire.

My instructions to the river fleet, under Captain Stephenson (see attached document A), were to lie in stream above the raft, with such boats as had stern guns, in order to assist the forts with their fire in case the enemy should attempt the passage, as well as to turn in and ram at all hazards all such vessels as might succeed in getting above the raft. He was also required to take entire control of the fire barges (see attached document B), to reconnoiter the enemy above the Head of the Passes, and to keep a watch boat below every night, near the point of woods, to signal the approach of the enemy. The accompanying diagram will illustrate all the points referred to in this report.

The same instructions were given to Captains Kennon and Grant, and upon his arrival Captain Renshaw was duly informed of the arrangements made, in which he promised heartily to co-operate.

While the enemy remained at the Head of the Passes, 22½ miles below the forts, and subsequently, when he came up to the Jump, or Wilder's Bayou, the boats of the river fleet took turns in running down and watching his movements. For a few nights, also, at this time one of them was kept below as a guard boat. We had telegraphic communication, besides, down to within half a mile of the Jump, 9 miles below the forts, which, together with scouts operating in the bays to the east and west of the river in skiffs and pirogues, kept us duly posted meanwhile of the enemy's movements below as far down as the Southwest Pass.

The enemy was not idle in the interim. His larger vessels were worked over the Southwest Bar after failing to make an entrance at Pass à l'Outre, and the mortar fleet was brought up as far as the Southwest Pilot Station, where the mortars were scaled and afterward tested. From seven to thirteen steam sloops of war and gunboats were constantly kept at the Head of the Passes or at the Jump, to cover his operations below and to prevent our observing his movements by way of the river. By gradual and regular approaches he carefully closed upon the forts day by day, and opened the attack as hereinafter detailed.

April 9.—One of our reconnoitering steamers was chased and followed up by two of the enemy's gunboats as far as the point of woods below Fort Jackson, but was soon forced to retire by a few shots from our batteries. This was his first reconnaissance, and our fire was not returned.

April 13.—Several of the hostile gunboats again came up to make observations. They would occasionally show themselves singly or in pairs above the point of woods and exchange a few shots with the forts and then retire again behind the point. Our sharpshooters obtained a few shots on this occasion, but with very partial success, owing to the lowness of the country and the extreme rise in the river. Many of the men were up to their waists in water, and in consequence sickness prevailed among them and unfitted them for duty. The enemy spent the principal part of the day in firing grape and canister and in shelling the woods to drive them out. This was repeated the following day, the enemy not coming within range or sight of the forts, but confining himself to shelling the woods below. The sharpshooters were all driven out by this second day's firing. Our telegraphic communication below was also broken up, as the wires were removed and many of the posts cut and torn down by the enemy.

There being no other point above or below where the sharpshooters could profitably act in that capacity, and as many of them were unfit for duty from exposure, I deemed it advisable to dispense with their services and send them to the city, which was accordingly done.

It being of the highest importance, however, to keep up the telegraphic connection below, Lieut. T. J. Royster, company of sappers and miners Twenty-second Regiment Louisiana Volunteers, volunteered his services, with 15 men of his company, to act as sharpshooters in pirogues, and cover the operator in repairing the line and re-establishing the connection with the forts above as well as to annoy the enemy. This also failed from the great difficulty of managing the pirogues effectively in the dense undergrowth of the swampy woods below, and the telegraph and the sharpshooters had to be abandoned in consequence.

April 15.—The enemy brought up his whole fleet, extending the same from the Head of the Passes to the point of woods below the forts.

Orders were repeatedly given to Captain Stephenson, of the river fleet, to cause the fire barges to be sent down nightly upon the enemy; but every attempt seemed to prove a perfect abortion, the barges being cut adrift too soon, so that they drifted against the banks directly under the forts, firing our wharves and lighting us up, but obscuring the position of the enemy. In consequence, I turned the control of them, as well as the boats employed to tow them into the stream, over to Captain Renshaw, the senior naval officer present. I also directed Captains Kennon and Grant to report to him for orders, as I found great difficulty in communicating with or controlling the vessels afloat, and directed Captain Stephenson, with his four boats, to co-operate with Captain Renshaw in every possible way. These boats of the river fleet, it seemed, could not be turned over directly to the immediate command of naval officers, owing to certain conditions imposed by the Navy Department.

April 16.—From 7.30 a. m. the enemy's gunboats came around the point repeatedly for observation, but were invariably forced to retire by our fire. In the mean time he was locating the position of the mortar flotilla, composed of twenty-one schooners, each mounting one 13-inch mortar and other guns, close against the bank on the Fort Jackson side and behind the point of woods.

At 4.15 p. m. the enemy ran out a gunboat and fired upon the fort, under the cover of which two of the mortar-boats were brought out into the stream.

These boats opened fire upon Fort Jackson at 5 p. m., which was continued for an hour and a half, the enemy under our fire retiring behind the point of woods.

April 17.—One fire barge sent down successfully against the enemy at 4 a. m., which drifted in among his vessels and was fired upon by them, creating considerable movement and perturbation.

During the day Captains Renshaw, Beverly Kennon, Grant, Stephenson, and Hooper passed in turns with their boats below the raft, now very much disconnected and scattered, and exchanged a few shots with the hostile gunboats and mortar boats.

Two more abortive attempts were made to send down fire barges against the enemy during the night.

April 18.—At 9 a. m. the enemy opened upon Fort Jackson with his entire mortar fleet of twenty-one vessels and with rifled guns from his gunboats. Fifteen of them were concealed behind the point of woods and the other six hauled out in the stream at an angle with them (see diagram), just at the extreme range of our heaviest guns. Our fire disabled one gunboat and one mortar boat, causing those in the stream to retire behind the cover of the woods. Generally our shots fell short for lack of elevation and in consequence of the inferiority of our powder compared to that of the enemy. Even our nearest gun, a 10-inch sea-coast mortar, would not reach his boats with the heaviest charges.

The enemy ceased firing at 7 p. m., having fired this day 2,997 mortar shells.

The quarters in the bastions were fired and burned down early in the day, as well as all the quarters immediately without the fort. The citadel was set on fire and extinguished several times during the first part of the day, but later it became impossible to put out the flames, so that when the enemy ceased firing it was one burning mass, greatly endangering the magazines, which at one time were reported to be on fire. Many of the men and most of the officers lost their bedding and clothing by these fires, which greatly added to the discomforts of the overflow. The mortar fire was accurate and terrible, many of the shells falling everywhere within the fort and disabling some of our best guns.

I endeavored to get the naval forces to carry down fire barges against the enemy so as to disperse them, but they were all let go above the raft, and with such a lack of judgment that they only lodged under the forts and did not reach the enemy. (See attached document C.)

None of the boats acted as a guard boat below the raft at night, so that, in consequence, the enemy sent up two launches to examine the character of the raft obstructing the river.

April 19.—The mortar fleet again opened at 6 a. m. and the fire was constantly kept up throughout the day. Gunboats constantly came above the point during the day to engage the forts, but were as constantly driven back by our fire. One of them we crippled, which was towed behind the point of woods. The enemy's fire was excellent, a large proportion of his shells falling within Fort Jackson. The terreplein, parade plain, parapets, and platforms were very much cut up, as well as much damage done to the casemates. The magazines were considerably threatened, and one shell passed through into the casemate containing fixed ammunition. One 10-inch and one 8-inch columbiad, one 32 and one 24 pounder, and one 10-inch siege-mortar were disabled in the main work, also two rifled 32-pounders in the water battery. Bombardment continued very regularly and accurately all night. Failures again were made in sending down fire barges.

April 20.—Some rain in the morning. Bombardment constant throughout the day, with occasional shots from the gunboats around the point. Wind very high. No fire barges sent down to light up the river or distract the attention of the enemy at night. In consequence, between 11 and 12 p. m., under cover of the heaviest shelling during the bombardment thus far, one of the enemy's gunboats came up in the darkness and attempted to cut the chains of the raft and drag off the schooners. A heavy fire was opened upon her, which caused her to retire, but not until she had partially accomplished her purpose. The raft after this could not be regarded as an obstruction. The fire continued uninterruptedly all night.

April 21.—Firing continued all day and night without interruption. Several guns were disabled. Disabled guns were repaired as far as practicable as often as accidents happened to them or their platforms. Fort Jackson by this time was in need of extensive repairs almost everywhere, and it was with extreme pleasure that we learned of the arrival during the night of the iron-clad steamer Louisiana, under the cover of whose heavy guns we expected to make the necessary repairs.

April 22.—By the direction of the major-general commanding the department everything afloat, including the tow-boats and the entire control of the fire barges, was turned over to Capt. John K. Mitchell, C. S. Navy, commanding the Confederate States naval forces Lower Mississippi River. I also gave Captain Mitchell 150 of our best men from Forts Jackson and Saint Philip, under Lieutenants Dixon and Gandy and Captain Ryan, to serve a portion of the guns of the Louisiana and to act as sharpshooters on the same vessel.

In an interview with Captain Mitchell, on the morning of this date, I learned that the motive power of the Louisiana was not likely to be completed within any reasonable time, and that in consequence it was not within the range of probabilities that she could be regarded as an aggressive steamer or that she could be brought into the pending action in that character. As an iron-clad invulnerable floating battery, with sixteen guns of the heaviest caliber, however, she was then as complete as she would ever be.

Fort Jackson had already undergone and was still subjected to a terrible fire of 13-inch mortar shells, which it was necessary to relieve at once to prevent the disabling of all the best guns at that fort, and, although Fort Saint Philip partially opened out the point of woods concealing the enemy and gallantly attempted to dislodge him or draw his fire, he nevertheless doggedly persisted in his one main object of battering Fort Jackson. Under these circumstances I considered that the Louisiana could only be regarded as a battery, and that her best possible position would be below the raft, close in on the Fort Saint Philip shore, where her fire could dislodge the mortar boats from behind the point of woods and give sufficient respite to Fort Jackson to repair *in extenso*. This position (X on the accompanying diagram) would give us three direct cross-fires upon the enemy's approaches and at the same time insure the Louisiana from a direct assault, as she would be immediately under the guns of both forts. Accordingly, I earnestly and strongly urged these views upon Captain Mitchell in a letter of this date (copy lost), but without avail, as will be seen by his reply, attached as document D.

Being so deeply impressed myself with the importance of this position for the Louisiana and of the necessity of prompt action in order to insure the success of the impending struggle, I again urged this subject upon Captain Mitchell, during the latter part of the same day, as absolutely indispensable and imperative to the safety of New Orleans and to the control of the Lower Mississippi. My efforts were ineffectual to get him to move the boat from her original position above the forts. His reply is attached as document E, in which he is sustained by all the naval officers present having the command of vessels.

I also addressed him two other notes through the day—one in regard to sending fire barges against the enemy and the other relative to keeping a vigilant lookout from all his vessels, and asking for co-operation should the enemy attempt to pass during the night. (See attached document F.)

Bombardment continued throughout the day and night, being at times very heavy. During the day our fire was principally confined to shelling the point of woods from both forts, and apparently with good results, as the mortar fire was slackened towards evening. The casemates were very much cut up by the enemy's fire, which was increased at night.

There was little or no success in sending down fire barges as usual, owing in part to the condition of the tow-boats Mosher, Music, and Belle Algerine, in charge of the same, explained by attached document G. This does not excuse the neglect, however, as there were six boats of the river fleet available for this service, independent of those alluded to, and fire barges were plentiful.

April 23.—The day broke warm, clear, and cloudless. No immediate relief being looked for from our fleet, the entire command was turned out to repair damages under a very heavy fire of the enemy.

The bombardment continued without intermission throughout the day, but slackened off about 12 m., at which hour there was every indication of an exhaustion on the part of the mortar flotilla; hence it became evident that the tactics of the enemy would necessarily be changed into an attack with broadsides by his larger vessels. In consequence, these views were laid before Captain Mitchell, and he was again urged to place the Louisiana at the point before mentioned, below the raft and near the Fort Saint Philip bank of the river, to meet the emergency. (See attached document H.) Captain Mitchell's reply is attached, in documents E, I, J, and K, wherein he positively declines again to assume the only position which offered us every possible chance of success, and Captains [Chas. F.] McIntosh, [Thomas B.] Huger, and Warley sustain Captain Mitchell in his views of the case.

Just before sundown, under a very heavy mortar fire, the enemy sent up a small boat, and a series of white flags were planted on the Fort Saint Philip bank of the river, commencing about 350 yards above the lone tree upon that shore. (See diagram.)

This confirmed my previous views of an early and different attack from the usual mortar bombardment, especially as I presumed that these flags indicated the positions to be taken up by the several vessels in their new line of operations.

As nothing was to be expected from the Louisiana after the correspondence during the day, I could only inform Captain Mitchell of this new movement of the enemy (see attached document L), and particularly impress upon him the necessity of keeping the river well lit up with fire barges, to act as an impediment to the enemy and assist the accuracy of our fire in a night attack.

Lieutenant [Geo. S.] Shryock, C. S. Navy (Captain Mitchell's aide), came on shore about 9 p. m. to inform me that the Louisiana would be ready for service by the next evening—the evening of the 24th. I informed him that time was everything to us and that to-morrow would in all probability prove too late. Lieutenant-Colonel Higgins warmly seconded my opinion, and warned Lieutenant Shryock that the final battle was imminent within a few hours.

In regard to lighting the river, Lieutenant Shryock stated that fire barges would be regularly sent down throughout the night every two hours, and as none had been sent up to that hour (9.30 p. m.), he left, informing me that this matter would be attended to as soon as he arrived on board. To my utter surprise not one single fire barge was sent down the river, notwithstanding, at any hour of this night. It was impossible for us to send them down, as everything afloat had been turned over to Captain Mitchell, by order of the major-general commanding, and the fire barges and the boats to tow them into the stream were exclusively under his control. In consequence of this criminal neglect the river remained in complete darkness throughout the entire night. The bombardment continued all night and grew furious towards morning.

April 24.—At 3.30 a. m. the larger vessels of the enemy were observed in motion, and, as we presumed, to take up the positions indicated by the small flags planted by them on the previous evening. I then made my last and final appeal to Captain Mitchell, a copy of which is attached as document M.

The Louisiana was still in her old position above Fort Saint Philip, surrounded by her tenders, on board of which was the majority of her cannoneers and crew, and the other boats of the fleet were generally at anchor above her, excepting the Jackson, Captain Renshaw, C. S. Navy, commanding, which had been sent the day before at my suggestion to prevent the landing of forces through the canals above.

The McRae lay near and above the Louisiana, and the steam ram Manassas, with her tender, remained in her constant position above Fort Jackson, both with steam up and ready for immediate action.

The enemy evidently anticipated a strong demonstration to be made against him with fire barges. Finding, upon his approach, however, that no such demonstration was made, and that the only resistance offered to his passage was the expected fire of the forts (the broken and scattered raft being then no obstacle), I am satisfied that he was suddenly inspired for the first time to run the gauntlet at all hazards, although not a part of his original design. Be this as it may, a rapid rush was made by him in column of twos *en échelon*, so as not to interfere with each other's broadsides.

The mortar fire upon Fort Jackson was furiously increased, and in dashing by each vessel delivered broadside after broadside of shot, shell, grape, canister, and spherical case to drive the men from our guns.

Both the officers and men stood up manfully under this galling and fearful hail, and the batteries of both forts were promptly opened at their longest range with shot, shell, hot shot, and a little grape, and most gallantly and rapidly fought until the enemy succeeded in getting above and beyond our range.

The absence of light on the river, together with the smoke of the guns, made the obscurity so intense, that scarcely a vessel was visible, and in consequence the gunners were obliged to govern their firing entirely by the flashes of the enemy's guns.

I am fully satisfied that the enemy's dash was successful mainly owing to the cover of darkness, as a frigate and several gunboats were forced to retire as day was breaking. Similar results had attended every previous attempt made by the enemy to pass or to reconnoiter when we had sufficient light to fire with accuracy and effect.

The passage by was of short duration, having been accomplished between 3.30 a. m. and daylight, under a very rapid and heavy pressure of steam.

Of the part taken in this action by the Louisiana, Manassas, and other vessels comprising the co-operative naval forces, I cannot speak with any degree of certainty, excepting that the Louisiana is reported to have fired but twelve shots during the engagement; but to the heroic and gallant manner in which Captain Huger handled and fought the McRae we can all bear evidence.

The Defiance, Captain McCoy commanding, was the only vessel saved out of the river fleet.

Shortly after daylight the Manassas was observed drifting down by the forts. She had been abandoned and fired, and was evidently in a sinking condition.

The McRae was considerably cut up in this action by shot and grape.

The Resolute was run on shore about a mile above the forts, where she hoisted a white flag, but by the prompt action of the McRae she was prevented from falling into the hands of the enemy. She was subsequently wrecked and burned.

The Warrior was run ashore and fired on the point just above Fort Saint Philip.

Nothing was known by us of the movements of the Stonewall Jackson, the Governor Moore, or the General Quitman.

The steamers Mosher, Music, and Belle Algerine, in charge of the fire barges, were all destroyed. So also was the Star.

The heroic courage displayed by the officers and men at both forts was deserving of a better success, especially after the fortitude which they constantly exhibited through the long tedium of a protracted bombardment, unsurpassed for its terrible accuracy, constancy, and fury.

Thirteen of the enemy's vessels out of twenty-three succeeded in getting by, viz: The Hartford, Pensacola, Richmond, Brooklyn, Mississippi, Oneida, Iroquois, Cayuga, Wissahickon, Sciota, Kineo, Katahdin, and Pinola.

In addition to the foregoing and to the Varuna and such other vessels as were sunk, there were 6 gunboats and 1 frigate engaged in this action besides the mortar flotilla. Heavy chains were flaked along the sides of the most of these vessels as an iron-proof protection.

The extent of the damage which was done to the enemy we had no means of ascertaining.

The vessels which passed all came to an anchor at or below the quarantine, 6 miles above the forts, where they remained until about 10 a. m., when they all passed slowly up the river, with the exception of two gunboats, left at the quarantine as a guard.

Shortly after the fleet above got under way a gunboat from below made her appearance with a flag of truce, and verbally demanded the surrender of the forts in the name of Commander D. D. Porter, U. S. Navy, commanding the mortar flotilla, under the penalty of reopening the bombardment (which had ceased shortly after the passage) in case of refusal.

The demand was rejected, and the bombardment was reopened about 12 m. It continued until near sundown, when it ceased altogether. The entire mortar fleet and all the other vessels except six gunboats then got under way, and passed down the river and out of sight under full steam and sail. A vigilant lookout was kept up above and below during the night, but all remained quiet. So long as the mortar fleet remained below, the position wherein the Louisiana could render the greatest assistance to the forts was the one below Fort Saint Philip, hereinbefore mentioned, where the fire of her batteries could dislodge the enemy from behind the point of woods.

After the mortar fleet had left, however, and when the enemy had got in force above the forts, the question was materially changed, in consequence of the fact that all of our heavy guns at both forts had been mounted to bear upon the lower approaches and not on those above. The most effective position which the Louisiana could then take as a battery was in the fight above Fort Jackson, where her guns could protect our rear and sweep the long reach of river above towards the quarantine. This would still insure her safety, as she would be under the guns of both forts. This is evident by a reference to the point (XX) on the diagram.*

In several personal interviews and by correspondence with Captain Mitchell, on this date (see attached documents N, O, P, Q, and R), I requested him during the morning of the 24th, while the mortar fleet was below, to place the Louisiana below the raft and dislodge it; and later in the day, when the mortar fire was nearly exhausted, to place her in the position (XX) above Fort Jackson, to assist in repelling an attack from the vessels above.

During the day she was in an unfit condition to assume either position, for the reasons given by Captain Mitchell in his letters to me.

The intoxicated volunteers referred to were none of my men, nor did they get their liquor at the forts, as there was none on hand there during the bombardment excepting the small supplies of hospital stores in the medical department.

April 25.—No attack attempted during the day by the enemy either from above or below. The gunboats from the quarantine above and from the point of woods below occasionally showed themselves for observation, but without firing.

During the day all the principal guns that would admit of it at both forts were prepared at once so as to traverse in a full circle and bear above or below, as necessity might require. Some of the 24-pounder barbette guns at Fort Jackson were also replaced by guns of heavier caliber to bear on the river above.

Permission was granted by the enemy to the Confederate States steamer McRae to proceed to New Orleans under a flag of truce with the wounded. Availing ourselves of the offer of Captain Mitchell, the seriously wounded of both forts were sent on board of her. As it was late when the wounded were all gotten on board, the McRae did not get off until the next morning.

Still failed during the day in getting Captain Mitchell to place the Louisiana in the bight above Fort Jackson, where she could act against the enemy from above.

One of the raft schooners was burned during the night to light the river, and all remained quiet.

April 26.—A gunboat, with a white flag, dropped down from the quarantine to escort the McRae on her mission. The McRae did not return again to the forts.

Four of the enemy's steamers were in sight at the quarantine at dawn. A gunboat occasionally showed herself below to reconnoiter.

In the direction of Bird Island, and back of the salt-works, a large steam frigate and an ordinary river steamer appeared in sight, the latter working her way up the bay behind Fort Saint Philip, apparently towards the quarantine.

During the day Captain Mitchell communicated with the enemy above under a flag of truce, and learned that the city had surrendered, and that the Confederate States steam ram Mississippi had been burned by our authorities. The wreck of the floating dock or battery drifted by the forts about 4 p. m.

The Louisiana was not placed in the position required of her during the day, Captain Mitchell promising to put her there the next day, the 27th. Another raft schooner burned for light, and all quiet during the night. No shots exchanged during the day.

April 27.—At daylight the steamer which had been observed the day

---

* See p. 546.

before working her way up in the back bays was in view, immediately in the rear of Fort Saint Philip, and near the mouth of Fort Bayou. A frigate and five other vessels were also in sight towards Bird Island, one of which was seen working her way up the bay. From ten to thirteen launches were visible near the boat back of Fort Saint Philip, by means of which troops were being landed at the quarantine above us.

About 12 m. one of the enemy's gunboats from below made her appearance under a flag of truce, bearing a written demand for the surrender of the forts, signed by Commander David D. Porter, U. S. Navy, commanding mortar flotilla. (See attached document S.) The forts refused to surrender. (See attached document T.)

About 4 p. m. the French man-of-war Milan, Captain Clouet, commanding, passed up to the city, after asking and obtaining permission of the forts to do so. The position of the Louisiana still remained unchanged.

So far, throughout the entire bombardment and final action, the spirit of the troops was cheerful, confident, and courageous. They were mostly foreign enlistments, without any great interests at stake in the ultimate success of the revolution. A reaction set in among them during the lull of the 25th, 26th, and 27th, when there was no other excitement to arouse them than the fatigue duty of repairing our damages and when the rumor was current that the city had surrendered and was then in the hands of the enemy.

No reply had been received from the city to my dispatches sent by couriers on the 24th and 25th, by means of which I could reassure them. They were still obedient, but not buoyant and cheerful. In consequence, I endeavored to revive their courage and patriotism by publishing an order to both garrisons, attached hereto as document U.

I regret to state that it did not produce the desired effect. Everything remained quiet, however, until midnight, when the garrison of Fort Jackson revolted in mass; seized upon the guard and posterns; reversed the field pieces commanding the gates, and commenced to spike the guns, while many of the men were leaving the fort in the mean time under arms. All this occurred as suddenly as it was unexpected. The men were mostly drawn up under arms and positively refused to fight any longer, besides endeavoring by force to bring over the Saint Mary's Cannoneers and such other few men as remained true to their cause and country.

The mutineers stated that the officers intended to hold out as long as possible, or while the provisions lasted, and then blow up the forts and everything in them; that the city had surrendered, and that there was no further use in fighting; that the enemy were about to attack by land and water on three sides at once, and that a longer defense would only prove a butchery. Every endeavor was made by the officers to repress the revolt and to bring the men to reason and order, but without avail. Officers upon the ramparts were fired upon by the mutineers in attempting to put a stop to the spiking of the guns.

I am greatly indebted to the Rev. Father Nachon for his efforts to quell the mutineers, through some of whom he learned that the revolt had been discussed among them for two days, and yet there was no one man among them true enough to communicate the fact to his officers. Signals also were said to have been passed between the forts during the night and while the mutiny was at its height. Being so general among the men, the officers were helpless and powerless to act. Under these circumstances there was but one course left, viz, to let those men go who wished to leave the fort, in order to see the number left and to ascertain what reliance could be placed upon them. About one-half of the garrison left immediately, including men from every company excepting the Saint Mary's Cannoneers, volunteers and regulars, non-commissioned officers and privates, and among them many of the very men who had stood last and best to their guns throughout the protracted bombardment and the final action when the enemy passed. It was soon evident that there was no further fight in the men remaining behind; that they were completely demoralized, and that no faith or reliance could be placed in the broken detachments of companies left in the forts.

In the mean time we were totally ignorant of the condition of affairs at Fort Saint Philip, and as all our small boats had been carried away by the mutineers, we could not communicate with that fort until the next morning. As the next attack upon the forts was likely to be a combined operation by land and water, and as Fort Saint Philip was the point most threatened, from the nature of the country around it and from the character of the work itself, with narrow and shallow ditches, and but little relief to the main work, it was self-evident that no reduction could be made in its garrison to strengthen that of Fort Jackson, even if all the men there remained true. In fact, two additional regiments had been asked for at the quarantine in anticipation of such an attack, to act as a reserve to strengthen the garrisons of both forts.

With the enemy above and below us, it will be apparent at once to any one at all familiar with the surrounding country that there was no chance of destroying the public property, blowing up the forts, and escaping with the remaining troops. Under all these humiliating circumstances there seemed to be but one course open to us, viz, to await the approach of daylight, communicate then with the gunboats of the mortar flotilla below under a flag of truce, and negotiate for a surrender under the terms offered us by Commander Porter on the 26th instant, and which had previously been declined.

April 28.—A small boat was procured and Lieutenant Morse, post adjutant, sent over to convey the condition of affairs at Fort Saint Philip, as well as to Captain Mitchell, on the Louisiana. Captain Mitchell and Lieutenant Shryock, C. S. Navy, came on shore and discussed the whole question, after which they left, remarking that they would go on board and endeavor to attack the enemy above, at the quarantine, notwithstanding that reasons had been given from time to time for not moving this vessel into her proper position, only a few hundred yards distant.

Captains Squires and Bond, Louisiana Artillery, and Lieutenant Dixon, commanding the company of Confederate States regular recruits, came on shore shortly afterwards from Fort Saint Philip, and concurred with us that, under the circumstances, we could do nothing else than surrender, as they were not at all confident of the garrison there after the unlooked-for revolt at Fort Jackson, although none of their men had left or openly revolted. For these reasons a flag of truce was sent down to communicate with the enemy below and to carry a written offer of surrender under the terms offered on the 26th instant. (See attached document V.)

This communication brought up the Harriet Lane and three other gunboats opposite the forts, with white flags at the fore, white flags being displayed from the yards of the flag-masts at both forts, while the Confederate flags waved at the mast-heads.

While negotiations were pending on the Harriet Lane, it was reported that the steamer Louisiana, with her guns protruding, and on fire, was drifting down the river towards the fleet. As the wreck in descending kept close into the Fort Saint Philip shore, the chances were taken by the enemy without changing the position of his boats. The guns of the

Louisiana were discharged at random as she floated down, and the boat finally blew up near Fort Saint Philip, scattering its fragments everywhere within and around the fort, killing 1 of our men and wounding 3 or 4 others.

Captain McIntosh, C. S. Navy, who had been severely wounded in the discharge of his duty on the night of the enemy's passage, and who was then lying in a tent at that fort, was nearly killed also.

As far as I could learn, however, the Louisiana was fired prior to the time that the enemy's boats with white flags came to an anchor abreast of the forts to negotiate. She was fired in her first and original position without a change of any kind since her arrival at the forts.

The terms of the capitulation are attached hereto as document W; in addition to which Commander Porter verbally agreed not to haul down the Confederate flag or hoist the Federal until the officers should get away from the forts.

The officers of Fort Jackson and the Saint Mary's Cannoneers left about 4 p. m. for the city, on board of the United States gunboat Kennebec, and arrived on the morning of the 29th in New Orleans. The officers of Fort Saint Philip, were sent up the next day, and all the men subsequently within a few days, as transportation could be furnished, excepting the men who revolted on the night of the 27th, many of whom enlisted with the enemy.

Upon my arrival in the city I found that the enemy's vessels were lying off the town, and that no flag, excepting that of the State of Louisiana, on the city hall, was visible upon the shore. I also learned that Flag-Officer Farragut had directed it to be hauled down and the United States flag hoisted in its stead, upon the penalty of shelling the city within forty-eight hours if the demand was not complied with, and that he had warned the city authorities to remove the women and children within the time specified. I therefore deemed it my duty to call at once upon the mayor at the city hall and inform him of the fate of the forts below, which I did accordingly.

Learning there from one of his aides that the major-general commanding the department was still in the city, I called upon him in person and verbally reported the main incidents of the bombardment, the passage of the enemy, and the capitulation of the forts.

I have the honor to inclose herewith the report of Lieut. Col. E. Higgins, Twenty-second Regiment Louisiana Volunteers, commanding Forts Jackson and Saint Philip, as well as the several reports of Capt. M. T. Squires, Louisiana Artillery, senior officer in charge of Fort Saint Philip, and those of the different company and battery commanders, together with the surgeons' reports of the killed and wounded.

The report of Colonel Szymanski, commanding the Chalmette Regiment at the quarantine, has not been received by me, so that I am unable to report upon his operations.

I fully indorse the just praise bestowed in the inclosed reports upon all the officers at both forts, and warmly return them my thanks. They all distinguished themselves by cool courage, skill, and patriotism throughout the entire bombardment, and by the patient fortitude with which they bore the several trying ordeals of water, fire, and the energetic fury of the enemy's protracted and continuous fire.

I must also bear testimony to the cheerful courage and prompt and willing obedience with which the men performed their duties throughout the bombardment and up to the sad night when they took the rash and disgraceful step of rising against their officers, breaking through all discipline, and leading to such disastrous and fatal consequences. I can charitably account for it only on the grounds of great reaction after the intense physical strain of many weary days and nights of terrible fire. through which they were necessarily subjected to every privation from circumstances beyond our control, but which they had not the moral courage to share and sustain with their officers, all of whom were subjected to the same hardships in every particular.

To Lieut. Col. E. Higgins, commanding the forts, my thanks are especially due for his indefatigable labors in preparing his heavy batteries preparatory to the attack, almost in the face of the enemy, and for the quiet, skillful, and judicious manner in which he caused them to be fought. He was present everywhere, and did his whole duty well and thoroughly.

Capt. M. T. Squires, Louisiana Regiment of Artillery, as senior officer in charge of Fort Saint Philip, under the orders of Lieutenant-Colonel Higgins, commanding, fully sustained every anticipation entertained of his gallantry, skill, and efficiency.

During the first day's bombardment, when Captain Anderson was wounded, my aide-de-camp (Lieut. William M. Bridges, Louisiana Artillery) volunteered to command the two 10 inch columbiads on the main work, and I return him my thanks for the gallant and efficient manner in which he fought them during the rest of the action.

I take great pleasure in making personal mention of my volunteer aides, Capts. William J. Seymour and J. R. Smith, for the valuable assistance which they rendered me at all times.

My thanks are also due to Drs. Bradbury and Foster, who volunteered their services to assist Assist. Surgs. S. Burke and C. D. Lewis at Forts Jackson and Saint Philip, respectively, and most efficiently did they aid in this department. Dr. Bradbury remained at Fort Jackson until its fall, and was paroled. Dr. Foster, at my request, accompanied the wounded soldiers to the city on the Confederate States steamer McRae.

Messrs. Fulda and Stickney and Sergt. J. R. Poindexter, Fourth Mississippi Volunteers, telegraph operators, rendered the most valuable services in keeping open our communication above and below under the most dangerous and difficult circumstances.

Although we have failed in our mission of keeping the enemy's fleet from passing the forts, and have been subjected to the deep humiliation of surrendering the charge intrusted to our keeping to the enemies of our country, I must nevertheless state, in common justice to myself and those under my command, that to the very best of our ability, with the means at our disposal, our whole duty was performed faithfully, honestly, and fearlessly. If all had to be gone through with again, under similar events and circumstances, I know that we should be forced to the same results and consequences.

Great as the disaster is, it is but the sheer result of that lack of cheerful and hearty co-operation from the defenses afloat which we had every right to expect and to the criminal negligence of not lighting up the river at night when the danger was imminent and the movements of the enemy absolutely known almost to the hour of the final attack. Except for the cover afforded by the obscurity of the darkness I shall always remain satisfied that the enemy would never have succeeded in passing Forts Jackson and Saint Philip.

I am, very respectfully, your obedient servant,

J. K. DUNCAN,

Brigadier-General, late Commanding Coast Defenses.

Maj. J. G. PICKETT,

Asst. Adjt. Gen., Department No. 1, Camp Moore, La.

NEW ORLEANS, LA., *May* 13, 1862.

MAJOR: In addition to the foregoing report, I wish to add that upon the arrival of the paroled enlisted men from Forts Jackson and Saint Philip in the city I endeavored, to the best of my ability, to see that they were properly cared for until such time as they could be sent out of town.

As far as it could be done, they were paid in part for the time due, and arrangements were also made through the city authorities and the city safety committee to have them boarded and lodged temporarily, all with the view of preventing them from going over to the enemy through distress and starvation. In this I was very much assisted by Capt. M. T. Squires and First Lieut. L. B. Taylor, Louisiana Regiment of Artillery. Notwithstanding that they were thus amply provided for, scores of them have been daily going over to the enemy and enlisting since, until now there are but a very few left from either fort not in the ranks of the enemy. Although I really did think at the time of the surrender that some few of the men were loyal, the facts which have since come to light have perfectly satisfied me that nearly every man in both forts was thoroughly implicated and concerned in the revolt on the night of April 27, with the exception of the company of Saint Mary's Cannoneers, composed mostly of planters.

Very respectfully, your obedient servant,

J. K. DUNCAN,
Brigadier-General, late Commanding Coast Defenses.

Maj. J. G. PICKETT,
Asst. Adjt. Gen., Department No. 1, *Camp Moore, La.*

[Inclosure A.]

FORTS JACKSON AND SAINT PHILIP, LA.,
April 6, 1862.

CAPTAIN: Keep your boats in constant readiness at all times for the enemy's approach. Should he attack, all of your fleet must be kept above the raft, and such of your boats as have stern guns should lie in the middle of the stream, above the raft and without the field of our fire, and use these guns against the enemy. Should any boat of the enemy by any means get above the raft, you must instantly ram it with determination and vigor at all risks and every sacrifice. All signal mast-head lights should be kept extinguished at night or never hoisted.

Trusting to your known energy and to the great expectations anticipated of the river fleet by your friends, I have every confidence that your whole duty will be thoroughly performed.

Very respectfully, your obedient servant,

J. K. DUNCAN,
Brigadier-General.

Capt. JOHN A. STEPHENSON,
Commanding River Fleet, present.

[Inclosure B.]

HDQRS. FORTS JACKSON AND SAINT PHILIP, LA.,
April 9, 1862.

CAPTAIN: Keep one of your boats constantly below night and day opposite the wooded point, where you can watch the movements of the enemy. Signal us his approach and the number of vessels seen coming up, and give me a copy of the signals for our government at the forts.

I wish you to take the entire control of the fire rafts, and you will be assisted therein by the steamers Star, Algerine, and such other boats as I can procure from the city for the purpose. Your own knowledge of the river and the currents will enable you to set them adrift at such time as your judgment warrants.

Very respectfully, your obedient servant,

J. K. DUNCAN,
Brigadier-General, Commanding Coast Defenses.

Capt. JOHN A. STEPHENSON,
Commanding River Fleet, present.

[Inclosure C.]

GUNBOAT JACKSON, *April* 18, 1862.

DEAR SIR: Yours just received. The fire barge was sent down, as I supposed, by your order. Captain Grant accompanied me to select a proper place to let her go. She was fired by my order, but was not aware that she was too close to the fort; but the eddy current, after firing, probably brought her into close proximity to the fort. I regret the affair was an abortion.

Respectfully,

F. B. RENSHAW,
C. S. Navy.

Colonel HIGGINS.

[Inclosure D.]

CONFEDERATE STATES STEAMER LOUISIANA,
Off Fort Jackson, La., April 22, 1862.

GENERAL: I have the honor to acknowledge the receipt of yours of this date, asking me to place the Louisiana in position below the raft this evening, if possible. This vessel was hurried away from New Orleans before the steam power and batteries were ready for service, without a crew, and in many other respects very incomplete, and this condition of things is but partially remedied now. She is not yet prepared to offer battle to the enemy, but should he attempt to pass the forts we will do all we can to prevent it, and it was for this purpose only that she was placed in position where necessity might force her into action, inadequately prepared as she is at this moment.

We have now at work on board about 50 mechanics as well as her own crew and those from other vessels, doing work essential to the preparation of the vessel for battle. Under these circumstances it would, in my estimation, be hazarding too much to place her under the fire of the enemy. Every effort is being made to prepare her for the relief of Fort Jackson, the condition of which is fully felt by me, and the very moment I can venture to face our enemy with any reasonable chance of success, be assured, general, I will do it, and trust that the result will show you that I am now pursuing the right course.

I am, very respectfully, your obedient servant,

JNO. K. MITCHELL,
Commanding C. S. Naval Forces Lower Mississippi.

General JOHNSON K. DUNCAN,
Commanding Coast Defenses, Fort Jackson, La.

P. S.—The Jackson, with launch No. 3, will go up to the quarantine this afternoon to watch the enemy, as suggested in your note this morning.

Respectfully, &c.,

J. K. M.

[Inclosure E.]

CONFEDERATE STATES STEAMER LOUISIANA,
Near Fort Jackson, La., April 23, 1862.

GENERAL: On the receipt last night of your second communication of yesterday's date, asking me to place this vessel under the fire of the enemy, I consulted the commanding officers of the Confederate States naval vessels present on the subject, and herewith annex a copy of their opinion, sustaining my own views on the subject.

I feel the importance of affording relief to your command as soon as possible; but, general, at the same time I feel, and I believe that I know, the importance to the safety of Forts Jackson and Saint Philip and the city of New Orleans of having this vessel in proper condition before seeking an encounter with the enemy. If he seeks one or attempts the passage of the forts before this vessel is ready I shall meet him, however unprepared I may be.

We have an additional force of mechanics from the city this morning, and I hope that by to-morrow night the motive power of the Louisiana will be ready, and that in the mean time her battery will be in place and other preparations will be completed so as to enable her to act against the enemy. When ready you will be immediately advised.

I have the honor to be, very respectfully, your obedient servant,

JNO. K. MITCHELL,
Commanding C. S. Naval Forces Lower Mississippi.

General JOHNSON K. DUNCAN,
Commanding Coast Defenses, Fort Jackson, La.

CONFEDERATE STATES STEAMER LOUISIANA,
Near Fort Jackson, La., April 22, 1862.

Two communications having this day been received from Brigadier-General Duncan (herewith attached, marked Nos. 1 and 3, and also the answer of Commander J. K. Mitchell, No. 1, marked No. 2), requesting that the Louisiana be placed in position below the raft in the river, near Fort Jackson, a consultation was held by Commander J. K. Mitchell with Commander McIntosh and Lieutenants Commanding Huger and Warley, who fully sustained the views of Commander Mitchell, as expressed in his reply (marked No. 2), declining to comply with the request of Brigadier-General Duncan.

C. F. McINTOSH,
Commander, C. S. Navy.
T. B. HUGER,
Lieutenant Commanding.
A. F. WARLEY,
Lieutenant Commanding.

Lieut. GEORGE S. SHRYOCK, C. S. NAVY,
Aide to Commanding Officer.

[Inclosure F.]

CONFEDERATE STATES STEAMER LOUISIANA,
Fort Jackson, La., April 22, 1862.

GENERAL: Your two notes of this date have been received. A fire has been ordered to be built below Saint Philip, as you requested, except that it will be on the beach, and a raft will be kept ready to fire and turned adrift, as you requested, near Fort Jackson, in the event of the apprehended attack being made by the enemy to-night. I shall also direct a vigilant lookout to be kept by all the vessels, and co-operate with you to prevent his passage of the forts at every hazard.

Your request respecting the report of the bad condition of the engines of the Mosher will claim my attention as soon as possible.

I have the honor to be, very respectfully, your obedient servant,

JNO. K. MITCHELL,
Commanding C. S. Naval Forces Lower Mississippi.

Brig. Gen. JOHNSON K. DUNCAN,
Commanding Coast Defenses at Fort Jackson, La.

[Inclosure G.]

CONFEDERATE STATES STEAMER LOUISIANA,
Off Fort Jackson, La., April 22, 1862.

GENTLEMEN: The steamers Mosher and Belle Algerine having been represented as being unfit for service, you will please to examine them carefully without delay, and report to me in duplicate their condition. In the performance of this duty please state the cause of any damage you may discover, with such recommendations as in your judgment you may deem proper.

I am, very respectfully, your obedient servant,

JNO. K. MITCHELL,
Commanding C. S. Naval Forces Lower Mississippi.

Lieutenant HUGER,
Asst. Engr., Comdg. C. S. Steamer McRae, off Fort Jackson, La.

P. S.—Lieutenant Huger will fill up the blanks with the names of the two engineers he thinks most suitable for the service belonging to the McRae.

J. K. M.

CONFEDERATE STATES STEAMER LOUISIANA,
April 22, 1862.

SIR: In obedience to your order we have held a survey upon the steamer Belle Algerine and the tug Mosher. The latter has, we think, loosened the after-bearing of her shaft. This we can, I think, obviate in a few hours. The Belle Algerine leaks badly in the bows, from two holes knocked in her, the captain reports, while working at the raft and also while landing guns at Fort Saint Philip. This we can also remedy, and are now doing so. I trust by to-night both vessels will be serviceable.

Very respectfully, your obedient servant,

T. B. HUGER,
Commanding the McRae.
SAMUEL BROCK,
Senior Engineer McRae.

GENERAL: Above you will see the report on the vessels reported to you as unfit for service. I send it for your information.

Respectfully, your obedient servant,

JNO. K. MITCHELL,
Commanding C. S. Naval Forces.

Brig. Gen. JOHNSON K. DUNCAN,
Commanding Coast Defenses.

[Inclosure H.]

FORT JACKSON, LA., *April* 23, 1862.

CAPTAIN: I am of the opinion that the mortar practice of the enemy against Fort Jackson must be nearly exhausted, and that there is every indication that the enemy, as the next plan of attack, is about to move his large vessels to the point of woods and open upon us with his broadsides. One of the large vessels has already been brought up and placed in position. Should the above prove to be the case, it is imperatively and absolutely necessary that the batteries of the Louisiana should be brought into action at all hazards, as well as those of Forts Jackson and Saint Philip.

A proper position for the Louisiana would be on the Fort Saint Philip side, a short distance below the raft and close to the shore, which will give us three direct and cross fires upon the point of attack.

Earnestly calling your attention to this subject, as you can see from your position the movements of the enemy, and can consequently know when to act, I remain, very respectfully, your obedient servant,

J. K. DUNCAN,
Brigadier-General, Commanding Coast Defenses.

Capt. J. K. MITCHELL,
Commanding Naval Forces Lower Mississippi River.

[Inclosure I.]

CONFEDERATE STATES STEAMER LOUISIANA,
Near Fort Jackson, La., April 23, 1862.

GENERAL: I am in receipt of your letter of this date, in which you express your belief that the enemy is about to change his place of attack and open the broadside of his larger ships on the forts, and in which you make certain suggestions as to the position to be taken by this ship.

By reference to a letter of mine to you of yesterday's date, and of No. 1 of this date, you will be apprised of the condition of this ship. Should an attack be made, as anticipated, I shall be governed by circumstances and do all I can against the enemy.

I have the honor to be, very respectfully, your obedient servant,

JNO. K. MITCHELL,
Commanding C. S. Naval Forces Lower Mississippi.

Brig. Gen. JOHNSON K. DUNCAN,
Commanding Coast Defenses, Fort Jackson, La.

[Inclosure J.]

CONFEDERATE STATES STEAMER LOUISIANA,
Off Fort Jackson, La., April 23, 1862.

SIR: I inclose herewith a copy of a communication received on the 21st instant from Captain Stephenson, from which you will perceive that, notwithstanding General Lovell's order to him, this letter so qualifies my authority as to relieve me from all responsibility as to the movements of the vessels of the river fleet under his command.

I have the honor to be, very respectfully, your obedient servant,

JNO. K. MITCHELL,
Commanding C. S. Forces Lower Mississippi.

Brig. Gen. JOHNSON K. DUNCAN,
Commanding Coast Defenses, Fort Jackson, La.

[Inclosure K.]

RIVER DEFENSES, C. S. GUNBOAT WARRIOR,
Fort Jackson, La., April 21, 1862.

SIR: I am in receipt of an order from Maj. Gen. M. Lovell, dated 20th instant, in which I am directed to place myself and my whole command at this point under your orders.

Every officer and man on the river defense expedition joined it with the condition that it was to be independent of the Navy, and that it would not be governed by the regulations of the Navy or be commanded by naval officers. In the face of the enemy I will not say more.

I will co-operate with you and do nothing without your approbation, and will endeavor to carry out your wishes to the best of my ability, but in my own way as to details and the handling of my boats; but I expect the vessels under my charge to remain as a separate command. All orders for their movements addressed to me will be promptly executed if practicable, and I undertake to be responsible for their efficiency when required.

I suppose this is all that is intended by the order of Major-General Lovell or that will be expected from me by you.

Respectfully, yours, &c.,

JNO. A. STEPHENSON,
Senior Captain, Comdg. River Fleet at Fort Jackson, La.

Commander J. K. MITCHELL,
C. S. Navy.

P. S.—Our signals should be made to assimilate at once. Captain Renshaw and myself could arrange this if you wish, as no doubt you are greatly fatigued and still have much to do and arrange. Anything I can do, rely on its being done promptly and cheerfully.

Yours, &c.,

J. A. S.

[Inclosure L.]

FORT JACKSON, LA., *April* 23, 1862.

CAPTAIN: The enemy has just sent up a small boat and planted a series of white flags on the Fort Saint Philip side, commencing about 350 yards above the lone tree. It is the probable position of his ships in the new line of attack, which in my opinion he contemplates for attacking Fort Jackson with his large vessels. As you may not have seen this operation, I furnish you with the information.

Please keep the river well lit up with fire rafts to-night, as the attack may be made at any time.

Very respectfully, your obedient servant,

J. K. DUNCAN,
Brigadier-General, Commanding Coast Defenses.

Capt. J. K. MITCHELL,
Commanding Naval Forces Lower Mississippi River.

[Inclosure M.]

FORT JACKSON, LA., *April* 24, 1862—3.30 a. m.

CAPTAIN: As I anticipated and informed you yesterday, the enemy are taking up their position at the present moment with their large ships on the Fort Saint Philip shore, to operate against Fort Jackson. They are placing themselves boldly, with their lights at their mast-heads. You are assuming a fearful responsibility if you do not come at once to our assistance with the Louisiana and the fleet. I can say no more.

Very respectfully, your obedient servant,

J. K. DUNCAN,
Brigadier-General, Commanding Coast Defenses.

Capt. J. K. MITCHELL,
Commanding Naval Forces Lower Mississippi River.

[Inclosure N.]

CONFEDERATE STATES STEAMER LOUISIANA,
Near Fort Saint Philip, La., April 24, 1862.

GENERAL: On returning to the Louisiana I find that we have no tender on whose steam power we can rely, and many of the volunteer troops on board of the W. Burton are intoxicated. These circumstances, as well as the exhausted condition of our own crew and excessive difficulty in handling the vessel, will prevent our taking the position, at least to-day, that I proposed and was arranged between us this forenoon. I will, however, as you suggested in your communication, take up a position above to protect the approaches in that direction. Having no adequate motive power of our own, it will be an easy matter for the enemy's vessels that have it to take up such a position that our guns cannot reach him for want of elevation or be brought to bear upon him. I will, however, do all I can to keep him back from above. The McRae has lost her 9-inch guns; of course we cannot expect much assistance from her.

I have the honor to be, very respectfully, your obedient servant,

JNO. K. MITCHELL,
Commanding C. S. Naval Forces, Lower Mississippi.

Brig. Gen. JOHNSON K. DUNCAN,
Commanding Coast Defenses, Fort Jackson, La.

[Inclosure O.]

CONFEDERATE STATES STEAMER LOUISIANA,
Fort Saint Philip, La., April 24, 1862.

GENERAL: Your second and third notes of this date are at hand. We are in a helpless condition for the want of tug-boats. The W. Burton is crippled and the Landis also, and the gunboat Defiance will not do anything for us. If she comes within my reach I will deprive her captain of his command by force, if necessary. The anchor we have down cannot purchase, and we are afraid to ship it to move about 300 yards higher up, where we can be better secured. We shall probably remain where we are, and do all we can to defeat the enemy should he attack us again. It will be out of our power, I am afraid, to light up the bank below Saint Philip to-night or to set adrift fire boats, as none are at hand and they have all disappeared, apparently.

I have the honor to be, very respectfully, your obedient servant,

JNO. K. MITCHELL,
Commanding C. S. Naval Forces, Lower Mississippi.

Brig. Gen. JOHNSON K. DUNCAN,
Commanding Coast Defenses, Fort Jackson, La.

[Inclosure P.]

FORT JACKSON, LA., *April* 24, 1862.

CAPTAIN: From all we can see and learn, the enemy, with the exception of one or two gunboats, has passed up the river, so that there will be no use in changing your present position to one farther above. I regret to learn the condition of the volunteer troops on board the W. Burton; this, together with the exhausted condition of your crew, will prevent your taking up the position below which was agreed upon this morning for the present. You may be able to take it up, however, when your crew recover from their fatigue and when you are able to control the irregularities of the volunteers.

Very respectfully, your obedient servant,

J. K. DUNCAN,
Brigadier-General, Commanding Coast Defenses.

Capt. J. K. MITCHELL,
Commanding C. S. Naval Forces, Lower Mississippi River.

[Inclosure Q.]

FORT JACKSON, LA., *April* 24, 1862.

CAPTAIN: As I have no boats of any kind, I must ask of you to light up the river with fire barges to-night if it possibly lies in your power. The absence of light greatly impairs the accuracy and effectiveness of our fire upon the enemy.

Very respectfully, your obedient servant,

J. K. DUNCAN,
Brigadier-General, Commanding Coast Defenses.

Capt. J. K. MITCHELL,
Commanding C. S. Naval Forces, Lower Mississippi River.

[Inclosure R.]

FORT JACKSON, LA., *April* 24, 1862.

CAPTAIN: The lower schooner will be lighted by firing her from a row-boat from Fort Saint Philip at early dusk. As this light dies away the next one above will be fired, and so on all night.

Unless you can better yourself materially, I would not advise any movement on your part from your present position, owing to all the adverse circumstances mentioned in your letter.

In regard to the Defiance, the authority over her which I formerly had has been transferred to you, but we will freely lend you any assistance which you may require in deposing her commander or in exercising your authority over her.

Keep a vigilant lookout for another attack to-night, when we will mutually support each other and do all that we possibly can.

Captain Squires has been directed by Colonel Higgins to furnish you such assistance as you may require.

Very respectfully, your obedient servant,

J. K. DUNCAN,
Brigadier-General, Commanding Coast Defenses.

Capt. J. K. MITCHELL,
Commanding C. S. Naval Forces, Lower Mississippi River.

[Inclosure S.]

U. S. STEAMER HARRIET LANE,
Mississippi River, April 26, 1862.

SIR: When I last demanded the surrender of Forts Jackson and Saint Philip I had no positive assurance of the success of our vessels in passing safely the batteries on the river. Since then I have received communications from Flag-Officer Farragut, who is now in possession of New Orleans. Our troops are or will be in possession of the prominent points on the river, and a sufficient force has been posted outside of the bayous to cut off all communication and prevent supplies.

No man could consider it dishonorable to surrender under these circumstances, especially when no advantage can arise by longer holding out, and by yielding gracefully he can save the further effusion of blood. You have defended the forts gallantly, and no more can be asked of you.

I feel authorized to offer you terms sufficiently honorable to relieve you from any feeling of humiliation. The officers will be permitted to retire on parole, with their side-arms, not to serve again until regularly exchanged. All private property will be respected; only the arms and munitions and the vessels lying near the forts will be surrendered to the United States Government. No damage must be done to the defenses. The soldiers also will be paroled and be permitted to return to their homes, giving up their arms.

I am aware that you can hold out some little time longer, and am also aware of the exact condition, as reported to us by a deserter, which convinces me that you will only be inflicting on yourself and those under you unnecessary discomforts without any good results arising from so doing.

Your port has long been closed to the world, by which serious injury has been experienced by many loyal citizens. I trust that you will not lend yourself to the further injury of their interests, where it can only entail calamity and bloodshed without any possible hope of success or relief to your forts.

Your surrender is a mere question of time, which you know is not of any extent; and I therefore urge you to meet my present proposition. By doing so you can put an end to a state of affairs which will only inflict injury upon all those under you, who have strong claims upon your consideration.

I remain, very respectfully, your obedient servant,

DAVID D. PORTER,
Commanding Mortar Fleet.

Col. EDWARD HIGGINS,
Comdg. Confederate Forces in Forts Jackson and Saint Philip.

[Inclosure T.]

HEADQUARTERS FORTS JACKSON AND SAINT PHILIP,
April 27, 1862.

SIR: Your letter of the 26th instant, demanding the surrender of these forts, has been received. In reply thereto I have to state that no official information has been received by me from our own authorities that the city of New Orleans has been surrendered to the forces of Flag-Officer

Farragut, and until such information is received no proposition for a surrender can be for a moment entertained here.

Very respectfully, your obedient servant,

EDWARD HIGGINS,
Lieutenant-Colonel, Commanding.

Commander DAVID D. PORTER, U. S. Navy,
Commanding Mortar Fleet.

[Inclosure U.]

FORT JACKSON, LA., *April* 27, 1862.

To the Soldiers of Forts Jackson and Saint Philip:

You have nobly, gallantly, and heroically sustained with courage and fortitude the terrible ordeals of fire, water, and a hail of shot and shell wholly unsurpassed during the present war. But more remains to be done. The safety of New Orleans and the cause of the Southern Confederacy, our homes, families, and everything dear to man yet depend upon our exertions. We are just as capable of repelling the enemy to-day as we were before the bombardment. Twice has the enemy demanded your surrender and twice has he been refused. Your officers have every confidence in your courage and patriotism, and feel every assurance that you will cheerfully and with alacrity obey all orders and do your whole duty as men and as becomes the well-tried garrisons of Forts Jackson and Saint Philip. Be vigilant, therefore, and stand by your guns, and all will yet be well.

J. K. DUNCAN,
Brigadier-General, Commanding Coast Defenses.

[Inclosure V.]

HEADQUARTERS FORTS JACKSON AND SAINT PHILIP,
April 28, 1862.

SIR: Upon mature deliberation it has been decided to accept the terms of surrender of these forts under the conditions offered by you in your letter of the 26th instant, viz, that the officers and men shall be paroled, officers retiring with their side-arms. We have no control over the vessels afloat.

Very respectfully, your obedient servant,

EDWARD HIGGINS,
Lieutenant-Colonel, Commanding.

Commander DAVID D. PORTER, U. S. Navy,
Commanding Mortar Fleet.

[Inclosure W.]

U. S. STEAMER HARRIET LANE,
Forts Jackson and Saint Philip, Mississippi River, April 28, 1862.

By articles of capitulation entered into April 28, 1862, between Commander David D. Porter, U. S. Navy, commanding the United States mortar flotilla, of the one part, and Brig. Gen. J. K. Duncan, commanding the coast defenses, and Lieut. Col. Edward Higgins, commanding Forts Jackson and Saint Philip, of the other part, it is mutually agreed:

First. That Brigadier-General Duncan and Lieutenant-Colonel Higgins shall surrender to the mortar flotilla Forts Jackson and Saint Philip, the arms, munitions of war, and all the appurtenances thereunto belonging, together with all public property that may be under their charge.

Second. It is agreed by Commander David D. Porter, commanding the mortar flotilla, that Brigadier-General Duncan and Lieutenant-Colonel Higgins, together with the officers under their command, shall be permitted to retain their side-arms, and that all private property shall be respected. Furthermore, that they shall give their parole of honor not to serve in arms against the Government of the United States until they are regularly exchanged.

Third. It is further agreed by Commander David D. Porter, commanding the mortar flotilla, on the part of the United States Government, that the non-commissioned officers, privates, and musicians shall be permitted to retire on parole, their commanding and other officers becoming responsible for them, and that they shall deliver up their arms and accouterments in their present condition, provided that no expenses accruing from the transportation of the men shall be defrayed by the Government of the United States.

Fourth. On the signing of these articles by the contracting parties the forts shall be formally taken possession of by the United States naval forces composing the mortar flotilla, the Confederate flag shall be lowered, and the flag of the United States hoisted on the flag-staffs of Forts Jackson and Saint Philip.

In agreement of the above we, the undersigned, do hereunto set our hands and seals.

DAVID D. PORTER,
Commanding Mortar Flotilla.

W. B. RENSHAW,
Commander, U. S. Navy.

J. M. WAINWRIGHT,
Lieutenant-Commander, U. S. Steamer Harriet Lane.

J. K. DUNCAN,
Brigadier-General, Commanding Coast Defenses.

EDWARD HIGGINS,
Lieutenant-Colonel, C. S. Army,
Commanding Forts Jackson and Saint Philip, La.

Witnessed by—

ED. T. NICHOLS,
Lieutenant-Commander, U. S. Gunboat Winona.

J. H. RUSSELL,
Lieutenant-Commander, U. S. Gunboat Kennebec.

Diagram of the Bombardment of
FORTS JACKSON AND ST. PHILIP, LA.
from April 16th to April 24th 1862.

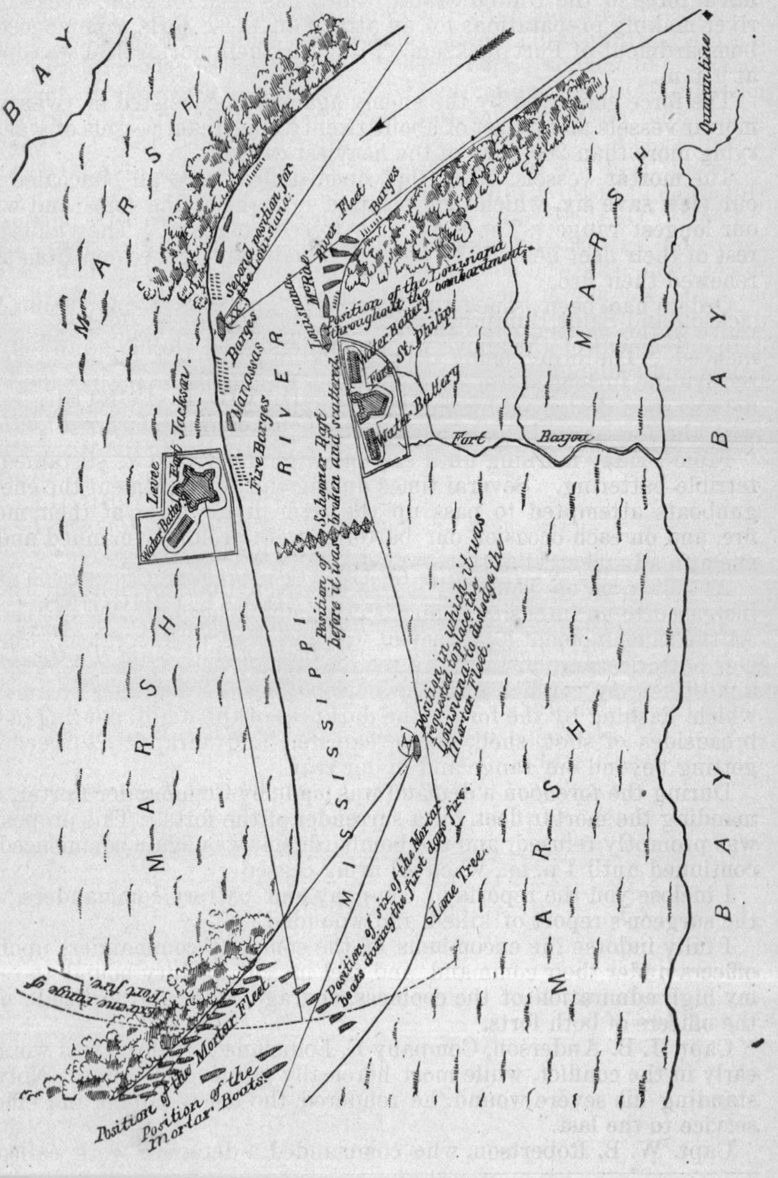

No. 5.

Reports of Lieut. Col. Edward Higgins, C. S. Army, of the bombardment and capture of Forts Jackson and Saint Philip.

HDQRS. FORTS JACKSON AND SAINT PHILIP, LA.,
April 27, 1862.

SIR: I have the honor to report that on Friday, the 18th instant, the naval force of the United States, which has been for some weeks in the river making preparations for an attack on these forts, commenced the bombardment of Fort Jackson. Fire from their mortar fleet was opened at 9 a. m.

The force employed by the enemy against us consisted of twenty-one mortar vessels and a fleet of about twenty-one steam vessels of war, carrying more than 200 guns of the heaviest caliber.

The mortar vessels, when they opened fire, were all concealed from our view save six, which took position in sight of the forts and within our longest range. These we soon forced to retire. They joined the rest of their fleet behind the point of woods, and, concealed from sight, renewed their fire.

Orders had been issued to the officers and men of my command to retire to the casemates of the fort the moment the bombardment commenced. The order being obeyed, nothing was left for us to do but receive the furious storm of shell which was hailed upon us. Our citadel was soon destroyed by fire. All buildings around and in connection with the fort shared the same fate.

From Friday morning until the following Thursday we sustained this terrible battering. Several times during the bombardment the enemy's gunboats attempted to pass up the river under cover of their mortar fire, and on each occasion our batteries were promptly manned and the enemy's advance gallantly repelled.

At 3.30 a. m. on Thursday it was observed that the mortar fire was increased to an intensity of fury which had not been previously reached. At the same moment a movement was observed in the steam fleet below. Our batteries were instantly in readiness and were at once engaged in a most terrific conflict with the enemy's fleet of fourteen steamships, which, dashing by the fort in the darkness of the night, pouring in their broadsides of shot, shell, grape, canister, and shrapnel, succeeded in getting beyond our range and in our rear.

During the forenoon a demand was made by Commander Porter, commanding the mortar fleet, for a surrender of the forts. This proposition was promptly refused, and the bombardment was again commenced and continued until 4 p. m., when all firing ceased.

I inclose you the reports of company and battery commanders,* also the surgeon's report of killed and wounded.†

I fully indorse the encomiums of the company commanders upon the officers under their command, and feel myself in duty bound to record my high admiration of the coolness, courage, skill, and fortitude of all the officers of both forts.

Capt. J. B. Anderson, Company E, Louisiana Artillery, was wounded early in the conflict, while most heroically fighting his guns. Notwithstanding his severe wound, he rendered the most gallant and efficient service to the last.

Capt. W. B. Robertson, who commanded a detached work called the

* Not found. † Tabulated on p. 550.

water battery, remained with his command during the whole of this protracted ordeal without cover of any kind, although suffering from severe physical disease and scarcely able at times to walk around his battery. He was most ably and gallantly assisted by Capt. R. J. Bruce, of the Louisiana Artillery.

First Lieut. Eugene W. Baylor, Louisiana Artillery, who was in command of the 42-pounder barbette battery, and First Lieut. Richard Agar, of the same battery, did all that gallant officers and men could.

The officers stationed at the heaviest batteries on the river front were the greater part of the time, fatigued as they were, obliged to be constantly with their detachments at their guns to prevent surprise. Lieuts. A. N. Ogden, Beverly C. Kennedy, and William T. Mumford, of the Louisiana Artillery, particularly distinguished themselves in this service.

Although not under my immediate command, I cannot omit to mention the devoted conduct of your aide-de-camp, Lieut. William M. Bridges, who upon the disability of Captain Anderson immediately volunteered his services, and took charge of the two 10-inch columbiads, and fought them night and day with ceaseless energy.

Lieut. J. W. Gaines, in command of the 32-pounder battery on the river front, assisted by Lieut. E. D. Woodlief; Capt. S. Jones, Company I, Twenty-third Regiment Louisiana Volunteers; Capt. F. Peter, Company I, Twenty-second Regiment Louisiana Volunteers, fought their batteries gallantly and well.

Lieut. Thomas K. Pierson, Twenty-third Regiment Louisiana Volunteers, was killed in the thickest of the fight, while gallantly fighting his guns.

The Saint Mary's Cannoneers, Capt. F. O. Cornay, have my warmest gratitude and admiration for their whole conduct, both in face of the enemy and in the severe and arduous fatigue duties, which they discharged always and at all times, day and night, with alacrity and energy. They are an honor to the country, and well may their friends and relatives be proud of them.

The report of Capt. M. T. Squires, who was the senior officer at Fort Saint Philip, is inclosed, with the reports of the other officers. Captain Squires fought the batteries of Fort Saint Philip most gallantly. He was in charge of that fort during the whole bombardment, the severe work at Fort Jackson requiring my constant presence there. I had every confidence in the coolness, courage, and skill of Captain Squires and his officers, and most satisfactorily did they discharge their duties. I refer you to his report for the mention of the individual conduct of his officers.

The floating battery Louisiana, the steam ram Manassas, and the Confederate steamer McRae, together with a number of vessels which had been fitted up by the Confederate and State Governments, were in the river above the forts at the time the enemy dashed by. I am unable to state what assistance, if any, was rendered by the greater portion of these vessels.

At daylight I observed the McRae gallantly fighting at terrible odds—contending at close quarters with two of the enemy's powerful ships. Her gallant commander, Lieut. Thomas B. Huger, fell during the conflict severely but, I trust, not mortally wounded.

The Manassas I observed under way, apparently in pursuit of one of the vessels of the enemy, but I soon lost sight of her.

I would here observe that I think an investigation should be demanded into the conduct of the authorities afloat, whose neglect of our urgent entreaties to light up the river during this sad night contributed so much to the success of our enemies.

My adjutant, Lieut. C. N. Morse, was indefatigable in the discharge of his important duties, which required his constant presence near my person, and has my sincere thanks.

Surg. Somerville Burke, C. S. Army, and Dr. Bradbury, who kindly volunteered his services when he became aware of the attack on the forts, were unremitting in their attention to the wounded, fearlessly exposing themselves at all times in the discharge of their duties.

Lieut. Charles Wermes, ordnance officer, distinguished himself by the most self-sacrificing attention to arduous and important duties. Day and night he was at his post, and by his great exertions our magazine was saved from being flooded, the water having risen considerably above the floor.

Lieutenants Mann and Royster, of Captain Ryan's company, rendered fearless and efficient service. Captain Ryan was, with a detachment of his company, on board the Louisiana during a portion of the bombardment and in the fight of Thursday morning. At all times his services were most promptly rendered.

Mr. James Ward rendered me the most important services during the bombardment. In charge of the firemen, he made almost superhuman exertions during the burning of the citadel. He has my warmest gratitude.

I have the honor to remain, very respectfully, your obedient servant,

EDWARD HIGGINS,
Lieutenant-Colonel, C. S. Army,
Commanding Forts Jackson and Saint Philip, La.

Lieut. WILLIAM M. BRIDGES,
A. A. A. G., Second Brig., Dept. No. 1, New Orleans, La.

NEW ORLEANS, LA., *April* 30, 1862.

SIR: I have the honor to report that on the morning of April 27 a formal demand for a surrender of Forts Jackson and Saint Philip was made by Commander David D. Porter, commanding United States mortar fleet.

The terms which were offered were of the most liberal nature; but so strong was I in the belief that we could resist successfully any attack which could be made upon us, either by land or water, that the terms were at once refused.

Our fort was still strong; our damage had been to some extent repaired; our men had behaved well, and all was hope and confidence with the officers, when suddenly at midnight I was aroused by the report that the garrison had revolted, had seized the guard, and were spiking the guns. Word was sent us through the sergeants of companies that the men would fight no longer. The company officers were immediately dispatched to their commands, but were driven back. Officers were fired upon when they appeared in sight upon the parapet. Signals were exchanged by the mutineers with Fort Saint Philip. The mutiny was complete, and a general massacre of the officers and a disgraceful surrender of the fort appeared inevitable.

By great exertions we succeeded, with your influence, in preventing this disgraceful blot upon our country, and were fortunate in keeping the passions of the men in check until we could effect an honorable surrender of the forts, which was done by us jointly on the morning of the 28th instant.

As the facts and documents relating to this matter are in your possession, it is unnecessary for me to dwell longer on this humiliating and unhappy affair.

I wish to place on record here the noble conduct of Capt. S. O. Cornay's company, the Saint Mary's Cannoneers, which alone stood true as steel when every other company in Fort Jackson basely dishonored its country.

I have the honor to remain, very respectfully, your obedient servant,

EDWARD HIGGINS,
Lieutenant-Colonel, C. S. Army,
Late Commander Forts Jackson and Saint Philip.

Lieut. WILLIAM M. BRIDGES,
Aide-de-Camp and Actg. Asst. Adjt. Gen., Second Brigade.

Return of casualties in the Confederate garrisons of Forts Jackson and Saint Philip, April 18-25, 1862.

Command.	Killed.	Wounded
Fort Jackson	9	35
Fort Saint Philip	2	4
Total	11	39

No. 6.

Report of Capt. M. T. Squires, Louisiana Artillery, of the bombardment of Fort Saint Philip.

FORT SAINT PHILIP, LA., *April* 27, 1862.

SIR: I have the honor respectfully to submit the following report:

Early on the morning of Friday, the 18th instant, perceiving by the movements of the enemy that they were about taking up their position, the heavy guns were ordered to open upon them, to annoy them in the execution of their purpose as much as possible, but, the distance being great and the range extreme, with but very little success, the enemy taking little or no notice of our fire, only answering by a few rifle shells at long intervals. The 13-inch mortar, after the thirteenth round, became useless, the bed giving way under it, breaking in two, and the mortar coming upon the ground. The enemy retired from our sight at 8 p. m. and nothing more was heard of him that night.

At an early hour on the morning of the 19th instant the enemy again took up a position identical with that of the day previous, excepting that no mortar boats were on this shore, all keeping close behind the point of woods, and opened fire upon Fort Jackson, which was allowed to continue without interruption from this side until 11 a. m., when, finding the fire concentrated upon the other side, fearing the effect, and having ascertained the exact range and distances, I determined to open upon them and draw off some of the fire to this side if possible. It was immediately done and with partial success, three of the mortar boats opening upon us with but little effect.

On the 20th, 21st, and 22d the fire of the enemy still continued from their mortar boats, with an occasional shot from the gunboats. The only damage done during these days was the damaging of the platform of the 24-pounder gun in the salient near the main magazine, the shell passing under and throwing it up, but not rendering it useless. Our fire was slow and deliberate, with no visible results more than the driving back of two of the mortar boats, which were partially exposed, around the wooded point. The fire of the enemy, although warm, well directed, and sustained, was for the most part either short or very much over.

Up to this time the only guns used were the columbiad battery, in the main work, and the 13-inch mortar, disabled on the first day. In the lower water battery one 8-inch columbiad and one 7-inch rifled gun, worked by Capt. R. C. Bond's company, and four 10-inch sea-coast mortars, by Capt. J. H. Lamon's company.

On the 23d the enemy still kept up a regular fire, to which we did not reply all day.

At 3.30 o'clock on the morning of the 24th the men were ready and standing at their guns, having received information that there was a movement by the enemy. No vessels were to be seen, and the first notice of an enemy nearing us was the reply to the shots from Fort Jackson, and the gunners were ordered to fire by the flashes of the enemy's guns, which was done; but the fire was entirely too high and passed over them.

Immediately after this a vessel came in sight, and they followed each other in rapid succession, seemingly in pairs, one of the two keeping back far enough to enable her to deliver her fire from her broadsides. The fire from our guns was rapid, and from the little that could be seen and heard was accurate; but after the first discharge the smoke almost hid them from sight, and we were again compelled to judge by the flashes of their guns. As to the effect of the fire, it is impossible to state what it was, as the darkness, aided by the smoke, rendered seeing out of the question.

A three-masted propeller ran ashore during the engagement above the upper water battery, and, remaining there several minutes, with a fire barge alongside, her rigging had caught fire, but was immediately extinguished. We were not able to open upon her, as one of the columbiads had been previously dismounted and the other could not be brought to bear; besides, their hands were full with other vessels coming up, and the 24-pounder in the salient of the upper water battery, bearing directly upon her, had been broken in two near the trunnions. The vessels passed close under our guns, taking advantage of the eddy which runs up with considerable force, and it was found impossible to get more than one or two shots at any one vessel, they passed with such rapidity.

All our guns were worked with courage, energy, and skill, excepting the upper water battery, where some confusion arose, caused by the men not being so thoroughly drilled as they should have been. Company C of the Confederate recruits, Lieut. J. K. Dixon, was fully prepared to work the guns of this battery, and would have done so with effect, but was two days before ordered on board the floating battery Louisiana, and its place was supplied by Captain Assenheimer's company (B), Twentieth Regiment Louisiana Volunteers, which had only been drilled a few times, and Captain Massicott's company (D), Chalmette Regiment, which was raw, undrilled, perfectly ignorant even of the use of the shot-guns with which it was armed, and had never been drilled as artillery.

As soon as it was seen that the guns did not open, Lieut. A. J. Quigley, with such men as could be gathered, was sent to attend to them, which was done, so far as they were concerned, to the satisfaction of that officer.

The company of Confederate recruits, under Lieutenants Dixon and Blow, were detailed to report to Captain Mitchell, C. S. Navy, for duty on board the Louisiana, as per instructions dated Headquarters Forts Jackson and Saint Philip, April 21, 1862, where they remained until the evening of the 24th instant.

Captain Lartigue's company did good service as scouts and sharpshooters, many of them being out both night and day, and some of them being out at all times. On the night of the 23d seven of them were sent to ascertain the movements of the enemy, and all returned without accomplishing anything. Two other scouts, one from Company K and the other from Company F, were out on the same mission, and had it not been for the failure of the rocket, which by an accident became wet, would have signaled their approach much sooner. As it was, the only intimation I received was the firing of one of their muskets.

The following is the number of projectiles used, &c.:

8-inch solid shot	675
8-inch shells	171
13-inch shells from columbiad battery, &c., in main work	13
10-inch mortar shells from lower mortar battery	142
Shot, shell, and grape from lower water battery	470
Shot, grape, and canister from upper water battery	120

Capt. R. C. Bond, assisted by First Lieuts. Carleton Hunt and William C. Ellis, and his company (K); Capt. J. H. Lamon, with the assistance of First Lieut. H. W. Fowler, with his company (C), in the lower battery, manning the 42 and 32 pounders respectively; Lieuts. Lewis B. Taylor and W. B. Jones, with Company F, at the columbiad battery, and Lieut. A. J. Quigley, with supernumeraries of Company F, taken from the main work to man the guns of the upper battery, behaved with gallantry, energy, coolness, and bravery worthy of imitation; and all, both officers and men, deserve the highest praise that could be given to any one for the honorable part they performed during the whole time since the commencement of this trying conflict.

Capt. Charles Assenheimer's company (B) did their best, both his officers and men.

Individual acts of heroism are numerous, but where all did so well it would appear invidious to mention names. Suffice it to say that were everything to be done again, or anything else required to be performed, one could ask no other privilege than to have the same men to do it, feeling satisfied it would be as well carried out as possible.

The injury to the fort was slight. Of the guns, one banded 7-inch rifle was burst by the explosion of a shell in its bore near the muzzle, and one 24-pounder gun was broken in two, about 14 inches in front of the trunnions, by being struck by a solid shot. An 8-inch columbiad was dismounted, but only temporarily useless, the gun being uninjured and soon remounted. The platform of one 24-pounder gun was undermined by a shell, but was not rendered entirely useless. One of the uprights of a 42-pounder gun-carriage was partially shot away, but can still be of service.

With many thanks to all officers and men for their assistance and efficient aid, and humbly bowing before the will of Almighty God, I am, very respectfully, your obedient servant,

M. T. SQUIRES,
Captain, Louisiana Artillery.

Lieut. CHARLES N. MORSE,
Post Adjutant, Fort Jackson, La.

No. 7.

Report of Brig. Gen. M. L. Smith, C. S. Army, of operations on the "Chalmette and McGehee Lines."

CAMP MOORE, TANGIPAHOA, LA., *May* 6, 1862.

MAJOR: I herewith submit a report of the operations of the troops under my command at the Chalmette and McGehee lines on the approach of the enemy's vessels from Forts Jackson and Saint Philip to the city of New Orleans. These interior lines of defense are constructed with special reference to an attack by land, but terminating them at the river banks were two batteries, calculated for twelve and twenty guns, respectively, and at the time of the action containing five and nine. Ten 42-pounders, intended for this battery, were turned over to the Navy for the defense of the city by water.

As you are aware, the defense of New Orleans by water has been considered as depending upon the forts mentioned, which are well constructed permanent works, rather well armed, and far stronger than any others that could be hastily erected. With this view all the available material, both of guns and ammunition, had been concentrated there prior to the bombardment, and during its continuance was being added to in such quantities daily as the means of the department admitted of, it being evident that the decisive struggle was there to be made.

As soon, therefore, as it became certain that the large vessels of the enemy had succeded in passing, there no longer existed a chance of preventing them from reaching New Orleans, and the short resistance made by the few guns mounted on the two batteries of the interior lines was made through a sense of duty, but without any expectation of success, the enemy numbering as many vessels, less one, as we had guns.

On the side of the river where I was in person during the action were stationed three companies of Lieutenant-Colonel Pinkney's battalion, to man the nine guns, and one company of sharpshooters. With the five guns on the other side were Captain Patton's company of the Twenty-second Louisiana Volunteers; one company from Fort Pike, under Lieutenant Butler, and one company of the Beauregard Battery, besides two battalions of infantry collected in camp for instruction, as well as to guard the line in case of the enemy's landing and attacking by land, all under the immediate command of General Buisson.

The enemy's vessels had approached to within about the fourth of a mile before we opened on them, the first gun being from Colonel Pinkney's battery, and immediately followed by several from the battery on the opposite side, and as promptly replied to from the enemy's vessels. The engagement lasted until every round of ammunition on hand was fired, both officers and men displaying a coolness and intrepidity that was gratifying, especially as regards the men, who then for the first time in their lives discharged a heavy gun. The firing on our side was spirited, perhaps a little uncertain; on the enemy's, heavy and rather well directed. During the engagement their vessels gradually lessened the distance until near enough to open with grape and canister. The ammunition being expended and every sense of duty satisfied, permission was given to Colonel Pinkney to withdraw his command along the line of field works affording shelter, which was done deliberately, officers and men retiring together.

The casualties were 1 killed and 1 wounded.

The battery on the Chalmette side seemed well served, and no doubt was so, judging from the character of the officers present.

The enemy, steaming up between us and the city, prevented the retreat of the troops to that point. They were accordingly directed to gain the Opelousas Railroad and reach Camp Moore via La Fourche or such route as might be found best. Lieutenant-Colonel Pinkney has already reported with his command, but somewhat reduced in numbers.

In concluding the report I wish particularly to call attention to the admirable assistance rendered by Lieutenants MacDonald and B. M Harrod, on engineer duty, both before and after the action. Their conduct could not have been better.

Lieutenant Frost, on special duty, was also of material assistance, but in carrying out some instructions was accidentally absent during the engagement.

Having received no report from General Buisson concerning the operations on his side of the river, I am unable to refer to them more particularly.

Respectfully submitted.

M. L. SMITH,
Brigadier-General, Commanding Third Brigade.

Maj. J. G. PICKETT,
Assistant Adjutant-General.

No. 8.

Proceedings of the Court of Inquiry upon the fall of New Orleans.

RICHMOND, VA., *June* 8, 1864.

To the House of Representatives:

In response to a resolution of the House of Representatives, of January 15, 1864, I herewith transmit for your information a communication from the Secretary of War, covering a copy of the proceedings of the Court of Inquiry relative to the capture of New Orleans.

JEFFERSON DAVIS.

[Inclosures.]

WAR DEPARTMENT,
Richmond, Va., June 6, 1864.

His Excellency the PRESIDENT:

SIR: In response to a resolution of the House of Representatives, adopted at its last session, I have the honor to forward for transmission to Congress a copy of the record of the Court of Inquiry on the fall of New Orleans, with accompanying documents, the preparation of which was not quite completed at the adjournment of the last Congress.

Very respectfully, your obedient servant,

JAMES A. SEDDON,
Secretary of War.

PROCEEDINGS OF A COURT OF INQUIRY, ASSEMBLED AT JACKSON, MISS., PURSUANT TO THE FOLLOWING ORDERS:

SPECIAL ORDERS, No. 41 } ADJT. AND INSP. GENERAL'S OFFICE, *Richmond, Va., February* 18, 1863.

* * * * * * *

XVI. By direction of the President, on the application of Maj. Gen. Mansfield Lovell, a Court of Inquiry, to consist of Brig. Gens. I.* T. F. Drayton, T. C. Hindman, and W. M. Gardner, will assemble at Jackson, Miss., on the 10th day of March next, or as soon thereafter as practicable, to examine into the facts and circumstances attending the capture of the city of New Orleans by the enemy in April, 1862, and the defense of the city and the evacuation of the same by our troops, under the command of Maj. Gen. Mansfield Lovell. Maj. L. R. Page, assistant adjutant-general, is appointed judge-advocate and recorder of the court. The Court of Inquiry appointed in Special Orders, No. 177, Adjutant and Inspector General's Office, July 31, 1862, paragraph XX, is hereby revoked.†

* * * * * * *

By command of the Secretary of War:

JNO. WITHERS,
Assistant Adjutant-General.

SPECIAL ORDERS, No. 43. } ADJT. AND INSP. GENERAL'S OFFICE, *Richmond, Va., February* 20, 1863.

* * * * * * *

XXIV. The Court of Inquiry directed in paragraph XVI, Special Orders, No. 41, current series, will sit without regard to hours, and will consider itself authorized to adjourn from place to place for the convenience of taking testimony of witnesses serving with the Army, in the field or elsewhere, and whose testimony may not be otherwise conveniently obtained, without embarrassment to the interests of the service.

The court will finally report the facts resulting from the investigation, together with their opinion thereon, for the information of the President.

* * * * * * *

By command of the Secretary of War:

JNO. WITHERS,
Assistant Adjutant-General.

SPECIAL ORDERS, No. 46. } ADJT. AND INSP. GENERAL'S OFFICE, *Richmond, Va., February* 24, 1863.

* * * * * * *

XXIV. A mistake having occurred in paragraph XVI, Special Orders, No. 41, current series, designating General T. C. Hindman as brigadier-general, he is hereby announced as major-general, and senior officer of the Court of Inquiry convened in said order and paragraph.

* * * * * * *

By command of the Secretary of War:

JNO. WITHERS,
Assistant Adjutant-General.

---

* An error; see proceedings of the court of April 6, 1863.

† Under that order Maj. Gens. L. Polk and Sam. Jones, and Col. B. Huger constituted the court.

APRIL 4, 1863—12.30 p. m.

The court met pursuant to the above orders.

Present, Maj. Gen. T. C. Hindman, Brig. Gens. T. F. Drayton and W. M. Gardner, and Maj. L. R. Page, judge-advocate. Maj. Gen. Mansfield Lovell also present.

The judge advocate, having read the orders convening the court, asked Maj. Gen. Mansfield Lovell if he had any objections to any member named therein, to which he replied he had none. The court was then duly sworn by the judge-advocate, and the judge-advocate was duly sworn by the presiding officer of the court in the presence of Maj. Gen. Mansfield Lovell. It was then resolved by the court to sit with closed doors, and ordered that W. H. Houston be employed as clerk to aid the judge-advocate.

The court adjourned to meet at 11 a. m. the 6th instant.

JACKSON, MISS., *April* 6, 1863—11 a. m.

The court met pursuant to adjournment.

Present, all the members of the court, the judge-advocate, and Major-General Lovell.

The proceedings of yesterday were read over. It was then ordered by the court that the letter "I," prefixed to the name of Brig. Gen. T. F. Drayton in the order convening the court, should be hereafter omitted in the records, it appearing to the satisfaction of the court that the insertion of the said letter "I" was a clerical error.

It was then ordered by the court that the word "accused" should not be used to designate Maj. Gen. Mansfield Lovell in these proceedings, there being no accusation or imputation against him before the court; and it was further ordered that the evidence in the case should be introduced without regard to the mode or order of proof governing in courts-martial or courts of inquiry when charges are made and an issue joined.

Maj. Gen. MANSFIELD LOVELL was then sworn and examined as a witness.

By the JUDGE-ADVOCATE:

Question. When did you assume command of the city of New Orleans?

Answer. On October 18, 1861, pursuant to paragraph VIII, Special Orders, No. 173, Adjutant and Inspector General's Office, October 7, 1861.

(The original of the order was read to the court and a copy thereof appended as document No. 1.)

Question. State for the information of the court the limits and extent of Department No. 1, its topographical features, and the various approaches to the city of New Orleans.

Answer. Department No. 1 embraced the State of Louisiana and the southern half of the State of Mississippi, except that part of the latter State on the Mississippi River included between the New Orleans, Jackson and Great Northern Railroad and the river, on which are situated Natchez and Vicksburg, they belonging to Department No. 2. Department No. 1 extended on the sea-coast more than 300 miles, from Texas on the west to Pascagoula Bay on the east. The city of New Orleans is situated in an alluvial delta on the left or northern bank of the river, about 100 miles from the mouth. From below New Orleans to Donaldsonville, a distance of about 90 miles, the river runs in nearly an east course, almost parallel with the Gulf coast. Bounding the city limits on the north lies Lake Pontchartrain, which is almost 40 miles long by 25 broad, its southern shore being nearly parallel to the Mississippi River for more than 20 miles, thus forming a strip of land between the two of an average width of 5 or 6 miles, on which New Orleans is situated, thus placing it on an island, except this narrow strip of land, through which runs the New Orleans, Jackson and Great Northern Railroad; the only line of land communication the city has with the interior. The river, before reaching New Orleans, finds its way through the alluvial country in various channels to the sea (as will be further described), which in high water offer facilities for navigation. Lake Pontchartrain is also in immediate connection with the Gulf of Mexico, independent of all other approaches to the city. Lake Borgne, likewise connected with the Gulf, gives us water approach to within a few miles of the Mississippi River at a point not far below the city. This was the route taken by the British in 1815. These are the general features of the location of New Orleans.

The coast line of Department No. 1 is penetrated by passes and streams navigable in high-water season at not less than twelve or fifteen different points, many of which, as the enemy had entire command of the sea, required immediate attention. Commencing at Pascagoula, on the east, the coast could be entered by water at Biloxi Bay and [Bay] Saint Louis and Pearl Rivers, which latter empties itself into the Gulf of Mexico by two mouths outside that entrance to Lake Pontchartrain, on which Fort Pike was located, to be hereafter described. A short distance up the Pearl River a bayou connected the river with the lake, thus avoiding entirely the guns of Fort Pike, beside which a fair road led west to the Mississippi River, giving access to the Jackson Railroad, as well as the whole northern shore of Lake Pontchartrain. This lake was connected with the Gulf by two outlets—the Rigolets and Chef Menteur Pass—on the former of which was located Fort Pike and on the latter Fort Macomb, formerly called Fort Wood. From the shore of Lake Borgne four bayous put into the land, through which access could be had by water to points near to and convenient for attack on the city. Two of them had small works upon them (Bienvenue and Phillippon) and others (Gentilly and Ciletche) were unguarded. Proceeding west, three large streams gave access directly from the ocean to firm ground near the river more than 40 miles above Forts Jackson and Saint Philip, viz: Bayous l'Outre, Terre aux Bœuff, and Aux Chène, the enemy occupying Breton Isle with land forces directly off the mouths of these bayous. The next main point of entrance is the Mississippi River, which enters the Gulf by five mouths or passes. Forts Jackson and Saint Philip are located on opposite sides of the river, about 25 miles above the Head of the Passes and 75 below New Orleans. Further west is Barataria Bay, at the entrance of which is an island, on the west end of which Fort Livingston is situated. The pass at the east end is not defended. From Barataria Bay there is a direct water communication with the river just above New Orleans via Bayous Barataria and Familles and a short canal. The next principal inlets are Bayous La Fourche and Grand Caillou, the former of which is one of the mouths of the Mississippi River, from which it offsets at Donaldsonville and crosses the Opelousas Railroad at Thibodeaux; the other heads near that railroad. Atchafalaya Bay and River afford the next important water approach. This river also connects with the Mississippi through Bayou Plaquemine above Donaldsonville, and, besides, gives access, via Bayou Teche and other streams, to a very rich and important section of country, as well as to the terminus of the Opelousas Railroad at Brashear City. West of this are Bayous Sayle and Dead Cypress, and Calcasieu Bay, the latter of which gave entrance to a large cattle-range country. Besides these important points there are numerous smaller creeks and bayous through which an enterprising enemy could penetrate and obtain access to important approaches above the defenses.

West of Lake Pontchartrain, and between it and the Mississippi River, is situated Lake Maurepas, connected with Pontchartrain by the North and South Manchac Passes, which are separated by an island, and with the river by Bayou Manchac, in former years leveed so as to destroy the river connection. The New Orleans, Jackson and Great Northern Railroad runs through the narrow strip of land between Lake Pontchartrain and the river, skirting the southern and western shores of the lake, and passing between it and Maurepas across the North and South Manchac Passes goes northward into the interior. The New Orleans and Opelousas Railroad starts from Algiers, opposite New Orleans, and runs westward, crossing Bayous La Fourche, Des Allemandes, and others, terminating at Brashear City, on the Atchafalaya, about 80 miles, where the great road led to Texas. This road was the principal means of transportation for beef cattle and supplies from Texas for New Orleans and the East, and its security was a matter of great importance.

The Mexican Gulf Railroad connected the city with Proctorsville, on Lake Borgne, distant 28 miles. There were also two short railroads from the compact part of the city to Lake Pontchartrain, besides a water connection with the lake by the new canal and the Bayou Saint John, both of which led into the heart of the city. Through the latter the Confederate States steamers Bienville and Carondelet were taken from their place of building to the lake. There were two good roads from the city to Lake Pontchartrain, one along the Bayou Saint John and the other on the Metairie Ridge. Also a road following Gentilly Ridge to Fort Macomb, near which road heads Bayou Gentilly, emptying into Lake Borgne, by which route the forts would be avoided. The city could also be approached by the enemy's fleet from the Upper Mississippi descending the river.

New Orleans is situated on low, flat ground, which is the character of all the surrounding country. To protect it against the annual rise of the river, which commences usually in January and lasts through the spring, embankments of earth, called levees, have been thrown up along its course, which levees extend from a long distance above the city in its front and for 30 miles below. The tops of these levees are much above the surface of the country, so that when the river rises to the height of the levees it is above the level of the adjacent land. Below these levees the river, in years of very high water, overflows the adjoining country almost entirely. The land above the city, with the exceptions indicated, is generally low and swampy, the city itself extending for miles immediately along the banks of the Mississippi River, but the inhabited part not extending far back towards the swamp.

For further answer of this question, and as explanatory of the above, I submit the accompanying map, which, while not correct in all minor details, gives all the general features of the country with sufficient accuracy to enable the court to understand the numerous routes by which the department could be entered.

(The map above referred to was inspected by the court, and is hereto appended as document No. 2.*)

The court adjourned to meet at 11 a. m. 7th instant.

JACKSON, MISS., *April* 7, 1863—11 a. m.

The court met pursuant to adjournment.

Present, all the members of the court, the judge-advocate, and Maj. Gen. Mansfield Lovell.

The proceedings of yesterday were read over.

Examination of Maj. Gen. MANSFIELD LOVELL continued.

By the JUDGE-ADVOCATE:

Question. What instructions, if any, did you receive on assuming command, from the War Department? What report was made to you by your predecessor of the existing state of affairs at the time; and what was the general military condition of Department No. 1 as you found it?

Answer. I received no specific instructions whatever from the War Department. The subject was referred to by the Secretary of War and Adjutant-General Cooper, but they seemed to think it not necessary, expressing confidence in my judgment and ability to do what was right and proper. I requested authority to control all matters for the defense of my department, naval and military, on the water as well as on land, assigning my reason therefor; but this authority was declined, as will appear by the letters of the President and Secretary of War hereunto appended. (Marked documents Nos. 3 and 4.) When I arrived in New Orleans, my predecessor, Major-General Twiggs, made no official report of the condition of affairs, but stated to me verbally that the department was almost entirely defenseless; that he had been unable to get anything done, and that at many points we could not make an hour's fight. He dwelt particularly upon the want of guns and ammunition. He gave me little or no information, as he said his feeble state of health had prevented him from making personal inspections of the various points of the department.

I assumed command on October 18, and in order to acquaint myself with the exact condition of the defenses, the topography of the country, the approaches, &c., of all of which I was entirely ignorant, I made personal inspections and critical examinations throughout the whole extent of the department. These inspections, together with the details of the office, occupied me night and day for more than two weeks. I found matters generally so deficient and incomplete, that I was unwilling to commit their condition to paper for fear of their falling into wrong hands, and so stated to the Secretary. The troops (three regiments) on the Mississippi coast were badly armed and had very little ammunition—one of the regiments not more than five rounds per man. The entrances to Pearl River were entirely unobstructed, as, indeed, were all the other inlets and approaches into the country. In addition to the works hereafter to be named, there was an open battery of ten 24-pounders on Bayou Bienvenue, one of five on Phillippon, and two small earthworks, intended for five guns each, had been thrown up guarding the approaches to Berwick Bay, but had not been completed.

The forts in the department viz, Pike, Macomb, Saint Philip, Jackson, and Livingston, were originally small works of a very inferior class, built of brick and earth,

*Not found.

and, having been unoccupied for many years, had become much dilapidated, and in places I found them crumbling with their own weight. On inspection I found them armed principally with smooth-bore 24 and 32 pounders, there not being in the whole department more than nine guns mounted of a greater caliber than a 32-pounder, and, indeed, but twenty-six of them mounted. Seven or eight of the 32s had been rifled, but there was neither shot nor shell for them. The gun-carriages were generally old and defective from long exposure to the weather. Many of them were so decayed that I could insert a penknife with ease into the wood. There was likewise a very great deficiency in all the implements and equipments necessary for the service of heavy guns, as sponges, rammers, priming-wires, friction-tubes, primers, haversacks, handspikes, hot-shot implements, budge-barrels, &c. The ammunition did not average more than twenty rounds per gun.

Forts Jackson and Saint Philip, owing to the exertions of General (then Colonel) Duncan, were in a better state of preparation than the other works, but still sadly deficient in very many respects for their full defense, and much of the ammunition on hand was so inferior in quality as not to give more than half range. The Macomb had nothing but 24-pounders, which, indeed, composed the main armament of all the works. There were no guns or works at Pass Manchac, or Bayou La Fourche, Grand Caillou, or on the approaches, or Barataria Bay, to the river near the city. No measures had been taken for obstructing any of the rivers or passes, either by felling timber, driving piles, or making rafts, except that the materials had been collected in part for making a raft, to be placed in the Mississippi River at the forts, and work on it had been commenced. A line of intrenchments around the city itself had been planned, and was commenced some weeks before my arrival, by Maj. (now General) M. L. Smith, but it was entirely unfinished; not a gun was mounted, a magazine built, nor a platform laid. The length of this line was more than 8 miles. General Twiggs had, shortly before being relieved, received from the Norfolk navy-yard more than 100 old navy guns, many of which had been long in use and the rest so worn as to be unfit for friction tubes. Many of the guns had been cast more than forty years. There were none above a 42-pounder, and a number were 32-pounder carronades, a gun entirely useless except for firing grape and canister at short distances. No carriages, chassis, or implements came with these guns, and none of them were mounted when I took command. There was a vast amount of engineer and ordnance work to be done, and both of these important branches were imposed upon Major Smith, who found it impossible to do justice to them both.

On the water there were two small vessels, the McRae and the Joy, and the ram Manassas, with one gun. Two river steamboats were being strengthened and ironed for service, the keels of two iron-clad ships—the Louisiana and Mississippi—had been lately laid, and two smaller gunboats, for service on Lake Pontchartrain, were on the stocks in the Bayou Saint John.

This is about the condition of the preparations on November 1, about the time I assumed command. I would add that several new regiments were in process of organization and preparation at Camp Moore, 78 miles north of the city, but were only partially armed and equipped. There were in all five new regiments, which were unfit to take the field.

The court adjourned to 10 a. m. the 8th instant.

JACKSON, MISS., *April* 8, 1863.

The court met pursuant to adjournment.

Present, all the members, the judge-advocate, and Major-General Lovell.

The proceedings of yesterday were read over.

Examination of Major-General LOVELL continued.

By the JUDGE-ADVOCATE:

Question. What steps did you take to organize and perfect the defenses of the department? Give a full account of your preparations and administration up to the time of the evacuation of the city.

Answer. Thinking it probable that an attack would be made some time in January, I commenced at once, with all the available means at my disposal, to supply the deficiencies and to provide against the dangers indicated in my last answer. In making these preparations, however, I was materially delayed by the want of a sufficient number of competent officers of experience and detailed knowledge. This deficiency was made known to the War Department and relief asked on several occasions, but without success. (See my letters to the War Department of various dates.)

Having completed my inspection in the early part of November, I telegraphed on the 5th to Colonel Gorgas, Chief of Ordnance, at Richmond, for mortars and columbiads. He replied the next day that he had no mortars or columbiads to spare at present. I then telegraphed General Bragg, at Pensacola, to send me, if possible, some 10-inch guns and mortars. He answered, "Not a gun to spare." Knowing that there was no other point to look to for guns, I then turned my attention to making arrangements in New Orleans with Messrs. Leeds & Co., Bennett & Surges, and S. Wolfe & Co. for putting up reverberating furnaces and making other preparations for casting 8 and 10 inch columbiads and 10-inch sea-coast mortars. I procured all the large chains and anchors that could be had from Pensacola, Savannah, and other places, for the purpose of constructing rafts and booms to place in the various water approaches, giving particular attention to that in the Mississippi River; contracted for the building and sinking of an obstruction in Pearl River; had Salt Bayou, as also Gentilly and Ciletche Bayous, with rows of piles driven across the channels, and Bayous l'Outre, Terre Aux Bœuff, and Aux Chène obstructed by felling the timber on the banks, and eventually, with the assistance of the Safety Committee of New Orleans, had two rows of piles, each more than 1,000 yards long and braced at the top, driven in the channel, under the guns of Fort Pike, where the water was nearly 50 feet in depth. The channel leading into Atchafalaya Bay was also filled up by sinking green live-oak trees, forming an obstruction 40 feet wide at the base and 8 at the tops, and a raft was placed on the river just below Fort Berwick. Judge Baker, of Louisiana, superintended this latter work.

I replaced the 24-pounders *en barbette*, bearing on the water, at Forts Jackson, Saint Philip, Pike, and Macomb, with the 42 and 32 pounders received from Norfolk, and added materially to the strength of the various garrisons. Obtaining sulphur and saltpeter wherever it could be found, I pressed to completion a large powder-mill, under charge of Messrs. Hobart & Foster, and soon commenced the manufacture of powder, which was submitted to the *éprouvette* test before it was received. Having arrangements made with the founderies in New Orleans for casting shot and shell, I proceeded, with the permission of the Secretary of War, to convert one-half of the large new Marine Hospital into an arsenal, where I had a steam-engine put up for driving the machinery, small-arms prepared, and the various implements, equipments, and munitions made for the service of heavy guns. A cartridge manufactory was established, in which a number of hands were employed, and which not only supplied my department, but enabled me to send more than 1,000,000 rounds to the army in Tennessee.

A considerable quantity of powder was brought in by the steamers Vanderbilt, Miramon, and Victoria, but it was all old and unfit for use, and every pound was remanufactured in New Orleans; and from this source I transferred to the Navy 25,000 pounds, sent 17,000 pounds to other departments, and 12,000 pounds to Richmond, besides furnishing ammunition to all the troops sent to General A. S. Johnston in Tennessee, and giving the river-defense fleet what they required.

Earthwork forts, mounting from two to six guns each, were commenced on the Grand Caillou and on Bayou La Fourche; on Bayou Barataria, at the Manchac Passes, and at Proctorsville; and two forts on Berwick Bay were almost entirely reconstructed. On the Mississippi River works were also put up above the city and on the southern and western shores of Lake Pontchartrain.

The general plan adopted was to have two lines of works—an exterior line passing through the forts and earthworks erected to defend the various water approaches, and an interior line, embracing New Orleans and Algiers, which was intended principally to repel an attack by land. Commencing at the swamp on the west side of the river, about 4½ miles below Algiers, this interior line extended across the firm ground of the right bank of the river, and from the right bank, at a point just opposite across the dry ground, to a swamp which occupied the space between it and Gentilly Ridge, where the line extended across the ridge to the adjoining swamp. It was resumed at the various points of firm ground on the railroad, canal, and roads, when they issued through the swamp in rear of the city, towards Lake Pontchartrain. Above the city it also extended from the swamp to the left bank of the river again, and from the opposite side it ran along the Barataria Canal from the bank of the river to the swamp above Algiers. The total length of the intrenchments on this line was more than 8 miles, and, when completed, it, in connection with the swamp, put New Orleans in an impregnable position so far as regarded any attack by land. It mounted more than sixty guns, of various calibers, and was surrounded by wide and deep ditches.

One regiment of troops was taken from the Mississippi coast and stationed at Berwick Bay, a point of vital importance, where I also located a battery of field artillery and a company of cavalry. Twenty independent companies of infantry, raised by my predecessor, were organized by me into regiments, placed as garrisons in the various works of the exterior line, and thoroughly drilled in the heavy artillery service. The infantry at Camp Moore was brought to the city and placed in camp, and when General Ruggles (after four weeks of severe illness) reported for duty he was charged with the organization of a brigade out of these troops. They were, after much difficulty, well armed, equipped, and provided in all respects, and held at the central position, to be sent to any point of the exterior line required or to defend the interior line if attacked. I laid a railway track in the city between the Pontchartrain and Mexican Gulf Railroads, so as to transfer troops rapidly from point to point, and established telegraph lines to Proctorsville and to Brashear City, on Berwick Bay. We were already in telegraphic communication with Forts Pike, Macomb, Saint Philip, and Jackson, and the Passes at the mouth of the Mississippi River. I also made every effort, through the citizens, to endeavor to accumulate a supply of flour and meat sufficient for sixty days for the whole city, to enable the inhabitants to stand a siege; but from causes beyond my control their efforts failed entirely, and this want of provisions for more than 150,000 inhabitants was an important element in determining the evacuation of the city in April. In addition to the great amount of labor imposed upon myself and the small number of experienced officers with me, by the details of the works above indicated, I received orders about January 15, 1862, from the Secretary of War, to seize fourteen steamers, then at New Orleans, which were to be strengthened, protected with cotton bales, armed, mounted, and equipped, under my general supervision, by Captains Montgomery, Townsend, and others named by them. For this purpose $1,000,000 was placed to my credit, and, although not favorably impressed with the plan myself, I labored assiduously to carry out the view of the Department. Montgomery and Townsend were sent from Richmond, and the twelve other captains were selected by them, the matter being placed in their hands by instructions from the Secretary of War. All these vessels were completed and put in service before April 1, eight of them being sent up the river to Fort Pillow and the other six retained for reasons indicated by me in my letter of March 10 to the Secretary of War, hereto appended.

Immense requisitions of all kinds were constantly made on my department, and provisions, clothing, camp and garrison equipage, powder, and munitions of war of various kinds were sent to the different parts of the Confederacy. My chief quartermaster, chief commissary, and ordnance officer not only performed their department duties, but acted as agents for the heads of their respective bureaus at Richmond. I had twelve launches fitted up and armed with one gun each, for service on the small bayous and canals by which the department is intersected in all directions. This was mainly for the purpose of preventing marauding expeditions and to keep negroes and others from communicating with the enemy.

I reported, quite in detail, to the War Department my progress in the duties of my command on December 5, 1861. During the succeeding four weeks I was directed from Richmond to send out of the department twenty-two heavy guns to Tennessee and Charleston, S. C. (see dispatches herewith, marked 5, 6, and 7), and to provide one gun each for the fourteen vessels of the river-defense fleet intended for service on the upper river. I also turned over to the Navy ten 42-pounders for arming the steamers Bienville and Carondelet for service in Lake Pontchartrain and Mississippi Sound; besides which I supplied them with powder and the men to serve their guns, as they had neither guns, powder, nor crews to make the ships available. I reported to the Secretaries of War and the Navy that I had turned over these ten guns. I also notified the former that I had sent two regiments of troops to Columbus, Ky., upon the urgent request of the general in command there.

In February I was ordered by the War Department to send 5,000 men also to Columbus, which took away all my available force in New Orleans, leaving me without a single armed regiment of Confederate troops in the city. Every vessel of war ready for service in the river was also ordered up to the same point, and the department left without ships or men, except the garrisons of the works on the exterior line.

On February 25 I made requisitions on the governor of Louisiana for 10,000 militia for the defense of the city, but the adjutant-general of the State reported that, in November, 1861, he had only about 6,000 armed militia available, and that since that time 3,000 of the best armed of these troops had been sent to re-enforce the army in Tennessee upon there quisition of General Beauregard. This gave me for the defense of New Orleans less than 3,000 militia, of which 1,200 had muskets, and the remainder very indifferent shot-guns. These troops were commanded by their own State officers, and a part of them, when ordered to the support of Fort Jackson, mutinied and refused to go, and had to be forced on board the transports by other regiments.

I reported to the War Department the manner in which my district had been stripped of men, guns, and ships, and objected thereto. (See my letters to the Secretary of War, February 12 and March 6, 9, 10, and 22, hereto appended, marked documents Nos. 8, 9, 10, 11, and 12, as well as subsequent letters to the Department.*)

The strength of the land defenses around the city was, however, so great that I felt confident of repelling, even with the troops at my disposal, any attack that might be

* See dispatches of dates indicated in "Correspondence, etc.—Confederate," *post.*

made by land, and I felt sure that the enemy was well posted as to the strength of our works.

With regard to the water approaches, I had put every gun in position that I could get and had obstructed every river of any size leading into the department, relying upon the Navy to have such iron-clad ships and other gunboats as would enable us to oppose successfully every attack by water.

I desire to state that there were two separate and distinct organizations for the defense of Department No. 1, viz, that under the control of the Secretary of War, of which I was the senior officer, and that under the Secretary of the Navy, of which Commodore Hollins and afterwards Commander Whittle were the seniors. We were entirely independent of each other, but were directed to co-operate cordially for the defense of the city. I had no control whatever over them, but the best feeling existed, and there was very seldom any difference of opinion between us as to what should be done. I made requests at various times of them that they were unable to comply with. They complained frequently of the inadequacy of the means and material placed at their disposal to assist me, and regretted that they had no power to hasten the completion of the proper ships for our defense. What few they had were sent up the rivers, and the others were directed to follow as soon as completed. Against this I protested by telegram on April 11 to the Secretary of War. (See dispatches, hereunto appended, marked document No. 13.) These vessels, however, were never entirely finished. On land we had, for the defense of the department, sixteen different forts, large and small (seven of which were built before the war), upon the various water approaches, besides an intrenched line, with numerous batteries, around the city, in all of which there were in position nearly 300 guns of various calibers, while on April 24 there was not a single war vessel of any great size or power afloat on the Mississippi River in serviceable condition for the defense of Department No. 1.

There was an additional part of my administration of affairs which cost much time and labor.

On March 15, 1862, by direction of the President, New Orleans and the adjacent parishes were placed under martial law. Eight provost-marshals were appointed, four for the city and four for the parishes, and for valid reasons I felt compelled to give a good deal of time and attention personally to their plans and course of action.

In the latter part of February the great raft in the Mississippi River began to show signs of giving way. The drift had accumulated greatly and the river was higher than ever known before. I employed steamboats and skiffs to remove the drift, but it gained on us so rapidly that the attempt was given up. The raft gave way at various points, and by the end of the first week in March the main chains snapped, and it ceased to be any longer an obstruction. I determined, therefore, to detain six of Montgomery's boats at New Orleans, contrary to orders from the War Department, but reported the fact and the reasons therefor on March 10 by letter to the Secretary of War.

Previous to taking command at New Orleans I had verbally stated, both to the President and Secretary of War, that, in my opinion, batteries on shore could be passed by ships of war under steam with the loss of but few vessels, and had repeated this opinion to the latter in my letter of November 19, 1861.

As soon as the raft had given way I applied for and got $100,000 from the city council of New Orleans, by whom the money for the previous raft had been furnished, and sent Colonel Higgins, an able and efficient officer, formerly of the U. S. Navy, down, to endeavor to repair the raft. I gave him full authority to take or hire steamers, employ men, and do anything that might be necessary to accomplish his purpose. It was found impossible to restore the raft; but a new obstruction was made of parts of the old raft and with schooners anchored and fastened together by chains. This obstruction was, however, far inferior to the other, and was by no means satisfactory; but heavy chains for anchoring a more formidable obstruction could not be obtained by the most strenuous endeavors. I had prepared and sent down forty or fifty fire rafts loaded with lightwood and mixed with cotton, rosin, and tar oil, which were placed above and below the new obstruction. This second obstruction was pretty much broken up and carried away before the final attack. I also sent to Memphis and procured the services of Mr. J. B. Cook, who had much experience with torpedoes, and endeavored to have them placed in the river; but the great depth (more than 130 feet) and the powerful current rendered such attempts nugatory. I ordered a Drummond light to be made and sent to Fort Jackson; but it was destroyed by one of the enemy's shells during the bombardment.

Governor Moore, at my request, took two steamers, lying in the river, had them strengthened with cotton bales and provided with officers and crews, which he placed under my orders. I armed them with two heavy guns each and furnished them with ammunition, &c., and sent them to Fort Jackson, under Captains Kennon and Grant.

The arrangements for casting heavy guns were meanwhile pressed forward under my frequent supervision, but many difficulties presented themselves. Pits for casting could not be used on account of water, which in that low, flat country rapidly filled them. It became necessary to make casings in the pits to exclude the water, but I succeeded, just before the evacuation, in having two 8-inch columbiads and two 10-inch mortars completed and the model for 10-inch columbiads was ready.

Learning by accident in the early part of March that Pensacola was to be abandoned, I renewed my application to the War Department for some of the columbiads and mortars, of which there was a large number there. I telegraphed Mr. Benjamin, Secretary of War, March 7, 1862, as follows: "In case of evacuation of points now fortified, please order 10-inch guns and mortars here." To this telegram I received no reply. On March 15 I telegraphed to Maj. Gen. S. Jones, commanding at Mobile, to send me 10-inch mortars, and also wrote on the 21st. (See letter marked document No. 14.) Receiving no answer, I telegraphed the Secretary of War, requesting him to order General Jones to send the columbiads and mortars promptly; to which he replied by telegraph that he had ordered them to be sent as requested. On the 29th I telegraphed the Secretary of War that the enemy were in force at the mouth of the river, and to please order the commanding officer at Mobile to send immediately. General Randolph, who in the mean time had become Secretary of War, telegraphed me on March 29 to know what guns I meant, whether guns in battery or guns on the way to me. I replied, "A part of the 10-inch columbiads and sea-coast mortars which were at Pensacola;" that New Orleans had only one of the former and none of the latter. On April 4 the Secretary of War telegraphed me that he had endeavored to get from Pensacola columbiads and sea-coast mortars, but found that all had been sent to Mobile that could be spared. Finding I could not obtain guns by authority, I sent Major Duncan, an energetic officer, to get possession of as many guns of that caliber as he could and to bring them through unless stopped by some superior officer. Major Duncan is now dead. He reported to me that General Jones, at Mobile, would let me have two 10-inch guns if he were in command, but that he had been ordered away; that he telegraphed General Bragg, who replied that the commanding officer was authorized to give the guns if he thought proper, but that they regarded the points above Memphis as the best for the defense of New Orleans. The commanding officer at Mobile refused to give them. Major Duncan then went to Pensacola and took three guns, which he brought to New Orleans. I also telegraphed and wrote to General Beauregard to request General Bragg to order me the guns. (See letters hereunto appended, marked documents Nos. 15, 16, and 17.) I borrowed some guns from Commander Whittle in the latter part of March, which were intended for the iron-clads Louisiana and Mississippi, and on April 4 suggested that the remaining guns of the Louisiana be sent to Fort Jackson, as I feared that vessel would not be ready in time for the fight. On the 11th the commodore demanded the return of the guns, against which I protested. (See letters on these points hereunto appended, marked documents Nos. 18, 19, 20, 21, and 22.) I urged the completion of the Louisiana and Mississippi upon Commander Whittle; but he replied that they were not under his control, the contracts being made independent of his order by the Secretary of the Navy.

I sent a regiment of troops, under Colonel Szymanski, to the quarantine to prevent an approach to the river bank above Fort Saint Philip by the enemy; but the unprecedented high water dislodged the troops, who were removed to the west bank, where they were located until they were captured by the enemy's fleet. Sharpshooters were also organized by my orders for service on the banks of the river below the forts. Obtaining a few heavy guns from Pensacola, I got 120 negroes from the planters on the river and sent them to General Duncan for mounting those guns in an additional water battery outside of Fort Jackson. General Duncan, lately promoted, had been placed by me in command of all the works of the exterior lines and made his headquarters at Fort Jackson. I also sent to General Beauregard for the ram Manassas, which he finally sent down, and she took part in the battle of the 24th.

Commodore Hollins came down in April with the McRae, and, after consultation with Commander Whittle, I telegraphed the Secretary of War, on April 17, to try and have Hollins put in command afloat below until he could strike a blow. (See document No. 23, hereunto appended.) This, however, was not done. The water meanwhile had risen in the river to an extraordinary height. Places heretofore free from overflow were entirely submerged, and the water was nearly 2 feet deep even in Fort Jackson. For miles above the forts the river formed one vast sheet of water in connection with the Gulf of Mexico, and nearer the city, where the banks are leveed, the surface of the river was not less than 8 or 9 feet above the level of the land adjacent. Maj. M. L. Smith, whose promotion I had urged for some time, was promoted a brigadier-general in April, and assigned by me to the command of the interior line. Ten 32-pounders, smooth bore, and two 8-inch columbiads, just finished in New Orleans, were mounted at the interior line where it abuts upon the river below the city (half the guns on each side), and they were provided with seventy rounds of ammunition per gun.

On April 20, Commander Whittle informed me that the Louisiana, although not entirely ready with her motive power, would go down at once to the forts, but he could get no powder for the guns, except the 3,000 pounds which I had already turned over to him. As she was an iron-clad ship, mounting sixteen guns, a number of which were rifled, of the heaviest caliber and longest range, I determined, in the emergency, to take 50 rounds from my battery of smooth-bore 32s on the lower line, which would give the Louisiana 5,000 pounds additional, but only left 20 rounds at the interior line battery. I thought that the powder would do better service on the Louisiana than, with my light guns and new recruits, on the inner line. I issued no ammunition to the militia at the camp near the interior line because they were utterly useless against ships; no land attack was anticipated, and, above all, they had, in some regiments, manifested such an insubordinate disposition, that I felt unwilling to put ammunition in their hands. I had, however, 600,000 rounds of shot-gun cartridges made up for their use, and put in the arsenal ready for use when the proper time should arrive.

I employed two small steamers, with officers selected by myself, and sent them to General Duncan, for towing the fire-rafts into position for setting them adrift. Several other steamers were also employed to carry down sand bags, already filled, for protection to the magazines, &c., of the forts. For full particulars of the long and arduous contest at Forts Jackson and Saint Philip reference is made to General Duncan's official report.

On April 20, in consequence of the heavy fire, I turned over to Captain Mitchell the control of the fire rafts, the steamers for towing them, and all other floating defenses at the forts, as General Duncan found it impossible to take proper charge of them. I sent orders to that effect to Captain Stephenson, the senior officer of the six boats of the river-defense fleet, and to the captains of the two ships turned over to me by Governor Moore.

This, I believe, answers the question in the most material points. A vast number of smaller matters gave me much trouble and labor and took up a great deal of my time. I refer the court especially to my correspondence with the War Department for additional particulars as to all that was done by me in the administration of the affairs of Department No. 1.

The court adjourned to meet at 10 a. m. the 9th instant.

JACKSON, MISS., *April* 9, 1863.

The court met pursuant to adjournment.

Present, all the members of the court, the judge-advocate, and also Maj. Gen. Mansfield Lovell.

Examination of Major General LOVELL continued.

By the JUDGE-ADVOCATE:

Question. Describe particularly the obstruction of the Mississippi River near Forts Jackson and Saint Philip, and state what, if any, confidence you placed in that obstruction as a permanent work.

Answer. The obstruction in the Mississippi River was placed just under the guns of Forts Jackson and Saint Philip, and work upon it had been begun before my arrival. It consisted of cypress trees 40 feet long and averaging 4 to 5 feet at the larger end. These were placed longitudinally in the river, about 3 feet apart, so as to leave a water-way. They were held together by (or rather strung upon) two $2\frac{1}{2}$-inch chain cables, which were passed through mortises in the under side of the logs and held in place by heavy iron staples. To give it stiffening large timbers, 6 by 4 inches, were securely pinned down transversely to the upper side of the logs. This raft was placed in the river by securing the chains on the left bank to large trees, and on the right bank, where there were no trees, they were fastened to crab capstans and to immense anchors buried in the ground and held by heavy timbers. In addition, all the anchors that could be had were got from various points in the Confederacy, and the raft was anchored up stream, the large anchors being laid singly and the smaller ones backed by a second anchor. The depth of the river being about 130 feet at that point, this required an immense amount of chain, which was difficult to procure, as well as a sufficiency of anchors.

The difficulty of anchoring a heavy mass in the Mississippi arises from the fact that the bottom is a shifting sand, and in high water the swift current soon cuts out the anchors or other obstruction placed on the bottom. In this manner the raft began to sag by the drifting of the anchors, and the whole weight was thrown upon the chains; and, when an immense amount of drift-wood had accumulated above the raft, these eventually parted. This occurred about the early part of March. I employed steamers to remove the drift, but it accumulated much faster than it could be removed. I then authorized General Duncan to employ 50 or 100 boatmen, with skiffs, to assist in the operation; but only a few boats could be obtained. Persons well acquainted with the river told me that any obstruction of such character could not be made to hold in the Mississippi River for the reason above indicated; but I thought it possible that I could make it so that it would hold for several months; at all events until the middle of January, at which date I was informed by those superintending their construction that the iron-clad vessels would be completed.

In constructing this raft I employed the best engineering and nautical ability at my command, Major Smith and Colonel Duncan, and Colonel [W. S.] Lovell (formerly of the U. S. Navy), being charged with its construction and anchorage. Its position was fixed upon after consultation with General Beauregard, who, as an engineer in the U. S. Army, had been in service in that country for many years. I had a long boom constructed to stretch diagonally across the river above the forts, so as to shed the drift over through the opening; but all my endeavors to get chains and anchors to secure it in position proved futile.

I omitted stating that on April 23 I requested Commander Whittle to order the iron-clad steamer Louisiana to take position just below Fort Saint Philip, and endeavor to dislodge the enemy's mortar boats, so as to give some relief to the garrisons and enable them to repair damages. He said she was not in condition for effective service, and she would probably be lost. I told him we had better lose her than the city of New Orleans, and he telegraphed Captain Mitchell to strain a point to endeavor to comply with my request. The naval commanders held a consultation on the subject, and, for reasons which they considered satisfactory, declined to place the vessel in the position indicated.

The court adjourned to meet at 10 a. m. to-morrow, the 10th instant.

JACKSON, MISS., *April* 10, 1863.

The court met pursuant to adjournment.

Present, all the members of the court, the judge-advocate, and Major-General Lovell.

The proceedings of yesterday were read over.

Examination of Major-General LOVELL continued.

By the JUDGE-ADVOCATE:

Question. State your reasons for the evacuation of the other forts and works of the exterior line and the city of New Orleans after the passage of Forts Jackson and Saint Philip by the enemy's fleet; the measures you adopted for the removal of public property; the amount of such property, and the number of troops removed from the city; state also the facts and circumstances attendant upon the evacuation.

Answer. I was present in a small river steamboat at the engagement which resulted in the passage of the forts by the enemy's fleet on the morning of April 24, and proceeded immediately to the city. I had taken down on the boats with me to Fort Jackson a number of large cartridges, already made up, for General Duncan's heavy guns, which I was unable to deliver On my return I directed them to be left at the batteries on the lower interior line, stopped there myself, and told the officers that the cartridges must be reduced to 8 pounds each for service with their guns, which were 32-pounders, which, I believe, was not done. I had already determined upon the course to be pursued in case of the passage of the forts, and had made arrangements to meet the emergency, having particularly directed my chief commissary (Major Lanier) to send out quietly from the city several hundred thousand rations, which were deposited at Covington and at points on the Jackson Railroad. I had also, through Colonel Lovell, of my staff, made arrangements to have several large steamers kept in such a state of preparation that they could be made available at a few hours' notice.

I determined to evacuate the city when the enemy succeeded in passing the forts for the following reasons: The principal concentration in men, guns, and ships had been made at this point. It had been selected as the spot where the battle for the defense of New Orleans against a fleet coming up the Mississippi River should be fought, and everything available for the defense below, both ashore and afloat, had been collected there, except the twelve guns on the river at the lower interior line, which were put there to flank that line. The obstacles had been placed there and swept away and had been a complete bar to the passage of a hostile fleet, and the naval and river defense officers had brought to bear at that point all the available strength, and although New Orleans was still in a condition to resist an attack by land, yet when, after six days and nights of incessant conflict, the forts were passed and all our defenses afloat were either burned or sunk, I knew there was no material obstacle to prevent the fleet from proceeding at once to the city, and that all the guns, forts, and men on the other ten or twelve water approaches would go for naught. The twelve guns in the upper earthworks on the lower line had but 20 rounds of powder each (the remainder having been given to the steamer Louisiana, for reasons which I have already stated), and could offer no serious resistance to a fleet which had already passed more than 100 guns in masonry works, better mounted and amply supplied with powder. The city was surrounded by swamps, and there was but one outlet by land, viz, through the narrow neck, heretofore described, between the river and Lake Pontchartrain.

At Kenner, on the Mississippi, 10 miles above the city, the firm ground between the river and the swamp which borders the lake is narrowed to about three-quarters of a mile, through which passes the Jackson Railroad. The river at this time was full to the top of the levees, and a single one of their large ships of war anchoring at this point would have commanded with her broadside, at point-blank range, the only land exit from the city, sweeping with her guns (which would have been higher than the surface of the country) every foot of land between the river and the lake. The obstructions placed across the Rigolets at Fort Pike had been swept away in a storm shortly before, by some vessels which had broken adrift, and there was an open channel, fully as wide as the Mississippi River, into Lake Pontchartrain, which could easily be passed by the enemy at night. Such a movement, in connection with the placing of one or more ships at Kenner, would have completely surrounded New Orleans, cutting off all communication, by land or water, with the interior. (See the map heretofore submitted.) My efforts to accumulate provisions enough in the city to feed the population had proved abortive, and an examination, made a few days previous to the evacuation, had satisfied me that there were not in the city provisions enough to sustain the population for more than eighteen days. Taking it for granted that the enemy would occupy Kenner, as indeed he did, in a few days, we should have been starved into a surrender in less than three weeks; for when the hostile fleet anchored in front of the city we were entirely cut off from Texas and the Red River, our main source of supply. I had more than three months' rations available for my troops (less than 3,000 men), but this would have answered but a few days for a population of more than 150,000 persons. Some of the steamers on the levee had been destroyed and a number had fled up the river, so that the Jackson Railroad was the only means of transportation for removing the women, children, and non-combatants from the city, which removal it would have required months to accomplish.

In the vicinity of New Orleans and for many miles above there was nothing but swamps filled with water, in which the families could take refuge, and, moreover, a great portion of the male protectors of these families were absent with our armies in Tennessee and Virginia, and of course could not superintend their removal. The plan, therefore, of removing the non-combatants and remaining with the troops was entirely impracticable. Thirteen of the enemy's ships were anchored abreast of the city, with their guns looking down upon the streets, which they could have swept to the swamps in rear of the houses or set on fire at a number of points; and, had I continued to occupy it with troops, they would have been justified, by the laws of war, in opening fire, after due notice to the women and children to withdraw from danger. I knew that they had not, and could not have for several days, land forces to take possession, and having determined, for the reasons above stated, to evacuate the city, I thought it best to remove the troops at once and speedily, and thus convert New Orleans from a military position into that of an ungarrisoned city. By so doing I should deprive the enemy of all pretext for a wanton and useless sacrifice of life and property, and, as they were unable to occupy it, I would have a number of days for the undisturbed removal of the vast amount of public property which was on hand at the time. My troops, however, were placed at Camp Moore, only four hours' run from the city by rail, and I could have reoccupied it at any time for several days after the evacuation, if it had been deemed advisable. Had I regarded the outside popular clamor that would ensue, I should have subjected the people of New Orleans to a bombardment; but I did not think myself justified, for such a purpose, in spilling the blood of women and children, when I knew that in two or three weeks at furthest want of food for the inhabitants would compel me to evacuate the city, or, if that had been impossible, to surrender. I spoke to the mayor, several members of the city council, and many prominent citizens on the subject, and, while none seemed unwilling to undergo the dangers, if by so doing they could arrive at favorable results, yet all, without exception, under the circumstances, approved of and advised the withdrawal of the troops. In determining upon the evacuation, I, necessarily, as soon as the enemy's fleet had passed the forts, regarded the position the same as if both their Army and Navy were present before the city, making due allowance simply for the time it would take them to transport their army up. Inasmuch as their ships had passed Forts Jackson and Saint Philip, they could at once place themselves in open and uninterrupted communication with their army at points from 6 to 20 miles above the forts through various small water communications from the Gulf, made more available by the extraordinary height of the river, and which, while they were in possession of the latter, I had easily and without risk defended with launches and a part of the river-defense fleet. I had also stationed Szymanski's regiment at the quarantine for the same object. These were, however, all destroyed or captured by the enemy's fleet after they got possession of the river between the forts and the city. There was a further and very important reason for the course which I pursued. I knew that if I remained in New Orleans we should, in all probability, lose, in a short time, troops, guns, and supplies of all kinds, and the enemy would then be in full possession of the river as far as Memphis, which eventually fell also into their hands. By withdrawing my command, however, I would be enabled to fortify, arm, and organize Vicksburg, a strong and defensible position.

On April 17 I had written to General Beauregard (see document No. 24, hereunto appended) recommending the fortification of Vicksburg, and asking him for an engineer officer, and two days after the evacuation I advised the Adjutant-General at Richmond, General Cooper, that I should occupy that place and Jackson. (See document No. 25, hereunto appended).* I sent thither a number of heavy guns and quantities of ammunition with the artillerists from the various forts near New Orleans, and sent General Smith, with a brigade of infantry, to take command of the whole. The officers, troops, and guns which held Vicksburg last summer were almost entirely the same which I withdrew from New Orleans rather than remain and submit to an inevitable surrender. Results have fully proved the wisdom of the military policy pursued by me of collecting all the means in Department No. 1 and taking a new and stronger position on the Mississippi River. The evacuation of New Orleans and its occupation by the enemy would necessarily be followed sooner or later by the abandonment of the various forts and small works of the exterior line, which were erected principally to defend the approaches to that city, and after its evacuation could no longer serve any useful purpose. As the position of the enemy (in the river abreast of the city) gave him control of the Opelousas Railroad, thus enabling him to get in rear of the works on Barataria Bay, Grand Caillou, Bayou La Fourche, and at Berwick Bay, by which he could cut off and capture all the garrisons, with small-arms, ammunition, and stores, all of which were greatly needed at that time, I directed them to be abandoned at once. The officers in command were ordered to report with their troops and all transportable supplies at Camp Moore or Vicksburg. Some of them complied with this order, but a portion of the garrisons, after marching part of the way, refused to go farther and, in spite of their officers, disbanded and went to New Orleans.

Forts Jackson and Saint Philip surrendered in consequence of a mutiny among the men on April 28. (See General Duncan's report).† Forts Pike and Macomb were abandoned without my orders. When I returned to the city from the lower forts, on the 24th, I directed Colonel Fuller, who was in command of the works on the lakes, which comprised Forts Pike and Macomb, to have everything ready to abandon those forts in case I should order it.

Supposing that the enemy would occupy Kenner and thus deprive me of the use of the Jackson Railroad, it was my intention to remove the troops, supplies, &c., across Lake Pontchartrain to Pass Manchac and Madisonville, holding the entrance to that lake by forts as long as possible. The enemy, however, did not interfere with the railroad at Kenner, and the greater part of the men and public property were removed by rail.

I went to Camp Moore on the night of the 25th to arrange matters there, and on the morning of the 27th received information that Colonel Fuller had arrived at Covington, La., with the garrisons of Forts Pike and Macomb. This was the first knowledge I had of the abandonment of those works. I immediately directed them to be reoccupied, and sent a letter to Captain Poindexter, of the Navy, in command of the ships on the lake, requesting his co-operation in this movement. Colonel Fuller replied, on the 28th, that the forts had been dismantled, the guns spiked, and the carriages destroyed, and that it was impossible to reoccupy them.

I was officially informed of the surrender of Forts Jackson and Saint Philip on the 29th, and deemed it, therefore, useless to make any further attempts to reoccupy Forts Pike and Macomb. The cisterns in the two last-named works only held water enough to serve the garrison a short time, and had to be supplied by steamer from a distance. They could not have held out for any great length of time for this reason, and I deemed it best to save their garrisons (composed of well-drilled artillerists) for the works at Vicksburg, where they have ever since rendered such good service, but it was not intended to abandon them so soon, nor, indeed, until I had transferred all the public property from New Orleans.

The court adjourned to meet to-morrow at 10 a. m.

---

*A duplicate of report printed on p. 510. †Page 521.

APRIL 11, 1863—10 a. m.

The court met pursuant to adjournment.

Present, all the members of the court, the judge-advocate, and Maj. Gen. Mansfield Lovell.

It was ordered by the court that the examination of Maj. Gen. Mansfield Lovell as a witness be suspended, so that the testimony of S. L. James, an important witness, now *en route* to Europe, might be taken.

S. L. JAMES was then duly sworn and examined as a witness.

By the JUDGE-ADVOCATE:

Question. Were you an officer in the C. S. Army, under the command of General Mansfield Lovell, at the time of the evacuation of New Orleans? If yea, how long had you been under his command and what position did you hold?

Answer. I was in New Orleans at that time and in the service, but only as a volunteer aide to General Lovell, with the nominal rank of major. My services as such began April 24, 1862, the day before the evacuation.

Question. State what orders you received from General Lovell; what services were rendered by you in obedience to those orders, and the circumstances attendant upon their execution.

Answer. On the afternoon of April 24 General Lovell ordered me to detain all the steamboats at the landing until they could be loaded with Government stores. I gave notice of this at once to the captains and owners of these steamboats. During the day there were large quantities of Government stores placed upon these boats by the ordnance officers, but during the excitement of the evacuation some of the engineers and pilots deserted their posts and left the boats at the mercy of the enemy or the people. Those that were loaded went up the river, leaving some nine or ten at the levee. During that evening General Lovell, to gratify the people, ordered me to call for 1,000 men to man these boats for a hand-to-hand fight with the enemy's vessels, although General Lovell said it was impracticable.

The citizens promised to have the men ready the next morning at 9 o'clock. I was authorized to take the boats that were left and make such arrangements as I thought necessary to carry out the plan. I published this order (with an appeal of my own to the people) in all the city papers. In the mean while I sent down cotton bales to protect the boats, and molasses barrels to put in their hulls to keep them afloat in the event they were penetrated by shot. I called upon General Lewis and other militia officers to assist me in carrying out this scheme, which they failed to do, and I only received in response to the call 140 men, without arms, under Captain Dupiere.

Hearing that the enemy's vessels were at Camp Chalmette, about 5 miles below the city, I sent an officer to the landing, who ascertained that the citizens had burned a number of the boats and the owners of the others had gone off with them. I then ordered these 140 men to proceed to the Jackson Railroad depot to go to Camp Moore, and I then went to Camp Moore.

The morning of my arrival at Camp Moore General Lovell ordered me to return to New Orleans, and take with me Major Bell, Captain Venable, and Mr. Caul Rives, and remove what Government property there was in the city, stating that the railroad authorities would give me every facility for its removal. I went to New Orleans the same day in a special train, and hired drays, wagons, &c., to remove the Government property to the depot, whence it was removed out of the city by the railroad authorities. There were many citizens who assisted me and pointed out private property which would be of use to the Government, which was also removed. I obtained funds from the Committee of Public Safety to pay for drayage and other charges incident to the removal. I also used the mayor's office.

After delivering at the depot all the Government property I could find, I ordered the military property of the State to be seized and removed. After that I removed such supplies as were in the hands of contractors for the Government. We also moved two batteries belonging to the State, two guns of which had been spiked. We were engaged four days and nights in removing from the city property available for military purposes. Some 18 or 20 mounted men were sent over to the city to get such military supplies as might have been taken by citizens. There was, however, but little found in this way.

I requested the mayor to give me an order upon General Paul Juge for the arms in the hands of the Foreign Brigade. This he would not do, but gave me a request for them to the general, which was refused. All the property available for military uses that I could find was removed, except some heavy guns, which had to be left because I could not get the men and sling-carts necessary to their removal.

Question. Did you make any communications with the mayor and council of New Orleans on behalf of General Lovell? If so, what was the substance of those communications and what was their result?

Answer. On April 28 General Lovell telegraphed me to inform the mayor and council that he would return with his forces to the city if they desired it, provided they would incur the hazards of a bombardment. They replied that General Lovell could do nothing further with his troops; that if they were brought back it would only cause a bombardment of the city, which would result in the death of many women and children; but they told me they would like the general to come down. I notified the general, and he came down that night. We went together to the mayor's house, where the general repeated the proposition he had made to him through me. He replied as before, and asked the general to remain, so that he might have the benefit of his counsel.

During the morning of the 29th the mayor received a communication from the commander of the Federal fleet, stating that it was useless to hold out longer, that the forts had fallen, and demanding the surrender of the city. In the afternoon the enemy landed their forces to take down the State flag. General Duncan also arrived in the city, a paroled prisoner of war. About this time a policeman told me that the mayor of the city was anxious to see me. I immediately called upon him, when he asked me for God's sake to get General Lovell out of town.

Question. Were you present at any interview between General Lovell and Commander Whittle in reference to the location of the steamer Louisiana? If yea, state where such interview occurred and what passed between them.

Answer. On the morning of April 23 I was present at such an interview, in which General Lovell stated to Commander Whittle, commanding the naval station, that he had received intelligence to the effect that the forts and magazines had been very much damaged and the sand bags over the magazines, and that the latter were in danger of being blown up by the enemy's shells, and that the sally-ports were injured to such an extent that it was impossible to replace the sand bags under the enemy's heavy fire. General Lovell then said he was satisfied that by placing the iron-clad gunboat Louisiana on the Fort Saint Philip side, about half a mile below the raft, where she would be under the protection of the cross-fire of both forts, she could enfilade the position of the enemy's fleet and drive them off, when the men in the forts could get some rest and replace the sand bags. The commander replied that he had every confidence in the officers in command of our fleet below, and that he did not like to interfere with them. General Lovell then stated to him that Captain Mitchell had already refused to make the desired change, and that he came to him as chief in command. Commander Whittle replied that the vessel was not entirely ready with her motive power, and that by placing her there he was afraid she would be lost. The general answered, saying that he did not wish her to be sent down amid the enemy's fleet, but that she could be towed down and placed in position as a battery; that the necessity was such that it was better to lose the vessel than the city of New Orleans. Commander Whittle then dispatched Captain Mitchell, which dispatch I saw and heard read. As near as I can recollect it was in these words: "I am informed by General Lovell that the garrisons need relief, and that by placing the Louisiana in position in the eddy on the Fort Saint Philip side of the river, below the fort, under the protection of the cross-fire of both forts, she can dislodge the mortar boats and relieve the garrison. If in your judgment this can be accomplished strain a point to do so." He then turned to General Lovell and asked if that would do. The general replied that nothing short of placing her in the position indicated would answer his purposes, and remarked to the commander that he was going down in a special boat to the forts that afternoon, and asked him to go with him and judge for himself. The commander replied that his business in the office was such that he could not spare the time.

Question. Were the steamboats that you say were burned by the citizens at the levee private property? State how many there were, and whether other vessels than those steamboats, private property, were destroyed.

Answer. The gunboat Yankee was also burned, and, to the best of my knowledge and belief, with her armament aboard. I do not know by whose, if anybody's, order she was burned. The remaining vessels were private property.

The court adjourned to meet at 10 a. m. April 13.

JACKSON, MISS., *April* 13, 1863—10 a. m.

The court met pursuant to adjournment.

Present, all the members of the court, the judge-advocate, and Maj. Gen. Mansfield Lovell.

The proceedings of the 11th instant were read over.

Examination of General M. LOVELL resumed.

Answer (continued). In answer to the latter part of the question asked previous to the examination of Major James, as to the removal of public property, I will state, in general terms, that I gave orders to my staff officers to employ every means, by vessels on the Mississippi River and the lake, and by the Jackson Railroad, to remove the public property in their charge. I also sent from Camp Moore several active and energetic officers, who were well acquainted with the city, to search out and to transport from thence all the Government property and all property of the State of Louisiana available for war purposes. Before the arrival of the enemy's fleet several steamers had been sent up the river loaded with ordnance and commissary stores and with the machinery of the rifle factory and powder-mills. I took possession of all the rolling stock of the Jackson Railroad, and, with the co-operation and assistance of the superintendent, Mr. Williams, kept the whole force of the road moving night and day, employed in bringing out such property as my agents collected for transportation. Majors James, Venable, and Bell, with Captains McDonald and Caulkins, were busily employed in this matter under my orders until they reported to me that they had brought everything that could be found belonging either to the State of Louisiana or the Government, or that was in the hands of contractors, that could be made available for military purposes. For details I will have to refer the court to other witnesses. I know that an enormous amount of property was brought from New Orleans, which I should estimate to be worth several millions of dollars. I advised the officer in command of the gunboats on the lake to take his ships to Mobile, but he determined, for his own reasons, to destroy them. I then got from there ten or twelve heavy guns, with ammunition, which I sent up and put in position at Vicksburg.

On the afternoon of April 24, after my return to the city, it was intimated to me that 1,000 volunteers might be got, who, if placed on steamers, partly protected by cotton bales, would undertake to board and take possession of the enemy's ships by a hand-to-hand fight. I did not think it practicable, because I did not believe that the requisite number of desperately bold men could be had; but I concluded to make the attempt, and published an order calling for the volunteers, placing the whole matter in charge of Maj. S. L. James. Advertisements to that effect were published in all the papers of the city, but less than 150 men volunteered for the enterprise, and it was accordingly abandoned.

I returned to the city from Camp Moore on the evening of the 28th, three days after the evacuation, as it was intimated to me that the citizens intended to resist the enemy at all hazards, and had they concluded to do so, I determined to support and assist them at any cost. I found, however, that no such idea was entertained. I was at the mayor's house when Commodore Farragut announced by letter the surrender of Forts Jackson and Saint Philip and demanded the surrender of the city. Soon after I met General Duncan, who confirmed the news of the surrender of the forts. The flag was taken down from the city hall on the same day and replaced by the United States flag while I was yet in the city. I remained six or eight hours after that event took place, and finally returned to Camp Moore on the night of the 29th, as my presence could no longer be of any use in New Orleans. Three days later I addressed the following letter to the Adjutant-General:

CAMP MOORE, LA., *May* 2, 1862.

General S. COOPER,
Adjutant and Inspector General, Richmond, Va.:

SIR: I have the honor to request that the Department will appoint a board of competent officers to examine into and report upon the circumstances preceding and attendant upon the evacuation of the city of New Orleans, as well as the passage of the forts (Jackson and Saint Philip) by the fleet of the enemy, which brought about the evacuation. This is necessary as an act of justice to myself and officers, as well as to vindicate the truth of history.

Respectfully, your obedient servant,

M. LOVELL,
Major-General, Commanding.

No official notice was taken of this application.

The court adjourned to meet at 12 m. the 14th instant.

JACKSON, MISS., *April* 14, 1863—12 m.

The court met pursuant to adjournment.

Present, all the members of the court, the judge-advocate, and Major-General Lovell.

The proceedings of yesterday were read over.

The judge-advocate then read in evidence to the court a certified copy of the official correspondence between Maj. Gen. M. Lovell and the War Department (hereto appended, and marked document A),* and certified copies of the official reports of Major-General Lovell and Brigadier-General Duncan upon the fall of New Orleans and the passage of Forts Jackson and Saint Philip. (Hereto appended, and marked documents B and C.†)

General Lovell then offered in evidence the letter-book of Department No. 1, for the purpose of supplying the omission of certain letters he had written to the War Department, already referred to and hereafter to be mentioned in his testimony, and to show his conduct while in command of said Department No. 1, special reference to be made to such of its contents as will be used for the purposes indicated.

The judge-advocate admitted the genuineness of said letter-book, when it was received in evidence by the court.

The court adjourned to meet at 7 p. m. the 15th instant.

JACKSON, MISS., *April* 15, 1863—7 p. m.

The court met pursuant to adjournment.

Present, all the members of the court, the judge-advocate, and Major-General Lovell.

The proceedings of yesterday were read over.

It was ordered by the court that Mr. R. Hammett be employed as an additional clerk, to aid the judge-advocate.

The judge-advocate then stated to the court that a question would arise as to the jurisdiction of this court to inquire into the conduct of naval officers on duty in Department No. 1, at the time Forts Jackson and Saint Philip were passed by the enemy's fleet, and that he was of opinion that the court had no jurisdiction to make such inquiry. It was thereupon ordered by the court that the judge-advocate communicate the question for decision to the Adjutant and Inspector General by telegraph, and in the following words:

General S. COOPER,
Adjutant and Inspector General, Richmond, Va.:

GENERAL: The court of inquiry instruct me to ask whether it is intended to restrict them in their investigation and opinion to the conduct of officers of the Army, or is it their duty to inquire into and express their opinion upon the conduct of the officers of the Navy, so as to embrace the whole subject of the capture, defense, and evacuation of New Orleans?

L. R. PAGE,
Major, Adjutant-General's Department, Judge-Advocate.

The court adjourned to meet at 10 a. m. to-morrow.

APRIL 16, 1863—10 a. m.

The court met pursuant to adjournment.

Present, all the members of the court, the judge advocate, and Maj. Gen. Mansfield Lovell.

The proceedings of yesterday were read over.

---

* Not found. This is probably the correspondence referred to in message of President Davis. See No. 9, p. 654.

† See pp. 510, 521.

The examination of Maj. Gen. MANSFIELD LOVELL continued.

By the JUDGE-ADVOCATE:

Question. State what preparations, if any, were made by you, and, if so, when begun, to resist the progress of the enemy's fleet up the river, after the raft ceased to be an obstruction, and when you believed the passage of the forts could be accomplished.

Answer. I made my preparations, from the beginning, on land, to resist the passage of the fleet up the river to the city, precisely as if there had been no obstructions in the river, and brought everything to bear that I could obtain for that purpose. I never did believe that the forts could have been passed if those who had charge of the construction of the vessels of war which were intended to co-operate with me in the defense had had them ready at the time named to me by themselves, as two powerful iron-clad steamers, heavily armed and manned, could have averted the necessity of any obstructions; with this assistance, which I was informed would undoubtedly be afforded, I did not think the enemy could get up the river. When the first obstructions were carried away, having done all I could by way of defense on land, I endeavored to urge forward the completion of the iron-clad steamers, and was told by the builders that they would undoubtedly be ready about April 1. Previous to this time I endeavored to get the heavy guns from Pensacola, as mentioned already in my testimony.

Question. When you considered the passage of the fort practicable, did you then or at any time urge upon the Government the speedy completion of the iron-clads, which were then being built in New Orleans, as necessary to its successful defense, and did you at any time advise the War Department of any tardiness on the part of those building them?

Answer. I did not. I had been distinctly informed by the Secretary of War and President that I was to have no control over those matters. The Navy Department had experienced officers at New Orleans in charge of its affairs, and I should have considered it a reflection upon these officers for me to undertake their duties. I did, however, represent the matter frequently and forcibly to the naval officer in command of New Orleans, who informed me that it had been represented by him to Richmond. It was also stated day after day that the Louisiana would be ready, and she did go down the river on the 20th to the forts, and I supposed that with her assistance the enemy could be driven off. When she got there she proved not to be ready.

Question. What officers informed you from day to day that the Louisiana would be ready; and did you not know before she went down that she was not ready?

Answer. Various persons connected with her construction and her crew. I did know that she was not entirely ready, but supposed she was all prepared, except some works upon the propellers, for the completion of which work she took down a number of mechanics, and I was informed that she would be entirely ready in less than two days by some of her officers or master-mechanics.

Question. When it became evident to you that the security of New Orleans required that the Louisiana should be placed as indicated by you to Commander Whittle, and that officer declined to give a positive order to that effect, did you or not communicate the fact to the War Department? If not, what were your reasons?

Answer. I did not. From information received I felt convinced that the final passage would be attempted within twenty-four hours, and, if so, I knew it was too late to communicate with Richmond, and went down myself to endeavor to effect the change by personal application to Captain Mitchell, and arrived a few moments before the battle commenced, and was unable to see him.

Question. By what considerations were you induced not to attempt the construction of defensive works on the river between Forts Jackson and Saint Philip and your interior line?

Answer. I had no guns wherewith to arm them and could get none. I had concentrated almost all the guns for the defense of the river at those forts after consultation with General Beauregard, who understood well the nature of the country, because I could put men and guns there under the protection of masonry works, and because I intended to obstruct the river at that point, and wished to bring to bear upon the enemy's fleet, when checked by such obstructions, the greatest possible weight of metal. The country for many miles above the forts offered no location for guns in high stages of the river, and nearer to New Orleans, where the banks are leveed, guns aboard ship in high water would command guns ashore. There was also great deficiency of earth for the erection of works, and had I located guns there the position could have been overflowed by breaking the levees; besides, I had not troops enough to act as a protecting force to a number of detached works.

Question. When did you make the arrangements with Leeds & Co. and S. Wolfe & Co. in regard to the erection of the reverberating furnaces? State what those arrangements were, and, if you know, where S. Wolfe & Co. and Leeds & Co. are.

Answer. I cannot state the precise time. It was soon after I became satisfied that if I wanted heavy guns I must have them made myself in New Orleans, The arrangements were to put up the necessary furnaces, and to get for S. Wolfe & Co. the large lathe at the Bellville Iron Works. Mr. Leeds, the member of Leeds & Co., with whom I made the arrangements, is since dead, and Mr. Wolfe is at Columbus or Athens, Ga.

Question. Did not the War Department uniformly approve and, when necessary, ratify every step taken by you in perfecting the defenses of New Orleans, and were you not authorized to adopt such measures as you deemed essential to its safety?

Answer. In answer to the first part of the question, I answer yes; to the latter part I answer that I was authorized by the department to adopt many, but not all, of the measures which I thought essential to the safety of New Orleans. I wanted control of the defenses afloat as well as ashore, and of their preparations, and I wanted guns transferred from points that I considered of minor importance (for instance, Pensacola) to New Orleans. There were other smaller points of difference, which appear fully in my correspondence. I had no funds placed under my control for river obstructions, although I directed Major Smith to make estimates, who reported that they had been made and sent forward. He may have obtained some money for this purpose, but the bulk of the money expended upon the obstructions was obtained from the city of New Orleans, amounting in all to nearly a quarter of a million of dollars. The estimates made by General Smith were not forwarded until I had been in New Orleans some months, because when I assumed command the city had already placed at my disposal nearly $100,000, which I could apply to the making of obstructions.

Question. Did not the Safety Committee of New Orleans repeatedly desire to know your necessities, and tender you money and every other means in their power to strengthen and perfect its defenses?

Answer. The Safety Committee several times offered me any assistance in money that I might desire, or their personal services, and desired to know more of the necessities of my position than I thought proper to confide to fifty persons (the number of the committee), many of them unknown to me. I availed myself of their personal services in many instances, and got from them about $250,000 in money. They offered me more money, to which I replied that I could not use the additional funds, as the articles of which I stood most in need—to wit, guns of heavy caliber, anchors, chains and small-arms—were not to be had in the Confederacy; but I urged them to obtain these things by running the blockade and to apply their funds to laying in a sufficient store of provisions to supply the population in case of a siege. In reply to my last call on them for funds, which they stated that I should have immediately upon my requisition, they waited several days, and then sent a sub-committee to me to know what I intended to do with the money before they would grant the request. This I declined to do, as I did not wish to make public the weak points of my department.

Question. When you ceased to feel secure as to the defense of the city why did you not begin the removal of public stores; and did you or not advise the removal of the iron-clads, particularly the Mississippi, to some other point?

Answer. Believing that the iron-clads would probably be completed before the enemy would make his final attack, I did not feel so insecure as to justify me in removing the public stores, which removal I knew would not be kept secret and would create a great panic among our own people, and also convey to the enemy the impression that we despaired of holding our position. I did not advise the removal of the iron-clads, because there were naval officers of age and experience present who were as well or better able than myself to decide as to what steps should be taken with regard to the property intrusted to their charge. I did, however, make arrangements, as already stated, to remove the property under my control in case of disaster at the lower forts.

Question. Give the names of the officers commanding the exterior lines of defense in your department and the names of the officers upon your staff. State also their rank and specific duties.

Answer. The whole exterior line was under the command of Brig. Gen. J. K. Duncan (now dead), Colonel Fuller commanding, under him, the works on Lakes Pontchartrain and Borgne. Major Clinch commanded at Fort Pike; Captain Capers at Fort Macomb; Captain Robertson at Battery Bienvenue; Captain Plaznier at Tower Dupré; Captain Patton at Proctorsville works; Colonel Higgins at Forts Jackson and Saint Philip, the latter being under the immediate command of Captain Squires; Colonel Heard at Fort Livingston and Little Temple. The works on Bayou La Fourche and Grand Caillou were under the command of two captains named Marks. Major Fry commanded at Forts Berwick and Chêne, and Captain Davis commanded at Calcasieu Pass, where I had placed two guns, which fort I omitted to state previously in my testimony. General Duncan's headquarters were at Fort Jackson.

My staff was composed as follows: Majors Pickett and Palfrey, assistant adjutants-general; Lieut. J. G. Devereux, acting assistant adjutant-general; Major Pickett disbursed recruiting funds for the army generally; Maj. M. L. Smith was my engineer and ordnance officer for several months, and acted also as the agent of the Ordnance Department at Richmond, purchasing supplies for the Army at large; Lieut. Col. W. S. Lovell relieved him subsequently as ordnance officer, and, in addition, was charged by me with the general supervision of the preparations of the river-defense fleet; Maj. W. L. Larice, my chief commissary, acted also as the general agent of the Commissary Department; Major Winnemore was the chief quartermaster, assisted by Captains Powell and Banks, the latter acting as paymaster; my quartermaster was the general agent of the department at Richmond for the supplies pertaining to his office, which devolved an immense additional labor upon him; Surgeon Hayden was the medical director, and Surg. Howard Smith the general medical purveyor. My aides were First Lieuts. J. Lovell and A. J. Toutant, besides whom I had several volunteer aides.

Question. Who informed you that the iron-clads would be finished by the January rise of the river?

Answer. One of the Messrs. Tift, shortly after I assumed command.

Question. What were the names of the contractors building the iron-clad steamers, and who was the principal naval constructor?

Answer. Mr. Pearce was the principal naval constructor, as I was informed. I do not know the names of the contractors.

Question. Who were the Navy officers who regretted that they had not sufficient means at their disposal to assist you in hastening the completion of the iron-clad steamers?

Answer. Commodore Hollins, Commander Whittle, and Captain Mitchell often spoke of the insufficiency of the means under their control.

The court adjourned to meet at 10 a. m. to-morrow, the 17th instant.

APRIL 17, 1863—10 a. m.

The court met pursuant to adjournment.

Present, all the members of the court, the judge-advocate, and Maj. Gen. Mansfield Lovell.

The proceedings of yesterday were read over.

Examination of Maj. Gen. M. LOVELL continued.

By a MEMBER OF THE COURT:

Question. Did you at any time order all non-combatants, women, and children to leave the city of New Orleans?

Answer. I did not.

The following statement was then made by General Lovell:

I desire to add, that when I have stated in my testimony I have done thus and so, it is to be understood that in many instances these matters were personally attended to by officers of my staff or members of the Safety Committee, but under my orders or with my knowledge and advice.

A certified copy of certain letters, a part of the official correspondence between the War Department and Maj. Gen. M. Lovell, was then offered in evidence by the judge-advocate, which said copy was read to the court, and is hereto appended as document N.*

Surg. D. W. BRICKELL was then duly sworn and examined as a witness.

By the JUDGE-ADVOCATE:

Question. Were you in New Orleans during the six months prior to its capture by the enemy in April, 1862? If yea, state what, if any, public duties were devolved upon you in that time.

Answer. I was in New Orleans during that time, and my only public duty was as a member of the Committee of Public Safety, from its organization to the fall of the city, a period of about sixty days.

Question. State by what authority this committee was organized, the number and character of its members, and what it did or endeavored to do while in existence.

Answer. The committee consisted originally of about fifty persons; several members of the city council and other persons were, however, added to it, until the number was probably more than sixty. It consisted of persons from all classes and pursuits, selected for their worth, usefulness, and intelligence, and was created by authority of the city council. Its object was to co-operate in every possible way with the Confederate and State authorities to defend and preserve the city. The first act of the committee was to tender to the commanding general its services, pecuniary aid, and every other aid in its power to render. The committee took charge of and urged the piling of the passage of the Rigolets. It also waited upon and urged the governor to have Messrs. Cook & Brothers' factory of small-arms enlarged so as to have 100, instead of 25, Enfield rifles turned out per day, and to this end we induced the governor to appropriate $40,000; but this he would not do until the committee had appropriated a like sum. The establishment at that time was making guns for the State of Alabama alone. We wanted that contract executed in the shortest time, so that the State of Louisiana might have the benefit of its works. The committee ascertained that the work on the Mississippi, an iron-clad gunboat, was almost at a dead stand, and we proposed to the Messrs. Tift money without limit. We proposed also to light up the sides of the vessel at night, so that the work might be pressed forward both day and night, and also tendered them mechanics, both white and black, to relieve their hands and to be entirely under their control. It was offered to do these things at the expense of the city, without cost to them; but every single proposal was rejected, and we were uniformly assured that the vessel would be completed within thirty days after our organization. They declined the service of negro mechanics, stating that the hands would not work in the day if negroes were employed at night. To this we replied that we would form military organizations and compel his hands to work.

As a member of the sub-committee to inquire into the condition and progress of the Mississippi, I found that the contracts made for engines, sheet-iron work, and other material of construction by the Messrs. Tift were with men altogether secondary in their lines, of limited capital, generally in great need of money, and wholly unable to fulfill their contracts. There were two or three machinists in the city of much larger capital and works—Messrs. Leeds & Co. and Bennett & Surges—who stood much higher with the citizens than these men. The committee sent an agent—Mr. James Beggs—to various places between Atlanta and New Orleans to collect the iron that was being made for plating the vessel, who brought it to the city. The committee also sent Major James to Richmond to bring the center shaft, which he did bring to the city. A large quantity of lightwood was collected by the agents of the committee for the purpose of making fire rafts to send down to the forts. Large quantities of iron and other metals were brought by the agents from various points on the Mississippi, contributed by the planters, and turned over to the military authorities. Every requisition for money made by the commanding general and his subordinates was promptly

*Not found.

complied with by the committee. The same course was pursued towards those in charge of naval affairs; their bills were paid and money furnished them to go ahead. We discovered that the naval department was largely indebted, without credit, and we sent a special agent to Richmond to obtain for it the necessary relief. The committee also sent out agents through the country obtaining food for the citizens, keeping a capital of $250,000 in circulation, and selling the supplies thus secured at cost. The committee never refused assistance to any reliable man who was endeavoring to develop the strength of the city.

By the COURT:

Question. Did the Committee of Safety communicate to any persons in authority the result of their inquiries as to the contractors Tift & Co.? If so, to whom, when, and what was the exact purport of such communication?

Answer. The committee did communicate the results of their investigations, particularly in regard to the Mississippi, to Captain Mitchell, Commander Whittle, and General Lovell. They all replied it was a matter not under their control. The Tifts replied to the sub-committee, after they had waited upon them many times, that they were responsible to nobody in New Orleans, and exhibited a paper to that effect.

By the JUDGE-ADVOCATE:

Question. State all you may know, and your means of knowing, of the ability of the founderymen in New Orleans to cast guns of heavy caliber.

Answer. When the committee organized, some of our earliest efforts were directed to obtain such guns. We found all the founderymen willing to undertake the manufacture of large guns, but Bennett & Surges was the only firm ready to go to work upon them immediately, and they would only work upon condition that no army officer should have anything to do or say about the matter, except to test the guns after they were complete. They might subject them to any test they pleased; if the guns stood the test we should pay for them; if they burst it should be their loss entirely. They were then ready to make 8-inch guns, and they were willing to make models for and begin the manufacture of guns of any caliber that we might call for. We at once contracted with them, without stipulation as to price, for all the 8-inch guns they could make until ready to make larger ones. At the time the city fell they had cast five 8-inch guns, two or three of which were completed and the others on the lathes in process of completion. The models for 9-inch rifle guns were in a forward state. The guns that where completed were immediately turned over to the military authorities. I was on the sub-committee that superintended the construction of the heavy 8-inch guns; not at first, but taking the place of a member who had retired. I was in the foundery nearly every day and saw the work progressing. Messrs. Bennett & Surges complained that they had not been patronized by the Government. In my opinion heavy guns could have been made in the city from the beginning of the war. Bennett & Surges were most anxious to engage in such work. They had made a heavy gun, which was mounted at Columbus and Island No. 10. They complained that they had always been willing and able to make heavy guns, but had received no encouragement from the Government. Messrs. Bujac & Bennett, by their individual efforts, built air-furnaces, had six lathes all abreast for making guns up to 11 inches in caliber, and when the city fell they were engaged in casting their first heavy guns. Their machinery and works had been begun and completed within the six months prior to the fall of the city.

Question. Were you present in the city during the evacuation and the removal of public stores by our troops? If yea, state all you may know on these subjects.

Answer. I was there. On the day in which the enemy's vessels were coming up to the city, hearing that the Marine Hospital, which had been converted into a factory for the repairing of arms and the making of cartridges, had been broke open by the populace, I went in that direction. I found them carrying off arms and everything pertaining to an establishment of that sort. In the foundery of Bennett & Surges several brass pieces, nearly completed, were left, also a heavy gun, and these should have been removed. After the troops under General Lovell had been removed, the foreign guard, at the instance of the city council, was keeping guard over many of the Government warehouses, to prevent the people from breaking into them. This is all I know of my own knowledge on these subjects. On the day of the arrival of the enemy's ships, but previous to their arrival, I saw large quantities of sugar, molasses, bacon, and some corn being seized and carried off from the town by the populace—men, women, and children; black and white—and all without restraint; on the contrary, with the encouragement of a man on horseback, dressed in Confederate uniform. This same man on horseback ordered a pile of corn to be burned. I personally remonstrated, telling him it was corn, the bread the people required. He repeated his order, and the corn was burned. I saw private individuals trying to save the sugar, &c., from the depredations of the populace, claiming some of it as their own, but they were disregarded.

Cross-examination by Major-General LOVELL:

Question. What was the quality of the iron offered by Messrs. Leeds & Co., Bennett & Surges, and others for casting heavy guns when you made inquiries on the subject, and what amount had they on hand that was fit for that purpose?

Answer. The best opinion I can offer as to the quality of that used by Bennett & Surges is that it was good, as a gun made by them had been tested by the military authorities and approved. Messrs. Bujac & Bennett had a large amount of Tennessee iron, part of which they tendered to us to be used by other founderies, so as to expedite the making of heavy guns in the event of such shops getting out of iron. I know nothing more as to the quantity and quality of iron to be used in making heavy guns.

Question. How many such lathes and furnaces had Bennett & Surges, and what time is necessary to cast and bore an 8-inch columbiad?

Answer. They had no lathes completed, but one was nearly done for boring large guns. I do not know that they had more than one furnace. A lathe in the machine-shop of the Jackson and Great Northern Railroad and another in the Shakspeare foundery, through the exertions of the committee, were placed at their disposal. I am a novice in such matters, but should think that thirteen days would be sufficient to cast and bore such a gun—five days and nights.

Question. Do you know whether the committee advised and consulted with General Lovell on the subject of engaging Bennett & Surges in making heavy guns?

Answer. I cannot say whether they did or not. Bennett & Surges said that they would not make a heavy gun under the direction of a military officer.

Question. Did Bennett & Surges inform the officers engaged in the removal of property that they had some unfinished guns?

Answer. I cannot say.

Question. Do you know whether any attempts were made to carry away heavy guns, and why those attempts did not succeed?

Answer. I do not.

Question. Were Bennett & Surges largely engaged in making other war material for the Government?

Answer. They were.

Question. Are you aware that the piling at Fort Pike was carried away on April 9?

Answer. I never heard.

By the COURT:

Question. Did the Committee of Safety delegate any person to represent to the Confederate Government at Richmond the condition of the defenses of New Orleans? If so, state the name of the person sent, with the date, what representations he was instructed to make, and what action, if any, was taken by the Government or any Department thereof in consequence of such representations.

Answer. About six weeks before the fall of the city the committee sent Mr. William Henderson to Richmond, to represent to the President and other authorities their conviction that the city was insecure and the deplorable condition of naval affairs, the want of credit from which that department suffered, and its extraordinary indebtedness, which the committee ascertained to amount to $600,000. This latter point received the attention of the President and the matter was arranged. I do not know that any other action was taken upon the representations of the committee.

Question. Did the Committee of Safety urge the launching of the steamer Mississippi? When and by whom was it undertaken? State all the facts connected with the launching of this vessel from first to last, with names of the parties engaged.

Answer. About four weeks before the city fell the Committee of Safety, through the sub-committee, as well as various members who certainly visited the Mississippi, became convinced that the vessel should be launched without delay, and for the following reasons:

1st. That the vessel was in such a condition of completion that to launch her would not at all interfere with subsequent work on her, and then, in case of the fall of the city, she could at any moment be towed off to a place of safety.

2d. That the river was rising rapidly; the stern of the vessel was being deeply immersed in the water; the bottom on which she lay was being softened, and the least giving way of the mud would result in "logging" her on the ways, thereby rendering it impossible to launch her.

They made these representations to Mr. Tift, and repeatedly urged him to launch her. He positively refused. Desiring to do only that which was right, and willing to admit the judgment of Mr. Tift in opposition to their own, they called his constructor (Mr. Pearce) before them, and asked his opinion on the subject. He unqualifiedly approved our recommendation to launch her, and assured the committee that he had personally urged the launching of the vessel. He expressed the greatest anxiety for the safety of his vessel, and expressed his fears that she would never be launched. The committee then appointed a special committee, composed of eminently practical and intelligent men, mostly outside the committee, to survey the vessel and report forthwith. The survey was cheerfully and promptly made, and the committee unanimously reported in favor of launching, and for the reasons stated. This report was sent to Mr. Tift, with renewed application for the launch. He refused ultimately, and, as I firmly believe, under the pressure of public opinion, a few days before the city fell he attempted the launch by attaching steamers to the ram, which steamers were to pull her off her ways. He worked all day before a large crowd, of which I was one, and utterly failed. That he would fail was the opinion of every intelligent man I met on the ground, as the vessels pulling were lower than the vessel pulled, and the mechanical effect was to pull the ram more and more firmly down on her ways at every effort. A conference was held with our practical men, and the result was that they went to the ship next morning with hydraulic rams and pushed her right out into the river. Bitterly disappointed by the persevering refusal of Mr. Tift to launch the vessel, and despairing of even her safety, the committee was on the eve of making a public announcement of the condition of things and calling on them to take the matter in hand, when one of its members (Mr. J. M. Marks, if I am not greatly in error as to name) received a private note from the commanding general, telling him that he was apprised of the probable action of the committee; that such an act on their part would apprise the enemy of our weakness, and intimating clearly that he would not permit such an act on the part of the committee. This note was read to the committee and I read it personally. The committee then abandoned all idea of the safety or utility of the ram.

The court adjourned to meet at 10 a. m. the 18th instant.

APRIL 18, 1863—10 a. m.

The court met pursuant to adjournment.

Present, all the members of the court, the judge-advocate, and Maj. Gen. Mansfield Lovell.

The proceedings of yesterday were read over.

T. S. WILLIAMS was then sworn and examined as a witness.

By Maj. Gen. M. LOVELL:

Question. What is your present occupation and how long have you been engaged in it?

Answer. I am general superintendent of the New Orleans, Jackson and Great Northern Railroad; have been such for four years, and engaged on the road for the last ten years.

Question. Describe the country for the first 10 or 12 miles above New Orleans, over which the New Orleans, Jackson and Great Northern Railroad runs.

Answer. From the city limits to the four-mile post on the railroad the country is a swamp; from that mile-post, which is about a mile and a half from the river, the road passes over a narrow strip of firm land; from the six to the seven mile post it is about a mile in width; and at Kenner the railroad is about 1,500 feet from the river. From the river to Lake Pontchartrain the distance at Kenner is about 4 miles, 3 miles of which country is a swamp. The ridge upon which the road runs extends 2 miles north of Kenner.

Question. State when the enemy's ships of war took position at or near Kenner and cut off the communication from New Orleans by the New Orleans, Jackson and Great Northern Railroad.

Answer. I think it was about seven days after the city was evacuated before the enemy's vessels compelled the stoppage of the trains at Kenner.

Question. State what arrangements were made with you by General Lovell, or by his order, and what work was done in removing public property and military stores at and after the evacuation of New Orleans.

Answer. On Thursday, April 24, I received orders to hold everything in readiness for the removal of troops and Government property, and as it was necessary that this should first be removed, to allow no citizens or private property to be transported upon the trains. The next morning I ordered all trains coming south to be unloaded and sent to Kenner to await further orders. For four days and nights we had every train and engine on the road at work for the Government, removing its property. Some of this property was put on at Kenner, Carrollton Crossing, and Manchac; that at Manchac having been brought across the lake.

Question. Give, if you can, a general idea of the value of the property removed over your road.

Answer. I do not know its value, but it required three or four trains a day for three weeks to take from Camp Moore the property which we had removed from the city.

Cross-examination by the JUDGE-ADVOCATE:

Question. Was there any unnecessary delay or confusion in loading the trains at the depot?

Answer. There was some confusion, but it was unavoidable. No delay. The trains were sometimes loaded before I was able to move them.

Question. Was the property it took three or four trains a day for three weeks to move from Camp Moore all of it Confederate and State property?

Answer. It was.

Col. J. SZYMANSKI was then sworn and examined as a witness.

By Maj. Gen. MANSFIELD LOVELL:

Question. Where were you at the time of the fall of New Orleans, and what, if any, position did you hold in the C. S. Army?

Answer. I commanded a regiment, which was then located about 5 miles above Forts Saint Philip and Jackson, on both sides of the river. One of my largest companies was in Fort Saint Philip.

Question. Where were you first located and what were your instructions?

Answer. I arrived at the quarantine station, on the left bank of the river, on April 5. I was ordered there to guard the approaches to the city from the sea through the bayous and canals. Afterwards Brigadier-General Duncan ordered one of my companies at Fort Saint Philip; the others were assigned to duty at the various bayous and canals that intersect the country that lies above the forts.

Question. Was it practicable for the enemy, after the forts had been passed, to transport his army through these bayous and canals to New Orleans without encountering the forts?

Answer. It was practicable to do so. A portion of the enemy did come that way after his fleet passed the forts.

Question. How long have you lived in that country, and what was the state of the river at that season compared with other years?

Answer. I have lived in Louisiana upwards of a quarter of a century, and for many years owned a plantation 15 miles below the city. I was very familiar with the whole country. I never have known the river so high as it was that year.

Question. What was the condition of the country above the forts for 30 or 40 miles in regard to the overflow?

Answer. On the left bank of the river the whole country was one vast sheet of water from the river to the Gulf, commencing at Point à la Hache, about 40 miles below New Orleans. On the other side the country was not overflowed, but, on account of the high water and the transpiration resulting therefrom, the road (there being but the one) was impassable. The country was such that when the river was high no earth could be had for a levee in the rear without letting in water from the Gulf. In the front an alluvial mud from the river, when low, might be had for levees. While General Lovell was in command at New Orleans the water was high, and no earthworks could be put up in that neighborhood. Even at Fort Jackson, at the time of the bombardment, the water was from a foot and a half to two feet deep.

Cross-examination by the JUDGE-ADVOCATE:

Question. State the reasons for the surrender of yourself and a portion of your command.

Answer. When the forts were passed, just about break of day, the fleet came upon my small camp and opened fire. After losing some 30 men killed and wounded, without a possibility of escape or rescue—perfectly at the mercy of the enemy, he being able to cut the levee and drown me out—I thought it my duty to surrender. A single shell could have cut the light embankment.

Question. Could not earthworks have been put up on the river banks a distance of 20 or 25 miles below New Orleans?

Answer. They might have been put up at English Turn, a commanding position, where the river makes a sharp turn, commanding, not from its height, but from the course of the river.

Question. State the elevation of that point above the water in high stages of the river.

Answer. It was not more than 6 inches above high water, but the ground was firm, and would have supported heavy works.

Question. Is English Turn above the debouches of the bayous and canals through which the enemy might have turned Forts Saint Philip and Jackson?

Answer. It is; but there is above that point water communication through Lake Borgne with the Gulf of Mexico by other bayous and canals of the same character, principally by Bayou Bienvenue.

Examination by Maj. Gen. M. LOVELL:

Question. In that high stage of water, during the year 1861, was not the river higher than the surface of the country below New Orleans? If so, state about how much.

Answer. It was, varying in depth from 2 to 14 feet.

The deposition of R. F. NICHOLS, a citizen, taken at Jackson, Miss., pursuant to an order of the court, Maj. Gen. M. Lovell and the judge-advocate being present at the time, was then read to the court.

JACKSON, MISS., *April* 18, 1863.

R. F. NICHOLS, having been duly sworn by the judge-advocate, testified as follows:

Question. Where did you reside in the years 1861 and 1862, up to the time of the evacuation of New Orleans, and what was your occupation previous to October 18, 1861?

Answer. I resided in New Orleans. My occupation was that of a merchant, engaged in the Mediterranean trade. About the month of August, 1861, I was solicited by Governor Moore to procure chains and anchors for him. I was engaged in this when General Lovell took command of New Orleans.

Question. State, when General Lovell took command at New Orleans, whether you were employed by him in any capacity; if so, what; and state fully what steps were taken by you under his orders or under those of his staff to procure chains and anchors, cordage, and other materials.

Answer. Immediately on General Lovell's taking command I was introduced to him by Governor Moore, and General Lovell thereupon employed me at once to procure chains, anchors, cordage, and other necessary materials which would be required for constructing and anchoring rafts or obstructions that might be necessary for the protection of New Orleans in the water approaches. I immediately proceeded to procure all the chains and anchors suitable in the city of New Orleans which could be found in all the stores or otherwise, and also all on board of each and every ship, bark, schooner, and steamboat in port, as well as on all the plantations and saw-mills on the coast and in the city of New Orleans. I further was authorized and did take one of the tow-boats for the purpose of taking the mooring chains from all the crafts afloat then in port, which I did, securing these vessels by such other means as I could, to wit, by cordage and chains of smaller dimensions. I continued incessantly at this business day by day up to the time of the passage of the forts, having in my employ a large number of seamen and stevedores to assist me. Oftentimes I encountered serious difficulty in effecting my object by the parties owning or controlling the chains and anchors concealing them from me. In several ships I found from 500 to 600 fathoms of chains laid under 10 to 15 feet of ballast, and some were sunk in the Mississippi River under the wharf, which I discovered and obtained. I further state that it was then, and is now, my firm belief that, through the means I adopted, I did obtain and turn over to General Lovell all the articles above named which were in and about the city of New Orleans that were in any way useful for the purposes required. After I had exhausted all that could be found, and more being required, as a last resort I did, under the advice of General Lovell, procure from the mayor of the city permission to take the chains from around the parks in the city, which, although far too small and not suitable for the purpose, was thought to be the best that could be done in our extremity.

The court adjourned to meet at Vicksburg, Miss., on Tuesday, the 21st instant, at 12 m. or as soon thereafter as practicable.

VICKSBURG, MISS., *April* 22, 1863—10 a. m.

The court met pursuant to adjournment.

Present, Maj. Gen. T. C. Hindman, Brig. Gen. T. F. Drayton, and W. M. Gardner, Maj. L. R. Page, judge-advocate, and Maj. Gen. Mansfield Lovell.

The proceedings of the 18th instant were read over.

Maj. Gen. M. L. SMITH was then sworn and examined as a witness.

By the JUDGE-ADVOCATE:

Question. Were you in the Army of the Confederate States during the years 1861 and 1862? If yea, state what was your rank, where you were located, and to what duty you were assigned from May, 1861, to May, 1862.

Answer. I entered the service early in April, 1861, as a major of engineers. I was located in New Orleans from May, 1861, until April 26, 1862. I was assigned to engineer and ordnance duty until April 11, 1862, when I was made a brigadier-general, and placed in command of the interior line of works around New Orleans.

Question. State generally your knowledge of the condition of the defenses in Department No. 1 at the time General Lovell assumed command of it.

Answer. The defenses consisted of Forts Pike and Macomb, guarding the approaches to New Orleans by way of Lake Pontchartrain; of Battery Bienvenue and Tower Dupré, guarding the streams leading from Lake Borgne to the main-land between the city; of a field work at Proctorsville, prepared for six guns, but not armed, guarding the approach to the city by way of the Proctorsville Railroad; of Forts Jackson and Saint Philip, guarding the approach to the city by way of the river from the Gulf; of Fort Livingston, guarding the approach by way of Barataria Bay; of Forts Berwick and Chène, on Berwick Bay, guarding the approach by the Opelousas Railroad, and a little work called Fort Guion, on La Fourche, was nearly completed and ready for guns. These constituted the outer line of defense.

In July, 1861, the inner line of defense was projected and in about the following condition when General Lovell assumed command, viz: It consisted of a continuous line across the Gentilly Ridge, prepared for artillery and infantry (this work was, I think, finished, but no guns mounted); of a continuous line at Chalmette, stretching from the swamp to the Mississippi, also intended for artillery and infantry (about half completed, the contractor, with his full power, being at work upon it); of a continuous line on the right bank of the river, known as the McGehee line, also stretching from the river to the swamp, and prepared for artillery and infantry (not more than one-sixth of the line was finished, but the contractor was at work upon it); of a line above the city, known as the Barataria line, on the right bank of the river, also stretching from the river to the swamp (not more than a sixth of the line was completed; the contractor at work upon it); of a continuous line of works about a mile and a half above Carrollton, on the left bank of the river, then known as the Victor line, intended to mount fourteen guns between the bank and the swamp (this work was about half done; the contractor at work with full force; no guns mounted); of a two-gun battery, guarding the Carrollton Railroad from Lake Pontchartrain, together with supporting infantry works (I do not think this work was then commenced); of a battery and short infantry line, guarding the shell road and canal leading from Lake Pontchartrain to the city (no work had been done upon this line); of a battery and infantry line guarding the road Bayou Saint John, from Lake Pontchartrain to the city (the contractor had just commenced upon this, he being the same who had finished the Gentilly work); of a battery and supporting infantry works guarding the Pontchartrain Railroad, leading into the city (I do not think this work had been commenced). These works constituted the interior line.

A raft was projected, to prevent the ascent of the river, by Colonel (now Brigadier-General) Hébert and myself, in July, 1861, which was completed and swung into place about the middle of September, stretching from Fort Jackson to Saint Philip, where it remained until March or April, when it was swept away. Much labor was expended by General Lovell in securing this obstruction by additional chains and anchors; in keeping it stretched in position; in additionally securing it to the banks, and in preventing a too great accumulation of drift against it. Fort Pike, guarding the Rigolets, was a complete work in April, 1861, as originally designed, as also Forts Macomb and Jackson. The inner or main work of Saint Philip had once been complete, but on account of the insecure foundation it had settled; the walls had cracked and were insecure in the rear. An encircling outwork had been projected by the Engineer Department of the United States, upon which about one season's work had been done. This was unfinished at the time General Lovell assumed command.

At Fort Livingston one cistern had been repaired; the other two were incapable of repair; the pintle-block and traverse circles were laid, and it had five or six guns mounted. The fort was gradually sinking, and the counterscarp gallery was constantly filled with water, and remained so. All these forts on the exterior line were armed, except Fort Guion. Their precise armament you can better ascertain from the officers stationed there at that time, as also the amount of ammunition on hand. The materials of war—guns, powder, projectiles, &c.—had to some extent been sent away from New Orleans and Baton Rouge to Pensacola, and, I think, everything of material remaining, except some guns, recently arrived from Richmond for the interior line, had been distributed to the forts before mentioned. The department was originally poorly supplied.

Question. State your knowledge of the causes of the fall of New Orleans, and how it might have been prevented, if at all, with the means at the disposal of the commanding general.

Answer. New Orleans, in my judgment, fell of necessity when thirteen of the enemy's vessels succeeded in passing Forts Jackson and Saint Philip. These vessels, in my judgment, were able to pass at any time after the river was free from obstructions.

Owing to the narrowness of the neck of land above Carrollton, separating the Mississippi from the impassable swamp and marsh bordering Lake Pontchartrain, New Orleans may be considered as situated on an island and subject to all the conditions of a place surrounded by water. The force controlling the water controls the supplies which subsist the island, and it can neither be approached nor left except by consent. This I understand to have been precisely the case with the city. Not a barrel of flour, not a pound of bacon or beef, could have been brought there with the Federal vessels in possession of the river above the forts and of the lakes as they practically were. Without firing a gun, without making a single hostile demonstration other than keeping out supplies, the city would most probably have been surrendered in a month or two from starvation. Had the fall of New Orleans depended upon the enemy's first taking Forts Jackson and Saint Philip, I think the city would have been safe against an attack from the Gulf. The forts, in my judgment, were impregnable so long as they were in free and open communication with the city. This communication was not endangered while the obstruction existed. The conclusion, then, is briefly this: while the obstruction existed the city was safe; when it was swept away, as the defenses then existed, it was within the enemy's power. I do not now think it was possible for General Lovell or any other person to have kept the obstruction in place during the continuance of high water and drift, and after it was swept away there was neither time nor materials for building another on a different plan.

Question. In the evacuation of New Orleans were any means neglected which should have been taken to save the public property or any part thereof, and was the evacuation well conducted?

Answer. My command lay below the city. I was not in it during the evacuation; in fact, was not aware that it was evacuated until after the soldiers and officers had all left. As to public property, I had none in charge, and am not sufficiently familiar with the means used to save it to give an opinion as to whether or not any means necessary to save it were neglected.

Question. Was it possible to save the gunboat Mississippi, and could she not have been removed to some other point when the raft ceased to be an obstruction?

Answer. I have no positive knowledge of my own regarding the gunboat Mississippi, was never on board of her, and am not cognizant of the efforts made to remove her.

Cross-examination by Maj. Gen. MANSFIELD LOVELL:

Question. What kind of works were Forts Berwick and Chène, and what were their condition and that of their armament when General Lovell assumed command?

Answer. They were the ordinary class of field works, intended to mount three or four guns. The parapet had sunk considerably at the time of his arrival and required fitting up again. From the character of the soil they required a good deal of work from time to time, and had already been repaired once or twice. After his arrival one or more gun-carriages had been substituted, and the equipments, upon his order, had been duplicated. There were three, perhaps four, guns mounted. There was one rifled 32-pounder; whether the others were all 32-pounder smooth bores or 24-pounders I do not recollect. There were no projectiles for the rifled 32-pounder in the department, the kind of projectile having not then been decided upon. These pieces had been but recently rifled by direction of General Twiggs.

Question. Were any platforms for guns laid, magazines built, or hot-shot furnaces erected for the interior line at that time?

Answer. I think not.

Question. You say Fort Jackson was completed as originally designed. Was there not a water battery, which was subsequently put in order, guns mounted, and used by direction of General Lovell?

Answer. I believe there was an advanced outwork, not then ready for use, put in order and guns mounted by General Lovell; but not being done under my directions I cannot say positively.

Question. What orders were given by General Lovell at Fort Livingston in relation to the preparation of the covered way for guns, and what time did the work occupy?

Answer. He directed the gallery to be pumped out and prepared for two flank howitzers, which were mounted. This took the garrison two or three weeks, but the water continued to flood the gallery.

Question. What was the general caliber of guns mounted at the various forts when General Lovell took charge of the department?

Answer. The general armament of Forts Pike and Macomb was 24-pounders; of Forts Jackson and Saint Philip 24 and 32 pounders, the majority, I think, being 24-pounders, together with seven 8-inch columbiads; Battery Bienvenue and Tower Dupré had 24-pounders; Fort Livingston had 24-pounders and a rifled 32-pounder.

The court adjourned to meet at 10 a. m. to-morrow.

APRIL 23, 1863—10 a. m.

The court met pursuant to adjournment.

Present, all the members of the court, the judge-advocate, and Maj. Gen. Mansfield Lovell.

The proceedings of yesterday were read over.

Examination of Maj. Gen. M. L. SMITH continued.

Cross-examined by Major-General LOVELL:

Question. Did you make any attempt to have heavy guns made by Leeds & Co.; and if so, with what success? Was their foundery employed to its full capacity by the Government, without intermission, in other work?

Answer. About June, 1861, Leeds & Co. cast an 8-inch columbiad for a private party in New Orleans. This fact becoming known, I was directed by the Ordnance Bureau to test it with a specified charge and continue the firing until it burst, the object being to ascertain the quality of the metal used. The charge was the ordinary service charge—single shot. This was done by laying the gun upon a piece of timber in the ordinary way. It burst at the sixty-third or sixty-fifth round. In proofs of this kind metal is unhesitatingly condemned that will not stand from 800 to 1,000 discharges. It is considered inferior if not standing over 1,200; fair when standing from 1,800 to 2,000, and excellent when beyond this last number of discharges. I reported against that firm as being unable at that time to cast guns of that caliber. The firm subsequently conceded that without changing their furnace they could not cast heavy guns. My report was fully indorsed, I believe, by the Ordnance Bureau. I think that foundery, during my entire stay in New Orleans, had about all it could do making light guns, casting shot, shell, &c., for the Confederate Government; but about the time of the evacuation they were putting up reverberatory furnaces.

Question. Why were not arrangements made with Bennett & Surges and Bujac & Bennett to cast heavy guns in New Orleans?

Answer. Bujac & Bennett were erecting works with a view of making small-arms, and would not take contracts for making heavy guns until near the time the city was evacuated. Bennett & Surges were fully employed by the Navy. These, I think, were the only founderies of any capacity in the city.

Question. Was any foundery and rifle factory set on foot in New Orleans subsequent to the arrival of General Lovell and used entirely for Government work? If so, whose was it, and did it furnish any heavy ordnance?

Answer. Subsequent to General Lovell's arrival Wolfe & Co. had undertaken the manufacture of heavy ordnance exclusively for the Government, as far as I know. There was in connection with this foundery a rifle factory, manufacturing exclusively for the Government. At the time of the evacuation they had made two mortars and were making other heavy guns.

Question. What was the condition of the interior line of works at the time of the evacuation as to guns, magazines, hot-shot furnaces, implements, and equipments? State your opinion as to its impregnability against land attacks.

Answer. This line of works was all completed; provided with magazines and hot-shot furnaces on the river. On the whole series of works there were probably from fifty-five to sixty guns mounted. I considered them of the very best class of field works, and, if manned and properly defended, capable of resisting any force that could be brought against them. The implements and equipments for the pieces that were mounted were generally in duplicate.

Question. What works were constructed after the arrival of General Lovell?

Answer. There was one inclosed field work opposite the Victor line; there were two advanced works higher up the river, about half completed at the time of the evacuation; a work about midway between New Orleans and Fort Livingston, known as the Little Temple; three batteries were put up at Pass Manchac, mounting two guns each, and five one-gun batteries on the western shore of Lake Pontchartrain. There was a large brick fire-proof magazine erected below the city and inclosed with substantial walls, with a railroad leading from it to the river, a well-constructed breakwater protecting the river bank where the Chalmette line touched it. Pearl River was obstructed and three bayous leading from Lake Borgne in the direction of the city. These were the main works that I now recall.

Question. At the time of the evacuation were there more platforms, pintles, and traverse circles ready in position bearing on the river below New Orleans than there were guns to mount on them?

Answer. There were.

Question. What orders in regard to the occupation of Vicksburg did you receive from General Lovell shortly after the evacuation of New Orleans, and what means were placed at your command to carry out those orders?

Answer. About May 2 or 3 I was directed to send the Twenty-sixth Louisiana to Jackson and the Twenty-seventh Louisiana to Vicksburg. About May 7 I was directed to proceed to Vicksburg and take command of the line from Vicksburg to Jackson. In addition to these two regiments mentioned there was placed at my disposal, about May 20, the Twenty-eighth Louisiana, the First Louisiana Artillery, and the Eighth Louisiana Battalion, also what was left of the Twenty-second and Twenty-third Louisiana Regiments and the Third Mississippi, in all about 2,632 men, and about 23 heavy guns, ranging from 32-pounders to 8 and 10 inch columbiads, all of which were mounted by me except some six or eight.

Re-examined by the JUDGE-ADVOCATE:

Question. Where were you on the day the city was evacuated?

Answer. I was in command of the forces on the Chalmette and McGehee lines, about 4 miles below the city. These forces numbered about 1,000 infantry and five companies of artillery.

Question. At or near the time of the evacuation did you receive any orders from General Lovell in regard to the abandonment of the Chalmette line and the removal of the troops under your command? If so, state what those orders were.

Answer. I received no orders from General Lovell at any time on these subjects; no guns or implements were brought away; the ammunition was exhausted in resisting the passage of the gunboats; the camp equipage was not saved because we had no wagons and were dependent upon the river for transportation, which was in possession of the enemy.

Question. Was it practicable for General Lovell to communicate with you after the enemy's fleet passed the Chalmette fortifications?

Answer. I cannot say that it was impracticable, as I crossed the river myself, as did also three other officers. I did not consider that I ran any risk in making the crossing. Orders would not probably have reached me after the enemy's fleet passed Chalmette.

Question. Did you see and have conversation with General Lovell after the enemy's fleet had passed Forts Saint Philip and Jackson?

Answer. I saw him on the afternoon of April 24, 1862, the evacuation being on the 25th.

By a MEMBER OF THE COURT:

Question. Were you at any time delayed or embarrassed in the discharge of your duties as engineer and ordnance officer by the want of funds?

Answer. As ordnance officer I was embarrassed for want of funds, but not materially delayed, because I borrowed money of the State of Louisiana. I made no requisition for money to expend on obstructions already alluded to, the expenses being borne by the State of Louisiana. Subsequent to General Lovell's arrival I did receive funds from the Government on requisitions, which were applied to obstructions and defense of the river; the amount received was, I think, $25,000.

Maj. HENRY A. CLINCH was then sworn and examined as a witness.

By the JUDGE-ADVOCATE:

Question. Were you in command of Forts Pike and Macomb at the time General Lovell assumed command of New Orleans? If so, state their condition at that time.

Answer. On January 19, 1861, I was ordered to the command of Fort Pike, and a few days thereafter I took possession of Fort Macomb also and garrisoned it. The armament and general condition of these works were nearly similar. They each mounted some thirty smooth bore 24-pounders *en barbette* and casemate, together with nine 24-pounder howitzers in flank defenses. For several years these forts had been under charge only of military storekeepers, and their general condition was far from good. I at once made every effort to place them in fighting order, but owing, doubtless, to the then deranged condition of our Ordnance Bureau the work progressed slowly. Major-General Lovell assumed command of the department in October of that year. At that time I had received from Ship Island one 9-inch Dahlgren and one 8-inch shell gun. These were in position, but required several fixtures and appurtenances for their proper working. The garrison consisted of two companies, A and I, First Artillery. I at once urgently requested General Lovell as well for heavier guns as a general outfit for the fort. These, I think, were supplied to me as fast as possible. He sent me two rifled 32-pounder guns and four 42-pounders, together with a 10-inch sea-coast mortar. The carriages and chassis were replaced by new ones; new cisterns sent down and the old ones repaired, and a full supply of ammunition of all kinds and implements supplied. The garrison was also re-enforced by three companies, making five in all—all large companies. Such was the condition of Fort Pike on the date of its evacuation in April, 1862.

Question. If you know, state what, if any, work was done in obstructing the Rigolets and the bayous in the vicinity of Fort Pike after October, 1861.

Answer. The Rigolets at Fort Pike was 3,750 feet wide and ranging in depth from 15 to 50 feet. In February, 1862, General Lovell determined to throw a raft as an obstruction across the pass, and charged me with the general superintendence of the work. It was extremely difficult to obtain logs of sufficient size and buoyancy for our purpose. These were obtained at a heavy cost and from long distances. One or two steamers were placed at my disposal by General Lovell, and the work went on night and day. When nearly ready to be laid across the channel, it was ascertained that a sufficiency of chains and anchors could not be had to secure it in its destined position. About this time several members of the Safety Committee, as it was called, came down, took soundings, and proposed to secure the raft by driving heavy piling on either side. A few days after they returned with all necessary apparatus for piling, and with orders from General Lovell for me to furnish them all the assistance in my power—an order very cheerfully, and to a large extent, obeyed by me. After a month's work, and only a very few days after the raft had been got into position, there came on a heavy blow of wind. One or two steamers and schooners lying above the raft dragged anchor and lodged against the structure. The consequence was that by next morning the whole affair was a wreck, and at least one-half of the piling broken off and washed away. I at once reported to General Lovell. He promised assistance, and we were in a fair way to renew the experiment, when further labor was rendered futile by the fall of New Orleans. By orders from department headquarters I obstructed, by very heavy piling, Salt Bayou, connecting West Pearl River with Lake Pontchartrain, and avoiding the guns of Fort Pike. This bayou was some 10 miles long, 60 feet in width, and with an average depth at high tide of 9 or 10 feet. There was also Mill Bayou, connecting West Pearl and West Middle Rivers. The mouth of West Pearl having been obstructed by rafting, it became important to secure the approaches to it from other rivers not so obstructed. Mill Bayou, 3½ miles long, 40 feet wide, and 10 feet deep, was thoroughly obstructed under my personal direction, by cutting down heavy trees on either bank across the channel for nearly its whole length.

Question. From whom did you receive orders to evacuate Fort Pike? State also the condition of that fort at the time of its evacuation.

Answer. It was on the morning of April 26, I think, that I received a telegraphic order to prepare to evacuate my fort. This I prepared to do by impressing one or two steamboats and schooners lying at the wharf or in the stream, and holding them in readiness for any emergency. I do not remember exactly how the order referred to was signed, but it must have been signed by order of Major-General Lovell, as otherwise I would have paid no attention to it. On the same afternoon I received another telegraphic order, I think, to the effect that I was to spike my guns and abandon the fort at once. This order was signed by C. A. Fuller, colonel, commanding First Louisiana Artillery, and dated New Orleans. I declined obeying this order, for the reason that I had never reported to or received orders from Colonel Fuller in my official capacity as commander of the fort, and I refused to recognize his authority in so grave a matter as abandoning a fortified position without fighting for it. I at once telegraphed Major Devereux, assistant adjutant-general, for written orders, and, if it was decided to abandon the fort, I asked for transportation, if possible, for my best guns at least. About 12 o'clock that night a steamer arrived from the city, and the officer in charge handed me a written order to immediately evacuate the fort. This order was signed by C. A. Fuller, colonel, commanding Third Brigade. I supposed that some accident had occurred to General Duncan, and that Colonel Fuller had assumed command of the brigade by seniority. Regarding, therefore, the order to be in form and from an authoritative source, nothing was left to me but to obey it. I embarked on board the transport all of my ammunition, implements, &c., all quartermaster and commissary stores (ninety days' supply), and in fact everything of value save the guns, for which I had no room on board. These, the moment before leaving the fort, I thoroughly spiked and destroyed in various ways—burning the carriages and chassis and setting fire to all the outbuildings. I left the fort with my whole command at daylight on the 27th.

At the date of its abandonment Fort Pike was in as good fighting trim as it was possible to place it, with the serious exception of the lightness of most of its armament. Had the raft held its intended position all water craft would have been forced within 50 yards of the walls of the fort in order to effect a passage, which fact would have rendered each 24-pounder gun nearly as destructive as guns of much heavier caliber. My orders had been to fight the fort to the last extremity. These orders I would at least have obeyed, and with the most sanguine confidence of a successful result.

Lieut. WILLIAM M. BRIDGES was then duly sworn and examined as a witness.

By the JUDGE-ADVOCATE:

Question. What position did you hold at the time of the evacuation of New Orleans in April, 1862, and where were you stationed for the previous six months?

Answer. I was first lieutenant in the First Regiment Louisiana Artillery, and aide-de-camp to General J. K. Duncan; stationed at Fort Jackson at the time General Lovell assumed command, and was there at the time the fort was surrendered.

Question. What additions, if any, were made in new guns and munitions of war to Forts Jackson and Saint Philip after General Lovell assumed command of Department No. 1?

Answer. Several companies of artillery were added to their garrisons. Three 10-inch columbiads, five 8-inch columbiads, two 7-inch rifled guns, two unbanded rifled 32-pounders, twelve 42-pounders, some smooth-bore 32-pounders (their exact number I do not recollect), and five 10-inch sea-coast mortars were added to the armament of both forts. A large quantity of implements were added to these after General Lovell assumed command, amply sufficient for the working of his guns. When General

Lovell assumed command we had about 18,000 or 20,000 pounds of powder, some of which was worthless, and was sent to New Orleans and reworked. This supply was trebled by him.

The court adjourned to meet at 10 a. m. the 24th instant.

APRIL 24, 1863—10 a. m.

The court met pursuant to adjournment.

Present, all the members of the court, the judge-advocate, and Maj. Gen. Mansfield Lovell.

The proceedings of yesterday were read over.

Col. EDWARD HIGGINS was then sworn and examined as a witness.

By the JUDGE-ADVOCATE:

Question. When did you first enter the service of the Confederate States? State your rank at that time; your present rank; where and to what duty you have been assigned from date of your entry into service.

Answer. I think I entered the service in April, 1861, as captain of the First Louisiana Artillery. I served as aide-de-camp to General Twiggs during his command of New Orleans. After this general was relieved I was placed in command of a light battery. About this time I resigned and remained out of service for about a month, when I was reappointed lieutenant-colonel of the Twenty-second Regiment Louisiana Volunteers. My first duty as lieutenant-colonel was, in obedience to orders from General Lovell, to save the raft between Forts Saint Philip and Jackson. I was assigned by General Duncan to the command of those forts. I was engaged upon this raft about two weeks with all the force that could be possibly had; it was a tremendous job.

Question. Were you in the service of the United States before the secession of the South? If so, in what capacity and for what length of time?

Answer. I was in the Navy of the United States from 1836 to 1854, when I resigned, a lieutenant. The last two years of my service under that Government was spent in commanding an ocean steamer, in which command I remained four years after leaving the United States service.

Question. State generally your knowledge of the causes of the fall of New Orleans, and whether or not the same might have been prevented by Major-General Lovell with the means at his disposal.

The judge-advocate, being told informally by the witness that the inefficiency and incompetency of the naval officers in command at or near Forts Jackson and Saint Philip was the principal cause of the fall of New Orleans, here asked the court to direct the witness to exclude from his reply to the foregoing question the expression of any opinion touching the efficiency or inefficiency of the officers of the C. S. Navy, because the court has no jurisdiction to inquire into and pronounce an opinion upon the official conduct of such officers.

In support of this proposition the judge-advocate submitted the following

ARGUMENT.

The ninety-first article of war, by which courts of inquiry are authorized, declares that they are "to examine into the nature of any transaction, accusation, or imputation against an officer or soldier." Their jurisdiction, both as to subject-matter and person, is thus clearly defined. The person must be an officer or soldier; the subject-matter must be the transaction of such officer or soldier or the accusation that may be made against him; but, as if to remove all doubt or uncertainty as to parties within the jurisdiction of army courts, their character is specifically designated in the ninety-sixth article of war, and in that specification naval officers are not mentioned. It should also be observed that the Articles of War are acts of Congress, declared to be for the government of the armies of the Confederate States. If, however, this court, composed exclusively of army officers, can go beyond these limits to hear testimony impeaching the official conduct of naval officers and pronounce judgment upon such conduct, the solecism in law and justice is presented of men being tried without notice and condemned without a hearing. Such a construction of the order convening this court is less to be justified when it is borne in mind that officers of the Navy belong to another and different arm of the service, and are responsible by law to a separate and distinct Department, clothed with full power and every facility to ascertain and punish its own delinquents. Again, such a course is not necessary to determine whether or not General Lovell has discharged the duties devolved upon him, nor does he ask it to be taken. He was directed by the President to concert and co-operate with the naval officers on duty in his department. If he obeyed this direction and was faithful to his other well-known trusts he should be acquitted of blame. The President and the Secretary of War also informed him that he had no control over officers of the Navy, which fact of course exempts him from all responsibility for their acts or failure to act. It is admitted that the witness may testify that General Lovell sought the co-operation of naval men and suggested certain measures for their adoption, and that this co-operation was refused and the proposed measures designated. To be more specific, it may be shown, and the court may report, if proven, that the Louisiana was not placed in the position desired by General Lovell, and that Commander Mitchell did not make such use of the fire rafts and guard boats as he had been requested and had promised to make. Should such facts appear in the report of the court, the basis of future action is furnished to the Government. It is submitted that this line of procedure is in accordance with the law, the requirements of the order, and substantial justice. The court does that which all courts of inquiry are designed to do; it enables the Government to determine whether or not further proceedings shall be had. A different course tends to excite strife and contention, arraying one arm of the service against the other when the public defense demands unity of spirit and action.

The court, however, declined to make the direction, as requested by the judge-advocate, for reasons set forth in the following opinion:

OPINION OF THE COURT.

On the 16th instant, with the view to remove all doubt upon the point raised by the judge-advocate, a telegram was sent by the order of this court to the Adjutant-General at Richmond, asking specific instruction in the premises. No reply has been received. It therefore remains for the court to act upon its own judgment. The order convening the court does not restrict its investigations to the conduct of Maj. Gen. Mansfield Lovell and the troops of his command except as to the mere evacuation of New Orleans. In relation to the capture of the city the words of the order preclude the idea of such restriction, and they do not imply it in respect to the defense. It is required of the court, too, in those matters, to examine into the attending facts and circumstances, without any limit as to persons or arm of the service. If a partial examination were intended, that intention would doubtless have been expressed. It is the duty of the court to obey the order under which it acts. It does not belong to it to account for the consequences of so doing.

The witness then answered as follows:

Answer. I have no personal knowledge as to the extent of General Lovell's authority over the defenses afloat. The inefficiency and incompetency of a majority of those commanding the defenses afloat were, in my judgment, the causes of its fall, but among them were some exceptions. The chief officer in command of the Confederate States steamer Louisiana, and all of those in command of the river fleet, they being unused to heavy guns and ships, with no idea of discipline, are those whom I consider inefficient and responsible for the fall of the city. On the day and evening of the passage of Forts Jackson and Saint Philip I sent three verbal communications to Capt. J. K. Mitchell, C. S. Navy, informing him that the enemy's vessels of war were making disposition to unite with his mortar fleet in an attack upon the forts or in an attempt to pass them that night, and requested him to place the steamer Louisiana in position before Saint Philip so that she could enfilade the mortar fleet, thereby enabling the men in the forts to stand to their guns to resist the passage of the enemy's vessels of war. The last of these communications was under these circumstances and to this effect. I went into General Duncan's quarters, who remarked to me that Commander Mitchell had sent him word that he (Mitchell) would move the Louisiana in twenty-four hours. The message was brought by Commander Mitchell, and I immediately turned to the latter officer and said to him: "Tell Commander Mitchell that there will be no to-morrow for New Orleans unless he immediately takes up the position assigned to him with the Louisiana; if he does not do so the city is gone, and he will be responsible to the country for its loss. The forts are powerless to prevent it." The commanding officer afloat turned a deaf ear to all our warnings and entreaties, and did not coincide with us in the belief that the enemy would have the temerity to attempt the passage of the forts, and that they were not prepared to resist it. It was fully twenty minutes from the time that the enemy rounded the point below the forts before the vessels of our fleet could move; most of these were run ashore and burned as the enemy passed.

I am of the opinion that if the vessels sent down from New Orleans to co-operate with the forts in the defense of the city had been properly officered and commanded, and had been under the control of an efficient head, we would now be in possession of New Orleans. The Louisiana was invulnerable, as was demonstrated by the fact that one of the heaviest of the enemy's ships poured broadside after broadside into her at a distance of 20 or 30 feet without the least damaging effect. The fleet would render us no assistance. We entreated Commander Mitchell to draw the enemy's fire for a short time, to enable us to secure one of our magazines, which was in danger, and to repair our damages and remount guns. He refused. One reason which he assigned for not taking up his position was that he had but two weeks' provisions. Another was that he was not bomb proof above, and a shell might hit him. I was obliged to move the powder from one of the magazines under fire of the enemy and when their shells were bursting every two or three minutes in the fort. The river fleet, commanded by Stephenson, refused to obey orders from Mitchell; there was no authority and no concert of action afloat. There were twelve vessels in all, including the Louisiana. Three of these were commanded by Commander Mitchell; six by a New Orleans merchant and former steamboat captain, named Stephenson; one by Capt. Beverly Kennon, formerly of the U. S. and C. S. Navies, and one by Captain Grant, a steamboat captain. They were all placed under the command of Mitchell, but he failed in making the river fleet yield obedience to him.

Question. Was anything done by you in preparing launches for additional defense of water approaches in Department No. 1, and under whose orders?

Answer. I was ordered by General Lovell to seize twelve fishing boats and fit them up as small gunboats. I seized them, and his orders for fitting them up were being carried into execution when I was assigned to other duty in fitting up the raft. I know that some of them were completed.

By the COURT:

Question. State what was done in the forts after the enemy's fleet had passed up the river. Were any preparations made to defend the forts from an attack above; and what co-operation, if any, did you receive from the defenses afloat?

Answer. All damages were repaired as far as possible; dismounted guns were remounted; the heavy guns in the lower front were traversed round so as to bear upon the fleet above in case of attack; a return of all the provisions in the forts was made; a demand for surrender by Commodore Porter was refused, and Commander Mitchell was requested by me to move his vessel to the opposite side of the river, above Fort Jackson, to assist in the defense from an attack which was expected from above, which he would not do or attempt to do.

Question. Under whose command were the fire rafts and guard boats before and after the time of the passage of the forts, and were they used as they should have been?

Answer. Previous to the arrival of Commander Mitchell (the second or third day of the bombardment) the river fleet was under the order of General Duncan; when he came down, the fire rafts, gunboats, the river fleet, and everything afloat was turned over to him. The fire rafts were not lighted up the night of the passage of the enemy's fleet, although Commander Mitchell had promised to have it done. While General Duncan commanded the floating defenses fire rafts and guard boats were regularly sent down, but not afterwards, to the best of my knowledge.

Question. Did General Lovell ever send you to Baton Rouge to induce the legislature of Louisiana to make appropriations for the building of gunboats for the defense of New Orleans? If yea, state at what time this mission was undertaken, and was it practicable to have constructed the gunboats and had them ready for service before the fall of the city?

Answer. General Lovell did send me to Baton Rouge on such duty in December, 1861. There was ample time and material obtainable to have provided a fleet sufficient for such purpose. A bill making an appropriation of $2,500,000 passed the senate and was defeated in the house.

Question. Were you sent by General Lovell, in the early part of March, 1862, to endeavor to replace the obstructions at Fort Jackson? If so, state what were your instructions, and give a general idea of what was done by you.

Answer. Yes; about that time. At the time spoken of I was informed by General Lovell that the raft had broken from its fastenings, on the Fort Jackson side of the river, and left about one-third of the river open. He instructed me to go down with a number of barges and fill up the gap, by placing them in the open space and using them as buoys to stretch chains across from the raft on the shore. Upon arriving at the fort I found the raft had also broken from the Fort Saint Philip side, and had dragged several hundred yards below its first position (it was then hanging by its heaviest anchors, which held it lengthwise of the river). I commenced immediately to cut it into sections, and telegraphed to the general to send me tow-boats to assist in replacing it by sections. I found it impossible, however, on account of the strength of the current, to hold all the sections in position after replacing them; the immense weight of the chains, together with the pressure of the water, forced them under the surface, and slowly dragged them down the river, except three sections, of about 100 yards each, one on the Fort Jackson side and two on the Fort Saint Philip side, which remained where placed. I then went up to New Orleans and reported the fact to General Lovell, who directed me to seize a number of vessels, take them down between the forts, and anchor them in line across the river, stretching chains across over them. I accordingly seized a number or heavily-built vessels, and carried out my instructions. They were anchored across the river, as nearly as possible, in the position occupied by the raft, and dismantled, their masts and rigging left to trail astern in order to catch the propellers of any vessel which might attempt to pass. Each vessel had two anchors down and 60 fathoms of chain to each anchor, and three 1-inch chains were stretched across all of them, connecting them with the raft sections remaining in position, forming a barrier which I am confident none of the enemy's ships could have forced under fire from the forts.

Question. What number of fire rafts were sent to Fort Jackson for use by General Lovell?

Answer. I do not remember the number; there were a great many.

Question. What was the immediate cause of the surrender of the forts on April 28, 1862?

Answer. Mutiny of the garrison.

Question. What amount of powder was expended in the fight at Forts

Jackson and Saint Philip and what amount turned over to the enemy; what the number of the garrisons, and the amount of provisions on hand?

Answer. About 70,000 pounds of powder; I think about 30,000 remained in our magazines when we left the fort. There were about 1,100 men in the two forts. Provisions for sixty days were on hand at the time of the passing up of the Federal fleet.

Question. Did you supply the artillerists to serve the guns on the steamer Louisiana? If so, how many?

Answer. Yes; about 150 picked men, under Captain Ryan and Lieutenant Dixon.

Question. Were the defenses strengthened by sand bags, &c., previous to and during the bombardment, and at what time and under what circumstances were the last heavy guns mounted?

Answer. Yes; very considerably by sand bags and cotton bales. The last heavy guns were mounted a few days before the bombardment by the Northern fleet and under fire from the gunboats.

Question. Was it possible to place sharpshooters on the bank of the river near the enemy's fleet to endeavor to dislodge them?

Answer. We placed sharpshooters in the swamp below, but they could not exist there on account of the high stage of water. The river at this time was so high that the parade ground of the fort was covered with water, and we had 9 inches of water in the casemates. Traverses were built around the magazine doors, and an engine and a large detail of men with buckets were kept constantly at work day and night during the bombardment to keep the water out of the magazines.

Capt. EDWARD HOBART was next sworn and examined as a witness.

By Maj. Gen. MANSFIELD LOVELL:

Question. What business were you engaged in at New Orleans while General Lovell was in command of Department No. 1?

Answer. Mercantile profession. We also furnished capital for the erection of the Louisiana powder-mills.

Question. What assistance, if any, did you receive from General Lovell in getting into operation the powder-mills near New Orleans?

Answer. General Lovell rendered important aid in enlarging and hastening the erection of the mills, ordering the founderies to give the necessary work precedence. He also, through means at his disposal, afforded material aid to complete the re-erection after the first explosion. By his direction the mills, originally located at Handsborough, Miss., were removed to New Orleans, the former location being deemed insecure. He also rendered valuable assistance in supplying the mills with materials.

Question. Was the machinery of these mills removed at the time of the surrender? If so, how was that effected and what has become of the mills?

Answer. The machinery of the powder-mills was entirely removed after the passage of the enemy's ships by the forts. It was taken by steamer to Vicksburg, and subsequently located at Selma, Ala., where it has been since in operation when material could be obtained. The boat was furnished by General Lovell.

Question. What was the daily capacity of your mills when completed?

Answer. Five thousand pounds of powder in twenty-four hours. The mills were never pushed to their capacity for want of material.

Capt. J. BRIEN was next sworn and examined as a witness.

By the JUDGE ADVOCATE:

Question. What position did you hold in New Orleans at the time of the evacuation in April, 1862?

Answer. I held the position of assistant ordnance officer and had charge of the main magazine, and was charged by Maj. Gen. M. Lovell with the proof of all powder manufactured and imported at New Orleans.

Question. Did you bring away the powder, cartridges, and other public property belonging either to the State of Louisiana or the Confederate Government?

Answer. I brought away every pound of ammunition and other public property in my charge. The following is a list thereof:

Barrels of cannon powder, 100 pounds each	182
Kegs of musket powder, 25 pounds each	245
Boxes of cannon powder, 100 pounds each	62
Boxes of damaged Spanish powder, 100 pounds each	150
Boxes of small-arm ammunition, 1,000 cartridges each	1,110

and a number of wagon loads of implements, tools, and Government property of all kinds.

Question. What was the quality of the powder brought to New Orleans by the steamers Vanderbilt, Merrimac, and Victoria in the winter of 1861? What was done with it?

Answer. The powder brought by these steamers was damaged and totally unfit for service. A portion was reworked, and the saltpeter extracted from the remainder and made into new powder.

Capt. W. C. CAPERS was next sworn and examined as a witness.

By the JUDGE-ADVOCATE:

Question. What command did you have previous to and at the time of the evacuation of New Orleans?

Answer. I was in immediate command of Fort Macomb, one of the defenses of Lake Borgne.

Question. What additions, if any, had been made to the strength of Fort Macomb after General Lovell assumed command of Department No. 1, in guns, powder, munitions, &c.?

Answer. The additions to my armament were one 8-inch columbiad, four 42-pounder guns, six 32-pounder smooth-bore guns, one 32-pounder rifled gun, and one 10-inch sea-coast mortar, all in place of 24-pounder guns. I also received, in place of old and worthless powder, an ample supply of the best powder then to be had, with all the munitions necessary for the complete equipment and defense of the fort. In addition to these, all the timber bordering the pass above the fort, and which would have completely masked the enemy's vessels, thereby rendering my fire comparatively ineffective, was felled, presenting an open field of fire, both by land and water, to the mouth of the pass. General Lovell furnished me everything necessary for placing the fort on a firm war footing.

Question. Under what orders did you evacuate Fort Macomb?

Answer. On the morning of April 25, 1862, I received an order from Colonel Fuller to hold myself in readiness to abandon the fort, which was signed by order of General Lovell. This order I did not obey, as I wished the order to come through General Lovell's assistant adjutant-general. During that afternoon I received another order, signed C. A. Fuller, colonel, commanding Second Brigade, requiring me to destroy my guns and report to him at Madisonville. This order I had to obey, as my fort was in his district.

Question. What official conversation, if any, took place between yourself and General Lovell relative to the evacuation of Forts Pike and Macomb immediately after your arrival at Camp Moore, after that evacuation?

Answer. I had a conversation with General Lovell at Camp Moore on the subject of the evacuation of the forts, sought by myself, as I desired to know whether Colonel Fuller really had authority for his act. During that conversation General Lovell informed me that he had not issued any such order, and that Colonel Fuller had only been required to have the forts in readiness in the event it became necessary to abandon them. He also said that, hearing the forts had been evacuated, he issued orders to have them reoccupied. This is as near as the frailties of memory will allow me to say concerning this particular point.

Lieut. Col. EDWARD FRY was next sworn and examined as a witness.

By Maj. Gen. MANSFIELD LOVELL:

Question. What position did you occupy in October, 1861, when General Lovell took command of Department No. 1?

Answer. I was assistant adjutant-general at Camp Moore, the camp of organization and instruction in Louisiana.

Question. What was the condition of the troops at Camp Moore at that time as to numbers, arms, equipments, and ammunition? Were they subsequently put in complete order, and what became of them?

Answer. The Thirteenth, Sixteenth, Seventeenth, Eighteenth, and Nineteenth Regiments Louisiana Volunteers, averaging 900 men each, were organized at Camp Moore, rather poorly armed and equipped, and transferred to the Confederate States service during October, November, and December, 1861. They were not supplied with ammunition when transferred. I know nothing, of my own knowledge, in regard to these troops after they were transferred to the Confederate States service.

Question. Were you stationed, at the time of the evacution of New Orleans, at Forts Berwick and Chène? If yea, what was the condition of those works when abandoned?

Answer. I was in command of both forts. The works were in fair condition.

Question. What property was brought away and what disposition was made of the remainder?

Answer. About 5,000 pounds of powder, over 12,000 rounds of musket cartridges, all of the infantry arms and accouterments, and fully two months' supply of commissary stores for about 160 men. All this property was turned over to the proper officers at Camp Moore, La. The remainder—the heavy guns, carriages, chassis, &c.—was destroyed or rendered unfit for service in obedience to orders from General Duncan.

Maj. W. H. DEVEREUX was then duly sworn and examined as a witness.

By Maj. Gen. MANSFIELD LOVELL:

Question. What position did you hold at the time General Lovell took command of Department No. 1 and from that date to the evacuation of New Orleans?

Answer. I held the position of chief of staff to Major-General Twiggs at the time General Lovell arrived to take command of Department No. 1, and continued in that capacity under Major-General Lovell until his own staff was organized, when, being ranked by Major Palfrey, I performed the duties of acting assistant adjutant-general in immediate and confidential connection with Major-General Lovell.

Question. What was the general condition of the department as to its defenses, as shown by the official reports, when General Lovell took command?

Answer. The general condition of the defenses of the department when General Lovell assumed command was not one of strength commensurate with the interests to be protected, nor yet hopelessly inadequate to encounter the force of the enemy then in the Gulf. The armament of the forts on the exterior line was light in caliber and insufficient in the number of guns; some of the gun-carriages were reported weak; implements were wanting, and the ammunition was inferior and very scarce. The interior line of defense for the immediate protection of the city of New Orleans was well advanced, but not completed. For this interior line a number of guns, perhaps 125, were arriving from Richmond, but unaccompanied by any equipment; these guns were also of light caliber. They had been secured by General Twiggs, and their equipment ordered to be prepared before the arrival of Major-General Lovell.

Question. Were you present at interviews between General Lovell and members of the Safety Committee? If so, state substantially what passed at these interviews.

Answer. I was present at many interviews between General Lovell and members of the Committee of Public Safety, and affirm, as the substance of their conversations, that the general accepted their offers of material, anchors and chains for rafts, iron and copper for castings, and, briefly, those articles for military purposes and construction which at that time could only be obtained readily by private enterprise, but declined a part of their tenders of money, as he was not embarrassed for want of funds, but retarded by the deficiency of procuring through Government agents articles of prime necessity, which had grown to be scarce. The general also declined many suggestions of military plans.

Question. What was the number and composition of the troops in the city at the time of the evacuation and how were they armed?

Answer. There were two brigades of State troops, under Generals Tracy and Buisson, in New Orleans at the time of its evacuation. These numbered in all, perhaps, 3,000 men; were new levies, chiefly composed of the men of the families resident in and about the city. They were indifferently armed, shot-guns being I believe the prevailing weapon. Two-thirds of them belonged to the French class of the population. Included in the above estimate was a battalion of some 400 men, Orleans Guards, which was well armed and equipped. There were, besides, the Confederate Regiment State Troops, about 700 strong, well armed and equipped, and the Pinkney Battalion (now Eighth Louisiana Battalion), heavy artillery, 500 unarmed men, newly enlisted, occupying the works on the river above and below the city; also the Thomas Battalion Confederate Troops, numbering about 350 men, also unarmed.

Question. State what was General Lovell's habitual routine of business while in command of Department No. 1. Was he ever absent from his office a single day during his administration except while engaged in personal inspections of the troops or works of his department?

Answer. General Lovell's hours of business were habitually from 9 a. m. to 3 p. m., during which he was always in his office. Most frequently he returned at 7 or 8 p. m. and continued in the transaction of public affairs until very late hours of the night. During the interval between 3 and 8 p. m. General Lovell was ordinarily occupied in personal inspections of the troops and lines of defense, visits to the founderies and work-shops, examinations of proper means in the construction of Montgomery's and the State fleets and the rams Mississippi and Louisiana. His tours of inspection through his department were frequent, and I believe thorough. The restless activity displayed by the department commander was a subject of general remark.

Question. What was the general military character of the population in New Orleans at the time of its fall?

Answer. It was indifferent. The better part of the fighting material had volunteered and been ordered elsewhere. The young men were all gone from the city with a few glaring exceptions.

The court adjourned to meet at 10 a. m. the 25th instant.

VICKSBURG, MISS., *April* 25, 1863—10 a. m.

The court met pursuant to adjournment.

Present, all the members of the court, the judge-advocate, and Maj. Gen. Mansfield Lovell.

Capt. W. B. ROBERTSON was then sworn and examined as a witness.

By the JUDGE-ADVOCATE:

Question. Where were you when the Federal fleet passed Forts Saint Philip and Jackson, in April, 1862, and what, if any, position did you hold in the Army of the Confederate States?

Answer. I was in command of the water battery at Fort Jackson; a captain in the First Regiment Louisiana Artillery.

Question. What orders did you receive from Colonel Higgins on the afternoon previous to the passage of the forts by the enemy's fleet on the morning of April 24, 1862?

Answer. I received a written order from Lieutenant-Colonel Higgins, commanding Forts Jackson and Saint Philip, that there was a movement among the enemy's gunboats and ships of war below his mortar boats and that he was planting signals on the Saint Philip shore, indicating that they would probably take up position and bombard in conjunction with the mortar boats, and, if a favorable opportunity presented, would attempt the passage of the forts. He charged me to prepare for such events. He also stated that the river would be lit up. The order from Lieutenant-Colonel Higgins is now in Louisiana, near the enemy.

The court adjourned to meet at Jackson, Miss., April 27, 1863, at 10 a. m.

JACKSON, MISS., *April* 27, 1863.

The court met pursuant to adjournment.

Present, all the members of the court, the judge-advocate, and also Maj. Gen. Mansfield Lovell.

The proceedings of the 25th instant were read over.

The following communication was then read to the court by the judge-advocate, to wit:

RICHMOND, VA., *April* 21, 1863.

Maj. L. R. PAGE:

The court is required by the order to examine into the facts and circumstances attending the capture of New Orleans, the defense of that city, and the evacuation of the same. The inquiry is broad and not restrictive, and will embrace every fact and every officer, whether of Army or Navy, connected with the object of inquiry. It is fully competent for the court, and it is expected of it, to report all the facts of the whole subject of the capture, defense, and evacuation of New Orleans, which included the defenses on the river below the city, and to report their opinion thereon.

S. COOPER,
Adjutant and Inspector General.

Lieut. Col. W. S. LOVELL was then sworn and examined as a witness.

By Maj. Gen. MANSFIELD LOVELL:

Question. What duty were you assigned to in New Orleans by General Lovell in November, 1861? State what was done by you.

Answer. I reported for duty to General Lovell at New Orleans on or about November 8, 1861. Was ordered immediately to take charge of the raft between Forts Jackson and Saint Philip; to repair, replace it in position, and anchor it properly. I found the raft had, by either dragging its anchors or parting its moorings, drifted so far down the river that the end towards the Fort Jackson side was about the middle of the river, leaving the river open between them about 400 yards; many of the gum rails, which were joined on top of the logs forming the raft, were broken, and the end towards the Saint Philip side very much broken up. Most of the anchors which had been used in mooring the raft were very small, and had rope attached to them instead of chain. Some of the ropes were so short as to lead almost up and down, not having sufficient scope. A number of the anchors were not recovered, having parted the moorings. Most of the gum rails, or stringers, were broken or wrenched out of place. I pinned down new ones. I secured the end on the Fort Saint Philip side by planting a large anchor, about 3,000 pounds, with what are called "dead men," or longer logs placed in front of each arm. The anchor was then backed by chains to a stump, and the stump backed by a small anchor from the main anchor. Mooring chains were secured to the end of the raft; there were no other means of securing the raft to the shore. The raft was then hauled back into position on this side by steamers and anchored. The heaviest anchors, from 2,500 to 3,000 pounds, were placed in the deepest water, with chains from 45 to 60 fathoms each. To the best of my recollection there were between twenty-five and thirty anchors used in anchoring the raft, and each with a sufficient scope of chain. A number of the anchors were between 2,000 and 3,000 pounds. The end of the raft on the Fort Jackson side was secured by two heavy chains running to two "crabs," also by heavy chains, made fast to a large anchor, planted as the one on the other side, so that they might be slacked up or lengthened if necessary. When the drift got to be heavy against the raft steamers were employed to endeavor to haul it out, which was found impossible. I built, by General Lovell's order, a raft or boom above the city of New Orleans, about 1,000 yards long, which was ready to be thrown across should it be required. I had charge, for a time, of a raft to be placed across the lake at Fort Pike. I also fitted up the steamers Oregon and Arrow as gunboats for the lake. The former vessel carried two guns, one 8-inch gun and one 32-pounder rifled; the latter, one 32-pounder. I also fitted up the yacht Corypheus with one gun, to be used in the lake.

Question. What duty was performed by you, under orders of General Lovell, in connection with the river-defense fleet; also with ships fitted out at the expense of the State of Louisiana?

Answer. I was appointed ordnance and disbursing officer of the river-defense fleet by General Lovell. As ordnance officer, I superintended the necessary work on vessels of the fleet, to receive and place in position their armament, 32 or 24 pounders, furnished by General Lovell. I also furnished them ammunition and small-arms, and established a system of signals. As disbursing officer, I had to examine and pay the many bills incurred in fitting out the fleet. When the steamers Charles Morgan, Galveston (afterwards the Governor Moore), and General Quitman were taken by Governor Moore to be fitted out as gunboats, they were immediately, by General Lovell's consent, turned over to me, to be altered, protected, armed, officered, and manned as I might deem proper. I had the whole charge of these two steamers. All that was done by the State was to pay the bills approved by me. The captains appointed by me (and confirmed by Governor Moore) to the command of these vessels were Capts. Beverly Kennon, of the Governor Moore, and Alexander Grant, of the General Quitman.

Question. When the raft at the lower forts was completed and put in position did you consider it an effective obstacle to ships ascending the river as long as it remained in place?

Answer. When the raft was in position, after I had taken charge of it, I considered it an effective obstruction to vessels coming up the river, and that it would have so remained had it not been for the extraordinary high water and drift. By the water overflowing the banks the ground was softened, which prevented the anchors from holding. I did not think it possible for the enemy to remove the raft under the guns of Forts Jackson and Saint Philip. If the raft had not been carried away I do not believe it possible for the enemy to have passed the forts.

Question. What measures were taken by you under authority of General Lovell previous to the passage of the forts, previous to the evacuation in case of such passage, and what use was made of such means at the time of the evacuation?

Answer. Some days before the enemy passed the forts, by General Lovell's directions, I got ready, for any move that might be necessary, the three steamers Magenta, Peytona, and Pargoud. These vessels were in such condition that they could all be ready to move at four hours' notice. I ordered these three vessels to get ready to move at 7 o'clock the morning the enemy passed the forts—April 24, 1862. I turned over the largest steamer (the Magenta) to Major Lamar, for the purpose of removing Government commissary stores. The next largest steamer (the Peytona) I turned over to Captain St. Clair, at his urgent request, to assist in towing the Mississippi. The third steamer (the Pargoud) was used to remove commissary and ordnance stores. Among the latter stores she had one 32-pounder and a number of battery forges; I think six. The cabin of the boat was filled with persons—many women and children—who wished to leave the city.

Cross-examination by the JUDGE-ADVOCATE:

Question. What was your occupation before April, 1861?

Answer. I was an officer in the Navy of the United States for nearly twelve years. I resigned from that service in 1859. I entered the Naval School at Annapolis as a midshipman in 1847 and graduated in 1853. During the last three years of my service in the U. S. Navy I was in command of steamers.

Question. Did you not succeed General M. L. Smith as ordnance officer of Department No. 1? If you were acting as such at the time of the evacuation of New Orleans, state the amount of ordnance you then had on hand and what became of it.

Answer. I did succeed him as such. I cannot state the amount on hand without reference to my ordnance papers; there was a great deal of ordnance stores at the various forts. Of that in the city, under my immediate charge, the larger proportion was saved; very little was lost. Many supplies of ordnance stores were furnished to various works for which I received no receipts, and had to report them in my return as lost. To illustrate my meaning, the powder reported by me to be lost was sent to the fort below the city (Chalmette) and to the upper batteries, and two or three 8-inch columbiads reported as lost were used at Chalmette in the fight.

Question. State your knowledge as to the effectiveness of the river-defense fleet. In what respect and by what means, if any, might the same have been made more efficient in the defense of the city?

Answer. The boats were fitted up generally very well for use as rams. I considered most of them as better for that purpose than the Queen of the West, a ram taken from the enemy, which I have well examined since her capture. There was no discipline, no organization, but little or no drill of the crews. I frequently requested the commanding officers (Montgomery and Townsend) to drill their men at a gun I placed on one of the vessels expressly for that purpose. I offered to employ a Navy officer to drill them. I also employed a person who had been a gunner in the U. S. Navy to act as such to the fleet; to mount the guns; to have a general superintendence of everything belonging to the gunner's department; also to teach the officers and men of the fleet how to use and manage the guns. I do not believe one of the officers in command of any of the vessels of the fleet knew how to load or manage heavy guns. Some of the vessels had men employed as gunners. Some of the captains told me they knew nothing about heavy guns and must have gunners.

Question. Were there in Department No. 1 any vessels not of the river-defense fleet which might have been fitted up similarly for resisting the enemy?

Answer. In my opinion the best steamers were taken and fitted out for the river defense; there were a number of other steamers that might have been fitted out as rams and gunboats.

Question. Were the rams of the river-defense fleet and such other vessels as were in Department No. 1 capable of being fitted out as rams or gunboats? Was it practicable, after October 1, 1861, to have prepared a fleet sufficient to cope with the war vessels of the Federal fleet or which passed the forts?

Answer. In my opinion no fleet could have been fitted out in New Orleans since October 1, 1861, out of the steamers there, to be able to cope with that of the enemy. One might have been fitted out to assist greatly regular gunboats like the Mississippi had they been properly officered and manned.

Question. Were as many shipwrights employed upon the Mississippi as could have been worked to advantage and could they have worked at night?

Answer. I am unable to say how many were employed. Work could have been done at night on the vessel with great advantage. She could have been lighted up very easily with gas or by light-wood torches from a steamboat anchored on the outside of her and by torches from the shore or the inside. I suggested this latter plan to Mr. Tift two or three times. I have seen the workmen quit the vessel by sundown, when they ought to have worked an hour or two longer.

Question. Could the Mississippi have been saved; if so, how?

Answer. My opinion is that she could and ought to have been saved by having vessels ready to tow her off, and there was an ample number of steamers at New Orleans that could have been used for that purpose. In my opinion, had they begun to make these steamers ready as soon as the report of the passage of the forts had reached the city, the Mississippi could have been removed. I received information about 5 o'clock on the morning of the 24th that the enemy's fleet had passed the forts; it anchored before the city about 12 m. the next day. About 11 a. m. on the 24th Captain St. Clair applied to me for the steamers I had gotten ready. I refused him all but one—the second largest of the three; the largest was, I think, then being loaded with commissary stores.

Question. Was the Star of the West at New Orleans at that time; if so, describe her, as also the Peytona and St. Charles.

Answer. She was there, a regular sea-going side-wheel steamer, of good power for towing. The Peytona was a river steamboat of fine power. The St. Charles was an old tow-boat, one that I had discharged as not strong enough to work on the rafts, and the two were, in my opinion, unable to tow the Mississippi. The Star of the West, the Peytona, and another strong boat could have done it.

Question. As the result of your knowledge, military and nautical, what is your opinion as to the ability of land defenses to resist vessels of war under steam?

Answer. My opinion has always been that steam vessels of war can pass forts in an open channel free from obstruction.

Question. How many guns of caliber of 8-inch and above that were mounted for the defense of Pensacola Harbor?

Answer. When I left Pensacola, about November 5, 1861, there were at least fifteen 8 and 10 inch columbiads; also a number of 10-inch and two 13-inch mortars. Three of the 10-inch guns were brought to New Orleans after April 1, 1862.

Capt. BEVERLY KENNON was then sworn and examined as a witness.

By Maj. Gen. MANSFIFLD LOVELL:

Question. What position did you hold when General Lovell assumed command of Department No. 1, in October, 1861?

Answer. I was in charge of the Ordnance Department of the Navy.

Question. Did you make arrangements with Bennett & Surges to cast heavy guns? If so, how many, and when were they to begin work?

Answer. I did make arrangements with the firm of Bennett & Surges to cast guns. This was about October 1, 1861. They could not make the guns I wanted then because they had not the proper iron. I ordered fifty heavy 8-inch smooth-bore guns. This party was to commence work when they procured the proper material, but the Secretary of the Navy broke all my contracts before any one firm was really ready to commence work.

By the JUDGE-ADVOCATE:

Question. Why was not the arrangement spoken of in regard to heavy guns executed by Bennett & Surges? State all the facts connected with this matter.

Answer. Because the Secretary of the Navy ordered that all work that I had ordered should be stopped. He gave as a reason that the expenditures in the Ordnance Department were enormous and must be curtailed. This note, or order, or whatever it may be termed, came from the Confederate States Naval Ordnance Department I suppose with Mr. Mallory's indorsement.

Question. State generally what other contracts made by you, if any, were stopped by order of the Secretary of the Navy.

Answer. All contracts were stopped, and in the majority of cases all purchases returned. By all contracts, I mean the manufacture of guns and carriages, shot, shell, spherical case, and pretty much everything belonging to an ordnance department. Mr. Mallory or his subordinates would not take the lead, copper, block tin, zinc, and flannel that I had purchased. As an instance of my purchases, in the line of flannel I must have gotten $50,000 worth, yet Mr. Mallory would not take it. I procured it at an average price of 45 cents per yard. He afterwards bought the same article at four times the price. All other articles rose in price in the same ratio. He found he had to have them, but paid a much greater price for them. Had Mr. Mallory allowed the founderies and other establishments in New Orleans then working for the Navy to continue their work, I am sure the city would not have fallen. There was an abundance of guns and projectiles of all sorts making and made when he stopped work. Among the contracts or work in progress I had 300 submarine batteries, which Mr. Mallory would not use or allow to be completed for use. I furnished General Polk with 150 of them. I know not what became of the rest. I made no contract for fuses, fire-works, rockets, &c., as they were made in the Confederate States naval laboratory. I started a powder-mill, which was broken up by order from Richmond. To bring this answer to a close, every contract was more or less broken in upon by Mr. Mallory's order until just before New Orleans fell, when it was too late to repair damages.

Question. Did you take part in the engagement with the Federal fleet before the passage of the forts? If so, in what capacity and with what result?

Answer. I did take part in the engagement below New Orleans with the Federal fleet. I was then commander of the steamer Governor Moore, and with her sunk the

United States steam sloop-of-war Varuna. I afterwards destroyed my ship to prevent her falling into the hands of the enemy. I lost 74 men out of 93; besides this, the ship was completely disabled.

Question. What assistance that was not rendered might have been given by the vessels of the C. S. Navy or of the river-defense fleet or by fitting out vessels then at New Orleans belonging to private parties?

Answer. There were no Confederate States naval ships of war in our neighborhood; therefore no assistance could come from them, unless, of course, I except those in the fight. Had all our vessels been at the forts, and had all the vessels alongside the wharves been fitted up properly, I am sure that the enemy would not have passed us. All the assistance was given by the Confederate States naval vessels present that could be given, but Mr. Mallory ordered Commander Mitchell to take command near the forts at an hour too late to do much service. As to the river-defense fleet, they behaved very shamefully; every single vessel ran away or was deserted by all hands without fighting. The vessels belonging to private parties or companies at New Orleans in the fall of 1861 numbered somewhere in the neighborhood of twenty tow-boats, strong and comparatively fast, which would and could have made excellent rams. There were about as many large ocean steamers, which in smooth water could have carried on an average twenty heavy guns. There were also about a dozen ships, brigs, &c., which on an average could have carried six heavy guns each; yet Mr. Mallory did not take any of these vessels. They were taken by the State, but it was then too late. I was making preparations to arm and equip all these vessels when I was relieved of my command in New Orleans and ordered to Richmond. I then resigned my commission as a naval officer. After I resigned, the State of Louisiana took many of these vessels, but there was too little time then to fit them, man, and officer them. Regular naval officers, even at that late hour, would have done better than the river steamboat captains who were on board of them.

Question. What was the character of the vessel you commanded, and what was the character of the Federal vessel Varuna, as to construction, armament, &c.?

Answer. My ship was an ordinary merchant mail steamer—strong, fast, and of much weight. Her battery was only two 32-pounder rifles. The Varuna was a regular man-of-war built ship, with a crew of 259 men, and eight 8-inch guns, four heavy 32-pounders, two 20-pounder Parrotts, and one 12-pounder howitzer.

The court adjourned to meet at Charleston, S. C., at 12 m. May 15, 1863, or as soon thereafter as practicable.

CHARLESTON, S. C., *May* 18, 1863—10 a. m.

The court met pursuant to adjournment.

Present, Maj. Gen. T. C. Hindman, Brig. Gens. T. F. Drayton and W. M. Gardner, Maj. L. R. Page, judge-advocate, and Maj. Gen. Mansfield Lovell.

The proceedings of the 27th ultimo were read over.

Gen. G. T. BEAUREGARD was then sworn and examined as a witness.

By Maj. Gen. MANSFIELD LOVELL:

Question. What was your rank in the U. S. Army, and were you while in that service stationed at or near New Orleans, and what were your opportunities to form an acquaintance with the topography of that section of country?

Answer. I was a brevet major of Engineers in the United States service, and in charge for about fifteen years of the works defending the approach to New Orleans, which made me thoroughly acquainted with the topography of that section of Louisiana.

Question. From your knowledge of the country and its peculiarities would you think it the proper plan to concentrate the main strength in artillery at Forts Jackson and Saint Philip in connection with obstructions at that point, rather than to place the guns at many points along the river which the enemy would have to pass in succession?

Answer. The true plan for the defense of a river from the passage of steamers, &c., is, when practicable, to obstruct its navigation with rafts, piles, torpedoes, &c., at the most favorable points for such obstructions; then to defend the latter by a concentration of the greatest number of heaviest guns at one's command, separating them, however, from each other by traverses when necessary to protect them from enfilade fires. Such was the system proposed by Generals Bernard and Patton, Majors Chase, Delafield, &c., when they planned Forts Jackson and Saint Philip and the batteries contiguous to those works. Detached batteries are very good when properly located and supported; otherwise they are apt to be overpowered successively by a naval attack or to be taken in rear by a land force. It is evident that since the enemy's steamers and gunboats passed the concentrated fires of Forts Jackson, Saint Philip, &c., without much injury, they would have done so even more easily if our guns had been scattered over 75 miles from those works to New Orleans. Moreover, the river being very high and the country between those two points being low, it could easily have been submerged by cutting the levees at night near any batteries which might have been constructed along the river, thereby cutting off their garrisons from succor or retreat. I will remark that Forts Jackson and Saint Philip were placed that low down the river to protect from the enemy's depredations as much of the country liable to cultivation as practicable, and also to increase the obstacles to a regular siege resulting from the lowness of their sites, which does not admit of the construction of bayous and parallels, especially when the river is high.

Question. The battle having been fought at the forts, and the fleet having passed, do you consider New Orleans a tenable military position, and did its evacuation by the infantry forces necessarily follow as a matter of course when the enemy was in full possession of the river?

Answer. The forts commanding the river having been passed, New Orleans necessarily lay at the mercy of the enemy's heavy guns afloat, which, owing to the high stage of the river, commanded the banks on both sides to the swamps skirting the river at a distance varying from a half to one mile. An army of 50,000 men or more could not then have saved the city from destruction. Whether the latter was desirable at the time before New Orleans had experienced Butler's iron rule could only have been determined by the State or Confederate authorities, who should have considered whether the destruction of so large a city would have done more injury to the enemy than to ourselves. It is evident that to him Baton Rouge is a better strategic point than New Orleans, and the destruction of the latter would have relieved him of the necessity of keeping a garrison of 5,000 or 6,000 men there to guard it. This act would have been a mere empty bravado, a wanton destruction of an immense amount of private and public property, which would have shaken at the time the Confederacy to its very foundations and thrown upon its Government a helpless population of about 160,000 non-combatants (men, women, and children) to feed and provide for when already overburdened to supply the wants of the armies in the field. When the Russians burned Moscow it was for the purpose of annihilating Napoleon's army of 300,000 or 400,000 men, which had invaded their country. When they again consented to the slow but certain destruction of Sevastopol it was to prevent the allies from taking possession of its immense docks, arsenals, military stores, and the fleet which had sought refuge under the guns of its forts. The possession of the harbor of Sevastopol would also have afforded them a magnificent base for their future operations in the Crimea. As I have already stated, the Mississippi River being extremely high, the streets of New Orleans could have been swept from one extremity to the other by the heavy guns of the enemy's fleet; or had Commodore Farragut preferred reducing the place to submission without using his guns, it would have been only necessary to have cut the levee above and below the city, and the whole population would have been utterly defenseless and in a starving condition in a few days. Without the command of the Mississippi River New Orleans is not worth holding as a military or strategic position.

By a MEMBER OF THE COURT:

Question. Was the land on the sugar plantations below New Orleans high enough for the construction of batteries upon them?

Answer. From Point à la Hache, about 40 miles below the city, batteries could have been constructed along both sides of the river, provided there were no crevasses. Such batteries would be liable to be submerged by breaks in the levee.

Question. What was the width of the levee in front of New Orleans?

Answer. Immediately in front of the center of the city the levee will average about 150 feet in width. Opposite the extremities of the city the levee varied from 5 feet in width at the crest to 10 or 12. The slopes of the levee have about an angle of 45 degrees; their height varies from 5 to 8 feet.

Question. Would the water let in from above the city through a crevasse have submerged the whole city or only that portion next the swamp and lakes?

Answer. The crevasse at Carrollton, about 6 miles above the city, several years ago, submerged the city to about Bourbon street, the fifth street on Canal street from the river. A crevasse nearer to the city than Carrollton would probably have submerged it to a greater extent. The water would have remained in the city as long as the river remained at high stage. I have known the city to be in danger of submersion without any crevasse of the levee, owing to the exceeding high stage of the river, and, in the event of a crevasse, the depth of water arising from the submersion would be proportioned to the height of the river and the width of the crevasse.

Question. Could Forts Jackson and Saint Philip have held the river against a hostile fleet without obstructions in the channel? What should have been the character of these obstructions? By what means could the accumulation of drift have been prevented?

Answer. I am decidedly of the opinion that Forts Jackson and Saint Philip could not have prevented a certain number of steamers out of a fleet from passing up the river in a dark night or a foggy day. A boom obstruction is, in my opinion, the only kind that could have answered the purpose of preventing the enemy's steamers from passing those forts; but the problem of constructing those booms so as to enable them to resist the pressure of the drift-wood is a difficult one, which would require very thorough examination and study to solve it satisfactorily. Knowing the importance of a boom for the defense of New Orleans, when the State seceded I had made the drawings and estimates of a boom to be put across the river between these two forts. When, in February, 1861, I left New Orleans for Montgomery, at the call of the Confederate States Government, I placed the drawings and plans referred to in the hands of Col. Paul Hébert, for the use of the State Military Board, calling their attention to the urgent necessity of having the boom constructed and put in position at the earliest moment practicable; but I am informed that it was never done, on account of its cost (less than $100,000), and the time required for its construction, probably three months. It was designed to make it in two sections, of several layers of logs, strongly bolted together; each section strongly anchored at one extremity to each bank of the river; their other extremities were then to be brought together down-stream, near the Fort Jackson side, about one-third the width of the river, by means of steam power, chains, and anchors; these chains were to be slackened when the drift-wood accumulated too much above the boom, and hauled taut again after its passage.

Question. As against a naval force of, say, twenty mortar vessels and thirty steam vessels and a land force of 15,000 men, what works, guns, obstructions, and troops would be necessary to the successful defense of New Orleans, and what naval co operation would be required?

Answer. This question is so important and difficult that I do not feel competent, away from the locality, to give it a reliable or satisfactory answer. In October, 1861, when General Lovell was ordered to Louisiana, he called upon me for my general views as to the defense of that State, which I furnished him in writing. He informs me that he has it now in his possession. It was hastily written, but it, or so much as may be deemed proper by the court, may be annexed as a part of this answer.

The court adjourned to meet at 10 a. m. to-morrow.

CHARLESTON, S. C., *May* 19, 1863—10 a. m.

The court met pursuant to adjournment.

Present, all the members of the court, the judge-advocate, and Maj. Gen. Mansfield Lovell.

Lieut. A. F. WARLEY, C. S. Navy, was then sworn and examined as a witness.

By the JUDGE-ADVOCATE:

Question. State your rank in the Navy, and where you were on duty in April, 1862.

Answer. I am first lieutenant in the C. S. Navy, and was in command of the Confederate States ram Manassas, between Forts Saint Philip and Jackson, in April, 1862.

Question. State, if you know, the condition of the Confederate States steamer Louisiana at the time the forts were passed by the enemy's fleet.

Answer. I was not attached to her, but joined her the morning after the fight, when my vessel had been destroyed. The Louisiana was without motive power, and was made fast to the bank and had an anchor down. She was to have been propelled by a submerged wheel and two propellers. The submerged wheel had proved to be useless and the propellers were unfinished. I know but little of her armament. There are other persons who can give you full information on this subject. Commander Mitchell and Lieutenants Shryock and Bowen were attached to the vessel.

Question. Were you one of the officers of the naval council convened to consider and determine a location for the Louisiana in the effort to resist the attack of the enemy's fleet upon and their passage of Forts Jackson and Saint Philip? If so, state why she was not placed in the position desired by Generals Lovell and Duncan.

Answer. I was one of that council. The vessel was not put in the position desired by Generals Lovell and Duncan because the vessel had no propelling power of her own, and to have taken that position she would have been under the fire of the mortar boats of the enemy, while she would not have been able to have reached them. Her port-holes were so constructed that her guns could not have had sufficient elevation to bring their fire within range. In my opinion she would have been sunk in that position in half an hour without effecting a particle of good. In that opinion the senior officers of the council concurred without a dissenting voice. I was the junior member of the council. The practice of the enemy's mortar fleet was perfect. As an illustration, I was satisfied before the bombardment commenced that they had been taking observations of the Manassas. I had orders to remove my vessel to the other side of the river as soon as the fight commenced. At the explosion of the first shell I hauled out of my position, but had not removed a ship's length before two mortar shells fell in the position I had held, and I subsequently counted sixty shots that struck within a short time the place the Manassas had retired from. The Louisiana presented a much larger surface than the Manassas, and one shell falling perpendicularly upon her upper deck would have been sufficient to have sunk her. The upper deck was flat and only covered with very thin iron. She was built to fight against vessels throwing broadsides at close range. We hoped to be able in three or four days to propel her at the rate of three knots an hour, which, if done, would have enabled her to have destroyed everything in the river. The port-holes were small, so as to present as small an aperture as possible to the guns and musketry of the enemy. Her range was not designed to be greater than 1,500 or 1,600 yards.

Question. Could the Louisiana have been finished had she not been removed from New Orleans in time to have resisted the passage of the forts or to have protected the city? State also why she was removed to the forts before her motive power was effective.

Answer. I think she could have been completed sufficiently to have protected the city had she not been removed. The day she was blown up (April 25) she was to have been finished at 12 m. I think the mechanics could have worked to better advantage at the city than while the vessel was in motion and at the forts. I had telegraphed Commander Whittle that it was necessary to make a naval demonstration in order to save the forts. He, I presume, sent her down, hoping that she might be got ready on her way down and assist in such demonstration. I also informed him at the same time that the Montgomery fleet was giving the forts no assistance whatever.

Question. If the ram Manassas and one or two other war steamers had been placed in position at the bar below the forts, do you think the enemy would have attempted to lighten over their ships of war while thus exposed to our fire?

Answer. I do not think they would; but at that time the Manassas had been sent up the river and had her propellers broken to pieces.

Question. What measures, not adopted, might have been taken that would have been effective for holding the Mississippi River against the Federal fleet?

Answer. If the river-defense fleet with the Governor Moore and General Quitman had co-operated with the Manassas as rams, they might have prevented the passage of the forts. One of the river fleet (the Defiance) never left the bank, and all the other boats, except the McRae, steamed up the river without firing a gun or taking any part in the fight. The next morning the Stonewall Jackson and Governor Moore came down to the quarantine and ran into a Yankee gunboat and sunk her. Had they acted in the same manner the night before, making their power available, they could have kept the enemy's fleet under the fire of the forts, and the city would have been saved. If the fleet could have been held fifteen minutes under the fire of the forts I believe we might have sunk every vessel they had. Had there been proper use of the fire rafts it would have conduced greatly to the safety of the city. I know of but one fire raft carried down to the fleet, which came near destroying the Hartford, the flag-ship of the enemy. This was taken down by the Mosher, commanded by a Captain Sherman, who was wounded and had his vessel sunk. There were a large number of these rafts (thirty or forty of them) which were not used, and which, even if not set on fire, would have been useful in blockading the channel had they been sent down. Stephenson (generally called Commodore Stephenson), of the Montgomery fleet, in attempting to carry down some fire rafts on the other side of the obstructions, permitted them to drift upon the obstructions, which caused them to be broken in the center, so that the middle of the river was a free and open channel.

Captains Grant, of the General Quitman, and Hooper, commanding the Resolute, of the river-defense fleet, came aboard the Manassas the evening before the fight, and, in the course of conversation, denied that they were under the command of Generals Lovell and Duncan, or of any one except the Secretary of War; that they were there to show naval officers how to fight.

Cross-examination by Maj. Gen. MANSFIELD LOVELL:

Question. If the Montgomery defense fleet had been properly officered and manned would they not have been of very great effect in resisting the passage of the forts?

Answer. It would have been very effective to that end.

Question. State in general terms your opinion of the means placed at the disposal of the naval officers at New Orleans to enable them to co-operate with the land forces in preventing the passage of the forts on April 24, 1862, mentioning each vessel and its efficiency.

Answer. We had the Louisiana, a formidable vessel, with a powerful battery, but without motive power. Her crew was of mixed character, some good men and some indifferent; at least such is my opinion, based upon the fact that some of her crew were from the Army, others from the lake fleet, &c. The McRae was a light vessel, with a fine crew; her battery consisted of one heavy 9-inch gun and six light 32-pounders; the 9-inch gun burst early in the action; for her size she was a very efficient vessel. The Jackson was only a river boat, with two 32-pounders; she was not in the fight; and the Manassas, a tug-boat that had been converted into a ram, covered with half-inch iron, and had a 32-pounder carronade; her crew consisted of thirty-five persons, officers and men. She was perforated in the fight by shot and shell as if she had been made of paper. These vessels constituted the entire naval force.

By a MEMBER OF THE COURT:

Question. Were any torpedoes placed in any of the passes leading into the Mississippi, and could they have been there used to advantage?

Answer. I do not know of any being used there; if they could have been used to advantage anywhere they might have been there.

The court adjourned to meet at 10 a. m. to-morrow.

CHARLESTON, S. C., *May* 20, 1863—10 a. m.

The court met pursuant to adjournment.

Present, all the members of the court, the judge-advocate, and Maj. Gen. Mansfield Lovell.

The proceedings of yesterday were read over.

Lieut. C. B. POINDEXTER, C. S. Navy, was then sworn and examined as a witness.

By Maj. Gen. M. LOVELL:

Question. State your rank and position at and before the evacuation of New Orleans, in April, 1862.

Answer. I was a lieutenant in the C. S. Navy, and in command of Confederate States gunboat Bienville, on Lake Pontchartrain, at that time.

Question. What assistance, if any, was furnished by General Lovell in arming and fitting the Bienville for service?

Answer. General Lovell furnished five of the six guns that she carried and the powder, and was always willing and anxious to assist me in every way.

Question. At the time of the evacuation of the city what services were you requested to render in assisting General Lovell?

Answer. When I came up to the city from Fort Pike I found the naval commandant of the station had left, when I in company with Lieutenant Gwathmey, of the Carondelet, tendered my services to General Lovell, who requested me to detain the gunboats at the lake end of the Pontchartrain Railroad, and to seize all the private steamers I could find in the neighborhood, and there to await further directions from him. That took place on the night of April 24.

Question. From whom did you receive the order or request which induced you to go to Forts Pike and Macomb and bring away the troops, and were you ever requested by General Lovell to do more than hold yourself in readiness for that duty?

Answer. From Colonel Fuller. I received no order from General Lovell to remove the troops until after they had been withdrawn.

Question. Did you observe any indecision, confusion, or want of coolness and energy on the part of General Lovell in your interviews with him during the evacuation of the city?

Answer. I did not. He was so cool and collected that I congratulated him.

Question. Were you ever requested by General Lovell to re-enter the lake in connection with a proposed reöccupation of the forts by our troops?

Answer. I was, on April 27 or 28.

Question. What disposition, if any, of the vessels under your command was suggested by General Lovell after the evacuation of the city?

Answer. General Lovell advised me by letter to go to Mobile, if I deemed it practicable.

Question. What disposition did General Lovell request you to make of the guns and ammunition of the gunboat Bienville, and when were they destroyed, and what was done with them?

Answer. On my arrival at Camp Moore, when I reported to General Lovell, I had the guns (eleven in number), ammunition, and projectiles saved from the gunboats. He asked me to take them immediately to Vicksburg, which I did, and assisted in putting them in position.

By the COURT:

Question. Did you command the Confederate naval forces on Lake Pontchartrain?

Answer. I did not; I commanded the Bienville.

Question. How many steamers were you able to collect at the Pontchartrain end of the railroad, and what services did you render in compliance with General Lovell's request?

Answer. I collected three or four steamers, which were used in withdrawing the troops from the forts, but under the immediate orders of Colonel Fuller. I also carried over two batteries of artillery and 1,500 or 2,000 troops from the city to Covington.

Question. Why did you not carry out the instructions of General Lovell to re-enter the lake?

Answer. The withdrawal of the troops, the dismantling of the forts, the burning of the gun-carriages, &c., rendered it unnecessary; besides, I believed at the time that entrance was completely obstructed by the sinking of the Oregon.

SAMUEL WOLFE was then sworn and examined as a witness.

By Maj. Gen. M. LOVELL:

Question. What business were you engaged in at New Orleans for some months prior to its evacuation, in April, 1862?

Answer. I was first a merchant and then engaged in the foundery business.

Question. State what suggestions and aid you received from General Lovell in your operations, and what results, if any, were achieved.

Answer. General Lovell suggested that the necessities of the Government were such as to require the full use of the foundery. We set a number of men at work to make the patterns for field pieces and 10-inch mortars, and at last patterns for 10-inch columbiads; also the requisite shot and shell for those guns. The patterns of the 10-inch mortars and field pieces were begun in November, 1861. The patterns for the columbiads were completed about the time the city fell. We cast quite a number of field pieces (probably six were finished) and several 10-inch mortars, one of which was completed. We had employed over 100 men. I was not acquainted with the business myself, but my employés were. Among them was an artillery officer, who was skilled in the fabrication of arms, &c. General Lovell called very frequently at the foundery and urged forward the completion of the guns ordered by him and the ordnance officer. Our supply of iron best suited for guns was quite limited, and General Lovell gave us an order for 100 very large water-pipes, a portion of which we used. General Lovell also found that we needed a very large lathe for the working of heavy guns, and provided us with one from the other side of the river, by permission of the Government. General Lovell, early in March, issued an order to the effect that the foundery was in the hands of the Government and the employés in its service, for the purpose of protecting them from the militia officer and to secure the entire services of the foundery; but that was unnecessary, as it had been purchased for Government use alone. At the suggestion of General Lovell we were putting up reverberatory furnaces, which were nearly completed when the city fell. General Lovell frequently tendered me money, which I declined to take.

Question. Were any attempts made to remove the property at your works at the time of the evacuation? State what was removed and your reasons for not removing the whole.

Answer. We were ordered on April 24 or 25, 1862, to remove all work at our shop, finished or unfinished. There were, I think, about eight brass pieces (part finished and part unfinished) sent up the Jackson Railroad. The mortars that were unfinished were thrown into the basin of the new canal. Some of the mortar beds were buried in the ground at the foundery. The reasons for these acts were that we could not get men and vehicles to carry them to the railroad depot. Men were afraid to be seen working about such an establishment upon the arrival of the enemy.

The court adjourned to meet at 10 a. m. to-morrow.

CHARLESTON, S. C., *May* 21, 1863—11 a. m.

The court met pursuant to adjournment.

Present, all the members of the court, the judge-advocate, and Maj. Gen. M. Lovell.

The proceedings of yesterday were read over.

The judge-advocate then informed the court that certain witnesses whom he had summoned from Savannah, Ga., had left that city for Richmond before the arrival of the summons, and that there were no other witnesses to examine at Charleston.

The court was then adjourned to meet at Richmond, Va., June 1, 1863, or as soon thereafter as practicable.

RICHMOND, VA., *June* 2, 1863—10 a. m.

The court met pursuant to adjournment.

Present, Maj. Gen. T. C. Hindman, Brig. Gens. T. F. Drayton and W. M. Gardner, Maj. L. R. Page, judge-advocate, and Maj. Gen. Mansfield Lovell.

Lieut. W. H. WARD, C. S. Navy, was then sworn and examined as a witness.

By the JUDGE-ADVOCATE:

Question. State your profession and what duty you were on in April, 1862.

Answer. I was a lieutenant in the Navy, on duty at New Orleans; attached to the Confederate States steamer Louisiana at that time.

Question. Were you on duty aboard the Louisiana when the enemy's fleet passed Forts Jackson and Saint Philip? If yea, state what part she bore in resisting its passage and her location during the action.

Answer. She was fought to the best advantage under the circumstances; her guns were fired with her bow down-stream, the starboard battery bearing upon the channel. She had no effective motive power, and her location on the east side of the river was the best, in my judgment, that she could have taken.

Question. State all you know touching the request of Generals Lovell and Duncan to have the vessel placed in a particular position before the passage of the forts; and, if you know, why their suggestions were not heeded. State, also, when and why the Louisiana was destroyed by our forces.

Answer. I know nothing of my own knowledge as to such request being preferred by those gentlemen. On the morning of April 28, about 6 o'clock, Commander Mitchell sent for the commissioned officers of the vessel, and said to them, when they had assembled, that he had just received a communication from Fort Jackson, stating that General Duncan was about to surrender the forts to the enemy; that he had no previous information that such a course would be pursued; that a large Federal fleet had passed up the river; that if the forts surrendered we would be immediately under the fire of their guns; that we would be attacked from above and below by the enemy's vessels; that we had no motive power of our own, being dependent altogether upon two high-pressure river steamboats, which would have most likely been disabled or destroyed by the enemy's first fire, and could not, therefore, withdraw from the fire that would be opened upon us by the forts. He then asked the officers what was the best course to pursue. The unanimous opinion was that the vessel should be destroyed rather than that she should fall into the hands of the Federals. In pursuance of this conclusion, she was fired about 10 o'clock that morning and in a short time blown to pieces. The Louisiana was the only vessel of the defenses afloat that was left, except a tow-boat (the Defiance), which had been abandoned by her officers and crew.

Question. State the condition of the Louisiana with respect to her fighting capacity at the time she was destroyed; and state how long it would have required to have completed her for effective service.

Answer. When we left New Orleans, by some mistake or mismanagement some of the guns—about three or four—were mounted on carriages that did not belong to them, and could not be worked efficiently in the forts. All the time we had was devoted to the correction of the mistake. There was also one gun lying in the dock that was not mounted at all. In my division, owing to an improper mounting of an 8-inch shell gun, it was ineffectual. The facilities for mounting the guns were very indifferent; it had to be done by blocking them up. Her motive power was also incomplete. She had to depend on wooden tugs to give her motion. Her wheels, which were designed as her chief motive power, were wholly inadequate, and I think they could never have been made serviceable. Her propellers, which were merely auxiliary, it was said would have been done that day, but I do not think they would have moved her; their chief value would have been to assist in steering the vessel. I looked upon her as a total failure, except that she might have been used as a floating battery; but even then her accommodations were so inferior that it would have been difficult to have lived on her. It may be well to state that the crew of the Louisiana was not full, and of a mixed and indifferent character. A company of artillery from the Crescent Regiment constituted a larger part of the crew, and were not skilled in the use of heavy guns.

Cross-examination by Major-General LOVELL:

Question. In your opinion was the Louisiana, or could she have been made within a reasonable time, an efficient war vessel for service in the Mississippi River?

Answer. I do not think she could have been made efficient for such purposes within a reasonable time. I regarded her an entire failure.

Commander ARTHUR SINCLAIR, C. S. Navy, was next sworn and examined as a witness.

By the JUDGE-ADVOCATE:

Question. State your rank in the C. S. Navy; your length of service as a naval officer, and the duty you were on in April, 1862.

Answer. I am a commander in the C. S. Navy, and held the same rank when I resigned from the Federal service. I have been forty years in the Navy, twenty of which I spent at sea. In the early part of April, 1862, I was ordered by the Secretary of the Navy to New Orleans, to superintend the fitting out of the Confederate States steamer Mississippi, then on the ways, and when finished I was to take command of her.

Question. State generally the condition of the Mississippi upon your arrival at New Orleans, your means of knowing such condition, and the length of time you deemed requisite to complete her for service.

Answer. She was on the ways at that time, and was not launched until about April 20; she was not near complete then nor at the time of her destruction. She had been ironed as high as her knuckle, but had no iron upon her flush deck, either forward or aft, at the time she was destroyed. I was daily aboard superintending her construction—often three or four times a day. A small part of the iron for her roof or shield had been laid down, but not bolted; one of three propellers was in position, the others lying upon the wharf; her rudder was just commenced; a box had been just begun to fit around the vessel (a sort of dry-dock and a very tedious and heavy piece of work), which had to be constructed to enable the remaining propellers to be shipped. A portion of her machinery was on board; her armament had not arrived; shot and shell were in process of manufacture, but only a small quantity cast; not a grain of powder was on board; her port frames had not arrived, which had to be put in before the plating was bolted down. The day the vessel was launched I borrowed from Commander Whittle, commanding the station, four old-fashioned smooth-bore 32-pounders and mounted them, and from General Lovell I borrowed 1,000 pounds of powder, and endeavored to get them ready, so that if the enemy came up I might, if possible, make some resistance with the workmen aboard, she having no crew, not a man having been shipped for her, no complement of men had been assigned; but I thought 500 men requisite for her crew. In attempting to mount these guns I found there was not a ring-bolt, or eye-bolt, nor any iron work on the ship by which a gun could have been secured. To be within bounds I have said that six or seven weeks were required to finish the vessel, but I believe it would have taken three months. In support of this opinion I may mention that I left a ship at Savannah recently which I had observed for three months; when I was ordered there the work upon her was much more advanced than that of the Mississippi, and, although she is scarcely one-fourth the size of the Mississippi, she is not yet done, though the work upon her has been prosecuted with energy.

Question. Was the work upon the Mississippi prosecuted with diligence and effect by those charged with her construction during the time that you superintended her?

Answer. The work during that time was pushed forward with great zeal, energy, and skill; all was done that could be done to finish her.

Question. As the officer supervising her construction and to command her when completed, what, if any, authority or control had you over the constructors and builders of the Mississippi?

Answer. I had no authority over them, but could and did make suggestions, which were followed. I could also have reported them to the commander of the station or the Navy Department for any dereliction of duty.

Question. Did General Lovell ever say to you that there was a probability of the enemy's fleet passing the forts, and did he ever recommend to you precautionary measures for the removal of the Mississippi in such event?

Answer. He never did, that I remember.

The court adjourned to meet at 10 a. m. to-morrow.

RICHMOND, VA., *June* 3, 1863—10 a. m.

The court met pursuant to adjournment.

Present, all the members of the court, the judge-advocate, and Maj. Gen. M. Lovell.

The proceedings of yesterday were read over.

Examination of Commander ARTHUR SINCLAIR continued.

By the JUDGE-ADVOCATE:

Question. State what measures were taken to remove the Mississippi, and whether or not she could have been saved.

Answer. The Mississippi might doubtless have been launched and towed up the river many days previous to the enemy's passing the forts, and there finally completed, but her completion would have been greatly retarded, as all the workshops, material, workmen, in fact the whole naval establishment, would have had to be transferred from New Orleans to the place of transfer, and there was no place of safety above, that I know of, short of Fort Pillow, and all above on the river was then menaced by the enemy. Her completion was a momentous affair, and therefore the work was prosecuted up to the last moment with all the energy within our power. I received no orders from the commander of the station, Commander Whittle, under whose orders I was, or from the Navy Department, to remove her until the morning of April 24, the day upon which the enemy passed the forts. On that day Commander Whittle sent for and informed me that the enemy had passed the batteries and were coming up, at the same time directing me to take the ship up the river, if possible, to some place of safety, but not to let her fall into the hands of the enemy. I immediately sent orders to the steamers engaged by the Messrs. Tift to proceed at once up to the ship-yard for the purpose of taking the ship in tow. The officers sent by me upon this duty returned and informed me that the steamers referred to had been detained by order of General Lovell. I called myself upon Colonel Lovell, the general being out of his office upon business, and obtained from him the release of two of the three, which were engaged for this purpose, the Peytona and the St. Charles. Although directed to proceed at once, they did not reach the ship-yard until late in the evening. The captains of these boats showed every disposition, in fact, determination, to thwart me in my wishes, and to accomplish my ends I had, with my own officers, to lash and secure them alongside, and furnished one of them, the steamer St. Charles, with an engineer, as the captain said he had only one. I finally succeeded in getting off, but found, after many hours of hard tugging against a powerful current, that I could not succeed. Assistance was promised me by Colonel Baggs (or Biggs) of the Safety Committee, but none was received. Still unwilling to give up the ship, I went myself back to the city in the Peytona, and urged the aid of the steamers, but in vain. Every variety of excuse was offered by their captains, and no disposition manifested to help me; in fact, a fixed determination not to move in the matter. While thus negotiating the enemy hove in sight, and I at once started back for the ship, 4 miles above, intending to fire her, but the officer in charge, Lieutenant Waddell, anticipated me and applied the torch. After remaining in the stream until the ship was nearly consumed I held a council of war with my officers, and it was determined to return to the city and offer our services to General Lovell. I was on my way back when I met Lieutenant McCorkle, of the Navy, who informed me that the enemy were off Canal street, and that General Lovell had marched his troops out. I then proceeded up the river with my officers to Vicksburg. I will also state that the assistance of several steamers, which passed up the river, while engaged in towing the Mississippi, was asked and refused. I also engaged the services of Navy workmen to accompany me up in the ship to try and finish her, and put on board, while awaiting the arrival of the steamers, much of the material for her completion. Some was afterwards put aboard the steamer St. Charles, before firing the ship, and taken up to Vicksburg and saved.

The Mississippi was launched on Saturday, April 19, and burned the Friday following. In this connection I would state that on my arrival at New Orleans there was a great desire upon the part of many persons expressed that the ship should be launched. The Tifts objected, and I agreed with them that to launch her in her then condition would cause much delay in shipping her propellers and involve the expense of building the box or dry-dock for that purpose of which I have already spoken; but finding the attack about to be commenced I recommended her being launched to her builders, the Tifts, in which Commander Mitchell joined me; the suggestion was heeded, but not until many days after, for reasons which they assigned.

Question. If the Mississippi had been completed, and with her armament and men on board, could she alone have held the river against the entire Federal fleet coming up from below?

Answer. I think she could. She would have been the most formidable ship that I ever knew or heard of—very creditable to her projectors, builders, and country.

Cross-examination by Maj. Gen. MANSFIELD LOVELL:

Question. You have been asked whether General Lovell recommended to you precautionary measures for the removal of the Mississippi. Did you consider that he was the proper person to give you advice or instructions as to your official acts and duties and did you look to him for such?

Answer. I did not. Although I would have respected very highly his suggestions, I should have felt it my duty to lay them before Commander Whittle, my immediate commander, before acting upon them. My orders were to report to Commander Whittle for the command of the ship.

Capt. GEORGE N. HOLLINS was next sworn and examined as a witness.

By Maj. Gen. MANSFIELD LOVELL:

Question. What position did you hold at New Orleans and in the West in the latter part of 1861 and the first part of 1862?

Answer. At New Orleans I commanded all the vessels afloat and the naval station. In the West, near New Madrid and Island No. 10, I only commanded the vessels afloat. I left New Orleans in January or February, 1862, Commander Whittle then assuming command of the station, but not the vessels afloat.

Question. State the force you took with you from New Orleans above and what force you left there.

Answer. I took with me from New Orleans eight vessels, averaging six guns each, except the Manassas; that had but one gun. I left no naval force at New Orleans. General Lovell urged me to leave some of the vessels there, but this I could not do, as my orders from the Navy Department were to take them all above.

Question. What conversation, if any, passed between General Lovell and yourself shortly before the fall of New Orleans relative to a proposed co operation of your fleet with his forces for the purpose of driving the enemy from the Lower Mississippi River?

Answer. General Lovell, Commander Whittle, and myself had a conversation at that time, in which we agreed that such an expedition should be made. I had often passed the Yankee batteries and knew that they could pass ours, and I was anxious that my squadron, which was up the river, should be ordered down to resist Farragut, feeling satisfied that I could have cut him up. I should have fought him to the greatest advantage. Farragut's ships would have been exposed bow foremost to my broadsides and the sides of his vessels to the fire of the forts. Had he exposed the sterns of his vessels to the fire of the forts they would have been sunk in a short time. I had previously presented this plan to the Secretary of the Navy, but it was rejected, he replying that the main attack on New Orleans was to be from above and not below. The enemy had never passed our fortifications until they had been reduced, and I know there would have been time enough to have gone below and returned to assist the land forces at Fort Pillow.

Question. State, if you know, what steps were taken by General Lovell, in connection with Commander Whittle, to have your fleet ordered below for such purpose.

Answer. Being detached from the command of the squadron, General Lovell and Commander Whittle prevailed upon me to remain a day longer in New Orleans while they could communicate with the Secretary of the Navy and urge his consent to such an expedition. I did remain twenty-four hours, but no reply was received.

Cross-examined by the JUDGE-ADVOCATE:

Question. While you were in command of the naval station at New Orleans had you opportunity of observing General Lovell's official conduct? If so, state his habits as an officer in command.

Answer. I had good opportunities of observing him, living in the same house with him and seeing him day and night. I thought him active, zealous, and most attentive to his duties.

Question. While in command of the defenses afloat at New Orleans were your requisitions promptly filled, and were zeal and energy manifested by the Navy Department in perfecting the naval defenses at that point?

Answer. All the powder I used was obtained from General Lovell. I could scarcely ever get money. I borrowed from the merchants of the city $45,000 in bankable funds, which the Departments, after a delay of four months, wanted to refund in Confederate bonds, which were then at a heavy discount, and I believe the debt was so settled. I was all the time cramped to pay even the smallest debts due to the wives of soldiers who were making cartridge-bags. I had no control whatever of the Louisiana or Mississippi. The work generally seemed to progress well, although I think at one time it was delayed for want of iron. There was but little energy or promptitude displayed by the Navy Department in the conduct of naval affairs at that station. My ordnance officer (Lieut. Beverly Kennon) made contracts for naval supplies of all sorts at low rates, but many of these contracts were annulled by the Secretary of the Navy. Such articles would now bring seven or eight times the price that they were contracted for then. I rather avoided any close inspection of the working upon the Louisiana and Mississippi; special agents, not naval officers, were assigned to that duty. The general custom is that bills for construction of ships are always to be approved by the officer commanding the station, who has a general supervision of ships building within the limits of his command; but such was not the case with regard to these steamers.

Question. From what failure, if any, to take necessary and possible measures of defense did the capture of New Orleans result?

Answer. Had my squadron been at the mouth of the river I could have kept the enemy from crossing the bar; their heavier ships had to be lightened very greatly; their armament, &c., taken out before they could have been put over; I could then have whipped their smaller craft with my squadron, and have prevented their larger vessels from getting over if it had not been in my power to have destroyed them. Subsequently, when the enemy's fleet was in the river, if I had been permitted, I could have taken my squadron and have driven him back at the time he passed the forts. The refusal of the Secretary of the Navy to allow these measures to be carried out is the cause, in my judgment, of the fall of New Orleans.

Commander J. K. MITCHELL was then duly sworn and examined as a witness.

By the JUDGE-ADVOCATE:

Question. State when and by whose order you were assigned to the command of the defenses afloat at or near Forts Saint Philip and Jackson.

Answer. On April 10 I received my orders from Commander Whittle.

Question. State the number of vessels, their armament, condition, &c., constituting your command.

Answer. The principal vessel of my command was the steamer Louisiana, iron clad, mounting sixteen guns; was without sufficient motive power even to stem the current of the Mississippi without the aid of her two tenders, the Landis and W. Burton. Her two propellers were not ready for use, and were designed more to assist in steering than in the expectation of adding to her speed, and her rudders had little, if any, power to control her movements. Most of her guns had to be dismantled after arriving at Fort Saint Philip and shifted to points where they could be worked, and one of them was not in position in the action of April 24, being dismounted. The crew of the Louisiana, aided by men from the McRae, was employed constantly, night and day, in arranging the battery for action. The decks were thus, from this cause and the presence of numerous mechanics employed in completing machinery for the propellers, the ironing of the decks, and calking wheel-houses, much incumbered, and being very cramped at best for room, prevented the proper exercise of the men at their guns. This condition of her motive power and battery rendered her not only unfit for offensive operations against the enemy, but also for defense, as, being immovable, her guns all around could only command about 40 degrees of the horizon, leaving 320 degrees of a circle on which she could have been approached by an enemy without being able to bring a gun to bear upon him. Her guns, from the small size of her ports, could not be elevated more than 4 to 5 degrees, which with our best guns would not have given a range probably of more than 2,000 yards. The means for purchasing her anchors were inadequate, and it was utterly impossible to weigh them, when once they were let go, either from the bow or stern, and, indeed, her steering apparatus prevented her being anchored by the stern in the middle of the river, a position, under all the circumstances, I should have preferred to being tied to the river bank, by which more guns might have been used against the enemy, and the vessel might have been warped or sprung, so as to bring some of her guns to bear upon any given point. The quarters for the crew of the Louisiana were wholly insufficient, and for her officers there were none at all, except on the shield deck or roof, under a tented awning. Most of the officers and crew had to live on board two tenders, which were also required as tugs, without which the vessel could not be moved at all. The shield of the Louisiana was effective, for none of the enemy's projectiles passed through it; but as it only extended to the water line, a shot between wind and water must have penetrated the perpendicular pine sides. In addition to the Louisiana, the following vessels of the C. S. Navy were under my command at the forts, viz: The steamer McRae, Lieut. Commanding Thomas B. Huger, with six light 32-pounder smooth-bore broadside guns, and one 9-inch shell gun pivoted amidships—total, seven; the steamer Jackson, Lieut. Commanding F. B. Renshaw, two pivoted smooth-bore 32-pounders, one forward and one aft; the iron-plated ram Manassas, Lieut.-Commanding A. F. Warley, one 32-pounder in bow; launch No. 3, Acting Master Telford, and one howitzer, 20 men; launch No. 6, Acting Master Fairbanks, one howitzer, and 20 men. Also the following converted sea steamers into Louisiana State gunboats, with pine and cotton barricades to protect the machinery and boilers, viz: The Governor Moore, Commander Beverly Kennon, two 32-pounder rifled guns; the General Quitman, Captain Grant, two 32-pounder guns. All the above steamers, being converted vessels, were too slightly built for war purposes. The following unarmed steamers belonged to my command, viz: The Phœnix, Captain ———, tender to the Manassas; the W. Burton, Captain Hammond, tender to the Louisiana, and the Landis, Captain Davis, tender to the Louisiana. The following-named steamers, chartered by the Army, were placed under my orders, viz: The Mosher, Captain Sherman, a very small tug; the Belle Algerine, Captain ———, a small tug; the Star, Captain La Place, used as telegraph station, and the Music, Captain McClellan, tender to the forts. The two former were in bad condition, and were undergoing such repairs as could be made below previous to the 24th. On arriving below I delivered to Captain Stephenson written orders from Maj. Gen. M. Lovell, requiring him to place all the river-defense gunboats under my orders, which consisted of the following converted tow-boats, viz: 1st, the Warrior, under the immediate command of Captain Stephenson; 2d, the Stonewall Jackson, Captain Philips; 3d, the Resolute, Captain Hooper; 4th, the Defiance, Captain McCoy; and, 5th, the General Lovell, ——— ———. The R. J. Breckinridge, ——— ———, joined the evening before the action. All of the above vessels mounted from one to two pivot 32-pounders each, some of them rifled. Their boilers and machinery were all more or less protected by thick double pine barricades, filled in with compressed cotton, which, though not regarded as proof against heavy solid shot, shell, and incendiary projectiles, would have been a protection against grape and canister, and ought to have inspired those on board with sufficient confidence to use their boats boldly as rams, for which they were in a good measure prepared with flat bar-iron casing around their bows. In thus using them their own safety would be best consulted, as well as the best way of damaging the vessels of the enemy.

Question. Did you have any control or authority over the Montgomery or river-defense fleet?

Answer. None. Captain Stephenson, who commanded them, on receiving General Lovell's orders, addressed me a communication to the effect that all the officers and crews of the vessels under his command had entered the service with the distinct understanding or condition that they were not to be placed under the orders of naval officers; and, therefore, while willing to co-operate with my forces, he could receive no orders from me himself, nor allow any vessel of his command to do so; that he reserved to himself the right of obeying or not any orders I might issue. His attitude with respect to my authority was one of absolute independence of action and command, and very embarrassing in the face of the enemy. A copy of his communication was sent by me to General Duncan, and one, through Commander W. C. Whittle, to General Lovell, informing them at the same time that the position assumed by Captain Stephenson relieved me from all responsibility for the conduct of the vessels under his command. Not knowing what moment an attack might be made by the enemy, I endeavored to agree upon a plan of co-operation with his forces by the arrangement of signals and concert of action, and the particular service to be performed by him—an endeavor which he himself seemed disposed zealously to second in many respects.

Question. If the fire rafts and guard-boats were under your command, state why they were not used to watch the enemy's movements the morning the enemy's fleet passed the forts.

Answer. The fire boats were under my control, and Captain Stephenson reported to me the evening of the 23d that each one of his vessels and the two tugs had a fire boat secured to her, ready for firing, and to be towed against the enemy's vessels in the event of an attack. I was getting, however, most of the fire boats into position to be chained or strung together, and so made to form a cordon, if possible, entirely across the river on the enemy's attempting to pass the forts, for which purpose they had been specially prepared, chiefly under my direction, and with some aid from General Smith, before they were sent down from New Orleans, the chains for which had, however, been scattered about so that the fire boats could not be made ready in this manner before the attack of the enemy. The little unarmed tug Mosher, it is thought, was the only one that succeeded in towing one of the fire boats against a vessel of the enemy by which she was set on fire, but it was soon extinguished, and the Mosher sunk by the enemy's shot. I am not aware of more than one or two of the fire boats having been fired during the passage of the enemy. The night of April 20, on my way down in the Louisiana, the enemy's boats are said to have visited the raft obstructions and cut the chain. To prevent further injury to it, and to break up the night reconnaissances of the enemy, and to watch and report all his movements, I was unsuccessful in my efforts to get Captain Stephenson to employ one or two of his gunboats below the obstructions at night. Although favoring the idea, he seemed to have no confidence in the fitness of his commanders for the service, and I could not induce him to give the necessary orders to them. I had no suitable vessels for this duty under my command—the only one that would have answered (the Jackson) having been sent with launch No. 3 5 miles above to the quarantine station, at the request of General Duncan, to watch the enemy in that neighborhood and prevent his approach through any of the adjacent bayous and canals. The vessels under Captain Stephenson having guns aft, and being converted tow-boats, were well calculated for the duty of making reconnaissances or keeping guard below from their light draught, easy management in the river, and being comparatively low in the water. The McRae, Manassas, Governor Moore, and the General Quitman were all converted sea steamers of a deep draught, great length, high out of the water, except the Manassas, and very difficult to handle, and none of them, I think, had after guns. One of the two launches (No. 6) was kept near me, for the special purpose of acting as a guard boat for the two nights preceding the action, and was well provided with the means for signaling the approach of any unusual movement of the enemy by firing its howitzer and setting off rockets. She was stationed below Saint Philip, but on the appearance of the enemy, or sooner, her commander deserted his station, returned clandestinely to the Louisiana, made no report of it, and, consequently, no alarm was given, at least by him.

Question. Was the river-defense fleet of any service in resisting the enemy's fleet in passing the forts?

Answer. I am not aware that the river-defense fleet did any service in resisting the enemy; if they did, it did not come under my observation, nor has it in any way been brought to my notice. I understand that four were destroyed by the enemy or set on fire and abandoned by their own crew; also the Louisiana State gunboat General Quitman. The Resolute was run ashore and abandoned, and finally burned by my order, to prevent her falling into the enemy's hands, as it was impossible to float her off, on account of shot-holes through her bows. The Defiance was discovered in our immediate vicinity after the action, having escaped without any material damage.

Question. State why you did not comply with the request of Generals Lovell and Duncan to place the Louisiana in the position they desired her to take prior to the passage of the forts.

Answer. The chief reasons for not placing the Louisiana in the position desired by Generals Lovell and Duncan below Fort Saint Philip were that she would at once be under the fire of the enemy's mortar fleet, the position proposed being about the same distance from his fleet as Fort Jackson, and he would only have to change slightly the direction of his fire to throw his shells with speedy and fatal effect on the deck of the vessel, while her guns, as stated in my answer to the first question, would not have a range probably greater than 2,000 yards, which was of course too short to reach his mortar fleet; for the 7-inch navy rifle in Fort Jackson, mounted on high parapets, and with an elevation of about 13 degrees, could not reach them, as I was credibly informed. For these reasons alone the position proposed would have been an improper one for the Louisiana; but her battery was not ready for use, and parties of mechanics were busy day and night preparing the propellers for service, and, besides, the strong current, deep water, and coming immediately under fire of the enemy, she could not have been secured properly. I made a reconnaissance the afternoon of the 23d, and determined that the proper position for the ship was below Fort Jackson, where the current and anchorage would admit of her being secured before the enemy could open his fire with effect, and from whence he could be in effective enfilading range of the Louisiana's guns. This position I purposed taking with the Louisiana as soon as she was in condition to be placed under fire of the enemy, which I hoped would have been the next day.

Question. Who was in immediate command of the Louisiana in the conflict with the enemy's fleet, and was the ship, in your opinion, fought to advantage?

Answer. Commander Charles F. McIntosh was in immediate command of the Louisiana, and the ship, in my opinion, was fought to the best advantage, under the very disadvantageous circumstances which have been detailed in my previous answers.

Question. Why was the Louisiana destroyed? Could she not have been saved?

Answer. The Louisiana was destroyed by my order on the unanimous advice of all the commissioned sea officers within my reach, because the forts were about being surrendered to the enemy, under the close fire of which she lay, with a heavy naval force both above and below her, from which it would have been impossible to escape or to attack, for want of motive power, and, if not destroyed, she must inevitably have fallen into his hands, as she could have been approached from many points by his vessels without being able to return his fire with effect from a single gun.

The court adjourned to meet at 11 a. m. to-morrow.

RICHMOND, VA., *June* 4, 1863—11 a. m.

The court met pursuant to adjournment.

Present, all the members of the court, the judge-advocate, and Maj. Gen. Mansfield Lovell.

The proceedings of yesterday were read over.

Examination of Commander J. K. MITCHELL continued.

Cross-examination by the JUDGE-ADVOCATE:

Question. While you were in charge of the naval station in New Orleans was not there a cordial co-operation between the military commanders and the naval officers at that point so far as was practicable?

Answer. There was, so far as I know. Applications were often made for powder, which were not always promptly satisfied, I suppose, for good reasons on the part of General Lovell. At all events the delays occasioned no unpleasant feeling. Nearly all the powder received came from the Army; all that was used on the Louisiana was supplied by General Lovell.

Question. In your judgment were the Confederate States naval forces, placed at your disposal for co-operation with Forts Jackson and Saint Philip, at all adequate to the requirements of the occasion?

Answer. Not at all adequate. The enemy had five first-class sloops of war, independent of seven or eight gunboats; every one of which sloops was a match for my entire force in the condition of the Louisiana at that time.

Question. Were you acquainted with the vessels of Commodore Hollins' squadron? In your opinion could these vessels, together with such others as could have been added, have prevented the enemy's passage over the bars at the mouths of the Mississippi, or could these vessels at any time afterward have driven the enemy's fleet out of the river?

Answer. I was acquainted with the squadron. I do not think it, with other vessels that might have been added, could have prevented the crossing of the bar, nor afterwards have driven the enemy's fleet out of the river.

Question. In the defense of New Orleans was anything omitted to be done by which the city might have been saved?

(This question was objected to by Major-General Lovell, because the witness is an officer of the Navy, and cannot be considered an expert as to army affairs, there being no proof to show him possessed of skill in military affairs, which alone would authorize an answer to the question. The court was then cleared for deliberation, and, when reopened, it was announced that the court overruled the objection.)

Answer. On the part of the Navy there was nothing omitted by which the city might have been saved; on the part of the Army I am unable to say that any step was omitted that should have been taken for its defense.

Lieut. W. GWATHMEY, C. S. Navy, was next sworn and examined as a witness.

By Maj. Gen. MANSFIELD LOVELL:

Question. Where and on what duty were you immediately before the fall of New Orleans?

Answer. I was the lieutenant commanding the C. S. gunboat Carondelet, in Lake Pontchartrain, at that time.

Question. What, if any, assistance did you receive from General Lovell in fitting out the Carondelet for service?

Answer. Her armament was furnished chiefly by the Army; five out of seven guns came from that source; also 30 men, as a part of her crew, were supplied from Fort Pike.

Cross-examination by the JUDGE-ADVOCATE:

Question. Did you see General Lovell after the passage of the forts and during the evacuation of New Orleans; if so, did he seem cool and collected, and competent for the duties devolved upon him by the disaster to the city?

Answer. I saw him in the evening after the enemy's fleet had passed the forts; he seemed to me very cool and collected, decidedly competent for the work on hand.

Maj. C. S. VENABLE, C. S. Army, was next sworn and examined as a witness.

By Maj. Gen. MANSFIELD LOVELL:

Question. What duty were you on at the time of the evacuation of New Orleans, in April, 1862? State what was done by you, under orders of General Lovell, in the removal of public property, army stores, &c.

Answer. On engineer duty. On Sunday morning, April —, after the evacuation, I was sent back, by order of Major-General Lovell, to act in conjunction with Major James and others in the removal of public property. After reaching the city I considered myself as acting under Major James, by General Lovell's orders. These orders were, as I understood, to remove all public property belonging to the Confederate States or State of Louisiana, which could be transported and be of any use to the Army; also the guns on the fortifications in the rear of the city, for use on works to be re-erected at Vicksburg; papers and other property of the engineer's department, &c. We arrived in New Orleans on Sunday afternoon in the train from Camp Moore. Arrangements were made that night by Major James and agents set to work. On Monday I took charge of the shipment of stores, hire of laborers, drays, &c. A large amount of public stores were shipped—light artillery, shot and shell from the arsenal; a great quantity of clothing, shoes, and blankets belonging to the State of Louisiana; medical stores, commissary stores, some machinery; leather and harness belonging to a Government contract; many new wagons and other articles of camp equipage; in fact, everything that could be found by the indefatigable search of Major James, who seemed to be well acquainted with the city and citizens. Lieutenant McDonald, of the Engineers, whom we found in the city, was engaged on the same duty. I sent drays down to Chalmette to bring away camp equipage, said to be left there by the troops, but found none. I made efforts to have the ammunition removed from Proctorsville, but failed, on account of the short time and some misunderstanding of orders by the sergeant in charge. We met with much difficulty in procuring labor, on account of the confusion and excitement of the people. This will account for the want of success in the removal of the guns on the fortifications (as this required a peculiar kind of transportation) and guns for shipping. Several guns and two mortars were carried to the depot, but I do not think they were shipped.

On Wednesday, the 30th instant, General Lovell, who was in the city at the time, ordered Lieutenant McDonald and myself to remain still longer, and urged especially the removal of the guns. We found it impossible to procure the necessary transportation and labor for this purpose, but found other stores of the Commissary Department, which had been overlooked, and succeeded in shipping some by the railroad and the rest by a schooner to Manchac. Many citizens aided us in our efforts, among them Mr. Bell, civil engineer, especially in bringing guns to the depot.

On Thursday or Friday I returned to Camp Moore, the transports of the enemy having reached the city. The confusion was great and there was an increasing timidity on the part of the citizens to act with us. I signed many receipts for goods delivered at the depot, made contracts, and offered rewards for the delivery of guns at Manchac, by order of Major-General Lovell, as the necessity of the occasion demanded. The stores saved were large in amount and value, and, so far as my information went, constituted by far the greater proportion of those which were in the city.

By the JUDGE-ADVOCATE:

Question. What was General Lovell's demeanor during the evacuation when you were with him? Did he seem confused and overwhelmed with the work before him or was he cool and collected?

Answer. I saw him with his staff riding to and fro in the streets at that time giving orders; he seemed on the occasions that I met him cool and collected. He gave me orders upon my application, and they were given in a clear and satisfactory manner.

(The judge-advocate here stated to the court that he had been summoned to appear to-day as a witness before a court martial, and that the only witnesses, as far as was then advised, remaining to be examined were not likely to arrive in the city for several days; thereupon the court adjourned to meet at 11 a. m. the 8th instant.)

RICHMOND, VA., *June* 8, 1863—11 a. m.

The court met pursuant to adjournment.

Present, all the members of the court, the judge-advocate, and Maj. Gen. Mansfield Lovell.

The proceedings of the 4th instant were read over.

PETER W. WOODLIEF, a citizen, was next sworn and examined as a witness.

By Maj. Gen. MANSFIELD LOVELL:

Question. What business were you engaged in prior to and at the time of the evacuation of New Orleans, in April, 1862?

Answer. I was a contractor with the Government for the furnishing of all sorts of military supplies.

Question. What amount of the property in your possession, available for military purposes, was brought out of the city and turned over to the Government agents?

Answer. I delivered to the Government agents for removal and removed myself from New Orleans at that time about $100,000 worth of such property, consisting of harness, saddles, valises, saddle-bags, horseshoes, clothing, blankets, &c. These steps were taken of my own motion, and not by order of General Lovell, though he knew I was engaged in the removal.

Commander WILLIAM C. WHITTLE, C. S. Navy, was next sworn and examined as a witness.

By the JUDGE-ADVOCATE:

Question. When and by whose order did you assume command of the naval station at New Orleans?

Answer. About March 28, by order of the Secretary of the Navy.

Question. Did you approve of the conduct of Commander Mitchell with reference to the disposition of the Louisiana during the fights at Forts Jackson and Saint Philip, in April, 1862?

Answer. I neither approved nor disapproved his conduct touching the management of the Louisiana at that time, not knowing the circumstances which surrounded his command.

Question. If you know, state whether the work upon the steamers Louisiana and Mississippi was pressed forward with energy and skill by the builders while you were in command of the naval station at New Orleans.

Answer. I cannot say that I had any personal knowledge as to the work upon those vessels; but from all I could learn from the builders and officers connected with the Mississippi the work must have progressed well. If I had not thought the work was getting on well I should have reported the fact to the Department, notwithstanding I had no authority over the builders of the Mississippi.

Question. If you had opportunities of observing, be pleased to state the demeanor of General Lovell during the evacuation of New Orleans.

Answer. We sat together at breakfast the morning after the enemy passed up. I saw nothing in his demeanor derogatory to him as an officer.

Cross-examination by Maj. Gen. MANSFIELD LOVELL:

Question. Was there cordial co-operation between yourself and General Lovell as far as the circumstances of the respective arms of service would allow and always good feeling between you?

Answer. There was. I believe the very best feeling existed between us.

Question. Were the naval means at your disposal for co-operation in the defense of the Mississippi River at all adequate for that purpose?

Answer. They were not, in my judgment. I only had command of the station on land. Commander Mitchell was placed by me temporarily in command of such defenses as we could muster for the fight at the forts.

Question. What steps were taken by you to have Commodore Hollins assist in the defense of the lower river?

Answer. I telegraphed Commodore Hollins that his presence with his fleet might be important at New Orleans if he could be spared for a few days from above. After Commodore Hollins had received a dispatch withdrawing him from the command afloat at New Orleans, General Lovell and myself had a conversation on the subject of his removal, and General Lovell was authorized by me to use my name in connection with his own in a communication to the Government requesting that Commodore Hollins might be permitted to remain there longer. There was time enough, in my opinion, for the fleet to have come down.

By the COURT:

Question. Did you make or cause to be made any inspection of the Louisiana? If so, when and what defects, if any, presented themselves? What steps were taken to remedy those defects? Was there sufficient time to remedy them before the vessel was destroyed?

Answer. I had daily reports of the condition of the Louisiana. She was deficient in motive power. All the workmen considered necessary and all requisites were placed upon her and used before she left New Orleans. There was not time enough to remedy this defect in view of the circumstances.

Question. What length of time would reasonably be required, under the circumstances existing since secession, to build and equip for service such a vessel as the Louisiana? Answer same question as to the Mississippi.

Answer. I have no idea of the time to build such vessels, not being acquainted with the building of such vessels, they being entirely new, and not being a naval constructor.

Question. Could Commodore Hollins' squadron, with such other vessels as might have been added, have prevented the enemy's vessels from crossing the bar at the mouths of the river, or when in the river have prevented the passage of the forts?

Answer. My impression is that if Commodore Hollins had been present with his fleet near Fort Jackson when they attempted to pass there, that, in connection with the naval force already there and the co-operation of the forts, they would have greatly embarrassed, if they had not succeeded in stopping, the passage of the enemy's fleet.

Question. In your opinion, was it practicable to save the Mississippi from the time the attack was commenced upon the forts and their passage with the means on hand?

Answer. I do not think she could have been saved.

The following communications were then read to the court by the judge-advocate:

RICHMOND, VA., *June* 4, 1863.

Maj. L. R. PAGE,
Judge-Advocate, &c.:

SIR: I respectfully request that the findings and opinion of the naval court of inquiry that has already examined into my conduct as a participant in the defense of New Orleans may be spread upon the record of the military court now investigating the same subject in this city. This request is made because I understand this latter tribunal is authorized to pronounce an opinion upon the conduct of naval officers on duty at New Orleans.

Very respectfully,

J. K. MITCHELL,
Commander, C. S. Navy.

RICHMOND, VA., *June* 8, 1863.

Maj. L. R. PAGE,
Judge-Advocate, Court of Inquiry, &c., Richmond, Va.:

SIR: I respectfully request that the findings and opinion of the naval court of inquiry in the case of the destruction by fire of the C. S. steamer Mississippi may be placed upon the record of the military court now in session in this city, as I learn that the conduct of naval officers is authorized to be pronounced upon by said tribunal.

Very respectfully, &c., your obedient servant,

A. SINCLAIR,
Commander, C. S. Navy.

It was thereupon ordered by the court that the foregoing communications be made a part of the record, and that the judge-advocate reply to Commanders Mitchell and Sinclair that this court will recommend that the same publicity be given to the findings and opinion of the naval court of inquiry referred to in their communications as to the findings and opinion of this court.

The court adjourned to meet at 11 a. m. to-morrow.

RICHMOND, VA., *June* 9, 1863—11 a. m.

The court met pursuant to adjournment.

Present, all the members of the court, the judge-advocate, and Maj. Gen. M. Lovell.

The proceedings of yesterday were read over.

Lieut. Col. E. F. PALFREY, C. S. Army, was next sworn and examined as a witness.

By the JUDGE-ADVOCATE:

Question. Where were you on duty in April, 1862, and for several months prior thereto? What was your rank and position at that time?

Answer. I was on duty as major, adjutant-general's department, on the staff of Major-General Lovell, in the city of New Orleans, from November 7, 1862, to the fall of the city.

Question. What were the business habits of Major-General Lovell during that time?

Answer. The office opened at 9.30 a.m., the general remaining in the office about three hours in the morning; from that time until 8 p.m. (excepting the interval for dinner) he was generally mounted, making an inspection of the camps and batteries. At 8 p.m. he returned to the office, where he met his staff. His duties generally detained him until 10 or 11 o'clock, and sometimes later. As well as I remember, the routine of duty that should obtain at headquarters was observed, business being dispatched with regularity and promptitude. I do not know that the general was ever absent a day from his office except on duty.

Question. Had you conversations with General Lovell touching the condition of the defenses of New Orleans and his ability to resist the attack of the enemy? If so, state the substance of those conversations.

Answer. He expressed confidence in his ability to resist the enemy so long as the obstructions at the forts might continue.

Question. Did General Lovell ever express to you any distrust as to the continuance of the obstructions?

Answer. About March 1, to the best of my recollection, he expressed some apprehension lest the accumulation of drift might destroy the raft.

Question. After the raft had been broken did he ever say to you that he considered the passage of the forts was practicable?

Answer. I do not think he ever did; but in a letter of March 10, to the Secretary of War, which came under my inspection, I think he said as much.

Question. Did General Lovell ever make known to you by word of mouth that the city of New Orleans could be taken by the enemy after the destruction of the raft between the forts, or from your conversations with him were you impressed with the belief that the city of New Orleans was likely to be captured?

Answer. I was not, that I remember.

Question. When was the piling begun at the Rigolets, when was it completed, and when washed away or destroyed?

Answer. It must have been begun and completed after February 18, and it was destroyed before the city fell.

Question. Do you know whether any preparations were made for an evacuation before the forts were passed or while the fight was there progressing?

Answer. As near as I remember, commissary stores were sent from the city to various points on the railroad and to Covington some ten or fifteen days before the passage of the forts. That is all that I can recollect, and I regarded it rather as a precaution in the event of disaster than a preparation for an evacuation.

Question. Was the evacuation conducted with as much order and effect as the circumstances would allow?

Answer. I saw but little of the evacuation; the little I did see was conducted in an orderly manner.

Question. Did you see General Lovell often during the evacuation? If so, state his demeanor on such occasions.

Answer. I saw General Lovell upon his arrival from the forts, immediately after their passage by the enemy. He placed me in charge of the office, and went out, I presume, to make ready to receive the enemy. I saw him late that night at the camp of the Confederate Guard Regiment; saw him again the next morning, between 9 and 10 o'clock, when he ordered me to pack up the records and proceed with them to the Jackson Railroad Depot. I saw him again at the depot just before the last train started, after all the troops had left the city or were leaving on that train, he being among the very last to leave. At no time did he exhibit anything like flurry or a want of presence of mind.

Question. Were the troops that left the city demoralized in their bearing or did they conduct themselves like disciplined soldiers?

Answer. I saw no further evidence of demoralization or want of discipline than is usual among raw, fresh levies.

Question. What forces were in the city and removed at the time of the fall?

Answer. There was but one company of Conf derate artillery, disciplined, Semmes' battery, and about 4,000 militia, turned over for local defense by the governor a short time before the city fell, armed chiefly with old altered muskets and double-barreled shot-guns—the shot-guns predominant. The majority of the militia and local defense troops remained in the city, and a large portion of the local defense force that went to Camp Moore returned to the city, being over age, and merely enlisted for duty in New Orleans.

Question. What was the character of the population in New Orleans, in a military point of view, when it was captured?

Answer. The best fighting material was off in the armies of the Confederate States; that left consisted of old men and foreigners. A large portion of the German population was disloyal. There were a good many others capable of bearing arms, but there were no arms for them.

Cross-examination by Major-General LOVELL:

Question. Was General Lovell in the habit of expressing his hopes, fears, plans, and views to those about him on duty?

Answer. He was not.

The court adjourned to meet at 11 a. m. to-morrow.

RICHMOND, VA., *June* 10, 1863—11 a. m.

The court met pursuant to adjournment.

Present, all the members of the court, the judge-advocate, and Major-General Lovell.

The proceedings of yesterday were read over.

ARCHIBALD MITCHELL was next sworn and examined as a witness.

By the JUDGE-ADVOCATE:

Question. Where did you reside and what was your occupation during the year 1861 and until May, 1862?

Answer. I resided in New Orleans, and was the principal foreman of the iron foundery of Leeds & Co. during that time.

Question. How long have you been in the iron-foundery business, and what was the character of the work made by Leeds & Co. in their establishment?

Answer. Since the year 1836. Sugar-mill machinery, steam-engines, boilers, saw-mills, and all sorts of machinery were made in their establishment. The works were the largest in the city, and had been in operation continuously since 1824 or 1825, and employed some 300 hands.

Question. Do you know who were the contractors for the engines, &c., which were to be placed upon the Mississippi, a gunboat or a ship of war, being completed in New Orleans at the time of its capture? If so, state their resources for a prompt compliance, with your opinion of their ability to fulfill such contract.

Answer. Mr. Kirk was the contractor, but he used the name of Jackson & Co. His establishment was next to that of Leeds & Co. in capacity, working 75 hands. He was generally reputed to be a man of limited pecuniary resources and of inferior mechanical capacity, but I have no personal knowledge on these points. It was a mechanical impossibility for him to have finished such a contract in the time agreed upon, to wit, three months. No establishment in the city could have performed the contract within that time. From my knowledge of the machinery of that vessel, and the fact that Leeds & Co. could not, with greater facilities for the dispatch of such work, have completed the contract in less than four months, I am of opinion that Kirk, with far inferior force, could not have complied with the terms of contract as to time. The contract was made about the latter part of September, and when the city fell the machinery was not then completed. When the enemy were assembling at Ship Island in force, some weeks previous to the fall of the city, much of the work of the Mississippi was distributed among other establishments. Leeds & Co. had about $6,000 worth of it to do.

Question. Did Leeds & Co. make a bid for the construction of the machinery for the Mississippi? If so, state their proposals with reference to the amount for which they would do the work and the time at which they would complete it.

Answer. They did make such a bid, and, to the best of my recollection, they agreed to make the entire machinery of the vessel for $65,000. I do not think they proposed any definite time as to the completion of the work, but expressed the opinion confidently that it could be done in four months. We could have made closer estimates, but we had no drawings or specifications. I believe we would have bound ourselves to have finished the work within five months. The capacity of an establishment like that of Kirk and Leeds & Co. was limited by the quantity of machinery they had. Leeds & Co. could not have made available a greater force than they had.

Question. Do you know who were the builders of the machinery of the Louisiana?

Answer. I do not know of my own knowledge, though I am well satisfied that Kirk and a machinist named John McLean did the work. I do not know where they are.

Question. How long had Kirk been established in the city, and what, if you know, was his general reputation as a business man?

Answer. He had not been long in the city before the war began. His reputation was that he was a man destitute of principle, though it was not generally so reputed at the time he took the contract for the machinery of the Mississippi.

Question. Did General Lovell ever visit the works of Leeds & Co. and manifest an interest in the progress of the Government works?

Answer. He visited there frequently and urged the progress of the work.

Question. Were any heavy guns made at Leeds & Co.'s establishment or were any rifled or banded?

Answer. We made a few heavy guns for the Navy and one for the Army. We rifled quite a number of old 32 and 42 pounders for the Army, and we banded one 7-inch gun. I do not recollect whether any more were banded.

Question. Were Leeds & Co. ever applied to by General Lovell to make heavy guns on an extensive scale or could they have done it?

Answer. I do not know that he did. He did business with Mr. Thomas Leeds, who is now dead.

Question. Was the establishment of Leeds & Co. in constant employment for the Government?

Answer. It was steadily employed for the Confederate States and the State of Louisiana from within a short time after the war began. The proprietors refused to undertake work for planters, &c.

Question. Were you in New Orleans when it was evacuated? If so, state, if you know, whether Leeds & Co. removed their machinery and such material of war as might have been then in their establishment.

Answer. None of the machinery was removed, but all the Government work was sent off that could be. Much the larger portion was removed under the order of Colonel Lovell, received on the morning of April 24, 1862. About 200 tons of shot and shell were all that was left, and that could have been got off, but the railroad became gorged up, and its agents refused to receive more. From experiments and authorities on the subject we found that heavy guns could not be well made with the machinery we had. The iron was much injured by being fused in a cupola furnace, but we went to work and had nearly completed a reverberatory furnace when the city fell.

Question. Did you ever inspect the machinery being erected on board of the Mississippi? If so, when, under what circumstances, and what time, in your opinion, would have been required for its completion?

Answer. I did, about April 15, 1862, in company with Mr. Cook, a well-known machinist of New Orleans, who had been requested to make the inspection by a committee in the city. We were of the opinion that, with the best assistance of other establishments in the city, aside from Kirk's, it might have been done in six weeks.

Hon. C. M. CONRAD was next sworn and examined as a witness.

By the JUDGE-ADVOCATE:

Question. Have you not been a member of Congress from the city of New Orleans since the organization of the Confederate States Government and for the same time have you not been chairman of the House Committee on Naval Affairs? If so, state all you may know touching the defenses of New Orleans, particularly its naval defenses, its capture by the enemy, and its evacuation.

Answer. I know very little about the defenses of New Orleans generally, being absent most of the time from the commencement of the war until it was taken, first at Montgomery and afterwards in this city. I will state, however, from the commencement of the war a great deal of anxiety was felt by the citizens for its safety, as there was no defense whatever from an attack from above, either by land or naval force, and the only defenses below were the two forts (Jackson and Saint Philip), which were known to have a very insufficient armament, and which it was known the highest military or naval officers regarded, even with a complete armament, inadequate to prevent the passage of steamers. At that time no preparations whatever had been begun to resist an attack by land. Under these circumstances the city authorities determined to provide, as far as possible, for the defense of the city, aided also by the governor of the State. They made a large appropriation in money, and, I think, also the governor assumed the responsibility of advancing some on behalf of the State for the purpose of erecting fortifications around the city. Engineers were employed for this purpose. These works were commenced, but they seemed to advance very slowly, and I was requested to see the President, to have one or more engineers assigned to duty there. A committee of the council came or sent to procure guns for the works, and some guns were obtained, but not as many as were demanded for these works were supplied. Still, however, great complaints were made as to a want of energy in the construction of the works, and great anxiety manifested lest they would not be done in time. Under these circumstances the Government determined to send General Lovell to take command. I returned to New Orleans about the time the general did. I had myself but little opportunity of judging of the manner in which he discharged his duties, as I only remained four or five weeks and returned to Richmond; but I must say that it was a subject at the time of general congratulation among the citizens that more energy seemed to be infused into the work of defense than had previously prevailed. He immediately visited all the forts (which General Twiggs' infirmities prevented him from doing), and it was understood that he had made important changes in the land defenses. I left there favorably impressed with his administration, although without accurate knowledge on the subject, and so stated on my arrival here. I observed, however, that the iron-plated gunboats were progressing slowly. I went up to look at them. The work on one of them (I think it was the Mississippi) had been suspended for ten or twelve days. While I was there this was a subject of remark among the citizens generally. During the course of that winter I received frequent letters from my constituents complaining of the slowness with which the work advanced, and requested that I should urge the adoption of measures to expedite the work. Either before I left New Orleans or after arriving, some one suggested that arrangements should be made to have the vessels worked upon at night and on Sundays, as there were many mechanics idle in the city that could relieve each other. I saw the Secretary of the Navy frequently upon the subject of these vessels; told him that I considered that the safety of New Orleans depended mainly, if not entirely, upon them, so far as a naval attack was concerned, which was the only one I apprehended, and I informed him of the anxiety that was felt by the people of New Orleans on the subject. The Secretary did not, however, seem to be alive to the magnitude of the danger, although I read him an extract from a New York newspaper containing a description of iron-plated vessels that were being built at Saint Louis and Cincinnati expressly to descend the Mississippi, and spoke of similar gunboats being built at New York. I mentioned the suggestion, which I thought a good one, that the work upon these vessels should be continued at night and on Sundays. I do not remember what he said about night work, but in regard to working on Sundays he said it would shock the religious sensibilities of the people. I told him, in reply, that so far as my constituents were concerned there were none of them that would be at all shocked; that the enemy would not hesitate to attack us on Sunday, and I did not see why we should not prepare to defend ourselves on Sunday. The letters to me also mentioned, on several occasions, that the mechanics employed on the naval works were not punctually paid, and, in consequence, they were greatly dissatisfied and much indisposed to work for that arm of the service. I think they stated that numbers had left on that account, refusing to work. I invariably informed the Secretary of the Navy of these complaints or read him that portion of the letter. He did not seem at all surprised at this information, but stated that the Treasury Department failed to supply him the funds as fast as they were needed. On one occasion I was somewhat excited, because I thought he treated such information too lightly, and I told him I did not know anything more important to which money could be applied than the completion of the two vessels upon which the safety of New Orleans depended, and that as he was responsible for the proper prosecution of the work I thought it was his duty to insist that the money should be so applied. Finally a committee of several prominent citizens of New Orleans was deputized to come on here to urge the Government to more energetic measures in regard to the two gunboats. They came to me, and I introduced the chairman (Mr. William Henderson, a respectable merchant of the city, a very zealous and energetic man) to the President and the Secretary of the Navy, and he represented to them the delay attending the building of these vessels, and made some suggestions on the subject, the nature of which I do not now recollect. He spoke particularly of the backwardness of paying the workmen as one cause of the delay. After the interview he said orders had been given to remedy the financial troubles, and also for the shipment of the shaft, that had been here for some time. This was in January or February, 1862. After this, however, the complaints about the slow progress of the work still continued, and I frequently saw the Secretary and informed him of the uneasiness felt by the citizens for the safety of New Orleans, in which I fully participated. I at last came to the conclusion that New Orleans would be taken, the only question in my mind being whether by the gunboats from above or the fleet from the sea. So strong was my belief that I mentioned it confidentially to several of my friends, though I did not publicly declare it, not deeming it prudent. Mr. Mallory having addressed a letter to the chairman of the Committee on Naval Affairs, recommending the construction of a foundery and naval depot at New Orleans, I mentioned to the committee my opinion on this subject as a reason why the suggestion should not be adopted, as I thought New Orleans would probably be taken that spring, and, accordingly, I wrote a letter to the Secretary in reply to his note, in which I mentioned, as our reason why his suggestion was disapproved by the committee, the belief or the apprehension felt by them that New Orleans would be captured owing to the backwardness of the naval preparations at that place. This was some five or six weeks before the attack on the forts. I also felt it my duty, both as the Representative from New Orleans and as chairman of the Committee on Naval Affairs, publicly to proclaim in Congress my conviction of the incapacity or inefficiency of the Secretary of the Navy.

The court adjourned to meet at 11 a. m. to-morrow.

RICHMOND, VA., *June* 11, 1863.

The court met pursuant to adjournment.

Present, all the members of the court, the judge-advocate, and Major-General Lovell.

The proceedings of yesterday were read over.

Examination of Hon. C. M. CONRAD continued.

By the JUDGE-ADVOCATE:

Question. Did not the President grant the request preferred by you on behalf of the citizens of New Orleans for engineers to take charge of the fortifications there in process of construction?

Answer. There was already a Confederate States engineer officer there, a Maj. M. L. Smith, but General Twiggs had expressed to me doubts of his activity and energy, although he spoke highly of him in other respects, and expressed a wish that some officer of more distinction should be given the superintendence of the works at New Orleans. On my arrival here I conferred with the President upon the subject, and he expressed very great willingness to comply with the request as far as practicable, but stated that very few engineers had resigned and come over to us from the old service, and that there was a great deficiency in our Army as to that corps. He looked over the list, and found that some had already been assigned to important duty, and of those that remained he said he would send any of them that General Twiggs would prefer, but expressed the opinion, from what he had heard of Major Smith, that he was as competent as either of those that were mentioned as disposable. I informed General Twiggs of the result of my interview, but am unable to say whether or not any change was made.

Question. Do you know any particular facts touching the defenses of New Orleans not before stated which you deem important? If so, state them.

Answer. I know nothing further on the subject than I have stated, except the condition of Fort Jackson before or shortly after General Lovell's arrival, and that shortly after the commencement of the first session of the Provisional Congress, at Montgomery, in February, 1861, before the President was inaugurated, either Major (now General) Beauregard or some one else sent me a slip from a paper containing a letter from General Beauregard in regard to the defenses of New Orleans. In this letter he expressed the opinion that the forts below the city would not be sufficient to prevent the passage of steam vessels of war, even if their armament was complete and the guns of the heaviest caliber, but added that the armament was not complete nor the guns of the heaviest caliber. He recommended, therefore, that some measures should be adopted retarding the progress of such vessels—keeping them under the fire of the forts. He suggested two modes that might be adopted to accomplish this end: the one was the stretching of heavy chain cables across the river; the other, which he considered most effective, the construction of a raft in the channel, and stated that he had prepared a plan of such a raft, and gave an estimate of its cost. Considering this communication a very important one, I summoned the Committee on Naval Affairs and laid it before them. They agreed with me, and it was determined that we should summon naval officers of the highest rank in order to lay this subject before them, and I applied for and obtained authority from Congress to summon them. The summons was issued to Captains Ingraham, Rosseau, Tatnall, Randolph, and Commander Semmes. They all obeyed the summons, and at the time appointed came to Montgomery and appeared before the committee, when I laid before them the communication of General Beauregard, and requested them carefully to consider it and furnish the committee with their views in writing at the next meeting. They did so, and sent me a report, expressing their entire concurrence in the view of General Beauregard as to the ability of steam vessels of war to pass the forts even with a complete armament of heavy guns. A day or so after the inauguration I laid this communication of General Beauregard and the report of the naval officers before the President. My belief that New Orleans would be taken was based mainly upon this paper of General Beauregard's and the report of the naval officers.

Question. Were you at Camp Moore shortly after the evacuation of New Orleans? If so, state the condition of military affairs there at that time.

Answer. I arrived at Camp Moore a day or two after the evacuation. I found General Lovell there with such force as he had brought out of the city, very small in number; I should not think it exceeded over 2,500 men; the troops seemed to be very much disorganized. The general's main attention seemed to be directed to getting the military supplies from the city, large quantities of which were constantly arriving. With the exception of Colonel De Clouet's regiment, which had been raised but a few days, and a battalion of Zouaves, the force was mainly composed of militia and troops raised for local defense. General Lovell, while I was there, was making arrangements for the destruction of cotton up the river, and informed me that he had given instructions for the fortification of Vicksburg. There was no greater confusion than was natural and to be expected; there was no military confusion. General Lovell gave no evidence of embarrassment; was perfectly cool, and told me he was willing to go back to New Orleans if the authorities desired it.

Cross-examination by Maj. Gen. M. LOVELL:

Question. Was not General M. L. Smith in immediate command of the troops at Camp Moore, General Lovell merely having his department headquarters in the vicinity of those troops?

Answer. He was in the immediate command, General Lovell merely having his headquarters there.

NELSON TIFT was next sworn and examined as a witness.

By the JUDGE-ADVOCATE:

Question. What were your relations to the Government with reference to the Confederate States steamer Mississippi?

Answer. I was the inventor of the plan of that vessel, and with my brother, Mr. A. F. Tift, brought a model to Richmond, submitted it to the Navy Department, and tendered our services without compensation to construct such a vessel. As a means of showing to the country our true relations to the Government I here submit our proposition to the Secretary of the Navy and his acceptance and instructions.

Question. Had you or your brother any experience as constructors of vessels?

Answer. Neither of us are practical mechanics; both of us are familiar with the character and qualities of vessels and the manner in which they are constructed. My brother has, as proprietor and superintendent, during the past twenty-five years, had many vessels built and repaired. In the case of the Mississippi I furnished the plan. My brother and myself superintended the entire work as agents of the Government, and Mr. Joseph Prim, a practical naval constructor, had the charge of her construction.

Question. Did you make the contracts for the construction of the Mississippi? If so, state with whom the more important contracts were made.

Answer. As the agents of the Government we made all the contracts that were made. We contracted with Jackson & Co., represented by Robert Kirk, for the machinery; with Schofield & Markham, at Atlanta, Ga., for the iron plating, &c.; with Winship & Co., of Atlanta, Ga., for bolts for plating and for making port doors; with Wells, Poitevant, Cary, Hammond & Co., Garland, and others, for timber; with Slocomb, Bean & Sons, Slark, Stauffer & Co., Folger & Co., and others, for iron fastenings, tools, &c.; with Leeds & Co., John Clarke, Barringer, Cosgrove, McCan & Harrold, Beanmiller, D. H. Fowler, Purseglove, Wheeler & Forestall, and others, for iron work of various kinds and machinery. Besides these, we purchased elsewhere, where we could get them, such articles as could not be obtained in New Orleans; bolt-iron, spikes, oarlocks, &c., in Mobile; bolt-iron in Macon, Atlanta, and Etowah, Ga., and in Chattanooga, Tenn., &c.

The court adjourned to meet at 11 a. m. to-morrow, the 12th instant

RICHMOND, VA., *June* 12, 1863—11 a. m.

The court met pursuant to adjournment.

Present, all the members of the court, the judge-advocate, and Maj Gen. Mansfield Lovell.

The proceedings of yesterday were read over.

Examination of NELSON TIFT continued.

By the JUDGE-ADVOCATE:

Question. What obstacles had you to encounter in the progress of the work, and what delays were you subjected to, and what means were used to overcome such obstacles?

Answer. We arrived at New Orleans on September 18, 1861. There was no shipyard suitable for the building of the Mississippi; they were all on the west bank of the river; were too small and inconvenient, the bank high, and the water deep alongside of it. We selected a suitable place on the east side of the river, at Jefferson City, where we prepared a yard with suitable buildings, sheds, blacksmith shops, a saw-mill, &c. We found no timber in New Orleans suitable for building the vessel. We contracted as soon as possible with all the responsible parties we could for the necessary timber, and, though it was brought to us by the contractors as fast as they could prepare it, we were sometimes delayed in the early part of the work for want of timber. Our contracts covered a space of more than 100 miles from the city. We sometimes had obstacles in the carpenter's department. There was a strike of all the ship carpenters in New Orleans for a few days. We first appealed to the authorities, and finding no remedy we raised the wages from $3 to $4 per day. All the workmen were called out by Governor Moore one or more days for military parade, and at other times some of our men were taken from their work by military officers for duty. This was remedied as far as possible by appeals to the authorities. Sometimes we had more men than we could continue to work and discharged them, and at other times we lacked men for a short time. When the Louisiana was being prepared for service we let them have 50 carpenters when we did not need them. Subsequently, when we did need them we could neither get them nor hire others. We then procured the necessary men from other ship-yards. When we commenced putting on the iron casting and could use laboring force at night we procured, through the aid of Captain Elmore, from neighboring plantations, between 200 and 300 negroes, who were worked as a night gang. We had obstacles in the procurement of bolt-iron, spikes, and other materials which could not be obtained in New Orleans; these were procured with some difficulty from distant points in Alabama, Georgia, and Tennessee. We had difficulty in procuring the iron plating. The Tredegar Works in Richmond was the only establishment doing that kind of work in the Confederacy, and this was fully occupied to supply the wants of the Government here. We tried to induce other establishments to prepare for and execute this work without effect, and were preparing to use railroad iron, when Schofield & Markham, of Atlanta, Ga., one of the parties to whom we had applied, concluded to consider our proposition. I went to Atlanta, and, on November 15, 1861, concluded a contract with them to roll and prepare the plating for the vessel, and through them a contract with Winship & Co. for the bolts for the plating. This being a new character of work, Schofield & Markham had to change the rolls of their establishment, erect new drills, and otherwise prepare for it. These arrangements were completed, I think, early in December, and they went on rapidly with the work. They encountered difficulties for want of hands and sometimes for want of coal, in both of which cases we aided them by appeals to the Government and the railroad agents.

We had obstacles in the transportation of plating and other materials. Our first shipments from Atlanta were by the way of Memphis and the river; finding delay by this route, we arranged to send through by railroad to Grand Junction and New Orleans. Subsequently a part of this line was occupied by the army of General Johnston, and transportation by that route rendered impossible. We then arranged to send by way of Montgomery and Mobile and thence by railroad to New Orleans. On this route delays were encountered at Mobile and Montgomery, which were as soon as possible removed by personal effort, by appeal to the Government, and by aid of friends. The cars containing the best of our iron plating arrived at New Orleans, I think, on April 23. We encountered many obstacles in the machinery department. Our final contract with Jackson & Co. was that they should complete the machinery on board the vessel by January 30.

In view of the fact that it might be impossible to procure wrought-iron shafting, we could make no positive contract for it. The contract, therefore, was for cast-iron shafting, with a provision that if the contractors could obtain wrought-iron shafting we were to pay the difference in cost. Under ordinary circumstances our duties and responsibilities in this department ended here and were assumed by the contractors; but finding extraordinary difficulties in the way of procuring shafting and other materials and suitable mechanics, and looking only to the final success of our labors, we made every effort in our power to aid the contractors to fulfill their contract. We aided as far as possible in furnishing men. They could get no skilled propeller molder. We procured one in Norfolk. We appealed to the Committee of Public Safety to aid them in men. They could get no wrought-iron shafting. We made diligent search in New Orleans and throughout the Confederacy. There was no establishment which could forge the shafting, and we could find but one shaft which could be adapted to our purpose. That was the shaft of a burned steamer at Richmond. It was procured for us by the Secretary of the Navy, and fitted, with great trouble and expense, at the Tredegar Works, and transported to New Orleans, where it arrived on April —. It was immediately put into the shop of Jackson & Co., turned and fitted with couplings, and was placed in its position, with its propeller, on board the ship before she was launched.

We continued our efforts to find material which would make the two long pieces of our side and quarter shafts (which were 32½ feet long each and 9 inches in diameter at the journals), or to engage parties to prepare the proper furnaces and hammer, and forge them. We applied several times to Leeds & Co., who as often answered us that they could neither procure the shafting nor forge it. We supposed it could be made in Richmond or at the Norfolk navy-yard, but ascertained that it could not. At one time we supposed that we had secured the making of these shafts by Ward & Co., of Nashville, but were disappointed. In the latter part of December we learned that Mr. John Clarke had taken a contract from the Government for making the Armstrong gun, and was about to erect a building, furnaces, and hammer for that purpose. We saw him, induced him to make some necessary changes in the plan of his works, and to agree to make our side shafting. On January 10 we wrote to the Secretary of the Navy:

"We have been much troubled about the side shafts. Mr. Clarke, of this place, has agreed to make them, and we hope will have them done in February."

This hope was derived from the opinion of Mr. Clarke, expressed to us; but he was unavoidably delayed in the erection of the building and works by much rainy weather and a scarcity of suitable mechanics. I think that his works were completed about the middle of March. He could get no person who had experience with such work; but with perseverance he succeeded in forging them—the first in about fifteen days and the second in about eight days. By our previous arrangement with Leeds & Co. these shafts, as soon as they were forged, were taken to their shop, and worked upon day and night until they were finished. The last of these shafts were put on board the vessel, I think, April 23. We frequently visited the foundery and workshop of Jackson & Co. to urge forward the work and to render all the assistance in our power. When we were convinced that the machinery would be the cause of delay, we urged the distribution of such parts as could be removed, and thus finished earlier, to other shops, and promised to pay any extra cost. We also, on April 3, promised Jackson & Co. to pay them $5,000 extra if they would have the machinery completed according to the specifications of their contract by the 25th of that month. Parts of the machinery were distributed to Leeds & Co., Clarke, Barringer, and other shops. We purchased two small auxiliary engines and a steam pump, which were a part of the machinery contract, and charged them to the contractor. We procured hands to aid in putting the machinery up in the ship, and did all we could in every way to remove every obstacle and forward the work. I have mentioned only the more important obstacles and our efforts to remove them. The Committee of Public Safety attempted to make us launch the vessel before she was ready. We convinced them that they were wrong, and they desisted. Mr. V. Sheldon, a member of the committee, refused to let us have his sub-marine armor to examine the ways of the ship, which was necessary to her safety in launching. We sent a steamer 25 miles to procure another, which was cheerfully furnished by Captain Whiting. We found it impracticable, in the early part of the work, to get from the authorities an armed guard for the protection of the vessel. These are samples of the minor difficulties.

Question. Was not Leeds & Co. a larger and better establishment than that of Jackson & Co.? If so, why did you not give the contract to Leeds & Co.? Did you know the character of Kirk as a business man? State also the reason that influenced you in giving the contract.

Answer. Leeds & Co. had a larger, and I think a better, establishment, all things considered; but I think the establishment of Jackson & Co., known as the Patterson foundery, was, for the purpose of building the machinery of the Mississippi, the equal of Leeds & Co. in point of capacity, tools, lathes, steam-hammers, foundery, &c. Jackson & Co., or Kirk, as their representative, had, I think, recently removed from Mobile to New Orleans, where they purchased the Patterson foundery, and were doing work for the Government when we arrived there. I know nothing of his character as a business man. He occupied a position as the head and proprietor of a machine shop and foundery second only to that of Leeds & Co. in New Orleans, which was calculated to recommend him, and I heard nothing objectionable to his character or capacity as a mechanic.

Our reasons for making the contract with Jackson & Co. and not with Leeds & Co. were:

1st. The lowest price of Leeds & Co. was $65,000 and the shortest time four months. The bid of Jackson & Co. for the same work was $45,000 and the time three months.

2d. Leeds & Co. were pressed with work, and they did not seem at all confident that they could do our work in the time mentioned. Jackson & Co. had but little work on hand, and this they promised to dispose of in a few days, and to devote the whole capacity of the establishment exclusively to our work.

Under these circumstances, with a saving of $20,000 to the Government and one month in time and with an apparent superior capacity for doing the work, we did not hesitate to make the contract with Jackson & Co. With continued, earnest, and zealous efforts I believe that Jackson & Co. could have completed the machinery earlier than they did, and yet I doubt whether any other establishment in New Orleans, with their other engagements, could have completed it earlier than they did. I have mentioned the case of Mr. Clarke, a first-rate business man, who was delayed in making our side shafts some two months beyond the time he calculated. Leeds & Co., on February 18, agreed to make the iron rudder for the Mississippi; it was not completed on April 25. I doubt whether they or any other similar establishment in New Orleans performed any important contract within the time contemplated when they undertook it. I mention these facts to show that the difficulties encountered by these establishments were common to all.

Question. How many working days were lost from the commencement of the Mississippi to the passage of the forts, including Sundays as lost days?

Answer. Not one working day was lost except that already referred to, when the men were called out to military parade by the governor, and this was done against my personal request that they should be allowed to go on with the work. There were some rainy days, when the men could not work outside, but work was continued in the shops and under the sheds. I do not remember how many Sundays we worked, but, as a general rule, we worked every Sunday when we thought it necessary to forward the work. We also worked nights in the shops when necessary and we could get hands for the purpose.

Question. In how many days would the Mississippi have been completed, beyond all doubt, had not the city fallen?

Answer. In my opinion two weeks as the extreme. I know that some other men entertain a very different opinion, but it will be found on examination that they have formed their opinion without a sufficient knowledge of the particulars necessary to her completion. All the iron below the deck line was on; the iron for the upper works had all been cut, fitted, and assorted to its place. About one-third of it had been put on within two days, and the opinion of the workman in charge was that the remainder could be put on and bolted in six days. In less than that time the machinery could have been connected ready for steam, and the port doors, which were completed and hinged, put in place, and the rudder hung. The dock for putting in the side propeller shafts was completed and launched. The shafts had been completed and the propellers fitted to them, and the side bearings were completed ready to be bolted up. I suppose that ten days would be a full allowance for this work. We had men enough, including a large force of negroes, which we worked as a night gang, to handle iron plating and other labor, to carry on all the departments of the work together, and it could have been done without interference with each other. It will be seen, therefore, that in fixing the time of completion at two weeks I have allowed four days to cover contingencies.

I know that the public mind has been prejudiced against my brother and myself by unfounded rumors and mistaken reports, but I state, without fear of contradiction by those who know the facts, that our best energies of mind and body were devoted to this work from the beginning to the end, and that we accomplished all that it was possible for us or for any other persons, with the means at our command, to do; and in this connection it is proper to state that the Secretary of the Navy, under whose orders we were acting, furnished us with all the means and facilities in his power, with repeated instructions to spare neither money nor men to forward the work, and that we obeyed the order in letter and spirit.

The court adjourned to meet at 11 a. m. to-morrow.

RICHMOND, VA., *June* 13, 1863.

The court met pursuant to adjournment.

Present, all the members of the court, the judge-advocate, and Maj. Gen. M. Lovell.

The proceedings of yesterday were then read over.

The judge-advocate then read to the court, prepared according to its directions, the following letter:

RICHMOND, VA., *June* 13, 1863.

General S. COOPER,
Adjutant and Inspector General, Richmond, Va.:

GENERAL: I have advised the court that it has in law the right to summon before it any member of the Cabinet whose testimony may be deemed important; but it is to be borne in mind that the court exercises its functions for the information of the President, and it may be considered a work of supererogation on its part to ascertain from members of the Cabinet, who are but parts of the Executive, facts which in law the President is presumed already to know. I am instructed by the court to ask your opinion as to the propriety of issuing a summons as above indicated, and whether such a step is in accordance with the custom of the service.

I have the honor to be, your obedient servant,

L. R. PAGE,
Major, Adjutant-General's Department, and Judge-Advocate.

It was then ordered by the court that the judge-advocate forward the said letter to General Cooper.

The judge-advocate then informed the court that the Adjutant and Inspector General had advised him that orders were in preparation, affecting the investigations of the court, which would render it expedient for the court to suspend its proceedings until said orders were issued.

The court thereupon adjourned to meet on Monday, the 15th instant, at 11 a. m.

RICHMOND, VA., *June* 15, 1863—11 a. m.

The court met pursuant to adjournment.

Present, all the members of the court, the judge-advocate, and Maj. Gen. M. Lovell.

The proceedings of the 13th instant were read over.

The following communication to Maj. Gen. T. C. Hindman, president, was then read to the court by the judge-advocate:

ADJUTANT AND INSPECTOR GENERAL'S OFFICE,
Richmond, Va., June 15, 1863.

Maj. Gen. T. C. HINDMAN,
President of Court of Inquiry, Richmond, Va.:

GENERAL: I have the honor to refer to you the inclosed copy of a letter of the Secretary of the Navy, with the President's indorsement thereon, on the subject of the examination of navy operations by the court over which you preside. Recurring tc my answer of April 21 last to the telegram of the judge-advocate on this subject, I find that my language was not as precise as could be wished, and in order that there may be no misunderstanding I desire now to state my views:

The court of inquiry, being an army court, is, of course, without authority to express any opinion upon the conduct of any officers of the Navy Department; but where the general whose conduct is under investigation alleges that the fall of the city was attributable to the misconduct or failure of any person not under his control, it is perfectly proper to examine as witnesses all that are cognizant of the facts, even if they be officers of the Navy. The inquiry is to be directed solely to the purpose of ascertaining whether the defense of the general is true; if it be so, the court will pronounce, of course, that the failure to defend the city arose from causes not within his control, but will not express any opinion as to the conduct of the officers of another department of the service. If, on the contrary, the defense of the general is rebutted by the evidence, the court will give its opinion that his defense is not sustained. In this way the truth may be reached without the court touching at all on the province of a naval court. It is plain that no opinion of the conduct of an officer connected with the Navy can be expressed by the court, because, if the court desires to examine into the conduct of any other officer than General Lovell, the court would be compelled to cite the officer before it, and it has no power to do so with a Navy officer, whose conduct can only be inquired into by a naval court.

Very respectfully, your obedient servant,

S. COOPER,
Adjutant and Inspector General.

NAVY DEPARTMENT,
Richmond, Va., June 8, 1863.

To the PRESIDENT:

SIR: I learn to-day, from an authentic source, that the court of inquiry, convoked by the War Department, at the request of General Lovell, and now in session in Richmond, for the ostensible purpose of investigating his conduct as connected with the defense and fall of New Orleans, is engaged in taking testimony, formally, as to the official conduct of the Navy Department and that of all its officers, civil and military, in any way connected with its operations in New Orleans and on the Mississippi River, embracing within the field of its inquiry the manner in which this Department transmitted funds from Richmond, how it met its expenditures, its correspondence with its subordinates, the construction and equipment of vessels, &c.

A court of inquiry is a tribunal whose results necessarily shape public opinion, and obvious justice demands that if this court could properly enter upon such investigation at all, the parties whose conduct is to be inquired of, and whose fame may be disparaged by its results, should have notice of its purpose and opportunity for explanation and defense. I will not dwell upon the evils which may follow a precedent thus established of subjecting the conduct of one Department of the Government and its officers to the formal inquiry of the officers of a different Department, and this, too, without notice; but I cannot refrain from saying that, in my judgment, the proceeding is illegal and is fraught with mischief to both branches of the military service. The naval officer in command afloat at New Orleans has been subjected to a court of inquiry formed of his peers, and the entire operations of the Department connected with the defense of New Orleans have been investigated by a committee of Congress, and the testimony in both cases is of record. I respectfully submit these facts to your attention as the Commander-in-Chief of the Army and Navy.

I have the honor to be, very respectfully, &c.,

S. R. MALLORY,
Secretary of the Navy.

JUNE 9, 1863.

Respectfully referred to the Adjutant and Inspector General, that proper notice may be given to the court.

JEFFERSON DAVIS.

Examination of NELSON TIFT resumed.

Cross-examination by Maj. Gen. M. LOVELL:

Question. Did you suppose when you laid the keel of the Mississippi, in October, 1861, that it would take so long a time to get her ready?

Answer. We did not suppose that it would take so long a time to get her ready. We could not anticipate the many difficulties we had to encounter. We thought then that we could get her ready in about four months.

Question. If the machinery had been finished in proper time would the other work on the vessel have been ready for it?

Answer. The wood work would have been ready, but the iron plating would not have been.

By the COURT:

Question. Have you or your brother ever received any compensation from the Government for your services as agents for the construction of the Mississippi?

Answer. None whatever; nor would we have received any had it been tendered.

Question. When you made the contract for machinery with Jackson & Co., how did the number of workmen they could usefully employ in their shops compare with the number in Leeds & Co.'s establishment?

Answer. I do not know the relative capacity of the two establishments as to the number of workmen they could employ on other work. Leeds & Co.'s was certainly much the larger, but as to their capacity for work on the machinery of the Mississippi, I think they were equal.

Upon application of Messrs. A. F. & N. Tift to inspect the testimony of Surg. D. W. Brickell, who appeared before the court as a witness, no member of the court objecting thereto, it was ordered that the application be granted.

It was then ordered that H. L. Coll be employed as a clerk to aid the judge-advocate, his compensation to begin from the 12th instant.

The court adjourned to meet at 11 a. m. to-morrow, the 16th instant.

RICHMOND, VA., *June* 16, 1863—11 a. m.

The court met pursuant to adjournment.

Present, all the members of the court, the judge-advocate, and Maj. Gen. Mansfield Lovell.

The proceedings of yesterday were read over.

It was ordered by the court that the following communication, addressed to the president of the court, should be read to the court and made a part of the record:

——, —— —, 1863.

General T. C. HINDMAN, C. S. A.,
President Court of Inquiry:

SIR: Having perused, by the courteous permission of the court, the testimony given before it by Dr. D. W. Brickell, and found that his testimony is calculated to create an erroneous judgment as to our conduct in the construction of the Mississippi and a judgment adverse to our skill, energy, good faith, and loyalty as agents of the Government; and that in his testimony he refers particularly to the Committee of Public Safety of New Orleans, whereof he was a member, and to Mr. Pearce, the naval constructor, we respectfully ask the court, in justice to ourselves thus assailed: 1st, to take the testimony of Mr. Pearce, the naval constructor of the Mississippi, as to building and launching her; 2d, the testimony of Naval Constructor Murray, the builder of the Louisiana, as to the work upon and the launching of the Mississippi; and, 3d, to receive and place on record the correspondence between ourselves and the Committee of Public Safety of New Orleans, referred to by Dr. Brickell, touching the completion and launching of the ship, and our correspondence with Commanders Mitchell and Sinclair, of the Navy, Constructor Pearce, and others, relative to the launching of the Mississippi, together with our correspondence upon the same subject with the Navy Department. By this testimony we expect to show, beyond all rational question or doubt, not only that Dr. Brickell's testimony as to our action is erroneous, and that he is mistaken both in his facts and his conclusions in relation to ourselves, but that the course we adopted and pursued had the sanction and approval of the men to whom he refers, and that any other course than the one we did pursue would have been wrong.

NELSON TIFT.
A. F. TIFT.

The request of the Messrs. Tift to introduce testimony, as indicated in the foregoing letter, being considered by the court, it was ordered that the same be refused: 1st, because the admission of such testimony would be contrary to the instructions of the Adjutant and Inspector General, set forth in the record of yesterday; and, 2d, because the proposed testimony has already been taken before a committee of Congress, and is likely thereby to have the same or a greater publicity than the proceedings of this court.

Lieut. D. P. MCCORKLE, C. S. Navy, was then sworn and examined as a witness.

By the JUDGE-ADVOCATE:

Question. State all you may know touching the defense, capture, and evacuation of New Orleans in April, 1862.

Answer. I know nothing of the fight at the forts, except that I sent a good deal of ordnance to them. I was the ordnance officer of the naval station. I witnessed the fight at Chalmette from the city. Two vessels were at first turned back. I know nothing of the evacuation under General Lovell. Between 3 and 4 p. m. of April 24, being anxious to mount and fight some guns on a floating battery, I applied to General Lovell for powder; he gave me an order for 1,000 pounds. The order was returned with the indorsement that all the powder had been sent up the river. I forget the name of the person who made the indorsement. This is all I know of my own knowledge upon the subject.

Cross-examination by Maj. Gen. MANSFIELD LOVELL:

Question. From what source was all the powder procured for the use of the Navy while you were the naval ordnance officer at New Orleans?

Answer. From General Lovell.

Question. State in general terms your opinion, as ordnance officer, of the adequacy of the means at your disposal for purposes of co-operation with the land forces in the defense of New Orleans.

Answer. We had everything we needed except powder. The guns were at Jackson, Miss., on their way to New Orleans. The carriages had been made in the city, under my direction, and were ready for use. We had to get our powder from General Lovell, as we would not compete in the market with the Army.

It was ordered by the court that the judge-advocate prepare interrogations to be propounded to A. D. Kelley, summoned as a witness before this court, but unable to appear on account of his health, and that he give notice of the taking of such deposition to Major-General Lovell.

The court then adjourned to meet at 11 a. m. to-morrow, the 17th instant.

RICHMOND, VA., *June* 17, 1863—11 a. m.

The court met pursuant to adjournment.

Present, all the members of the court, the judge-advocate, and Maj. Gen. Mansfield Lovell.

The proceedings of yesterday were read over.

JOSEPH STINSON, a citizen, was next sworn and examined as a witness.

By the JUDGE-ADVOCATE:

Question. Were you in New Orleans from October, 1861, to May, 1862? If so, state your occupation during that time.

Answer. I was there during that time keeping a hotel.

Question. State all you may know, of your own knowledge, concerning the evacuation of New Orleans. Was there much property of the Government lost that might have been saved with ordinary efforts? And, if you know, state what sort of property it was.

Answer. A few tents were left on Lafayette Square; the bells sent by the planters to make cannon were also left, and some heavy cannon with gun-carriages were left, which fell into the hands of the enemy.

Question. Do you know, of your own knowledge, that any property of the Government was left at Camp Lewis when our troops evacuated the city?

Answer. Only from hearsay.

Question. Did you see General Lovell during the evacuation? If so, state whether or not he was cool and self-possessed.

Answer. I saw him the day after the fleet passed the forts. I did not see him again. I went to see him about removing Government property, which I understood was left at Camp Lewis. Some one had told him that I had reported he had run away. He told me that he would cut the throat of any man who said so. His manner was excited then, and he passed right on. I do not know where he went to. This is all I know of my own knowledge. I have spoken of other things on various occasions, but spoken from rumor.

Question. State, if you know, the feeling of the citizens of New Orleans when the forts were passed. Was it for resistance or for a surrender?

Answer. I am under the impression that a majority were for resistance. The best of the French held out very well. The Germans took no active part either way.

Question. What were your opportunities for forming an opinion as to the feeling of the citizens? Did you know of any meetings that were held counseling resistance? If so, were you present?

Answer. My opinion was formed from mixing with the people. I heard of such a meeting, but it fell through. I was not at it.

Question. Do you know of any persons volunteering with the Army to defend the city after the passage of the forts? If yea, state their number, and whether or not they were able-bodied men.

Answer. It was calculated that we could get 25,000 or 30,000 men, including those under arms, for the purpose at that time. Some 400 or 500 of us were ready to join the Army for that purpose, and applied to Governor Moore for arms. He said that he had none, and referred us to General Lovell; but we could not see General Lovell, and abandoned our effort. A majority of the men referred to by me were too old to go into camp, but could have done good fighting. I do not know the number of men under arms.

Question. Was there much private property destroyed or left in the city that would have been valuable for military uses?

Answer. I saw a pile of corn burned and some sugar and molasses. This property might have been saved if the steamboats that were at the levee could have been used to transport it; but the boats were made ready to leave by their owners as soon as they knew the forts had been passed.

Cross-examination by Maj. Gen. MANSFIELD LOVELL:

Question. Did the heavy guns that you saw lying at the custom-house belong to the Army or the Navy?

Answer. I do not know.

Question. Did not General Lovell stop on the city hall steps directly after his conversation with you and address the people for some time, attempting to allay their excitement?

Answer. My impression is that he did, though I cannot say whether it was before or after our conversation. I was too far off to hear or see well. The crowd was very great.

Question. On the morning after the day in which you say 400 or 500 of your crowd were willing to fight, did not General Lovell publish an order and appeal in all the papers of the city calling for 1,000 men to board the enemy's vessels? Did any of that crowd volunteer for that service that you are aware of?

Answer. I did not, nor did any of our crowd that I know of.

Question. You say that you think 25,000 or 30,000 men could have been obtained in New Orleans to defend it; did not General Lovell, through Governor Moore, call for 10,000 men from the city at least six weeks before the fall of New Orleans?

Answer. I do not recollect.

The court adjourned to meet at 11 a. m. to-morrow.

RICHMOND, VA., *June* 18, 1863—11 a. m.

The court met pursuant to adjournment.

Present, all the members of the court, the judge-advocate, and Maj. Gen. Mansfield Lovell.

F. W. C. COOKE, a citizen, was then sworn and examined as a witness.

By the JUDGE-ADVOCATE:

Question. Were you a resident of New Orleans from October, 1861, to May, 1862? If so, what was your occupation?

Answer. I was, and, with my brother, engaged in the manufacture of small-arms. I have lived in New Orleans for seventeen years.

Question. Was your machinery removed from the city at the time of its capture, in April, 1862? If so, was it done in pursuance of orders from or with the assistance of General Lovell?

Answer. I saved all the machinery connected with the armory, except the motive power. I did not save all the work. I left 130 tons of wrought iron, which I could not bring away. We lost the tools and machinery of the machine shop. Afterwards, on or about April 29, I received a schooner laden with steel and iron. At Madisonville the Yankee sentinel permitted her to pass through the canal for $20. On Thursday morning, April 24, 1862, at 11 o'clock, Major Smith sent for me, and told me the fleet had passed the forts, and to save what I could. I asked him to put it down in writing, which he did; the paper I have not here with me. It was to the effect that, by the wish and consent of the general commanding, Cooke & Brother were requested to remove their machinery from New Orleans. After setting the men to work I sought for General or Colonel Lovell to get an order for a steamboat; the order was received from Colonel Lovell the same day. In obedience to it I took and used the steamer Newsboy, but had to pay $2,600 for freightage. On the morning of the 25th, not finding the enemy at the city, and not being able to find any one to give me an order for another steamer, I wrote one myself and signed General Lovell's name to it, per my own name, which I subsequently reported to General Lovell at Camp Moore. That boat left the wharf about 12 o'clock that day. While at Camp Moore General Lovell gave me another order to the effect that steamboat men and railroad agents should give every facility for removing the machinery throughout the country after we had brought it from New Orleans. This order was given on April 28.

Question. When you applied to Colonel Lovell for an order for the steamboat had you any difficulty in obtaining it, and did you then consider one steamboat sufficient for the removal of your machinery?

Answer. I only asked for one steamer. At first Colonel Lovell told me he could not give me an order, but upon my telling him that I had taken down my machinery in obedience to orders, he gave me an order.

Question. After getting the order did you have difficulties in obtaining and using the steamboat? If yea, state what those difficulties were.

Answer. I got the steamboat without trouble, but there was no one on board but the captain. I had to furnish the crew, engineers, and pilot. There was a general stampede among all the steamboat-men, as far as came under my observation.

Question. After the bombardment commenced why did you not take earlier measures for the removal of your stock and machinery from the city?

Answer. Because Major Smith had promised me forty-eight hours' notice of the time when the removal should be made. Messrs. Leeds & Co. had applied with me for permission to remove our shops some six weeks before the city fell. Major Smith, whom we saw, said he would see General Lovell. After leaving me in his office a short time, he returned and said that the removal of our establishment would create too much excitement, but said he would give us forty-eight hours' notice, the time in which I told him I could remove my works, &c.

Question. State all you may know touching the testing of a heavy gun made by Leeds & Co.

Answer. The gun was an 8-inch columbiad, and when tested it was placed on the levee at the end of the shell road, at an elevation of from 15 to 20 degrees, the breach placed against heavy piling fastened by strong horizontal timber, thus depriving it of ——— *; it burst, I think, about the seventy-sixth charge. I do not remember the name of the officer who was superintending the test; he was a Frenchman, belonging to an artillery company from the city. I was present at intervals during the day when the gun was tested.

Question. State all you know concerning the evacuation of New Orleans.

Answer. There seemed to be a decided panic in the city. I was only enabled to obtain wagons and teams to remove my machinery by seizure made by Deputy Provost-Marshal McCann, who with such force as I could furnish was engaged all of Thursday in seizing teams. While removing the machinery, I delivered to Major Smith, on his order, 200 rifles, retaining 200 for the use of my hands. There were several steamboats at the levee when I went to procure one, but they had been deserted by the crew and all the officers but the captains. Of three of these boats one fell into the hands of the enemy, another was burned, and the third went up the Ouachita River. As I was leaving on the boat on Friday evening, April 25, we were hailed by some Irishwomen at the Marine Hospital, with guns in their hands; we stopped and

* The blank is in the original.

got the guns, some ten or twelve in number. I do not know whether there were others there. I met a good many soldiers the evening I left; they were very greatly disordered and moving in squads. I was closely occupied at work in removing my machinery after the passage of the forts, and did not see a great deal. This is about all I can remember on this subject. When I left the wildest confusion prevailed upon the levee; men, women, and children were removing sugar and molasses up the streets to their houses.

Question. In the foregoing testimony have you omitted any material fact bearing upon the fall of New Orleans or the loss of property during the evacuation?

Answer. I recollect nothing more. I have stated about all I know of my own knowledge.

Cross-examination by Maj. Gen. M. LOVELL:

Question. Do you know whether or not many of the stores of which you speak as being in the city on April 25, the day you left, were not subsequently brought out on railroads and by the lake by Majors James, Venable, and others?

Answer. They might or might not have been saved. I do not know.

The deposition of Capt. E. POWELL, assistant quartermaster, duly attested, was then offered in evidence by General Lovell, it being within the knowledge of the court that the witness had been summoned before the court at Vicksburg, and in obedience to its summons had reached Jackson, Miss., when he was ordered to return to his post at Natchez, by Lieutenant-General Pemberton, who informed the court that the services of Captain Powell could not be spared at that time, and since then the state of affairs being such in Mississippi that the witness' attendance could not be procured, although all proper efforts had been made to that end.

To the reading of this deposition the judge-advocate objected, because depositions of officers in the line or staff of the Army are not admissible as evidence before courts of inquiry.

The court having considered the objection, decided that under the circumstances it should be received.

By Major-General LOVELL:

Question. What position did you hold before and at the evacuation of New Orleans, in April, 1862?

Answer. I was an assistant quartermaster in the C. S. Army, with the rank of captain, and was in charge of the clothing, camp and garrison bureau, in the city of New Orleans.

Question. What amount of public property in your charge was saved at that evacuation and what was its estimated value?

Answer. I saved the whole of the public property in my charge, with the exception of a few castings, and would have saved them also if Major Winnemore, assistant quartermaster, had not taken my means of transportation from me. I am unable to state the value of the property saved, my books and papers having been removed from here (Natchez) for safety, and I cannot refer to them. I also saved all my books, papers, and funds at New Orleans; a considerable quantity of stores, &c., was stolen from the cars while *in transitu* from New Orleans to Camp Moore and above.

Question. Was there any other property of the same kind belonging to the State of Louisiana or other parties brought out that was turned over to you; if so, what was the value of the same as estimated by you?

Answer. There was no other property turned over to me that was brought out of New Orleans belonging to the State of Louisiana or others, but I picked up a portion of the clothing, camp and garrison equipage, which I believe belonged to the State of Louisiana, and for which I gave credit on my papers, together with a large quantity of quartermaster's stores, for which I believe Major Winnemore, assistant quartermaster, was responsible, the whole amounting to about $125,000.

The court adjourned to meet at 11 a. m. to-morrow.

RICHMOND, VA., *June* 20, 1863—11 a. m.

The court met pursuant to adjournment.

Present, all the members of the court, the judge-advocate, and Maj. Gen. M. Lovell.

The proceedings of yesterday were read over.

Lieut. A. J. TOUTANT was then sworn and examined as a witness.

By Maj. Gen. M. LOVELL:

Question. What position did you hold in New Orleans from October, 1861, to May, 1862?

Answer. I held the position of aide-de-camp to Major-General Lovell.

Question. What were your opportunities for knowing the routine business habits of General Lovell in New Orleans? If you know, state what they were.

Answer. I was with General Lovell more regularly than any of his staff officers, not only in the office, but also in all outdoor duty. I, in fact, accompanied him on all his tours of inspection out of town, which gave me full opportunities to judge of his business habits. He was industrious, attentive, punctual, and energetic in dispatching all business connected with his department.

Question. Was he ever absent from his office or from duty for any cause whatever a single day while in command at New Orleans?

Answer. He was never absent from his office while in command at New Orleans except on duty, which duties consisted in the inspection of camps, fortifications, also founderies and all other Government works about the city, also a thorough inspection of forts and defenses commanding the different entrances to it. On these occasions he took particular pains to examine thoroughly the arms, ammunition, and clothing of the garrison, and pointed out, if any, the deficiencies to the commanding officer of the post. The visit to the founderies, &c., in the city was generally done after dinner, say 4 p. m., when the general could more easily be spared from the office. His time then was entirely devoted to the investigation and to the urging of the completion of public works; this lasted until dark, when he again returned to the office to finish his correspondence or attend to some other business matters, which invariably kept him there until 10 p. m. and often later. The different officers of the staff were also required to be in their respective offices until that hour.

Question. Did you have occasion to observe General Lovell during the engagement of Fort Jackson, when the enemy's fleet passed, and at various times during the evacuation? If so, state what was his demeanor as to calmness, coolness, and decision.

Answer. As on almost all other occasions, I accompanied the general to the forts below the city. He left New Orleans the evening previous to the passage of the enemy's gunboats and arrived there probably half an hour before the attempt was made. He had gone down for the express purpose of trying to have the position of the Louisiana changed; also to verify for himself the amount of damage done to Fort Jackson by the enemy's shells. We observed, as we arrived, that the fort was being slowly shelled by the enemy's mortar fleet, when all of a sudden the number seemed to increase, and Forts Jackson and Saint Philip both opened fire. It was not until one of the Federal vessels, the Varuna, had got close by us that General Lovell ordered the captain of the packet boat we were on, the Doublon, to steam up the river as fast as possible, so as to get out of the reach of the gunboat that was pursuing us. While under the fire of that boat, which was gaining on us, Captain Kennon engaged and sunk her. General Lovell was coolly delivering orders to some of the river-defense fleet, which, to his great contempt, seemed to be getting out of the enemy's way. He ordered them to go back and fight him. After reaching about 30 miles from the city, the general, knowing that by taking a carriage he could get to the city sooner, concluded to proceed by land; his presence he knew would be needed there as soon as possible during the excitement of this sad news. I continued with some of the other members of the staff on the boat, again joining the general that afternoon. I found him engaged in giving orders in reference to the removal of Government property; also in giving orders for what defense could be made at Chalmette in case the enemy should make his appearance. I noticed no change in his manner, decision, or coolness. I was with him pretty near the whole of the next day (April 26), with the only exception of the moments that I was conveying his orders. And again I must say he gave the orders of the evacuation with the same coolness, determination, and precision that characterized his demeanor during the whole time. When it was found that the fortifications at Chalmette could not check the enemy's fleet, orders were immediately given by him to the different commands to proceed to the New Orleans and Jackson Railroad, where the cars were held in readiness to remove them from the city in case of need. Due notice was also given to the boats remaining in the river and employed in removing Government property, he himself leaving the city in the last train. General Lovell subsequently returned to the city on the 28th, but I did not accompany him.

Major-General LOVELL was then recalled and examined.

By the JUDGE-ADVOCATE:

Question. In your testimony you speak of many deficiencies in Department No. 1 which are not mentioned in your correspondence with the War Department. Why were you silent as to these points?

Answer. I did not particularize all the deficiencies in my letters to the War Department because before I assumed command, and while in Richmond, I learned from conversations with the Secretary of War and heads of bureaus, in substance, that, as the Department and its various bureaus had been but lately set on foot, there were in almost all the kinds of material required for war purposes many deficiencies, not only in the materials, but in the mechanical means and appliances for erecting them; and I was informed that my predecessor had made persistent appeals for things which as yet the Department had no means of furnishing, which was a source of some annoyance, and I stated that I should make the most of the means at my disposal, without bothering the Department about deficiencies in which I knew they could not help me. When, therefore, I ascertained these deficiencies I set to work as rapidly as possible to supply them, and was in a fair way to make my department self-sustaining when New Orleans fell, both as to guns, powder, munitions of war, and supplies of all kinds.

By the COURT:

Question. Was not the impression created upon the pubic mind that you had at New Orleans shortly before its fall a force of 20,000 or 25,000 men? If so, state, if you can, by whom it was created and for what purpose.

Answer. In February, 1862, Governor Moore and his major-general of militia, Lewis, proposed a grand turn-out of all the militia in the city, saying that they could parade about 25,000 men, and asked my opinion as to the policy of such a display. I asked how many of them could be furnished with arms of any description, even pistols and sabers, to which they replied about 5,000 or 6,000. I then objected strongly to parading 18,000 or 20,000 men without a weapon as an uncalled-for display of weakness. They replied that the papers, in giving an account of it, need not speak of their arms and equipment, but would mention their numbers. I said we would only deceive our own people, as the enemy had, without a doubt, spies among us, who would give him correct information. A parade was, nevertheless, made of 25,000 or 26,000 men, and the adjutant-general of Louisiana, at my request, furnished me a return of all those in any manner armed, who numbered about 6,000 men. This was before the troops were sent to Beauregard. The next morning all the papers gave glowing accounts of the magnificent parade of 25,000 men that occurred on the day previous. This was doubtless the origin of the impression. Had I had 25,000 additional infantry I should have still evacuated the city, as numbers would only have added to the slaughter. They could have inflicted no damage to gunboats anchored off the city, while they themselves would have been within point-blank range.

General Lovell then submitted to the court the following copies of letters from the official letter-book and telegram-book of Department No. 1, already in evidence, viz: A letter from Colonel Gorgas, Chief of Ordnance, on the subject of establishing a laboratory at New Orleans, and disapproving the same; appended as document No. 26. A letter to Gov. T. O. Moore, suggesting the seizure and fitting up of two ocean steamers for the defense of New Orleans; appended as document No. 27. A letter to Gov. T. O. Moore, calling for militia to the number of 10,000 men for defense; appended as document No. 28. Two letters from General R. E. Lee, relative to the evacuation of New Orleans by

General Lovell and his occupation of Vicksburg; appended as documents Nos. 29 and 30. A telegram and his reply to Governor Pettus, of Mississippi, relative to sending heavy guns to Vicksburg; appended as document No. 31. A letter of General Randolph, Secretary of War, omitted in the printed correspondence relative to New Orleans; appended as document No. 32.

The said letters and telegrams were admitted by the judge-advocate to be correct copies and were read to the court.

The deposition of W. L. LANIER was then read to the court.

By Maj. Gen. M. LOVELL:

Question. What position did you hold in New Orleans at and for some months prior to its evacuation, in April, 1862?

Answer. I was post commissary.

Question. Did you, under orders of General Lovell, make an examination and estimate, a short time before the evacuation, of the amount of provisions in the city at that time available for the support of the population? If so, please state how many days' provisions were on hand at the time of the evacuation.

Answer. I was ordered by General Lovell to ascertain, as near as possible, the amount of provisions in the city not belonging to the Government for the support of the population. I did so, and reported supplies for from sixteen to twenty days' subsistence.

Question. Was the great bulk of the commissary stores in your charge saved at the time of the evacuation? Did any amount thereof that was fit for issue fall into the hands of the enemy? Were any such destroyed?

Answer. It was. No stores fit for issue fell into the hands of the enemy, as all sound stores left in the city, by order of General Smith, during the absence of General Lovell at Fort Jackson, the day previous to the evacuation, were turned over to the Committee of Safety, for sale to the citizens, proceeds of which to be placed to the credit of the Government, except fifty hogsheads of sugar, which had been sent to the New Orleans and Jackson Railroad depot some days before the evacuation, for shipment to Summit, Miss., where General Lovell had ordered me to establish a depot for stores some time previous. This sugar, on the evening of the evacuation, as I learn, was either destroyed or taken by the mob from said depot.

Cross-examination by the JUDGE-ADVOCATE:

Question. Were any preparations made by you, under orders of General Lovell, for supplying the people of New Orleans with provisions in the event of a siege?

Answer. None that I remember.

Question. Were you present during the evacuation of New Orleans? If so, state the manner in which it was conducted; and if you saw General Lovell during that period state whether or not he was self-possessed and seemingly equal to the emergency.

Answer. I was in the city until about 2 o'clock of the day of the evacuation. I did not see General Lovell more than once during the day, and then only a very short time. He seemed to be a good deal excited.

The court adjourned to meet at 12 m. the 24th instant.

RICHMOND, VA., *June* 24, 1863—12 m.

The court met pursuant to adjournment.

Present, all the members of the court and the judge-advocate.

To enable the judge-advocate to prepare a summary of the evidence the court adjourned until 11 a. m. the 28th instant.

RICHMOND, VA., *June* 28, 1863—11 a. m.

The court met pursuant to adjournment.

Present, all the members of the court and the judge-advocate.

The evidence adduced in this investigation was then read over to the court by the judge-advocate.

The court adjourned to meet at 11 a. m. to-morrow.

RICHMOND, VA., *June* 29, 1863—11 a. m.

The court deliberated upon the evidence in this case.

The court received notice from the Adjutant-General (General S. Cooper) to continue in session until the deposition of A. D. Kelley arrived.

The court then adjourned to meet at 11 a. m. July 9, 1863.

RICHMOND, VA., *July* 9, 1863—11 a. m.

The court met pursuant to adjournment.

Present, all the members of the court and the judge-advocate.

The deposition of A. D. Kelley is hereto appended, and marked document A.*

The court, having maturely considered the evidenced adduced, submits the following report of facts and opinion thereon. (Report of the following furnished Secretary of State October 17, 1863:)

REPORT OF FACTS.

Department No. 1 is intersected by numerous streams, which in high water afford ten or twelve different approaches to New Orleans, and render its defense difficult without a strong naval force. When General Lovell assumed command of the department, on October 18, 1861, but little had been done in constructing the land defenses of New Orleans. Two lines of intrenchments had been laid off, but were wholly incomplete, without platforms, guns, magazines, ammunition, and all necessary implements and equipments. Forts Jackson, Saint Philip, Pike, Macomb, and Livingston were in great need of repair, the two first named in better condition than the others, but all of them deficient in armament, requiring an increase in the number and caliber of their guns. There was also needed at these works ammunition and all the implements necessary to the use of heavy guns. The keels of two iron-clad gunboats had been recently laid. Under the direction of General Lovell the forts mentioned were strengthened and the number and caliber of guns composing their armament increased. An exterior line passing through the forts, with earthworks to defend the various water approaches, and an interior line, embracing New Orleans and Algiers, designed chiefly to repel attacks by land, were pressed to completion. The best guns that could be had were mounted upon these lines, magazines constructed, and ammunition and all the necessary implements supplied. In a word, everything was done that could be to render them first-class works of their kind. The various water approaches were obstructed by piling, &c., and launches prepared and put in service to protect several of them from navigation by the enemy.

An immense raft was constructed in December, 1861, to serve as an obstruction in the Mississippi River between Forts Jackson and Saint Philip, but owing to the strong current of that river in its highest stages and the great accumulation of drift it was swept away in the latter part

*Found as document No. 2.

of February following. From its fragments and such other material as could be obtained it was attempted, but without success, to make another effectual obstruction.

Mills were erected for the manufacture of powder, considerable quantities of which article were turned out, and much that had been received at New Orleans in a damaged condition was reworked and made fit for use. At the time of the fall of the city more than one establishment was ready for the manufacture of heavy guns, which until then had been impracticable for the want of suitable furnaces.

Such was the condition of the department when the enemy, on April 18, 1862, opened fire upon Fort Jackson from a fleet of twenty-one mortar boats. The bombardment continued, with but slight intermission, until the morning of April 24, when, between 3 and 4 o'clock, the enemy's vessels of war and gunboats succeeded in passing the forts. One of his vessels was sunk; his loss in killed and wounded is not known. Our loss in the fight and during the bombardment did not exceed, at the forts, more than 50 in killed and wounded. Owing to the high stage of water, the river being higher than it had been before for twenty-five years, the efforts to employ sharpshooters outside the forts proved ineffectual. In the forts the water rose to a height of from 12 to 18 inches, causing great discomfort to the garrisons, and requiring the men in Fort Jackson to work day and night to prevent the magazines from being flooded. The damage done by the enemy had also to be repaired under heavy and incessant fire, which added much to the suffering of the men. While the bombardment continued, and when the enemy were making the passage of the forts, with a fleet consisting of five steam sloops of war and eight or nine gunboats, the men fought with great courage and determination; but at midnight on April 27 it was discovered that they were in open mutiny at Fort Jackson. This mutinous spirit pervaded the entire garrison at Fort Jackson, except the Saint Mary's Cannoneers. It was also soon discovered that the garrison of Fort Saint Philip was similarly affected. The officers, however, by their coolness managed to hold the men in check until the morning of April 28, when the forts were surrendered to the enemy upon liberal terms. For this strange revolt no cause could be ascertained. A large part of the enemy's fleet, after passing the forts, proceeded up the river. At Chalmette and from the opposite bank its farther advance was resisted by two batteries of six guns each, until their ammunition was exhausted, but with little or no effect, the enemy having nearly as many vessels of war and gunboats as we had guns in position at that point. More than half of the ammunition designed for these batteries had been given to the iron-clad steamer Louisiana. Six vessels of the river-defense fleet were at the forts at the time they were passed, but rendered no assistance in checking the enemy.

To meet this attack it is shown that General Lovell's plan was to concentrate as many heavy guns as possible at the forts, and there, by obstructions, to detain the enemy's vessels under their fire, as well as the fire of such defenses afloat as we could bring to bear.

The country between the forts and New Orleans is of a character most unfavorable for the construction of batteries, the banks of the river in its highest stages being below the surface of the water, and only protected from inundation by levees, which might easily be destroyed by an enemy. It also shows that there were no suitable guns in Department No. 1 for such batteries, and no infantry forces adequate for their protection against a land attack.

On the morning of April 25 several of the enemy's gunboats anchored off New Orleans, about which time General Lovell gave up the city to the control of the municipal authorities, by whom, on April 29, it was surrendered to the enemy.

It is shown that but little or no provision was made for an evacuation before the passage of the forts. After that event the work of removing supplies was prosecuted with energy, and a vast amount of property belonging to the Confederate and State Governments, as well as that of private individuals, was saved.

Forts Pike and Macomb were evacuated by the order of Colonel Fuller, and without the knowledge or approval of General Lovell, on the morning of April 27. Brig. Gen. M. L. Smith, commanding the forces at the McGehee and Chalmette lines, numbering about 1,000 infantry and five companies of artillery, received no orders as to their removal, although he and General Lovell were together on the afternoon of April 24. The troops withdrawn from New Orleans by General Lovell did not exceed 4,000 in number, and, with slight exceptions, were raw levies, belonging to the militia and organizations for local defense. A large proportion of this force was unfitted for service in the field. In their movement from the city there was no greater confusion manifested than is usual among such bodies of men. The best troops in Department No. 1 had been sent to re-enforce General A. S. Johnston after the fall of Fort Donelson. General Lovell had also sent many supplies from his department to the army of that general. Between General Lovell and the naval officers on duty in Department No. 1 there existed good feeling and a desire to co-operate for the public defense. General Lovell often supplied the Navy with guns and ammunition. During the bombardment it was designed by Generals Lovell and Duncan that the Louisiana should be placed in a position from which they thought she could enfilade and drive off the mortar fleet of the enemy, but this request was not complied with—Capt. J. K. Mitchell, commanding the defenses afloat, alleging, in reply, that the Louisiana was without motive power, but in the position indicated her guns could not be given sufficient elevation to reach the enemy, while she would be in full range of his mortar fleet, and that her top deck was flat and vulnerable. These statements are proven to be true. He also added, as his opinion, sustained by a council of naval officers, that the desired movement would result in the destruction of the vessel by the enemy. The guard boats and fire rafts were not used to any advantage, if at all, on the night preceding the passage of the forts. General Lovell left New Orleans for Camp Moore on April 25, but returned on the 28th, and proposed to bring back his command to the city if the authorities would incur the risk of a bombardment, which he thought might and would ensue if the city were occupied by his troops. The proof shows that General Lovell's demeanor was cool and self-possessed during the evacuation.

OPINION OF THE COURT.*

1st. As against a land attack by any force the enemy could probably bring, the interior line of fortifications, as adopted and completed by Major-General Lovell, was a sufficient defense of the city of New Orleans, but his ability to hold that line against such an attack was greatly impaired by the withdrawal from him by superior authority of nearly all his effective troops.

2d. The exterior line, as adopted and improved by him, was well devised, and rendered as strong as the means at his command allowed.

*Published, without comment, in G. O., No. 152, A. and I. G. O., Nov. 24, 1863.

3d. Until the iron-clad gunboats Louisiana and Mississippi should be ready for service, it was indispensably necessary to obstruct the navigation of the Mississippi River between Forts Jackson and Saint Philip. The raft completed under General Lovell's direction was adequate for the purpose while in position, but it was swept away, and left the river unimpeded, either by reason of some error in its construction or neglect in preventing the accumulation of drift, or because of insuperable mechanical difficulties, as to which this court feels unprepared to give an opinion. General Lovell communicated to the Government no opinion as to the insecurity of the raft nor any apprehension that it might be swept away, nor did he immediately make known that fact when it occurred. In this it is considered that he was remiss in his duty.

4th. When the raft was swept away, General Lovell, with great energy, immediately endeavored to replace it, and partially succeeded, but, without fault on his part, this last obstruction was broken by the carelessness of vessels of the river-defense fleet colliding with it and by fire rafts drifting against it, and by the failure of the guard boats to protect it against night expeditions of the enemy.

5th. The non-completion of the iron-clad gunboats Louisiana and Mississippi made it impossible for the Navy to co-operate efficiently with General Lovell.

6th. The so-called river-defense fleet was wholly useless as a means of resistance to the enemy, for which General Lovell was in nowise responsible.

7th. Under the existing circumstances the passage of the forts by the enemy's fleet could not have been prevented by General Lovell with any means under his control, and, the forts being passed, the fall of New Orleans was inevitable and its evacuation a military necessity.

8th. When the first raft was broken, and the danger of New Orleans thus became imminent, all necessary preparations should have been made for removing the public and private property available for military uses, and when the second obstruction was swept away the removal of such property should have been commenced immediately. The failure to take these timely steps caused the losses of property that occurred, but there was comparatively little property lost for which General Lovell was responsible.

9th. The failure of General Lovell to give proper orders to Brig. Gen. M. L. Smith for the retirement of his command from Chalmette is not sufficiently explained, and is therefore regarded a serious error.

10th. The proposition of General Lovell to return to New Orleans with his command was not demanded by his duty as a soldier, involving, as it did, the useless sacrifice of himself and his troops, though it explains itself upon the ground of sympathy for the population and a natural sensitiveness to their reproaches.

11th. General Lovell displayed great energy and an untiring industry in performing his duties. His conduct was marked by all the coolness and self-possession due to the circumstances and his position, and he evinced a high capacity for command and the clearest foresight in many of his measures for the defense of New Orleans.

The court respectfully reports that its assembly was delayed by the failure of its president to receive his orders in due time, and that its session was protracted by the taking of testimony, under the order of the War Department, as to the conduct of naval officers on duty in Department No. 1. This order was rescinded, thus rendering irrelevant and useless much of the labor of the court. The testimony referred to, although appearing of record, was not considered by the court in determining its findings and opinion.

There being no further business before them, the court adjourned *sine die.*

T. C. HINDMAN,
Major-General and President of Court.
L. R. PAGE,
Major, Adjt. Gen.'s Dept., Judge-Advocate and Recorder.

RICHMOND, VA., *July* 13, 1863.

General S. COOPER,
Adjutant and Inspector General, Richmond, Va.:

GENERAL: I have the honor herewith to transmit the record of proceedings of the court of inquiry convened to examine into the facts and circumstances attending the capture of New Orleans, &c., and accompanying documents.

I have the honor to be, your obedient servant,

L. R. PAGE,
Major, Adjt. Gen.'s Dept., Judge-Advocate and Recorder.

APPENDIX.

Documents 1 *to* 32, *and deposition of A. D. Kelley, accompanying and referred to in record of the Court of Inquiry on the capture of New Orleans.*

[Document No. 1.]

SPECIAL ORDERS, No. 173. } ADJT. AND INSP. GENERAL'S OFFICE, *Richmond, Va., October* 7, 1861.

* * * * * * *

VIII. Maj. Gen. Mansfield Lovell, Provisional Army, will proceed to New Orleans, La., and relieve Maj. Gen. D. E. Twiggs, Provisional Army, in command of Department No. 1.

* * * * * * *

By command of the Secretary of War:

JNO. WITHERS,
Assistant Adjutant-General.

[Document No. 2.]

RICHMOND, VA., *June* 17, 1863.

Interrogations to be propounded to A. D. Kelley, a citizen, at Columbia, S. C., which, with the answers thereto, will be read as evidence before the Court of Inquiry convened pursuant to paragraph XXI, Special Orders, No. 41 (current series), Adjutant and Inspector General's Office, now in this city.

By the JUDGE-ADVOCATE:

Question. Where were you residing from October, 1861, to May, 1862, and what was your occupation during that time?

Question. State whether or not you were a member of the Safety Committee of New Orleans; and, if yea, what duties were devolved upon you as such.

Question. State whether or not you have had conversations, official or otherwise, with General Lovell touching the defenses of New Orleans; if yea, state the substance of such conversations, when they occurred, and in whose presence.

Question. State all you may know, of your own knowledge, touching the defense, fall, and evacuation of New Orleans.

Cross-examination by Maj. Gen. M. LOVELL:

Question. Were the conversations between yourself and General Lovell official or casual private conversations? If both, state what information you derived from official and what you inferred from private conversations.

(I object to the third question asked by the judge-advocate, asking for conversations other than official between General Lovell and Mr. A. D. Kelley, as a member of the Safety Committee. A general officer in command of a department is frequently asked officious questions by very respectable citizens in relation to public affairs, to which he may give inaccurate or incorrect replies, either as a matter of policy or to avoid making known matters which he wishes kept secret. Such answers, if spread upon the record as testimony, might unjustly produce a prejudicial effect. I claim that the witness should first establish the fact of the existence of such relations between himself and the commanding general as to entitle him to his confidence, and not give casual conversations as testimony bearing upon his official conduct of affairs.

M. LOVELL.)

The answer of A. D. Kelley to the interrogations propounded to him by L. R. Page, major, &c., and judge-advocate, in the case of Maj. Gen. M. Lovell, on trial in Richmond, and which interrogations were forwarded in a letter dated June 17, 1863.

1st question. Where were you residing from October, 1861, to May, 1862, and what was your occupation during that time?

Answer. I resided in New Orleans from October 1, 1861, to April, 1862. My occupation was that of commission merchant, though during that time was much and earnestly engaged or occupied in all efforts or aid that I could give for the protection of New Orleans.

2d question. State whether or not you were a member of the Safety Committee of New Orleans; and, if yea, what duties where devolved upon you as such.

Answer. I was a member of the Safety Committee of New Orleans, which committee was recognized by the citizens and the city authorities. The duties of said committee were to confer with the military, naval, and city authorities in all matters in relation to the defense of the city, and to tender and appropriate any money from the city that might be needed in promoting the safety and defense of New Orleans.

3d question. State whether or not you have had conversations, official or otherwise, with General Lovell concerning the defense of New Orleans; if yea, state the substance of such conversations, when they occurred, and in whose presence.

4th question. State all that you may know, of your own knowledge, touching the defense, fall, and evacuation of New Orleans.

Answer to 3d and 4th questions. By direction of the Safety Committee, I, with Dr. G. W. Campbell and two other members, whose names I do not recollect now, were appointed and instructed by the Safety Committee to confer with the military and naval authorities about the defenses, and to tender all financial aid that might be required. We conferred with General Lovell; tendered to him all needful financial aid, and asked many questions about his plans of defense in certain places; also about his supply of arms, ammunition, &c. He replied explicitly to some of the minor questions, but declined replying to others, stating that the commanding general deemed it best not to give information to any one in certain matters. Some of the members appeared satisfied with the interview, though I was not, and so expressed myself to the other members, and in two or three days afterwards I sought another interview with General Lovell alone at his office, and promptly stated that I came to discuss more fully our city defenses, and at the same time I renewed the assurance that the city would furnish any money that he might need in making any defenses for the city. I renewed this assurance, because General Lovell had the day before complained much that his draft on the city was not promptly paid, which occurred because there was some officer in the city treasury department who was not aware of General Lovell's authority to draw such a draft when it was presented to him. During this interview with General Lovell I discussed many matters about the plan and the prospect of the successful defense of the city. In this discussion some of my inquiries were not answered, as he did not consider it proper for the commanding general to do so. In some of these positions he was perhaps correct; but the effect upon my mind during and after the discussion was that, if a vigorous attack was made by the enemy and the forts passed near the mouth of the river, I did not believe that the city would be held by our forces. This impression was confirmed after an interview with the naval commander. These views depressed me much, and I communicated my fears not only to my family, but to several friends, and we most decidedly condemned the administration for sending such an officer as General Lovell to defend New Orleans, the most important point in the Confederacy, when the Government had in the field two such generals as Beauregard and Bragg, both citizens of Louisiana. When the enemy commenced the attack on the forts I most anxiously watched the prospect. As I had before feared, I found that our reliance was altogether upon a successful defense at the forts, though I had been confident that a good general, with such resources as had been at the command of General Lovell, could and would have defended the city from the extensive and expensive fortifications a few miles below the city and on both sides of the river. I could not see or hear of any proper arrangements for defense at that point, and as our defense therefore was alone at the forts, I did expect to see the commanding general go promptly to that point and there see that all possible defense was made. Although the attack lasted several days, General Lovell made no effort to go to the forts until about the time the enemy's fleet passed them. I had many unofficial conversations with General Lovell, and none of them inspired me with confidence in the safety of New Orleans, if vigorously attacked by the enemy.

A. D. KELLEY.

MAYOR'S OFFICE,
Columbia, S. C., July 2, 1862.

Personally appeared before me A. D. Kelley, and made oath that the foregoing statements are facts, according to the best of his knowledge.

T. J. GOODWYN,
Magistrate ex officio.

[Document No. 3.]

RICHMOND, VA., *October* 17, 1861.

General MANSFIELD LOVELL:

SIR: I am induced by the impression made on the mind of the Secretary of War, in a conversation which you had with him just before your departure, to write to you on the subject of your relations to the officers of the Navy. When you mentioned the subject to me I supposed you referred to the case provided for in the sixty-first and sixty-second articles of war, as enacted by the Congress of the Confederate States; therefore it was that I read and commented on those articles, particularly the sixty-second.

The fleet maintained at the port of New Orleans and the vicinity is not a part of your command; and the purposes for which it is sent there or removed from there are communicated in orders and letters of a Department with which you have no direct communication. It must, therefore, be obvious to you that you could not assume command of these officers and vessels, coming within the limits of your geographical department, but not placed on duty with you, without serious detriment to discipline and probable injury to the public service. To promote harmony, to secure co-operation, and increase the power for public defense it will often be desirable that each arm should know the objects and means of the other. To this end it is hoped that there will be unrestrained intercourse and cordial fraternization.

Very respectfully, yours,

JEFFERSON DAVIS.

[Document No. 4.]

DEPARTMENT OF STATE,
Richmond, Va., January 19, 1863.

Maj. Gen. MANSFIELD LOVELL:

SIR: I state, at your request, that, while I was Secretary of War, in giving you orders to take charge of the defense of the Department of Louisiana, you requested authority to control the operations of the officers of the Navy within the department, and to order such dispositions of naval forces as you might deem best to aid in defense. I answered you that your request could not be granted; that the Department of War could assume no control over naval operations, which were confided by law to a distinct Department, and that you must rely for securing the aid of naval forces on endeavoring to establish concert of action through mutual understanding between yourself and the naval officer highest in rank in your department.

Your obedient servant,

J. P. BENJAMIN,
Secretary of State.

[Document No. 5.—By telegraph.]

RICHMOND, VA., *December* 17, 1861.

General MANSFIELD LOVELL:

The Secretary of War desires you to send seventeen 32-pounder guns, if you can spare them, to General A. S. Johnston.

J. GORGAS.

[Document No. 6.—By telegraph.]

RICHMOND, VA., *December* 17, 1861.

General MANSFIELD LOVELL:

Please send three 32 pounder guns to General Lee, at Charleston, S. C. No carriages required.

J. GORGAS.

[Document No. 7.—By telegraph.]

RICHMOND, VA., *January* 1, 1862.

General MANSFIELD LOVELL:

Please send two large 32-pounder navy guns for General A. S. Johnston, care of Lieut. M. H. Wright, ordnance officer, Nashville, Tenn.

L. GIBBON,
Captain (*for Chief of Ordnance*).

[Document No. 13.]

NEW ORLEANS, LA., *April* 11, 1862.

General RANDOLPH,
Secretary of War, Richmond, Va.:

With forty vessels in the lower river, please protest, in my name, against sending the Louisiana up the river. If she must go, let them leave her two 7-inch rifles, now at Fort Jackson. She has one on board, besides other heavy guns; all she can use in the upper river to advantage. We have not now as many guns of heavy caliber as at Mobile.*

M. LOVELL.

[Document No. 14.]

HEADQUARTERS DEPARTMENT NO. 1,
New Orleans, La., March 21, 1862.

General SAMUEL JONES,
Mobile, Ala.:

DEAR GENERAL: Learning that most of the guns at Pensacola were to be removed, I wrote to Bragg, and learned that he had requested some to be sent here. Major Duncan then went after them, and only succeeded in getting one 10-inch columbiad. There is not another one in this whole department to defend this the most important city on the great water communication from the Gulf to the Ohio River. The enemy is collecting his ships at the mouth of the river to combine his attack with the great effort from above, yet all the heavy guns are kept at places of minor importance. I shall send Major Duncan over again, and beg that you will give him every 10-inch columbiad and 10-inch sea-coast mortar that you can possibly spare. Time is passing rapidly. More than a dozen ships of war are at the mouth of the river, of which seven are inside the bar. If you can spare a dozen 10 inch columbiads, do let us have them. Beauregard telegraphed me that the heavy guns would be sent here. Duncan only got two, one of which he says you took from him. Give us a share. What is Mobile worth with the Mississippi in the hands of the enemy?

Yours, very truly,

M. LOVELL,
Major-General, C. S. Army.

[Document No. 15.]

HEADQUARTERS DEPARTMENT NO. 1,
New Orleans, La., March 7, 1862.

General G. T. BEAUREGARD,
Jackson, Tenn.:

DEAR GENERAL: I received your notes of February 24 and March 3. Have ordered the additional flags you wish. I have pushed forward to your support every available man. Seven companies of the Crescent Regiment left here yesterday; the remainder will leave on Saturday with the Washington Artillery. I shall also send you the Twentieth Regiment and the Orleans Artillery, with a battalion from that corps; Gibson's and Vaiden artillery has already been sent. You will have in all from me ten infantry regiments and four batteries of artillery. Full 40 rounds of ammunition (in some instances 100) have been furnished to every description of troops sent on. I shall have to hold up now and look out a little for New Orleans. I asked Bragg for some 10-inch guns, but he had none to spare. New Orleans has inferior caliber to Mobile, Pensacola, and even Galveston. People send here for everything, and I have literally stripped the department, but never get anything in return that I ask for. I wrote and urged General Polk to send me the anchors and chains from Columbus to obstruct the river at the forts below the city, but he never would send them, and finally

* See answer, of same date, in "Correspondence, etc.—Confederate," p. 873.

abandoned them at Columbus. I intend hereafter to hold on to what I have until I feel perfectly secure. If you can put me in the way of getting any large guns, chains, or anchors, I beg you will do so. In a few days we hope to be able to cast 10-inch columbiads and sea-coast mortars.

In haste, yours, truly,

M. LOVELL.

[Document No. 16.]

HEADQUARTERS DEPARTMENT NO. 1,
New Orleans, La., March 8, 1862.

General G. T. BEAUREGARD,
Jackson, Tenn.:

DEAR GENERAL: The current and drift have finally got the upper hand of my raft between Saint Philip and Jackson. This, taken in connection with the facts that Captain Hollins has taken up the river every vessel that mounts a gun, and that General Polk declined to ship me the chains and anchors at Columbus, which would have saved my raft, compels a new disposition as to the fourteen vessels of Montgomery's expedition. They will not be ready under ten days, but I will send up eight of them, with circles laid for one 32-pounder each, provided you can supply the guns up there. I cannot, under the circumstances, send a gun out of this department. The remaining six vessels I will have to keep here until I ascertain whether I shall be able to fix an obstruction in the river at Fort Jackson. Their fleet in the Gulf is much more formidable than that above, and the river is now open to them if they pass the lower forts. You will therefore see the necessity of my retaining every gun and a portion of the vessels until I can bar the river again. I should have to dismount guns from my works to put on these ships, and under the circumstances above set forth you will be able to do that with as little risk as I can. I can send no more ammunition up with men, as we have no caps. Calls are made upon this department from all parts of the Confederacy, but nothing is sent here in the way of materials to make up, and no facilities are given except what I take in opposition to the wishes of heads of bureaus.

Yours, truly,

M. LOVELL,
Major-General, C. S. Army.

[Document No. 17.]

HEADQUARTERS DEPARTMENT NO. 1,
New Orleans, La., March 9, 1862.

Maj. Gen. BRAXTON BRAGG,
Jackson, Tenn.:

MY DEAR GENERAL: I received your dispatch this afternoon, asking me to send up all the small-arm ammunition that I could manufacture. This I have already done. The department has been literally stripped of everything—men, arms, guns, and munitions of war—so much so, that evil-disposed persons do not hesitate to say that I am placing New Orleans in such a condition as to make it an easy prey to the enemy. More than 1,000,000 cartridges have been forwarded in the past few weeks, nearly ten regiments, well armed and equipped, and four batteries of artillery. I have literally nothing more to send, and must cast about to place myself in condition to defend this important position in case the enemy (informed of our situation) should return to attack. I have called upon the governor of the State for the militia, who are coming in slowly with shot-guns, for which I am having ammunition made, but we are out of caps; they were to have been furnished us from Nashville, but none came; nor, in answer to all my calls, has anything of any kind been sent here. Yesterday I sent 10,000 pounds of musket powder to Richmond, which leaves me none to make up, and I have no caps. The powder that came from Cuba is all inferior, and has to be reworked, but I can get no saltpeter; that which comes from Memphis has been sent to Augusta, and if the raw materials are sent elsewhere, the requisitions must be made in the same direction. With a large fleet concentrating on the coast and a force of the enemy collecting at Ship Island it behooves me to commence to make some preparations to defend my own position. In default of any definite information from your part of the country as to your supplies and necessities, I shall be compelled to use my best judgment as to what further can be spared of the supplies that I expect to get together. At this present moment I have nothing to send unless it may be a small amount of musket cartridges. I wrote to Beauregard to-day my reasons for applying everything here to my own use. If you can push some saltpeter here I will try to help you, but you must not rely upon me, as I have deficiencies here to make good before I can send off anything, except upon reasons of the most imperative necessity. Those reasons, if they existed, have been studiously withheld from me thus far.

Very truly, yours,

M. LOVELL,
Major-General, Commanding.

[Document No. 18.]

HEADQUARTERS DEPARTMENT NO. 1,
New Orleans, La., March 21, 1862.

Commander MITCHELL,
Commanding Naval Station:

SIR: The concentration of the enemy's ships of war at the mouth of the river induces me to suggest to you the propriety of putting in position at the forts below the two 7-inch rifled cannon lately received from Richmond by you. The heavy guns from Pensacola have mostly been placed on the river above, where the weight of metal against them is less than we may expect below. When Tift's vessel is ready for service the guns could be returned, if necessary.

Respectfully, your obedient servant,

M. LOVELL,
Major-General, Commanding.

[Document No. 19.]

HEADQUARTERS DEPARTMENT NO. 1,
New Orleans, La., March 30, 1862.

Commander WHITTLE,
Commanding Naval Station:

SIR: I learn that you have four rifled 32-pounder guns, intended for a gunboat not yet completed. As the enemy is collecting in force at the mouth of the river, and may attack at any moment, I should like to get the four guns alluded to to place temporarily on my boats to assist in repelling attack. They will be returned when your vessel is ready.

Respectfully, your obedient servant,

M. LOVELL,
Major-General, Commanding.

[Document No. 20.]

HEADQUARTERS DEPARTMENT NO. 1,
New Orleans, La., April 4, 1862.

Commander WHITTLE,
Commanding Naval Station:

SIR: Would it not be well to place the guns lately arrived for the Navy in position on the floating battery until such time as the Louisiana can be ready to receive them? They would make a formidable addition to the strength of our defenses at the lower forts, and I fear that the Louisiana will not be ready for them in time to take part in the approaching contest.

Respectfully, your obedient servant,

M. LOVELL,
Major-General, Commanding.

[Document No. 21.]

HEADQUARTERS DEPARTMENT NO. 1,
New Orleans, La., April 11, 1862.

Commander WHITTLE,
Commanding Naval Station:

SIR: I have telegraphed General Duncan to send up the 7-inch rifles and three 32-pounder rifles. I regret that these guns have been taken, as in my judgment the safety of this city does not warrant the withdrawal from below of a single gun while so many vessels of war are within the mouth of the river.

Respectfully, your obedient servant,

M. LOVELL,
Major-General, Commanding.

[Document No. 22.]

NEW ORLEANS, LA., *April* 11, 1862.

Major-General LOVELL,
Commanding, &c.:

SIR: I have received your note of this date. You cannot regret more than I do the necessity which compels me to ask the return of the guns loaned you by the Navy, but I am ordered, with emphasis, to send the Louisiana with all dispatch up the river, and these guns are absolutely necessary to arm her partially.

May it not be that the city is in as much danger from above as from below? This opinion, it would seem, is entertained in a high quarter at Richmond; I mean at the Navy Department.

I am, sir, respectfully, your obedient servant,

W. C. WHITTLE.

[Document No. 23.—Copy of telegram.]

NEW ORLEANS, LA., *April* 17, 1862.

General RANDOLPH,
Secretary of War, Richmond, Va.:

After conversation with Commander Whittle we beg that Captain Hollins may be allowed to remain in command afloat, at least until he can strike a fair blow at the enemy, which he is ready to do.

M. LOVELL.

[Document No. 24.]

HEADQUARTERS DEPARTMENT NO. 1,
New Orleans, La., April 17, 1862.

General G. T. BEAUREGARD,
Commanding Army of the Mississippi:

DEAR GENERAL: I telegraphed and subsequently wrote you in reference to fortifying the vicinity of Vicksburg, for the double purpose of protecting the river and giving you a *point-d'appui* for the left of your line in case you are compelled to occupy a position in rear of your present one. I have some twelve or fifteen guns in position above New Orleans, and in case others could be got we might, as soon as the works were finished and the platforms laid, transfer our batteries to that point. There is no engineer officer here to be sent on that duty, or I should have fortified Vicksburg long since. Have you any one in your army who, with the help of a few thousand negroes, could put up the works, and thus, perhaps, delay the enemy until we can finish Tift's iron-clad steam ram? I will give you all the assistance in my power in pushing forward the matter; but with the limited means at my command and the enemy knocking at the door below I cannot give it personal attention. M. L. Smith, now a brigadier-general, is now on duty here with me, organizing troops and attending also to the engineer duties of the department. The subject of fortifying Vicksburg strikes me as of pressing importance, and if you agree with me I will endeavor to push it as much as possible.

Yours, truly,

M. LOVELL,
Major-General, Commanding.

[Document No. 25.]*

[Document No. 26.]

ORDNANCE OFFICE,
Richmond, Va., February 15, 1862.

General MANSFIELD LOVELL,
New Orleans, La.:

GENERAL: I received this morning a letter from Richard Lambert, ordnance officer on your staff, inclosing an estimate for $66,000, copy of which I inclose. We have already one disbursing officer at New Orleans (Maj. M. L. Smith), and it is deemed advisable not to have more than one for the department at the same post. The estimate indicates the intention of erecting a laboratory, shop, &c. This has not been contemplated by the Department.

Very respectfully, your obedient servant,

J. GORGAS,
Lieutenant-Colonel, and Chief of Ordnance.

[Document No. 27.]

HEADQUARTERS DEPARTMENT NO. 1,
New Orleans, La., February 19, 1862.

Gov. THOMAS O. MOORE:

SIR: I would suggest the propriety and necessity of your taking possession of the steamers Charles Morgan, Galveston, and W. H. Webb, or two of them, for the immediate defense of the city, and to be used as

---

* Is a duplicate of report on p. 510.

transports for troops in case the occasion should require it. One gun might be put on each to prevent small parties of the enemy from annoying them with boat howitzers, sent up the river by launches from the shoal water to the eastward.

Respectfully, your obedient servant,

M. LOVELL,
Major-General, Commanding,

[Document No. 28.]

HEADQUARTERS DEPARTMENT NO. 1,
New Orleans, La., February 25, 1862.

His Excellency Gov. THOMAS O. MOORE:

SIR: I have the honor to make requisition upon you for volunteers and militia to the number of 10,000 men, to be placed in camp and held ready for defense at short notice.

Very respectfully, your obedient servant,

M. LOVELL,
Major-General, Commanding.

[Document No. 29.]

HEADQUARTERS,
Richmond, Va., May 8, 1862.

Maj. Gen. MANSFIELD LOVELL,
Commanding, &c., Camp Moore, La.:

GENERAL: Your letter of the 26th ultimo to the Adjutant-General, containing a report of the circumstances attending the fall of New Orleans, is received. The loss of this city is a very severe blow to us, and one that we cannot fail to feel most sensibly, but it is believed that with the means of defense at your disposal you have done all in your power.

Your plan of collecting all the troops you can and taking a position which will enable you to defend the rear of General Beauregard and protect his communications is fully approved, and I regard it as a matter of great moment. You will endeavor to collect as large a force as possible, and collect all the arms that you can procure. The want of arms is very severely felt at this time, and I hope you will spare no efforts to collect all that can be obtained in the hands of the people that can be made serviceable. You will organize and prepare the troops that you may be able to collect, to act most efficiently against the enemy, should he expose himself in any manner, and protect, as far as it is possible, the army of General Beauregard from any movement that may endanger his communications or threaten his rear.

I am, general, very respectfully, your obedient servant,

R. E. LEE,
General.

[Document No. 30.]

HEADQUARTERS,
Richmond, Va., May 24, 1862.

Maj. Gen. MANSFIELD LOVELL,
Commanding, &c., Camp Moore, La.:

GENERAL: I have had the honor to receive your letter of the 11th instant. My reply to your former communication will have made known to you the opinion I entertain of your course in evacuating New Orleans. That opinion is confirmed by the additional particulars contained in your letter just received. After the enemy succeeded in passing the forts it seems there was nothing left for you to do but to withdraw the troops. I think you may confidently rely upon the judgment of intelligent and reflecting men for the justification of your course as soon as the facts, as they actually existed, shall be known. The city being lost, I approve of your purpose to confine the enemy to its limits as closely as possible and to protect the State from his ravages. The means with which you propose to accomplish this seem to be the best that you can now employ, and I must urge you to put them in operation without delay, soliciting bold and judicious partisans who can raise proper corps, and whose appointment, when recommended by you, will be subject to the approval of the President. In the mean time set them vigorously to work. The want of arms is much felt everywhere, and no exertions should be spared to procure all of serviceable kind. I hope to be able to send you 1,000 rifles from a cargo lately arrived at Charleston, should it embrace arms for the Confederacy.

I am, general, very respectfully, your obedient servant,

R. E. LEE,
General.

[Document No. 31.]

CAMP MOORE, LA., *April* 28, 1862.

GOV. JOHN J. PETTUS,
Jackson, Miss.:

Please send cannon from Mobile intended for New Orleans to Vicks burg; also any powder. General Jones says he sent both from Mobile

M. LOVELL.

[Answer.]

JACKSON, MISS., *April* 29, 1862.

General LOVELL:

Five army guns here from Mobile; nine navy guns without carriages. Do you want many guns sent to Vicksburg?

JOHN J. PETTUS.

[Document No. 32.]

HEADQUARTERS DEPARTMENT NO. 1,
New Orleans, La., April 12, 1862.

General GEORGE W. RANDOLPH,
Secretary of War:

SIR: I have the honor to report that we shall in a few days have about 5,000 men in this part of the State enlisted for the war for whom I have no arms. All the troops for the interior lines about the city that I had organized were sent to Corinth, and the defense of those lines left in the hands of a few badly-organized volunteers, very poorly armed. The forces of the enemy at Ship Island and Isle Breton cannot be less than 10,000 or 12,000 men, and I deem it my duty to lay before you the entirely defenseless condition of the city against any attack by land. Should the enemy attempt to land at Bay Saint Louis, and march a column of 12,000 or 15,000 men to Jackson, Miss., he would cut off all communication with Beauregard without the possibility of my preventing it. Learning that a large number of arms had arrived in the country, I telegraphed and wrote at once for them, as I have only about 200, but have received nothing.

The condition of our defenses, so far as regards artillery, has been represented to the Department, yet upon the evacuation of Pensacola the greater portion of the heavy guns were sent to Mobile and other points, and that, too, at a time when the whole mortar fleet of the enemy and twelve steamers were in the river below the forts. I wrote to General Jones, at Mobile, and telegraphed the Department, and received the reply that some of the heavy guns were ordered here. I learn that fourteen 10-inch columbiads were kept at Mobile while three were sent here. Mr. Benjamin also wrote me that 44,000 pounds of powder had been sent from Columbus, but it was depleted on the road to less than half that amount. With powder-mills that have an abundance of sulphur and charcoal and facilities for making 3,000 pounds of powder per day, saltpeter has been sent from Arkansas to Georgia, while Memphis and Corinth were making requisitions on me for powder. Not a pound of saltpeter has been sent here for three months.

I mention these things, not that I am by any means discouraged or disheartened, but to account in some measure for the dissatisfaction that exists among the people here, who, having sent men, arms, and everything they had to Virginia and Tennessee, now find the enemy at their doors, both by land and water, while they can obtain neither heavy guns nor small-arms, which they learn by the papers are being sent to places which certainly are not considered so important as the city of New Orleans and the mouth of the Mississippi. The whole city is in a fever of anxiety about the finishing of the Louisiana and Mississippi, which they consider as their salvation against the fleet below, and I should not regard it as wise to send them above, unless we could place in position at Fort Jackson such a number of guns of heavy caliber as would insure that New Orleans could not be taken by a bold dash. It is scarcely probable that the gunboats of the enemy would come down the river much in advance of their army. Meanwhile we might clear the mouth of the river, and then send the whole fleet above and drive them back to Cairo; but, in any event, we require several more 10-inch guns and at least 4,000 or 5,000 stands of small-arms. I would also earnestly urge the confirmation of Colonel Smith as a brigadier-general. I have but one officer of that rank in the department, which compels me to do a great deal of work that should devolve upon subordinate officers.

Very respectfully, your obedient servant,

M. LOVELL,
Major-General, Commanding.

No. 9.

Message from the President of the Confederate States, transmitting correspondence with the Governor of Louisiana and General Lovell.

RICHMOND, VA., *March* 11, 1863.

To the House of Representatives:

In response to your resolution of the 3d ultimo I herewith transmit for your information a copy of my correspondence, together with that of the Secretaries of War and of the Navy, with the governor of Louisiana and Major-General Lovell, during the period beginning October 25, 1861, and ending with the date of the capture of the city of New Orleans, in reference to the defenses of that city.*

JEFFERSON DAVIS.

---

*Such of the correspondence referred to as does not relate to mere matters of detail or to subjects embraced in the Fourth Series of this publication, will follow, in chronological order, in the "Correspondence, etc.—Confederate," *post.*

[Inclosures.]

WAR DEPARTMENT,
Richmond, Va., February 27, 1863.

To the PRESIDENT OF THE CONFEDERATE STATES:

SIR: I have the honor to submit, under a resolution of the House of Representatives, copies of the correspondence between Major-General Lovell and the War Department, in reference to the defense of New Orleans, from October 25, 1861, to the date of the surrender of that city; also copies of the correspondence on file in this Department between the President and Secretary of War and the governor of Louisiana on the same subject. A copy of General Lovell's report has been already submitted to Congress. It is believed that all the correspondence pertinent to the subject is embraced in the volume now placed before you.

Very respectfully, your obedient servant,

JAMES A. SEDDON,
Secretary of War.

EXECUTIVE DEPARTMENT,
Richmond, Va., February 4, 1863.

To the Hon. SECRETARY OF WAR:

SIR: I am directed by the President to forward for your attention and the proper action the following resolution of the House of Representatives of the 3d instant:

Resolved by the House of Representatives, That the President be requested to furnish this body, if not incompatible with the public interests, with copies of the correspondence between Major-General Lovell and the War Department in reference to the defenses of New Orleans from October 25, 1861, to the date of the surrender of that city; also copies of all correspondence between the President or Secretaries of War and the Navy and the governor of Louisiana on the same subject.

Your obedient servant,

BURTON N. HARRISON,
Private Secretary.

NAVY DEPARTMENT,
Richmond, Va., February 9, 1863.

The PRESIDENT:

SIR: In response to the following resolution, adopted by the House of Representatives on the 3d instant—

Resolved by the House of Representatives, That the President be requested to furnish this body, if not incompatible with the public interests, with copies of the correspondence between Major-General Lovell and the War Department in reference to the defenses of New Orleans from October 25, 1861, to the date of the surrender of that city; also copies of all correspondence between the President or Secretaries of War and the Navy and the governor of Louisiana on the same subject—

I have the honor to state that this Department had no correspondence with the governor of Louisiana in reference to the defenses of New Orleans from October 25, 1861, to the date of the surrender of that city. I transmit, however, copy of a letter addressed to the governor of Louisiana on September 18, 1861,* by the Department, to which no reply was received.

With much respect, your obedient servant,

S. R. MALLORY,
Secretary of the Navy.

---

*Not found.

APRIL 27-MAY 8, 1862.--Evacuation of Fort Quitman, La., by the Confederates, and capture of blockade runner in Bayou Grand Caillou.

Report of Maj. Gen. Mansfield Lovell, C. S. Army.

HEADQUARTERS DEPARTMENT NO. 1.
Jackson, Miss., June 19, 1862.

GENERAL: In reply to your letter of the 10th instant [following], requesting the reasons for evacuating Fort Quitman, on the Bayou Grand Caillou, I have to state that it was a little earthwork, with two smoothbore 32-pounders, established by me to prevent ingress for marauding parties by the enemy in small vessels through the Caillou and other inlets into the northern parishes of Louisiana.

The fall of New Orleans laid open the route to those parishes, and as the troops stationed in the fort were supplied from the city, and were at any moment liable to be taken in the rear and captured by way of the Opelousas Railroad, which was in the enemy's hands, I ordered the guns to be spiked and the garrison (a small company of twelve-months' volunteers) to bring away their small-arms, ammunition, and stores, and to rejoin me at Camp Moore. The enemy did not go down, it is true, for some days, but they could have gone at any hour and any day and taken the men with their arms, which I was anxious to preserve. The order I gave was not obeyed. Instead of joining me at Camp Moore, the men mutinied and disbanded, and both officers and men returned to New Orleans. It would be well, as your correspondent suggests, to punish the officers, but as they are now in New Orleans such a step is impracticable.

A glance at the map which I sent to the Department some months ago will show that after the city fell the little works on the coast must be abandoned, being altogether unnecessary.

The report of the cargo of the vessel and her capture, as in all other instances, is grossly exaggerated.

Some few citizens fired upon two or three Federals; in retaliation a number of them were taken prisoners and threatened with death if they did not produce the parties who had committed the act, but the penalty was not inflicted.

I had no force to protect the people in that district of country, but sent an officer to raise a partisan corps for that purpose, yet the prominent citizens earnestly entreated that the corps should not be raised there unless I could send a large body of troops to protect them from the additional outrages to which they would be subject from the Yankees for having raised such a corps. Having no large force to send, and objections being raised to a small one, I countermanded the order.

The fact is that that part of the country is inhabited by two classes of people—the rich, fearful of their property and not anxious to resist unless supported by an army in every parish; and the poor, miserable mixed-breed, commonly called Dagos or Acadians, on whom there is not the slightest dependence to be placed. I gave authority to several persons to raise partisans there, but they met with no success. When I urged that the bridges over the railroad be destroyed, a parish delegation entreated that it be not done, as it would bring down upon them Yankee vengeance. They would only consent to assist on condition that I should send a large body of troops there. Moreover, if the railroad had been destroyed, the stage of water was such that free access could have been had to Thibodeaux through Bayou La Fourche. I therefore concluded, at the request of many of the most influential citizens, to delay operations until the subsiding water should have deprived the enemy of the means of entering the interior at pleasure.

Had a contrary course been pursued the whole country would have been devastated without a possibility of preventing it. Nine out of every ten persons from that part of the country warmly approved of my decision.

I trust that the Department will not give ear to the many false and absurd rumors that are set afloat by persons who think that there should be an army stationed on every plantation for its protection.

I am satisfied that our present condition is to be attributed in a great measure to the fact that we have followed this plan too much already, dispersing instead of concentrating our troops, and thus rendering them an easy prey to the enemy.

Very respectfully, your obedient servant,

M. LOVELL,
Major-General, Commanding.

Hon. GEORGE W. RANDOLPH,
Secretary of War.

[Indorsements.]

Respectfully submitted to the President for his information.

G. W. RANDOLPH,
Secretary of War.

Read. It might be well to furnish the complainant with a copy of this reply. The abandonment of the fort was a necessary consequence of the fall of New Orleans and the subsequent events. Whether it was possible to save the armament for use elsewhere was a question which the commanding general of course duly considered. As he established the post under the discretionary power conferred on him, the application of his remark about the error of dispersion is not perceived.

J. D.

WAR DEPARTMENT,
Richmond, Va., June 10, 1862.

Maj. Gen. MANSFIELD LOVELL,
Camp Moore, Tangipahoa, La.:

GENERAL: Your attention is respectfully called to the annexed copy of a letter received from a person in Louisiana in regard to the evacuation of the forts at Grand Caillou, and you are requested to report to this Department the facts of the case.

Very respectfully, your obedient servant,

G. W. RANDOLPH,
Secretary of War.

[Inclosure.]

OPELOUSAS, LA., *May* 21, 1862.

President DAVIS:

DEAR SIR: * * * A steamer (name not known) reached Grand Caillou on the night of the 7th, with 350,000 pounds of powder and 4,500 rifles. The Federals, duly informed of it by telegraph, which has not been cut from Terre Bonne to New Orleans, came by the Opelousas Railroad, which has not been interrupted, and took possession of her on the night of the 8th. A party of determined citizens started on the 10th to recapture her. Eight hundred Federals were sent out from New Orleans and secured her, and have sent her to the city. They have taken with them sixteen citizens, four of whom they threaten to hang, declaring they are not prisoners of war, but persons taken in rebellion since the authority of the Union has been restored.

The fort at Grand Caillou had been evacuated on April 27 by order of General Lovell, the guns spiked, and the powder thrown into the bayou. Eleven days after the enemy made their first appearance there. This is the manner in which all our forts (of course I do not include Jackson and Saint Philip) were evacuated. There was not a Yankee near one of them until more than a week after the powder was all destroyed and the interior of the fort burned. Ample time was had to save the guns as well as powder, &c. If for these acts some of the officers are not cashiered or shot, we need not expect either a brave or a disciplined Army. The Navy emulated this conduct of the Army, the fleet in Pontchartrain being run up the bayous and scuttled or burned.*

* * * * * * *

I am, very respectfully, &c.

[The above from Governor Moore. In copy furnished General Lovell his name was omitted.]

MAY 9-12, 1862.—Pensacola, Fla., abandoned by the Confederates and occupied by the Union forces.

REPORTS.

No. 1.—Brig. Gen. Lewis G. Arnold, U. S. Army.

No. 2.—Col. Thomas M. Jones, Twenty-seventh Mississippi Infantry.

No. 1.

Reports of Brig. Gen. Lewis G. Arnold, U. S. Army.

HDQRS. WESTERN DISTRICT, DEPT. OF THE SOUTH,
Pensacola, Fla., May 10, 1862.

MAJOR: I have the honor to report that about 12 o'clock last night it was reported to me that Fort McRee, the navy-yard, Marine Hospital and Barracks, and several other buildings, and two rebel steamboats were on fire, which, being simultaneously ignited, indicated that they had been abandoned by the rebels and purposely fired by them. To prevent the spread of these fires and to disperse these wicked destroyers of property, I opened my batteries with a very happy effect. I directed my aide-de-camp and acting assistant adjutant-general, Lieutenant Jackson, to go on board a small naval schooner lying off the harbor, to run in, and summon the city of Pensacola to surrender, which the mayor did to the extent of his authority, which has been very limited.

Commodore Porter arrived here this morning on board the gunboat Harriet Lane. With his kind assistance in transporting my men across the bay I have been enabled to take military possession of Forts Barrancas and McRee, Barrancas Barracks, and the navy-yard, over which the flag of the Union now waves. Fort Barrancas is very little injured by the fire and Barrancas Barracks not at all. Fort McRee is seriously

* The portions of Governor Moore's letter here omitted relate to events in Louisiana subsequent to May 12, 1862, and will appear in another chapter.

damaged, Marine Hospital destroyed, and several store-houses in the navy-yard were burned.

I am, major, respectfully, your obedient servant,

L. G. ARNOLD,
Brigadier-General, U. S. Volunteers, Commanding.

Maj. CHARLES G. HALPINE,
Assistant Adjutant-General, U. S. Vols., Dept. of the South.

HDQRS. WESTERN DISTRICT, DEPT. OF THE SOUTH,
Pensacola, Fla., May 15, 1862.

MAJOR: I have the honor to report that, with a portion of my command (1,000 strong), I took military possession of Pensacola on the 12th instant.

The march from Fort Barrancas was uninterrupted, excepting that the vedettes of some rebel cavalry that were hovering around the city fired two shots at my advanced guard. I had the troops formed in square around the flag-staff in the center of the plaza, and raised the flag of the United States amid the cheers of the soldiers, mingled with those of many citizens.

I take pleasure in adding that the United States schooner M. A. Wood, Anthony Chase master (U. S. Navy), commanding, was the first vessel that had the honor to run into the harbor of Pensacola since the attack on Sumter. He with his officers and crew participated with much spirit in reeving new halyards on the flag-staff and in raising the flag.

Capt. David D. Porter, U. S. Navy, ordered the sloop-of-war Vincennes from Mobile Bay to Pensacola. She arrived off the city a short time after I had entered it with my command, where she now lies.

The citizens seem orderly and quiet, and the acting mayor, Brosenham, zealous and apparently loyal. I have had posted up at different points of the city the inclosed circular,* which I considered necessary and proper to promulgate for the information of all good and loyal citizens.

A stronger force is very necessary here to guard the city and my new line from Pensacola to Fort McRee, a distance of 10 miles. A regiment of cavalry should be ordered here immediately for scouting and picket service, and to capture or drive to their homes the irregular cavalry in this vicinity, and to enable me to carry on other important military operations that I have in view. I have neither horses, mules, nor transportation of any kind for this new business; scarcely sufficient mules and carts for the wants of Fort Pickens, where my depot of supplies is established. My small force in its new position—very different from that on Santa Rosa Island, within striking distance of Mobile and Pollard, which place I understand they are fortifying and occupy in force—might invite an attack; all of which makes it important that re-enforcements should be sent here immediately.

The steam propeller General Meigs has just arrived for service in this district, which facilitates very much keeping up communications with Forts Barrancas and Pickens and my depot of supplies on Santa Rosa Island.

I am, major, very respectfully, your obedient servant,

L. G. ARNOLD,
Brigadier-General, U. S. Volunteers, Commanding.

Maj. CHARLES G. HALPINE,
Assistant Adjutant-General, Department of the South.

---

*Not found.

No. 2.

Reports of Col. Thomas M. Jones, Twenty-seventh Mississippi Infantry.

MOBILE, ALA., *May* 14, 1862.

SIR: In accordance with your instructions I have the honor respectfully to tender the following report of my evacuation of the forts, navy-yard, and position at and near Pensacola, Fla.:

On being placed in command of that place by Brig. Gen. Samuel Jones, March 9 last, his instructions were to move, as fast as my transportation would allow, the machinery and other valuable property from the navy-yard. This was kept up steadily until the night of the evacuation.

On receiving information that the enemy's gunboats had succeeded in passing the forts below New Orleans with their powerful batteries and splendid equipments, I came to the conclusion that, with my limited means of defense, reduced as I have been by the withdrawal of nearly all my heavy guns and ammunition, I could not hold them in check or make even a respectable show of resistance. I therefore determined, upon my own judgment, to commence immediately the removal of the balance of my heavy guns and their ammunition, and dispatched to you for your approval, which was answered by one advising me to continue doing so. On receipt of General Lee's written instructions on the subject I pushed on the work with renewed vigor, and night and day kept up the removal of guns and valuable property.

On the afternoon of the 7th instant I received a dispatch from your adjutant-general stating that there were a number of mortar and gunboats off Fort Morgan, and that the fort had fired ten shots at them. Conceiving that the contingency named in General Lee's instructions had arrived, viz, to bring all my available force to this point in the event of an attack, I concluded to promptly leave my position. I therefore sent to Montgomery a regiment of unarmed troops.

On the next day I ordered the Eighth Mississippi Regiment, Lieutenant-Colonel Yates commanding, to proceed at once to this place and report to you, and on the 9th I prepared my plans for generally evacuating.

On the night of the 8th three companies of cavalry arrived from Montgomery. With these and two companies I already had I determined to destroy the public property, &c., which I had not been able to remove, and which might prove of benefit to the enemy. As the few troops were so disposed that any reduction in the day-time would attract the notice of the enemy, I merely withdrew the camp and garrison equipage and sick, in accordance with an order from General Lee, to keep the army mobilized.

On the morning of the 9th, all the work of removing sick and baggage having been completed, I published orders that my forces should present themselves to the best advantage to the enemy, and as soon as it was dark they were quietly marched out of their camps and started on the road to Oakfield. Sentinels were posted as usual on the beach, and they were withdrawn one hour after the other troops had left. All these instructions were obeyed to the letter, and much to the credit of the comparatively raw troops under my command.

When my infantry were well on the road, and out of range of the enemy's guns, the cavalry were assigned their places to commence the necessary destruction at a signal previously agreed upon, to be given from the cupola of the hospital, and one answering at the navy-yard, Barrancas, and Fort McRee. Precisely at 11.30 o'clock, when everything was perfectly quiet, both on the enemy's side and ours, the most painful duty it ever fell to my lot to perform was accomplished, namely, the signalizing for the destruction of the beautiful place which I had labored so hard night and day for over two months to defend, and which I had fondly hoped could be held from the polluting grasp of our insatiate enemies. The two blue-lights set off by Colonel Tattnall and myself at the hospital were promptly answered by similar signals from the other points designated, and scarcely had the signals disappeared ere the public buildings, camp tents, and every other combustible thing from the navy-yard to Fort McRee were enveloped in a sheet of flames, and in a few moments the flames of the public property could be distinctly seen at Pensacola. The custom-house and commissary storehouses were not destroyed for fear of endangering private property, a thing I scrupulously avoided.

As soon as the enemy could possibly man their guns and load them, they opened upon us with the greatest fury, and seemed to increase his charges as his anger increased. But in spite of bursting shell, which were thrown with great rapidity and in every direction, the cavalry proceeded with the greatest coolness to make the work of destruction thorough and complete, and see that all orders were implicitly obeyed. Their orders were to destroy all the camp tents, Forts McRee and Barrancas, as far as possible, the hospital, the houses in the navy-yard, the steamer Fulton, the coal left in the yard, all the machinery for drawing out ships, the trays, shears—in fact everything which could be made useful to the enemy. The large piles of coal were filled with wood and other combustibles and loaded shells put all through it, so that when once on fire the enemy would not dare to attempt to extinguish it. Loaded shell were also placed in the houses for the same purpose, and the few small smooth-bore guns I was compelled to leave were double-shotted, wedged, and spiked, and carriage-chassis burned. The shears in the navy-yard were cut half in two, and the spars and masts of the Fulton were cut to pieces.

By the most unremitting labor I succeeded, with my little force and limited transportation, in saving all the heavy guns and nearly all the small-sized guns. I took away all the flanking howitzers from Barrancas and the redoubt.

In removing the large columbiads from the batteries which were in full view of the enemy, I was compelled to resort to General Johnston's plan of replacing them with wooden imitations as they were removed.

All of the powder and most of the large shot and shell were removed; the small-sized shot were buried. I succeeded in getting away all the most valuable machinery, besides large quantities of copper, lead, brass, and iron; even the gutters, lightning-rods, window weights, bells, pipes, and everything made of these valuable metals were removed; also cordage, blocks, cables, chain cables, and a large number of very valuable articles of this character which I cannot here enumerate.

All the quartermaster and commissary stores, except such as were not worth the transportation, were sent away. As soon as this was completed I set hands to work taking up the railroad iron at Pensacola and others to reeling up the telegraph wires, under the protection of a strong guard of cavalry, infantry, and one piece of light artillery. Having received orders not to destroy any private property, I only destroyed at Pensacola a large oil factory, containing a considerable quantity of resin, the quartermaster's store-houses, some small boats, and three small steamers used as guard boats and transports. The steamers Mary and Helen were the only private property of their kind burned.

The steamboat Turel, which we had been using as a transport, was sent up the Escambia River, she being of very light draught, well loaded with stores, machinery, &c., with orders to cut down trees and place every obstruction possible in the river behind her. She has arrived safely at a point I deem beyond the enemy's reach, and she has been unloaded of her freight. The casemates and galleys of Fort McRee were filled with old lumber and many loaded with shell and fired. The galleries and implement rooms at Barrancas were similarly dealt with, and the destruction at both places was as complete as it could be without the use of gunpowder. This I did not deem it necessary or proper to use for this purpose. The enemy's furious cannonade only served to make the havoc more complete. There was no damage done by it to man or horse.

When it is remembered that all this work has been done by a mere handful of raw troops, with but few arms, and many of them without any arms at all, and this, too, in the very face of a formidable force, I deem it but simple justice to my men to say that the conduct of each and all of them was worthy of the highest praise. It not unfrequently happened that after standing guard all night they cheerfully labored all the next day and night. I have not room to make distinctions where all did so well, but I feel constrained to make particular mention of Capt. J. H. Nelson, of the Twenty-seventh Mississippi Regiment, who commanded at Fort McRee, the most exposed and dangerous point; Major Kilpatrick, who commanded at the navy-yard, and Lieutenant-Colonel [J. F.] Conoley, who commanded at Pensacola. These gentlemen deserve the greatest credit for their zeal and watchfulness in the management of their respective stations. I feel that I am also authorized in saying of the Twenty-seventh, under Captain Hays, that during the frequent and terrible alarms, so unavoidable with new troops, it was always cool and ready for serious work.

The unwearied exertions, both night and day, of my personal staff officers have received my personal thanks, and I feel called upon to remark that they deserve great credit, as they were so zealous and unremitting in their exertions to assist me in carrying out my orders and of serving the country, that I frequently had to insist on their taking rest, for fear that they would completely wear themselves down.

On the completion of my work I proceeded to rejoin my army at Oakfield, 6 miles north of Pensaçola, on the railroad, leaving five companies of cavalry, in command of Capt. J. T. [F. J.?] Myers, an efficient and daring officer, to watch the enemy's movements.

The next morning I proceeded, with the Twenty-seventh Mississippi Regiment, to Mobile, leaving Lieutenant-Colonel Conoley, with the Twenty-ninth Alabama Regiment, and Lieutenant-Colonel Tullen, with five companies of Florida Volunteers, two of which companies were armed, to guard the railroad while the iron was being removed.

I regret to acknowledge the receipt of a telegraphic dispatch from the honorable Secretary of War, dated subsequent to my evacuation, directing me not to burn the houses in the navy-yard. I received one from him the day before the evacuation, directing me to spare all private dwellings not useful to the enemy for war purposes, which was done. The first-named dispatch reached me after my arrival in the city.

I am, sir, very respectfully, your obedient servant,

THOS. M. JONES,
Acting Brigadier-General, C. S. Army.

Brig. Gen. JOHN H. FORNEY,
Commanding Department of Alabama and West Florida.

[Indorsement.]

HDQRS. DEPT. OF ALABAMA AND WEST FLORIDA,
May 15, 1862.

I have the honor to transmit, with my approval, the foregoing report of Brig. Gen. T. M. Jones of the evacuation of Pensacola.

I am, sir, very respectfully, your obedient servant,

JNO. H. FORNEY,
Brigadier-General, Commanding.

General S. COOPER,
Adjutant and Inspector General, Richmond, Va.

HEADQUARTERS ARMY OF MOBILE,
May 24, 1862.

SIR: I have the honor respectfully to acknowledge the receipt of the following dispatch from the Hon. Secretary of War, referred to me by the general commanding the department:

The President desires that you inquire into the reported destruction of the dwelling-houses in the navy-yard at Pensacola and many houses in the town on its evacuation. He is determined to punish the wanton, useless destruction of property by our officers (which we fear has reached a great and most injurious extent to property) which would merely prove a convenience to the enemy, the loss of which inflicts great and lasting injury to our own people, and should not be destroyed. Cotton, tobacco, and navy stores should always be destroyed if in danger of falling into the hands of the enemy.

In answering this dispatch I might rely, I think, on the plain statement of facts set forth in my report of the evacuation, as it meets the requirements made upon me by yourself, but something further in relation to the orders under which I acted may not be improper.

On assuming command at Pensacola, 9th of March last, written and verbal instructions were given me by Maj. Gen. Samuel Jones, in both of which the property the War Department desired to be destroyed was particularly and specially designated. In these instructions the dwelling-houses in the navy-yard were not only named, but were actually prepared for conflagration by having combustibles placed in them. Certain private and public property in Pensacola was also named. A dispatch from the honorable the Secretary of War, dated 6th instant, so modified my instructions as to require me not to destroy private property and dwellings at Pensacola. This dispatch was literally obeyed and respected, for not a single dwelling was touched intentionally in the town; one very small house which stood near the oil factory was consumed, I learn, in spite of the most strenuous efforts to prevent it. So decided and specific were my instructions to the officer in command at Pensacola, that several houses embraced in the orders for destruction were not fired at all for fear of endangering private property.

That the President is displeased at the houses belonging to the Government in the navy-yard being burnt I most sincerely regret, since my most ardent desire was so to execute my orders as to give entire satisfaction to those above me, and for this I labored unremittingly for two months, sleeping only at intervals in the day-time at such moments as I could snatch, as it were, from the incessant demands made upon my energies. I flattered myself that I had succeeded until the telegram from the Hon. Secretary of War was received, three days after the evacuation, ordering that the dwellings in the navy-yard be not destroyed. Having served as a soldier for fourteen years, I scarce know how to disobey orders; and in destroying this property (the propriety of which I never entertained a doubt), though the task was a painful one, it was nevertheless imperative.

As an evidence of how scrupulous I was in carrying out my orders in respect to private property I refer you to the inclosed copies of dispatches which passed between the commanding officer at Pensacola and myself in reference to this subject.

In conclusion I ask leave respectfully to say that, from the tenor of this dispatch in reference to my official acts in evacuating Pensacola, I am constrained to believe that representations have been made by evil-minded, designing persons—with little regard for veracity and much less for the interest of our cause and country than their own—with the view of injuring me before I had an opportunity of placing myself and my actions properly before those to whom I am responsible. Though it is discouraging and disheartening to an officer whose highest aim has been to serve his country and merit the approbation of his superiors, I have yet the consolation to feel that I did my duty to the very best of my knowledge and ability, and only ask for an impartial hearing before punishment or censure is inflicted upon me. Knowing that the task of evacuating was a difficult and thankless one, I asked that an older and wiser officer might be assigned to it, but this was refused, and if the manner in which I have executed it has not given satisfaction, I can only say that it was not for want of effort on my part or of the little army I had the honor to command.

With the hope that this communication may be received in the respectful spirit it is intended, I have the honor to be, very respectfully, your obedient servant,

THOS. M. JONES,
Acting Brigadier-General.

General JOHN H. FORNEY.

[Indorsement.]

HDQRS. DEPT. OF ALABAMA AND WEST FLORIDA,
May 25, 1862.

General S. COOPER,
Adjutant and Inspector General, Richmond:

SIR: I have the honor respectfully to state that on assuming the command of the department at this point I found Col. T. M. Jones in command of the Army of Pensacola. Knowing him to be an officer of discretion and capacity, and being myself heavily pressed with work, I did not think it necessary to be very particular in giving him instructions; in fact I placed the greatest confidence in his integrity and judgment, and therefore did not interfere particularly with his operations. I was well aware that he was better acquainted with what was necessary to be done at that point than I, as he had long been stationed there.

If, therefore, any blame is to attach to him for what he did there, and I candidly think there should not, I feel that it should rest on me rather than on him, and if any one is to be punished for anything that occurred there let it fall on me, for if any one is guilty it is myself.

In conclusion I beg to be permitted to say that I consider General Jones' conduct as highly creditable to him as an officer and a gentleman, and that he will receive praise instead of censure when his instructions and the difficulties by which he was surrounded are considered.

I have the honor to be, very respectfully, your obedient servant,

JNO. H. FORNEY,
Brigadier-General, Commanding.

[Inclosure No. 1.]

O'BANNONVILLE, *May* 9, 1862.

Lieut. Col. J. F. CONOLEY,
Pensacola:

In destroying public property and such as General Sam. Jones has ordered of private property, remember that there is an act of Congress prohibiting the destruction of private property other than what can be used against us for war purposes. Tell your men that much of their reputation as honorable men and true patriots is at stake, and that coolness and judgment must characterize the destruction, and no more than what is absolutely necessary must be burned.

THOS. M. JONES,
Brigadier-General.

[Inclosure No. 2.]

COOPER'S, *May* 23, 1862.

General THOMAS M. JONES:

GENERAL: No private dwellings were destroyed by my order and none were destroyed known to me, except one near the oil factory, which was unavoidable.

J. F. CONOLEY.

CORRESPONDENCE, ORDERS, AND RETURNS RELATING TO EVENTS IN WEST FLORIDA, SOUTHERN ALABAMA, SOUTHERN MISSISSIPPI, AND LOUISIANA FROM SEPTEMBER 1, 1861, TO MAY 12, 1862.

UNION CORRESPONDENCE, ETC.

HEADQUARTERS DEPARTMENT OF FLORIDA,
Fort Pickens, Pensacola, September 3, 1861.

Lieut. Col. E. D. TOWNSEND,
Assistant Adjutant-General:

COLONEL: The rebels have endeavored to occupy and remove the dry-dock, and, having notified General Bragg that I should consider his doing either as an act of hostility, I last night ordered it to be burned, which was done.

I am, colonel, very respectfully, your obedient servant,

HARVEY BROWN,
Colonel, Commanding.

ORDERS, No. 82. } HDQRS. U. S. TROOPS AT KEY WEST, FLA.,
September 6, 1861.

1. Within ten days from this date all male citizens of the Island of Key West who have taken the oath of allegiance will send their names to these headquarters to be registered.

2. Within thirty days from this date all the citizens of this island are required to take the oath of allegiance to the United States.

3. At the termination of sixty days all citizens of this island who

have failed and refused to take the oath of allegiance to the United States will be removed from Key West. This will also apply to their families and the families of those who have left the island to join the Confederate States.

WM. H. FRENCH,
Brevet Major, U. S. Army, Commanding.

HEADQUARTERS DEPARTMENT OF FLORIDA,
Fort Pickens, September 10, 1861.

Lieut. Col. E. D. TOWNSEND,
Assistant Adjutant-General:

COLONEL: Yesterday morning nine men, being the crew of one of the enemy's guard boats, deserted to this post, bringing their boat and arms. They belonged to a rebel company of marines. I have closely questioned them and obtained valuable information.

The same morning two citizens arrived here. They have been contractors for supplying saw-mills with logs, and have staid in the country, vainly hoping to get the money due on their contract. They have been living the last eighteen weeks at or near Milton, 30 miles up the bay. They represent there being many Union men in this country, but the expression of Union sentiments to be dangerous. I shall send all North by the first opportunity.

I am, very respectfully, your obedient servant,

HARVEY BROWN,
Colonel, Commanding.

NEW YORK, *October* 1, 1861.

Hon. SIMON CAMERON,
Secretary of War:

SIR: At the recent cutting out and destruction of the Judah, at Pensacola, by boats from the Colorado, it is noticed that, although the boats were fired at and a considerable force rushed forward to beat them off, no gun was fired from Fort Pickens. It seems, too, that the fort could at any time have destroyed the Judah.

A large gang of mechanics are now reported finishing the steam-frigate Fulton for launching at Pensacola as a war vessel, within reach of the guns from the fort, or by the aid of those guns capable of being reached by our boats and seamen.

Colonel Brown refers to old orders to act at the fort strictly on the defensive. I beg to call your attention to this point, in order that you may see if there is not some oversight or miscarriage or change of circumstances requiring a correction of the apparent inconsistency of the Navy acting offensively and the fort defensively on the same ground and at the same time, so that they cannot unite in a common object. Whether Colonel Brown already has sufficient liberty by his orders to use his discretion, or whether he needs some prompting to insure co-operation with the naval officers—often a difficult thing between Army and Navy—or whether any other officer would be better at that place, we of course leave wholly to the Government. But we are here deeply interested that no effort of either Army or Navy be omitted to prevent privateers or steamships from being built or fitted out to prey upon our commerce besides our general interest in success, and suppose such intimations as the present, based upon distinct information which may not be so open to you, are what you wish us to make.

In behalf of underwriters, yours, very respectfully,

CHAS. B. MOORE.

[OCTOBER 6, 1861.—For General Butler's order assuming command of the Department of New England, see Series III, Vol. I, p. 511.]

FORT PICKENS, *October* 12, 1861.

Brigadier-General MEIGS,
Quartermaster-General:

MY DEAR GENERAL: The prediction contained in my letter to you of the 15th July* has been sooner fulfilled than I expected. If Barry's battery had been here not one hundred of the enemy would have left the island alive on the morning of the 9th instant.

If the companies of Barry, Hunt, and Duane had not been with so little ceremony taken from me I should have had a much better account to render than I now have; and if I had sat down and grieved over what I considered great wrongs in being so inconsiderately weakened and done nothing, instead of exerting every nerve and taking responsibilities that few under existing circumstances would have taken in sending three Zouave companies away and replacing them by two regular companies, what would now be our condition? We would have been disgracefully whipped and this fort at this moment would be closely beleaguered by the rebels—all our batteries being lost—for I could not then have had the means of sending a man from the fort to sustain and support the batteries and to repel the invaders; and Billy Wilson's Zouaves, I am sorry to say, disgracefully ran and took shelter under our batteries.

I do not say this, my dear general, in a spirit of self-laudation, but as re-expressing to the fullest extent the opinions and fears I so fully and freely expressed at the time and for which I was so much condemned.

I must also add that in the coming conflict, which the defense of the honor of our insulted flag imposes on me, if I had these companies of which I have been deprived, and especially the officers, I should probably be able to give a better account of my stewardship than I can now hope for; but my command is in good condition and good spirits.

We have a just and noble cause, and may humbly hope for the blessing of God, which I daily fervently invoke.

I am, my dear Meigs, yours, truly,

HARVEY BROWN.

HEADQUARTERS DEPARTMENT OF FLORIDA,
Fort Pickens, October 12, 1861.

Lieut. Col. E. D. TOWNSEND,
Assistant Adjutant-General U. S. Army, Washington, D. C.:

COLONEL: All my letters, all my suggestions, and all my requests, written and made since I have been in command of this post, having

---

* See p. 438, Vol. I.

met with so mortifying, and I must add such undeserved neglect, not once having received the slightest notice, that I now only write you at any time from a sense of duty. I do so now to report that this fort, with its appendant batteries, is now as ready for service as it probably will at any future time be, and that the enemy are still erecting batteries and arming them with guns of heavy caliber, so that the relative strength is constantly changing to our loss. If I had not been confined by positive orders to defensive operations, and which I have in vain tried to have rescinded, I would open my batteries on the enemy, believing that at this time true policy and the best interest of the service and of the country demand it.

I fired the dry-dock with the hope and expectation that the enemy would open on me, but he has not yet thought proper to do so. I can therefore only patiently wait the course of events, while the strength of my command is constantly and rapidly diminishing by disease and orders.

I am, very respectfully, your obedient servant,

HARVEY BROWN,
Colonel, Commanding.

HEADQUARTERS OF THE ARMY,
Washington, October 14, 1861.

Brig. Gen. HARVEY BROWN,
Fort Pickens, Pensacola, Fla.:

SIR: The General-in-Chief directs me to say that your several communications from the time of your assuming command of Fort Pickens have been duly read to him, and such as required such reference have been laid before the War Department.

Your operations have been approved and your zeal and energy appreciated.

The usual punctuality in acknowledging your letters has been unavoidably departed from because of the incessant pressure of matters which demanded immediate attention and left no time for anything else.

The circumstances which prevented offensive operations on your part changed with your ability to assume them, the cause of the prohibition having been evidently removed by the state of active and open war which now exists.

More regular troops as well as officers would have been gladly sent you if they were to be had, but the pressing need of regulars can hardly be appreciated except by the authorities, on whom urgent requisitions are made for them from all quarters. At some posts there is not one officer to a company. The General could not give you leave of absence when you asked it or since, because he had no one to relieve you to whom he could confide your responsible command.

The Commissary-General reports that a vessel left New York loaded with beef and ice in September, and one is now preparing with live cattle, stores, and vegetables. The subject of pay for your command has been brought to the attention of the Paymaster-General.

I am, sir, very respectfully, your obedient servant,

E. D. TOWNSEND,
Assistant Adjutant-General.

HEADQUARTERS DEPARTMENT OF FLORIDA,
Fort Pickens, October 15, 1861.

Col. E. D. TOWNSEND,
Assistant Adjutant-General, Washington, D. C.:

COLONEL: I have to report to you that I sent the McClellan with dispatches to Flag-Officer McKean on the 9th instant, proposing a joint attack on the enemy, to which he readily acceded, and on the 11th he, with the Niagara and Colorado, arrived here. After consultation we agreed on a plan of attack, which was to have been carried into execution to-morrow morning at daybreak. At the request of the flag-officer I had lent him two Parrott rifled guns and the steamer to carry them to the Mississippi. She returned this morning, bringing the commodore a report of the unfortunate affair at the mouth of the Mississippi, which, as you will perceive by his letter (A), renders his immediate presence at the Southwest Pass necessary; and as I am thus deprived of his assistance, I have been compelled to listen to his suggestion to suspend operations until he can co-operate with me. I need not say with what feelings of disappointment I have been compelled now the third time to forego an attack on the enemy.

I intended to have sent the prisoners taken on the 9th to New York by the McClellan, but the captain represents that he cannot take them with safety to his vessel.

I am, colonel, very respectfully, your obedient servant,

HARVEY BROWN,
Colonel, Commanding.

[Inclosure A.]

U. S. FLAG-SHIP NIAGARA,
Off Fort Pickens, October 15, 1861.

Col. HARVEY BROWN,
Commanding Department of Florida, Fort Pickens.

SIR: The information received by the McClellan is such as to make it indispensable that I should proceed immediately to the Mississippi. The Richmond is leaking badly, having three planks stove in below the water line by the ram. The Vincennes has thrown overboard all her guns but four. At one of the passes there is not a sufficient force to contend with that of the enemy. It is exceedingly mortifying and trying, but my duty seems plain. I ought to be there at this time. I would suggest that you defer your operations until I can assist you with a suitable naval force. The Colorado I will leave here. Lieutenant May will give you particulars, as I am much hurried.

I am, very respectfully, your obedient servant,

WM. W. McKEAN,
Flag-Officer, Commanding Gulf Squadron.

[OCTOBER 21, 1861.—For General Butler's General Orders, No. 2, of this date, see Series III, Vol. I, p. 521.]

HEADQUARTERS DEPARTMENT OF FLORIDA,
Fort Pickens, October 29, 1861.

Col. E. D. TOWNSEND,
Assistant Adjutant-General:

COLONEL: I herewith inclose you three letters which passed between General Bragg and myself. The two first were published by him in the

Pensacola Observer, with a very laudatory editorial notice of him, and one not so very much so of me, in which I am accused, among other delinquencies, of being in cold blood a murderer of a sick enemy.

I am, very respectfully, your obedient servant,

HARVEY BROWN,
Colonel, Commanding.

[Inclosures.]

HEADQUARTERS DEPARTMENT OF FLORIDA,
Fort Pickens, October 9, 1861.

General BRAXTON BRAGG,
Commanding Troops near Pensacola.

SIR: I observe this morning for the first time a yellow flag hoisted over a large building directly in front of my batteries. I also understand that officers' wives and children are in the adjoining buildings. I do not make war on the sick, women, or children. These buildings will necessarily be exposed to my fire should there be a bombardment, and, besides, they are subject under this flag to be used as a protection to any of your troops that may take shelter behind or before them. I therefore give you this notice, that the sick, the women, and the children may be removed, so that if fired on the responsibility may rest where it belongs.

I am, very respectfully, your obedient servant,

HARVEY BROWN,
Colonel, Commanding.

HDQRS. TROOPS C. S., NEAR PENSACOLA, FLA.,
October 10, 1861.

SIR: I received late last evening your communication of that date with profound astonishment. The building on which you had for the first time observed a yellow flag has been well known to you and all your command, as well as to the United States Navy, as the military hospital of this station, and you could not help knowing that it is now used for that purpose.

Dealing with one who had been an old brother soldier of high reputation, I had hoped that our intercourse and conduct in the hostile attitude in which we are placed would be marked by all the courtesies and amenities of civilized warfare; but it seems from your communication that you claim the right to violate a hospital flag because it may be abused. Admit this principle, and we revert to a state of barbarism. The sick, the women and the children, and prisoners must become the objects of vengeance; the white flag must be abolished; "booty and beauty," "rape and rapine," must follow in the track of a victorious commander. I decline your invitation to make these the objects of war. Your hospital flag has been and shall be respected. In the affair of Tuesday night your hospital with its inmates was in our possession for at least one hour, and as far as I can learn my orders to scrupulously respect both were rigidly enforced.

Our hospital and the two adjacent buildings occupied by medical officers will continue to be used for legitimate purposes. Nothing has been or will be done to attract your fire. If, under these circumstances, you should put your threat into execution, which would only be in accordance with the acts of some of your brother commanders of little experience in the customs of war, I shall take care that the facts shall be made known, that it may receive, as it will deserve, the execration of the civilized world.

I have the honor to be, your obedient servant,

BRAXTON BRAGG,
Major-General, Commanding.

HEADQUARTERS DEPARTMENT OF FLORIDA,
Fort Pickens, October 16, 1861.

Maj. Gen. BRAXTON BRAGG,
Commanding Troops near Pensacola.

SIR: Your letter of the 10th instant was duly received, and I should deem it unworthy of an answer had you not thought proper to publish it to the world and to countenance an editoral in a Pensacola paper every way worthy of it.

You have knowingly and willfully misconstrued my letter, for the evident purpose of having your Christian answer published, so as to make capital with your deluded followers. You have, in the very face of my declaration that I did not make war on women, the children, and the sick, declined an invitation that I never made, and which you knew I never made, to make those the objects of war. You knew that in calling to your notice that these buildings would necessarily be exposed to my fire I was influenced by a desire to save the sick, women, and children from danger, for previously to writing the letter to which yours is an answer I mentioned to your inspector-general, who was here with a flag, my intention to do so, and then, on the spot where the batteries and buildings could be plainly seen, I pointed out that I could not fire from certain batteries of mine at some of yours without endangering your hospital, which is in a direct line with them (and this is perfectly obvious to your own sight). You therefore knew that I must either omit to fire on particular batteries of yours or it must necessarily be exposed to my fire, and yet your Christian philanthropy is such that you declare your intention of keeping your sick, your women, and your children in this dangerous situation. And for what motive but in the hope of fixing on me the stigma of firing on your hospital or killing women, children, and the sick? Your conduct shall not influence mine. I intend to prosecute this war as a Christian man who has an account to give to his Maker. I will do my duty as I construe it, regardless of your calumny and that of the wretch who edits the Pensacola Observer.

I have had three of your officers prisoners. They have notified you that they were treated as brother officers by mine. I have had some thirty of your privates prisoners. They have, with one solitary exception (and he said nothing), in writing to their friends, declared that they were well and kindly treated, and I have your sick in my hospital, and they have also reported that they receive the same attention as my own. I have released three of your medical officers without parole. I have collected and buried your dead with the same decency as my own. I have done much more. At your special request I have for two days employed my soldiers in disinterring and carting to the wharf your dead, so that their friends might have the satisfaction of knowing their bodies were cared for, and this has been done with the full knowledge of the entirely different treatment our prisoners and our dead have received and are receiving from your hands at Manassas and Richmond. And you, knowing all this, have malignantly and falsely accused me of inviting you to make war on the sick, women, and children.

I will hold no terms of courtesy with a man who so far forgets what is due to an honorable profession, and who so well knows, yet so little practices, the principles of honorable warfare. I decline all further communications with you unless it be by verbal message and strictly on official subjects.

I am, sir, very respectfully, your obedient servant,

HARVEY BROWN,
Colonel, Commanding.

Abstract from return of the Department of Florida, Col. Harvey Brown, Fifth U. S. Artillery, commanding, for the month of October, 1861.

Stations.	Present for duty.		Aggregate present.	Memoranda.				
						Prisoners of war.		
	Officers.	Men.		Aggregate killed or missing in action.	Aggregate wounded in action.	Officers.	Men.	Pieces of field artillery.
Fort Pickens, Fla	21	709	833	4	20	1	8	.....
Camp Brown, Santa Rosa Island	12	243	370	10	9	....	13	.....
Total in Pensacola Harbor	33	952	1,203	14	29	1	21	.....
Fort Jefferson, Fla	10	238	330	.....	.....	.....	.....	.....
Fort Taylor, Fla	9	190	273	.....	.....	.....	.....	4
	52	1,380	1,806	14	29	1	21	4

ADJUTANT-GENERAL'S OFFICE,
Washington, November 1, 1861.

Brig. Gen. HARVEY BROWN,
U. S. Forces, Commanding Department of Florida:

SIR: Your letter of the 12th ultimo has been received and referred to the Headquarters of the Army, and in reply I am directed to transmit to you the indorsement there made upon it. You will perceive that a letter was addressed to you on the 14th of October, two days subsequent to the date of yours, which has doubtless reached you by this time, and will contain the answer to your inquiries.

I am, sir, very respectfully, your obedient servant,

A. BAIRD,
Assistant Adjutant-General.

[Indorsement.]

HEADQUARTERS OF THE ARMY,
Washington, October 28, 1861.

This letter having been handed me by the Adjutant-General, I respectfully report that Colonel Brown's letters were all promptly communicated to the General-in-Chief as they were received. On the 14th of October a letter was addressed to Colonel Brown from this office which is believed to cover all the points in the correspondence, a copy of which was forwarded to the Adjutant-General at its date. Owing to the secrecy with which General Brown's expedition was fitted out no copies of the instructions to him are found in this office. I was not informed on a single point touching the expedition, nor have I been able to gain any information concerning Colonel Brown's orders, &c., until furnished a day or two since with a rough copy in his possession by General Meigs.

E. D. TOWNSEND,
Assistant Adjutant-General.

[NOVEMBER 9-19, 1862.—For Secretary of War to General Butler (November 9), in relation to transportation; General McClellan to Butler (November 15), calling for reports of strength and condition of command; Butler's reply of November 18, and order suspending the embarkation of the expedition, see Series III, Vol. I, pp. 545, 552, 555, 559.]

HDQRS. OF THE ARMY, ADJT. GEN.'S OFFICE,
Washington, December 20, 1861.

Col. HARVEY BROWN, U. S. A.,
Comdg. Department of Florida, Fort Pickens, Fla.:

SIR: I have the honor to acknowledge the receipt of your highly important dispatches, as follows:

October 9 and 11, with inclosures, reporting the attack of the rebels and their disastrous repulse on the 9th October.

October 15, in relation to joint attack intended to be made by you with the naval force.

Three letters of November 25, and report, with inclosures, of December 2, in relation to the bombardment of the rebel forts and batteries around Pensacola by the fort and fleet of the United States on the 22d and 23d November.

Letter of December 3, remarking upon bravery and good conduct of officers and men of your command.

The brilliant and successful operations detailed in these dispatches have been read with lively satisfaction by the President, Secretary of War, and General-in-Chief. The General will not forget to bring specially to notice the valuable services thus rendered by yourself, your officers, and your whole command, and to urge an appropriate recognition of them by the Government.

Your suggestions in relation to armament, &c., have already been brought to the attention of the Ordnance and also of the Navy Departments. The regiment sent to re-enforce you has doubtless arrived before this, and it is hoped that some if not all the absent officers of your regular companies have also joined by this time.

I am, sir, very respectfully, your obedient servant,

L. THOMAS,
Adjutant-General.

HEADQUARTERS DEPARTMENT OF FLORIDA,
Fort Pickens, December 27, 1861.

Brig. Gen. LORENZO THOMAS,
Adjutant-General U. S. Army, Washington, D. C.:

GENERAL: Nothing of special import has occurred at this fort since the bombardment. The Seventy-fifth New York Volunteers, whose arrival I duly reported, are encamped and industriously engaged in drilling. The Sixth [N. Y.] Regiment, I am sorry to say, so far as the officers are concerned, is in a state of disorganization; criminations, recriminations, charges, and countercharges, between the officers, and especially between the colonel and two or three espousing his side and the other officers of the regiment, became of such daily occurrence, that I had peremptorily to stop it, and to notify all concerned that I would entertain no more complaints until the result of those forwarded had been acted on at Washington. I ordered a court, which is now in session, for the trial of two of the captains and some privates, and since then charges against almost every officer of the regiment have been sent me.

I do not deem it expedient to exercise the authority vested in me by your letter of the 18th November, unless in marked cases, but I must reiterate the opinion expressed in my letter of the 12th October, that the good of the service requires some stringent action in reference to the officers of this regiment.

And while on this subject I desire to call the especial attention of the Department to the fact that Colonel Wilson is the next to me in rank, and if I am rendered unserviceable the command will devolve on him, and this, serious under almost any circumstances, but remote and isolated as we are, might be of the most vital consequence, and I therefore think it my duty to call your attention to it.

Some more appropriate and efficient means of unloading vessels is a subject of serious consideration. The boats we have answered tolerably well the purpose in summer when the sea was smooth, but in the heavy surf which now almost constantly prevails they are nearly or quite useless. A receiving vessel and good surf-boats are almost of indispensable and immediate necessity.

I respectfully again submit that an officer of more rank than I have should be stationed here, and I beg leave to state that, while willing to devote my whole being to the service, I know that I cannot endure another summer in this enervating climate, and that my health and probably my life will be sacrificed by it. I have now spent upwards of fifteen years in Florida, and I require the bracing influences of a Northern climate. If, therefore, consistent with the good of the service, it will be gratifying to me to be relieved by one of the many efficient general officers now in service, and to be ordered to duty in the North.

The rebels have been for some six weeks busily engaged with a large force in putting up batteries on Oak Island, at Deer or Town Point, and are putting heavy (10-inch columbiads) guns in them, and since the bombardment they have erected a battery at the mouth of the Big Lagoon and put one or two heavy guns in it, and have, besides, greatly strengthened their existing batteries.

I have never doubted but that with three or four gunboats and 5,000 men the navy-yard at Pensacola could at any time until October have been taken, and I think the day after the bombardment, such was their panic, it might even with a smaller force have been successfully assailed, but since October they have so materially strengthened their works and erected so many batteries that I should consider an attack as hazardous without strong land and naval forces. We are now strong enough for defense (unless in case of bombardment, when we ought to have more artillery troops), and more will be useless unless a sufficient number is sent to act offensively; and this can only be done with the co-operation of gunboats of light draught of water.

I respectfully renew my application for Parrott's rifle guns and for a large supply of ammunition for those I have. I would also report that there are two 10-inch sea-coast mortars here, but no beds.

I am, general, very respectfully, your obedient servant,

HARVEY BROWN,
Colonel, Commanding.

Abstract from return of the Department of Florida, Col. Harvey Brown, Fifth U. S. Artillery, commanding, for month of December, 1861.

Stations.	Troops.	Present for duty. Officers.	Present for duty. Men.	Aggregate present.
Santa Rosa Island:				
Fort Pickens	Detachments 1st and 2d Artillery and 3d Infantry.	19	568	704
Camp Lincoln	6th New York Infantry	13	228	474
Camp Seward	75th New York Infantry	32	711	829
Fort Jefferson	Detachments 1st Artillery and 6th New York Infantry.	10	307	347
Fort Taylor	Detachments 1st Artillery, and 1st Infantry,	6	209	261
	Total	80	2,023	2,615

SHIP ISLAND, MISS., *January* 3, 1862.

Maj. Gen. BENJAMIN F. BUTLER,
Commanding New England Division, Boston, Mass.:

SIR: The last few days have been occupied with muster of the troops. As these troops are raw, much time and attention have been necessary to examine the rolls. To show how raw these troops are, I may state that three men have already been wounded in one month by the careless use of fire-arms.

The transport-ships George Green and Bullion arrived on the 31st ultimo. The former landed 138 horses, 6 of which are private property, in good condition. Twelve died on board, and 1 has died since coming ashore. The captain of the George Green (Fairbanks) stopped at Key West, when it is thought there was no necessity for it.

Captain Clouét, of the French steamer Milan, came into the harbor recently, and is receiving facilities to go to New Orleans, being detained at this present moment by a fog, which appears to continue day and night. He informed me that the French have some twenty vessels of war in the Gulf. I should feel more at ease if we had our Sawyer guns mounted, for we need them to insure respect, if for nothing else.

JANUARY 7, 1862.

From some cause or other the captain of the Milan went to New Orleans in one of his own ship's boats. I should have been very glad to supply him with the small steam-tug belonging to the Quartermaster's Department, which has been sent us from Pensacola by Colonel Brown, but I understood from the flag-officer that he intended to send the Water Witch gunboat on this service, and hence gave the subject no further attention until I incidentally learned that the captain had gone. Should I see him again, I shall express to him my regret at not having the pleasure of giving him a passage by one of our vessels.

I had designed making use of the occasion to gain some knowledge as to the defenses of the Rigolèts, with a view to ascertain whether our long-range rifle guns might reach them from the sound. I have suggested to the flag-officer to make use of the Lewis, the captured light-draught high-pressure steamer, for making reconnaissances. She went over to Biloxi the other day, and from all I can learn I should judge that a great deal of property lies exposed to us on the northern shore of the sound. If so, the condition of affairs presents the curious spectacle of a rebel army lying in wait to seize upon Washington, staking everything upon the hazard of seizing upon our capital and its capital influences with the unrelenting determination of accomplishing our ruin, while at the same time they leave their rear comparatively unprotected, and their property exposed in a way that appeals rather to mercy and pity than to the ordinary visitations of war. I may possibly be mistaken in this view of things. The waters of the opposite coast are very shallow, and may be regarded as unnavigable for all our vessels except the Lewis, which for various reasons has not been in condition for reconnoitering till within the last week or fortnight. I shall endeavor to extend our knowledge of this region of country by all the means in my power, which, however, are exceedingly limited. It might become desirable to transfer our camp to the northern shore, and especially if the rebellion should continue through the summer. The glare and heat of the sand of which the island is composed would probably be intolerable during that season. The depot, however, must be here, whatever direction the forces may take.

So convenient thus far have we found the harbor, admitting easily of large vessels of war, that, taken together with the modern tendency of building large vessels, I think that it must become of more importance than New Orleans. By means of railroads terminating on the other shore, and large vessels, like the Constitution, I think that it would be cheaper to dispatch a cargo of rice or cotton from this point than it would be from the mouth of the Mississippi. The question is whether we ought not to adopt a plan from the very beginning with regard to this point and begin its execution at once; for under any circumstances, holding in view even a temporary independence of the South, the possession of the island would be valuable to us. The opposite shore is comparatively healthy, and by means of long wharves and light-draught steamers vessels could be expeditiously laden at this point in almost any weather that we have had since being here. It would be economy in the long run to have a plan to follow. The plan should be well matured, covering at least a period of thirty years, and be left with the head of the Engineer Corps for preservation and execution.

JANUARY 8, 1862.

I am informed that the mail will leave to-day for the North.

It may be well to state that the Schenkl shot that have been supplied to the battery appear to be too large in their paper envelopes, these envelopes or cylinders fitting too close for a foul piece. The only means that I have of reducing them is to pass them through a hot ring.

Just previous to my leaving Newport News I applied for two officers, viz, Lieutenant Tyler, of the Second Vermont, and Lieutenant Holbrook, of the Fourth Vermont, as staff officers. I have heard nothing from them since, but I trust that the application has been favorably entertained and the officers authorized to report to me for duty. Without either a staff or the usual blank forms to do business by, my duties are rendered more difficult than they need be.

I am, sir, very respectfully, your obedient servant,

J. W. PHELPS,

Brigadier-General, Commanding.

WAR DEPARTMENT,
Washington, D. C., January 24, 1862.

Brig. Gen. LORENZO THOMAS,
Adjutant-General:

Ordered, That the general commanding report without delay his opinion whether the expedition proposed by General B. F. Butler shall be prosecuted, abandoned, or modified, and in what manner.

By order of the Secretary of War:

P. H. WATSON,
Assistant Secretary.

ADJUTANT-GENERAL'S OFFICE,
Washington, January 25, 1862.

To the Hon. SECRETARY OF WAR:

SIR: In compliance with your instructions of yesterday, I have the honor to report in reference to the expedition of Maj. Gen. B. F. Butler, U. S. volunteers, as follows:

It appears that on the 10th of September a general authority was given in the following terms:

WAR DEPARTMENT, *September* 10, 1861.

Maj. Gen. B. F. Butler is hereby authorized to raise, organize, arm, uniform, and equip a volunteer force for the war in the New England States, not exceeding six regiments of the maximum standard, of such arms, and in such proportions, and in such manner as he may judge expedient; and for this purpose his orders and requisitions on the Quartermaster's, Ordnance, and other staff departments of the Army are to be obeyed and answered, provided the cost of such recruitment, armament, and equipment does not exceed in the aggregate that of like troops now or hereafter raised for the service of the United States.

SIMON CAMERON,
Secretary of War.

This authority was extended, and an object for the expedition indicated by an order from the Secretary dated two days after, as follows:

WAR DEPARTMENT, *September* 12, 1861.

Major-General Butler is authorized to fit out and prepare such troops in New England as he may judge fit for the purpose, to make an expedition along the Eastern Shore of Virginia, via the railroad, from Wilmington, Del., to Salisbury, and thence through a portion of Maryland, Accomac and Northampton Counties, of Virginia, to Cape Charles.

Transportation agents, quartermasters, and commissaries of subsistence will answer General Butler's requisitions for this purpose.

SIMON CAMERON,
Secretary of War.

The object of General Butler's expedition, as given in these last-quoted orders, seems to have been soon after abandoned, and the general seems to have contemplated an attack on Mobile.

Again, on the 2d of December, he submitted a plan for invading the coast of Texas, and he appears to have had in view an ultimate attempt to capture New Orleans.* On the 2d of December he reports that a part of his expedition sailed in the steamer Constitution from Portland for Ship Island on the 23d of November, touching at Fort Monroe the 27th of November, to take on board Brig. Gen. J. W. Phelps, U. S. Volunteers, who at the request of General Butler † was detached from Fort Monroe to command this detachment, consisting of nine companies Ninth Connecticut and the Twenty-sixth Massachusetts Infantry Regiments

---

* See Series III, Vol. I, p. 580. † Of November 13. See Series III, Vol. I, p. 548.

and the Fifth Massachusetts Light Battery, in all about 1,900 men. General Phelps' command landed and occupied Ship Island on the 5th to the 7th of December, and has since been fortifying itself there; a very proper measure, as it enables the Government to hold a very important point, interrupting a part of the communications of the rebels. General Phelps' command is the only part of General Butler's expedition that has so far gone to the Gulf coast.

The great points from which important operations are to be conducted are, first, the Department of the Potomac, in front of which is posted and strongly intrenched the largest and best-armed body of the insurgents guarding the approach to Richmond; second, the Department of the Ohio, opposed to the next great body of the rebels in Kentucky; third, the Department of the Missouri, the army in which, besides the clearing of the State of Missouri, has for a prime object the control of the Mississippi River and operations against New Orleans. Next to these the Department of Kansas is to furnish a heavy column, to move in co-operation with that in Missouri. There are other separate operations, designed to draw off and distract the enemy along the sea-coast. These are, Sherman's expedition, which has already occupied Port Royal, S. C., and which is to attack Charleston or Savannah or both; second, Burnside's, which, having entered Albemarle Sound, will be directed against North Carolina or Southern Virginia; third, the occupancy of Fort Jefferson, on the Tortugas, of Fort Taylor, Key West, and of Fort Pickens, Pensacola, together with demonstrations against the Florida coast. These outside operations are deemed to be the only ones that ought to be undertaken at this time in support of the main plan. It would be only a wise and necessary measure to hold in reserve the troops raised, but not yet assigned, to corps d'armée, ready to support and re-enforce in any quarter where they may be required, and which can only be determined by circumstances in the course of active operations. Thus they should not be withdrawn to raise General Butler's expedition to the number (not less than 30,000 men, and it is believed 50,000) which would be required to insure success against New Orleans in a blow to be struck from the Gulf. It is assumed that New Orleans, being the vital point on the Gulf, should be the object, rather than Mobile or the coast of Texas. Under all these circumstances it is clear to my mind that what is known as "General Butler's expedition" ought to be suspended. The part of it now at Ship Island is well placed, and is quite adequate, with the co-operation of the Navy, to hold that important position. The remaining troops of this expedition now at Fort Monroe cannot at present be better disposed of than by adding them to the command of Major-General Wool at that post. They will there have ample opportunity for discipline and instruction, and can be readily transferred thence to another point whenever required. The supplies intended for them under the supposition they were to go to Ship Island will serve them as well at Fort Monroe.

I have the honor to be, sir, very respectfully, your obedient servant,

GEO. B. McCLELLAN,
Major-General, Commanding U. S. Army.

[JANUARY 25, 1862.—For Governor Andrew's communication to the Secretary of War in relation to complications growing out of the organization of the Butler expedition, &c., see D. Andrew to Stanton, January 27, 1862, Series III, Vol. II.]

SHIP ISLAND, MISS., *January* 29, 1862.

General LORENZO THOMAS,
Adjutant-General, Washington, D. C.:

SIR: There is not much of importance to communicate from my command.

The period of maximum cold has passed; warm weather is approaching, and some provision must be made for it in any plan of operations that may be adopted for this region of country. The climate is so damp that our tents mildew speedily and threaten a rapid decay.

One of the regiments here, the Ninth Connecticut, is very much in want of clothing of all kinds. Instead of coats, blouses are the best for this climate.

At the hazard of frequent repetition I must again refer to the subject of blanks. Another muster day will soon be at hand, and if we are not soon supplied with blanks it will be difficult, if not impossible, to make out the rolls. Matters of this kind are of great importance to the discipline and accountability of the troops.

By the Milton we received a small engine, which is now at work unloading that ship. Temporary store-houses have been constructed, and a bake-house will soon go into operation. The 9-inch shell gun on navy carriages is being put up to the number of ten, but I am in hopes that Sawyer's rifled 24-pounder and 8 or 10 inch columbiads will be sent to replace them. I would take this occasion to state, as my opinion, that if the 42-pounder were bored for Sawyer's 24-pounder it would be the best heavy ordnance that we have, either for land or sea service.

Several of the men of the regiments and battery are considered unfit for service, and I have concluded to send them back to New England, with a view to their discharge. Three officers have tendered their resignations, which I shall forward to your office for acceptance, at the same time allowing them to return with the men to Lowell, Mass., where they will be directed to await action on their resignations from your office.

Some arrangement seems called for with a view to the regular transmission of intelligence between the posts of the Gulf station and the North. We have been here nearly two months, and have yet received no communication from any military source and but very few letters or papers of any kind.

Intelligence from Washington occasionally reaches us through the rebels and the Navy. We are thus informed that the Constitution has landed her troops at Old Point.

Our field of view and our sphere of action are both limited here, but from general appearances I should suppose it well to be provided against the contingency of collision with some foreign power—at least to the extent of having an unobstructed channel of communication open for the receipt of intelligence and supplies.

It might be well, perhaps, to fortify this point more strongly than I have proposed, even against immediate contingencies.

I remain, very respectfully, your obedient servant,

J. W. PHELPS.
Brigadier-General Volunteers.

SHIP ISLAND, MISS., *February* 3, 1862.

General LORENZO THOMAS,
Adjutant-General, Washington, D. C.:

SIR: I write on the occasion of the gunboat Massachusetts being about to sail for the North.

Some definite plan should be adopted with reference to this point. Few of the officers of the Government are aware, perhaps, of the character of the island on which we are situated, or what it is to be amid glaring white sand during the heats of summer. If troops remain here they must have wooden structures for shelter, and even then they will need some protection for the eyes, I think. I would beg to be informed, at as early a moment as may suit your convenience, whether there are any particular designs or not with respect to this point, or at least what direction I shall give to requisitions for carrying out such designs as I may entertain of my own. As it is, we are threatened with a shortness of provisions, having but about three weeks' of some articles on hand.

One of my instructions was to place the island in a state of defense, but I have not the means of rendering it as strong as I should desire. To this end there would be necessary a better class of guns and carriages, with a large supply of bricks and mortar, pintles, traverse-circles, materials for a magazine, &c. The magazine ought to be of peculiar structure, perhaps made of iron, and strong enough when buried in sand to resist 11-inch shells. It should exclude the air as much as possible, for the climate is very damp. It would be good economy to have a general plan, embracing a long period of time, and have everything done in accordance with it.

As I understand the policy of the Government with regard to this region it was to establish new sites for commercial centers in the place of New Orleans and Mobile, which were founded without any reference to cotton shipping and large vessels. As a war measure this could be done by the same means that would secure the most effective military operations, or, at all events, military points could be found, I think, which would threaten the trade of those two cities, and would have a great influence upon the security of slave property.

We now have 24 of the enemy's negroes, which we employ in lightering vessels at an unfixed rate of pay. They appear to be intelligent, and far more dignified and manly than many of their masters, whom they look upon with mingled feelings of pity and contempt as well as dread. Some of them crossed the sound to us, a distance of 10 or 11 miles. One of them came at night in a thunder-gust, finding that more friendly than the sympathies of his master. One of the mulattoes came originally from North Carolina, another from Virginia. They are aware of their alliance with the white race, and of the ties which have been snapped in their leaving home. They are ripe for manumission, and any measure to avert it may put off, but cannot long prevent, a revolution—a revolution of that kind where men are restored to their original rights.

In case that wooden structures should be put up upon the island for the two regiments and one battery now here, we should need some more lumber than we have on hand.

To take possession of a point on the main-land and hold it we should need more troops, I think, than we now have, since the conspirators might possibly be able to direct a large force against us. We should also need some siege and garrison artillery and the shallow-draught boats I have alluded to in former communications.

In conclusion, permit me to call your attention to the main point of this letter, which is the necessity of some channel through which my wants in the due form of requisitions and the intentions of the Government can be made known. Clothing, and probably provisions, will be needed as soon as they can be got here.

I remain, very respectfully, your obedient servant,

J. W. PHELPS,

Brigadier-General, Commanding.

HEADQUARTERS DEPARTMENT OF NEW ENGLAND,
Boston, February 6, 1862.

Maj. Gen. GEORGE B. MCCLELLAN,
Commanding Army of the United States, Washington, D. C.:

GENERAL: I have the honor to report the following matters existing at Ship Island, as reported by Brigadier-General Phelps, which will bear upon the necessities of our expedition, and which may be of interest to the Commanding General.

General Phelps reports that seventeen 9-inch guns upon navy carriages arrived at Ship Island from the Tortugas on the 18th of January, from which he has taken enough for the fortifications.

He further reports that the health of the troops is good, and that the intercourse through the sound between Mobile and New Orleans has been stopped.

I would desire respectfully to inquire when the Seventeenth Massachusetts Regiment, the Fifth New York Regiment, and Nims' battery will be at Fortress Monroe ready for embarkation.

The steamer Constitution can be ready to take these troops, with good fortune, in ten days from to-day, if this meets the approbation of the Commanding General. All other transportation has been and will be provided for.

I have the honor further to report that the Fourteenth Maine Regiment sailed on Saturday, and that the Thirteenth and Fifteenth Maine Regiments will sail within seven days from this date. The Twelfth Connecticut Regiment is expected to sail on board the steamer Fulton this week, and the Western Bay State Regiment upon the steamer Mississippi also within a week.

I take the liberty to urge the subject of the Maine cavalry. The regiment expects to be disbanded and there are now applications for a court-martial upon some of the officers. The keeping up of the regiment is attended with large expense, and it is very desirable, if the horses are to be turned over to me, that they should be shipped as soon as possible, that they arrive out in season for training and use. These circumstances make it desirable that such orders as may be considered necessary should be given at the earliest possible moment.

Very respectfully,

BENJ. F. BUTLER,
Major-General, Commanding.

HEADQUARTERS DEPARTMENT OF NEW ENGLAND,
Boston, February 6, 1862.

To the ADJUTANT-GENERAL OF THE ARMY:

GENERAL: In compliance with the order from the War Department of the 24th day of January, 1862, that General Butler report without delay—

1st. The present state and condition of the expedition now under his charge;

2d. The amount of expenditures made and liabilities incurred, specifying in detail the nature and amount of each expenditure;

3d. The probable expenditure required to place the expedition at its contemplated destination;—

General Butler has the honor to make the following report, which he prepared himself to do immediately upon his return to New England as soon as the necessary documents could be copied:

1st. There are now at Ship Island, in Mississippi Sound, the Twenty-sixth Regiment Massachusetts Volunteers and nine companies of the Ninth Regiment Connecticut Volunteers, together with the First Battery of light artillery of the New England Division (Fourth Massachusetts), armed with two 6-pounder rifled guns and four 12-pounder howitzers; in the aggregate about 2,000 men, all under the immediate command of Brigadier-General Phelps, whose various reports have been from time to time as received forwarded to the Department, to which reference is requested for particular information in regard to the condition of that portion of General Butler's command.

There are now *en route* for Ship Island, on board the Constitution, the Twelfth Regiment Maine Volunteers and nine companies of the Eastern Bay State Regiment, with three companies of mounted men; say 2,200 men in the aggregate.

There are embarked on board ship in Boston Harbor, ready to sail, the Fourteenth Regiment of Maine Volunteers and the Third Battery of light artillery, New England Division (Second Vermont), armed with six 6-pounder Sawyer guns, the Second Battery of said division (First Maine), armed with six 12-pounder rifled guns, and the Fourth Battery of said division, armed with two 6-pounder rifled and four 6-pounder smooth-bore guns, with the tenth company of the Eastern Bay State Regiment; say 1,500 men.

There are in Massachusetts the Western Bay State Regiment at Pittsfield, now ready to start at a moment's notice, waiting only for the paymaster, and the Eighth New Hampshire, now at Fort Independence, waiting for transportation, which will be ready immediately; say 1,900 men, to be 2,000 by the time of sailing.

In Connecticut the Twelfth Connecticut Volunteers at Hartford is full, and only awaits the paymaster to be ready to move as soon as necessary.

In Vermont the Eighth Vermont Volunteer Regiment is full at Brattleborough and ready to be mustered in and to march immediately, and the Seventh Vermont Regiment Volunteers will be ready as soon as transportation is obtained for them. By the last reports they contained about 1,800 men, and will be full by the time of sailing.

There are in the State of Maine, in various conditions of readiness, the Thirteenth Regiment Maine Volunteers, the Fifteenth Regiment Maine Volunteers, and five batteries of light artillery, to wit, the Second, Third, Fourth, Fifth, and Sixth Maine Batteries, which will be hurried to completion and ready for embarkation within ten days; in all about 2,500 men.

For an exact statement of the numbers and condition of the troops now in New England reference is made to the report marked A, forwarded herewith,* containing a summary of the latest reports from all in New England except from the Seventh and Eighth Vermont Regiments and the Second and Sixth Maine Batteries.

A *résumé* of these troops shows—

At Ship Island: Twenty-sixth Regiment Massachusetts Volunteers; Ninth Connecticut Volunteers (nine companies); First Battery N. E. D. (Fourth Massachusetts).

En route per Constitution: Twelfth Regiment Maine Volunteers; Eastern Bay State Regiment (nine companies); three companies mounted men.

On board ship in Boston Harbor: Fourteenth Regiment Maine Volunteers; Third Battery N. E. D. (Second Vermont); Second Battery N. E. D. (First Maine); Fourth Battery N. E. D.; tenth company of Eastern Bay State Regiment.

---

* Omitted in view of the *résumé* following.

At their camps ready: Twelfth Regiment Connecticut Volunteers, at Hartford; Seventh and Eighth Regiments Vermont Volunteers, at Brattleborough; Eighth Regiment New Hampshire Volunteers, at Fort Independence; Fifteenth Regiment Maine Volunteers, at Augusta.

To be ready: Thirteenth Regiment Maine Volunteers, at Augusta; Second, Third, Fourth, Fifth, and Sixth Batteries Maine Volunteers, at Augusta.

The aggregate of infantry and artillery now in New England, 8,500; on Constitution, 2,200; at Ship Island, 2,000; total, 12,700; eleven regiments infantry, three companies mounted men, and nine batteries of artillery. These troops as they are moved are fully armed and equipped for service.

2d. Quartermaster's department.—The amount of expenditures made in the quartermaster's department to the 1st of February, 1862, is $497,633.25, the details of which are fully set out in Schedule B,* forwarded herewith. (The original bills, with the accounts of the quartermaster, will be forwarded to Washington immediately.) The liabilities incurred in that department are, so far as they can be ascertained on that date, $422,911.52, as per Schedule C,* forwarded herewith.

Ordnance department.—The expenditures in this department to February 1, 1862, are $178,774.90, as per Schedule D,* herewith forwarded. For liabilities incurred, $39,730.87, as per Schedule E.*

Adjutant general's department.—The expenditures in this department to February 1, 1862, are $14,895.92, as per Schedule F* and Captain Goodhue's statement. These expenditures were for recruiting expenses, transportation of recruits, and rations of the several regiments. No liabilities.

Commissary department.—The expenditures in this department have been $191,897.51, as per Schedule G.* No liabilities.

Medical department.—The expenditures in this department have been $2,190.72. No liabilities.

To resume, the expenditures in all the departments to February 1, 1862, are:

Quartermaster's	$497,633 25	
Ordnance	178,774 90	
Adjutant general's	14,895 92	
Commissary	191,897 51	
Medical	2,190 72	
		$885,392 30
Liabilities incurred:		
Quartermaster's	422,911 52	
Ordnance	39,730 87	
The others none	....	
		462,642 39
Total cost to February 1		1,348,034 69

It will be observed that a very large proportion of all these expenditures should not be put to the account of the expedition, but are for the raising, arming, and equipping of some 6,000 men.

3d. The probable expenditure necessary to place the expedition at its contemplated destination must now substantially be the expenses of transportation and transport ships. The troops being now all armed, uniformed, and equipped, it will, of course, cost no more to feed and pay them in one place than in another, and the others may be fairly put

* See *résumé* following.

at $30 per man as the maximum, but a part of this expenditure for transportation has already been incurred.

Respectfully submitted.

BENJ. F. BUTLER,
Major-General, Commanding.

OFFICE CHIEF ENGINEER ARMY OF THE POTOMAC,
Washington, February 7, 1862.

Col. A. V. COLBURN,
Assistant Adjutant-General:

COLONEL: I do not know how General Butler proposes to operate. The memorandum I drew up was made for the use of Mr. Fox, and without consultation with others. It proposed to attack New Orleans and obtain command of the Mississippi River by a combined naval and land [force], operating through the mouths of the river, and making the capture of Forts Jackson and Saint Philip an essential feature of the plan.

I believe that any other way of approaching New Orleans is to run great risk and half do the work, and, under the most favorable issue, to protract the period of complete triumph of our arms in the Mississippi Valley. Take these works, and New Orleans falls, and our gunboats appear at once before Vicksburg, Natchez, and Memphis, and the rebel defense both ways (our armies and flotilla in the Upper Mississippi co-operating) is completely annihilated. The approaches to New Orleans by Lakes Borgne and Pontchartrain are very intricate; require the expeditionary force to be put in boats or barges and towed for 15 or 20 miles; then to attack works not easily taken; then to encounter the hazards of a defile through narrow bayous and over narrow causeways, &c.

Assuming the attack by the Mississippi adopted, I thought 10,000 men to be more than would be required for the capture of those works, in which I depended mainly upon a *coup d'instant* of the Navy, that it would be enough for the immediate capture (aided by the fleet) of New Orleans, and therefore that it would not be best to encumber the expedition with a larger mass of transports than that number of troops required, but that 20,000 men should be available in all, the balance being left, say, at Ship Island, to be brought up immediately or as soon as necessary. I thought a dozen siege 24-pounders enough; even this perhaps is excessive; for if the works fall at all they will fall at once, or they will be reduced more slowly by naval bombardment and cutting off of provisions and supplies. I should think the forces estimated in the "Memoranda of changes in General Butler's suggestions"* to come pretty near the mark, and that the cavalry, artillery, troops, and light batteries were sufficient. I look upon this expedition as one of immense importance. Its failure would be a terrible blow; its success would bring us almost to the close of the war. Hence I recommended in my memorandum that the Chief Engineer United States Army should be consulted on account of his thorough knowledge of the works and his great experience in such matters.

I am, very respectfully, your most obedient servant,

J. G. BARNARD,
Brigadier-General, and Chief Engineer.

---

*See pp. 687, 688.

OFFICE OF CHIEF ENGINEER ARMY OF THE POTOMAC,
Washington, February 7, 1862.

Col. A. V. COLBURN,
Assistant Adjutant-General:

COLONEL: I would add to what I addressed you this morning that I deem it very important that an Engineer officer thoroughly acquainted with the fortifications about New Orleans, and who has traveled through the intricate routes of approach, should accompany the expedition. There is (besides myself and General Totten) one such, viz, Lieutenant Weitzel. McFarland has some little acquaintance, not at all approaching to Weitzel's. Palfrey knows nothing of the works nor the country.

Yours, respectfully, &c.,

J. G. BARNARD,
Chief Engineer.

FEBRUARY 7, 1862.

General GEORGE B. MCCLELLAN:

MY DEAR GENERAL: I would be glad if you would find time to look over attentively the plan I submitted for taking Forts Jackson and Saint Philip. I do not care that that particular mode of operation be adopted, if any other as good or better offers, but what I do wish is, that the matter shall be carefully concerted and prepared for, with a full sense of the important consequences likely to ensue. Engrossed as I have been with local duties, I have not comprehended their consequences nor how attainable they were. To attack Port Royal or Charleston or Savannah successfully is to attain, indeed, a great moral effect, but to capture Forts Jackson and Saint Philip and take New Orleans is to conquer the whole Mississippi Valley, and I may add the whole Gulf coast. All would speedily fall. I would not, therefore, have this expedition fail or produce a mere half-way result.

I would add that besides myself there is one other Engineer officer, Lieutenant Weitzel, thoroughly acquainted with these works, and a most capital officer he is, too. McFarland was there a short time; he is much too inexperienced. I think some one ought to go. Beauregard has told them that New Orleans is safe from the Mississippi. I should confess to a personal gratification (besides my general interest in the matter) in seeing this region, so associated with Chase and Beauregard, recaptured. I believe that in three months we may have the rebellion by the throat.

Yours, respectfully, &c.,

J. G. BARNARD,
Chief Engineer.

HEADQUARTERS DEPARTMENT OF NEW ENGLAND,
Boston, February 7, 1862.

Maj. Gen. GEORGE B. MCCLELLAN,
Commander-in-Chief U. S. Army:

GENERAL: In reply to telegram from Lieutenant-Colonel Colburn I have the honor to state that the heavy artillery required by me (in addition to four Sawyer rifled guns, 5 and 8 inch, &c., which are being prepared here) is simply as follows:

1. Four 8-inch siege howitzers and carriages, now at Fort Jefferson, the shells for them at Fortress Monroe.
2. One battery of six 20-pounder Parrott guns, with carriages, ammunition, &c., complete.

The first were promised some time since by General Ripley. The Parrott guns will be required immediately, and could be shipped from New York, Baltimore, or Washington.

With First and Second [Vermont], First Maine, and Fourth and Sixth Massachusetts Batteries, all of which are recruits, if there can be given to us Nims' battery at Baltimore (understood to be a well-drilled corps), these six batteries might be sufficient of field artillery for my expedition. There remain five batteries in Maine which (when mounted from dismounted cavalry regiment there) might be sent to Fortress Monroe.

The above estimate for heavy artillery provides nothing for the fort at Ship Island, which it is understood will be furnished from Tortugas by navy guns there.

It will be seen, then, that we require but one more complete field battery (six guns—12-pounder howitzers preferred) to be furnished by the Ordnance Department, as I now have guns for five, if I include Nims', which I would be glad to have done within ten days.

I am, General, very respectfully, your obedient servant,

BENJ. F. BUTLER,
Major-General, Commanding.

HEADQUARTERS DEPARTMENT OF NEW ENGLAND,
Boston, February 12, 1862.

The Hon. SECRETARY OF WAR:

SIR: I have the honor to report that as fast as possible the troops and supplies are being dispatched to the Gulf.

The Eighth New Hampshire embarks to-morrow. The transportation for the remainder is in such progress that I hope to get all but two regiments off next week.

I propose to have 3,000 men sail on Tuesday next; one of the steamers to take me up at Fortress Monroe, where we are to get some ordnance stores. By taking the rail I can gain time enough to meet the ship there, and visit Washington for my final instructions, if you think that desirable.

In this connection I desire to call attention to the fact, but not complainingly, that I have as yet received no written instructions or information in regard to the details of the expedition, a memorandum of which I gave to the Commanding General, to which he was kind enough to signify his approval except as to the number of light batteries. I presume, in the press of more important matters, these details may have been overlooked. Fearing, however, that the memorandum may be mislaid, and, in order to refer to it, a duplicate is sent herewith.

I desire to be informed as to the disposition of the Seventeenth Massachusetts and Fifth New York and Nims' battery, which were to be detached from Major-General Dix's division at Baltimore and sent to Fortress Monroe. When will they be at the fortress and what are their numbers, so that I may prepare transportation for man and horse? Very early knowledge is needed upon this topic. Also a detail of signal officers for the service. I should like six at least, and could take them up at Fortress Monroe.

The preparation immediately of two light-draught steamers is an imperative necessity.

I have to thank the Commanding General and Ordnance Department for the battery of Parrott guns so promptly ordered.

I must again call attention to the Maine Cavalry Regiment—if I am to have the horses; if not, I must purchase others for battery and transportation purposes. I would most strongly advise the dismounting of that regiment, both in an economical and military point of view. I send this report directly to the Secretary of War because I hear of the absence of the Commanding General across the Potomac.

Most truly and respectfully, your obedient servant,

BENJ. F. BUTLER,
Major-General, Commanding.

[Indorsement.]

FEBRUARY 17, 1862.

The within letter is referred to the General Commanding, and his immediate attention requested to General Butler's expedition, and to the instructions to be given to him, if he is to command the expedition.

By order of the Secretary of War:

P. H. WATSON,
Assistant Secretary of War.

Memorandum.

It is suggested that a military geographical department be created, to be called the Department of the Gulf, coast west of Fort Pickens and so much of the adjoining States as may be occupied by the United States troops; headquarters wherever the commanding general may be.

That for the purpose of carrying on military operations there the following corps be put under the command of Major-General Butler, viz:

1. 12th Connecticut Volunteers	900
2. 13th Connecticut Volunteers	900
3. 7th Vermont Volunteers	900
4. 8th Vermont Volunteers	900
5. 8th New Hampshire Volunteers	900
6. 13th Maine Volunteers	900
7. 14th Maine Volunteers	900
8. 15th Maine Volunteers	900
9. 12th Maine Volunteers (*en route* to Ship Island)	900
10. 26th Massachusetts Volunteers (at Ship Island)	900
11. Eastern Bay State Regiment Volunteers (*en route* to Ship Island)	900
12. Western Bay State Regiment Volunteers	900
13. 9th Connecticut Volunteers (Battalion) Ship Island	600
14. 5th New York Volunteers (at Baltimore)	900
15. 17th Massachusetts Volunteers (at Baltimore)	900
	13,200
CAVALRY.	
Three companies of mounted men (*en route* to Ship Island)	275
LIGHT ARTILLERY.	
1st, 2d, 3d, 4th, 5th, and 6th Maine Batteries Volunteers (145 men each)	870
4th Massachusetts Battery Volunteers (at Ship Island)	145
1st and 2d Vermont Batteries Volunteers (145 men each)	290
Everett's Massachusetts battery volunteers	145
Nims' Massachusetts Battery Volunteers (at Baltimore)	145
Capt. P. A. Davis' company (unattached, at Fortress Monroe)	100
	15,170

That so much of the supplies of siege artillery now in depot at Fort Jefferson as may be needed by him be put at General Butler's direction, together with that suggested in General Butler's report of December 2, 1861.

That this force, with proper supplies, be transported with the greatest possible rapidity to Ship Island and the adjacent islands, there to be made ready for such movements as may be directed in concert with the naval forces in the Gulf. It is desirable that the First Maine Cavalry and a squadron of Connecticut cavalry be dismounted, the men being given the option either to be transferred to the regular dragoons or to enlist in any other arm of the service, either volunteers or regulars, or be discharged, the officers mustered out of service, and the horses taken either to mount the artillery or for the transport service.

It is desired that Capt. N. A. M. Dudley, Tenth Infantry, have leave of absence, for the purpose of taking command of the Western Bay State Regiment.

It is desired that Major Wallen, of the Seventh Infantry, have leave of absence, to take command of the Eastern Bay State Regiment. Also that the Signal Officer of the Army be permitted to detail a suitable force for signal service. That Lieutenant Palfrey, of the Engineers, be directed to report to the general commanding the Department of the Gulf.

It is desirable that a Treasury draft for $10,000, or $5,000 minimum, be passed in favor of the commanding general, on account of army contingencies, and charged to him as secret-service money. This money is designed to pay spies and purchase intelligence, without which the best schemes fail. So small a sum is asked for because there will be frequent means of communication with the War Department. It is absolutely essential.

It is desirable that at least two steamers, small size and of the lightest possible draught that can be got down to the Gulf, be chartered or purchased, for the purpose of towing barges and surf-boats into the bayous and creeks. The Navy have no such light-draught boats. It would be better to charter, with privilege of purchase during the charter. This would throw the risk of the sea voyage on the owners.

Respectfully submitted,

BENJ. F. BUTLER,
Major-General Volunteers.

Memoranda of changes in General Butler's suggestions.

Confine limits of proposed department to scene of projected operations.

Strike out Fifth New York and Seventeenth Massachusetts, and substitute two regiments to be determined hereafter. Add at least four Western regiments, making—

Minimum force of infantry	16,800
Cavalry, three companies	275
Two companies of artillery (to serve heavy guns)	290
Four light batteries	580
	17,945

General Butler to furnish specific list of heavy ordnance and ordnance stores required.

SHIP ISLAND, MISS., *February* 13, 1862.

General LORENZO THOMAS,
Adjutant-General, Washington, D. C.:

SIR: At length the Constitution arrived yesterday, with two regiments of infantry and a squadron of cavalry. The season is already pretty well advanced, and I had begun to doubt whether there was any definite plan to the movement in this quarter, or, if there was, whether it had not been abandoned. A plan ought rather to precede operations than follow them. What I am to do with four regiments, with such means as I possess, is more than I can conjecture.

Recent rains have so flooded part of the island that two regiments cannot well be maneuvered upon it in line without marching through water.

The troops which have just arrived have apparently suffered from the long continuance of their voyage since its first commencement. Two of their number have been carried to their graves to-day and another is reported as at the point of death. The mail which was to have been brought by the Constitution, but which was put on board the Pensacola, has not yet arrived, so that I am still without any military intelligence from the headquarters since our departure from the North.

I have to acknowledge the receipt of some blanks, but am sorry to find that they contain no company muster rolls nor quartermaster's returns. Another muster is close at hand, and I have no blanks for the occasion. There seems to be a want of system in furnishing blanks, which I cannot comprehend.

There are now in position upon the island twelve guns, viz, ten 9-inch guns on navy carriages and two 12-pounder rifled brass pieces, besides several smaller guns for a field battery. I have found it difficult to get enough cartridge-bags for the 9-inch guns, and am accordingly without a sufficient number of rounds for those guns.

I shall endeavor to improve the drill of the command as much as possible, as one sure advantage that may be derived from our condition. In other respects six shallow-draught boats, with a heavy armament of Sawyer guns, might enable us to move, and perhaps to effect something. We might, perhaps, be called upon by the people of New Orleans to assist them against the conspirators, though I have seen no evidence of such a spirit yet. Two of their boats have been reconnoitering us to-day, and with the usual timidity which they have displayed on every occasion that we have observed them. They are doubtless aware of the arrival of the Constitution, and came to see what she had brought. Our boats usually make towards them, and they run, occasionally firing a few ineffectual rounds.

I am mistaken in saying that I have received no military intelligence from the North. I have received one item, which is the refusal of certain staff officers for whom I applied several months since. As Captain Butler learns that his nomination as commissary has been rejected by the Senate, and expects soon to retire, I shall have to supply his place with such persons as I can find. I say persons, because he has been doing the duty of quartermaster as well as commissary, and the duties henceforward will be quite enough for two—quite enough for officers of the rank of captain, which I cannot appoint. I must choose lieutenants, and on comparatively short acquaintance. Had I been allowed my own choice, a particular object with me would have been to shut out as far as possible speculations upon public calamities, which I shall still endeavor to do as far as I am able.

As a summary of our military position I would state that the island is no place for so large a force as is here collected (upwards of 3,500 men), and that to take up any other position among the exceedingly shallow waters of this coast peculiar means beyond which we possess are necessary. Some of the wharves on the other side, I am told, are nearly a mile in length, with but 7 feet of water at the end. No landing could be effected on these against opposition without shallow-draught gunboats, to lie nearer shore on the flanks of the landing force. Such, I am told—for I have had no suitable boat to reconnoiter—is the case at Mississippi City, Biloxi, and Pascagoula. I have thought that the Rigolets would be a good point to attack, but my knowledge of that region is limited.

In fine, there does not appear to me to be any adaptation of means to any particular end in this quarter of the country. Many of the vessels are of an inferior class, and their armament generally behind the improvements of the times. With suitable vessels Mobile Harbor might be entered, it seems to me, and Fort Morgan taken in reverse.

I shall send by this opportunity estimates for clothing for the troops here, to include the entire year, and must also suggest that one good clerk would probably keep the army supplied with all the blanks that they would require.

A tug (the Reamy) was sent to this station in the month of December by Colonel Brown from Fort Pickens. I kept her until recently, when, as there was not much for her to do and as there appeared to be no prospect of more troops arriving, I sent her back to Fort Pickens, with instructions, if not wanted there, to go to Key West, and if not wanted there, to bring us a mail. She is too small for any considerable gun, carries none, and is deep-draught for her size. We used her part of the time in towing down rafts of logs from the upper end of the island for fire-wood. The pay of the crew is a considerable item of expense.

I must refer again to the necessity of greater powers than are possessed by any one at the Gulf stations. We may have some cases for general court-martial, and such as would render it convenient to have the Tortugas as a place of confinement.

Some cases of discharge and leaves of absence occur which are beyond any powers possessed in this region that I am aware of. I have felt compelled to transcend mine in the case of Surgeon Hooker, of the Twenty-sixth Massachusetts Volunteers, whom I have allowed permission to go home on sick leave.

I will endeavor to make the most of this expedition for the service, for it would be sad to see the energies and generous impulses of the people wasted in such movements. It would be better, perhaps, not to use them at all than to use them without a well-defined object. It is a quarter of the country that needs the attention of the Government, though it is a difficult region to operate in, as the British movement against New Orleans will prove. There is an iron English steamship in harbor, laden with cotton, which was taken by the Navy near the mouth of the Rio Grande. From what I hear, an ingenious question may arise as to whether she was at the time of capture in American or Mexican waters. The flag-officer is not here. If I had control in the case I would keep her until the occasion for making an issue out of her capture should be passed, for if we cannot settle our own affairs without the interference of foreign powers, we have lost not only self-government, but also our independence.

Out of some 40 mechanics who have been employed on the island I have decided to send home some 17 or more. Should their services be needed, their places can be supplied by soldiers.

I would suggest again that prompt communication between this region and the seat of Government is necessary, in order to derive the full value from what the Government has already done here.

I have written more at length than I proposed, indulging in words for want of action.

FEBRUARY 15, 1862.

A norther interferes with the coaling of the Constitution, so that she will not get off as early as I wish. She is a rather expensive transport unless there is constant and pressing employment for her. As several vessels laden with coal have arrived here recently from Philadelphia, I have thought it better for her to coal here than to stop at the Havana.

The flag-ship Niagara has arrived at her station to-day, but the mail of the Pensacola has not yet reached us.

In referring again to the subject of staff officers, I would express my regret that those whom I selected were not allowed to report to me. They were but two, whom, as aides-de-camp, I would have employed as adjutant general and quartermaster or commissary. In their stead it is not unreasonable that I should request the services of one quartermaster, one commissary, and one adjutant-general. To have such agents, however, selected for an officer instead of by him is so contrary to the nature of the case, that I would prefer that my original request might be reconsidered. It will be readily perceived that at a station like this the services of a quartermaster are needed.

I need not say, perhaps, that a person of questionable loyalty would be worse than useless—a mere hinderance in the way of business that he should advance.

I shall send together with this communication some estimates for clothing, &c., among which are requisitions for medicines, made out by the surgeons of regiments. There is no brigade surgeon present, and the battery and a squadron of cavalry, numbering some 260 men, have no medical attendance of their own.

FEBRUARY 17, 1862.

The Constitution is still delayed by an extraordinary storm of rain and fog from the southwest. At a late moment I have received from among her freight a box of blanks, including muster rolls, which will be all that I shall need for the present.

I have concluded to allow Lieutenant Salla, of the Fourth Battery Massachusetts Volunteers, to go to Boston, such services as he can render not being particularly required here. His name was not borne on the original muster roll of the battery, and he shows no commission. I do not see the necessity of such irregular appointments.

The Constitution I hope will get to sea to-day.

I am, sir, very respectfully, your obedient servant,

J. W. PHELPS,
Brigadier-General, Commanding.

WASHINGTON, *February* 15, 1862.

General GEORGE B. McCLELLAN:

DEAR GENERAL: Touching our conversation yesterday, I make a few remarks suggested by further thought. As to New Orleans, my estimate was made before I had seen any proposition from any quarter as to land or naval forces. For the former I think (using that number there) 20,000 is an ample number, and I would not hesitate to go with 15,000, if it was difficult to supply the greater number. Horse artillery and cavalry in very small proportions only. One thing I would suggest as to the naval preparations, prompted by the fact that Goldsborough sends word he has consumed his ammunition and cannot make another operation until he gets more. The bombardment of Fort Jackson will doubtless consume pretty much of the stock on board ships, and, when taken, the mortar vessels can do no more in the river, and a large part of the fleet can be spared. It should go at once to Mobile and bombard Fort Morgan. That work is much like Fort Jackson internally, and stands alone. Fort Gaines (Dauphin Island) is over 3 miles off. (If we had gunboats drawing not over 9 feet I cannot see what would prevent their entering Mobile Bay now and occupying it.)

For this bombardment a large surplus of shells and ships' ammunition should be collected at Ship Island. Forts Jackson and Morgan taken, whether the mortar fleet should go to Pensacola (a place of no importance, unless it be to release our fleet from blockade there), or to Charleston, or Pulaski (if that has not fallen), would depend on the situation at the time.

Now as to Savannah: If the city is so thoroughly fortified as to require a siege, it is not worth sieging. I did not know but Fort Jackson might be intended by Sherman, but that is a very insignificant work, and ought to be taken with a dash, combined with a gunboat operation, or let alone. We have the river above Pulaski, and have cut off all its communications. I don't see why the gunboats cannot ascend to Savannah; but if they cannot, or can only do it at the expense of a siege, there's no sufficient object. Looking at Fort Pulaski, I find it is a work of interior area about equal to Fort Jackson (Mississippi), with one casemate and one barbette tier. In the gorge are quarters; in front, a demi-lune. There is very little fire up in the faces of the demi-lune (not more than ten or twelve barbette guns could be put in each), being too oblique to act in positions where I have masked "gunboats," and if the rebels attempt to mount any on the gorge, a battery on its prolongation would enfilade it. The nearest point of Tybee Island is about a mile; here batteries of heavy rifled cannon would operate principally on the walls (and 24-pounder siege guns be good for nothing) and mortars behind. I think fifteen mortars (13-inch), with a few batteries of heavy guns and the co-operation of the fleet, would soon reduce Pulaski; and I think it quite likely the heavy ships of the fleet could, with the help of their land batteries, cross the southern (Tybee Island) channel and co-operate. One thing is certain, the work would soon use up all its ammunition, and would become a helpless recipient of our shot and shells, under the play of which it must surrender.

The capture of Pulaski is the capture of everything valuable—the port, the river, the city of Savannah; and I think the taking of such works is calculated to exert a powerful influence on public opinion abroad.

Woodbury has discussed the siege of Charleston, or rather the capture of the works (Sumter and Moultrie). It is a difficult undertaking, would require some preparation, and at least two iron-clad vessels, supposing Pulaski taken and Burnside to have taken Fort Macon (and perhaps Caswell).

I was just about to write that I did not approve of Burnside's march to Goldsborough as accomplishing nothing permanent, and running a risk for that nothing, while at Beaufort and Wilmington he could effect decisive results, but the news from Fort Donelson has come in, and we can march anywhere, I take it. This knocks all present calculations in the head, and we must try to do something off-hand, or the Army of the Potomac will find the war finished without its aid. Seems to me we ought not to lose a moment in siezing Norfolk, and then we can operate by the James, York, and Rappahannock, and be in Richmond in two weeks.

"God and Liberty."

I congratulate you with all my heart.

J. G. BARNARD.

P. S.—The occupation of Tennessee, as you indicated yesterday, seems to me judicious. Nashville (supplied by the Cumberland), Memphis (by the Mississippi), Florence (by the Tennessee, which great artery gives us control of the whole State), and the subordinate points—Grand Junction, Chattanooga, Knoxville, &c.—give us a grand citadel in the very heart of Secessia, from which we control all the railroads, and are able to march at will anywhere through Mississippi, Alabama, Georgia, and South Carolina, while from the seaports (soon to be ours) we hold all their external communications and routes inward. Can we not subjugate them? I have always maintained that we could, but hope the sober second thought of a cruelly deceived people will render subjugation unnecessary.

J. G. BARNARD,
Chief Engineer.

SHIP ISLAND, MISS., *February* 21, 1862.

General LORENZO THOMAS,
Adjutant-General, Washington, D. C.:

SIR: The steamer Saxon arrived to-day with provisions and will return to-morrow; a dispatch which I wish might be imitated by other vessels, but their charters are generally too much in favor of the ship, her loss, as I understand it, being at the risk of the Government, while there is not much extraordinary risk in sailing to and from a port like this. The want of a regular transmission of intelligence between this port and the North is so great and the failure in the receipt of letters long due is so marked, that I must be excused in referring to this point again as one of particular importance. A regular packet, it appears to me, ought to ply once a fortnight, say, between Old Point and the Gulf stations, and the public be informed of the arrangement. The mail service needs regulating in this quarter, as a means of regulating and invigorating other branches of the service. They are not pushed with sufficient vigor to prevent those collateral issues and perhaps speculating projects, in which direct purposes become lost and dissipated.

Owing to recent rains the island is so flooded that I should find it difficult to encamp more troops upon it. If more arrive soon those now here should be sent over to the main-land, but I have not suitable means for that object. Light-draught gunboats, heavily armed, of which I have often spoken, are necessary. Lieutenant Palfrey, of the Engineers, has arrived to-day, and he will require considerable room for his workmen and material. What from store-houses, troops, stores, and pools of water I am already too much encumbered for any suitable freedom of movement. I have thus far had the services of only one staff officer, viz, Capt. A. J. Butler, commissary and acting quartermaster. The Government will perhaps find it to its advantage to send two officers to perform those duties, Captain Butler soon expecting to leave. I would also like to have the services of an experienced adjutant-general.

Some difficulty is experienced for the want of a tariff of prices of clothing, and I would be greatly obliged for one.

To-morrow being the birthday of Washington, I propose to celebrate the occasion with a national salute of thirty-four guns, a parade of the troops, national airs, &c. Recent favorable news from the valley of the Mississippi, brought from New Orleans by a captured steamer, gives us particular satisfaction, and awakens new hopes of the speedy downfall of the conspirators.

I remain, very respectfully, your obedient servant,

J. W. PHELPS,
Brigadier-General, Commanding.

GENERAL ORDERS, No. 6. } HDQRS. DEPARTMENT OF FLORIDA,
Fort Pickens, February 22, 1862.

In compliance with the instructions of the General-in-Chief of the Army, dated Headquarters of the Army, Adjutant-General's Office, Washington, January 29, 1862 (directing Col. Harvey Brown to turn over the command of the Department of Florida to Brig. Gen. Lewis G. Arnold, U. S. Volunteers), the undersigned assumes command of the department.

* * * * * * *

L. G. ARNOLD,
Brigadier-General, U. S. Volunteers.

HEADQUARTERS OF THE ARMY,
Washington, February 23, 1862.

Maj. Gen. BENJAMIN F. BUTLER,
U. S. Volunteers:

GENERAL: You are assigned to the command of the land forces destined to co-operate with the Navy in the attack upon New Orleans. You will use every means to keep your destination a profound secret, even from your staff officers, with the exception of your chief of staff, and Lieutenant Weitzel, of the Engineers. The force at your disposal will consist of the first thirteen regiments named in your memorandum handed to me in person, the Twenty-first Indiana, Fourth Wisconsin, and Sixth Michigan (old and good regiments from Baltimore). The Twenty-First Indiana, Fourth Wisconsin, and Sixth Michigan will await your orders at Fort Monroe. Two companies of the Twenty-first Indiana are well drilled at heavy artillery. The cavalry force already *en route* for Ship Island will be sufficient for your purposes. After full consultation with officers well acquainted with the country in which it is proposed to operate, I have arrived at the conclusion that two light batteries, fully equipped, and one without horses, will be all that are necessary. This will make your force 14,400 infantry, 275 cavalry, 580 artillery—total, 15,255 men. The commanding general of the Department of Key West is authorized to loan you temporarily two regiments. Fort Pickens can probably give you another, which will bring your force to nearly 18,000.

The object of your expedition is one of vital importance—the capture of New Orleans. The route selected is up the Mississippi River, and the first obstacle to be encountered (perhaps the only one) is in the resistance offered by Forts Saint Philip and Jackson. It is expected that the Navy can reduce these works. In that case you will, after their capture, leave a sufficient garrison in them to render them perfectly secure; and it is recommended that on the upward passage a few heavy guns and some troops be left at the Pilot Station (at the forks of the river), to cover a retreat in the event of a disaster. The troops and guns will of course be removed as soon as the forts are captured. Should the Navy fail to reduce the works, you will land your forces and siege train, and endeavor to breach the works, silence their guns, and carry them by assault.

The next resistance will be near the English Bend, where there are some earthen batteries. Here it may be necessary for you to land your troops to co-operate with the naval attack, although it is more than probable that the Navy, unassisted, can accomplish the result. If these works are taken, the city of New Orleans necessarily falls. In that event it will probably be best to occupy Algiers with the mass of your troops; also the eastern bank of the river above the city. It may be necessary to place some troops in the city to preserve order; but if there appears sufficient Union sentiment to control the city, it may be best, for purposes of discipline, to keep your men out of the city.

After obtaining possession of New Orleans it will be necessary to reduce all the works guarding its approaches from the east, and particularly to gain the Manchac Pass. Baton Rouge, Berwick Bay, and Fort Livingston will next claim your attention. A feint on Galveston may facilitate the objects we have in view. I need not call your attention to the necessity of gaining possession of all the rolling stock you can on the different railways and of obtaining control of the roads themselves. The occupation of Baton Rouge by a combined naval and land force should be accomplished as soon as possible after you have gained New Orleans. Then endeavor to open your communication with the northern column by the Mississippi, always bearing in mind the necessity of occupying Jackson, Miss., as soon as you can safely do so, either after or before you have effected the junction. Allow nothing to divert you from obtaining full possession of all the approaches to New Orleans. When that object is accomplished to its fullest extent it will be necessary to make a combined attack on Mobile, in order to gain possession of the harbor and works, as well as to control the railway terminus at the city. In regard to this I will send more detailed instructions as the operations of the northern column develop themselves. I may briefly state that the general objects of the expedition are, first, the reduction of New Orleans and all its approaches; then Mobile and its defenses; then Pensacola, Galveston, &c.

It is probable that by the time New Orleans is reduced it will be in the power of the Government to re-enforce the land forces sufficiently to accomplish all these objects. In the mean time you will please give all the assistance in your power to the Army and Navy commanders in your vicinity, never losing sight of the fact that the great object to be achieved is the capture and firm retention of New Orleans.

I am, very respectfully,

GEO. B. McCLELLAN,
Major-General, Commanding in Chief.

GENERAL ORDERS, No. 20. } HEADQUARTERS OF THE ARMY, A. G. O.,
Washington, February 23, 1862.

I. A new military department, to be called the Department of the Gulf, is hereby constituted. It will comprise all the coast of the Gulf of Mexico west of Pensacola Harbor and so much of the Gulf States as may be occupied by the forces under Maj. Gen. B. F. Butler, U. S. Volunteers. The headquarters for the present will be movable, wherever the general commanding may be.

By command of Major-General McClellan:

L. THOMAS,
Adjutant-General.

SHIP ISLAND, MISS., *March* 9, 1862.

General LORENZO THOMAS,
Adjutant-General, Washington, D. C.:

SIR: The Fourteenth Maine, six companies of the Thirteenth Maine, and the Twelfth Connecticut arrived yesterday. Other vessels are in sight to-day, and probably with troops. The ship Idaho, containing the men of several batteries, has run aground, and we are trying to get her off. The force now here is made up as follows, viz: The Twenty-sixth Massachusetts, the Eastern Bay State Regiment, the Ninth and Twelfth Connecticut, the Twelfth and Fourteenth Maine, and six companies of the Thirteenth; Read's Second Massachusetts Cavalry (three companies), and Manning's battery, besides the troops on the Idaho, not yet landed; in all, some 6,500 men. It is rather late in the season to assemble so large a body of raw troops on such a spot as this, and it appears to me desirable that suitable transportation for its transference to some other point should be furnished as soon as possible. The British forces in their attack on New Orleans left here, if I am not mistaken, before the month of January.

Some days since a party from this command went over to Biloxi and examined the ground there. It is out of the way and not desirable for a military station. Another party went over yesterday to a point nearer Mississippi City. The wharf there is some 3,000 feet or more in length, of a light structure, and has been partly broken up. The reconnoitering party (about 100 men) went but a short distance from the wharf, and were fired upon from artillery. Returning to their boat (the steam gunboat Calhoun, taken from the enemy) the enemy's shots were replied to by three rounds from the boat. The number of troops there is probably not very considerable; the location would be better for a camp than this is. There are 9 feet of water at the end of the wharf. I wished to send back there to-day to make a further examination, but both of our steam lighters are broken down and the Calhoun is employed in getting off the Idaho.

It is useless for a force to attempt to do anything here without suitable transportation, and we need it now, if for nothing more than to procure room for the troops. It appears to me that the enemy at this moment ought to be kept in a state of alarm throughout this entire approach by the Rigolets and Lake Borgne to New Orleans, but it is seldom that a gunboat goes far in that direction. The superficies of that part of the island which is occupied by the troops is about one-half of a square mile, and at times nearly one-half of that, if not quite, is under water. Limits so narrow render the desired military instruction impracticable, and yet without that instruction we should be subject to external influences, as of the weather, the season, political demonstration, military necessity, &c., rather than be free to make our movements from inherent force. We should be in the dangerous condition of submitting to controlling influences ourselves, as all military bodies ought to do. To be the slave instead of the master of circumstances is not to promise much for any kind of measures, and least of all for military measures.

A step that is taken from impulsion cannot be otherwise than a stumbling one.

Had these troops arrived two months ago we might have gained some confidence and coherence by this time. No effort, however, shall be spared to render them effective. New Orleans appears to me to be a proper point to strike at. It is the center of the conspiracy. The perversity of Charleston, the pride of Richmond, and the honesty of the people along the Alleghanies have alike been made subordinate to the combinations of the conspirators there. New Orleans, the seat of the conspiracy, must have less respect for their work than any other quarter of the country. A few gunboats can reach the city from above by the river, even if we could not from this point. I can form no plan, for I have no means of executing one.

MARCH 11, 1862.

The several batteries which have arrived (four in all) have but a very few pieces of artillery among them, no harness, and hardly enough horses for one battery. With a volunteer force like this both artillery and engineering are likely to be necessary, and for the latter purpose we have a wholly inadequate supply of intrenching tools. The Navy seem to be making some preparations to ascend the river towards New Orleans, and if they expect to be backed by a land force in that direction, as they doubtless will, such tools will be indispensable. The forwardness of the season, the rawness of the troops, and the absence of means to render them efficient are calculated to fill one with concern. The fleet of mortar boats have been arriving to-day and will probably soon proceed to their destination. A party of machinists have also arrived, with a building and machinery for establishing a machine-shop, which numerous breakages in our gunboats render necessary. The materials for Lieutenant Palfrey's work on the fort are also beginning to arrive.

I am sorry to state that the Idaho is not yet got off, notwithstanding all the favoring efforts of steam-tugging, lightering, and extraordinarily high tides. She has thrown over a part of her cargo, chiefly provisions, of which our supply is not very considerable. There is something so remarkable in her running aground and in her conduct since, that I have appointed a board of survey of officers of rank to examine into it. A small lantern is kept burning in the light-house during the night, which may be announced, if thought necessary. The enemy's gunboats have not made their appearance for some time.

I have omitted no opportunity to write to you when I have thought that my communications might contain matters of interest. I have received no communications in return. Paymasters Watson and Locke have been engaged paying the troops for some time. They have probably met with some difficulties in deciding upon several cases, but they have presented others which might have been settled at the seat of Government before setting out on their tour. By and with my decision they are paying the men from the date of enrollment, and are including the 28th day of February, which I doubt not will be satisfactory to the Department. Other troops here cannot be paid at this time, but I am in hopes that funds will be sent as soon after the next muster as practicable.

The Eastern Bay State Regiment has been brought together with some degree of irregularity, and it contains a certain number of men who are not physically qualified for the proper performance of their duty. They should be discharged from the service, but I have neither time nor authority to attend to it. I shall in the mean time make such use of them as will render their services available. I have appointed Lieut. Charles S. Palmer, Ninth Connecticut Volunteers, acting assistant quartermaster, and Adjutant Hall, of the same regiment, aide-de-camp and acting assistant adjutant-general.

Very respectfully, your obedient servant.

J. W. PHELPS,
Brigadier-General, Commanding.

SHIP ISLAND, MISS., *March* 12, 1862.

General LORENZO THOMAS,
Adjutant-General, Washington, D. C.:

SIR: Since closing my letter this morning the Idaho has got off by her own efforts; how much of her cargo will prove a loss I have not yet ascertained. The steamer Constitution arrived this afternoon, with three regiments on board, under the command of General Williams. A rumor is current here that since the evacuation of Columbus the rebels are falling back upon New Orleans, with a view to its defense, and that troops have been called away from Pensacola for that purpose. If so, and we could get possession of the mouth of Red River and of a point in the line of communication between the city and Texas, the rebel forces would probably be reduced to great straits for the want of provisions.

The inconvenience attending a variety of calibers in our fire-arms is beginning to be felt. We have some of the caliber of .58 and others of the caliber of .54; for the latter caliber there should be a greater number of rounds than we have on hand here.

I regret that the elements of an organized expedition do not appear to be as far advanced as they should be. The Government party in this region must be assured of a strong, firm power to back them before they will decide in our favor; and it appears to me to be time to set our civil courts in operation, for they are the only power that can strike the traitors with wholesome dread. If the law does not assert its dignity amidst the arms that are raised for its defense, it will never do so. All our victories will prove useless unless the law is vindicated. Rebellions will occur as often as whirlwinds of a summer's day if defeats at arms are the only penalties to be incurred thereby. One execution at the right time and place would do more towards checking the rebellion than would whole holocausts upon the field of battle. The law has been disparaged and emasculated for many years, and if it does not arise in its majesty and wield the sword before war lays it down, it will never wield it under our present form of government. A victorious popular party would be prone to forget the wholesome severities of the law in the congratulations of success when their arms were once laid down.

I would be permitted to state once more that I have received no communication from headquarters covering the period of our stay here—going on four months—and only two of official character from the seat of Government. They are from the Light-House Board. So far as this silence may imply confidence in me I shall strive to merit, but it would not be out of place to let an officer have some knowledge of what he is to do or else the means of deciding for himself.

Very respectfully, your obedient servant,

J. W. PHELPS,
Brigadier-General, Commanding.

ON BOARD STEAMER MISSISSIPPI,
Off Hilton Head, S. C., March 12, 1862.

Maj. Gen. GEORGE B. MCCLELLAN,
Commander-in-Chief U. S. Army:

GENERAL: I have the honor to report the causes of my detention at this port, which will be fully set forth in the extracts from the itinerary herewith inclosed.

It will be seen that after a series of most unparalleled marine disasters I am at last ready for sea, and shall sail as soon as the weather permits.

I inclose also a copy of an order of arrest of the master of the steamer, by whose faults and mismanagement our misfortunes have been caused. A competent master and coast pilot have been detailed from the naval squadron to command the ship on the rest of the voyage.

I desire to express my deep sense of obligation both to General Sherman and officers of his command for every aid in our distressed condition. Thanks are especially due to Commander Boutelle, assistant, U. S. Coast Survey, for the very efficient assistance given by the steamer Bibb, under his command, and the untiring personal exertions in giving his services and those of his officers, at my request, to get this ship in a condition for sea, and also in acting as pilot to get her off a shoal on which she had grounded in our attempt to get to sea.

A board of survey of competent naval officers have pronounced the ship fit for sea, and I have no further fear of her, under a competent commander. No serious casualty has occurred amid all these dangers. We have lost two men from diseases contracted prior to their enlistment. The health of the command is good.

Of the conduct of nearly every officer and man during these perils, more trying and disheartening than the perils of any battle could be, I cannot speak too highly.

I am, General, very respectfully, your obedient servant,

BENJ. F. BUTLER,
Major-General.

[Indorsement.]

HEADQUARTERS ARMY OF THE POTOMAC,
Seminary, March 22, 1862.

Respectfully forwarded to the Adjutant-General.

By command of Major-General McClellan:

S. WILLIAMS,
Assistant Adjutant-General.

[Inclosure No. 1.]

Itinerary kept by Joe. M. Bell, major and aide-de-camp, at the order of Major-General Butler, U. S. Army.

On the morning of the 25th February the steamer Mississippi, having on board Major-General Butler, with his staff, and the Thirty-first Regiment Massachusetts Volunteers, under Col. O. P. Gooding, and four companies of the Thirteenth Regiment Maine Volunteers, under Col. Neal Dow, left Hampton Roads, with fair weather and every prospect of a pleasant voyage, for Ship Island, with intent to stop at Hatteras Inlet, to take on board Brig. Gen. Thomas Williams, assigned to General Butler, and at Key West. The run through the night was very pleasant, the motion of the ship being scarcely perceptible, the vessel making from 8 to 10 miles per hour.

The morning of the 26th broke beautiful, with a smooth sea. The vessel ran very easily, and under the regulations established by General Butler the troops had got into regular and comfortable position. The weather warm. In the afternoon it began to grow lowering and symptoms of bad weather; the vessel was making for Hatteras Inlet. When about 8 miles from the inlet the weather became such as to make it imprudent to attempt to proceed farther in that direction, and the vessel was put to sea; the sea and wind steadily increased during the night, with the wind from southwest, to a gale, the vessel behaving admirably.

On the morning of the 27th, at about 1 o'clock a. m., the wind shifted instantly to the northeast, blowing a hurricane. The head of the ship was brought to the wind, during which maneuver she shipped several seas, which brought into the cabin through the sky-light some water and some into the engine-room. The vessel behaved admirably, there being no perceptible strain or labor, though she rolled considerably, yet not so much as might have been expected.

The ship's crew being found insufficient to work the ship, a gang of sailors from Colonel Dow's command was detailed to aid, and rendered the most valuable assistance. The gale continued very severe through the morning until towards 10 o'clock it began to abate, and at about 11 o'clock the vessel's head was put to the southward. At 12 the sun was out and the captain took an observation, reporting to General Butler the position of the vessel to be 50 miles east of Hatteras. Vessel bowled along merrily, the sea and wind constantly subsiding, until evening, when no perceptible motion was apparent to the vessel. During the night everything quiet.

The morning of the 28th, at reveille, was dull and looked like rain, but before 7 o'clock it became bright and clear.

The vessel off Cape Fear after breakfast, and about 8.30 o'clock it was said she was aground.

Cape Fear light-house had been in sight for an hour or more and a buoy had been observed for some time. The vessel was moving about for some fifteen minutes, now backing, now going forward slowly, constantly striking, not very severely, the lead going. The captain ordered the anchor thrown over, and it was dropped on port bow. There was no wind or sea; boats were sent out to sound a passage off; under General Butler's direction buoys were prepared; the vessel was sounded all around and from certain points, her bow and various points on either side and from the stern; in all directions soundings were made and buoys set. The sailors and soldiers of the command were all put to use and worked cheerfully.

At about 11 o'clock a sail was seen from the southwest; the ensign was set, Union down, and a signal gun fired. The vessel hoisted American colors, but sent no boat and did not appear to be approaching. It was supposed her colors might be a ruse; a boat was sent off to her; she proved to be the U. S. steamer Mount Vernon, Commander Glisson. He promised all assistance and sent a boat to sound, and proceeded to work up to the Mississippi. He came up to within a quarter of a mile, and attempted to haul the head round with a hawser, without success.

Under General Butler's direction various plans for the immediate lightening of the ship had been put in progress, to be resorted to as a last necessity.

The troops began to be transferred to the Mount Vernon, Colonel Dow's command being first sent forward. The tide in the mean time was rising, to become full at about 8.30 o'clock p. m. The propeller was set to work at full speed, all the troops were moved rapidly from stern to stem and back again, and at about 7 o'clock she moved from her position and passed slowly ahead. At this time about 200 troops had been and were in the process of being transferred to the Mount Vernon. The Mount Vernon got under weigh and ran along with the vessel for a mile or more, when she passed ahead to lead the way to an anchorage. The Mississippi cast anchor to allow her boats to come up with the soldiers and then weighed and followed the Mount Vernon. It had been known that she leaked badly, and it was found that the water filled the lower hold and fore hold, and that it was fast coming in.

Details of soldiers were set to work bailing, and such pumps as could be worked were set going, with no apparent effect upon the leak. It was supposed that she had forced a hole in herself upon the anchor. All that could work were incessantly occupied with the leak. At about 10 o'clock anchored in Cape Fear River, below Fort Caswell; passed the night, which was clear and beautiful, in quiet.

In the morning of March 1 a survey was held upon the vessel, at the order of General Butler, by Colonel Dow, H. L. Sturgis, acting master of the Mount Vernon, who had been left on board of the Mississippi by Commander Glisson, and Captain Conant, of the Thirty-first Regiment. They reported in favor of proceeding under convoy to Port Royal. A quilted sail was placed under her bow; all hands arranged for bailing and pumping, and the captain of the Mount Vernon having agreed to accompany and having kindly detailed Acting Master Sturgis to proceed with us to Ship Island, the vessel—the chain having been brought aft and the gun amidships—at about 6 o'clock set out for Port Royal. She was very much down by the head and the leak remained as before, the water-tight compartments preventing the water from coming aft the forecastle. The night was pleasant, the sea smooth, with no wind, and the vessel ran at about 8½ knots an hour.

March 2, at 8 o'clock a. m., the vessel was off Charleston, S. C., with the Mount Vernon about 2 miles astern; weather delightful. Three blockading vessels just out; one ran down to the Mount Vernon; vessel kept steadily forward, and at about 5 o'clock arrived in harbor at Port Royal and anchored; leak as before. Sent ashore for leave to land troops that evening, but could not get it until morning.

Sent to Flag-Officer Boggs, of the Varuna, for assistance and survey. He, with Captains Boutelle and Renshaw, came immediately on board; promised all assistance in their power; lay at anchor all night.

March 3, proceeded according to orders to Skull Creek, Seabrook's Landing, about 7 miles up the river. In the forenoon landed the troops, and under charge of Captain Boutelle, of the Bibb, commenced searching for and endeavoring to stop the leak. A sail was bent over the bow, and all the pumps on board with several obtained from the land were set to work. This was continued from day to day without effect until on Friday, the 7th of March, a mattress cushion having been substituted for the sail, at evening the leak was got under.

On Saturday the 8th, just as the stoppage of the hole was supposed to have been effected, it burst out afresh.

Sunday, the 9th, renewed attempts were made with success, and the hole was stopped; a cushion of tarred oakum was wound around the hole; several sheets of tarred canvas laid on, then a thick sheet of rubber; a sheet of boiler iron was laid over this and screwed down with a jack-screw, and several barrels of heated rosin poured in, covering in to the depth of 8 inches. This caused the leak to nearly stop, and was pronounced sufficient for safety by nautical men of large experience.

On Monday, the 10th of March, the vessel was reladen and the troops brought on board—the Thirty-first Massachusetts Regiment.

Prior to this, on Saturday, the steamer Matanzas had been employed to take part of the troops, in case of necessity, and the Maine troops had been put on board her on Monday forenoon, and she had dropped down to Hilton Head, with orders to await the Mississippi. At about 2.30 p. m. the Mississippi cast off and began to clear the wharf preparatory to departure. In opposition to the opinion of several nautical gentlemen of skill the captain moved his boat by the stern; she backed against the shore, and, hitting the rudder, the tiller-rope parted just as she began to move forward; it being impossible to guide her, she ran directly upon shore about a half mile below the wharf, and became hard and fast. The tug-boat Mercury was sent for and the steamer Honduras to get her off. At high tide on the morning of 11th, at about 2.30 o'clock, the ship having been put under the charge of Captain Boutelle, of the Bibb, who had kindly volunteered his assistance, an attempt was made to tow her off, but unfortunately the tide was the lowest, with one exception, ever recorded in this creek.

Another attempt was made on the tide in the afternoon with the Mercury, the Locust Point, and the Parkersburg steamers, to tow her off, without success. Another attempt was advised. On the morning of the 12th, at about 4 o'clock, the attempt was successfully made, and she ran down to Hilton Head, and anchored there at about 5.30 o'clock a. m.

Our escape from this as from the other troubles is due to everybody but the master of our vessel and his crew. But for our own sailors and soldiers and the advice and assistance of others our fate would have been a sorry one.

ADDENDUM.—I have learned since it occurred that the vessel when approaching Hatteras Inlet got among the breakers and into less than a proper amount of water for safety. The facts appear clearly in the records of the board of inquiry.

[Inclosure No. 2.]

ON BOARD STEAM TRANSPORT MISSISSIPPI,
[Captain FULTON:] *March* 12, 1862.

CAPTAIN: I transmit herewith a copy of the proceedings and testimony of a board of inquiry ordered upon the causes of the disaster which have delayed our voyage and imperiled our lives. The results of careful examination of the evidence are these:

1st. That off Cape Hatteras we were in the most imminent peril from running over the shoals within 4 fathoms water, and that, too, in daylight. If we had struck there in the gale that followed every life must have been lost.

2d. Could competent foresight and seamanship have brought us into that position?

I cannot permit the statement made by yourself, that you learned in twelve or fifteen hours after leaving Fort Monroe that the general wished to stop at Hatteras, to be any excuse; it was told you in Hampton Roads that it was necessary to stop at Hatteras Inlet to take up General Williams. The testimony of William A. Drum, one of the quartermasters of the ship, shows that it was known at least to him.

3d. That in smooth water, with a clear sky, land in full sight, with a buoy and light-house in view, the vessel was run ashore upon Frying Pan Shoals in less than 3 fathoms water.

4th. That being hard and fast aground in less than 3 fathoms water and falling tide, the port anchor was let go, the ship heading southwest, the wind westerly, and the fore main-sail, spencer, forestay sail, and jib being set (see statement of chief officer), so that the ship was forced upon it, and a hole punched through her bottom.

I do not feel myself competent to examine the courses and distances had by the ship by which we were brought into this position, having only a landsman's acquaintance with navigation, but the facts above stated are too prominent to escape the most careless observation. I will call attention, however, to some of the discrepancies of your statement, both with itself and with the direct testimony of others. You say (page 15) that between 5 and 6 o'clock a. m. of the 28th February you judged yourself on the edge of the Gulf Stream. You say (page 17) that the edge of the Gulf Stream is from 30 to 40 miles from Frying Pan Shoals. You say (page 16) you were running 8½ knots per hour; that at 7 o'clock a. m. you were in sight of main-land. Now the eastern point of Frying Pan Shoals is shown by the charts to be about 22 miles from the main-land. How could you get in sight of main-land within two hours, and, finding yourself so much out of your place, not heave the lead until after the ship struck? Besides, you say (page 15) you did not "turn out" till between 6 and 7 o'clock. What means had you of judging where you were between 5 and 6 a. m.? You will observe also that your statement as to the depth of water off Hatteras, when the vessel was in the breakers, is expressly contradicted by at least four persons. You say there was not less than 7 fathoms at any time (page 16), while the concurrent testimony of at least four witnesses is that the lead showed 4 fathoms less.

These are but a small part of the discrepancies, which show to me that your mind is in such a state of confusion as to events that the lives of my men are not safe under the guidance of your nautical skill. I am forced to the conclusion, therefore, that through your neglect or incompetency the lives of 1,400 men have thrice been in peril; that the important interests of the Government in the speed of this voyage have been greatly injured and its objects much delayed, and perhaps thwarted.

After much detention we are now at anchor in Port Royal Harbor, about to again start upon our voyage. With the convictions above expressed I ought not, I cannot, permit the voyage to proceed with yourself in command of this ship.

It has been found impossible to get another to carry the troops within any reasonable time. There is but one course of duty left to me, a responsible and unpleasant one. You will therefore be placed under arrest, in your state-room, until you can be conveniently transferred to the Matanzas. You will be allowed to take from the ship with you your personal baggage only. Everything else will be left on board and a receipt will be given you for the ship, her tackle, equipment, and stores of every description; you will proceed to Ship Island on board the Matanzas.

After landing the troops there, if I determine to terminate the charter-party, the ship and crew will be again turned over to you, if the owners so desire.

Copies of the proceedings of the court of inquiry and of this order of arrest will be sent to the owners, together with a copy of the log since we left Fortress Monroe, with a report of the voyage from the itinerary kept by my order.

I am grieved to be obliged to this action, for our personal relations have been of the kindest character, and I know yourself will believe that only the sternest sense of duty would compel me to it.

I have the honor to be, your obedient servant,

BENJ. F. BUTLER,
Major-General, Commanding.

SAINT LOUIS, *March* 14, 1862.

E. M. STANTON,
Secretary of War, Washington:

General Bragg is at Memphis, and large re-enforcements are arriving from the South by railroad, to sustain General A. S. Johnston and prevent us from reaching Memphis. If an attack on Mobile is intended, now is the time. The capture of that place would assist us very much here. Moreover, gunboats could then ascend the Alabama River and open its commerce.

H. W. HALLECK,
Major-General.

GENERAL ORDERS, No. 1.

HDQRS. DEPARTMENT OF THE GULF,
Ship Island, March 20, 1862.

Pursuant to General Orders, No. 20, of February 23, 1862, from the Headquarters of the Army, Maj. Gen. B. F. Butler, U. S. Volunteers, assumes command of this department.

His staff is announced as follows:

Maj. George C. Strong, assistant adjutant-general, ordnance officer and chief of staff.

Capt. Jonas H. French, aide-de-camp and inspector-general.

Capt. Peter Haggerty, aide-de-camp.

First Lieut. J. W. Cushing, Thirty-first Massachusetts Volunteers, acting chief quartermaster.

First Lieut. J. E. Easterbrook, Thirtieth Massachusetts Volunteers, acting chief commissary.

Capt. George A. Kensel, chief of artillery.

First Lieut. Godfrey Weitzel, chief engineer.

First Lieut. J. C. Palfrey, assistant engineer.

First Lieut. C. N. Turnbull, chief of topographical engineers.

Surg. Thomas H. Bache, medical director.

Maj. J. M. Bell, volunteer aide-de-camp.

Capt. R. S. Davis, volunteer aide-de-camp.

First Lieut. J. B. Kinsman, aide-de-camp.

Second Lieut. H. C. Clarke, aide-de-camp.

By command of Major-General Butler:

GEO. C. STRONG,
Assistant Adjutant-General.

HEADQUARTERS DEPARTMENT OF FLORIDA,
Fort Pickens, March 22, 1862.

Brig. Gen. LORENZO THOMAS,
Adjutant-General U. S. Army, Washington, D. C.:

GENERAL: I deem it proper to report for the information of the General-in-Chief that the rebels at Pensacola and along their line of defense have been stampeded by our glorious Union victories elsewhere. This information (indefinite, however) was derived from two stupid white men and two negroes, who came over a few days since from Milton and East Bay, some 40 miles from Pensacola, but it is apparent that the enemy hold firm possession of Forts McRee and Barrancas and at least five sand batteries lining the shore between the former fort and the navy-yard. The four refugees could furnish no information but hearsay stories as to the force of the enemy in their forts, navy-yard, Pensacola, on Bayou Grande, Live Oak Plantation, &c. As my position is a defensive one, on an island, I am perfectly helpless for any offensive movement requiring water transportation for 50 men without naval co-operation. I have not under my command a dispatch steamer or sail vessel, and have scarcely enough surf-boats to land stores for the command.

I have made estimates on the Quartermaster's Department for a steamboat and surf-boats, which ought to be, and I am in hopes will be, furnished without delay. The sloop of war Vincennes, carrying two 9-inch and four 8-inch Dahlgren guns, two rifled guns—one 20-pounder and one 10-pounder—is the only vessel of war that has been lying off Santa Rosa for the past two weeks. She cannot be made available here for any successful movement against the enemy.

The General-in-Chief can rely upon the zeal and spirit of my command. I will do everything in my power, with my limited means, to aid in crushing out this senseless and wicked rebellion.

I am, general, very respectfully, your obedient servant,

L. G. ARNOLD,

Brigadier-General, U. S. Volunteers, Commanding.

GENERAL ORDERS, No. 8. } HDQRS. DEPARTMENT OF THE GULF, *Ship Island, March* 29, 1862.

The following-named regiments and corps will embark to-morrow, commencing at 8 a. m., in the following order, viz:

1. On board steamer Mississippi, the commanding general and staff; Fourth Regiment Wisconsin Volunteers; Durivage Cavalry (dismounted) and Manning's battery; Weitzel Pioneers.
2. On board steamer Matanzas: Brigadier-General Williams and staff; Twenty-first Regiment Indiana Volunteers.
3. On board steamer Lewis: Ninth Regiment Connecticut Volunteers.
4. On board ship North America: Twenty-sixth Massachusetts Volunteers; Everett's battery.
5. On board ship Wild Gazelle: Sixth Michigan Volunteers.
6. On board ship E. W. Farley: Twelfth Connecticut Volunteers.

Each regiment will take three tents, and the detached companies of cavalry, artillery, and pioneers one tent each. The remaining tents will be left standing. The troops will carry their camp kettles, mess-pans, cups, plates, knives and forks, and each soldier his knapsack, overcoat, blanket, one extra shirt, one extra pair of drawers, one extra pair of shoes, canteen, and in his haversack four days' cooked rations. They will also take all the axes, hatchets, picks, shovels, and spades they may have in possession.

Officers' baggage will be limited to bedding and one valise, bag, or knapsack; no trunks in any case to be taken. The remaining baggage of officers and men will be properly secured, as compactly as possible, marked, and turned over to the division quartermaster.

Captains of companies will be held responsible that every soldier has in his cartridge-box 40 rounds of ammunition.

The troops will be inspected at 6 p. m. to-day, to see that this order has been complied with as far as may be necessary at that hour, to insure promptness in the embarkation to-morrow. One con-commissioned officer for each regiment will be left behind to turn over the baggage, tents, &c., to the chief quartermaster.

By command of Major-General Butler:

GEO. C. STRONG,
Assistant Adjutant-General.

HEADQUARTERS, ETC., *March* 30, 1862.

Flag-Officer FARRAGUT,
Commanding West Gulf Squadron:

SIR: I am now ready to put on board ship six regiments and two batteries, and will be able to be in the "passes" in twelve hours. I am still of opinion that an effort be made to land above the fort as soon as you can get the gunboats by. Its moral, not to say actual, effect would aid the attack, if not compel surrender. If the Navy are not to be ready for six or eight days I ought not to sail, as my coal is running short, and I cannot carry more than eight days' for sailing. May I ask that you send me word so as to reach me by Tuesday morning, and I will be embarked in waiting. If you prefer, I will be in time to attempt the landing off Isle Breton. If I can aid you in any way please command me. I shall wait your advices. If it is of importance that you advise me, please do not fail.

I am, with much respect, your obedient servant,

BENJ. F. BUTLER,
Major-General, Commanding.

Organization of the troops in Department of the Gulf, March 31, 1862.

First Brigade.

Brig. Gen. JOHN W. PHELPS.

9th Connecticut.
12th Connecticut.
13th Connecticut.
8th New Hampshire.
7th Vermont.
8th Vermont.
4th Massachusetts Battery.
1st Vermont Battery.
2d Vermont Battery.
2d Battalion Massachusetts Cavalry (one company).

Second Brigade.

Brig. Gen. THOMAS WILLIAMS.

21st Indiana.
26th Massachusetts.
31st Massachusetts.
6th Michigan.
4th Wisconsin.
2d Massachusetts Battery.
6th Massachusetts Battery.
2d Battalion Massachusetts Cavalry (one company).

Third Brigade.

Col. GEORGE F. SHEPLEY, Twelfth Maine Infantry.

12th Maine.
13th Maine.
14th Maine.
15th Maine.
30th Massachusetts.
1st Maine Battery.
2d Battalion Massachusetts Cavalry (one company).

Abstract from return of the Department of the Gulf, commanded by Maj. Gen. B. F. Butler, U. S. Army, for March, 1862.

Command.	Present for duty.		Aggregate present.	Aggregate present and absent.	Pieces of artillery.
	Officers.	Men.			
1st (Phelps') Brigade:					
Infantry	97	2,298	2,584	2,718	......
Artillery	8	250	270	291	6
Cavalry	3	69	81	86	......
2d (Williams') Brigade:					
Infantry	163	4,126	4,908	4,380	......
Artillery	4	89	115	145	......
Cavalry	3	79	95	95	......
3d (Shepley's) Brigade:					
Infantry	128	2,862	3,619	3,872	......
Artillery	5	124	141	143	6
Cavalry	3	65	80	82	......
Total	414	9,962	11,893	12,412	12

The Thirteenth Connecticut, Fifteenth Maine, and Seventh and Eighth Vermont Regiments of Infantry, and the Second Massachusetts and First Vermont Batteries reported on original as "not arrived."

APRIL 2, 1862.

Maj. GEORGE C. STRONG,
Assistant Adjutant-General, &c.:

MAJOR: Taking with you on board the steamer Lewis the Ninth Regiment of Connecticut Volunteers and a section of Captain Everett's battery, and acting in conjunction with the Navy, you will proceed to Biloxi, and demand and obtain an ample apology for the firing into a flag of truce upon an errand of humanity under your command upon the 1st instant.

The apology must be an ample one, and you will demand and obtain a guarantee against such occurrences in the future, signed by the mayor, the principal inhabitants, and the colonel commanding the forces there.

You will inform the authorities and the citizens that no flag of truce must be hereafter sent to this island unless accompanied by a commissioned officer, in full uniform, with proper credentials; that civilians cannot be received under such flag, or if received will be detained.

You will land and compel any force there to retire, and take such measures to secure and enforce the foregoing as you may deem best, either by seizing and bringing off the principal inhabitants or whatever else may seem advisable.

You will also proceed to Mississippi City and Pass Christian, if desired by the Navy, and co-operate with it in any demonstrations deemed advisable against those places.

By command of Major-General Butler:

JOS. M. BELL,
Major and Aide-de-Camp.

BILOXI, MISS., *April* 3, 1862.

To the Mayor of Biloxi:

SIR: I am directed by Major-General Butler, commanding the Department of the Gulf, to call your attention to the fact that on the 1st instant a party of men under my command, bearing a flag of truce and on an errand of mercy, were fired into in a most cowardly manner while their schooner was aground and just after they had left your shore.

An apology was made by a person claiming to be an officer of the Third Mississippi Volunteers, but General Butler has ordered that the repetition of such or similar outrageous action be the signal for the destruction of your town.

I am directed, moreover, to inform you that all persons in citizens' dress who visit the lines of the United States forces on this coast under a flag of truce will be detained if suspected. All such flags, to be respected, must be accompanied by a military officer in uniform and with proper credentials.

Respectfully, &c.,

GEO. C. STRONG,
Assistant Adjutant-General.

GENERAL ORDERS, No. 9. } HDQRS. DEPARTMENT OF THE GULF,
Ship Island, April 10, 1862.

The following-named regiments and corps will embark, commencing at —— m., and in the following order:

On board ship Great Republic: Twenty-first Regiment Indiana Volunteers; Fourth Regiment Wisconsin Volunteers; Sixth Regiment Michigan Volunteers.

On board steamer Mississippi: Twenty-sixth Regiment Massachusetts Volunteers; Thirty-first Regiment Massachusetts Volunteers; Brown's sappers and miners; Everett's battery.

On board steamer Matanzas: Ninth Regiment Connecticut Volunteers; Second Vermont Battery.

On board ship North America: Thirtieth Regiment Massachusetts Volunteers; Read's cavalry; Durivage's cavalry; Manning's battery.

On board ship E. Wilder Farley: Twelfth Regiment Connecticut Volunteers.

The amount of provisions, baggage, &c., to be carried by the troops will be the same as heretofore designated in General Orders, No. 8, current series. No knapsack will be unslung during embarkation or disembarkation or on board a lighter in going to or from any transport.

By command of Major-General Butler:

GEO. C. STRONG,
Assistant Adjutant-General.

HEADQUARTERS DEPARTMENT OF THE GULF,
Ship Island, April 13, 1862.

To the Hon. SECRETARY OF WAR:

SIR: I have the honor to report my safe arrival at Ship Island on the 21st of March, after a series of casualties set forth in my last report from Port Royal to the General commanding the Army, but from thence no further accident. For three days after my arrival a storm prevented a landing of either troops or stores. Upon consultation with Flag-Officer Farragut, I was informed by him that he would probably be able to move in seven days. Accordingly, by dint of most strenuous labor of my troops day and night, I had embarked and ready for embarkation 6,000 of my best men to support his operations—a force judged to be sufficient for the advance, to be at once supported by the remainder of my disposable force. After waiting four days, with troops on shipboard, I learned from the flag-officer that the storms and low water at the bar had prevented his getting his ships into position. For sanitary reasons I disembarked the troops, and shall re-embark to-morrow, and shall sail for the Head of the Passes when I am informed that the Navy will be ready for operations.

I have pleasure in reporting the safe arrival of all the troops assigned to this department (the last regiment from the North, the Thirteenth Connecticut Volunteers, arriving last night), except Nims' battery, the only drilled corps of artillery given me, which has for some unexplained reason been detained at Fortress Monroe.

During my enforced delay by shipwreck, General Phelps had sent away both the Constitution and Fulton steamers, so that I am much crippled for transportation. But "where there is a will there is a way," and I shall be able by means of sailing vessels under tow to make my way up the Mississippi, but for ulterior movements on the coast one at least of those steamers will be of the last necessity, as well as several light-draught steamers, for which I had made requisition upon the Quartermaster-General.

In the mean time I have sent a regiment and section of a battery, under the direction of Major Strong, my chief of staff, to co-operate with the Navy, to demand an apology for an insult to our flag of truce, sent on an errand of mercy, with a shipwrecked passenger, as well as to destroy the position of a regiment of the enemy at Pass Christian. This service was gallantly performed; the proper apology was made at Biloxi, the town surrendered into our hands, and the rebels at Pass Christian, an equal force, with four pieces of artillery, driven from their camp, which, with its material, was burned. No lives were lost, and only 2 of our men were wounded. I trust my next dispatch, by the first opportunity of sending by a mail steamer, will give account of larger and as successful operations.

I think it due to the good conduct of the brave men of that expedition to ask to have published the general order upon that subject inclosed.

I put myself in communication with General Arnold, and have no doubt, in conjunction with him, of the easy capture of both Mobile and Pensacola, were it not that I felt bound as well by my instructions as my own judgment not to hazard the success of the main object of the demonstration in the Gulf.

I have the honor to be, most respectfully, your obedient servant,

BENJ. F. BUTLER,
Major-General, Commanding.

[Inclosure.]

GENERAL ORDERS, No. 10. } HDQRS. DEPARTMENT OF THE GULF, *Ship Island, April* 12, 1862.

The major-general commanding desires publicly to testify his admiration of the gallant courage and good conduct of the Ninth Regiment of Connecticut Volunteers, Colonel Cahill commanding, and a section of the Sixth Massachusetts Battery, under Captain Everett, in the recent expedition to Biloxi and Pass Christian, as exhibited by the report of the staff officer in command of that expedition.

Of their bravery in the field he felt assured, but another quality more trying to the soldier claims his admiration. After having been for months subjected to the privations necessarily incident to camp life upon this island, these well-disciplined soldiers, although for many hours in full possession of two rebel villages, filled with what to them were most desirable luxuries, abstained from the least unauthorized interference with private property and all molestation of peaceful citizens.

This behavior is worthy of all praise. It robs war of half its horrors. It teaches our enemies how much they have been misinformed by their designing leaders as to the character of our soldiers and the intention of our Government. It gives them a lesson and an example in humanity and civilized warfare much needed, however little it may be followed.

The general commanding commends the action of the men of this expedition to every soldier in this department. Let it be imitated by all in the towns and cities we shall occupy—a living witness that the United States soldier fights only for the Union, the Constitution, and the enforcement of the laws.

By command of Major-General Butler:

GEO. C. STRONG,
Assistant Adjutant-General.

HEADQUARTERS DEPARTMENT OF THE GULF,
Off the Passes, Mississippi Delta, April 17, 1862.

To the Hon. SECRETARY OF WAR:

SIR: I have the honor to report that I am now off the passes with eight regiments and three batteries of artillery of my best troops, under command of Brigadier-Generals Phelps and Williams, ready to co-operate with the fleet, who move to-day or, as I believe, to-morrow upon Forts Saint Philip and Jackson. These are all for which I have possible means of transportation, owing to the circumstances stated in my dispatch of 13th instant, and all that I believe will be needed for the present emergency. You may think that we have delayed, but I beg to assure you that, with the storms and winds and the means at our disposal, we made every haste and are ready as soon as we are needed.

The health of the command is very good, and their equipments as to arms and provisions abundant. It was especially fortunate that I made so large a provision for coal, as I have been enabled to spare the Navy more than a thousand tons, without which they would have been very much embarrassed. I have taken the means to keep up my own supply, and now there will be enough for all for the present. Steamers are much needed of light draught.

Very respectfully, your obedient servant,

BENJ. F. BUTLER,
Major-General, Commanding.

HEADQUARTERS DEPARTMENT OF FLORIDA,
Fort Pickens, April 24, 1862.

Brig. Gen. LORENZO THOMAS,
Adjutant-General U. S. Army:

GENERAL: I have the honor to state for the information of the War Department that the relations between my command and the rebels have (to the extent of my knowledge) undergone very little change since my last report.

Their forts and batteries and the navy-yard opposite appear nearly as formidable as they did three months ago. The spirit, discipline, and instruction of my troops have improved. I would have attacked the enemy before this if I had not been separated from him by a broad bay and having no naval co-operation nor water transportation for anything like an adequate force. I was in hopes that General Butler would have co-operated with me in attacking the rebels in their rear, by landing two regiments of infantry and a field battery on the Perdido and by furnishing me with a steam gunboat to attack them at or above Pensacola, thus making a joint attack; but unfortunately the necessities of the service prevented this, as a copy of General Butler's letter, herewith inclosed, will explain.

The position of the enemy is a very strong one from fortuitous circumstances. Occupying two strong forts and a redoubt and a line of batteries for at least 3 miles and separated from us by a broad bay, and being within easy communication with Mobile and Montgomery by rail and telegraph, he can be re-enforced, and having but a small force to oppose him with, not a naval vessel to co operate, nor water transportation to aid our land forces—such is and has been for two months past the military status in this department.

I inclose copies of correspondence between Flag-Officers Farragut and McKean and General Butler and myself on this subject.

I am, general, very respectfully, your obedient servant,

L. G. ARNOLD,
Brigadier-General, U. S. Volunteers, Commanding.

[Inclosures.]

HEADQUARTERS DEPARTMENT OF FLORIDA,
Fort Pickens, March 15, 1862.

Flag-Officer D. G. FARRAGUT,
Commanding Gulf Squadron:

DEAR SIR: I have under my command on this island 1,200 volunteers and 600 regular soldiers, but I am perfectly helpless for offensive movements without naval co-operation, being on an island, and having no water transportation. If you can spare two or three gunboats to run in by the Swash Channel, they, together with the land force that I will furnish, can, I think, take Town Point, on Live Oak Plantation, which (as reported by some rebel deserters) was defended by five heavy guns behind sand batteries, supported by 2,000 men; but subsequent information, derived from runaway negroes, leads me to believe that all the guns and men, except one 10-inch columbiad and 400 men, have been removed, probably to Mobile.

The rebels have, and will have, entire control of the bay and inner harbor as long as they hold this point and their line of forts and batteries; but if we can take this point, your gunboats can pass out of range of their heaviest guns—from Four Mile Point, on Santa Rosa Island, to Milton, on the main-land, which would enable you to capture or destroy all the rebel steamers and sail vessels in those waters, and more perfectly blockade the harbor of Pensacola.

Town Point is an initial and decisive point necessary to be taken in any future operations for the recapture of the navy-yard and their line of defensive works.

I am in hopes you will soon be here, when we can discuss the whole subject.

I am, commodore, very respectfully, your obedient servant,

L. G. ARNOLD,
Brigadier General, U. S. Volunteers, Commanding.

U. S. FLAG-SHIP HARTFORD,
Mississippi River, Head of Passes, April 8, 1862.

Brig. Gen. ARNOLD,
Commanding Fort Pickens, Fla.:

DEAR GENERAL: Nothing would give me more pleasure than to co-operate with you in your designs against Pensacola, but you must be aware that I am on the eve of attacking New Orleans, and my orders are such that I cannot look at any other place until I succeed or fail in this.

If I succeed, Pensacola comes in turn, but not the first; still I hope to be able to gratify your wishes soon.

Until then I remain, very respectfully, your obedient servant,

D. G. FARRAGUT,
Flag-Officer Western Gulf Blockading Squadron.

HEADQUARTERS DEPARTMENT OF THE GULF,
Ship Island, April 10, 1862.

Brig. Gen. LEWIS G. ARNOLD,
Commanding Department of Florida:

GENERAL: I regret that we are unable to co-operate with you at present in the capture of Pensacola, as the presence of my troops and transports is necessary, as soon as possible, in the Mississippi River.

Should you not have taken that place before my return hither I shall take pleasure in sending you any assistance that may be necessary, and I trust you will not fail to call upon me at all times for any aid I can render you.

I am, very respectfully, your obedient servant,

BENJ. F. BUTLER,
Major-General, Commanding.

HEADQUARTERS DEPARTMENT OF FLORIDA,
Fort Pickens, April 13, 1862.

Maj. Gen. BENJAMIN F. BUTLER,
Commanding Department of the Gulf, Ship Island:

GENERAL: I have just received your note of the 10th instant. I regret that the "fortune of war" will not permit you to co-operate with me in the taking of Pensacola, &c., at this time, for I am convinced that if the co-operation suggested by your assistant adjutant-general could have been afforded me the expedition would have been entirely successful; and so hopeful was I, that my orders have been issued and arrangements made with that view.

I must thank you for the patriotic and soldierly tender of your aid and co-operation at any future time, as expressed in the closing paragraph of your note, and I take this occasion to reciprocate the same kind and delicate sentiments, by offering you anything that you may require within my limited command that will benefit the public service.

I am, general, very respectfully, your obedient servant,

L. G. ARNOLD,
Brigadier-General, U. S. Volunteers, Commanding.

HEADQUARTERS DEPARTMENT OF FLORIDA,
Fort Pickens, April 13, 1862.

Flag-Officer W. W. MCKEAN,
Commanding Eastern Division U. S. Gulf Squadron:

DEAR SIR: Our recent victories in Tennessee, North Carolina, &c., having caused the rebels to remove the most of their best troops from the navy-yard and their whole defensive line from Fort McRee to Pensacola, I am confident (although they apparently present a bold front as respects their forts and batteries) that if you will co-operate with me, by furnishing one or two gunboats, I can land a sufficient force, with your aid, to retake Pensacola, the navy-yard, and their entire line of forts and batteries. Moreover, you can capture four of their steamers and several schooners.

I have under my command from 1,800 to 2,000 available troops on this island, but I am perfectly helpless for any offensive movement off the island without naval co-operation and water transportation.

Flag-Officer Farragut writes to me that he cannot assist me against Pensacola till he has taken New Orleans. Then the opportune moment may have passed.

I am in hopes you will come here immediately and bring one or two gunboats, for I would be most happy to co-operate with Flag-Officer McKean.

The Navy has not a single vessel off Pensacola Harbor.

I am, commodore, very respectfully, your obedient servant,

L. G. ARNOLD,

Brigadier-General, U. S. Volunteers, Commanding.

HEADQUARTERS DEPARTMENT OF THE GULF,
Steamer Mississippi, April 24, 1862.

Flag-Officer FARRAGUT,
Commanding Western Gulf Squadron:

SIR: Allow me to congratulate you and your command upon the bold, daring, brilliant, and successful passage of the forts by your fleet this morning. A more gallant exploit it has never fallen to the lot of man to witness.

Captain Porter, with whom I have had a conference, agrees that it was best we should at once proceed to carry out the plan agreed upon by yourself and me, to wit, that I should immediately land troops to co-operate with you at the quarantine station and so hem in the forts.

When I left the mortar fleet, at about 8 o'clock this morning, the rebel flag was still flying upon the forts; the ram had floated down on fire and was consumed; another rebel steamer was burning. A signal had been made to cease firing by Captain Porter; the Portsmouth had returned to her anchorage unhurt; the Winona had been badly crippled, a shot through her boilers and several in her hull, making water fast; the Itasca had been badly used, but had lost no men, and was in an effective condition—all other men unhurt save trifling casualties; the Harriet Lane had but one killed and wounded, beside, in all, so far as I could learn.

Captain Porter will forward you ammunition and supplies through the quarantine station should you desire. I will be able to aid you from the same point immediately. Please send directions as to your wishes by the bearer or otherwise.

I send this by Captain Conant, of the Thirty-first Massachusetts Regiment, who goes to communicate with you. He is the gentleman of whom I spoke to you as having made a reconnaissance in the rear of Lieutenant Philips night before last. He knows the contents of this dispatch, for fear of accident, and may be most implicitly relied upon and trusted. I hope he may be able to report to me off Point Salle, when I will immediately communicate with Captain Porter. If in danger, Captain Conant has been ordered to destroy this and remember its contents, and will do the same with any dispatches you may give him.

If you design proceeding up the river, will you leave, say, two gunboats at the quarantine station to protect our landing?

Respectfully, yours,

BENJ. F. BUTLER,
Major-General, Commanding.

GENERAL ORDERS, No. 14. } HDQRS. DEPARTMENT OF THE GULF,
Head of Mississippi Passes, April 24, 1862.

The transports Mississippi, Matanzas, Lewis, Saxon, and Great Republic, with all the troops now on board, will proceed, under convoy of U. S. steamers Miami and Sachem, and without delay, to Sable Island, with a view to reaching quarantine station in rear of Fort St. Philip. All of the above-named troops will be under the command of Brigadier-General Williams until further orders.

II. Brigadier-General Phelps will remain in command of all the troops on board transport ships North America and E. W. Farley, and hold himself in readiness to occupy the forts as soon as they shall have been reduced.

By order of Major-General Butler:

GEO. C. STRONG,
Assistant Adjutant-General.

HEADQUARTERS DEPARTMENT OF THE GULF,
Off Fort Saint Philip, on Gulf Side, April 26, 1862.

Actg. Brig. Gen. GEORGE F. SHEPLEY,
General, Commanding at Ship Island:

GENERAL: The fleet passed by the forts on the morning of the 24th instant with but little loss, leaving the mortar fleet and a few gunboats below, without reducing the forts. They have substantially cleared the river of boats above the forts, but have left the ram and two rebel boats under the cover of the forts. These are proving troublesome to the remnant of our fleet below in the river.

The flag-officer has gone up with twelve vessels of his fleet to New Orleans, leaving us to reduce the forts.

I am endeavoring to effect a landing on the Gulf side, at the quarantine grounds. I am sadly in want of means of light transportation.

The Lewis is broken down for want of coal. She very foolishly came away with only five days' coal, having lain alongside the Idaho while mending her smoke-stacks without taking any. I must have soft coal. I suppose the coal, or a large portion of it, from the Idaho is now in a schooner. If so, send her at once, either under tow of the Saxon or under sail, or both, but send the coal at all events; make every possible dispatch. Send also all the light draught schooners you have there not drawing more than 4 feet, say four; the little one I used to have, the Gipsey, if repaired, and all the boats possible; all are needed at once. Have the Parliament ready to sail at a moment's notice, with everything on board for thirty days' provision for us, with plenty of rice. Send fresh meat if any has arrived. Do not send the Parliament until further orders. You may send beef at once.

If the Washington or Butler has a large quantity of lumber on board, send her at once. Dispatch is of the first moment. If you have a light-draught steamer, send her by all means. The devil is in the Saxon and he is trying to break her down. Have her sent down here under sail if she does break down, so that I may get the Government property out of her.

Very respectfully, &c.,

BENJ. F. BUTLER,
Major-General, Commanding.

Send on board one of the schooners a large supply of medical and surgical stores suitable for wounded men.

No great haste required as regards this.

By order:

GEO. C. STRONG,
Assistant Adjutant-General.

HEADQUARTERS DEPARTMENT OF FLORIDA,
Fort Pickens, Fla., April 28, 1862.

Brig. Gen. M. C. MEIGS,
Quartermaster-General U. S. Army, Washington, D. C.:

GENERAL: I feel it my duty to report to you (that the evil complained of may be remedied as soon as possible) the great injustice that has been done my command, about 2,000 strong, by being located on an island without having suitable boats to transport at one time 100 men off of it for any offensive movement against the enemy, and without a steamer or sail vessel belonging to the Quartermaster's Department at my control to keep open communications with the army stationed at other points in the Gulf, to convey or bring any intelligence of the movements of our own troops or of the rebels, to tow flats loaded with troops and munitions for any military operation of this island. A requisition was made by my order on your department in February last for a steamer of 200 or 300 tons burden, as a dispatch boat, twelve surf-boats, 30 feet long, and 100 oars, to which no reply has yet been received.

The condition of military affairs within the limits of my command for the past two months can be summed up in brief as follows: 2,000 men have been stationed on an island without sufficient or suitable means to get off of it, with scarcely enough surf-boats, &c., to land stores for the command, without a steamer or sail vessel belonging to the Quartermaster's Department to communicate with other posts in the Gulf, receiving a mail about once a month or six weeks, and, I will add, almost abandoned by the Navy, as no vessel of war has been off this harbor for the major part of that time; this notwithstanding I have applied to Flag-Officers Farragut and McKean to co-operate with me in attacking the rebels opposite. They were compelled to decline for the time being, as they were employing every available vessel in their squadrons in the grand attack on New Orleans and in blockading.

I have been thus particular in stating the condition of things here to impress you with the importance and necessity of immediately furnishing my chief quartermaster with the boats, &c., called for in the requisition referred to.

I am, general, very respectfully, your obedient servant,

L. G. ARNOLD,
Brigadier-General, U. S. Volunteers, Commanding.

HEADQUARTERS DEPARTMENT OF THE GULF,
Quarantine Station, La., April 30, 1862.

Col. E. F. JONES,
Twenty-sixth Mass. Volunteers, U. S. Army,
Commanding Forts Jackson and Saint Philip, La.:

SIR: You will, as soon as possible, place Forts Jackson and Saint Philip in a proper state of police and defense.

In addition to the general regulations of the Army relating to the care of fortifications and their armament, you will be guided by the following instructions:

At both works all frame buildings and everything combustible must at once be removed to the outside of the main work or be placed under bomb-proof cover; the ammunition, carefully assorted, placed in the magazine nearest to the batteries to which such ammunition belongs, and the magazine kept well ventilated, dry, and bomb-proof. The serviceable guns left at the works will be arranged in position mostly for up-river defense. All the provisions will be carefully stored in as dry places as possible. Temporary bridges will be constructed only at the main entrance. The damage to the earthwork at Fort Jackson will be repaired as much as possible. The ruins of the citadel will be removed to the outside of the work, and the material used for walks wherever necessary. Colonel Jones will establish a strict quarantine at this station, allow no vessel to pass (save ships of war of the United States) until the strictest surgical examination, and with a clean bill of health. No communication will be had with vessels by any person of his command without his express order and after the examination of the surgeon.

BENJ. F. BUTLER,
Major-General, Commanding.

HEADQUARTERS DEPARTMENT OF THE GULF,
April 30, 1862.

Brigadier-General SHEPLEY,
Ship Island:

GENERAL: I send you the Tennessee for a transport. You will at once take so many troops as she can carry and proceed to Fort Saint Philip, there delivering the camp equipage of Colonel Jones, and then proceed to New Orleans, or wherever I may be, and report to me. I want three regiments—Eighth Vermont, Twelfth Maine, and Thirteenth Connecticut. Leave the ablest colonel you have in charge at the island. Have provisions for us all for thirty days. I send Quartermaster Monroe for all the camp equipage of the regiments here and reasonable baggage. Send all baggage and horses for self and staff, so far as they have distinctive horses. If any accommodation, bring Mrs. Butler with you; if not, take the Saxon. I send the Great Republic for horses, all she can take, and Thompson's battery, with ammunition. She can take one of the regiments. Do not put her below 15 feet, or 6 inches more, if possible; she cannot get over the bar. Get a tow for her.

Organize a number of men, say 250, with provisions for sixty days, and a competent commander, to take possession of Fort Wood. Lieutenant Reed, in the naval force at the island, will convey the expedition. I have very direct information from thence of the evacuation, but not official. Send Geo. Washington or some other ship with forage sufficient for present need at least, and as much as possible. Bring an invoice of the supplies at Ship Island, and take all the unissued clothing not absolutely needed at the island. Let the brig Yankee Blade sail at once, without unloading; bring her invoice. Let the postmaster transfer himself to near New Orleans.

Everything is so far successful and everything requires dispatch.

2 P. M.

I am now at the passes. I find the Great Republic ashore there, *hors de combat.* I am tired of waiting for her any longer. Take the Ocean Pearl, or any other ship that does not draw more than 15 feet, for the horses; use your own discretion; the river is now open and free.

I am, your obedient servant,

BENJ. F. BUTLER,
Major-General, Commanding.

Abstract from return of the Western District, Department of the South, Brig. Gen. Lewis G. Arnold, U. S. Army, commanding, for April, 1862.

Garrisons.	Troops.	Present for duty. Officers.	Present for duty. Men.	Aggregate present.
Santa Rosa Island, Fla.:				
Fort Pickens	Detachments 1st and 2d Artillery and 3d Infantry	18	527	640
Camp Lincoln	6th New York Infantry	22	449	676
Camp Seward	75th New York Infantry	26	655	803
	Total	66	1,631	2,119

GENERAL ORDERS, No. 15. } HDQRS. DEPARTMENT OF THE GULF, *New Orleans, May* 1, 1862.

I. In anticipation of the immediate disembarkation of the troops of this command, amid the temptations and inducements of a large city, all plundering of public or private property, by any person or persons, is hereby forbidden, under the severest penalties.

II. No officer or soldier will absent himself from his station without arms or alone under any pretext whatever.

III. The commanders of regiments and companies will be held responsible for the strict execution of these orders and that the offenders are brought to punishment.

By command of Major-General Butler:

GEO. C. STRONG,
Assistant Adjutant-General.

PROCLAMATION.

HEADQUARTERS DEPARTMENT OF THE GULF,
New Orleans, May 1, 1862.

The city of New Orleans and its environs, with all its interior and exterior defenses, having been surrendered to the combined naval and land forces of the United States, and having been evacuated by the rebel forces in whose possession they lately were, and being now in occupation of the forces of the United States, who have come to restore order, maintain public tranquillity, enforce peace and quiet under the laws and Constitution of the United States, the major-general commanding the forces of the United States in the Department of the Gulf hereby makes known and proclaims the object and purposes of the Government of the United States in thus taking possession of the city of New Orleans and the State of Louisiana, and the rules and regulations by which the laws of the United States will be for the present and during a state of war enforced and maintained, for the plain guidance of all good citizens of the United States, as well as others who may heretofore have been in rebellion against their authority.

Thrice before has the city of New Orleans been rescued from the hand of a foreign government, and still more calamitous domestic insurrection, by the money and arms of the United States. It has of late been under the military control of the rebel forces, claiming to be the peculiar friends of its citizens; and at each time, in the judgment of the commander of the military forces holding it, it has been found necessary to preserve order and maintain quiet by the administration of law martial. Even during the *interim* from its evacuation by the rebel soldiers and its actual possession by the soldiers of the United States, the civil authorities of the city have found it necessary to call for the intervention of an armed body known as the European Legion, to preserve public tranquillity. The commanding general, therefore, will cause the city to be governed, until the restoration of municipal authority and his further orders, by the law martial, a measure for which it would seem the previous recital furnishes sufficient precedents.

All persons in arms against the United States are required to surrender themselves, with their arms, equipments, and munitions of war. The body known as the European Legion, not being understood to be in arms against the United States, but organized to protect the lives and property of the citizens, are invited still to co-operate with the forces of the United Statess to that end, and, so acting, will not be included in the terms of this order, but will report to these headquarters.

All flags, ensigns, and devices tending to uphold any authority whatever, save the flag of the United States and the flags of foreign consulates, must not be exhibited, but suppressed. The American ensign, the emblem of the United States, must be treated with the utmost deference and respect by all persons, under pain of severe punishment.

All persons well disposed towards the Government of the United States who shall renew their oath of allegiance will receive the safeguard and protection, in their persons and property, of the armies of the United States, the violation of which by any person is punishable with death. All persons still holding allegiance to the Confederate States will be deemed rebels against the Government of the United States, and regarded and treated as enemies thereof.

All foreigners not naturalized and claiming allegiance to their respective governments, and not having made oath of allegiance to the supposed Government of the Confederate States, will be protected in their persons and property as heretofore under the laws of the United States.

All persons who may heretofore have given their adherence to the supposed Government of the Confederate States or have been in their service, who shall lay down and deliver up their arms and return to peaceful occupations and preserve quiet and order, holding no further correspondence nor giving aid and comfort to the enemies of the United

States, will not be disturbed either in person or property, except so far, under the orders of the commanding general, as the exigencies of the public service may render necessary.

The keepers of all public property, whether State, National, or Confederate, such as collections of art, libraries, museums, as well as public buildings, all munitions of war, and armed vessels, will at once make full returns thereof to these headquarters. All manufacturers of arms and munitions of war will report to these headquarters their kind and places of business.

All rights of property, of whatever kind, will be held inviolate, subject only to the laws of the United States.

All inhabitants are enjoined to pursue their usual avocations; all shops and places of business are to be kept open in the accustomed manner, and services to be had in the churches and religious houses as in times of profound peace.

Keepers of all public houses, coffee houses, and drinking saloons are to report their names and numbers to the office of the provost-marshal; will there receive license, and be held responsible for all disorders and disturbance of the peace arising in their respective places.

A sufficient force will be kept in the city to preserve order and maintain the laws.

The killing of an American soldier by any disorderly person or mob is simply assassination and murder and not war, and will be so regarded and punished. The owner of any house or building in or from which such murder shall be committed will be held responsible therefor, and the house will be liable to be destroyed by the military authority.

All disorders and disturbances of the peace, done by combinations and numbers and crimes of an aggravated nature, interfering with the forces or laws of the United States, will be referred to a military court for trial and punishment; other misdemeanors will be subject to the municipal authority, if it chooses to act. Civil causes between party and party will be referred to the ordinary tribunals. The levy and collection of all taxes, save those imposed by the laws of the United States, are suppressed, except those for keeping in repair and lighting the streets and for sanitary purposes. Those are to be collected in the usual manner.

The circulation of Confederate bonds, evidences of debt, except notes in the similitude of bank notes issued by the Confederate States, or scrip, or any trade in the same, is strictly forbidden. It having been represented to the commanding general by the city authorities that these Confederate notes in the form of bank notes are in a great measure the only substitute for money which the people have been allowed to have, and that great distress would ensue among the poorer classes if the circulation of such notes were suppressed, such circulation will be permitted so long as any one may be inconsiderate enough to receive them till further orders.

No publication, either by newspaper, pamphlet, or handbill, giving accounts of the movement of soldiers of the United States within this department, reflecting in any way upon the United States or its officers, or tending in any way to influence the public mind against the Government of the United States, will be permitted, and all articles of war news, or editorial comments or correspondence making comments upon the movement of the armies of the United States or the rebels, must be submitted to the examination of an officer who will be detailed for that purpose from these headquarters. The transmission of all communications by telegraph will be under charge of an officer from these headquarters.

The armies of the United States came here not to destroy but to make good, to restore order out of chaos, and the government of laws in place of the passions of men; to this end, therefore, the efforts of all well-disposed persons are invited to have every species of disorder quelled; and if any soldier of the United States should so far forget his duty or his flag as to commit any outrage upon any person or property, the commanding general requests that his name be instantly reported to the provost guard, so that he may be punished and his wrongful act redressed.

The municipal authority, so far as the police of the city and crimes are concerned, to the extent before indicated, is hereby suspended.

All assemblages of persons in the street, either by day or night, tend to disorder, and are forbidden.

The various companies composing the fire department in New Orleans will be permitted to retain their organizations, and are to report to the office of the provost-marshal, so that they may be known and not interfered with in their duties.

And, finally, it may be sufficient to add, without further enumeration, that all the requirements of martial law will be imposed so long as, in the judgment of the United States authorities, it may be necessary. And while it is the desire of these authorities to exercise this government mildly and after the usages of the past, it must not be supposed that it will not be vigorously and firmly administered as occasion calls.

By command of Major-General Butler:

GEO. C. STRONG,
Assistant Adjutant-General, Chief of Staff.

GENERAL ORDERS, No. 19. } HDQRS. DEPARTMENT OF THE GULF, *New Orleans, May 3, 1862.*

The commanding general of this department has been informed that there is now at Mobile a stock of flour, purchased by the city of New Orleans for the subsistence of its citizens. The suffering condition of the poor of this city for the want of this flour appeals to the humanity of those having authority on either side.

For the purpose of the safe transmission of this flour to this city the commanding general orders and directs that a safe-conduct be afforded to a steamboat to be laden with the same to this place. This safe-conduct shall extend to the entire protection of this boat in coming, reasonable delay for discharge, and return to Mobile. The boat will take no passengers save the owners and keepers of the flour, and will be subject to the strict inspection of the harbor master detailed from these headquarters, to whom its master will report its arrival.

The faith of the city is pledged for the faithful performance of the requirements of this order on the part of the agent of the city authorities, who will be allowed to pass each way with the boat, he giving no intelligence or aid to Confederates.

By command of Major-General Butler:

GEO. C. STRONG,
Assistant Adjutant-General.

GENERAL ORDERS, No. 20. } HDQRS. DEPARTMENT OF THE GULF, *New Orleans, May 3, 1862.*

The president, directors, &c., of the Opelousas Railroad are authorized and required to run their cars over the road for the purpose of bringing to the city of New Orleans provisions, marketing, and supplies of food which may be offered in order to supply the wants of the city.

No passengers, other than those having the care of such supplies as owners or keepers, are to be permitted to come into the city and none others are to leave the city. All other supplies are prohibited transportation over the road either way, except cotton and sugar, which may be safely brought over the road, and will be purchased at the fair market value by the United States in specie. The transmission of live stock is especially enjoined. An agent of the city government will be allowed to pass over the road either way, stopping at all points, on the faith of a pledge of such government agent that he transmits no intelligence and affords no aid to the Confederates.

The officer commanding the post having the terminus of such road within his pickets will cause a thorough inspection of the cars and boats for the purpose of furthering this order, and will offer no further hinderance, so long as this order is in good faith complied with.

By command of Major-General Butler:

GEO. C. STRONG,
Assistant Adjutant-General.

GENERAL ORDERS, No. 21. } HDQRS. DEPARTMENT OF THE GULF, *New Orleans, May 4, 1862.*

The commanding general of the Department of the Gulf has been informed that live stock, flour, and provisions, purchased for subsistence of the inhabitants of the city of New Orleans, are now at the junction of the Red and Mississippi Rivers. The suffering condition of the poor of the city for want of these supplies appeals to the humanity of those having authority on either side. For the purpose, therefore, of the safe transmission of these supplies to the city, the commanding general orders and directs that a safe-conduct be afforded for two steamers, to be laden with provisions, cattle, and supplies of food, either alive or slaughtered, each day, if so many choose to come.

This safe-conduct shall extend to their entire protection by the forces of the United States during their coming, reasonable delay for discharge not exceeding six days, unless in case of accident to their machinery, and in returning to or near the junction of the Red and Mississippi Rivers.

And safe-conduct is further granted to boats laden as beforesaid with provisions for New Orleans from any point above the junction of such rivers, if at any time during which these supplies are needed the forces of the United States should be at or above said junction.

The boats will take no passengers save the owners and keepers of the freight aforesaid, and will be subject to strict inspection by the harbor master detailed from these headquarters, to whom they will report their arrival.

The faith of the city is pledged for the faithful execution of the requirements of this order on the part of the agent of the city authorities, who will be allowed to pass the boats either way, he giving no intelligence or aid to the Confederates.

By command of Major-General Butler:

GEO. C. STRONG,
Assistant Adjutant-General, Chief of Staff.

GENERAL ORDERS, No. 22. } HDQRS. DEPARTMENT OF THE GULF, *New Orleans, May* 4, 1862.

The commanding general of the department having been informed that rebellious, lying, and desperate men have represented, and are now representing, to honest planters and good people of the State of Louisiana that the United States Government, by its forces, have come here to confiscate and destroy their crops of cotton and sugar, it is hereby ordered to be made known, by publication in all the newspapers of this city, that all cargoes of cotton and sugar shall receive the safe conduct of the forces of the United States; and the boats bringing them from beyond the lines of the United States forces may be allowed to return in safety, after a reasonable delay, if their owners so desire, provided they bring no passengers except the owners and managers of said boat and of the property so conveyed, and no other merchandise except provisions, of which such boats are requested to bring a full supply for the benefit of the poor of this city.

By command of Major-General Butler:

GEO. C. STRONG,
Assistant Adjutant-General.

GENERAL ORDERS, No. 23. } HDQRS. DEPARTMENT OF THE GULF, *New Orleans, May* 6, 1862.

A military commission, of not less than five commissioned officers of and above the rank of captain, with a recorder and legal adviser, is constituted and appointed, for the trial of all high crimes and misdemeanors which by the laws of any State in the Union, or the United States, or the laws martial, are punishable with death or imprisonment for a long term of years.

The sentence of such courts will be assimilated to those provided by such laws, due regard being had to the necessity of severity and for prompt punishment incident to the crimes and disorders arising from a state of war.

The commission will sit at all convenient hours for the dispatch of business, will be attended by the provost-marshal or his assistants, all its orders respected and obeyed, and its summonses complied with.

As the motives of men make so largely the element of the crimes cognizable by this commission, the rules of evidence of the English common law may be so far relaxed as to allow the accused to be questioned in presence of the commission, always leaving it to his free choice to respond or not to the questions proposed.

The accusation will be substantially in the form used in courts-martial, excepting that it should fully set forth a description of the accused, his residence and business, whether or not he has been a loyal citizen, his antecedents, character, and acts in that regard, so far as known, which portion of the accusation may be put in controversy at the trials, provided the accused be not a soldier of the United States.

All proceedings, findings, and sentences of this commission are to be subjected to the approval of the commanding general, and will be carried into effect upon his order.

The following-named officers are detailed for and will constitute such commission:

1. Col. Henry C. Deming, Twelfth Regiment Connecticut Volunteers.
2. Col. N. A. M. Dudley, Thirtieth Regiment Massachusetts Volunteers.

3. Lieut. Col. C. M. Whelden, Thirty-first Regiment Massachusetts Volunteers.
4. Maj. F. A. Boardman, Fourth Regiment Wisconsin Volunteers.
5. Capt. Peter Haggerty, aide-de-camp.

Maj. J. M. Bell, volunteer aide-de-camp, recorder and legal adviser.

By command of Major-General Butler:

GEO. C. STRONG,
Acting Chief of Staff.

HEADQUARTERS DEPARTMENT OF THE GULF,
New Orleans, May 8, 1862.

WM. H. SEWARD,
Secretary of State:

MY DEAR SIR: I write this note simply as a remembrance of your kindness and support to the expedition which has accomplished such fortunate results.

I find that the British consul here has complicated himself and his fellow-countrymen with the rebels in every form. The precise contrary course, I believe, has been taken by the French consul. The British Guard, now all claiming protection as British subjects, having organized themselves into a company on the night of the occupation of the city by our troops, voted to send their arms and uniforms to Beauregard, and a portion of them were sent.

For this violation of neutrality I have ordered every man who cannot produce his arms and uniform to leave the city in twenty-four hours.

Allow me to suggest for your consideration whether the port of New Orleans might now be opened.

Most truly, your friend,

BENJ. F. BUTLER.

HEADQUARTERS DEPARTMENT OF THE GULF,
New Orleans, May 8, 1862.

Brigadier-General PHELPS:

SIR: I am directed by the major-general commanding the department to ask if you have seized the Carrollton and Lake Railroad; if you have not, that he desires it to be done, and that pickets be thrown out the shore of the lake, so that schooners and other means are not used to carry or send people away in that direction.

I have the honor to be, very respectfully, your obedient servant,

P. HAGGERTY,
Captain and Aide-de-Camp.

HEADQUARTERS DEPARTMENT OF THE GULF,
New Orleans, May 9, 1862.

To the Mayor and Common Council of the City of New Orleans:

MESSRS.: I desire to call your attention to the sanitary condition of your streets. Having assumed, by the choice of your fellow-citizens and the permission of the United States authorities, the care of the city of New Orleans in this behalf, that trust must be faithfully administered. Resolutions and inaction will not do. Active, energetic measures, fully and promptly executed, are imperatively demanded by the exigencies of the occasion. Specially the present suspension of labor furnishes ample supplies of starving men who can be profitably employed to this end. A little of the labor and effort spent upon the streets and public squares which was uselessly and inanely wasted upon idle fortifications, like that about the United States mint, will place the city in a condition to insure the health of its inhabitants. It will not do to shift the responsibility from yourselves to the street commissioners, from them to the contractors, and then to the sub-contractors through all the grades of civic idleness and neglect of duty.

Three days since I called the attention of Mr. Mayor to this subject, and nothing has been done.

Respectfully,

BENJ. F. BUTLER,
Major-General, Commanding.

GENERAL ORDERS, No. 24. } HDQRS. DEPARTMENT OF THE GULF, *New Orleans, May* 10, 1862.

Acting Brig. Gen. George F. Shepley, Colonel Twelfth Maine Volunteers, is hereby appointed military commandant of New Orleans.

All officers on duty in this city or in Algiers, except officers of the division staff, will report to him.

By command of Major-General Butler:

GEO. C. STRONG,
Assistant Adjutant-General.

GENERAL ORDERS, No. 25. } HDQRS. DEPARTMENT OF THE GULF, *New Orleans, May* 9, 1862.

The deplorable state of destitution and hunger of the mechanics and working classes of this city has been brought to the knowledge of the commanding general. He has yielded to every suggestion made by the city government, and ordered every method of furnishing food to the people of New Orleans that government desired. No relief by those officials has yet been afforded. This hunger does not pinch the wealthy and influential, the leaders of the rebellion, who have gotten up this war, and are now endeavoring to prosecute it without regard to the starving poor, the workingman, his wife and child. Unmindful of their suffering fellow-citizens at home, they have caused or suffered provisions to be carried out of the city for Confederate service since the occupation by the United States forces.

Lafayette Square, their home of affluence, was made the depot of stores and munitions of war for the rebel armies, and not of provisions for their poor neighbors. Striking with the vile, the gambler, the idler, and the ruffian, they have destroyed the sugar and cotton which might have been exchanged for food for the industrious and good, and regrated the price of that which is left by discrediting the very currency they had furnished while they eloped with the specie; as well that stolen from the United States as the banks, the property of the good people of New Orleans, thus leaving them to ruin and starvation. Fugitives from justice many of them, and others their associates, staying because too puerile and insignificant to be objects of punishments by the clement Government of the United States. They have betrayed their country; they have been false to every trust; they have shown themselves incapable of defending the State they had seized upon, although they have forced every poor man's child into their service as soldiers for that purpose, while they made their sons and nephews officers.

They cannot protect those whom they have ruined, but have left them to the mercies and assassinations of a chronic mob. They will not feed those whom they are starving. Mostly without property themselves, they have plundered, stolen, and destroyed the means of those who had property, leaving children penniless and old age hopeless.

Men of Louisiana, workingmen, property-holders, merchants, and citizens of the United States, of whatever nation you may have had birth, how long will you uphold these flagrant wrongs, and by inaction suffer yourselves to be made the serfs of these leaders?

The United States have sent land and naval forces here to fight and subdue rebellious armies in array against her authority. We find substantially only fugitive masses, runaway property-burners, a whisky-drinking mob, and starving citizens, with their wives and children. It is our duty to call back the first, to punish the second, root out the third, feed and protect the last.

Ready only for war, we had not prepared ourselves to feed the hungry and relieve the distressed with provisions. But to the extent possible within the power of the commanding general it shall be done.

He has captured a quantity of beef and sugar intended for the rebels in the field. A thousand barrels of these stores will be distributed among the deserving poor of this city, from whom the rebels had plundered it, even although some of the food will go to supply the craving wants of the wives and children of those now herding at Camp Moore and elsewhere in arms against the United States.

Capt. John Clark, acting chief commissary of subsistence, will be charged with the execution of this order, and will give public notice of the place and manner of distribution, which will be arranged as far as possible so that the unworthy and dissolute will not share its benefits.

By command of Major-General Butler:

GEO. C. STRONG,
Assistant Adjutant-General, Chief of Staff.

CONFEDERATE CORRESPONDENCE, ETC.

Abstract from field return of troops of the Confederate States near Pensacola, Fla., commanded by Brig. Gen. Braxton Bragg, on the 1st day of September, 1861.

Troops.	Present for duty.		Aggregate present.	Aggregate present and absent.
	Officers.	Men.		
1st (Chalmers') Brigade	76	1,314	1,761	1,895
2d (Wood's) Brigade	81	1,272	2,004	2,177
3d (Tyler's) Brigade	81	1,487	1,804	1,922
4th (Jackson's) Brigade	52	892	1,096	1,126
Alabama Mounted Rifles	2	72	84	101
Walton Guards	4	51	55	55
Total	296	5,088	6,804	7,276

ENGINEER BUREAU,
Richmond, September 2, 1861.

Capt. S. H. LOCKETT,
Corps of Engineers, Fort Gaines, Mobile, Ala.:

SIR: Five columbiads and rifled guns have been ordered for arming Fort Gaines and thirteen for Fort Morgan. Two of those for Fort Gaines and some of those for Fort Morgan have been forwarded. Please inform me how many of the latter have come to hand. The order for armament of Fort Morgan consists of five guns, of the size and form of the 8-inch columbiad, bored as 24-pounders and rifled. The shot has about the weight of an 8-inch shot, with greater range, accuracy, and power; one 10-inch gun, bored to a 32-pounder caliber and rifled; the remainder smooth-bore 10-inch. At Fort Gaines you are to have two 8-inch guns rifled as a 32. These guns are not yet made, but will be forwarded one or two at a time as fast as finished. Their carriages will be made here. It is said that four flank casemate guns and carriages have been sent forward to Fort Gaines, and had strayed from the road. They have been found and ordered on to Mobile. The remainder of these flank guns are being made at Lynchburg.

The Secretary informs me that he has ordered from North Carolina to Mobile thirty 32-pounders. For these the carriages must be made at Mobile. The elevating screws, male and female, will be made here and sent on. As the 32-pounders differ in size, it will not be well to put together any one of their upper carriages until the gun for it shall have come to hand. It is expected that your armament will be improved by rifling the 32-pounders on hand, and these improved guns should be placed where they are most needed. For example, one should be added to the armament at Grant's Pass as soon as possible. These guns should unquestionably be reinforced with wrought-iron bands, so as to make up one an inch and a half thick and 8 or 10 inches wide. The gun should be perfectly clean, and the band be shrunk on at a light heat. The preponderance of the breech does no great harm. The shells ought not to be longer than two calibers probably, nor to weigh more than 40 or 45 pounds. The charge of powder will not exceed 5 pounds. I will send to Messrs. Skates a sketch showing the mode of rifling adopted here and the form of the shell most approved. There are many varieties. The heavy guns bored with small calibers carry heavier shot and higher charges. There are some old guns lying at Forts Morgan and Gaines. You are authorized to have them rebored, and to build carriages for them if found fit for service, such as firing round or grape shot for the defense of redoubts or of the city.

I have prevailed on the Ordnance Bureau to order of Messrs. Skates & Co. four batteries of field guns, with harnesses. These may help in your defensive arrangements for the city. For additional means of defense you will proceed to construct the following: Drive a row of piles, beginning at the west bank and running over to the point of Dauphin Island Spit, as shown in the sketch herewith. The piles should be as large as those at the Fort Morgan wharf, be driven as deep as possible, 10 feet apart, and cut off 2 or 3 feet under water. The piles should be lashed together with chain cables. By beginning at the west bank and working westerly the enemy will be pushed towards Fort Gaines in proportion as the work progresses. It is expected that the armament of Fort Morgan will be such as to take care of the main ship channel. You can build two redoubts on the peninsula in advance of Fort Morgan. You will also build a battery to mount four or five guns on piles driven at the point (*a*) on the Southeast Spit of Pinto's Island. This may be done mostly by contract (say with Mr. John King or Mr. Gregg).

On Dauphin Island you will want some batteries, and should consult the commanding officer as to their dispositions. One or two rifled 32-pounders opposite Pelican Island, another of the same kind half way thence to the point of woods, and a strong battery across the island at that point, would seem advisable. For the armament of all these redoubts and batteries you have available fourteen 32-pounders at Fort Morgan, and thirty to be sent from North Carolina—44.

You will want for the advanced redoubts at Fort Morgan, say, 12 guns, including several rifled batteries; on Dauphin, 12; at Grant's Pass, rifled, 7; at Fort Gaines 2 additional on each curtain—10; at battery near Choctaw Point, rifled, 4; in all required, 39. The remaining 5, together with the old guns rebored, should be mounted on siege carriages, and be placed at the disposal of the city troops, to serve as batteries of position for defense of the city. These, with the light artillery disposable there, would be sufficiently formidable. You will go on with Fort Gaines as rapidly as possible, finish the bastions and curtains, with the privy, and the opening there should be closed at once. Make the rampart, the parapet, and the breast-height wall continuous. The breast-height of the covered way will be revetted with planks, and the glacis should be brought essentially to its proper height and shape as well as the covered way. Above all, make carriages and mount guns (green heart pine will answer very well), say, the traverse circles at the flank casemates.

It has proved impossible to get funds, probably because of the sickness of the President. They will be sent at the earliest possible moment. Up to the end of August it will be best to pay in my name, and I will sign and certify the accounts here.

Very respectfully, your obedient servant,

D. LEADBETTER,

Major Engineers, Acting Chief of Bureau.

ENGINEER BUREAU,

Richmond, Va., September 4, 1861.

Capt. S. H. LOCKETT,

Corps of Engineers, Mobile, Ala., Fort Gaines:

SIR: I have now every prospect of getting all the irons for 32-pounder gun-carriages made here, and I propose, therefore, to send them on to you. You should go on in the shortest possible time to have the timber sawed and all the sticks got out of the proper sizes, the chassis made, and for the upper carriages everything done but the assembling, for the guns on the carriages can be furnished. The Department is now very anxious to push forward the rifling of guns, and I am sure you will see that there is no delay in that of our 32-pounders. A few of those not yet mounted should be sent first to Mr. Skates, and as soon as one is finished let it be returned and substituted on the carriage of a smooth-bore and try it. This matter should go on night and day, Sundays and week days, cheap or costly.

Presuming that you are to have the 32-pounders from North Carolina, (30), 14 on hand, and, say, 6 old guns, you will have 50 in all. You have on hand a few carriages, but how many I don't know. Telegraph me the number of carriages for which you want me to provide irons. The columbiad carriages lately received do not fit the guns. Let all of them be made to fit, and this without delay, for you will get no carriages in lieu of them.*

Very truly, yours,

D. LEADBETTER,
Major Engineers, Acting Chief of Bureau.

NAVY DEPARTMENT, CONFEDERATE STATES,
Richmond, Va., September 6, 1861.

Hon. L. P. WALKER,
Secretary of War, Richmond, Va.:

SIR: I have the honor to request that Capt. George N. Hollins, commanding naval station at New Orleans, may be supplied as early as practicable with 100,000 pounds of cannon and 1,500 pounds of musket powder, required for the defense of New Orleans.

With much respect, your obedient servant,

S. R. MALLORY,
Secretary of the Navy.

HEADQUARTERS DEPARTMENT No. 1,
New Orleans, La., September 6, 1861.

Hon. L. P. WALKER,
Secretary of War, Richmond, Va.:

SIR: Ship Island is now in the best condition for defense that my means allow. Col. J. K. Duncan, with four officers of the Regiment of Louisiana Artillery as instructors, has been detailed for temporary duty on the island. I beg leave again to remind the Department that I have not one officer of any army experience at my disposal.

I do not wish to appear pettish or to be importunate in the matter of powder, but if it cannot be obtained the sad spectacle will be presented to the Confederacy of the Mississippi Valley falling into the hands of the enemy because of the lack of ammunition. There is not in my mind the slightest doubt that this city will be attacked early in the autumn. One company of Louisiana troops has been moved to the Grand Caillou, and another will be sent to-morrow. If I had ammunition I would order a gun to be sent with these companies.

I have the honor to be, very respectfully, your obedient servant,

D. E. TWIGGS,
Major-General, C. S. Army.

ENGINEER BUREAU,
Richmond, Va., September 11, 1861.

H. B. WARREN, Esq.,
Fort Gaines, Mobile, Ala.:

SIR: Captain Lockett was long ago ordered to relieve me at Mobile, and I have taken it for granted that he was there; but hearing nothing from him, I conclude that he has been delayed by some cause. You were telegraphed on the 5th instant to open the letters of this bureau to Captain Lockett, and to act in accordance with the instructions to him as far as possible.

*Some matters of detail omitted.

The most urgent matter is first to have the 32-pounders rifled and put in position, with shells fit for their use. I have written to Mr. Skates to hurry up this business. Next get cement from New Orleans, and finish the bastions and close up the north curtain. The postern arch at the main entrance and other interior masonry are of comparatively small account. Lay the traverse rails in the flank casemates as they are laid at Fort Morgan. Make the rampart and parapet as nearly continuous as possible, revetting the breast-height of the latter with planks, as in case of the covered way, if cement is not to be had.

At Fort Morgan the walls of the addition to the citadel (which was intended by me as a privy in case of siege) should be strengthened by an additional thickness of masonry at the northeast end and at the partition walls. A barrier gate of iron bars should be hung inside of the south postern gate, lest the existing gate there be blown in. The outer end of the passage leading under the glacis coupe into the open field should be bricked up just inside the gate by a 6-foot wall.

Of course many last things remain to be done—protecting the magazines with sand bags; substituting these for the board revetment of bomb-proof of citadel, and having arrangements for plenty of water to drink, and everywhere in vessels to extinguish fire. In the casemates the quartermaster's stores should not be piled against the scarp wall. Leave a free passage for defense of embrasures and loop-holes.

General Withers takes command. Show this to him, or at least to Captain Lockett.

Very truly, yours,

D. LEADBETTER,
Major Engineers, Acting Chief of Bureau.

WAR DEPARTMENT, C. S. A.,
Richmond, September 12, 1861.

Hon. S. R. MALLORY,
Secretary of the Navy:

SIR: I have the honor to submit the following copy of a letter just received at this Department:

RICHMOND, *September* 11, 1861.

Hon. L. P. WALKER,
Secretary of War:

SIR: The thirty guns (32-pounders) cannot be had elsewhere than from the Portsmouth navy-yard. May I request that you will procure an order from the Secretary of the Navy directing the officer in charge to forward to my address at Mobile, Ala., the thirty guns of the caliber named, or, if those cannot be had, then such others as may be designated by me and not necessary for the Norfolk defenses,

J. M. WITHERS,
Brigadier-General, &c.

Your compliance with this requisition would oblige,

Very respectfully,

L. P. WALKER,
Secretary of War.

HEADQUARTERS DEPARTMENT NO. 1, C. S. A.,
New Orleans, La., September 12, 1861.

Hon. L. P. WALKER,
Secretary of War, Richmond, Va.:

SIR: Mr. Ford, a citizen of Memphis, informs me that he met in Louisville a few days ago Mr. Walworth, son of Chancellor Walworth, recently from Washington, and learned from him that he had been told by the Secretary of the Navy that a person near General Dahlgren, at Pass Christian, was in close communication with the powers at Washington, had given them all the information that they wished, and had told them of our want of guns and ammunition in and near New Orleans. From the same source Mr. Walworth knew that extensive preparations were making to invade Louisiana early this fall. General Dahlgren is in command of a camp of Mississippi troops at Pass Christian, and has a brother in Washington, an officer in the Black Republican Navy. The Secretary of the Navy seemed well aware of our position on Ship Island.

Col. J. K. Duncan, whom I sent to Ship Island in the absence of Lieutenant-Colonel Allen, has made a lengthy report upon the importance and capabilities of the island, and declares the place wholly untenable. His report, together with the opinion of Maj. M. L. Smith, chief of engineers, is transmitted herewith.*

I hope to have in operation within two or three weeks a powder-mill, now erecting at the barracks. This is my only real dependence for powder, and yet its success hangs upon an uncertain promise of a supply of saltpeter. I have but 120 rounds for each gun on Ship Island; at the other fortifications not more than 40 rounds. To send this supply I have almost emptied the magazine. If I can obtain ammunition I have no doubts of the result of an invasion in this quarter. I would respectfully suggest, in view of a very probable necessity, that a camp be established near this city as a rendezvous for troops. The assembling of men from their homes is a work of much time.

I have the honor to be, very respectfully, your obedient servant,

D. E. TWIGGS,
Major-General, C. S. Army.

HEADQUARTERS DEPARTMENT NO. 1,
New Orleans, La., September 12, 1861.

SIR: I have the honor to inclose herein a report by Col. J. K. Duncan upon the defenses of Ship Island, together with the opinion of Maj. M. L. Smith, Engineers. I have never been on the island, but every intelligent person whom I meet, acquainted with the locality, concurs with the views of Colonel Duncan, that there are several other entrances to the sound besides Ship Island Channel, and that small steamers and gunboats can pass through them without difficulty. I shall hold the island until ordered to relinquish it.

I have the honor to be, very respectfully, your obedient servant,

D. E. TWIGGS,
Major-General, C. S. Army.

[Inclosure No. 1.]

NEW ORLEANS, LA., *September* 9, 1861.

Second Lieut. J. G. DEVEREUX,
Louisiana Regt. Art., A. A. A. G., New Orleans, La.:

SIR: In accordance with Special Orders, No. 82, dated Headquarters Department No. 1, New Orleans, September 3, 1861, I proceeded to Ship Island, to take temporary command of that post, accompanied by four officers of the Louisiana Regiment of Artillery, to take charge of the

* See inclosures to letter following.

drills at the heavy guns, as called for by Special Orders, No. 81, from the same headquarters.

After a thorough examination of the island and the fortifications commenced at its westerly extremity, its capabilities for defense, character of the guns, implements, equipments, and ammunition, together with the condition and discipline of the troops composing the command, I have the honor to report thereon as follows, viz:

1st. The fortification is a half circle, or horseshoe, closed at the gorge with a half-bastion front, as a flanking arrangement for land defense. It was originally intended to carry up the walls sufficiently high for one tier of casemate and one tier of barbette guns, and to have a moat, with a glacis without, to protect the masonry.

The brick work generally was only found to be carried up as high as the soles of the embrasures, however, and in this unfinished state it has been attempted to complete the work for temporary defense.

This has been done by carrying up the piers between the embrasures by brick work in offsets from the outside, which is to be protected by sand bags. To complete the covering over the guns brick piers are being built within the work, and heavy timbers thrown thence to the walls, to be covered by 3-inch planking and sand bags. Hence, from every direction in which a shot or shell can reach the interior of the fort, they will be almost certain to strike one of the piers in question, and chances are that they will be brought down, together with the timber and sand bags over them, burying the guns and increasing the number of casualties from the splinters and scattering brick work.

To have much strength, or to be able to maintain anything like a determined attack, this fort must be completed after its original plans. If progressed with after the present method of temporarily completing it, a few heavy men-of-war will pelt it to ruins in a very short space of time. I regard it as affording the least possible protection to the men and guns, and totally incapable of resisting any formidable force.

If the island must be fortified, and if possible be held at all hazards, I would earnestly suggest that Fort Twiggs and all work upon it be abandoned at once, and that the only attempt made at fortification be the ordinary resort to sand-bag batteries. The embrasures of the latter can be carefully revetted with sand bags and the parapets carried up above the height of the tallest men. Bomb-proof shelters, built close up to the parapets, will afford ample protection to the reliefs and to the men not employed at the guns, who can crawl into them for protection and shelter during an actual engagement. Such a work can be constructed at one-tenth of the cost of the present work, can be completed within a very few days comparatively, and will afford ten times the resistance of the unfinished brick fort. All the labor can be done by the command, and the material is all ready to hand, excepting a few more sand bags.

2d. The present armament is composed of two 24-pounders in position on the flanking front and one 8-inch shell gun completely exposed on the same front; eight 32-pounders within the circular work and one 32-pounder and one 9-inch Dahlgren shell gun without the fort and behind a sand-bag parapet. The fire of the two latter is partially masked by the masonry of the fort, as is shown, together with the positions of all of the guns, by the following diagram.*

The guns are all good enough of their several classes, but the 32-pounders, being mounted upon barbette gun-carriages on casemate

*Omitted, as of no present importance.

chassis, the barbette wheels strike against the scarp walls, and materially interfere with pointing the guns, and intercept their full elevation in consequence.

But taking the 9-inch Dahlgren gun, however, the best gun, with full charge and elevation, its extreme range falls short of Cat Island about a mile and a half. Within this mile and a half of the channel, I am informed by pilots familiar with the sound, there is 18 feet of water. Hence, admitting that the fortification is completely defensible within itself and mounted with the best guns, yet nevertheless it could not prevent the passage of large-class ships through the very channel which it is built to guard. This, however, is but one passage leading into the sound.

Between Ship and Horn Islands there is another, with a depth of 14 feet of water, and between the eastern end of Horn Island and Pêtit Bois still a third, which several pilots agree in stating had deepened to 18 feet during the heavy storms of last year.

Now, the coast line is about 15 miles distant from these island keys, which partly lock and protect the main-land. About midway between them, a line drawn from east to west and generally parallel with the coast, will represent the 13-foot line of water, and from this line to the main-land the water shoals very rapidly, becoming extremely shallow as the coast line is approached.

It is hence evident that gunboats of light draught can alone be used by the enemy against the coast. Upon this coast there are only two points of so much consequence as to require a vigilant guard. These are, 1st, New Orleans, through the Rigolets, and, 2d, Mobile, through Dog and Pascagoula Rivers; for, if the war is to be prosecuted by the enemy regardless of all the rules governing civilized communities, it will be utterly impracticable without a navy to protect all the watering places and residences along the sound, and indemnity must be looked for either by the confiscation of Northern property within our borders or by a like retaliation across them.

But with the cities mentioned the case is different, as their possession by the enemy may change the destinies of the war. Through Dog and Pascagoula Rivers light transports and gunboats can pass to within 20 or 25 miles of Mobile, thus throwing men and material to within a single day's march of that city, with fair roads leading thence through an open pine country. A few batteries erected at suitable points on those rivers can prevent this, and the guns used need only be of the caliber of 24 or 32 pounders.

In a like manner Fort Pike, on the Rigolets, can be strengthened and one or two other points fortified, which will prevent an entrance into Lake Pontchartrain. If the enemy obtains possession of Fort Pike, and thus a foothold on the lake, by operating thence as a base with the boats and material to be collected upon its shores, the capture of New Orleans becomes almost certain in time, and consequently Forts Jackson and Saint Philip and the control of the entire mouth of the Mississippi River, by starving those forts into capitulation.

The occupation of Ship Island even by the most powerful fortifications, fully capable of resisting a combined land and naval attack, does not benefit either of the two important points mentioned, nor yet protect them in the least. Neither does it protect the sound coast, as gunboats can pass between Ship Island and the main-land with impunity, passing thereto through any of the channels in and around the islands.

Nothing, for instance, would be more easy for the enemy than the capture of the small steamers and other craft now plying in the sound by merely passing between any of the channels around the islands and heading them off with two or more gunboats. Again, it is perfectly practicable for the few hostile gunboats to lie off of Ship Island, and merely by preventing the landing of stores and material to starve them into capitulation without firing a single gun. Its present condition certainly makes it a temptation to a bold and active enemy where the prize is thirteen guns, seven companies, and the glory and *éclat* of the achievement.

If, however, our inferior gunboats had Fort Pike on the one hand and the forts proposed upon Dog and Pascagoula Rivers upon the other to act upon as bases, they would always have strong points upon which to retreat, and whence, working by combined movements, the sound might be kept comparatively free from the enemy's gunboats, which alone can operate there, if, indeed, many of these boats could not be captured.

At all events, Ship Island affords no protection to those boats now, their only point of refuge now being behind Fort Pike; but the fort on Ship Island is wholly incapable of resisting a combined land and water attack like that which the enemy threatens. The two detachments of regulars are more than sufficient to man all of the guns and afford the necessary reliefs. The other five companies should be deployed in open order without the fort and behind the line of sand hills, at from 300 to 400 yards from it, where they would be within good supporting distance of the regulars in the fort. Being in open order, they would be less liable to casualties from the enemy's shells, and whence, from under cover, a heavy rifle fire could be opened upon a landing party above or they could form and charge from behind the sand hills, as occasion might require. This would probably be the best plan of resisting an attack from an insignificant force. Should the enemy land 4,000 or 8,000 men beyond the range of the fort guns, however, and thence attack simultaneously with the bombardment of a considerable fleet, with the guns on every ship equal to the two best in the fort and superior to all of the rest, the result of the engagement would not differ materially from that at Cape Hatteras, and would not, in my opinion, last an hour.

In short, I consider the works now on Ship Island totally incapable of formidable defense, and feel confident that they cannot be made so within any reasonable period of time. Furthermore, I am satisfied that, however much they may be strengthened, they can still be starved into submission without firing a single shot.

The occupation of the island is objectless, as there is no control over any channel nor of the sounds at best. Hence great expense is unnecessarily incurred, besides the risk of the men and material now there in a shameful and humiliating manner, and all without even intimidating the enemy or of being productive of one particle of good in any direction.

Strongly advocating the superiority of land batteries over superior naval attacks, I cannot, nevertheless, without a strong protest, stand by and encourage an impracticable project, which has not a single object of importance to recommend it. Such an impracticability, aimless and objectless, is now being projected at Ship Island, and, if prosecuted to the end, I predict for it disgrace, from starvation on the one hand or butchery and capture on the other, in case of any considerable combined attack.

I would, therefore, most seriously and earnestly urge the immediate abandonment of the island. The troops, guns, and important material can be removed in a single night, as the present enemy would probably prevent their removal in the day-time.

Instead of the useless occupation of this island, I would respectfully recommend that the smaller guns be taken and placed in intrenchments to be thrown up near the mouths of Dog and Pascagoula Rivers and the heavier ones to strengthen Fort Pike, for the reasons before given. These points are important and there is an object in holding them, whereas Ship Island has no object or importance, and its occupation is more likely to prove highly disastrous than to be productive of good.

I found at the island only about 15 rounds to each gun, but powder and cartridge-bags sufficient to increase the number to each gun to about 120 rounds. Lieutenant Devereux, an active and skillful officer, was appointed ordnance officer, and details were made from the several companies to assist him in making cartridges, lining the magazine, keeping the guns in order, and to look after the implements and equipments. The men of the several companies were drilled at the heavy guns by the officers of the Louisiana Artillery who accompanied me, and among them were found a number of detachments sufficiently well drilled to man the guns; besides, the regular detachments there are in command of Lieutenants Semmes and Barnes, from West Point, and as they requested permission to drill their own companies at the heavy guns I of course granted it, these officers being fully competent to the task. These two companies alone can furnish all the necessary reliefs and gun detachments to man and fight the battery at any time. In view of this I have directed the officers of the Louisiana Artillery mentioned to repair to their several posts, and they consequently accompanied me to town this evening. They are of much less use at Ship Island than at Forts Jackson and Saint Philip.

The sand-bag revetting in front of the five 32-pounder guns was carried up to the top of the wall, with proper embrasures left, the masonry and wood work not being quite ready for the sand bags at other points. The planking over the guns I directed to be parapeted around with sand bags and then the interior space to be filled with loose sand.

Colonel Barrow had improved the discipline on the island for the few days he was there before my arrival, and I am satisfied that he would get along very well shortly and as satisfactorily as circumstances admit of. He ran a sand-bag traverse in rear of the five 32-pounders looking to the westward on the line *a b* of great importance. Similar traverses will have to be thrown in the rear of all the guns for their protection. Both of the shell guns are very much exposed to be dismounted by the enemy's fire, but especially the 8-inch gun, which is wholly unprotected. Trusting that the island will be speedily abandoned and the men and material moved elsewhere, I am, very respectfully, your obedient servant,

J. K. DUNCAN,
Colonel, C. S. Army.

[Inclosure No 2.]

ENGINEER'S OFFICE,
New Orleans, September 11, 1861.

Maj. Gen. DAVID E. TWIGGS,
Comdg. Military Department No. 1, New Orleans, La.:

SIR: I have the honor to acknowledge the reference to this office of the report of Colonel Duncan upon the defenses on Ship Island, and return it with the following remarks:

The report discusses the defenses from two points of view: First, the particular manner of fortifying the island; second, the policy of occupying it at all.

On the first point the views expressed in the report are not concurred in. First, I see no reason for abandoning a position inclosed by the heavy scarp wall of a regular fort and building up the same height of wall of sand bags, the embrasures in both instances to be made alike. Again, it is not apparent to me that the labor required to protect a gun placed behind a wall capable of resisting shot can be less than if the same gun is placed on the open ground; hence, that a new work can be commenced as suggested and sooner finished than the present one. The timber bomb-proofs rest upon low piers built upon the scarp wall, protected on the outside by sand bags, and upon piers run up from the ground in rear of the gun carriages. It but remains to inclose the rear of these timber casemates, as they may be termed, by piling up sand bags to the height of the brick piers, and we have not only a perfect bomb-proof, but a comfortable place for the soldiers, inasmuch as the roof above has designedly been made water-tight.

In regard to the use of sand bags, it may be remarked that their efficiency is of a temporary character, five and six weeks being sufficient for them to become so decayed as to admit of little or no strain being put upon them.

But it is proper to remark here that the work at Ship Island has progressed unusually slowly, and that much remains to be done. The engineer office here has not from the first had one single dollar at its disposal to expend there, and has not up to this day ever been able to get any funds. The few bills and laborers that have been paid the quartermaster department has provided for.

Owing to the impossibility of my being at the island after the first week of the occupancy, and there being no engineer officer to send, considerable work has been done having no special bearing upon the proper defense of the fort. This, under the circumstances, was doubtless unavoidable. The two guns remaining outside are the two rapidly pushed ashore under fire and mounted on our first arrival at the island, and bear so handsomely upon the entrance and sound that it has not been thought desirable to attempt their removal to the inside until more important work is finished.

In regard to the armament of the fort, I have but to remark that every available gun of any size has been sent there.

In respect, then, to the defense of Ship Island, if it is to be held, my opinion is decidedly in favor of continuing the occupation of the work, incomplete as it is, and for perfecting its interior arrangements. I believe the garrison can be more readily sheltered there than elsewhere. The work is, to a certain extent, ready for an attack at any moment, and I regard it as less liable to be taken by an assaulting force, consequently stronger than a work of the same size as suggested in Colonel Duncan's report.

As to the policy of attempting to hold Ship Island at all, my views were officially given in a communication dated May 16, 1861, and forwarded to Montgomery by the commanding officer of this department. In a subsequent one, dated May 25, a course to be pursued to defend Mississippi Sound was recommended, and this also forwarded.

I have nothing to add to-day to the reasoning and conclusions of those reports, which were essentially the same as those now submitted by Colonel Duncan, and should the enemy appear in force at any time within the next three weeks the relative positions of the combatants will be as there indicated. But notwithstanding the views then expressed, the occupation of Ship Island was understood to have been directed by the President of the Confederate States. The necessity that existed then for its occupation exists, as far as I am aware of, now, and I do not perceive how, under this condition of things, its abandonment can be determined upon without the express authority of the President himself. Should it be decided to vacate the island, then the proper defense of the sound is a question to be taken in connection with the gunboat force that is or will be available.

I am, very respectfully, your obedient servant,

M. L. SMITH,
Major of Engineers.

HDQRS. FIRST DIV. LOUISIANA VOLUNTEER INFANTRY,
New Orleans, La., September 12, 1861.

Maj. Gen. DAVID E. TWIGGS,
Commanding Department No. 1, *C. S. Army:*

GENERAL: In accordance with the wish expressed by you verbally, on the 9th instant (the day I visited you at your house), that I should proceed to Berwick Bay and examine the fortifications and other means of defense that could be made available in the event of an attack upon that place, I proceeded thither the next morning, accompanied by three of my staff, Majors Farish, Hyllested, and Fago. During my journey on the Opelousas Railroad I had every possible assistance from the gentlemen in the employment of the company, and, upon arriving at my destination, each seemed to vie with the other in the desire to afford me information. To Captain Carr my thanks are particularly due for the handsome and generous manner in which he placed not only his steamer, the Sigle, but his own valuable services as a pilot, at my disposal.

Immediately after my arrival I proceeded to inspect Forts Berwick and Chène. Fort Berwick is situated about 4 miles from Brashear City, at the junction of Wax Bayou and the Atchafalaya River. The depth of water on the bar of Wax Bayou, as I was informed, is about 7 feet. The fort is a common earthen one, quadrangular in shape, with earthen parapets 5 feet high on three sides, the rear being protected only by palisades about 7 feet high, loop-holed for musketry, the whole surrounded by a moat about 6 feet wide in front and 3 feet in the rear. On the front face two 24-pounder pivot guns are mounted, which command the outlet of Wax Bayou, where boats of only very light draught can be used, but which would be of little avail in protecting the Atchafalaya.

To render Fort Berwick capable of resisting only a moderate force the parapets would require strengthening. The magazine also requires protection, which can be done by covering the same with earth to the thickness of several feet. I would recommend three additional guns being sent to Fort Berwick, to arm the right and left parapets, which are at present defenseless; also a light gun (9 or 12 pounder) to aid in protecting the rear, which is open to attack by a land force.

The ammunition consists of 21 24-pounder cartridges, 200 shot, and 4,000 musket-ball cartridges. Rammers, port-fires, primers, and flannel for cartridges and swabs are much needed; but I do not enter into the particulars, as I am assured a list has already been furnished by the officer in command. The garrison consists of two companies, one of infantry and one of sappers and miners.

Fort Chène is in all respects a counterpart of Fort Berwick, situated at a point commanding two bayous, admitting only vessels of light draught of water, and consequently of much less importance than Fort Berwick. The armament is two 24-pounder pivot guns. The ammunition consists of 90 24-pounder cartridges, 193 shot, 30 charges of canister, and 3,000 musket cartridges. The garrison consists of one company of infantry.

My next visit was to Shell Island, which is 15 miles from Brashear City, and is at the junction of the main channel of the Atchafalaya River and Shell Island Bayou. The depth, as I was informed, of the former is 9 feet on the bar at high water and never less than 7 feet; and of the latter 6 feet on the bar at high water and never less than 4 feet.

Shell Island, as its name would indicate, is composed of shells, but only in part, raised about 2 to 3 feet above high-water mark. In the rear is an impenetrable marsh, but on its front, and facing Atchafalaya River and Shell Bayou, is a shell bank, extending 400 yards in length by 60 in depth.

I am of opinion that a strong fort ought as soon as possible to be constructed upon Shell Island, commanding, as it does, the most important channel to Berwick Bay, the main channel of the Atchafalaya River at this point being only about one-quarter of a mile wide, and consequently easily commanded by a battery. In urging the establishment of a fort on Shell Island for the protection of Berwick Bay I do not think I overestimate the value of the position, while it will render it unnecessary to maintain Fort Chêne, the garrison and armament of which could be removed to Shell Island.

A fort situated upon Shell Island ought not to contain less than ten guns, some of heavy caliber. I am informed that the planters in this section of country will furnish any number of hands for works of defense.

I would also call your attention to the companies composing the garrisons of Forts Berwick and Chêne. They are infantry, some of which, especially in Fort Berwick, are but imperfectly acquainted with the musket exercise, while all, both officers and men, are entirely ignorant of the management of heavy artillery. A competent instructor of artillery is a most pressing necessity.

The great number of fishermen, or men of doubtful avocations, who reside in the numerous bayous, quite out of reach of the forts, renders a coast guard necessary. The steamer Mobile, which is now being altered into a gunboat, will not be ready for two weeks, and I would recommend the employment in the mean time of Captain Carr's steamer, the Teazer, and which, being of light draught of water, could act as a tender to the Mobile, and render effective service in clearing the bayous of all such as may be rendering aid and comfort to the enemy. I would also urge the employment of Captain Carr upon this service, for which his intimate knowledge of Berwick Bay and its bayous make him so well fitted.

The commanders of the forts have represented to me the necessity, to the proper carrying out of their duty in preventing the passage of small craft, that they each be supplied with a 6 or 8 oared barge, the small boats they are at present using being loaned them by citizens.

In laying before you the foregoing result of my examination of the means of defense at Berwick Bay, permit me to again call your attention to the serious results that would arise from this point falling into the hands of the enemy. We should be completely cut off from the valuable supply of cattle from Texas, while 60,000 barrels of coal, which is an article of almost incalculable advantage to the enemy's shipping, would be sacrificed. No time or means ought, therefore, to be lost in properly defending a point of so much importance.

Respectfully submitted.

JNO. L. LEWIS,
Major-General, Comdg. First Div. La. Volunteer Infantry.

SPECIAL ORDERS, No. 151. } ADJT. AND INSP. GENERAL'S OFFICE.
Richmond, Va., September 12, 1861.

* * * * * *

18. The State of Alabama and that portion of Mississippi east of the Pascagoula River will hereafter constitute a separate command, which is assigned to the charge of Brig. Gen. Jones M. Withers, Provisional Army.

* * * * * *

By command of the Secretary of War:

JNO. WITHERS,
Assistant Adjutant-General.

RICHMOND, *September* 13, 1861.

General DAVID E. TWIGGS,
New Orleans, La.:

Take immediate measures to evacuate Ship Island, and cause the guns to be removed at once.

S. COOPER,
Adjutant and Inspector General.

HEADQUARTERS DEPARTMENT NO. 1, C. S. A.,
New Orleans, September 16, 1861.

The Hon. SECRETARY OF WAR,
Richmond, Va.:

SIR: There will no doubt be an invasion of this place by the Black Republicans early in the fall. I respectfully ask that two brigadier-generals be ordered to report to me at as early a day as possible. The works around the city are extensive, and it is impossible for one person to attend to all matters pertaining to the service.

I am, very respectfully, your obedient servant,

D. E. TWIGGS,
Major-General, Commanding.

MOBILE, *September* 16, 1861.

Hon. L. P. WALKER,
Secretary of War:

SIR: In view of the opposition manifested here to the assignment of Brigadier-General Withers to the command at Mobile, I deem it proper to state that in my opinion the public good will be promoted by the order which it is understood the Department has given to that effect.

I have just returned from a visit to General Twiggs at New Orleans.

I received official confirmation of an important fact, report of which had previously reached me; that is, that there are less than 50 rounds of powder at the three forts at the mouth of this bay. Two hours of active fighting will exhaust the supply, and then the repetition of the *contretemps* at Hatteras is open, and Mobile is at the mercy of a naval power holding these forts and commanding the bay.

General Moore is here, and I at once advised him of the fact. He appeared surprised. New Orleans is equally destitute of powder. If it be possible I trust that these works will be supplied at once.

Pardon me for expressing the opinion that the five regiments constituting the garrison at Ship Island may be cut off whenever the enemy commanding the sea wills it. The waters of the Mississippi Sound can only be defended by guns afloat, and without them the Ship Island forces are at the mercy of the Black Republican fleet. That garrison cannot command the Ship Island Pass. If it could, there are several others by which gunboats may enter. I am aware of the presumption of my opinion. A sense of duty prompts it, for after the misfortune shall have befallen us I should reproach myself if I remained silent.

I am greatly indebted to the Government for the presence and instructions of Captain Lockett. I am doing all in my power to aid him in carrying his plans into execution.

I am, very respectfully, your obedient servant,

JOHN FORSYTH, *Mayor.*

NEW ORLEANS, *September* 17, 1861.

SECRETARY OF WAR:

Ship Island is evacuated. Two heavy frigates, two steamers, a brig, and two tenders were 8 miles off Ship Island at dark yesterday. As the last boat departed the steamers were bearing down upon the island.

D. E. TWIGGS.

MOBILE, *September* 17, 1861.

Hon. SECRETARY OF WAR:

I am just informed that there is very little powder at Forts Gaines and Morgan, Ala. Have but little. It is of the utmost importance that cannon powder be sent immediately to these forts.

A. B. MOORE.

RICHMOND, *September* 18, 1861.

His Excellency A. B. MOORE,
Governor Alabama:

Supplies of powder will be sent to the forts designated as soon as possible.

J. P. BENJAMIN,
Acting Secretary of War.

NEW ORLEANS, *September* 18, 1861.

SECRETARY OF WAR:

The enemy's fleet did considerable shelling yesterday at, as they supposed, a masked battery on Ship Island.

D. E. TWIGGS,
Major-General.

ENGINEER BUREAU,
Richmond, Va., September 19, 1861.

General JONES M. WITHERS,
Mobile, Ala.:

GENERAL: At the last moment the Ordnance Department has laid hands on our big rifled gun and sent it to Memphis. The programme is that we are to have the next one. We are able, therefore, to send only a 10-inch smooth bore, with its appurtenances, carriage, implements, and a few shot and shells. Our main reliance for the present must be the seven columbiads at the two forts and the rifled 32-pounders. I am satisfied that these last will prove to be formidable guns. They weigh 7,000 pounds each, I think, and with a shell of about 50 pounds weight each of those guns should be better (more effective) than a 10-inch columbiad. Sights should be adapted to them. I had hoped to send some friction-primers, but they are not ready, and must be sent by express.

Lieutenant Withers has a list of the articles which you have asked for, with a note of the establishment from which they have been ordered by the Ordnance Department. Lieutenant Withers has been very active in his efforts to promote the interests of the public service.

Very respectfully, your obedient servant,

D. LEADBETTER,
Major Engineers, Acting Chief of Bureau.

HEADQUARTERS LOUISIANA MILITIA,
New Orleans, September 20, 1861.

Hon. JEFFERSON DAVIS,
President Confederate States:

DEAR SIR: I am now endeavoring to organize the militia of my State, in order that we may be in some state of preparation for an attack. The generals and some of their subordinates, at a recent meeting to concert measures to this end, adopted the following resolution, which at their request I forward to you:

Resolved, That the governor of this State be requested respectfully to write immediately to the President of the Confederate States and ask his excellency to appoint and send to New Orleans two competent superior officers, one of the Corps of Engineers and one of the Artillery, to form with General Twiggs a board of defense.

Without sanctioning the request contained in the last part of the resolution concerning the board of defense, which appears to me not consonant to military usage or propriety, I have already represented to you the necessity of having an officer here who, with youth, energy, and military ability, would infuse some activity in our preparations and some confidence in our people. I hope ere this General Van Dorn has acquainted you with my views, which from motives of delicacy I preferred to deliver to him verbally in a confidential conversation.

The generals of my militia have designated the corps from which the officers to be sent here should be selected. I leave that to your good judgment, asking only that this city, the most important to be preserved of any in the Confederacy, and our coast, the most exposed of all the States, be no longer neglected.

I am, very respectfully, your obedient servant,

THO. O. MOORE.

WAR DEPARTMENT, C. S. A.,
Richmond, September 21, 1861.

Hon. JOHN FORSYTH,
Mayor of Mobile, Ala.:

SIR: In reply to your letter of the 16th instant I am directed by the Secretary of War to say that the Government is aware of the deficiency of powder at the forts below Mobile, and is using every effort to supply it as promptly as possible.

The garrison at Ship Island has been withdrawn, to prevent the possibility of its being cut off by the enemy.

This Department will be pleased to receive your suggestions on all occasions.

Respectfully,

A. T. BLEDSOE,
Chief of Bureau of War.

HEADQUARTERS LOUISIANA MILITIA,
New Orleans, La., September 21, 1861.

Maj. Gen. JOHN L. LEWIS,
And the other Field Officers of the First Division of Militia of Louisiana:

GENTLEMEN: I have examined the proceedings of your meeting held on the 19th instant, of which a copy was presented to me by your committee. I immediately addressed a letter to President Davis, and inserted the resolution of request for the appointment of an additional engineer and artillery officer at New Orleans.

I must decline complying with the request contained in your first resolution. Passing by the consideration of the question of my power or right to declare martial law, I cannot perceive, in the present state of public affairs, any justification for the adoption of so stringent a measure. Martial law suspends the functions of the civil magistrate, and makes the will of him who declares it the supreme and only law. If he has the power—the military force—to compel subjection to his will, no one can question the propriety or necessity of any of his orders. It is true it may be restricted in its operations as to locality, but it cannot be modified as to character. It may be declared in a district or portion of country, and has in some instances been accompanied with qualifications of its operation; but these qualifications may be altered or dispensed with at the pleasure of the person who has the supreme power. It is therefore the substitution of the uncontrolled rule of one man for the government of law as administered by civil officers. I do not think the exigencies of the State and its people at the present moment demand or require the assumption and exercise of such power. I have in contemplation issuing general orders for the enrolling and organization of the militia, in the enforcement of which I shall expect, and know I will receive, your active co-operation.

I am, very respectfully, your obedient servant,

THO. O. MOORE,
Governor of Louisiana.

NEW ORLEANS, *September 22, 1861.*

J. P. BENJAMIN,
Acting Secretary of War, Richmond, Va.:

DEAR SIR: * * * I am looking anxiously for the officers you promised to send us. A gentleman by the name of Smith, I believe from New

York, is much desired here, or Captain Boggs, at Pensacola. I have felt considerable anxiety (but never have mentioned it except to Moise) about assistance here when it should be required. You are now in a situation not to send off a man from Virginia, Kentucky, or Missouri. What should we do in Louisiana if we should be attacked by even 30,000 men when all are gone and arms too? Our fortifications are very backward. We have but one engineer here (Major Smith), and he is not an active one, according to my judgment. I am not satisfied with our situation—not at all; and, should we be attacked by any strong force, I am fearful of the result. My arms have all been given out and all gone. We could get the men, but they would be of no use. I sent to Cuba for guns long since and made a failure. I have now 1,800 there if I could get them; besides I have sent a considerable amount to another point, but whether I shall ever get them or not I do not know, and as for our reliance on the assistance of any volunteers now in those States where hostilities exist, whether from our State or others, it is very poor.

It is high time ample provision was made for the reception of our enemies. If they cannot raise soldiers rapidly, they can, it is said, raise any number of sailors and marines. Dr. Mackie writes from Nashville (just arrived there from the North) that gigantic measures are being adopted at the North for a move on Louisiana, and no secret in the matter, and that he believes it will be made soon. Now, my dear sir, do at once what may be necessary for our State. I can't say any more, as my office is filled with talkers.

I am anxious for saltpeter. I am alarmed to death for want of powder. Aid us in these materials, as we could fight but a short time with present supply.

By the very earnest solicitations of General Polk, General Twiggs has consented to send the Third Regiment to him, so you can, if agreeable, leave the Fourth here; but if it remains across the lake it would do no good for the defense of the city.

General Dahlgren is over the lake with 1,500 or 2,000 men. Is that force not sufficient? I desire to write you relative to the gentleman above and may do so. If I do not, another will.*

Yours, very truly,

THO. O. MOORE.

NEW ORLEANS, LA., *September* 22, 1861.

Hon. J. P. BENJAMIN,
Richmond, Va.:

Letters of the 16th received. Third Regiment ordered to Columbus. Cannot the Fourth remain? Send officers at once. I dispatched you for saltpeter. None yet received.

THO. O. MOORE.

RICHMOND, VA., *September* 23, 1861.

Gov. THOMAS O. MOORE,
New Orleans, La.:

I shall not move the Fourth Regiment from Louisiana without the most urgent necessity. Shall send one or two brigadier-generals to New

*Some matters of detail omitted.

Orleans this week. Two tons of saltpeter were ordered from Augusta to New Orleans on the 19th instant.

J. P. BENJAMIN,
Acting Secretary of War.

NEW ORLEANS, *September* 23, 1861.

SECRETARY OF WAR:

I have countermanded the movement of the Third Regiment to General Polk at the wish and with the concurrence of Governor Moore.

D. E. TWIGGS.

ENGINEER BUREAU,
Richmond, Va., September 23, 1861.

HON. SECRETARY OF WAR:

SIR: The defensive works for the protection of Mobile Bay and city consist of Forts Morgan and Gaines, a battery at Grant's Pass, and other batteries now under construction in the immediate neighborhood of the city. Fort Morgan has five 10-inch columbiads, two of them known to be mounted; two others probably so; the fifth on the way, not arrived. Some ten other heavy guns (rifled) and columbiads ordered by Mr. Secretary Walker are anxiously expected, and are believed to be under fabrication in this city. There are also about thirty-eight 32-pounders mounted on the work, which are now being rifled. From these last we cannot expect the full range and power of guns made for rifling, but when the full armament shall have been received it will be formidable. Two redoubts are under construction on the land side in advance of Fort Morgan. Present garrison, one regiment.

Fort Gaines is opposite Fort Morgan, $3\frac{1}{4}$ miles distant, and the two are required to protect the intervening channel. This work was intended to mount one columbiad in each bastion (five of them) and fifty 32-pounders in barbette on the curtains. It has two 10-inch columbiads, probably not yet mounted, as their carriages (new iron) do not fit the old and usual form of traverse circle. The alteration is being made. Two rifled guns and one 8-inch smooth bore are required there, and will be made in this city. Ten 32-pounders are mounted on the curtains. Four of its flanking guns have been received, and are probably mounted. Sixteen more of the last-named guns (howitzers) are required, and are being made at Florence, Ala. The present garrison of Fort Gaines is supposed to be three companies.

Fort Morgan and Fort Gaines are permanent works, with walls of brick masonry. The battery at Grant's Pass mounts three 32-pounders, which will soon be rifled; garrison, one company. Near the city, in the neighborhood of Choctaw Pass, a battery is being built in the water to command the channel in case small vessels should run past the forts or armed launches be hauled across the peninsula of Mobile Point. Some batteries are being thrown up on the land front of the city, for which guns were ordered by Mr. Secretary Walker. The labor for this last work is understood to be furnished gratuitously by the citizens.

The great want of Mobile Bay is an armed steamer, to cope with any armed small craft which might steal into the bay at night or be hauled over land, as already mentioned. A single armed launch could cut off communication between the city and the forts, for there is literally nothing in which to make head against such an invader. A steamer like the Miramon should be immediately bought for that service, and be armed with one or two heavy guns.

Very respectfully, sir, your obedient servant,

D. LEADBETTER,
Major of Engineers, Acting Chief of Bureau.

RICHMOND, *September* 23, 1861.

General DAVID E. TWIGGS:

Will send you an active and competent brigadier-general this week. Will send you powder as fast as we can procure it.

J. P. BENJAMIN,
Acting Secretary of War.

RICHMOND, *September* 25, 1861.

JOHN FORSYTH,
Mayor, Mobile, Ala.:

I have ordered 50 barrels of cannon powder sent from Nashville to Mobile, also 100 barrels to New Orleans, also 12 tons of saltpeter to New Orleans for immediate manufacture. Further supplies will be sent at the earliest possible moment.

J. P. BENJAMIN,
Acting Secretary of War.

HEADQUARTERS TROOPS CONFEDERATE STATES,
Near Pensacola, Fla., September 25, 1861.

Hon. J. P. BENJAMIN,
Acting Secretary of War, Richmond, Va.:

SIR: You will pardon me for the freedom of addressing you, but the subject is of vital importance, and requires prompt attention. For some time a growing dissatisfaction has existed here among the regular officers of the Army from the old United States service, which has culminated in a number of resignations. They have seen themselves overlooked by their Government, while their juniors in years and service, and I think their inferiors in many cases, were put over them in rank in other armies. To this they submitted without a murmur, and labored incessantly, doing what their superiors in rank here could not do, but for which they were receiving the credit. The last feather, however, has broken the camel's back. The Department, just before your entrance on its duties, came into their midst, and selected one of the very youngest of their number for the grade of colonel. Lieutenant (Colonel) Wheeler is a very excellent officer, and none envy him his good fortune, but they cannot see the justice of the apparent reflection on themselves. The jealousy with which professional soldiers look upon military rank is second only, my dear sir, to that of honor. For whatever success I have attained in my efforts for the organization and instruction of this army I am indebted to these officers. You can see, then, how keenly I may share the mortification which has been inflicted on them, and I sincerely trust the Department will be able to assist me in averting the calamity which threatens, for they clearly see that my personal influence heretofore exerted has availed them nothing.

I am, sir, very respectfully, your obedient servant,

BRAXTON BRAGG.

RICHMOND, *September* 25, 1861.

General DAVID E. TWIGGS,
New Orleans:

I cannot spare any rifled cannon for New Orleans. You have one transferred from Hollins. Have the others rifled as fast as possible at the New Orleans founderies. There are but two large-sized rifled guns received at Savannah and twelve rifled field pieces. The coast of Georgia will be attacked in a few days, and I cannot withdraw guns. I have appointed Mansfield Lovell a brigadier-general, and ordered him to New Orleans. He will be with you this week. Have ordered 10 more tons of saltpeter from Augusta to New Orleans, and 100 barrels of cannon powder from Nashville to New Orleans and 50 barrels to Mobile.

J. P. BENJAMIN,
Acting Secretary of War.

NEW ORLEANS, LA., *September* 25, 1861.

Hon. J. P. BENJAMIN,
Richmond, Va.:

General Twiggs requests me to seize all the pork in the city, about 2,500 barrels. Shall I do it?

THO. O. MOORE.

RICHMOND, VA., *September* 25, 1861.

Gov. THOMAS O. MOORE,
New Orleans, La.:

I know of no necessity for seizing the pork. Do you see any need of it?

J. P. BENJAMIN,
Acting Secretary of War.

ENGINEER BUREAU,
Richmond, September 26, 1861.

SECRETARY OF WAR:

The letter of Hon. F. B. Shepard, under date of September 4,* has been referred to this office for information. At that date the condition of Fort Gaines in the matter of armament and munitions was very unsatisfactory. The fort itself was scarcely defensible with any armament, though all the guns available had been mounted. Two 10-inch guns had been received, but not mounted for want of carriages. These have been supplied, and it is hoped that these guns are now mounted. The bastions are now finished, their traverse circles laid for a columbiad in each; the scarp wall by this time must be everywhere to its proper height; the magazines are undoubtedly available; the rampart and parapet are rapidly approaching entire continuity, and the glacis wants but little to give efficient cover to the masonry. There are still wanted three heavy guns for the three bastions now unarmed and sixteen flanking howitzers. These guns have been ordered by the Hon. Secretary of War, and are supposed to be under fabrication. They are urgently needed, as well as others, at Fort Morgan. The lack of munitions and implements at Fort Gaines lies between the commander of the post and

---

* Not found.

that of Fort Morgan. The latter place, though insufficiently supplied for the exigencies of war, can well spare more largely to the other. Most likely General Withers, now in command, has corrected the unequal ratio of distribution. At Fort Gaines the guns are supplied with friction-primers. There are six 32-pounders bearing favorably on the land. The Fort Gaines channel is from 9 to 10 feet deep.

D. LEADBETTER,
Major Engineers, Acting Chief of Bureau.

NEW ORLEANS, *September* 26, 1861.

TO SECRETARY OF WAR:

We are ready to make powder at once if we get saltpeter.

D. E. TWIGGS,
Major-General.

RICHMOND, VA., *September* 26, 1861.

GOV. THOMAS O. MOORE,
Louisiana:

SIR: Yours of the 20th instant, containing a copy of a resolution which you informed me was adopted by the generals and some of the subordinates of the militia of Louisiana, has been received. I concur in your objection to a proposition for a board of defense; and in relation to the other point would say that long since one of the best officers in the Engineer Corps, and of superior rank (Maj. M. L. Smith), was sent to Louisiana to perform the duties of chief engineer there. If from any cause he has been found incompetent, I regret that the evidence was not laid before me, so that he might have been removed.

General Van Dorn has not communicated to me the views which you intrusted to him to be orally delivered; but from various sources I have learned that General Twiggs has proven unequal to his command. As in his selection I yielded much to the solicitation of the people of New Orleans, I think they should sooner have informed me of the mistake they had made. Your own recent letter was the first information received by me. I have, however, directed Mansfield Lovell, who is no doubt known to you by reputation, to be appointed a brigadier-general, and assigned to duty in connection with the defenses of New Orleans and the adjacent coast. It is some weeks since I met a committee from your city, charged with propositions for the defenses of New Orleans, and had hoped the needful works for defense were under construction and repair. In the mean time I have endeavored to provide the necessary armament and munitions.

Should your worst apprehensions be realized—which I cannot bring myself to believe when I remember how much has been done for the defense of New Orleans since 1815, both in the construction of works and facilities for transportation—I hope a discriminating public will acquit this Government of having neglected the defenses of your coast and approaches to New Orleans.

I am, very respectfully, your obedient servant,

JEFFERSON DAVIS.

MONTGOMERY, *September* 27, 1861.

General S. COOPER:

There is misapprehension as to my requisition for troops. It was for three regiments, independent of Mobile organizations, which were only considered for an emergency. If governor of Alabama cannot furnish the three, have I authority to accept deficiency from Mississippi if tendered? Answer to Mobile.

J. M. WITHERS,
Brigadier-General.

NEW ORLEANS, *September* 27, 1861.

To SECRETARY OF WAR:

Mississippi troops on lake shore will muster in for eleven months only. Hollins has orders from Secretary of Navy not to turn over the guns to me. Can Colonel Duncan be appointed brigadier-general, to report to me?

D. E. TWIGGS.

NEW ORLEANS, LA., *September* 27, 1861.

Hon. J. P. BENJAMIN,
Richmond, Va.:

No pork here except amount mentioned. What are we to do for our volunteers here? Answer.

THO. O. MOORE.

NEW ORLEANS, LA., *September* 28, 1861.

Hon. J. P. BENJAMIN,
Richmond, Va.:

My guns are gone—are all distributed. Can any be had? I telegraphed you about pork I seized. Answer.

THO. O. MOORE.

WAR DEPARTMENT, C. S. A.,
Richmond, September 28, 1861.

His Excellency THOMAS O. MOORE,
Governor of Louisiana, New Orleans:

SIR: In reply to your letter of the 22d instant I am directed by the Secretary of War to say that 12 tons of saltpeter and 100 kegs of powder have been ordered to New Orleans, in compliance with your request for those articles. The President has written to you relative to the other points touched upon in your letter.*

Respectfully,
A. T. BLEDSOE,
Chief of Bureau of War.

NEW ORLEANS, LA., *September* 29, 1861.

Hon. J. P. BENJAMIN:

MY DEAR SIR: I have about 3,500 men in camp, organized into companies, and three regiments formed, including the Thirteenth, Colonel

---

* Mr. Davis' letter not found.

Gibson's, and have not arms for them all. I am now sorry that I ever sent off so many, as they, with the volunteers who took them off, are so occupied I fear I shall not get them back when needed. It seems that all will be wanted that are in Virginia, Tennessee, Kentucky, and Missouri, where they are; if so, we are here certainly in rather an unpleasant situation, for if we could raise the men we could not arm them. Our fortifications have progressed slowly, it having rained almost every day since they were commenced, but now we are getting on more rapidly, the weather improved, and more force put on the works. We are much in need of engineers and other officers, as I before wrote you. I see the necessity for them daily. General Twiggs' age precludes the possibility of his doing the labor necessary to a command of the magnitude and importance of this, and an officer here should be able to visit and inspect every place. Even were I possessed of the military qualifications, with my present official duties I could do nothing in that way. The raft was placed across the river at the forts on yesterday, I think; it was all ready, and the engineer went down to place it three days since, so I trust nothing can pass the forts.

We have not heard of the fleet that has left with the 20,000 men, but I have no doubt, and that is the impression generally, that it is destined to other points besides Brunswick. We can be greatly harassed here on our entire coast, and no doubt will be, and I am kept constantly distressed at the incompetency, as I consider, of our commander. If anything is to be done here you must send us officers and more arms. The Fourth Regiment, I trust, will not be sent off, but that it will be brought over. Cannot General Dahlgren take care of the lake coast? I fear he is not the man that should be there.

I am now waiting for the saltpeter, as I am informed the mill is ready, but everything by rail moves so slow, so slow. I have had Major Ramsey to dispatch the whole line to forward it as fast as possible. The amount of powder here is very small compared to what is necessary, and a knowledge of that fact keeps up a constant excitement among our people.

I, notwithstanding your advice to the contrary, seized the pork in the city, and telegraphed you (but have had no reply), and shall hold it, unless requested by you to act otherwise, as I see no way to feed our troops without it, but hope you do, as your advice was to that effect. Write me fully on that point.

Is the Government doing anything to clothe and shoe our troops? I do not learn that it is. I have sent a suit of clothes and underclothes, blankets, and shoes to our regiment in Missouri, and blankets for our entire force in Virginia, and clothing for the First and Second Regiments, with shoes also for the whole force, but provision ought to be made for another pair of shoes, as some of those I sent I fear will not last very well, but they were the best to be had.

Have arrangements been made by the Government for arms in Europe? Certainly arms ought to have been procured before this. I have about 1,600 in Havana, and have $150,000 in England to purchase more. The only trouble is to get them here. Cannot Mr. Slidell, who leaves soon, give some aid and advice in the matter? He knows the parties acting for me. I expect something done, indeed everything that is necessary for us, for I have tried to do so for the Confederacy. I hardly know what I have written, I am so constantly troubled by visitors on business.

Yours, truly,

THO. O. MOORE.

NEW ORLEANS, LA., *September* 29, 1861.

Hon. J. P. BENJAMIN,
Richmond, Va.:

I seized pork against your advice. Will release if not wanted. Generals not arrived. Have not arms for volunteers in camp. Have you any? What am I to do? Answer.

THO. O. MOORE.

RICHMOND, VA., *September* 30, 1861.

Gov. THOMAS O. MOORE,
New Orleans, La.:

I can conceive no possible reason for seizing pork and cannot approve it. There is an abundance of food in our country, and private rights ought not to be invaded except in cases of necessity for public defense.

J. P. BENJAMIN,
Acting Secretary of War.

RICHMOND, *September* 30, 1861.

General DAVID E. TWIGGS,
New Orleans:

Do not accept the Mississippi troops for less than twelve months, unless they are simply for local defense, under law passed last session. Captain Hollins was only ordered to turn over to you a single rifled gun as a model for rifling other guns at the foundery. If he refuses this, let me know. Terry has already been ordered to join General Johnston with his regiment. Do as you please about assigning Higgins to ordnance duty. It is said here that young Palfrey, recommended by you for your staff, is not twenty-one years old. If this is so he cannot be appointed an officer in the Army.

J. P. BENJAMIN,
Acting Secretary of War.

RICHMOND, VA., *September* 30, 1861.

Gov. THOMAS O. MOORE,
New Orleans, La.:

Your several dispatches about arms and generals received. Pray have a little patience. I am doing the best I can with the means at my disposal, and you do not allow me time to concert the arrangements necessary to satisfy you. In two or three days I will inform you fully of what is to be done.

J. P. BENJAMIN,
Acting Secretary of War.

Abstract from field return of troops of the Confederate States near Pensacola, Fla., Maj. Gen. Braxton Bragg commanding, for October 1, 1861.

Commands.	Present for duty.		Aggregate present.
	Officers.	Men.	
1st (Ruggles') Brigade	150	2,778	3,686
2d (Anderson's) Brigade	125	2,061	2,698
Alabama Mounted Rifles (Jenkins)	2	76	94
Walton Guards (McPherson)	4	51	55
Total	281	4,966	6,533

NEW ORLEANS, *October* 4, 1861.

TO SECRETARY OF WAR:

Black Republicans assembling a fleet at Head of Passes. The Richmond, a sloop of war, a schooner, a captured pilot-boat, and the Water Witch were there yesterday evening. I will send some powder and re-enforcements to Colonel Duncan immediately. I do not think Fort Jackson is the point that will be attacked. I will try to be ready to meet them at all points.

D. E. TWIGGS.

ENGINEER BUREAU,
Richmond, Va., October 7, 1861.

Capt. S. H. LOCKETT,
Corps of Engineers, Mobile, Ala.:

SIR: Your letter of the 1st instant has been received.* The commanding general being responsible for the defense, he decides what works shall be built and when. Your own responsibility ends when your views have been made known to him officially.

With regard to armament, I had supposed that having the Secretary's order for thirty guns from North Carolina we were sure to get them, but there is no hope in that quarter. From present appearances I would not recommend you to rely on getting any more heavy guns or carriages from this quarter. The demands from all directions are urgent, and the Secretary says he cannot give what he has not got. If you do not get heavy guns for the remaining bastions of Fort Gaines—and I see no probability of getting them—you will have to mount a rifled 32 in each. If the flank guns fail (and I can gain no information of them) you had better fasten the embrasure shutters firmly, and make a loop-hole for musketry in each. Of course you will have the guns rifled for Grant's Pass, and another gun ought to be added there. When I left, the magazine at that place was not sufficiently covered.

I see you have had a broadside. One heavy rifled gun left on the 3d.

Very truly, yours,

D. LEADBETTER,
Major Engineers, Acting Chief of Bureau.

---

*Not found.

SPECIAL ORDERS, No. 173. } ADJT. AND INSP. GENERAL'S OFFICE, *Richmond, Va., October* 7, 1861.

* * * * * * *

IX. The command of Maj. Gen. Braxton Bragg, Provisional Army, is extended to embrace the coast and State of Alabama.

* * * * * * *

By command of the Secretary of War:

JNO. WITHERS,
Assistant Adjutant-General.

GENERAL ORDERS, No. 110. } HEADQUARTERS TROOPS OF C. S., *Near Pensacola, Fla., October* 12, 1861.

I. Brig. Gen. Daniel Ruggles, Provisional Army, is relieved from duty with this command, and will proceed to New Orleans, and report to Major-General Twiggs, in conformity to special orders from the War Department.

The regret of the commanding general in parting with General Ruggles, whose labors have been so untiring and efficient with this army, is lessened by the knowledge of his transfer to a more extended field in Louisiana, where he is commended to the confidence of many friends.

II. Brigadier-General Gladden, Provisional Army, is assigned to the First (Ruggles') Brigade. Col. J. Patton Anderson is relieved from the command of his regiment, the First Florida, and will relieve Brigadier-General Gladden in command of the Second (Anderson's) Brigade.

III. The habit again growing up in the army of an indiscriminate waste of ammunition must be discontinued. No guns will be loaded except on the advanced and beach picket guards, and their guns will be discharged at a target the next morning at sunrise under their respective officers. The discharge of a gun at any other hour will subject the offender to arrest and trial. Captain Jenkins' company, mounted volunteers, will patrol the camps of the whole army for the enforcement of this order, and all officers will be held accountable for any infringement. Not only our success but our safety depends on a preservation of our very limited supply of ammunition.

By command of Major-General Bragg:

GEO. G. GARNER,
Assistant Adjutant-General.

WAR DEPARTMENT,
Richmond, Va., October 13, 1861.

GOV. THOMAS O. MOORE,
New Orleans, La.:

MY DEAR SIR: I snatch a moment this (Sunday) evening to answer your favor of the 29th ultimo. Matters have been so changed since the date of that letter that it is scarcely necessary to do more than say that I have used every effort in my power to put [you] in such a position as shall allay all fears relative to the defenses of New Orleans.

Maj. Gen. Mansfield Lovell, a brilliant, energetic, and accomplished officer, has been assigned to the command of your department. Powder, saltpeter, and cannon have been forwarded, and will be still further supplied as fast as they can be possibly spared, and the recent gallant dash of Captain Hollins at the blockading fleet must have infused new life and spirit into our people.

The Government is fast providing, to the extent of its ability, shoes and clothing for our troops, and is greatly relieved in this herculean task by the patriotic and generous aid of just such governors of States as our own Tom Moore.

I am sure you will be persuaded that nothing I can do shall be left undone for the defense of Louisiana, while you would not wish, I am equally sure, that I should neglect the defenses of other points of importance in order to concentrate all our resources in New Orleans alone.

Yours, very truly,

J. P. BENJAMIN.

GENERAL ORDERS, No. 1. } HDQRS. DEPT. OF ALA. AND WEST FLA., *Near Pensacola, Fla., October* 14, 1861.

I. The command of Major-General Bragg, extended by Special Orders, No. 173, Adjutant-General's Office, October 7, 1861, to include the coast and State of Alabama, will be known as the Department of Alabama and West Florida. All returns and reports from troops stationed therein will be rendered to the headquarters, near Pensacola.

II. The following officers compose the staff of the major-general commanding:

1. Maj. George G. Garner, assistant adjutant-general.
2. First Lieut. Towson Ellis, aide-de-camp.
3. First Lieut. J. E. Slaughter, acting inspector-general.
4. Capt. W. R. Boggs, chief of engineers and artillery.
5. Capt. H. Oladowski, chief of ordnance.
6. Maj. L. W. O'Bannon, chief quartermaster.
7. Capt. Thomas M. Jones, chief of subsistence and paymaster.
8. Surg. A. J. Foard, medical director.
9. First Lieut. H. W. Walter, acting judge-advocate.

III. Brig. Gen. J. M. Withers will continue in the execution of his present command, to be known as the District of Alabama.

* * * * * * *

By command of Major-General Bragg:

GEO. G. GARNER,
Assistant Adjutant-General.

NEW ORLEANS, LA., *October* 14, 1861.

Hon. J. P. BENJAMIN,
Secretary of War, Richmond, Va.:

We want muskets without delay. Send us some.

THO. O. MOORE.

RICHMOND, VA., *October* 16, 1861.

Gov. THOMAS O. MOORE,
New Orleans, La.:

Will send you the very first muskets that I can dispose of.

J. P. BENJAMIN,
Acting Secretary of War.

ENGINEER BUREAU,
Richmond, Va., October 18, 1861.

Col. J. GORGAS,
Chief of Ordnance:

DEAR SIR: Fort Gaines, at Mobile, Ala., yet requires for its armament sixteen 24-pounder howitzers and carriages for flank casemate defense. Three of its bastions are yet without guns in barbette, and require a columbiad in each—say three 8-inch columbiads, with barbette carriages.

Very truly, your obedient servant,

D. LEADBETTER,
Major Engineers, Acting Chief of Bureau.

HEADQUARTERS DEPARTMENT NO. 1,
New Orleans, La., October 18, 1861.

Hon. J. P. BENJAMIN,
Acting Secretary of War:

SIR: As this city, the first in importance in the Confederacy, has been greatly drained of arms, ammunition, medical stores, clothing, and supplies for other points, I would respectfully suggest that the heads of bureaus be requested to order nothing further of that description to be forwarded from here until we have provided ourselves with a fair supply for the force required for the defense of this city. Anything that in my judgment could be spared I would readily send forward; but it will require great exertions to put ourselves in a proper state of defense, and nothing should be diverted from that purpose until the object is gained. The actual state of preparation I shall not put on paper.

When companies or regiments enlisted for twelve months have been in service under State authority for a portion of the time and are then transferred to the Confederate service, persistent objection is made in some instances to being mustered for a longer period than the balance of the original twelve months. Most of these have fully nine months to serve, and as the fate of New Orleans for this season must be settled within that time, I shall not stand upon that point, unless you direct me by telegraph to do so.

I am greatly in need of two things, viz, an assistant adjutant-general, acquainted with the details of office matters, forms, &c., who can instruct the volunteers and keep the records in such shape that claims may be settled at some indefinite future period, and some saltpeter for the manufacture of powder. While the first would greatly facilitate matters here, it is not indispensable; the latter is.

We are daily expecting funds, without which we cannot get on a great while.

Respectfully, your obedient servant,

M. LOVELL,
Major-General, Commanding.

GENERAL ORDERS, No. 120. } HDQRS. TROOPS CONFEDERATE STATES,
Near Pensacola, Fla., October 22, 1861.

The major-general commanding, intending to be absent for a few days on a tour of inspection, the command of the troops at and near Pensacola will devolve upon Brigadier-General Gladden, pending the disability of Brig. Gen. R. H. Anderson.

The official designation of the forces at and near Pensacola will in future be, "Army of Pensacola."

By command of Major-General Bragg:

GEO. G. GARNER,
Assistant Adjutant-General.

NEW ORLEANS, LA., *October* 23, 1861.

Hon. J. P. BENJAMIN:

Is it impossible to give us powder or saltpeter in quantity immediately?

M. LOVELL.

RICHMOND, VA., *October* 23, 1861.

General MANSFIELD LOVELL,
New Orleans, La.:

We calculate that we have sent in powder and saltpeter to New Orleans within the last month the equivalent of 500 barrels of powder, to be added to the stock previously on hand. We can spare no more at present without urgent necessity. Telegraph me what your whole supply is.

J. P. BENJAMIN,
Acting Secretary of War.

HEADQUARTERS DEPARTMENT NO. 1, C. S. A.,
New Orleans, La., October 25, 1861.

Hon. J. P. BENJAMIN,
Acting Secretary of War:

DEAR SIR: I have received your telegram relative to the amount of powder and saltpeter sent to this point within the past month, but think it hardly advisable to make known our deficiency through the telegraph office.

Your dispatch says that "the equivalent of 500 barrels of powder has been sent here within a month." I find no correct returns of ordnance and ordnance stores from the various posts, but have sent a circular calling for them, and am getting them in. I know that the acting ordnance officer has several invoices of powder which have not yet come to hand. Admit, however, that we have 500 barrels. We have now at the various forts and approaches 210 guns in position and about 100 more that we shall soon have in place, giving in all 310 guns of the caliber of a 24-pounder and upwards. The average charge, large and small, will be 8 pounds for each gun, or 2,480 pounds for a single round apiece. Five hundred barrels contains 50,000 pounds, which would give us 20 rounds per gun, not more than enough for an hour's fight; but the powder received from Memphis was quite worthless. More than 30 barrels invoiced to us have not arrived, and we loaned Commodore Hollins the powder with which he made his attack upon the vessels above the passes a few days since. We have therefore less than 20 rounds per gun.

I am hurrying into operation two mills which will give us 6,000 or 8,000 pounds per day if we can get saltpeter, and have sent an agent to contract for working some of the idle saltpeter caves in the adjoining States. Of sulphur and charcoal we have a supply.

The want of powder is our only glaring deficiency. I do not allow an ounce to be burned unnecessarily, and am straining every nerve to add to our supply. If I can get saltpeter, and the enemy will give us a few weeks, which I think he will do, we shall be pretty well prepared to defeat him. With 100 rounds per gun I should feel pretty safe.

Respectfully, your obedient servant,

M. LOVELL,
Major-General, Commanding.

HDQRS. DEPARTMENT ALABAMA AND WEST FLORIDA,
Mobile, October 25, 1861.

ADJUTANT-GENERAL C. S. ARMY,
Richmond:

SIR: As indicated in my dispatch of the 22d, I left Pensacola that night, and arrived here on the 23d. After a long and free interview with General Withers on the state of his command, it was arranged to visit the defenses, which was done yesterday.

A small battery is being erected on piles at the junction of Mobile and Tensas Rivers, not far from the city, which may have a beneficial effect in preventing boat expeditions should the enemy enter the bay.

At Grant's Pass a small earthwork has been erected, and furnished with three guns and a garrison of one company. This is probably sufficient for the purpose of keeping this pass open to our steamers still allowed to run to New Orleans. As the place is not susceptible of successful defense against any large attacking force, I directed the hull of an old vessel we own here to be heavily ballasted and anchored there, ready to close the pass at a moment's notice, and a practicable ford to be staked out by which the garrison can reach the main-land.

Fort Gaines is rapidly approaching a condition for strong defense, but is almost destitute of guns and ammunition. Demands long since made for both meet no response. It is of little or no importance except to prevent the enemy from using the island against us, being about 2½ miles from the channel. With a view of preventing a landing on the island an outwork is in progress, some 3 miles off, and masked by intervening woods. Deeming this a weakness, by dispersing our forces and armament, I directed its discontinuance. The completion of the fort will be pushed vigorously, and the armament increased as rapidly as possible. Two large brick buildings, three stories high, built inside the fort, apparently as a mark for the enemy's fire, to mask the field of our guns, or to furnish splinters and brickbats for the destruction of the garrison, I have directed to be demolished at once. The temporary quarters, of wood, badly located and much dispersed, are to be concentrated in a proper position.

Fort Morgan is in a better condition, though not half armed, and with a very limited supply of ammunition. In rough weather, and especially during the north winds of winter, boats cannot land at the wharf at this post. Another wharf is being constructed some 3 miles off, at Navy Cove, and a railroad laid to it from the fort. Three sand batteries are being constructed for the defense of this position. Fort Morgan is the key to Mobile Bay, and must be held with a heavy armament and ample supplies. I shall at once reduce my position at Pensacola to one of defense strictly, and send what can be spared to this point, though it will be totally inadequate to the wants here.

The safety of this position is in the enemy's ignorance, if he be ignorant, for they seem to get late and correct information from us by illicit means through our own people. It may be that the very state of affairs so long existing on the Gulf has called out his heavy expedition not yet heard from, and which may strike us at any moment without warning. We must at every hazard force him to land and fight us in the open field. For this we are well prepared at Pensacola, except in light artillery, for which the Ordnance Department has persistently promised and as persistently withheld all supplies. Here we are equally deficient in that and not very well off with infantry, but in both we possess some elements of improvement not heretofore available to me. I shall at once commence the manufacture of artillery harness, carriages, guns, and ammunition at this point, and hope soon to increase our efficiency—or rather decrease our inefficiency—in this essential arm. We need more cavalry for defensive operations at both points, but it is useless to call for them unless we are assured of arms.

A recent order from General Pillow, if we are correctly informed, will paralyze this arm of our service, if it does not starve us all out. A heavy rise in the provision market is already the result of this unfortunate move. With a rigid blockade in front and a stringent embargo behind on both provisions and munitions we occupy rather a perilous position. It may be well to inform the author of this move of our presence here and of the fact that we are engaged in the same cause with himself. I inclose the report of Mr. Hessee, quartermaster's agent here, on this subject. We are confidently assured of railroad connection within three weeks hence to Pensacola. This will greatly increase our ability to meet an attack on either place. With unity of sentiment and concert of action between the commanders mutual aid could be received and given with great celerity between this and the department west; but one common superior, if the Government has an officer of the requisite rank, would more effectually secure the same object, and greatly strengthen the defenses of the whole Gulf coast. On this point I submit a communication, indorsed by Brigadier-General Withers, in regard to a telegraph line on the Mobile and Ohio Railroad. I shall encourage its construction. Our lines on the coast can be destroyed at any time by the enemy.

Would it not be more healthful and comfortable, and equally as cheap, to concentrate near this place and Pensacola the unarmed regiments in Alabama in suitable camps of instruction, where they could be ready to receive the arms of the twelve-months' men soon to be discharged? They might be learning the artillery drill, too, which they cannot do where they are. The discharges will commence in three months, and the subject is worthy of early attention. The effort to raise troops here for local defense, sedentary militia, is working badly, and should be abolished everywhere. Whenever we can get arms we can get men for the war unconditionally. The two regiments of Colonels Buck and Crawford have consented to change their times and tenure of service, and are mustered in for twelve months.

Brigadier-General Withers is laboring hard and successfully. He has very properly suspended the grand scheme for squandering money by digging ditches around the city, which would have required 40,000 men to defend them, and has concentrated his means and labor on important points requiring the promptest attention and all his resources.

I shall have to spare him a part of my regular officers from Pensacola, as his need is great and pressing. I shall return to Pensacola to-morrow.

I am, sir, very respectfully, your obedient servant,

BRAXTON BRAGG,
Major-General, Commanding.

HDQRS. DEPARTMENT ALABAMA AND WEST FLORIDA,
Near Pensacola, Fla., October 28, 1861.

ADJUTANT-GENERAL C. S. ARMY,
Richmond, Va.:

SIR: I arrived here yesterday from Mobile, and find no change to report. The enemy is in a constant state of excitement on Santa Rosa, and has frequent alarms. He has moved artillery up the island to our landing place of the late expedition. General Withers' command needs much to put it in an efficient condition. He has about 4,200 troops—which should be increased to 6,000—mostly raw, and inefficiently organized, armed, and equipped, and very destitute of military instructors. The positions of Forts Morgan and Gaines and Grant's Pass are occupied by his best troops, about 2,000, and in close proximity. The two senior officers commanding at the forts are very competent, but sadly addicted to drinking, and therefore unsafe for those exposed positions. The General cannot remain there and discharge his other duties, though he will visit them frequently. The remainder of his command, except two detached companies, will be concentrated in a suitable camp on the west of Mobile Bay, and some 15 or 20 miles below the city, where they will be away from dissipation, can be cheaply supplied, and will be available for any attack. These two positions require commanders of military knowledge and experience and capacity for command.

First Lieut. J. E. Slaughter, acting inspector-general; Capt. W. R. Boggs, Engineers; Lieut. Col. J. B. Villepigue, Georgia and Mississippi regiment, and Maj. L. W. O'Bannon, quartermaster, furnish material from which the President might select two brigadiers for those important positions, I can very well fill the vacancies on my staff from well-instructed volunteers, except in the Engineers. Should Colonel Villepigue receive one of the appointments, one of the others might fill his vacancy. I shall order First Lieut. G. W. Holt, C. S. Army, to report to General Withers, at Mobile, as depot quartermaster there, and discharge the agent now on that duty. Lieutenant Holt deserves and should receive promotion. First Lieutenant Hallonquist, C. S. artillery, will also be ordered to report to General Withers, as chief of artillery. As that command has several companies of light artillery, I suggest his appointment as major of them. Promotion could not fall on a more gallant or efficient officer. If it could be arranged so that Brigadier-General Ruggles could be my second in command here, or could assume my local duties, my services could be much more efficient, and from the hold he has on the confidence and affection of the troops here I know the consequences feared by the Department in my removal would not ensue. I should still be much with them.

I am, sir, very respectfully, your obedient servant,

BRAXTON BRAGG,
Major-General, Commanding.

O'BANNONVILLE, *October* 29, 1861.

General S. COOPER,
Adjutant-General:

In view of the heavy expedition now on its way South, we should develop all our resources. One regiment here and one at Mobile can be armed by using arms of the sick and disabled. Can they be sent from Huntsville? We have efficient light artillery. For want of supplies we have less than 2,000 effective men at Mobile outside of the forts.

BRAXTON BRAGG.

WAR DEPARTMENT, C. S. A.,
Richmond, October 29, 1861.

Maj. Gen. MANSFIELD LOVELL,
New Orleans:

SIR: Your letter of 18th instant was not received till yesterday, 28th. I telegraphed you to-day that we have no power to receive troops for less than twelve months, but where troops offer themselves specially for local defense they may be accepted in any proportion and for any term, as they are a mere improvised militia, not entitled to pay or subsistence except during actual service. (See act of 21st August, No. 229, of third session.)

I cannot restrain the heads of bureaus from purchasing or forwarding supplies from New Orleans. This interference with commerce exceeds my power except in case of extreme urgency. I much prefer that you should make requisitions for everything in the way of supply that you need, and have your purchases made in New Orleans, and thus it is easy to prevent the removal from the city of what is required for its defense without infringing on the rights of any one.

I anxiously await your letter about the supply of powder and saltpeter. I cannot conceive what has become of the quantity recently sent to New Orleans, say within the last six weeks. I hope your demand for supply was based on erroneous information from persons who did not know the facts.

I have ordered a young officer, said to be of high merit as an engineer, to report to you—First Lieutenant Cunningham, just appointed in artillery, with a view to assign him to Engineer Corps if he proves as competent as represented.

I am much gratified to learn from different sources that you have succeeded in inspiring general confidence in New Orleans, thereby justifying the confidence reposed by the Government in yourself.

Your obedient servant,

J. P. BENJAMIN,
Acting Secretary of War.

HDQRS. DEPARTMENT ALABAMA AND WEST FLORIDA,
Near Pensacola, Fla., October 30, 1861.

Hon. J. P. BENJAMIN,
Acting Secretary of War, Richmond, Va.:

SIR: On the receipt of your letter of the 6th instant a short reply was made to the first point and a further one promised on the main subject.

Though very grateful to my wounded feelings, yours was not entirely satisfactory to me, nor to those on whose behalf I had presumed to complain. I now propose to controvert your positions, knowing the danger I encounter.

Nothing, it seems, can be done for my neglected officers under the legislation as it now exists. How does it happen that so much has been done for others, their juniors, under this same legislation? You acknowledge this in your letter. You admit one case in Colonel Wheeler. Others present themselves to my mind. A private in one of my companies, a gentleman of high attainments and merit, only equaled by his modesty, was offered the colonelcy of a regiment. He declined it in favor of one of my regular officers, but saying, "If civilians must be appointed, then I will accept." He was at once commissioned, and removed from a position he adorned on my staff to one he was unprepared to fill. He will in time make a fine officer, but those he preferred seeing appointed were already made. Other regiments raised at the same time were officered by civilians in the same way. All of my staff officers here of the old Regular Army, the first to quit it, some even before their States seceded, were allowed to rest in subordinate positions, while their inferiors in rank, of the eleventh-hour converts and civilians, were placed over their heads. Certainly the legislation of Congress never required this. You now propose that whenever I can spare them you will find means to give them increased rank in the Provisional Army. I will not spare them if I can help it, nor are they desirous of leaving me, but I claim consideration for them equal to that accorded to their inferiors in other armies. My officers and myself have remained at our posts faithfully laboring in the cause we so early espoused. We have not united in the "On to Richmond," seeking high places. We considered it unmilitary and unbecoming. We were ardently serving the cause, not ourselves, but, nevertheless, we did not suppose our Government would so soon forget we were in its service and degrade us. This state of things, my dear sir, we believe has been brought about to some extent without the knowledge of the President and against his wishes, but it is nevertheless a rankling sore, which he only can cure. I am candid, perhaps harsh, but I am doing him more service than by permitting the evil to grow while he is in ignorance. I do not hesitate to say, "I impugn the action of your predecessor." He has done the service more harm in the Cabinet than he will ever repair in the field.

Let me now appeal to you for an old brother soldier, who is more aggrieved and with more cause than any of us. Brigadier-General Ruggles first reported to me as second in command under the impression derived from the Adjutant General, and I believed it from the precedence given his name in his order. We soon learned that Brigadier-General Anderson, his junior by many years in the old service, and it is no disparagement to say very far his inferior as a soldier, was his senior in rank. General Ruggles, soon after raising this question, was ordered to New Orleans, as a means, we hoped, of removing this cause of complaint. What was his and our dismay, then, to learn that another junior, just from the enemy, who had been up to a late hour lecturing them on the art and science of war, was promoted over his head, and assigned to a command the highest and most important in the Southern country. That command includes my home and fireside, and all that is dear to me in life. I can appreciate the feeling of sullen dissatisfaction which pervades my neighbors. The appointee is competent, but he does not and cannot possess the confidence of many who look with distrust on his eleventh-hour conversion. A great element of strength is thus lost to us. You will never preserve the *morale* of this army by thus degrading the commanders they so much admire and love. The feeling of discontent has reached the rank and file intelligent enough to read and digest these things, and where I expected to re-enlist hundreds for the war tens cannot be found. They will not abandon the cause, but will try and find a service less obscure and more appreciated—one in which their commanders possess sufficiently the confidence of the Government to justify them in expecting more consideration.

The result of all your deliberations has not been to preserve the *morale* of this army. Soldiers who have confidence in and respect for their commanders are never demoralized by seeing them advanced in rank or command or by seeing their sphere of usefulness increased, nor will you encourage the zeal of those commanders by making known to them that success in their arduous labors of organization and instruction is to consign them to inferior positions, as mere drill-masters.

Feeling so deeply it was due to myself, to you, and the President that I should give free expression to my sentiments, it is done in no spirit of insubordination. All that I have, all that I am, shall remain in this cause whenever and wherever it may please the Government to employ me.

I am, sir, very respectfully and truly, yours,

BRAXTON BRAGG,
Major-General, Commanding.

HEADQUARTERS DEPARTMENT No. 1,
New Orleans, La., October 31, 1861.

His Excellency President DAVIS:

DEAR SIR: The works for the defense of this city are progressing rapidly, and I think in a couple of weeks we can defeat any force that shall attempt invasion, if we can provide ourselves with powder. I have now one mill in operation which will turn out 1,200 pounds per day, another which can make 1,500, and in two weeks hope to have a third in full blast which will make 3,000 or 3,500 pounds per day. I have your dispatch about saltpeter and am looking for it daily; but we ought to have to-day 50 tons of cannon powder on hand besides what we can make.

My letter to Mr. Benjamin of the 25th instant will give you an idea of what we require to serve our guns.

I think we can fix the raft between Forts Jackson and Saint Philip so as to make a complete obstruction under the fire of those works. I send you inclosed a sketch of the works and raft.* The dotted black lines above the latter, running diagonally to Saint Philip, represent an arrangement which I propose to shed the drift over towards the opening in the raft on the Fort Jackson shore.

With your permission I will urge strongly upon you the appointment of Col. J. K. Duncan as a brigadier-general; he is worth a dozen of Ruggles, and has rendered most efficient service, with a zeal, untiring industry, and ability which entitle him to your high consideration. Had he more rank he could be of great assistance to me in organizing and giving directions, and I can assure you that help would not be unacceptable, as I have to keep driving all day and frequently the larger part of the night. If you have serious objections I will not press it, but the public service would be advanced by giving him rank enough to direct, and if necessary order, the colonels of volunteer regiments in this department, who require a great deal of dry-nursing.

---

* Not found.

General Bragg consents to the removal of Major Lovell to service here. I have two armed boats which he could use to material advantage on the coast of Mississippi, where, I am sorry to say, there are many disaffected persons, who will communicate with the enemy at every opportunity.

I receive every assistance here, except from some of the speculators, who endeavor to secure materials that the Government must have. The first operation I can fix upon them I shall publish their names to the community.

I am inclined to think that the attack on this coast will be on Mobile from East Pascagoula by land, with a strong demonstration by water. Is that city defended by intrenchments on the land side?

Respectfully, your obedient servant,

M. LOVELL.

O'BANNONVILLE, *October* 31, 1861.

General S. COOPER,
Adjutant-General:

Does my command include General Walker's brigade at Huntsville? In an emergency I might use a part of it with the arms of my sick and wounded. The measles at Mobile has disabled many.

BRAXTON BRAGG,
Major-General Commanding.

RICHMOND, *October* 31, 1861.

General BRAGG,
Pensacola:

You are authorized to take two of the Alabama regiments from Huntsville, to be armed with the spare arms at Mobile and Pensacola. If the expedition should make its attack elsewhere you must not expect to retain them with you.

J. P. BENJAMIN,
Acting Secretary of War.

BOWLING GREEN, *October* 31, 1861.

J. P. BENJAMIN:

By special messenger General Lovell writes from New Orleans, October 24:

There is an absolute, immediate necessity for powder or saltpeter for the defense of New Orleans, and the ordnance officer at Nashville reports 15 or 20 tons of saltpeter at each of the mills, and 20 tons on the way from Georgia; also 1,500 pounds of cannon powder on hand now, being prepared for General Zollicoffer. Twenty-four hundred pounds will yet be required by General Polk from the first manufactured. Great as seems the pressure at New Orleans, I do not feel authorized to make demands on the ordnance department at Nashville except for the wants of my own department, and therefore give you information of the call and the supply.

The messenger of General Lovell is waiting, and I wish for instructions. Can the 20 tons of saltpeter from Georgia expected be sent to New Orleans?

A. S. JOHNSTON,
General.

RICHMOND, *November* 1, 1861.

General A. SIDNEY JOHNSTON,
Bowling Green, Ky.:

Your dispatch received. Send nothing to General Lovell without orders from this Department. I have ordered 10 tons of saltpeter sent to him from Augusta.

J. P. BENJAMIN,
Acting Secretary of War.

O'BANNONVILLE, *November* 1, 1861.

Hon. J. P. BENJAMIN:

I shall be ready to spare the two regiments and a considerable portion of my other force for any point the enemy may assail. My railroad connection with Mobile will be completed in twelve days.

BRAXTON BRAGG,
Major-General, Commanding.

SPECIAL ORDERS, No. 200. } ADJT. AND INSP. GENERAL'S OFFICE,
Richmond, Va., November 1, 1861.

* * * * * * *

17. The two Mississippi regiments, known as or called the Fourth Mississippi Brigade, now at Camp Pettus, near Enterprise, Miss., will proceed to Pensacola, Fla., and report to Major-General Bragg, commanding.

By command of the Secretary of War:

* * * * * * *

JNO. WITHERS,
Assistant Adjutant-General.

Abstract from field return of the Army of Pensacola, Maj. Gen. Braxton Bragg commanding, for November 1, 1861.

Commands.	Present for duty. Officers.	Present for duty. Men.	Aggregate present.
1st (Gladden's) Brigade	167	2,970	3,813
2d (Anderson's) Brigade	135	2,063	2,639
Alabama Mounted Rifles (Jenkins)	4	87	99
Walton Guards (McPherson)	4	51	55
Total	310	5,171	6,606

WAR DEPARTMENT, C. S. A.,
Richmond, November 4, 1861.

Major-General BRAGG,
Pensacola:

MY DEAR SIR: I have ordered two and shall probably order a third Mississippi regiment to Pensacola. These regiments are not yet organized with field officers. The men are recovering from measles, and it is thought imprudent to send them north at this season. This will give you an opportunity to reward such of your officers as you may think most worthy with field appointments. Send in a list of recommendations for appointments of field officers for these regiments, and I doubt not the President will be glad to avail himself of the opportunity of testifying his sense of the merits of those officers who have cheerfully borne with you the dull routine and cheerfully watch at Pensacola without a murmur. You know that such appointments are made under act No. 155, second session, and are temporary in their character. They expire at the end of the war, and the officers then resume their regular position in the permanent Army. As soon as it is ascertained that no attack is to be made on you by the enemy's naval expedition, I hope you will send us in the place of those new regiments those of your present forces who have served longest and seem to you best to merit removal to more active field service.

Yours of 25th ultimo* to Adjutant-General, with its inclosures, is received. I have written to General A. S. Johnston on the subject of the interference by General Pillow with the forage collected for General Withers' command. I recognize the justice of his complaint, and trust that no further occasion of like character will require action on the part of the Department.

I fully concur in your strictures on the local-defense system, but you are mistaken in supposing that the Confederate Government can do anything to prevent it. The difficulty lies with the governors of the States, who are unwilling to trust the common defense to one common head. They therefore refuse arms to men who are willing to enlist unconditionally for the war, and put these arms in the hands of a mere home militia, who are not bound to leave the State. It is a very untoward condition of things, but as we have no arms, and the State authorities will not give us the control of the matter, we are forced to accept from them just what they choose to give. Still worse, they are accepting and arming men for local defense for six or twelve months, and thus breaking up our volunteer regiments that were offering for the war, in order to get from us such arms as we could supply. All this is sad, but I know not how to avoid it. Each governor wants to satisfy his own people, and there are not wanting politicians in each State to encourage the people to raise the cry that they will not consent to be left defenseless at home. The voice of reason, which would teach them that their home defenses would be best secured by a vigorous attack on the enemy on his own frontier is unheeded, and a clamor is raised against us for not attacking the enemy in front by the very men who are depriving us of the possibility of such a movement, by witholding the arms necessary for re-enforcing our little Army, that is so fearfully outnumbered that I dare not give you the figures. I have entire confidence that you will do all that skill and energy can effect with your own insufficient means, and will to the utmost of my power aid in all measures that you may devise for the security of the department committed to your charge.

I am, your obedient servant,

J. P. BENJAMIN,
Acting Secretary of War.

---

*Not found.

NEW ORLEANS, LA., *November* 4, 1861.

Hon. J. P. BENJAMIN:

Will the Secretary of the Treasury allow us to use the Marine Hospital for military purposes? Shall I recognize foreign consuls?

M. LOVELL.

RICHMOND, VA., *November* 4, 1861.

General MANSFIELD LOVELL,
New Orleans, La.:

Foreign consuls are recognized by our Government in all commercial matters. What kind of military use do you propose to make of the Marine Hospital? Answer, and I will apply to the Secretary of the Treasury. I ordered 10 tons of saltpeter sent to you by express from the Augusta Arsenal.

J. P. BENJAMIN,
Acting Secretary of War.

HUNTSVILLE, *November* 4, 1861.

J. P. BENJAMIN,
Secretary of War:

Orders have been received from General Bragg, saying by authority of the Secretary of War. Do these orders supersede the orders to report to General Sidney Johnston? Answer at once.

L. P. WALKER,
Brigadier-General.

RICHMOND, *November* 5, 1861.

General L. P. WALKER,
Huntsville, Ala.:

General Bragg was authorized to call down to the coast any organized regiments that he could arm until we are relieved from the alarm about the naval expedition. It is useless to keep your regiments idle in camp whilst waiting arms. As soon as General Johnston can arm them your brigade will be put on the march for his headquarters. General Bragg had arms enough of the sick on hand to arm two regiments in Mobile and Pensacola, and for this reason was allowed to call them to his aid. I write you in full.

J. P. BENJAMIN,
Acting Secretary of War.

HDQRS. DEPARTMENT ALABAMA AND WEST FLORIDA,
Near Pensacola, November 5, 1861.

ADJUTANT-GENERAL C. S. ARMY,
Richmond, Va.:

SIR: From the delay in hearing from the enemy's fleet, which sailed south on the 29th ultimo, we infer it is intended for some point in the Gulf. With a view of being ready with all our available means, I have ordered General Walker to send one regiment of his command to Mobile and one here to be armed with the weapons of our sick. Colonel Deas' regiment and Colonel Beck's, already armed by private enterprise and by the State of Alabama, I have ordered to report to General Withers, at Mobile.

This will give an efficient force of about 7,000 here and 5,000 at Mobile. From what I learn of the force in Louisiana from private sources I suppose we could calculate on assembling 15,000 men at any point the enemy might assail from this to New Orleans.

If nothing intervenes, we shall pass a train from here to Mobile on the 11th. By giving assistance and working at night this result is accomplished some days sooner than we expected.

I am much in need of some young and active navy officers for my small gunboats. They were promised me verbally last summer, and I have since applied for them. Our landsmen are but poor substitutes.

I am, sir, very respectfully, your obedient servant,

BRAXTON BRAGG,
Major-General, Commanding.

HUNTSVILLE, *November* 7, 1861.

Hon. J. P. BENJAMIN:

I have ordered the troops under my command to Pensacola and Mobile, and shall, unless otherwise directed, proceed to Mobile myself.

L. P. WALKER.

NEW ORLEANS, LA., *November* 8, 1861.

Hon. J. P. BENJAMIN,
Secretary of War, Richmond, Va.:

Mill here now ready. Can make 3,000 pounds of powder per day, but without an ounce of saltpeter. Cannot you send it from Memphis?

THO. O. MOORE.

RICHMOND, VA., *November* 8, 1861.

Gov. THOMAS O. MOORE,
New Orleans, La.:

It is impossible for me to comprehend what has become of the saltpeter sent to New Orleans. I have sent 24 tons, and cannot learn that one pound has been received or one pound of powder made. On September 26, 3 tons were sent by freight; on September 27, 1 ton was sent by express; on October 1, 3 tons were sent by express; on October 2, 7 tons were sent by express; on November 2, 10 tons were sent by express. All this was sent from Augusta, and I cannot get the acknowledgment that one pound was ever received, and you now say you have not one ounce. This mystery must be explained before I can send any more.

J. P. BENJAMIN,
Acting Secretary of War.

HEADQUARTERS DEPARTMENT NO. 1, C. S. A.,
New Orleans, La., November 8, 1861.

Hon. J. P. BENJAMIN,
Secretary of War:

DEAR SIR: Governor Moore has just handed me your dispatch of to-day relative to saltpeter. The amount named therein (24 tons) will all have been received when the 10 tons now on their way from Augusta shall arrive. The acting ordnance officer, Captain Rawle, informs me that he has not yet acknowledged the receipt of the 14 tons already received, because he has had no invoices with the greater part of it, and does not know from whom it came. The only invoice we have from Augusta is that for 10 tons now on the way. Every pound we have on hand is being made up into powder, but a good deal of it is so mixed with foreign matter that it does not give more than pound for pound of powder; but when all made up it will only make about 50,000 pounds, which when distributed will give us about 20 rounds per gun, as fully explained in my letter to you of the 25th ultimo.

We have a battery of light artillery here, raised by order of General Twiggs, composed of Confederate recruits under Captain Higgins, with a complement of four horses to each gun and caisson. He applies to me for a farrier, which I consider necessary and a judicious economy, but find no legal authority for employing one. I am satisfied that a good farrier would more than pay for himself, especially here, where the price of horses is so high. Will you authorize his employment?

I have been requested to ask your attention to the case of Dr. S. Burke, now on duty at Fort Jackson. He was the surgeon on duty with the Louisiana Regiment of Artillery when it was mustered into the Confederate service on 1st June, but by some oversight on the part of the mustering officer he was not transferred. He nevertheless remained at his post on severe duty from that time up to 21st September, when he received his commission. This he hesitates to accept, as he thereby loses nearly four months' rank and pay and one of his juniors takes precedence of him. He asks that his appointment may date 1st June, the day of transfer of the regiment with which he has been serving since its entry into service. His zeal and attention to duty are highly spoken of by his commander, Colonel Duncan, who intercedes for him in this act of justice.

I have the honor to acknowledge the receipt of your printed circular of instructions, as also of your letter of 29th ultimo. I have to thank you for the expression of confidence therein contained, and shall do my utmost to prove that the administration has made no mistake in my case. We are progressing rapidly towards a good state of defense. The interior line of works will soon be complete and the guns mounted. I have increased the armament of Forts Pike and Macomb by four 42s each, and have sent twelve to Colonel Duncan for the forts below. I think we shall make a complete obstruction of the raft (see the sketch I sent the President), and if we stop the enemy's ships we can hammer them to pieces, if the powder holds out.

I have sent 1,000 men to Berwick Bay, and have called for four companies of mounted men (local-defense men) from Saint Mary's Parish, mainly to show themselves occasionally among the negroes.

Respectfully, your obedient servant,

M. LOVELL,
Major-General, Commanding.

O'BANNONVILLE, *November* 11, 1861.

General COOPER:

Railroad to Mobile completed this morning. It is equal to 3,000 men at each end.

BRAXTON BRAGG.

WAR DEPARTMENT, C. S. A.,
Richmond, November 17, 1861.

Maj. Gen. MANSFIELD LOVELL,
New Orleans:

DEAR SIR: I have your letter of the 8th instant, and am happy to learn that the saltpeter has been received in New Orleans. I beg your special attention to the manufacture, as from imperfect refining of the saltpeter much of the powder made at different points absorbs moisture so rapidly as quickly to become worthless. Our supply of powder and of material for its manufacture is so small, that it would be really a calamity to exhaust our material and find the powder valueless.

I received your former letter in regard to the quantity of powder required in your department, and am anxiously awaiting the promised report of the ordnance stores on hand, for there was, of course, quite a quantity of powder on hand before the saltpeter was sent. I beg you will have made for me as early as possible a complete official return of all "ordnance and ordnance stores" in your department, as it is impossible for me to introduce regularity into the administration of this Department without such returns. I always feel a suspicion when they are not furnished that makes me reluctant to respond to requisitions.

I have also learned to regard with great distrust the statements of manufacturers of what they are going to make. A statement of the actual results of one week's work in the powder-mills in New Orleans would be far more satisfactory than any number of assurances of prospective efficiency. I see no objection to your employing a farrier, if necessary, for your company of light artillery. The law, however, does not permit the enlisting of such an artificer to any other than cavalry companies. In regard to Dr. Burke's case, I beg you to inform him that many such cases exist, but I cannot remedy them until I get authority from Congress, which I am now about to ask and hope to obtain. As some additions have been made to my printed circular I send you another copy as amended. I am much gratified to hear of your rapid progress in perfecting the defenses of New Orleans, and especially from different friends of your success in inspiring confidence amongst our people.

Your obedient servant,

J. P. BENJAMIN,
Acting Secretary of War.

HEADQUARTERS ARMY OF PENSACOLA,
Near Pensacola, Fla., November 17, 1861.

ADJUTANT-GENERAL C. S. ARMY,
Richmond:

SIR: In a letter from the Secretary of War I am informed that the three regiments of Mississippi volunteers to be ordered here are not organized, and I am desired to make recommendations for field officers. The inclosed rosters of field officers will show you there is some grave misunderstanding about the two regiments which have arrived.* They claim, too, that their service dates from August 24 last, when called out by the State, leaving them only nine months to serve.

In regard to the companies to compose the other regiment for the war I sent you a telegram from Major Hessee, reporting their refusal to come. Yesterday I was called on by Colonel Dowd, claiming to be colonel of

* Not found.

the regiment referred to. He informs me there are nineteen companies in all—ten organized as a regiment under him and nine other independent companies; that they construed the order variously, but that his companies would refuse to come except as an organized regiment. The other nine, however, would move under the order and soon be here.

With these facts before you, it is for the Department to solve the question. Col. T. H. Watts' Alabama regiment for the war arrived yesterday; aggregate about 900.

I am, sir, very respectfully, your obedient servant,

BRAXTON BRAGG,
Major-General, Commanding.

[Indorsement.]

NOVEMBER 23, 1861.

Respectfully submitted to the Secretary of War. Colonel Dowd's regiment has since been ordered to Savannah, to report to General Lee. I have no recollection of the telegram of Major Hessee.

S. COOPER,
Adjutant and Inspector General.

HEADQUARTERS ARMY OF PENSACOLA,
Near Pensacola, Fla., November 19, 1861.

ADJUTANT-GENERAL C. S. ARMY,
Richmond, Va.:

SIR: The process of reorganizing the twelve-months' men in this army for the war, under a suggestion from the President, had been commenced, and a few companies were in progress. The plan was to allow the men of the same regiment to form companies and elect their officers, when they would be mustered in for the war and discharged on their old engagements. These companies to be attached to their old regiments until a sufficient number were obtained for a regiment, when the companies would be aggregated, and the field officers appointed by the President.

A letter from the Secretary of War, of the 9th of November, in reply to my request for the discharge of Captain Posey's company, First Alabama Regiment, lays down a principle, necessary in that case to make it conform to law, which I fear is incompatible with the course proposed by me, and I must therefore suspend my action until further advised. If the men must be first discharged and then re-enlisted, but few will be secured. Most of them having the option will insist on going home, and nothing but the presence of an enemy in sight will prevent it; and if their re-enlistment is postponed until near the time of their discharge the same desire to get home, with an immediate prospect of gratifying it, will have the same result. The arrival of a goodly number of unarmed men, ready to receive all guns as soon as turned in, will stimulate re-enlistments; and one company of the instructed and disciplined soldiers of the oldest force here will be worth any two just formed.

I am, sir, very respectfully and truly, your obedient servant,

BRAXTON BRAGG,
Major-General, Commanding.

HEADQUARTERS DEPARTMENT NO. 1, C. S. A.,
New Orleans, La., November 19, 1861.

Hon. J. P. BENJAMIN,
Secretary of War:

DEAR SIR: Since my last communication we have steadily progressed in our preparations for defense. Six tons of powder have been made, and distributed to the various works in due proportion. I have increased the armament of Fort Pike by four 42-pounders, Fort Macomb with four 42s and one 8-inch shell gun, Fort Livingston with one 8-inch columbiad, and Forts Jackson and Saint Philip with six 42-pounders each. The raft in the river between the last-named forts has been further secured by four anchors of 3,000 pounds each and fastened by heavy chains to either shore, and I think will stop a fleet under the close fire of more than 100 heavy guns (with Commodore Hollins' assistance about 150). Feeling satisfied that ships under steam can pass forts in an open channel, I am taking prompt measures to obstruct the passage at Forts Pike and Macomb, at Berwick Bay, and in the Mississippi above the city at a point where I shall concentrate the fire of 50 guns of heavy caliber.

I have ordered the Marine Hospital to be fitted up for army use by the quartermaster. On inquiry I found that we could not rent a hospital for less than $3,000 per annum, and it would cost half as much more to fit it up. Besides this, we hire three or four buildings for ordnance stores. The sum of these rents laid out on the hospital will enable it to answer all purposes, and the improvements will belong to the Government. Nothing will be lost in rent.

We shall have in operation in a few days three powder mills, two of which are private property and one belongs to the city. They will turn out more than 3 tons per day. The powder is proved, and rejected if much under range. We will want all the saltpeter that can be had, as we will be able to work up about 3 tons a day. Permit me to call your attention to the necessity of a telegraph line between Meridian and Mobile; also between Meridian and Montgomery. The line hence to Mobile runs along the coast, and can be cut at any time by a force from the enemy's fleet, to say nothing of the largely disaffected population on the southern coast of Mississippi. I inclose you a letter received from Mr. Douglass on this subject.* It requires immediate attention.

General Pillow telegraphed me to send him 5,000 men to Columbus. This I declined, as I have no more than are necessary for the defense of New Orleans and its approaches. If the river had been obstructed above, so as to prevent a fleet from passing down, I might have felt justified in giving him some assistance, but I should have attached more weight to the call if it had come from General Johnston.

I regret that I cannot have some columbiads and mortars in addition to my present armament. Some of the detached companies, transferred from the State service under General Twiggs' orders, have become much reduced and disorganized by bad management and poor officers, and I should wish to have power to disband some and consolidate others, so as to make the force more effective; also authority, under your sanction, to discharge men in certain cases of hardship, family affliction, or where they are required for important work—as, for instance, some cases of widows' only sons, or where parents have died since entry into service, or where they are required in founderies or workshops where Government work is being done. I should exercise such authority very sparingly, and only in cases where I feel satisfied you would approve.

* Not found.

Colonel Preston, who was to join my staff, has gone to South Carolina. Am I not entitled to two officers in the adjutant and inspector general's department—one lieutenant colonel and one major?

I have received the appointments of Majors Palfrey and Lanier. General Ruggles has been sick since his arrival here, which has devolved all the inspection of troops upon me from Berwick to Mississippi City. I was in hopes that the President would act on my request in relation to Colonel Duncan. Matters, however, by dint of incessant attention, are progressing favorably, and I hope soon to be able to report myself as beyond the chances of an attack.

Has your attention been called to the fact that the enemy can land near East Pascagoula and march 24 miles over a good road into Mobile? I understand that there are no intrenched lines on the land side around that city, but can hardly think it possible that it has not been done. If so, it is an easy road from Ship Island to Mobile.

Respectfully, your obedient servant,

M. LOVELL,
Major-General, C. S. Army.

CIRCULAR.] HEADQUARTERS ARMY OF PENSACOLA,
Near Pensacola, Fla., November 21, 1861.

With a view of preserving to our cause the invaluable services of those soldiers he has so long commanded with pride, the general is desirous of reorganizing his old regiments for the war. The advantages to be obtained by the officers and men themselves are so apparent as to give the strongest hope of a large success. But few of us, if any, can contemplate retiring from the field to the inglorious occupation of idly witnessing the labors of our mothers, wives, and daughters, nobly working for their defenders in the field.

To receive a discharge and go home temporarily, with a view of again enlisting in some other command, will subject the soldier to many annoyances he has probably not contemplated. He will never again be as well satisfied, mixed up, as he will be, with strangers and raw men, where he will have to go through all the drudgery of elementary instruction, so essential to them, but irksome to him. All his former acquaintances and *esprit de corps* will be lost, and he will be looked on as a raw recruit instead of a veteran of one campaign. Above all, he will lose his arms, for the army is now full of men eager to see him depart, that they may secure his gun, with which to win a name. To return with an old shot-gun, or perhaps with no gun at all, and wait a chance opportunity to secure what has been thrown away, will be the fate of those who thus depart. Those who remain may confidently rely on soon being employed actively—if not here, at some other point to which they can now be sent, their places being supplied by the new troops; and as far as he can do so, consistently with his sense of duty, the general will allow to those who re-enlist and require it an opportunity to visit home and arrange their business affairs. This indulgence will be granted to re-enlisted men in preference to all others.

1. Companies of not less than 64 privates (a larger number would be preferred), with their proper officers, non-commissioned officers, and musicians, will be received and mustered for the war, retaining their present arms and equipments, when they will be discharged from their old engagements and paid off to that date.

2. Such companies will be attached to their old regiments until a sufficient number is obtained to constitute a new regiment, when they

will be aggregated, and field officers will be appointed by the President. In making these appointments he will no doubt be influenced by a known desire of a large majority of a regiment, ascertained through the proper military channel; but no elections will be held and no electioneering will be tolerated. Merit, not popularity, will control the selections.

Such of his veterans as are willing to join him for the war the general will be proud to receive, as evincing a confidence he has labored to deserve. It may not be his good fortune to lead them against the enemy, but on any field and against any foe he will answer for their conduct, and predict for them a brilliant victory or a glorious death.

By command of Major General Bragg:

GEO. G. GARNER,
Assistant Adjutant-General.

O'BANNONVILLE, *November* 23, 1861.

General S. COOPER:

General Withers should have the assistance of two regular officers of rank and experience. Dissipation and a want of experience and organization will cause me to tremble for the result if he is vigorously attacked now.

BRAXTON BRAGG.

HDQRS. DEPARTMENT ALABAMA AND WEST FLORIDA,
November 28, 1861.

ADJUTANT-GENERAL C. S. ARMY,
Richmond, Va.:

SIR: The arrival of an unorganized regiment of Mississippians yesterday gives us at this place now four new regiments, 3,000 men at least, with only about 600 efficient arms between them. About the same state of affairs exists at Mobile. These men will at once be put to a rigid course of instruction, and, with the example and influence of our well-instructed, well-disciplined veterans, will soon be made into good soldiers. When arms can be had for them I shall be able to spare a considerable portion of my gallant little army for more active, and therefore more gratifying, service elsewhere.

I am, sir, very respectfully, your obedient servant,

BRAXTON BRAGG,
Major-General, Commanding.

HEADQUARTERS ARMY OF PENSACOLA,
Near Pensacola, Fla., November 29, 1861.

ADJUTANT-GENERAL C. S. ARMY,
Richmond, Va.:

SIR: To transmit some letters to our prisoners of war and send over the free negro in my possession to his friends I yesterday sent a flag to Fort Pickens, with a communication to Colonel Brown, a copy of which I inclose.* He refused to receive my communication or to reply, and only consented to take the negro after one of his officers specially waited on him to represent the urgency of the case. Fort Pickens is not seriously injured, of course, as my fire was not directed at the fort, which is ours, but at those inside of it. The armament and garrison seem to

*Not found.

have suffered, and the commander is by no means as courteous and amiable as he was after the infliction on his outside *confrere*, Colonel Wilson. My lookouts report that escorts to their grave-yard, which is immediately under our glasses, are very frequent, and that two officers certainly have been buried. Yesterday a small boat attempted to enter the harbor from the fleet—a privilege heretofore accorded them, as our steamers were allowed to run freely to the yard. We fired on it, when the crew precipitately abandoned it and swam ashore, leaving the boat to float off. Some of our shots went very near the fort, but they declined the invitation. We infer they are satisfied. One of their ships (the Hartford) was towed off yesterday by a gunboat, thus proving her disability. Some operation is going on by them far up Santa Rosa Island, but what we cannot exactly conjecture. An expedition leaves to-day to ascertain.

Captain Thom's company of Marines, 100 men, leaves to-day for Virginia, by request of the Secretary of the Navy. This is the third draft made on me, and while it gives me great pleasure to discipline and instruct his men, the Secretary must excuse me for declining any longer to furnish him arms, &c. It is a depleting process I cannot stand.

As early as last spring and frequently since I have asked for some young navy officers, but without success. I have two steam gunboats commanded by landsmen. A rifled ship gun promised for one of them some weeks ago is not yet heard from. These points are of importance.

I am, sir, very respectfully, your obedient servant,

BRAXTON BRAGG,
Major-General, Commanding.

SPECIAL ORDERS, No. 14. } HDQRS. DEPT. OF ALA. AND WEST FLA., *Near Pensacola, Fla., December* 1, 1861.

Brig. Gen. L. P. Walker, having reported in person at these headquarters for duty, is assigned to the District of Alabama, and will report to Brigadier-General Withers, at Mobile.

By command of Major-General Bragg:

GEO. G. GARNER,
Assistant Adjutant-General.

Abstract from field return of the District of Alabama, commanded by Brig. Gen. Jones M. Withers, December 2, 1861.

Troops.	Present for duty. Officers.	Present for duty. Men.	Aggregate present.	Aggregate present and absent.
1st Alabama Battalion	15	202	367	406
18th Alabama	36	594	858	942
19th Alabama	35	625	940	992
20th Alabama	34	474	836	916
22d Alabama	37	376	709	783
Beck's Alabama regiment	30	333	674	728
Company infantry Alabama volunteers	4	62	66	66
Battalion infantry Mississippi volunteers (3 companies)	11	196	238	267
Companies (5) mounted Alabama volunteers	14	371	410	461
Battalion Light Artillery (5 companies)	23	407	471	506
Fort Gaines	61	991	1,144	1,263
Fort Morgan	82	1,223	1,596	1,691
Total	382	5,854	8,309	9,021

NEW ORLEANS, LA., *December* 2, 1861.

Hon. J. P. BENJAMIN,
Acting Secretary of War:

MY DEAR SIR: I desire to introduce to you Capt. John A. Stephenson. Captain S. is a commission merchant of New Orleans of high standing. He constructed and built the Manassas. He is a man of large river experience, having for many years had command of steamboats on the Mississippi. Great confidence is felt by our community in his skill, energy, and ability, so much so, that they are ready to advance the means to build, under his superintendence, another ram. This, however, they will not do without some assurance that the Government will not take the boat out of the possession and control of Captain S. The fact is that, while great confidence is felt here in Commodore Hollins as a naval officer, our people are convinced that he is led astray in his judgment of individuals, as he has no just means of forming a correct estimate of their character and ability. It is no disparagement to his ability as an officer to say this much of him, and it is said in the best and friendliest spirit. We all hope you will aid in carrying out the wishes of our people, and do all in your power to further the object in view. Captain Stephenson will communicate freely with you. You can rely upon him.

Very truly, yours,

THO. O. MOORE.

WAR DEPARTMENT, C. S. A.,
Richmond, December 2, 1861.

Maj. Gen. BRAXTON BRAGG,
Pensacola:

SIR: I am sorry to say that I was in error in supposing certain Mississippi regiments ordered to your command to be without organization. I supposed the companies to have been tendered to us independent companies under a call made by this Department, but it turns out that they were called into service by General A. S. Johnston, under an unlucky proclamation which he issued for twelve months' men before he was fully aware of the policy of the Government on the subject.

I have, however, ordered to you one regiment of independent companies, which you will be able to organize and to provide with field officers, when the President will take pleasure in nominating on your recommendation.

I see no objection to your getting the men of the different twelve-months' regiments in your command to re-enlist for the war, as suggested in your letter of the 19th ultimo.

In the precise case referred to in my letter of November 9 I did not see how it could be done without violating the rights of some of the parties, but in the way you propose no one is injured. We have a right to discharge any one whose services are no longer needed. The only modification I suggest is that when you muster in the new companies "for the war," as they are formed, you make the muster to take effect at some future day, on which day you will discharge the men from their former contract.

I do not see why a man may not be mustered in to-day for service "for the war," his term of service to commence on the 1st January next. He would then remain in his present organization until the 1st January, and on that day be discharged from his old obligation and become bound by the new one. If you think this plan objectionable, pray point out the difficulty, as I am most anxious to effect the object, and I am sure Congress (now in session) would grant any legislation necessary for the purpose.

A law will, I doubt not, be passed in a day or two, offering a bounty for re-enlistment that will afford you great help in getting your volunteers to remain in service.

Let me congratulate you and your gallant command on the successful repulse of the recent attack. I await your official report for submission to Congress, and in hopes of hearing that their vessels were effectually crippled.

Your obedient servant,

J. P. BENJAMIN.

P. S.—I never thought of asking whether General Withers had taken any measures to defend Mobile against a *coup de main* via Pascagoula. A few thousand men landed there could make a rapid night march and surprise the city, if I remember the distance aright. According to my recollection it is not more than 18 or 20 miles.

HEADQUARTERS DEPARTMENT NO. 1, C. S. A.,
New Orleans, La., December 5, 1861.

Hon. J. P. BENJAMIN,
Secretary of War:

SIR: I avail myself of Colonel Davis' trip to Richmond to send you a map and description, which will give you some definite idea of the existing condition of affairs in this department.

Commencing at Calcasieu Bay, we have one company with two 24-pounders, which are now being put up and will prevent foraging parties from reaching the cattle-grazing prairies around the head of that lake.

At Grand Chenier there is a company of militia that I am furnishing with one 6-pounder gun. In Saint Mary's Parish there are two companies of infantry and one battery (at Franklin). I have also mustered one company of cavalry for local defense. These troops are also intended for moral effect in that densely slave-populated section.

Passing east to Atchafalaya Bay, I have placed there a regiment of 1,000 men (less two companies at Franklin), having one company each at Forts Berwick and Chène, at each of which forts are mounted one 32-pounder rifled gun and four 24-pounders. I have thus strengthened this point because the railroad which supplies us with Texas cattle here approaches very near to the coast and is accessible with 8 feet of water. I have also ordered the main channel of the Atchafalaya to be filled by sinking live-oak trees, leaving open an intricate channel 80 feet wide for the entrance of vessels running the blockade. Flats loaded with live-oak will be kept in readiness to sink in this channel at a moment's warning. Rafts are also being prepared to obstruct the bayou under the guns of Forts Berwick and Chène. We can support this point in four hours, by the Opelousas road, by troops from the city.

There is no navigable bayou until we reach Grand Caillou, on which I have a work with two 32-pounders and two full companies. The other bayous are unnavigable except La Fourche, on which I have also located a work with two 32s and two companies of men. These works extend from swamp to swamp on either side of the bayous.

At Fort Livingston are four companies (about 300 men), with one rifled 32, one 8-inch columbiad, seven 24s, and two flank howitzers (24s), with four 12-pounders on the land side. Should this work be passed, all the inlets converge at the Little Temple, where a work is just finished, where I shall put two 32s and 100 men.

On the Mississippi, Forts Jackson and Saint Philip are in good order and garrisoned by ten companies—nearly 1,000 men. They are armed as follows:

Fort Jackson: six 42-pounders, twenty-six 24-pounders, two 32-pounder rifles, sixteen 32-pounders, three 8-inch columbiads, one 10-inch columbiad, one 10-inch and two 8-inch mortars, with two 48-pounder and ten 24-pounder howitzers.

Fort Saint Philip: six 42-pounders, nine 32-pounders, twenty-two 24-pounders, four 8-inch columbiads, one 8-inch and one 10 inch mortar, and three field guns.

Between the forts the river is completely obstructed by a raft of logs securely chained to both banks and held by fifteen large anchors weighing from 2,500 to 4,000 pounds each, and laid in 25 fathoms of water with 60 fathoms of strong chain. This raft is a complete obstruction, and has an enfilading fire from Fort Jackson and a direct fire from Saint Philip.

On the Lake Borgne side we have, first, a work 1 mile back from Proctorsville, with six guns (two 32s and four 24s), with 100 men. They can be re-enforced from the city by the Mexican Gulf Railroad. I have contracted for a telegraph line from here to the work, to be paid for by the city.

At Tower Dupré there is one large company, with five 24-pounders. The adjoining bayou has been obstructed by piles. At Battery Bienvenue I have 100 men, with ten 24-pounders.

Fort Macomb is garrisoned by three companies (250 men), and armed with four 42s, one 8-inch columbiad, twenty-one 24-pounders, and four flank howitzers (24s). The live-oak grove, which grew within 300 yards of the fort and offered a secure approach for the enemy, I have had felled at a cost of $1,000, of which the State paid half and the city half.

Fort Pike has a garrison of 350 men, and the following armament: Four 42s, one 9-inch and one 8-inch gun, two 32-pounder rifled guns, twenty 24-pounders, and five 24-pounder flank howitzers. I have had logs cut and chains and anchors bought, to obstruct the channel both at Forts Macomb and Pike. I have also contracted to shoal the mouths of West and East Pearl Rivers to 4 feet by sinking obstructions. I keep a regiment and a field battery in advance, at Bay Saint Louis and Pass Christian, and have made a depot of 15,000 rations at Gainesville, in case they are driven back suddenly from the coast by a large force of the enemy.

The foregoing comprises the exterior line, with which I am in communication by telegraph to Berwick Bay, Fort Jackson, Fort Macomb, and Fort Pike. Instructors have been sent to the various forts requiring it, and the garrisons are all quite proficient in the drill of the sea-coast gun.

The interior line, as you will observe on the map, composes, with the intervening swamps, a complete continuous line around the city, including Algiers within its limits. It is almost entirely finished. Ten 32s are mounted on the line below the barracks, at its junction with the river, and ten 42s will soon be up on the opposite side, giving a cross-fire of twenty guns at that point. The lines extend to the swamp on each side, and have flanking arrangements for 32-pounder carronades to sweep the whole point. Their development is 8½ feet, with a wide ditch, which is filled with water. On the Gentilly Ridge the same kind of work, with four guns; on the Pontchartrain Railroad five guns, the canal four guns, the Bayou Saint John four, and the Jefferson Railroad two guns—all with flanking arrangements for infantry. The guns of these small works will all be mounted within ten days.

Above the city the line extends from the swamp to the river, with flanking arrangements for artillery, and terminates at the river with a powerful battery of fourteen 42-pounders. At this point Major Lovell is building an obstruction under the fire of this battery, which, I think, will prevent any vessel from passing down the river. On the Algiers side the line is just behind the Barataria Canal, and runs from the river to the swamp. It is all complete except the battery on the river, where it is intended to mount ten 32-pounders. The whole should be finished and mounted in two weeks, when New Orleans will be a citadel.

The exterior line is manned by about 4,500 men, and I have about 3,500 for the interior line, besides about 6,000 well-armed volunteers in the city, who are uniformed and drilled. With 15,000 men I can defend the city against any force that can be brought, unless we are attacked on all sides at once. I have also had two sham parapets made in the city and some guns mounted, as schools of practice for the volunteers. In enumerating the troops I do not reckon two regiments (1,600 men) that I sent up to Columbus last week to General Polk's aid.

The two powder-mills are in running order, one at the barracks and one at the old Marine Hospital. Major Rains came down last week, and after a full inspection reports that they can easily turn out 2 tons of powder per day, and I am making a contract with responsible parties here for 200 tons of saltpeter. Sulphur and charcoal we have in abundance. The new marine hospital is being fitted up at a small cost, one-half for a hospital and the other for a laboratory and store-rooms for munitions of war, implements, arms, &c.

With a sufficiency of powder I should consider myself in a position to hold New Orleans for an indefinite length of time. The only point, then, for consideration would be provisions. I am endeavoring silently, through other parties, to induce holders to lay in not less than 60,000 barrels of flour, of which the city consumes about 800 *per diem*. This, with beef cattle from Texas and from Mississippi via Mandeville, would enable us to stand a siege of two or three months, if it should be necessary.

I have thus endeavored to give you a rough sketch of the progress that has been made in the work assigned me by the administration. There are a thousand minor matters which have taken up a great deal of time and given much trouble, but the heaviest part of the work is done. The amount of labor involved has been more than I anticipated, as matters were in a much worse condition than I could have supposed possible; but I have no hesitation in saying that I regard New Orleans at present as strong enough to withstand any attack that is likely to be made.

Respectfully, your obedient servant,

M. LOVELL,

Major-General, Commanding Department No. 1.

HEADQUARTERS ARMY OF PENSACOLA,
Near Pensacola, Fla., December 10, 1861.

Hon. J. P. BENJAMIN,
Secretary of War, Richmond, Va.:

SIR: The transfer of Colonel Wood's regiment, Seventh Alabama, to East Tennessee leaves me little over 6,000 arms here. With this number and my present means of rapid re-enforcement from Mobile I have no apprehension, but it leaves me a large number of men, near 3,000, without arms, and renders it impossible for me to comply with the wish expressed in yours of the 4th November for a transfer of some of my oldest and best troops to more active service. Could I give an assurance of such a move to these men I am satisfied it would have a happy effect in causing many to re-enlist "for the war." Without such assurance and a short furlough to visit their homes but few can be secured. It would be a great misfortune to lose them, for they are the best troops I have ever known, all inferior men having been culled out. The artillery will be an especial loss, for it takes time and much labor to teach the duties of that arm. As most of my artillery officers of the regular service have been transferred to other and higher duties, I shall have to ask of the Department to allow me in some way to retain some of the best of those in the volunteers here, when their men are discharged, to act as instructors. The time of some of the companies of one of my best regiments (the First Alabama) expires in January, six weeks from now, as they claim from the time they entered the State service, and not their transfer to the Confederacy in March.

I am, sir, very respectfully, your obedient servant,

BRAXTON BRAGG,
Major-General, Commanding.

HEADQUARTERS DEPARTMENT NO. 1,
New Orleans, La., December 10, 1861.

General S. COOPER,
Adjutant and Inspector General C. S. Army:

SIR: When I assumed command in this department I found that a number of independent companies, originally mustered into the State service, had been transferred to the Confederate service at the request of General Twiggs.

Some of these companies had very poor officers, and in some cases the ranks were filled in part with men wholly unfit for military service; and the sifting out of these companies has in some instances reduced them below the number required.

What I desire to know is, whether, in companies thus reduced, and when the officers are manifestly incompetent, I cannot have the authority to break them up or to transfer the good men and let the officers be turned over again to the State authorities. I could thus add much to the efficiency of the service, while materially diminishing the expense in getting rid of inefficient and supernumerary officers.

Respectfully, your obedient servant,

M. LOVELL,
Major-General, Commanding Department.

HEADQUARTERS DEPARTMENT NO. 1,
New Orleans, La., December 10, 1861.

General S. COOPER,
Adjutant and Inspector General:

SIR: After great delay and many blunders I have succeeded in getting up a return* of the troops in my department for the month of October. It is not as accurate as it should be, but will give you an approximate idea of the force here. I have sent the Thirteenth Louisiana and Third Mississippi Regiments to Columbus at the earnest instance of the generals in command there, but have called upon Governor Moore for two regiments to replace them, which I have ordered to be mustered. I do not know whether this exceeds my authority or not; if it does, please give me the necessary orders, as I want all the men I can arm. The November returns shall not be delayed so long.

Respectfully, your obedient servant,

M. LOVELL,
Major-General, Commanding Department.

HEADQUARTERS ARMY OF PENSACOLA,
Near Pensacola, Fla., December 11, 1861.

Hon. J. P. BENJAMIN,
Secretary of War:

SIR: Yours of the 2d only reached me yesterday. It will relieve some embarrassment with the two Mississippi regiments which had elected field officers. Upon a critical examination of all the new regiments recently received, they were found to contain many men utterly unfit for service. All such have been promptly discharged. It does not weaken our strength, and materially lightens our expenses, especially in the medical department.

The regiment of independent companies was on the eve of organization when your order for one company (Captain Coopwood's) to join Colonel Dowd's regiment at Savannah checked it. Some imposition has been practiced in this case. I shall apply to the governor of Mississippi to send me another company to fill the regiment. It is suffering much for want of organization.

Great difficulties are being encountered in reorganizing our old men for the war. I inclose a circular issued to them some three weeks since. It produced some effect for a while, but no result so far. Our fight, I fear, has injured the prospect. Men wish to go home and talk over their deeds with friends and families. I shall now try by liberal offer of furloughs. As they are to go anyhow, it will be as well to let them go on furlough, and they will not be able to stay. The women will not tolerate it. Many return who have gone off sick, and say it is impossible to stay at home. It is a mere indefinite fancy to get away, and be clear of the restraints of military control for a while. They will soon repent and rejoin the service, but the loss of organization and expense of getting them back will be great. Though my discipline has been rigid, I think I can safely say it has not driven a desirable man from the service, and most of them are now better men and better soldiers, and more attached to me, than if they had been allowed liberty and license.

*Not found.

A letter from Colonel Chalmers, Ninth Mississippi Regiment (a very good officer), who was requested by me to try and reorganize his admirable regiment, may throw some light on the points of difficulty. If we had arms for my new men the promise they desire could be made, but in the absence of Colonel Wood's regiment we have only about 6,000 stand of guns. My reply to the colonel tries to combat the idea of going north now. Wood's regiment is clamorous to return already. I shall not despair of success nor cease to strive, but the prospect is not very encouraging. Your plan of fixing a future date for discharge and commencement of new service will be tried.

The danger to Mobile which you suggest is provided for. Mounted men are stationed at the points where the enemy might land, with instructions to report any hostile demonstration, and all our infantry out of the forts and light artillery are in readiness for concentration on any point, and the telegraph could secure re-enforcements from here in ten hours. A thorough inspection by my staff officers is now going on in all the departments of General Withers' command, and I shall soon pay him another visit myself. I inclose a copy of a letter just received from him, upon which I ordered the closing of Grant's Pass effectually and unconditionally. The defenses of the sound have been sadly overlooked. As early as last May I called the attention of our friends in Louisiana to the subject. They replied the Navy Department had it in hand. If I may judge from what they have done here, but little has been accomplished. But this is a matter not within my province, though I can but lament results.

I am, sir, very respectfully, your obedient servant,

BRAXTON BRAGG,
Major-General, Commanding.

[Inclosure.]

HEADQUARTERS DISTRICT OF ALABAMA,
Mobile, December 9, 1861.

Maj. GEORGE G. GARNER,
Assistant Adjutant-General, Pensacola, Fla.:

SIR: The coast guard between this place and New Orleans is not such as the policy and interest of the Confederate Government demands. Several schooners and steamers have been captured of late. The steamer Lewis, from New Orleans to this place, with cargo of sugar and molasses, was captured about ten days since, and a part of her crew have returned here. From the engineer of the boat, a Mr. Haley, who has the reputation of being entirely reliable, I learn that, besides the cargo of the Lewis, Ship Island was covered with barrels of sugar, turpentine, molasses, and resin, and with lumber and cattle. The character of the lumber and cattle was such as to preclude the thought of those articles having been brought out from the North. When taken on board the enemy's vessel, he found the New Orleans papers of the preceding day's date on the table in the cabin. During his detention expeditions were sent out nightly, and which he believes were intended to keep up communication with the shore. A steamer to carry off freight runs regularly between the island and New York. This report is corroborated by all the information I have been able to gather from other sources. To crush out this evil I would suggest the propriety of closing Grant's Pass, as the most effectual way of removing all pretext for a coast trade so advantageous to the enemy. The battery there, removed to Cedar Point and strengthened, would command those waters, and not be subject to the objections to Grant's Pass, as Cedar Point is part of the main-land, with good road leading into the back country.

The idea of our caricature gunboats being a protection to the coast trade is to me simply ridiculous. In truth I should look on our Navy Department as an amusing fancy sketch but for the waste of money and corruption for which it is the excuse.

In that I am tormented by hourly applications from selfish boat-owners for permits through Grant's Pass, you will oblige me by telegraphing me at the earliest moment the decision of the general as to this trade being stopped promptly and finally. The railroad communication and reduced charges prevent the necessity for all undue risks to keep the coast trade open. We cannot, therefore, afford to furnish the enemy the low-water transportation, which they can only get by taking our boats, as well as the produce of our country.

The coast being within General Lovell's department, I have nothing to recommend for its being properly guarded.

Very respectfully, major, your obedient servant,

J. M. WITHERS,
Brigadier-General, &c.

SPECIAL ORDERS, No. 264. } ADJT. AND INSP. GENERAL'S OFFICE, *Richmond, Va., December* 12, 1861.

* * * * * * *

16. The command of Major-General Bragg is extended west, so as to include Pascagoula Bay and that portion of Mississippi east of the Pascagoula River.

* * * * * * *

By command of the Secretary of War:

JNO. WITHERS,
Assistant Adjutant-General.

JACKSON, MISS., *December* 12, 1861.

His Excellency JEFFERSON DAVIS:

Lincoln boats continually harassing our sea-coast. Our people will be driven from their homes and their property destroyed. Third Regiment Mississippi Volunteers have been ordered from the coast to Kentucky; many of them sailors, and much needed. Please order them back to seaport and keep them there.

JOHN J. PETTUS.

RICHMOND, VA., *December* 13, 1861.

Gov. JOHN J. PETTUS,
Jackson, Miss.:

Keep the regiment to which you refer on the sea-coast until further orders. There is a confusion in numbering the regiments, so that I cannot tell which one it is. We will endeavor to organize a force better adapted to sea-coast defense than an infantry regiment, and duly inform you.

JEFFERSON DAVIS.

JACKSON, MISS., *December* 14, 1861.

His Excellency JEFFERSON DAVIS,
President, Richmond:

DEAR SIR: I am earnestly requested by the people of the Mississippi Gulf coast and by Governor Pettus to ask the attention of the President and the Secretary of War to the defense of the coast by a military force on shore sufficient to protect property and repel invasion by the enemy. The governor requests me to ask that three regiments shall be accepted into the Confederate service under the act authorizing troops to be accepted for local defense, to be stationed on the coast; also a battalion which he has now organized and equipped, and which could be sent there immediately. It is also requested by him and by the Hon. R. Seale, Representative from the coast, that the Third Regiment, Colonel Deason's, shall be one so accepted, and that it be ordered back to the coast, from which it was by recent order of General Johnston removed to Columbus, Ky., where it now is. The reason for this is that this regiment is composed mainly or in large part of men familiar with the coast, its bays and bayous, and accustomed to the management of water-craft. This is very important, and the governor authorizes me to say he will supply its place at Columbus with another regiment at the earliest practicable day. The legislature has made an appropriation of $250,000 to build gunboats on the coast, and force will be required to protect the points at which they are to be constructed. The necessity of a military force for our coast protection and defense is imperious, and I earnestly and respectfully urge it upon the President and Secretary of War.

Most respectfully, your obedient servant,

JOHN J. McRAE.

The Seventh Regiment, Colonel Goode's, is now upon the coast at Bay Saint Louis and in the Confederate service, under command of General Lovell. This to be one of three.

HEADQUARTERS DEPARTMENT NO. 1,
New Orleans, La., December 16, 1861.

Hon. J. P. BENJAMIN,
Secretary of War:

SIR: I have the honor to acknowledge the receipt of yours of the 7th instant, inclosing a letter from Dr. Cartwright to the President, relative to the Mexican Gulf Railroad. I am not aware that the Government or the parties who claim to have purchased the road have any intention of using the iron for ship-building purposes, nor do I believe that any such purpose exists. Had any plan of that railroad been laid before me, I should have weighed the respective advantages to the Government of using the iron on the road or on the ships and decided accordingly. I am well satisfied that the whole scheme is to make a grand speculation for private purposes, either by selling the iron in this market or by forcing the road upon the Government at an exorbitant price.

I have a work at Proctorsville, across the railroad, mounting six 32-pounders, and manned by 100 men, distant from the city 27 miles, which covers the valuable plantations along the left bank of the river. To re-enforce this work rapidly I have constructed a switch from the Pontchartrain to the Mexican Gulf road, at a cost of $1,600, and am putting up telegraph lines between the city and Proctorsville, which will enable me to receive early notice, and, by using the rolling stock of the Pontchartrain road, to send down 4,000 men in four hours.

It is this arrangement that I do not wish to be interfered with by what I consider a "rail speculation." The only order I have given in the case is to say that the road shall not be torn up so as to prevent the passage of troops. I have told them they may take up the present rail and put down the T-rail, but they decline. Of one thing I am sure, the Government has no prospective benefit in what the company proposes to do.

To avoid, however, the exercise of military authority, if possible, I sought other means of obtaining the end in view, by ordinary process of law. Learning that the State has mortgages upon the road, I consulted with the attorney-general, who is now taking the necessary steps to prevent, by an injunction, any damage being done to it, so as to preserve it intact for the better security of the claims that the State has upon it. I consider it, therefore, hardly necessary to discuss the propriety of military interference as long as the matter is, or forthwith will be, with the civil authorities, but have merely mentioned the foregoing facts to give you the correct data in the premises.

Respectfully, your obedient servant,

M. LOVELL,
Major-General, Commanding.

HEADQUARTERS ARMY OF PENSACOLA,
Near Pensacola, Fla., December 17, 1861.

ADJUTANT-GENERAL,
Richmond, Va.:

SIR: On the 14th instant the enemy landed about 1,000 men on Santa Rosa Island, and they are now encamped near the fort. No movement of any sort on their part indicates a renewal of the attack. Should their ships again attempt to take position against McRee, they will be received by a masked battery of five heavy shell and three rifled guns, which will teach them a lesson. This battery was projected last spring, but abandoned after an examination of the Coast Survey charts. It seems the depth of water has increased or the chart was wrong.

I am, sir, very respectfully, your obedient servant,

BRAXTON BRAGG,
Major-General, Commanding.

NAVY DEPARTMENT, C. S. A.,
Richmond, Va., December 17, 1861.

Hon. J. P. BENJAMIN,
Secretary of War:

SIR: This Department is unable to obtain any powder for the naval service at New Orleans, and Flag-Officer Hollins reports that he is without a grain. The daily produce of the mills at New Orleans, I am informed, may be sufficient for its naval as well as for its military defenses; and I have the honor to request, if you can possibly do so, that you will be pleased to instruct General Lovell to supply Flag-Officer Hollins with cannon powder upon his requisitions as it may be required for the public service.

I am, respectfully, your obedient servant,

S. R. MALLORY,
Secretary of the Navy.

WAR DEPARTMENT,
Richmond, Va., December 18, 1861.

Maj. Gen. MANSFIELD LOVELL,
Commanding Department, &c., New Orleans, La.:

SIR: In compliance with a request addressed to this Department by the Hon. Secretary of the Navy, you are instructed to do all in your power, consistent with the exigencies of the military service in your department, towards supplying Flag-Officer Hollins, C. S. Navy, with cannon powder, upon his requisition therefor.

I am, respectfully, your obedient servant,

J. P. BENJAMIN,
Secretary of War.

HEADQUARTERS DEPARTMENT NO. 1,
New Orleans, La., December 19, 1861.

Governor MOORE:

DEAR SIR: I return Colonel Fontaine's letter. I do not disapprove of fortifying Vicksburg. I said in my previous letter we had no officer of Engineers and no guns to spare, and I thought it too late to commence a self-protecting work. If they wish to build it, however, let them do so, although I must adhere to my previous opinion, that it is better to concentrate the forts and obstructions at the points where the batteries already exist. If this cannot be done, I would grant permission to go to work on the Louisiana side, but I can give them no competent officer, no guns, and no powder.

Yours, very truly,

M. LOVELL,
Major-General, Commanding.

[Inclosure.]

HEADQUARTERS ARMY OF THE MISSISSIPPI,
Ordnance Office, Jackson, Miss., December 18, 1861.

His Excellency THOMAS O. MOORE,
Governor of Louisiana:

DEAR SIR: I hope you will pardon me for again calling your attention to the subject of the defense of New Orleans. I have entire confidence in your wisdom and patriotism and the ability of the officers to whom you have intrusted the safety of our great metropolis; but persons at a distance from an object can see its position, with all its bearings, more distinctly than those who are in close contact with it. The plans of the enemy are now clearly developed. They intend to attempt the descent of the Mississippi without attacking Columbus or Fulton at all. Their object will be to reach Memphis and Nashville by movements up the Tennessee and Cumberland Rivers and from Bowling Green, so as to compel General Polk to fall back upon Memphis and General Johnston upon Nashville. I believe they will be whipped if they attempt it, but they may not, and we should not let our hopes lull us into supineness and a neglect of our security. As soon as their army moves upon Bowling Green and their flotilla commences the ascent of the Tennessee from Paducah, you may expect their gunboats to enter Lake Pontchartrain and attempt the capture of Manchac and the occupancy of all the positions on Lake Maurepas and above your city accessible to a land force put ashore from their transports. Unless every pass is fortified on both sides and obstructed the attempt may succeed, for no batteries can stop the passage of steamers, unless their headway can be checked while they are held under fire. I shall go to Vicksburg to-morrow, to lay out our fortifications and to make an estimate of the number of negroes it will take to finish them. I feel confident that a large force will descend the Mississippi, if one is moved up the Tennessee River, as soon as the latter succeeds in reaching a proper point for debarking for Memphis. I will fortify Vicksburg and prevent its capture, but I cannot prevent the enemy from burning it and passing it. I can keep them from entering the corporation, but they can shell it from the river and from the Louisiana side. A fort constructed at the bend above would guard the railroad approach to Vicksburg and the interior of your State, and prevent them from cutting a canal and turning the river through the narrow neck between the bends, which a small army could do in a single day. I believe that their designs will be thwarted by a kind Providence. God seems to fight our battles for us and to turn our very blunders into advantages against our foes; but still I should feel more confident if the Tennessee and Cumberland Rivers were closed on the military line between Generals Johnston and Polk; if a fort was opposite Columbus, two others opposite above Memphis, and two on the opposite banks of the bend above Vicksburg. This, with obstructions between Forts Saint Philip and Jackson, and all the approaches from the Mississippi Sound, east of the city and above it, similarly guarded, would insure the safety of New Orleans, if we had one strong brigade, with a thousand cavalry and two batteries of horse artillery, about the Bay of Saint Louis and the mouth of Pearl River. I think your greatest immediate danger threatens you from that direction.

With the highest regard for your excellency, and with the deepest regret that I have to differ in opinion with General Lovell, I am, respectfully, your obedient servant,

EWD. FONTAINE,
Lieutenant-Colonel and Chief of Ordnance, Mississippi Army.

HEADQUARTERS ARMY OF PENSACOLA,
Near Pensacola, Fla., December 20, 1861.

ADJUTANT-GENERAL,
Richmond, Va.:

SIR: We were getting on finely in re-enlisting the twelve-months' men here, having some 450 in the Ninth Mississippi Regiment and a fair prospect in the First Alabama, a well-instructed body of artillery, when the unfortunate law of bounties and universal suffrage upset everything. Men who were perfectly willing to accept good and competent field officers, especially necessary in artillery, are now torn and tossed about by the intrigues of designing men, seeking their own advancement or revenge upon others who have made them do their duty. Discord now reigns where all was harmony, and our very best officers are sure to be sacrificed to this fell spirit. The men did not ask this privilege, did not desire it, and would not now claim to exercise it, but for these demagogues, who are misleading them from anything but pure motives. We shall still labor to overcome this evil, greater than all others combined, and hope yet to reorganize a part under the old law. In one month we should have secured 5,000 of the 6,000 twelve-months' men here. Now if we get 2,000 we shall do well. Our best field officers are certainly sacrificed; a poor reward for past faithful services. They would have cheerfully met this fate at the hands of the enemy, but from their own Government it is hard to bear.

I am, sir, very respectfully, your obedient servant,

BRAXTON BRAGG,
Major-General, Commanding.

GENERAL ORDERS, No. 18. } HDQRS. DEPT. OF ALA. AND WEST FLA., *Near Pensacola, Fla., December* 20, 1861.

The command of Brig. Gen. J. M. Withers is extended westward, so as to include Pascagoula Bay and that portion of Mississippi east of Pascagoula River.

By command of Major-General Bragg:

GEO. G. GARNER,
Assistant Adjutant-General.

WAR DEPARTMENT, C. S. A.,
Richmond, December 23, 1861.

Maj. Gen. MANSFIELD LOVELL,
New Orleans:

SIR: I have the honor to acknowledge receipt of your two letters of 10th instant and one of 16th.

1. I entirely approve your forwarding the Thirteenth Louisiana and Third Mississippi Regiments to the aid of our commanders in Kentucky. While I do not feel at liberty, under present circumstances, to order unconditionally any troops to be sent from your department, I shall be most happy to learn that you can spare any for the aid of the generals in Kentucky, who are sadly outnumbered. Of course it is useless to call out any troops that you cannot arm, unless they are willing to enlist for the war, in which event the Government is willing to pay the expense of holding them in camp of instruction until armed. We want all the men that will enlist for the war and we want all armed men that will enlist for twelve months. I only require that you keep your returns up to date, so that I may be at all times advised of the entire resources at command of the Government in your department.

2. In relation to your question about the power to break up and reorganize companies, so as to get rid of incompetent officers, I have to say that under the acts of Congress company officers are always elective, and this right of the men must be kept steadily in view and always respected. Now you have done well to sift out the men unable to do duty and discharge them from the service. The companies thus reduced below the standard number may be disbanded at our pleasure if not filled up by other able men. We have no right to assign them to commanders whom they have not elected, but we have a right, with their consent, to consolidate them into new companies, and have new elections of officers. The best plan, it seems to me, is to get the men to agree to form new companies and re-enlist. On getting their agreement, muster the old companies out of service and new companies into service at the same time, and let the latter elect their new officers. With your advice and influence they could readily be induced to elect competent officers; but the whole matter must be managed by concert with the men, and not by exercise of authority, for we have none.

3. On the subject of the iron of the Mexican Gulf Railroad I will write you again in a day or two. Mr. Gordon is here, and it is possible an

arrangement may be made advantageous to the Government and satisfactory to the company.

4. I have now to ask your attention to the subject of the coast defense of Mississippi. The interception of your communication with that portion of your department has caused us to take into serious consideration the formation of a new district, extending from the mouth of Pearl River to East Pascagoula, and detaching it from your command, as it must be almost impracticable for you to give it any personal attention. In the mean time, however, our concern has been awakened by news that there is considerable communication kept up between our coast and the enemy by small traders running with sloops and schooners out of the different streams that empty into the Mississippi Sound, and supplying the enemy at Ship Island and the Chandeleurs with all the intelligence they can gather, as well as the daily papers of New Orleans. I inclose you for examination and reflection a paper on this subject, prepared by Hon. J. J. McRae, who is intimately acquainted with the whole coast, and on which the President has written an indorsement that I also recommend to your attention.* We must, as far as possible, protect our people against marauders, and the proclamation issued by the Yankee general, as contained in the papers, is so open an invitation to the slaves to revolt, that they ought, in my opinion, at once be removed out of the reach of the incendiary gang, who are not simply our enemies, but the enemies of the human race. If you think you cannot communicate with the southern coast of Mississippi with sufficient facility to supervise efficiently defensive measures, you will be good enough so to inform me at once, and we must try to find a commander for it as a separate district.

Please inform me how the powder factory is getting on and what quantity of powder you have. Major Rains tells me that the mills thus far are not making over 1,500 pounds a day, although capable of making about twice that quantity.

I am, your obedient servant,

J. P. BENJAMIN,
Secretary of War.

HEADQUARTERS DEPARTMENT NO. 1, C. S. A.,
New Orleans, La., December 24, 1861.

Hon. J. P. BENJAMIN,
Secretary of War:

SIR: I have the honor to acknowledge the receipt of your letter of the 18th instant relative to furnishing Commodore Hollins with cannon powder. I have made it a point, without instructions, to aid him to the extent of my ability, and he has already been furnished by us with nearly 4 tons of powder. I have collected materials at great trouble and expense and urged to completion a large mill for making powder for the purpose of supplying my own wants, and they are yet far from being in a satisfactory condition. I have already turned over to the Navy more powder than in justice to the Army I should have done, and it will require more than I have on hand to give a half allowance to the guns I have mounted. If I can be supplied with saltpeter in large quantities I can easily furnish Captain Hollins and myself, or if he will procure the saltpeter I will have it worked up. As matters now stand he cannot rely upon me for a pound. I must supply myself

* See McRae to Davis, p. 781; indorsement not found.

first, and I feel satisfied that you will indorse my action when you are made acquainted with all the circumstances.

I beg leave to ask your attention to my recommendation in reference to Colonel Duncan. There are nearly 5,000 men in the works on the exterior line, without any competent brigade commander, who should be a thorough artillerist and understand well the nature of the coast. It is utterly impossible for me to visit these works while keeping up the affairs of the department in this city.

Respectfully, your obedient servant,

M. LOVELL,
Major-General, Commanding.

HDQRS. DEPARTMENT ALABAMA AND WEST FLORIDA,
Mobile, December 24, 1861.

ADJUTANT-GENERAL C. S. ARMY,
Richmond, Va.:

SIR: The senior officer of the Navy here, having charge of such forces of that department as operate in Mobile Bay, declines to recognize any military authority. It is not my desire to encroach on the province of this department, but it occurs to me our service would be more efficient under one than two heads. At sea, beyond the range of my guns, no question would be raised of the supremacy of this department, but inside the bay harmony and efficiency are both sacrificed by this division of authority. At Pensacola a senior naval officer to the one here acknowledges my jurisdiction.

I am, sir, very respectfully, your obedient servant,

BRAXTON BRAGG,
Major-General, Commanding.

HEADQUARTERS DEPARTMENT NO. 1, C. S. A.,
New Orleans, La., December 25, 1861.

HON. J. P. BENJAMIN,
Secretary of War:

SIR: I have received your letter stating that Major Lovell could not be put on duty here with rank of field officer except to command troops. I was led into mistake in the matter by having in mind the case of Colonel Duncan.

I cannot spare Major Lovell, whose services in obstructing the channels have proved invaluable, and the objection as to command can easily be obviated. There are in this department on duty twenty-one separate companies of volunteers, who cause as much office detail at department headquarters as twenty-one regiments would do. With your permission I will organize these troops into regiments and battalions, and assign field officers to them. I can thus place Major Lovell on duty here with troops as a field officer, and his position with General Bragg's army can be filled by another officer. Shall I thus assign him?

I have mustered in regiments in place of the troops that I sent to General Johnston, and have called upon Governor Moore for an additional regiment to man the guns on the interior line. If in this I have been in error, please let me know. In conversation with the President before leaving Richmond, I understood him to say that I could call for such troops as the case might require, taking care not to create more expense for maintaining men than was absolutely necessary.

As the enemy is congregating at Ship Island, I shall organize the forces here as rapidly as possible. The governor, at my request, has ordered all the independent volunteer companies to form into regiments and elect their field officers, which will give about 6,000 pretty well armed men in the city subject to call. Do they bring their general officers when called into service? A militia law has also been draughted and presented, which I think will make about one-third of the militia available at short notice.

Respectfully, your obedient servant,

M. LOVELL,
Major-General, Commanding.

NEW ORLEANS, LA., *December* 27, 1861.

Hon. J. P. BENJAMIN,
Secretary of War:

I have made into good powder all the saltpeter sent. Can you spare any more?

M. LOVELL.

WAR DEPARTMENT, C. S. A.,
Richmond, December 27, 1861.

Maj. Gen. BRAXTON BRAGG,
Pensacola:

MY DEAR SIR: When we sent General A. S. Johnston to take command of the Western Department it was believed that he would proceed at once to the west of the Mississippi and conduct the campaign in Arkansas and Missouri. The obtaining possession of the latter State is of such supreme importance, that I need not say to you a word on the subject. Before, however, General Johnston reached the Mississippi the threatened invasion of Tennessee and the advance of the Federal forces into Kentucky rendered it necessary to detain him in this latter State, equally important as Missouri to the Confederacy, and threatening more immediate danger, especially when considered in connection with the menaced attack on our lines of communication by railroad through East Tennessee. At that time, too, the Department of Missouri was committed by the enemy to General Frémont, whose incompetency, well known to us, was a guarantee against immediate peril. All this is now changed. Missouri is under command of an able and well-instructed military commander. Dissensions exist between General Price and General McCulloch which prevent their cordial co-operation. We are threatened with grievous disaster. McCulloch has put his army (of about 9,000 excellent troops) into winter quarters in Northwestern Arkansas. Price has advanced alone, and we fear with fatal rashness, into a district of country where he is likely to be surrounded and cut off by overwhelming forces, and the Army of Missouri is represented to be a mere gathering of brave but undisciplined partisan troops, coming and going at pleasure, and needing a master mind to control and reduce it into order and to convert it into a real army.

After long and anxious consultation with the President we can find no one but yourself on whom we feel we could rely with confidence as commander-in-chief of the Trans-Mississippi Department; yet we do not know how to fill your place at Pensacola. Missouri, however, must not be lost to us, even at some risk of misfortune at Pensacola.

You have so thoroughly and satisfactorily prepared the defenses at the latter point that we scarcely believe another attempt will be made on your defenses, and we hope that by sending Kirby Smith to take your place, if you should leave, that important point will be successfuly defended.

You see already that my purpose is to ask you if you would consent to go to the West. In that event General Johnston's command would be limited by the Mississippi River, giving him as much even then as he can efficiently attend to, and your command would embrace everything west of the Mississippi except the coast defenses. Your campaign would comprehend the States of Arkansas and Missouri, together with Northern Texas and the Indian Territory. General Price will probably be continued in the command of the Missouri troops when mustered into our service. Their number, of course, I cannot approximate, but we could scarcely have less than 20,000 or 25,000 men from that State. In Arkansas and the Indian Territory our forces amount to about 12,000. A number of other regiments are now nearly organized in Texas and Arkansas, and we would find means of arming two or three of the new regiments at Pensacola, and thus disengaging for your command the two best Mississippi regiments.

With all these resources, aided, of course, by our hearty and cordial co-operation, it seems to me that we may confidently look for brilliant results. If the tide of battle should turn towards the Mississippi River your operations would be conducted in concert with General Johnston's, and of course, in that event, he would rank you; but, unless in case of joint operations on the river, your command would be entirely independent, and such joint operations would only be undertaken by special order of the President or by your own concert with General Johnston.

Will you undertake this work? I tell you frankly I believe you owe it to your country in this her hour of peril, but it will not be urged on you against your will. If we cannot now make available your name and reputation as a soldier, I confess I know not where else to look at this time. The President and myself have anxiously scanned every name on our army list, and under all the circumstances (many of which it is not possible to communicate in this letter) we invariably fell back on yours as the name. The circumstances are pressing. I could not say all that was important for your consideration by telegraph, but I must beg you, as soon as it is possible, to answer me by telegraph "I refuse," if such be your conclusion. If you say in reply, "I refuse," I must see what next best can be done.

I am, yours, very truly,

J. P. BENJAMIN.

HDQRS. DEPARTMENT ALABAMA AND WEST FLORIDA,
Mobile, Ala., December 29, 1861.

ADJUTANT-GENERAL C. S. ARMY,
Richmond, Va.:

SIR: An occurrence of the 27th instant at Fort Morgan illustrates the absolute necessity of the military commander here having control of the guard boats in the harbor. On that morning a small vessel from Havana attempted to run the blockade with supplies for us. Pressed by the enemy, she was beached under the guns of Fort Morgan. The enemy attempted to cut her out or destroy her, and the guns of our fort had difficulty in keeping them off until a small unarmed steamer went to her assistance, and under the fire of the enemy's gunboats relieved and brought her in. She brought in 150 bags of coffee, with some sulphur and other small stores. During all this time the Florida, an armed steamer, is lying at the moorings of the city, unoccupied and independent. An armed schooner is also lying in the harbor here utterly useless. It would be economy to give her away and discharge the crew.

I am, sir, very respectfully, your obedient servant,

BRAXTON BRAGG,
Major-General, Commanding.

HEADQUARTERS DEPARTMENT NO. 1, C. S. A.,
New Orleans, La., December 29, 1861.

Hon. J. P. BENJAMIN,
Secretary of War:

SIR: At 12 o'clock last night Hobart & Foster's powder-mill, in the old Marine Hospital, exploded. One charge of powder (4,000 pounds) was in the drying-room, and another of the same amount was in the cylinders, all of which was lost. I had taken out 4,000 pounds the same day. The mill was turning out this amount daily.

The mill that I brought over from Handsborough will be put up in twenty days, and this, together with the city mill, will enable us to turn out 2,500 or 3,000 pounds daily. Hobart & Foster will proceed immediately to rebuild their mill, and I shall drive it through with all the means at my control, and hope to have it in operation again in six weeks.

The total amount of saltpeter invoiced to this point since the middle of last September is 82,506 pounds gross, of which only 62,000 ever came to hand. The weight of the casks and sacks is to be deducted, besides which some of it was very impure. Hobart & Foster had three days' supply on hand at the time of the explosion (10,000 pounds), which was not injured.

The enemy has now at Ship Island twenty-two vessels, large and small, and is landing troops in large numbers. They have been sounding and staking out the channels leading towards the Rigolets and Chef Menteur Pass, but I think this is only a blind to draw our attention from Mobile, which I think is their object of attack. They cannot take New Orleans by a land attack with any force they can bring to bear.

I should much like to have for an inspector-general an officer of knowledge and experience. I am almost entirely deficient in the way of officers. General Ruggles and Colonel Duncan are the only two serving with troops who can render me aid. No other department is so deficient, and certainly none is more important.

Respectfully, your obedient servant,

M. LOVELL,
Major-General, Commanding.

MOBILE, *December* 30, 1861.

General S. COOPER,
Adjutant-General:

The enemy's vessels, some twenty, are below, landing supplies and large bodies of troops on Ship Island.

BRAXTON BRAGG.

RICHMOND, VA., *January* 1, 1862.

General MANSFIELD LOVELL,
New Orleans, La.:

Can give you no more saltpeter, but expect large supply very soon. Send me return of your entire stock of ammunition.

J. P. BENJAMIN,
Secretary of War.

NEW ORLEANS, LA., *January* 1, 1862.

Hon. J. P. BENJAMIN:

DEAR SIR: I must earnestly request that the Thirteenth Louisiana Regiment, as well as the Third Mississippi, be ordered back to New Orleans. The wretchedly-armed green troops sent here from Mississippi cannot supply the place of Gibson's regiment, armed by me. We are here entitled to that regiment, and I should have urged that they should not have been permitted to leave if the implied promise of General Polk had not been given that they would be returned when needed. They are needed.

Yours, very truly,

THO. O. MOORE.

HEADQUARTERS DEPARTMENT NO. 1,
New Orleans, La., January 1, 1862.

Hon. J. P. BENJAMIN,
Secretary of War:

SIR: I have the honor to acknowledge the receipt of your letter of the 23d ultimo, with its inclosure, relative to the defense of the Mississippi coast. You have suggested the propriety of making a new department out of the district between Pearl River and Pascagoula, and have asked my views about it. I do not see the necessity of such a step, as Pearl River is of necessity a part of Department No. 1, and Pascagoula of General Bragg's department. The country between (the piney woods district of Mississippi) is a sandy barren, running back 40 or 50 miles, with a poor, sparse population, and is utterly destitute of any supplies which might be necessary for troops. Nearly all that is of value is the line of fine summer residences just on the beach, and as long as the enemy has full command of the water he can at any time land under fire of his heavy guns and take possession of these houses at Biloxi, Mississippi City, &c. The companies of infantry to be stationed as suggested by Mr. McRae would be more than useless, as a couple of light-draught gunboats with a few 8-inch shells could at any time drive them back from the beach, leaving in the enemy's possession all that is really of any value, viz, the fine houses, &c., on the shore, and the opposition, inefficient though it would be, would give the enemy, in their own judgment, good cause for committing excesses.

We can, however, station troops in such a manner as to prevent much communication with the enemy by our own people; but in this we should have the assistance of the Navy Department, as we have no armed vessels to use for that purpose.

I have telegraphed General Johnston to send me back the Third Mississippi Regiment from Columbus, so that I can again place them on the sound coast. I have a regiment of infantry and a battery of artillery at Bay Saint Louis and Pass Christian. The regiment that I removed was stationed at Mississippi City and Handsborough, and when I sent them away I wrote to Governor Pettus to ask if he could furnish more men to replace them. I learn that he has ordered some cavalry down there, but if you will look on the map I sent you by Colonel Davis you will observe that this section of the country is so cut up with streams that it is very difficult for troops to move through it, and no use could be made of it by the enemy.

All that I ask is to give me some competent and experienced subordinate officers that I can place some reliance on, and the supervision and management of the affairs of the department between Pearl River and Pascagoula will be an easy matter; but I do not think that in any event it should be made a separate department. If you have a competent officer to spare to place over that section of the country let him report to me, and I will put him in position to do all that can be done there by infantry and light artillery, and can keep in hand here in New Orleans a force sufficient to throw upon the enemy should he presume to make a flank march towards Covington.

The coast is beyond a question untenable should the enemy land in considerable force, which I do not think he will do, east of Bay Saint Louis, unless it be with a view to Mobile. The part between that bay and Pascagoula is valueless in a military point of view except to use the houses on the coast for quarters, and this cannot be prevented without a naval force of some kind.

I will have the return of powder made up and send it as soon as possible. I wrote you fully about powder a few days since.

Respectfully, your most obedient servant,

M. LOVELL,
Major-General, C. S. Army.

Abstract from field return of the Army of Pensacola, commanded by Maj. Gen. Braxton Bragg, on the 1st day of January, 1862.

Troops.	Present for duty.		Aggregate present.	Aggregate present and absent.
	Officers.	Men.		
1st (Gladden's) Brigade	198	2,970	3,896	4,793
2d (Anderson's) Brigade	201	3,093	3,947	4,103
Alabama Mounted Rifles	3	78	88	94
Walton Guards	4	56	60	64
Grand total	406	6,197	7,991	9,054

RICHMOND, VA., *January* 3, 1862.

GOV. JOHN J. PETTUS,
Jackson, Miss.:

Orders were sent some time since to General Lovell for the defense of the coast of Mississippi, and I hope he has taken measures which it would now be too late for me to initiate. The movement no doubt is intended against Mobile or New Orleans, but I shall much regret if any successful raid be made against the villages on our coast.

JEFFERSON DAVIS.

HDQRS. DEPARTMENT ALABAMA AND WEST FLORIDA,
Near Pensacola, Fla., January 4, 1862.

ADJUTANT-GENERAL,
Richmond, Va.:

SIR: After completing my inspections at Mobile I reached here on the morning of the 2d instant. Affairs in that part of my command are not in a very encouraging state, and I regret to say I see but little hope of improvement with the means at my command.

The question of rank between Colonels Powell and Maury was settled in favor of the former, and the latter, found off duty in Mobile, has returned to his post. Colonel Powell appears to be an intelligent, energetic, and faithful officer, but for want of experience in army service has great difficulties to contend with. The forts are in much better condition than when I visited them in October, and with ammunition would be in condition to prevent any entrance to Mobile Bay. The services of a good gunboat, in conjunction with Forts Morgan and Gaines, would be of great service; but they are utterly useless at the city of Mobile, where they are now kept. The health of the troops at the forts is very good, and everything indicates improving discipline and a close attention to duty.

The infantry brigade under Brig. Gen. L. P. Walker, encamped on the main-land, some 12 or 15 miles from Mobile, on the road to Pascagoula, I regret to report in a very bad condition. The commander had established himself in the city of Mobile with a large and useless staff at a heavy expense, whilst his troops were suffering in crowded tents and huts, without hospitals or any of those essentials for the comfort and health of raw men. There was no organization, no system, and no instruction. Each regimental and battalion commander was independent of all the rest. The necessary consequence is disease, demoralization, and great mortality, about one-third of the command being sick, with a great deficiency of hospital accommodation.

I ordered General Walker sent to his command before I left here; but under various pretexts he was still absent from his command on the 1st instant. Except as a matter of principle, I attach no importance to this absence of the general, as his want of knowledge and experience, and it appears to me an inaptitude for military command, render it impossible for him to supply the wants in that brigade. I consequently look for little improvement without a change.

The Department cannot but see the great importance of this position at the present time, and the necessity of having a well-organized, well-instructed, disciplined, and equipped command at such an exposed point. The recent movements of the enemy render it more important than ever. Had my former recommendations been adopted our strength would have been much greater; it may not be too late to retrieve a part of what is lost; but time is precious, and prompt and decided action necessary.

Cannon, powder, and small arms and accouterments are the great essentials for our strength, provided we can get proper commanders to have them used.

I am, sir, very respectfully, your obedient servant,

BRAXTON BRAGG,
Major-General, Commanding.

RICHMOND, *January* 5, 1862.

General BRAXTON BRAGG,
O'Bannonville, Fla.:

My private letter to you [of December 27, 1861] was written before the enemy had landed at Ship Island and Biloxi, and it is not just that you should now be asked to accede to the proposal contained in my letter.

J. P. BENJAMIN,
Secretary of War.

WAR DEPARTMENT, C. S. A.,
Richmond, Va., January 5, 1862.

Maj. Gen. BRAXTON BRAGG,
Pensacola, Fla.:

SIR: I ought sooner to have replied to your several letters of the 10th, 11th, 17th, and 29th ultimo, but I was extremely anxious to give you definite information in relation to the subject of re-enlistment of twelve-months' men; and after the act of Congress on the subject I was much engrossed, in concert with the President and Adjutant-General, in the attempt so to execute the law as to prevent the disorganization of the Army.

No one can deprecate more sincerely than I do the obvious consequences of what you well denominate the system of universal suffrage in the Army; but the lawgivers have spoken, and we must do the best we can. I send you herewith a circular copy of the regulations we have devised, which will appear in a few days in the shape of a general order from the bureau of the Adjutant-General.

I know in advance that, however contrary to your own ideas of a proper system, the Department can rely with confidence on your cordial co-operation, and at least one point is gained, viz, that after the first election all vacancies will be filled by promotion.

I regret the total impossibility of supplying you with arms for your unarmed regiments. We have a large cargo near at hand, but Heaven knows when we will receive it, if at all; and until we can get in some arms from abroad we cannot put another man in the field. It is a cruel necessity that forces this avowal, but it is due to you to state the facts. In the mean time our enemy, with free intercourse abroad and full control of the sea-coast, augments his forces at pleasure, and leaves us a desperate struggle, to be maintained only by heroic effort and unconquerable will. Everywhere we are outnumbered, and while demagogues and newspaper squibblers are clamorous for offensive movements, we are scanning the horizon with anxious eyes and praying for no other succor than arms and powder—for nothing but weapons with which to fight in defense of our rights. If the winter closes upon the campaign without serious disaster all will be well, for it is impossible, with the varied efforts already made, with the large supplies already purchased, and with the numerous expedients now in progress, that some successful venture shall fail to occur, and thus put into our hands all that is wanted to wrest from the foe the admission that our subjugation is impossible.

The President has ordered the appointment of Major Jones to be colonel of the new regiment of Mississippians organized by you, which you will please to number as the Twenty-seventh Mississippi; but he does not seem entirely to concur in your recommendation of the lieutenant-colonel. As soon as he determines that point Lipscomb will be appointed major, as you advise. In Colonel Bullock's regiment the field officers are, if I am not mistaken, to be filled up under the laws of Alabama, the regiment being, I believe, one that was tendered by the State with its field officers already elected. Where regiments are formed by us out of separate companies we appoint the field officers, and vacancies are filled by promotion; but where the State organizes and tenders the regiment, the field officers are appointed by the State.

Your letters of the 24th and 29th, in relation to the right of commanding the naval forces in the harbor, have been submitted to the President, and he concurs in your opinion. As the matter, however, is somewhat delicate, and we all desire to avoid unpleasant conflicts of authority, I will converse with Mr. Mallory on the subject and write you again.

I am, yours, respectfully,

J. P. BENJAMIN,
Secretary of War.

WAR DEPARTMENT, C. S. A.,
Richmond, Va., January 5, 1862.

Major-General LOVELL,
New Orleans, La.:

SIR: Your letters of the 24th and 25th ultimo, have been received.

1st. My request in relation to the powder asked for by Commodore Hollins was of course subordinate to your discretion, but I am anxious to accommodate the Navy on all proper occasions and to keep up cordial relations in all branches of the service.

2d. I will call the President's attention again to your recommendation in favor of Colonel Duncan.

3d. Your suggestion as to organization of independent companies into regiments and battalions is entirely approved. I had no idea that the condition of your forces was such as you represent. We never permit an accumulation of independent companies. We consult their wishes, however, in throwing them together, and you are requested, with this view, to organize two regiments out of these twenty-one companies, and to send to this Department a return of the organization, with muster rolls and a recommendation for appointment of field officers. In this way provision can be made for Major Lovell within your department.

4th. Your muster-in of other regiments in place of those sent to Kentucky is approved; indeed, until further orders, you are authorized to receive and muster into the Confederate service all companies, battalions, or regiments that tender themselves for the war, or three years; but bear in mind we will accept no men for a less term, unless they arm themselves at their own expense. In this event you may accept them for not less than twelve months.

5th. The militia, when called out as such, bring their generals with them.

6th. I hope soon to hear of your having been able to do something to check the enemy and encourage our people on the sea-coast of Mississippi, though of course I cannot and do not expect you to weaken your command in New Orleans for the purpose of punishing marauders on the sea-coast. If you could get up a small local organization, however, with a flying battery, equipped with good, reliable horses, for rapid movements, so as to prevent the landing of small parties of plunderers, it would have a happy effect and give pleasure and confidence to our people in Southern Mississippi.

Your obedient servant,

J. P. BENJAMIN,
Secretary of War.

WAR DEPARTMENT, C. S. A.,
Richmond, Va., January 6, 1862.

Hon. S. R. MALLORY,
Secretary of the Navy:

SIR: I have the honor to inclose, for your perusal, two letters* from General Bragg, which I beg may be returned to me.

Without desiring for a moment that any authority should be assumed over the vessels and officers of the Navy by any military commander, it does seem to me that small craft in harbors and shore waters should to some extent be made subordinate to commanders of departments charged with the coast defenses, and I beg to call your attention to the subject and to ask for your views.

I may be permitted to add that General Withers on a former occasion represented the naval officers in command of the gunboats in Mobile Bay as being utterly inefficient and unreliable. I do not even know their names, and of course have no knowledge on the subject beyond the report of the military commanders; but as you cannot have chosen your best officers for such unimportant commands, I think it not improbable that there is ground for the complaints.

Yours, very respectfully,

J. P. BENJAMIN,
Secretary of War.

WAR DEPARTMENT, C. S. A.,
Richmond, Va., January 6, 1862.

Maj. Gen. MANSFIELD LOVELL,
New Orleans, La.:

SIR: Your letters of the 24th and 29th ultimo are received. I have to announce to you that the President has authorized the appointment of Colonel Duncan as brigadier-general, and his nomination will be sent to Congress to-morrow.

The President desires that you assign General Trimble to the command of the district stretching from the Rigolets to Pascagoula, and confide to him that part of your department, furnishing him one or two light batteries, well equipped, for active movement, and such number of troops as may be sufficient for checking marauding parties that may attempt plunder. It is not, of course, expected that he can resist an army; but you can furnish him with sufficient force to encourage and inspirit the people on the sea-shore, cut off communication of evil-disposed persons with the enemy, and check boating parties attempting to carry on a predatory warfare.

I am sorry to hear of the destruction of the powder-mill, with its contents, as we have not a pound to spare. You will be good enough to send me at once a statement by which I can discover which of the saltpeter shipments have failed to reach you, as you seem to be short at least 20,000 pounds by your letter of the 29th.

I will see if I can send you a good inspecting officer. I think Major Pickett is disposable, and the only one we have at present not in active and important service.

I have taken all the powder (said to be 45 tons) just arrived by the Vanderbilt and telegraphed you to that effect. Please have it inspected, so as to be sure that we are not paying such an enormous price as $2 per pound for damaged powder, and aid the owners in having it all brought

* Probably those of December 29, 1861, and January 4, 1862, pp. 789, 793.

for distribution to New Orleans, except 5 tons of cannon and 1 of rifle powder, which I desire sent to Galveston.

Your obedient servant,

J. P. BENJAMIN,
Secretary of War.

RICHMOND, VA., *January* 6, 1862.

Major-General LOVELL,
New Orleans, La.:

I have taken all the powder by the Vanderbilt. Arrange with the owners for bringing it all to New Orleans, except 5 tons of cannon powder and 1 ton of rifle powder, ordered to Galveston.

J. P. BENJAMIN,
Secretary of War.

HEADQUARTERS ARMY OF PENSACOLA,
January 6, 1862.

Hon. J. P. BENJAMIN,
Secretary of War, Richmond, Va.:

MY DEAR SIR: Your private and confidential dispatch of the 27th ultimo reached me on the evening of the 4th instant, and has had my most earnest consideration. I could not reply yesterday by telegraph, but do so this morning, and shall anxiously await the President's decision.

The aspect of affairs has so far changed within my present command that I feel greatly embarrassed by the alternative presented and the responsibility imposed. Had the President issued his order to me, I should have promptly obeyed without a murmur; but the alternative requires that, while I make no objection, I should submit a few considerations which impress me, and which the Department probably did not fully know at the date of the dispatch.

A portion of my command is now powerfully menaced by a large force, constantly increasing. Our force, at best, is very weak, and a part of it in very bad condition, so that I really cannot consider the city of Mobile perfectly safe. This place, to which you seem only to refer, is in no danger, unless from an incompetent commander; a danger we have just escaped. But it will take time, labor, and all the influence I can bring to bear to produce so good a result in the western part of my department. Much valuable time is already lost there, and but little progress is now being made, owing to the means I am compelled to use. This state of affairs is seen, felt, and deplored by those who have all at stake. A feverish state of excitement and much alarm exists in Mobile, where the danger is greatest, and it is no egotism in me to say I am looked to as their hope and support. The influence I have gained over the minds of the people in this section of the country, as well as over my troops, is considerable, and I do not believe any other could now fill my place to their satisfaction. You will readily see, then, my embarrassment.

The field to which you invite me is a most important one, but, under present aspects, not enticing. So much has been lost there, and so little done in organization and instruction, that the prospect of retrieving our ground is most gloomy. Troops so long accustomed to the freedom and license they have enjoyed will be more difficult to command than raw men; and though I have succeeded to some extent in making soldiers here of raw levies of volunteers, and at the same time retaining their good will and confidence, I distrust my ability to accomplish the same in the new field offered me.

Without a base of operations, in a country poorly supplied at best, and now exhausted by being overrun by both armies in mid-winter, with an unclad, badly-fed, and badly-supplied mass of men, without instruction, arms, equipments, or officers, it is certainly a most unpromising field for operations. But should the President decide on it, after knowing the state of affairs here, I will bend all my energies and faculties to the task, and offer myself (as a sacrifice, if necessary) to the great cause in which we are engaged.

I shall need and must receive from the Department great assistance in the way of staff and general officers. Upon them depends, as much as upon the commander, the success of all his efforts. Many of the volunteers here are now so well instructed that this may be granted without materially weakening this department.

Could you possibly send 3,000 stand of arms here? I should desire to take from this army Chalmers' Ninth Mississippi, Adams' Louisiana Regulars, and Jackson's Fifth Georgia Regiments. These would give me a nucleus upon which to form, would set an example of discipline, and would give me the support of excellent officers, who know and trust me, and in whom I place unlimited confidence. I should desire Brigadier-General Gladden to command them; Colonel Chalmers might be made a brigadier, to remain here in place of Gladden, and Lieutenant-Colonel Autrey would make an excellent colonel for his regiment, now nearly reorganized for the war. Jackson I should desire to see advanced to the command of a brigade.

Major Slaughter, my acting inspector-general, is on a short official visit to Richmond. He possesses my entire confidence in every respect, and may be fully and freely consulted by the Department, as he knows my views in regard to matters here, and is as fully posted as I am.

Most respectfully, your obedient servant,

BRAXTON BRAGG,
Major-General, &c.

HEADQUARTERS DEPARTMENT NO. 1,
New Orleans, La., January 7, 1862.

HON. J. P. BENJAMIN,
Secretary of War:

SIR: After reading the letter of Mr. McRae, relative to the use of launches on the coast of Mississippi Sound, I suggested to Commodore Hollins to make some arrangements with that purpose in view. Nothing has been done, nor is it likely that anything will be done, by the Navy Department there unless under orders from Richmond. You will recollect our conversation the evening before I left Richmond, in which you took a different view from myself. I felt satisfied that if the protection of the navigable streams running up into the country was removed from my control it would in all probability not be properly arranged in connection with the land defenses, while the general commanding the department would be considered by the people at large as responsible for inroads into the territory of his command. This is just what has happened.

I should have had light-draught armed vessels or launches at numerous points along the coast had I not kept in view your expressed wish that all clashing, even in appearance, should be avoided between the two arms of service. I have now on Lake Borgne a larger armed force than the Navy has, but it is kept up under the name of supplying our posts on the sound, it being necessary that the vessels should be armed for their own protection. I hope that, in connection with Mr. Mallory, you may be able to devise some plan by which either the entire matter may be placed under my control or the naval officer in command may have orders to afford such aid as I may officially require of him. The blame of want of protection will rest upon me in any event, and I should therefore have some power to say what should be done.

Respectfully, your obedient servant,

M. LOVELL,
Major-General, Commanding.

HEADQUARTERS DEPARTMENT NO. 1,
New Orleans, La., January 8, 1862.

Hon. J. P. BENJAMIN,
Secretary of War:

SIR: Some six weeks since, at the urgent call of an officer in Kentucky, and believing that I would be safe from attack until January, I sent two regiments to Columbus, with the distinct understanding on my part, and so expressed both to Generals Johnston and Polk, that when the enemy appeared here they should be returned. General Polk now, in answer to my call, telegraphs me that he has asked you to send me other troops, and you have consented. I hope that this is not so. The troops I sent him are natives of this part of the country and cannot be replaced by others. The Third Mississippi Regiment is composed largely of the fishermen, oystermen, and sailors of Louis Bay, Biloxi, Ocean Springs, &c., and are well acquainted with all the inlets, bayous, and soundings of that intricate and difficult coast, and can be of more service there than any other body of men. I have therefore written to General Polk to insist that the Third Mississippi Regiment, at all events, shall be sent down. They can as well be replaced there as here by fresh troops, but none can supply their place to me on the Mississippi coast. The regiment was raised particularly for that service, about half of it being amphibious, and I shall want to put a number of them in boats. The country troops will not answer my purpose. I beg, therefore, that even if you permit General Polk to retain the Thirteenth Louisiana you will telegraph him to send me the Third Mississippi Regiment immediately. He does me great injustice by leaving me until this late hour under the impression that when I wanted these two regiments they should be returned, and I have so written him.

Respectfully, your obedient servant,

M. LOVELL,
Major-General Commanding.

NAVY DEPARTMENT, C. S. A.,
Richmond, January 9, 1862.

Hon. J. P. BENJAMIN,
Secretary of War:

SIR: I have the honor to acknowledge the receipt of your letter of the 6th instant, inclosing two communications from General Bragg.

When the vessel to which General Bragg refers crossed the Mobile bar the Confederate steamer Florida was at the city, 30 miles off, and of course could render no assistance.

The Florida had recently gone there from the lake after an engagement with a Federal steamer, and on observing her arrival in the public papers I directed Flag-Officer Hollins to prevent her from lying at the city a moment beyond what her necessities might require.

General Bragg complains that the little guard boat did not go out to the vessel's assistance, which he says was pursued by the enemy's gunboats. This is a small sailing schooner, mounting one gun, commanded by an active and zealous young naval officer, and I trust that he would have sailed out against the enemy's gunboats could he have rendered any service. I will call upon him to explain his apparent neglect of duty.

I concur with you in the necessity of securing perfect harmony of action between the land and naval forces, and so soon as the steamers now nearly completed for service in the waters near Mobile shall go into commission I will give such instructions as will, I think, certainly secure it. At present there is but one small sailing schooner and two barges. The naval officer in charge, and who is reported by General Withers as "unreliable and inefficient," Lieut. Jas. D. Johnston, is regarded by the service and the Department as one of the best officers of the old service. Perhaps the cause of General Withers' report may be found in the letter of Lieutenant Johnston, a copy of which is inclosed.

General Bragg's letters are herewith returned.

I have the honor to be, very respectfully, your obedient servant,

S. R. MALLORY,
Secretary of the Navy.

[Inclosures.]

MOBILE, *December* 9, 1861.

Hon. S. R. MALLORY,
Secretary of the Navy, Richmond:

SIR: On the morning of the 4th instant I was accosted by Brigadier-General Withers, commanding this military division, in the presence of Major Hessee and Lieutenant Holt, assistant quartermaster at this place, in these words: "Some of your marines have been overpowering one of my sentinels and taking coal from Hitchcock's press." I replied, "Yes, sir, I have heard something of that, and intend to reprimand Lieutenant Mills for it." To this General Withers replied, "Reprimand him, sir! You must arrest him, sir; my orders to you are to arrest him, sir, at once," using a highly excited tone and manner. I then said, "That is a matter for me to attend to, general, and not you." Whereupon he replied, "I don't care, sir; my instructions to you are to investigate the matter and to arrest him, and if you don't I'll arrest the whole of you;" and then left me without waiting for a reply. He spoke throughout in an exceedingly angry and offensive tone, and did not seem disposed to listen to anything I had to say.

I immediately directed Lieutenant Mills to furnish me with a written explanation of his conduct in the case; and in the afternoon of the same day I addressed a communication, inclosing Lieutenant Mills' statement, to General Withers, informing him that I had investigated the circumstances connected with the occurrence which had so seriously excited his displeasure, and that the charge made against Lieutenant Mills of having overpowered one of his sentinels was entirely groundless.

A copy of this letter is herewith inclosed;* and I have only to say, in addition to the explanation therein given, that Lieutenant Mills was entirely ignorant of the fact that the press referred to was under military rule, and that I had informed him before that coal was stored there belonging to the Navy Department, which he could obtain for use on board the receiving-ship under his charge when he required it, taking it for granted that with his knowledge of naval regulations he would understand the necessity of making a requisition upon me for the coal before sending for it. His conduct in going to the press with a dozen armed men, to take the coal by force if resisted, and in using a dray and bags belonging to the press without consent of the agent in charge, was certainly reprehensible and altogether unnecessary; but his offense was against naval and not military rule, as he encountered no sentinel, nor had any been placed over the coal, as I am confident the military authorities were not even aware of its being there.

I have made a report to Flag-Officer Hollins of the whole affair, sending copies of my letters to General Withers and Mr. Mills' statement. No one can regret more sincerely than myself that any misunderstanding should occur between officers charged with the duties belonging to the separate branches of the public defense at this time; and I have always regarded the requests of General Withers as of equal force with his orders when it has been in my power to comply with them; but when he threatened to arrest me and the whole force under my command for an infraction of discipline on the part of one of my subordinates, and that without even giving me an opportunity to investigate the nature of this offense, I considered it my duty, not only to myself but to the service to which I belong, to inform him that I was not placed under his orders, especially as I received on the 9th ultimo an order from Flag-Officer Hollins to obey no orders but those coming from him, and to use my own judgment about complying with the requests of General Withers.

Under these circumstances I hope the Department will sustain me in having made what I intended as a respectful remonstrance against an unwarrantable assumption of authority and a gross violation of the rule of courtesy which should govern all officers in their official intercourse.

I have the honor to be, very respectfully, your obedient servant,

J. D. JOHNSTON,

Lieutenant in Charge of Naval Station.

MOBILE, *December* 4, 1861.

Brig. Gen. JONES M. WITHERS,

Commanding Military District of Alabama:

SIR: I inclose herewith the statement of Lieut. T. B. Mills relative to the occurrence at Hitchcock's press, of which you took occasion to speak to me this morning in the presence of two officers of the Army in a manner not only offensive to my feelings as an officer and a gentleman, but altogether unwarrantable between officers holding our relative positions.

You will perceive by Lieutenant Mills' statement that the charge you made against him of having overpowered one of your sentinels and taken coal which was under his charge is entirely groundless, inasmuch as the coal in question belongs to the Navy Department, and is stored in a part of the warehouse not in use for army purposes and in which no sentinel is stationed.

* Lieutenant Mills' letter not found.

The only person with whom Mr. Mills came in collision was a watchman at the warehouse, appointed by the agent of the owners of the press.

The conduct of Lieutenant Mills in the taking of an armed force to procure the coal and making use of property belonging to the press without first obtaining the consent of the agent was highly reprehensible and altogether unnecessary.

I shall make an official report of the facts to the commandant of this naval station, located at New Orleans, under whose orders I am placed in charge of naval affairs here.

With regard to your threat to "arrest the whole of us" (meaning, I suppose, the entire naval force here), I take this occasion to inform you that, although you may be clothed with the military power to execute it, you certainly have not the authority; and that, while I shall always be happy to comply with any request you may make to me, I shall by no means hold myself amenable to your orders, as I am attached to a branch of the public service over which you have no command.

I am, sir, respectfully, your obedient servant,

J. D. JOHNSTON,
Lieutenant, C. S. Navy, in Charge of Naval Station.

WAR DEPARTMENT, C. S. A.,
Richmond, Va., January 9, 1862.

Maj. Gen. BRAXTON BRAGG,
Pensacola, Fla.:

SIR: Your several favors of the 3d* and 4th instants are before me. I regret very much to hear of the deficiencies in your means of defense at Mobile, and will do everything I can to aid you. I have ordered the Chief of Ordnance to forward you every musket he can gather together as fast as possible; but we are so sadly deficient, that I fear it will be two or three weeks before you receive a quantity sufficient to arm one or two regiments.

I bought all the powder that arrived per the Vanderbilt, and hope soon to have it in New Orleans, when you shall have enough of it to relieve your most pressing wants. I am in daily hopes of a large additional supply from another source. In the mean time, if the attack is made on you first, I shall telegraph General Lovell to send you a part of his stock, to be replaced when that by the Vanderbilt reaches the city.

We are sadly pressed for competent officers, and I am equally surprised and indignant to learn of the conduct of General Anderson, and heartily concur in your decision not to overlook it.

On consultation with the President, and after a survey of all our resources, we have detached General Samuel Jones from the Army of the Potomac, and shall order him at once to report to you for service at Pensacola. I think you will feel safe when compelled to absent yourself from Pensacola.

To aid you in Mobile we have nominated Colonel Jackson brigadier-general, as recommended by you; and, although he is ranked of course by General Walker, you will find means to give him such command as will enable him to relieve you of much anxiety in getting your troops in proper order.

---

*See p. 497.

The landing of the enemy in force in your neighborhood of course puts an end to all idea of assigning you to other duty, as equally unjust to the country and yourself; and in this connection I will remark that a petition is here from Mobile asking that your headquarters be changed to that city. As I consider you entirely at liberty to place your headquarters where you deem best in your own department, I make no answer to this petition.

I have ordered Lieutenant Slaughter to be appointed to temporary rank as colonel, to be assigned to duty by you.

I am, your obedient servant,

J. P. BENJAMIN,
Secretary of War.

WAR DEPARTMENT, C. S. A.,
Richmond, Va., January 12, 1862.

Maj. Gen. BRAXTON BRAGG,
Pensacola, Fla.:

MY DEAR SIR: I have received yours of the 6th instant, and anticipated the answer a day or two ago. I merely write now to say that the President requests me to assure you of his appreciation of your readiness to serve your country wherever you could render yourself most useful, and that neither he nor myself would have thought of making to you the proposal contained in my letter if we had anticipated that the enemy would land in any force within your department.

The people there would have every reason to complain of your withdrawal under such circumstances, and the dissatisfaction would be such as to produce a very bad state of feeling as regards their defense.

We have concluded to send Maj. Gen. Earl Van Dorn to the district west of the Mississippi.

Yours, very truly,

J. P. BENJAMIN,
Secretary of War.

EXECUTIVE DEPARTMENT,
Montgomery, Ala., January 13, 1862.

Hon. J. P. BENJAMIN,
Secretary of War:

SIR: I have recently visited the forts and encampments of our troops at and near Mobile, and deem it my duty to the people of Alabama to report to your Department the great need of munitions for the defense of our coast, both guns for the fortifications and small-arms for the land forces. I hope to be able to specify at an early day the description and number of guns needed for the forts; the land forces there are now wanting several thousand muskets or rifles.

I beg to hand you inclosed a letter from Hon. P. Hamilton, chairman of the Executive Committee of Safety for the city of Mobile, in reference to certain arms in Havana, and to call your attention to the suggestions contained in it, and respectfully to ask your compliance with the same. In our opinion I am sorry to say that, in view of the increasing armaments and numbers of the enemy in the Gulf and his threatening attitude towards our coast, we are perhaps as unprepared, for want of guns and arms, for his reception as any point in the Confederacy.

I hope I may be pardoned for reminding the Department of the many thousand arms which Alabama promptly and cheerfully contributed and sent into distant States in the hands of her own volunteers for the common defense, and for further advising that, under the recent requisition of General A. S. Johnston, we have forwarded over two regiments of armed troops to Tennessee and Kentucky. We make no boast of these achievements; on the contrary, we profoundly regret that we had it not in our power to do far more than has been accomplished. While, however, the enemy is now seriously threatening our own soil, which has thus far been spared the pollution of his foot-print, and in view of our own destitution by reason of a surrender of arms for the defense of other prior exposed localities, I am sure you will most favorably consider the sincere and urgent appeal I here make. I have the means with which to procure additional arms and am making contracts for their manufacture within the State, but the emergency is now so pressing that we are unwilling to await the delays of delivery months hence, and have no other alternative but to appeal to your Department to afford us prompt and timely relief.

Awaiting, I trust, your early and favorable response, I am, with high regard, your obedient servant,

JNO. GILL SHORTER.

[Inclosure.]

MOBILE, *January* 9, 1862.

To His Excellency J. G. SHORTER,
Governor of Alabama:

SIR: I learn from Mr. Murrell, who derived his information from the master of a schooner recently from Havana, that there are 2,500 stand of arms at that place awaiting shipment to the Confederate States. They are the property of the Government, and might have reached this place before now by some of the schooners recently in this port from Havana. In the present condition of things here may it not be in your power to procure an order for said arms being shipped to Mobile for the use of troops here?

I respectfully suggest that a representation of the matter from you to the Secretary of War might secure these arms for this point.

Very respectfully, your obedient servant,

P. HAMILTON,
Chairman Executive Committee of Safety.

HEADQUARTERS DEPARTMENT NO. 1,
New Orleans, La., January 13, 1862.

Hon. J. P. BENJAMIN,
Secretary of War, Richmond, Va.:

SIR: I have the honor to state, in reply to your telegram, that the amount of powder in this department, in round numbers of pounds, is as follows:

	Pounds.
At Forts Jackson and Saint Philip	55,000
At Fort Pike	11,500
At Fort Macomb	6,900
At Fort Proctorsville	750
At Bienvenue	2,200
At Tower Dupré	500
At Fort Livingston	4,500
At Grand Caillou	1,350

	Pounds.
At Fort Berwick	1,100
At Fort Chêne	1,100
At Fort Guyon or Bayou La Fourche	1,000
At Calcasieu Pass	850
In magazine in and around New Orleans	30,000
Total	116,750

The quarterly returns are coming in slowly, and when received will enable me to report exactly the quantity of powder on hand; but I have caused the above estimate to be made out carefully, and am convinced that it will not vary materially from the aggregate of the official returns.

Considering New Orleans to be in a condition to resist an attack, I am turning my attention particularly to the coast of Mississippi. I had received no notice of the assignment of General Trimble to my command. If the Third Mississippi Regiment, which was raised mainly on that coast, be returned to me from Columbus, I can easily provide him with a force sufficient to prevent communication with the enemy and repel predatory parties.

The water communication between here and the eastern portion of this department being somewhat precarious, I have organized trains for supplying the troops to be located in that section by land.

I have ordered an accurate reconnaissance and topographical map to be made of the country between the Jackson Railroad and Mississippi City, which will enable me to select the most defensible positions for General Trimble's command to hold the enemy in check should he attempt to push up to the Jackson Railroad. Meanwhile I have in hand a well-organized movable column (General Ruggles' brigade), of about 5,000 men, including artillery, which I can throw over Lake Pontchartrain at a few hours' notice, to operate against his column should he be foolish enough to attempt such a flank movement.

If, however, he should attempt to land at Pascagoula and strike for Mobile, I could move Trimble's brigade, re-enforced by Ruggles', against his base of operations at Pascagoula, and thus, perhaps, compel an abandonment of the attack. These movements will, of course, depend upon my ability to transport troops and supplies through that section of country by land.

I shall probably have on that coast two batteries, of four guns each, and two mounted companies—all from this city; and if the naval department will give me half a dozen launches to place in Biloxi Bay, Bay Saint Louis, and Pearl River, I think we can obtain all necessary results on that coast. We cannot, of course, prevent an army from landing under cover of their gunboats.

Respectfully, your obedient servant,

M. LOVELL,
Major-General, Commanding.

NEW ORLEANS, LA., *January* 13, 1862.

Hon. J. P. BENJAMIN:

A party will contract to deliver here 75 tons of powder, if we advance the money, under bonds satisfactory to me, at 84 cents per pound, specie, or $1.14 in Confederate notes. If approved, notify and enable me to raise the money.

M. LOVELL.

HDQRS. DEPARTMENT ALABAMA AND WEST FLORIDA,
Near Pensacola, Fla., January 14, 1862.

Hon. J. P. BENJAMIN,
Secretary of War, Richmond, Va.:

SIR: I have to acknowledge yours of the 5th instant, covering a copy of your circular regulations based on the law for encouraging re-enlistments.

The subject shall have my earliest attention, none the less cordial because I doubt the policy of parts of the law. And I will add, that though my opinions will be freely expressed at all times, as due to us both, it is only necessary for me to know the policy of the Government to secure my efforts in carrying it out. In no other way can military operations be successfully conducted.

From what I can see and learn there seems to be a prospect of reaction taking place, and our success may yet be greater than anticipated when I last wrote. The governor of Alabama is giving me cordial assistance, and the people at home, as a general rule, are prompting their neighbors and friends to remain in the service. Many who had gone on furlough are back before their times are up, bringing their comrades; the strongest assurances that they cannot stay at home.

We confidently rely, then, on securing eventually a very large proportion of all we have had. The great question now is to keep up their organization, for one of our well organized and instructed regiments, under good officers, is worth any two which could be made up of a heterogeneous mass fresh from the country, and they require but half the number of arms.

The circumstances in which we are placed in regard to arms impose upon us a sacred duty of preserving to the greatest extent those we have. New troops are particularly destructive, and the closest attention from officers of all grades is necessary to preserve what we possess. The officer or man who by neglect or inattention destroys an efficient weapon now does the cause more harm than if he abandoned it in battle. With what we have I cannot but regard our cause as safe, though a larger supply would render its vindication less tedious.

In nominating the lieutenant-colonel of the Twenty-seventh Mississippi, I was influenced solely by the reputation that officer has established here in his nine months' service. He was assigned temporarily to these companies on their arrival here, and has done much already towards putting them in shape. He is an excellent disciplinarian, a very good drill officer, and has no superior, if an equal, of his grade, in this army. Of his antecedents I know nothing, and it may be the President there finds cause to object. I intended assigning this regiment, thus admirably officered, to Fort McRee and adjacent batteries, to replace Colonel Villepigue's regiment, which will not be reorganized as such, the companies being from three different States.

I strongly desire to retain the colonel, with his present rank, as chief of artillery and engineers on my staff, in place of Captain Boggs, resigned.

You are mistaken in regard to Colonel Bullock's regiment. It was organized, and the field officers appointed by the President, or the vacancy would at once have been filled, as in other cases, under the State law. The lieutenant-colonel (Shorter) is a gentleman and man of character, and will faithfully apply himself to learn and discharge his duties.

I am, sir, very respectfully, your obedient servant,

BRAXTON BRAGG,
Major-General, Commanding.

HDQRS. DEPARTMENT ALABAMA AND WEST FLORIDA,
Near Pensacola, Fla., January 14, 1862.

ADJUTANT-GENERAL C. S. ARMY,
Richmond, Va.:

SIR: By information from Ship Island to the 11th instant we learn the enemy are quiet and making no attempt yet at a location on the main-land. But few vessels remained there, and the number of troops was not as large as had been supposed. Their gunboats are hovering about Pascagoula, Bayou Labatre, and Grant's Pass, probably to cut off our water communication with the troops at the former place.

Should they make a lodgment anywhere between Pascagoula and the Rigolets, it can only be for the mere name of the thing, as no movement could be made thence against any assailable point.

Should he land at Pascagoula or east of it, whatever numbers, I shall fight him at the earliest possible moment, and with confidence in the result.

I am, sir, very respectfully, your obedient servant,

BRAXTON BRAGG,
Major-General, Commanding.

HEADQUARTERS DEPARTMENT NO. 1,
New Orleans, La., January 15, 1862.

Hon. J. P. BENJAMIN,
Secretary of War:

SIR: I have the honor to acknowledge the receipt of your two letters of the 5th and 6th instant.

I sent you on December 5, by Col. J. Davis, aide to the President, a map, with a descriptive letter, giving a summary of the defenses of the department as arranged at that date. I hope it reached you safely, as it has important information.

In my letter of the 13th instant the powder in this department was placed, in round numbers, at 115,000 pounds. A considerable quantity of this is not cannon powder, and, by reference to the letter of the 5th ultimo, you will see that there are more than 300 heavy guns in this department, scattered from Calcasieu to Pearl River. I mention this in reference to the distribution of the powder by the Vanderbilt.

There is not a single 10-inch gun in this department. I can have some cast here in a few days, provided machinery can be had to bore them. The Belleville Foundery has two lathes large enough to bore 12 inches, but the foundery is shut up, and the parties will neither sell, hire, nor lend the lathes, hoping to compel the Government to purchase the works. In case I fail to negotiate for them, shall I take them, appraise, and pay for them?

Through Mr. Dunn and other sources I have collected (by purchase mainly) about 900 small-arms, half of which are double-barreled shot-guns. After perfecting as far as possible the arming of the war men, I should propose to exchange the shot-guns for some miserable muskets and carbines in the hands of twelve-months' troops. It would look badly to go into action with poor guns, while better ones were in our possession, merely because the men were not enlisted for the war. Besides, the war men generally are an inferior class of shots, while the twelve-months' men are nearly all well skilled in the use of arms, and should be intrusted with the best weapons. The rifles that I have collected have been cut off to equal lengths and bored out to the caliber of the old United States rifle (54th of an inch). [.54.]

It was reported yesterday that Lieutenant Foster, of the United States Navy, had been in the city as a spy some days since. Should I arrest a Federal officer under such circumstances is he to be punished with death? I ask, having in view Tyler's case, of our Army, who was arrested in Cincinnati last summer, but has never been tried as a spy.

When our large powder-mill blew up we got to work upon the machinery of the mill that I ordered to be removed from Handsborough, and yesterday a charge was put in. This mill turned out on its old site about 1,200 or 1,500 pounds per day. The city mill has had a 20-horse-power engine placed in it, which will increase its capacity considerably. I sent Mr. Thomas B. Lee, of this city, agent to Texas, to bring over the Vanderbilt powder as soon as I got your dispatch.

Feeling satisfied some time since that letters were being sent to the United States conveying intelligence by the private expresses carrying mails via Havana and Mexico, I ordered all such letters to be examined, and appointed Messrs. Greenwood and Benochi, two gentlemen of high standing here, as an examining committee.

In addition to the defenses stated in my letter of the 5th ultimo, we are now erecting eight small batteries at Manchac and on the lake shore where the Jackson Railroad skirts the water, so as to prevent interruptions of that line of communication by the enemy. These batteries are for two guns each—sixteen in all.

Major Rains took on a proposition from me about the steamer Tennessee. He telegraphed that you approved the plan; but I have had no official authority to guarantee half the value of the ship or to raise funds for the purchase of our half of the return cargo.

I am engaged in organizing the independent companies into two regiments, and will send on the names of the officers in a few days. It is difficult to find good officers who will take the positions for the short time (six months) that these troops will have to serve.

Respectfully, your obedient servant,

M. LOVELL,
Major-General, Commanding.

RICHMOND, *January* 15, 1862.

General MANSFIELD LOVELL,
New Orleans:

I have ordered back the Third Mississippi Regiment, but cannot take the Louisiana regiment away from Columbus at this moment.

J. P. BENJAMIN,
Secretary of War.

RICHMOND, VA., *January* 15, 1862.

General MANSFIELD LOVELL,
New Orleans, La.:

Will take the powder if delivered at an early day. Will let you know to-morrow whether we will send you specie or notes.

J. P. BENJAMIN,
Secretary of War.

RICHMOND, VA., *January* 16, 1862.

General MANSFIELD LOVELL,
New Orleans, La.:

One hundred and ninety-five thousand dollars will be placed to your credit to-morrow in Treasury notes for completing the contract for the 75 tons of powder. Make the contract for delivery as soon as possible, and let it be all cannon powder.

J. P. BENJAMIN,
Secretary of War.

HEADQUARTERS DEPARTMENT NO. 1,
New Orleans, La., January 16, 1862.

Hon. J. P. BENJAMIN,
Secretary of War:

SIR: In compliance with your telegram, I took possession yesterday of the following steamers, viz: Mexico, Texas, Orizaba, Charles Morgan, Florida, Arizona, William Heines, Atlantic, Austin, Magnolia, Matagorda, William H. Webb, Anglo Saxon, and Anglo Norman—fourteen in all. Captain Huger, of the Navy, who accompanied the party that took possession of the ships, thinks the Atlantic will hardly answer as a war vessel, and I telegraphed yesterday to know whether I should substitute the Galveston for her. After the ships were seized I asked Commodore Hollins to take charge of them until further orders.

In this connection permit me to call attention to Captain Higgins, who lately resigned with a view of fitting out some of these vessels for war purposes under State authority. This seizure puts an end to his business. He is an officer of the old Navy, of experience, skill, and high reputation as a bold and efficient officer. His services would be of great value in assisting to fit out a fleet here and in fighting it afterwards.

I see various reports about the occupation of Biloxi by the enemy. This is a mistake. Some 60 men landed there last week, remained for a few hours, doing no damage, and returned to the fleet. They have no footing on the main shore as yet.

We have here about 500 prisoners of war, who are a serious nuisance. Is there a prospect of exchanging them?

Respectfully, sir, your obedient servant,

M. LOVELL,
Major-General, Commanding.

HDQRS. DEPARTMENT ALABAMA AND WEST FLORIDA,
Near Pensacola, January 17, 1862.

Hon. J. P. BENJAMIN,
Secretary of War Richmond, Va.:

SIR: I inclose you a copy of a letter from an agent in Mobile, who is keeping up pretty constant communication with Ship Island.

No doubt the enemy gain information from our employés, but as they get the same anyhow in spite of us, we lose nothing by employing even doubtful agents.

The first report of the enemy's strength was no doubt exaggerated, and it may be a portion of their force is on some marauding expedition.

Should Burnside's force join them a demonstration may be made against us, but none which I can now look upon as formidable, unless they are willing to run greater risks than heretofore, by passing our forts and batteries. Such an attempt is hardly probable, and any move upon Mobile or this point by land is scarcely within the bounds of Yankee enterprise.

Affairs about Mobile are improving, and the information you give me in yours of the 9th, received yesterday, is cheering. With the cheerful and cordial aid of Governor Shorter we shall probably get out at least 1,000 armed militia—men who have held back, but will come out rather than give up their army.

On the arrival of General Jones I propose turning over to him the immediate command here, so as to give my entire time to the affairs of the department. But I shall be much here, not intending to change my headquarters, but to be more free to move and to be more at Mobile.

General Walker's superior rank to General Jackson will embarrass the use of the latter somewhat, but I will try to arrange them so as to make both as serviceable as possible. Jackson is a man of great nerve and energy, and with a good staff, which I hope to give him, will soon make his mark on any raw command.

I am happy to report a decided improvement in our prospects of re-enlisting the twelve-months' men. So far as I have been able to visit and address the regiments orally, they are doing finely. It will be continued until I see them all. One thousand will be allowed to be absent at a time, and their arms are being reserved for them—to be used, of course, in case of emergency by the unarmed men here. This seems to be a *sine qua non*, and has more effect than all else in securing them. So great is the disposition for change, that but few would remain if they felt confidence in getting arms elsewhere.

The question of transferring the regiment, Louisiana infantry, Colonel Adams, for the balance of their three years, from the State to the Confederate service, is exciting much interest with the officers. I trust it may soon be settled. The twelve-months' men, about half the regiment, are freely re-enlisting.

I am, sir, very respectfully, your obedient servant,

BRAXTON BRAGG,
Major-General, Cammanding.

[Inclosure.]

MOBILE, *January* 14, 1862.

MY DEAR GENERAL: I wrote you on the 11th instant, since when the first two men we sent off for information have returned and confirmed the report made by telegraph from Ocean Springs, particulars of which I gave you in my last, and they further state that on their way from Ocean Springs they landed last Saturday on Ship Island, some 6 miles to the eastward of the Ship Island anchorage, and on Sunday were within 4 miles of the west end of Ship Island; that but four vessels were there; these were war steamers; that from information they obtained from the sailors of the launch of the French war steamer Milan, with 18 men and 4 officers, which landed at Pass Christian, but about 5,000 troops were then on the island, as far as they could judge from the mast head of their vessel, and that the sailors understood that much sickness prevailed among the Yankee troops. Our men speaking French fluently, the Frenchmen communicated freely with them. They are much exasperated against the Yankees for firing into their ship, the ball passing through both wheel-houses, causing much damage, which they are repairing at Ship Island anchorage.

The object of the French launch making a landing at Pass Christian was to communicate with the French consul at New Orleans.

The officers inform our men that some twenty-two war vessels, English and French, were in the Gulf and on our coast.

The Yankee transports (large sailing ships) being towed out while the wind was blowing from the *westward* would seem to indicate an *eastward* destination.

While on this cruise our men purchased 12,000 pounds of lead back of Biloxi, at 8 cents per pound, which they will have here in a few days. They return to-day for this lead and to make further reconnaissance about the enemy's headquarters on Ship Island.

The man Frederic, of Pascagoula, failed in his first trip to Ship Island (could not get there) to obtain information; but he returned this morning to the island with two old ladies of Pascagoula, who go over for their runaway slaves. He expected to be allowed to land at the fort, and will be back in a day or two with information which I will report to you.

Very respectfully, your obedient servant,

[No signature.]

WAR DEPARTMENT,
Richmond, Va., January 19, 1862.

Maj. Gen. MANSFIELD LOVELL,
New Orleans, La.:

SIR: A few days ago I sent you a telegram requesting the seizure for account of the Government of fourteen steamships, and received your reply informing me that the request had been complied with.

These instructions were sent you in consequence of the passage by Congress of two laws, Nos. 344 and 350, herewith forwarded, providing $1,000,000 for application to floating defenses for the Western rivers, to be expended at the discretion of the President by the Secretary of War or Secretary of the Navy, as he shall direct, and authorizing a corps of not more than 6,000 men to be raised for temporary and special service on the Western waters.

The terms of the acts will at once suggest to you that the force intended is a peculiar one. It is not to be part of the Navy, for it is intended for service on the rivers, and will be composed of the steamboatmen of the Western waters.

It will be subject to the general command of the military chief of the department where it may be ordered to operate, but the boats will be commanded by steamboat captains and manned by steamboat crews, who will be armed with such weapons as the captains may choose, and the boats will be fitted out as the respective captains may desire. The intention and design are to strengthen the vessels with iron casing at the bows, and to use them at high speed to run down or run over and sink, if possible, the gunboats and mortar rafts prepared by the enemy for attack at our river defenses. These gunboats and mortar rafts have been so far protected by iron plates and by their peculiar construction as to offer, in the judgment of the President and of Congress, but small chance of our being able to arrest their descent of the river by shot or shell, while at the same time their weight, their unwieldy construction, and their slow movement, together with the fact that they show very little surface above the water line, render them peculiarly liable to the mode of attack devised by the enterprising captains who have undertaken to effect their destruction by running them down, if provided with swift and heavy steamers, so strengthened and protected at the bows as to allow them to rush on the descending boats without being sunk by the first fire.

Captains Montgomery and Townsend have been selected by the President as two of those who are to command these boats. Twelve other captains will be found by them and recommended to the President for appointment. Each captain will ship his own crew, fit up his own boat, and get ready within the shortest possible delay. It is not proposed to rely on cannon, which these men are not skilled in using, nor on fire-arms. The men will be armed with cutlasses. On each boat, however, there will be one heavy gun, to be used in case the stern of any of the gunboats should be exposed to fire, for they are entirely unprotected behind, and if attempting to escape by flight would be very vulnerable by shot from a pursuing vessel.

I give you these details as furnishing a mere outline of the general plan to be worked out by the brave and energetic men who have undertaken it. Prompt and vigorous preparation is indispensable. The Department relies confidently on your co-operation in rendering effective this plan, which may, perhaps, not only be of vast importance for the peculiar service now hoped for on the Upper Mississippi, but may prove very formidable aids to your future operations in the lower part of the valley.

I shall at once place to your credit $300,000, to be expended for the purpose of preparing and outfitting these vessels as rapidly as possible, and shall renew the remittances as far as required while the appropriation will permit. It is expected that you will allow a very wide latitude to the captains in the preparation of these vessels, merely exercising such general supervision as to prevent the throwing away of money in purely chimerical experiments and checking any profligate expenditure.

Your chief quartermaster can keep the accounts, so as to relieve you of the responsibility of a disbursing officer, and you can discharge yourself any money liability by simply taking his receipt as your voucher for turning over this money.

To a commander of your intelligence and capacity it is deemed sufficient thus generally to sketch the outline of a scheme of defense, without attempting to lay down any minute rules or details for carrying out what is necessarily a novel experiment, yet one from which much is hoped by the Government.

This letter will be delivered to you by Captain Townsend in person, he being one of the two already elected by the President for the command of boats.

I am, your obedient servant,

J. P. BENJAMIN,
Secretary of War.

[Inclosures.]

CHAP. XXXIV.—AN ACT making appropriations for certain floating defenses.

Be it enacted by the Congress of the Confederate States of America, That the sum of one million of dollars be, and the same is hereby, appropriated for floating defenses for the Western rivers, to be expended, at the discretion of the President, by the Secretary of War or Secretary of the Navy, as he shall direct.

Approved January 9, 1862.

CHAP. XLIII.—AN ACT supplementary to an act entitled "An act to authorize the appointment of additional officers of the Navy," approved December twenty-fourth, eighteen hundred and sixty-one.

The Congress of the Confederate States of America do enact, That the President is authorized to appoint officers of the Regular Navy to any higher grade under the act above mentioned, without prejudice to their position under their original appointment.

Approved January 16, 1862.

NEW ORLEANS, LA., *January* 20, 1862.

Hon. J. P. BENJAMIN,
Secretary of War:

SIR: I have the honor to acknowledge the receipt of your "unofficial" of the 12th instant, and this evening, by Captain Montgomery, your note of the 13th. I fear I have gone almost too far with the Tennessee matter to withdraw.

On December 17 Major Rains wrote me that the plan proposed was acceptable to the President and yourself, and I authorized the parties to go to work at once, notifying you by telegraph and also by letter. The Tennessee was bought for $100,000, of which we are to guarantee one-half in case of capture. Saltpeter in Europe is 10 cents per pound, here 40 cents, and in case she brought us only 100 tons, we should save not less than $60,000; but by the terms of the proposed agreement we are to have half of her storage on the return voyage, which, in case of success, will net us a large amount. If it is impossible to obtain the necessary credit abroad, I may be able to make arrangements with parties here to make the purchases, we to pay them at such rate as, in case of success, to reimburse the $50,000 which we risk by way of guarantee. I inclose you a copy of a letter received from Major Rains to-night, which confirms me in my favorable view of the proposed plan. Please telegraph me on receipt of this, and say whether I shall make the best terms I can, taking it for granted that it will be impossible to obtain the necessary credits abroad. The party who offered to bring in 75 tons of powder, if we advance the money, under bonds, offers E. Gautherin & Co., of New Orleans, as bondsmen. I objected to the security, but he says their status is well known to you and to the President, and wished me to advise with you.

Mr. Lee, whom I sent to Texas for the Vanderbilt powder, reports that General Hébert had taken half of it without examination. Acting under orders from me, he examined 135 boxes of the remainder, rejecting 30 boxes as being some wet, some damp, and others lumpy. When he gets through with half, he will go to General Hébert to carry out your instructions with reference to the balance of the cargo. The part that passed inspection was shipped to me on the 13th instant from Beaumont, Tex., via New Iberia.

I was in Mississippi Sound yesterday; made a close reconnaissance of the enemy's fleet, and found twenty-four vessels at the island. Two of their steamers got under way and drove us back to Pass Christian. Biloxi is not and never has been occupied by the enemy. They came ashore with 60 men, staid for a few hours, and left. The reports about outrages and communications with the enemy are grossly exaggerated. With the Third Mississippi Regiment and a few launches I can do all that we propose; *i. e.*, prevent marauding parties from landing, negroes from escaping, or any communication with the enemy.

Governor Pettus, under authority from Richmond, is mustering in and sending here some companies rather poorly armed and equipped. I shall have to complete them from the Government stores in such manner as to make them effective. I have sent one of my staff to Jackson, to endeavor to make such arrangements with the governor as will conduce to some more systematic concert of action. Some of the State organizations allow more officers to a company than the Confederate law permits, and where the companies are first mustered into the State service and then transferred we are compelled to drop one or more of the officers. I had much rather send an officer from here to muster in the companies, as it saves trouble in the end.

If I do not need the $195,000 placed to my credit I will advise you at once.

I have to thank you for your prompt and considerate attention and assistance in my duties here. It gives me unbounded satisfaction.

Respectfully, your obedient servant,

M. LOVELL,
Major-General, C. S. Army.

[Inclosure.]

NASHVILLE, TENN., *January* 17, 1862.

"MY DEAR L.: I feel very anxious about a certain matter. The amounts received now are less than what they were two months since. It is absolutely necessary that we should receive supplies from other sources, and I trust the arrangements to that effect will be speedily put into operation. I am in a better position to know the situation of the Confederacy in the matter in question than any other person, and you will understand me when I urge the absolute necessity of increasing our store. It is in vain for one portion of the country to be placed in a secure state of defense and broad openings left at the other places. The safety of each part depends at last on the security of the whole. You may feel entirely safe from successful attack, but other vital points have not your resources, and their necessities must be looked after without delay. The Secretary gave me full powers to make and authorize any contract I might deem necessary in my department, but I have seen no prospect so promising wherever I have been as the one we spoke of. I trust you will bring your energy to assist in the matter. It is more vital to the country than anything else at this period."

[Indorsement.]

The "certain matter" referred to in the beginning of the above extract was the proposed plan for obtaining saltpeter, which I submitted to you, through Major Rains, in December.

M. L.

NEW ORLEANS ARSENAL, LA., *January* 24, 1862.

Lieut. Col. J. GORGAS,
Chief of Ordnance C. S. Army, Richmond:

COLONEL: I am instructed by Maj. Gen. M. Lovell to request that you please order from Nashville, Tenn., 10,000,000, or such a number as you can spare, of percussion musket caps, which are absolutely needed here, there being none on hand to complete the cartridges already made.

Very respectfully, your obedient servant,

RICHARD LAMBERT,
Military Storekeeper, Commanding.

WAR DEPARTMENT, C. S. A.,
Richmond, Va., January 27, 1862.

Maj. Gen. MANSFIELD LOVELL,
New Orleans, La.:

SIR: The overwhelming pressure of business in this Department causes some unavoidable delay in correspondence. I now acknowledge the receipt of your letters of 13th, 15th, 16th, and 17th instant.

1st. Your letter of the 13th instant disclosed to me the fact that, by some unaccountable hallucination, I used the name of General Trimble instead of that of General Ruggles in my letter of the 6th instant. My intention was to say that the President desired you to place General Ruggles in command of the Mississippi coast, and I congratulate myself that this strange error of mine has not produced any disastrous result. I have read in the same letter with great interest your plans for the defense of your department, and am rejoiced to find that your vigilance leaves no exposed point without protection. Your powder returns show less supply than I had hoped, but still sufficient, I think, to relieve us of apprehension till some of the supplies daily expected shall reach us from some quarter.

2d. You are authorized to use your own discretion in relation to the planing machine and lathe in the Belleville Iron Works. If the owners are unwilling to part with them by sale or hire, they must be impressed, if necessary for the public service, and on impressment you should give the owners the choice whether the impressment shall be by hire or purchase. If the owners wish, however, to use these machines themselves, I do not think the impressment would be justifiable.

3d. The map and letter by Colonel Davis were duly received, and I thought I had acknowledged their receipt some time since.

4th. In relation to the distribution of arms between war men and twelve-months' men, although as a general rule we desire the best arms given to the former, we do not intend to preclude you from the exercise of a sound discretion in any exceptional cases, such as you suggest.

5th. If you arrest a Federal officer as a spy he is to be put to death without the slightest hesitation, in accordance with the Articles of War. Tyler's case, to which you refer, was not that of a spy; he did not go to a city threatened with attack, nor for any hostile purpose; he went simply to see and bring away his wife, and it would have been a barbarous outrage to have considered or treated him as a spy.

6th. I have instructed General Joseph E. Johnston to open negotiations with McClellan, by flag of truce, for a general exchange of prisoners. As soon as I know the result I will try to relieve you of your prisoners.

7th. I have organized the two regiments, and made the nominations as proposed in your letter of the 17th instant.

I am, your obedient servant,

J. P. BENJAMIN,
Secretary of War.

GENERAL ORDERS, } HDQRS. DEPT. ALA. AND WEST FLA.,
No. 23. } *Near Pensacola, Fla., January 27, 1862.*

I. The command of Brig. Gen. J. M. Withers will in future be known as the Army of Mobile, to include all troops in and about that city and south of it. Brigadier-General Withers is specially charged with the defense of the coast from Perdido to Pascagoula Rivers.

II. Brig. Gen. L. P. Walker, P. A., is relieved from his present duties near Mobile, and is assigned to the command of all troops at and near Montgomery, where he will select a proper location and establish a depot for the instruction of new troops. In the selection of a site, the general will consult convenience for transportation, health, and economy.

III. Brig. Gen. A. H. Gladden, P. A., is relieved from duty with the Army of Pensacola, and will proceed to Mobile, Ala., and report to Brig. Gen. J. M. Withers, commanding Army of Mobile, for duty.

IV. Col. J. B. Villepigue, Thirty-sixth Regiment Georgia Volunteers, is announced as chief of artillery and engineers on the staff of the commanding general, in place of Capt. Wm. R. Boggs, C. S. Engineers, resigned.

By command of Major-General Bragg:

GEO. G. GARNER,
Assistant Adjutant-General.

GENERAL ORDERS, No. 5. } HEADQUARTERS ARMY OF PENSACOLA,
Near Pensacola, Fla., January 27, 1862.

* * * * * * *

III. Brig. Gen. J. K. Jackson is assigned to the command of the First Brigade, and will immediately relieve Brigadier-General Gladden.

IV. Brig. Gen. Samuel Jones, Provisional Army, having reported for duty, is assigned to the command of the Army of Pensacola. The regret of the major-general at yielding the immediate command of this army, which he has exercised with so much pleasure and pride, is lessened by a knowledge that he devolves it on a tried veteran, every way worthy of confidence.

By command of Major-General Bragg:

GEO. G. GARNER,
Assistant Adjutant-General.

HEADQUARTERS DEPARTMENT NO. 1,
New Orleans, La., January 28, 1862.

Hon. J. P. BENJAMIN,
Secretary of War:

SIR: I have the honor to acknowledge the receipt of your letter of the 19th instant, by Captain Townsend, relative to the plan for floating defenses on the Western waters.

The fourteen vessels named in your telegram were seized and appraised by a board consisting of Messrs. Bogart, Stephenson, Frost, Grinnel, Milliken, and the naval constructor, Porter. Several of the vessels were costly and could be replaced by others equally well adapted to the contemplated service at much less expense. I have therefore caused those changes to be made, reducing the value of the seizures from $900,000 to $620,000, and the ships we have are as good, or better, for what we want, than those named. The parties owning these ships are anxious to be paid at once, as in some instances agreements had been made for their sale. Are these appraised values to be paid out of the appropriation of $1,000,000 made by act of January 9, 1862, or is that money to be expended for altering, fitting up, payment, and subsistence of officers and men? If the latter, how shall I pay the owners, who are clamorous for their money? If the former, $1,000,000 is not enough. The fourteen vessels named in your telegram would alone have cost nearly that sum.

I think it advisable that the captains should recommend to the President some competent person to have general control of the fleet in fitting it out, and making general rules and orders for its control and management. Fourteen Mississippi River captains and pilots will never agree about anything after they once get under way. Moreover, as each ship will carry one gun, there will be some necessary arrangements for munitions of war, signals, &c.

They have already got to work upon some of the ships. I will send you a list of their names, with valuations, as soon as I receive the official report of the appraisers.

I sent Mr. Lee to Texas for the Vanderbilt powder. General Hébert, acting, as he says, under necessity, had taken half the powder, and, taking into consideration all the circumstances, of their distance, their want of local means, and other facilities, I think it is about as well that he has done so. The other half is *en route* for this point, and will arrive in a week or ten days. Some forty boxes are wet, but these can be worked over at our mills.

The securities proposed by Mr. Angoman (Charles Koch & Co.) have withdrawn their names, as they consider it impossible for him to bring in the 75 tons of powder.

The steamer Calhoun, on her way here from Havana, with 50,000 pounds of powder, 400 bags of coffee, &c., was abandoned last week near the mouth of the river most unnecessarily and timidly, and fell into the hands of the enemy. She will prove a great pest on the coast, as she is very fast and of light draught. Her crew tried to set her on fire, but in their fright and haste they failed to do so effectively. It was an unfortunate piece of business.

I sent General Johnston, after the defeat of Crittenden, 200,000 cartridges, 400 double-barreled shot-guns, and 16 tons of lead, as he telegraphed me that he was out of that article. I will also send up to him the five Mississippi companies that Governor Pettus sent me for coast defense when it was understood that General Polk had declined to send back the Third Mississippi Regiment as soon as I can have them put through the measles; a process which they are now undergoing, one-half of them now being sick.

In your letter of the 6th instant you indicated particularly the duties which it was proposed to assign to General Trimble, but he has never made his appearance here as yet. The nature of the proposed duty requires a young and active man, but I will gladly receive any assistance that you can spare. General Cooper telegraphs, in reply to my question, that no order has been issued transferring General Trimble to this department. There must be some mistake about it.

I beg that you will advise me at your early convenience as to the time and means of paying for the steamers seized here, as the parties annoy me considerably.

Respectfully, your obedient servant,
M. LOVELL,
Major-General, Commanding.

RICHMOND, VA., *January* 28, 1862.

General MANSFIELD LOVELL,
New Orleans, La.:

Your letter of the 20th received. Make the best arrangements you can for the Tennessee. It is impossible to put credits abroad, but we can make any proper advances on this side.

J. P. BENJAMIN,
Secretary of War.

NEW ORLEANS, LA., *January* 30, 1862.

Hon. J. P. BENJAMIN:

Can the Navy Department give us any cutlasses and pistols for river flotilla; if so, how many?

M. LOVELL.

RICHMOND, VA., *January* 30, 1862.

General MANSFIELD LOVELL,
New Orleans, La.:

Remittance of $195,000 is now on the way to you to pay for powder. I write to-day.

J. P. BENJAMIN,
Secretary of War.

WAR DEPARTMENT,
Richmond, Va., January 30, 1862.

Maj. Gen. MANSFIELD LOVELL,
New Orleans, La.:

SIR: I have your letters of the 20th and 22d instant.* I sent you a dispatch in relation to the Tennessee, and now repeat the authority to make the best bargain you can with the owners for sharing in the adventure, so that we may have half of the return tonnage for saltpeter. Let me, however, caution you on one point. If they have all the profits of an outward cargo of cotton, we ought not to be expected to bear any of the risk of going out; if we take half of the risk, we must have half of the profits. If we are to share only in the return cargo, we must only share the return risk.

Your proposal of Charles Koch & Co. for sureties for the contract for powder is quite satisfactory. Before getting your letter I had drawn in your favor for $195,000 to cover cost of 75 tons of powder, and the money must now be in your hands. As, however, your advance is only $125,000, you will have a surplus of $70,000, most of which you will require for settlement for powder per Vanderbilt.

I got a letter from Mr. Sumner, proposing to receive in part payment of the powder per Vanderbilt $120,000 in 8 per cent. bonds. This suits us much better than issuing Treasury notes. I accordingly drew a warrant on the Treasury in your favor for $127,500, of which $120,000 in 8 per cent. bonds and $7,500 in Treasury notes. In settling with the owners of the Vanderbilt powder, therefore, you will give them the bonds, and the balance only in Treasury notes.

Your obedient servant,

J. P. BENJAMIN,
Secretary of War.

---

* That of 22d not found.

Abstract from return of Department No. 1, commanded by Maj. Gen. Mansfield Lovell, for January, 1862.

Troops.	Present for duty.		Aggregate present.	Aggregate present and absent.	Artillery.	
	Officers.	Men.			Heavy.	Field.
Forts Jackson and Saint Philip	26	682	838	892	112	5
Fort Pike, La	8	193	245	277	32	......
Fort Livingston, La	9	248	275	294	12	4
Fort at Little Temple, La	3	80	83	96	......	......
Camp Benjamin, New Orleans	204	3,231	4,060	4,520	......	6
Arsenal, New Orleans	2	70	79	81	......	......
Battalion Mississippi Volunteers, New Orleans	11	124	260	291	......	......
Baton Rouge Barracks	1	4	5	5	......	......
Fort Guion	8	93	110	140	2	......
District of Lake Borgne	17	398	484	513	......	......
District of Berwick	42	807	943	1,040	......	......
Fort Quitman	5	137	150	157	......	......
Bay Saint Louis, Miss	34	594	750	1,003	......	......
Handsborough, Miss	24	386	532	896	......	......
Calcasieu Pass, La	2	68	83	91	......	......
Total	396	7,115	8,897	10,296	158	15

Abstract from field return of the Department of Alabama and West Florida, commanded by Maj. Gen. Braxton Bragg, February 1, 1862.

Troops.	Present for duty.		Aggregate present.	Aggregate present and absent.
	Officers.	Men.		
Army of Pensacola, Brig. Gen. Sam. Jones, commanding	377	5,254	6,790	8,150
Army of Mobile, Brig. Gen. J. M. Withers, commanding	440	6,777	9,278	10,056
Grand total	817	12,031	16,068	18,206

Organization of troops in the Department of Alabama and West Florida, commanded by Maj. Gen. Braxton Bragg, February 1, 1862.

Army of Pensacola.

Brig. Gen. SAM. JONES, commanding.

1st Alabama.
17th Alabama.
1st Florida.
5th Georgia.
36th Georgia.
1st Louisiana.
5th Mississippi.
8th Mississippi.
9th Mississippi.
10th Mississippi.
27th Mississippi.
Independent Alabama mounted companies (2).
Independent Florida mounted company.
Company Alabama State artillery.
Robertson's company light artillery.
Detachment C. S. Marines.

Army of Mobile.

Brig. Gen. J. M. WITHERS, commanding.

2d Alabama.
18th Alabama.
19th Alabama.
20th Alabama.
21st Alabama.
22d Alabama.
23d Alabama.
24th Alabama.
25th Alabama.
2d Alabama (Battalion).
Alabama infantry (1 company).
Battalion Mississippi volunteers.
Mississippi infantry (1 company).
Alabama Mounted volunteers (6 companies).
First Battalion Alabama Artillery.
Second Battalion Alabama Light Artillery.

HEADQUARTERS DEPARTMENT NO. 1,
New Orleans, La., February 1, 1862.

Hon. J. P. BENJAMIN,
Secretary of War:

SIR: I received a telegram from you yesterday stating that $195,000 was now on the way here for me to pay for powder. The fact that this is the exact amount placed to my credit already, in answer to my request for money to carry out the arrangement with the steamer Tennessee for arms and powder, induces me to write and say that I have already entered into the arrangement with the Tennessee, and that this sum is not available to pay for the powder by the Vanderbilt. It may be that the coincidence is accidental; but I think it safest to advise you. I will send on a copy of my agreement with the owners of the Tennessee in a few days, by which you will see that we got $200,000 in Havre by depositing $100,000 here and insuring half of the ship ($50,000) in case of capture. On the return cargo we take the risk of first cost and half the value of the ship in case of capture, the powder to be delivered at 100 per cent. and the arms at 50 per cent. above invoice price. As a money transaction I have calculated that it results in our favor largely more than in risk.

Respectfully, your obedient servant,

M. LOVELL,
Major-General, Commanding.

HDQRS. DEPARTMENT ALABAMA AND WEST FLORIDA,
Near Pensacola, Fla., February 1, 1862.

ADJUTANT-GENERAL C. S. ARMY,
Richmond, Va.:

SIR: As you will perceive by my orders [February 27], on the arrival of Brigadier-General Jones, delayed some days on the route by sickness, the immediate command of the troops here was transferred to him. This will enable me to devote more time to other parts of my command, which, I regret to say, sadly need supervision. From General Jones' high character as an officer and his experience as an artillerist there is every reason to hope for entire success in his new command, which is in fine order, though somewhat disorganized at present by re-enlistments and furloughs.

Brigadier-General Anderson having been relieved, another to command his brigade is necessary here. My previous recommendations of Cols. J. E. Slaughter, and J. B. Villepigue, P. A., and J. Patton Anderson, First Regiment Florida Volunteers, are brought to your notice. The promotion of Col. S. A. M. Wood, Seventh Regiment Alabama Volunteers, over Colonel Anderson, his senior, and much his superior as a soldier, has been very mortifying to the latter. Colonel Wood, for his opportunities, is a very good soldier, and no doubt made a very favorable impression in Kentucky with his well-drilled and well-equipped regiments; but Colonel Anderson was more deserving of the honor. To enable me to progress at all in my labors at Mobile it was necessary to dispose of Brigadier-General Walker, whose rank rendered him an incumbrance. You will see he was sent to Montgomery, to command the unarmed men concentrated near that place. I have no idea he will be of any service; but he can do less harm there. To command his important brigade at Mobile Brigadier-General Gladden was ordered to report to General Withers. From his energy, zeal, great efficiency as a disciplinarian and infantry instructor, an indomitable will to execute what he knows to be my purpose, I hope for the happiest results. Brig. Gen. J. K. Jackson, at whose prompt appointment I felt greatly gratified, replaces General Gladden here, and will fill his place with credit.

I shall in a few days go over to Mobile, to remain some two or three weeks, with a view of putting things in a better condition there; and if necessary shall assume the immediate command, though not with a view of making it my permanent headquarters. Such action might look like a violation of the right of rank in case of General Withers; but, as in the case of General Walker, if the public good, which must be paramount to all other considerations now, demands it, my action will be prompt and decided. I trust, however, that my presence, and the services of Brigadier-General Gladden, with the excellent staff he carried from here, strengthened by the approval the Department has so far extended to my exertions, will fully accomplish the desired object.

Recent advices from Ship Island represent the enemy as having some 8,000 or 10,000 men, but making no preparations for a descent on us at this time. Expeditions are apparently sent from there to other points, and probably the one to Cedar Keys was of the number. Should no move against us take place in the next four weeks, I shall look upon their force as merely intended to hold us in check by threatening our positions, and would recommend the withdrawal of a portion of the oldest and best forces in this department for service elsewhere. Could such an assurance be given, re-enlistments in our twelve-months' men would be greatly stimulated.

We continue to receive supplies from Havana by small vessels running the blockade, both here and at Mobile. A good invoice of some very essential medicines was obtained last week by an arrival here.

I am, sir, very respectfully, your obedient servant,

BRAXTON BRAGG,
Major-General, Commanding.

[FEBRUARY 2, 1862.—Requisition made by the Confederate Government upon the State of Louisiana for five and a half "war regiments." Requisition appears in Series IV, Vol. I.]

HEADQUARTERS DEPARTMENT NO. 1,
New Orleans, La., February 4, 1862.

Hon. J. P. BENJAMIN,
Secretary of War:

SIR: On the 30th ultimo your telegram stated that $195,000 was on its way to me to pay for powder. When the drafts arrived one was for $120,000 and the other for $7,500, instead of $75,000, the sum necessary to make up the total stated by you. I have no doubt that it was the intention to make it the latter sum, as the estimated value of the cargo of the Vanderbilt was more than $180,000, which, with the transportation to this point, would bring it up to the sum named by you. As General Hébert has taken half of the powder, I shall not pay for the whole until I hear from him what part of his half was damaged. In the part received by me there were forty boxes more or less damaged.

The draft for $120,000 was drawn upon the Treasurer at Richmond, and Mr. Guirot will not, of course, pay it here. I return it to Mr. Elmore to-day.

Respectfully, your obedient servant,

M. LOVELL,
Major-General, Commanding.

O'BANNONVILLE, *February* 6, 1862.

General SAMUEL JONES:

SIR: A large naval expedition left Hampton Roads on 4th with additional land forces for the Gulf; supposed destination Mobile and Pensacola. Suspend all furloughs, and prepare to receive them.

BRAXTON BRAGG.

HEADQUARTERS DEPARTMENT NO. 1,
New Orleans, La., February 6, 1862.

Hon. J. P. BENJAMIN,
Secretary of War:

SIR: I have the honor to acknowledge the receipt of your letters of the 27th and 30th ultimo.

1st. With regard to General Ruggles' assignment to the duty of caring for the Mississippi coast, I think it would be exceedingly unadvisable. His services in organizing a brigade of five regiments as a movable force to any point of the department are more valuable than they would be on the coast. Neither his age nor his rank are exactly in conformity with outpost duty in command of two regiments. He would feel mortified, I am sure, at such an assignment. I can manage matters better by leaving them as at present. With 10,000 men in this department, and a long extent of coast to guard, I would recommend the appointment of a brigadier-general from Mississippi for duty on that part of the line. I have but two here, while in the Department of Mobile (General Bragg's) I learn there are not less than five or six officers of that grade.

2d. I have just received the first installment of powder by the Vanderbilt, and on testing it I found it much below range. In justice to the service it should be worked over again. I will probably reject it; certainly at $2 per pound.

3d. The Federal prisoners, 493 in number, will leave to-day for Salisbury, N. C., pursuant to telegraphic order from General Cooper.

4th. I look daily for appointments of officers in the new regiments. Major Lovell's resignation has been accepted, but not his new appointment. As he is constantly on important duty, giving orders, &c., it is a little awkward, but he continues at work. At the written request of Captains Montgomery and Townsend I have placed him in charge of the ordnance and disbursements of their expedition.

5th. After careful search and inquiry we can find nothing of Capt. W. F. McLean, alluded to in your letter of January 27. When found I will act as advised by you.

6th. Your impressions about the arrangement with the steamer Tennessee are not quite correct. We take no risk on the cotton at all, but guarantee $50,000 on the ship in case of capture on outward voyage; and in case she arrives in Havre (the chances of which are largely in our favor) we receive $50,000 in the shape of exchange, as the parties buy for us there $200,000 worth of arms and munitions. We thus risk the loss of $50,000 for the certain receipt of that amount in case of success, as it would cost us that sum to get a credit of $200,000 in France. On the return we take a risk of $50,000 on the ship and $200,000 on the cargo; but the prices, if delivered, are so arranged that in case of success we should save more than $300,000 on present prices of arms and powder.

7th. I had no knowledge of the arrangement with Mr. Sumner about the bonds, and therefore got the draft for $120,000 cashed here. No bonds came to me, nothing but two drafts; one for $7,500, on the Assistant Treasurer here, the other for $120,000, on the Treasurer at Richmond. There must have been a mistake on his part in carrying out your views.

Respectfully, your obedient servant,

M. LOVELL,
Major-General, Commanding.

WAR DEPARTMENT, C. S. A.,
Richmond, February 8, 1862.

Maj. Gen. MANSFIELD LOVELL,
New Orleans:

SIR: The President desires that as soon as possible on receipt of this letter you dispatch 5,000 men to Columbus to re-enforce that point, sorely threatened by largely superior forces. The menacing aspect of affairs in Kentucky has induced the withdrawal from points, not in immediate danger, of every man that can be spared to prevent the enemy from penetrating into Tennessee or passing Columbus. A draft has been made on General Bragg; four regiments have been ordered from Virginia, together with several batteries, and with the number now required from your command we hope to stem the tide till the new levies called out from the State shall be in condition to take the field.

New Orleans is to be defended from above by defeating the enemy at Columbus; the forces now withdrawn from you are for the defense of your own command, and the exigencies of the public defense allow us no alternative.

Your obedient servant,

J. P. BENJAMIN,
Secretary of War.

WAR DEPARTMENT, C. S. A.,
Richmond, Va., February 8, 1862.

Maj. Gen. BRAXTON BRAGG,
Mobile, Ala.:

SIR: The President desires that you will as soon as possible send to Knoxville all the troops you can spare from your command without immediate danger, and he hopes that the number will be at least four regiments. The condition of affairs in Kentucky and Tennessee demands from us the most vigorous effort for defense, and General A. S. Johnston is so heavily outnumbered, that it is scarcely possible for him to maintain his whole line without large additional re-enforcements. We have ordered to his aid four regiments from Virginia and 5,000 men from New Orleans, and by thus subtracting something from other points, where the pressure is not so great, we hope to enable him to defend his lines until the new levies ordered from all the States shall be in condition to take the field.

I am happy to inform you that the President has ordered the nomination of J. Patton Anderson to be brigadier-general, as well as that of Colonel Chalmers. There was no reason for any sensitiveness on the part of Colonel Anderson, as the nomination of Col. S. A. M. Wood was not made with any reference to the comparative merits of these gentlemen, but solely from the portentous circumstances that the services of a brigadier were urgently needed at the point where Colonel Wood was serving and not so with you. The President and myself have both a very high opinion of the merits and soldierly qualities of Colonel Anderson.

We got in a small cargo the other day on the Southern coast with 6,000 rifles and 50,000 pounds of powder, together with other valuable munitions. I mention this, as the supply of powder will enable us to furnish Generals Lee and Huger without drawing on any that may be received in New Orleans or made in Nashville. I hope ere this you have had your supply replenished from New Orleans.

Please telegraph me what troops and what number you will dispatch to Knoxville as soon as you receive this letter.

Your obedient servant,

J. P. BENJAMIN,
Secretary of War.

RICHMOND, VA., *February* 8, 1862.

Maj. Gen. MANSFIELD LOVELL,
New Orleans, La.:

I have written you to-day, by the President's direction, to send immediately 5,000 of your best-equipped men to Columbus, to re-enforce General Beauregard.

J. P. BENJAMIN,
Secretary of War.

MOBILE, *February* 10, 1862.

Hon. J. P. BENJAMIN:

SIR: I send a regiment to-day to Decatur, Ala., to save our railroad bridge.

If Farragut and Butler are destined for this point my force is too weak to spare more.

BRAXTON BRAGG.

[Confidential.]

HDQRS. DEPARTMENT ALABAMA AND WEST FLORIDA,
Mobile, February 12, 1862.

General SAMUEL JONES,
Commanding Army of Pensacola:

Our necessities are so great that we have been compelled to make large drafts on your command and may have to reduce you still more. The President has called on me for four regiments for Tennessee, and, though I am not yet decided to send them, you must be prepared to spare one more, the Ninth Mississippi, in case I do.

To prepare you for this, and also to secure you from danger by too great a dispersion of your command, I deem it prudent to withdraw from Deer Point all the force there except, say, two companies, to act as a mere picket, in conjunction with your gunboats. A small detachment of mounted men, too, would be well there. Your largest gunboat (Bradford) should be at or near this position every night, to bring off this small force in case of a heavy attack. Withdraw the two guns, one 8-inch and one 10-inch, and send both to this place, with carriages and implements, at once.

I have information, considered perfectly reliable, that the enemy will attack this place by a large fleet of gunboats in a very short time. Forts Gaines and Morgan, 3 miles apart, cannot prevent their entrance of a dark night, and the whole width is open to them—9 feet water from fort to fort. We are erecting some batteries around the city and one at Blakely, to keep them off in case they enter, and preserve our railroad connection with you. I would abandon the hospital at Deer Point and send the sick daily to the hospital in Pensacola, putting Surgeon Gamble, Florida regiment, in charge. Surgeon Flewellen, Fifth Georgia, should go on and join his regiment, which will go to East Tennessee as soon as the people of the country in North Alabama can be rallied to the defense of their own homes.

General A. S. Johnston, from whom I heard yesterday, feels confident of holding Fort Donelson and driving the enemy from the Tennessee soon. Our disaster at Roanoke Island is much more serious.

Yours, respectfully and truly,

BRAXTON BRAGG,
Major-General.

HEADQUARTERS DEPARTMENT NO. 1,
New Orleans, La., February 12, 1862.

Hon. J. P. BENJAMIN,
Secretary of War:

SIR: I received yesterday your dispatch directing me to send 5,000 men to Columbus. I have already sent one (the Thirteenth), and shall move five more regiments in two days (Ruggles' entire brigade) with a field battery. I shall order General Ruggles to go on in command of them, and shall go to work at once to endeavor to organize a force for the defense of the interior lines from the volunteers and militia of this city and State. Unfortunately, the legislature passed a law at its late session reorganizing the whole militia, which has to be done at a very inconvenient moment, but I am in hopes that most of the volunteeers will elect their company and field officers on the instant, so that we shall soon have a force on hand. I regret the necessity of sending away my only force at this particular juncture, and feel sure that it will create a great panic here, but will do my best to restore confidence by a show of strength.

You have never sent me any orders about the distribution of the Vanderbilt's powder. General Hébert has one-half, and a part of the remainder arrived here lately. On proof, it was found to lack 15 per cent. of saltpeter; but I can work it all over in twelve days and make it into good powder. We shall have about 40,000 pounds. I gave Commodore Hollins 3,500 pounds of my own stock to go up the river, and General Bragg has sent to me for some of that by the Vanderbilt. I shall make it go as far as I can.

Respectfully, your obedient servant,

M. LOVELL,
Major-General, Commanding.

P. S.—I borrowed from the Navy two launches, armed with one gun each, which I manned with crews from the Third Mississippi Regiment, and stationed one in Bay Saint Louis and one in Biloxi Bay. The Secretary of the Navy requires that they be returned to Mobile, whence they came. Such accessories are very necessary on that coast, and I should like to have authority to use any funds that may be in my hands to construct two more, to replace those I have. I can get no assistance from the Navy, as they have no funds.

HDQRS. DEPARTMENT ALABAMA AND WEST FLORIDA,
Mobile, Ala., February 15, 1862.

Hon. J. P. BENJAMIN,
Secretary of War, Richmond, Va.:

SIR: You will excuse me, at this time of great danger to our cause, for presuming to depart from my usual course and to offer a few suggestions on our future military policy.

1. Our means and resources are too much scattered. The protection of persons and property, as such, should be abandoned, and all our means applied to the Government and the cause. Important strategic points only should be held. All means not necessary to secure these should be concentrated for a heavy blow upon the enemy where we can best assail him. Kentucky is now that point. On the Gulf we should only hold New Orleans, Mobile, and Pensacola; all other points, the whole of Texas and Florida, should be abandoned, and our means there made available for other service. A small loss of property would result from their occupation by the enemy; but our military strength would not be lessened thereby, whilst the enemy would be weakened by dispersion. We could then beat him in detail, instead of the reverse. The same remark applies to our Atlantic seaboard. In Missouri the same rule can be applied to a great extent. Deploring the misfortunes of that gallant people, I can but think their relief must reach them through Kentucky.

2. The want of success with our artillery everywhere is deplorable; but I believe it can be explained and remedied. This arm requires knowledge, which nothing but study and experience combined can give. Unfortunately, many of our higher officers and a larger proportion of our men consider there is no duty to be done in this contest but to fight. Gallant to a fault, they ignore preparation, and exhaust their energies and time in clamoring for this fight. Calamitous results teach them too late the unfortunate error.

The enemy's light-draught gunboats require of us different defenses for our assailable points. An old-fashioned artillery will not answer. We must have long range guns to reach them, and they must be properly mounted, supplied, and served. Our 8 and 10 inch shell guns have my preference. The rifle gun I consider yet an experiment, not a success, except the light field piece—bronze; still I use them as an auxiliary. Whenever the enemy has brought his shell guns against our lighter metal, we have had to yield. But at Pensacola we crippled and drove off two of his largest and heaviest armed ships with only two 8-inch guns in an open sand battery, served, it is true, by brave men, thoroughly instructed and directed by a competent artillery officer.

We must then oppose the enemy's heavy metal by the same, and put competent men to mount, supply, and serve our own guns. If we have not the guns, it is better to yield the positions than to sacrifice our men and means in a futile attempt at defense. And when you have the guns, it is equally futile if they are handled by incompetent troops. From reports which reach us, it would appear that at least half our guns are rendered useless after the first hour, from different accidents, not attributable to the enemy, but to a want of knowledge, skill, or attention on our own part.

We have the right men, and the crisis upon us demands they should be in the right places. Our little army at Pensacola could furnish you hundreds of instructors competent to build batteries, mount guns, and teach the use of them. Our commanders are learning by bitter experience the necessity of teaching their troops; but a want of instructors is sadly felt.

Pardon me if I have been too free in the expression of my feelings and opinions, and attribute any error to an overzeal in the great cause we all have at heart.

I am, sir, very respectfully, your obedient servant,

BRAXTON BRAGG,
Major-General, Commanding.

RICHMOND, VA., *February* 16, 1862.

General MANSFIELD LOVELL,
New Orleans:

Your letter of the 6th instant received. Your course in relation to General Ruggles approved. If you have not yet sent the troops to Columbus, as advised by my dispatch, let them stop at Memphis, and send telegram so informing General A. S. Johnston. The great line of attack by the Cumberland River may make it necessary to send the troops eastward from Memphis instead of sending them to Columbus.

J. P. BENJAMIN,
Secretary of War.

RICHMOND, VA., *February* 16, 1862.

General MANSFIELD LOVELL,
New Orleans:

Send every musket by the Victoria at once to Grand Junction, subject to orders of General A. S. Johnston. Send an agent with them to force them forward by express. Inform General Johnston of what you have done and of the kind of arms and such details as will enable him to prepare ammunition for them in advance. Inform me of what you do and the number of arms sent.

J. P. BENJAMIN,
Secretary of War.

RICHMOND, VA., *February* 18, 1862.

General BRAXTON BRAGG,
Mobile:

Your dispatch just received.* Commence immediately the movement you suggest for aiding General Johnston. I will send you our views and plans by messenger to-morrow.

J. P. BENJAMIN,
Secretary of War.

---

* See p. 894.

WAR DEPARTMENT, C. S. A.,
Richmond, Va., February 18, 1862.

Maj. Gen. BRAXTON BRAGG,
Mobile, Ala.:

SIR: The heavy blow which has been inflicted on us by the recent operations in Kentucky and Tennessee renders necessary a change in our whole plan of campaign, as suggested in your dispatch of this date, just received.

We had had in contemplation the necessity of abandoning the seaboard in order to defend the Tennessee line, which is vital to our safety; but I am still without any satisfactory information from General A. S. Johnston. I know not the nature nor extent of the disaster at Fort Donelson, nor the disposition of his troops, nor his plans, and am only aware of the very large loss we have suffered in prisoners through the dispatches in the Northern papers.

However, all this is beside the question. The decision is made, and the President desires that you proceed as promptly as possible to withdraw your forces from Pensacola and Mobile and hasten to the defense of the Tennessee line. In doing this, of course the first care will be to save, as far as possible, all our artillery and munitions of war. It is not feasible, perhaps, to save all the artillery, but the munitions are invaluable to us.

It is not proposed to leave any force at all at Pensacola—a weak garrison would inevitably be captured—but it is deemed advisable to leave an effective garrison in the forts in Mobile Harbor and provide an ample supply of food for them. The continuance of the occupation of the forts would probably defer for some time a movement against Mobile, and it is possible might prevent the capture of that city; but the risk of its capture must be run by us.

All the Confederate forces in Mobile, as well as those in Pensacola, are to be moved as rapidly as possible to the Tennessee line, and by the time you can reach the Memphis and Charleston Railroad we will be able to determine towards what point they are to move.

We suppose it will be necessary to abandon Columbus and fall back to Island No. 10, or possibly to Memphis. Five thousand men have been ordered from New Orleans to the latter point. Until we hear from General Johnston, however, it will not be possible to determine upon this retrograde movement from Columbus. It is almost certain that he has agreed with General Beauregard upon the movements now to be made; but we grope in the dark here, and this uncertainty renders our own counsels undecided and prevents that promptness of action which the emergency requires. Enough, however, is known to satisfy us that without additional supplies of arms we cannot hold our entire exposed coast and frontier, and we must withdraw from the defense of the whole Gulf coast except New Orleans. I shall order all troops from Eastern Florida also to Tennessee. At Savannah an immediate attack is anticipated, and it is perhaps best to endeavor to give the enemy a decisive repulse there before withdrawing the troops at that point.

Your obedient servant,
J. P. BENJAMIN,
Secretary of War.

NEW ORLEANS, LA., *February* 21, 1862.

Hon. J. P. BENJAMIN:

There are but 150 guns and 20,000 pounds of powder on the Victoria. Have sent four regiments to Corinth.

M. LOVELL.

NEW ORLEANS, LA., *February* 21, 1862.

Hon. J. P. BENJAMIN:

The steamer Miramon has arrived, with 20,000 pounds of powder and 400 guns.

M. LOVELL.

MOBILE, ALA., *February* 22, 1862.

Hon. J. P. BENJAMIN:

Dispatch 18th received this evening. Railroads washed away. Prompt movement impossible.

BRAXTON BRAGG.

RICHMOND, VA., *February* 23, 1862.

General MANSFIELD LOVELL,
New Orleans, La.:

Seize all the powder on the Victoria and Miramon, paying for it $2 per pound, if of full proof, and making a ratable deduction if not proof. Send 20,000 pounds of cannon powder here by special agent, with instructions to force it through without an hour's delay.

J. P. BENJAMIN,
Secretary of War.

WAR DEPARTMENT, C. S. A.,
Richmond, Va., February 23, 1862.

Maj. Gen. MANSFIELD LOVELL,
New Orleans, La.:

SIR: I am in arrears with my correspondence, but the pressure on this Department is so intense that I cannot always be punctual. I have your letters of the 28th ultimo and 6th and 12th instant. I await your returns of the list and appraisement of the steamers prepared for the defense of the Mississippi River. I will then take immediate measures for payment. Pray let me know immediately on receipt of this, and by telegraph, if necessary, when the boats will be ready, and if they have full crews and their armament; also the names of commanders, &c.

2d. The change you have made in regard to General Ruggles is fully approved. The orders for the defense of the Mississippi coast were issued against my judgment, but the urgency of the members from that State on the President was so great that it was not politic to refuse at the time to gratify their wish. Events have shown how unreasonable was their demand, and we must dismiss all idea of scattering our forces in defense of unimportant points and concentrate them at vital lines.

3d. The appointments of the officers in the new regiments are all complete, but the number submitted to Congress and confirmed at the last session was so great that I am not yet able to send them all. They are confirmed, however, and you can assign to them their commands.

4th. I am very much pleased with your arrangement about the Tennessee, and hope she has got out safely.

5th. You are authorized to use any funds in your hands for the construction of two launches, to replace those borrowed from the Navy, for guarding the Mississippi coast.

6th. I dispatched to-day to impress all powder by Miramon and Victoria. I do not want you to let an ounce of powder, any arms, or munitions of war escape you at any time. They are a matter of life and death to us, and scarcely any price is too much to pay till our people are armed, although, of course, I desire to save every dollar we can.

I inclose you a letter for General Hébert, which you will please forward by special express. I leave it open, that you may understand the policy of the Government.

Your obedient servant,

J. P. BENJAMIN,
Secretary of War.

[Inclosure.]

WAR DEPARTMENT C. S. A.,
Richmond, Va., February 23, 1862.

Brig. Gen. P. O. HÉBERT,
Galveston, Tex.:

SIR: Our recent disaster in Tennessee has greatly exposed our line of communication with the West, and the importance of this line is so great, that it must be held at any sacrifice. You are therefore instructed at once to send forward to Little Rock, there to report to Maj. Gen. Earl Van Dorn, all the troops in your command, for the defense of the coast, except such as are necessary to man your batteries.

No invasion of Texas is deemed probable, but if any occurs its effects must be hazarded, and our entire forces must be thrown towards the Mississippi, for the defense of that river and of the Memphis and Charleston Railroad.

I do not desire that you withdraw such troops as you may have on the Rio Grande or western frontier, but only the troops you may have gathered for defending the Gulf coast. If at any point where you have batteries you deem there is danger of losing the guns by the withdrawal of the land forces, you will remove the guns; but the troops are to be pushed forward with all possible rapidity to Little Rock by such routes as you deem best.

I am, your obedient servant,

J. P. BENJAMIN,
Secretary of War.

NEW ORLEANS, *February* 26, 1862.

Hon. J. P. BENJAMIN:

Raising war troops is extremely difficult and slow. If Beauregard's need of re-enforcements be as great as we here consider it, and you will accept volunteers for that special service for a few months, I can send him relief immediately. Answer quickly,* and state shortest time.

THO. O. MOORE.

EXECUTIVE OFFICE,
New Orleans, La., February 26, 1862.

His Excellency JEFFERSON DAVIS,
President of the Confederate States, Richmond, Va.:

SIR: This letter will be delivered to you by Mr. William Henderson, a citizen of this place, and a gentleman of probity, integrity, and excel-

* Answered March 1, p. 837.

lent standing. I have deputed him as a special messenger to place in your hands a memorial from the Executive Sub-committee of a Committee of Safety appointed by the city council to render such aid as it may be able to the State and Confederate authorities in this department. I refer you to the memorial itself for its design and to Mr. Henderson for any explanations you may desire not embodied in the memorial.

I cannot suppose that your excellency has been fully apprised of the evils which the memorial presents to your attention and consideration, and I most earnestly recommend it to you. Your excellency will no doubt appreciate the necessity for immediate action to preserve not only the dignity and credit of the Navy Department, but also to provide such defenses as we are in absolute and immediate need of.

Citizens as well as the incorporated banks of the city are generous in their support of the Government, and I have no fears that this generosity will be abused.

I am, sir, with great respect, your obedient servant,

THO. O. MOORE,
Governor of Louisiana.

[Inclosure.]

NEW ORLEANS, LA., *February* 26, 1862.

To the PRESIDENT OF THE CONFEDERATE STATES:

SIR: In the present disturbed condition of our country it has been deemed expedient by our city council to appoint a committee of some sixty persons, to be styled the Committee of Safety.

The object of said committee is to aid and co-operate with the State and Government authorities in rendering this department as complete and effectual as possible. The committee is composed of gentlemen of standing and influence, and who have appointed the undersigned their executive committee, and who are not insensible of the labors and responsibilities placed upon them. They feel that your excellency will not be offended at their desire to co-operate with the constitutional authorities in this our struggle for liberty and independence.

They find, from investigation, that the naval department at this station, as far as finances are concerned, is in a most deplorable condition, retarding by this course manufactures of all kinds for that department; also preventing the enlisting of men for that branch of the public service.

The undersigned committee have been led to believe that your excellency could not be aware of the extent to which the naval department at this station has been reduced.

They therefore beg leave respectfully to represent some of the bad effects which will naturally and certainly follow in case this defect is not promptly remedied, by placing an adequate amount of funds at the disposal of that department to liquidate its present indebtedness and provide for future contingencies.

The present outstanding indebtedness, judging from facts placed before this committee, cannot be less than $600,000 or $800,000. A large portion of this is owing to the founderies for shells, fuses, &c., to the machine-shops, draymen, &c. Many of the bills have been approved by the proper officers, and still no means provided for their payment, although some of them have stood over for four or six months. It has come to the positive knowledge of this committee that some of these establishments (so much needed in the present emergency) have given notice that, for want of the requisite means, they are forced to decline any further orders from the Government.

It has also come to the knowledge of this committee that private citizens have repeatedly been forced to raise funds for this department in order to prevent the mechanics in the employ of the Government from stopping work. Indeed, so low has the credit of that particular department sunk, that draymen, whose bills are yet unpaid, have refused to do further work.

Your excellency will doubtless agree with the committee that this is a deplorable state of things. The committee have been careful to investigate the facts, so as not to place before your excellency anything which cannot be substantiated.

For months and months a sign has been hanging over the paymaster's office of that department, "No funds." The committee feel confident that, unless the proper remedy is at once supplied, workmen cannot longer be had.

The committee most respectfully submit this statement of facts to your consideration, and for the interest of our common cause and the safety of our city would respectfully request that you will give our citizens, through this committee, some assurance that the present state of affairs in that department will be changed for the better.

S. L. JAMES.
S. O. NELSON.
J. P. HARRISON.
R. C. CUMMINGS.
T. GREENFIELD.

[Indorsement.]

Secretary of the Navy, for prompt attention and report.

JEFFERSON DAVIS.

HEADQUARTERS DEPARTMENT NO. 1,
New Orleans, La., February 27, 1862.

Hon. J. P. BENJAMIN,
Secretary of War:

I have the honor to report that since my last letter I have sent forward to Tennessee Ruggles' brigade, of four regiments, with a battery of six field guns; also a new company of artillery (Vaiden's), with six guns and their harness and equipments. Yesterday the Fourth Louisiana and to-day the Seventh Mississippi moved to the same destination. The Twentieth Louisiana Regiment was mustered for State service, but, not wishing to remain behind, eight companies have reorganized for the war, and I shall send that regiment on in a few days. This will make a total of eight regiments and two batteries from the department, besides a quantity of shot-guns (500) and 1,000,000 cartridges. People are beginning to complain that I have stripped the department so completely, but I have called upon Governor Moore for 10,000 volunteers and militia for State service. Raw troops, with double-barreled shot-guns, are amply sufficient to hold our intrenchments against such troops as the enemy can send to attack them. Besides, I regard Butler's Ship Island expedition as a harmless menace so far as New Orleans is concerned. A black Republican dynasty will never give an old Breckinridge Democrat like Butler command of any expedition which they had any idea would result in such a glorious success as the capture of New Orleans.

He will not have 10,000 men for a demonstration by land upon any of the Gulf cities.

2d. Bowling Green has been turned by the Cumberland River, as I predicted, in the plan which I submitted to you early in October, although at that time they had no such men there as Buell and Halleck to command such an operation.

3d. I transmitted to you in January a letter of Captain Buchel in reference to a draft that he had drawn in Texas for supplies to subsist troops, and asked your instructions. Since then the draft was presented, and I paid it in specie out of the funds in my hands. Had it been protested, our troops on the Rio Grande could not have received provisions. I hope it meets your approval.

4th. The river defense expedition is progressing favorably, but considerable dissatisfaction has been expressed here at some of the appointments made by Montgomery and Townsend. The matter will be put before you by some citizens of this place. I have disbursed about half of the $300,000 placed to my credit on that appropriation, and large amounts are due. I trust that there will be no delay from want of funds to keep the works from being driven forward with all dispatch. Time is an important element at this juncture.

5th. In view of the constant demands from all points upon me for munitions, repairs of arms, &c., and the defenseless condition of our workshops and machinery at Nashville and Baton Rouge, I ordered preparations at the new Marine Hospital to be made for carrying on all such operations on a considerable scale, and directed an estimate for funds to be made by Captain Lambert, which was returned by Colonel Gorgas, with the remark that he did not contemplate having a laboratory here. The necessities of the public service, in my judgment, demand all and much more than I have done to keep pace with the requisitions daily made. I have fifteen gunsmiths at work putting in order the old weapons of all kinds collected from the country, and am preparing ammunition and implements for artillery, which I cannot get elsewhere; indeed, I have furnished Generals Johnston and Polk with large supplies, and hope that nothing will be permitted to interfere with operations so necessary to our salvation. If I cannot get the funds from Richmond I must throw myself upon the generosity of the people of the city. The work must go on unless you order it to be suspended. Knowing the immense pressure upon your time, and trusting that you had confidence in my judgment, I have assumed a good deal of responsibility and gone on with matters which I conceived to be important for the public good without referring every trifle to you for consideration. If you wish me to pursue a different course please indicate your view. Whatever has been done has been upon principles of a sound and wise economy, and has thus far produced beneficial results.

6th. The Tennessee has been unable as yet to get out of the river. The Magnolia, Florida, Whitmore, and Vanderbilt got to sea last week, but one of them (supposed to be the Magnolia) has been captured and taken to Ship Island. The powder by the Victoria turns out to be musket powder, although it seems to be of good quality. That by the Miramon, which came in at the Grand Caillou, has not yet reached the city. As soon as I work over 20,000 pounds of the Vanderbilt powder I will dispatch it to Richmond, as ordered by you in a telegram.

7th. Some of the parties who met with heavy losses on the Calhoun, J. L. Day, and Magnolia owned several of the boats seized by us for Montgomery's fleet, and are very anxious, in their straitened circumstances, to be paid for the vessels that we took. Can funds be placed at my disposal for that purpose? The total value of the steamers seized is about $600,000. I will inclose a schedule of the appraisements, with the remark that some of the owners have protested that the amounts allowed are not a fair price. Those objected to I had reappraised, and the board adhered to its first decision. No more should be allowed.

8th. I turned over to the Navy ten 42-pounders to arm their two gunboats for lake service, and hope that they will get them out pretty soon; but whether from want of funds or lack of systematic expenditures the credit of that branch of the public service here is so bad that it is almost impossible for them to get anything done. A few days since I wanted a crew for a boat to work on the lower rafts, but could not get a man until they were satisfied that it was not intended for service in the naval department. This is a serious embarrassment to them in their work.

9th. With some funds that I got from the city I bought, and am fitting up as launches, with one light gun each, twelve luggers, for a coast guard, to watch the enemy and prevent communication with the shore.

10th. I am a good deal delayed by the want of competent officers to assist me in the laborious details of this department. We want an ordnance officer here badly. Many things are necessarily kept back by having Major Smith perform the duties of engineer and ordnance officer, either one of which would tax a competent man to the utmost. It is neither justice to him nor to the service to make him responsible for such an immense and varied amount of detailed work.

With much respect, your obedient servant,

M. LOVELL,
Major-General, Commanding.

MOBILE, *February* 27, 1862.

J. P. BENJAMIN:

SIR: My troops are pressing forward. I leave to-morrow to join General Beauregard. There is the great danger.

BRAXTON BRAGG.

HDQRS. DEPARTMENT ALABAMA AND WEST FLORIDA,
Mobile, February 27, 1862.

Hon. J. P. BENJAMIN,
Secretary of War:

SIR: Your written dispatch of the 18th, by the hands of Major Lewis, only reached me this morning, four days at least behind its time, and as much behind others who left Richmond on that day. The major tells me he did not start till the 21st, and as he is at best a very slow man, perhaps he has done his best. Heavy movements of troops had already been made as far as our damaged roads would permit; but as your telegram did not indicate the extent to which we were to go, no arrangements had been made for abandoning any point.

Instructions to General Jones, commanding at Pensacola, go over to-day, and he will be urged to a hasty execution of the orders. Everything, public and private, is ordered to be destroyed which he is unable to remove and which might prove useful to the enemy; and the railroad as far as the junction to this city is to be destroyed, and the iron sent to Montgomery. By this means we may hold the enemy in check for some weeks at least.

Last week I sent a messenger to confer with General A. S. Johnston, that I might be able to act with some knowledge of the state of affairs. He has returned this morning, and I regret to hear the deplorable state of affairs. As he is an officer of great prudence, caution, and good judgment, I am the more concerned at his report. Officers of rank and standing having already gone on to lay before the Department this information, it is unnecessary, perhaps improper, that I should enter upon the subject.

The past we cannot recall, but it will be a cruel sacrifice to expose what is left of our gallant men to the same fate. Confidence is lost on all hands, from the private to the major-general, and nothing but a change can restore it.

It were futile to waste our time inquiring whether this is deserved. We must deal with facts as we find them, promptly and energetically, or we are lost.

I propose sending my heavy guns from Pensacola to General Beauregard, to enable us to hold the Mississippi, reserving only such as may be necessary to enable me to give some confidence to the people here and in the interior should the enemy pass our forts.

Very respectfully your obedient servant,

BRAXTON BRAGG,
Major-General, Commanding.

MOBILE, *February* 27, 1862.

Brig. Gen. SAMUEL JONES,
Commanding at Pensacola:

SIR: In the great strait to which we are reduced it has become necessary to concentrate our resources even at the cost of giving up some of our important positions.

You will make all dispositions at the earliest moment, working day and night, to abandon Pensacola. Send to this place all the heavy shell guns, rifle guns, and carriages, &c., complete, with the ammunition for them; all other supplies to Montgomery, to be located a few miles this side, for safety, in case the enemy should reach there by gunboats.

This movement should be made with all the secrecy possible; removing your guns at night, and masking the positions, taking the most advanced first. Keep sufficient troops in position to deceive the enemy until all is ready.

As you can do so, send forward all bodies which can be spared, only reserving enough to do the work, and hold your positions until the last, when one regiment can wind up all, and leave by the railroad.

I desire you particularly to leave nothing the enemy can use; burn all from Fort McRee to the junction with the Mobile road. Save the guns, and if necessary destroy your gunboats and all other boats. They might be used against us. Destroy all machinery, &c., public and private, which could be useful to the enemy; especially disable the sawmills in and around the bay and burn the lumber. Break up the railroad from Pensacola to the Junction, carrying the iron up to a safe point.

Your troops, except Captain Amos' mounted company, and the six companies First Confederate Regiment, ordered here, will move as rapidly as you can spare them to Chattanooga, Tenn., and await orders. All that you can spare should go at once. The enemy is not in condition to assail you at this point.

Much depends, general, on active and prompt measures. Our armies in Tennessee, are fearfully outnumbered, and I regret to say, from information just received, utterly demoralized, having no confidence. A timely arrival and intermixture of our troops may tend to restore confidence.

Very respectfully and truly, BRAXTON BRAGG,
Major-General, Commanding.

Report as you progress. Seize all transportation on railroads. Captain Oladowski comes to your aid in ordnance department.

MOBILE, *February* 27, 1862.

General BEAUREGARD:

MY DEAR GENERAL: Hearing by telegraph from the governor of this State that you had called on him for re-enforcements to be sent to Corinth, Miss., I directed a portion of those I was sending to General A. S. Johnston, and inclose you a copy of my order directing them to rendezvous at Corinth. I trust they will be of timely assistance and prove worthy of your command. The Louisiana infantry is one of our regiments of regulars, and is finely equipped and instructed. Brigadier-General Ruggles has assumed command, at my request, of the troops of my command in North Alabama, one regiment mounted men and three companies infantry. These I have requested him to call into Corinth and hold subject to your order. The people of the country will guard our bridges.

I am acting on my own responsibility, and doing what it seems to us ought to have been done long ago—concentrating our limited means at some important point to resist a vital blow. We should cease our policy of protecting persons and property, by which we are being defeated in detail.

Wishing you all success, I am, without occupation, restless and sad, but hopeful.

BRAXTON BRAGG.

[Inclosure.]

SPECIAL ORDERS, No. 62. } HDQRS. DEPT. ALA. AND WEST FLA.,
Mobile, Ala., February 26, 1862.

* * * * * * *

II. The regiment of Louisiana infantry, Colonel Adams; the Eighteenth and Twenty-second Regiments of Alabama Volunteers, Colonels Shorter and Deas, will immediately proceed to Corinth, Miss., there to receive further orders.

* * * * * * *

By command of Major-General Bragg:

GEO. G. GARNER,
Assistant Adjutant-General.

GENERAL ORDERS, No. 38. } HDQRS. DEPT. ALA. AND WEST FLA.,
Mobile, Ala., February 28, 1862.

Maj. Gen. Braxton Bragg relinquishes the command of this department to Brig. Gen. Samuel Jones.*

By command of Major-General Bragg:

GEO. G. GARNER,
Assistant Adjutant-General.

---

*Brig. Gen. Samuel Jones seems to have assumed command, under this order, March 3, 1862.

RICHMOND, VA., *March* 1, 1862.

GOV. THOMAS O. MOORE,
New Orleans:

You may accept all armed men that will go to re-enforce General Beauregard for a term of six months, under the law for local defense and special service.

J. P. BENJAMIN,
Secretary of War.

HEADQUARTERS SECOND BRIGADE,
New Orleans, March 1, 1862.

Major-General LEWIS,
Commanding Louisiana State Troops:

GENERAL: The following troops are out under my command this day in obedience to your order, No. 19:

Continental Regiment, Colonel Clark, 320 men.
Jeff. Davis Regiment, Colonel Smith, 150 men.
Beauregard Regiment, Colonel Bartlett, 400 men.
Sumter Regiment, Colonel Breaux, 200 men.
Lewis Battalion, Major Tenbrink, 80 men.
Washington Artillery, Captain Hodgson, 140 men.
Wilson Cavalry, Captain Moore, 50 men.

The Crescent Regiment has been excused from parade.

Colonel Clark has five companies without arms, Colonel Smith has nine companies without arms, Colonel Bartlett has six companies without arms, Major Tenbrink has two companies without arms, Colonel Breaux has three companies without arms.

I have the honor to be, &c.,

E. L. TRACY,
Brigadier-General.
THOS. F. WALKER,
Brigade Inspector.

HDQRS. DEPARTMENT ALABAMA AND WEST FLORIDA,
Mobile, Ala., [*March* 1?.]

General SAMUEL JONES:

SIR: Such is the pressing necessity in West Tennessee that I have concluded, at the request of General Beauregard, to proceed immediately to his assistance. Brigadier-General Withers having been relieved here, you will assume command of the department, remaining, however, at Pensacola to complete the work there. Press forward the troops and heavy guns. We must have them to hold the Mississippi. Should you find yourself unable to accomplish your work in ten days, destroy your smooth-bore guns and send me your troops. I would not thus press you, but our fate may depend on two weeks in the valley of the Mississippi.

Colonel Villepigue remains to complete the defenses here. Send him to me as soon as you come over, and if you can relieve Major Hallonquist from Fort Gaines I shall be much pleased to have him.

With every confidence in your zeal, industry, and ability, I part with you with great regret, well knowing all will be done your limited means will allow.

I am, general, very respectfully and truly, yours,

BRAXTON BRAGG,
Major-General, Commanding.

HEADQUARTERS ARMY OF PENSACOLA,
Near Pensacola, Fla., March 4, 1862.

Mr. C. L. LE BARRON,
Pensacola, Fla.:

SIR: You are aware that a number of troops have been recently detached from this army. It is important that I should have the services of every available soldier on this side of Bayou Grande. It is also important that I should keep a good and efficient guard in Pensacola. I have a battalion of volunteers now on that duty in Pensacola. I am convinced that the people of Pensacola are fully able to guard their own town quite as well as it is now guarded if the men will organize and volunteer for that service. I desire that you confer with the mayor and such citizens as you may think proper, and endeavor to organize a sufficient guard for the town. If that can be done, I can then avail myself of the services of the Fourth Battalion Alabama Volunteers here to defend the most important point.

Communicate to me with as little delay as possible what you can do to carry out the foregoing suggestion.

Very respectfully, your obedient servant,

SAM. JONES,
Brigadier-General.

[MARCH 4, 1862.—Maj. Gen. Braxton Bragg, at Jackson, Tenn., issues an order resuming command of the Department of Alabama and West Florida, and assuming, in addition thereto, command of the troops in North Mississippi and south of Jackson in West Tennessee. See operations, November 19, 1861–March 4, 1862, in Kentucky, Tennessee, &c. Vol. VII, p. 920.]

HDQRS. DEPARTMENT ALABAMA AND WEST FLORIDA,
Pensacola, Fla., March 5, 1862.

[General BRAGG:]

GENERAL: My movements here to carry out your orders have been greatly retarded—more, I presume, than you apprehended—by the want of transportation and the necessary facilities for moving guns.

The first train of cars from Pensacola to Mobile since the damage to the road started yesterday, and both the road to Mobile and that to Montgomery are in such bad condition that cars are not permitted to run on them at night. The president and superintendent of the Montgomery road, who came here this morning at my request to confer with me, promised to do all in their power to expedite the public business. I have directed that the superintendent of the Mobile road shall remain at Pollard, to direct the movements on all the roads meeting at that point. I am establishing a depot there, and will after to-day have a special train twice a day from Pensacola to that place, to carry such stores as cannot be immediately sent to Montgomery and Mobile. I have directed some supplies to be sent to Greenville, and will deposit others at Evergreen and Brewton, where I can procure storage temporarily, with a view of collecting them at the most suitable point as soon as practicable. The First Alabama Regiment is now in Pensacola, and will leave for Memphis via Mobile this evening. I will send forward the troops ordered to Corinth as rapidly as possible, and I am making and will continue to make every preparation to carry out fully your orders respecting this place.

I telegraphed you to-day that I had sent 96 mules by wagon road to Hall's Landing, thence via Mobile to Corinth. I had no harness or wagons for them. I also asked to be allowed to retain Colonel Jones and the Twenty-seventh Mississippi Regiment a few days beyond the time you have allowed me to accomplish the work in hand, and I trust that you will allow me to do so. My reason for asking this I will explain more fully in another letter, probably to-night. The mail will close before I could give my reasons in this. In your telegram of yesterday for 32-pounder barbette carriages to be sent to Memphis you did not say if you wanted the guns and ammunition with them.

Your telegram (the only one I have received since you left Mobile) I received late last night, and of course have not yet forwarded the carriages, as it was necessary to dismount the guns at night.

I shall look most anxiously for news from West Tennessee, and hope you will keep me advised of your movements in that quarter.

Most respectfully, your obedient servant,

SAM. JONES,
Brigadier-General.

O'BANNONVILLE, FLA., *March* 5, 1862.

General BRAXTON BRAGG,
Jackson, Tenn.:

Shall I send with the 32-pounder barbette carriages the guns and ammunition pertaining to them?

SAM. JONES,
Brigadier-General.

O'BANNONVILLE, FLA., *March* 5, 1862.

General BRAXTON BRAGG,
Jackson, Tenn.:

Your telegram of yesterday received. Barbette carriages and all ordnance and stores called for will be forwarded as rapidly as possible. No railroad communication with Mobile until yesterday. First Alabama started to-day for Memphis. Ninety-six mules left yesterday for Corinth, Miss. Negro laborers arrived last night and this morning. Do let me keep Colonel Jones and his regiment a few days at least beyond the time you have allowed me. My movements here have been greatly retarded by want of transportation and laborers.

SAM. JONES,
Brigadier-General.

NEW ORLEANS, LA., *March* 5, 1862.

Hon. J. P. BENJAMIN:

Vanderbilt powder had to be reworked, Victoria powder was all musket, and Miramon powder not arrived. Shall I send musket powder?

M. LOVELL.

RICHMOND, VA., *March* 5, 1862.

Maj. Gen. MANSFIELD LOVELL,
New Orleans, La.:

Your dispatch of the 5th received. Send 10,000 pounds of musket powder and 10,000 pounds of cannon powder, with an agent, to force it on by express.

J. P. BENJAMIN,
Secretary of War.

RICHMOND, VA., *March* 6, 1862.

Gov. THOMAS O. MOORE,
New Orleans, La.:

The Nashville brought no arms.

J. P. BENJAMIN,
Secretary of War.

HDQRS. DEPARTMENT ALABAMA AND WEST FLORIDA,
Near Pensacola, Fla., March 6, 1862.

Maj. Gen. BRAXTON BRAGG,
Jackson, Tenn.:

GENERAL: I telegraphed you yesterday asking that I might be allowed to retain the Twenty-seventh Regiment Mississippi Volunteers, Colonel Jones, a few days beyond the time you fixed for the evacuation of this post, and mentioned the same in my letter of yesterday, but had not time to give my reasons. I am convinced that the enemy on Santa Rosa Island is not prepared to attack this place at present. I have never believed the force as large as reported, and I have reason to believe it has been recently reduced. A large transport steamer came in some days since and left the next day. A large sailing vessel left the same day, and between the arrival and departure of the steamer a large number of the tents on the island were struck. I have watched the island carefully, and see very few men there.

I believe if we keep up even the appearance of being prepared to defend the place the enemy will not attack it. The governor of Alabama informs me that by the end of this week he can send me 1,000 men engaged to serve for thirty days, and by the middle of next week more, engaged for the same period, and before their time expires he can replace them by more than double the number of war troops. Under these circumstances I believe that Colonel Jones, with his regiment and the men who can be collected here before I can possibly send off all the troops you have called for, can keep up such an appearance of preparation to defend the place as to deter the enemy from attacking. The importance of holding this point is so great that it will, I think, justify the risk of allowing the navy-yard in its present dilapidated condition and a few 24, 32, and 42 pounder smooth-bore guns to fall uninjured into the hands of the enemy.

Your instructions are, that I shall destroy the guns, except the shell and rifled guns, and burn everything from Fort McRee to the Junction that can be of service to the enemy. These guns would be of but little value to an enemy who has an abundance of much better guns, and the houses could only contribute a little to their comfort, and you know how readily they can make thousands comfortable at this place. But there is no reason why the guns and houses should fall uninjured into their hands. I am making every preparation to destroy them, so that whenever an attack is made, and it becomes necessary to retire, a few men can disable the guns, apply the torches, do the work of destruction, and escape unhurt. The enemy has no mounted troops on the island. If they had, it would take time to land them, and if the men left here, nearly all unarmed, could not escape, I think their capture would not be a very serious loss to the country.

My plan only differs from your instructions to me in this, that I shall withhold from you Colonel Jones and the 350 armed men he has for duty, and leave the work of destruction to be done when an overpowering attack is made, instead of before and when there is no indication of an attack. I have explained my views fully to General Anderson and Colonel Jones, and they approve them. Colonel Jones is willing to undertake the task I propose to assign him, and believes he can manage it successfully. I submit it for your consideration.

The people of Pensacola and Mobile and all Alabama and West Florida, I hear, are greatly alarmed at the report that this place is to be abandoned to the enemy. I am sorry to say that the report of the intended evacuation reached Pensacola before your first instructions in the matter reached me. It seems impossible to keep any military secrets in this country.

I am, general, very respectfully, your obedient servant,

SAM. JONES,
Brigadier-General.

HEADQUARTERS DEPARTMENT NO. 1,
New Orleans, La., March 6, 1862.

Hon. J. P. BENJAMIN,
Secretary of War:

SIR: I have the honor to acknowledge the receipt of your letters of the 23d, 24th, and 26th ultimo, which reached me yesterday.

1st. The river expedition is progressing well. Seven of the boats will be ready, except the gun, on Saturday, the 8th, and the remainder in a week from that time. We are working under many disadvantages, but no time is being lost. I shall be out of funds for that purpose in a few days. The appraisement of the ships was forwarded in my letter of the 27th ultimo.

2d. I received your telegram directing 20,000 pounds of cannon powder to be sent to Richmond. All the powder that came in the Vanderbilt, Victoria, and Miramon is small-grained, not cannon powder, and that by the first and last of those vessels requires to be reworked, with an addition of 15 per cent. of saltpeter. This department is being completely drained of everything, and I trust that the arrival of the Nashville will enable you to leave here all the powder that we have on hand. We have filled requisitions for arms, men, and munitions until New Orleans is about defenseless. In return we get nothing. Mobile and Pensacola—even Galveston—are defended by 10-inch columbiads, while this city has nothing above an 8-inch, and but few of them. The fortified line about the city is complete, but I have taken ten of the guns for the Navy and sixteen for the vessels that we are fitting up for the river expedition. My reliance to defend these lines will be upon militia, with double-barreled guns and 32-pounder carronades. If now you take the powder from me we shall be in no condition to resist. The only thing to provide is a sufficiency of powder to enable us to resist a prolonged attack by ships and mortar boats upon two points—Forts Pike and Macomb and Forts Jackson and Saint Philip. If the first are passed we still have a land defense to make; if the last, a fleet can proceed at once to the city.

3d. I shall send up this week the Crescent Regiment, the Twentieth Regiment, two batteries of artillery, four companies of Mississippi volunteers, besides several separate companies, which will make eight regiments, four batteries of field artillery, and several companies, armed, equipped, and provided with a good supply of ammunition. I cannot organize the militia left here without the assistance of a general officer of experience and detailed knowledge. The circumstances of the case render it imperative. You will see by the letter accompanying this that I have urged upon the President the appointment of Major Smith as the proper person to fill that position. His engineer duties are drawing towards a condition which will enable him to be of great service in command of troops. He knows the whole country from personal observation, and, moreover, is fairly entitled, from his great and faithful labors, to be put more nearly on a par with his classmates at the Military Academy, all of whom are in high position—mostly general officers. He is willing to act as the engineer officer of the department in connection with a command in the line. My desire is to place him in charge of the troops intended for the defenses of the interior lines, which as an engineer he has constructed, and as ordnance officer armed and provided. His appointment would be acknowledged by the community here as a just tribute to faithful merit and valuable services rendered. They feel much indebted to him for their present condition of defense. Major Smith is a classmate of Smith, Van Dorn, Longstreet, Anderson, McLaws, D. H. Hill, A. P. Stewart, myself, and others high in rank. He alone, one of the first in the field, has been left in a position of inferior rank. The absence of General Ruggles demands a brigadier here, and there is every reason, public as well as private, that Major Smith should receive the appointment. I hope you will urge it upon the President, and let me know by telegraph his answer. I want the services of a general officer at once.

4th. Several persons here are refusing to take Confederate notes. They do not come under military supervision or I would put an end to it in short order. What do you think should be done? I am almost daily urged by prominent citizens to declare martial law here. It would, however, only remedy a few evils, while causing much inconvenience. I think that every desirable end could be attained by a military police and a registry of all comers. I would like to have your views about the propriety of having martial law here. Thus far I have steadily declined to do so.

5th. After the disasters in Tennessee, and when I became satisfied that Columbus could not be held, I ordered all the stores on hand at Baton Rouge to be sent here, as that city could be taken and all the public property there destroyed by half a dozen gunboats at a dash. Meanwhile I am enlarging the laboratory and arsenal here, so as to be prepared, in some small measure, in case the Baton Rouge works should be destroyed. It does not seem to meet with the approval of Colonel Gorgas, who regards it rather with the eye of the head of a bureau than as a military commander. Meanwhile I must go ahead with preparations which I consider to be of vital importance until you put a stop to them. I have at the Marine Hospital a steam-engine and a large number of hands employed in repairing arms, making ammunition, &c., and had it not been for this we never could have forwarded eight regiments and four batteries to aid them in Tennessee, for nothing of any description has been sent here except some saltpeter.

6th. I am hunting all over the Confederacy to procure saltpeter to rework the powder lately arrived from Cuba. They are sending it from Memphis to Augusta. I have, however, sent an agent to Texas to get some that I heard was at Houston, and there is a lot of 6,000 pounds *en route* here from Georgia. Until I get some the powder must remain *in statu quo*.

7th. Permit me again to urge upon you the necessity of sending here an officer of ordnance to attend to the numerous requisitions constantly made upon this department from all quarters. Much delay and difficulty have arisen from the want of such a person here. This duty has been performed by Major Smith, in addition to his other duties; but by this arrangement injustice is done both to him and to the public service.

8th. I am somewhat fearful that a little too much latitude has been given to the steamboat captains and pilots in charge of the river expedition. If the current of opinion here should set against them they will be unable to get crews, and I would recommend a responsible head to the expedition when it is ready to move, otherwise there will be discussion, confusion, and consequent inaction.

9th. The Calhoun runs up the river below the forts, and we have nothing to keep her back. I hope the Secretary of the Navy will keep at least one vessel here to prevent the enemy from making reconnaissances under our very guns.

10th. I allow no arms or powder arriving to escape me, but have no need to impress, as I will not give a permit to go out until I have the promise of the refusal of the cargo. The arrangement works smoothly.

Respectfully, your obedient servant,

M. LOVELL,
Major-General, Commanding.

[Confidential.]

HDQRS. DEPARTMENT ALABAMA AND WEST FLORIDA,
Pensacola, March 7, 1862.

Lieutenant-Colonel BEARD,
First Florida Regiment, Commanding Deer Point:

COLONEL: The brigadier-general commanding directs me to say that the steamer Tom Murray has been chartered and will be placed under your orders at Deer Point. You will hold your battalion in readiness to move at a moment's warning. Send your tents and heavy baggage, in charge of a commissioned officer and 3 men, to Brewton, there to await further orders from you. You will keep constantly on the alert, and if attacked by an overpowering force, or if you should discover two or more buildings in the navy-yard to be on fire, you will take your men on the steamer, first firing the buildings, if possible, and proceed immediately to Bagdad and Milton, and there burn every foot of lumber, the saw-mills, and boats, including the steamer Tom Murray, and everything that can be of any service to the enemy. If the saws and machinery can be moved to the interior, it may be done; otherwise the saws and machinery must be broken and destroyed. Having accomplished the work assigned you, you will march your command to Brewton and there await further orders. You will keep your battalion supplied with forty rounds of ammunition and five days' rations, three of which should be cooked.

The general expects that you will not hesitate or falter an instant in carrying out thoroughly and effectually the foregoing instructions, in order that, if we are forced to abandon this place, nothing of value, except the position itself, will fall into the hands of the enemy.

It is presumed that you have already moved the 8-inch columbiad, with carriage, ammunition, and implements, to Pensacola, as directed some days since. If not, you will lose no time in so doing.

This communication you will regard as strictly confidential.

I am, colonel, yours, very respectfully,

CHARLES S. STRINGFELLOW,
Assistant Adjutant-General.

HDQRS. DEPARTMENT ALABAMA AND WEST FLORIDA,
Pensacola, March 7, 1862.

Lieutenant-Colonel CONOLEY,
Fourth Alabama Battalion, Commanding at Pensacola:

COLONEL: The brigadier-general commanding directs that you hold your battalion in readiness to move at the shortest notice out of Pensacola, either by railroad or marching on the Mill road towards Pollard, as circumstances may require. You will send your heavy baggage to Pollard as soon as you can do so without retarding the transportation of troops and ordnance stores ordered to Mobile and Montgomery. On receiving an order from the general or officer commanding here to retire, whether such order may be in writing or through a staff officer, you will immediately destroy and burn all public buildings, including the railroad depot, and all factories, machine-shops, machinery, boats, and lumber, whether public or private, and then retire, destroying the railroad, and removing the iron to the interior. A sufficient number of laborers and an engine and platform cars will be placed at your disposal to do this latter work. The destruction of property in Pensacola must be done by your own men.

I am, colonel, very respectfully, your obedient servant,

CHARLES S. STRINGFELLOW,
Assistant Adjutant-General.

(These instructions were given in compliance with orders from General Bragg.)

NAVY DEPARTMENT,
Richmond, Va., March 8, 1862.

To the PRESIDENT:

SIR: For your information I have the honor to make the following statement in reference to the communication of the Committee of Safety of New Orleans,* submitted to me this day:

The credit of the Government has doubtless suffered in New Orleans from the failure of the Treasury to meet the requisitions of the Department, and this has been a constant source of embarrassment to the Department and of annoyance to its creditors and disbursing agents in that city. I have repeatedly brought the subject to the attention of the Secretary of the Treasury and invoked prompt payment, though I

---

*Of February 26. See p. 831.

have felt that with his limited power to produce Treasury notes and under the rule adopted giving priority to certain disbursements for the Army he was powerless to correct the evil. Here is my last letter to him upon the subject. (Letter to the Secretary of the Treasury, dated February 22, 1862.)

The requisitions of this Department upon the Treasury for money to meet payments in New Orleans have usually been made immediately upon hearing from its disbursing officers the amount required, and always, I think, within twenty-four hours thereafter; but the delay of the Treasury in paying them has been from twenty-five to forty days. In some cases the Treasury Department has, after long delay, instead of sending notes for which our creditors were waiting, sent drafts for Confederate bonds payable in Richmond, and which drafts were useless to our agents and creditors there, and which therefore had to be returned to Richmond for payment and then sent to New Orleans, thus still further protracting payment.

This has been a source of great embarrassment to this Department and complaint of its creditors. In one of these cases a requisition for $42,000 was dated December 24, 1861, payable to Navy Agent William B. Howell on February 6, 1862. He received a draft—one-half in notes and one-half in bonds—at Richmond. His letter of advice was received February 15, and on February 17 I called upon the Treasurer for the requisition—forty-eight days afterwards.

When the Department draws its requisition in favor of its creditors upon an existing appropriation its duty and its power are alike exhausted, and though the Department has endured the embarrassment consequent upon these delays, and which it had not the power to avert, it has felt that the condition of the Treasury rendered them inevitable, and that the responsibility for them was with that Department. Our agents are instructed to make all contracts they can payable partly in bonds, and they do so, and in such cases our requisition calls for the amount of bonds to be sent; but the Treasury, as you will see by the Secretary's letter, deems it proper to send bonds when not required and when we cannot use them, and embarrassment to the Department and losses to creditors inevitably follow. Our agents, from the nature of their disbursement, can dispose of bonds only to a very limited extent.

The following telegram from our Navy agent and the Treasury comments thereon will thus show the character of these transactions:

[Telegram.]

Ordnance money received; one-half in drafts on Richmond, payable in bonds, which I cannot use. Shall I pay for what stores received, as advised you in my letter of February 8?

ANSWER OF SECRETARY.

I return you the telegram of Navy Agent Howell. If you will examine the acts of Congress you will find that a large amount of the means furnished by Congress to pay the expenditures consists of bonds. These must be distributed among these expenditures, for which alone they can be used, and I see no remedy but to require your agents to make their contracts accordingly. It is not possible to supply the means, except in the form provided by Congress, and if the agents, instead of complaining, would set themselves to aid the Government by disposing of the bonds there would be no difficulty.

Similar cases are constantly occurring, and this day I am notified by telegram that upon a requisition to pay a debt due in notes drawn by me one month ago one-third of the amount was sent to New Orleans in bonds, which of course the creditor declines to receive.

Embarrassment to creditors has also arisen in New Orleans from the following circumstances: Captain Hollins, without the knowledge or authority of the Department, without acquainting it with his actions, and when no appropriation existed for meeting the payment, made contracts for ordnance and ordnance stores amounting to about $500,000. The amount of these contracts was for a long time unknown to the Department, and information of their extent was first acquired through the contractors themselves. The navy agent and an officer sent especially for the purpose were instructed to ascertain their amount, and an estimate was submitted to Congress and an appropriation obtained to pay them at the earliest possible moment thereafter, and on the very day I received the act of Congress I made a requisition for the funds, and they have been placed in New Orleans to meet all demands which have come to hand.

The statement of the Committee of Safety as to the amount of indebtedness is totally incorrect. No such amount as from $600,000 to $800,000 has been outstanding, and if the Treasury Department has sent to the disbursing agents of this Department the money for its requisition of March 1 for $300,000, they have funds in hand more than sufficient to meet every cent due by the Department and of which it has any knowledge. I annex copies of my letters to the Treasury Department,* and herewith return the communication of the Committee of Safety.

I am, respectfully, your obedient servant,

S. R. MALLORY,
Secretary of the Navy.

RICHMOND, VA., *March* 6, 1862.

A copy of the foregoing report was forwarded to the Committee of Safety, by the President's direction, by his private secretary, as soon as received.

BURTON N. HARRISON,
Private Secretary.

HDQRS. DEPARTMENT ALABAMA AND WEST FLORIDA,
Pensacola, Fla., March 8, 1862.

Capt. THOMAS W. BRENT, C. S. N.,
Pensacola, Fla.:

SIR: The naval storekeeper in Pensacola was informed on the 4th instant, by my direction, that the naval stores in Pensacola should be removed to the interior and those now 15 miles out of town could remain where they are for the present. All the transportation at my disposal has been for some days and is now required to move troops and military stores to points where they are needed. I suggest, therefore, that you put such naval stores now in Pensacola as you can on the steamer Time. They can be placed on her while she is at the wharf in Pensacola, and continue to perform the service she is now engaged in. If it becomes necessary to evacuate this place (and I trust no such necessity will arrive), the captain of the Time has been ordered to run his boat as far up the Escambia as possible. At present and for some weeks it is believed that he can run her to within a few miles of the State line, to a point within a mile or two of the railroad. From that point the naval stores could be moved to the railroad for transportation elsewhere if necessary. The stores 15 miles from Pensacola should be moved

*Not found.

farther to the interior as soon as transportation by railroad can be provided.

I hear that an officer of the Navy has been for some time engaged in building two gunboats at or near Milton, and that they are now nearly ready for service. He should be immediately informed of the condition of things as you know them to be here, and warned to be constantly on the alert, to prevent them falling into the hands of the enemy. If he cannot take them up the Escambia or place them beyond the reach of the enemy, he should burn them as soon as he hears that this place has fallen into the hands of the enemy, and measures should be taken to give him the earliest possible information on the subject.

It is probable that an attempt will be made to run the Bradford and Nelms into Mobile Bay, and it may be that they could tow the two gunboats on a dark night into Mobile Bay. You are better able to judge of that than I can. Under no circumstances should they be allowed to fall into the hands of the enemy.

No time should be lost in carrying out the foregoing suggestions. The quartermaster in Pensacola will give you all the aid he can in moving the naval stores.

I am, sir, very respectfully, your obedient servant,

SAM. JONES,
Brigadier-General, Commanding.

HEADQUARTERS DEPARTMENT NO. 1,
New Orleans, La., March 9, 1862.

Hon. J. P. BENJAMIN,
Secretary of War:

SIR: In obedience to your orders, I have sent forward to Tennessee, besides the Thirteenth Louisiana, already detached, the following regiments, viz: the Sixteenth, Seventeenth, Eighteenth, Nineteenth, and Fourth Louisiana, and the Seventh Mississippi Regiments. The Twentieth will leave on Tuesday. Gibson's and Vaiden's field batteries have also gone forward. In addition, Governor Moore has sent the Crescent Regiment and Fifth Company Washington Artillery, and the Orleans Guard Battery, with three companies of that battalion, will go in a few days, all nominally for ninety days; but there is every reason to believe that once in the field they will remain. These troops have all been fitted out completely by the State. I have only furnished ammunition, subsistence, and transportation. One or two independent companies will probably join Beauregard in the same manner.

The four Mississippi companies of Hardcastle's battalion which were here I have ordered to join their own corps, now with General A. S. Johnston.

You will thus perceive that this department has been completely stripped of every organized body of troops. To replace them I have called upon Governor Moore for 10,000 volunteers and militia for the defense of the lines about New Orleans, which call, I hope, will meet with the approval of the Government. Persons are found here who assert that I am sending away all troops so that the city may fall an easy prey to the enemy.

All requisitions for ammunition have been filled until I have none left except what is in the hands of troops; neither have I funds placed at my disposal to create supplies in place of those sent off.

If the enemy intends an attack here he will make it soon, and I trust no further calls will be made until we are placed in a defensible condition.

Respectfully, your obedient servant,

M. LOVELL,
Major-General, Commanding.

HDQRS. DEPARTMENT ALABAMA AND WEST FLORIDA,
Pensacola, Fla., March 9, 1862.

Col. THOMAS M. JONES:

SIR: You will receive with this an order assigning you to the command of the troops remaining here. You are aware that by instructions from Major-General Bragg preparations have been made to evacuate this post.

I have ordered Lieutenant-Colonel Conoley, commanding Fourth Battalion Alabama Volunteers in Pensacola, on receiving an order from the commanding officer here, or if attacked by an overpowering force, or on discovering buildings of the navy-yard to be on fire, immediately to burn and destroy all public buildings, including the railroad depot, all machinery and machine-shops, cotton, lumber, the wharves, and all boats of every description in Pensacola, then retire to Pollard, destroying as far as possible the railroad, and moving the iron to the interior. An engine and sufficient number of platform cars will be placed at his command for this service.

I have ordered Lieutenant-Colonel Beard, commanding battalion Florida regiment at Deer Point, if attacked in force, or if he should discover two or more buildings in the navy-yard to be on fire, immediately to fire his huts, take his men on the steamer Tom Murray, which is placed at his disposal and ordered to remain at Deer Point constantly subject to his orders, proceed to Crigler, Bagdad, and Milton, burn the Tom Murray and all boats of every description, every foot of lumber and the saw-mills, breaking and destroying the machinery, then to march across the country to Brewton, 7 miles above Pollard, on the railroad, and there await further orders. Preparations have been made for burning all the buildings of any value from Fort McRee to Pensacola, and for disabling all the guns and their carriages. You will keep constantly on the alert, and, if attacked in such force as to render it impossible in your judgment to defend the place, you will immediately cause the guns remaining in the batteries to be disabled and all the buildings fired; then retire with all your troops, and proceed as rapidly as possible to Mobile. Florida Railroad and rolling stock are at your command. In the mean time you will continue with all possible dispatch to dismount the remaining shell and rifled guns, and send them, with the carriages, ammunition, and implements, to Pensacola, for transportation to Mobile, and all other guns and supplies to Montgomery.

You are aware that I still have some hope of being able to hold this place. The governor of Alabama has promised to send here by the middle or end of this week about 1,500 men. Five hundred are expected to arrive to-night. As they arrive they will report to you. By distributing them judiciously at the different batteries you may prevent the enemy from discovering that other troops have been withdrawn.

The Eighth Regiment of Mississippi Volunteers has been ordered to proceed on Tuesday next, the 11th instant, to Corinth, Miss. As soon thereafter as transportation can be provided you will send first the Mississippi Battalion, then the Florida Battalion, then the Fourth Alabama Battalion to Corinth, Miss., to report to the commanding officer at that place. If the Florida Battalion moves before it becomes necessary to evacuate this place, Lieutenant-Colonel Beard will hand over his written instructions in regard to the destruction of property at Milton and other places to Lieutenant-Colonel Conoley, who will assign that duty to two companies of his battalion.

If, as I trust will not be the case, you are forced to evacuate the place, you will proceed with your command as rapidly as possible to Mobile, and thence to Corinth, Miss., and report to the commanding officer at that place.

I am, sir, very respectfully, your obedient servant,

SAM. JONES,
Brigadier-General.

[Inclosure.]

SPECIAL ORDERS, No. 62. } HEADQUARTERS ARMY OF PENSACOLA,
Near Pensacola, Fla., March 8, 1862.

* * * * * * *

II. Col. Thos. M. Jones, Twenty-seventh Regiment Mississippi Volunteers, is assigned to the command of the First Brigade. Staff officers will report to him accordingly.

By command of Brig. Gen. S. Jones:

CHAS. S. STRINGFELLOW,
Assistant Adjutant-General.

HEADQUARTERS ARMY OF PENSACOLA,
Pensacola, Fla., March 10, 1862.

Lieutenant-Colonel BEARD,
First Florida Regiment, Deer Point:

SIR: You will proceed to-night to execute the orders given you in my letter of instructions a few days since.* You will take only 100 men, the best and most reliable you have, with three officers. You will start in time to reach the Point, where your work is to begin, by daylight to-morrow morning, and will not commence the work of destruction until it is light, lest some injury might result to persons not aware of your mission. You will burn every saw-mill, planing-mill, sash factory, every foot of lumber, and all boats of every description. If there is any cotton at any of the places you will not fail to destroy it.

You will communicate with the officer or agent having charge of the gunboats, and deliver a letter which I will send you. If those can be towed up the Escambia, you will, after having completed thoroughly the destruction of the property I have mentioned, give such assistance in towing them out of danger up the Escambia as you can. If that cannot be done you will destroy the gunboats also.

Instead of burning the Tom Murray, as directed in my former letter, you will, after having burned all the property I have mentioned, proceed with your command in the Tom Murray up the Escambia as near to Pollard as you can approach, leave the steamer, and go to Pollard, to act as a guard temporarily of the public property at that place.

Take four days' rations, and as many more as you may have on hand, and 40 rounds of ammunition. It is not supposed that you will meet with any opposition, but should there be, you will carry out your orders by force of arms. I rely upon you so to execute your orders that nothing of material value to the enemy shall be left in that vicinity.

---

* See p. 843, Stringfellow to Beard, March 7.

The following is a list of the mills as far as I can ascertain them:*

* * * * * * *

The remainder of your force you will leave at Deer Point for to-night, with orders, if attacked in force, to burn the hut and come to this side in the Bradford, which will be near the Point all night.

Very respectfully, your obedient servant,

SAM. JONES,
Brigadier-General.

HEADQUARTERS DEPARTMENT NO. 1,
New Orleans, La., March 10, 1862.

HON. J. P. BENJAMIN,
Secretary of War:

SIR: The steamer Tennessee has been unable to get out of the river so far. When she went down to make the attempt, it was understood that she would be assisted to the extent of calling off the attention of the blockaders by one of our gunboats. These, however, have all been ordered up the river, and she still remains at the lower forts.

Since the river expedition (Montgomery's) was set on foot circumstances have so materially changed as to require, in my judgment, at least a temporary change in the programme. The evacuation of Columbus puts an end to any attack upon the enemy's fleet at Cairo. Still, I should have sent the whole number, fourteen, up as soon as they were ready, notwithstanding the Secretary of the Navy had ordered every gun afloat up the river, had not the heavy drift and current broken up, in a great measure, the river obstructions at Fort Jackson. Under these circumstances, with the enemy's fleet collecting and beginning to enter the mouths of the river with boldness, and having an open passage to New Orleans if the batteries below are passed, I have written to General Polk that I could put no guns on the boats of the expedition, and that until I could replace some obstructions in the river I should feel compelled to keep here six of the steamers. The fleet threatening us below is much more formidable than that above, and I object strongly to sending every armed vessel away from New Orleans at this time. This city has been already too much weakened by the detachments of all kinds. Loud complaints are made on all hands, and until we are placed in security below I do not think it advisable to draw anything further from this point except the eight ships, strengthened and prepared for their guns, which can be furnished above as well as here.

Respectfully, your obedient servant,

M. LOVELL,
Major-General, Commanding.

HDQRS. ELEVENTH BRIGADE, M. L. T. [L. M. T.?],
Bastrop, La., March 10, 1862.

Major-General LEWIS,
New Orleans:

GENERAL: I am in receipt of your General Orders, No. 14, referring to Order 191 of the governor and commander-in-chief, exempting from militia duty one white man on each plantation in the parish where there are slaves.

---

* List omitted, as well as an accompanying "estimate" of the value ($764,500) of the property to be destroyed.

I shall endeavor to organize the militia in this brigade and give due effect to the exemption therein prescribed, but permit me most respectfully to suggest that I fear the task will prove a fruitless one, and for these reasons: The population subject under the law to militia duty (male between the ages of 18 and 45), in the parishes composing this brigade, with the exception of the two parishes lying west of the Ouachita River, consists chiefly of planters who are slave-owners, their sons, and the overseers on the larger plantations; the non-slave-owners (not including overseers), comprising but a small class of the population. All these parishes have contributed most liberally in volunteers for the war, and the number subject to militia duty is now greatly reduced.

The volunteers have been drawn from all classes of our citizens, but the non-slaveholders are most largely represented in the Army. The young or single men of all classes have nearly all gone, and such has been the drain on our population, that you can now rarely find any one plantation with two able-bodied men upon it.

Under these circumstances I apprehend that the exemption referred to would cover a large majority of those otherwise subject to duty, and its enforcement would, I fear, defeat anything like a general or efficient organization of the militia. In some parishes of the brigade I doubt whether a single company could be raised of persons not entitled to the exemption, and in only two of them could a sufficient number be enrolled to form a regiment.

The planters and their overseers would in a large majority of instances be exempt, and the burden of militia duty would fall almost exclusively upon the non-slaveholders; a class least able to bear the sacrifice of time and labor required, and whose numbers are already greatly reduced by their patriotic contributions of soldiers for the war. Should such be the effect of it, this class might be impressed with the inequality if not injustice of its operation, and this might tend to defeat that harmony and cordial co-operation for the public defense among all classes so very necessary in the present great emergency. This I deem an important consideration. I have, besides, some practical experience in regard to the working of this exemption. Up to the time of my recent appointment as brigadier-general I was colonel of the Morehouse Regiment of Militia. Notwithstanding the defects in the law of 1853, I had succeeded in effecting a thorough organization of the regiment, and was progressing rapidly in perfecting the militia of the parish both in the company and battalion drill. After the order of the governor referred to was issued I could never secure a sufficent "turn-out" for a battalion drill, and in several of the company beats the companies were completely broken up, owing entirely to the number of persons claiming exemption under this order. In short, the regiment was disorganized. Such, I fear, would be the practical effect of the exemption in nearly every other parish in the brigade.

I hope these considerations may lead to a rescinding of the order. I am duly sensible that the order was prompted by a desire to secure the slave-holding communities from the dangers arising from insubordination among the slaves, and the apprehension lest the absence of the owner or overseer from the plantation on militia duty might tend to produce such insubordination. This consideration would, perhaps, make some provision of the kind necessary, in case the militia is called into active service, but even in such a case I do not think the exemption need be as broad as that provided by the order. Many plantations are very small and have but few slaves upon them, and in many instances one man could conveniently take charge of several of them; but until the contingency referred to arises I am fully satisfied, from actual observation, that the mustering and drilling of the entire militia force, notwithstanding the temporary absence of the owners and overseers from the plantations it would involve, so far from having a tendency to encourage a spirit of insubordination among the slaves, would have the contrary effect, to keep them in awe and subjection; and to these military displays and the drilling of volunteer and militia troops I attribute in a great measure that remarkable state of discipline and subordination that has been observed among the slave population in this section since the commencement of the war.

Military rule of implicit obedience to the orders of superiors debars, perhaps, the privilege of in any manner questioning the propriety of those orders, and if I have seemingly departed from it in this instance, I trust I shall be pardoned for the motive that prompts it; which is the extreme anxiety felt to see the proper strength and efficiency imparted to the militia system, now so important an arm of the public defense.

Your communication of the 3d instant, with the accompanying order, was also received, and shall be promptly attended to.

Very respectfully, your obedient servant,

R. B. TODD.

NEW ORLEANS, LA., *March* 11, 1862.

Hon. J. P. BENJAMIN:

Quartermaster, commissary, river defense, engineer, and medical funds exhausted. Time is important. Cannot move rapidly without money.

M. LOVELL.

JACKSON, *March* 11, 1862.

General JONES:

Relieve Colonel Villepigue and send him here as soon as possible.

BRAXTON BRAGG,
Major-General.

PENSACOLA, FLA., *March* 11, 1862.

General S. COOPER,
Adjutant-General, C. S. Army:

SIR: You know, I presume, General Bragg's instructions to me. There is a large quantity of most valuable war material here yet, including several rifled and shell guns, and machinery in the navy-yard, which can be moved and used in making guns. I am convinced the enemy's force on Santa Rosa Island is much smaller than has been supposed. All seems quiet there. I believe Col. T. M. Jones, with from 700 to 1,000 armed men, with the volunteers who are coming in, can hold the place long enough to move all that is particularly worth moving, and perhaps much longer. He agrees with me, and desires to undertake it. May I make the necessary arrangements and try it? If not, our loss of material will be heavy.

SAM. JONES,
Brigadier-General.

HEADQUARTERS ARMY OF PENSACOLA,
Pensacola, Fla., March 12, 1862.

Col. THOMAS M. JONES:

SIR: I have just received the following telegram from the Adjutant and Inspector General C. S. Army:

RICHMOND, *March 12, 1862.*

Your dispatch of yesterday just received. You are fully authorized to use your own discretion, making all necessary arrangements for the safety of material referred to by you.

S. COOPER,
Adjutant and Inspector General.

Let me know by Lieutenant Noble, who will hand you this, the number of armed men, as shown by your morning report of this morning. Do not include any of the Fourth Alabama Battalion. The few arms they have belong to the Florida regiment, and the lieutenant-colonel is ordered to turn them over. You will keep the battalion as so many over and above the number of armed men left you. The governor of Alabama has just telegraphed me that five companies will leave Montgomery for Pensacola to-morrow, and he will send 1,000 here.

Make your arrangements as we agreed on last evening. Encourage your men; tell them they are engaged in most important service. If they can hold Pensacola even long enough to save the public property and move it to a place of security they will have rendered most valuable service, which will not fail to be properly noticed and appreciated. If they can hold it permanently they will immortalize themselves.

Put some men with axes to cutting up all the masts and spars of the Fulton and all such. They are in one of the store-houses of the navy-yard, and some of them are piled against the wall near the officers' quarters. In arranging for the destruction of machinery, do not forget to overlook that used for drawing vessels into the dock.

General Bragg telegraphed me last night again to relieve Villepigue and send him to him. I must therefore go to Mobile. Will leave to-morrow if the road is practicable. I leave most important and responsible duties to you, and have full faith in your ability and will to perform them if they can be performed.

Do all you can to quiet and reassure your officers and men. Represent to them—what is really the case, I believe—that from the apparent condition of things on Santa Rosa the enemy is not prepared to make a serious attack; that from reports which they may have heard of the movements here they may attempt to feel us to ascertain our true condition, and if met boldly and repelled all will be quiet, at least until they are strongly re-enforced.

In haste, respectfully, &c.,

SAM. JONES,
Brigadier-General.

WAR DEPARTMENT,
Richmond, Va., March 12, 1862.

General MANSFIELD LOVELL,
New Orleans, La.:

SIR: I have your letter of the 27th ultimo, together with its inclosures. I have also received several communications in relation to the command of the river steamer defenses, and both the President and myself have felt much embarrassed by them. The expedition was planned and gotten up by Captains Montgomery and Townsend, recommended by the whole Mississippi delegation and General Polk, and the objections made to them now appear to us of the most vague and inconclusive character.

The President has great confidence in Capt. T. P. Leathers, and if he can be induced to go as commander of the expedition you are requested to put him in command of the whole, Captain Montgomery second, Captain Townsend third, and the remainder in such order as may be fixed by Captain Montgomery.

The list of captains recommended by Montgomery and Townsend is as follows, viz:

January 15, Capt. John A. Stephenson.
January 26, Isaac Hooper.
January 27, Burdett Paris.
January 28, John H. Burke.*
January 29, James Beverly Smith.
January 30, James C. Delancy.
January 31, Joseph Davis McCoy.
February 1, William H. H. Leonard.*
February 2, James Henry Hurt.
February 3, George Willholland Phillips.
February 4, William W. Lamb.
February 5, Joseph A. Sturtevant.*

The three against whose names stars (*) have been placed are said by some of the citizens of New Orleans to be unreliable. If you could replace them (the last especially) by some captains acceptable to our people, with the consent of Montgomery and Townsend, it would be well. I do not myself find sufficient reason for distrusting the parties, but public opinion ought to be satisfied if possible. In relation to these three parties you will use your own discretion.

The expedition ought to go as promptly as possible, subject to the orders of General Beauregard as regards the service required of it (but of course without any interference in their organization), and the relative rank of each officer settled in a general order, which you are hereby authorized and requested to issue to them in conformity with the foregoing instructions.

I have sent you $300,000 on account of the expenses of this expedition, and will send you further remittances very promptly. As soon as I can get one moment I will answer the rest of your letter; but I conclude by saying that your whole conduct of your department justifies the confidence reposed in you, and that I have not yet found a single act of yours which I disapprove in the smallest degree.

Your obedient servant,

J. P. BENJAMIN,
Secretary of War.

P. S.—If Captain Leathers will not go, then give the command to Montgomery. If you can get Captain Holmes to take charge of one of the boats I would be gratified. He is an excellent officer. The expedition is in no event to be put under control of officers of the Navy.

HDQRS. SECOND GRAND DIVISION, ARMY OF THE MISS.,
Jackson, Tenn., March 12, 1862.

Brig. Gen. SAMUEL JONES,
Comdg. Dept. Ala. and West Fla., near Pensacola, Fla.:

GENERAL: Your letter of the 5th instant was not received until this morning. Owing to a heavy pressure of business the general has instructed me to reply.

He feels confident everything has been done by you to carry out his instructions. He is aware of the many difficulties under which you are laboring. With the utmost confidence in your ability, zeal, and industry, the general knows nothing will be neglected by you which can possibly be performed.

He directs that by all means the large shell guns, ammunition, and implements, with the most important stores, be collected and saved. Abandon nothing that can possibly be secured.

Also that you relieve Colonel Villepigue, Captain Gibbs, and Lieut. W. F. Johnson, C. S. Marine Corps, as soon as you can spare them, and direct them to report here. The services of Colonel Villepigue are much needed. Would it not be well to relieve him immediately, and assign Col. W. L. Powell, at present commanding Second Brigade, to the temporary command of the Army of Mobile?

You can retain such forces as you deem necessary to carry out instructions.

The general has the pleasure of knowing that you have been nominated for a major-general. As soon as the appointment is received you will be assigned to the command of one of the divisions of this army.

We shall endeavor to keep you advised of important events transpiring in this quarter.

I am, general, very respectfully, your obedient servant,

GEO. G. GARNER,
Assistant Adjutant-General.

HEADQUARTERS ARMY OF PENSACOLA,
Pensacola, Fla., March 12, 1862.

Capt. F. J. MYERS,
First Florida Regiment, Commanding at Deer Point:

CAPTAIN: You must not suppose that you and the companies with you are left at Deer Point merely to let the enemy see that the Point is still held, and to retreat on the first demonstration of an attack. A much smaller guard would better serve that purpose.

I am convinced that the enemy on Santa Rosa is by no means so strong as has been supposed, and I do not believe they are prepared to make a serious attack on us. It is not improbable that they have received reports of our movements here which will induce them to reconnoiter and perhaps feel you, without any intention of attacking seriously, but only to ascertain the condition of things. If they are met boldly and driven off they will let you alone, at least until they are strongly re-enforced. You must not give up your position unless attacked by overpowering numbers. Your position is such that the enemy can only approach you by boats or by crossing high up and coming down the beach, which is so narrow that a few men judiciously placed, sheltered by sand hills and trees, can drive off five times their numbers if they will keep cool and fight bravely. Extend your sentinels 3 or 4 miles up the beach, as far as Live Oak Plantation if practicable, so as to give you timely warning of the approach of the enemy if he presents himself, and be sure they are too many for you before you retreat.

The Floridians at Deer Point have an important duty to perform, and I expect them so to perform it as to reflect credit upon themselves and their State. You will be withdrawn and your places supplied in a day or two.

Very respectfully, &c.,

SAM. JONES,
Brigadier-General.

RICHMOND, VA., *March* 13, 1862.

GOV. THOMAS O. MOORE,
New Orleans, La.:

You are requested to proclaim martial law in my name over the parishes of Orleans, Jefferson, Saint Bernard, and Plaquemine.

JEFFERSON DAVIS.

[Repeated March 15.]

FORT MORGAN, *March* 14, 1862.

General SAMUEL JONES:

The temporary command of the Army of Mobile having been turned over to me by Colonel Villepigue by telegraph, I respectfully report the same and await your instructions.

W. L. POWELL,
Colonel, &c.

HEADQUARTERS ARMY OF MOBILE,
Mobile, Ala., March 15, 1862

General BRAXTON BRAGG,
Jackson, Tenn.:

GENERAL: On the receipt of your telegram ordering me to relieve Colonel Villepigue and send him to you as soon as possible I left Pensacola on the morning of the 13th, and arrived here about midnight. Colonel Villepigue, to whom I telegraphed my intention of starting on the 13th, left here *en route* for your headquarters a few hours before I arrived.

I left Col. Thomas M. Jones at Pensacola to carry out your instructions, ordering him to hold the place, if possible, until all the public property is removed. The damage to the railroads, and the panic produced in the community by the report that the place was to be evacuated, which got abroad before your instructions reached me, greatly retarded my operations. I trust that Colonel Jones will be able to move all the most valuable stores remaining there when I left. Besides the ordnance and other stores that you directed to be first moved there was in Pensacola and about 15 miles out of town a quantity of very valuable navy stores, the loss of which could probably not be supplied, which I thought it proper to remove; also a quantity of valuable machinery in the navy-yard, which, if moved to a place of security, might be used in the manufacture of guns, which I was removing. As the railroad could not furnish sufficient transportation, the steamer Time was loaded and sent up the Escambia, which was so unusually high as to enable the steamer to reach Bluff Springs on the 13th in about forty hours from Pensacola. She would return and carry up another load. All necessary preparations were made before I left to disable the guns, burn all the buildings, and carry out fully the work of destruction you directed. On the night of the 10th I ordered Lieutenant Colonel Beard, of the First Florida Regiment, to take with him 100 men of his regiment and proceed by steamboat up to East Bay, Blackwater, and the Escambia, and burn and destroy all saw-mills, lumber. and boats that he could find. I directed him not to commence burning the mills until after daylight on the 11th. He was ordered to communicate with the officer having charge of the two gunboats nearly completed at or near Milton, and, if practicable, tow them up the Escambia, but if that could not be done, and the officer having charge of them had any doubt of his ability to destroy the boats if necessary to prevent them falling into the hands of the enemy, then to burn them also. Having performed this duty, Colonel Beard was ordered to take his command to Brewton, on the railroad, about 7 miles above Pollard, where his regiment would be concentrated and then ordered to Corinth.

You are aware that a very small number of the men of the First Florida Regiment were with the army when you left. The interruption to travel and excessive rains retarded the Floridians somewhat in rejoining the regiment. Most of them had returned the day before I left, and as soon as they could collect their arms, which had been issued to other troops, they would go to Brewton and Pollard. As only about 320 of the Twenty-seventh and 450 of the Eighth Mississippi Regiments were present for duty, it was necessary to leave the latter with Colonel Jones or give up all idea of moving the remaining stores. They will be ordered to you as soon as possible. The telegraphic communication with Pensacola is interrupted by the storm of last night, or I would order them to start immediately. Failing to hear from you in reply to my letter of the 6th, and as your telegrams were very long on the way, I took the liberty of telegraphing the Adjutant-General, presuming, of course, that he was informed of the instructions under which I was acting, and asked if I could be permitted to leave from 700 to 1,000 armed men with Colonel Jones, to hold the place as long as possible, and move, as far as practicable, all the remaining war material. He replied promptly, telling me to use my discretion, and make the necessary arrangements for saving the war material remaining at Pensacola.

I write in great haste to get this off by a special express, which starts with a part only of the small ammunition, all I could furnish, called for by Colonel Slaughter's telegram of the 13th, which I received about 12 o'clock to-day.

Most respectfully, your obedient servant,

SAM. JONES,
Brigadier-General.

JACKSON, *March* 15, 1862.

General SAMUEL JONES:

Your letter of 6th received. Suggestions approved. Carry them out. Where is Florida regiment and Eighth Mississippi?

BRAXTON BRAGG.

GENERAL ORDERS, No. 10. } HEADQUARTERS DEPARTMENT NO. 1, *New Orleans, La., March* 15, 1862.

By authority of the President of the Confederate States, and in his name, martial law is hereby declared in the parishes of Orleans, Jefferson, Saint Bernard, and Plaquemine.

All grown white males in the aforesaid parishes, except unnaturalized foreigners, will be required to take the oath of allegiance to the Confederate States, and all persons, whether foreigners or not, who are unfriendly to our cause, are notified to leave the district embraced by this order without delay.

A system of registry and passport will be established, and no one will be permitted to sojourn in the above-mentioned parishes without satisfying the provost-marshals of their loyalty; and all good citizens are requested to report to those officers all who are suspected of hostility to the Government.

All places for the sale of liquor will be closed by 8 o'clock p. m. Any found open after that hour will be closed permanently and the liquor seized.

A number of persons who have no ostensible business, nor any interests in the city or State, have recently arrived in New Orleans. They must satisfy the provost-marshals of their good intentions and objects here or leave immediately.

The following-named persons are appointed provost-marshals for Orleans Parish:

William Freret, first district; Cyprian Dufour, second district; Hon. Pierre Soulé, third district; Col. H. D. Ogden, fourth district. For Algiers, Capt. Norbert Trepagnier; for Jefferson Parish, Judge Victor Burthe;—who will enter upon the discharge of the duties of their offices immediately.

The provost-marshals for the parishes of Plaquemine and Saint Bernard will be announced in a few days.

By command of Major-General Lovell:

J. G. PICKETT,
Assistant Adjutant-General.

HEADQUARTERS ARMY OF MOBILE,
Mobile, March 16, 1862.

Col. THOMAS M. JONES,
Commanding, Pensacola:

COLONEL: Before leaving Pensacola I directed Captain Bird and a sergeant of Captain McDowell's company, First Florida Regiment, to take the men of their respective companies, which had just arrived, to Brewton, and report to Lieutenant-Colonel Beard, commanding the regiment, who I supposed would have arrived there with 100 men of his regiment, which he had taken with him on special service, by the 14th instant. I had intended to order the eight organized companies of that regiment to assemble at Brewton or Pollard as soon as they had collected their arms which had been issued to other troops, but in the pressure of business on me I omitted to give the order. Send the four companies of that regiment (two at Deer Point and Captains Gee's and Cropps') to report to Lieutenant-Colonel Beard as soon as possible, and order him as soon as his companies are together to proceed to Corinth, Miss., and report to the commanding officer there.

It will not do as yet to leave Deer Point entirely unguarded. Direct Lieutenant-Colonel Conoley to keep a guard of about 30 men of his battalion there, having a steamer always ready near at hand to bring them off if attacked in such force that they cannot hold the Point. The guard can be relieved as often as you think proper, only be sure to have a guard always there. They should keep up camp-fires enough to indicate 300 or 400 men were in the camp, and they should use the material of which the huts are built as fuel, pulling the huts down for the purpose, but they must not make anything like a conflagration.

Continue to send forward as rapidly as you can the guns you do not absolutely need to keep up appearances. If there are any more rifled or shell guns, send them here; also the 10-inch mortars. The smoothbore guns, send to Montgomery. Do not suppose that I have given up or wish you to give up the idea of holding the place permanently. I hope we may be able to hold it. But you will not want the 10-inch mortars or the guns in the redoubt. After all the columbiads, rifled guns, and sea-coast howitzers are moved move the mortars, then the smooth-bore guns.

Captain Merchant says there are several bars of lead at the store-house by the magazine, and some more about the quartermaster's office or store-house; if so, send it all here by the first train; it is greatly needed; and have the roofs of the houses in the navy-yard and hospital examined, and if any lead can be found send it here.

Telegraphic communication with Pensacola and Montgomery has been cut off for two days, and I therefore do not know how many volunteers you have received. If you want more, telegraph Governor Shorter, and ask him to send them. There are reports here of fighting in West Tennessee, but nothing positive.

Very respectfully and truly, &c.,

SAM. JONES,
Brigadier-General.

PENSACOLA, *March* 16, 1862.

Capt. C. S. STRINGFELLOW,
Assistant Adjutant-General:

CAPTAIN: I have the honor to report that, in obedience to orders from you by letters dated respectively the 7th and 10th instant,* I proceeded with two companies (Captains Means' and Baker's) of the First Regiment Florida Volunteers, in the steamer Tom Murray, from Deer Point, at 8 o'clock p. m. on the 10th, arriving at Miller's Mills, in East Bay, at 11 o'clock. I called at once on Colonel Miller, but not finding him at home, I advised Mrs. Miller of the object of my mission. At daylight I commenced the execution of your orders by firing the mills and other property, boats, &c.

Having finished here, I proceeded without delay up the Blackwater River, destroying everything in my route embraced in my instructions until I reached Milton. There, at the earnest solicitation of the citizens, I deferred burning anything until my return from General Jackson Morton's, at the head of Blackwater, they thinking that they could destroy one of the mills, the burning of which at that time would have endangered a large portion of the city, and it making no material, if any, difference whether destroyed then or on my return. Returning, I destroyed everything at Milton embraced in your order.

I reached the mouth of the Escambia about 11 o'clock a. m. on Wednesday, and proceeded up the river, burning as I went all that could be burned. A large amount of square (ship) timber which could not be burned was turned adrift. I found it necessary to burn the gunboats at Bagdad and Milton, it being impracticable to tow them up the Escambia, as they could not pass the bar; in fact, only one of them was launched.

I reached Bluff Springs at about 10 o'clock a. m. on Saturday, after a fatiguing and unremitting labor in the performance of my duties. At this point I received your note from Pollard, dated the 13th. The duties had required so much longer time than had been anticipated that our provisions were entirely out on reaching the Springs; indeed, they gave out on Tuesday evening, and it became necessary to purchase supplies, which I did at Milton. But these again gave out, and I had to

---

* Letter of the 7th not found.

get some at another point on the river, but was only able to procure a small quantity. Being entirely out of provisions, I marched my men to Pollard, and on arriving there could obtain none, so was forced to go on to Brewton. I took to-day 10 men and a sergeant, under a lieutenant, and placed them on the steamer Murray at Bluff Springs, with order to proceed immediately to Deer Point, to await further orders.

For particulars of the property destroyed I beg to refer you to the accompanying paper, marked Exhibit A.* This, of course, could not be perfect, as much of my work was done after night, and again so hurriedly that a correct statement could not be made. It will afford you some idea of the extent of my operations, and account for the time consumed in the execution of your orders.

I cannot close this report without remarking upon the sacrificing patriotism of those whose property—in many cases all they had—was destroyed. While they regretted the necessity none shrank from the sacrifice, and in many cases were prepared themselves to apply the torch to all they possessed. A more loyal and spirited people I have not met during our troubles. I am happy in being able to state that no dwelling or property other than that embraced in your order was destroyed, except at Bagdad, where the proximity of the dwellings to the mills caused three houses—Overman's, Simpson's, and Bushnell's—to be burned. The furniture, I believe, was saved, as I had a detail from my command to aid in removing it, though of course damaged to some extent.

My command conducted themselves with marked decorum, being sensible of the delicate and unpleasant duty in which they were engaged. I am much indebted to Mr. A. McVoy, who accompanied me throughout, and without whose assistance I could not have carried out my orders, being unacquainted with the topography of the country and the location of the mills. He was otherwise of great assistance to me.

I am, captain, your obedient servant,

W. K. BEARD,

Lieutenant-Colonel First Fla. Regt., Commanding Expedition.

GENERAL ORDERS, No. 11. } HDQRS. DEPARTMENT NO. 1, C. S. A., *New Orleans, La., March* 18, 1862.

In order to carry into effective operations the requirements of General Orders, No. 10, current series, from these headquarters, the provost-marshals will each establish an office in their respective districts for the transaction of business. Due notice of the localities will be given in the public prints.

Each office will be provided with such assistants and clerks as may be necessary for the transaction of business.

Every white male above the age of sixteen years, residing temporarily or otherwise in the parishes of Orleans and Jefferson, whether he be a citizen of the Confederate States or an alien, shall, within six days from the publication of this order, present himself before the provost-marshal of this district, to have his name registered and to furnish as far as able such information as may be required.

Those who claim to be citizens of the Confederate States, by birth or otherwise, shall be required to subscribe an unconditional oath of alle-

---

*Exhibit omitted. Among its more important items are two gunboats, four other steamboats, and a number of sailing vessels.

giance to said States, and such as claim to be aliens shall be sworn to the effect that they will abide by the laws of this State and of the Confederate States as long as they are permitted to reside therein, and that they will, under no circumstances, convey to our enemies any information relative to the military or political affairs of the country.

Persons who came to this city or State since the 21st of May, 1861, from any of the States at war with the Confederate States, shall be subject to arrest and imprisonment, unless they procure within six days from the date hereof a permit to remain, signed by the commanding general or the provost-marshal of the district in which they reside, which permit will be renewed from time to time by an indorsement setting forth the time of extension.

The foregoing requirements will go into effect as above in the parishes of Saint Bernard and Plaquemine within six days after the appointment of the provost-marshals of those parishes. Every person who desires to go beyond the limits of the aforesaid districts or parishes shall provide himself with a passport signed by the commanding general or the provost-marshals of the district or parish in which said person resides.

All orders issued by provost-marshals in the execution of their offices will be promptly obeyed, and any disobedience of summons emanating from any of them will be dealt with summarily, and all officers in command of troops are hereby directed to comply promptly with any requisitions made on them by the provost-marshals, and to furnish them such aid and assistance as they may require. The police of the city will in like manner, render every assistance in their power when called on.

The commanding general confidently expects that the friends of order, all those who have at heart the success of our glorious cause, will cordially co-operate with the provost-marshals and furnish them every possible assistance in the performance of the onerous duties devolved upon them for the general welfare. Circumstances have rendered these measures necessary for our safety and success, and it becomes each and every good citizen to contribute all in his power to the promotion of such desirable ends.

Martial law has not been declared for the purpose of annoying unnecessarily the true and loyal citizens. No greater restrictions will be imposed upon the community than are deemed absolutely necessary by those in authority to attain the objects in view, which are mainly to ascertain and remove from among us those who, acting under the instigation of the enemy, are endeavoring by word and deed to impede our onward progress towards independence and self-government, and to rid ourselves of able-bodied loyal men liable to military duty, who have fled to New Orleans from the presence of the enemy, leaving others to perform the duty which they are seeking to avoid.

By command of Major-General Lovell:

E. A. PALFREY,
Major, and Assistant Adjutant-General.

CORINTH, *March* 18, 1862.

General SAMUEL JONES:

Your letters of 6th and 15th received. All dispositions approved. Transportation coming back for all stores. Send forward medicines and hospital property and heavy guns.

BRAXTON BRAGG.

HEADQUARTERS ARMY OF MOBILE,
Mobile, March 21, 1862.

General BRAXTON BRAGG:

GENERAL: Colonel Jones has not yet informed me if all the rifled and shell guns at Pensacola have been dismounted and forwarded as you directed, but I presume it has all been done by this time. The bad condition of the roads, and the fact that I was obliged to send a few of the guns you want up the Escambia and land them a mile or two from the railroad, have caused some delay in the delivery of the guns and ammunition at Corinth. I have made every effort to forward with the least possible delay all ordnance and ordnance stores called for by you.

I am glad to learn by your telegram received yesterday that my suggestions and operations communicated to you in my letters of the 6th and 15th instant met with your approbation. I have never been entirely without hope of holding Pensacola, even with the very limited means left me, until some favorable change in our affairs should enable us to gather a sufficient force there to hold it permanently. The governor of Alabama has sent there something over a thousand volunteers, and will send more. Colonel Jones wrote me on the 16th instant that all was going on well; that the new troops, though unarmed, were full of energy and zeal, and he adds, "With the army I now have, had I arms, I could defy the attempt of the enemy to dislodge me." The colonel, you see, enters upon his work with spirit. Since he wrote, the governor of Alabama has sent him 300 arms, and I have strong hope of being able to send him a sufficient number to arm nearly all the new troops. I am more and more convinced that the enemy's force in the Gulf, and especially on Santa Rosa, has been greatly overestimated. When I left Pensacola only 96 tents could be seen on the island. The season for operations on a large scale on the Gulf is fast passing away, and if we can hold our ground a month or two longer all may yet be well on the Gulf coast.

In view of all the circumstances I respectfully suggest and urge upon you to permit all the smooth-bore guns and the troops now at Pensacola to remain there, hold the place as long as possible, and never give it up without a fight. If forced to abandon it, the guns, which would be of little value to the enemy, can be first disabled, and the other work of destruction carried out as directed by you. I feel so deeply the importance of this matter that I venture to urge it upon your consideration, notwithstanding the pressure of business immediately around you.

Most respectfully, &c.,

SAM. JONES,
Brigadier-General.

MOBILE, ALA., *March* 22, 1862.

Hon. J. P. BENJAMIN,
Secretary of War, Richmond, Va.:

Your telegram of yesterday received. The powder delivered to Flag-Officer Randolph. Would like much to have it replaced. Supply here very inadequate; only a small quantity remaining at Pensacola. Railroad communication with Pensacola will not be open sooner than eight or ten days. I believe enemy's force in the Gulf, especially on Santa Rosa, greatly overestimated. Governor Shorter has sent about 2,000 volunteers to Pensacola and can send more. If permitted to keep the troops and ordnance now there, we may be able to hold the place permanently. Colonel Jones says he can hold it if 700 or 800 muskets or rifles are sent him. I have some hope of getting them for him. Have ordered him not to abandon the place unless forced. Shall we go on dismounting all smooth-bore guns and sending them to Montgomery and then abandon the place, or shall we hold it as long as possible? Beg you to excuse my telegraphing you directly. It is difficult and takes time to communicate through General Bragg. Will inform him that I have telegraphed you. Telegraph.

SAM. JONES.
Brigadier-General.

WAR DEPARTMENT,
Richmond, Va., March 22, 1862.

Maj. Gen. MANSFIELD LOVELL,
New Orleans, La.:

SIR: Before turning over the affairs of this Department to my successor I am anxious to give you full replies to your letters of the 6th, 9th, and 10th instant, as well as those remaining unanswered in your letter of the 27th ultimo.

1st. I send you a remittance of $350,000, which will enable you to pay 60 per cent. of the value of the fourteen steamers seized for the public use. I applied to Congress for a further appropriation of $500,000, which will, it is hoped, suffice to complete all payments for these vessels.

2d. I have seen Colonel Gorgas on the subject of the works at the Marine Hospital. Your action in this matter is fully approved, and nothing is more gratifying than the zeal and activity you have so intelligently applied to remedying the deficiency under which we labor in the conduct of this war. Exercise your discretion in concentrating all our resources for the public defense, and feel assured of executive support and approval.

3d. The nomination of Colonel Smith as brigadier-general was sent to the Senate more than a week ago, but from some cause it has not yet been confirmed. I shall inquire into the difficulty immediately.

4th. No more calls will be made on you for any supplies. Your assistance to the army in Tennessee has been most timely and valuable, and exceeded what I had hoped. I informed you by telegraph this morning that I had ordered 44,000 pounds of powder from Columbus to you. This is part of the cargo of the Florida, which brought 64,000 pounds. The remaining 20,000 pounds have been sent to Mobile, so that the whole cargo goes to the Gulf. My main purpose in sending it was to enable you to supply the new iron-clad steamers just about to be completed. From the recent experiment of the Virginia and what I hear of the steamers at New Orleans I feel confident that, if even one of them can be got ready before you are attacked, she will disperse and destroy any fleet the enemy can gather in the river above or below. The naval officers say that Tift's steamer is far superior to the Virginia, and the Virginia's performances were more extraordinary than the printed reports exhibit. If she had only drawn 5 feet less water she would certainly have captured the Minnesota. She is in perfect order and will soon make another dash, and our officers are confident of taking or sinking the Monitor.

5th. We have received from the Gladiator and Economist altogether 190,000 pounds of powder. The Florida's I send to New Orleans and Mobile. A large quantity of powder, nearly 100,000 pounds, was lost in our disasters at Forts Henry and Donelson and the evacuation of Nashville. If, with the powder from the Florida, you are still short, I must try and have part of that received from England forwarded to you; but I hope this will not be necessary. We have contracts out for several thousand tons of saltpeter, and ought now very soon to receive one or two cargoes. This would put us on our legs completely. There is saltpeter in Mexico, and Mr. Oliver came here to make contracts with me, but I could do nothing with him. He wanted large advances and to bind himself to nothing. He was so fearful of responsibilities, that it was impossible to agree on anything. See his agents, Messrs. Avendain Brothers, in New Orleans. They may, perhaps, procure you promptly a saltpeter supply.

6th. I ought to have mentioned, in regard to powder by the Florida, that the parties telegraphed that they required for it $2 a pound, cash, delivered in Marianna, Fla., the Department to take the risk and expense of getting it to Columbus. I consider this extortionate, in view of the fact that they had called on the Government for help to save it and get it to Columbus. I ordered General Pemberton to impress it at that rate. I advise you of these facts for information. The parties complain that they have only received $120,000 on account of the powder per Vanderbilt. Pray settle up with them for that cargo.

7th. Your call on Governor Moore for troops to replace those sent to Tennessee is approved.

8th. In view of the great extent to which you have been weakened by sending aid up the river you are right in retaining some of the steamboat fleet below. I hope, however, that the iron-clad boats will soon be under way and relieve you from all fear of a river attack.

Your obedient servant,

J. P. BENJAMIN,
Secretary of War.

NEW ORLEANS, LA., *March* 22, 1862.

Hon. J. P. BENJAMIN:

Please order General Jones, at Mobile, to send me some 10-inch columbiads and sea-coast mortars promptly.

M. LOVELL.

NEW ORLEANS, LA., *March* 22, 1862.

Hon. J. P. BENJAMIN,
Secretary of War:

Seven vessels of the enemy inside of the mouth of the river. All naval ships at Memphis. I will have to retain six of Montgomery's fleet for service below.

M. LOVELL.

HEADQUARTERS DEPARTMENT NO. 1,
New Orleans, La., March 22, 1862.

Hon. J. P. BENJAMIN,
Secretary of War:

SIR: I have the honor to acknowledge the receipt of your letter of the 12th relative to Montgomery's expedition. The evacuation of Columbus overturns his original intentions of destroying the enemy's fleet at Cairo, and in my judgment they can now be used only as assistants to the land and naval forces in defending our own positions. The people of New Orleans thought it strange that all the vessels of the Navy should be sent up the river, and were disposed to find fault with sending in addition fourteen steamers, leaving this city without a single vessel for protection against the enemy, who was collecting heavy fleets near the mouth of the river. Within the past few days they have had thirteen ships near the mouth, and have succeeded in towing inside several large steamers, which in my opinion only await the arrival of the mortar fleet to attempt to come up the river to New Orleans and operate as a diversion for the column descending from Cairo. Under these circumstances I shall retain here six of Montgomery's ships to assist in repelling any attack upon the forts below.

At my request Governor Moore is also fitting up with bulkheads of cotton two vessels, which will give us eight here. This will be of material service and will quiet the people, who think that they have been too much neglected. In guns of large caliber we are greatly deficient, as I have mentioned before. It was to be hoped that in the evacuation of Pensacola some 10-inch columbiads would be sent here, but I have only succeeded in getting one, and that by sending a persevering officer after it.

I inclose you two orders on the subject of martial law.* Affairs here have reached a crisis (which Mr. Yancey will explain to the President), and it became necessary for some one to seize the helm with a strong hand, or we should have had trouble, perhaps bloodshed, between men who were all friendly to the cause. A city composed of such heterogeneous elements as this, with an excitable population, who are easily led into excesses, is difficult to govern, as there are so many interests to consult, each jealous of the other. This rendered the appointment of provost-marshals a matter of great difficulty, more especially as I knew that there were large and influential associations in existence whose leaders were desirous to take control. The universal approval of my appointments throughout the city and the satisfaction and quiet so apparent to all lead me to infer that the difficulty has been entirely solved, and everything seems to have settled back into its proper channel. We shall encourage our friends, root out our enemies, guard the public interests, and keep the speculators well in hand. No movement has been made since martial law was proclaimed that has not been received with approval by the people at large. I feel sure that the administration and our cause have been saved from a terrible embarrassment here in New Orleans.

We are called upon here from all quarters to furnish everything—powder, food, equipments, and ordnance stores of all kinds—and it is utterly impossible to make any estimate which will suit the requirements of the bureaus. We must have money here in large quantities, for we know not what urgent requisition may come upon us by telegraph at a moment's notice. Bragg telegraphed to-day for 500,000 pounds of hard bread, yet the estimate of my commissary, approved by me, has been returned from Richmond for details of what we would require. Such red tape will kill us. We had to borrow money to keep troops from suffering. This point being recognized as a great source of supply, I hope you will see the importance of placing large amounts of money here for all the bureaus—commissary, ordnance, quartermaster, and medical purveyors. It is utterly impossible to foresee what we will require. Money will have to be borrowed to keep our troops in Tennessee from wanting bread. This certainly could not have been forseen by the assistant commissary of this department.

I thank you very warmly for the confidence expressed in the last paragraph of your letter, and trust that nothing will occur to abate it. My position here is one of labor and difficulty, without much chance for

* Nos. 10 and 11, March 15 and 18, pp. 857, 860.

glory; but I shall do my duty as I understand it, without "partiality, favor, or affection."

Respectfully, your obedient servant,

M. LOVELL,
Major-General, Commanding.

RICHMOND, VA., *March* 23, 1862.

Major General LOVELL, *New Orleans, La.:*

I have ordered 44,000 pounds of cannon powder sent to you from Columbus, to enable you to supply gunboats. Have also sent orders for heavy guns, as requested in your dispatch of yesterday.

J. P. BENJAMIN,
Secretary of War.

RICHMOND, VA., *March* 23, 1862.

Maj. Gen. SAMUEL JONES, *Mobile:*

Send to General Lovell as promptly as possible some 10-inch columbiads and sea-coast mortars.

J. P. BENJAMIN,
Secretary of War.

RICHMOND, VA., *March* 23, 1862.

Maj. Gen. SAMUEL JONES, *Mobile:*

The President desires that you proclaim martial law in his name over Mobile and the surrounding country.

J. P. BENJAMIN,
Secretary of War.

RICHMOND, *March* 23, 1862.

Major General JONES:

Your dispatch of yesterday received. Reserve the guns, forces, and ammunition necessary, as suggested by you, to hold the place against the small force you believe the enemy to have. Communicate further, if necessary. You will be further advised.

J. P. BENJAMIN,
Secretary of War.

RICHMOND, VA., *March* 27, 1862.

C. J. MCRAE, *Mobile, Ala.:*

I understood the purpose of the governor. General Jones was intended to remain in command, and orders have been given accordingly.

JEFFERSON DAVIS.

HDQRS. SECOND GRAND DIVISION, ARMY OF THE MISS.,
Corinth, Miss., March 28, 1862.

Maj. Gen. SAMUEL JONES,
Commanding Department Alabama and West Florida.:

GENERAL: Your dispatch of 19th instant, from Mobile,* reached the major-general commanding after some delay, owing to his change of

*Not found, but see that of March 21, p. 862.

position, who directs me to say that the dispositions you have made under the orders of the War Department appear to be judicious, and he has no doubt the position at Pensacola may be held by Colonel Jones without danger, especially as we may expect no active operations from the enemy in the Gulf during the approaching summer season.

As his instructions for the destruction of property were based entirely on the orders of the War Department to "abandon Pensacola," he is gratified to find you exercised a proper discretion in that matter, though rumors have reached here that the order had been executed in part on private property.

The breaking of the railroad again is very unfortunate. Our defenses on the Mississippi are very imperfect, and require all the guns we can command. Will you please hurry forward those behind. There were in all at least twenty heavy shell guns, besides 8-inch howitzers and rifle guns. Half were ordered via Memphis and the other half to New Orleans. But seven have yet reached Memphis. Please urge them forward, sending everything complete with each one.

The general directs that you will change the destination of those to New Orleans, too, and send them to Jackson, Miss., to be used on the river near Vicksburg.

As soon as you can ascertain how many can be sent in each direction please advise us.

It is perfectly useless to send guns to New Orleans. If we lose the river, New Orleans must fall; no defenses can save it; the railroads would be cut immediately, and starvation would do its work.

In resuming his old command, in addition to the one here, the general did not intend to interfere with your command of the department, and requests you to resume it. His command is a larger, and only includes the smaller one. The object was to give us control of means.

It is a subject of regret that the Department should have interfered to prevent your coming here. The most important command in this army was assigned you, and the one on which the general considers the safety of our cause depends.

I am, general, very respectfully, your obedient servant,

GEO. G. GARNER,
Assistant Adjutant-General.

NEW ORLEANS, LA., *March* 29, 1862.

Hon. J. P. BENJAMIN:

I cannot get heavy guns from Mobile. The enemy is in large force at the mouth of the river. Please order commanding officer at Mobile to send immediately.

M. LOVELL.

RICHMOND, VA., *March* 29, 1862.

General MANSFIELD LOVELL,
New Orleans, La.:

What guns do you mean; guns in batteries or guns on their way to you?

G. W. RANDOLPH,
Secretary of War.

NEW ORLEANS, LA., *March* 31, 1862.

Hon. GEORGE W. RANDOLPH:

A part of the 10-inch columbiads and sea-coast mortars which were at Pensacola. New Orleans has only one of the former and none of the latter.

M. LOVELL.

HEADQUARTERS,
Richmond, March 31, 1862.

General SAMUEL JONES,
Commanding at Pensacola:

GENERAL: In answer to certain inquiries made in behalf of Col. Thomas M. Jones, as the commanding officer at Pensacola, by Capt. John B. Sale, I have the honor to state that you are desired to hold Pensacola, the navy-yard, &c., provided you have the ability to do so, and to save all the public property of value. Should you be opposed by an irresistible force, you are expected to bring off your command in good order, with their arms, &c. It is therefore suggested that you at once make arrangements for sending to places of security all property not necessary for your purpose, to mobilize your troops, and be prepared for any emergency.

All the arms that are available have been sent to the governor of Florida. Nine hundred will be sent to you by him. Possibly he may supply you with more. The commanding officer at Tallahassee has been written to to send you a company of cavalry and a company of light artillery, if he can procure them. As regards the field officers of the Twenty-seventh Mississippi Regiment, I learn from the Adjutant and Inspector General's Office that Thomas M. Jones has been appointed colonel, James L. Autrey lieutenant-colonel, and George H. Lipscomb major.

Very respectfully,

R. E. LEE,
General.

Abstract from field return of the Army of Mobile, commanded by Maj. Gen. Samuel Jones, for March, 1862.

Troops.	Present for duty.		Aggregate present.	Aggregate present and absent.
	Officers.	Men.		
2d Brigade	78	1,548	1,945	2,104
9th Brigade Alabama Militia	53	599	735	1,041
1st Confederate Regiment	13	196	235	270
Gracie's regiment	14	282	296	296
Ketchum's regiment	9	157	166	166
McKinstry's regiment	16	579	616	638
Smith's regiment	21	398	419	419
Boyle's company Mobile Dragoons	3	94	107	131
Semple's company light artillery	5	104	119	121
Waters' company light artillery	4	113	129	141
Total	216	4,070	4,767	5,327

NEW ORLEANS, LA., *April* 1, 1862.

President DAVIS,
Richmond, Va.:

I purchased eight months ago 1,880 rifles and 30,000 cartridges, and have just succeeded, after infinite trouble and over $60,000 of outlay, in having them landed on the Florida coast. They were at once seized by Governor Milton, and I telegraphed they must be sent to me. I have received his reply, in which he coolly informs me he has taken one-half and your Secretary of War the other. This unpardonable and unparalleled outrage is nothing less than robbery and just as bad. I cannot use Louisiana's money to buy arms when they are to be seized by the first freebooter that meets them. I have given out all the arms I had, expecting that these would be in the hands of my own troops. Now that thirty-seven sail of the enemy are in the river, in God's name, in the name of my State, I ask you to order them to be sent to me immediately.

THO. O. MOORE.

RICHMOND, VA., *April* 2, 1862.

Governor MOORE,
New Orleans, La.:

I was not aware that the arms in the hands of Governor Milton belonged to the State of Louisiana. One-half of them, sent to Pensacola, have been ordered to be placed subject to your order, and I have requested Governor Milton to make the same disposition of the remainder. He took them supposing that they were arms given him by Mr. Benjamin, when in fact they were part of a different cargo. I did not know until Mr. Benjamin informed me of it that the arms held by Governor Milton were a part of the cargo of the Florida. Col. T. M. Jones, commanding at Pensacola, will communicate to you the arrival of the arms at that place.

G. W. RANDOLPH,
Secretary of War.

MOBILE, *April* 2, 1862.

Col. THOMAS M. JONES,
Pensacola:

I have resumed command of this department. Nine hundred rifles on the way to you for war troops.*

* * * * * * *

SAM. JONES.

O'BANNONVILLE, *April* 2, 1862.

General SAMUEL JONES:

Ten 10-inch, seven 8-inch columbiads, nine sea-coast howitzers, four rifle guns, and two 8-inch sea-coast howitzers have been shipped. Lieutenant Aldrich is absent at East Pass, and there may be more; when he returns I'll let you know. The enemy shelled Captain McPherson's camp, in order, I think, to enable him to land re-enforcements behind the island, which I think was done yesterday, as 160 cavalry were seen on island to-day. I think there is mischief intended. They have been

*Some matters of detail omitted.

re-enforced. More than 225 men seen landed near Pickens. I think they will make an attack.

The negro is in prison; he has implicated a white man with his evidence and corroborative circumstances.

THOS. M. JONES,
Colonel, Commanding.

NEW ORLEANS, LA., *April* 3, 1862.

General GEORGE W. RANDOLPH:

The seizure of Governor Moore's guns by the War Department leaves me in a precarious condition. We sent off all our men, relying upon those guns to arm others. Please order them here.

M. LOVELL.

RICHMOND, VA., *April* 4, 1862.

General LOVELL,
New Orleans:

I have already ordered Colonel T. M. Jones at Pensacola, and requested Governor Milton, of Florida, to hold the arms subject to Governor Moore's order, and have notified him of the fact. I have also endeavored to get columbiads and sea-coast mortars for you from Pensacola, but find that all have been sent to Mobile that could be spared.

G. W. RANDOLPH,
Secretary of War.

PENSACOLA, *April* 4, 1862.

General JONES:

I am confident that the enemy now know my true condition, two men having escaped to Fort Pickens.

THOS. M. JONES.

EXECUTIVE OFFICE,
Montgomery, Ala., April 5, 1862.

General GEORGE W. RANDOLPH,
Secretary of War, C. S. A., Richmond:

DEAR SIR: I consider the maintenance of the possession of Pensacola a matter of such prime importance, not only to Alabama and Florida, but to the cause at large, that I must claim your attention to a few thoughts and suggestions upon the subject.

Pensacola is, next to Norfolk, the most important point on our entire seaboard to hold at this time. To us as a possession it may not be of any great importance, but to the Yankee Government its importance, in view of their manifest designs, is incalculable. They want a spacious and safe harbor far South for their vast naval armament. Here they have it. It is the only one in the Gulf to which their large ships can find access. When they get it, there is the spacious bay to ride in, the navy-yard to repair at, the fine hospital, and other appointments, which cost the old Government millions of dollars, the extensive fortifications, all ready to their hands.

But, again, they cannot summer at New Orleans, nor Mobile, nor Savannah, nor Charleston. The yellow fever will be a terror to them and repel them; but at Pensacola they can make safe and pleasant summer quarters. The healthfulness of the place has been tested by time and experience and is established, and the Yankees who have already spent one summer at Pickens will feel every confidence in making Pensacola summer quarters. No other place on the Southern coast with a roadstead for ships can compare with it for such a purpose.

Put these two great facts together, and it is needless to elaborate an argument. They speak for themselves. I will not weary you nor myself in amplifying.

This great and important point can be securely held with 5,000 men, properly armed and trained, against any force the Yankee Government can detach for its capture; perhaps by less, but certainly by 5,000 men.

But we are now ill provided, and if provision be not made, and that soon, our comparatively naked condition will be known to the invaders, and they will make a stroke at us and take us, as I fear, almost without a show of resistance.

Let me state to you plainly what is needed to put the place in condition of defense:

1st. We want a good brigadier-general—some man who will inspire confidence and effect speedy organization. The gallant and worthy colonel who now commands the post himself feels this want.

2d. We want small-arms for nearly half the troops; now have about 3,200, and we need permanently at the post 5,000 small-arms.

3d. We want now one or two artillery companies and several companies of cavalry.

Alabama is doing all she can, and she will readily furnish the men if she can have the effective co-operation of the C. S. A.

I have this suggestion to make both for present and future operations in respect to Pensacola. Being a point of so great importance, a healthy location, and accessible for stores and provisions, let it be made a camp of instruction for the Confederate service. Send new regiments or companies, as they are formed, to Pensacola for drill; when sufficiently trained, retire them where they may be needed and bring in others, keeping the complement at 4,000 or 5,000 men. In this way the post can be maintained and the new levies of Alabama and adjoining States furnished with a most eligible camp of instruction.

I do not wish to seem importunate, but feeling persuaded, as I do, that 50,000 men will not be able to repair the loss of a post which 5,000 could now hold safely, I hope I will be excused for any seeming importunity. From Pensacola, in the hands of the enemy, the whole great producing country of Middle Alabama can be so menaced as to put a serious check to ordinary agricultural labor at little or no cost to the invader. With Kentucky, Tennessee, and parts of North Carolina, South Carolina, and Virginia lost to us, what are we to do for food if Middle Alabama is seriously disturbed?

I remain, with very great respect,

JNO. GILL SHORTER.

P. S.—If the Secretary will furnish arms, I will furnish 5,000 more troops for the post without delay, with the troops already there included.

NEW ORLEANS, LA., *April* 10, 1862.

General GEORGE W. RANDOLPH:

Can you possibly order here 4,000 or 5,000 small-arms? I have sent all my troops to Corinth, but have several unarmed war regiments.

M. LOVELL.

RICHMOND, VA., *April* 10, 1862.

Maj. Gen. MANSFIELD LOVELL,
New Orleans, La.:

Are the cotton-lined boats ready, and where are they?

G. W. RANDOLPH,
Secretary of War.

RICHMOND, VA., *April* 10, 1862.

To the GOVERNORS OF MISSISSIPPI, LOUISIANA, SOUTH CAROLINA, GEORGIA, AND ALABAMA:

General Beauregard must have re-enforcements to meet the vast accumulation of the enemy before him. The necessity is imminent; the case of vital importance. Send forward to Corinth all the armed men you can furnish.

JEFFERSON DAVIS.

NEW ORLEANS, LA., *April* 11, 1862.

JEFFERSON DAVIS:

Can troops be armed if I send them? I have no arms here except those General Lovell thinks we should keep—those just received from Pensacola.

THO. O. MOORE.

RICHMOND, VA., *April* 11, 1862.

Gov. THOMAS O. MOORE:

No arms to furnish. You will not fail to appreciate the necessity which caused the application to you. If you could spare armed troops for a few weeks they might then be returned to you.

JEFFERSON DAVIS.

NEW ORLEANS, LA., *April* 11, 1862.

Hon. GEORGE W. RANDOLPH,
Secretary of War, Richmond, Va.:

Governor Milton will not forward my guns. John Leeds, my agent, has been waiting at Columbus, Ga., one week. Order them sent. I am greatly annoyed.

THO. O. MOORE,
Governor of Louisiana.

RICHMOND, VA., *April* 11, 1862.

General MANSFIELD LOVELL,
New Orleans, La.:

We have just had a call for arms from Corinth, which we cannot supply, but hope soon to be able to do so and to send you some. Did you receive my telegram yesterday asking where the cotton-lined boats are?

G. W. RANDOLPH,
Secretary of War.

NEW ORLEANS, LA., *April* 11, 1862.

General RANDOLPH,
Secretary of War:

Five cotton boats have gone up; three more will go to-night. The other six are to go below—four being ready.

M. LOVELL.

NEW ORLEANS, *April* 11, 1862.
(Received April 12.)

Hon. S. R. MALLORY:

I am here and will leave soon. The Louisiana will be ready in three days. My boats are not able to meet the enemy without losing them. Enemy march down the banks and erect fortifications, trying to cut off our boats. Island 10 was given up the 8th, losing all the guns. Our boats brought off 500 of the army. The floating battery was sunk by a shell from a mortar.

GEO. N. HOLLINS,
Flag-Officer.

RICHMOND, VA., *April* 11, 1862.

Major-General LOVELL,
New Orleans, La.:

The Louisiana was ordered up the river to meet three iron-clad boats which have succeeded in passing Island No. 10, and her presence there is deemed very important to the defense of New Orleans. The guns were intended expressly for her, and the Secretary of the Navy is unwilling to give them up.*

You have not answered my two telegrams asking where the cotton-lined boats were.

G. W. RANDOLPH,
Secretary of War.

WAR DEPARTMENT, C. S. A.,
Richmond, Va., April 12, 1862.

His Excellency J. G. SHORTER,
Governor of Alabama, Montgomery, Ala.:

SIR: I beg to tender you my thanks for the valuable suggestions contained in your letter of the 5th instant, and to inform you, in reply, that the Department fully appreciates the importance of Pensacola, and has been making every possible effort to arm troops for its defense.

Very respectfully, your obedient servant,

G. W. RANDOLPH,
Secretary of War.

WAR DEPARTMENT, C. S. A.,
Richmond, Va., April 14, 1862.

Maj. Gen. SAMUEL JONES,
Commanding Department of Alabama and West Florida:

GENERAL: Your letter to the Adjutant-General of the 5th instant has been referred to me, and I have the honor to inform you that there

* This was in answer to dispatch printed as document No. 13, in record of the Court of Inquiry. See p. 646.

is no general prohibition of the exportation of produce from the ports of the Confederate States. Whenever a military commander thinks that it will fall into the hands of the enemy he may stop it, and even destroy it if necessary, such authority having been expressly granted by Congress; or where he thinks that the exportation is a violation or evasion of the law against trading with the enemy, he may prohibit it; but he should bear in mind that it is good policy to exchange produce for arms and munitions of war with any one willing to make such exchange.

Persons suspected of disloyalty, and yet suffered to go at large for the want of evidence against them, should not be allowed to export cotton or other produce, of which the enemy stand in need, unless you are satisfied that it will not be carried directly or indirectly to the enemy's ports.

After exported produce gets into circulation you cannot, of course, prevent its going to the ports of the United States; but if you have reason to think that it is exported for that purpose, you would be justified in stopping it.

Very respectfully, your obedient servant,

G. W. RANDOLPH,
Secretary of War.

RICHMOND, VA., *April* 14, 1862.

Governor MOORE,
New Orleans, La.:

I have telegraphed to Governor Milton to deliver the arms to your agent on his exhibiting his authority from you and identifying the arms as the property of Louisiana. If, however, the arms were originally taken by the agents of the governor of Florida and not by our own, we have no control over them. Under the circumstances of the landing it was impossible to distribute the cargo at the time.

G. W. RANDOLPH,
Secretary of War.

HDQRS. DEPARTMENT ALABAMA AND WEST FLORIDA,
Mobile, Ala., April 15, 1862.

General S. COOPER,
Adjutant and Inspector General C. S. Army:

GENERAL: Before relinquishing command of this department, as I have been ordered by General Lee to do, I desire to place on file in your office copies of the principal instructions I received and gave in regard to Pensacola. The copies will be inclosed with this.*

The damaged condition of the railroads and other causes made it impracticable to move the shell and rifled guns and other property specified as rapidly as General Bragg supposed it could be; and when I undertook to hold Pensacola beyond the time appointed for its evacu-

*For documents referred to see Bragg to Jones, February 27 and March 1, pp. 835, 837; Jones to Le Barron, March 4, p. 838; Jones to Bragg, March 5 and 6, pp. 838, 840; Jones to Brent, March 8, p. 846; Jones to Jones, March 9, p. 848; Jones to Beard, March 10, p. 849; Bragg to Jones, March 11, p. 852; Jones to Cooper, March 11, p. 852; Jones to Jones and Myers, March 12, pp. 853, 855; Jones to Bragg and Bragg to Jones, March 15, pp. 856, 857; Jones to Jones, March 16, p. 858; Beard to Stringfellow, March 16, p. 859; Bragg to Jones, March 18, p. 861; Jones to Bragg, March 21, p. 862; Jones to Benjamin, March 22, p. 862; Benjamin to Jones, March 23, p. 866; and Lee to Jones, March 31, p. 868.

ation it was not alone for the purpose of saving much valuable public property, but I hoped whilst doing so to gather a sufficient force to repel any attack I believed the enemy capable of making at that time, and to hold the place until the men I hoped to collect could be armed, organized, and instructed, and put in condition to hold it against any attack the enemy might be induced to make after ascertaining that nearly all the troops that had so long held it securely had been withdrawn. About 1,000 armed and 500 unarmed men were retained. Of these only about 330 had any experience or instruction in the use of heavy artillery. The governor of Alabama has sent to Pensacola about 2,000 unarmed and unorganized men. Other unarmed men might have been and may now be sent there, but I have not thought it advisable to do so without some assurance that I could procure arms for them. One hundred very inferior old Spanish muskets, brought in by a schooner that ran the blockade, and 200 or 300 shot-guns and rifles furnished by Governor Shorter, are the only arms I have yet been able to procure. Col. T. M. Jones, commanding at Pensacola, has now about 3,500 men, including one cavalry company. More than half of them are unarmed, and he has no field artillery. If the Government can furnish arms, this force can, I believe, be very soon increased to 5,000 or 6,000 men, and if to that is added the two companies (one of artillery and one of cavalry) which General Lee informs me, by letter of the 31st October, the commanding officer at Tallahassee had been ordered to send to Pensacola, if they could be procured, Colonel Jones would, I think, be able to defend his post successfully against a formidable attack. The effectiveness of his force would be increased beyond the mere addition of numbers by the encouragement and confidence it would inspire in the officers and men. Heretofore they have been greatly discouraged and depressed, regarding themselves as detained at their post only to keep up the appearance of holding it, but in reality to offer but a feeble resistance if attacked, and then to escape or fall into the hands of the enemy, whilst their more fortunate companions were sent to Tennessee to meet the enemy. But unless the garrison can be increased to near 5,000 infantry, and one or two companies each of light artillery and cavalry added, the place is constantly in imminent danger of falling into the hands of the enemy.

It is for the Department to judge whether it is better to hold it by so uncertain and insecure a tenure, or to move to a place of security the large armament of heavy guns remaining there and then abandon the place. Colonel Jones undertook the task I assigned him in the best possible spirit, and has had many difficulties to contend with. He has held his post more than a month beyond the time appointed for its evacuation, and has thus saved a large amount of valuable Government property. He has performed the duty assigned him so far in a manner deserving high commendation.

This place is but little, if at all, more secure than Pensacola. When the Army of Mobile was withdrawn garrisons were left in Forts Morgan and Gaines, and two companies with the battery at Cedar Point; two cavalry companies, one patrolling from Fort Morgan to the Perdido, the other, near Old Portersville on Bayou Labatre, patrolling the coast; one light artillery company, just organized and ready for service, and another with field guns, but no horses. A battalion of the First Confederate Regiment, now reduced to two companies, was sent over from Pensacola to man the batteries near this city, the total present for duty being about 2,360. Of this force, one regiment—the Twenty-fourth

Alabama, aggregate present 680—is now under orders from Fort Morgan to Corinth.

There are here now about 1,500 unarmed and unorganized war troops. I have ordered a portion of them to Fort Morgan, to take the place of the Twenty-fourth Alabama. Besides these I have about 1,000 ninety-day volunteers from the country, armed with shot-guns, and about the same number of armed militia can be turned out in this city on an emergency. I do not speak accurately as to numbers, because the returns are exceedingly inaccurate, and we have no blank forms.

While the garrisons of Forts Morgan and Gaines may be able to repel any attack likely to be made on them soon, there is little or nothing to resist a land attack on the city if made in force.

You will see, general, from the foregoing statement that not only Pensacola, but this city and bay and the large and valuable armaments of Forts Gaines and Morgan, and the batteries at Cedar Point and nearer the city, are very much at the mercy of the enemy. From what the governor of this State tells me, I believe that if arms can be procured the force here can easily be so increased as to defend this place against any attack the enemy is likely to make soon.

A few weeks more and the climate will probably deter the enemy from undertaking extensive operations on the Gulf coast. In the mean time a few thousand arms here and at Pensacola might be of incalculable service to us. I have not received a gun of any sort from the Government since I have commanded this department.

You will not, I am sure, general, understand me as writing this in any spirit of complaint. This is not at all my intention. The Department knows its own resources and the best way of applying them far better than I do. I only desire before turning over my command to state the condition of things here and at Pensacola.

I am, very respectfully, your obedient servant,

SAM. JONES,
Major-General.

HEADQUARTERS DEPARTMENT NO. 1, C. S. A.,
New Orleans, La., April 15, 1862.

General GEORGE W. RANDOLPH,
Secretary of War:

SIR: I beg leave to report that the funds for the river-defense fleet which were sent me are nearly exhausted. The enormous price of every kind of materials has made the preparation very expensive, in addition to which the river pilots (Montgomery and Townsend), who are at the head of the fleet, are men of limited ideas—no system and no administrative capacity whatever. I very much fear, too, that their powers of execution will prove much less than has been anticipated. In short, unless some competent person, of education, system, and brains, is put over each division of this fleet, it will, in my judgment, prove an utter failure. No code of laws or penalties has been established, and it is difficult to decide how deserters from the fleet are to be tried and punished. There is little or no discipline or subordination, too much "steamboat," and too little of the "man-of-war," to be very effective. The expenses of fitting up, provisioning, coaling, and paying advances so far on the fourteen ships are about $800,000. I have received $950,000, but have paid nothing as yet towards the $563,000, at which sum the vessels seized were appraised. The original appropriation was $1,000,000. Captain Montgomery informs me that half a million more has been voted; if so, it should be sent on at once, so as to pay off the liabilities on the vessels.

I trust that the results to be derived from this fleet will compensate for the outlay, but unless some good head is placed in charge of it I fear such will not be the case. The expenses of outfit, payment for ships, and months' wages will consume one and a half millions. It is due, however, to Montgomery to say that for everything he has been compelled to pay nearly 300 per cent. over current piece prices. Eight of these vessels are up the river and four below; the remaining two will go below in a few days.

I telegraphed General Beauregard some time since about fortifying at Vicksburg, although we have no guns to put up there, but in case we fall back from the Corinth and Memphis line we might make a fair stand on a line running from Vicksburg through Jackson and Meridian. I have no officer of engineers to send there, but think the subject of importance.

The enemy has forty vessels just below Fort Jackson, and has been firing occasionally for two days past. I think they will locate their mortar ships, shell the forts for several days or weeks, and then try to dash by with their steamers. They have four ships of the class of the Hartford, and twelve or fifteen gunboats, besides twenty-one mortar schooners. If we can manage to obstruct the river so as to retain them thirty minutes under our fire I think we can cripple the fleet.

We have several regiments here which have enlisted for the war, but are entirely destitute of small-arms, I having sent all I had to Corinth with Ruggles' brigade.

Heavy requisitions, entirely unforeseen, are constantly made on this department for supplies of all kinds, and when they come are generally very urgent. To meet such calls large amounts of funds should be kept here, either in the hands of the different disbursing officers or placed at my disposition. It is too late after the requisition is received to make estimates; neither can we give details in advance.

I received a telegram from the President that the Secretary of War had, in answer to my dispatches about the necessity of martial law in some of the adjoining parishes, written me fully on the subject. I have not received his letter. The good citizens in many of the neighboring parishes are sending petitions constantly to have martial law extended over them. It should be done, in order to make it effective in those parishes where it exists. Please inform me on this point, as also how are the expenses of provost-marshals to be paid hereabouts.

Respectfully, your obedient servant,

M. LOVELL,
Major-General, Commanding.

NEW ORLEANS, LA., *April* 15, 1862.

General RANDOLPH:

The enemy is preparing for a formidable attack on the forts below. He shelled them a little for the past two days; no harm done. Twenty-seven vessels in sight from forts.

M. LOVELL.

RICHMOND, VA., *April* 17, 1862.

Governor MILTON,
Tallahassee:

I wish 1,500 arms sent to Pensacola or 1,500 armed troops. The rest of the arms will receive such destination as General Lee may think proper after returning to the governor of Georgia what were taken from him. I will submit your dispatch to General Lee, and request him to telegraph you.

G. W. RANDOLPH,
Secretary of War.

NEW ORLEANS, LA., *April* 17, 1862.

President DAVIS:

Forts bombarded an hour and a half yesterday. General Duncan telegraphs none of our guns will reach them. Commodore Whittle has orders from the Secretary of the Navy to send the Louisiana to Tennessee. Duncan and Higgins both telegraph she is absolutely a necessity at the forts for the safety of New Orleans, and that it is suicidal to send her elsewhere. With the enemy's plan of attack our safety may depend upon her timely arrival there. I earnestly beg her destination may be changed and protest against her being sent up the river. Excitement among the people great on the subject.

THO. O. MOORE,
Governor of Louisiana.

RICHMOND, VA., *April* 17, 1862.

GOV. THOMAS O. MOORE:

A dispatch was sent yesterday to General Lovell on the subject of the attack on the forts below. His answer was required in connection with the question proposed by you. The wooden vessels are below; the iron gunboats are above. The forts should destroy the former if they attempt to ascend. The Louisiana may be indispensable to check the descent of the iron boats. The purpose is to defend the city and valley. The only question is as to the best mode of effecting the object. Military men must decide, and to-day their discretionary power has been enlarged.

JEFFERSON DAVIS.

HEADQUARTERS DEPARTMENT NO. 1,
New Orleans, La., April 17, 1862.

General GEORGE W. RANDOLPH,
Secretary of War:

SIR: The occupation of Tennessee by the enemy, the low water in Red River, the interruption of the railroads at Decatur, and the want of communication by rail with Texas, all combined, have brought about a scarcity of provisions here. Mr. E. Salomon goes hence to Richmond as special agent, to endeavor to remedy this evil, if possible. I beg that you will cause all necessary orders to be given to facilitate his mission, as you will perceive at once it is one of vital importance. He takes letters from Governor Moore and several of our most prominent citizens.

Very respectfully, your obedient servant,

M. LOVELL,
Major-General, Commanding.

HEADQUARTERS DEPARTMENT NO. 1.
New Orleans, La., April 17, 1862.

General SAMUEL JONES,
Commanding Department of Alabama:

DEAR SIR: We are threatened here with a scarcity of flour and other provisions. Mr. Salomon goes from here as a special agent to Richmond to endeavor to procure supplies. Please give him every facility in his business and endeavor to push forward by every possible means any provisions that he may succeed in obtaining. It is a matter of vital importance, and there is no time to be lost. I wish you would give the requisite orders in your department to enable Mr. Salomon to succeed in his mission.

The great importance of this matter will strike you at once.

Yours, truly,

M. LOVELL,
Major-General, C. S. Army.

HDQRS. DEPARTMENT ALABAMA AND WEST FLORIDA,
Mobile, Ala., April 20, 1862.

General S. COOPER,
Adjt. and Insp. Gen. C. S. A., Richmond, Va.:

GENERAL: The occupation by the enemy of points on the Memphis and Charleston Railroad enhances so much the importance of holding this place, that I deem it my duty to bring it prominently to your notice.

As I am at present informed, the only railroad and telegraphic communication between the Atlantic States and those bordering on the Mississippi, between the Army of the Valley of the Mississippi and the seat of Government, passes through this city. The supply of flour and grain in New Orleans is so reduced, that the general commanding and the governor of Louisiana regard that city as in more danger from famine than from the guns and troops of the enemy.

Special messengers are sent from Louisiana to procure flour from the Atlantic States, whilst those States are in great want of the molasses and sugar of Louisiana.

If this place is occupied by the enemy steam and telegraphic communication between the Atlantic and Western States is cut off, and there is little or nothing to prevent its falling into the hands of the enemy, as I have stated in my letter to you of the 15th instant, if it is attacked in force by land and water.

The governor and people of Alabama are fully alive to the importance of holding Mobile. If arms can be procured, the men can be found to use them here; if additional arms cannot be procured, it becomes a question for the Government to decide whether the interest of the service does not demand that some armed troops be sent here from some other point.

So far as I am informed, the enemy's land force in the Gulf is not such as to indicate any intention on their part of undertaking extensive operations by land in this quarter, but I believe it to be large enough, if the commander is active and energetic, to enable them to seize Mobile. So important do I regard this place that I would now carry out my instructions to abandon Pensacola, if by so doing I could so increase the force here as to afford any security for its defense against a formidable attack. If the troops here and at Pensacola were all armed and organized this place might be rendered comparatively secure for a time by combining the armies of Pensacola and Mobile, but under existing circumstances that combination would not add more than about 1,500 muskets and shot-guns to the force here. I have therefore preferred to continue the occupation of Pensacola, trusting that our affairs in Tennessee would take such a turn as to enable the Government to transfer a part of the force now there to the Gulf coast.

This place has labored under other embarrassments than the want of men and arms; one of these has been the frequent change of commanders. Until about the 5th of February General Withers was in command. During the last three weeks of February General Bragg was here in person. On the 28th of February he assigned me to the command of this department, directing me to carry out certain instructions at Pensacola and then come here. In the mean time Colonel (now Brigadier-General) Villepigue was left in command. On the 4th of March General Bragg issued an order resuming his former command of this department, but subsequently explained that he did not intend thereby to take the command from me, but only to attach the department to his command in Tennessee and Mississippi.

I arrived here and assumed command on the 14th March. Ten days later General Bragg ordered me to turn over my command and report to him in person at Corinth. I did so, and on the 31st March was ordered to return here and resume command of this department. Ten days after my return (on the 11th April) I received a telegram from General Lee, ordering me to turn over the command of the department to Brigadier-General Forney, who had been ordered to report to me, and to report myself in person to General Beauregard.

Forney arrived, but with his wound and general health such that he could not enter on duty, but applied for and obtained leave of absence on surgeon's certificate. I so telegraphed General Lee, who replied that I could not leave here until relieved by General Forney. In the mean time General Bragg telegraphed me that if I could not go immediately to Corinth and report to General Beauregard I need not go at all. So the matter now stands.

I am under orders from General Lee to report to General Beauregard when Forney is able to relieve me, and from General Bragg not to do so unless I can do it immediately. This state of uncertainty is embarrassing, and prevents me from carrying out some plans which I thought would add to the security of this place.

I am at present the only general officer of the Confederate Army on duty in the department, and I, as you see, am under rather uncertain orders. I respectfully suggest that there should be at least two; one here and one in Pensacola. It would be desirable that another should command the department if one can be spared for that service.

I shall be glad if you will lay the substance of this letter before the Secretary, and communicate to me such instructions as may be thought proper.

I am, very respectfully, your obedient servant,

SAM. JONES,
Major-General.

HDQRS. DEPARTMENT ALABAMA AND WEST FLORIDA,
Mobile, April 21, 1862.

General R. E. LEE, C. S. A.,
Richmond, Va.:

GENERAL: I am under somewhat conflicting orders at present. By your telegram of the 9th instant, received on the 11th, I am ordered to turn over this department to Brigadier-General Forney and report in person as soon as practicable to General Beauregard. General Forney arrived and reported to me, but with his wound and general health such that he could not enter on duty, but on surgeon's certificate applied for and obtained a leave of absence—sick leave. I so telegraphed you, and you replied on the 17th that I could not leave here until relieved by Forney. An hour or so before I received this last telegram of yours I received one from General Bragg, this department being attached to his command, saying if I could not go immediately to Corinth not to go at all; from which I inferred that if I could not go on to Corinth immediately, it was intended to assign some other officer to the command to which it had been intended to assign me, and I presume that has been done, as I have since received various telegrams from Generals Bragg and Beauregard, and no allusion is made to my leaving here. One just now received from General Bragg directs me to do certain things in this department which he would not direct me to do if he contemplated my going to Corinth.

But as matters now stand I am under orders from you to go to Corinth and report to General Beauregard when General Forney can relieve me, and from General Bragg not to do so, and both orders were received within a few hours of each other.

Under the circumstances I shall await further orders from you, and I shall be glad if you will give them as soon as you can conveniently do so. It is not probable that General Forney will be well enough to enter on duty before I can hear from you, particularly if you reply to this by telegraph, and I shall be glad if you will do so; and if before answering you will have the kindness to read a letter of yesterday's date which I addressed to General Cooper I shall be obliged. It contains some suggestions which I desire you to see. It is rather long and I have not time now to recapitulate it.

I am, very respectfully, your obedient servant,

SAM. JONES,
Major-General.

HEADQUARTERS,
Richmond, Va., April 22, 1862.

General SAMUEL JONES,
Commanding, &c., Mobile, Ala.:

GENERAL: It is represented by General Lovell that he needs heavy guns for the defenses of the city of New Orleans. He states that but three of those removed from Pensacola were sent him, while fourteen 10-inch columbiads were kept at Mobile. I desire to know if you cannot spare him some of those in your command, and, if so, request that you will cause them to be forwarded to New Orleans without delay. It is all the more important that he should have them, because, when in position, he will be able to send the iron-clad steamers up the river, where they would render most efficient service. You will therefore please send such as are not positively necessary for the defense of your department.

I am, very respectfully, your obedient servant,

R. E. LEE,
General.

NEW ORLEANS, *April* 22, 1862.

General JONES:

Bombardment still goes on day and night; casualties few, but forts much cut up. Can you send two 10-inch columbiads in haste, or spare any powder?

M. LOVELL.

HEADQUARTERS,
Richmond, Va., April 22, 1862.

Maj. Gen. MANSFIELD LOVELL,
Commanding Department No. 1, New Orleans, La.:

GENERAL: Your letter of the 12th instant to the Hon. Secretary of War has been referred to General Lee, who directs me to say that he has ordered that such heavy guns as are here available be sent you. The Chief of Ordnance Bureau informs him that he can send four or five; in addition, General Samuel Jones has been written to and instructed to send you some of the guns taken from Pensacola, if they can possibly be spared from the defense of Mobile. As regards the small-arms you desire, he regrets there are none on hand for issue. The demand is great from all sides and the supply inadequate. There are some afloat, however, and it is hoped they will soon arrive, when, as far as practicable, your wants in this respect will be supplied.

The nomination of Brig. Gen. M. L. Smith has been confirmed, of which fact you are perhaps already aware.

I am, general, very respectfully, your obedient servant,

W. H. TAYLOR,
Assistant Adjutant-General.

NEW ORLEANS, LA., *April* 22, 1862.

General RANDOLPH:

In case the city should be occupied, should the cotton and tobacco belonging to foreigners be destroyed? I require funds for river-defense fleet immediately or cannot keep it up.

M. LOVELL.

RICHMOND, VA., *April* 23, 1862.

Major General LOVELL,
New Orleans:

You will not destroy foreign property unless it is necessary to insure the destruction of our cotton and tobacco. Your telegram about funds is not intelligible and had better be repeated, but in case of necessity, before receiving further instructions, you may borrow such funds as are necessary for the defense of the city.

G. W. RANDOLPH,
Secretary of War.

RICHMOND, VA., *April* 23, 1862.

General LOVELL,
New Orleans, La.:

Confine the functions of your provost-marshals to subjects proper to military police. Revoke orders to banks to issue notes in conformity with views of provost-marshals, and leave all State institutions as far as possible undisturbed by military power.

JEFFERSON DAVIS.

NEW ORLEANS, LA., *April* 23, 1862.

General S. COOPER:

Bombardment continues with unabated vigor; now five days and nights. We still hold out, with 4 casualties, but Fort Jackson much cut up. Want more powder, if it can be had.

M. LOVELL.

NEW ORLEANS, *April* 24, 1862.

General SAMUEL JONES:

The enemy has passed our forts. It is too late to send any guns here; they had better go to Vicksburg.

M. LOVELL.

RICHMOND, VA., *April* 24, 1862.

Gov. THOMAS O. MOORE,
New Orleans, La.:

I sent dispatch to General Lovell on receipt of yours in relation to the banks. From his reply find that orders were revoked.

Your dispatch in relation to enemy's ships this day received. I am hopeful that, whilst the forts divide the fleet, the Louisiana will not lose the opportunity. In painful anxiety wait further intelligence.

JEFFERSON DAVIS.

RICHMOND, VA., *April* 24, 1862.

Gov. THOMAS O. MOORE,
New Orleans, La.:

We will take the coin of the banks and be responsible for it. The Secretary of the Treasury will take action immediately.

JEFFERSON DAVIS.

RICHMOND, VA., *April* 25, 1862.

Maj. Gen. MANSFIELD LOVELL,
New Orleans, La.:

It has been determined to burn all the cotton and tobacco, whether foreign or our own, to prevent it from falling into the hands of the enemy. You will therefore destroy it all, if necessary, to prevent them from getting it.

G. W. RANDOLPH,
Secretary of War.

HEADQUARTERS,
Richmond, Va., April 27, 1862.

General SAMUEL JONES,
Commanding, &c., Mobile, Ala.:

GENERAL: In reply to that portion of your letter to the Department of the 15th instant which relates to the public property and defenses at Pensacola I would state that it is deemed expedient to remove at once all Government property, including guns, munitions of war, &c., not necessary for present service, to some place of security, and to make every preparation for concentrating the whole available force of your command at Mobile, should occasion require it.

Such of the heavy guns as are not needed in your department could be sent to Montgomery or other safe point and a portion of them assigned to defense of the interior of Florida. General Joseph Finegan, commanding the Department of Florida, can inform you what may be required for the defense of the Saint John's, Chattahoochie, and other rivers.

Everything of value that it is possible to remove should be sent away, and what cannot be secured should be destroyed when you withdraw from the position, to prevent its falling into the hands of the enemy. As much as in your power deceive the enemy as to your real intent, keeping a bold front and doing the work of the removal with all the secrecy possible.

I am, general, very respectfully, your obedient servant,

R. E. LEE,
General, Commanding.

CAMP MOORE, LA., [*April*] 27, 1862.

General SAMUEL JONES:

I evacuated New Orleans, the fleet having anchored opposite the city. Send all heavy guns you can to Vicksburg with great dispatch.

M. LOVELL.

RICHMOND, VA., *April* 28, 1862.

Mayor MONROE,
of New Orleans, La.:

I deeply sympathize with your situation, and recognize with pride the patriotism of the citizens of New Orleans.

Your answer to Commander Farragut leaves to you all the chances and rights of war. General Duncan may prevent re-enforcements to the enemy, and General Beauregard has been informed of your condition, and will aid you as he may.

My prayers are with you. There is no personal sacrifice I would not willingly make for your defense. Maintain firmly the position you took in your reply, and let us hope for a successful issue.

JEFFERSON DAVIS.

TANGIPAHOA, LA., *April* 30, 1862.

General VAN DORN:

Just returned from New Orleans. The men at forts refused to hold out longer, and Duncan had to surrender. The enemy will therefore occupy the city under his guns. All seems quiet and orderly, and I think there will be no trouble for citizens and families. The only fear is a scarcity of provisions.

I shall occupy Vicksburg, and support Beauregard with all the men I can organize and arm.

M. LOVELL.

CAMP MOORE, LA., *May* 1, 1862.

General RANDOLPH,
Secretary of War:

Have received no instructions about destruction of cotton. Shall I destroy all that can be reached by the enemy, leaving each planter a portion for supplies; if so, what percentage shall be left? Shall I burn the barracks and arsenal at Baton Rouge?

M. LOVELL.

CAMP MOORE, LA., *May* 2, 1862.

General RANDOLPH:

Butler occupied New Orleans to-day. Cannot enroll men there. What is to be done about destroying cotton?

M. LOVELL.

RICHMOND, VA., *May* 2, 1862.

General LOVELL:

The following dispatch was sent to you on the 25th ultimo:

> It has been determined to burn all the cotton and tobacco, whether foreign or our own, to prevent it from falling into the hands of the enemy. You will therefore destroy it all, if necessary, to prevent them from getting it.
>
> G. W. RANDOLPH,
> *Secretary of War.*

A. T. BLEDSOE,
Assistant Secretary of War.

RICHMOND, VA., *May* 3, 1862.

Major-General LOVELL,
Camp Moore, La., via Mobile, Ala.:

This is the third telegram which has been sent to you about burning cotton—the last two copies from the first. It is this:

> It has been determined to burn all the cotton and tobacco, whether foreign or our own, to prevent it from falling into the hands of the enemy. You will therefore destroy it all, if necessary, to prevent them from getting it.

Acknowledge receipt of this at once.

G. W. RANDOLPH,
Secretary of War.

CAMP MOORE, LA., *May* 4, 1862.

General RANDOLPH:

Dispatch about cotton received. Immediate steps taken to carry out the instructions of yesterday. Want copy of law to organize guerrilla parties, with authority to act. This is the only available force in the swamps of South Louisiana.

M. LOVELL.

RICHMOND, VA., *May* 5, 1862.

Governor MOORE,
Camp Moore, La.:

Notice that you were going to Monroe caused my failure to reply to your former dispatch. With regret I afterwards learned that the enemy had occupied New Orleans. Concur with you as to the changes necessary because of that event. I had previously concluded to form a department west of the Mississippi. It is now a necessity, but we must further delay action, because the troops and higher officers are concentrated for a battle in Tennessee.

My present opinion is that it will be better to have one of your camps on each side of the river.

JEFFERSON DAVIS.

(Repeated May 7.)

MONTGOMERY, *May* 5, 1862.

Hon. GEORGE W. RANDOLPH,
Secretary of War:

Have furnished General Forney with all the arms I have. If he can get 500 of those at Charleston, brought by Nashville and Cecilia, he believes he can defend Mobile successfully. Its fall involves the arsenal at Mount Vernon, perhaps this place, and cuts off communication with Corinth. Shall send immediately an agent to Charleston to bring them, and most earnestly urge they be supplied. Alabama, in addition to turning over 21,000 stand taken at Mount Vernon, has armed over 18,000 troops now in other States. She asks but for 500.

JNO. GILL SHORTER,
Governor of Alabama.

[Indorsement.]

I have only heard of 3,000 arms having been brought to Charleston by the Cecilia; 2,000 were ordered to General Pemberton for Georgia troops and 1,000 to Chattanooga for the Alabama troops.

So far as I know there are no arms in Charleston.

R. E. LEE.

RICHMOND, VA., *May* 5, 1862.

General JOHN H. FORNEY,
Mobile:

Governor Shorter suggests that in case of an attack upon Mobile the prisoners at Montgomery should be removed to Columbus or Macon, Ga. As you may be too much occupied in case of attack to attend to their removal, I have requested the governor to advise with and assist you in the matter. You had better communicate with him.

G. W. RANDOLPH,
Secretary of War.

RICHMOND, VA., *May* 6, 1862.

Col. THOMAS M. JONES,
Commanding at Pensacola:

In case you have to evacuate Pensacola, destroy cotton, tobacco, and military and naval stores, but avoid the destruction of buildings and other private property as much as possible. Only such things as could be used by the enemy in the prosecution of the war are required by the act of Congress to be destroyed.

G. W. RANDOLPH,
Secretary of War.

RICHMOND, VA., *May* 6, 1862.

Maj. Gen. MANSFIELD LOVELL,
Camp Moore, La.:

I see no reason for the destruction of the barracks and arsenal at Baton Rouge. You will therefore preserve them, unless, in your opinion, there is some urgent reason for their destruction.

G. W. RANDOLPH,
Secretary of War.

NEW ORLEANS, *May* 8, 1862.

[The SECRETARY OF WAR:]

In the perilous and entirely isolated position in which we find ourselves in this once glorious city of New Orleans, and under the pressure of the calamities which have befallen us, bearing, as it were, by common consent, the burden and responsibility of a trust so complex and arduous as that which it imposed upon me, I feel authorized, in the absence and during the flight of all our State authorities, to address myself to Major-General Lovell, commanding at Camp Moore, and to Major-General Beauregard, commanding at Corinth, and, through the latter, to the President of the Confederate States, for the purpose of obtaining some information concerning the ulterior designs of the Government with reference to this doomed city, that the good citizens, in whose breast still lingers not only hope, but faith in the success of the great struggle in which we are engaged, may have some direction to guide them in the course which coming events may command them to adopt and in the efforts which they may be disposed to make in vindication of their independence.

The city has been deserted by all such as had moneys or other resources of the Government under their control, and is left without official direction and without means for supplying the necessities which that desertion has left unprovided for.

Vast amounts of property, such as coal, guns, small-arms, and ammunitions of every shape and form, have been abandoned without any steps having been taken to protect them from the grasp of the invader and secure their possession to the Confederate Government. They still lie in the places where they had been stored up, at the mercy of the enemy, without a word of instruction from any quarter as to what should have been done with them, and without a single cent being left anywhere to provide security for the same.

The entire crew of the McRae, 108 in number, and the scattered remnants of the soldiers that retreated from Camps Lovell and Chalmette, and from the forts below and around New Orleans, are dispersed throughout the city, prowling about in the streets asking for their pay, and having no bread to put in their mouths or to give to their families, and exposed to the temptations which the enemy fails not to hold out to them, to entice them into the Federal ranks.

We are threatened with measures on the part of the Federal commander which look to a servile insurrection as the means of crushing the indomitable energy supposed still to exist in many hearts, and if the threat be carried out we will have to encounter a much harder question than that of a bombardment: the sack of our houses and the slaughter of our women and children by the hand of our own slaves will be the next issue we may have to face. We do know what this supreme contingency will exact from us, and we will, I hope, be prepared for the dire dilemma which may arise out of it.

But are we not to be remembered by those who have assumed charge of our destinies? Shall we be left without assistance, nay, without a word of comfort and encouragement, to the tender mercy of our infuriated negroes, and will not the hand of the Government manifest itself in some form or shape, if it were but to protest that they have not yet given us up to the enemy?

I repeat again that we are left entirely to ourselves, with a State government in shameless flight, and with the supreme Government in an apparent state of torpescence and forgetfulness!

The messenger who takes charge of this communication is recommended to me as an intelligent, skillful, and reliable medium of intercourse. His name is James D. Brylan. He may be freely trusted. I send him at the earnest instance of our friends here, that my message may be carried safely, and that he may be the means of bringing back to us, either from General Beauregard or the Government at Richmond, such intelligence and instructions as will relieve our minds from doubt and perplexity as to what best should be done.

PIERRE SOULÉ.

[Indorsement.]

MAY 22, 1862.

Read and returned to Secretary of War for assurance to the citizens of New Orleans that the Confederate States Government has not been unmindful of their condition, and had its power but been equal to its will, would have long since rescued the city from the brutal invader. On both the east and west side of the river efforts are being made to organize forces, &c.

JEFFERSON DAVIS.

RICHMOND, VA., *May* 8, 1862.

Governor MOORE,
Camp Moore, La.:

Dispatch received. Concur in your wish for prompt organization west of river, and gladly accept your offer to proceed at once in enrollment. Let the first camp be at Opelousas, if you so choose; how would Camp Moore do for the other? I have no authority to appoint, but only to detail, officers to command the encampments. General Beauregard has been called on to name officers for encampments in the West. A general to command department will be sent as soon as practicable.

JEFFERSON DAVIS.

RICHMOND, VA., *May* 12, 1862.

Governor MOORE,
Camp Moore, La.:

Dispatches of 10th received. Let a third camp be located at Monroe. Martial law, if declared by me, can be administered only by Confederate officers or agents. It is not intended to interfere with your powers as executive of the State.

I will wait for further communication from you.

JEFFERSON DAVIS.

RICHMOND, *May* 12, 1862.

General JOHN H. FORNEY,
Mobile, Ala.:

Your dispatch of yesterday received. In the contingency referred to, burn all the cotton of foreign subjects except in cases where exemption has been granted by our Government. Where the consul applies for exemption on cotton the property of foreign government, immediately advise this office by telegraph for action here.

S. COOPER,
Adjutant and Inspector General.

HEADQUARTERS DEPARTMENT NO. 1,
Camp Moore, May 12, 1862.

General G. T. BEAUREGARD,
Corinth:

DEAR GENERAL: I received your dispatch asking for my regiments here, which I declined sending. In my judgment the most energetic steps should be taken to confine the enemy to New Orleans, where he must suffer more from sickness than in the country adjoining. Besides, it would have a very bad moral effect upon the State to abandon it entirely, and might operate to prevent the burning of the cotton, which act will show the world that we are in earnest, and put an effectual stopper on the promises of the Federals "to send out the cotton in thirty days." If it is destroyed, it certainly cannot be delivered in Europe, even though they should hold every seaport in the Confederacy. The troops in New Orleans are already suffering much from sickness, and they will, beyond a question, endeavor to occupy Baton Rouge, the lake shore, or this railroad. To prevent this, I propose to have a considerable number of partisan rangers, with 5,000 or 6,000 men well armed and provided, in some central position, who can prevent their troops from leaving New Orleans except in very large force.

I was raising and arming five regiments here under the last call of the President, and by the aid of Governor Moore was getting along very well, when I learned that 800 guns, for which I had an order from the governor, were seized and carried to Corinth, thus depriving me of the means of arming a fine regiment. I must protest against this method of procedure. Everything intended for the defense of New Orleans for the past six months has been stopped and seized in every direction until it was left literally defenseless.

If the enemy occupies Baton Rouge I shall attempt to dispossess him, but cannot do it without guns.

I beg you will do me the favor to say to persons who ask where General Lovell and his army were when New Orleans fell, that all the troops that I had organized and prepared were sent to Corinth in March, and took a prominent part in the battle of Shiloh, leaving me with the heterogeneous militia of the city, armed mostly with shot-guns, against 9 and 11 inch Dahlgrens. Not that 20,000 well-armed infantry would have made any difference against ships of war, but the people, not understanding this, cast censure upon me.

The city fell from three causes:

1st. The carrying away of the river obstructions at the forts by the storm and flood a few nights before the attack.

2d. The want of a sufficiency of heavy guns, which I tried in vain to procure from Mobile and Pensacola.

3d. From inefficiency and want of proper co-operation on the part of those who were building and those who were to use the naval defenses when ready.

I have asked for an official investigation. My conscience is clear.

Yours, truly,

M. LOVELL,
Major-General.

RICHMOND, VA., *May* 13, 1862.

Col. THOMAS M. JONES,
Pensacola, Fla.:

In case you evacuate the navy-yard, destroy such machinery as cannot be removed, but do not destroy the dwelling-houses.

G. W. RANDOLPH,
Secretary of War.

BROOKSVILLE, MISS., *June* 20, 1862.

General S. COOPER,
Adjutant and Inspector General C. S. Army, Richmond, Va.:

GENERAL: I send with this a letter in reply to one addressed to me by the Secretary of War, calling on me to report the facts regarding the burning of two unfinished gunboats by my order in Pensacola Bay, on the 11th of March last. When I wrote the letter I was preparing to leave Mobile and go to Corinth in obedience to an order from General Lee, and in the press of business on me just then in turning over the command of the department and other matters I omitted to forward the letter to its address. It was sent in my valise to the rear a short time after I reached Corinth, and I now avail myself of the first opportunity to forward it with this explanation of the delay, which I have to ask you to make known to the Secretary.

Events which have transpired since my letter was written show, I think, that if the destruction of the unfinished gunboats was uncalled for on the 11th of March, it would have been called for a little later, and that by destroying them when I did I at least saved the Government the additional expense which would have been incurred by longer work on the boats, which could not have been completed before Pensacola was in the hands of the enemy.

I have been detained here a week by an attack of sickness, but expect to rejoin my division in a few days.

Very respectfully, your obedient servant,

SAM. JONES,
Major-General.

[Inclosure No. 1.]

HDQRS. DEPARTMENT ALABAMA AND WEST FLORIDA,
Mobile, April 25, 1862.

Hon. GEORGE W. RANDOLPH,
Secretary of War, Richmond, Va.:

SIR: I have the honor to acknowledge the receipt of your letter of the 17th instant, inclosing copies of two letters, one from Commander Farrand, C. S. Navy, to the Secretary of the Navy, and one from the latter to the President.

Commodore Farrand reports correctly to the Secretary of the Navy that two unfinished gunboats were burned in Pensacola Bay on the 11th ultimo by my order, and adds that when he was at Pensacola he could not discover the necessity for the destruction of the gunboats. The Secretary of the Navy communicates this report to the President, and adds that, so far as he is advised, "the destruction of these vessels was uncalled for," and asks that the officer under whose authority they were burned may be called upon to report why it was done.

You request me to make a report of the facts of the case. They are these:

On the 1st of March I received from Major-General Bragg, commanding this department, a letter dated 27th February last, in which he says: "You will make dispositions at the earliest moment, working day and night, to abandon Pensacola." And after giving certain directions he adds:

> I desire you particularly to leave nothing the enemy can use; burn all from Fort McRee to the junction with the Mobile road. Save the guns, and, if necessary, destroy your gunboats and all other boats; they might be used against us, &c.

On the 2d or 3d of March I received another letter from Major-General Bragg. It has no date, but could not have been written later than the 1st of March, as it was written in this city and he left here on that day. He says:

> Press forward your troops and heavy guns; we must have them to hold the Mississippi. Should you find yourself unable to accomplish your work in ten days, destroy your smooth-bore guns and send me your troops. I would not thus press you, but our fate may depend on two weeks in the valley of the Mississippi.

On the evening of the 10th of March I considered that the time appointed by Major-General Bragg for the evacuation of Pensacola had arrived. My force had by that time been so reduced by sending off troops to Corinth that I could not have held my post if attacked in force.

I had reason, too, to believe that the enemy was informed of the reduction of my force and the preparations to abandon the place. The report that it was to be abandoned was known in Pensacola before the first instructions on the subject reached me and caused a great panic. The inhabitants were flying from the town, and some persons had succeeded in escaping to Fort Pickens, and no doubt informed the enemy of the condition of things; and though I determined, for reasons not now necessary to state, to hold the place as long as possible, I thought it incumbent upon me to carry out the work of destruction ordered by General Bragg as far as it could be done without attracting the attention of the enemy to what I was doing. I therefore directed Lieutenant-Colonel Beard to proceed up the bay and the next morning to commence the work of destruction. In my instructions to him I said in regard to those unfinished gunboats:

> You will communicate with the officer or agent having charge of the gunboats and deliver a letter which I will send you. If they can be towed up the Escambia, you will, after having completed thoroughly the destruction of the property I have mentioned, give such assistance as you can in towing them out of danger up the Escambia. If that cannot be done, you will destroy the gunboats also.

Lieutenant-Colonel Beard reported to me that it was found impracticable to tow the gunboats up the Escambia or put them out of reach of the enemy, and he therefore burnt them.

I was reluctant to give any orders for the destruction of these unfinished gunboats, and would have much preferred leaving them to the naval officers. But I was informed there was no naval officer present in charge of them. Commander Farrand, who had charge of them, was, by his own statement, in Jacksonville, Fla., and did not return to Pensacola until a week after they were destroyed. I was informed that there were no engines or machinery ready for the boats; that they had been commenced early the previous autumn, and it was supposed would be ready to receive the machinery, if it could be procured, some time in May; that they were at that time in the hands of contractors and ship-carpenters, and that the mechanics and laborers employed about them could not be relied on to destroy them to prevent their falling into the hands of the enemy. Under all the circumstances of the case, therefore, I thought it my duty to prevent the enemy from profiting by the results of so many months of labor bestowed on those unfinished gunboats, and accordingly ordered their destruction.

The Secretary of the Navy, in his letter of the 12th of April to the President, says: "So far as I am advised, the destruction of those vessels was uncalled for." I entertained at the time no doubt that the Secretary of the Navy knew that I was ordered to abandon Pensacola, and that the unfinished gunboats must either be destroyed or fall into the hands of the enemy; for I supposed that Major-General Bragg had ordered the abandonment of Pensacola under instructions from the War Department, or that he had communicated to the Department his instructions to me, and that the evacuation of so important a place as Pensacola would necessarily be known to the Secretary of the Navy. It not only contained much valuable naval property, but was the place of the Secretary's private residence, where much of his property was located. A number of his slaves were hired by my quartermaster, and a day or two after I received the order to prepare for the evacuation, and while I was calling upon the governor of Alabama for slaves to aid in removing public property, the Secretary's agent called upon me for his slaves, to be removed, as I was informed, with his furniture, to a place of security.

From all of these circumstances I was convinced that the Secretary was advised of the order for the evacuation of the place, and the consequent necessity of destroying the unfinished gunboats, to prevent them from falling into the hands of the enemy. I regret that I did not know at the time that the Secretary was not advised of the orders in the case, that I might have brought the matter to his notice.

I am, respectfully, sir, your obedient servant,

SAM. JONES,
Major-General.

[Inclosure No. 2.]

WAR DEPARTMENT, C. S. A.,
Richmond, April 17, 1862.

Maj. Gen. SAMUEL JONES,
Commanding Dept. Alabama and West Florida, Mobile, Ala.:

SIR: The inclosed copies of a report from Commander E. Farrand, C. S. Navy, and a letter from Secretary of the Navy to the President, in reference to the destruction of two unfinished gunboats at the head of Pensacola Bay by your order, have been referred to me by the President, and you are requested to make a report of the facts of the case.

Very respectfully, your obedient servant,

G. W. RANDOLPH,
Secretary of War.

[Inclosure No. 3.]

NAVY DEPARTMENT, C. S.,
Richmond, April 12, 1862.

The PRESIDENT:

SIR: I have the honor to submit for your information the report of Commander Farrand. He was charged with the duty of constructing naval vessels on the inland waters of Florida, and he details the destruction, under the orders of the military commandant at Pensacola, of two fine gunboats on the bay of Escambia.

So far as I am advised the destruction of these vessels was uncalled for, and I have the honor to request that the officer under whose authority they were burned may be called upon to report why it was done.

The Government loses the entire value of the vessels; but apart from this, they were built with express reference to service in the waters near Pensacola and Mobile, and would have been of important service.

I have the honor to be, with great respect, your obedient servant,

S. R. MALLORY,
Secretary of Navy.

[Inclosure No. 4.]

NAVY DEPARTMENT, C. S.,
Richmond, April 11, 1862.

Hon. S. R. MALLORY,
Secretary of the Navy:

SIR: Upon my return from Jacksonville to Pensacola, on the 17th ultimo, I found that the two gunboats that were being constructed at the head of Pensacola Bay, under my superintendence, had been burned by military authority on the 11th of March. It was done by an armed force of 100 men, under the command of Lieut. Col. W. K. Beard, of the First Regiment Florida Volunteers, and, as Colonel Beard informed me, by order of Brig. [Maj.] Gen. Samuel Jones, commanding the Confederate forces at Pensacola.

The progress and condition of the gunboats at the time they were destroyed were as follows:

The one that was being built by F. G. Howard was yet on the stocks, but might have been, if necessary, put into the water at the moment, and would, in her regular course of progress, have been ready to launch in six or eight days, and, with the exception of machinery, would have been ready for her armament in twenty or twenty-five days, and would have carried two 10-inch guns of 9,000 pounds.

The one building by Ollinger & Bruce had been in the water about ten days, and, with the exception of machinery, would have been ready for her guns in ten days; she would have carried one 10-inch and one rifled 32-pounder.

These gunboats [were] well, strongly, and thoroughly built, and for sails or steam, and would, in my opinion, have rendered important service in case of an attack by the enemy upon Pensacola. These vessels were being constructed about 35 miles from Fort Pickens, and in case of an attack upon Pensacola were in a condition to have been, and might have been, removed up the Escambia River, out of reach of the enemy's gunboats.

When I was at Pensacola I saw no unusual number of enemy's ships off the port, nor could I discover the necessity for the destruction of the gunboats.

I am, sir, very respectfully, your obedient servant,

EBEN FARRAND,
Commander, C. S. Navy.

MOBILE, *February* 18, 1862.*

Hon. J. P. BENJAMIN:

Yours of the 8th just received. Fifth Georgia, Ninth Mississippi, Twentieth and Twenty-third Alabama Regiments on way to Knoxville. Should we not give up the seaboard now and concentrate all our means on the vital point?

BRAXTON BRAGG.

---

* Found too late for insertion in regular sequence.

INDEX.

Brigades, Divisions, Corps, and Armies are "Mentioned" under name of commanding officer; State and other organizations under their official designation.

*Claimed for Florida.

* Includes affairs at Buckingham and Hunting Island, S. C.

* Originally 36th Georgia Infantry.

*State Militia. †Claimed for Alabama.

* State Militia.

---

*Includes bombardment and capture of Forts Jackson and Saint Philip.

*Designation changed from 8th, November 14, 1861.

* Includes capture of blockade-runner in Bayou Grand Caillou, La.

*State Militia.

* Prior to March 19, 1862, embraced in Fourth District.
† Prior to March 19, 1862, designated Fifth District.

*Improvised. †Designated at this date Expeditionary Corps.

O